Quick Tax Facts
American Recovery and Reinvestment Act of 2009

Key Provisions At A Glance

The chart below summarizes the key tax provisions of the American Recovery and Reinvestment Act of 2009. See the explanation in CCH's *American Recovery and Reinvestment Act of 2009: Law, Explanation, and Analysis*, for a complete discussion.

Individuals

Provision	In Effect	Impact
General Tax Relief		
Making Work Pay Credit	2009-2010	Provides individuals with a refundable credit equal to the lesser of 6.2% of the taxpayer's earned income or $400 ($800 in the case of joint filers), phased out for modified AGI above $75,000 ($150,000 in the case of joint filers).
First-Time Homebuyer Credit	1/1/09-11/30/09	Extends the credit for purchases before 12/1/09, increases the maximum credit amount to $8,000 ($ married taxpayers filing separately), and generally waives the repayment requirement for purchases
Child Tax Credit	2009-2010	Provides that refundable portion of child credit is calculated to apply to 15% of earned income in excess
Deduction for Tax on Purchase of Vehicle	2/17/09–12/31/09	Allows itemizers and non-itemizers to deduct state and local sales and excise taxes incurred on the most new motor vehicles. Purchase price limitation and phase-out based on income apply.
Suspension of Tax on Unemployment Compensation	2009	Excludes up to $2,400 of unemployment compensation from gross income.
Education		
American Opportunity Tax Credit	2009-2010	Increases Hope credit to 100% of first $2,000 and 25% of next $2,000 of qualified expenses for first post-secondary education; extends it to apply to course materials; increases AGI limits; allows credi and makes a portion refundable.
Computer Technology Treated as Higher Education Expense	2009-2010	Enables taxpayers to use distributions from Section 529 accounts to purchase computer technology or Internet access and services while beneficiary is enrolled at educational institution.
AMT Relief		
AMT Exemptions	2009	Increases the exemption amounts for 2009 to $70,950 for married individuals filing jointly and surviv $46,700 for other unmarried individuals, and $35,475 for married individuals filing separately.
Non-refundable Credits Offset AMT	2009	Allows individuals to offset non-refundable personal credits against the AMT through 2009.

Quick Tax Facts
American Recovery and Reinvestment Act of 2009

Businesses

Provision	In Effect	Impact
Bonus Depreciation	2009	Extends 50% first-year bonus depreciation deduction to property placed in service during 2009 (2010 for certain property having longer production periods and aircraft).
Section 179 Expensing	2009	Increases the Code Section 179 deduction to $250,000 for 2009. Phase-out starts at $800,000.
NOL Carryback	For Applicable 2008 NOL	Allows eligible small businesses to elect up to a five year carryback of a net operating loss for a tax year ending or beginning in 2008.
Estimated Tax Payments	2009	The required annual estimated tax payments of a qualified individual are reduced to the amount not greater than 90% of the tax liability shown on the return for the preceding tax year. A qualified individual has adjusted gross income for the preceding tax year of less than $500,000, more than 50% of which is income from a small business.
Small Business Stock	Stock acquired after 2/17/09 and before 1/1/11	Increases to 75 percent the amount of gain excluded from an individual's income from the sale or exchange of small business stock acquired after February 17, 2009, and before January 1, 2011, and held for more than five years.
Work Opportunity Credit	2009-2010	Expands the work opportunity credit to cover unemployed veterans and disconnected youth hired in 2009 and 2010.

Energy

Provision	In Effect	Impact
Plug-in Vehicles	After 2009 (modified existing credit); 2/18/09 – 2011 (new credits)	Modifies the existing credit, adds a new 10% credit (up to $2,500) for plug-in electric vehicles that are low-speed or two- or three-wheeled vehicles; adds a new 10% credit (up to $4,000) for the cost of converting a motor vehicle into a qualified plug-in vehicle.
Credit for Nonbusiness Energy Property	2009-2010	Extends the credit through 2010, modifies the calculation of the credit, and updates the efficiency standards (effective as of 2/18/09).
Residential Energy Efficient Property	2009-2016	Eliminates the credit caps for solar hot water, geothermal, and wind property.
Alternative Motor Vehicle Credit	After 12/31/08	Treats the credit as a personal credit allowed against the AMT.

TAX LEGISLATION 2009

AMERICAN RECOVERY and REINVESTMENT ACT of 2009

(P.L. 111-5)

As Signed by the President
on February 17, 2009

Law, Explanation and Analysis

CCH Editorial Staff Publication

This publication is designed to provide accurate and authoritative information in regard to the subject matter covered. It is sold with the understanding that the publisher is not engaged in rendering legal, accounting, or other professional service. If legal advice or other expert assistance is required, the services of a competent professional person should be sought.

ISBN 978-0-8080-2149-0

©2009 CCH. All Rights Reserved.

4025 W. Peterson Ave.
Chicago, IL 60646-6085
1 800 248 3248
www.CCHGroup.com

No claim is made to original government works; however, within this Product or Publication, the following are subject to CCH's copyright: (1) the gathering, compilation, and arrangement of such government materials; (2) the magnetic translation and digital conversion of data, if applicable; (3) the historical, statutory and other notes and references; and (4) the commentary and other materials.

Printed in the United States of America

American Recovery and Reinvestment Act of 2009
President Signs Economic Stimulus Bill

President Obama, on February 17, 2009, signed into law a massive economic stimulus package titled the American Recovery and Reinvestment Act of 2009 (P.L. 111-5). On February 13, 2009, the House approved the measure by a vote of 246 to 183. The Senate followed suit on February 13, 2009, and passed the bill by a vote of 60 to 38. The total $787 billion cost of the bill includes nearly $300 billion in tax relief. The legislation includes a new Making Work Pay Credit, enhancements to the child tax credit and first-time homebuyer credit, an alternative minimum tax (AMT) patch for 2009, and energy incentives. In addition, the legislation provides extensions for 2008 bonus depreciation and increased Code Sec. 179 expensing, a limited five-year net operating loss (NOL) carryback for small businesses, and tax relief for state and local governments. The package also contains:

1. a one-time stimulus payment of $250 to retirees, disabled individuals, social security recipients and disabled veterans;

2. a temporary increase of the earned income credit for working families with three or more children;

3. an above-the-line deduction for interest expenses and state and local taxes paid on the purchase of a new automobile; and

4. a suspension of federal income tax on the first $2,400 of unemployment benefits per recipient for 2009.

On February 4, 2009, President Obama signed legislation that renews and expands the State Children's Health Insurance Program (SCHIP). The Senate passed the bill on January 26, 2009, by a vote of 66 to 32. The House, which passed a similar measure on January 14, 2009, agreed to the Senate version on February 4, 2009. The Children's Health Insurance Program Reauthorization Act of 2009 (P.L. 111-3) funds investment in the SCHIP program with a 61-cent increase in federal tax on cigarettes, with proportional increases on other tobacco products. The increases will raise approximately $65 billion over 10 years.

About This Work and CCH

Following the passage of the American Recovery and Reinvestment Act of 2009 (P.L. 111-5) and the Children's Health Insurance Program Reauthorization Act of 2009 (P.L. 111-3), CCH is providing practitioners with a single integrated law and explanation of the tax provisions of this legislation. As always, CCH Tax and Accounting remains dedicated to responding to the needs of tax professionals in helping them quickly understand and work with these new laws as they take effect. Other products and tax services relating to the new legislation can be found at CCH's website http://tax.cchgroup.com.

Contributors

Jean M. Baxley, J.D., LL.M.
Crowell & Moring LLP
Washington, D.C.

Debra J. Bennett, CPA, M.S.T.
Ernst & Young LLP
Dallas, Texas

Katherine Breaks
KPMG LLP
Washington, D.C.

Dale Collinson
KPMG LLP
Washington, D.C.

David Culp
KPMG LLP
Washington, D.C.

Kip Dellinger, CPA
Kallman And Co. LLP
Los Angeles, California

Jeffrey D. Eicher, J.D., CPA
Clarion University of Pennsylvania
Clarion, Pennsylvania

John Everett, Ph.D., CPA
Virginia Commonwealth University
Richmond, Virginia

Deanna Flores
KPMG LLP
San Diego, California

John Gimigliano
KPMG LLP
Washington, D.C.

Charles R. Goulding, J.D., CPA, MBA
Energy Tax Savers, Inc.
Syosset, New York

Glenn A. Graff, J.D.
Applegate & Thorne-Thomsen, P.C.
Chicago, Illinois

Kurt Hanway
KPMG LLP
Washington, D.C.

Leo N. Hitt, J.D., LL.M.
Reed Smith LLP
Pittsburgh, Pennsylvania

Cherie Hennig, Ph.D., CPA
Florida International University
Miami Beach, Florida

Charles C. Hwang, J.D., LL.M.
Crowell & Moring LLP
Washington, D.C.

Paul C. Lau, CPA, CMA, CFM
Blackman Kallick
Chicago, Illinois

Vincent O'Brien, CPA
Vincent J. O'Brien, CPA, PC
Lynbrook, New York

Pam Perdue, J.D.
Summers, Compton, Wells & Hamburg
St. Louis, Missouri

Mark Price
KPMG LLP
Washington, D.C.

William A. Raabe, Ph.D., CPA
Ohio State University
Bexley, Ohio

Jennifer A. Ray, J.D.
Crowell & Moring LLP
Washington, D.C.

Michael Schlesinger, J.D., LL.M.
Schlesinger and Sussman
New York, New York

Denise Schwieger
KPMG LLP
New York, New York

John A. Sikora, J.D.
Weiss Berzowski Brady LLP
Milwaukee, Wisconsin

Sandy Soltis, CPA, CFP
Blackman Kallick
Chicago, Illinois

Robert B. Teuber, J.D.
Weiss Berzowski Brady LLP
Delafield, Wisconsin

Scott Vance
KPMG LLP
Washington, D.C.

Jon Zelnik
KPMG LLP
Washington, D.C.

CCH Tax and Accounting Publishing
EDITORIAL STAFF

Gene McGovern, *Vice President, Publishing, M.B.A.*
Tracy Gaspardo Mortenson, *Director, Federal and State Tax, J.D., C.P.A.*
Mark L. Friedlich, *Director, International and Accounting, J.D.*
Elizabeth Albers, *Director, Production and Processes*

Explanation and Analysis

Jennifer M. Lowe, *Senior Managing Editor & Legislative Coordinator, J.D.*
Karen Heslop, *Managing Editor & Legislative Coordinator, J.D.*
Linda J. O'Brien, *Managing Editor & Legislative Coordinator, J.D., LL.M.*

Louis W. Baker, J.D., M.B.A.
David Becker, J.D.
Dan Billings, J.D.
Maureen Bornstein, J.D., *Managing Editor*
Glenn L. Borst, J.D., LL.M.
Anne E. Bowker, J.D., LL.M.
John Buchanan, J.D., LL.M.
Edward T. Bryant, J.D.
Barbara L. Bryniarski, C.P.A., M.S.T.
Managing Editor
Mildred Carter, J.D.
Maurice M. Cashin, J.D.
James A. Chapman, J.D., LL.M.
Tom Cody, J.D., LL.M., M.B.A.
Torie D. Cole, J.D.
Casie Cooper
Eileen Corbett, J.D., LL.M.
Heather Corbin, J.D.
Donna J. Dhein, C.P.A.
Kurt Diefenbach, J.D., *Managing Editor*
Liliana Dimitrova, LL.B., LL.M.
Zisl Edelson, J.D., M.B.A.
Karen Elsner, C.P.A.
Alicia C. Ernst, J.D.
Bernita J. Ferdinand, J.D.

Shannon Jett Fischer, J.D.
Donna M. Flanagan, J.D.
Mary Jo Gagnon, C.P.A.
Hilary Goehausen, J.D.
Brant Goldwyn, J.D.
Irene Goodman, J.D.
Bruno L. Graziano, J.D., M.S.A.
Joy A. Hail, J.D.
Harold Hancock, J.D., LL.M.
Carmela Harnett, *Senior Manager*
Kay L. Harris, J.D.
Michael Henaghan, J.D., LL.M.
Kathleen M. Higgins
Dem A. Hopkins, J.D.
Caroline L. Hosman, J.D., LL.M.
David M. Jaffe, J.D.
George G. Jones, J.D., LL.M., *Managing Editor*
Geralyn A. Jover-Ledesma, LL.B., LL.M., C.P.A.
Carol Kokinis-Graves, J.D.
Lynn S. Kopon, J.D., LL.M. *Managing Editor*
Mary W. Krackenberger, J.D.
Thomas K. Lauletta, J.D.
Laura A. LeeLun, J.D.
Ian S. Lesch, J.D., M.B.A., LL.M.

Adam R. Levine, J.D., LL.M.
Laura M. Lowe, J.D., *Managing Editor*
Mark A. Luscombe, J.D., LL.M, C.P.A.
Principal Analyst
Jerome A. Maes, J.D.
Rocky Mengle, J.D.
Michael Menzhuber, J.D., LL.M.
Jela Miladinovich, J.D.
Sheri Wattles Miller, J.D.
Ellen Mitchell, EA
Sherri G. Morris, J.D., LL.M.
Robert A. Morse, J.D.
John J. Mueller, J.D., LL.M., *Managing Editor*
Kieran Murray, J.D., LL.M.
Anita I. Nagelis, J.D., LL.M.
Jean T. Nakamoto, J.D.
Jerome Nestor, J.D., C.P.A., M.B.A., *Managing Editor*
Ron Newlin, J.D., M.S.T., C.P.A.
Karen A. Notaro, J.D., LL.M., *Portfolio Managing Editor*
John Old, J.D., LL.M.
Lawrence A. Perlman, C.P.A., J.D., LL.M.
Deborah M. Petro, J.D., LL.M.
Joseph E. Rebman, Jr., J.D.

Robert Recchia, J.D., M.B.A., C.P.A.
John W. Roth, J.D., LL.M.
Linda Scharf, J.D.
Carolyn M. Schiess, J.D.
Michael G. Sem, J.D.
James Solheim, J.D., LL.M.
Raymond G. Suelzer, J.D., LL.M.
Kenneth L. Swanson, J.D., LL.M.

Mary P. Taylor, J.D.
Deanna Tenofsky, J.D., LL.M.
Laura A. Tierney, J.D.
David Trice, J.D., CFP®, EA
Tulay Turan, J.D.
Chandra Walker, J.D.
James C. Walschlager, M.A.

Kelley Wolf, J.D.
Victor Woo, J.D., LL.M.
George L. Yaksick, Jr., J.D.
Denis Yurkovic, J.D.
Ken Zaleski, J.D.
Susan M. Zengerle, J.D., LL.M.
Managing Editor

Washington News Staff

Sarah Borchersen-Keto
Jeff Carlson, M.A.
Stephen K. Cooper

Paula L. Cruickshank
Kathryn Hough
Catherine Hubbard, M.G.

Rosalyn Johns-Thomas
Joyce Mutcherson-Ridley
William Pegler

Electronic and Print Production

Aisha Arif
Linda Barnich
Molly Bennett
Marsha Blase
Jeffrey Bosse
Douglas Bretschneider
Stella Brown
Kimberly D. Burns
Angela D. Cashmore
Deepti Chennupati
Lou Dagostino
Katherine Edwards
Amelia Eslava

Tara K. Farley
Jane Fridman
Lien Giang
Mary Ellen Guth
Ann Hartmann
Jennifer Jones
Linda Kalteux
Catherine A. Koenig
Kathy Kowalski
Faina Lerin
Chantal M. Mahler
Andrejs Makwitz

Tina Medina
Helen Miller
Samantha Munson
Jennifer Nelson
Elaine Ogawa,
Managing Editor
Jennifer K. Schencker
David Schuster
Monika Stefan
Jim F. Walschlager
Jennifer Youngless
Christopher Zwirek

¶1 Features of This Publication

This publication is your complete guide to the tax and accounting-related provisions of the *American Recovery and Reinvestment Act of 2009* (P.L. 111-5), signed by President Obama on February 17, 2009; and the *Children's Health Insurance Program Reauthorization Act of 2009* (P.L. 111-3), signed by President Obama on February 4, 2009. The core portion of this publication contains the CCH Explanations of the Acts. The explanations outline all of the law changes and what they mean for you and your clients. The explanations also feature practical guidance, examples, planning opportunities and strategies, as well as pitfalls to be avoided as a result of the law changes.

The law text and committee reports are reproduced following the explanations. Any new or amended Internal Revenue Code sections appear here, with changes highlighted in *italics*. The law text for portions of this Act that did not amend the tax code appear here. The committee reports that provide the legislative history of each provision follow the law text.

The book also contains numerous other features designed to help you locate and understand the changes made by these Acts. These features include cross references to related materials, detailed effective dates, and numerous finding tables and indexes. A more detailed description of these features appears below.

HIGHLIGHTS

Highlights are quick summaries of the major provisions of the *American Recovery and Reinvestment Act of 2009* (P.L. 111-5) and the *Children's Health Insurance Program Reauthorization Act of 2009* (P.L. 111-3). The Highlights are arranged by taxpayer type and area of interest, such as tax credits and deductions for individuals and businesses, energy conservation and economic development bonds, and health insurance provisions. At the end of each summary is a paragraph reference to the more detailed CCH Explanation on that topic, giving you an easy way to find the portions of the publication that are of most interest to you. *Highlights starts at ¶5.*

TAXPAYERS AFFECTED

The first chapter of the book, *Taxpayers Affected*, contains a detailed look at how the new laws affect specific categories of taxpayers. This chapter provides a quick reference for readers who want to know the immediate impact that the laws will have on their clients. The chapter also identifies the state tax consequences of the new laws. *Taxpayers Affected starts at ¶101.*

CCH EXPLANATIONS

CCH Explanations are designed to give you a complete, accessible understanding of the new laws. Explanations are arranged by subject for ease of use. There are two main finding devices you can use to locate explanations on a given topic. These are:

- A detailed table of contents at the beginning of the publication listing all of the CCH Explanations of the new laws;
- A table of contents preceding each chapter.

Each CCH Explanation contains special features to aid in your complete understanding of the new laws. These include:

- A summary at the beginning of each explanation providing a brief overview of the new laws;
- A background or prior law discussion that puts the law changes into perspective;
- Editorial aids, including examples, cautions, planning notes, elections, comments, compliance tips, and key rates and figures, that highlight the impact of the new laws;
- Charts and examples illustrating the ramifications of specific law changes;
- Captions at the end of each explanation identifying the Code sections added, amended or repealed, as well as the Act sections containing the changes;
- Cross references to the law and committee report paragraphs related to the explanation;
- A line highlighting the effective date of each law change, marked by an arrow symbol; and
- References at the end of the discussion to related information in the Standard Federal Tax Reporter, Tax Research Consultant and Practical Tax explanations.

The CCH Explanations begin at ¶205.

AMENDED CODE PROVISIONS

Changes to the Internal Revenue Code made by the *American Recovery and Reinvestment Act of 2009* (P.L. 111-5) and the *Children's Health Insurance Program Reauthorization Act of 2009* (P.L.111-3) appear under the heading "Code Sections Added, Amended or Repealed." *Any changed or added law text is set out in italics.* Deleted Code text, or the Code provision prior to amendment, appears in the Amendment Notes following each reconstructed Code provision. An effective date for each Code change is also provided.

The amendment notes contain cross references to the corresponding committee reports and the CCH Explanations that discuss the new laws. *The text of the Code begins at ¶5005.*

Sections of the Act that do not amend the Internal Revenue Code, appear in full text following "Code Sections Added, Amended or Repealed." *The text of these provisions appears in Act Section order beginning at ¶7003.*

COMMITTEE REPORTS

The Conference Report (H. Rept. 111-16) of the *American Recovery and Reinvestment Act of 2009* (P.L. 111-5), explains the intent of Congress regarding the provisions of the *American Recovery and Reinvestment Act of 2009* (P.L. 111-5). The relevant portions of the Conference Report for the *American Recovery and Reinvestment Act of 2009* are included in this section. At the end of each section, references are provided to the corresponding CCH explanations and the Internal Revenue Code provisions. *The pertinent sections of the Conference Report appear in Act Section order beginning at ¶10,010.*

¶11

The Joint Committee on Taxation (JCT) Description of the Revenue Provisions of the Children's Health Insurance Program Reauthorization Act of 2009 (JCX-1-09, the *Children's Health Insurance Program Reauthorization Act of 2009,* explains the intent of Congress regarding the revenue provisions of the *Children's Health Insurance Program Reauthorization Act of 2009.* There was no conference report issued for the *Children's Health Insurance Program Reauthorization Act of 2009.* The relevant portions of the Description of Revenue Provisions from the JCT are included in this section to aid the reader's understanding, but may not be cited as the official House, Senate or Conference Committee Report accompanying the *Children's Health Insurance Program Reauthorization Act of 2009.* At the end of each section, references are provided to the corresponding CCH explanations and the Internal Revenue Code provisions. *The pertinent sections of the Description of Revenue Provisions appear in Act Section order beginning at ¶15,010.*

EFFECTIVE DATES

Tables listing the major effective dates provides a reference bridge between Code Sections and Act Sections. The tables also indicate the retroactive or prospective nature of the laws. *The effective dates table for the American Recovery and Reinvestment Act of 2009 (P.L. 111-5) begins at ¶20,001. The effective dates table for the Children's Health Insurance Program Reauthorization Act of 2009 (P.L. 111-3) begins at ¶20,005.*

SPECIAL FINDING DEVICES

Other special tables and finding devices in this book include:

- A table cross-referencing Code Sections to the CCH Explanations (*see ¶25,001*);
- A table showing all Code Sections added, amended or repealed (*see ¶25,005*);
- A table showing provisions of other acts that were amended (*see ¶25,010*);
- A table of Act Sections not amending the Internal Revenue Code (*see ¶25,015*); and
- An Act Section amending Code Section table (*see ¶25,020*).

CLIENT LETTERS

Sample client letters allows you to quickly communicate the changes made by the *American Recovery and Reinvestment Act of 2009* to clients and customers (*see ¶27,001*).

TREASURY AND IRS GUIDANCE

Selected items of Treasury and IRS guidance that address the federal tax issues faced by taxpayers as a result of the downturn in the housing market and U.S. economy are provided (*see ¶28,001*).

PROVISIONS DROPPED IN CONFERENCE

A listing of provisions is from the House and Senate versions of the American Recovery and Reinvestment Act that were not included in the Conference Committee Report for the *American Recovery and Reinvestment Act of 2009 (see ¶29,001).*

¶2 Table of Contents

¶1	Features of This Publication
¶5	Highlights

EXPLANATION

¶105	Chapter 1	Taxpayers Affected
¶205	Chapter 2	Individual Income and Deductions
¶305	Chapter 3	Individual Related Tax Credits
¶405	Chapter 4	Business Income and Deductions
¶505	Chapter 5	Business-Related Tax Credits
¶605	Chapter 6	Tax Bonds
¶705	Chapter 7	Group Health Insurance and Other Provisions

LAW

¶5001	Code Sections Added, Amended or Repealed
¶7003	Act Sections Not Amending Code Sections

COMMITTEE REPORTS

¶10,001	American Recovery and Reinvestment Act of 2009
¶15,001	Children's Health Insurance Program Reauthorization Act of 2009

SPECIAL TABLES

Effective Dates Table

¶20,001	American Recovery and Reinvestment Act of 2009
¶20,005	Children's Health Insurance Program Reauthorization Act of 2009

Other Tables

¶25,001	Code Section to Explanation Table
¶25,005	Code Sections Added, Amended or Repealed
¶25,010	Table of Amendments to Other Acts
¶25,015	Table of Act Sections Not Amending Internal Revenue Code Sections
¶25,020	Act Sections Amending Code Sections

APPENDICES

¶27,001	Client Letters
¶28,001	Treasury and IRS Guidance
¶29,001	Provisions Dropped in Conference

Page 673	Topical Index

¶3 Detailed Table of Contents

CHAPTER 1. TAXPAYERS AFFECTED

AMERICAN RECOVERY AND REINVESTMENT TAX ACT OF 2009

¶101	Overview

INDIVIDUALS

¶105	Effect on Individuals Generally
¶107	Effect on First-Time Homebuyers
¶109	Effect on Homeowners
¶111	Effect on Individuals Subject to the AMT
¶113	Effect on Purchasers of Automobiles, Motorcycles, Light Trucks, and Motor Homes
¶115	Effect on Owners of Alternative Powered Vehicles
¶117	Effect on Parents
¶119	Effect on Recipients of Social Security and Other Benefits
¶121	Effect on the Unemployed
¶123	Effect on Residents of U.S. Possessions
¶125	Effect on Students
¶127	Effect on Small Business Owners
¶129	Effect on Investors Generally
¶131	Effect on Investors in Tax Credit and Tax-Exempt Bonds
¶133	Effect on Veterans
¶135	Effect on "Disconnected" Youth
¶137	Effect on Commuters
¶138	Effect on Tobacco Users
¶139	Effect on Certain Employees of TARP Participants

BUSINESSES

¶151	Effect on Business Generally
¶153	Effect on Small Business
¶155	Effect on Corporations
¶157	Effect on Partnerships
¶159	Effect on S Corporations
¶161	Effect on Financial Institutions
¶163	Effect on Regulated Investment Companies
¶165	Effect on Renewable Energy Producers and Facilities

¶167 Effect on Government Contractors
¶171 Effect on Low-Income Housing Industry
¶173 Effect on Computer Industry
¶175 Effect on Auto Industry
¶177 Effect on Aviation Industry
¶179 Effect on Tobacco Industry
¶181 Effect on Manufacturers of Intangibles
¶183 Effect on Railroad Industry
¶185 Effect on Building Contractors

TAX-EXEMPT ORGANIZATIONS AND GOVERNMENT ENTITIES

¶187 Effect on State and Local Government Entities
¶189 Effect on Indian Tribal Governments
¶191 Effect on State Housing Agencies
¶193 Effect on U.S. Possessions
¶195 Effect on the IRA and Treasury

STATE TAX CONSEQUENCES

¶197 Effect on State Tax Law

RECOVERY ACT SAMPLE SCENARIOS

¶199 Sample Scenarios for Individuals

CHAPTER 2. INDIVIDUAL INCOME AND DEDUCTIONS

GROSS INCOME AND DEDUCTIONS

¶205 Partial Exclusion of Unemployment Compensation Benefits
¶210 Qualified Small Business Stock
¶215 Limitation on Qualified Transportation Fringe Benefits
¶220 Qualified Expenses for Qualified Tuition Programs
¶225 Economic Recovery Payments for Recipients of Certain Federal Benefits
¶230 Deduction of Taxes on the Purchase of Certain Motor Vehicles

ALTERNATIVE MINIMUM TAX

¶235 Alternative Minimum Tax Exemption Amount
¶240 Use of Nonrefundable Personal Credits Against AMT Liability

CHAPTER 3. INDIVIDUAL RELATED TAX CREDITS

¶305 Making Work Pay Credit
¶310 First-Time Homebuyer Credit
¶315 Refundable Portion of Child Tax Credit
¶320 Increase in Earned Income Tax Credit
¶325 $250 Credit for Government Retirees

¶3

¶330	Hope Scholarship Credit
¶335	Residential Energy Property Credit
¶340	Residential Alternative Energy Credit
¶345	Plug-in Electric Drive Motor Vehicle Credit
¶350	Plug-in Electric Vehicle Credit
¶355	Plug-in Electric Drive Motor Vehicle Conversion Credit
¶360	Alternative Motor Vehicle Credit
¶365	Qualified Alternative Fuel Vehicle Refueling Property Credit

CHAPTER 4. BUSINESS INCOME AND DEDUCTIONS

¶405	Deferral of Discharge of Indebtedness Income Resulting From Reacquisition of Business Indebtedness
¶410	Code Sec. 179 Expense Election for 2009
¶415	Availability of Bonus Depreciation for 2009
¶420	Recognition Period for S Corporation Built-In Gains Tax
¶425	Maximum Five-Year Carryback Period for 2008 Net Operating Losses of Small Businesses
¶430	Clarification of IRS Guidance Related to Limitations on Certain Built-In Losses Following an Ownership Change
¶435	Treatment of Certain Ownership Changes for Purposes of Limitations on NOL Carryforwards and Certain Built-In Losses
¶440	Original Issue Discount on High-Yield Discount Obligations
¶445	Financial Institution De Minimis Safe Harbor Exception for Deducting Tax-Exempt Interest Expense
¶450	Temporary Expansion of Small Issuer Exception to Tax-Exempt Interest Expense Allocation Rules for Financial Institutions
¶455	$500,000 Executive Compensation Deduction Limit Extended to All Entities That Take TARP Assistance
¶460	Withholding on Certain Payments Made by Government Entities
¶465	Estimated Tax of Qualified Individuals
¶470	Corporate Estimated Tax Payments

CHAPTER 5. BUSINESS-RELATED TAX CREDITS

¶505	Election to Claim Accelerated Credits in Place of Bonus Depreciation
¶510	Energy Credit Portion of Investment Credit
¶515	Grant for Investment in Specified Energy Property
¶520	Renewable Electricity Production Credit
¶525	Credit for Investment in Advanced Energy Facilities
¶530	New Markets Tax Credit

¶3

¶535 Grants to Provide Financing for Low-Income Housing
¶540 Incentives to Hire Unemployed Veterans or Disconnected Youth
¶545 Carbon Dioxide Capture Credit

CHAPTER 6. TAX BONDS

TAX-CREDIT BONDS

¶605 Build America Bonds
¶610 Credit for Qualified Bonds
¶615 Pass-Through of Tax Credit Bond Credits to Mutual Fund Shareholders
¶625 Recovery Zone Economic Development Bonds
¶630 Qualified School Construction Tax Credit Bonds
¶635 Qualified Zone Academy Bonds (QZAB)
¶640 Qualified Energy Conservation Bonds
¶645 New Clean Renewable Energy Bonds

TAX-EXEMPT BONDS

¶650 Alternative Minimum Tax Limitations on Tax-Exempt Bonds
¶652 Recovery Zone Facility Bonds
¶655 Exempt Facility Bonds for High-Speed Intercity Rail Facilities
¶660 Industrial Development Bond Financing for Production of Intangible Property
¶665 Tribal Economic Development Bonds

CHAPTER 7. GROUP HEALTH INSURANCE AND OTHER PROVISIONS

¶705 COBRA Premium Assistance
¶710 Penalty for Failure to Notify Health Plan of Cessation of Eligibility for COBRA Premium Assistance
¶715 Extension of COBRA Benefits for Certain TAA-Eligible Individuals and PBGC Recipients
¶720 Special Enrollment Period for Group Health Plans for Medicaid or CHIP Coverage
¶725 Health Coverage Tax Credit
¶730 Tobacco Tax Rates and Treasury's Authority Over Permits

¶5 Highlights

INDIVIDUAL INCOME AND DEDUCTIONS

¶205 **Unemployment compensation.** Up to $2,400 of unemployment compensation is excludable from gross income for 2009.

¶210 **Excludable gain on small business stock.** Individuals can exclude up to 75 percent of their gain on the sale of qualified small business stock they acquire after the date of enactment and before 2011.

¶215 **Public transportation fringe benefits.** Through 2010, the limit on excludable fringe benefits for vanpools and transit passes increases to match the limit applicable to parking benefits.

¶220 **Qualified tuition programs.** Excludable qualified tuition program distributions can be used for some computer equipment and internet access costs that are paid or incurred during 2009 and 2010.

¶225 **Economic recovery payments.** The Treasury Department will make one-time payments of $250 to adults who are eligible for benefits under certain social security, Railroad Retirement, veterans and supplemental security income (SSI) programs.

¶230 **New car purchases.** Most individuals who purchase qualified motor vehicles before 2010 can claim an additional standard deduction for some state and local sales and excise taxes.

¶235, ¶240 **AMT.** The increased alternative minimum tax (AMT) exemption amounts and the use of nonrefundable personal tax credits against regular tax and AMT liability are both extended to tax years beginning in 2009.

INDIVIDUAL-RELATED TAX CREDITS

¶305 **Making Work Pay Credit.** Most workers with earned income can claim a refundable credit of up to $400 ($800 on a joint return) for 2009 and 2010.

¶310 **First-time homebuyer credit.** The credit for first-time homebuyers is extended through November 30, 2009. For qualified purchases during 2009, the maximum credit increases to $8,000 and the repayment requirement is generally waived.

¶315 **Refundable child credit.** For 2009 and 2010, the refundable child credit is calculated to apply to 15 percent of earned income in excess of $3,000.

¶320 **Earned income credit.** For 2009 and 2010, the phaseout amounts for the earned income credit increase by $5,000 for married taxpayers who file joint returns, and the credit percentage for taxpayers with at least three qualifying children increases to 45 percent.

¶325 **Government retiree credit.** Certain retired government workers whose work was not covered by social security can claim a refundable $250 tax credit.

¶330 **American Opportunity Credit.** For 2009 and 2010, the Hope Scholarship Credit is replaced by a more generous American Opportunity Credit.

¶335 **Nonbusiness energy property credit.** The residential energy property credit is modified and increased through 2010, and the efficiency standards for qualifying property are updated.

¶340 **Residential energy efficient property credit.** The annual maximum limits applicable to the residential alternative energy credit are eliminated for solar hot water heaters, wind turbine property, and geothermal heat pumps.

¶345, ¶355 **Plug-in electric drive motor vehicles.** The qualified plug-in electric drive motor vehicle credit is overhauled and made permanent. A new credit applies to the cost of converting a vehicle into a plug-in electric vehicle.

¶350 **Plug-in electric vehicles.** A new credit applies to two-wheeled, three-wheeled and low-speed plug-in electric vehicles acquired before 2012.

¶360, ¶365 **Alternative vehicles and refueling property.** For 2009, the alternative motor vehicle credit can be claimed against the alternative minimum tax. The alternative fuel vehicle refueling property credit is increased for 2009 and 2010.

BUSINESS INCOME AND DEDUCTIONS

¶405 **Cancellation of debt income.** A taxpayer can elect to defer cancellation of indebtedness income arising from a qualified reacquisition of certain corporate or business debt instruments issued by the taxpayer or a related person.

¶410 **Code Sec. 179 expensing.** The increase in the Code Sec. 179 expensing allowance (to a $250,000 dollar limitation and $800,000 investment limitation) that applies to tax years beginning in 2008 is extended to tax years beginning in 2009.

¶415 **Bonus depreciation.** The 50-percent bonus depreciation deduction that applies to tax years beginning in 2008 is extended for one year.

¶5

¶420 **S corporations.** For tax years beginning in 2009 and 2010, no tax is imposed on an S corporation's net unrecognized built-in gain if the seventh tax year in the corporation's 10-year recognition period preceded its 2009 or 2010 tax year.

¶425 **NOL carrybacks.** Eligible small businesses can elect to use an extended three-, four-, or five-year carryback period for 2008 net operating losses (NOLs).

¶430 **Bank acquisitions.** The Treasury Department's controversial Notice 2008-83, which exempts banks from the Code Sec. 382 limitations on certain built-in losses following an ownership change, is revoked after January 16, 2009.

¶435 **Corporate restructurings.** The loss limitation rules are not triggered by ownership changes occurring under certain restructuring plans required by loan agreements or line of credit commitments with the Treasury Department under the Emergency Economic Stabilization Act of 2008.

¶440 **Corporate OID.** Rules limiting corporate deductions of original issue discount (OID) on high-yield discount obligations are suspended for certain obligations issued in a debt-for-debt exchange, including an exchange resulting from a significant modification of a debt instrument, after August 31, 2008, and before January 1, 2010.

¶445, ¶450 **Exempt interest expenses.** For 2009 and 2010, financial institutions can deduct certain tax-exempt interest expenses. The small-issuer exception to the normal disallowance of the deduction is also expanded.

¶455 **TARP limits on executive pay.** The $500,000 deduction limitation on executive compensation applies to all entities that take troubled asset relief program (TARP) assistance.

¶460 **Withholding on government contracts.** Required tax withholding and reporting on certain government payments to contractors is delayed until 2012.

¶465 **Individual estimated tax payments.** For certain individuals with qualified small business income, estimated tax payments for tax years beginning in 2009 may be based on 90 percent of the prior year's tax liability.

¶470 **Large corporation's estimated tax payments.** Corporations with at least $1 billion in assets must increase their estimated tax payments for July, August and September of 2013 to 120.25 percent of the amount otherwise due.

¶5

BUSINESS-RELATED TAX CREDITS

¶505 **Accelerated credits.** A corporation that elects to claim an accelerated alternative minimum tax credit or research credit in lieu of bonus depreciation may increase its credit limitation by the amount of bonus depreciation claimed with respect to certain extension property placed in service in 2009.

¶510 **Energy credit.** The energy credit is modified with respect to small wind energy property and subsidized energy financing or industrial development bonds. Taxpayers can elect to claim the energy credit portion of the investment tax credit in lieu of the production tax credit for certain qualified energy production facilities.

¶515 **Renewable energy grants.** Certain electricity production facilities and other property eligible for the energy credit can qualify for federal grants worth up to 30 percent of the basis of the property.

¶520 **Renewable electricity production credit.** The placed-in-service date for property to qualify for the electricity production credit is generally extended through 2013 (2012 for wind facilities).

¶525 **Qualifying advanced energy project credit.** The investment credit includes a 30-percent credit for investment in qualified property used in a qualifying advanced energy manufacturing project.

¶530 **New markets credit.** The new markets credit is expanded and modified for 2009 and 2010.

¶535 **Low-income housing grants.** States may elect to receive federal grants in exchange for a portion of their unused low-income housing credit allocations for 2008 and 2009. The states must use the grants to make subawards to finance low-income housing.

¶540 **Work opportunity credit.** The work opportunity credit is expanded to include unemployed veterans and disconnected youth who begin work during 2009 and 2010.

¶545 **Carbon sequestration credit.** To qualify for the $10 per-metric-ton carbon sequestration credit, carbon dioxide used as a tertiary injectant must be sequestered by the taxpayer in permanent geological storage.

TAX BONDS

¶605, ¶610 **Build America bonds.** State and local governments may issue taxable build America bonds before January 1, 2011, that provide bondholders with both taxable interest and a federal tax credit. For certain qualifying bonds, the issuer may elect to receive a federal cash payment that replaces the bondholder's credit.

¶5

Highlights 23

¶615 Tax credit bonds and RICs. Certain regulated investment companies (RICs) that hold tax credit bonds can elect to pass through the bond credits to their shareholders; they are no longer required to do so.

¶652, ¶625 Recovery zone bonds. To fund qualified activities in economically distressed areas, certain counties and large municipalities can issue recovery zone facility bonds (similar to exempt facility bonds) and recovery zone economic development bonds (a type of build America bond).

¶630 Qualified school construction bonds. A new category of tax credit bonds, qualified school construction bonds, can be issued in 2009 and 2010 to fund the construction, rehabilitation, or repair of public schools, or the purchase of land on which a funded school will be built.

¶635 Qualified zone academy bonds. The authority for qualified zone academy bonds is extended through 2010, and additional bonds are authorized to fund renovations, equipment, course materials and training.

¶640 Energy conservation bonds. The qualified energy conservation bond program is expanded, additional bonds are authorized, the definition of "qualified conservation purpose" is broadened, and rules applicable to green community programs are liberalized.

¶645 CREBs. The new clean renewable energy bonds (CREBs) program is expanded, and additional bonds are authorized to finance qualified renewable energy facilities that generate electricity.

¶650 Exempt bond interest and AMT. For purposes of the alternative minimum tax (AMT), tax-exempt interest on private activity bonds issued in 2009 and 2010 is not treated as a tax preference item or included in a corporation's AMT income for purposes of computing its adjusted current earnings.

¶655 High-speed intercity rail. Speed requirements are modified for high-speed intercity rail facilities that can be financed with exempt facility bonds.

¶660 Industrial development bonds. For industrial development bonds issued in 2009 and 2010, the definition of manufacturing facilities is expanded with respect to intangible property and facilities that are directly related and subordinate to a manufacturing facility.

¶665 Tribal bonds. Indian tribal governments may issue up to $2 billion in tax-exempt bonds nationally for projects to spur economic development on tribal lands, without regard to the usual "essential government function" requirement

¶5

GROUP HEALTH INSURANCE AND OTHER PROVISIONS

¶705, ¶710 **COBRA premium assistance.** Certain involuntarily terminated employees can qualify for a 65-percent reduction in their premiums to maintain health insurance through their former employers under COBRA (Consolidated Omnibus Budget Reconciliation Act of 1985). A penalty is imposed on workers who fail to notify the health plan when they cease to be eligible for the assistance.

¶715 **COBRA extension.** COBRA continuation coverage is extended for certain workers who are eligible for benefits from the Pension Benefit Guaranty Corporation (PBGC) or under the Trade Adjustment Assistance Act (TAA).

¶720 **Group health plan enrollment.** A special 60-day period for enrollment in an employer's group health plan is triggered by certain determinations regarding the eligibility of an employee or dependent for Medicaid or children's health insurance program (CHIP) benefits.

¶725 **HCTC.** The health coverage tax credit (HCTC), a benefit under the Trade Adjustment Assistance Act, is increased to 80 percent of the taxpayer's premiums for qualified health insurance through 2010.

¶730 **Tobacco excise taxes.** Excise taxes on several tobacco products are increased, and the Treasury Department's regulatory and enforcement authority of with respect to tobacco and alcohol is strengthened.

Taxpayers Affected

AMERICAN RECOVERY AND REINVESTMENT TAX ACT OF 2009

¶101 Overview

INDIVIDUALS

¶105 Effect on Individuals Generally
¶107 Effect on First-Time Homebuyers
¶109 Effect on Homeowners
¶111 Effect on Individuals Subject to the AMT
¶113 Effect on Purchasers of Automobiles, Motorcycles, Light Trucks, and Motor Homes
¶115 Effect on Owners of Alternative Powered Vehicles
¶117 Effect on Parents
¶119 Effect on Recipients of Social Security and Other Benefits
¶121 Effect on the Unemployed
¶123 Effect on Residents of U.S. Possessions
¶125 Effect on Students
¶127 Effect on Small Business Owners
¶129 Effect on Investors Generally
¶131 Effect on Investors in Tax Credit and Tax-Exempt Bonds
¶133 Effect on Veterans
¶135 Effect on "Disconnected" Youth
¶137 Effect on Commuters
¶138 Effect on Tobacco Users
¶139 Effect on Certain Employees of TARP Participants

BUSINESSES

¶151 Effect on Business Generally
¶153 Effect on Small Business
¶155 Effect on Corporations

¶157 Effect on Partnerships
¶159 Effect on S Corporations
¶161 Effect on Financial Institutions
¶163 Effect on Regulated Investment Companies
¶165 Effect on Renewable Energy Producers and Facilities
¶167 Effect on Government Contractors
¶171 Effect on Low-Income Housing Industry
¶173 Effect on Computer Industry
¶175 Effect on Auto Industry
¶177 Effect on Aviation Industry
¶179 Effect on Tobacco Industry
¶181 Effect on Manufacturers of Intangibles
¶183 Effect on Railroad Industry
¶185 Effect on Building Contractors

TAX-EXEMPT ORGANIZATIONS AND GOVERNMENT ENTITIES

¶187 Effect on State and Local Government Entities
¶189 Effect on Indian Tribal Governments
¶191 Effect on State Housing Agencies
¶193 Effect on U.S. Possessions
¶195 Effect on the IRS and Treasury

STATE TAX CONSEQUENCES

¶197 Effect on State Tax Law

RECOVERY ACT SAMPLE SCENARIOS

¶199 Sample Scenarios for Individuals

AMERICAN RECOVERY AND REINVESTMENT TAX ACT OF 2009

¶101 Overview

The American Recovery and Reinvestment Property Tax Act of 2009 is part of a massive $787 billion legislative vehicle comprised of tax breaks, spending on infrastructure, health care, and alternative energy, in addition to aid to the states and local governments. For individuals, the legislation includes the $400 ($800 for joint filers) Making Work Pay Credit (¶305) while Social Security recipients, disabled veterans, and retired railroad workers will instead receive a $250 economic stimulus payment (¶225), and certain recipients of government pensions or annuities can qualify for a separate credit (¶325). Also included is a "patch" to protect against the alternative minimum tax for 2009 (¶235) and the extension and modification of the first-time homebuyer credit (¶310). Hopefully, auto sales will be spurred by a deduction for sales and excise taxes paid on the purchase of a new car, light truck, motorcycle, or motor home (¶230). Additional changes expand application of the refundable Child Tax Credit (¶315) and the Earned Income Tax Credit (¶320). A new form of education tax credit, the American Opportunity Tax Credit, which will be partially refundable, will also be available (¶330). Unemployed persons will benefit from suspension of income tax on up to $2,400 of unemployment benefits for 2009 (¶205). Parents and students will appreciate the expansion of eligible expenses for 529 plans to include computers and related technology (¶220). However, executives and some other employees of banks participating in the Troubled Asset Relief Program may not be happy with new restrictions on their compensation (¶455). With respect to alternative energy vehicles, there is an increase in the credit for alternative fuel vehicle refueling property (¶365) and modifications to the plug-in electric drive motor vehicle credit (¶350), a new credit for two or three wheel and low-speed plug-in electric vehicles (¶345), and the availability of a credit for plug-in conversions (¶355).

Businesses did receive at least some benefits, including the extension of bonus depreciation and increased Code Sec. 179 expensing through 2009 (¶410). The carryback period for net operating losses has been raised to up to five-years (¶425), but in last-minute negotiations, the provision was scaled back to cover only businesses with gross receipts under $15 million. The categories of qualified workers under the Work Opportunity Tax Credit were expanded to include unemployed veterans and "disconnected" youth (¶540). The capital gain exclusion percentage for qualified small business stock is increased from 50 to 75 percent (¶210) and the built-in gain holding period applicable to an S corporation is dropped to seven years from 10 (¶420). Controversial Notice 2008-83, concerning the utilization of net operating losses of acquired companies has been repealed (¶430). However, this action was tempered with new rules under Code Sec. 382 applicable to restructurings pursuant to agreements with the Treasury Department that should benefit certain financially troubled companies (e.g., General Motors) (¶435). The legislation also includes a number of new or enhanced bond provisions aimed at economic recovery and alternative energy (¶605, ¶610, ¶615, ¶625, ¶630, ¶635, ¶640, ¶645, ¶650, ¶652, ¶655, ¶660, and ¶665).

INDIVIDUALS

¶105 Effect on Individuals Generally

Making Work Pay Credit.—For 2009 and 2010, new Code Sec. 36A provides a credit against income computed as the lesser of 6.2 percent of earned income or $400 ($800 for joint filers) (¶305). The credit phases out at two percent of modified adjusted gross income (MAGI) in excess of $75,000 ($150,000). Accordingly, the phase out would be complete at $95,000 ($190,000 for joint filers). The amount of the credit must be reduced by the amount of a payment received pursuant to another provision of the American Recovery and Reinvestment Act of 2009, such as the economic recovery payments available to Social Security recipients, disabled veterans, and railroad workers (¶ 225) or the credit for certain government retirees (¶ 325). The credit is not available to nonresident aliens, dependents, or an estate or trust. In addition, taxpayers must satisfy taxpayer identification number (TIN) requirements similar to those applicable to the earned income tax credit in order to be eligible for the credit. Special provisions are applicable to residents of U.S. possessions. It remains to be seen how fast this credit will impact the overall economy.

¶107 Effect on First-Time Homebuyers

First-time homebuyer credit.—The amount of the first-time homebuyer credit is increased to $8,000 and the availability of the credit is extended through November 2009 (¶ 310). The repayment requirement is eliminated for purchases made after December 31, 2008, and before December 1, 2009. Recapture rules will apply if the home is disposed of or ceases to be treated as a principal residence within 36 months of the date of purchase. The prohibition against claiming the credit if the residence was financed by proceeds from a mortgage revenue bond is lifted. Taxpayers eligible for the first-time homebuyer credit will not be eligible for the first-time homebuyer credit under Code Sec. 1400C for purchases in the District of Columbia. Taxpayers contemplating an election to accelerate the benefit of the credit by treating a purchase made in 2009 as one having been made on December 31, 2008, should consider the potential negative ramifications of doing so because a strict reading of the amendments would indicate that the increased credit amount and modified financing rule would no longer be allowed.

¶109 Effect on Home Owners

Residential energy efficient property credit.—Present law caps on the Code Sec. 25D residential energy efficient property credit would be eliminated beginning in 2009 for solar hot water, geothermal, and wind property (¶ 340). Any reduction in the credit due to the use of subsidized energy financing is also eliminated.

Alternative fuel vehicle refueling property credit.—The maximum credit for installing qualified refueling property on nonbusiness property is doubled to $2,000 and the percentage is increased from 30 to 50 percent for property placed in service in 2009 and 2010 (¶ 365).

Non-business energy property tax credit.—A number of enhancements are made to the Code Sec. 25C credit for non-business energy property, including raising the rate of the credit from 10 percent to 30 percent (¶ 335). Energy property that would have been allowed a $50, $100, or $150 credit is instead eligible for a credit of 30 percent of qualifying expenditures and the aggregate amount of the cap on such expenditures is raised to $1,500 for property placed in service during 2009 and 2010. Modified standards are imposed for energy-efficient building property including electric heat pumps, central air conditioning units, and water heaters, as well as for oil furnaces, hot water boilers, and for energy efficiency improvements (e.g., windows, doors, skylights, insulation, etc.).

¶111 Effect on Individuals Subject to the AMT

AMT exemption amount.—The alternative minimum tax (AMT) exclusion amounts for tax years beginning in 2009 will be $70,950 in the case of married persons filing a joint return and surviving spouses, $46,700 for single filers, and $35,475 for married persons filing separately (¶235).

Use on nonrefundable personal credits against AMT.—The ability to fully utilize nonrefundable credits (e.g., the adoption credit, the child tax credit, and the retirement savings contribution credit) against the AMT is extended through 2009 (¶240).

Interest on private activity bonds.—Tax-exempt interest on private activity bonds issued in 2009 and 2010 will not be treated as a tax preference item for purposes of the AMT (¶650). This change will not apply to tax-exempt interest on private activity bonds issued in 2009 and 2010 used to refund a private activity bond that was issued after 2003 and before 2009.

Alternative motor vehicle credit treated as personal credit.—For 2009 and 2010, the Code Sec. 30B alternative motor vehicle credit will be treated as a nonrefundable personal credit for purposes of the alternative minimum tax (¶360).

¶113 Effect on Purchasers of Automobiles, Motorcycles, Light Trucks, and Motor Homes

Deduction for sales tax.—Purchasers of automobiles, motorcycles, and trucks with a gross vehicle weight of no more than 8,500 pounds, and motor homes, will be entitled to a deduction for state and local sales or excise taxes paid on purchases of such vehicles between the date of enactment and January 1, 2010 (¶230). The sales tax deduction will be limited to taxes imposed on an amount of $49,500 or less. Accordingly, the total price of the vehicle purchased could exceed $49,500, but only the sales tax attributable to the first $49,500 would be eligible for the deduction. An additional limitation will phase out the deduction for those individuals with modified adjusted gross incomes in excess of $125,000 ($250,000 for a married couple filing jointly) and the deduction will not be available to a taxpayer who itemizes deductions and makes an election under Code Sec. 164(b)(5) to deduct state and local sales taxes in lieu of state income taxes. The deduction for qualified motor vehicle taxes will be allowed against the alternative minimum tax and could prove to be particularly valuable for purchasers in states with relatively high tax rates on auto purchases, such as California, Illinois, Indiana, Massachusetts, Nevada, New Jersey, Rhode Island, Tennessee, and Washington.

¶115 Effect on Owners of Alternative Powered Vehicles

Alternative fuel vehicle refueling property credit.—The maximum credit for installing qualified refueling property on nonbusiness property is doubled to $2,000 and the percentage is increased from 30 to 50 percent (¶365).

Plug-in electric drive motor credit.—Effective for vehicles acquired after 2009, the maximum plug-in electric drive motor credit will be $7,500 except, in the case of a vehicle with a battery having less than a five kilowatt hour capacity, the maximum credit will be $2500 (¶345). The aggregate number of vehicles sold by a manufacturer that will trigger the phase-out of eligibility for the plug-in electric drive motor vehicle credit is changed to 200,000.

Low-speed vehicles.—Code Sec. 30 is amended to provide a credit for new categories of qualified plug-in electric vehicles, which will include certain "low-speed" and two or three-wheeled vehicles (¶350). The maximum credit is $2,500.

Plug-in conversions.—A new 10-percent credit of up to $4,000 will be available for the conversion of existing vehicles into plug-in electric drive motor vehicles before 2012 (¶355).

Alternative motor vehicle credit treated as personal credit.—For 2009 and 2010, the Code Sec. 30B alternative motor vehicle credit will be treated as a nonrefundable personal credit for purposes of the alternative minimum tax (¶360).

¶117 Effect on Parents

Earned income tax credit.—In the case of a family with three or more children, the earned income tax credit percentage is increased to 45 percent of the first $12,570 of earned income for 2009 and 2010 (¶320). In addition, the marriage penalty phase out threshold will be $5,000 more for married couples filing jointly than for single filers, surviving spouses, and heads of households and will be adjusted for inflation beginning in 2010.

Refundable child credit.—The refundable portion of the child credit will be available for 2009 and 2010 based on a formula of 15 percent of earned income in excess of a floor amount of $3,000 (¶315).

American opportunity tax credit.—A modified Hope credit, referred to as the American Opportunity Tax Credit, would be available for 100 percent of the first $2,000 of qualified tuition and related expenses (including course materials) and 25 percent of the next $2,000 of expenses (for a maximum credit of $2,500) per student for each of the first four years of post-secondary education (¶330).

The credit may be claimed against the alternative minimum tax and 40 percent of the credit would be refundable although no portion would be refundable if the individual claiming the credit is subject to the "kiddie tax." Phase out of the credit begins at $80,000 ($160,000 for joint filers) of MAGI and ends at $90,000 ($180,000 for joint filers). Special provisions are applicable to residents of U.S. possessions. In addition, the Treasury is instructed to conduct a study of coordinating the Hope and Lifetime

Learning credits with the Pell grant program along with a study of whether community service should be required of students taking advantage of these credits.

Qualified expenses for 529 programs.—The cost of computers and certain computer equipment, software, and services will be considered a qualified expense for purposes of Code Sec. 529 qualified tuition programs, effective for expenses paid or incurred in 2009 and 2010 (¶220).

¶119 Effect on Recipients of Social Security and Other Benefits

Economic recovery payments to certain individuals.—Seniors, individuals receiving Social Security supplemental income payments, disabled veterans, and retired railroad employees will be entitled to one-time payments of $250 (¶225). The payment will reduce the amount of any allowable Making Work Pay Credit. Certain federal and state pension recipients, who are not entitled to Social Security, will instead be eligible for a one-time $250 refundable credit (¶325).

¶121 Effect on the Unemployed

Exclusion of unemployment compensation.—For 2009, the first $2,400 of unemployment compensation would be excluded from gross income (¶205).

COBRA premium assistance.—The American Recovery and Reinvestment Tax Act of 2009 includes a provision granting assistance with the payment of COBRA health insurance continuation coverage over nine months for unemployed persons and their families, if the individual pays 35 percent of the premium amount and was involuntarily terminated between September 1, 2008, and December 31, 2009 (¶705). Individuals who were involuntarily terminated between September 1, 2008, and February 17, 2009, but did not elect COBRA coverage, will have an additional 60 days to make an election and receive the subsidy. Persons receiving assistance under this provision will not be considered eligible individuals for purposes of the health insurance cost deduction under Code Sec. 35. The Recovery Act also imposes a penalty for the failure of an assistance eligible individual to notify a group health plan as to the cessation of eligibility for COBRA premium assistance (¶710). The penalty is equal to 110 percent of the amount of any premium reduction after eligibility for such reduction terminated. COBRA continuation coverage is also extended with respect to certain covered employees who are "PBGC recipients" or "TAA-eligible individuals" (¶715).

Special enrollment period for group health plans.—Under the Children's Health Insurance Program Reauthorization Act of 2009 (P.L. 111-3), a group health plan must permit an employee or dependent of the employee who is eligible, but not enrolled, to enroll in the plan if the employee or dependent applies for coverage not later than 60 days after either: (1) the employee's or dependent's Medicaid or Children's Health Insurance Program coverage is terminated as a result of loss of eligibility for such coverage; or (2) the employee or dependent is determined to be eligible for employment assistance under Medicaid or Children's Health Insurance Program to help pay for coverage under the plan (¶720).

Trade Act assistance.—Under the Trade Act Assistance Health Coverage Improvement Act of 2009 (P.L. 111-5), the amount of the Health Coverage Trade Credit is increased to 80 percent for eligible coverage months beginning before 2011 (¶725). The amount of the credit that may be paid in advance directly to a health care provider will also be 80 percent of the amount paid by a taxpayer for eligible coverage months beginning before 2011.

¶123 Effect on Residents of U.S. Possessions

Payments similar to Making Work Payment Credit.—Residents of U.S. possessions having either a "mirror Code" or non-mirror Code tax system will be entitled to payments in amounts similar to that provided under the Making Work Pay Credit for U.S. citizens (¶305).

¶125 Effect on Students

American opportunity tax credit.—A modified Hope credit, referred to as the American Opportunity Tax Credit, would be available for 100 percent of the first $2,000 of qualified tuition and related expenses (including course materials) and 25 percent of the next $2,000 of expenses (for a maximum credit of $2,500) per student for each of the first four years of post-secondary education (¶330).

The credit may be claimed against the alternative minimum tax and 40 percent of the credit would be refundable although no portion would be refundable if the individual claiming the credit is subject to the "kiddie tax." Phase out of the credit begins at $80,000 ($160,000 for joint filers) of MAGI and ends at $90,000 ($180,000 for joint filers). Special provisions are applicable to residents of U.S. possessions. The Treasury is also instructed to conduct a study of coordinating the Hope and Lifetime Learning credits with the Pell grant program along with a study of whether community service should be required of students taking advantage of these credits.

Qualified expenses for 529 programs.—Recognizing the increased importance of computer technology for college students, the cost of computers and certain computer equipment, software, and services will be considered a qualified expense for purposes of Code Sec. 529 qualified tuition programs, effective for expenses paid or incurred in 2009 and 2010 (¶220).

¶127 Effect on Small Business Owners

Estimated tax payments.—The applicable safe-harbor percentage governing estimated tax payments of an individual who has an adjusted gross incomes of less than $500,000 ($250,000 for married persons filing separately) and who receives more than 50 percent of his or her gross income from a small business (those with an average of less than 500 employees), is lowered from 100 percent to 90 percent for 2009 (¶465).

¶129 Effect on Investors Generally

Exclusion of gain from qualified small business stock.—For qualified small business stock acquired after the date of enactment and before 2011, the exclusion percentage applicable to gain on the sale of such stock is increased from 50 percent to 75 (¶210).

¶131 Effect on Investors in Tax Credit and Tax-Exempt Bonds

AMT break for private activity bonds.—The American Recovery and Reinvestment Tax Act of 2009 provides that tax-exempt interest on private activity bonds issued in 2009 and 2010 will not be treated as a preference item for purposes of the alternative minimum tax (¶650).

Pass-through to mutual fund investors.—The pass-through of credits attributable to tax credit bonds to shareholders of registered investment companies (mutual funds) will be elective rather than mandatory, effective for tax years ending after the date of enactment (¶615).

New and expanded bond programs.—Additional amounts have been allocated for clean renewable energy bonds (¶645), qualified conservation bonds (¶640), and qualified zone academy bonds (¶635). Rules governing industrial development bonds (¶660) and exempt facility bonds for high-speed rail (¶655) have been clarified in an effort to expand the reach of these bond programs. New categories of bonds include qualified school construction bonds (¶630), Build America bonds (¶605), recovery zone facility bonds (¶652) and recovery zone economic development bonds (¶625). In addition, a new category of tax-exempt bonds called tribal economic developments bonds (¶665) have been created that temporarily eliminates the "essential governmental function" requirement ordinarily imposed on tax-exempt bonds issued by tribal governments.

¶133 Effect on Veterans

Economic recovery payments to certain individuals.—Disabled veterans will be entitled to a $250 one-time payment (¶225). The payment will reduce the amount of any allowable Making Work Pay Credit.

New category for work opportunity credit.—The categories for which employers may claim the work opportunity tax credit are expanded to include unemployed veterans released from active duty during the five-year period prior to hiring and who received unemployment compensation for more than four weeks during the year preceding hiring (¶540).

¶ 135 Effect on "Disconnected" Youth

New category for work opportunity credit.—The categories for which employers may claim the work opportunity tax credit are expanded to include "disconnected" youth (¶ 540). This would include individuals between 16 and 25 who have not been regularly employed or attended school within the past six months prior to hiring and who are not readily employable due to a lack of basic skills.

¶ 137 Effect on Commuters

Exclusion of qualified transportation fringe benefits.—In a change aimed at promoting more environmentally friendly commuting, the monthly exclusion for employer-provided vanpool and transit benefits is increased to the same level as that applicable to employer-provided parking ($230 in 2009) (¶ 215).

¶ 138 Effect on Tobacco Users

Tobacco users hit.—Tobacco users are again the target of increased federal excise taxes (¶ 730). Cigarette smokers in particular will face an excise tax increase of over 61 cents per pack. At a rate of $50.33 per thousand this equates to a tax of more than $1 per pack.

¶ 139 Effect on Certain Employees of TARP Participants

Incentive compensation limited.—New limits would apply to the compensation paid by financial institutions and other entities participating in the Troubled Asset Relief Program (TARP) (¶ 455). First, the $500,000 compensation deduction limit imposed by the Emergency Economic Stabilization Act of 2008 (P.L. 110-343) is now extended to all entities, not just financial institutions, that receive TARP assistance, for the period financial assistance under the program remains outstanding. Additional (nontax) changes would effectively limit bonuses and other incentive compensation paid to certain employees. This provision could have a serious impact on the hiring and retention policies of employees by entities participating in TARP. The provision is effective upon enactment.

The applicability of the new bonus restrictions is dependent on how much money the firm has received in government assistance. If the entity received less than $25 million, the limits would apply to only the highest-paid employee. For those entities that received $25 million to $250 million, the restriction would apply to at least the five highest-paid employees. For entities that received $250 million to $500 million, it would apply to senior executives and at least the next ten highest-paid employees. Finally, for entities that received more than $500 million, the prohibition would be applicable to senior executives and at least the next 20 highest paid employees. The

Secretary of the Treasury would have the discretion to increase the number of employees covered by this provision. Separate limits are also imposed on "golden parachute" payments to departing executives.

BUSINESSES

¶151 Effect on Business Generally

Although a number of business tax breaks were eliminated or reduced in the final negotiations leading up to enactment of the American Recovery and Reinvestment Tax Act of 2009, there remain a wide variety of provisions, many of which will apply to most businesses, some of which are particularly aimed at small business, and a number of which will primarily impact particular industries.

Bonus and other depreciation.—Additional ("bonus") first-year depreciation would be extended by the American Recovery and Reinvestment Tax Act of 2009 for an additional year through 2009 (through 2010 for certain longer-lived and transportation property) (¶415). The election to accelerate the alternative minimum tax and research credits in lieu of bonus depreciation is extended through 2009 and transition rules for extension property are added (¶505).

Deferral of cancellation of indebtedness income.—An election is provided for a taxpayer to elect to defer cancellation of indebtedness income with respect to debt repurchased in 2009 or 2010 (¶405). The legislation also temporarily suspends the limitation on the interest deduction for certain applicable high yield discount obligations issued by a corporation issued in a debt for debt exchange (¶440).

Advanced energy project credit.—A new credit under Code Sec. 48C is provided for 30-percent of the qualified investment in projects relating to renewable energy, energy storage and conservation, efficient transmission and distribution of electricity, carbon capture and sequestration, and plug-in electric drive motor vehicles. This would include projects that re-equip, expand, or establish a manufacturing facility for the production of property designed to produce energy from sun, wind, geothermal, or other renewable sources, as well as, the manufacture of fuel cells, microturbines, electric grids, or energy conservation technologies such as energy-saving lighting or smart grids. However, the advanced energy project credit is not available for taxpayers receiving the enhanced credit for energy research under Code Sec. 48(¶525).

Work opportunity tax credit.—The group of employees for which an employer may claim the Work Opportunity Tax Credit is expanded for 2009 and 2010 to include unemployed veterans and "disconnected" youth (¶540).

New markets tax credits.—The total of new markets tax credits allocated to 2008 and 2009 is increased to $5 billion for each of those years. A special rule provides for allocation of the increased amount for 2008 for qualified community development entities (CDEs) that submitted an allocation application and did not receive the full allocation requested (¶530).

Carbon dioxide sequestration credit.—In order to be eligible for the $10 per metric ton credit under Code Sec. 45Q, carbon dioxide used as a tertiary injectant must be sequestered in permanent geologic storage (¶545).

COBRA premium assistance.—New Code Sec. 6432 provides a reimbursement to employers for the amount of premiums not paid by plan beneficiaries as a result of the COBRA premium assistance amendments made by the Recovery Act. Generally, the reimbursement will be in the form of a credit against payroll taxes, but any excess would be paid to the employer (¶705). There will also be a penalty imposed for the failure of an assistance eligible individual to notify a group health plan as to the cessation of eligibility for COBRA premium assistance (¶710).

Parity for transportation fringe benefits.—The monthly exclusion for employer-provided transit and vanpool benefits is temporarily increased to $230 per month (¶215).

Making Work Pay Credit.—Businesses will be required to adjust their payroll systems and payroll deductions to accommodate the Making Work Pay Credit (¶305).

Plug-in electric vehicles.—The legislation changes the vehicle limit for the plug-in electric vehicle credit to a 200,000 per manufacturer limit (¶345), creates a new credit for low-speed and two or three wheel plug-in electric vehicles (¶350), and extends the plug-in electric vehicle credit to conversion kits (¶355). The legislation also specifies that there is no recapture under Code Sec. 30B if the conversion is to a plug-in electric vehicle. A credit for a qualified plug-in electric vehicle used for business is treated as a business credit under Code Sec. 38(b).

Alternative fuel vehicle refueling property credit.—The maximum credit for installing qualified refueling property on business property is increased to $200,000 for hydrogen refueling property and $50,000 for other refueling property, In addition, the applicable percentage is increased from 30 to 50 percent, except it remains at 30 percent for hydrogen refueling property (¶365).

Recovery zone bonds.—An additional $15 billion of bonds have been created for investments in economic recovery zones (¶652). An additional $10 billion in recovery zone economic development zone bonds are authorized (¶625).

¶153 Effect on Small Business

Net operating losses.—The carryback period for a net operating loss (NOL) is increased from two to three, four, or five years for the 2008 tax year. The provision applies to businesses with gross receipts of $15 million or less (¶425).

Expensing.—The $250,000 maximum amount of property eligible for expensing is extended through 2009 as is the $800,000 aggregate threshold on qualifying property triggering reduction of the $250,000 amount (¶410).

Qualified small business stock.—The Code Sec. 1202 exclusion for gain from the sale of certain small business stock held for more than five years is increased from 50 percent to 75 percent (¶210).

Estimated tax payments.—The required estimated tax payment safe harbor for certain small businesses for 2009 is reduced to 90 percent of the tax due on the prior year's return (¶465). To qualify an individual's return must show adjusted gross income for the prior year of less than $500,000 and more than 50 percent of the gross income must be from a business which employed less than 500 employees.

¶155 Effect on Corporations

Built-in gains of S corporations.—The recognition period governing the tax imposed on built-in gains that are recognized following the transformation of a C corporation to an S corporation is temporarily reduced from 10 years to seven (¶420).

Estimated tax.—Corporations with assets of $1,000,000,000 or more will face a 0.5 percentage point increase in the percentage amount applicable to estimated taxes that will be due in July, August, or September of 2013 under the Children's Health Insurance Program Reauthorization Act of 2009 (P.L. 111-3) (¶470).

Deferral of cancellation of indebtedness income.—An election is provided for a taxpayer to elect to defer cancellation of indebtedness income with respect to debt repurchased in 2009 or 2010 (¶405). The legislation also temporarily suspends the limitation on the interest deduction for certain applicable high yield discount obligations issued by a corporation issued in a debt for debt exchange (¶440).

Election in lieu of bonus depreciation.—The election available to a corporation to accelerate the alternative minimum tax and research credits in lieu of bonus depreciation is extended through 2009 and transition rules for extension property are added (¶505).

Tax-exempt bonds.—Bonds issued in 2009 and 2010 are not private activity bonds for alternative minimum tax purposes and no adjustment need be made to a corporation's adjusted current earnings for such interest (¶650).

¶157 Effect on Partnerships

The legislation specifies how the deferral of cancellation of indebtedness income is passed through to partners from the partnership (¶405). There is also an acceleration provision that would apply on the sale of a partnership interest. The election is to be made at the entity level.

¶159 Effect on S Corporations

Deferral of COD income.—The new provision in the legislation on the deferral of cancellation of indebtedness specifies that the election is to be made at the entity level, rather than the shareholder level (¶405). There is also an acceleration provision that would apply on the sale of an interest in the S Corporation.

Built-in gain holding period.—The built-in gains holding period for C Corporations converting to S Corporation status is reduced temporarily from ten to seven years (¶420).

¶161 Effect on Financial Institutions

Limits on executive compensation.—The new legislation puts limits on the compensation that may be received by financial institutions that receive financial assistance from the government under the troubled asset relief program. Restrictions would be applied on up to 25 of the most highly compensated employees. The restrictions apply to both past and future recipients of government assistance (¶455).

Limitation on built-in losses following ownership change.—The application of IRS Notice 2008-83 (I.R.B. 2008-42, 905) with respect to the acquisition of entities having built-in losses is restricted to changes of ownership occurring on or before January 16, 2009, unless the change of ownership was subject to a written binding agreement or was disclosed in a public announcement or Securities and Exchange Commission filing prior to that date. Notice 2008-83 received critical scrutiny following a number of high profile acquisitions, such as that of National City Corp. by PNC Financial Services Group, that occurred after the federal government intervened to save a number of financial entities during the fourth quarter of 2008 (¶430). In addition, new rules would govern the application of Code Sec. 382 to certain company restructurings pursuant to the Emergency Economic Stabilization Act of 2008. This provision appears to have been inserted primarily to benefit General Motors Corporation (¶435).

Tax-exempt interest safe harbor.—The American Recovery and Reinvestment Tax Act of 2009 provides a de minimis safe harbor for the tax-exempt interest expense of financial institutions with respect to tax-exempt obligations issued in 2009 and 2010 that do not exceed two percent of adjusted basis of the financial institutions assets. Tax-exempt obligations issued in 2009 and 2010 that are not taken into account in computing that portion of the financial institution's interest expense that is subject to disallowance under Code Sec. 265(b) will be deemed to be financial institution preference items, thus reducing the amount allowable as an interest deduction for carrying such obligations by 20 percent (¶445). The definition of a "qualified small issuer" under Code Sec. 265(b)(3)(G)(i) is modified to increase the annual limit from $10 million to $30 million. Further modifications are made in applying the $30 million limit to a "pooled financing issue" under Code Sec. 265(b)(3)(G)(iv) (¶450).

¶163 Effect on Regulated Investment Companies

The legislation provides an election for passing through credits on tax credit bonds to the shareholders of an electing regulated investment company in place of a mandatory pass through (¶615).

¶165 Effect on Renewable Energy Producers and Facilities

Production credit tax extended.—The Code Sec. 45 credit for electricity produced from renewable energy resources is extended through 2012 for wind facilities and through 2013 for qualifying closed-loop and open-loop biomass facilities, as well as those providing power from geothermal, solar, hydroelectric, landfill gas, trash, marine, and hydrokinetic renewable resources (¶520).

Temporary election to claim investment tax credit.—Under the American Recovery and Reinvestment Tax Act of 2009, qualified renewable energy facilities may elect the 30-percent investment tax credit available under Code Sec. 48 instead of the production tax credit. The election is available for qualified wind facilities placed in service in 2009 through 2012 and through 2013 for qualifying closed-loop and open-loop biomass facilities, and for those providing power from geothermal, solar, hydroelectric, landfill gas, trash, marine, and hydrokinetic renewable resources (¶510). The Recovery Act would also eliminate the credit cap for small wind energy property and also eliminate a provision that reduces the credit for taxpayers who finance their facility with subsidized energy financing or the proceeds from private activity bonds (¶510).

Energy property subject to grant.—If the property is subject to a grant authorized by the Recovery Act, the property is not eligible for the Code Sec. 45 or Code Sec. 48 credit (¶515).

Credit for alternative refueling property.—The alternative refueling property credit for businesses for 2009 and 2010 is increased to 50 percent, with a $50,000 cap, except for hydrogen refueling property, at 30 percent, with a $200,000 cap (¶365).

Carbon dioxide sequestration credit.—In order to be eligible for the $10 per metric ton credit under Code Sec. 45Q, carbon dioxide used as a tertiary injectant must be sequestered in permanent geological storage (¶545).

Clean Renewable Energy Bonds.—An additional $1.6 billion in Clean Renewable Energy Bonds is authorized to finance qualified renewable energy facilities that generate electricity (¶645).

¶167 Effect on Government Contractors

Withholding rules.—The three-percent withholding rate that was set to apply to payments made to government contractors after 2010 is pushed back one year to December 31, 2011 (¶460).

¶171 Effect on Low-Income Housing Industry

Low-income housing grants.—An election is created under the American Recovery and Reinvestment Tax Act of 2009 to substitute grants to states for low-income housing projects in lieu of a low-income housing credit allocation for 2009. Builders of low-income housing may be entitled to a subaward for the construction or acquisition and rehabilitation of low-income properties from a state receiving a grant under a program to substitute grants for the low-income housing credit allocation (¶535).

¶173 Effect on Computer Industry

Computer technology and equipment is allowed as a higher education expense for Code Sec. 529 plans (¶220).

¶175 Effect on Auto Industry

Plug-in electric vehicles.—The legislation changes the vehicle limit for the plug-in electric vehicle credit to a 200,000 per manufacturer limit (¶345), creates a new credit for low-speed and two or three wheel plug-in electric vehicles (¶350), and extends the plug-in electric vehicle credit to conversion kits (¶355). The legislation also specifies that there is no recapture under Code Sec. 30B if the conversion is to a plug-in electric vehicle.

Tax deduction for auto purchase.—A new deduction is created for sales and excise taxes with respect to the purchase of a new automobile (¶230).

Use of net operating loss carryforwards.——General Motors and similarly situated automakers were protected from Code Sec. 382 limits on the use of net operating losses with respect to a restructuring resulting from an agreement with the Treasury Department under the Emergency Economic Stabilization Act of 2008 (¶435).

¶177 Effect on the Aviation Industry

The placed-in-service deadline for bonus depreciation for commercial aircraft and certain noncommercial aircraft, as well as other property with a longer production period, is extended to January 1, 2011 (¶415).

¶179 Effect on Tobacco Industry

The legislation providing funding for the supplemental children's health insurance program includes an increase in the excise tax on tobacco products—the Children's Health Insurance Program Reauthorization Act of 2009 (P.L. 111-3) (¶730).

¶181 Effect on Manufacturers of Intangibles

Manufacturing facilities producing intangible property can now qualify for industrial development bonds if the facility producing intangible property is functionally related to, subordinate to, and on the same site as the manufacturing facility for tangible property (¶660).

¶183 Effect on Railroad Industry

High speed rail.—Facility bonds available for high speed trains and rail facilities require only a maximum speed in excess of 150 miles per hour rather than an operating speed at that level (¶655).

Economic stimulus payments.—Railroad retirees are eligible for a $250 one-time economic stimulus payment (¶225).

¶185 Effect on Building Contractors

Schools.—An additional $22 billion in new tax credit bonds have been made available for school construction and repair (¶630).

Build America.—New build America bonds are authorized that provide both an interest payment and a tax credit (¶605).

TAX-EXEMPT ORGANIZATIONS AND GOVERNMENT ENTITIES

¶187 Effect on State and Local Government Entities

New and expanded bond programs.—The American Recovery and Reinvestment Tax Act of 2009 adds a number of new categories of tax credit and tax-exempt bonds. The Recovery Act also makes a number of beneficial modifications to existing bond programs.

Build America bonds.—The Recovery Act gives state and local governments the option of issuing a tax credit bond in lieu of a tax exempt bond (¶605) and, for bonds issued in 2009 and 2010, allows the state or local government to receive a direct payment from the federal government equal to the credit they would otherwise have received (¶610.

Clean renewable energy bonds.—An additional $1.6 billion is authorized to finance qualifying closed-loop and open-loop biomass facilities, and those providing power from geothermal, solar, hydroelectric, landfill gas, trash, marine, and hydrokinetic renewable resources (¶645). This amount will be divided in three equal portions among states and local government entities, public power companies, and electric cooperatives.

Qualified energy conservation bonds.——The limitation on bonds used to facilitate a reduction in energy consumption and the emission of greenhouse gases is increased to $3.2 billion (¶ 640).

Qualified zone academy bonds.—Qualified zone academy bonds are extended through 2010 and the limitation for 2009 and 2010 is raised to $1.4 billion (¶ 635).

Qualified school construction bonds.—A new category of tax credit bonds is created for the construction, rehabilitation, or repair of a public school facility or for the acquisition of land on which such a facility is to be constructed (¶ 630). National limits are placed on the total amount of such bonds and a specific allocation limit is applicable to Indian schools.

Recovery zone facility bonds and economic development bonds.—The Recovery Act creates new categories of tax credit and exempt facilities bonds (¶ 625 and ¶ 652). Each state will receive at least 0.9 percent of the national allocation limitation on such bonds, plus an additional amount based on the degree of job loss suffered in the state during 2008. States may then allocate these bonds to counties and large municipalities based on each county's or large municipality's employment decline. Bonds must be issued prior to 2011 to qualify.

Exempt facility bonds for high-speed rail.—The Recovery Act clarifies that vehicles used in high-speed intercity rail lines need not necessarily operate at speeds in excess of 150 miles per hour, but only that they be capable of attaining such speeds (¶ 655).

Industrial development bonds.—Modifications intended to expand the reach of industrial development bonds amend the definition of a manufacturing facility to include those used in the manufacture, creation, or production of intangible (e.g., patents, copyrights, formulas, processes, designs, patterns, etc.), as well as tangible property (¶ 660). In addition, the new law clarifies application of a limitation on the issuance of bonds for "ancillary" components of a manufacturing facility.

Grants in lieu of low-income housing credit allocations.—States may elect to receive a grant for low-income housing rather than the credit allocation otherwise available as determined under Code Sec. 42(h). Builders of low-income housing may be entitled to a subaward for the construction or acquisition and rehabilitation of low-income properties from a state receiving a grant under the program (¶ 535).

¶ 189 Effect on Indian Tribal Governments

Tribal economic development bonds.—A new category of tax-exempt bonds have been created that temporarily eliminates the "essential governmental function" requirement ordinarily imposed on tax-exempt bonds issued by tribal governments. The overall cap on the issuance of such bonds is $2 billion (¶ 665). A Treasury Department study of the impact of this modification is required. The new bonds will not be available to finance the cost of gaming facilities or any facility outside of the tribe's reservation.

¶191 Effect on State Housing Agencies

Grants.—State housing agencies may be entitled to a grant from the Treasury in lieu of low-income housing credit allocation (¶535).

¶193 Effect on U.S. Possessions

Payments to possessions.—The U.S. Treasury will make payments to U.S. possessions (e.g., Commonwealth of Puerto Rico, U.S. Virgin Islands, Guam, and the North Mariana Islands) to make up for the make work pay credit available to residents of possessions (¶305) and the American Opportunity Tax Credit (¶330).

¶195 Effect on the IRS and Treasury

Treasury Studies.—The Treasury is instructed to conduct a study of coordinating the Hope and Lifetime Learning credits with the Pell grant program along with a study of whether community service should be required of students taking advantage of these credits (¶330). In addition, the Treasury is instructed to study the impact of the issuance of new "tribal development bonds" (¶665).

STATE TAX CONSEQUENCES

¶197 Effect on State Tax Law

The American Recovery and Reinvestment Act of 2009 (P.L. 111-5) poses a significant dilemma for the states. Although a state may wish to attempt to boost its economy by adopting some of the Act's provisions (like the above-the-line deductions for certain motor vehicle purchases), they cannot afford to create deeper revenue shortfalls. The majority of the states are, or will soon be, in legislative session, and how they decide to respond to the 2009 Recovery Act will greatly impact taxpayers in the 2008 and subsequent tax years. Some states that have traditionally adopted federal tax law for purposes of computing taxable income have already introduced legislation that would not incorporate the 2009 Recovery Act (Oregon, H.B. 2157, for example). The state tax consequences of a number of these provisions are discussed, below.

Bonus depreciation.—The extension of the allowance of first-year 50 percent bonus depreciation through 2009 would affect only those states that have not decoupled from Code Sec. 168(k) and that have Code conformity dates that would not include the extension of the provision. For those states like Delaware, Idaho, and Louisiana, the extension will not apply unless/until they update their conformity dates. However states that allow bonus depreciation and that conform to the Code annually (including Virginia) will most likely conform to the extension during their next legislative sessions. However, more states have been decoupling from bonus depreciation to alleviate further state revenue shortfalls. The majority of states have decoupled from federal bonus depreciation and they will not be affected by the extension (¶415).

Code Sec. 179 asset expense election.—The extension through 2009 of the increased Code Sec. 179 expense allowance and limitation amounts for property placed in service in 2008, will not impact states, including California, Florida, Indiana, New Jersey, and Wisconsin that have decoupled from the federal expensing allowance and limitation. For states like Connecticut, Illinois, Massachusetts, Michigan, and Pennsylvania that adopt the federal allowance and limitation amounts, whether they adopt this amendment will depend on their Code conformity dates. Those states that update their Code conformity dates annually will most likely conform during their next legislative sessions. However, more states have been decoupling from the increased expense allowances and limitations to alleviate further state revenue shortfalls (¶410).

Five-year NOL carryback for small businesses.—The five-year carryback provision for small business losses incurred for any tax year beginning or ending in 2008 will impact states that allow a net operating loss (NOL) carryback. Some states, including Florida, Illinois, Massachusetts, New Jersey, Ohio, and Pennsylvania do not allow NOL carrybacks. Most states, including Delaware, Indiana, Kansas, Louisiana, and Maryland that do allow NOLs to be carried back limit the carryback to two or three years. Most of these states have not conformed to prior special carryback periods and in any event, most will be out of conformity until they update their Code conformity dates during their next legislative sessions. Taxpayers should check the 2008 appropriate state form instructions for guidance as to whether a state adjustment must be made if 2008 losses were carried back for federal tax purposes (¶425).

Election to accelerate AMT/R&D credits in lieu of bonus depreciation.—The extension through 2009 of the Code Sec. 168(k) provision that allows a taxpayer to accelerate its federal alternative minimum tax and research and development credits in lieu of claiming bonus depreciation will not be available in most states. The vast majority of states do not incorporate either of these federal credits. Therefore, the credit alternative will not be allowed even in states like Colorado, Delaware, Idaho, Louisiana, Montana, and New Mexico that incorporate Code Sec. 168(k) and allow bonus depreciation. Because the starting point for computing taxable income in these states is federal taxable income, if a taxpayer elects to claim the credits in lieu of bonus depreciation on the federal return, the amount of bonus depreciation that could have been claimed will not flow through to the state return. This raises a planning issue for a taxpayer that is taxable in one or more of these states. The taxpayer will have to determine whether the tax benefit gained on the federal return by claiming the credits will offset the loss of the bonus depreciation deduction that could be claimed on these state returns (¶505).

COBRA premium assistance—new Code Sec. 139C.—The exclusion from gross income under new Code Sec. 139C for COBRA premium assistance payments will impact states that do not adopt federal tax law as currently amended or that only incorporate specific Code sections. For those states without conforming legislation, either updating their Code conformity dates or specifically incorporating Code Sec. 139C, the amounts excluded from federal adjusted gross income would have to be added back for state income tax purposes. However, because the exclusion applies to tax years ending after the date of enactment, most states will likely conform by the time the exclusion takes effect (¶705).

Tax credits.—Generally, states do not incorporate federal tax credits. Therefore, the Making Work Pay credit, the increases to the earned income and child tax credits, the American Opportunity credit (HOPE Scholarship credit), the first-time homebuyers credit, the extension of the work opportunity tax credit to veterans and disconnected youth, the credit for government retirees, the tax credit for taxable government bonds, the energy credits, and the modifications to the new markets credit will not impact the states (¶305 et seq. and ¶505 et seq.).

Although the states do not incorporate the energy credits, several states have similar independent credits, including Arizona, Colorado, Kansas, Kentucky, Louisiana, Maryland, New York, Oklahoma, Oregon, and Virginia (¶335, ¶340, ¶515, ¶520 and ¶525).

Interest from private activity bonds excluded from AMT.—The majority of states do not impose an alternative minimum tax (AMT). Most of the states that impose an AMT based on, or paralleling federal AMT provisions for personal income tax purposes (including California and New York) generally already exclude tax-exempt interest from their list of preference items (¶650).

Withholding tax on payments made by government entities.—The delay of the requirement on government entities to withhold on payments for certain property or services does not impact the states because the states generally do not adopt the federal withholding provisions, but have their own withholding provisions (¶460).

AMT patch.—The majority of states do not impose an alternative minimum tax (AMT). Most of the states that impose an AMT based on, or paralleling federal AMT provisions for personal income tax purposes (including California and New York) provide their own exemption amounts. Therefore, the increase in the federal AMT exemption amounts would have no state tax impact.

Additionally, because the states generally do not adopt federal credits, the extension of the use of personal credits against the AMT would have no impact on state taxation (¶235 and ¶240).

Expansion of Code Sec. 529 qualified distribution to include computer technology and equipment.—The expansion of tax-exempt distributions from a Code Sec. 529 college plan to include distributions used for computer technology and equipment will impact states, like California, Pennsylvania, and Wisconsin, which follow federal tax law with regard to expenses that qualify a distribution for tax exemption, but that may have Code conformity dates that would not include this amendment. Some states, such as Connecticut, define "qualified withdrawals" or "qualified distributions" without reference to the Code and, therefore, would not include expenses used for computer technology and equipment without conforming legislation (¶220).

Exclusion of UI benefits.—The provision that would allow up to $2,400 of unemployment compensation to be excluded from federal gross income would require an addition to federal adjusted gross income in states that adopt Code Sec. 85, but that have Code conformity dates that would not incorporate the exclusion. Most states do follow federal law with regard to taxation of unemployment compensation and those states that update their Code conformity date annually will most likely continue to conform. California, Virginia, and Pennsylvania do not tax any unemployment compensation, while Arkansas, Indiana, and Wisconsin tax some, but not all unemployment compensation (¶ 205).

Deferral of income from cancellation of debt.—Most states conform to Code Sec. 108 regarding the exclusion from income of a discharge of indebtedness. Therefore, unless a state has a Code conformity date that would not incorporate the amendment that requires a discharge of indebtedness in connection with the reacquisition of a debt instrument in 2009 and 2010 to be included in gross income ratably over five taxable years, most states will conform. In addition, because the provision applies to discharges after 2008, most state will conform by the time the provision takes effect. However, some states (California and Illinois, for example) require adjustments to other items such as net operating losses, capital losses and carryovers, and basis for discharges of indebtedness. If those states do not conform to the new deferral provision for 2009 and 2010, the taxpayer may have to make different adjustments to such items for federal and state tax purposes (¶ 405).

Small business stock—increased exclusion.—The increased exclusion from 50 percent to 75 percent from gains on the sale of small business stock will impact those states that incorporate the federal exclusion (like Kentucky, Louisiana, and Oregon), but that have a Code conformity date that would not adopt the increase. Most states that update their conformity dates on an annual basis will conform during their next legislative sessions and, therefore, will conform for the 2009 tax year. For states like Wisconsin that do not allow the exclusion, amounts excluded on the federal income tax return will continue to be added back to federal income (¶ 210).

S corporations—reduced holding period for built-in gains.—The majority of states conform to the federal tax treatment of S corporations, including the taxation of built-in gains. Those conforming states that have Code conformity dates before the reduced holding period for avoiding tax on built-in gains when a C corporation elects S corporation status will most likely conform by updating their conformity dates. Thus, these states will adopt the new holding period for C corporations that convert to S corporations in 2009 and 2010. Some states, like Alabama, have similar but separate provisions regarding built-in gains that specify the existing 10-year holding period. These states would require additional legislation to conform the seven-year holding period (¶ 420).

Transportation fringe benefits—increased exclusion for van pooling and transit passes.—Most states adopt the federal income tax exclusion for employer-provided fringe benefits. The increase in the exclusion for van pooling and transit passes for 2009 and 2010 will impact states that have Code conformity dates that do not, or will not, include the increase by the 2009 tax year. For those states that do not conform, amounts not included in federal adjusted gross income will have to be added back for state tax purposes. Several states, including New Jersey, have separate provisions that are not tied to the federal exclusion. The increase will have no impact on those states (¶ 215).

Economic recovery payments.—Because the exclusion from gross income of the one-time payment to certain recipients of SSI, Social Security, Veterans, and Railroad Retirement benefits is uncodified, the states will have to conform through specific legislation or administrative act. For those states that fail to do so, the payments will have to be added back to federal adjusted gross income for state tax purposes (¶ 225).

Deduction of taxes on certain vehicles.—Most states will not adopt the itemized deduction for state sales or excise taxes on certain vehicles purchases after 2008, because most states do not allow a deduction for state sales taxes and such deductions taken on the federal income tax return must be added back for state income tax purposes. Those states that do allow the itemized deduction for states sales taxes in lieu of income taxes, under Code Sec. 164, would not necessarily adopt the additional standard deduction for nonitemizers. Most states either do not allow a standard deduction or have their own standard deduction, which is independent of the federal standard deduction. Without legislation adopting the additional standard deduction for nonitemizers, taxpayers will have to check the 2009 appropriate form instructions for guidance as to whether a state adjustment will have to be made on the 2009 state return (¶230).

Treatment of certain ownership changes for purposes of Code Sec. 382 limitations.—The exception to the Code Sec. 382 limitation for ownership changes occurring pursuant to certain restructuring plans required under loan agreements or line of credit commitments entered into with the Treasury Department under the Economic Emergency Stabilization Act of 2008 (P.L.110-343) will impact those states that adopt Code Sec. 382, but that have Code conformity date that would adopt the exception. Taxpayers should check the 2009 appropriate state form instructions for guidance as to whether a state adjustment must be made (¶435).

RECOVERY ACT SAMPLE SCENARIOS

¶199 Sample Scenarios for Individuals

The following are sample scenarios illustrating the impact of the American Recovery and Reinvestment Tax Act of 2009 on various hypothetical individual taxpayers.

Scenario 1

Single taxpayer, renter, age 67, $30,000 of AGI including Social Security benefits

	2009 Present Law	2009 Under P.L. 111-x	Difference
Adjusted Gross Income	30,000	30,000	
Standard Deduction	(7,100)	(7,100)	
Personal Exemptions	(3,650)	(3,650)	
Taxable Income	19,250	19,250	
Regular Tax	2,470	2,470	
Economic Recovery Payment		(250)	(250)
Tax Due/(Refund)	2,470	2,220	(250)

¶199

Scenario 2
Head of household, one child under age 17, $30,000 of earned income

	2009 Present Law	2009 Under P.L. 111-x	Difference
Adjusted Gross Income	30,000	30,000	
Standard Deduction	(8,350)	(8,350)	
Personal Exemptions	(7,300)	(7,300)	
Taxable Income	14,350	14,350	
Regular Tax	1,555	1,555	
Making Work Pay Credit		(400)	(400)
Earned Income Credit	(873)	(873)	
Child Credit	(1,000)	(1,000)	
Tax Due/(Refund)	(318)	(718)	(400)

Scenario 3
Married couple, four children under age 17, $30,000 of earned income

	2009 Present Law	2009 Under P.L. 111-x	Difference
Adjusted Gross Income	30,000	30,000	
Standard Deduction	(11,400)	(11,400)	
Personal Exemptions	(21,900)	(21,900)	
Taxable Income	0	0	
Regular Tax	0	0	
Making Work Pay Credit		(800)	(800)
Earned Income Credit	(2,825)	(3,850)	(1,025)
Child Credit	(2,618)	(4,000)	(1,382)
Tax Due/(Refund)	(5,443)	(8,650)	(3,207)

Scenario 4
Single taxpayer, renter, age 67, $30,000 of AGI including Social Security benefits and $5,000 of earned income

	2009 Present Law	2009 Under P.L. 111-x	Difference
Adjusted Gross Income	30,000	30,000	
Standard Deduction	(7,100)	(7,100)	
Personal Exemptions	(3,650)	(3,650)	
Taxable Income	19,250	19,250	
Regular Tax	2,470	2,470	
Economic Recovery Payment		250	(250)
Making Work Pay Credit		60	(60)
Tax Due/(Refund)	2,470	2,160	(310)

¶199

Scenario 5
Married couple, two children under age 17, $50,000 of earned income

	2009 Present Law	2009 Under P.L. 111-x	Difference
Adjusted Gross Income	50,000	50,000	
Standard Deduction	(11,400)	(11,400)	
Personal Exemptions	(14,600)	(14,600)	
Taxable Income	24,000	24,000	
Regular Tax	2,765	2,765	
Making Work Pay Credit		(800)	(800)
Child Credit	(2,000)	(2,000)	
Tax Due/(Refund)	765	(35)	(800)

Scenario 6
Single taxpayer, no children, $50,000 of earned income

	2009 Present Law	2009 Under P.L. 111-x	Difference
Adjusted Gross Income	50,000	50,000	
Standard Deduction	(5,700)	(5,700)	
Personal Exemptions	(3,650)	(3,650)	
Taxable Income	40,650	40,650	
Regular Tax	6,350	6,350	
Making Work Pay Credit		400	(400)
Tax Due/(Refund)	6,350	5,950	(400)

Scenario 7

Married couple, two children under age 17, $100,000 of income, first-time home purchase in 2009. Purchased home in Jan. 2009 and purchase price exceeded $80,000. Itemized deductions include $7,000 in taxes, $9,000 of mortgage interest expense, and $1,500 in charitable contributions

	2009 Present Law	2009 Under P.L. 111-x	Difference
Adjusted Gross Income	100,000	100,000	
Itemized Deduction	(17,500)	(17,500)	
Personal Exemptions	(14,600)	(14,600)	
Taxable Income	67,900	67,900	
Regular Tax	9,350	9,350	
Alternative Minimum Tax	2,220		(2,220)
Making Work Pay Credit		(800)	(800)
Child Credit	(2,000)	(2,000)	
First Time Homebuyer Credit	(7,500)	(8,000)	(500)
Tax Due/(Refund)	2,070	(1,450)	(3,520)

Note that under prior law, the $7,500 homebuyer credit in not a true credit but an interest free loan which may need to be repaid. Under the new law, the credit is not required to be repaid if the home remains the taxpayer's principal residence for three years.

¶199

Scenario 8

Married couple, with $100,000 of income with two children in college. Children are juniors in college and each incurred $5,000 of tuition and educational expenses. The couple also purchases a new car for $25,000 pays $1,750 of sales tax on the car. Itemized deductions include $7,000 in taxes, $9,000 of mortgage interest expenses, and $1,500 in charitable contributions.

	2009 Present Law	2009 Under P.L. 111-x	Difference
Wages	100,000	100,000	
Less Tuition and Fees Deduction	(4,000)		4,000
Adjusted Gross Income	96,000	100,000	
Itemized Deduction	(17,500)	(19,250)	(1,750)
Personal Exemptions	(14,600)	(14,600)	
Taxable Income	63,900	66,150	2,250
Regular Tax	8,750	9,088	338
Alternative Minimum Tax	1,780		(1,780)
Making Work Pay Credit		(800)	(800)
American Opportunity Tax Credit		(5,000)	(5,000)
Tax Due/(Refund)	10,530	3,288	(7,242)

Note that the prior law scenario claimed a $4,000 tuition and fees deduction. This is because under prior law, the taxpayer would be subject to the alternative minimum tax and would have received no tax benefit for claiming the lifetime learning credit.

Scenario 9

Single taxpayer, $100,000 of earned income. Itemized deductions include $7,000 in taxes, $9,000 of mortgage interest expense, and $1,500 in charitable contributions.

	2009 Present Law	2009 Under P.L. 111-x	Difference
Adjusted Gross Income	100,000	100,000	
Itemized Deduction	(17,500)	(17,500)	
Personal Exemptions	(3,650)	(3,650)	
Taxable Income	78,850	78,850	
Regular Tax	15,900	15,900	
Making Work Pay Credit		(0)	
Tax Due/(Refund)	15,900	15,900	(0)

Scenario 10

Married couple, with two children in college, $300,000 in earned income. Taxpayer has $40,000 in itemized deductions, including $5,000 in charitable contributions, $15,000 in state and local taxes, $20,000 mortgage interest.

	2009 Present Law	2009 Under P.L. 111-x	Difference
Adjusted Gross Income	300,000	300,000	
Itemized Deduction	(38,668)	(38,668)	
Personal Exemptions	(12,653)	(12,653)	
Taxable Income	248,679	248,679	
Regular Tax	59,885	59,885	
Alternative Minimum Tax	9,765	(2,499)	(7,266)
Making Work Pay Credit		(0)	
Tax Due/(Refund)	69,650	62,384	(7,266)

¶199

Individual Income and Deductions

GROSS INCOME AND DEDUCTIONS

¶205 Partial Exclusion of Unemployment Compensation Benefits
¶210 Qualified Small Business Stock
¶215 Limitation on Qualified Transportation Fringe Benefits
¶220 Qualified Expenses for Qualified Tuition Programs
¶225 Economic Recovery Payments for Recipients of Certain Federal Benefits
¶230 Deduction of Taxes on the Purchase of Certain Motor Vehicles

ALTERNATIVE MINIMUM TAX

¶235 Alternative Minimum Tax Exemption Amount
¶240 Use of Nonrefundable Personal Credits Against AMT Liability

GROSS INCOME AND DEDUCTIONS

¶205 Partial Exclusion of Unemployment Compensation Benefits

SUMMARY OF NEW LAW

An individual may exclude up to $2,400 of unemployment compensation received from gross income for 2009.

BACKGROUND

Unemployment compensation benefits are includible in gross income in the same manner as wages and other ordinary income for federal income tax purposes (Code Sec. 85(a)). Unemployment benefits include payments under federal or state law, disability payments received as a substitute for unemployment benefits, and payments under certain legislative acts and other benefit programs (Code Sec. 85(b); Reg. §1.85-1(b)). State unemployment agencies are required to permit a recipient an

BACKGROUND

election to have federal income tax withheld from their benefit payment at a 10 percent rate by filing Form W-4V, Voluntary Withholding Request (Code Sec. 3402(p)(2)). States may also (but are not required to) allow individuals who apply for unemployment benefits to elect to have state and local income tax withheld from their benefits.

Although unemployment benefits are fully includible in income, in limited situations a taxpayer may reduce the amount that is required to include in gross income. For example, if the taxpayer contributed to a governmental unemployment compensation program, and the contributions are not deductible, then amounts received under that unemployment compensation program are not included in income until the taxpayer recovers his contribution. Similarly, unemployment benefits from a private fund to which the taxpayer voluntarily contributes are taxable only to the extent that the amounts received exceed the taxpayer's total payments into the fund.

A taxpayer who is required to repay some of his unemployment benefits to qualify for trade readjustment allowances under the Trade Act of 1974 may reduce the total benefits by the amount repaid, provided that the repayment is in the same tax year as the year of receipt of the benefits. Repayments of $3,000 or less that are made in a later tax year are taken as an adjustment to gross income on Form 1040 in the year of repayment. Repayments of more than $3,000 may be claimed either as a deduction or as a credit under the Code Sec. 1341 claim of right rules.

NEW LAW EXPLAINED

Partial exclusion of unemployment benefits from gross income—Effective for tax years beginning in 2009, an individual may exclude up to $2,400 of unemployment compensation benefits received during the year from gross income (Code Sec. 85(c), as added by the American Recovery and Reinvestment Tax Act of 2009 (P.L. 111-5)).

> **Comment:** The rationale for taxing unemployment benefits is to treat the benefits the same as wages since they are essentially wage replacement payments. By not taxing them, an individual may have less of an incentive to work (if such work is available). However, when an individual losses their job, their earned income will most likely be less, even if unemployment benefits are received. The decline may result in an increase, or enable the individual to claim, the earned income tax credit.

▶ **Effective date.** The provision applies to tax years beginning after December 31, 2008 (Act Sec. 1007(b) of the American Recovery and Reinvestment Tax Act of 2009 (P.L. 111-5)).

Law source: Law at ¶5200. Committee Report at ¶10,070.

— Act Sec. 1007(a) of the American Recovery and Reinvestment Tax Act of 2009 (P.L. 111-5), adding Code Sec. 85(c);

— Act Sec. 1007(b), providing the effective date.

Reporter references: For further information, consult the following CCH reporters.

— Standard Federal Tax Reporter, ¶5507.031, and ¶6412.01
— Tax Research Consultant, COMPEN: 6,064 and INDIV: 6,208
— Practical Tax Explanation, § 3075

¶210 Qualified Small Business Stock

SUMMARY OF NEW LAW

The percentage exclusion for qualified small business stock sold by an individual is increased from 50 to 75 percent for stock acquired after February 17, 2009 and before January 1, 2011.

BACKGROUND

To encourage investment in small businesses, individuals may exclude 50 percent of the gain from the sale of qualified small business stock held at least five years. The exclusion is increased to 60 percent in the case of the sale of certain empowerment zone stock. In both cases, the taxable portion of the gain is taxed at a maximum rate of 28 percent and seven percent (forty-two percent after 2010) of the excluded gain is an alternative minimum tax preference. There is a cumulative limit on the gain from a single issuer of stock that a taxpayer may exclude. The amount of gain eligible for the exclusion by an individual with respect to any corporation is the greater of (1) ten times the taxpayer's basis in the stock or (2) $10 million.

To be eligible for the exclusion, the small business stock must be acquired by the individual at its original issue (directly or through an underwriter), for money, for property other than stock, or as compensation for services. Stock acquired through the conversion of stock (such as preferred stock) that was qualified stock in the taxpayer's hands is also qualified stock in the taxpayer's hands. However, small business stock does not include stock that has been the subject of certain redemptions that are more than de minimis. When the stock is issued, the gross assets of the issuing corporation may not exceed $50 million. In addition, Thee corporation also must have at least 80 percent of the value of the it's assets used in the active conduct of one or more qualified trades or businesses.

NEW LAW EXPLAINED

Increased exclusion for qualified small business stock sales—The percentage exclusion for qualified small business stock sold by an individual is increased to 75 percent for stock acquired after February 17, 2009 and before January 1, 2011 (Code Sec. 1202(a)(1), as amended by the American Recovery and Reinvestment Tax Act of 2009 (P.L. 111-5)). The percentage exclusion increase does not apply to the sale or exchange of certain empowerment zone stock.

Practical Analysis: Paul C. Lau and Sandy Soltis, Tax Partners at Blackman Kallick in Chicago, point out that under existing law, 50 percent of the gain on the sale of

NEW LAW EXPLAINED

qualified small business stock is excluded from income. If the corporation is located in an empowerment zone, the excluded amount is 60 percent of the gain. This exclusion is only available to noncorporate taxpayers. The 50-percent portion of the gain included in income is subject to tax at the 28-percent capital gains tax rate. A portion of the excluded gain is also subject to alternative minimum tax at a maximum 28-percent tax rate.

Qualified small business stock is stock of a C corporation that is owned by a noncorporate taxpayer and held by that taxpayer for more than five years. The stock must have been acquired in the original issue or in certain nontaxable transactions. The amount of gain eligible for this exclusion with respect to any corporation is the greater of (1) 10 times the taxpayer's basis in the stock, or (2) $10 million.

To qualify as a small business, the aggregate gross assets (*i.e.*, cash and the aggregate adjusted bases of other property) of the corporation may not exceed $50 million at the time the stock is issued. The corporation must also meet certain active trade or business requirements.

Under the American Recovery and Reinvestment Tax Act of 2009, the exclusion of gain on the sale of qualified small business stock sold by an individual in 2009 or 2010 is increased from 50 percent (60 percent for certain empowerment zone business) to 75 percent.

Comment: As a result of the increased exclusion, gain from the sale of qualified small business stock to which the provision applies is taxed at effective rates of seven percent under the regular tax and 12.88 percent under the alternative minimum tax (Conference Report on P.L. 111-5, American Recovery and Reinvestment Act of 2009 (H. Rept. 111-16).

Practical Analysis: Robert B. Teuber, Tax Attorney with Weiss Berzowski Brady, LLP in Milwaukee, Wisconsin and author of the *www.federaltaxlawforum.com* tax law blog, notes that Act Sec. 1241 of the American Recovery and Reinvestment Tax Act of 2009 ("2009 Recovery Act") is likely to encourage additional investment in Qualified Small Business Stock in the years 2009 and 2010.

The modification to Code Sec. 1202 is simple: the exclusion for 50 percent (60 percent in certain empowerment zone businesses) of gain on the sale or exchange of Qualified Small Business Stock is increased to 75 percent. The impact of the change is, however, much larger than the small modification to the code's text.

While other requirements may apply, to qualify for the exclusion (both before and after 2009 Recovery Act), the stock must be that of a domestic C corporation acquired at original issue from a business that uses 80 percent of its assets in a qualified trade or business and having gross assets that do not exceed $50 million before or after the issuance of the stock.

Prior to the 2009 Recovery Act, Code Sec. 1202 allowed a noncorporate taxpayer to exclude from gross income 50 percent of the gain on the sale or exchange of qualified small business stock held for more than five years. The gain included in gross income is taxed at a maximum rate of 28 percent. A percent of the pre-2009

NEW LAW EXPLAINED

Recovery Act 50 percent exclusion from gross income is an AMT preference. The conference report reconciling the House and Senate bill summarizes the pre-2009 Recovery Act effective rates of tax on the total gain as 14 percent of the regular tax and a range of 14.98 percent and 19.98 percent under the AMT depending on the acquisition and disposition dates.

Under 2009 Recovery Act, the 50-percent exclusion is increased to 75 percent. This results in a reduction in the effective tax on the entire gain to seven percent of the regular tax and 12.88 percent under the AMT.

This change in effective rates is likely to encourage additional investment in Qualified Small Business Stock during the balance of 2009 and in 2010. The 75 percent exclusion will only be available for such stock purchased in these years. Qualified Small Business Stock acquired before enactment of 2009 Recovery Act or after December 31, 2011, will only be eligible for the 50-percent exclusion from gross income. This investment incentive will likely provide capital to small businesses in the short run while the investors will have to hold onto their stock for at least five years (under the holding period rules) to receive the benefits from their purchases.

▶ **Effective date.** The provision applies to stock acquired after February 17, 2009 (Act Sec. 1241(b) of the American Recovery and Reinvestment Tax Act of 2009 (P.L. 111-5)).

Law source: Law at ¶5290. Committee Report at ¶10,290.

— Act Sec. 1241(a) of the American Recovery and Reinvestment Tax Act of 2009 (P.L. 111-5), adding Code Sec. 1202(a)(3);

— Act Sec.1241(b), providing the effective date.

Reporter references: For further information, consult the following CCH reporters.

— Standard Federal Tax Reporter, ¶30,375.01

— Tax Research Consultant, SALES:15,302.05

— Practical Tax Explanation, § 16,605.05

¶215 Limitation on Qualified Transportation Fringe Benefits

SUMMARY OF NEW LAW

The limitation on the amount employees may exclude for transportation in a commuter highway vehicle and transit passes provided by an employer is temporarily increased to equal the limitation on the exclusion for qualified parking ($230 for 2009).

BACKGROUND

The costs of commuting to and from work are not deductible as a business expense or an expense incurred in the production of income. Instead, they are nondeductible personal expenses. However, transportation fringe benefits are sometimes provided by employers to their employees in addition to cash compensation. Although compensation for services is generally taxable, qualified transportation fringe benefits provided by an employer to an employee are excluded from an employee's gross income for income tax purposes and from wages for payroll tax purposes. The exclusion is limited to those who are employees, including only common law employees and statutory employees, such as corporate officers, at the time the benefit is provided (Reg. § 1.132-9). If a fringe benefit is not specifically excluded, it is treated as taxable income.

Qualified transportation fringe benefits include transportation in a commuter highway vehicle (i.e., van pooling), transit passes, qualified parking, and for tax years beginning after December 31, 2008, qualified bicycle commuting reimbursement (Code Sec. 132(f)(1)). An employer can generally provide an employee with any combination of these benefits simultaneously, with the exception that a qualified bicycle commuting reimbursement cannot be given in any month in which any other transportation fringe benefit is given (Code Sec. 132(f)(5)(F)(iii)(II)). For tax years beginning in 2009, the inflation-adjusted amounts an employee can exclude as a qualified transportation fringe benefit per month is limited to $120 for qualified van pooling, transit passes and $230 for qualified parking (Code Sec. 132(f)(2) and (6); Rev. Proc. 2008-66, I.R.B. 2008-45)).

To be excluded, transportation in a commuter highway vehicle (i.e., van pooling) must be provided by an employer in connection with travel between the employee's residence and place of employment. "Commuter highway vehicle" is defined as any highway vehicle that has a seating capacity of at least six adults, excluding the driver, that can reasonably be expected to be used to transport employees in connection with travel between their residences and their place of employment and on trips during which the number of employees transported for such purposes is at least one-half of the adult seating capacity of such vehicle (excluding the driver) for at least 80% of the mileage use of such vehicle. Transportation includes cash reimbursements for transportation. No amount exceeding this limitation is excludable under other fringe benefit provisions (Code Sec. § 132(f)(5)(B)).

A "transit pass" is a pass, token, fare card, voucher or similar item (including an item exchangeable for fare media) that entitles a person to transportation or transportation at a reduced price on public or private mass transit facilities or in a highway vehicle with a seating capacity of at least six adults, not including the driver. The IRS does not require any substantiation if an employer distributes transit passes. Unless the employer chooses to require it, employees receiving passes need not certify that they will use the passes for commuting (Code Sec. 132(f)(5)(A); Reg. § 1.132-9).

NEW LAW EXPLAINED

Limitation on van pool benefits and transit passes temporarily increased.— Effective for any month beginning on or after February 17, 2009, the monthly exclusion

¶215

Explanation 57

NEW LAW EXPLAINED

for van pool benefits and transit passes provided by an employer to an employee is increased to match the exclusion amount for qualified parking Code Sec. 132(f)(2), as amended by the American Recovery and Reinvestment Tax Act of 2009 (P.L. 111-5). The exclusion amount for 2009 is $230 per month (Rev. Proc. 2008-66, I.R.B. 2008-45, 1107)). The increased exclusion amount will not apply to any month beginning on or after January 1, 2011 (Code Sec. 132(f)(2), as added by the 2009 Recovery Act).

> **Comment:** According to RideFinders, a regional rideshare program, commuters who drive alone may experience an expensive, frustrating workday commute that increases traffic congestion and air pollution. Van pool riders lower their commuting stress by not driving, which reduces traffic congestion and improves the region's air quality. Additionally, public transportation can make a significant contribution toward job creation, reducing our dependence on foreign oil, and becoming carbon efficient. According to the American Public Transportation Association, public transportation use in America saves 4.2 billion gallons of fuel and 37 million metric tons of carbon dioxide emissions per year while supporting two million jobs.

▶ **Effective date.** The provision applies to months beginning on or after February 17, 2009 (Act Sec. 1151(b) of the American Recovery and Reinvestment Tax Act of 2009 (P.L. 111-5)).

Law source: Law at ¶5210. Committee Report at ¶10,210.

— Act Sec. 1151(a) of the American Recovery and Reinvestment Tax Act of 2009 (P.L. 111-5), amending Code Sec. 132(f)(2);

— Act Sec. 1151(b), providing the effective date.

Reporter references: For further information, consult the following CCH reporters.

— Standard Federal Tax Reporter, ¶7438.054

— Tax Research Consultant, COMPEN: 36,350, COMPEN: 36,352, COMPEN: 36,354 and PAYROLL: 3,200

— Practical Tax Explanation, § 21,125.05

¶220 Qualified Expenses for Qualified Tuition Programs

SUMMARY OF NEW LAW

For purposes of a qualified tuition plan, the definition of qualified higher education expenses is expanded to include expenses for computer equipment and technology in tax years beginning in 2009 and 2010.

¶220

BACKGROUND

A qualified tuition program is a program set up to allow you to either prepay, or contribute to an account established for paying, a student's qualified education expenses at an eligible educational institution. Qualified tuition programs (also known as "qualified tuition plans" or "529 plans") were originally limited to state programs, but they have been expanded to include prepaid tuition programs that are established and maintained by eligible private institutions that satisfy the Code Sec. 529 requirements (Code Sec. 529(b)(1)). As a result, there are actually two types of qualified tuition plan (QTP): one is a "savings account program" and the other is a "prepaid tuition program."

Contributions to a QTP must be in cash, and are generally treated as completed gifts for purposes of the annual gift tax exclusion. Persons who contribute to a private eligible educational institution's QTP prepaid tuition plan are not allowed to make contributions to a college savings account plan. The income earned on the funds in a QTP account is not subject to current income tax. And distributions from a QTP account are excludable from the beneficiary's gross income to the extent that the total distribution does not exceed the qualified higher education expenses incurred for that beneficiary.

The term "qualified higher education expenses" (QHEE) means the tuition, fees, books, supplies, and equipment required for the enrollment or attendance of a designated beneficiary at an eligible educational institution and, in the case of a special needs beneficiary, expenses for special needs services which are incurred in connection with such enrollment or attendance. Qualified higher education expenses also include room and board, provided that the student is: (1) enrolled in a degree, certificate, or other program leading to a recognized educational credential at an eligible institution; and (2) carrying at least half of the normal full-time work for the course of study the student is pursuing (Code Sec. 529(e)(3)).

NEW LAW EXPLAINED

Definition of education expenses temporarily expanded to include computer expenses.—The definition of qualified higher education expenses for a qualified tuition program is expanded to include expenses for computer equipment and technology, or for internet access and related services, paid or incurred in 2009 and 2010 (Code Sec. 529(e)(3)(A)(iii), as added by the American Recovery and Reinvestment Tax Act of 2009 (P.L. 111-5)). This includes computer software, computer or peripheral equipment, and fiber optic cable related to computer use (Code Sec. 170(e)(6)(F)(i)). However, such equipment, technology or services may be included in qualified higher education expenses provided they will be used by the beneficiary or his family during the years he is enrolled at an eligible educational institution. The expanded definition of qualified higher education expenses specifically excludes any computer software that is designed for games, sports or hobbies unless that software is "predominantly educational in nature" (Code Sec. 529(e)(3)(A), as amended by the 2009 Recovery Act).

¶220

NEW LAW EXPLAINED

Practical Analysis: Vincent O'Brien, President of Vincent J. O'Brien, CPA, PC, Lynbrook, New York, observes that two relatively recent changes have made Code Sec. 529 plans even more attractive. First, the Pension Protection Act of 2006 (P.L.109-280) made permanent the provision allowing distributions from Code Sec. 529 plans to be free of federal income tax, if such distributions are used for qualified post-secondary education expenses of the beneficiary for whom the plan was established.

Second, effective for 2008 and later years, the "kiddie-tax" generally applies to the unearned income of children who are under the age of 19 or under the age of 24 and a full-time student. Since investments held by college-age students will now generally be taxed at their parents' higher income tax rates, the use of Code Sec. 529 plans, which offer tax-free treatment of the earnings portion of qualified distributions, becomes even more useful.

Some states also offer tax incentives for certain contributions to Code Sec. 529 plans maintained for those states.

The change made by the American Recovery and Reinvestment Tax Act of 2009 adds a small and temporary "sweetener" to Code Sec. 529 accounts. For 2009 and 2010 only, distributions made for certain qualified computer and technology expenses will be treated as qualified.

Practical Analysis: Michael Schlesinger, a partner in Schlesinger & Sussman of New York, New York and author of *Practical Guide to S Corporations* (4th edition), notes that while the amendment to Code Sec. 529 plans to allow expenditures for computer expenses will help individuals with their education, it is important to remember that Congress has still not addressed a trap for the unwary that lurks in Code Sec. 529(c)(5). Code Sec. 529(c)(5) prescribes that if an account owner changes beneficiaries in the plan and the newly designated beneficiary is one generation below the prior beneficiary, the change will be deemed a gift from the prior designated beneficiary to the newly designated beneficiary, unless the newly designated beneficiary is a member of the family of the old beneficiary. This gift situation arises even though the prior designated beneficiary's consent is not obtained. If the newly designated beneficiary is at least two generations below the prior beneficiary, then generation-skipping tax consequences will also arise. Thus, if the Code Sec. 529 plan owner wants to be spiteful, mean, *etc.* to a designated beneficiary, all the account owner has to do is with a single stroke of the pen change the designated beneficiary to at least one generation below and make sure that the beneficiary is not a member of the family of the old beneficiary as that term is defined in Code Sec. 529(e)(2).

▶ **Effective date.** This provision applies to expenses paid or incurred after December 31, 2008 (Act Sec. 1005(b) of the American Recovery and Reinvestment Tax Act of 2009 (P.L. 111-5)).

¶220

NEW LAW EXPLAINED

Law source: Law at ¶5270. Committee Report at ¶10,050.

— Act Sec. 1005(a) of the American Recovery and Reinvestment Tax Act of 2009 (P.L. 111-5), amending 529(e)(3)(A);

— Act Sec. 1005(b), providing the effective date.

Reporter references: For further information, consult the following CCH reporters.

— Standard Federal Tax Reporter, ¶22,945.021
— Tax Research Consultant, INDIV: 60,204.15
— Practical Tax Explanation, § 1,810.25

¶225 Economic Recovery Payments for Recipients of Certain Federal Benefits

SUMMARY OF NEW LAW

Economic recovery payments of $250 will be made to adults who are eligible for certain Social Security benefits, Railroad Retirement benefits, veterans compensation or pension benefits, or supplemental security income (SSI) benefits.

BACKGROUND

For 2008, individual taxpayers could qualify for a refundable recovery credit of up to $600 ($1,200 for joint returns), plus $300 for each qualifying child (Code Sec. 6428). The credit was paid out to most recipients in the form of rebates issued during 2008. To be eligible for the credit, a taxpayer had to have a threshold amount of qualifying income or of net income tax liability and gross income (Code Sec. 6428(b)(2)). Qualifying income included earned income and certain Social Security, Railroad Retirement and veterans' benefits (Code Sec. 6428(e)(1)). The credit began to phase out for adjusted gross income levels in excess of $75,000 ($150,000 for joint returns) (Code Sec. 6428(d)).

The expansive definition of qualifying income meant that many lower-income taxpayers could qualify for a minimum credit of $300, even if they had little or no tax liability. For instance, a taxpayer whose only income was $3,000 in nontaxable Social Security benefits was eligible for the $300 credit, even though the taxpayer had no taxable income and no federal tax liability.

NEW LAW EXPLAINED

Recipients of certain federal benefits can receive $250 payments.—Eligible adults will receive a one-time economic recovery payment of $250 (Act Sec. 2201 of the Assistance for Unemployed Workers and Struggling Families Act (P.L. 111-5)).

NEW LAW EXPLAINED

Comment: Individuals who receive certain government pensions or annuities can qualify for similar economic assistance through a tax credit, discussed at ¶325.

Eligible individuals. To receive an economic recovery payment, the individual must satisfy both of the following tests:

(1) During any of the months of November 2008, December 2008 or January 2009, the individual must have been eligible to receive benefits under a "qualifying program" (generally, Social Security benefits, Railroad Retirement Act benefits, veterans compensation or pension benefits, or supplemental security income (SSI) benefits) (Act Sec. 2201(a)(1) of the Struggling Families Act).

(2) The individual's current address of record under the qualifying program must be in one of the 50 states, the District of Columbia, Puerto Rico, Guam, the U.S. Virgin Islands, American Samoa, and the Northern Mariana Islands (Act Sec. 2201(a)(2) of the Struggling Families Act).

Comment: Although the payments are aimed at adults, the group of individuals who are eligible for veterans compensation or pension benefits includes, because of administrative constraints, a small number of persons under the age of 18. Also, the group of individuals who are eligible for SSI benefits includes SSI recipients who are under age 18 (Joint Committee on Taxation, Description of the American Recovery and Reinvestment Tax Act of 2009, January 23, 2009 (JCX-10-09)).

Caution: An individual who is eligible for benefits under more than one of the qualifying programs will receive only one economic recovery payment (Act Sec. 2201(a)(3) of the Struggling Families Act).

Ineligible individuals. An individual who falls into any of these categories is not eligible to receive an economic recovery payment:

- if the individual receives SSI benefits while in a Medicaid institution (and is not eligible for economic recovery payments under any of the other qualifying programs) (Act Sec. 2201(a)(1)(C) of the Struggling Families Act);

- if, during the most recent month in which the individual is entitled to a qualifying benefit during the three-month qualification period (November 2008 through January 2009) (i) the individual's Social Security benefits (including those authorized by the Railroad Retirement Board) are suspended because the individual is imprisoned, a fugitive or a probation or parole violator; made false or misleading statements with respect to his or her right to the benefit; or is no longer lawfully present in the United States; (ii) the individual's veterans benefits are suspended or reduced because the individual has been imprisoned or incarcerated or is a fugitive felon; or (iii) the individual's SSI cash benefits are suspended because the individual is an inmate, a fugitive, or a probation or parole violator, or made false or misleading statements with respect to his or her right to the benefit;

- if the individual dies before the date of certification to receive the economic recovery payments (as discussed below under "Certification of recipients") (Act Sec. 2201(a)(4) of the Struggling Families Act).

¶225

NEW LAW EXPLAINED

Qualifying programs. Eligible individuals must qualify for payments under one of the following benefit programs:

- Social security payments that make an individual eligible for an economic recovery payment are benefits generally known as Title II benefits. These are monthly insurance benefits payable under certain provisions of the Social Security Act (42 U.S.C. Sec. 401 *et seq.*), but without regard to sections 202(j)(1) and 223(b) (42 U.S.C. 402(j)(1) and 423(b)). These benefits are payments under Social Security Act sections 202(a), 202(b), 202(c), 202(d)(1)(B)(ii), 202(e), 202(f), 202(g), 202(h), 223(a), 227, or 228 (42 U.S.C. 402(a), 402(b), 402(c), 402(d)(1)(B)(ii), 402(e), 402(f), 402(g), 402(h), 423(a), 427, or 428) (Act Sec. 2201(a)(1)(B)(i) of the Struggling Families Act).

- Railroad retirement benefits that make an individual eligible for an economic recovery payment are monthly annuity or pension payments that are payable under certain provisions of the Railroad Retirement Act of 1974, but without regard to section 5(a)(ii) (45 U.S.C. 231d(a)(ii), which has to do with the commencement of certain disability annuities). These benefits are payments under sections 2(a)(1), 2(c), 2(d)(1)(i), 2(d)(1)(ii), 2(d)(1)(iii)(C) to an adult disabled child, 2(d)(1)(iv), 2(d)(1)(v), or 7(b)(2) with respect to any of the Social Security Act benefits listed above (45 U.S.C. 231a(a)(1), 231a(c), 231a(d)(1)(i), 231a(d)(1)(ii), 231a(d)(1)(iii)(C), 231a(d)(1)(iv), 231a(d)(1)(v), 231f(b)(2))) (Act Sec. 2201(a)(1)(B)(ii) of the Struggling Families Act).

- Veterans benefits that make an individual eligible for an economic recovery payment are compensation or pension payments that are (i) payable under 38 U.S.C. 1110, 1117, 1121, 1131, 1141, 1151, 1310, 1312, 1313, 1315, 1316, 1318, 1513, 1521, 1533, 1536, 1537, 1541, 1542, 1562, 1805, 1815 or 1821, and (ii) payable to a veteran, surviving spouse, child or parent (as defined at 38 U.S.C. 101(2), (3), 4(A)(ii) or (5)) during November 2008, December 2008, or January 2009 (Act Sec. 2201(a)(1)(B)(iii) of the Struggling Families Act).

- SSI cash benefits that make an individual eligible for an economic recovery payment are cash benefits payable under section 1611 (other than 1611(e)(1)(B), which provides payments to patients in Medicaid institutions) or 1619(a) of the Social Security Act (42 U.S.C. 1382 and 1382(h)) (Act Sec. 2201(a)(1)(C) of the Struggling Families Act).

Certification of recipients. The Commissioner of Social Security, the Railroad Retirement Board, and the Secretary of Veterans Affairs are directed to certify the individuals who are entitled to receive economic recovery payments, and provide the Treasury Department with the information necessary to disburse the payments. The certification of an individual is not affected by any subsequent determination or redetermination of the individual's entitlement to or eligibility for benefits under a qualifying program (Act Sec. 2201(b) of the Struggling Families Act).

Timing and delivery. The Secretary of the Treasury is directed to begin making the payments as soon as possible, but no later than 120 days after February 17, 2009, the date of enactment. No economic recovery payments can be made after December 31, 2010. A payment may be made electronically to an individual as if it was a benefit

NEW LAW EXPLAINED

payment or cash benefit under the applicable qualifying program (Act Sec. 2201(a)(5) of the Struggling Families Act).

Representative payees. If benefits under the qualifying program are paid to an eligible individual's representative payee or fiduciary, the economic recovery payment is also made to the representative payee, and can be used only for the benefit of the eligible individual (Act Sec. 2201(d)(1) of the Struggling Families Act). Economic recovery payments are treated like benefits paid under a qualifying Social Security or SSI program for purposes of the penalties that apply to representative payees who convert such benefits to uses other than for the entitled recipient's welfare (Act Sec. 2201(d)(2)(A) of the Struggling Families Act). Similarly, economic recovery payments are treated like qualifying veterans benefits for purposes of the rules governing the payment of benefits to fiduciaries and the restitution of misused benefits (Act Sec. 2201(d)(2)(C) of the Struggling Families Act). Finally, economic recovery payments are treated like qualifying Railroad Retirement Act benefits for purposes of the penalties for persons who fail or refuse to make required reports or provide required information, or who knowingly make or cause to be made any false or fraudulent report (Act Sec. 2201(d)(2)(B) of the Struggling Families Act).

Coordination with MWPC. If the individual is also eligible for the new Making Work Pay Credit (MWPC) (discussed at ¶305), the amount of that credit is reduced by the amount of the individual's economic recovery payment (Code Sec. 36A(c), as added by the American Recovery and Reinvestment Act of 2009 (P.L. 111-5).

> **Comment:** For 2009 and 2010, individual taxpayers with earned income can qualify for the MWPC, which is equal to the lesser of 6.2 percent of the taxpayer's earned income, or $400 ($800 on a joint return). The credit effectively refunds the employee's share of Social Security taxes on an individual worker's first $6,450 in wages.

> **Example:** Mike is eligible for veterans benefits and Social Security benefits during January 2009. Even though he is eligible under two federal programs, he receives only one $250 economic recovery payment. Mike also earns $9,000 from his part-time job, which entitles him to the maximum $400 MWPC. He must deduct the full amount of his economic recovery payment from his MWPC for 2009, reducing it to $150. Note, however, that the economic recovery payments are made only for one year, while the MWPC applies to both 2009 and 2010. Thus, if Mike's situation is the same in 2010, he can claim the entire amount of the MWPC for 2010, because he will not receive an economic recovery payment in that year.

> **Planning Note:** Congress intends for the MWPC to be implemented via adjusted withholding tables that reduce the taxes withheld from workers' paychecks for the remainder of 2009 and for 2010. Thus, individuals like Mike, who must reduce the amount of their MWPC for 2009, might want to increase the amounts withheld from their pay in 2009 after the new tables take effect.

¶225

NEW LAW EXPLAINED

Coordination with other provisions. The economic recovery payments are not considered gross income for income tax purposes. Similarly, for purposes of determining any individual's eligibility for, or the amount or extent of, benefits or assistance under any federal program or any state or local program financed in whole or in part with federal funds, the economic recovery payments are not taken into account as income or taken into account as resources for the month of receipt and the following nine months. The payments are generally protected by the assignment and garnishment provisions of the qualifying programs. However, they are subject to administrative offset to collect delinquent federal debts under 31 U.S.C. 3716 (Act Sec. 2201(c) of the Struggling Families Act).

▶ **Effective date.** No effective date is provided by the Act. The provision is therefore, considered effective on February 17, 2009, the date of enactment.

Law source: Law at ¶7070. Committee Report at ¶10,490.

— Act Sec. 2201 of the Assistance for Unemployed Workers and Struggling Families Act (P.L. 111-5).

Reporter references: For further information, consult the following CCH reporters.

— Standard Federal Tax Reporter, ¶38,869.021

— Tax Research Consultant, INDIV: 57,900

— Practical Tax Explanation, § 1,030

¶230 Deduction of Taxes on the Purchase of Certain Motor Vehicles

SUMMARY OF NEW LAW

Taxpayers are allowed a deduction from gross income for state sales and excise taxes on new motor vehicles purchased for use by the taxpayer before January 1, 2010.

BACKGROUND

A deduction is allowed under Code Sec. 164 for certain taxes, even if those taxes are not directly connected with a trade or business or with property held for production of income. Among the taxes that may be deducted are state and local income taxes, as well as state or local personal property taxes. For tax years beginning before January 1, 2010, a taxpayer may elect to deduct state and local sales taxes in lieu of deducting state and local income taxes. The sales tax, however, must be a general rate of tax that is imposed on the retail sale of a broad range of classes of items (Code Sec. 164(b)(5)). Personal property taxes are deductible only if they are ad valorem (substantially in proportion to the value of the property) and imposed on an annual basis. For example, payment for car registration and licensing or a motor vehicle tax may be

BACKGROUND

deductible as a personal property tax if it is imposed annually and assessed in proportion to the value of the car (Reg § 1.164-3(c)).

Taxes unrelated to a trade or business are only deductible as an itemized deduction on Schedule A of Form 1040. Generally, itemized deductions are only allowed if the taxpayer elects to forgo claiming the standard deduction. Furthermore, an individual whose adjusted gross income (AGI) exceeds a threshold amount must reduce the amount of allowable itemized deductions by a reduction equal to the lesser of: (1) three percent of the excess over the threshold amount; or (2) 80 percent of allowable deductions (Code Sec. 68). The phaseout threshold amount for 2008 is $159,950 (or $79,975 for a married individual filing a separate return) (Rev. Proc. 2007-66). The 2009 threshold amount is $166,800 (or $83,400 for married taxpayers filing separate returns) (Rev. Proc. 2008-66). However, the reduction in the amount of itemized deductions that high-income taxpayers may claim is being phased out. For 2008 and 2009, only one-third of the reduction will apply (Code Sec. 68(f) and (g)). In 2010, high-income taxpayers will not be required to reduce the amount of itemized deductions they can claim. However, the full limit on itemized deductions will apply for tax years after 2010. In contrast to itemized deductions, deductions from gross income are not generally subject to phaseouts based on a taxpayer's income level regardless of the year.

NEW LAW EXPLAINED

Deduction from gross income for state sales and excise taxes on the purchase of certain motor vehicles.—A taxpayer is permitted to claim a deduction from gross income with respect to "qualified motor vehicle taxes" (Code Sec. 164(a)(6), as added by the American Recovery and Reinvestment Tax Act of 2009 (P.L. 111-5)). The deduction may be claimed in calculating the taxpayer's regular income tax and alternative minimum tax liability (Code Sec. 56(b)(1)(E), as amended by the 2009 Recovery Act). The amount of the deduction is limited to the portion of the state sales or excise tax imposed on the first $49,500 of the purchase price of the vehicle. (Code Sec. 164(b)(6)(B), as added by the 2009 Recovery Act). Qualified motor vehicle taxes are not included in the cost of an acquired vehicle under Code Sec. 164(a) (Code Sec. 164(b)(6)(E), as added by the 2009 Recovery Act).

Qualified motor vehicle taxes are defined as any state or local sales, or excise tax imposed on the purchase of a "qualified motor vehicle" (Code Sec. 164(b)(6)(A), as amended by the 2009 Recovery Act). A qualified motor vehicle is a passenger vehicle, light truck, or motorcycle that has a gross vehicle weight rating of 8,500 pounds or less, or a motor home of any gross vehicle weight. Original use of the vehicle must commence with the taxpayer (i.e., the purchase must be of a new, not a used, vehicle) and the taxpayer must purchase the vehicle on or before December 31, 2009 (Code Sec. 164(b)(6)(D) and (G), as added by the 2009 Recovery Act).

> **Comment:** The terms *passenger vehicle* and *light truck* have the same meanings given such terms in regulations prescribed by the Administrator of the Environmental Protection Agency for purposes of the administration of title II of the

¶230

NEW LAW EXPLAINED

Clean Air Act (Code Sec. 30B(e)(2)). The terms *motorcycle* and *motor home* have the same meaning given such terms under section 571.3 of title 49 of the Code of Federal Regulations (as in effect on February 17, 2009, the date of the enactment of the 2009 Recovery Act) (Code Sec. 164(b)(6)(D)(ii), as added by the 2009 Recovery Act).

The motor vehicle sales tax deduction is treated as an increase in the standard deduction (Code Sec. 63(c), as amended by the 2009 Recovery Act). The amount of the deduction is subject to a phaseout for high-income taxpayers. The phaseout begins to apply when a taxpayer's modified adjusted gross income (MAGI) exceeds $125,000 ($250,000 for joint filers). The amount of the deduction is reduced in the same ratio as the excess of the taxpayer's MAGI in excess of the threshold amount bears to $10,000 (Code Sec. 164(b)(6)(C), as added by the 2009 Recovery Act). MAGI for this purpose is the taxpayer's AGI increased by any amount excluded from the taxpayer's gross income as income of a citizen or resident of the United States living abroad under Code Sec. 911, income from sources within Guam, American Samoa or the Northern Mariana Islands under Code Sec. 931, and income from sources within Puerto Rico under Code Sec. 933.

Planning Note: Due to the phaseout, the deduction will be reduced to zero when the taxpayer's MAGI reaches $135,000 ($260,000 for joint filers).

No double benefits. If a taxpayer elects to deduct state or local general sales taxes in lieu of deducting state and local income taxes, then he may not "double dip" and also claim the deduction for qualified motor vehicle taxes (Code Sec. 164(b)(6)(F), as added by the 2009 Recovery Act).

▶ **Effective date.** The provision applies to purchases on or after February 17, 2009 in tax years ending after that date (Act Sec. 1008(e) of the American Recovery and Reinvestment Tax Act of 2009 (P.L. 111-5)).

Law source: Law at ¶5185, ¶5195 and ¶5235. Committee Reports at ¶10,080.

— Act Sec.1008(a) of the American Recovery and Reinvestment Tax Act of 2009 (P.L. 111-5), adding Code Sec. 164(a)(6);

— Act Sec. 1008(b), adding Code Sec. 164(b)(6);

— Act Sec.1008(c), amending Code Sec. 63(c);

— Act Sec. 1008(d), amending Code Sec. 56(b)(1)(E);

— Act Sec. 1008(e), providing the effective date.

Reporter references: For further information, consult the following CCH reporters.

— Standard Federal Tax Reporter, ¶6081.01, ¶9502.031, ¶9502.037 and ¶9502.0385

— Tax Research Consultant, FILEIND: 9,050, FILEIND: 12,050, FILEIND: 12,056 and INDIV: 45,100

— Practical Tax Explanation, §5,001, §7,015, §7,301, and §7,320

ALTERNATIVE MINIMUM TAX

¶235 Alternative Minimum Tax Exemption Amount

SUMMARY OF NEW LAW

The alternative minimum tax (AMT) exemption amount for individuals has been increased for tax years beginning in 2009.

BACKGROUND

In addition to all other tax liabilities, an individual is subject to an alternative minimum tax (AMT) to the extent that his or her tentative minimum tax exceeds the amount of regular income tax owed (Code Sec. 55). An individual's tentative minimum tax is generally equal to the sum of: (1) 26 percent of the first $175,000 ($87,500 for a married taxpayer filing a separate return) of the taxpayer's alternative minimum taxable income (AMTI); and (2) 28 percent of the taxpayer's remaining AMTI (Code Sec. 55(b)(1)(A)).

AMTI is the individual's regular taxable income recomputed with certain adjustments and increased by certain tax preferences (Code Sec. 56). However, a specified amount of AMTI is exempt from tax based on the taxpayer's filing status. For example, the exemption amount for tax years prior to 2001 was: (1) $45,000 for married individuals filing a joint return and surviving spouses; (2) $33,750 for unmarried individuals; and (3) $22,500 for married individuals filing separate returns. The exemption amount is phased out by an amount equal to 25 percent of the amount by which the taxpayer's AMTI for the tax year exceeds: (1) $150,000 in the case of married individuals filing a joint return, surviving spouses and corporations; (2) $112,500 in the case of unmarried individuals; and (3) $75,000 in the case of married individuals filing separate returns, or an estate or trust.

Neither the exemption amounts, nor the threshold amounts, are indexed for inflation. Thus, the number of individuals affected by the AMT has increased each tax year. To alleviate this problem, the exemption amounts have been periodically increased by legislation. The latest change increased the exemption amounts for tax years beginning in 2008 to: (1) $69,950 for married individuals filing a joint return and surviving spouses; (2) $46,200 for unmarried individuals; and (3) $34,975 for married individuals filing separate returns (Code Sec. 55(d)(1)). However, for tax years beginning after 2008, the exemption amounts for individuals are scheduled to revert to the amounts that applied prior to 2001.

> **Comment:** The exemption amount for corporations, and estates or trusts, have remained unchanged during this period. The exemption amount is $40,000 for a corporation and $22,500 for an estate or trust.

¶235

NEW LAW EXPLAINED

Extension of AMT exemption amounts.—The alternative minimum tax (AMT) exemption amount for individuals is increased for tax years beginning in 2009, to:
- $70,950 for married individuals filing a joint return and surviving spouses;
- $46,700 for unmarried individuals; and
- $35,475 for married individuals filing separate returns (Code Sec. 55(d)(1)(A) and (B), as amended by the American Recovery and Reinvestment Tax Act of 2009 (P.L. 111-5).

The $40,000 exemption amount for corporations and the $22,500 exemption amount for estates or trusts remains unchanged for tax years beginning in 2009.

> **Caution:** Absent another legislative extension, the AMT exemption amounts for individuals are scheduled to revert back to the amounts that applied prior to the 2001 tax year. Thus, the exemption amounts for tax years beginning after 2009 are schedule to be: (1) $45,000 for married individuals filing a joint return and surviving spouses; (2) $33,750 for unmarried individuals; and (3) $22,500 for married individuals filing separate returns.

> **Practical Analysis:** Jeffrey D. Eicher, J.D., CPA, Professor of Finance at Clarion University of Pennsylvania, and Leo N. Hitt, J.D., LL.M., Tax Partner in the Pittsburgh office of Reed Smith, LLP, observe that the exemption amount for noncorporate taxpayers subject to the alternative minimum tax is increased and extended for an additional year in the American Recovery and Reinvestment Tax Act of 2009. The exemption amount is increased from $69,950 to $70,950 for joint returns or surviving spouse returns, from $46,200 to $46,700 for single returns, and from $34,975 to $35,475 for returns for married individuals filing separately. This is yet another one-year patch, and effectively allows an estimated 24 million taxpayers to avoid the alternative minimum tax for another year. Because the increased exemption amounts apply only through 2009, they are scheduled to return to the substantially lower amounts applicable in pre-2001 tax years, beginning in 2010, unless additional legislation is enacted which continues the enhanced exemptions.

> **Caution:** Although the AMT exemption amounts for individuals are increased for 2009, the threshold levels for the calculation of the phase out remain unchanged. Thus, the exemption amount for tax years beginning in 2009 is still reduced by 25 percent for each $1 of alternative minimum taxable income (AMTI) in excess of: (1) $150,000 in the case of married individuals filing a joint return, surviving spouses and corporations; (2) $112,500 in the case of unmarried individuals; and (3) $75,000 in the case of married individuals filing separate returns or an estate or a trust.

> **Practical Analysis:** John O. Everett, Ph.D., CPA, tax professor at Virginia Commonwealth University, Cherie J. Hennig, Ph.D., CPA, tax professor at Florida Interna-

NEW LAW EXPLAINED

> tional University, and William A. Raabe, Ph.D., CPA, tax professor at the Ohio State University, note that the American Recovery and Reinvestment Tax Act of 2009 extends through tax year 2009 the identification of certain tax credits as refundable when applied against the AMT. It also allows an indexing of the AMT exemption amount for non-corporate taxpayers for one more year.
>
> Extension of the existing AMT patches means that the underlying problems presented by the AMT will go unaddressed by Congress for one more year. The AMT may be "too big to repeal," and too politically sensitive to allow in its unpatched form. It is estimated that the 2009 patch effectively exempts more than 25 million taxpayers from an AMT liability, reducing federal revenues by about $70 billion for the 10-year scoring period.
>
> The corporate AMT does not generate significant amounts of annual revenues. Tax reductions from the 2009 AMT patch are likely to accrue largely to the middle and upper-middle income individuals who are may be subject to the AMT or may newly to fall into AMT status. Very little of the tax effects from this amendment will be available to lower and middle income individuals, or to the uppermost levels of AGI.
>
> The AMT is found by most tax professionals to be very difficult to plan around. Individuals might use the 2009 tax year to reallocate investments away from municipal bonds, if they hold legacy private activity bonds, and to exercise incentive stock options if the market has significantly reduced the taxable spread upon election.

▶ **Effective date.** The amendments made by this section apply to tax years beginning after December 31, 2008 (Act Sec. 1012(b) of the American Recovery and Reinvestment Tax Act of 2009 (P.L. 111-5).

Law source: Law at ¶5180. Committee Reports at ¶10,090.

— Act Sec. 1012(a) of the American Recovery and Reinvestment Tax Act of 2009 (P.L. 111-5), amending Code Sec. 55(d)(1)(A) and (B);

— Act Sec. 1012(b), providing the effective date.

Reporter references: For further information, consult the following CCH reporters.

— Standard Federal Tax Reporter, ¶5101.035 and ¶5101.036
— Tax Research Consultant, FILEIND: 30,400
— Practical Tax Explanation, § 15,015

¶240 Use of Nonrefundable Personal Credits Against AMT Liability

SUMMARY OF NEW LAW

The use of nonrefundable personal tax credits against an individual's regular tax and alternative minimum tax liability is extended to tax years beginning in 2009.

¶240

BACKGROUND

An alternative minimum tax (AMT) is imposed on an individual taxpayer to the extent his or her tentative minimum tax liability exceeds his or her regular income tax liability (Code Sec. 55(a)). An individual's tentative minimum tax is the sum of: (1) 26 percent of the first $175,000 ($87,500 for married individuals filing separately) of the taxpayer's alternative minimum taxable income (AMTI) in excess of an exemption amount; and (2) 28 percent of any remaining AMTI in excess of the exemption amount (Code Sec. 55(b)(1)(A)). AMTI is the individual's regular taxable income recomputed with certain adjustments and increased by certain tax preferences (Code Sec. 56).

For tax years beginning before 2009, the amount of nonrefundable personal tax credits available to an individual may be claimed to the extent of the full amount of the taxpayer's combined regular tax and AMT liability. The taxpayer's regular tax liability, however, must first be reduced by the amount of any applicable foreign or U.S. possession tax credit (Code Sec. 26(a)(2)). The nonrefundable personal tax credits include the dependent care credit, the credit for the elderly and disabled, the adoption credit, the child tax credit, the credit for interest on certain home mortgages, the HOPE Scholarship and Lifetime Learning credits, the retirement savings contributions credit, the credit for certain nonbusiness energy property, the credit for residential energy efficient property, and the District of Columbia first-time homebuyer credit.

> **Comment:** An individual is eligible to claim the alternative motor vehicle credit and alternative fuel vehicle refueling property credit for business as well as nonbusiness use. However, the personal use portions claimed by an individual is limited to the excess of the taxpayer's regular tax liability, reduced by all other nonrefundable credits plus the foreign and possessions tax credit, over his or her tentative minimum tax liability (Code Secs. 30B(g)(2) and 30C(d)(2)). Thus, the rule that allows nonrefundable personal credits to be claimed against the sum of the taxpayer's regular and AMT liability for tax years beginning before 2009 does not apply to these credits.

Without further legislative action, the amount of nonrefundable personal credits that may be claimed by an individual for tax years beginning after 2008, (except for the adoption credit, the child tax credit and the retirement savings contributions credit) is limited to the excess of the taxpayer's regular tax liability over tentative minimum tax liability, determined without regard to the AMT foreign tax credit (Code Sec. 26(a)(1)). Thus, all nonrefundable personal credits (except for the child tax credit, the adoption credit and the retirement savings contributions credit) will only be able to offset regular tax liability in 2009 and only to the extent it exceeds his or her tentative minimum tax unless further legislative action is taken.

> **Comment:** The adoption credit, the child tax credit and the retirement savings contributions credit are allowed to the full extent of the taxpayer's regular tax and AMT liability. Thus, without further legislative action, only these three credits may be claimed against both the regular tax and minimum tax liability for those years for tax years beginning after 2008.

¶240

Explanation 71

NEW LAW EXPLAINED

Nonrefundable personal credits allowed against regular tax and AMT liability for tax years beginning in 2009.—For tax years beginning in 2009, the nonrefundable personal tax credits are allowed to the full extent of the taxpayer's regular tax and AMT liability. For this purpose, the regular tax liability is first reduced by the amount of any applicable foreign tax credit (Code Sec. 26(a)(2), as amended by the American Recovery and Reinvestment Act of 2009 (P.L. 111-5).

> **Practical Analysis:** Jeffrey D. Eicher, J.D., CPA, Professor of Finance at Clarion University of Pennsylvania, and Leo N. Hitt, J.D., LL.M., Tax Partner in the Pittsburgh office of Reed Smith, LLP, observe that the temporary provision which permits the offset of nonrefundable personal credits against the sum of an individual's regular income tax and alternative minimum tax is extended for an additional year to years that begin during 2009.

Comment: The extension does not apply to the personal use portion of the alternative fuel vehicle refueling property credit. The personal use portion may only be used against the excess of the taxpayer's regular tax liability, reduced by all other nonrefundable credits plus the foreign or U.S. possession tax credit, over the tentative minimum tax (Code Secs. 30B(g)(2) and 30C(d)(2)).

However, for tax years beginning in 2009, the personal use portion of the alternative motor vehicle credit will be treated as a nonrefundable personal credit that may be claimed against a taxpayer's regular tax and AMT liabilities (see ¶360). The personal use portion of the new qualified plug-in electric vehicle credit will be treated as a nonrefundable personal credit that may be claimed against a taxpayer's regular tax and AMT liabilities (see ¶350). Finally, the personal use portion of the qualified plug-in electric drive motor vehicle placed in service after 2009 will be treated as a nonrefundable personal credit that may be claimed against a taxpayer's regular tax and AMT liabilities (see ¶345).

▶ **Effective date.** The amendments made by this section apply to tax years beginning after December 31, 2008 (Act Sec. 1011(b) of the American Recovery and Reinvestment Act of 2009 (P.L. 111-5)).

Law source: Law at ¶5035. Committee Reports at ¶10,090.

— Act Sec. 1011(a) of the American Recovery and Reinvestment Tax Act of 2009 (P.L. 111-5), amending Code Sec. 26(a)(2);

— Act Sec. 1011(b), providing the effective date.

Reporter references: For further information, consult the following CCH reporters.

— Standard Federal Tax Reporter, ¶3851.021

— Tax Research Consultant, INDIV: 57,200

— Practical Tax Explanation, § 15,005

¶240

Individual Related Tax Credits

¶305 Making Work Pay Credit
¶310 First-Time Homebuyer Credit
¶315 Refundable Portion of Child Tax Credit
¶320 Increase in Earned Income Tax Credit
¶325 $250 Credit for Government Retirees
¶330 Hope Scholarship Credit
¶335 Residential Energy Property Credit
¶340 Residential Alternative Energy Credit
¶345 Plug-in Electric Drive Motor Vehicle Credit
¶350 Plug-in Electric Vehicle Credit
¶355 Plug-in Electric Drive Motor Vehicle Conversion Credit
¶360 Alternative Motor Vehicle Credit
¶365 Qualified Alternative Fuel Vehicle Refueling Property Credit

¶305 Making Work Pay Credit

SUMMARY OF NEW LAW

For 2009 and 2010, most individuals with earned income can claim a refundable Making Work Pay Credit of up to $400 ($800 for joint returns).

BACKGROUND

A worker's *tax liability* has three components: tax on the worker's income; old-age, survivors and disability insurance (OASDI) taxes, also known as social security taxes; and hospital insurance (HI) taxes, also known as Medicare taxes. The tax on the worker's income is progressive, meaning that the tax rate rises as income increases (Code Sec. 1). For most workers, the personal exemption (Code Sec. 151) and the basic standard deduction (Code Sec. 63) also effectively exempt the first few thousand dollars of wages from the income tax. Social security taxes and Medicare taxes (collectively known as FICA taxes, for the Federal Insurance Contribution Act) are

American Recovery and Reinvestment Act of 2009

BACKGROUND

both regressive; they are imposed at a flat rate beginning with the first dollar of the worker's wages, and social security taxes are not imposed on wages that exceed an annual threshold ($106,800 for 2009) (Code Sec. 3101; Notice 2008-103). Social security and Medicare taxes are imposed on both the employer and the employee at a rate of 6.2 percent and 1.45 percent, respectively. Self-employed workers must pay both the employer's and the employee's share of the taxes; thus, they pay Self-Employment Contribution Act (SECA) taxes equal to 15.3 percent of their net self-employment income (Code Sec. 1401).

Lower-income and moderate-income workers can receive substantial benefits from the *earned income credit* (EIC). Eligibility for and the amount of the EIC depend on the taxpayer's earned income, adjusted gross income, investment income, filing status, and number of children (Code Sec. 32).

For purposes of the EIC, *earned income* is generally taxable compensation from employment, including wages, salaries and tips. Earned income does not include: amounts received as pensions or annuities; a nonresident alien's income that is not connected with U.S. business; amounts earned for services provided by an inmate at a penal institution; and workfare payments that are subsidized under a state workfare program (such as Temporary Assistance for Needy Families (TANF)) (Code Sec. 32(c)(2)). Net earnings from self-employment are included, but earned income is reduced by any net loss from self-employment (Code Sec. 32(c)(2); Reg. § 1.32-2(c)(2)). Most nontaxable compensation, such as excludable dependent care and adoption benefits, is not earned income, but there are two exceptions (IRS Publication 596, "Earned Income Credit"). First, a taxpayer may elect to treat combat pay that is otherwise excluded from gross income under Code Sec. 112 as earned income for purposes of the EIC (Code Sec. 32(c)(2)(B)(vi)). Second, an excludable parsonage allowance is included in the determination of the taxpayer's net earnings from self-employment and, thus, is indirectly included in earned income (Code Sec. 32(c)(2)(A)(ii)).

The EIC is *refundable* to the extent it exceeds the taxpayer's income tax liability. Tax liability for this purpose includes the taxpayer's share of self-employment taxes, but it does not include the taxpayer's share of regular employment taxes, such as FICA taxes and Federal Unemployment Tax Act (FUTA) taxes (Code Sec. 32(a)). Thus, lower-income taxpayers who pay regular employment taxes can receive a tax refund arising from the EIC, even if they have little or no normal income tax liability (that is, non-employment tax liability).

NEW LAW EXPLAINED

New "Making Work Pay Credit" for 2009 and 2010.—For tax years beginning in 2009 and 2010, eligible individuals are allowed a refundable Making Work Pay Credit (MWPC) that is applied against the income tax liability imposed by Subtitle A of the Internal Revenue Code (that is, Code Secs. 1 through 1563 (Code Sec. 36A, as added by the American Recovery and Reinvestment Tax Act of 2009 (P.L. 111-5)).

Amount. The MWPC is equal to the lesser of:

¶305

NEW LAW EXPLAINED

(1) 6.2 percent of the taxpayer's earned income, or

(2) $400 ($800 for married couples filing a joint return) (Code Sec. 36A(a), as added by the 2009 Recovery Act).

Comment: The MWPC effectively eliminates the 6.2-percent employee share of social security tax on about the first $6,450 of a single worker's wages.

Reduction for economic recovery payments and government retiree credits. The MWPC is reduced by the amount of the taxpayer's economic recovery payment (discussed at ¶225) or government retiree credit (discussed at ¶325) (Code Sec. 36A(c), as added by the 2009 Recovery Act). A failure to reduce the claimed MWPC by the amount of the taxpayer's economic recovery payment or government retiree credit is a mathematical or clerical error on the return, which allows the IRS to assess any resulting additional tax without using deficiency procedures (Code Sec. 6213(g)(2)(N), as added by the 2009 Recovery Act).

Comment: The MWPC is limited to taxpayers with earned income, while the economic recovery payments and government retiree credits are available to individuals who are eligible for certain governmental benefits and pensions.

Phaseout. The amount of the MWPC (before any reduction for economic recovery payments or government retiree credit) is reduced (but not below zero) by two percent of the taxpayer's modified adjusted gross income (AGI) that exceeds $75,000 (or $150,000 on a joint return) (Code Sec. 36A(b)(1), as added by the 2009 Recovery Act). For this purpose, modified AGI is the taxpayer's AGI for the tax year, plus any amounts excluded from gross income under Code Sec. 911 (relating to foreign earned income), Code Sec. 931 (relating to income from sources within Guam, American Samoa, or the Northern Mariana Islands) and Code Sec. 933 (relating to income from sources within Puerto Rico) (Code Sec. 36A(b)(2), as added by the 2009 Recovery Act). Thus, the $400 MWPC is phased out completely at modified AGI of $95,000, and the $800 credit on a joint return is phased out at modified AGI of $190,000.

Practical Analysis: Robert B. Teuber, Tax Attorney with Weiss Berzowski Brady, LLP in Milwaukee, Wisconsin and author of the *www.federaltaxlawforum.com* tax law blog, observes that Act Sec. 1001 of the American Recovery and Reinvestment Tax Act of 2009 adds the new Code Sec. 36A. This new "Making Work Pay Credit" will put a maximum of $400 ($800 for joint filers) in the pockets of eligible individuals in each of the years 2009 and 2010.

To be eligible for the credit, a taxpayer must have earned income and may not be claimed as a dependent on another taxpayer's return. Moreover, a taxpayer may only receive the credit if they have a Social Security number. This effectively makes the credit available only to those that are legally permitted to work in the United States. (Only one taxpayer on a joint return is required to have a social security number to claim the credit.)

Unlike the earlier stimulus packages, this credit will not be paid out by the government by check. Rather, the credit will be advanced to taxpayers through reduced income tax withholding. Conceptually, the additional funds available to consumers

¶305

NEW LAW EXPLAINED

> with each paycheck will provide a steady and continuous stream of spending into the economy. This may provide more favorable economic results than a stimulus check as the tax savings are less likely to be paid in a lump sum against outstanding debts. The reduced withholding, however, may cause difficulty in applying the requirement that the taxpayer have a valid social security number. While the IRS may more easily determine whether a taxpayer that files a return has a valid social security number, it is more difficult to make this determination at the point of withholding. By advancing the credit through reduced withholding, the likelihood that those without valid Social Security numbers receive the credit will be greater than where a stimulus check is sent to taxpayers.

Eligible individuals. All individual taxpayers are eligible for the credit, except for:

- a nonresident alien,
- an individual who can be claimed as another taxpayer's dependent for a tax year beginning in the calendar year in which the individual's tax year begins,
- an estate or trust, or
- a taxpayer whose return does not include his or her social security number (or, on a joint return, a social security number for at least one of the spouses). A taxpayer identification number (TIN) issued by the IRS does not qualify as a social security number (Code Sec. 36A(d)(1), as added by the 2009 Recovery Act). An omission of a correct social security number is treated as a mathematical or clerical error on the return, which allows the IRS to assess any additional tax arising from the omission without using deficiency procedures (Code Sec. 6213(g)(2)(N), as added by the 2009 Recovery Act).

Earned income. Earned income is defined as it is for purposes of the EIC, with two modifications:

(1) Earned income includes amounts excluded from gross income under Code Sec. 112 (relating to compensation received by members of the Armed Forces for active service in a combat zone, or while hospitalized for injuries incurred while serving in a combat zone) regardless of whether the taxpayer elects to include combat pay in earned income for purposes of the EIC.

(2) Earned income does not include net earnings from self-employment that are not taken into account in computing taxable income (Code Sec. 36A(d)(2), as added by the 2009 Recovery Act; see Code Sec. 32(c)(2)).

Coordination with government benefits, calculations. For purposes of calculating a deficiency, the MWPC is taken into account as a negative tax (Code Sec. 6211(b)(4)(A), as amended by the 2009 Recovery Act).

For purposes of determining any individual's eligibility for benefits or assistance, or the amount or extent of benefits or assistance, under any federal program or under any state or local program financed in whole or in part with federal funds, MWP credits and refunds allowed or paid (including credits and refunds under the U.S. possession rules discussed below) are not taken into account as income, or taken into account as

¶305

NEW LAW EXPLAINED

resources for the month of receipt and the following two months (Act Sec. 1001(c) of the 2009 Recovery Act). Thus, MWP credits and refunds do not count toward or negatively impact an individual's eligibility for other income-based government benefits, such as social security benefits, food stamps and other programs.

Termination. The credit does not apply in tax years beginning after December 31, 2010 (Code Sec. 36A(e), as added by the 2009 Recovery Act).

> **Comment:** Congress anticipates that the MWPC will be expeditiously implemented through revised income tax withholding schedules that will reduce income tax withheld for each remaining pay period in 2009 by an amount equal to the amount that withholding would have been reduced had the proposal been reflected in the income tax withholding schedules for the entire tax year (Conference Report on P.L. 111-5, American Recovery and Reinvestment Act of 2009, (H. Rept. 111-16)). In other words, Congress hopes to heighten the stimulus effect of the credit by effectively paying it out quickly via small increases in taxpayers' paychecks, rather than in a lump sum when they file their returns. However, many lower-income workers, who are considered to be the most likely to spend their additional funds quickly, have little or no income tax liability and, therefore, will not be affected by lower withholding tables. Instead, the MWPC will increase the refunds these taxpayers, and taxpayers who do not receive the full amount of the credit via decreased withholding, can claim on their 2009 and 2010 returns.

U.S. possessions. Some special provisions apply to U.S. possessions which, for this purpose, include the Commonwealth of Puerto Rico and the Commonwealth of the Northern Mariana Islands (Act Sec. 1001(b)(3)(A) of the 2009 Recovery Act).

- Payments by Treasury to mirror code possessions.—The U.S. Treasury will pay each mirror code possession an amount equal to that possession's loss caused by the MWPC for tax years beginning in 2009 and 2010. The amount is based on information provided by the government of the possession (Act Sec. 1001(b)(1)(A) of the 2009 Recovery Act). A mirror code possession is one that determines the income tax liability of its residents by reference to U.S. income tax laws as if the possession were the United States (Act Sec. 1001(b)(3)(B) of the 2009 Recovery Act). Mirror code possessions are the United States Virgin Islands, Guam, and the Commonwealth of the Northern Mariana Islands (Conference Report on P.L. 111-5, American Recovery and Reinvestment Act of 2009, (H. Rept. 111-16)).

- Payments by Treasury to non-mirror code possessions.—The U.S. Treasury will pay each non-mirror code possession an amount estimated to be equal to the aggregate benefits that would have been provided to its residents by reason of the MWPC if the possession had a mirror code tax system. In order to receive payment, the possession must have a plan, approved by the Treasury Secretary, to promptly distribute the payment to its residents (Act Sec. 1001(b)(1)(B) of the 2009 Recovery Act). Non-mirror code possessions are Puerto Rico and American Samoa (Conference Report on P.L. 111-5, American Recovery and Reinvestment Act of 2009, (H. Rept. 111-16)),

¶305

NEW LAW EXPLAINED

- Restriction on MWPC claims against U.S. tax liability.—A taxpayer who is allowed a MWPC against taxes imposed by a possession, or who is eligible for a MWPC-related payment from a non-mirror code possession, cannot claim a MWPC against U.S. income tax liability (Act Sec. 1001(b)(2) of the 2009 Recovery Act).

- Treatment of Treasury payments to possessions.—For purposes of the rules permitting the U.S. Treasury to disburse refunds arising from tax credits, payments made under these provisions are treated as refunds due from the MWPC (Act Sec. 1001(b)(3)(C) of the 2009 Recovery Act).

   Comment: The MWPC shares several similarities with the Code Sec. 6428 recovery credit, which most taxpayers received in the form of rebates of up to $600 (plus $300 for each qualifying child) during 2008. The definition of earned income is the same; the definition of eligible individuals is the same except for the income and tax thresholds that applied to the recovery credit; the treatment of the credit for purposes of eligibility to participate in other government programs is the same; and the provisions governing U.S. possessions are the same.

▶ **Effective date.** The provision is effective for tax years beginning after December 31, 2008 (Act Sec. 1001(f) of the American Recovery and Reinvestment Tax Act of 2009 (P.L. 111-5)).

Law source: Law at ¶5075, ¶5375 and ¶5380. Committee Report at ¶10,010.

— Act Sec. 1001(a) of the American Recovery and Reinvestment Tax Act of 2009 (P.L. 111-5), adding Code Sec. 36A;

— Act Sec. 1001(b) and (c);

— Act Sec. 1001(d), adding Code Sec. 6213(g)(2)(N);

— Act Sec. 1001(e) amending Code Sec. 6211(b)(4)(A) and 31 U.S.C. Sec. 1324(b)(2);

— Act Sec. 1001(f), providing the effective date.

Reporter references: For further information, consult the following CCH reporters.

— Standard Federal Tax Reporter, ¶3270.01, ¶4082.032 and ¶33,506.01

— Tax Research Consultant, INDIV: 57,000

— Practical Tax Explanation, § 1,020

¶310 First-Time Homebuyer Credit

SUMMARY OF NEW LAW

For homes purchased after 2008 and before December 1, 2009, the first-time homebuyer credit increases to $8,000, it does not have to be repaid unless the taxpayer sells the home within 36 months, and it can apply to homes that are financed by exempt mortgage revenue bonds or located in the District of Columbia.

BACKGROUND

The Housing Assistance Tax Act of 2008 (P.L. 110-289) created a tax credit for first-time homebuyers who purchase a principal residence in the United States after April 8, 2008, and before July 1, 2009, and who did not have an ownership interest in a principal residence in the prior three years (Code Sec. 36). The refundable income tax credit is equal to 10 percent of the purchase price of the home, up to a maximum credit of $7,500 ($3,750 for a married taxpayer filing a separate return). The credit is phased out for higher-income taxpayers (Code Sec. 36(b)). Taxpayers may elect to claim the credit on a purchase made during the eligible period in 2009 on their 2008 income tax returns (Code Sec. 36(g)).

> **Compliance Tip:** The credit is claimed on Form 5405, First-Time Homebuyer Credit.

Credit exceptions. No first-time homebuyer credit is allowed if:

- the Code Sec. 1400C credit for first-time homebuyers in the District of Columbia is allowable to the taxpayer or the taxpayer's spouse for the tax year of the purchase or any prior tax year;
- the purchased residence is financed by the proceeds of a tax-exempt mortgage revenue bond;
- the taxpayer is a nonresident alien; or
- before the end of the tax year of the purchase, the taxpayer disposes of the residence or it ceases to be the principal residence of the taxpayer (and, if married, the taxpayer's spouse) (Code Sec. 36(d)).

> **Caution:** The rule that prohibits the Code Sec. 36 first-time homebuyer credit when the Code Sec. 1400C District of Columbia first-time homebuyer credit is *allowable* to the taxpayer (or spouse) effectively forces first-time homebuyers in Washington, D.C. to claim the Code Sec 1400C credit even though, at a maximum of $5,000, it is less generous than the Code Sec. 36 homebuyer credit.

Recapture. Although labeled a credit, the first-time homebuyer credit actually amounts to a no-interest loan, because a taxpayer who claims the credit must repay it in equal installments over a 15-year recapture period, beginning with the second tax year following the tax year of purchase). The recapture operates by increasing the taxpayer's federal tax liability by 6 2/3 percent (or 1/15th) of the credit amount for each year during the recapture period (Code Sec. 36(f)).

> **Comment:** According to the National Association of Realtors, the repayment requirement was the biggest obstacle to the credit's effectiveness during 2008.

Accelerated recapture. If, before the end of the recapture period, the taxpayer sells the home, or the taxpayer (and spouse, if married) ceases to use the home as a principal residence, the portion of the credit that has not yet been recaptured must be recaptured on the return for the year in which the sale occurs or the use as a principal residence ceases (Code Sec. 36(f)(2)). However, if the taxpayer sells the home to an unrelated person, the accelerated recapture amount may not exceed the taxpayer's gain from the sale (Code Sec. 36(f)(3)).

Recapture exceptions. The recapture and accelerated recapture rules do not apply after the taxpayer's death. The accelerated recapture rules also do not apply if there is an

¶310

BACKGROUND

involuntary or compulsory conversion of the home, as long as the taxpayer acquires a new principal residence within two years; or if the taxpayer transfers the home to a spouse or former spouse incident to divorce (Code Sec. 36(f)(4)).

NEW LAW EXPLAINED

Credit increased and extended; recapture generally waived.—For purchases made after December 31, 2008, the first-time homebuyer credit is expanded in five respects:

(1) The credit is extended to apply to homes purchased before December 1, 2009 (Code Sec. 36(h), as amended by the American Recovery and Reinvestment Tax Act of 2009 (P.L. 111-5)).

(2) The maximum amount of the credit is increased to $8,000 ($4,000 for a married taxpayer filing a separate return) (Code Sec. 36(b), as amended by the 2009 Recovery Act).

(3) The recapture of the credit is generally waived. However, the accelerated recapture rules apply if, within 36 months after the purchase, the taxpayer disposes of the home, or the taxpayer (and spouse, if married) ceases to use the home as a principal residence (Code Sec. 36(f)(4)(D), as added by the 2009 Recovery Act).

(4) The credit is available even if the purchased residence is financed by the proceeds of a tax-exempt mortgage revenue bond (Code Sec. 36(d), as amended by the 2009 Recovery Act).

(5) The taxpayer cannot claim the Code Sec. 1400C credit for first-time homebuyers in the District of Columbia if the Code Sec. 36 first-time homebuyer credit is allowable to the taxpayer or the taxpayer's spouse (Code Sec. 36(d), as amended by the 2009 Recovery Act; Code Sec. 1400C(e)(4), as added by the 2009 Recovery Act). Thus, first-time homebuyers who purchase homes in Washington, D.C. after 2008 and before December 1, 2009, can claim only the Code Sec. 36 credit; they cannot claim the Code Sec. 1400C credit.

Practical Analysis: Vincent O'Brien, President of Vincent J. O'Brien, CPA, PC, Lynbrook, New York, observes that eligible taxpayers who purchased a home during 2008 will still receive the same first-time homebuyer credit that was originally established by The Housing Assistance Tax Act of 2008 (P.L.110-289). However, eligible taxpayers who purchase a home during 2009 will receive a substantially improved credit.

2008 Purchases. Eligible taxpayers who purchased a home after April 8, 2008, and before January 1, 2009, and claim the credit in 2008 must still begin repaying the credit over a 15-year period, beginning in 2010. In addition, if the taxpayer sells the home or stops using it as his or her principal residence, he or she must repay the entire remaining unpaid balance of the credit in the year in which the sale or change of use occurs. This provision can be especially burdensome for taxpayers who cease to use a home as a principal residence but do not sell it. Practitioners should

NEW LAW EXPLAINED

> thoroughly warn their clients about the repayment requirements that still apply when the credit is claimed for 2008 purchases.
>
> *2009 Purchases.* Eligible taxpayers who purchase a home after December 31, 2008, and before December 1, 2009, as long as they continue to own and use the home as their principal residence for at least three years after the date of purchase, will not have to repay the credit at all.
>
> *Eligibility for Credit.* The eligibility rules for the credit were unchanged by the new law. To claim the credit, taxpayers cannot have owned a home within the three-year period ending on the date of the purchase of the new home.
>
> *Use of Special Election.* Eligible taxpayers who purchase a home after December 31, 2008, and before December 1, 2009, can elect to claim the credit on their 2008 returns. The Committee Report for the American Recovery and Reinvestment Tax Act of 2009 indicates the waiver of repayment will apply to all homes purchased during 2009, even if the credit is claimed on a 2008 return.
>
> *Timing of Filing 2008 Returns.* A taxpayer who elects to claim the credit for a 2009 purchase on a 2008 return can do so on an originally filed return or on an amended return filed within the normal statute-of-limitations period. A taxpayer that expects to purchase a home before October of 2009 should consider obtaining an extension for his or her 2008 return, which is far simpler than amending it later.
>
> However, taxpayers who purchase a home near the October 15, 2009, extended due date for filing 2008 returns, or after that date (and before December 1, 2009), will have to make a choice of whether to amend their 2008 returns or simply wait and claim the credit on their 2009 returns.
>
> *New Instructions for Form 5405.* It is likely that the IRS will issue revised instructions for Form 5405, *First-Time Homebuyer Credit*, to reflect the new provisions. Therefore, even if an eligible taxpayer purchases a home in early 2009, he or she should wait until the new instructions are available before filing a 2008 return that claims the credit.

Comment: According to the Conference Committee Report for American Recovery and Reinvestment Act of 2009, a taxpayer cannot claim the Code Sec. 36 credit if the taxpayer claimed the Code Sec. 1400C credit for any prior year (Conference Report on P.L. 111-5, American Recovery and Reinvestment Act of 2009 (H. Rept. 111-16)). However, that restriction existed under prior law, but now has been removed from the statute (Code Sec. 36(d)(1), prior to removal by the 2009 Recovery Act).

Caution: These amendments are not retroactive. Thus, none of these modifications apply to taxpayers who claim the credit for homes purchased to the first-time homebuyer credits during 2008.

> **Practical Analysis:** Kip Dellinger, CPA, Senior Tax Partner at Kallman And Co. LLP in Los Angeles, observes that at first blush, a tax benefit such as the new homebuyer credit appears to provide significant incentive to prospective homebuyers to jump

¶310

NEW LAW EXPLAINED

> into the market. However, to the extent clients seek advice from tax professionals about the purchase of a residence in situations where the credit applies, any advice must be tempered with advising the client that the economics of the particular marketplace where the home is located should dictate whether or not to purchase a home. While the tax credit is designed to generate home buying activity and place a floor under falling prices, the problems of the housing market and the related credit markets are of such magnitude that the benefits of the credit may not outweigh the potential for significant market declines in the neighborhood of a client's target property.

A taxpayer's election to accelerate the benefit of the credit by treating a purchase made during the eligible period in 2009 as having been made on December 31, 2008, does not apply for purposes of the waiver of the repayment requirement and the modifications to the accelerated recapture rules (Code Sec. 36(g), as amended by the 2009 Recovery Act). Thus, a first-time homebuyer who purchases a home after 2008 and before December 1, 2009, can elect to claim the credit for the 2008 tax year, and still be excused from repaying the credit, unless the taxpayer sells the home within 36 months.

> **Caution:** Under a strict reading of the amendments, an election to accelerate the credit by treating a 2009 purchase as having been made in 2008 would cause the original 2008 credit to apply in all respects except for the recapture rules. Under this interpretation, the election would cause the maximum credit to revert to $7,500, and would make it unavailable with respect to homes that are financed by the proceeds of a tax-exempt mortgage revenue bond or located in the District of Columbia.

▶ **Effective date.** The amendments apply to residences purchased after December 31, 2008 (Act Sec. 1006(f) of the American Recovery and Reinvestment Tax Act of 2009 (P.L. 111-5)).

Law source: Law at ¶5070 and ¶5305. Committee Report at ¶10,060.

— Act Sec. 1006(a) of the American Recovery and Reinvestment Tax Act of 2009 (P.L. 111-5), amending Code Sec. 36(g) and (h);

— Act Sec. 1006(b), amending Code Sec. 36(b);

— Act Sec. 1006(c), adding Code Sec. 36(f)(4)(D) and amending (g);

— Act Sec. 1006(d), adding Code Sec. 1400C(e)(4) and striking Code Sec. 36(d)(1);

— Act Sec. 1006(e), striking Code Sec. 36(d)(2), and redesignating former Code Sec. 36(d)(3) and (4) as Code Sec. 36(d)(1) and (2), respectively;

— Act Sec. 1006(f), providing the effective date.

Reporter references: For further information, consult the following CCH reporters.

— Standard Federal Tax Reporter, ¶4190.05

— Tax Research Consultant, INDIV: 57,950

— Practical Tax Explanation, § 13,010

¶315 Refundable Portion of Child Tax Credit

SUMMARY OF NEW LAW

In 2009 and 2010, individuals are eligible for a refundable child tax credit equal to 15 percent of their earned income in excess of $3,000, up to the per child credit amount, if their allowable child tax credit exceeds their total tax liability (regular and alternative minimum).

BACKGROUND

Individuals who have dependent children under age 17 at the close of a calendar year may be eligible for a child tax credit (CTC) in the amount of $1,000 per child through 2010 (Code Sec. 24). The CTC is subject to income phase out rules and is limited to *qualifying* children (Code Sec. 24(b)(1), (b)(2), and (c)). The CTC is generally a nonrefundable credit that may be used to offset both an individual's regular and alternative minimum tax liabilities (Code Secs. 24(b)(3) and 26(a)(2)).

The CTC does have a refundable component when the total amount of the CTC exceeds the individual's total tax liability minus nonrefundable credits previously taken. The CTC is refundable to the extent of 15 percent of the individual's earned income in excess of $10,000, as adjusted annually for inflation, up to the per child credit amount, as long as the individual has a total tax liability of less than his or her allowable CTC (Code Sec. 24(d)(1)).

The 15 percent of earned income refundable CTC is subject to a sunset provision and will not apply for tax years beginning after December 31, 2010. Furthermore, taxpayers with three or more children may calculate the refundable portion of the credit using the excess of their social security taxes over their earned income credit, instead of the 15 percent method, if it results in a greater refundable credit (Code Sec. 24(d)(1)).

The refundable credit amount will reduce the nonrefundable credit otherwise allowable (*i.e.*, converting some or all of the nonrefundable credit into a refundable credit), and the refundable credit is not taken into account in applying the tax liability limitation on nonrefundable personal credits (Code Sec. 24(d)(1)). These rules apply regardless of whether the refundable credit is computed under the 15 percent of earned income method or the additional credit for families with three or more children method.

The refundable component's $10,000 base amount of earned income is subject to cost-of-living adjustments (Code Sec. 24(d)(3)). In 2009, the inflation adjusted base amount of earned income is $12,550 (Rev. Proc. 2008-66, I.R.B. 2008-45, 1107).

Example: Joe and Paula Hart have three children and earned income of $25,000 in 2009. They have no other income and no alternative minimum tax liability. They are not entitled to any nonrefundable personal credits other than the CTC. Since they file jointly, they are entitled to a standard deduction of $11,400. They

BACKGROUND

> are also entitled to a personal exemption of $3,650 for each family member, or $18,250. They have no taxable income after the deduction and exemptions are applied, therefore, their tax liability is $0. Their allowable nonrefundable CTC is equal to $3,000 ($1,000 per child). However, the nonrefundable credit is limited to the amount of tax liability, or $0.
>
> The refundable credit is equal to the lesser of either the unclaimed portion of the nonrefundable credit amount, $3,000 ($3,000 − $0), or 15 percent of the Harts' earned income that exceeds $12,550, $1,868 (($25,000 − $12,550) × .15), since the additional credit for families with three or more children does not result in a greater refundable credit. Their total refundable credit amount is $1,868. Joe and Paula receive a little over 50 percent of their otherwise allowable CTC in 2009.

The Emergency Economic Stabilization Act of 2008 (P.L. 110-343) lowered the base amount of earned income to $8,500 for 2008 only. Taxpayers with earned income of less than the base amount are not eligible for the refundable CTC.

NEW LAW EXPLAINED

Refundable child credit income threshold reduced in 2009 and 2010.—In 2009 and 2010, the child tax credit (CTC) is refundable to the extent of 15 percent of the taxpayer's earned income in excess of $3,000, up to the per child credit amount, if the taxpayer has a total tax liability (regular and alternative minimum) of less than his or her allowable CTC minus nonrefundable credits previously taken (Code Sec. 24(d)(4), as amended by the American Recovery and Reinvestment Tax Act of 2009 (P.L. 111-5)).

In 2009 and 2010, the threshold requirements for the 15 percent of earned income refundable component of the CTC are:

(1) a total tax liability (regular plus alternative minimum), minus nonrefundable credits previously taken, of less than the taxpayer's allowable CTC ($1,000 per qualifying child); and

(2) earned income in excess of $3,000.

> **Comment:** Eligibility for the refundable portion of the CTC previously required that an individual have earned income *in excess* of $12,550 in 2009. The reduction in the refundable component's base amount of earned income to $3,000 is only effective for tax years 2009 and 2010.

> **Example:** In 2009, Pam and Jim Allen have three children and earned income of $25,000. They have no other income, no alternative minimum tax liability, and are not entitled to any nonrefundable personal credits other than the CTC. As joint filers, they are entitled to a standard deduction of $11,400. In addition, they are entitled to a personal exemption of $3,650 for each family member, or $18,250. This results in no taxable income and no tax liability. Their allowable

NEW LAW EXPLAINED

> nonrefundable CTC is equal to $3,000 ($1,000 per child). However, the nonrefundable credit is limited to the amount of tax liability, or $0.
>
> The refundable credit is equal to the lesser of either the unclaimed portion of the nonrefundable credit amount, $3,000 ($3,000 − $0), or 15 percent of the Allens' earned income in excess of $3,000, $3,300 (($25,000 − $3,000) × .15), because the additional credit for families with three or more children does not result in a greater refundable credit. Pam and Jim are entitled to a refundable credit of $3,000.
>
> The inflation adjusted earned income threshold would have been $12,550 in 2009 absent the amendment reducing the earned income threshold to $3,000. This would have given the Allens a total CTC of $1,868 consisting of a refundable credit of $1,868 (($25,000 − $12,550) × .15) and a nonrefundable credit of $0 (no tax liability) which is $1,132 less than the $3,000 credit amount.

Comment: By reducing the earned income threshold for computing the refundable CTC, more low-income taxpayers will be eligible for the refundable CTC. The maximum increase in the refundable CTC for any taxpayer in 2009 will be $1,432.50 (($12,550 − $3,000) × .15).

▶ **Effective date.** The amendment applies to tax years beginning after December 31, 2008 (Act Sec. 1003(b) of the American Recovery and Reinvestment Tax Act of 2009 (P.L. 111-5)).

Law source: Law at ¶5005. Committee Report at ¶10,030.

— Act Sec. 1003(a) of the American Recovery and Reinvestment Tax Act of 2009 (P.L. 111-5), amending Code Sec. 24(d)(4);

— Act Sec. 1003(b), providing the effective date.

Reporter references: For further information, consult the following CCH reporters.

— Standard Federal Tax Reporter, ¶3770.03

— Tax Research Consultant, INDIV: 57,454.10

— Practical Tax Explanation, § 12,120.15

¶320 Increase in Earned Income Tax Credit

SUMMARY OF NEW LAW

For tax years beginning in 2009 and 2010, the maximum amount of the earned income tax credit is increased, and the AGI phaseout range is broadened, for taxpayers with three or more qualifying children. Also, for joint filers, regardless of the number of qualifying children, the AGI phaseout amounts are increased.

BACKGROUND

A refundable earned income credit is available to certain low-income individuals (Code Sec. 32). The amount of credit varies depending on the number of the taxpayer's qualifying children (Code Sec. 32(b)).

The credit amount is determined by multiplying an individual's earned income that does not exceed a maximum amount (called the earned income amount) by the applicable credit percentage. The credit is reduced by a limitation amount determined by multiplying the applicable phaseout percentage by the excess of the amount of the individual's adjusted gross income (AGI) (or earned income, if greater) over a phaseout amount. The earned income amount and the phaseout amount are adjusted yearly for inflation.

The threshold amount at which the phaseout of the earned income credit begins for taxpayers whose filing status is married filing jointly increases by $3,000 for tax years beginning in 2008 and thereafter (Code Sec. 32(b)(2)(B)). The $3,000 amount is adjusted for inflation (Code Sec. 32(j)).

Under present law, for tax years beginning in 2009, the following amounts were scheduled to be used in determining a taxpayer's earned income credit (Rev. Proc. 2008-66, I.R.B. 2008-45, 1107):

Single, Surviving Spouse, or Head of Household

Number of Qualifying Children	Earned Income Amount	Credit Percentage	Maximum Credit Amount	AGI Phaseout Range
One	$8,950	34%	$3,043	$16,420—$35,463
Two or More	$12,570	40%	$5,028	$16,420—$40,295
None	$5,970	7.65%	$457	$7,470—$13,440

Married Filing Jointly

Number of Qualifying Children	Earned Income Amount	Credit Percentage	Maximum Credit Amount	AGI Phaseout Range
One	$8,950	34%	$3,043	$19,540—$38,583
Two or More	$12,570	40%	$5,028	$19,540—$43,415
None	$5,970	7.65%	$457	$10,590—$16,560

NEW LAW EXPLAINED

Increase in earned income tax credit.—For tax years beginning in 2009 and 2010, the applicable credit percentage for taxpayers with three or more qualifying children is 45 percent (up from 40 percent) (Code Sec. 32(b)(3)(A), as added by the American Recovery and Reinvestment Tax Act of 2009 (P.L. 111-5). Also, the phaseout amount is increased by $5,000 for joint filers, regardless of the number of qualifying children. This $5,000 amount is adjusted for inflation for tax years beginning in 2010 (Code Sec. 32(b)(3)(B), as added by the 2009 Recovery Act).

¶320

NEW LAW EXPLAINED

Thus, for tax years beginning in 2009, the following amounts are used in determining a taxpayer's earned income credit (see, also, Rev. Proc. 2008-66, I.R.B. 2008-45, 1107):

Single, Surviving Spouse, or Head of Household

Number of Qualifying Children	Earned Income Amount	Credit Percentage	Maximum Credit Amount	AGI Phaseout Range
One	$8,950	34%	$3,043	$16,420—$35,463
Two	$12,570	40%	$5,028	$16,420—$40,295
Three or More	*$12,570*	*45%*	*$5,657*	*$16,420—$43,281*
None	$5,970	7.65%	$457	$7,470—$13,440

Married Filing Jointly

Number of Qualifying Children	Earned Income Amount	Credit Percentage	Maximum Credit Amount	AGI Phaseout Range
One	$8,950	34%	$3,043	*$21,420—$40,463*
Two	$12,570	40%	$5,028	*$21,420—$45,295*
Three or More	*$12,570*	*45%*	*$5,657*	*$21,420—$48,281*
None	$5,970	7.65%	$457	*$12,470—$18,440*

In light of the required annual inflation adjustments to the "earned income amount" and "phaseout amount" used in determining a taxpayer's credit, the maximum credit amounts cannot be currently computed for tax years beginning in 2010.

> **Comment:** Increasing the credit percentage from 40 to 45 percent, for taxpayers with three or more qualifying children, yields not only a higher maximum credit amount but also a broader AGI phaseout range for those taxpayers, even if they do not file a joint return.
>
> **CCH Caution:** Rev. Proc. 2008-66, I.R.B. 2008-45, 1107, which provides the maximum earned income credit and phaseout ranges for the 2009 tax year was issued prior to February 17, 2009. The Act provides an increased credit percentage for taxpayers with 3 or more qualifying children and increases the credit phaseout range by $5,000 for married taxpayers filing joint returns. Presumably, the IRS will issue a modification to Rev. Proc. 2008-66 to reflect these changes.

▶ **Effective date.** The provision applies to tax years beginning after December 31, 2008 (Act Sec. 1002(b) of the American Recovery and Reinvestment Act of 2009 (P.L. 111-5)).

Law source: Law at ¶5060. Committee Report at ¶10,020.

— Act Sec. 1002(a) of the American Recovery and Reinvestment Tax Act of 2009 (P.L. 111-5), adding Code Sec. 32(b)(3);

— Act Sec. 1002(b), providing the effective date.

Reporter references: For further information, consult the following CCH reporters.

— Standard Federal Tax Reporter, ¶4082.01

— Tax Research Consultant, INDIV: 57,250

— Practical Tax Explanation, § 12,601

¶320

¶325 $250 Credit for Government Retirees

SUMMARY OF NEW LAW

Individuals who receive certain government pensions and annuity payments will receive a $250 credit for 2009.

BACKGROUND

Adults who are eligible for benefits under certain social security, Railroad Retirement and veterans compensation programs, or for supplemental security income (SSI) cash benefits, will receive a one-time economic recovery payment of $250 (Act Sec. 2201 of the Assistance for Unemployed Workers and Struggling Families Act (P.L. 111-5)). These payments are discussed at ¶225.

For 2009 and 2010, individuals with earned income can qualify for a refundable Making Work Pay Credit of up to $400 ($800 on a joint return) (Code Sec. 36A, as added by the American Reinvestment and Recovery Tax Act of 2009). This credit is discussed at ¶305.

NEW LAW EXPLAINED

Government retirees can qualify for $250 credit for 2009.—Certain government retirees can claim a refundable $250 tax credit for their first tax year beginning in 2009. The credit increases to $500 on a joint return if both spouses are eligible (Act Sec. 2202(a) of the Assistance for Unemployed Workers and Struggling Families Act (P.L. 111-5)).

Eligible individuals. A person eligible for the credit must meet all of these tests:

(1) During his or her first tax year beginning in 2009, the individual must receive some amount as a pension or annuity for service performed in the employ of the United States, any state, or any instrumentality thereof, which is not considered employment for purposes of the Federal Insurance Contributions Act (FICA, or Code Secs. 3101 through 3128) (Act Sec. 2202(b)(1)(A) of the Struggling Families Act). Thus, the worker's government employment must not have been covered by social security (Conference Report on P.L. 111-5, American Recovery and Reinvestment Act of 2009 (H. Rept. 111-16)).

(2) The individual must not receive an economic recovery payment during the tax year (as discussed at ¶225) (Act Sec. 2202(b)(1)(B) of the Struggling Families Act).

(3) The individual's tax return must include his or her social security number. A joint return must include the social security number of at least one of the spouses. For this purpose, a social security number does not include a taxpayer identification number (TIN) issued by the IRS. Any omission of a correct social security number is treated as a mathematical or clerical error on the return under Code Sec.

NEW LAW EXPLAINED

6213(g)(2), which allows the IRS to assess any additional tax arising from the omission without using deficiency procedures (Act Sec. 2202(b)(2) of the Struggling Families Act).

Treatment of the credit. The credit is treated as a refundable credit allowed by the Internal Revenue Code, Chapter 1, subchapter A, part IV, subpart C. Thus, it is refundable to the same extent as the new Code Sec. 36A Making Work Pay Credit (MWPC) (discussed at ¶ 305). For purposes of the rules permitting the U.S. Treasury to disburse refunds arising from tax credits, refunds of the credit are treated as refunds due from the MWPC (Act Sec. 2202(c)(1) of the Struggling Families Act). For purposes of calculating a deficiency, the credit is taken into account as a negative tax; see Code Sec. 6211(b)(4)(A), as amended by the American Recovery and Reinvestment Tax Act of 2009 (P.L. 111-5), and Code Sec. 36A, as added by the 2009 Recovery Act (Act Sec. 2202(c)(2) of the Struggling Families Act).

Coordination with government benefits, calculations. For purposes of determining any individual's eligibility for benefits or assistance, or the amount or extent of benefits or assistance, under any federal program or under any state or local program financed in whole or in part with federal funds, credits and refunds allowed or paid are not taken into account as income, or taken into account as resources for the month of receipt and the following two months (Act Sec. 2202(d) of the Struggling Families Act). Thus, the credit and refunds arising from it do not count toward or negatively impact an individual's eligibility for other income-based government benefits, such as social security benefits, food stamps and other programs.

▶ **Effective date.** No effective date is provided by the Act. The provision is therefore, considered effective on February 17, 2009, the date of enactment.

Law source: Law at ¶7071. Committee Report at ¶10,500.

— Act Sec. 2202 of the Assistance for Unemployed Workers and Struggling Families Act (P.L. 111-5).

Reporter references: For further information, consult the following CCH reporters.

— Standard Federal Tax Reporter, ¶38,869.021

— Tax Research Consultant, INDIV: 57,900

— Practical Tax Explanation, § 1,030

¶330 Hope Scholarship Credit

SUMMARY OF NEW LAW

In 2009 and 2010, the Hope Scholarship Credit is increased to a maximum of $2,500 per eligible student, text books and course materials are included as qualifying expenses, the credit can be claimed for up to four years per eligible student, the income phase out range is increased to $80,000 - $90,000 for single taxpayers and $160,000 - $180,000 for joint filers, and 40 percent of the credit is refundable.

¶330

BACKGROUND

The Hope Scholarship Credit generally allows individual taxpayers to claim a nonrefundable credit against federal income taxes for tuition and related expenses paid for the first two years of post-secondary education for each eligible student. The Hope credit could offset both regular and alternative minimum tax liabilities in tax years beginning in 2000 through 2008 (Code Sec. 26(a)(2)). For tax years beginning after 2008, the Hope credit cannot exceed the excess of the taxpayer's regular tax liability for the tax year over the taxpayer's tentative minimum tax liability (Code Sec. 26(a)(1)).

The Hope credit is equal to 100 percent of the first $1,000 of qualified tuition and related expenses and 50 percent of the next $1,000 of such expenses (Code Sec. 25A(b)(1) and (4)). The $1,000 amount is subject to adjustment for inflation annually (Code Sec. 25A(h)(1)). In 2009, the inflation adjusted cap on qualified tuition and related expenses is $1,200, therefore, the maximum amount of the Hope credit for each eligible student is $1,800 (Rev. Proc. 2008-66, I.R.B. 2008-45, 1107).

In order to qualify for the credit, the tuition must be paid on behalf of the taxpayer, the taxpayer's spouse or the taxpayer's dependent (Code Sec. 25A(f)(1)(A)). An eligible student for purposes of the credit is an individual who is enrolled in a degree, certificate or other program leading to a recognized educational credential at an eligible educational institution. The individual must be enrolled at least half-time and must not have been convicted of a federal or state felony for possession or distribution of a controlled substance (Code Sec. 25A(b)(2)). An eligible educational institution is an accredited post-secondary educational institution offering credit towards a bachelor's degree, associate's degree or another recognized post-secondary credential. Proprietary institutions or vocational schools may also be eligible (Code Sec. 25A(f)(2); Reg. §1.25A-2(b)).

The credit can only be claimed with respect to expenses incurred for qualified tuition and related expenses, which includes the tuition and fees required to be enrolled at or attend a particular institution. Expenses incurred with respect to classes relating to sports or hobbies are not considered unless the courses are a part of the degree program. Nonacademic fees such as student activity fees, athletic fees or insurance expenses are also not considered for purposes of the credit (Code Sec. 25A(f)(1)). The IRS has specifically stated that expenses for room and board are not included in "qualified tuition and related expenses" (Reg. §1.25A-2(d)(3)). Typically, books and classroom supplies and equipment are not considered "qualified tuition and related expenses" unless payment for such expenses must be made directly to the educational institution in order for the student to enroll and attend classes at the institution (Reg. §1.25A-2(d)(2)).

The Hope credit is subject to several restrictions. The credit is only available for the first two years of post-secondary education for an eligible student (Code Sec. 25A(b)(2)(C)). The credit is phased out ratably for taxpayers with modified adjusted gross income (AGI) between $40,000 and $50,000 ($80,000 and $100,000 for joint filers) (Code Sec. 25A(d)). The modified AGI amounts are adjusted for inflation (Code Sec. 25A(h)(2)). For 2009, the phase-out range is $50,000 to $60,000 for single taxpayers and $100,000 to $120,000 for joint filers (Rev. Proc. 2008-66, I.R.B. 2008-45, 1107).

¶330

BACKGROUND

For tax years beginning in 2008 and 2009, students enrolled in and paying tuition at an eligible education institution located in the Midwestern disaster area may be eligible for 100 percent of the first $2,400 in qualified tuition and related expenses and 50 percent of the next $2,400, up to a maximum Hope credit of $3,600 under Code Sec. 1400O(2) (Division C, Act Sec. 702(a)(1)(B) and (d)(8) of the Emergency Economic Stabilization Act of 2008 (P.L.110-343)). Qualified tuition and related expenses can be determined by using the broader standard for withdrawals from Code Sec. 529 plans which includes qualifying expenses for books, room and board, and for special needs students pursuant to Code Sec. 1400O(1) (Division C, Act Sec. 702(a)(1)(B) and (d)(8) of P.L.110-343).

NEW LAW EXPLAINED

Hope credit increased, expanded and made partially refundable.—For tax years 2009 and 2010, the Hope Scholarship Credit is modified. The modifications are entitled the American Opportunity Tax Credit and are effective only for 2009 and 2010. The Hope credit is increased to the sum of 100 percent of the first $2,000 of qualified tuition and related expenses and 25 percent of the next $2,000, for a total maximum credit of $2,500 per eligible student per year in 2009 and 2010 (Code Sec. 25A(i)(1), as added by the American Recovery and Reinvestment Tax Act of 2009 (P.L. 111-5)). The credit is expanded to apply to the first four years of a student's post-secondary education for tax years 2009 and 2010 (Code Sec. 25A(i)(2), as added by the 2009 Recovery Act).

The adjusted gross income (AGI) phase-out limits for taxpayers claiming the Hope credit in 2009 and 2010 are also increased. The Hope credit is ratably reduced by the amount bearing the same ratio to the credit as the excess of the taxpayer's modified AGI over $80,000 bears to $10,000. These amounts double to $160,000 and $20,000 for joint filers (Code Sec. 25A(i)(4), as added by the 2009 Recovery Act).

> **Example:** Opie was a full-time student in 2009 at a university with tuition and related expenses of $10,000. Opie's unmarried father, Andy, paid for Opie's tuition at the college and wishes to claim a Hope tax credit on behalf of Opie. Andy's AGI as a small-town sheriff for 2009 was $82,000. The ratio of the excess of Andy's AGI over $80,000 ($2,000) to $10,000 is $1/5$ ($2,000/$10,000 = $1/5$). The $2,500 Hope tax credit claimed by Andy is reduced by $1/5$, so Andy can only claim a $2,000 credit ($2,500–($1/5 \times $2,500) = $2,000).

The Hope credit retains most qualification requirements and definitions in 2009 and 2010, such as the half-time enrollment requirement and the definitions of an eligible student and an eligible educational institution. While the Hope credit applied to qualified tuition and related expenses prior to 2009, it can be claimed for tuition, fees and course materials in 2009 and 2010 (Code Sec. 25A(i)(3), as added by the 2009 Recovery Act). This allows claimants of the credit to include the cost of books and other required course materials in the determination of the credit amount in 2009 and 2010.

¶330

NEW LAW EXPLAINED

Compliance Pointer: Note that the increased credit amount is only available for tuition and related expenses paid in 2009 or 2010 for education furnished to the student in an academic period beginning in 2009 or 2010 (Code Sec. 25A(i)(1), as added by the 2009 Recovery Act). Many institutions require payment for a spring semester before the end of December in the prior year. For example, the tuition for a spring semester beginning in January, 2009 may be due in December, 2008. Under these circumstances, the tuition paid in December, 2008 would not be eligible for the increased Hope credit because it was not paid in 2009.

Practical Analysis: Robert B. Teuber, Tax Attorney with Weiss Berzowski Brady, LLP in Milwaukee, Wisconsin and author of the *www.federaltaxlawforum.com* tax law blog, observes that Act Sec. 1004 of the American Recovery and Reinvestment Tax Act of 2009 modifies Code Sec. 25A to increase the amount of the Hope Scholarship Credit and to rename it the American Opportunity Credit.

Previously, the Hope Scholarship Credit had only been available to students in their first two years of post-secondary education. For the years 2009 and 2010, the credit will be made available to those students in their first four years of post-secondary education. Additionally, the maximum amount of credit is temporarily increased to $2,500 (from $1,800 in 2008). Under the new section the phase-out of the credit is pushed back by approximately $30,000. That is, the phase-out, which in 2008 began at an Adjusted Gross Income of $48,000 ($96,000 for joint-filers) starts at an AGI of $80,000 ($160,000 for joint filers) for 2009 and 2010.

An additional benefit provided by the American Opportunity Credit is that 40 percent of the credit is refundable. That is, up to $1,000 (40 percent of maximum $2,500 credit) may be refunded to a taxpayer that otherwise has a zero tax liability.

The increase in the credit will sunset with the numerous expiring provisions under the Economic Growth and Tax Relief Reconciliation Act of 2001 after December 31, 2010, until that time, however, the expanded Hope credit provides an increased incentive for individuals to go to, or stay in, college. Those students in Midwestern Disaster Areas, however, may opt to take advantage of the expanded Hope Scholarship Credit provisions granted by the disaster area relief in lieu of the American Opportunity Credit under the stimulus package.

Forty percent of a taxpayer's otherwise allowable Hope credit is refundable in 2009 and 2010. However, if the taxpayer claiming the credit is a child who has unearned income subject to the "kiddie tax" under Code Sec. 1(g), none of the credit is refundable (Code Sec. 25A(i)(6), as added by the 2009 Recovery Act). The nonrefundable portion of the credit may be offset against both regular and alternative minimum tax (AMT) liabilities in tax years when Code Sec. 26(a)(2) does not apply (tax years after 2009) (Code Sec. 25A(i)(5), as added by the 2009 Recovery Act). Code Sec. 26(a)(2) is amended by the 2009 Recovery Act to apply to tax years beginning in 2009 (see ¶ 240).

Comment: Since Code Sec. 25A(i) only applies in tax years 2009 and 2010 and Code Sec. 26(a)(2), as amended by the 2009 Recovery Act, applies in 2009, the offset of the nonrefundable portion of the Hope credit against regular tax and

¶330

NEW LAW EXPLAINED

AMT in tax years when Code Sec. 26(a)(2) does not apply means that the offset under Code Sec. 25A(i)(5) only applies in 2010.

> **Example:** In 2009, Sue and Tim McComb have two children and taxable income of $13,100. Their regular tax is $1,310 and they have alternative minimum tax of $100. They paid $5,000 in college tuition for their son Jim in 2009. Jim has no unearned income in 2009. The McCombs are entitled to a Hope credit of $2,410, $1,000 refundable and $1,410 nonrefundable. Their otherwise allowable credit is $2,500 ($2,000 × 1 + $2,000 × .25). Forty percent of $2,500 (.40 × $2,500 = $1,000) is refundable and the remaining $1,500 is nonrefundable, but limited to the total of their regular and alternative minimum tax liabilities, or $1,410. Under prior law, they would have only been entitled to a $1,410 nonrefundable credit, but due to the addition of a refundable portion to the Hope credit, they can now claim a credit of $2,410 ($1,410 + $1,000).

Any reference in Code Secs. 24, 25, 25A, 25B, 26, 904 or 1400C to the increased Hope credit is treated as a reference to the amount of the education credits under Code Sec. 25A(a) attributable to the Hope Scholarship Credit (Code Sec. 25A(i)(5), flush language, as added by the 2009 Recovery Act).

In 2009, taxpayers who qualify for a Hope credit of up to $3,600 resulting from the student's enrollment in and tuition being paid to an eligible education institution located in the Midwestern disaster area may elect to waive application of Code Sec. 25A(i) in favor of the larger Hope credit under Code Sec. 1400O(2) as determined by Division C, Act Sec. 702(a)(1)(B) of the Emergency Economic Stabilization Act of 2008 (P.L.110-343) (Code Sec. 25A(i)(7), as added by the 2009 Recovery Act).

The conforming amendment providing that the child tax credit (CTC) can be offset against regular tax and alternative minimum tax liability reduced by the foreign tax credit and all other nonrefundable credits except the CTC, the adoption credit, the American opportunity credit (Hope credit in 2009 and 2010), the saver's credit, the residential alternative energy credit, and the plug-in electric drive motor vehicle credit will sunset for tax years beginning after 2010 (Code Sec. 24(b)(3)(B), as amended by the 2009 Recovery Act; Act Sec. 1004(e) of the 2009 Recovery Act).

The refundable portion of the Hope credit is generally available to bona fide residents of U.S. possessions (including the Commonwealths of Puerto Rico and the Northern Mariana Islands), but cannot be claimed by those residents in the U.S. (Act Sec. 1004(c)(2) of the 2009 Recovery Act). A bona fide resident of a possession with a mirror code tax system may claim the refundable portion of the credit in the possession in which the individual is a resident. The Secretary of the Treasury is required to provide payment for the amount of loss incurred by that possession due to the refundable portion of the Hope credit, based upon information provided by the possession (Act Sec. 1004(c)(1)(A). A mirror code tax system exists if the income tax liability of the residents of the possession is determined by reference to the income tax laws of the U.S. as if the possession were the U.S. (Act Sec. 1004(c)(3)(B)). A bona fide resident of a possession

¶330

NEW LAW EXPLAINED

that does not have a mirror code tax system can also claim the refundable portion of the credit in the possession, but only if the possession establishes a plan for permitting the claim under internal law (Act Sec. 1004(c)(1)(B) of the 2009 Recovery Act; Conference Committee Report for American Recovery and Reinvestment Act of 2009). The Secretary of the Treasury is also required to provide a payment to non-mirror code tax system possessions equaling the aggregate benefits provided to residents of the possession due to the application of the refundable portion of the credit, but only if the possession has a plan in effect to promptly distribute such payments to residents of the possession (Act Sec. 1004(c)(1)(B) of the 2009 Recovery Act).

> **Comment:** The Commonwealth of the Northern Mariana Islands, Guam and the U.S. Virgin Islands employ a mirror code tax system. The Commonwealth of Puerto Rico and American Samoa do not (Conference Committee Report for American Recovery and Reinvestment Act of 2009).

The Secretary of the Treasury and the Secretary of Education, or their delegates, are required to perform studies on the coordination of the Hope and Lifetime Learning credits with the Federal Pell Grant program to maximize their effectiveness of promoting college affordability, and on ways to expedite delivery of the tax credit. They are also required to study the feasibility of requiring students to perform community service as a condition of taking tuition and related expenses into account for purposes of the Hope and Lifetime Learning credits. The results of these studies must be reported to Congress not later than one year after the date that the 2009 Recovery Act is enacted (Act Sec. 1004(f) of the 2009 Recovery Act).

▶ **Effective date.** The provision applies to tax years beginning after December 31, 2008 (Act Sec. 1004(d) of the American Recovery and Reinvestment Tax Act of 2009 (P.L. 111-5)).

Law source: Law at ¶5005, ¶5010, ¶5015, ¶5020, ¶5035, ¶5280, ¶5305 and ¶5375. Committee Report at ¶10,040.

— Act Sec. 1004(a) of the American Recovery and Reinvestment Tax Act of 2009 (P.L. 111-5), redesignating Code Sec. 25A(i) as Code Sec. 25A(j) and adding Code Sec. 25A(i);

— Act Sec. 1004(b), amending Code Secs. 24(b)(3)(B), 25(e)(1)(C)(ii), 25B(g)(2), 26(a)(1), 904(i), 1400C(d)(2), 6211(b)(4)(A) and 31 U.S.C. 1324(b)(2);

— Act Sec. 1004(c);

— Act Sec. 1004(d), providing the effective date;

— Act Sec. 1004(e) and (f).

Reporter references: For further information, consult the following CCH reporters.

— Standard Federal Tax Reporter, ¶3830.01, ¶3830.031

— Tax Research Consultant, INDIV: 60,152

— Practical Tax Explanation, § 12,405

¶335 Residential Energy Property Credit

SUMMARY OF NEW LAW

The residential energy property credit is extended to include expenditures for certain energy property placed in service during 2010. The credit amount is 30 percent of the sum of expenditures for *qualified energy efficiency improvements* (building envelope components) and *qualified energy property* (furnaces and certain fans, central air conditioners, water heaters, certain heat pumps, biomass stoves) placed in service in 2009 and 2010. The credit is limited to $1,500 for tax years 2009 and 2010. Energy efficiency standards for windows, doors, skylights, insulation, natural gas, propane, or oil hot water boilers, oil furnaces, electric heat pumps, central air conditioners, water heaters, and biomass fuel stoves are modified.

BACKGROUND

Individuals who own a dwelling unit in the United States and use it as their principal residence are eligible for a nonrefundable personal tax credit of up to $500 over all tax years for certain residential energy property installed in or on the dwelling unit and originally placed in service by the individuals in 2006, 2007, or 2009 (Code Sec. 25C(a), (b)(1), (d) and (g)). The amount of the credit is equal to the sum of:

(1) 10 percent of the amount paid for qualified energy efficiency improvements (building envelope components) installed during the tax year, and

(2) the amount of the residential energy property expenditures (on certain heat pumps, furnaces, central air conditioners, water heaters, biomass fuel stoves (2009 only), and advanced main air circulating fans) paid or incurred during the tax year (Code Sec. 25C(a)).

A *qualified energy efficiency improvement* is an energy efficient building envelope component that meets the criteria set forth in the 2000 International Energy Conservation Code (IECC), as in effect on August 8, 2005, or a metal or asphalt roof that meets the Energy Star Program requirements (Code Sec. 25C(c)(1)). Building envelope components include insulation materials, exterior windows and skylights, exterior doors, and any metal roof with appropriate pigmented coatings, or any asphalt roof with appropriate pigmented coatings or cooling granules in 2009 only (Code Sec. 25C(c)(2)).

> **Comment:** The IECC prescribes R-values for insulation at various locations in the building and U-factors for windows and doors. The U-factor is a composite value of the ability of window, skylight or door components, including the actual glass, air space and frame components, to resist the transmission of cold and heat. Less heat and cold will pass through a window, skylight or door with a lower U-factor. R-value is the inverse of U-factor, therefore, insulation with a higher R-value allows less heat and cold to pass through the insulation.

BACKGROUND

Residential energy property expenditures are expenditures made for qualified energy property. Qualified energy property includes the following items that meet prescribed performance and quality standards in effect at the time of acquisition:

(1) a qualified natural gas, propane or oil furnace or hot water boiler that achieves an annual fuel utilization efficiency rate of at least 95,

(2) an advanced main air circulating fan (certain furnace fans), and

(3) energy-efficient building property (Code Sec. 25C(d)(2)).

Energy-efficient building property includes:

(1) electric heat pump water heaters yielding an energy factor of at least 2.0 in the standard Department of energy test procedure,

(2) electric heat pumps with a heating seasonal performance factor (HSPF) of at least 9, a seasonal energy efficiency ratio (SEER) of at least 15, and an energy efficiency ratio (EER) of at least 13,

(3) certain geothermal heat pumps only in 2006 and 2007,

(4) central air conditioners that achieve the highest efficiency tier established by the Consortium for Energy Efficiency (CEE) in effect on January 1, 2006,

(5) natural gas, propane or oil water heaters with an energy factor of at least 0.80 or a thermal efficiency of at least 90 percent, and

(6) beginning in 2009, stoves using biomass fuel to heat U.S. residential dwelling units or heat water for use in the units, and that have a thermal efficiency rating of at least 75 percent (Code Sec. 25C(d)(3)).

The IECC provides specifications for heating and cooling systems, including duct systems and related insulation, temperature and humidity controls, and water heating systems. Measurements of the EER for central air conditioners and electric heat pumps must be based on published data that is tested by manufacturers at 95 degrees Fahrenheit, and may be based on the data of the Air Conditioning and Refrigeration Institute prepared in partnership with the CEE (Code Sec. 25C(d)(2)(C)).

Comment: Geothermal heat pumps qualify as alternative energy equipment for purposes of the residential alternative energy credit under Code Sec. 25D beginning in 2008. The amount of the alternative energy credit is 30 percent of the qualified geothermal heat pump property expenditures up to an annual maximum of $2,000. The residential alternative energy credit applies through 2016.

The residential energy property credit is limited to $500 over tax years 2006, 2007 and 2009, but no more than $200 of the credit can be based on expenditures for windows (Code Sec. 25C(b)). The credit amount is also limited to:

(1) $50 for an advanced main air circulating fan,

(2) $150 for any qualified natural gas, propane, or oil furnace or hot water boiler, and

(3) $300 for any energy-efficient building property item (Code Sec. 25C(b)(2) and (3)).

¶335

NEW LAW EXPLAINED

Residential energy credit extended, amount increased and certain energy efficiency standards modified.—The residential energy property credit is extended to include qualifying property placed in service in 2010 (Code Sec. 25C(g)(2), as amended by the American Recovery and Reinvestment Tax Act of 2009 (P.L. 111-5)). The credit amount in 2009 and 2010 is 30 percent of the sum of the amount paid or incurred by an individual for *qualified energy efficiency improvements* and *residential energy property expenditures* (Code Sec. 25C(a), as amended by the 2009 Recovery Act).

> **Comment:** For building envelope components such as windows and doors, the credit percentage has been increased from 10 to 30 percent for 2009 and 2010. For residential energy property expenditures such as furnaces, furnace fans, central air conditioners, water heaters and certain heat pumps, 30 percent of the expenditure is used to compute the credit in 2009 and 2010. There was no percentage applied to residential energy property expenditures when computing the credit in 2006 and 2007.

Practical Analysis: Charles R. Goulding, J.D., CPA, MBA, and President of Energy Tax Savers Inc. of Syosset, New York, notes that Act. Sec. 1121 of the American Recovery and Reinvestment Tax Act of 2009 extends the residential efficiency credit for two years for 2009 and 2010 and triples what was a $500 credit into a $1,500 credit. The previous 10-percent credits and the $50, $100 and $150 sub-capped items are now all eligible for the full 30-percent credit up to $1,500. The residential credits are limited to HVAC (heating ventilation and air conditioning) and building envelope items and exclude lighting. Since the price of residential energy efficient lighting has fallen drastically and is readily available on store shelves, it is logical to focus the incentive on larger-ticket HVAC and building envelope items. This is good tax policy because investing in energy efficient HVAC and building envelope items provides the largest long-term energy cost savings. These credits support the new policy trend towards funding for more weatherization measures, which permanently reduce home heating costs as opposed to continuously subsidizing annual heating costs which is a perpetual expense. Another complimentary portion of the stimulus package provides funding for residential weatherization aimed at low income homeowners.

It is important to note that although the residential credit is now larger and simpler, the efficiency standards for much of the qualifying property have been increased to very high January 1, 2009, building code standards. Many HVAC and building envelope dealers do not stock equipment at these high energy efficiency levels so residential taxpayers planning upgrades may need to build extra delivery time into their project planning schedules.

Although this tax credit provision is for existing residences, purchasers of new homes may want to consider incorporating the designated energy standards into their new home specifications.

¶335

NEW LAW EXPLAINED

For tax years beginning in 2009 and 2010, the residential energy property credit is limited to $1,500 over both tax years (Code Sec. 25C(b), as amended by the 2009 Recovery Act).

> **Planning Point:** If the previous $500 lifetime maximum has already been used by an individual for qualifying expenditures in 2006 and/or 2007, that person can now incur additional qualifying property costs in 2009 and/or 2010 and be eligible for a residential energy property credit of up $1,500 over both years.

> **Comment:** All credit limitations applicable to specific property, such as the $200 maximum credit for window expenditures and the $150 maximum credit for furnaces, have been removed for qualifying expenditures in 2009 and 2010.

Example: In 2007, Tom spent $3,500 to have energy-efficient windows put in his home. He also replaced his gas furnace with an energy-efficient model at a cost of $4,000. Tom was entitled to a residential energy property credit of $350 (($3,500 × .10 = $350, but limited to $200 maximum) + ($4,000, but limited to $150 maximum) in 2007. If the same energy-efficient property was purchased and installed in 2009, the credit would be $1,500 ($3,500 + $4,000 × .30 = $2,250, but limited to $1,500 maximum) since there are no specific property limitations.

Energy efficiency standards have been modified for certain qualified energy efficiency improvements (building envelope components), certain qualified energy property (natural gas, propane, and oil hot water boilers and oil furnaces), and certain energy efficient building property (electric heat pumps, central air conditioners, water heaters) placed in service after February 17, 2009, as follows.

(1) Qualified energy efficiency improvements

- Exterior windows, skylights and doors must have a U-factor and a solar heat gain coefficient (SHGC) of 0.30 or less (Code Sec. 25C(c)(4), as added by the 2009 Recovery Act).

- Insulation installed in or on a dwelling unit must be designed to reduce heat loss or gain of the dwelling unit and must meet the criteria established by the 2009 International Energy Conservation Code (IECC) as in effect (with any supplements) on February 17, 2009 (Code Sec. 25C(c)(2)(A), as amended by the 2009 Recovery Act).

(2) Qualified energy property

- A minimum annual fuel utilization efficiency rate (AFUE) of at least 90 is required for any natural gas, propane or oil hot water boiler, or oil furnace; the preexisting rate of at least 95 required for any natural gas or propane furnace remains unchanged (Code Sec. 25C(d)(4), as amended by the 2009 Recovery Act).

(3) Energy efficient building property

NEW LAW EXPLAINED

- An electric heat pump must achieve the highest efficiency tier established by the Consortium for Energy Efficiency (CEE) as in effect on January 1, 2009 (Code Sec. 25C(d)(3)(B), as amended by the 2009 Recovery Act).

- A central air conditioner must achieve the highest efficiency tier established by the CEE as in effect on January 1, 2009 (Code Sec. 25C(d)(3)(C), as amended by the 2009 Recovery Act).

- A natural gas, propane or oil water heater must have either a minimum energy factor of 0.82 or a thermal efficiency minimum of 90 percent (Code Sec. 25C(d)(3)(D), as amended by the 2009 Recovery Act).

In addition, the minimum thermal efficiency rating of 75 percent for a stove burning biomass fuel to heat a residence (or water for such residence) must be measured using a lower heating value beginning in 2009 (Code Sec. 25C(d)(3)(E), as amended by the 2009 Recovery Act; Act Sec. 1121(f)(1) of the 2009 Recovery Act). Biomass fuel is any fuel that is derived from plants on a renewable or recurring basis. Most commonly this would be wood, but it also includes wood waste and residues such as wood pellets, agricultural crops, and plants such as aquatic plants, grasses, residues and fibers (Code Sec. 25C(d)(6)).

Comment: The solar heat gain coefficient (SHGC) is the fraction of incident solar radiation admitted through a window, absorbed, and subsequently released inward. The SHGC is expressed as a number between 0 and 1. The lower the SHGC, the less solar heat it transmits.

The annual fuel utilization efficiency (AFUE) rating reflects how efficiently a furnace converts fuel to energy. An AFUE of 90 means that approximately 90 percent of the fuel provides heat to the dwelling and the remaining 10 percent goes up the flue. The minimum AFUE rate of at least 95 continues to apply for a natural gas or propane furnace placed in service after February 17, 2009.

The CEE is a nonprofit public benefits corporation that promotes the manufacture and purchase of energy-efficient products and services. Members include utilities, environmental groups, state energy offices, manufacturers, retailers and the U.S. Department of Energy and the Environmental Protection Agency. The HSPF, SEER and EER requirements applicable to electric heat pumps placed in service after February 17, 2009, are incorporated in the CEE highest efficiency tier.

Compliance Pointer: The efficiency standard modifications applicable to certain energy property only apply to such property placed in service after February 17, 2009. For example, if Joe has a central air conditioner installed at his principal residence in January of 2009, that unit must achieve the highest efficiency tier established by the CEE as in effect on January 1, 2006, in order for Joe to qualify for a residential energy credit based on the cost of the unit. If Joe waits until 2010, the central air unit must achieve the highest efficiency tier established by the CEE as in effect on January 1, 2009, pursuant to Code Sec. 25C(d)(3)(C), as amended by the 2009 Recovery Act.

¶335

NEW LAW EXPLAINED

Subsidized energy financing. The rule that any expenditures made with funds obtained from subsidized energy financing are ineligible for the residential energy property credit has been eliminated, effective for tax years beginning after December 31, 2008 (Code Sec. 25C(e)(1), as amended by the 2009 Recovery Act; Act Sec. 1103(c)(2) of the 2009 Recovery Act). For further discussion of this change, see ¶510.

▶ **Effective date.** All amendments except efficiency standard changes other than as to wood stoves apply to tax years beginning after December 31, 2008 (Act Sec. 1121(f)(1) of the American Recovery and Reinvestment Tax Act of 2009 (P.L. 111-5)). The efficiency standard amendments, except as to wood stoves, apply to property placed in service after February 17, 2009 (Act Sec. 1121(f)(2) of the 2009 Recovery Act).

Law source: Law at ¶5025. Committee Report at ¶10,160.

— Act Sec. 1121(a) of the American Recovery and Reinvestment Tax Act of 2009 (P.L. 111-5), amending Code Sec. 25C(a) and (b);

— Act Sec. 1121(b), amending Code Sec. 25C(d)(3)(B), (C), (D) and (E);

— Act Sec. 1121(c), amending Code Sec. 25C(d)(2)(A)(ii) and Code Sec. 25C(d)(4);

— Act Sec. 1121(d), amending Code Sec. 25C(c)(2)(A) and adding Code Sec. 25C(c)(4);

— Act Sec. 1121(e), amending Code Sec. 25C(g)(2);

— Act Sec. 1121(f), providing the effective date.

Reporter references: For further information, consult the following CCH reporters.

— Standard Federal Tax Reporter, ¶3843.01, ¶3843.021 and ¶3843.07

— Tax Research Consultant, INDIV: 57,800 and INDIV: 57,808

— Practical Tax Explanation, § 13,205

¶340 Residential Alternative Energy Credit

SUMMARY OF NEW LAW

The annual maximum limits applicable to the residential alternative energy credit are eliminated for solar hot water heaters, wind turbine property, and geothermal heat pumps effective for tax years 2009 through 2016.

BACKGROUND

An individual is entitled to a nonrefundable personal tax credit equal to 30 percent of the cost of eligible solar water heaters, solar electricity equipment, fuel cell plants, wind energy property, and qualified geothermal heat pumps installed on or in connection with a dwelling unit located in the United States and used as a residence by the taxpayer (Code Sec. 25D(a) and (d)). Expenditures for fuel cell property qualify for the credit only if the property is installed on or in connection with a dwelling unit located in the United States that is used as a *principal* residence by the taxpayer (Code Sec. 25D(d)(3)).

BACKGROUND

The maximum annual credit is:

(1) $2,000 for solar water heaters,

(2) $500 for each half kilowatt of electric capacity from fuel cell plants,

(3) $500 for each half kilowatt of electric capacity generated by a wind turbine, up to $4,000, and

(4) $2,000 for geothermal heat pumps (Code Sec. 25D(b)(1)).

There is no annual credit limit for qualified solar electric property expenditures.

> **Example:** Joe and his family have an eight room home located on five acres in Arkansas. In 2008, Joe purchased a GeoExchange heat pump to meet the heating and cooling needs for the family home. The cost was $9,500. He also spent $20,500 on a 7 kilowatt output PEM (Proton Exchange Membrane) fuel cell power plant for his home. Joe did not finance any of these costs with low interest utility loans. Since both the heat pump and the power plant are qualified property under Code Sec. 25D, Joe is entitled to a residential alternative energy credit of $9,000 (($9,500 × .30 = $2,850, but limited to $2,000 maximum) + ($500 × 14 = $7,000)) in 2008.

When there is joint occupancy of a dwelling unit by two or more individuals, the maximum amount of expenditures that may be used by all such individuals in calculating the residential alternative energy credit is $6,667 per tax year for qualified solar water heating equipment, $6,667 per tax year for geothermal heat pump property expenditures, $1,667 per tax year for each half kilowatt of capacity of fuel cell property, and $1,667 per tax year for each half kilowatt of capacity of wind turbine property (Code Sec. 25D(e)(4)(A)). In effect, the tax credit is split among all of the co-owners, and the total credit claimed by the combined owners cannot exceed $2,000 per tax year for solar water heating property or geothermal heat pump property, and $500 for each .5 kW of capacity for qualified fuel cell property per tax year or for wind turbine property.

NEW LAW EXPLAINED

Credit caps for solar hot water, wind and geothermal property removed.—The residential alternative energy annual credit maximums of $2,000 for solar hot water heaters, $500 for each half kilowatt of electric capacity generated by a wind turbine (not to exceed $4,000 annually), and $2,000 for geothermal heat pumps are eliminated for tax years 2009 through 2016 (Code Sec. 25D(b)(1) and (e)(4), as amended by the American Recovery and Reinvestment Tax Act of 2009 (P.L. 111-5)).

> **Comment:** The maximum annual credit for each half kilowatt of electric capacity from fuel cell plants remains at $500.

¶340

NEW LAW EXPLAINED

> **Example:** Ron purchased a GeoExchange heat pump for his family home in January of 2009 at a cost of $9,500. In June of 2009, he spent $20,500 on a 7 kilowatt output PEM (Proton Exchange Membrane) fuel cell power plant for his home. Ron did not finance any of these costs with low interest utility loans. In 2009, Ron is entitled to a residential alternative energy credit of $9,850 (($9,500 × .30 = $2,850) + ($500 × 14 = $7,000)) since both the heat pump and the power plant are qualified property under Code Sec. 25D.

In the case of joint occupancy of a dwelling unit with regard to which qualified fuel cell property is installed, the maximum annual amount of fuel cell expenditures by all occupants cannot exceed $1,667 for each half kilowatt of capacity of the qualified fuel cell property (Code Sec. 25D(e)(4), as amended by the 2009 Recovery Act). This is the equivalent of the annual credit maximum of $500 for each half kilowatt of electric capacity from fuel cell plants.

> **Practical Analysis:** Charles R. Goulding, J.D., CPA, MBA, and President of Energy Tax Savers Inc. of Syosset, New York, notes that Act Sec. 1122 of the American Recovery and Reinvestment Tax Act of 2009 eliminates the $2,000 cap on the 30-percent residential tax credits for solar and geothermal and the cap on small wind energy property. These are major changes. The solar residential thermal cap removal makes this solar credit consistent with the both the solar PV and solar thermal 30-percent commercial solar credit tax regime and the residential solar PV credit where the $2,000 cap was also removed in recent tax legislation. Many solar vendors sell both commercial and residential solar PV and solar thermal systems and these changes will enable them to simplify the economic payback formulas in their customer proposal software with a simple consistent methodology. For mixed use commercial and residential properties, this new straightforward solar tax credit system eliminates complicated solar system tax credit allocations. As with any sales process, the ability to both keep it simple while offering more financial incentives will enable solar sellers to sell more solar systems.
>
> Geothermal systems are very energy efficient because, unlike solar and wind, they provide uninterrupted low-cost energy. However, geothermal systems have high upfront cost making a 30-percent credit very relevant.
>
> It is very important to note that this new section also eliminates the previous alternative energy credit reductions for subsidized energy financing. The prior reductions for subsidized energy financing were difficult to interpret and acted as disincentive for projects that only met investment criteria with both subsidized financing and tax incentives.

Subsidized energy financing. The rule that any expenditures made with funds obtained from subsidized energy financing are ineligible for the residential alternative energy credit has been eliminated, effective for tax years beginning after December 31, 2008 (Code Sec. 25D(e), as amended by the 2009 Recovery Act; Act Sec. 1103(c)(2) of the 2009 Recovery Act). For further discussion of this change, see ¶ 510.

¶340

Explanation

NEW LAW EXPLAINED

▶ **Effective date.** The amendment applies to tax years beginning after December 31, 2008 (Act Sec. 1122(b) of the American Recovery and Reinvestment Tax Act of 2009 (P.L. 111-5)).

Law source: Law at ¶5030. Committee Report at ¶10,170.

— Act Sec. 1122(a)(1) of the American Recovery and Reinvestment Tax Act of 2009 (P.L. 111-5), amending Code Sec. 25D(b)(1);

— Act Sec. 1122(a)(2), amending Code Sec. 25D(e)(4);

— Act Sec. 1122(b), providing the effective date.

Reporter references: For further information, consult the following CCH reporters.

— Standard Federal Tax Reporter, ¶3847.01, ¶3847.02, ¶3847.021 and ¶3847.07

— Tax Research Consultant, INDIV: 57,850 and INDIV: 57,852

— Practical Tax Explanation, § 13,305

¶345 Plug-in Electric Drive Motor Vehicle Credit

SUMMARY OF NEW LAW

For taxpayers who acquire vehicles after December 31, 2009, the maximum amount of the plug-in electric drive motor vehicle credit is $7,500. If the plug-in vehicle does not have battery capacity of at least 5 kilowatt hours, the minimum credit of $2,500 applies. When a manufacturer has sold 200,000 plug-in vehicles for use in the United States after December 31, 2009, the phaseout period is triggered applicable to vehicles from that particular manufacturer. The gross weight for a qualified vehicle must be under 14,000 pounds.

BACKGROUND

A taxpayer is eligible for a credit against tax for qualified plug-in electric drive motor vehicles placed in service in 2009 through 2014 (Code Sec. 30D, as added by the Emergency Economic Stabilization Act of 2008 (P.L. 110-343). A qualified plug-in electric drive motor vehicle is a motor vehicle that draws propulsion using a traction battery with at least 4 kilowatt hours of capacity, can be recharged from an external electricity source, and meets certain emission standards except for heavy weight vehicles (Code Sec. 30D(c)).

The credit is equal to the applicable amount for each new qualified plug-in electric drive motor vehicle placed in service during the eligible tax year (Code Sec. 30D(a)). The applicable amount is the sum of the $2,500 base amount, plus an additional $417 for each kilowatt hour of traction battery capacity in excess of four kilowatt hours (Code Sec. 30D(a)(2)). The maximum amount of the credit is between $7,500 and $15,000 depending upon the weight of the motor vehicle from under 10,000 pounds to over 26,000 pounds (Code Sec. 30D(b)(1)).

BACKGROUND

The credit amount is also limited by the number of vehicles sold. Sale for use in the United States of 250,000 new qualified plug-in electric drive motor vehicles triggers the phaseout of the credit. The phaseout period begins with the second calendar quarter following the calendar quarter in which the 250,000th unit is sold. For the first two quarters of the phaseout period, the credit is cut to 50 percent of the full credit amount. The credit is cut to 25 percent for the third and fourth quarters of the phaseout period. Thereafter, there is no credit allowed (Code Sec. 30D(b)(2)).

NEW LAW EXPLAINED

Credit maximum reduced; maximum vehicle weight prescribed; credit phaseout triggered on sale of 200,000th vehicle per manufacturer.—The American Recovery and Reinvestment Tax Act of 2009 (P.L. 111-5) overhauls the qualified plug-in electric drive motor vehicle credit and makes the credit permanent (Code Sec. 30D, as amended by the 2009 Recovery Act).

> **Compliance Note:** The requirements of Code Sec. 30D, prior to amendment by the 2009 Recovery Act, apply for taxpayers claiming the plug-in electric drive motor vehicle credit based on plug-in vehicles placed in service in 2009. For qualified plug-in electric drive motor vehicles acquired after December 31, 2009, the requirements of Code Sec. 30D, as amended by the 2009 Recovery Act, apply.

The credit for each new qualified plug-in electric drive motor vehicle placed in service by the taxpayer in the tax year is equal to the sum of:

(1) a base amount of $2,500, and

(2) $417 for a vehicle drawing propulsion energy from a battery with at least 5 *kilowatt hours* of capacity plus $417 for each additional kilowatt hour of capacity in excess of 5 kilowatt hours, up to a maximum aggregate of $5,000 based on kilowatt hour capacity (Code Sec. 30D(a) and (b), as amended by the 2009 Recovery Act).

The minimum credit amount is $2,500 if the vehicle battery has 4 but less than 5 kilowatt hours of capacity. The credit maximum is $7,500 consisting of the $2,500 base amount plus the $5,000 maximum predicated on battery kilowatt hour capacity.

> **Comment:** In 2009, the credit minimum is $2,500 and the maximum is between $7,500 and $15,000 depending upon gross vehicle weight in combination with kilowatt hour battery capacity in excess of 4 *kilowatt hours*.

> **Practical Analysis:** Charles R. Goulding, J.D., CPA, MBA, and President of Energy Tax Savers Inc. of Syosset, New York, observes that doubling the number of vehicles eligible for the plug-in electric vehicle credit comes at an opportune time. Media reports indicate that GM has spent over $750 million developing the plug-in Chevy Volt. Clearly, to obtain an adequate return on investment of this magnitude, it needs to sell a large volume of plug-ins. With both new car sales and the number of scrapped cars falling to historic lows, presumably there is tremendous pent-up demand building for new cars. In one of its first initiatives, the Obama administration

¶345

NEW LAW EXPLAINED

> has removed the prohibition on state fuel mileage standards greater than Federal standards, making plug-ins even more desirable.
>
> It is anticipated that some of the first mover large volume purchasers of plug-ins will be Federal and State and Local government organizations. Automobile dealers will be able to take the credits on sales to tax-exempt entities provided they make full disclosure to the tax exempt entity. This provision is clearly intended to create an economic transfer resulting in a lower price point for the government plug-in purchaser. This incentive will give a dealer with taxable income an economic advantage and may require dealers with tax losses to consider restructuring and other tax planning techniques.

New qualified plug-in electric drive motor vehicle. In order for a motor vehicle to qualify as a new plug-in electric drive vehicle after 2009, the vehicle must be made by a manufacturer, acquired for use or lease, but not resale, the original use must begin with the taxpayer, and the motor vehicle must:

(1) have a gross vehicle weight rating of less than 14,000 pounds,

(2) be a self-propelled vehicle designed for transporting persons or property on a street or highway (section 216(2), title II of the Clean Air Act), and

(3) be propelled to a significant extent by an electric motor drawing electricity from a battery having a capacity of at least 4 kilowatt hours that can be recharged from an external source (Code Sec. 30D(d)(1), as amended by the 2009 Recovery Act).

Furthermore, the vehicle must be in compliance with the applicable provisions of the Clean Air Act for the vehicle's particular make and model year (or applicable air quality State law provisions where a Clean Air Act waiver is in effect) and the motor vehicle safety provisions of 49 U.S.C. 30101-30169 (Code Sec. 30D(f)(7), as amended by the 2009 Recovery Act).

> **Comment:** A taxpayer who places a motor vehicle in service in 2010 with a battery capacity of 4 kilowatt hours and meets the other requirements for a new qualified plug-in electric drive motor vehicle will only qualify for the minimum credit of $2,500.

A *motor vehicle* is any vehicle manufactured primarily for use on public streets, roads, and highways that has at least 4 wheels (Code Sec. 30D(d)(2), as amended by the 2009 Recovery Act). The term *manufacturer* has the meaning set forth in Environmental Protection Agency regulations prescribed for purposes of administering title II of the Clean Air Act (Code Sec. 30D(d)(3), as amended by the 2009 Recovery Act). *Battery capacity* is the quantity of electricity the battery can store, expressed in kilowatt hours measured from a 100 percent charge state to a 0 percent state of charge (Code Sec. 30D(d)(4), as amended by the 2009 Recovery Act).

Phaseout of credit. When 200,000 new qualified plug-in electric drive motor vehicles have been sold for use in the United States after December 31, 2009 by a manufacturer, the phaseout will be triggered as to that manufacturer's vehicles. For purposes of this phaseout, consolidated groups of corporations and foreign controlled corporations will be considered one manufacturer (Code Sec. 30D(e)(4), as amended by the

NEW LAW EXPLAINED

2009 Recovery Act). The phaseout period begins with the second calendar quarter following the calendar quarter that includes the date the 200,000th unit is sold (Code Sec. 30D(e)(2), as amended by the 2009 Recovery Act). For the first two quarters of the phaseout period, the credit is cut to 50 percent of the otherwise allowable full credit amount. The credit is cut to 25 percent for the third and fourth quarters of the phaseout period. Thereafter, there is no credit allowed (Code Sec. 30D(e)(1) and (e)(3), as amended by the 2009 Recovery Act).

Disqualified property. No new qualified plug-in electric drive motor vehicle credit is allowed for property used predominately outside of the United States except for property detailed in Code Sec. 168(g)(4), such as aircraft, rolling stock, and motor vehicles of U.S. persons that are operated to and from the U.S. (Code Sec. 30D(f)(4), as amended by the 2009 Recovery Act). In addition the amount of any deduction or other credit allowable for a new qualified plug-in electric drive motor vehicle must be reduced by the amount of the new qualified plug-in electric drive motor vehicle credit allowed under Code Sec. 30D (Code Sec. 30D(f)(2), as amended by the 2009 Recovery Act).

Business or personal use. If the plug-in electric drive motor vehicle is used in a trade or business and, is therefore, subject to depreciation, the credit allowed for the business use portion is treated as part of the general business credit and that portion is not allowed to calculate the new qualified plug-in electric drive vehicle credit (Code Secs. 30D(c)(1) and 38(b)(35), as amended by the 2009 Recovery Act). If the plug-in electric drive motor vehicle is considered personal property, the credit will be treated as if it is part of the nonrefundable personal credits under subpart A of the Internal Revenue Code (Code Sec. 30D(c)(2)(A), as amended by the 2009 Recovery Act). This treatment allows the credit to be claimed against a taxpayer's regular tax and alternative minimum tax (AMT) liabilities in years that Code Sec. 26(a)(2) applies. In years when Code Sec. 26(a)(2) does not apply (after 2009), the plug-in credit must be offset against the excess of the taxpayer's regular tax plus AMT liabilities over the sum of the nonrefundable personal credits allowable (except this credit, the adoption credit, the residential alternative energy property credit) and the foreign tax credit (Code Sec. 30D(c)(2)(B), as amended by the 2009 Recovery Act). For a discussion of the use of nonrefundable personal credits against AMT liability, see ¶240.

Property used by tax-exempt entity. If the plug-in electric drive motor vehicle will be used by a tax-exempt organization, governmental unit or foreign person or entity and is not subject to a lease, the seller of the vehicle can claim the credit provided the seller clearly discloses in writing to the entity the amount of any credit allowable with respect to the vehicle (Code Sec. 30D(f)(3), as amended by the 2009 Recovery Act).

Basis. The basis of any property for which the new qualified plug-in electric drive motor vehicle credit is allowable must be reduced by the amount of the credit allowed (Code Sec. 30D(f)(1), as amended by the 2009 Recovery Act).

Election. Taxpayers can elect to not have the new qualified plug-in electric drive motor vehicle credit apply to their vehicle (Code Sec. 30D(f)(6), as amended by the 2009 Recovery Act).

NEW LAW EXPLAINED

Regulations. The Secretary of the Treasury is to issue regulations providing for the recapture of the new qualified plug-in electric drive motor vehicle credit benefit in the event the property ceases to be eligible property (Code Sec. 30D(f)(5), as amended by the 2009 Recovery Act).

▶ **Effective date.** The amendments apply to vehicles acquired after December 31, 2009 (Act Sec. 1141(c) of the American Recovery and Reinvestment Tax Act of 2009 (P.L. 111-5)).

Law source: Law at ¶5045, ¶5055, ¶5080, ¶5285, and ¶5400. Committee Report at ¶10,200.

— Act Sec. 1141(a) of the American Recovery and Reinvestment Tax Act of 2009 (P.L. 111-5), amending Code Sec. 30D;

— Act Sec. 1141(b), amending Code Sec. 30B(d)(3)(D), Code Sec. 38(b)(35), Code Sec. 1016(a)(25), and Code Sec. 6501(m);

— Act Sec. 1141(c), providing the effective date.

Reporter references: For further information, consult the following CCH reporters.

— Standard Federal Tax Reporter, ¶4059P.01

— Tax Research Consultant, INDIV: 58,000

— Practical Tax Explanation, § 12,915

¶350 Plug-in Electric Vehicle Credit

SUMMARY OF NEW LAW

A new credit against tax is available for the cost of acquiring 2-wheeled, 3-wheeled and low-speed plug-in electric vehicles.

BACKGROUND

Since 2005, Congress has enacted numerous tax incentives to encourage development of alternative fuels for motor vehicles. The Energy Tax Incentives Act of 2005 (P.L. 109-58) created the alternative motor vehicle credit and the alternative fuel vehicle refueling property credit (Code Secs. 30B and 30C), and the Emergency Economic Stabilization Act of 2008 (P.L. 110-343) added a credit against tax for qualified plug-in electric drive motor vehicles placed in service in 2009 through 2014 (Code Sec. 30D, as added by the Emergency Economic Act of 2008).

The credit for qualified plug-in electric drive motor vehicles is equal to the applicable amount for each new qualified plug-in electric drive motor vehicle placed in service during the eligible tax year (Code Sec. 30D(a)). A qualified plug-in electric drive motor vehicle is a 4-wheeled motor vehicle that draws propulsion using a traction battery with at least 4 kilowatt hours of capacity (Code Sec. 30D(c)). The applicable amount is the sum of the $2,500 base amount, plus an additional $417 for each kilowatt hour of traction battery capacity in excess of four kilowatt hours (Code Sec.

BACKGROUND

30D(a)(2)). The maximum amount of the credit is between $7,500 and $15,000 depending upon the weight of the motor vehicle (Code Sec. 30D(b)(1)).

NEW LAW EXPLAINED

Creation of new of plug-in electric drive motor vehicle credit for low speed vehicles, 2-wheeled vehicles and 3-wheeled vehicles.—

The American Recovery and Reinvestment Tax Act of 2009 (P.L. 111-5) adds a new credit against tax that is generally modeled on the plug-in electric drive motor vehicle credit in Code Sec. 30D, as amended by the 2009 Recovery Act. The new law provides a credit for 10% of the cost of acquiring certain electrically powered 2-wheeled vehicles, 3-wheeled vehicles and low-speed vehicles. To qualify for the credit, which is capped at $2,500, a vehicle must be a "qualified plug-in electric vehicle." The credit is available for the tax year in which the qualifying vehicle is put into service. Note, however, that a taxpayer may elect not to have the credit apply (Code Sec. 30(a), (b), and (e)(6), as amended by the 2009 Recovery Act).

"Qualified plug-in electric vehicle". In order to qualify as a "qualified plug-in electric vehicle", the vehicle must meet all of the following requirements:

- the vehicle must be a *specified vehicle*. A specified vehicle is either (1) any vehicle with 2 or 3 wheels, or (2) a "low speed vehicle" as defined in the Federal Motor Vehicle Safety Standards (section 571.3 of title 49 of the Code of Federal Regulations) in effect on February 17, 2009. Under the safety standards, a low speed vehicle must have:

— four wheels,

— a minimum speed attainable in 1 mile of more than 20 miles per hour and a maximum speed attainable in 1 mile of no more than 25 miles per hour, on a paved level surface, and

— a gross weight of less than 3,000 pounds.

- the vehicle must be made by a "manufacturer" (defined below), acquired for use or lease, but not resale and the original use must begin with the taxpayer;
- the vehicle must be manufactured primarily for use on public streets, roads and highways;
- the vehicle must have a gross vehicle weight rating of less than 14,000 pounds; and
- the vehicle must be propelled to a *"significant extent"* by an electric motor drawing power from a battery that can be recharged from an external source with a "battery capacity" (defined below) of not less than

— 4 kilowatt hours in the case of low speed vehicles; or

— 2.5 kilowatt hours in the case of a 2 or 3 wheeled vehicle (Code Sec. 30(d)(1) and (2), as amended by the 2009 Recovery Act).

NEW LAW EXPLAINED

Definitions. The rules governing "qualified plug-in electric vehicles" utilize the following defined terms:

- "Manufacturer" has the same meaning given such term in regulations prescribed by the Administrator of the Environmental Protection Agency for purposes of administering title II of the Clean Air Act (Code Sec. 30(d)(3), as amended by the 2009 Recovery Act).
- "Battery capacity" means the quantity of electricity the battery can store expressed in kilowatt hours, as measured from a 100 percent state of charge to a 0 percent state of charge (Code Sec. 30(d)(4), as amended by the 2009 Recovery Act).

Business versus personal use. If the "qualified plug-in electric vehicle" eligible for the credit is used in a trade or business and, therefore, is subject to depreciation, then the amount of the credit is treated as a business credit under Code Sec. 38(b) and is not allowed under Code Sec. 30(a) (Code Sec. 30(c)(1), as amended by the 2009 Recovery Act). If the vehicle is considered personal property, the credit is treated as part of the non-refundable personal credits under subpart A of the Internal Revenue Code. The credit can offset regular tax and alternative minimum tax (AMT) liabilities in 2009 (Code Sec. 26(a)(2), as amended by the 2009 Recovery Act). In tax years when Code Sec. 26(a)(2) does not apply (after 2009), the credit is limited to the excess of the

- sum of the regular tax liability (as defined in Code Sec. 26(b)) plus the alternative minimum tax imposed under Code Sec. 55, over
- the sum of credits allowable under Code Secs. 21, 22, 24, 25, 25A, 25B, 25C, and 27 (Code Sec. 30(c)(2)(B), as amended by the 2009 Recovery Act) (see LEA¶ 240 for discussion of the use of nonrefundable personal credits against AMT).

Reduction of basis for amount of credit. The taxpayer's adjusted basis in the "qualified plug-in electric vehicle" is reduced for the amount of credit claimed under the new Code Sec. 30 (Code Sec. 30(e)(1), as amended by the 2009 Recovery Act).

Reduction of other benefits. The amount of credit claimed under Code Sec. 30 for a specific vehicle reduces the amount of *any* other credit or deduction the taxpayer may take on the same vehicle.

> **Comment:** The statute specifically states that the Code Sec. 30 credit reduces the amount of "any deduction or credit allowable under this chapter". Thus, any deduction or credit found in Code Secs. 1 through 1400T that can be claimed with regards to a "qualified plug-in electric vehicle" is reduced by the amount of any credit taken under Code Sec. 30 (Code Sec. 30(e)(2), as amended by the 2009 Recovery Act).

Recapture. The IRS is required by the statute to prescribe regulations that will recapture any benefit claimed under Code Sec. 30 if the vehicle in question no longer qualifies as a "qualified plug-in electric vehicle" (Code Sec. 30(e)(5), as amended by the 2009 Recovery Act).

Sale of qualifying vehicle to tax exempt entity, government entity or foreign persons/entities. The special rules of Code Sec. 50(b)(3) and (4) prevent certain taxpayers from fully using the credits found in Code Secs. 46 through 50. If a "qualified plug-in electric

¶350

NEW LAW EXPLAINED

vehicle" is sold to a taxpayer subject to Code Sec. 50(b)(3) or (4), the *seller* of the vehicle may claim the Code Sec. 30 credit. However, the seller must disclose the credit amount to the buyer of the "qualified plug-in electric vehicle" (Code Sec. 30(e)(3), as amended by the 2009 Recovery Act).

> **Caution:** The title of Code Sec. 30(e)(3) only references tax exempt entities, but the language of the subparagraph refers to both Code Sec. 50(b)(3) and (4) which cover government entities and foreign taxpayers as well as tax-exempt entities.

Foreign property. The Code Sec. 30 credit is generally not allowed to a vehicle used predominantly outside of the United States (Code Sec. 30(e)(4), as amended by the 2009 Recovery Act).

Termination date and transition rules. Code Sec. 30 generally applies to vehicles purchased after February 17, 2009 (Act Sec. 1142(c) of the 2009 Recovery Act). However, the credit is subject to the following termination and transitional rules:

- the credit is not available for any vehicle acquired after December 31, 2011; and
- the credit is not available for a vehicle purchased before January 1, 2010 if the same vehicle qualifies for a credit under Code Sec. 30D (Code Sec. 30(f), as amended by the 2009 Recovery Act; Act Sec. 1142(d) of the 2009 Recovery Act).

▶ **Effective date.** The amendments made by this section shall generally apply to vehicles acquired after February 17, 2009 (Act Sec. 1142(c) of the American Recovery and Reinvestment Tax Act of 2009 (P.L. 111-5)).

Law source: Law at ¶5040. Committee Report at ¶10,200.

— Act Sec. 1142(a) of the American Recovery and Reinvestment Tax Act of 2009 (P.L. 111-5), amending Code Sec. 30;

— Act Sec. 1142(b), amending Code Secs. 24(b)(3)(B), 25(e)(1)(C)(ii), 25B(g)(2), 26(a)(1), 30B(h), 30C(d)(2)(A), 53(d)(1)(B), 55(c)(3), 904(i), 1016(a)(25), 1400C(d)(2), 6501(m);

— Act Sec. 1142(c), providing the effective date;

— Act Sec. 1142(d), providing the transitional rules; and

— Act Sec. 1142(e), applying a sunset provision.

Reporter references: For further information, consult the following CCH reporters.

— Standard Federal Tax Reporter, ¶4059P.01

— Tax Research Consultant, INDIV: 58,000

— Practical Tax Explanation, § 12,915

¶355 Plug-in Electric Drive Motor Vehicle Conversion Credit

SUMMARY OF NEW LAW

A new credit against tax is available for the cost of converting any motor vehicle into a qualified plug-in electric drive motor vehicle.

BACKGROUND

Prior to passage of the Energy Tax Incentives Act of 2005 (P.L. 109-58), the only tax incentives to encourage development of alternative fuels for motor vehicles were the credit for qualified electric vehicles and the deduction for the cost of clean-fuel vehicles and related property (Code Secs. 30 and 179A). The Energy Act of 2005 changed the landscape for developing alternative fuels by creating the alternative motor vehicle credit and the alternative fuel vehicle refueling property credit (Code Secs. 30B and 30C). There are actually four different credits under the alternative motor vehicle credit of Code Sec. 30B, each of which deals with a different type of alternative fuel currently being developed or already available in the marketplace. The benefit of any credit claimed under Code Sec. 30B must be recaptured if the property in question no longer qualifies for the credit (Code Sec. 30B(h)(8)).

The incentive to encourage alternative fuels for motor vehicles was expanded by the Emergency Economic Stabilization Act of 2008 (P.L. 110-343) which added a credit against tax for qualified plug-in electric drive motor vehicles placed in service in 2009 through 2014 (Code Sec. 30D, as added by the Emergency Economic Act of 2008). A qualified plug-in electric drive motor vehicle is a motor vehicle that draws propulsion using a traction battery with at least 4 kilowatt hours of capacity, can be recharged from an external electricity source, and meets certain emission standards except for heavy weight vehicles (Code Sec. 30D(c)).

NEW LAW EXPLAINED

Credit for converting existing motor vehicles into plug-in electric drive motor vehicles.—A credit is available to taxpayers for the cost of converting an existing motor vehicle into a "qualified plug-in electric drive motor vehicle" (Code Sec. 30B(a)(5) and (i), as added by the American Recovery and Reinvestment Tax Act of 2009 (P.L. 111-5)). The plug-in conversion credit is equal to 10 percent of the cost of converting the vehicle, up to $40,000, for a maximum credit of $4,000, but will not apply to conversions made after December 31, 2011 (Code Sec. 30B(i)(1) and (i)(4), as added by the 2009 Recovery Act). The plug-in conversion credit is treated as part of the alternative motor vehicle credit and may be claimed even if another alternative motor vehicle credit under Code Sec. 30B(a)(1) through Code Sec. 30B(a)(4) was claimed for the same motor vehicle in any preceding tax year (Code Sec. 30B(a)(5) and (i)(3), as added by the 2009 Recovery Act).

Qualified plug-in electric drive motor vehicle. For purposes of the plug-in conversion credit, a "qualified plug-in electric drive motor vehicle" is defined by reference to the definition for any new qualified plug-in electric drive motor vehicle in Code Sec. 30D, with certain modifications. The 2009 Recovery Act, however, amends the definition of the term *new qualified plug-in electric drive motor vehicle* in Code Sec. 30D, effective for vehicles acquired after December 31, 2009. Therefore, in 2009 the definition in Code Sec. 30D prior to amendment applies, while the amended definition applies in 2010 and 2011. For further discussion on the amendments to the qualified plug-in electric drive motor vehicle credit, see ¶ 345.

¶355

NEW LAW EXPLAINED

Compliance Pointer: Since the plug-in conversion credit may be claimed for property placed in service after February 17, 2009, and in 2010 and 2011, the vehicle for which the credit is claimed must satisfy the qualified plug-in electric drive motor vehicle requirements in effect during the tax year the credit is being claimed.

In 2009, for purposes of the plug-in conversion credit, a "qualified plug-in electric drive motor vehicle" is a motor vehicle that:

(1) draws propulsion using a traction battery with at least 4 kilowatt hours of capacity,

(2) uses an offboard source of energy to recharge such battery,

(3) in the case of a passenger vehicle or light truck that has a gross vehicle weight rating of not more than 8,500 pounds, has received a certificate of conformity under the Clean Air Act and meets or exceeds the equivalent qualifying California low emission vehicle standard under section 243(e)(2) of the Clean Air Act for that make and model year, and

   (a) in the case of a vehicle having a gross vehicle weight rating of 6,000 pounds or less, meets the Bin 5 Tier II emission standard established in regulations prescribed by the Administrator of the Environmental Protection Agency under section 202(i) of the Clean Air Act for that make and model year vehicle, and

   (b) in the case of a vehicle having a gross vehicle weight rating of more than 6,000 pounds but not more than 8,500 pounds, meets the Bin 8 Tier II emission standard which is so established, and

(4) is acquired for use or lease by the taxpayer and not for resale (Code Sec. 30B(i)(2), as added by the 2009 Recovery Act; Code Sec. 30D(c)(1) through (c)(3) and (c)(5), prior to amendment by the 2009 Recovery Act).

In 2010 and 2011, for purposes of the plug-in conversion credit, a "qualified plug-in electric drive motor vehicle" is a motor vehicle that:

(1) is propelled significantly by an electric motor drawing electricity from a battery with a capacity of at least 4 kilowatt hours,

(2) uses an external source of electricity to recharge such battery,

(3) has a gross vehicle weight rating of less than 14,000 pounds,

(4) is treated as a motor vehicle under title II of the Clean Air Act (a self-propelled vehicle designed for transporting persons or property on a street or highway), and

(5) is acquired for use or lease by the taxpayer and not for resale (Code Sec. 30B(i)(2), as added by the 2009 Recovery Act; Code Sec. 30D(d)(1), as added by the 2009 Recovery Act).

Comment: The qualified plug-in electric drive motor vehicle credit requirements that the original use of the vehicle must commence with the taxpayer and that the vehicle must be made by a manufacturer do not apply to the plug-in conversion credit.

¶355

Explanation   113

NEW LAW EXPLAINED

No alternative motor vehicle credit recapture for conversion. Under the alternative motor vehicle credit general rules, if property that generated the credit no longer qualifies, any benefit derived from the claimed credit must be recaptured. However, recapture is not required if the property ceases to qualify for any credit described in Code Sec. 30B(a)(1) through (4) because the property is converted to a qualified plug-in electric drive motor vehicle (Code Sec. 30B(h)(8), as amended by the 2009 Recovery Act).

▶ **Effective date.** The conversion credit applies to property placed in service after February 17, 2009 (Act. Sec. 1143(d) of the American Recovery and Reinvestment Tax Act of 2009 (P.L. 111-5)).

Law source: Law at ¶5045. Committee Report at ¶10,200.

— Act Sec. 1143(a) of the American Recovery and Reinvestment Tax Act of 2009 (P.L. 111-5), adding Code Sec. 30B(i) and redesignating Code Sec. 30B(i) and (j) as Code Sec. 30B(j) and 30B(k);

— Act Sec. 1143(b), amending Code Sec. 30B(a);

— Act Sec. 1143(c) amending Code Sec. 30B(h)(8);

— Act Sec. 1143(d), providing the effective date.

Reporter references: For further information, consult the following CCH reporters.

— Standard Federal Tax Reporter, ¶4059E.01 and ¶4059P.01

— Tax Research Consultant, INDIV: 57,700 and INDIV: 58,000

— Practical Tax Explanation, § 12,905 and § 12,915

¶360 Alternative Motor Vehicle Credit

SUMMARY OF NEW LAW

The alternative motor vehicle credit is treated as a nonrefundable personal credit for tax years beginning after December 31, 2008 and before January 1, 2011. This will allow a taxpayer to use the credit to offset both regular tax liability and alternative minimum tax liability.

BACKGROUND

A taxpayer may claim an alternative motor vehicle credit (Code Sec. 30B). The credit amount is equal to the sum of the following component credits: (1) a qualified fuel cell motor vehicle credit; (2) an advanced lean burn technology motor vehicle credit; (3) a qualified hybrid motor vehicle credit; and (4) a qualified alternative motor vehicle credit. There are distinct requirements for each of the four components of the credit, including vehicle weight, vehicle fuel efficiency, lifetime fuel savings, etc. However, three requirements are common to each of the components: the original use of the vehicle must commence with the taxpayer; the vehicle must be acquired for use

¶360

BACKGROUND

or lease by the taxpayer and not for resale; and the vehicle must be made by a manufacturer.

The credit claimed is the sum of the components applicable to a particular vehicle, whether used for personal or business purposes. Taxpayers with qualified motor vehicles that are used in a trade or business and subject to depreciation will claim the alternative motor vehicle credit as a part of, and subject to, the rules of the general business credit (Code Sec. 38). Thus, any unused credit in a tax year will be eligible to be carried back three years and forward 20 years. If the alternative motor vehicle credit is claimed by an individual as a personal credit, the credit cannot exceed the excess of their regular income tax liability reduced by the sum of the nonrefundable personal credits (other than the adoption credit, the child tax credit, and the credit for residential energy efficient property expenditures, the foreign tax credit, and the credit for electric automobiles, over the individual's tentative minimum tax (Code Sec. 30B(g)).

NEW LAW EXPLAINED

Alternative motor vehicle credit treated as a nonrefundable personal credit.—For tax years beginning in 2009, the alternative motor vehicle tax credit will be treated as a nonrefundable personal tax credit. This means that it can be used to offset regular tax liability and alternative minimum tax (AMT) liability the same as other nonrefundable personal credits to the extent permitted (see ¶ 240) (Code Sec. 30B(g)(2)(A), as amended by the American Recovery and Reinvestment Tax Act of 2009 (P.L. 111-5)). For this purpose, the regular tax liability is reduced by the amount of any applicable foreign tax credit.

> **Comment:** The rule which allows nonrefundable personal credits to offset both regular and AMT liability has been extended to 2009 (Code Sec. 26(a)(2), as amended by the 2009 Recovery Act). See ¶ 240.

For any tax year in which nonrefundable personal credits are not allowed to offset both regular and AMT liability under Code Sec. 26(a)(2), the alternative motor vehicle credit claimed by an individual as a personal credit cannot exceed their regular and AMT liability, reduced by the sum of all nonrefundable personal credits claimed (other than the adoption credit, the residential energy efficient property credit, the qualified plug-in electric vehicle (see ¶ 350), and the new the qualified plug-in electric drive motor vehicle credit (see ¶ 345)), plus the foreign tax credit for the tax year (Code Sec. 30B(g)(2)(B), as amended 2009 Recovery Act).

> **Comment:** Effective for property placed in service after February 17, 2009, the alternative motor vehicle credit includes a credit for the cost of converting an existing motor vehicle into a qualified plug-in electric drive motor vehicle (see ¶ 345).

Practical Analysis: Jeffrey D. Eicher, J.D., CPA, Professor of Finance at Clarion University of Pennsylvania, and Leo N. Hitt, J.D., LL.M., Tax Partner in the Pittsburgh

¶360

NEW LAW EXPLAINED

> office of Reed Smith, LLP, observe that the credit for alternative motor vehicles, including qualified fuel cell, qualified advanced lean burn technology, qualified hybrid and certain other qualified alternative motor vehicles will be allowed as a credit against the alternative minimum tax for tax years beginning after 2008. This provision adds the Alternative Motor Vehicle Credit to the list of nonrefundable personal credit that may offset the alternative minimum tax.

▶ **Effective date.** The amendments apply to tax years beginning after December 31, 2008, subject to the sunset provisions of the Economic Growth and Tax Relief Reconciliation Act of 2001 (P.L.107-16) (Act Sec. 1144(c) of the American Recovery and Reinvestment Tax Act of 2009 (P.L. 111-5)).

Law source: Law at ¶5045. Committee Report at ¶10,200.

— Act Sec. 1144(a) of the American Recovery and Reinvestment Tax Act of 2009 (P.L. 111-5), amending Code Sec. 30B(g)(2);

— Act Sec. 1144(c), providing the effective date.

Reporter references: For further information, consult the following CCH reporters.

— Standard Federal Tax Reporter, ¶3851 and ¶5101.04
— Tax Research Consultant, INDIV: 57,700
— Practical Tax Explanation, § 15,125 and § 15,315

¶365 Qualified Alternative Fuel Vehicle Refueling Property Credit

SUMMARY OF NEW LAW

The qualified alternative fuel vehicle refueling property tax credit percentage for qualified non-hydrogen–related property increases to 50 percent for tax years beginning in 2009 and 2010. The maximum dollar amount of the credit for such non-hydrogen–related property which is subject to an allowance for depreciation increases to $50,000 and to $200,000 for hydrogen-related property. The maximum credit amount that may be claimed for non-hydrogen–related property not subject to an allowance for depreciation increases to $2,000 for these tax years.

BACKGROUND

The Energy Tax Incentive Act of 2008 (P.L. 109-58) added two key tax credits to encourage American automobile manufacturers and consumers to manufacture and use motor vehicles powered by alternative fuels. The credit which received the most attention was the alternative motor vehicle credit which allowed purchasers of the Toyota Prius to claim a credit against tax of up to $3,150. To insure the continued development of this technology, the second credit was the alternative fuel vehicle

BACKGROUND

refueling property credit. This credit is to encourage fuel distributors to develop more refueling locations as an additional incentive to drive an alternative fuel vehicle. The credit allowed is equal to 30 percent of the cost of a qualified alternative fuel vehicle refueling property placed in service by the taxpayer during the tax year. The maximum dollar amount of the credit that can be claimed in any one year is $30,000 for property subject to an allowance for depreciation and $1,000 for all other property.

> **Comment:** The qualified alternative vehicle fuel refueling property credit replaced the Code Sec. 179A deduction for clean-fuel vehicle refueling property, which terminated for property placed in service after December 31, 2005.

If qualified alternative fuel vehicle refueling property is subject to an allowance for depreciation, the credit is considered to be a part of and subject to the limitation of the general business credit (Code Sec. 30C(d)(1)). The amount of the credit for property not subject to an allowance for depreciation cannot exceed the excess of regular tax liability reduced by the nonrefundable personal credits under Subpart A, the foreign tax credit (Code Sec. 27), the qualified electric vehicle credit (Code Sec. 30, prior to expiration) and the alternative fuels motor vehicle credit (Code Sec. 30B) over the taxpayer's tentative minimum tax (Code Sec. 30C(d)(2)).

The IRS issued Notice 2007-43 to provide interim guidance until the issuance of regulations regarding the alternative fuel vehicle refueling property credit (Notice 2007-43, I.R.B. 2007-22, 1318). The guidance includes definitions of qualified new refueling property, dual-status property, and converted property. The definition of qualified costs, allocation of costs regarding dual-status and converted property, the calculation and examples are included.

The credit for qualified alternative fuel vehicle refueling property is not applicable to hydrogen-related property placed into service after December 31, 2014 and for any other property placed into service after December 31, 2010 (Code Sec. 30C(g)).

NEW LAW EXPLAINED

Percentage and maximum dollar limitation increased.—The credit percentage of the alternative fuel vehicle refueling property tax credit for installation of non-hydrogen–related property is increased to 50 percent for property placed in service in tax years beginning after December 31, 2008, and before January 1, 2011 (Code Sec. 30C(e)(6)(A)(i), as added by the American Recovery and Reinvestment Tax Act of 2009 (P.L. 111-5)). For non-hydrogen–related property subject to an allowance for depreciation, the maximum dollar limitation of the credit increases to $50,000 for all qualified alternative fuel vehicle refueling property that the taxpayer places in service at a location during the above mentioned designated period (Code Sec. 30C(e)(6)(A)(ii), as added by the 2009 Recovery Act). For non-hydrogen–related property not subject to depreciation rules, the maximum dollar amount of the credit is increased to $2,000 for property placed in service during the designated period (Code Sec. 30C(e)(6)(A)(iii), as added by the 2009 Recovery Act).

¶365

Explanation 117

NEW LAW EXPLAINED

> **Practical Analysis:** Charles R. Goulding, J.D., CPA, MBA, and President of Energy Tax Savers Inc. of Syosset, New York, notes that to enable these alternative fuels to actually be utilized, it is crucial for the alternative fuel industry to be willing to make the large investments in the required new fuel distribution systems. For a commercial or retail refueling station the combination of the higher 50-percent credit up to $50,000 as compared to the previous 30-percent credit up to $30,000 is a substantial increase. This means that a taxpayer with $90,000 project cost would now receive a $45,000 tax credit, as compared to the previous tax credit of $27,000.
>
> The maximum credit for hydrogen refueling property increases to $200,000. As of the end of 2008, there were only 60 hydrogen refueling stations in the country and most of those are in California. Our nation cannot take advantage of the hydrogen fueled cars scheduled to be available in 2011 unless we have a national fueling station network.

For hydrogen-related property placed in service after December 31, 2008, and before January 1, 2011, the credit percentage remains the same at 30 percent. However, the maximum dollar limitation of the credit for such property, if it is subject to an allowance for depreciation, is increased to $200,000 (Code Sec. 30C(e)(6)(B), as added by the 2009 Recovery Act).

> **Comment:** For hydrogen-related property placed in service during this time period which is not subject to an allowance for depreciation, not only does the credit percentage remain at 30 percent but the maximum dollar amount of the credit also remains at $1,000.
>
> **Compliance Tip:** The credit is claimed on Form 8911, Alternative Fuel Vehicle Refueling Property Credit.

▶ **Effective date.** The amendments made by this section apply to tax years beginning after December 31, 2008 (Act Sec. 1123(b) of the American Recovery and Reinvestment Tax Act of 2009 (P.L. 111-5)).

Law source: Law at ¶5050. Committee Report at ¶10,180.

— Act Sec. 1123(a) of the American Recovery and Reinvestment Tax Act of 2009 (P.L. 111-5), adding Code Sec. 30C(e)(6);

— Act Sec. 1123(b), providing the effective date.

Reporter references: For further information, consult the following CCH reporters.

— Standard Federal Tax Reporter, ¶4059K.01

— Tax Research Consultant, INDIV: 57,750

— Practical Tax Explanation, §12,910

¶365

Business Income and Deductions 4

¶405 Deferral of Discharge of Indebtedness Income Resulting From Reacquisition of Business Indebtedness
¶410 Code Sec. 179 Expense Election for 2009
¶415 Availability of Bonus Depreciation for 2009
¶420 Recognition Period for S Corporation Built-In Gains Tax
¶425 Maximum Five-Year Carryback Period for 2008 Net Operating Losses of Small Businesses
¶430 Clarification of IRS Guidance Related to Limitations on Certain Built-In Losses Following an Ownership Change
¶435 Treatment of Certain Ownership Changes for Purposes of Limitations on NOL Carryforwards and Certain Built-In Losses
¶440 Original Issue Discount on High-Yield Discount Obligations
¶445 Financial Institution De Minimis Safe Harbor Exception for Deducting Tax-Exempt Interest Expense
¶450 Temporary Expansion of Small Issuer Exception to Tax-Exempt Interest Expense Allocation Rules for Financial Institutions
¶455 $500,000 Executive Compensation Deduction Limit Extended to All Entities That Take TARP Assistance
¶460 Withholding on Certain Payments Made by Government Entities
¶465 Estimated Tax of Qualified Individuals
¶470 Corporate Estimated Tax Payments

¶405 Deferral of Discharge of Indebtedness Income Resulting From Reacquisition of Business Indebtedness

SUMMARY OF NEW LAW

At the election of the taxpayer, income from the discharge of indebtedness in connection with the reacquisition after December 31, 2008, and before January 1,

¶405

SUMMARY OF NEW LAW

2011, of corporate or business debt instrument is includible in gross income ratably over a five-tax-year period.

BACKGROUND

Discharge of indebtedness income. When a loan is settled for less than the amount owed, discharge of indebtedness (DOI) income is realized by the debtor and usually must be included in the debtor's gross income (Code Sec. 61(a)(12)). The amount of DOI income is generally equal to the amount of loan forgiveness. DOI income also occurs when a debtor repurchases his own debt at a discount (meaning a price lower than the adjusted issue price of the debt instrument). In debt repurchase transactions, the amount of DOI income is generally equal to the difference between the adjusted issue price and the price paid for the debt instrument (Reg. § 1.61-12(c)(2)(ii)).

> **Comment:** DOI income is particularly burdensome because transactions that cause such income do not normally provide cash to pay the tax. Worse yet, when the economy is in recession a taxpayer who was counting on other assets and investments to pay taxes may find that severe declines in asset values or illiquid markets make it impossible to raise sufficient funds.

Exceptions for inclusion of DOI income. There are several exceptions, under Code Sec. 108(a)(1), to the general rule that DOI income must be included in the debtor's gross income, which are:

(1) if the debt is discharged under a Chapter 11 bankruptcy;

(2) if the debt is discharged when the taxpayer was insolvent;

(3) if the debt discharged is qualified farm indebtedness;

(4) if the debt discharged is qualified real property business indebtedness (except if the debtor is a C corporation); and

(5) if the debt discharged is qualified principal residence indebtedness, discharged before January 1, 2013 (Code Sec. 108(a)(1)).

In cases of debt discharged under a Chapter 11 bankruptcy, debt discharged due to insolvency or qualified farm indebtedness, tax attributes must be reduced by the amount of excluded DOI income in a specific order (Code Sec. 108(b)(1)). In cases of discharged qualified real property business indebtedness or qualified principal residence indebtedness, the bases of properties must be reduced by the amount of excluded DOI income (Code Secs. 1017(b)(3) and 108(h)(1)).

Acquisition of indebtedness by a related person. If outstanding debt is acquired from a third party by a person related to the debtor through certain family, business or fiduciary connections, the transaction is generally treated as if the debtor repurchased the debt himself (Code Sec. 108(e)(4)). Therefore, any DOI income which results from the transaction must generally be recognized as gross income by the *debtor* - and not by the person who acquired the debt. There are certain exceptions and limitations including if the debtor was in Chapter 11 bankruptcy or was insolvent (Reg. § 1.108-2(a)). In addition, the regulations provide further rules and limitations regard-

Explanation

BACKGROUND

ing disclosure, timing of acquisitions and subsequent transactions (Reg. §1.108-2). A person is generally considered to be a related person, for purposes of acquisitions of debt under Code Sec. 108(e)(4), under the same rules that are applied for disallowance of losses from transactions between related parties under Code Sec. 267(b) and controlled partnerships under Code Sec. 707(b)(1). Losses from transactions between related persons are not deductible, but a previously disallowed loss can later be used (to the extent of gain) by the original transferee if he sells the property to a non-related third party. (Code Sec. 267(a); Reg. §1.267(d)-1).

> **Comment:** There is great potential for tax fraud in transactions among related persons, so these transactions are heavily regulated under the Code. Creating false losses and undervaluing assets are among the more common tax avoidance schemes. For example, losses generated by a purchase and sale of property between related persons can produce paper losses which in fact have no economic substance, because of the relationship between the buyer and the seller. Such losses are disallowed under Code Sec. 267(a) and related provisions for good reason.

NEW LAW EXPLAINED

Limited deferral for discharge of indebtedness income from reacquisition of debt instruments.—At the election of the taxpayer, income from the discharge of indebtedness in connection with the reacquisition after December 31, 2008, and before January 1, 2011, of an applicable debt instrument is includible in gross income ratably over the five-tax-year period beginning with:

- The fifth tax year following the tax year in which the reacquisition occurs for a reacquisition occurring in 2009; and

- The fourth tax year following the tax year in which the reacquisition occurs for a reacquisition occurring in 2010 (Code Sec. 108(i)(1), as added by the American Recovery and Reinvestment Tax Act of 2009 (P.L. 111-5)).

Deferral of deduction for OID in debt-for-debt exchanges. If a debt instrument is issued for the applicable debt instrument being reacquired (or is treated as issued under Code Sec. 108(e)(4), which concerns acquisition of indebtedness by a person related to the debtor), and there is any original issue discount (OID) with respect to the debt instrument:

- no deduction otherwise allowable shall be allowed to the issuer with respect to the portion of such OID which (a) accrues before the first tax year in the five-tax-year period in which income from the discharge of indebtedness attributable to the reacquisition of the debt instrument is includible in gross income, and (b) does not exceed the income from the discharge of indebtedness with respect to the debt instrument being reacquired; and

- the aggregate amount of deductions disallowed shall be allowed as a deduction ratably over the five-tax-year period.

¶405

NEW LAW EXPLAINED

If the amount of OID accruing before the first tax year in which the OID income is to be recognized exceeds the income from the discharge of indebtedness with respect to the applicable debt instrument being reacquired, the deductions are to be disallowed in the order in which the OID is accrued (Code Sec. 108(i)(2)(A), as added by the 2009 Recovery Act).

Deemed debt-for-debt exchanges. If any debt instrument is issued by an issuer and the proceeds are used directly or indirectly by the issuer to reacquire an applicable debt instrument of the issuer, the newly issued debt instrument is treated as issued for the debt instrument being reacquired. If only a portion of the proceeds from a debt instrument are used for this purpose, the deferral rules apply to the portion of any OID on the newly issued debt instrument which is equal to the portion of the proceeds from such instrument used to reacquire the outstanding instrument (Code Sec. 108(i)(2)(B), as added by the 2009 Recovery Act). Thus, if a taxpayer makes the deferral election for a debt-for-debt exchange in which the newly issued debt instrument issued (or deemed issued, including by operation of Reg. § 1.108-2(g)) in satisfaction of an outstanding debt instrument of the debtor has OID, then any otherwise allowable deduction for OID with respect to such newly issued debt instrument that (a) accrues before the first year of the five-tax-year period in which the related, deferred discharge of indebtedness income is included in the gross income of the taxpayer, and (b) does not exceed such related, deferred discharge of indebtedness income, is deferred and allowed as a deduction ratably over the same five-tax-year period in which the deferred discharge of indebtedness income is included in gross income (Conference Committee Report for American Recovery and Reinvestment Act of 2009).

This rule can apply in certain cases when a debtor reacquires its debt for cash. If the taxpayer issues a debt instrument and the proceeds of such issuance are used to reacquire a debt instrument of the taxpayer, the newly issued debt instrument is treated as if it were issued in satisfaction of the retired debt instrument. If the newly issued debt instrument has OID, this rule applies. Thus, all or a portion of the interest deductions with respect to OID on the newly issued debt instrument are deferred into the five-tax-year period in which the discharge of indebtedness income is recognized. Where only a portion of the proceeds of a new issuance are used to satisfy outstanding debt, the deferral rule applies to the portion of the OID on the newly issued debt instrument that is equal to the portion of the proceeds of such newly issued instrument used to retire outstanding debt of the taxpayer (Conference Committee Report for American Recovery and Reinvestment Act of 2009).

Applicable debt instrument. An applicable debt instrument is any debt instrument issued by: (i) a C corporation, or (ii) any other person in connection with the conduct of a trade or business by such person (Code Sec. 108(i)(3)(A) as added by the 2009 Recovery Act). A debt instrument for these purposes is broadly defined to include bonds, debentures, notes, certificates, or any other instrument or contractual arrangement constituting indebtedness within the meaning of Code Sec. 1275(a)(1) (which excludes certain annuity contracts) (Code Sec. 108(i)(3)(B), as added by the 2009 Recovery Act).

¶405

NEW LAW EXPLAINED

Reacquisition. Reacquisition for these purposes includes any acquisition of an applicable debt instrument by (i) the debtor which issued (or is otherwise the obligor under) the debt instrument, or (ii) a related person to such debtor (Code Sec. 108(i)(4)(A), as added by the 2009 Recovery Act). The determination of whether a person is related to another person is made in the same manner as Code Sec. 108(e)(4) concerning acquisition of indebtedness by a person related to the debtor (Code Sec. 108(i)(5)(A), as added by the 2009 Recovery Act).

Acquisition. Acquisition for these purposes includes an acquisition of an applicable debt instrument for cash, the exchange of the debt instrument for another debt instrument (including an exchange resulting from a modification of the debt instrument), the exchange of the debt instrument for corporate stock or a partnership interest, the contribution of the debt instrument to capital, and the complete forgiveness of the indebtedness by the holder of the debt instrument (Code Sec. 108(i)(4)(B), as added by the 2009 Recovery Act).

Election. The election to defer OID income is to be made on an instrument by instrument basis. Once made, the election is irrevocable. A taxpayer makes an election with respect to a debt instrument by including with its return for the tax year in which the reacquisition of the debt instrument occurs a statement that: (a) clearly identifies the debt instrument, and (b) includes the amount of deferred income under this provision, plus any other information that may be prescribed by the IRS. The IRS is authorized to require reporting of the election (and other information with respect to the reacquisition) for years subsequent to the year of the reacquisition. In the case of a pass-through entity, such as a partnership or S corporation, the election is made at the entity level (Code Sec. 108(i)(5)(B), as added by the 2009 Recovery Act; Conference Committee Report for American Recovery and Reinvestment Act of 2009).

Coordination with other exclusions. If a taxpayer elects to defer discharge of indebtedness income, the exclusions for discharge under a Chapter 11 bankruptcy, when the taxpayer is insolvent, qualified farm indebtedness, and qualified real property business indebtedness (Code Sec. 108(a)(1)(A), (B), (C) and (D)) do not apply to the income from the discharge of indebtedness for the tax year of the election or any subsequent tax year (Code Sec. 108(i)(5)(C), as added by the 2009 Recovery Act). Thus, for example, an insolvent taxpayer may elect to defer income from the discharge of indebtedness rather than excluding the income and reducing tax attributes by a corresponding amount (Conference Committee Report for American Recovery and Reinvestment Act of 2009).

Acceleration of deferred items. In the case of the death of the taxpayer, the liquidation or sale of substantially all the assets of the taxpayer (including in a title 11 bankruptcy or similar case), the cessation of business by the taxpayer, or similar circumstances, any item of income or deduction which is deferred (and has not previously been taken into account) must be taken into account in the tax year in which such event occurs (or in the case of a title 11 bankruptcy or similar case, the day before the petition is filed). This rule applies in the case of the sale or exchange or redemption of an interest in a partnership, S corporation, or other pass-through entity by a partner, shareholder, or

¶405

NEW LAW EXPLAINED

other person holding an ownership interest in such entity (Code Sec. 108(i)(5)(D), as added by the 2009 Recovery Act).

> **Practical Analysis:** Paul C. Lau and Sandy Soltis, Tax Partners at Blackman Kallick in Chicago, point out that under Reg. § 1.61-12(a), a debtor has cancellation of debt (COD) income equal to the amount of debt reduction. Under Code Sec. 108, the debtor can exclude COD income to the extent it is insolvent or to the extent the debt is discharged in a Title 11 (bankruptcy) proceeding. Some debtors may also exclude the COD income if the debt is "qualified farm indebtedness" or "qualified real property indebtedness." The COD income exclusion is not a free lunch. The debtor is required to reduce certain tax attributes such as net operating losses, general business credits, basis of property (both depreciable and nondepreciable) and unused foreign tax credits. In certain reductions of property tax basis, Code Sec. 1017(b)(2) provides that any basis reduction cannot be more than the excess of the total adjusted basis of property over the total liabilities of the debtor immediately after the debt discharge.
>
> These COD income recognition and exclusion rules apply when a debt is forgiven, "significantly modified," exchanged for a new debt, or repurchased by the debtor. A significant modification of a debt is treated as an exchange of the old debt for a new debt. Significant modifications, subject to certain safe harbors, include a change in interest rate and/or a deferral of principal and interest payments. In addition, a debt that is repurchased by a related party of the debtor (as described in Code Sec. 108(e)(4)) is treated as repurchased by the debtor.
>
> *New Law.* The new law, Code Sec. 108(i), is intended to provide a debtor the ability to elect to recognize COD income on a deferred basis ratably over a five-tax year period. The election is made on a debt by debt basis and, once made, is irrevocable. If this election is made, both the COD income exclusion and tax attribute reduction rules are no longer applicable.
>
> The application of the COD income deferral election is far from clear, especially in a partnership context. Code Sec. 108(d)(6) currently provides that the general COD income exclusion and tax attribute reduction rules are applied at the partner level. The new COD income deferral election rule, however, is made and applied at the partnership level. Guidance is needed to coordinate the application and interaction of these rules.
>
> The election to recognize COD income on a deferred basis can be beneficial in most cases where the debtor is not a C corporation and does not qualify for any COD income exclusion (e.g., insolvency exclusion). In cases where a debtor qualifies for COD income exclusion, the debtor should compare the tax benefits and costs between the election and the COD income exclusion to make an informed decision.
>
> In the case of a C corporation, which does not qualify for the COD income exclusion under Code Sec. 108(a), it should analyze the interaction of the COD income deferral rules with the net operating loss (NOL) limitation rules under Code Sec. 382. If a debt discharge occurs in conjunction with a change in ownership subject to Code Sec. 382, the use of the NOL in subsequent years is limited by the "Code Sec. 382 limitation" described in Code Secs. 382(b) and (h). COD income recognized at the time of or within the five-year period beginning on an ownership change may be fully

NEW LAW EXPLAINED

offset by the NOL or may increase the Code Sec. 382 limitation and the use of the NOL against taxable income during the five-year period. Under Code Sec. 382(h)(6) and (7), COD income recognized after the five year period generally cannot increase the Code Sec. 382 limitation. Without further guidance, it appears that COD income recognized after the fifth year following the ownership change year may not be offset by any NOL carryover. If the deferral election were not made, the COD income could have been offset by the NOL. Following are more detailed discussion and analysis of the new provisions.

Under new Code Sec. 108(i), a taxpayer can elect to recognize and report COD income from a "reacquisition" of an "applicable debt instrument" that occurs after December 31, 2008, and before January 1, 2011, ratably over a five-tax year period. For a reacquisition occurring in 2009, the COD income is reportable as income starting in the fifth tax year following the tax year in which the debt is repurchased. For example, if a debtor repurchased a debt in 2009 and elected the new provision, it would recognize the COD income ratably from 2014 to 2018. For a reacquisition occurring in 2010, the COD income is reportable ratably over five tax years starting in the fourth tax year following the reacquisition year (i.e., 2014–2018).

An "applicable debt instrument" is defined as a debt instrument issued by a C corporation or by any other person in connection with the conduct of its trade or business. In essence, the debt must be issued or incurred in connection with a trade or business for a person other than a C corporation. Personal debt or debt incurred for investment purposes does not qualify for the election. It is unclear if a debt incurred by a partner or a shareholder (active or passive) to invest in a partnership or S corporation which conducts an active trade or business would qualify for the election.

A "reacquisition" is defined as an acquisition of the debt instrument by the debtor (or a related party) that issued (or is the obligor of) the debt. An acquisition is broadly defined to include: (1) a cash purchase of the debt, (2) an exchange of new debt for old debt (including an exchange due to significant modifications), (3) an exchange of debt for corporate stock or a partnership interest, (4) contribution of the debt to capital and (5) a complete debt forgiveness by the debt holder. A related party is any person described under the current law (i.e., Code Sec. 108(e)(4)).

If a taxpayer made the election to apply the COD income deferral recognition, the COD income exclusions (such as bankruptcy or insolvency exclusion) and tax attribute reduction rules will not apply to the debt discharge. A taxpayer makes the election by attaching a statement to the income tax return for the tax year in which the debt is reacquired. The statement must identify the debt instrument, the amount of COD income to be deferred, and any other information required by the IRS. The election, once made, is irrevocable. The IRS may issue regulations requiring information of the election on tax returns for subsequent tax years. For partnerships, S corporations, or other pass through entities, the election is made by the applicable entity.

If a debt with original issue discount (OID) is issued in exchange for the old debt as part of the repurchase of the old debt by the debtor, the debtor must defer the deduction of the amount of accrued OID equal to the amount of COD income attributable to the debt repurchase until the first tax year in which the COD income

¶405

NEW LAW EXPLAINED

(first COD income year) is includible in income. The deferred OID is deductible ratably over five tax years beginning with the first COD income year. If the amount of accrued OID for the period before the first COD income year exceeds the amount of COD income, the OID amount accrued in the earliest years is subject to deferral until the accrued OID amount equal to the COD income amount.

A debt is treated as issued for the repurchased debt if the proceeds are used directly or indirectly to acquire the repurchased debt. If only a portion of the proceeds are used to acquire the repurchased debt, the amount of accrued OID subject to deferral is the amount of OID on the new debt in proportion to the amount of new debt proceeds used to repurchase the old debt. The OID deferral rules are applicable to the repurchase of debt by a debtor or a related party of the debtor.

The amount of COD income that has not been includible in income becomes taxable income immediately upon: (1) the debtor's death; (2) the liquidation or sale of substantially all of the debtor's assets (including Title 11 or similar proceeding); (3) the closing of business; or (4) other similar events. Any accrued OID that has not been deducted also becomes deductible. These income and deduction acceleration rules also apply in the case of a sale or exchange or redemption of an interest in a partnership, S corporation, or other pass-through entity by a partner, shareholder, or owner. The IRS can issue regulations to expand the acceleration rules to other circumstances.

In the partnership context, presumably only a partner's distributive shares of COD income and OID deduction are accelerated and allocated to the partner whose interest is sold or redeemed. It is unclear what amounts should be accelerated when there is a constructive termination of the partnership under Code Sec. 708(b)(1)(B).

It is also unclear how the acceleration rules should apply in an S corporation context. If a shareholder's stock is sold or redeemed, presumably only the amounts of COD income and OID deduction in proportion to the percentage of stock sold or redeemed will be accelerated and allocated to all shareholders.

For purposes of allocating COD income and OID deductions to partners, the COD income and OID deductions will only be allocated to those who were partners at the time immediately before the debt repurchase. The allocable shares to the partners are the amounts that would have been allocated to these partners if the income and deductions were not deferred. Any decrease in a partner's share of partnership liabilities as a result of the debt repurchase is not taken into account under Code Sec. 752 to the extent that a deemed cash distribution (due to a reduction of partnership debt) would cause the partner to recognize gain under Code Sec. 731. Instead, the decrease in partnership liabilities that was deferred is taken into account by the partner at the same time, and to same extent, as the COD income is includible in income.

In essence, any gain that would have been recognized from a deemed cash distribution that is attributable to a debt reacquisition is also deferred. Again, clarification is needed on how the deemed cash distribution should interact with the deferred COD income rules in determining the amount of gain to be recognized under Code Sec. 731. COD income, if not deferred as taxable income, increases the tax basis of the partnership interest in the hands of the partners, which should, in turn, reduce the

NEW LAW EXPLAINED

> amount of gain recognized from the deemed cash distribution for purposes of Code Sec. 731. Therefore, the deferred COD income, when recognized, should increase a partner's tax basis for determining the amount of gain from the deemed cash distribution. Presumably, the deferred partnership liabilities will also be taken into account ratably over the five-year period as the COD income.

Special rule for partnerships. In the case of a partnership, any income deferred under this provision is to be allocated to the partners in the partnership immediately before the discharge in the manner such amounts would have been included in the distributive shares of the partners under Code Sec. 704 if the income were recognized at such time. Any decrease in a partner's share of partnership liabilities as a result of such discharge is not be taken into account for purposes of Code Sec. 752 (concerning the treatment of certain liabilities) at the time of the discharge to the extent it would cause the partner to recognize gain under Code Sec. 731. Thus, the deemed distribution under Code Sec. 752 is deferred with respect to a partner to the extent it exceeds such partner's basis. Amounts so deferred are taken into account at the same time, and to the extent remaining in the same amount, as income deferred under the provision is recognized by the partner (Code Sec. 108(i)(6), as added by the 2009 Recovery Act; Conference Committee Report for American Recovery and Reinvestment Act of 2009).

> **Practical Analysis:** Kip Dellinger, CPA, Senior Tax Partner at Kallman And Co. LLP in Los Angeles, notes that the decision whether or not to utilize the cancellation of indebtedness provisions will be very troublesome for partnerships. Because the election is made at the partnership level, and because it prohibits other beneficial option in Code Sec. 108 for bankruptcy, insolvency and qualified real property indebtedness, potentially conflicting desires of respective partners will likely come into play. In addition, partners may have decidedly different views of the benefit of deferral on the tax ramifications on their particular tax situations in the years of ratable inclusion of the income. This may create situations that place the tax matters partner between a rock and a hard place when contemplating the election.
>
> Also, the provision the deemed distribution that occurs by virtue of any decrease in a partner's share of partnership liabilities as a result of the discharge; however, the decrease is only to the extent it will cause a partner to recognize gain under Code Sec. 731 at the time of distribution. Accordingly, the deemed distribution for a partner only to the extent it exceeds the partner's basis; the effect is that a partner's basis for her partnership interest may be reduced as consequence of the reacquisition.

The Secretary of the Treasury may prescribe rules and regulations regarding the application of this provision, including: (a) extending the application of the rules regarding the acceleration of deferred items to other circumstances where appropriate, (b) requiring reporting of the election (and such other information as the Secretary may require) on returns of tax for subsequent tax years, and (c) rules for the application of the provision to partnerships, S corporations, and other pass-through entities including

¶405

NEW LAW EXPLAINED

for the allocation of deferred deductions (Code Sec. 108(i)(7), as added by the 2009 Recovery Act).

▶ **Effective date.** The provision applies to discharges in tax years ending after December 31, 2008 (Act Sec. 1231(b) of the American Recovery and Reinvestment Tax Act of 2009 (P.L. 111-5)).

Law source: Law at ¶5205. Committee Report at ¶10,270.

— Act Sec. 1231(a) of the American Recovery and Reinvestment Tax Act of 2009 (P.L. 111-5), adding Code Sec. 108(i);

— Act Sec. 1231(b), providing the effective date.

Reporter references: For further information, consult the following CCH reporters.

— Standard Federal Tax Reporter, ¶7010.01 and ¶7010.05

— Tax Research Consultant, SALES: 12,252

— Practical Tax Explanation, §3,420

¶410 Code Sec. 179 Expense Election for 2009

SUMMARY OF NEW LAW

The increased Code Sec. 179 expensing allowance provided for tax years beginning in 2008 is extended one additional year. Thus, for the years beginning in 2009, the Code Sec. 179 dollar limitation is $250,000, and the investment limitation is $800,000.

BACKGROUND

An expense deduction is provided for taxpayers (other than estates, trusts or certain noncorporate lessors) who elect to treat the cost of qualifying property, called section 179 property, as an expense rather than a capital expenditure (Code Sec. 179). Section 179 property is depreciable tangible personal property that is purchased for use in the active conduct of a trade or business. Off-the-shelf computer software placed in service in tax years beginning before 2010 is also treated as section 179 property.

A dollar limit is placed on the maximum amount of section 179 property a taxpayer may expense during the year. The annual dollar limitation is reduced dollar for dollar by the cost of section 179 property placed in service during the tax year in excess of an investment limitation. These limits are indexed annually for inflation. The inflation-adjusted dollar limitation and investment limitation for tax years beginning in 2008 were announced as $128,000 and $510,000, respectively (Rev. Proc. 2007-66, I.R.B. 2007-45). However, the Economic Stimulus Act of 2008 (P.L. 110-185) temporarily increased the maximum Code Sec. 179 deduction to $250,000 and the investment limitation to $800,000 for tax years beginning in 2008 (Code Sec. 179(b)(7), as added by the 2008 Stimulus Act). The inflation-adjusted dollar limitation and

BACKGROUND

investment limitation for tax years beginning in 2009 were announced as $133,000 and $530,000, respectively (Rev. Proc. 2008-56, I.R.B. 2008-45).

NEW LAW EXPLAINED

Increased Code Sec. 179 expensing extended to apply to tax years beginning in 2009.—The increased Code Sec. 179 dollar and investment limitations provided by the Economic Stimulus Act of 2008 (P.L. 110-185) for tax years beginning in 2008 have been extended an additional year and now also apply to tax years beginning in 2009 (Code Sec. 179(b)(7), as amended by the American Recovery and Reinvestment Tax Act of 2009 (P.L. 111-5)). Thus, for tax years beginning in 2008 and 2009 the dollar limitation is $250,000 and the investment limitation is $800,000, respectively.

Practical Analysis: David Culp, a senior manager in the Federal Tax group of the Washington National Tax practice of KPMG LLP, notes that the American Recovery and Reinvestment Tax Act of 2009 extends into 2009 the higher limitations on Code Sec. 179 expensing that were in effect for 2008.

Code Sec. 179 allows a taxpayer an election to expense, rather than capitalize and depreciate, its investment in Code Sec. 1245 tangible depreciable property and certain computer software that is purchased in the tax year for use in the active conduct of a trade or business. The election is limited to $125,000 of investment each tax year. The limitation is reduced when total investment for the tax year exceeds $500,000. These amounts are indexed for inflation.

Legislation enacted in 2008 provided a temporary increase in the annual limitation to $250,000 for eligible property placed in service in that tax year. The threshold at which the limitation begins to be reduced was raised to $800,000. These same limitations now apply for tax years beginning in 2009.

Without this extension, the expensing limitation for 2009 would be $133,000, and the phase-out would begin at $530,000 of investment.

(The views and opinions of this KPMG commentary, as well as all other KPMG commentaries throughout this publication, are those of the authors and do not necessarily represent the views and opinions of KPMG LLP.)

Practical Analysis: Michael Schlesinger, a partner in Schlesinger & Sussman of New York, New York and author of *Practical Guide To S Corporations* (4th edition), notes that advanced planning is required when an S corporation plans to utilize Code Sec. 179 to expense assets. The reason is multifaceted due to the fact that the operation of Code Sec. 179 occurs at two levels, first at the S corporate level to elect the deduction and then at the shareholder level to utilize the deduction. For instance, Code Sec. 179(d)(4) specifically prescribes that Code Sec. 179's expense deduction does not apply to estates and trusts. So, if an S corporation has an estate and/or a trust for a shareholder, Reg. § 1.179-1(f)(3) provides that the trust or estate may not

¶410

NEW LAW EXPLAINED

deduct its allocable share of the Code Sec. 179 expense elected by the S corporation and the S corporation's basis in Code Sec. 179 property shall not be reduced to reflect any portion of the Code Sec. 179 expense that is allocable to the trust or estate. However, the S corporation may claim a depreciation deduction under Code Sec. 168 or a Code Sec. 38 credit (if available) with respect to any depreciable basis resulting from the trust or estate's inability to claim its allocable portion of the Code Sec. 179 expense. Other key examples where planning is required under Code Sec. 179 are set forth below.

If an S corporate shareholder disposes of his or her stock where gain or loss is not recognized in whole or in part (including transfers of an S corporate interest at death) and the shareholder has not been able to fully utilize his or her Code Sec. 179 deduction due to Code Sec. 179's income limitation, Reg. §1.179-3(h)(2) states that immediately before the transfer of the shareholder's stock in the S corporation, the shareholder's basis is increased by the amount of the shareholder's outstanding carryover of disallowed deduction with respect to his or her S corporate interest.

Reg. §1.179-2(b)(4) states that Code Sec. 179's dollar limitation (Code Sec. 179(b)(1)'s current limit is $250,000) applies to the S corporation as well as to each S corporate shareholder. In applying the dollar limitation to a taxpayer that is an S corporate shareholder in one or more S corporations, the S corporate shareholder's share of Code Sec. 179 expenses allocated to the S corporate shareholder from each S corporation is aggregated with any non-S corporation Code Sec. 179 expenses of the taxpayer for the taxable year. So, assume that a calendar year S corporation owned equally by two individual shareholders, Mike and Laurie, purchases $250,000 of Code Sec. 179 property on January 1, 2009, and elects to expense all of it. On December 31, 2009, Mike individually for his sole proprietorship purchases $200,000 of Code Sec. 179 property. Mike cannot take a Code Sec. 179 deduction of $325,000 ($125,000 from the passthrough of 50 percent of the S corporation's Code Sec. 179 deduction and $200,000 from his proprietorship) on his 2009 Form 1040; rather, he can only take under Code Sec. 179(b)(1) a maximum of $250,000. Accordingly, $75,000 of a Code Sec. 179 deduction is wasted due to bad timing of purchases.

Code Sec. 179(d)(6) prescribes that members of a controlled group cannot expense totally more than $250,000 in a tax year. Code Sec. 179(d)(7) states that for purposes of determining a control group for Code Sec. 179 purposes, the group is determined using a "more than 50%" ownership test rather than "at least an 80%" one. So, if an S corporation owns more than 50 percent of the stock of another corporation, then care must be practiced so as not to run afoul of Code Sec. 179(b)(1)'s dollar limitation.

Practical Analysis: John O. Everett, Ph.D., CPA, tax professor at Virginia Commonwealth University, Cherie J. Hennig, Ph.D., CPA, tax professor at Florida International University, and William A. Raabe, Ph.D., CPA, tax professor at the Ohio State University, observe that the American Recovery and Reinvestment Tax Act of 2009 extends through 2009 the 2008 enhanced Code Sec. 179 immediate deduction

NEW LAW EXPLAINED

amount of $250,000, with the accompanying $1 for $1 phaseout for eligible property placed in service during 2009 that exceeds $800,000. This provision is also designed to stimulate investment in depreciable business properties, and is one of the centerpieces of the legislation aimed specifically at the small business taxpayer.

Taxpayers considering a Code Sec. 179 deduction should consider the following factors:

Any amounts expensed under Code Sec. 179 are not treated as depreciable property placed in service during the year for purposes of testing for the mid-quarter rule. Therefore, electing the Code Sec. 179 deduction on properties placed in service in the last quarter may provide some tax benefit in the year of acquisition.

Example: Brown Corporation, a calendar-year taxpayer, placed a $450,000 five-year MACRS asset in service on March 1, 2009, and another $450,000 five-year MACRS asset in service on November 1, 2009. Brown's maximum Code Sec. 179 deduction is $150,000 ($250,000 less a $100,000 phaseout for eligible property exceeding $800,000). If Brown elects Code Sec. 179 expensing on the first acquisition, the mid-quarter convention will apply (i.e., $450,000/$750,000 exceeds 40 percent). On the other hand, if Brown elects Code Sec. 179 expensing on the second acquisition, the half-year convention will apply (i.e., $300,000/$750,000 equals but does not exceed 40 percent).

The Code Sec. 179 deduction is limited to the taxable income of the taxpayer, whereas regular MACRS deductions are not. Foregoing the Code Sec. 179 deduction in the current year may allow the taxpayer to create a net operating loss with MACRS deductions. On the other hand, even though electing Code Sec. 179 may invoke the taxable income limitation, it may still be advisable because any Code Sec. 179 deduction not allowed in the current year due to the income limitation will carryover to the next year as an addition to that year's limitation (and recall that under the American Recovery and Reinvestment Tax Act of 2009, the Code Sec. 179 deduction will revert to the old $25,000 annual limit in 2011). This decision depends largely on the taxpayer's expected capital outlays in the coming years.

Example: Rita Ellis has Schedule C taxable income of $30,000 in 2009 before considering cost recovery on a $250,000, five-year MACRS asset placed in service during the year. If Rita foregoes the Code Sec. 179 election, she may deduct $50,000 MACRS on her 2009 return, generating a $20,000 net operating loss (which under the American Recovery and Reinvestment Tax Act of 2009 may be carried back for five years). If she elects Code Sec. 179, she will expense only $30,000 (limited to taxable income); however, the $220,000 excess will increase her Code Sec. 179 limit in 2010 dollar for dollar. If Rita had postponed the asset acquisition until 2010, her maximum Code Sec. 179 deduction will be only $25,000.

Reg. § 1.179-2(c)(7) states that when a husband and wife file a joint return, the taxable income limitation applies to the aggregate taxable income of each spouse. Furthermore, Reg. § 1.179-2(c)(6)(iv) defines "taxable income" for purposes of Code Sec. 179 as including wages, salaries, and commissions of a spouse received as an employee, since such individuals are "... engaged in the active conduct of the trade or business of their employment." The combination of these two factors suggests an additional planning possibility.

¶410

NEW LAW EXPLAINED

Example: Taxpayer A is self employed and earns net income from self-employment of $50,000 per year. B, Taxpayer A's spouse earns wage income of $50,000 per year. A and B file a joint return and have other income equal to their itemized deductions and personal exemptions. A purchased a new machine for $100,000 in the current year, eligible for the Code Sec. 179 deduction. Since the combined earned income of A and B is $100,000, they can claim the entire purchase price as a Code Sec. 179 deduction in year 1. In year 2 they will receive no tax benefit from the acquisition and will pay income tax on their wage and self-employment income. A will also pay self-employment tax in year 2. Their combined two year tax, assuming a five-percent discount rate is approximately $22,700. If A uses the Code Sec. 179 deduction to reduce self-employment income to $0 in year 1, the unused deduction can be carried forward to year 2. As a result, A and B will pay only income tax on B's wages. Their marginal tax rate would be 15 percent rather than 25 percent. In addition, A would pay no self-employment tax over the two-year period. As a result, they would save approximately $9,700 in tax over the two-year period by limiting the Code Sec. 179 deduction to self-employment income.

Code Sec. 179 Election Example

	Year 1	Year 2	Year 1	Year 2
Wages	$ -	$50,000	$50,000	$50,000
SE Income	$ -	$50,000	$ -	$ -
Taxable Income	$ -	$100,000	$50,000	$50,000
Income Tax	$ -	$16,800	$6,700	$6,700
SE Tax	$ -	$7,000	$ -	$ -
Total Tax	$ -	$23,800	$6,700	$6,700
Total 2-year Tax, at 5%	$ -	$22,700		$13,000
Tax Cost of Immediate Expensing				$(9,700)

▶ **Effective date.** The provision applies to tax years beginning after December 31, 2008 (Act Sec. 1202(b) of the American Recovery and Reinvestment Tax Act of 2009 (P.L. 111-5)).

Law source: Law at ¶5250. Committee Reports at ¶10,230.

— Act Sec. 1202(a) of the American Recovery and Reinvestment Tax Act of 2009 (P.L. 111-5), amending Code Sec. 179(b)(7);

— Act Sec. 1202(b), providing the effective date.

Reporter references: For further information, consult the following CCH reporters.

— Standard Federal Tax Reporter, ¶12,126.01

— Tax Research Consultant, DEPR: 12,000

— Practical Tax Explanation, §9,801

¶410

¶415 Availability of Bonus Depreciation for 2009

SUMMARY OF NEW LAW

The bonus depreciation deduction is extended one year to apply to property placed in service before January 1, 2010 (January 1, 2011, in the case of qualifying property with a longer production period and certain noncommercial aircraft).

BACKGROUND

A 50-percent bonus depreciation deduction is allowed for qualifying MACRS property acquired after December 31, 2007, and placed in service before January 1, 2009 (Code Sec. 168(k), as amended by the Economic Stimulus Act of 2008 (P.L. 110-185)). No written binding contract for the acquisition of the property may be in effect prior to January 1, 2008. Property acquired pursuant to a written binding contract entered into after December 31, 2007, and before January 1, 2009, and which is acquired after December 31, 2007, and placed in service before January 1, 2009, however, may qualify for bonus depreciation (Code Sec. 168(k)(2)(A)(iii)).

There is no limit on the total amount of bonus depreciation that may be claimed in any given tax year. The bonus depreciation deduction is allowed in full for alternative minimum tax (AMT) purposes. In addition, the regular depreciation deductions claimed on property on which bonus depreciation is claimed are also allowed in full for AMT purposes (Code Sec. 168(k)(2)(G)).

The bonus allowance is only available for new property (*i.e.*, property whose original use begins with the taxpayer) that is depreciable under MACRS and has a recovery period of 20 years or less, is MACRS water utility property, is off-the shelf computer software depreciable over three years under Code Sec. 167(f), or is qualified leasehold improvement property. Property that *must* be depreciated using the MACRS alternative depreciation system (ADS) does not qualify. If the taxpayer elects to depreciate the property under ADS, however, the property may qualify. A listed property (Code Sec. 280F), such as a passenger automobile, which is used 50 percent or less for business, does not qualify for bonus depreciation. Similarly, intangible property amortized under Code Sec. 197 does not qualify (Code Sec. 168(k)(2)(A) and (D)).

Property with a longer production period. The placed-in-service deadline is extended one year (to January 1, 2010) for property with a longer production period (Code Sec. 168(k)(2)(A)(iii)). Thus, property with a longer production period qualifies for bonus depreciation if it is not acquired pursuant to a binding contract that was entered into before January 1, 2008, or after December 31, 2008, and the property is placed in service before January 1, 2010. Property with a longer production period is property which:

(1) is subject to the Code Sec. 263A uniform capitalization rules;

(2) has a production period greater than one year and a cost exceeding $1 million; and

BACKGROUND

(3) has an MACRS recovery period of at least 10 years or is used in the trade or business of transporting persons or property for hire, such as commercial aircraft (Code Sec. 168(k)(2)(A)(iv)).

Only pre-January 1, 2009, progress expenditures are taken into account in computing the bonus deduction if the extended placed-in-service deadline applies to property with a longer production period.

Noncommercial aircraft. The extended January 1, 2010, placed-in-service deadline also applies to certain noncommercial aircraft acquired by purchase. Progress expenditures made in 2009 on noncommercial aircraft placed in service before January 1, 2010, are eligible for bonus depreciation (Code Sec. 168(k)(2)(A)(iv) and 168(k)(2)(C)).

Self-constructed property. If a taxpayer manufactures, constructs, or produces property for the taxpayer's own use, the requirement that the property be acquired after December 31, 2007, and placed in service before January 1, 2009, is deemed satisfied if the taxpayer begins manufacturing, constructing, or producing the property after December 31, 2007, and before January 1, 2009 (Code Sec. 168(k)(2)(E)(i)). The property, however, still needs to be placed into service before January 1, 2009 (unless the one year extension for property with a long production period discussed above applies).

NEW LAW EXPLAINED

Luxury car depreciation caps. Assuming that the election out of bonus depreciation is not made, the first-year Code Sec. 280F depreciation cap for passenger automobiles that qualify for bonus depreciation is increased by $8,000 for vehicles acquired after December 31, 2007, and placed in service in 2008 (Code Sec. 168(k)(2)(F), as amended by the Economic Stimulus Act of 2008 (P.L. 110-185). The first-year cap for a vehicle placed in service in 2008 if bonus depreciation is claimed is $10,960 for passenger automobiles and $11,160 for qualifying trucks/vans. If the vehicle does not qualify for bonus depreciation (e.g., the vehicle is used or an election out of bonus depreciation is made), the first year cap is $2,960 for passenger automobiles and $3,160 for qualifying trucks/vans (Rev. Proc. 2008-22, I.R.B. 2008-12).

Bonus depreciation extended one year to apply to property placed in service before January 1, 2010.—The Code Sec. 168(k) 50-percent bonus depreciation allowance is extended an additional year to apply to qualifying property acquired by a taxpayer after December 31, 2007, and placed in service before January 1, 2010 (Code Sec. 168(k), as amended by the American Recovery and Reinvestment Tax Act of 2009 (P.L. 111-5)).

> **Comment:** Prior to this one-year extension, the bonus allowance applied to property acquired after December 31, 2007, and placed in service before January 1, 2009. The rule which prevents property from qualifying if it is acquired pursuant to a written binding contract that was in effect prior to January 1, 2008, continues to apply. Thus, property acquired pursuant to a binding contract that was in effect before January 1, 2008, does not qualify for bonus depreciation even

¶415

NEW LAW EXPLAINED

if the property is placed in service in 2008 or 2009 (Code Sec. 168(k)(2)(A)(iii)(I)), as amended by the 2009 Recovery Act.

> **Example 1:** A taxpayer acquires new property in February 2009 pursuant to a binding contract that was entered into on December 1, 2007, and places the property in service in February 2009. The property does not qualify for bonus depreciation even though it was acquired after December 31, 2007, and placed in service before January 1, 2010, because it was acquired pursuant to a binding contract that was in effect before January 1, 2008.

> **Example 2:** A taxpayer acquires new property pursuant to a binding contract that was entered into on June 1, 2008, and places it in service in 2009. The property qualifies for bonus depreciation because it was acquired pursuant to a binding contract that was in effect after December 31, 2007, the property was acquired after December 31, 2007, and the property was placed in service before January 1, 2010.

Property with a longer production period. The placed-in-service deadline for property with a longer production period is one year longer than the placed-in-service deadline that applies to other qualified property (Code Sec. 168(k)(2)(B)). Taking into account the new law's one-year extension, property with a longer production period now only needs to be placed in service by the taxpayer before January 1, 2011 (Code Sec. 168(k)(2)(A)(iv), as amended by the 2009 Recovery Act).

> **Comment:** Prior to this one-year extension, property with a longer production period had to be placed in service before January 1, 2010.

> **Practical Analysis:** David Culp, a senior manager in the Federal Tax group of the Washington National Tax practice of KPMG LLP, notes that the American Recovery and Reinvestment Tax Act of 2009 extends the Code Sec. 168(k) 50 percent "bonus depreciation" deduction for one year, so that it applies to qualified property placed in service in 2009, as well as in 2008.
>
> Code Sec. 168(k)(1) allows a deduction of 50 percent of the basis of qualified property in the tax year it is placed in service, prior to the determination of any other depreciation on the remaining basis. Qualified property includes (1) MACRS property with a recovery period of 20 years or less; (2) water utility property; (3) certain computer software; and (4) qualified leasehold improvement property.
>
> The taxpayer must be the original user of the property. Under prior law, property was not qualified if there was a written binding contract for its acquisition before January 1, 2008, or, for property considered manufactured, constructed, or produced by the taxpayer for the taxpayer's own use ("self-constructed property"), if the self-construction was considered to have begun before January 1, 2008.

¶415

NEW LAW EXPLAINED

> Prior law also required, generally, that the property be placed in service by the taxpayer in calendar year 2008. Certain property placed in service in 2009 was still eligible for the bonus depreciation deduction if it was acquired in 2008, or there was a written binding contract in place in 2008, or self-construction had begun in 2008. This included certain long-production period property that has a MACRS recovery period of at least 10 years or that is to be used in commercial transportation activities. It also included certain aircraft not used in commercial aviation.
>
> The legislation extends the Code Sec. 168(k) bonus depreciation rules by allowing the deduction for otherwise qualified property placed in service before January 1, 2010. There is no change to the other requirements. The legislation provides a corresponding one-year extension of the extended placed in service deadline for long-production-period property and aircraft, if they were acquired (or there was a binding contract or self-construction that began) before 2010.
>
> The rules allowing the bonus deduction for certain long-production period property placed in service in 2009 limited the basis of the property to which the 50-percent deduction applied to the adjusted basis that was attributable to manufacture, construction, or production before January 1, 2009. With the extension, the full basis of such qualified property will be eligible for the bonus when placed in service in 2009. However, the same restriction will now apply to long-production period property that will be qualified property when placed in service in 2010, that is, only its pre-2010 basis will be allowed the 50-percent bonus depreciation deduction.
>
> During 2008, Code Sec. 168 was amended to provide a 15-year recovery period for "qualified retail improvement property" placed in service in 2009, and to expand the definition of "qualified restaurant property," for property placed in service in 2009. Some of this property would previously have been classified as qualified leasehold improvement property, which is eligible for bonus depreciation. The 2008 amendments specified, however, that qualified retail improvement property and qualified restaurant property placed in service in 2009 cannot be qualified property eligible for the 50 percent bonus depreciation deduction.

The current rule, which limits the bonus deduction for property with a longer production period to the adjusted basis attributable to manufacture, construction, or production before January 1, 2009, is also extended one year. Thus, only the pre-January 1, 2010, adjusted basis of such property is now eligible for bonus depreciation (Code Sec. 168(k)(2)(B)(ii), as amended by the 2009 Recovery Act).

> **Example 3:** A taxpayer enters into a contract for the purchase of a new commercial passenger plane (i.e., property with a longer production period) on February 1, 2008. The plane is delivered and placed in service on November 1, 2010. The plane qualifies for bonus depreciation because it was acquired pursuant to a contract entered into after December 31, 2007, and it was acquired after December 31, 2007, and placed in service before January 1, 2011. However, progress expenditures attributable to 2010 construction do not qualify for the bonus deduction.

¶415

NEW LAW EXPLAINED

Noncommercial aircraft. In addition to property with a longer production period, the placed-in-service deadline for certain noncommercial aircraft is one year longer than the placed-in-service deadline that applies to other qualified property (Code Sec. 168(k)(2)(C)). The new law also provides a one-year extension of this deadline. As extended, such noncommercial aircraft must be placed in service before January 1, 2011 (Code Sec. 168(k)(2)(A)(iv), as amended by the 2009 Recovery Act). The deadline was previously January 1, 2010.

> **Comment:** The rule which limits the bonus depreciation deduction for property with a longer production period to pre-January 1, 2010, adjusted basis (previously, pre-January 1, 2009, adjusted basis) does not apply to noncommercial aircraft. Thus, the entire adjusted basis of a qualifying non-commercial aircraft placed in service before January 1, 2011, qualifies for the additional depreciation allowance.

Example 4: A taxpayer enters into a contract for the purchase of a new noncommercial passenger plane on February 1, 2009. The plane is delivered and placed in service on September 1, 2010. The plane qualifies for bonus depreciation because it was acquired pursuant to a contract entered into after December 31, 2007, and it was acquired after December 31, 2007, and placed in service before January 1, 2011. Progress expenditures attributable to 2010 construction will qualify for the bonus deduction because the property is a noncommercial aircraft.

Self-constructed property. If a taxpayer manufactures, constructs, or produces property for the taxpayer's own use, the requirement that the property be acquired after December 31, 2007, and placed in service before January 1, 2010 (previously before January 1, 2009) is deemed satisfied if the taxpayer begins manufacturing, constructing, or producing the property after December 31, 2007, and before January 1, 2010 (previously before January 1, 2009) (Code Sec. 168(k)(2)(E)(i), as amended by the 2009 Recovery Act). The property, however, still needs to be placed into service before January 1, 2010 (unless the one year extension for property with a long production period discussed above applies).

Conforming amendments to provisions incorporating self-constructed property rule. Code Sec. 168(l) provides a separate 50 percent bonus depreciation allowance for cellulosic biofuel plant property placed in service before January 1, 2013. A non-substantive provision in Code Sec. 168(l) that incorporates a self-constructed property rule by cross reference to the regular bonus depreciation self-constructed property rule is amended to reflect the one year extension of the bonus depreciation provision (Code Sec. 168(l)(5)(B), as added by the 2009 Recovery Act). A similar conforming amendment is made to the separate provision that provides a 50 percent bonus depreciation allowance for qualified disaster assistance property (Code Sec. 168(n)(2)(C), as amended by the 2009 Recovery Act) and the bonus allowance for property placed in service in the Gulf Opportunity Zone (i.e., GO-Zone bonus depreciation) (Code Sec. 1400N(d)(3)(B), as amended by the 2009 Recovery Act).

¶415

NEW LAW EXPLAINED

Luxury car depreciation cap. The first-year depreciation cap for luxury cars placed in service in 2009 on which bonus depreciation is claimed is increased by $8,000. This $8,000 increase also applies to vehicles placed in service in 2008 if bonus depreciation is claimed (Code Sec. 168(k)(2)(F)).

> **Comment:** While the IRS has yet to release the official depreciation limits on luxury automobiles first put into use during the 2009 tax year for business and investment purposes, CCH has projected the unofficial depreciation limits using the "new cars" and "new trucks" components of the October 2008 Consumer Price Index. Based on those inflation-adjusted computations (as specified under Code Sec. 280F(d)(7)(B)), the 2009 Code Sec. 280F limits on the amounts of depreciation deductions for passenger automobiles first placed in service in 2009 will remain the same as in 2008 at $2,960. The depreciation limits for trucks and vans first placed in service in 2009 will drop to $3,060 when compared to 2008. Thus, the first-year cap for a vehicle placed in service in 2009 if bonus depreciation is claimed is projected to be $10,960 for passenger automobiles and $11,060 for qualifying trucks/vans.

Alternative minimum tax. The new law does not change the rule, discussed in the Background, that the bonus deduction, as well as regular depreciation deductions on bonus depreciation property, are allowed in full for AMT tax purposes (i.e., this rule continues to apply to bonus depreciation claimed on property placed in service in 2009, as well as 2008) (Code Sec. 168(k)(2)(G)).

Practical Analysis: John O. Everett, Ph.D., CPA, tax professor at Virginia Commonwealth University, Cherie J. Hennig, Ph.D., CPA, tax professor at Florida International University, and William A. Raabe, Ph.D., CPA, tax professor at the Ohio State University, point out that Act. Sec. 1201 of the American Recovery and Reinvestment Tax Act of 2009 generally extends for one additional year two temporary investment incentives that otherwise expired at the end of 2008: (1) the Code Sec. 168(k)(2) election to deduct as bonus depreciation 50 percent of the cost of qualifying personalty placed into service in 2008 (2009 for certain long-lived assets), and (2) the Code Sec. 168(k)(4) election to forego bonus depreciation on qualifying property placed in service after March 31, 2008, and before January 1, 2009, (2010 for the same long-lived assets under the bonus depreciation rules) in exchange for converting limited amounts of unused pre-2006 research credits and AMT credits into current refundable credits.

The extension of bonus depreciation for an additional year will be welcomed by small and large businesses alike as an incentive for increasing capital investments. All other aspects of the 2008 law remain in effect, including the provision allowing bonus depreciation for the alternative depreciation system (ADS) and the taxpayer's alternative minimum tax (AMT) computation. It is important to note that the new law retains the $8,000 increase in first-year depreciation on luxury autos under Code Sec. 280F(a)(1); although the annual limitations are adjusted for inflation each year, the $8,000 add-on is not subject to this adjustment.

¶415

NEW LAW EXPLAINED

▶ **Effective date.** The provision applies to property placed in service after December 31, 2008, in tax years ending after such date. Amendments to Code Sec. 168(k)(4)(D)(ii) apply to tax years ending after March 31, 2008 (Act Sec. 1201(c) of the American Recovery and Reinvestment Tax Act of 2009 (P.L. 111-5)).

Law source: Law at ¶5240 and ¶5310. Committee Reports at ¶10,220.

— Act Sec. 1201(a)(1) of the American Recovery and Reinvestment Tax Act of 2009 (P.L. 111-5), amending Code Sec. 168(k)(2);

— Act Sec. 1201(a)(2), amending Code Sec. 168(k), Code Sec. 168(l)(5)(B), Code Sec. 168(n)(2)(C) and Code Sec. 1400N(d)(3)(B);

— Act Sec. 1201(c), providing the effective dates.

Reporter references: For further information, consult the following CCH reporters.

— Standard Federal Tax Reporter, ¶11,279.058

— Tax Research Consultant, DEPR: 3,600

— Practical Tax Explanation, § 11,225.05

¶420 Recognition Period for S Corporation Built-In Gains Tax

SUMMARY OF NEW LAW

For a tax year beginning in 2009 or 2010, no tax will be imposed on an S corporation's net recognized built-in gain if the seventh tax year in the 10-year recognition period preceded the tax year.

BACKGROUND

A corporate-level tax is imposed on an S corporation's net recognized built-in gains attributable to assets that it held at the time it converted from a C corporation to an S corporation, if the gain is recognized during the statutorily defined recognition period (Code Sec. 1374(a)). The tax on built-in gains also applies if an S corporation sells, during the recognition period, assets that were acquired in a carryover basis transaction (e.g., a tax-free reorganization) in which the S corporation's basis in the assets is determined by reference to the C corporation's basis in the assets.

The term "net recognized built-in gain" means, with respect to any tax year in the recognition period, the lesser of (1) the amount that would be the taxable income of the S corporation if only recognized built-in gains and recognized built-in losses were taken into account or (2) the corporation's taxable income for the tax year (Code Sec. 1374(d)(2)).

For assets held by the S corporation as of the beginning of its first tax year, the recognition period is the 10-year period beginning with the first day of the first tax year for which the corporation was an S corporation (Code Sec. 1374(d)(7)).

¶420

BACKGROUND

For assets acquired from a C corporation in a carryover basis transaction, the recognition period is the 10-year period beginning on the day the assets were acquired by the S corporation instead of the beginning of the first tax year for which the corporation was an S corporation (Code Sec. 1374(d)(8)).

The recognition period is not limited to 10 years for income resulting from the Code Sec. 593(e) treatment of pre-1988 bad debt reserves of thrift and former thrift institutions that became S corporations. Thus, distributions that trigger Code Sec. 593(e) will be subject to corporate-level recapture even if the distributions occur more than 10 years after the beginning of the recognition period (Code Sec. 1374(d)(7)).

> **Comment:** The built-in gains tax was enacted to prevent a C corporation from electing S corporation status to avoid a corporate-level tax on gain from unrealized appreciation of C corporation assets or gain from C corporation assets on which depreciation deductions had been taken. To avoid the built-in gains tax, the S corporation must not sell the assets during the recognition period applicable to the assets. The built-in gains tax does not apply if the assets are sold after the recognition period.

NEW LAW EXPLAINED

Ten-year recognition period for built-in gains tax temporarily reduced.—For a tax year beginning in 2009 or 2010, no tax will be imposed on the net recognized built-in gain of an S corporation if the seventh tax year in the 10-year recognition period preceded that tax year. The reduction in the recognition period applies separately with respect to any asset acquired in a carryover basis transaction pursuant to Code Sec. 1374(d)(8) (Code Sec. 1374(d)(7)(B), as amended by the American Recovery and Reinvestment Tax Act of 2009 (P.L. 111-5)).

> **Practical Analysis:** Charles C. Hwang, Partner, and Jennifer A. Ray, Associate, in the Tax Group at Crowell & Moring LLP, note that the Code Sec. 1374(d)(7) recognition period for net recognized built-in gains of S corporations is temporarily reduced. Code Sec. 1374 imposes an entity-level tax on an S corporation's net unrealized built-in gains that arose before the corporation's conversion from a C corporation to an S corporation and that are recognized during the "recognition period." Generally, the recognition period is the 10-year period beginning with the first day of the first year the company was an S corporation. Act Sec. 1251 of the American Recovery and Reinvestment Tax Act of 2009 temporarily reduces the recognition period for built-in gains. New Code Sec. 1374(d)(7) provides that for tax years beginning in 2009 and 2010, no tax is imposed on an S corporation's net recognized built-in gain if the seventh year in the recognition period preceded such tax year. New Code Sec. 1374(d)(7) applies to tax years beginning after December 31, 2008, but (as with Code Sec. 1374(d)(7) before this revision) does not apply to any amount includible in income by reason of distributions to shareholders pursuant to Code Sec. 593(e).

¶420

NEW LAW EXPLAINED

Comment: Thus, for a tax year beginning in 2009 or 2010, in the case of gain that arose prior to the conversion of a C corporation to an S corporation, no built-in gain tax under Code Sec. 1374 will be imposed on the corporation after the seventh tax year that the S corporation election is in effect. With respect to built-in gain attributable to an asset received by an S corporation from a C corporation in a carryover basis transaction, no tax will be imposed on the corporation under Code Sec. 1374 if the gain is recognized after the date that is seven years following the date on which the asset was acquired. Shareholders will continue to take into account all items of gain and loss under Code Sec. 1366 (Conference Committee Report for American Recovery and Reinvestment Act of 2009).

> **Practical Analysis:** Kip Dellinger, CPA, Senior Tax Partner at Kallman And Co. LLP in Los Angeles, observes that the opportunity for existing corporations to dispose of assets in some circumstances that are otherwise subject to the built-in gains may be crucial to the survival of some companies; this is particularly true for companies dependent on the transportation industry that provide parts, services to, and repair and maintenance under subcontract to the larger companies in their industry. The built-in gains tax is often thought of as a tax if the company is sold within the 10-year conversion time frame (now seven years in some circumstances), but it actually operates to tax at the corporate level assets held at conversion and disposed of during the requisite time frames. Therefore, it can be triggered by downsizing, acting on survival decisions, or on a decision to dispose of unused assets to raise needed cash. Consequently, the relief provided in this provision should be very valuable and welcome to small family or privately-owned businesses. It may be especially valuable when coupled with the extended net operating loss carryback periods of Act Sec. 1211.

The special recognition rule for 2009 and 2010 does not apply to distributions to shareholders pursuant to Code Sec. 593(e), relating to pre-1988 bad debt reserves of thrift and former thrift institutions that became S corporations (Code Sec. 1374(d)(7)(C), as amended by the 2009 Recovery Act). Such distributions under Code Sec. 593(e) continue to be subject to corporate-level taxation without regard to when the distributions occur.

> **Practical Analysis:** Michael Schlesinger, a partner in Schlesinger & Sussman of New York, New York and author of *Practical Guide to S Corporations* (4th edition), points out that a reduction in Code Sec. 1374's conversion period to seven years is beneficial. However, the key to minimizing and possibly eliminating Code Sec. 1374's tax bite is planning both before the C corporation converts to S status and during the conversion period. An example of tax planning before conversion would be the sale of appreciated assets by the C corporation so that there is only one level of taxation instead of two as would possibly occur under Code Sec. 1374. Caution must be exercised however in that the sale of appreciated assets will generate earnings and profits exposing the S corporation to tax under Code Sec. 1375 if the S

NEW LAW EXPLAINED

corporation has at least one dollar of these earnings and profits at the time of conversion and has more than 25 percent of its gross receipts arising from passive investment income. Further, there could be loss of S status under Code Sec. 1362(d)(3) if the S corporation has at least 25 percent of gross receipts from passive investment income for three consecutive years and earnings and profits from a predecessor C corporation.

While there are various ways to avoid the trap generated by Code Secs. 1375 and 1362(d)(3), this requires advance planning. One means is to fail one of the tests under Code Secs. 1375 and 1362(d)(3) such as distribution of the C corporation's earnings and profits prior to or during conversion; however, to avoid a termination under Code Sec. 1362(d)(3), the distribution must occur before the expiration of three consecutive years where the corporation has more than 25 percent of its gross receipts from passive investment income in each of these years. Another is to eliminate any passive investment income for the S corporation by making it "active."

Reg. § 1.1362-2(c)(5)(ii)(B)(2) prescribes that in the case of rents (one of the categories of passive investment income), the income will be treated as "active" and lose its passive taint if the rents are "derived in an active trade or business of renting property." The determination of whether there is "an active trade or business" is a fact one and there are a slew of private letter rulings which address this issue. An example where "active income" was found for an S corporation was in LTR 200128025 (Apr. 12, 2001) where the corporation through its full-time and part-time employees, as well as through outside vendors and independent contractors, provided services to various properties including maintenance of common areas and facilities; maintenance and repair of structural portions of the properties, including foundations, exterior walls, and roofs; parking lot and sidewalk repair; making and supervising of tenant improvements.

During Code Sec. 1374's conversion period, various steps can be undertaken to minimize or eliminate Code Sec. 1374's tax. Some key means follow:

(1) Instead of selling appreciated assets, do tax-free exchanges.

(2) If there are C corporate net operating loss carryforwards, Code Sec. 1374 allows these losses to offset Code Sec. 1374's built in gains. Thus, if at the time of conversion, the S corporation did not dispose of appreciated assets, a sale of the appreciated assets before the expiration of the carryforward for the C net operating losses utilizing these losses will reduce Code Sec. 1374's tax.

(3) Engage in leasing or licensing the appreciated assets, mindful that the income generated will be passive investment income and subject to the tax effects of Code Secs. 1375 and 1362(d)(3) if these tax provisions apply, subject to the discussion as outlined above.

(4) Since one measure of Code Sec. 1374's tax is taxable income, minimize its effect by declaring bonuses to shareholder-employees. However, Code Sec. 1374's tax is geared to C corporate standards, so care must be utilized to prevent a challenge by the IRS for unreasonable compensation.

(5) Contribution of appreciated property to a charity. LTR 200004032 (Oct. 26, 1999) held that when an S corporation contributes appreciated property to a charity, there is no gain or loss recognition under Code Sec. 1374.

¶420

NEW LAW EXPLAINED

> (6) Allocation of the purchase price to non-Code Sec. 1374 items. An example of such an allocation occurred in *Martin Ice Cream Co.*, 110 TC 189, Dec. 52,624 (1998) where a sale of an oral distribution agreement was deemed personal to an S corporate shareholder and not a corporate asset subject to Code Sec. 1374.

> **Practical Analysis:** John A. Sikora, J.D., Partner in the Milwaukee and Delafield offices of Weiss Berzowski Brady LLP, notes that Act Sec. 1251 of the American Recovery and Reinvestment Act of 2009 temporarily reduces the "recognition period" applicable under the S corporation built-in gains tax rules from 10 to seven years. The revision applies only to built-in gains recognized in tax years beginning in 2009 and 2010.
>
> The rules relating to the tax on S corporation built-in gains were revised substantially in 1986. Before revision, a corporate-level tax generally applied for only a three-year period following conversion to S corporation status and then only if the corporation had relatively substantial net capital gain income.
>
> The 1986 change coincided with the repeal of provisions which, under certain circumstances, permitted liquidation of a corporation without incurring a "double-level" tax upon the prior sale of its assets or the distribution of its assets to the shareholders in liquidation, which (double tax) is now generally the case (except for certain complete liquidations of subsidiaries) under Code Secs. 331 and 336. See Code Secs. 336 and 337 as in effect prior to the Tax Reform Act of 1986 (P.L. 99-514).
>
> Following the effective date of the 1986 changes to the corporate liquidation provisions (beneficial transitional rules applied to certain small corporations for 1987 and 1988), corporations generally recognize all gains realized on the sale or distribution of their assets and a shareholder recognizes gain upon liquidation of the corporation if the value of the property distributed to the shareholder exceeds the basis in the stock (i.e., together the corporation and shareholders are potentially subject to a "double-level" tax). The principal reason for extending the built-in gains tax recognition period to 10 years and making the tax applicable to all gains recognized by an S corporation in 1986 was to prevent corporations contemplating liquidation, perhaps following a sale of the corporation's business, from circumventing the revised liquidation rules by electing S corporation status (and its general "single-level" tax regime) before the applicable transactions. The apparent expectation was that time period was sufficient because few corporations would plan a business sale or complete liquidation more than 10 years in the future (or that even if a corporation did so, waiting 10 years justified imposing essentially only a "single-level" tax).
>
> The 10-year built-in gains tax rule has inhibited sales of appreciated assets by S corporations subject to it. Depending on the nature of the asset, the character of any resulting gain and the tax rates then in effect, the combined effective built-in gains tax and shareholder tax rate on the corporation's disposition of an asset that it held at the time of the conversion to S status could exceed 50 percent. The post-1986 built-in gain tax provisions also often affect the overall structure of asset dispositions; for

NEW LAW EXPLAINED

example, an S corporations that converted from C corporation status is frequently willing to dispose of assets within 10 years only if it can do so in circumstances in which gain will not be recognized (such as, for example, under Code Sec. 1031). The provision has also motivated sellers of S corporation businesses to negotiate for the sale of the corporate stock, rather than the corporation's assets, if a business sale is under consideration during the built-in gains recognition period. Finally, the 1986 changes to the corporate liquidation and built-in gains tax provisions have motivated corporations for which sale of the business is a possibility in the relatively long term (i.e., more than 10 years in the future) to consider making an S election currently.

Act Sec. 1251 of the 2009 Recovery Act revises paragraph (7) of Code Sec. 1374(d) to add a new subparagraph (B) applicable to tax years of the S corporation beginning in 2009 or 2010. No built-in gains tax is imposed on gains recognized in such years if "the 7th tax year in the recognition period preceded" the 2009 or 2010 tax year. In other words, for 2009 and 2010, the recognition period under Code Sec. 1374 for imposition of the built-in gains tax has generally been reduced from 10 years to 7 years. By way of example, if a C corporation elected S status for its tax year beginning on January 1, 2002, it will be entitled to sell appreciated assets it held on that date during 2009 (and 2010) without being subject to tax under Code Sec. 1374. (Note, however, that in the case of assets described in Code Sec. 1374(d)(8), the recognition period runs from the date the assets are acquired by the S corporation rather than from the beginning of its first S corporation year.)

Because the change applies only to tax years beginning in 2009 or 2010, the principle that motivated extension of the built-in gains tax period to 10 years in 1986 will not be adversely affected. A corporation that elected S corporation status more than seven years prior to the 2009 tax year could not have anticipated the change included in the Act and, because the change applies only to gains recognized in 2009 and 2010, no C corporation now planning to sell its business or to liquidate can elect S status and obtain the benefit of the temporary changes made by the 2009 Recovery Act.

▶ **Effective date.** The amendment is effective for tax years beginning after December 31, 2008 (Act Sec. 1251(b) of the American Recovery and Reinvestment Tax Act of 2009 (P.L. 111-5)).

Law source: Law at ¶5295. Committee Report at ¶10,300.

— Act Sec. 1251(a) of the American Recovery and Reinvestment Tax Act of 2009 (P.L. 111-5), amending Code Sec. 1374(d)(7);

— Act Sec. 1251(b), providing the effective date.

Reporter references: For further information, consult the following CCH reporters.

— Standard Federal Tax Reporter, ¶32,203.021

— Tax Research Consultant, SCORP: 356

— Practical Tax Explanation, §28,305.15

¶425 Maximum Five-Year Carryback Period for 2008 Net Operating Losses of Small Businesses

SUMMARY OF NEW LAW

Eligible small businesses can elect to use an extended three-, four-, or five-year carryback period for 2008 net operating losses (NOLs). An eligible small business is generally a business that meets a $15 million average annual gross receipts test.

BACKGROUND

Taxpayers that sustain a net operating loss (NOL) for a tax year generally can take an NOL deduction to reduce income in another tax year (Code Sec. 172(a)). An NOL is the amount by which deductions exceed gross income, with modifications (Code Sec. 172(c) and (d)). Under the general rule, taxpayers can carry back an NOL to each of the two tax years preceding the loss year or carry over the NOL to each of the 20 tax years following the loss year (Code Sec. 172(b)).

Different NOL carryback and carryover periods can apply to losses incurred during specified periods of time. For example, NOLs that arose in a tax year ending in 2001 or 2002 can be carried back for five years, instead of the normal two years (Code Sec. 172(b)(1)(H)). Although 2001 and 2002 NOLs can be carried back for five years, taxpayers can elect not to use the five-year carryback (Code Sec. 172(k)).

In addition, different NOL carryback and carryover periods can apply to special kinds of losses, such as certain "eligible losses", farming losses, disaster losses, losses attributable to corporate equity reduction transactions (CERTs), and many others (Code Sec. 172(b)(1)(E), (F), and (G) and 172(j)). For example, taxpayers can use a three-year carryback period for the portion of an NOL that is an eligible loss (Code Sec. 172(b)(1)(F)(i)). An eligible loss, for an individual, is a loss of property due to fire, storm, shipwreck, or other casualty, or due to theft. An eligible loss, for a small business taxpayer or a taxpayer engaged in the trade or business of farming, is an NOL attributable to a federally declared disaster (Code Sec. 172(b)(1)(F)). An eligible loss does not include a farming loss, as defined in Code Sec. 172(i), or a qualified disaster loss, as defined in Code Sec. 172(j).

A CERT is a major stock acquisition by a corporation of stock in another corporation or an excess distribution by a corporation of its own stock (Code Sec. 172(h)(3)). Where a corporation's NOL was caused by a deduction for interest on debt attributable to a CERT, use of this corporate equity reduction interest loss is limited. A corporate equity reduction interest loss for a loss limitation year, which is the tax year in which the CERT occurred and the two succeeding tax years, generally cannot be carried back to a tax year that precedes the tax year in which the CERT occurred (Code Sec. 172(b)(1)(E)).

¶420

NEW LAW EXPLAINED

Carryback period for 2008 NOLs of small businesses lengthened.—The Act benefits small businesses experiencing financial difficulty by expanding their ability to use net operating losses (NOLs) attributable to 2008. Taxpayers can elect to carry back 2008 NOLs for three, four or five years, instead of the normal two years (Code Sec. 172(b)(1)(H), as amended by the American Recovery and Reinvestment Tax Act of 2009 (P.L. 111-5)). Changes have also been made to theCode Sec. 382 loss limitation rules, which apply following a corporate ownership change (see ¶ 430 and ¶ 435).

> **Comment:** The carryover period for 2008 NOLs remains at 20 years (Code Sec. 172(b)(1)(A)(ii)), whether or not the taxpayer elects to use an extended carryback period.

Extended carryback period for 2008 NOLs. Eligible small businesses that have an "applicable 2008 NOL" and have elected to apply the special carryback rule can use a carryback period of three, four or five years (Code Sec. 172(b)(1)(H)(i), as added by the 2009 Recovery Act). An "applicable 2008 NOL" is a taxpayer's NOL for any tax year ending in 2008 (Code Sec. 172(b)(1)(H)(ii)(I), as added by the 2009 Recovery Act).

> **Practical Analysis:** David Culp, a senior manager in the Federal Tax group of the Washington National Tax practice of KPMG LLP, notes that an eligible business is defined as a corporation, partnership or sole proprietorship that had average annual gross receipts of no more than $15 million for the tax year of the NOL and the two immediately preceding tax years (as determined under the principles of Code Sec. 448(c)). The taxpayer could also elect to apply the extended carryback period to NOLs incurred in a tax year beginning in 2008, rather than in a tax year ending in 2008.
>
> Alternative minimum tax NOLs (ATNOLs) would be subject to the same elective carryback period.
>
> Under current law, a taxpayer may elect to forego any carryback period for its NOLs, and to use them only as a carryforward. This election must be made on a timely filed return for the year of the NOL (determined with any filing extensions) and is irrevocable. The new elections to use a longer carryback period (or to apply the rules to a tax year beginning in 2008) would also generally need to be made on the timely filed original return and, once made, would be irrevocable. The legislation specifies, furthermore, that the election may be made "only with respect to one tax year." Thus, a taxpayer with more than one tax year beginning or ending in the 2008 period (because, for example, it uses a fiscal year or has a short tax year) would be allowed the extended carryback period for only one of them, and would need to determine which tax year's extended NOL carryback would provide the greatest benefit.
>
> However, the legislation would allow a taxpayer with a tax year ending in 2008 or in 2009 (before the date of enactment) until at least 60 days after the date of enactment to make the new carryback election available for NOLs from that tax year or to revoke an earlier election to forego any carryback of an NOL from that tax year. This 60-day grace period would also give the taxpayer additional time to apply for a Code

¶420

NEW LAW EXPLAINED

> Sec. 6411 tentative carryback adjustment of the 2008 or 2009 NOL (on Form 1139 or Form 1045).
>
> The availability of the election to use a three-, four- or five-year NOL carryback is targeted to smaller taxpayers. Code Sec. 448(c) requires certain corporations, partnerships, sole proprietorships, trusts and estates related to the taxpayer to be treated as a single taxpayer in applying the gross receipts test. (This aggregation generally applies to entities that have more than 50-percent common ownership.) This will reduce the availability of the election. Furthermore, because the $15 million gross receipts test is applied to the year of the NOL and the two preceding tax years, some taxpayers may need considerable time past the end of the NOL year to determine whether they are eligible for the election.
>
> The "small business" designation applies to partnerships as well as to corporations and sole proprietorships. It is not clear, for a partnership or an S corporation, what the effect of an election would be, as any NOL would be determined at the partner or S corporation shareholder level.

> **Example:** Acme, Inc. is a calendar-year small business with a 2008 NOL that is eligible for the extended carryback period. Acme had income in 2004 through 2007, a loss in 2003 that was carried back and used in its entirety, and no carryovers. Acme would elect a four-year carryback in this instance since a carryback cannot be used in the fifth preceding year, 2003. Thus, it would carry the NOL back to each of the four tax years preceding the tax year of the loss, that is to 2004, 2005, 2006 and 2007, until it is fully utilized (Code Sec. 172(b)(1)(H)(i), as added by the 2009 Recovery Act, and 172(b)(1)(A)(i)).

Eligible small businesses can elect to treat an NOL for any tax year *beginning* in 2008, instead of any tax year *ending* in 2008, as "an applicable 2008 NOL" (Code Sec. 172(b)(1)(H)(ii)(II), as added by the 2009 Recovery Act). This makes a difference for fiscal-year taxpayers, but not calendar-year taxpayers, because a calendar-year taxpayer's 2008 tax year both begins and ends in 2008. For information on making the election, see "Election procedures," below.

> **Example:** Benson Co., is an eligible small business that has a fiscal year that ends on September 30th. It has suffered losses for the past 18 months and the losses are expected to continue for at least another year. Benson's applicable 2008 NOL is its NOL for the tax year that began on October 1, 2007, and ended on September 30, 2008. In the alternative, it could elect to treat its NOL for the tax year that began on October 1, 2008, and will end on September 30, 2009, as its applicable 2008 NOL.

> **Comment:** By allowing small businesses either to treat an NOL for a tax year *ending* in 2008 as an applicable 2008 NOL or to elect to treat an NOL for a tax

¶425

NEW LAW EXPLAINED

year *beginning* in 2008 as an applicable 2008 NOL, fiscal-year taxpayers receive even more flexibility in choosing how to optimize their NOL carrybacks.

Eligible small business defined. An eligible small business is defined as a corporation or partnership that meets a $15 million gross receipts test for the tax year in which the loss arose (or a sole proprietorship that would meet such test if the proprietorship were a corporation) (Code Sec. 172(b)(1)(H)(iv), as added by the 2009 Recovery Act, and 172(b)(1)(F)(iii)). The $15 million gross receipts test is based on the gross receipts test in Code Sec. 448(c), with $15 million substituted for $5 million in that test.

The $15 million gross receipts test would be met for any tax year if the average annual gross receipts for the business for the three-taxable-year period ending with such tax year does not exceed $15 million (Code Sec. 172(b)(1)(H)(iv), as added by the 2009 Recovery Act, and Code Sec. 448(c)(1)). Gross receipts for a tax year are reduced by returns and allowances made during such year (Code Sec. 448(c)(3)(C)). Predecessors of the business are treated as the business for purposes of the test (Code Sec. 448(c)(3)(D)). Also, all persons treated as a single employer under Code Sec. 52(a) or (b) or Code Sec. 414(m) or (o) are treated as one person for purposes of the gross receipts test (Code Sec. 448(c)(2)).

> **Practical Analysis:** Kip Dellinger, CPA, Senior Tax Partner at Kallman And Co. LLP in Los Angeles, notes that the optional 3, 4 or 5-year net operating loss carryback—like bonus and Code Sec. 179 depreciation, along with the opportunity to monetize accumulated R&D and AMT credits in the 2008 Emergency Economic Stabilization Act of 2008 (P.L. 110-185) and extended in this legislation—presents businesses with a mathematical teaser that may require analysis of multiple available carryback tax benefit scenarios and predictions about the value of these items as future tax benefits. This becomes even more complex when carrybacks may free up tax credits claimed in those earlier years for carryback to even earlier tax years.
>
> A collateral issue with immediate consequences arises for qualifying 2008 C corporation financial statement issuers with gross revenues of less than $15 million. The net operating loss provision applies to 2008 net operating losses and the selection of the carryback period and amounts refundable will thus have impact in applying FAS 109, *Accounting for Income Taxes* with respect to 2008 financial statements that will soon be issued. Statement issuers may be required to disclose as a subsequent event the effects of the Act. In addition, there well may be FIN 48, *Accounting for Uncertain Tax Positions* ramifications arising from credit and NOL carrybacks; tax positions of years closed by statute may need to be evaluated under FIN 48 because the tax authorities may challenge those positions to the extent of the claimed NOL or tax credit carryback benefits in each affected year.
>
> Also, many business taxpayers in need of the urgent infusion of cash in the current economic environment will apply for tentative refunds under Code Sec. 6411 (the "quick carryback" provision). Practitioners are advised to inform taxpayers that if the IRS later decides to "disallow" all or some portion of the refund, the IRS has available as a collection option an action for erroneous refund under Code Sec. 6501, which provides for more limited administrative review than the normal deficiency process applied to claims for refund.

¶425

NEW LAW EXPLAINED

If the business was not in existence for the entire three-year period, then the test is applied for the period during which the business was in existence (Code Sec. 448(c)(3)(A)). Gross receipts for a short tax year of less than 12 months should be annualized by multiplying the gross receipts for the short period by 12 and dividing the result by the number of months in the short period (Code Sec. 448(c)(3)(B)).

Election procedures. Eligible small businesses that qualify for the extended carryback period for applicable 2008 NOLs must make an affirmative election to use the longer carryback period. Taxpayers can elect to use any carryback period of whole years that is more than two years and less than six years (Code Sec. 172(b)(1)(H)(i)(I), as added by the 2009 Recovery Act). Eligible small businesses that want to treat an NOL for any tax year *beginning* (rather than ending) in 2008 as an applicable 2008 NOL also must make an election to do so (Code Sec. 172(b)(1)(H)(ii)(II), as added by the 2009 Recovery Act).

Election: The procedure for making an election to use an extended NOL carryback period or to treat an NOL for a tax year beginning in 2008 as an applicable 2008 NOL will be set forth by the IRS. The election must be made by the due date, including extensions, for filing the taxpayer's return for the tax year of the NOL. Any such election is irrevocable and can only be made with respect to one tax year (Code Sec. 172(b)(1)(H)(iii), as added by the 2009 Recovery Act). In the case of a group of corporations filing a consolidated return, the common parent of the group makes the election, which is binding on all members of the group (Conference Committee Report for the American Recovery and Reinvestment Act of 2009).

Comment: Taxpayers that had a 2001 or 2002 NOL automatically were assigned a five-year carryback period. Such taxpayers had to elect to waive the five-year carryback period for 2001 and 2002 NOLs (Code Sec. 172(k), prior to being stricken by the 2009 Recovery Act). Taxpayers with an applicable 2008 NOL will do just the opposite. An applicable 2008 NOL can be carried back for two years, unless the taxpayer elects to use a longer carryback period.

Compliance Tip: Corporations carrying back an NOL can file Form 1120X, Amended U.S. Corporation Income Tax Return, or Form 1139, Corporation Application for Tentative Refund, to apply for a refund of taxes for the year to which the NOL is being carried. Individuals carrying back an NOL from their partnership or sole proprietorship can file Form 1040X, Amended U.S. Individual Return, or Form 1045, Application for Tentative Refund, to apply for their tax refund. Estates and trusts carrying back an NOL from a partnership can file an amended Form 1041, U.S. Income Tax Return for Estates and Trusts, or Form 1045, Application for Tentative Refund, to apply for their tax refund.

Practical Analysis: Jean M. Baxley, Counsel in the Tax Group of Crowell & Moring LLP, observes that by electing to carry back NOLs, small businesses will be able to apply for refunds for prior years in which it had net income and paid income taxes. If a business elects the four- or five-year carryback period, however, the loss limitation

¶425

NEW LAW EXPLAINED

> period for corporate equity reduction transactions is increased from two years to three or four years, respectively (in any case, plus the year in which the transaction occurs). The carryback election must be made by the due date for the return for the tax year of the NOL and is available for tax years ending after December 31, 2007. The provision gives the Treasury authority to prescribe anti-abuse rules and provides a transition rule for NOLs for tax years ending before the date of enactment of the American Recovery and Reinvestment Tax Act.
>
> Eligibility for this provision was scaled back heavily in final negotiations and, thus, the election for an expanded net operating loss carryback period will not have the broad effect that some originally hoped for.

Special rules for eligible losses and CERTs. Two special rules apply to taxpayers that have elected to use an extended carryback period for an applicable 2008 NOL and also have an eligible loss that normally is carried back for three years or an excess interest loss from a corporate equity reduction transaction (CERT). First, if a taxpayer has elected to use an extended carryback period for a 2008 NOL, then the three-year carryback period for eligible losses will not apply (Code Sec. 172(b)(1)(H)(i)(III), as added by the 2009 Recovery Act; Code Sec. 172(b)(1)(F)). Thus, for example, if a portion of a small business taxpayer's applicable 2008 NOL is an eligible loss and the taxpayer elects to use a five-year carryback period for the applicable 2008 NOL under the Act, then the eligible loss can also be carried back for five years, rather than three years.

> **Caution:** A small business is defined differently for purposes of the carryback of applicable 2008 NOLs (generally, a $15 million gross receipts test) than for the carryback of eligible losses (generally, a $5 million gross receipts test).

For corporate equity reduction transactions (CERTs), the Act changes the definition of a loss limitation year if a taxpayer has elected to use an extended carryback period. In general, a loss limitation year is the tax year in which the CERT occurred and the two succeeding tax years (Code Sec. 172(b)(1)(E)). If a taxpayer has elected to use an extended carryback period for an applicable 2008 NOL, the loss limitation year is the tax year in which the CERT occurred and each of the succeeding tax years, the number of which is one less than the number of years that has been elected as the extended carryback period (Code Sec. 172(b)(1)(H)(i)(II), as added by the 2009 Recovery Act). For example, if a taxpayer has elected to use a five-year carryback period for an applicable 2008 NOL, then the loss limitation year would be the tax year in which the CERT occurred and each of the four succeeding tax years.

Anti-abuse rules. The Secretary of the Treasury or the designee of the Secretary will prescribe anti-abuse rules to prevent misuse of the extended NOL carryback period for small businesses. Such anti-abuse rules could include anti-stuffing rules, anti-churning rules, and rules similar to the Code Sec. 1091 wash sales rules (Act Sec. 1211(c) of the 2009 Recovery Act).

Transitional rules. Transitional rules apply to NOLs for tax years ending before February 17, 2009. These transitional rules are as follows:

(1) Election to relinquish entire carryback period.—For NOLs for tax years ending before February 17, 2009, any election to relinquish the entire carryback period

NEW LAW EXPLAINED

for the NOL under Code Sec. 172(b)(3) can be revoked before the date that is 60 days after February 17, 2009, the date of enactment (Act Sec. 1211(d)(2)(A) of the 2009 Recovery Act).

(2) Election to use extended carryback.—For NOLs for tax years ending before February 17, 2009, any election to use an extended carryback period for the NOL or to treat such an NOL with a tax year beginning in 2008 as an applicable NOL (Code Sec. 172(b)(1)(H), as amended by the 2009 Recovery Act) will be treated as timely if it is made before the date that is 60 days after February 17, 2009, the date of enactment (Act Sec. 1211(d)(2)(B) of the 2009 Recovery Act).

(3) Application for tentative carryback adjustment.—For NOLs for tax years ending before February 17, 2009, any application for a tentative carryback adjustment of the tax for the prior tax year affected by the NOL (generally, on Form 1045, for individuals, estates, and trusts, or Form 1139, for corporate taxpayers other than S corporations) will be treated as timely if it is filed before the date that is 60 days after February 17, 2009, the date of enactment (Act Sec. 1211(d)(2)(C) of the 2009 Recovery Act).

Comment: Prior to enactment of the 2009 Recovery Act, an eligible small business might have elected to relinquish the entire carryback period for a 2008 NOL thinking that it could not be used during the normal two-year carryback period. For example, the taxpayer might not have had any income to offset in the two tax years preceding the NOL year. Since taxpayers now have up to a five-year carryback period under the 2009 Recovery Act and may be able use a 2008 NOL in the third, fourth or fifth preceding tax year, the transitional rules give them time to revoke a waiver of a carryback period and to elect to use an extended carryback period.

▶ **Effective date.** In general, the amendments made to the carryback rules for net operating losses (NOLs) apply to NOLs arising in tax years ending after December 31, 2007 (Act Sec. 1211(d)(1) of the American Recovery and Reinvestment Tax Act of 2009 (P.L. 111-5)). Transitional rules apply with respect to elections and applications for tentative tax adjustments related to NOLs for tax years ending before February 17, 2009 (Act Sec. 1211(d)(2) of the 2009 Recovery Act). See "Transitional rules," in the explanation above.

Law source: Law at ¶5245. Committee Report at ¶10,240.

— Act Sec. 1211(a) of the American Recovery and Reinvestment Tax Act of 2009 (P.L. 111-5), amending Code Sec. 172(b)(1)(H);

— Act Sec. 1211(b), striking Code Sec. 172(k) and redesignating former Code Sec. 172(l) as Code Sec. 172(k);

— Act Sec. 1211(c);

— Act Sec. 1211(d), providing the effective date;

Reporter references: For further information, consult the following CCH reporters.

— Standard Federal Tax Reporter, ¶5210.03, ¶12,014.01 and ¶12,014.073

— Tax Research Consultant, BUSEXP: 45,150, NOL: 12,100, NOL: 18,254 and FILEIND: 30,156.

— Practical Tax Explanation, § 15,415 and § 17,010.05

¶425

¶430 Clarification of IRS Guidance Related to Limitations on Certain Built-In Losses Following an Ownership Change

SUMMARY OF NEW LAW

Notice 2008-83, which exempts banks from the Code Sec. 382 limitation on certain built-in losses following an ownership change, will apply to ownership changes occurring on or before January 16, 2009, and will have no force or effect with respect to ownership changes after that date.

BACKGROUND

When a corporation experiences an ownership change, Code Sec. 382 may apply to limit the use of the corporation's pre-change net operating losses (NOLs), certain built-in losses and certain deductions attributable to the pre-change period. Because the Code Sec. 382 loss limitation rules are intended to prevent trafficking of losses through acquisitions, they are triggered only if an ownership change occurs in a loss corporation. A loss corporation includes a corporation that has an NOL carryforward or NOL incurred in the year of the change. It also includes a corporation that has a net unrealized built-in loss (NUBIL), which is the amount by which the aggregate adjusted basis of the corporation's assets immediately before the ownership change exceeds the fair market value of the assets at that time (Code Sec. 382(h)(3) and (k)(1)).

Under the loss limitation rules, the taxable income of the loss corporation for any post-change year that may be offset by its pre-change losses cannot exceed the Code Sec. 382 limitation for that year (Code Sec. 382(a)). The Code Sec. 382 limitation is generally determined by multiplying the value of the loss corporation's stock by the federal long-term tax-exempt rate. The Code Sec. 382 limitation is applied annually. Any unused limitation is carried over to the next year and increases the limitation for that year (Code Sec. 382(b)).

For purposes of the Code Sec. 382 loss limitation rules, an ownership change includes an owner shift involving a five-percent shareholder or an equity structure shift as a result of which the percentage of stock owned by one or more five-percent shareholders increases by more than 50 percentage points over the lowest percentage of stock owned by these shareholders at any time during a specified testing period (Code Sec. 382(g)). The testing period is the three-year period ending on the day of the ownership change (Code Sec. 382(i)). The date on which an owner shift involving a five-percent shareholder or equity structure shift occurs is the testing date for the ownership change (Code Sec. 382(j)).

If the loss corporation has a NUBIL, any loss recognized on the disposition of an asset (which was held by the corporation at the time of the ownership change) within the five-year period beginning on the change date and ending at the close of the fifth post-change year (the recognition period) is a recognized built-in loss (RBIL) that is

BACKGROUND

treated as a pre-change loss subject to the Code Sec. 382 limitation. An RBIL also includes any amount allowable as depreciation, amortization or depletion during the recognition period to the extent it is attributable to the excess of the adjusted basis of the asset over its fair market value on the ownership change date. In addition, any amount that is allowable as a deduction during the recognition period but which is attributable to periods before the ownership change date is treated as an RBIL for the tax year in which it is allowable as a deduction. If the corporation has a net unrealized built-in gain (NUBIG) at the time of the ownership change, then any built-in gain recognized on the disposition of an asset during the recognition period increases the Code Sec. 382 limitation (Code Sec. 382(h)). The IRS has provided two alternative safe harbor approaches for identifying built-in items for purposes of Code Sec. 382(h) (Notice 2003-65, 2003-2 CB 747).

Code Sec. 166 generally allows a deduction for a debt that becomes worthless, in whole or in part, during the tax year. In the case of a bank or other corporation that is subject to supervision by federal or state authorities, a presumption of worthlessness exists to the extent that a debt is charged off during the tax year pursuant to a specific order of such an authority or in accordance with the authority's established policies. The presumption does not apply if the taxpayer does not claim the charged off amount as a deduction for the tax year in which the charge-off takes place. A bank can make a conformity election under which debts charged off for regulatory purposes during a tax year are conclusively presumed to be worthless for tax purposes if certain conditions are met (Reg. § 1.166-2(d)).

Based on the regulatory authority granted by Code Sec. 382(m), the IRS issued Notice 2008-83, 2008-42 I.R.B. 905, to provide that, for purposes of Code Sec. 382(h), any deduction properly allowed after an ownership change of a bank (as defined in Code Sec. 581) with respect to losses on loans or bad debts, including any deduction for a reasonable addition to a reserve for bad debts, will not be treated as a built-in loss or a deduction attributable to periods before the change date. The IRS stated that it continues to study the proper treatment under Code Sec. 382(h) of certain items of deduction or loss allowed after an ownership change of a bank both immediately before and after the change date, and that banks may rely on this guidance unless and until additional guidance is issued. The guidance provided in Notice 2008-83 does not address the application of any Code provisions other than Code Sec. 382 (Notice 2008-83).

> **Comment:** Notice 2008-83, which is intended to provide incentives for the acquisition of struggling banks, has been controversial based on the perception that the IRS has exceeded its rule-making authority by exempting banks from the application of the statutory limitation on built-in losses following an ownership change.

NEW LAW EXPLAINED

Notice 2008-83 repealed.—The Congress has found that the delegation of authority to the Secretary of Treasury (the Secretary) under Code Sec. 382(m) does not authorize the Secretary to provide exemptions or special rules that are restricted to particular

¶430

NEW LAW EXPLAINED

industries or classes of taxpayers. It has further found that Notice 2008-83 is inconsistent with the congressional intent in enacting Code Sec. 382(m) and that the legal authority to prescribe Notice 2008-83 is doubtful. Based on these findings and on the fact that taxpayers should generally be able to rely on guidance issued by the Secretary, Congress has determined that legislation is necessary to clarify the force and effect of Notice 2008-83 and to restore the proper application under the Code of the limitation on built-in losses following an ownership change of a bank (Act Sec. 1261(a) of the American Recovery and Reinvestment Tax Act of 2009 (P.L. 111-5)).

> **Practical Analysis:** Debra J. Bennett, Partner in the Transaction Advisory Services Group of Ernst & Young LLP, observes that Congress viewed the issuance of Notice 2008-83 by the Treasury and the IRS as exceeding the authority granted the Secretary of the Treasury under Code Sec. 382(m) to provide regulations to carry out the purposes of Code Sec. 382. Congress did not interpret this grant of regulatory authority to include providing exemptions for certain industries or classes of taxpayers. Hence, in Act Sec. 1261 of the American Recovery and Reinvestment Tax Act of 2009, Congress provides clarification on the application of Notice 2008-83 to recognized built-in losses of banks following an ownership change. Notice 2008-83 will not apply to ownership changes of banks after January 16, 2009. The two exceptions are if (1) the event resulting in the ownership change is the subject of a binding, written contract on or before that date or (2) is the subject of a written, binding agreement entered into on or before that date where the ownership change was publicly announced or described in a filing with the Securities and Exchange Commission required for the ownership change.

As a result, the 2009 Recovery Act provides that Notice 2008-83 shall be deemed to have the force and effect of law with respect to any ownership change described in Code Sec. 382(g) that occurred on or before January 16, 2009, but will have no force or effect with respect to any ownership change after that date. However, Notice 2008-83 will apply with respect to any ownership change occurring after January 16, 2009, if the ownership change is:

(1) pursuant to a written binding contract entered into on or before that date; or

(2) pursuant to a written agreement that was entered into on or before that date and that was described on or before that date in a public announcement or in an SEC filing required as a result of the ownership change (Act Sec. 1261(b) of the 2009 Recovery Act).

> **Practical Analysis:** Paul C. Lau and Sandy Soltis, Tax Partners at Blackman Kallick in Chicago, observe that a loss corporation which has an NOL carryover or a net unrealized built-in loss (NUBIL) incurred before a "Code Sec. 382 ownership change" is limited on the use of these losses for period beginning after the ownership change. Under Code Sec. 382(a), the loss corporation can only deduct NOL (or NUBIL)

NEW LAW EXPLAINED

incurred or accrued before the ownership change to the extent it is not more than the Code Sec. 382 limitation.

Code Sec. 382 ownership change generally occurs if the percentage of the stock owned by any one or more "5% shareholders" has increased by more than 50 percentage points over the lowest percentage owned by these shareholders at any time during the preceding three years. The concept of a "5% shareholder" is highly complex and the regulations contain extensive rules in identifying such shareholders.

The Code Sec. 382 limitation is an amount equal to the "long-term tax-exempt rate" times the value of the corporation's stock immediately before the ownership change. Under Code Sec. 382 (h)(1), the Code Sec. 382 limitation can be increased by recognized "built-in gains" within a five-year period after the ownership change.

On October 1, 2008, the IRS issued Notice 2008-83, IRB 2008-42, 905 which provided that a bank's loss on loans or bad debts (including any deduction for a reasonable addition to reserve for bad debts) would not be treated as built-in losses incurred prior to an ownership change. The Notice had been a subject of debate as to whether the IRS had the legal authority to provide such an exemption.

New Law. The new law gave Notice 2008-83 the force and effect of law for any ownership change occurring on or before January 16, 2009, as well as any subsequent ownership change that is pursuant to a written binding agreement entered into on or before January 16, 2009 (or a written agreement entered into on or before such date and the agreement was described on or before such date in a public announcement or in a filing with the SEC), but denied any force or effect for any other ownership change.

▶ **Effective date.** No specific effective date is provided by the Act. The provision is, therefore, considered effective on February 17, 2009, the date of enactment.

Law source: Law at ¶7015. Committee Report at ¶10,310.

— Act Sec. 1261 of the American Recovery and Reinvestment Tax Act of 2009 (P.L. 111-5).

Reporter references: For further information, consult the following CCH reporters.

— Standard Federal Tax Reporter, ¶17,115.028

— Tax Research Consultant, NOL: 33,250

¶435 Treatment of Certain Ownership Changes for Purposes of Limitations on NOL Carryforwards and Certain Built-In Losses

SUMMARY OF NEW LAW

The Code Sec. 382 limitation will not be triggered by ownership changes occurring pursuant to certain restructuring plans required under loan agreements or line of

SUMMARY OF NEW LAW

credit commitments entered into with the Treasury Department under the Emergency Economic Stabilization Act of 2008 (P.L. 110-343).

BACKGROUND

When the ownership of a corporation changes, Code Sec. 382 may be triggered to limit the use of the corporation's pre-change losses. Because the Code Sec. 382 loss limitation rules are intended to prevent trafficking of losses through acquisitions, they are triggered only if an ownership change occurs in a loss corporation.

A loss corporation includes a corporation that has a net operating loss (NOL) carryforward, an NOL incurred in the year of the change, or a net unrealized built-in loss (NUBIL) (Code Sec. 382(k)(1)). An NUBIL is the amount by which the aggregate adjusted basis of the corporation's assets immediately before the ownership change exceeds the fair market value of the assets at that time (Code Sec. 382(h)(3)). The loss limitation rules refer to the corporation that is a loss corporation after the ownership change as the new loss corporation, while the corporation that was a loss corporation before the ownership change is referred to as the old loss corporation. The same corporation may be both the old and new loss corporations (Code Sec. 382(k)(2), (3)).

Under the loss limitation rules, the taxable income of the loss corporation for any post-change year that may be offset by its pre-change losses cannot exceed the Code Sec. 382 limitation for that year (Code Sec. 382(a)). The Code Sec. 382 limitation is generally determined by multiplying the value of the loss corporation's stock by the federal long-term tax-exempt rate. The Code Sec. 382 limitation is applied annually. Any unused limitation is carried over to the next year and increases the limitation for that year (Code Sec. 382(b)).

For purposes of the Code Sec. 382 loss limitation rules, an ownership change includes an owner shift involving a five-percent shareholder or an equity structure shift as a result of which the percentage of stock owned by one or more five-percent shareholders increases by more than 50 percentage points over the lowest percentage of stock owned by the these shareholders at any time during a specified testing period (Code Sec. 382(g)). The testing period is the three-year period ending on the day of the ownership change (Code Sec. 382(i)). The date on which an owner shift involving a five-percent shareholder or equity structure shift occurs is the testing date for the ownership change (Code Sec. 382(j)).

If the loss corporation has an NUBIL, any loss recognized on the disposition of an asset (held by the corporation at the time of the ownership change) within the five-year period beginning on the change date and ending at the close of the fifth post-change year (the recognition period) is a recognized built-in loss that is treated as a pre-change loss subject to the Code Sec. 382 limitation. If the corporation has a net unrealized built-in gain at the time of the ownership change, then any built-in gain recognized on the disposition of an asset during the recognition period increases the Code Sec. 382 limitation (Code Sec. 382(h)).

Based on the Treasury Department's authority granted by the Housing and Economic Recovery Act of 2008 (P.L. 110-289) to purchase any obligations and other securities

BACKGROUND

issued by certain entities (that is, Fannie Mae and Freddie Mac), the IRS announced that it will issue regulations under Code Sec. 382 providing that the date on which the U.S. government purchases obligations of Fannie Mae and Freddie Mac (or any date after that date) will not be considered a testing date for purposes of determining whether an ownership change has occurred under Code Sec. 382 (Notice 2008-76, I.R.B. 2008-39, 768). The IRS later announced that it will issue regulations that address the application of Code Sec. 382 in the case of certain acquisitions not described in Notice 2008-76 in which the United States becomes a direct or indirect owner of a more-than-50-percent interest in a loss corporation. For this purpose, a more-than-50-percent interest is generally stock of the loss corporation possessing more than 50 percent of the total value of shares of all classes of stock. The regulations will not treat as a testing date any date as of the close of which the United States directly or indirectly owns a more-than-50-percent interest in a loss corporation. Thus, the loss corporation will be required to determine whether there is a testing date and, if so, whether there has been an ownership change, on any date as of the close of which the United States does not directly or indirectly own a more-than-50-percent interest in the loss corporation (Notice 2008-84, I.R.B. 2008-41, 855).

The Emergency Economic Stabilization Act of 2008 (P.L. 110-343) authorized the Treasury Secretary to establish the Troubled Asset Relief Program (TARP) and to issue regulations and other guidance as may be necessary or appropriate to carry out the purposes of P.L. 110-343. In Notice 2009-14, I.R.B. 2009-7, dated January 30, 2009, the IRS provided guidance on the application of Code Sec. 382 to loss corporations (financial institutions and auto companies) whose instruments are acquired by the Treasury Department (the Treasury) under five programs established pursuant to P.L. 110-343 (the EESA programs): (1) the Capital Purchase Program for publicly-traded issuers (Public CPP); (2) the Capital Purchase Program for private issuers (Private CPP); (3) the Capital Purchase Program for S corporations (S Corp CPP); (4) the Targeted Investment Program (TARP TIP); and (5) the Automotive Industry Financing Program (TARP Auto). This Notice amplified and superseded Notice 2008-100, I.R.B. 2008-44, 1081, which provided guidance only with respect to the acquisition of instruments in financial institutions under the CPP program.

Notice 2009-14 provides that, with respect to any stock (other than preferred stock) acquired by the Treasury pursuant to the EESA programs, the ownership represented by such stock on any date on which it is held by the Treasury will not be considered to have caused the Treasury's ownership in the issuing corporation to have increased over its lowest percentage owned on any earlier date. Thus, the Treasury's acquisition of such stock pursuant to the EESA programs will not trigger the Code Sec. 382 loss limitation rules. The acquired stock will generally be considered outstanding for purposes of determining the percentage of stock owned by other five-percent shareholders on a testing date.

In addition, for all federal income tax purposes, any debt instrument issued to the Treasury pursuant to any of the EESA programs will be treated as an instrument of indebtedness and any preferred stock will be treated as Code Sec. 1504(a)(4) stock. Such instrument will not be treated as stock for purposes of Code Sec. 382 while held by the Treasury or by other holders, except that preferred stock will be treated as

¶435

BACKGROUND

stock for purposes of determining the old loss corporation's value under Code Sec. 382(e)(1).

Moreover, any warrant to purchase stock acquired by the Treasury pursuant to the Public CPP, TARP TIP, and TARP Auto will be treated as an option (not as stock) and will not be deemed exercised under Reg. § 1.382-4(d)(2) while held by the Treasury. Any warrant to purchase stock acquired by the Treasury under the Private CPP will be treated as an ownership interest in the underlying stock, which will be treated as Code Sec. 1504(a)(4) preferred stock, and any warrant acquired by the Treasury pursuant to the S Corp CPP will be treated as an ownership interest in the underlying indebtedness. Notice 2009-14 further provides that, for purposes of Code Sec. 382(l)(1), any capital contribution made by the Treasury pursuant to the EESA programs will not be considered to have been made as part of a plan a principal purpose of which was to avoid or increase any Code Sec. 382 limitation.

The IRS intends to issue regulations implementing the rules described in Notice 2009-14, but taxpayers may apply these rules until and unless additional guidance is issued. Any future contrary guidance will not apply to instruments (i) held by the Treasury that were acquired pursuant to the EESA programs prior to the publication of that guidance, or (ii) issued to the Treasury pursuant to the EESA programs under binding contracts entered into prior to the publication of that guidance (Notice 2009-14).

A number of Code provisions use the related person definition of Code Sec. 267(b), which describes a number of relationships. The following persons are related under Code Sec. 267(b):

(1) family members, including brothers and sisters (by whole or half blood), spouses, parents, grandparents, children and grandchildren;

(2) an individual and a corporation in which the individual owns, directly or indirectly, more than 50 percent of the value of the outstanding stock;

(3) two corporations that are members of the same controlled group;

(4) a grantor and a fiduciary of any trust;

(5) a fiduciary of a trust and a fiduciary of another trust, if the same person is the grantor of both trusts;

(6) a fiduciary and a beneficiary of any trust;

(7) a fiduciary of a trust and a beneficiary of another trust, if the same person is a grantor of both trusts;

(8) a fiduciary of a trust and a corporation of which more than 50 percent in value of the outstanding stock is owned directly or indirectly by or for the trust, or by or for a person who is the grantor of the trust;

(9) a person and a tax-exempt organization that is controlled directly or indirectly by the person or, if the person is an individual, by members of his family;

(10) a corporation and a partnership if the same persons own more than 50 percent in value of the outstanding stock of the corporation, and more than 50 percent of the capital interest or the profits interest in the partnership;

BACKGROUND

(11) an S corporation and another S corporation if the same persons own more than 50 percent in value of the outstanding stock of each corporation;

(12) an S corporation and a C corporation, if the same persons own more than 50 percent in value of the outstanding stock of each corporation; or

(13) an executor of an estate and a beneficiary of the estate, except when the sale or exchange is made in satisfaction of a pecuniary request.

Code Sec. 707(b) generally disallows losses and capital gain treatment on a sale or exchange between a partnership and a person who owns directly or indirectly more than a 50-percent interest in the partnership's capital or profits, or between two partnerships in which the same persons own more than 50 percent of the capital or profits interests.

A voluntary employees' beneficiary association is a tax-exempt organization that provides for the payment of life, sick, accident, or other benefits to the association members or their dependents or designated beneficiaries. Except for such payments, no part of the net earnings of the association may inure to the benefit of any private shareholder or individual (Code Sec. 501(c)(9)).

NEW LAW EXPLAINED

Code Sec. 382 limitation not triggered by ownership changes pursuant to certain restructuring plans.—The Code Sec. 382(a) limitation will not apply in the case of an ownership change occurring pursuant to a restructuring plan of a taxpayer that is (1) required under a loan agreement or a commitment for a line of credit entered into with the Department of the Treasury under the Emergency Economic Stabilization Act of 2008 (P.L. 110-343), and (2) intended to result in a rationalization of the costs, capitalization, and capacity with respect to the manufacturing workforce of, and suppliers to, the taxpayer and its subsidiaries (Code Sec. 382(n)(1), as added by the American Recovery and Reinvestment Tax Act of 2009 (P.L. 111-5)). This exception will not apply in the case of any subsequent ownership change unless the subsequent ownership change also meets the requirements of the exception (Code Sec. 382(n)(2), as added by the 2009 Recovery Act).

Practical Analysis: Debra J. Bennett, Partner in the Transaction Advisory Services Group of Ernst & Young LLP, observes that dealing with ownership changes under Code Sec. 382, Act Sec. 1262 of the American Recovery and Reinvestment Tax Act of 2009 provides a very limited exception to the application of the Code Sec. 382 limitation. The exception applies if an ownership change occurs under a required restructuring plan entered into as part of a loan agreement or a commitment for a line of credit with the Department of Treasury under the Emergency Economic Stabilization Act of 2008 and the restructuring plan is intended to result in the rationalization of costs, capitalization and capacity of the manufacturing workforce and suppliers of the corporation subject of the plan as well as its subsidiaries. Code Sec. 382 will still apply to the corporation, however, the annual limitation on the use of the net

¶435

NEW LAW EXPLAINED

> operating losses and recognized built-in losses will not. Moreover, this exception to the Code Sec. 382 limitation will not apply if after the ownership change, 50 percent of more of the voting power or value stock of the corporation is owned by one person, applying the related party rules of Code Sec. 267(b) and Code Sec. 707(b). Persons who are members of a group acting together or in concert, are treated as a single person.

An ownership change that would be otherwise excepted from the application of the Code Sec. 382(a) limitation will instead remain subject to the limitation if, immediately after such ownership change, any person (other than a voluntary employees' beneficiary association described in Code Sec. 501(c)(9)) owns stock of the new loss corporation possessing 50 percent or more of the total combined voting power of all classes of stock entitled to vote, or of the total value of the stock of such a corporation. In determining the stock ownership, related persons will be treated as a single person. For this purpose, a person will be treated as related to another person if (1) that person bears a relationship to the other person described in Code Sec. 267(b) or 707(b), or (2) such persons are members of a group of persons acting in concert (Code Sec. 382(n)(3), as added by the 2009 Recovery Act).

> **Comment:** The Conference Committee clarifies that the exception from the application of the Code Sec. 382 limitation does not change the fact that an ownership change has occurred for other purposes of Code Sec. 382 (such as, for example, for purposes of determining the testing period under Code Sec. 382(i)(2)) (Conference Committee Report for American Recovery and Reinvestment Act of 2009).

> **Practical Analysis:** Paul C. Lau and Sandy Soltis, Tax Partners at Blackman Kallick in Chicago not that under new Code Sec. 382(n), the Code Sec. 382 limitation does not apply to an ownership change that meets two requirements discussed below. While the Code Sec. 382 limitation does not apply, an ownership change would still be in effect for other Code Sec. 382 purposes.
>
> The Code Sec. 382 limitation does not apply if the ownership change (1) occurs under a restructuring plan required under a loan agreement or a commitment for a line of credit entered into with the U.S. Treasury under the Emergency Economic Stabilization Act of 2008 (EESA), and (2) is intended to result in a rationalization of the costs, capitalization, and capacity of the manufacturing workforce of (and suppliers to) the taxpayer and its subsidiaries. This exception does not apply to an ownership change if, immediately after the ownership change, any person (other than a VEBA under Code Sec. 501(c)(9)) owns 50 percent or more of the total voting power or total value of the loss corporation. Related parties are treated as one person. Related parties are persons bearing relationships described in Code Sec. 267(b) or 707(b), or persons acting in concert.
>
> The first requirement for the exception (i.e., a change pursuant to an EESA plan) is fairly clear. The second requirement, however, will need clarification and guidance, as the Committee Report does not provide any guidance or explanation on the

¶435

NEW LAW EXPLAINED

> application and interpretation of the required intent (a subjective state of mind) "to result in a rationalization of the costs, capitalization and capacity with respect to the manufacturing workforce of, and suppliers to, the taxpayer and its subsidiaries."

▶ **Effective date.** The amendment made by this provision applies to ownership changes after the date of the enactment (Act Sec. 1262(b) of the American Recovery and Reinvestment Tax Act of 2009 (P.L. 111-5)).

Law source: Law at ¶5265. Committee Report at ¶10,320.

— Act Sec. 1262(a) of the American Recovery and Reinvestment Tax Act of 2009 (P.L. 111-5), adding Code Sec. 382(n);

— Act Sec. 1262(b), providing the effective date.

Reporter references: For further information, consult the following CCH reporters.

— Standard Federal Tax Reporter, ¶17,115.021

— Tax Research Consultant, NOL: 33,050

¶440 Original Issue Discount on High-Yield Discount Obligations

SUMMARY OF NEW LAW

The rules that disallow a deduction to corporations for a portion of the original issue discount (OID) on any applicable high-yield discount obligation (AHYDO), and that defer, until paid, a deduction for the remainder of the OID, are, with certain exceptions, temporarily suspended. The suspension applies to any AHYDO issued, during the period beginning on September 1, 2008, and ending on December 31, 2009, in exchange for an obligation that is not an AHYDO, so long as the issuer (or obligor) of both the AHYDO and the non-AHYDO are the same.

BACKGROUND

In general, a deduction is allowed for all interest paid or accrued within a tax year on indebtedness (Code Sec. 163(a)). However, there are numerous provisions in both Code Sec. 163 and other Code sections that limit or preclude a taxpayer from deducting certain types of interest. One major limitation with respect to the interest deduction under Code Sec. 163 concerns debt instruments that have original issue discount (OID) and, in particular, certain high-yield discount obligations, referred to as "applicable high-yield discount obligations" (AHYDOs).

Ordinarily, a debt instrument is issued at a price approximately equal to its redemption price, and the return to the holder is in the form of periodic interest payments. Original issue discount debt instruments, however, are issued at prices below the

BACKGROUND

redemption price, and the return is in the form of appreciation in price. "Original issue discount" means the difference between the issue price of a debt instrument and its stated redemption price at maturity (Code Sec. 1273(a)(1)).

Original issue discount (OID) is generally deductible as interest by the issuer of a debt instrument and the OID recipient (the holder of the debt instrument) must also annually take into income the amount of accrued OID. The method of computing the amount of OID that is deductible by the issuer each year depends on the date the debt instrument was issued. For instruments issued after July 1, 1982, actual accrued OID (even though not yet paid) is deductible (Code Sec. 163(e)(1)). More specifically, the allowable deduction for any tax year is equal to the aggregate daily portions (as defined under Code Sec. 163(e)(2)(B)) of the OID for days during the tax year. This applies to both corporate and noncorporate issuers, regardless of whether the issuer uses the cash or the accrual method of accounting. For instruments issued after May 27, 1969, and before July 2, 1982, OID was calculated using the straight-line method and total OID was prorated over the life of the issue.

If a debt instrument is issued by a corporation, other than an S corporation (Code Sec. 163(e)(5)(D)), and is an applicable high-yield discount obligation (AHYDO) issued after July 10, 1989, special limitations apply. In such instances, the OID is divided between (1) a disqualified portion, and (2) the remainder of the discount (Code Sec. 163(e)(5)). The disqualified portion is treated as a nondeductible return on the equity of the debt instrument's issuer, eligible for the dividends-received deduction (Code Sec. 163(e)(5)(A)(i) and (B)). The remainder of the discount is treated as interest that is not deductible until paid in cash or property other than debt or stock of the issuer (but that is included in income by the holder) (Code Sec. 163(e)(5)(A)(ii), (i)(3)).

An AHYDO is a debt instrument where (Code Sec. 163(i)(1)): (1) the instrument's maturity date is more than five years from the date of issue; (2) the instrument's yield to maturity is five percentage points or more over the applicable federal rate (AFR) for the month it is issued; and (3) the instrument has "significant original issue discount." An instrument has significant original issue discount if the aggregate amount that would be included in gross income on the instrument for periods before the close of any accrual period (Code Sec. 1272(a)(5)) that ends more than five years after the date of issue exceeds the sum of (a) the aggregate amount of interest to be paid under the instrument before the close of such accrual period and (b) the product of the instrument's issue price (Code Secs. 1273(b) and 1274(a)) and its yield to maturity (Code Sec. 163(i)(2)).

> **Comment:** In 2008, the IRS issued Rev. Proc. 2008-51, I.R.B. 2008-35, 562, which described circumstances in which it will not treat a debt instrument as an applicable high yield discount obligation (AHYDO) for purposes of Code Sec. 163(e)(5). These circumstances involve: (1) a debt instrument issued for money pursuant to a financing commitment; (2) a debt instrument exchanged for a debt instrument issued pursuant to a financing commitment; and (3) a debt instrument indirectly exchanged for a debt instrument issued pursuant to a financing commitment. In describing why it issued the procedure, the IRS noted that corporations often obtain financing commitments in advance of borrowing money. Moreover, recent events have proven that market conditions can unex-

¶440

BACKGROUND

pectedly worsen between the time a binding financing commitment is obtained by a corporation and the time the corporation calls upon the lender to perform pursuant to the financing commitment. This can have certain collateral economic consequences, which can result in the issue price of a debt instrument being significantly less than the amount of cash actually received by the corporation for the debt instrument. Accordingly, the IRS believed that the circumstances described above should not result in the disallowance of interest deductions on the debt instrument under Code Sec. 163(e)(5).

The disqualified portion of the OID on an AHYDO issued by a corporation is the lesser of (1) the amount of the OID, or (2) the portion of the "total return" on the obligation that bears the same ratio to the total return that the "disqualified yield" on the obligation bears to the yield to maturity on the obligation (Code Sec. 163(e)(5)(C)(i)). The "disqualified yield" on an applicable high-yield discount obligation is the excess of the yield to maturity on the obligation over the sum of the applicable federal rate (AFR) for the calendar month in which the debt instrument is issued plus six percentage points. The "total return" is the amount that would have been the OID on the obligation if the stated redemption price at maturity of the debt instrument included all qualified periodic interest payments under the debt instrument (Code Sec. 163(e)(5)(C)(ii)).

The portion of the OID on an AHYDO issued by a corporation that exceeds the disqualified portion is not allowed as a deduction to the issuer until it is paid (Code Sec. 163(e)(5)(A)(ii)). The nondisqualified portion of the OID is not considered paid until it is paid in cash or property other than an obligation of the same issuer or of a person related to the issuer (Code Secs. 267(b) and 318(a)) or stock of the issuer or a related person (Code Sec. 163(e)(5)(A)(ii) and (e)(5)(A); Code Sec. 163(i)(3)(B) and (i)(3)).

NEW LAW EXPLAINED

Rules for OID on certain high-yield discount obligations temporarily suspended.—The rules that disallow a deduction to corporations for a portion of the OID on any AHYDO, and that defer, until paid, a deduction for the remainder of the OID, are, with certain exceptions, temporarily suspended (Code Sec. 163(e)(5)(F)(i), as added by the American Recovery and Reinvestment Tax Act of 2009 (P.L. 111-5)). In particular, the suspension applies to any AHYDO issued in exchange for an obligation that is not an AHYDO, during the period beginning on September 1, 2008, and ending on December 31, 2009. In order for the suspension to apply, the issuer (or obligor) of the AHYDO and the issuer (or obligor) of the non-AHYDO must be the same. For this purpose, an "exchange" includes an exchange resulting from a significant modification of the debt instrument.

The suspension does not generally apply to any newly issued debt obligation that is issued for an AHYDO (including any debt obligation issued as a result of a significant modification of a debt obligation) (Conference Committee Report to the American Recovery and Reinvestment Tax Act of 2009). However, any newly issued debt obliga-

¶440

NEW LAW EXPLAINED

tion for which the AHYDO rules are suspended under the new law is not treated as an AHYDO for purposes of a subsequent application of the suspension rule (Code Sec. 163(e)(5)(F)(ii), as added by the 2009 Recovery Act).

> **Comment:** For example, as cited in the Conference Committee Report, if a new debt obligation that would be an AHYDO under current law is issued in exchange for a debt obligation that is not an AHYDO, and the provision suspends application of Code Sec. 163(e)(5), another new debt obligation, issued during the suspension period in exchange for the obligation with respect to which the rule in Code Sec. 163(e)(5) was suspended, would be eligible for the relief provided by the provision, despite the fact that it is issued for an instrument that would be considered an AHYDO under current law.

The suspension also does not apply to any newly issued debt obligation (including any debt obligation issued as a result of a significant modification of a debt obligation) the interest on which is (1) contingent interest (as described in Code Sec. 871(h)(4), without regard to Code Sec. 871(h)(4)(D), which would otherwise exclude interest paid or accrued with respect to any indebtedness with a fixed term that was issued on or before April 7, 1993, or which was issued after such date pursuant to a written agreement that was binding before such date and at all times after that), or (2) issued to a person related to the issuer, within the meaning of Code Sec. 108(e)(4) (Code Sec. 163(e)(5)(F)(i), as added by the 2009 Recovery Act).

> **Comment:** Under Code Sec. 108(e)(4), parties related to the issuer include: (1) a member of a controlled group of corporations, as defined by Code Sec. 414(b), of which the issuer is also a member; (2) a trade or business under common control, within the meaning of Code Sec. 414(b) or (c); (3) a partner in a partnership controlled by the issuer or a controlled partnership under Code Sec. 707(b)(1); or (4) a family member or a person bearing a relationship to the debtor specified in Code Sec. 267(b), including a spouse of the debtor's child or grandchild.

Practical Analysis: Jonathan Zelnik, a Principal in the Federal Tax group of the Washington National Tax practice of KPMG LLP, observes that Act Sec. 1232 of the American Recovery and Reinstatement Tax Act of 2009 temporarily suspends the applicable high-yield discount obligation (AHYDO) rules for certain debt instruments issued in a debt-for-debt exchange after August 31, 2008, and before January 1, 2010. For a corporation that issues an AHYDO, (1) no deduction is allowed for the disqualified portion of the OID, and (2) no deduction is allowable for the remainder of the OID until paid. Under Reg. § 1.701-2(f), Example 1, the AHYDO rules also apply to corporate partners of a partnership that issued an AHYDO. However, the AHYDO rules do not apply to a debt instrument issued by a corporation for any period the corporation is an S corporation.

The suspension applies to an AHYDO issued in exchange, including an exchange resulting from a modification of the debt instrument, for a debt instrument that is not an AHYDO and the issuer of the AHYDO is the same as the issuer of the old debt instrument. The provision also provides that an AHYDO for which the AHYDO rules

NEW LAW EXPLAINED

are suspended is treated as a debt instrument that is not an AHYDO for purposes of applying the relief provision to a debt instrument issued in exchange for that AHYDO during the suspension period. Thus, although an AHYDO issued in exchange for an AHYDO generally will not be eligible for relief under the provision, that is not case if the old AHYDO benefited from the suspension of the AHYDO rules.

The suspension of the AHYDO rules does not apply to a debt instrument (1) the interest on which is interest described in Code Sec. 871(h)(4) (without regard to Code Sec. 871(h)(4)(D)), or (2) issued to a related person within the meaning of Code Sec. 108(e)(4). Code Sec. 871(h)(4) provides that portfolio interest does not include certain contingent interest. In general under Code Sec. 108(e)(4), a person is related to an issuer if the person bears a relationship to the issuer described in Code Sec. 267(b) or Code Sec. 707(b)(1).

The provision also amends Code Sec. 163(i)(1) to permit the Secretary to issue regulations that, on a temporary basis, allows a rate that is higher than the AFR for purposes of determining if a debt instrument is an AHYDO, if the Secretary determines that such rate is appropriate in light of distressed conditions in the debt capital markets.

The AHYDO suspension provision applies to debt instruments issued after August 31, 2008, in tax years ending after that date. The provision that allows the Secretary to issue regulations to use temporarily a rate that is higher than the AFR applies to debt instruments issued after December 31, 2009.

The AHYDO suspension is welcome relief for those issuers that would otherwise bear an often unexpected tax burden for refinancing or modifying existing debt during a depressed credit market. The tax impact on an issuer from a debt-for-debt exchange can vary greatly depending on the issue price of the new debt instrument. The issue price of the new debt instrument affects both the amount, if any, of cancellation of indebtedness income and the yield to maturity of the new debt instrument. In a depressed credit market, an issue price based on the fair market value of the debt, which is the rule if the old or the new debt is publicly traded under Reg. § 1.1273-2(f), can be markedly less than an issue price based on the principal amount of the new debt instrument. That means that an issuer seeking to modify publicly traded debt with a depressed fair market value faces not only the prospect of cancellation of indebtedness income on the exchange, but in some cases, a deferred or disallowed deduction for OID because the issue price was low enough to cause the modified debt to be an AHYDO. So for some issuers, solving a business problem would create an unexpected tax cost because of the AHYDO rules. Consequently, the provision's AHYDO relief complements the changes to the cancellation of indebtedness income (CODI) rules for debt-for-debt exchanges.

Issuers, however, should pay close attention to fact that the relief does not extend to debt issued to a related person under Code Sec. 108(e)(4). So, even though an issuer may be able to defer the recognition of CODI if its debt is acquired by a related person, the issuer may still confront the effect of the AHYDO rules on the deemed reissued debt instrument.

Finally, issuers that undertook a debt-for-debt exchange after August 31, 2008, but before passage of the Act and that modified terms so as to prevent the new debt

¶440

NEW LAW EXPLAINED

> from being AHYDO may want to evaluate those modifications and decide whether other changes, in light of the Act, are worth pursuing with the holders.

The new law provides authority to the IRS to apply the suspension rule to periods after December 31, 2009, if the IRS determines that such application is appropriate in light of distressed conditions in the debt capital markets (Code Sec. 163(e)(5)(F)(iii), as added by the 2009 Recovery Act). In addition, the IRS is granted authority to use a rate that is higher than the AFR for purposes of applying Code Sec. 163(e)(5) for obligations issued after December 31, 2009, in tax years ending after such date, if the IRS determines that the higher rate is appropriate in light of distressed conditions in the debt capital markets (Code Sec. 163(i)(1), as amended by the 2009 Recovery Act).

▶ **Effective date.** The amendments pertaining to the suspension of the rules in Code Sec. 163(e)(5) apply to obligations issued after August 31, 2008, in tax years ending after such date (Act Sec. 1232(c)(1) of the American Recovery and Reinvestment Tax Act of 2009). The amendments pertaining to the interest rate authority granted to the IRS is applicable to obligations issued after December 31, 2009, in tax years ending after such date (Act Sec. 1232(c)(2) of the 2009 Recovery Act (P.L. 111-5)).

Law source: Law at ¶5230. Committee Report at ¶10,280.

— Act Sec. 1232(a) of the American Recovery and Reinvestment Tax Act of 2009 (P.L. 111-5), redesignating Code Sec. 163(e)(5)(F) as Code Sec. 163(e)(5)(G) and adding new Code Sec. 163(e)(5)(F);

— Act Sec. 1232(b), amending Code Sec. 163(i)(1);

— Act Sec. 1232(c)(1) and (2), providing the effective dates.

Reporter references: For further information, consult the following CCH reporters.

— Standard Federal Tax Reporter, ¶9303.043 and ¶9303.044

— Tax Research Consultant, ACCTNG: 36,262

— Practical Tax Explanation, § 19,301

¶445 Financial Institution De Minimis Safe Harbor Exception for Deducting Tax-Exempt Interest Expense

SUMMARY OF NEW LAW

A temporary exception is added to the rule prohibiting financial institutions from deducting tax-exempt interest expenses. The exception applies with respect to tax-exempt bonds issued during 2009 and 2010 to the extent that these investments constitute less than two percent of the average adjusted bases of all the assets of the financial institution.

Explanation

BACKGROUND

There is a 100-percent deduction disallowance rule for interest on indebtedness incurred or continued in order to purchase or carry obligations the interest on which is exempt from tax (Code Sec. 265(a)). In general, an interest deduction is disallowed only if the taxpayer has a purpose of using borrowed funds to purchase or carry tax-exempt obligations. For individuals and certain nonfinancial corporations, in the absence of direct evidence linking a taxpayer's indebtedness with the purchase or carrying of tax-exempt obligations, the IRS will not infer that a taxpayer's purpose in borrowing money was to purchase or carry tax-exempt obligations if the taxpayer's investment in tax-exempt obligations is "insubstantial." A taxpayer's holdings of tax-exempt obligations are presumed to be "insubstantial" if during the tax year the average adjusted basis of the taxpayer's tax-exempt obligations is two percent or less of the average adjusted basis of the individual's portfolio investments and assets held by the individual in the active conduct of a trade or business (Rev. Proc. 72-18, 1972-1 CB 740, clarified by Rev. Proc. 74-8, 1974-1 CB 419, and modified by Rev. Proc. 87-53, 1987-2 CB 669).

Financial institutions. Since 1982, financial institutions have been subject to a somewhat stricter regime than other taxpayers. A 20-percent disallowance rule for financial institution preference items applies to interest on debt used to purchase or carry tax-exempt obligations acquired after 1982 but before August 8, 1986 (Code Sec. 291(a)(3)). A 100-percent disallowance rule applies to the interest expense allocable to tax-exempt obligations for most obligations acquired after August 7, 1986 (Code Sec. 265(b)). There is no "insubstantial" exception for this rule. For certain qualified tax-exempt obligations (which must not exceed $10 million under current law) acquired after August 7, 1986, the obligation is treated as being acquired on August 7, 1986. For these obligations, the 20-percent disallowance rule rather than the 100-percent disallowance rule applies (Code Secs. 265(b)(3)(A), 291(e)(1)(B)).

The dollar amount of the interest expense disallowed is determined as follows. For tax-exempt obligations acquired in either period, the amount of interest allocable to the obligations is equal to total interest expense multiplied by a fraction, the denominator of which is the average adjusted basis of all assets of the institution. For 20-percent disallowance assets, the numerator is the average adjusted basis of obligations acquired after 1982 but before August 8, 1986. For the 100-percent disallowance assets, the numerator is the average adjusted basis of all tax-exempt obligations acquired after that date (Code Secs. 265(b)(2), 291(e)(1)(B)(ii)).

NEW LAW EXPLAINED

Temporary de minimis safe harbor exception to 100-percent disallowance rule for financial institutions.—To improve the marketability of tax-exempt bonds, the American Recovery and Reinvestment Tax Act of 2009 (P.L. 111-5) adds a de minimis safe harbor exception for financial institutions to the 100-percent disallowance rule that prohibits them from deducting interest expenses associated with tax-exempt obligations. Under the safe harbor, the portion of interest expense is allocable to investments in tax-exempt municipal bonds does not include investments in tax-exempt municipal bonds issued during 2009 and 2010 to the extent that these investments constitute less

¶445

NEW LAW EXPLAINED

than two percent of the average adjusted bases of all the assets of the financial institution (Code Sec. 265(b)(7)(A), (B), as added by the 2009 Recovery Act).

Financial institution preference item disallowance applies. The portion of any obligation not taken into account under this rule is treated as having been acquired on August 7, 1986 (Code Sec. 291(e)(1)(B)(iv), as amended by the 2009 Recovery Act). Accordingly, the 20-percent deduction disallowance for interest on debt used by a bank to carry tax-exempt obligations applies (Code Sec. 291(a)(3)).

> **Example:** The Second National Bank acquires $50 million in Springfield municipal bonds issued in 2009, which is less than two percent of the bank's average adjusted bases for all its assets. The 100-percent disallowance rule does not apply, but the 20-percent disallowance rule does.

Refunding bonds. A refunding bond (whether a current or advance refunding) is treated as issued on the date of the issuance of the refunded bond (or in the case of a series of refundings, the original bond) (Code Sec. 265(b)(7)(C), as added by the 2009 Recovery Act). Accordingly, the safe harbor will not apply to bonds issued to retire or fund bonds issued prior to 2009.

> **Example:** The City of Springfield originally issued bonds in 2006, and would now like to use refunding bonds to take advantage of the current lower interest rates. If Springfield issues refunding bonds in 2009, the issuance will not qualify for the safe harbor. If, however, it originally issues bonds in 2009, and later wants to issue refunding bonds with respect to 2009 bonds, the refunding bonds will be treated as issued in 2009, and thereby may qualify for the safe harbor.

> **Comment:** A version of this safe harbor appeared in the Municipal Bond Market Support Act of 2008 (S. 3518, September 22, 2008; and H.R. 6333, June 24, 2008), which was not enacted. Senator Bingaman (D-N.M.), who introduced the bill in the Senate, noted that banks historically were permitted to deduct the full interest costs they incurred and that they made up a significant share of the demand for municipal debt. The safe harbor would restore bank demand and provide some stability by bringing this group of institutional investors back into the municipal market, as well as bring their treatment into parity with other taxpayers. See Introduction to Municipal Bond Market Support Act of 2008, S. 3518 (September 22, 2008).

> **Practical Analysis:** Mark Price and Denise Schwieger, Principals in the Financial Institutions and Products group of the Washington National Tax practice of KPMG LLP, observe that the American Recovery and Reinvestment Tax Act of 2009 added a provision to exempt newly issued tax-exempt obligations from a financial institu-

NEW LAW EXPLAINED

tion's *pro rata* interest expense disallowance rules under Code Sec. 265(b). Under the new provision, tax-exempt obligations issued during 2009 and 2010 are not treated as tax-exempt obligations issued after August 7, 1986, up to two percent of the adjusted basis of the financial institution's assets, and are thus excluded from a financial institution's Code Sec. 265(b) calculation. The new provision further requires that tax-exempt obligations excluded from the Code Sec. 265(b) calculation under this provision are subject to the interest expense disallowance rules of Code Sec. 291. Therefore, the new provision has the effect of reducing the interest expense disallowance attributable to these tax-exempt obligations from 100 percent to 20 percent.

It is important to note that the *de minimis* rule for financial institutions created by the American Recovery and Reinvestment Tax Act of 2009 operates differently than the *de minimis* rule under Code Sec. 265(a)(2) set forth in Rev. Proc. 72-18, 1972-1 CB 740. The Rev. Proc. 72-18 *de minimis* rule provides that, if a corporation that is not a financial institution holds tax-exempt obligations with an adjusted basis that does not exceed two percent of the average total assets held for use in a trade or business, then the holding of the tax-exempt obligations will be insubstantial and Code Sec. 265(a)(2) will not apply to disallow any interest expense absent direct evidence linking the indebtedness to the purchase or carrying of the tax-exempt obligation. Therefore, Code Sec. 265(a)(2) is not turned off if a corporation owns tax-exempt obligations that exceed two percent of the corporation's average total assets. The *de minimis* rule for financial institutions in the American Recovery and Reinvestment Tax Act of 2009, however, provides a blanket exclusion, up to two percent of a financial institution's assets, from the 100 percent disallowance rule of Code Sec. 265(b), regardless of whether the financial institution owns tax-exempt obligations issued in 2009 and 2010 in excess of two percent of its assets.

The fact that a financial institution can apply the *de minimis* rule even if it owns tax-exempt obligations issued during 2009 and 2010 that exceed two percent of the adjusted basis of the financial institution's assets creates open questions as to how the interest expense disallowance rules of Code Secs. 265(b) and 291 should be applied. Namely, it is not clear which tax-exempt obligations will be subject to the financial institution's Code Sec. 265(b) disallowance or the more favorable Code Sec. 291 disallowance provisions. Further, when calculating the average amount of tax-exempt obligations owned for purposes of the Code Sec. 265(b) calculation, financial institutions are required to average the amount of tax-exempt obligations owned at month end. It is not clear whether the amount of tax-exempt obligations subject to the *de miminis* rule are determined monthly and thus reduce the amount of tax-exempt obligations held at month end or whether the two-percent disallowance is determined at year end. It is also not clear how a financial institution should apply the *de minimis* rule when the taxpayer purchases and sells tax-exempt obligations issued during 2009 and 2010 throughout the year. Until further guidance is issued, financial institutions should consider separately tracking purchases and sales of tax-exempt obligations issued during 2009 and 2010.

Comment: The 2009 Recovery Act also provides an increase in the small issuer dollar limit from $10 to $30 million, plus relaxation of the pooled issuance rules for 2009 and 2010 issues. See ¶450.

¶445

NEW LAW EXPLAINED

▶ **Effective date.** The safe harbor provisions apply to obligations issued after December 31, 2008 (Act Sec. 1501(c), American Recovery and Reinvestment Tax Act of 2009 (P.L. 111-5)).

Law source: Law at ¶5255 and ¶5260. Committee Report at ¶10,390.

— Act Sec. 1501(a) of the American Recovery and Reinvestment Tax Act of 2009 (P.L. 111-5), adding Code Sec. 265(b)(7);
— Act Sec. 1501(b), amending Code Sec. 291(e)(1)(B);
— Act Sec. 1501(c), providing the effective date.

Reporter references: For further information, consult the following CCH reporters.
— Standard Federal Tax Reporter, ¶14,054.045 and ¶15,191.035
— Tax Research Consultant, RIC: 12,204.20 and SALES: 51,054.80
— Practical Tax Explanation, § 7,420.05

¶450 Temporary Expansion of Small Issuer Exception to Tax-Exempt Interest Expense Allocation Rules for Financial Institutions

SUMMARY OF NEW LAW

The limit for the small issuer exception to the 100-percent disallowance rule for deductions for tax-exempt interest expenses by financial institutions is increased from $10 million to $30 million for tax-exempt bonds issued during 2009 and 2010. The small issuer exception under this temporary expansion applies to a pooled financing issue if all of the ultimate borrowers in such issue would separately qualify for the exception.

BACKGROUND

A financial institution is not allowed to take a deduction for the portion of its interest expense that is allocable to the institution's investments in tax-exempt municipal bonds (Code Sec. 265(b)(1)). However, "qualified tax-exempt obligations" that are issued by a "qualified small issuer" are not taken into account as investments in tax-exempt bonds for these purposes (Code Sec. 265(b)(3)). Instead, only 20 percent of the interest expense allocable to qualified tax-exempt obligations is disallowed (Code Secs. 265(b)(3)(A), 291(a)(3) and 291(e)(1)). A "qualified small issuer" is any issuer that reasonably anticipates that the amount of its tax-exempt obligations (other than certain private activity bonds) will not exceed $10 million (Code Sec. 265(b)(3)(C)). A "qualified tax-exempt obligation" is a tax-exempt obligation that (1) is issued after August 7, 1986, by a qualified small issuer, (2) is not a private activity bond, and (3) is designated by the issuer as qualifying for the exception from the general rule (Code Sec. 265(b)(3)(B)).

BACKGROUND

Composite (or pooled) issues can qualify for the exception for qualified small issuers only if the requirements are met both with respect to the composite issue as a whole (determined by treating the composite issue as a single issue), and with respect to each separate lot of obligations that is a part of the issue (determined by treating each separate lot of obligations as a separate issue). Accordingly, a composite issue may qualify for the exception only if the composite issue itself does not exceed $10 million and if each issuer benefiting from the composite issue reasonably anticipates issuing $10 million or less of tax-exempt obligations (other than private activity bonds) during the calendar year, including bonds issued through the composite arrangement (Code Sec. 265(b)(3)(F)).

NEW LAW EXPLAINED

Dollar limit for small issuer exception for 2009 and 2010 issues increased to $30 million.—The American Recovery and Reinvestment Tax Act of 2009 (P.L. 111-5) increases the dollar threshold from $10,000,000 to $30,000,000 when determining whether a tax-exempt obligation issued in 2009 and 2010 qualifies for the small issuer exception (Code Sec. 265(b)(3)(G)(i), as added by the 2009 Recovery Act). The small issuer exception now also applies to an issue if all of the ultimate borrowers in such issue separately qualify for the exception (Code Sec. 265(b)(3)(G)(ii), as added by the 2009 Recovery Act).

Pooled financing issues. The small issuer exception applies to a pooled financing issue if all of the ultimate borrowers in such issue would separately qualify for the exception (Code Sec. 265(b)(3)(G)(iv), as added by the 2009 Recovery Act). Any obligation issued as a part of a pooled financing issue is to be treated as a qualified tax-exempt obligation if the requirements for the exception are met with respect to each qualified portion of the issue. This determination is made by treating each qualified portion as a separate issue. The rule that requires composite issues to qualify for the exception as a whole as well as in its parts (Code Sec. 265(b)(3)(F)) does not apply (Code Sec. 265(b)(3)(G)(iii), as added by the 2009 Recovery Act). A qualified portion is the portion of the proceeds which are used with respect to each qualified borrower under the issue (Code Sec. 265(b)(3)(G)(v), as added by the 2009 Recovery Act). A qualified borrower is a state or political subdivision thereof or a tax-exempt Code Sec. 501(c)(3) organization (Code Sec. 265(b)(3)(G)(vi), as added by the 2009 Recovery Act).

> **Example:** The proceeds from a $100 million pooled financing issued in 2009 are used to make four equal loans of $25 million to four qualified borrowers. The issue can qualify for the small issuer exception. However, if (1) more than $30 million were loaned to any qualified borrower, (2) any borrower were not a qualified borrower, or (3) any borrower would, if it were the issuer of a separate issue in an amount equal to the amount loaned to such borrower, fail to meet any of the other requirements of Code Sec. 265(b)(3), the entire $100 million pooled financing issue would fail to qualify for the exception (Joint Committee

NEW LAW EXPLAINED

on Taxation, Description of Title I of H.R. 598, the American Recovery and Reinvestment Tax Act of 2009 (JCX-5-09), January 21, 2009).

Practical Analysis: Mark Price and Denise Schwieger, Principals in the Financial Institutions and Products group of the Washington National Tax practice of KPMG LLP, observe that the American Recovery and Reinvestment Tax Act of 2009 provides financial institutions favorable tax treatment on certain tax-exempt obligations issued during 2009 and 2010. Specifically, the American Recovery and Reinvestment Tax Act of 2009 amends the definition of "qualified small issuer" for purposes of Code Sec. 265(b)(3). Under current law, a "qualified small issuer" is an issuer that reasonably expects to issue $10 million or less of tax-exempt obligations during the calendar year. The American Recovery and Reinvestment Tax Act of 2009 amends the definition by increasing the annual limit from $10 million to $30 million for tax-exempt obligations issued during 2009 and 2010. In addition, under the new provision, the $30 million cap is generally applied at the borrower level in the case of composite issues. The new provision also treats qualified 501(c)(3) bonds as issued directly by the 501(c)(3) organization that benefited from the issue for purposes of applying the $30 million limits.

Congress originally provided more favorable tax rules for tax exempt obligations issued by small issuers so that small localities could obtain the lowest possible borrowing costs. Small localities do not have access to the broad capital markets and thus rely on local financial institutions to buy the localities' bonds in order to fund *bona fide* governmental projects. By reducing a financial institution's interest expense disallowance allocable to the tax exempt obligations from 100 percent to 20 percent, financial institutions were given an incentive to lend to small issuers at a lower cost. By increasing the annual limit of funds raised from $10 million to $30 million, financial institutions will have an incentive to lend more money to a broader group of issuers of tax exempt obligations and those issuers will be able to benefit from a lower cost of borrowing.

Comment: A version of this modification appeared in the Municipal Bond Market Support Act of 2008 (S. 3518, September 22, 2008; and H.R. 6333, June 24, 2008), which was not enacted. Senator Bingaman (D-N.M.), who introduced the bill in the Senate, noted that the small issuers exception was added because small issuers' infrequent and small borrowing amounts make it too costly for them to sell debt in the national capital markets, leaving private placements with local banks the most feasible and cost-effective alternative. See Introduction to Municipal Bond Market Support Act of 2008, S. 3518, (September 22, 2008).

Comment: The 2009 Recovery Act also provides a temporary de minimis exception for financial institutions that hold less than two percent of their assets in tax-exempt obligations. See ¶445.

▶ **Effective date.** The provision applies to obligations issued after December 31, 2008 (Act Sec. 1502(b), American Recovery and Reinvestment Tax Act of 2009 (P.L. 111-5)).

¶450

NEW LAW EXPLAINED

Law source: Law at ¶5255. Committee Report at ¶10,390.

— Act Sec. 1502(a) of the American Recovery and Reinvestment Tax Act of 2009 (P.L. 111-5), adding Code Sec. 265(b)(3)(G);

— Act Sec. 1502(b), providing the effective date.

Reporter references: For further information, consult the following CCH reporters.

— Standard Federal Tax Reporter, ¶14,054.066 and ¶15,191.035

— Tax Research Consultant, RIC: 12,204.20 and SALES: 51,054.80

— Practical Tax Explanation, §7,420.05

¶455 $500,000 Executive Compensation Deduction Limit Extended to All Entities That Take TARP Assistance

SUMMARY OF NEW LAW

The $500,000 deduction limitation on executive compensation is extended to all entities that take TARP assistance until they repay it.

BACKGROUND

Under the Troubled Asset Relief Program (TARP) established pursuant to the Emergency Economic Stabilization Act of 2008 (P.L. 110-343), the federal government is authorized to purchase troubled assets from financial institutions, either through a public auction or directly from the institution. Such sales would trigger certain limits on executive compensation. Financial institutions that sell troubled assets to the Treasury Department by means of a public auction are restricted for a period of time from deducting more than $500,000 for compensation paid to certain executives (Code Sec. 162(m)(5), as added by the Emergency Economic Act). In addition, they are subject to the golden parachute rules for payments triggered by severance during this period (Code Sec. 280G(e)), and the firm is prohibited from contracting for new golden parachute payments (Division A, Act Sec. 111(c) of the Emergency Economic Act of 2008). A firm that sells troubled assets directly to the government is subject to certain executive compensation standards under which it cannot offer incentives for executive officers to take unnecessary risks, and must recover bonuses to senior executives based on materially inaccurate information, and must not make any golden parachute payments to senior executives while the government holds an equity or debt position in the firm (Division A, Act Sec. 111(b) of the Emergency Economic Act of 2008).

The first round of TARP money was spent purchasing preferred stock from certain financial institutions without the government taking troubled assets, and hence the executive compensation limits were not triggered. Some of the firms that took TARP

BACKGROUND

money paid their top executives jaw-dropping bonuses for 2008, provoking a political backlash.

$500,000 limit on executive compensation deduction. An applicable employer's deduction for executive remuneration for any applicable taxable year attributable to services performed by a covered executive during that tax year is limited to $500,000 (Code Sec. 162(m)(5)(A)(i)). An *applicable employer* is any employer from which one or more troubled assets are acquired under TARP if the aggregate amount of the assets so acquired for all tax years (including assets acquired through a direct purchase by the government) exceeds $300 million (Code Sec. 162(m)(5)(B)(i)). Employers that sell troubled assets to the Treasury solely through direct purchases are not included (Code Sec. 162(m)(5)(B)(ii)).

A modified version of the aggregation rules of Code Sec. 414(b) and (c) apply in determining whether an employer is an applicable employer. The rules are applied disregarding the rules for brother-sister controlled groups and combined groups in Code Sec. 1563(a)(2) and (3). Accordingly, this aggregation rule only applies to parent-subsidiary controlled groups (Code Sec. 162(m)(5)(B)(iii), as added by the Emergency Economic Act of 2008). Under the aggregation rules, all corporations in the same controlled group are treated as a single employer for purposes of identifying the covered executives, and all compensation from all members of the controlled group are taken into account for purposes of applying the $500,000 deduction limit. Further, all sales of assets under TARP from all members of the controlled group are considered in determining whether such sales exceed $300 million (Joint Committee on Taxation, Technical Explanation of Division A of P.L. 111-5424, the "Emergency Economic Stabilization Act of 2008" (JCX-79-08)).

An "applicable taxable year" with respect to an applicable employer is the first tax year that includes any portion of the TARP authorities period if the aggregate amount of troubled assets acquired from the employer under that authority during the tax year (when added to the aggregate amount so acquired for all preceding tax years) exceeds $300 million. Any subsequent tax year that includes any portion of the authorities period is also an applicable taxable year (Code Sec. 162(m)(5)(C), as added by the Emergency Economic Act of 2008).

Covered executives include the chief executive officer (CEO) and the chief financial officer (CFO) of an applicable employer (or an individual acting in that capacity), at any time during a portion of the tax year that includes the TARP authorities period. It also includes any employee who is one of the three highest compensated officers of the applicable employer for the applicable taxable year (other than the CEO and CFO), taking into account only employees employed during any portion of the tax year that includes the TARP authorities period. The three highest compensated employees are determined on the basis of the shareholder disclosure rules for compensation under the Securities Exchange Act of 1934 (without regard to whether those rules apply to the employer), and by only taking into account employees employed during the portion of the tax year during which TARP is authorized (Code Sec. 162(m)(5)(D)(i) and (ii), as added by the Emergency Economic Act of 2008). If an employee is a covered executive with respect to an applicable employer for any applicable taxable year, the employee remains a covered executive with respect to

BACKGROUND

that employer for all subsequent applicable taxable years, and for all subsequent tax years in which deferred deduction executive remuneration for services performed in all such applicable taxable years would be deductible (Code Sec. 162(m)(5)(D)(iii), as added by the Emergency Economic Act of 2008).

NEW LAW EXPLAINED

$500,000 compensation deduction limit applies to all TARP recipients.—During the period in which financial assistance under the Troubled Asset Relief Program (TARP) remains outstanding, each TARP recipient will be subject to the $500,000 compensation deduction limit (Code Sec. 162(m)(5)), as well as nontax compensation standards (Act Sec. 7001 of the American Recovery and Reinvestment Tax Act of 2009 (P.L. 111-5), amending Act Sec. 111(b)(1) of the Emergency Economic Stabilization Act of 2008 (P.L. 110-343)). Financial assistance under TARP is not treated as outstanding for a period in which the government only holds warrants to purchase common stock of the TARP recipient (Act Sec. 7001 of the 2009 Recovery Act, amending Division A, Act Sec. 111(a)(5) of the Emergency Economic Act of 2008).

Under the 2009 Recovery Act, the deduction limitation under Code Sec. 162(m)(5) applies "as applicable" to TARP recipients. TARP recipients include any entity (not just financial institutions) that has received or will receive financial assistance under TARP (Act Sec. 7001 of the 2009 Recovery Act, amending Division A, Act Sec. 111(a)(3) of the Emergency Economic Act of 2008). The deduction limit will apply during the period that the TARP obligation remains outstanding. There is no threshold amount of assistance an entity must receive to qualify for TARP recipient treatment for these purposes.

> **Comment:** This provision presumably overrides the "applicable employer" definition in Code Sec. 162(m)(5)(B), which defines applicable employers subject to the deduction limit as (1) employers from which one or more troubled assets are acquired under TARP, and (2) the aggregate amount of which for all tax years (including assets acquired through a direct purchase by the government) exceeds $300 million. It would also seem to affect the definition of "applicable taxable year" as the first tax year the aggregate amount of troubled assets acquired from the employer exceeds $300 million (Code Sec. 162(m)(5)(C)).

Timing. The compensation deduction limit will apply to entities that have taken or will take TARP assistance until they pay it back (Act Sec. 7001 of the 2009 Recovery Act, amending Division A, Act Sec. 111(b)(1) of the Emergency Economic Act of 2008).

> **Comment:** The nontax compensation standards that used to apply only to financial institutions that sold troubled assets directly to the government are also now applicable to any entity receiving TARP assistance, though there are phase-in amounts based on how much assistance a TARP recipient gets for how deeply into management the standards apply.

Compensation standards applicable to TARP recipients. The compensation standards are tougher than the standards included in the original TARP legislation. Among other restrictions, TARP recipients cannot pay or accrue any bonus, retention award, or

NEW LAW EXPLAINED

incentive compensation during the period in which any obligation arising from financial assistance provided under the TARP remains outstanding. There is a limited exception for long-term restricted stock that does not fully vest while any TARP obligation remains outstanding, so long as its value is not greater than 1/3 of the total amount of the employee's annual compensation (Act Sec. 7001 of the 2009 Recovery Act, amending Division A, Act Sec. 111(b)(3)(D)(i) of the Emergency Economic Act of 2008). The prohibition also does not prohibit bonuses required by a written employment contract executed on or before February 11, 2009 (Act Sec. 7001 of the 2009 Recovery Act, amending Division A, Act Sec. 111(b)(3)(D)(iii) of the Emergency Economic Act of 2008).

> **Practical Analysis:** Pamela D. Perdue, author of *Qualified Pension and Profit-Sharing Plans* and Of Counsel with Summers, Compton, Wells & Hamburg in St. Louis, Missouri, notes that while the restrictions have been extended to apply to any entity that receives or will receive financial assistance under TARP, the period in which TARP financing remains outstanding is not deemed to include any period in which the Federal government only holds stock warrants to purchase common stock in the entity.
>
> It is unclear what happens if the restrictions are imposed, and as a result, some or all of the 20 most highly compensated employees cease to fall within that category and are thus replaced by those who were previously below them in compensation. Do the restrictions now apply to those replacement employees or are the restrictions only applied once?

How deeply this prohibition penetrates the executive suite depends on how much TARP assistance the employer receives. For any financial institution that received less than $25 million, the prohibition applies only to its most highly compensated employee. For institutions receiving between $25 and $250 million, the prohibition applies to at least its five most highly-compensated employees (or more if the Secretary of the Treasury so determines). For institutions receiving $250 to $500 million, the prohibition applies to the senior executive officers and at least the 10 next most highly-compensated employees (or more if the Secretary so determines). For institutions receiving $500 million or more, the prohibition applies to the senior executive officers and at least the 20 next most highly-compensated employees (or more if the Secretary so determines) (Act Sec. 7001 of the 2009 Recovery Act, amending Division A, Act Sec. 111(b)(3)(D)(ii) of the Emergency Economic Act of 2008).

> **Comment:** Two common objections to such restrictions are that they won't work as companies are adept at getting around executive compensation limits, and at the same time they will work too well by encouraging a mass exodus of experienced talent from the banks to more highly paid positions elsewhere in the economy at a time when such talent is most needed. A common response is that if these limits do encourage the exodus of the management teams who have presided over these massive failures, maybe that's not so bad. And in any case, the financial industry is shrinking so rapidly there is likely little risk many will be able to secure highly paid positions elsewhere.

¶455

NEW LAW EXPLAINED

A more serious objection is that such compensation restrictions make it difficult for TARP to work as it discourages the people in charge of damaged banks from participating. This was Hank Paulson's objection, and reportedly Secretary of the Treasury Timothy Geithner shares these misgivings. Since it is he who will be enforcing the standards, it is reasonable to expect he will take as light a hand as he can.

▶ **Effective date.** No effective date is provided, so the change is effective upon enactment of the American Recovery and Reinvestment Act of 2009 (P.L. 111-5).

Law source: Law at ¶7075. Committee Report at ¶10,520.

— Act Sec. 7001 of the American Recovery and Reinvestment Act of 2009 (P.L. 111-5), amending Division A, Act Sec. 111(b)(1) of the Emergency Economic Stabilization Act of 2009 (P.L.110-343).

Reporter references: For further information, consult the following CCH reporters.

— Standard Federal Tax Reporter, ¶8636.0267

— Tax Research Consultant, COMPEN: 12,358

— Practical Tax Explanation, § 9,310.05

¶460 Withholding on Certain Payments Made by Government Entities

SUMMARY OF NEW LAW

The date after which federal, state and local government entities are required to begin withholding three percent on certain payments for property or services and reporting the withheld amounts to the IRS is changed from December 31, 2010 to December 31, 2011.

BACKGROUND

Beginning in 2011, the federal government, every state and local government, and all of their political subdivisions and instrumentalities (including multi-state agencies) will be required to withhold tax at the rate of three percent on certain payments to persons providing any property or services (Code Sec. 3402(t)). Any payment made in connection with a government voucher or certificate program that acts as a payment for services or property will be subject to the withholding requirement. The withholding requirement applies even if the government entity making the payment is not the recipient of the property or services.

The withholding requirement does not apply to any payment: (1) which is subject to withholding under any other provision of Chapter 1 regarding income taxes and surtaxes or under Chapter 3 regarding withholding of tax on nonresident aliens and foreign corporations, except as provided in (2) ; (2) which is subject to withholding

BACKGROUND

under Code Sec. 3406 and from which amounts are being withheld under such section; (3) of interest; (4) for real property; (5) to any governmental entity subject to the requirements of Code Sec. 3402(t)(1), any tax-exempt entity or any foreign government; (6) made pursuant to a classified or confidential contract described in Code Sec. 6050M(e)(3); (7) made by a political subdivision of a state (or any instrumentality thereof) which makes less than $100 million of such payments annually; (8) which is made with respect to a public assistance or public welfare program, eligibility for which is determined by a needs or income test; and (9) to any government employee not otherwise excludable with respect to their services as an employee.

Information reporting requirements. For purposes of the liability for the tax under Code Sec. 3403 and the return and payment requirements under Code Sec. 3404, payments to any person for property or services which are subject to withholding are treated as if such payments were wages paid by an employer to an employee. This same treatment applies for purposes of so much of subtitle F (Procedure and Administration), except Code Sec. 7205, as relates to the collection of income tax at source on wages under Chapter 24 (Code Sec. 3402(t)(3)).

NEW LAW EXPLAINED

Withholding and reporting requirements delayed one year.—The new law delays by one year the imposition of the withholding and reporting requirements on certain payments made by the federal government and every state and local government and their political subdivisions and instrumentalities, including multi-state agencies (Act Sec. 1511 of the American Recovery and Reinvestment Tax Act of 2009, P.L. 111-5). The withholding and reporting requirements under Code Sec. 3402(t) will now apply to payments made after December 31, 2011.

> **Practical Analysis:** Charles C. Hwang, Partner, and Jennifer A. Ray, Associate, in the Tax Group at Crowell & Moring LLP, note that the effective date of Code Sec. 3402(t) has been delayed. Code Sec. 3402(t), added to the Code by the Tax Increase Prevention and Reconciliation Act of 2005 (P.L. 109-222), generally requires a government entity to deduct and withhold three percent of the gross amount of any payment it makes to a person providing property or services. That section would have applied to payments made after December 31, 2010. Act Sec. 1511 of the American Recovery and Reinvestment Tax Act delays the effective date of Code Sec. 3402(t) for one year so that it will apply only to payments made after December 31, 2011. Please note that in December 2008, the IRS proposed regulations under Code Sec. 3402(t) (REG-158747-06). Among other things, the proposed regulations provide rules regarding which government entities are required to withhold, which payments are subject to withholding, when withholding is required, and how government entities pay and report tax to the IRS.

▶ **Effective date.** No specific effective date is provided by the Act. The provision is, therefore, considered effective on February 17, 2009, the date of enactment.

NEW LAW EXPLAINED

Law source: Law at ¶7024. Committee Report at ¶10,420.

— Act Sec. 1511 of the American Recovery and Reinvestment Tax Act of 2009 (P.L. 111-5), amending Act Sec. 511(b) of Tax Increase Prevention and Reconciliation Act of 2005 (P.L.109-222).

Reporter references: For further information, consult the following CCH reporters.

— Standard Federal Tax Reporter, ¶33,590S.01
— Tax Research Consultant, FILEBUS: 18,410
— Practical Tax Explanation, §22,405.05

¶465 Estimated Tax of Qualified Individuals

SUMMARY OF NEW LAW

Estimated tax payments of qualified individuals for tax years beginning in 2009 may be based on 90 percent of the individual's prior year's tax liability. An individual is a qualified individual if the adjusted gross income shown on the individual's return for the preceding tax year is less than $500,000 and more than 50 percent of the gross income shown on the return for the preceding tax year is from a business which employed less than 500 employees on average during the calendar year that ends with or within the preceding tax year of the individual.

BACKGROUND

No penalty for failure to pay estimated tax applies to an individual whose tax liability for the tax year, after credit for withheld taxes, is less than $1,000. Also, a U.S. citizen or resident need not pay estimated tax if he or she had no tax liability for the preceding tax year, provided the preceding tax year was a 12-month period. Under circumstances of hardship or following an individual's retirement or disability, the penalty may be waived (Code Sec. 6654(e)).

Individuals who do not qualify for any of these exceptions may generally avoid the penalty for failure to pay estimated tax by:

(1) paying at least 90 percent of the tax shown on the current year's return,

(2) paying 100 percent of the tax shown on the prior year's return (110 percent if adjusted gross income on the prior year's return exceeds $150,000), or

(3) paying installments on a current basis under an annualized income installment method.

An individual may not use the 100-percent-of-prior-year's-tax safe harbor if the prior year was not a 12-month period.

The required payments may be made either through withholding or payment of annual quarterly installments (Code Sec. 6654(d)).

NEW LAW EXPLAINED

Qualified individuals may base estimated tax payments in 2009 on 90 percent of prior year's tax.—In the case of a tax year of a "qualified individual" that begins in 2009, the exception to the estimated tax penalty that is based on paying 100 percent (or 110 percent) of the tax shown on the prior year's return will be satisfied if the qualified individual paid at least 90 percent of the tax shown on the prior year's return (Code Sec. 6654(d)(1)(D), as added by the American Recovery and Reinvestment Tax Act of 2009 (P.L. 111-5)).

A qualified individual means any individual if:

(1) the adjusted gross income shown on the individual's return for the preceding tax year is less than $500,000 ($250,000 for a married person filing separately in the tax year that the installment is being determined), and

(2) the individual certifies that more than 50 percent of the gross income shown on the return for the preceding tax year was "income from a small business" (Code Sec. 6654(d)(1)(D)(ii) and (iv), as added by the 2009 Recovery Act).

Income from a small business means income from a trade or business with an average number of employees of less than 500 persons for the calendar year ending with or within the preceding tax year of the individual (Code Sec. 6654(d)(1)(D)(iii), as added by the 2009 Recovery Act).

Practical Analysis: David Culp, a senior manager in the Federal Tax group of the Washington National Tax practice of KPMG LLP, notes that the American Recovery and Reinvestment Tax Act of 2009 reduces the estimated tax payments certain individuals are required to make for their tax years beginning in 2009. Under current law, individuals can base their estimated tax payments on 100 percent of the tax shown on the preceding year's tax return; this percentage is raised to 110 percent for individuals with more than $150,000 of adjusted gross income in the preceding year.

A "qualified individual" would avoid an estimated tax penalty for 2009 if it makes estimated tax payments based on 90 percent of the tax shown on the tax return for the preceding tax year.

A qualified individual is one who had less than $500,000 of adjusted gross income on the preceding year's tax return ($250,000 for a married individual filing a separate return), and who certifies that more than 50 percent of gross income on that return was from a small business. A small business is a trade or business that had fewer than 500 employees, on average, for the preceding calendar year. The Treasury and the IRS are authorized to issue regulations specifying the form of the certification and the time and manner for its filing.

This provision does not affect an individual's ability to base estimated tax payments on 90 percent of the current year's tax. Also, if a taxpayer does not determine that it is a "qualified individual" until after paying the first installment for 2009, and made a payment of more than 25 percent of 90 percent of the preceding year's tax, current

NEW LAW EXPLAINED

> law provides that later installments can be reduced to reflect the overpayment in the first installment.

The IRS will prescribe regulations that govern the form, manner, and time of certification.

In the case of estates and trusts, adjusted gross income is determined as provided in Code Sec. 67(e) (Code Sec. 6654(d)(1)(D)(v), as added by the 2009 Recovery Act).

▶ **Effective date.** No specific effective date is provided. The provision is, therefore, considered effective on February 17, 2009, the date of enactment.

Law source: Law at ¶5405. Committee Report at ¶10,250.

— Act Sec. 1212 of the American Recovery and Reinvestment Tax Act of 2009 (P.L. 111-5), adding Code Sec. 6654(d)(1)(D).

Reporter references: For further information, consult the following CCH reporters.

— Standard Federal Tax Reporter, ¶39,560.021

— Tax Research Consultant, FILEIND: 15,352

— Practical Tax Explanation, §1,425.10

¶470 Corporate Estimated Tax Payments

SUMMARY OF NEW LAW

The estimated tax payment required to be made by certain large corporations in July, August, September 2013 has been increased to 120.25 percent of the amount otherwise due.

BACKGROUND

A corporation is required to make quarterly estimated tax payments during its tax year based on its annual required payment. Generally, a corporation's required annual payment is 100 percent of the tax shown on its return for the current tax year or the preceding tax year. However, large corporations cannot base their estimated tax payments on the return for the preceding year.

The Tax Increase Prevention and Reconciliation Act of 2005 (P.L.109-222) (TIPRA) increased the estimated tax payment required to made in July, August or September of 2006, 2012 and 2013 for a corporation with assets of $1 billion or more (determined as of the end of the preceding tax year). The next required installment due in October, November, or December of those years was then reduced to offset the increased amount paid in the previous quarter. The amount of estimated tax required to be paid by a large corporation in July, August, or September of 2012 and 2013 has been changed a number of times since the enactment of TIPRA. Currently, the estimated

BACKGROUND

tax payment required to be made in July, August or September of 2013 by a corporation with assets of $1 billion or more is 119.75 percent of the amount otherwise due (Act Sec. 401(1)(C) of the TIPRA, as amended by as amended by P.L. 110-191, §4; P.L. 110-289, §3094(b); and P.L. 110-436, §6). The amount due in October, November, or December of 2013 is 80.25 percent of the amount otherwise due.

> **Comment:** The acceleration and deferral of estimated tax payments in these years is due to fact that the federal government's fiscal year begins on October 1. Thus, changing the amount of estimated tax payments due is designed to meet federal budgetary requirements.

> **Comment:** The increased estimated tax payment required to be made in July, August, or September of 2012 under TIPRA and all subsequent legislation was effectively repealed by Act Sec. 3094(a) of the Housing Assistance Tax Act of 2008 (P.L. 110-289). As a result, the estimated tax payment required to be made in July, August, or September of 2012 by a corporation with assets of $1 billion or more is 100 percent of the amount due.

NEW LAW EXPLAINED

Certain payment of corporate estimated taxes increased.—The estimated tax payment required to be made in July, August, or September of 2013 by a corporation with least $1 billion in assets is increased by 0.5 percentage point, to 120.25 percent, of the amount otherwise due (Act Sec. 704 of Children's Health Insurance Program Reauthorization Act of 2009 (P.L. 111-3)). The next required installment due in October, November or December of 2013 is reduced to 79.75 percent of the amount otherwise due.

> **Practical Analysis:** Kurt Hanway, a senior associate, and Scott Vance, a principal, both in the Federal Tax group of the Washington National Tax practice of KPMG LLP, observe that for corporations with assets of at least $1 billion, estimated tax payments required in July, August and September 2013 will be increased by 0.5 percentage points.
>
> Currently, corporations are required to make quarterly estimated tax payments of their income tax liability. For calendar-year corporations, estimated tax payments are due on April 15, June 15, September 15 and December 15. Fiscal-year corporations pay estimates on the 15th day of the fourth, sixth, ninth and 12th month of the corporation's tax year. In the case of a corporation with assets of at least $1 billion, the Tax Increase Prevention and Reconciliation Act of 2005 (P.L. 109-222) (TIPRA), as amended, increased the required estimated tax payments for payments made in July, August and September of 2013 to 120 percent of the payment otherwise due, and the next required payment is reduced accordingly.
>
> The Children's Health Insurance Program Reauthorization Act of 2009 changes the required estimated tax payment amount for 2013 for corporations with assets of $1 billion or more. The otherwise applicable percentage for estimated tax payments

¶470

NEW LAW EXPLAINED

> required in July, August and September 2013 (120 percent) is now increased by 0.5 percentage points. The amount of the next required estimated tax payment is reduced accordingly.
>
> By increasing the percentage required for estimated payments in July, August and September of 2013, Congress shifts revenue from the 2014 fiscal year into the 2013 fiscal year; affected corporations are allowed to reduce their next estimated tax payment by the amount of the increase. It is important for a corporation to monitor the applicable estimated tax payment percentage as each payment is required, especially given the repeated changes to the applicable percentage for July, August and September 2013 estimated tax payments.

▶ **Effective date.** No specific effective date is provided by the Act. This provision is, therefore, considered effective on February 17, 2009, the date of enactment.

Law source: Law at ¶7090. Committee Reports at ¶15,090.

— Act Sec. 704 of the Children's Health Insurance Program Reauthorization Act of 2009 (P.L. 111-3), amending Act Sec. 401(1)(C) of the Tax Increase Prevention and Reconciliation Act of 2007 (P.L. 109-222) (as amended by P.L. 110-191, §4; P.L. 110-289, §3094(b); and P.L. 110-436, §6).

Reporter references: For further information, consult the following CCH reporters.

— Standard Federal Tax Reporter, ¶39,575.01

— Tax Research Consultant, FILEBUS: 6,050

— Practical Tax Explanation, §26,015.10.

¶470

Business-Related Tax Credits

¶505 Election to Claim Accelerated Credits in Place of Bonus Depreciation
¶510 Energy Credit Portion on Investment Credit
¶515 Grant for Investment in Specified Energy Property
¶520 Renewable Electricity Production Credit
¶525 Credit for Investment in Advanced Energy Facilities
¶530 New Markets Tax Credit
¶535 Grants to Provide Financing for Low-Income Housing
¶540 Incentives to Hire Unemployed Veterans or Disconnected Youth
¶545 Carbon Dioxide Capture Credit

¶505 Election to Claim Accelerated Credits in Place of Bonus Depreciation

SUMMARY OF NEW LAW

A corporation that makes an election to claim an accelerated alternative minimum tax credit or research credit in lieu of claiming bonus depreciation for its first tax year ending after March 31, 2008, may increase its credit limitation by the amount of bonus depreciation claimed with respect to certain "extension" property placed in service in 2009.

BACKGROUND

A corporation that acquires "eligible qualified property" may make an election in its first tax year ending after March 31, 2008, to forgo the bonus depreciation deduction on such property and instead to claim a credit for a portion of its unused alternative minimum tax (AMT) and research credits that are attributable to tax years beginning before January 1, 2006 (Code Sec. 168(k)). Generally, "eligible qualified property" is property that is eligible for bonus depreciation under Code Sec. 168(k) except that it must be acquired after March 31, 2008 (rather than after December 31, 2007) and placed in service before January 1, 2009 (before January 1, 2010 in the case of property with a long production period and certain noncommercial aircraft).

BACKGROUND

The amount of the unused research and AMT credits attributable to tax years beginning before 2006 that may be claimed as an accelerated credit is limited to the "bonus depreciation amount" computed for the tax year. The "bonus depreciation amount" is 20 percent of the difference between:

- the aggregate bonus depreciation and regular depreciation that would be allowed on eligible qualified property placed in service during the tax year if bonus depreciation was claimed; and
- the aggregate straight-line depreciation that would be allowed on the eligible qualified property placed in service during the tax year if no bonus depreciation was claimed.

However, the bonus depreciation amount may not exceed the "maximum increase amount" which is the lesser of: (1) six percent of the sum of the corporation's unused AMT and research credits that are attributable to tax years beginning before January 1, 2006, or (2) $30 million. If the maximum increase amount is less than the otherwise applicable bonus depreciation amount the tax benefit of the accelerated credit election may be substantially diminished.

If a corporation elects to accelerate the AMT and research credits under this provision, it may not claim bonus depreciation on any "eligible qualified property" that it places in service in tax years ending after March 31, 2008. In addition, the electing corporation must use the MACRS straight-line method to depreciate any eligible qualified property placed in service in the tax year of the election and in any later tax year.

NEW LAW EXPLAINED

Election to accelerate AMT and research credits in lieu of bonus depreciation extended.—The rule providing that a corporation may increase its research credit or minimum tax credit limitation by the "bonus depreciation amount" with respect to "eligible qualified property" is extended for one year to apply to property that is placed in service in 2009 (2009 or 2010 in the case of certain longer-lived and transportation property) (Code Sec. 168(k)(4)(D)(iii), as amended by the American Recovery and Reinvestment Tax Act of 2009 (P.L. 111-5)).

However, a taxpayer that has made an election to increase the research credit or minimum tax credit limitation for its first tax year ending after March 31, 2008, may choose not to have the election apply to certain "extension property" (Code Sec. 168(k)(4)(H)(i), as added by the 2009 Recovery Act). In addition, a taxpayer that has not made an election for its first tax year ending after March 31, 2008, may make the election allowed under Code Sec. 168(k)(4) apply only to extension property for its first tax year ending after December 31, 2008 (Code Sec. 168(k)(4)(H)(ii), as added by the 2009 Recovery Act). In the case of a taxpayer electing to increase the research or minimum tax credit for both eligible qualified property and extension property, separate maximum increase amounts are applied to these two groups of property (Code Sec. 168(k)(4)(H)(i)(II), as added by the 2009 Recovery Act).

¶505

NEW LAW EXPLAINED

For this purpose, "extension property" is property that is "eligible qualified property" solely because it meets the requirements for which bonus depreciation may be claimed one additional year if acquired by the taxpayer after December 31, 2008, and before January 1, 2010 (see ¶ 415) (Code Sec. 168(k)(4)(H)(iii), as added by the 2009 Recovery Act).

The provision clarifies that eligible qualified property does not include property acquired pursuant to a written binding contract in effect before April 1, 2008 (Code Sec. 168(k)(4)(D)(ii), as added by the 2009 Recovery Act). For purposes of determining a deficiency, accelerated AMT and research and development credits claimed in lieu of bonus depreciation are taken into account as a negative tax (Code Sec. 6211(b)(4)(A), as amended by the 2009 Recovery Act).

> **Practical Analysis:** David Culp, a senior manager in the Federal Tax group of the Washington National Tax practice of KPMG LLP, notes that the American Recovery and Reinvestment Tax Act of 2009 (2009 Recovery Act) extends for one year the availability of an election corporations can make to forego the benefits of the Code Sec. 168(k) "bonus depreciation" deduction on certain qualified property and instead claim additional R & D or AMT tax credits.
>
> As originally enacted in 2008, a corporation making an election under Code Sec. 168(k)(4) would not take any "bonus depreciation" under Code Sec. 168(k)(1) for "eligible qualified property" acquired and placed in service after March 31, 2008, and such property would be depreciated using the straight-line method. The electing corporation is instead allowed an increase in the limitation under Code Sec. 38(c) on its use of R & D credits or the limitation under Code Sec. 53(c) on the use of AMT credits, or a combination thereof. Any increases in the allowable credits are refundable.
>
> "Eligible qualified property" is defined as qualified property that was acquired (or for which self-construction began) after March 31, 2008. Thus, as originally enacted, it included both qualified property placed in service in calendar year 2008 and certain property placed in service in calendar year 2009. (A discussion of the Code Sec. 168(k) bonus depreciation rules is provided above; those rules were also extended by the legislation.)
>
> The increased credit limitation for a tax year, if the election is made, can not exceed the taxpayer's "bonus depreciation amount." This is 20 percent of the excess of the depreciation deduction (including bonus depreciation) that would be allowed for eligible qualified property placed in service in the tax year, over the amount allowed if there was no bonus depreciation deduction (both amounts computed without regard to any election to use straight-line depreciation).
>
> The aggregate amount of increased credit limitations is the greater of $30 million or six percent of the sum of R & D credit carryforwards into the first tax year ending after March 31, 2008, from tax years beginning before January 1, 2006, and AMT credits allocable to the adjusted minimum tax imposed for tax years beginning before January 1, 2006. These increased limitations could potentially be used over several tax years, as additional eligible qualified property is placed in service. The taxpayer

¶505

NEW LAW EXPLAINED

may allocate the bonus depreciation amount as it chooses each tax year between the two credit limitations.

The members of a controlled group of corporations are treated as one taxpayer for purposes of the election; an election by any member of the group applies to all members of the group.

The 2009 Recovery Act allows a corporation to make a separate election under Code Sec. 168(k)(4) for its first tax year ending after December 31, 2008, that would apply only to eligible qualified property that became eligible for a bonus depreciation deduction solely because of 2009 Recovery Act's one-year extension of Code Sec. 168(k)(1). That is, only qualified property placed in service in calendar year 2009 or calendar year 2010 (other than property that, under prior law, would have been allowed a bonus depreciation deduction when placed in service in 2009) would be eligible qualified property. A new aggregate limitation of the greater of $30 million or six percent of pre-2006 credit carryovers of R & D credits and AMT is available, beginning with the first tax year ending after December 31, 2008. Any additional credits allowed by reason of an election in the first tax year ending after March 31, 2008, would have no bearing on the additional credit limitations generated by making this new election.

The legislation also clarifies that, in computing the bonus depreciation amount for the first tax year ending after March 31, 2008, property is not taken into account if there was a written binding contract in effect for its acquisition before April 1, 2008.

A corporation can choose to make an election under Code Sec. 168(k)(4) for the first tax year ending after March 31, 2008, or for the first tax year ending after December 31, 2008, or for both years. There will be potentially $30 million of additional credits allowed under each election. Because the earlier election would potentially allow additional credits to be used on account of eligible qualified property placed in service in 2009, it is possible that a corporation could claim more than $30 million of additional research credits and AMT credits in a 2009 tax year.

Practical Analysis: Glenn A. Graff, a partner at Applegate & Thorne-Thomsen, P.C., Chicago, notes that the American Recovery and Reinvestment Tax Act of 2009 reenacts 50-percent bonus depreciation which had previously expired. The reenactment has a few noteworthy points. First, the bonus depreciation is available for qualifying property placed in service before January 1, 2010, and for certain longer production period property placed in service before January 1, 2011. However, as with the prior bonus depreciation, property qualifying for placement in service after January 1, 2010, but before January 1, 2011, will only receive bonus depreciation on costs incurred prior to January 1, 2010. Second, the extension of bonus depreciation retains the requirement that the property have a depreciation recovery period. Thus for real estate projects bonus depreciation would not be available for building costs but would be available for personal property and site improvements. In addition, for site improvements that qualify for the longer production period provision described above, placement in service can occur during 2010 although bonus depreciation will be limited to costs incurred prior to January 1, 2010. Third, the requirement that construction or acquisition not occur prior to December 31, 2007, has not changed.

¶505

NEW LAW EXPLAINED

This is fortunate and avoids issues that could have occurred for assets which had been acquired but not placed in service or for which there was a binding agreement to acquire the asset but delivery had not yet occurred. For example, a contract to purchase equipment which was signed on January 1, 2009, should qualify for bonus depreciation as long as the assets are actually received and placed in service within the timing and other bonus depreciation requirements.

Practical Analysis: John O. Everett, Ph.D., CPA, tax professor at Virginia Commonwealth University, Cherie J. Hennig, Ph.D., CPA, tax professor at Florida International University, and William A. Raabe, Ph.D., CPA, tax professor at the Ohio State University comment that the extension of the credits acceleration election of Code Sec. 168(k)(4) provides for a more orderly planning of capital acquisitions during the tax year. The election has been subject to much confusion, since Congress enacted a powerful incentive to make capital investments right away (bonus depreciation) in February 2008, and then in July 2008 offered another powerful incentive to give up the previous "powerful incentive" of bonus depreciation for cash by monetizing unused credits. Taxpayers had only a nine-month window to analyze the effects of this election, and the IRS offered precious little guidance in two revenue procedures issued around year-end.

Despite this welcomed extension of the acceleration election, there remain significant unanswered questions about the credit that hopefully Treasury will address soon. These include the following:[*]

The computed "bonus depreciation amount" (*e.g.*, the maximum credits that may be monetized) is limited to the lesser of (1) $30 million or (2) six percent of the qualifying unused pre-2006 research and AMT credits. On the other hand, Code Sec. 168(k)(4)(A)(i) states that "... [bonus depreciation]shall not apply to *any* [emphasis supplied] eligible property placed in service by the taxpayer," and Code Sec. 168(k)(4)(A)(ii) states that "... the applicable depreciation method under this section with respect to such property shall be the straight line method." Does this mean that the taxpayer must use straight-line recovery on *all* eligible property placed in service during the qualifying period, even if this total exceeds the amount necessary to qualify for the maximum credit?

Example. Crane Corporation placed into service $10 million of qualifying five-year bonus depreciation property in 2009. Their allowable "bonus depreciation amount" is $800,000, or 20 percent of the excess of cost recovery with bonus depreciation ($6 million) over cost recovery without bonus depreciation ($2 million). However, six percent of Crane's unused research and AMT credits is only $600,000. If Crane makes the election, will Crane be required to use straight-line recovery on the entire $10 million, even though only $7.5 million of eligible property would have been required to provide the maximum $600,000 bonus depreciation amount?

---

[*] For a discussion of these and other unresolved issues with the 2008 provision, see William A. Raabe, Cherie J. Hennig and John O. Everett, *Congress: How About a Mulligan For the Acceleration Election?* CXXII TAX NOTES 2 (Jan. 12, 2009), at 222-26.

NEW LAW EXPLAINED

If a corporation's qualifying property placed in service in 2009 does not exceed $1.05 million, what is the interplay of the Code Sec. 179 election and the acceleration election? Under the Code, the Code Sec. 179 election is made first, and the amount of bonus depreciation amount seems to be computed after the Code Sec. 179 amount is claimed. This raises the question of whether the bonus depreciation amount is computed only "after Code Sec. 179," or must straight-line cost recovery be used on all of the year's acquisitions if the election is made?

If a research credit expired after 2005, will it still be available for the election as a "pre-2006" unused credit? Corporate taxpayers considering an acceleration election should consider the following observations:

The acceleration election appears to have been designed to help struggling loss companies to monetize credits that they may never be able to use. But the election may be advantageous to profitable companies as well. Present value analysis is needed for such an important decision, in that the value of the monetized credits received today must be compared with the cost of foregoing bonus and regular MACRS procedures on all eligible property placed into service. See the example provided below.

The "bonus depreciation amount" is a function of the MACRS asset classes of the eligible properties. Simple algebra can be used to determine the percentage of asset cost by class that is converted to a bonus depreciation amount. These percentages are:

3-year property—6.67 percent of total cost

5-year property—8.00 percent of total cost

7-year property—8.57 percent of total cost

10-year property—9.00 percent of total cost

15-year property—9.50 percent of total cost

20-year property—9.63 percent of total cost

However, if present value analysis is performed on the election and the no election options with a constant dollar amount of investment for a single MACRS class, the five-year class offers the largest tax savings. Using a present value model developed by the authors, investments in five-year MACRS class assets offer the highest projected cost savings.

$5 Million Investment—Expected Tax Savings by MACRS Class

Asset Class	Projected Tax Cost (Savings) of Election
3-year MACRS	($186,691)
5-year MACRS	($344,400)
7-year MACRS	($197,786)
10-year MACRS	($165,624)
15-year MACRS	($143,202)
20-year MACRS	($89,756)

Ironically, if the mid-quarter convention applies, the bonus depreciation amount actually increases the bonus depreciation amount. In the earlier example involving a

¶505

NEW LAW EXPLAINED

$10 million investment in five-year MACRS property, the bonus depreciation amount using a mid-quarter convention (assuming that the property is placed in service in the last three months of the year) increases from $800,000 to $950,000.

The American Recovery and Reinvestment Tax Act of 2009 allows taxpayers who did make the election in 2008 to opt out of making the election in 2009, and likewise allows taxpayers who did not make the election in 2008 to "opt in" in 2009. However, the revised statute is worded in such a way to prevent a taxpayer from doubling up on the same eligible property during the 21-month eligibility period.

Before deciding to elect bonus depreciation, corporations with unused tax credit carryforwards should consider whether to forego the bonus deduction and instead elect to accelerate its tax credits.

Example. Corporation A purchased two depreciable assets that qualify for the 50-percent bonus depreciation deduction. In addition A has unused Research and AMT credits that it has been carrying forward. Corporation A has the option to forego the bonus depreciation deduction and claim a portion of the unused business credits against its regular tax liability. If A claims the bonus depreciation deduction the net present value of the tax savings over the depreciable life of the assets is approximately $2,656,000. If A foregoes the bonus depreciation and depreciates the assets over their MACRS lives, it can claim an immediate credit against its regular income tax of $600,000. The present value of the immediate credit option is approximately $2,985,000 (i.e., the refundable credit plus straight-line recovery). The tax cost associated with the bonus depreciation deduction over the tax credit option is approximately $329,000.

Bonus Deduction Example

	Total Cost	*Maximum Credits*
5-year property	$3,000,000	$240,000
7-year property	$5,000,000	$428,500
Total Cost	$8,000,000	$668,500
Maximum Bonus Depreciation Deduction at 50%	$4,000,000	
Research credit carryforward		$8,000,000
AMT credit carryforward		$2,000,000
Total Unused Credits		$10,000,000
Maximum Allowable Credit at 6%		$600,000
PV Tax Savings, at 5% discount rate		
Bonus Depreciation		$2,656,000
Maximum Credit		$2,985,000
Tax Cost of Bonus Depreciation		$(329,000)

¶505

NEW LAW EXPLAINED

▶ **Effective date.** This provision applies to property placed in service in tax years beginning after December 31, 2008, in tax years ending after such date (Act Sec. 1201(c)(1) of the American Recovery and Reinvestment Tax Act of 2009 (P.L. 111-5)). The binding contract and deficiency provisions apply to tax years ending after March 31, 2008 (Act Sec. 1201(c)(2) of the 2009 Recovery Act).

Law source: Law at ¶5240 and ¶5375. Committee Report at ¶10,220.

— Act Sec. 1201(a)(3)(A) of the American Recovery and Reinvestment Tax Act of 2009 (P.L. 111-5), redesignating Code Sec. 168(k)(4)(D)(ii) as (iii) and adding Code Sec. 168(k)(4)(D)(ii);

— Act Sec. 1201(a)(3)(B) and (b)(2), amending Code Sec. 6211(b)(4)(A);

— Act Sec. 1201(b), amending Code Sec. 168(k)(4);

— Act Sec. 1201(c)(1) providing the effective date.

Reporter references: For further information, consult the following CCH reporters.

— Standard Federal Tax Reporter, ¶11,279.0583

— Tax Research Consultant, DEPR: 3,606

— Practical Tax Explanation, §11,225.25

¶510 Energy Credit Portion of Investment Credit

SUMMARY OF NEW LAW

The credit cap applicable to small wind energy property and the special basis reduction rule for energy property financed by subsidized energy financing or industrial development bonds have been eliminated. In addition, a taxpayer is provided a special temporary election to claim the energy credit portion of the investment tax credit in lieu of the production tax credit for certain qualified energy production facilities.

BACKGROUND

The Code Sec. 46 investment credit is composed of several separate credits: the rehabilitation credit, the energy credit, the qualifying advanced coal project credit, and the qualifying gasification project credit. The energy credit component equals a specified percentage of the basis of each qualified energy property placed in service during the tax year (Code Sec. 48(a)(1)). Qualified energy property includes solar property, geothermal property, qualified fuel cell property or stationary microturbine property, combined heat and power system property, qualified small wind energy property, and geothermal heat pump systems (Code Sec. 48(a)(3)).

The energy credit includes 30 percent of the basis of solar energy property, hybrid solar lighting systems, qualified fuel cell property, and "qualified small wind energy property" incurred by the taxpayer during the year (Code Sec. 48(a)(2)(A)). For this purpose, "qualified small wind energy property" is property that uses a qualifying

BACKGROUND

wind turbine to generate electricity. A "qualifying wind turbine" means a wind turbine of 100 kilowatts of rated capacity or less. The maximum credit that may be claimed for qualified small wind energy property placed in service during the tax year is limited to $4,000 (Code Sec. 48(c)(4)). The energy credit also includes 10 percent of the basis of stationary microturbine property, combined heat and power system property, geothermal property, geothermal heat pump systems.

The total amount of energy credit claimed by the taxpayer for the tax year for all qualified energy property must be reduced if the property is also financed with industrial development bonds or through any other federal, state, or local subsidized financing program. In determining the amount of the energy credit, the basis of energy property that is financed in whole or in part by the proceeds of tax-exempt private activity bonds or by subsidized energy financing must be reduced in the same proportion that the basis attributable to those sources bears to the basis of the property. This is computed by multiplying the basis of the property by (1 minus the above fraction) (Code Sec. 48(a)(4)). Similar rules apply for purposes of the qualifying advanced coal project credit (Code Sec. 48A) and the qualifying gasification project credit (Code Sec. 48B). In addition, any expenditures made with funds obtained from subsidized energy financing are ineligible for the residential energy property credit (Code Sec. 25C(e)(1)) or the residential alternative energy credit (Code Sec. 25D(e)).

> **Practical Analysis:** Glenn A. Graff, a partner at Applegate & Thorne-Thomsen, P.C., Chicago, explains that under prior law, the investment tax credit under Code Sec. 48 was reduced to the extent that property was financed by tax-exempt private activity bond bonds or by subsidized energy financing. Code Sec. 48(a)(4)(C) defined subsidized energy financing as "financing provided under a Federal, State, or local program a principal purpose of which is to provide subsidized financing for projects designed to conserve or produce energy." The result of such reduction was a decrease in the effectiveness of state programs designed to encourage renewable energy projects because the subsidy indirectly resulted in less federal credits. The elimination of such provisions will provide more federal credits (or grants) where such property also received subsidized energy financing or uses tax-exempt bonds. This increase in credits should increase the feasibility of such projects allowing more renewable energy projects to go forward. This achieves one of the stated purposes of the stimulus legislation, which was to increase the amount of the United States' electricity produced from renewable resources.

In addition to the energy investment credit, a taxpayer is allowed an income tax credit for the production of electricity from qualified energy resources at qualified facilities (Code Sec. 45). Qualified energy resources comprise wind, closed-loop biomass, open-loop biomass, geothermal energy, solar energy, small irrigation power, municipal solid waste, qualified hydropower production, and marine and hydrokinetic renewable energy (Code Sec. 45(c)(1)). Qualified facilities are, generally, facilities that generate electricity using qualified energy resources (Code Sec. 45(d)). To be eligible for the credit, electricity produced from qualified energy resources at qualified facilities must be sold by the taxpayer to an unrelated person (Code Sec. 45(a)).

¶510

NEW LAW EXPLAINED

Repeal of certain energy credit limitations; election to claim energy credit in lieu of production credit.—A number of changes have been made regarding the amount of energy credit that a taxpayer can claim. First, the energy credit cap for small wind energy property has been eliminated, as well as the requirement that energy property basis must be reduced for property acquired with subsidized energy financing or private bonds. Second, an election to treat certain qualified facilities producing electricity as energy property for purposes of the investment credit has been established.

Small wind energy property. The $4,000 credit cap applicable to qualified small wind energy property has been eliminated for periods after 2008, thus allowing an uncapped 30 percent credit to be claimed for such property (Code Sec. 48(c)(4), as amended by the 2009 Recovery Act).

Basis reduction for subsidized financing. The rule that reduces the basis of the property for purposes of claiming the energy credit if the property is financed in whole or in part by subsidized energy financing or with proceeds from private activity bonds is also eliminated for periods after December 31, 2008 (Code Sec. 48(a)(4)(D), as added by the American Recovery and Reinvestment Tax Act of 2009 (P.L. 111-5)). Thus, businesses and individuals will qualify for the full amount of the energy credit even if the property is financed with industrial development bonds or through any other subsidized energy financing. The basis reduction rule continues to apply for purposes of the qualifying advanced coal project credit and the qualifying gasification project credit (Code Secs. 48A(b)(2) and 48B(b)(2), as amended by the 2009 Recovery Act). The rules that any expenditures made with funds obtained from subsidized energy financing are ineligible for the residential energy property credit or the residential alternative energy credit have been eliminated (Code Secs. 25C(e)(1) and 25D(e), as amended by the 2009 Recovery Act). For discussions of additional modifications to the residential energy credit and the residential alternative energy credit, see ¶ 335 and ¶ 340, respectively.

Transition rules. The credit cap on small wind energy property and the basis reduction rule in the case of subsidized energy financing will not apply to the construction, reconstruction, or erection of property (small wind or energy) completed by the taxpayer after 2008 to the extent of the cost attributable to the construction, reconstruction or erection after 2008, and to acquisitions of small wind or energy property made after 2008 and placed in service after 2008 (Act Sec. 1103(c)(1) of the 2009 Recovery Act). For any small wind or energy property having a normal construction period of more than two years, the small wind energy cap and the basis reduction rule will not apply to expenditures made after 2008.

Practical Analysis: Charles R. Goulding, J.D., CPA, MBA, and President of Energy Tax Savers Inc. of Syosset, New York, notes that wind turbine facilities require large capital investments and that in the current financial environment it has been difficult to raise capital to fund these projects. While the production credit was instrumental in increasing return on investment and payback over the life cycle of these projects, an investment credit will help lower the first cost capital outlay and allow more projects

NEW LAW EXPLAINED

> to hurdle the current funding environment. Act Sec. 1603 of the American Recovery and Reinvestment Tax Act of 2009 provides a further financing alternative enabling an investor to receive an immediate grant in lieu of an investment tax credit. The grant provision is designed to mirror the tax credit alternative. The amount of the grant is not included in taxable income; however, the depreciable basis of the property is reduced by 50 percent of the grant, just as the depreciable basis is reduced by 50 percent of the tax credit.

Investment credit election. A taxpayer may make an irrevocable election to treat certain qualified property that is part of a qualified investment credit facility placed in service in 2009 through 2013 as energy property eligible for a 30-percent investment credit under Code Sec. 48(a)(5) (as added by the 2009 Recovery Act). If the election is made, no production credit will be allowed under Code Sec. 45 for any tax year with respect to any qualified investment credit facility (Code Sec. 48(a)(5)(B), as added by the 2009 Recovery Act).

For purposes of the credit, qualified investment credit facilities are facilities otherwise eligible for the Code Sec. 45 production tax credit with respect to which no credit under Code Sec. 45 has been allowed. Qualified facilities (within the meaning of Code Sec. 45) include those producing electricity using wind, closed-loop biomass, open-loop biomass, geothermal energy, landfill gas, municipal solid waste (trash), hydropower, or marine and hydrokinetic renewable energy. In order to qualify for the election, wind facilities must be placed in service in 2009 through 2012. All other facilities must be placed in service in 2009 through 2013 in order to qualify (Code Sec. 48(a)(5)(C), as added by the 2009 Recovery Act).

> **Caution:** Not all Code Sec. 45(d) facilities are eligible to make this election. Facilities producing electricity using refined coal, Indian coal, or solar energy are not qualified facilities for purposes of the election.

Qualified property is property that is (1) tangible personal property or (2) other tangible property (not including a building or its structural components), but only if such property is used as an integral part of the qualified investment credit facility and with respect to which depreciation (or amortization in lieu of depreciation) is allowable (Code Sec. 48(a)(5)(D), as added by the 2009 Recovery Act).

> **Comment:** The House Ways and Means Committee notes that because of the current market conditions, it is difficult for many renewable energy projects to find financing. The temporary election allows certain qualified facilities that are placed in service in 2009 through 2013 to claim the investment tax credit instead of the production tax credit (Committee on Ways and Means, Summary of the Tax Relief Included in the "American Recovery and Reinvestment Plan").

> **Practical Analysis:** Katherine Breaks, Director in the Federal Tax Legislative and Regulatory Services group of the Washington National Tax practice of KPMG LLP, observes that the American Recovery and Reinvestment Tax Act of 2009 permits qualified facilities to claim a 30-percent investment tax credit in lieu of the production

NEW LAW EXPLAINED

tax credit for the production of electricity from renewable resources ("production tax credit"). The election is available for qualifying projects placed in service in 2009, 2010, 2011, 2012 or 2013. In the case of wind, the election does not apply to projects placed in service after 2012. The decision whether to elect the investment credit in lieu of production tax involves a number of tax considerations.

Under current law, certain renewable energy projects may be eligible for the production tax credit for the production of electricity from renewable resources ("production tax credit.") The production tax credit for electricity produced from renewable resources is generally claimed over a 10-year period. This production tax credit is not refundable.

Developers of renewable energy projects often seek investors (so-called tax investors) that are allocated 99 percent of the income, gains, losses, deductions and tax credits of the project. See Rev. Proc. 2007-65, IRB 2007-45, 967, for a description of such structures.

In the current economic environment, potential tax investors may not be confident that they will be paying enough federal income tax over a 10-year period to be able to claim the production tax credit on a current basis. To alleviate that uncertainty, the provision permits tax investors to forego the 10-year credit in favor of a credit that can be claimed entirely in the year the facility is placed in service. The investment tax credit option may be attractive to tax investors that are not sure of their tax liability in the future.

Developers and investors that elect to claim the investment tax credit for energy property (ITC) in lieu of the production tax credit face a number of tax structuring challenges that are unique to the ITC.

For instance, developers will want to be mindful not trigger the five-year credit recapture rules that apply to the ITC. The ITC recapture provision applies if the project is sold within five years (Code Sec. 50). In addition, the recapture provision applies if a partner in a partnership that owns the facility reduces its interest in the partnership by more than a third (Reg. § 1.47-6(a)(2)).

For regulated utilities, the decision to claim the ITC presents unique issues as well. Specifically, the ITC yields a different result for ratemaking purposes. The ITC is required to be normalized, Reg. § 1.46-6, whereas most utility commissions will "flow through" the benefit of the production tax credit to the ratepayer.

Other special structuring decisions are raised by the choice of claiming the ITC. For instance, if the developer and investor decide to claim the ITC, they would have the additional option of entering into a sale-leaseback transaction for the investment. A sale leaseback transaction would have the effect of permitting the parties to allocate the tax credit to an investor who will be paying sufficient federal income tax in the year the facility is placed in service to claim the tax credit on a current basis. Sale-leaseback transactions cannot be used for projects that claim the production tax credit because the production tax credit rules require the owner of the facility to also be the operator of the facility.

Finally, the decision to choose the ITC would affect the depreciation calculations for the project. Under the ITC rules, adjusted basis of the facility must be reduced by one-half of the ITC claimed. Code Sec. 50(c)(3). Further, if bonus depreciation is

NEW LAW EXPLAINED

> available (see earlier discussion on bonus), the taxpayer needs to consider the basis adjustment ordering rules. The tax owner of the project would, first, adjust the basis of the project by one-half of the credit claimed. Next, the tax owner would calculate bonus depreciation using that adjusted basis. Finally, the tax owner would calculate regular depreciation for the tax year on the remaining basis.

▶ **Effective dates.** The investment credit election applies to facilities placed in service after December 31, 2008 (Act Sec. 1102(b) of the American Recovery and Reinvestment Tax Act of 2009 (P.L. 111-5)). The elimination of the small wind property credit cap and the termination of the basis reduction rule, along with conforming amendments to Code Secs. 48A, and 48B, apply to periods after December 31, 2008, under rules similar to the rules of Code Sec. 48(m), as in effect on the day before the enactment of the Revenue Reconciliation Act of 1990 (P.L. 101-508) (Act Sec. 1103(c)(1) of the 2009 Recovery Act). Conforming amendments under Code Secs. 25C and 25D apply to tax years beginning after December 31, 2008 (Act Sec. 1103(c)(2) of the 2009 Recovery Act).

Law source: Law at ¶5025, ¶5030, ¶5110, ¶5115, and ¶5120. Committee Report at ¶10,110 and ¶10,120.

— Act Sec. 1102(a) of the American Recovery and Reinvestment Tax Act of 2009 (P.L. 111-5), adding Code Sec. 48(a)(5);

— Act Sec. 1103(a), striking Code Sec. 48(c)(4)(B) and redesignating Code Sec. 48(c)(4)(C) and (D) as Code Sec. 48(c)(4)(B) and (C);

— Act Sec. 1103(b), adding Code Sec. 48(a)(4)(D) and amending Code Secs. 25C(e)(1), 25D(e), 48A(b)(2), and 48B(b)(2);

— Act Secs. 1102(b) and 1103(c), providing the effective dates.

Reporter references: For further information, consult the following CCH reporters.

— Standard Federal Tax Reporter, ¶4671.01

— Tax Research Consultant, BUSEXP: 51,100

— Practical Tax Explanation, § 13,710

¶515 Grant for Investment in Specified Energy Property

SUMMARY OF NEW LAW

Each person who places an electricity production facility otherwise eligible for the renewable electricity credit or qualifying property otherwise eligible for the energy credit into service during 2009 or 2010, or after 2010 but before the credit termination date if construction for the property began during 2009 or 2010, will receive a grant of up to 30 percent of the basis of that property.

BACKGROUND

A renewable electricity income tax credit is allowed for the production of electricity from qualified energy resources at qualified facilities (Code Sec. 45). Qualified energy resources comprise wind, closed-loop biomass, open-loop biomass, geothermal energy, solar energy, small irrigation power, municipal solid waste, qualified hydropower production and marine and hydrokinetic renewable energy. Qualified facilities are generally facilities that generate electricity using qualified energy resources. To be eligible for the credit, electricity produced from qualified energy resources at qualified facilities must be sold by the taxpayer to an unrelated person. The amount of the credit is 1.5 cents (adjusted annually for inflation) for each kilowatt hour of electricity sold by the taxpayer during the tax year that is produced from qualified resources at a qualified facility within ten years after the facility is originally placed in service.

In addition to the renewable electricity production credit, a taxpayer is allowed to claim a credit under Code Sec. 46 for the investment in certain property. The investment credit is composed of several separate credits: the rehabilitation credit, the energy credit, the qualifying advanced coal project credit, and the qualifying gasification project credit. The energy credit is allowed for certain energy property placed in service (Code Sec. 48). Qualifying property includes certain fuel cell property, solar property, geothermal power production property, small wind energy property, combined heat and power system property and geothermal heat pump property. The credit is generally equal to 30 percent of the taxpayer's basis in qualified fuel cell property, certain solar energy property, and qualified wind energy property; and 10 percent of the taxpayer's basis in other types of energy property.

Qualified energy property generally must be placed in service during the tax year. However, a taxpayer may elect to apply the credit percentage to qualified progress expenditures paid or incurred during the tax year, that is, construction expenditures for energy property with a normal construction period of two years or more. To qualify for the energy credit, the property must be either constructed, erected, or reconstructed by the taxpayer, or acquired by the taxpayer if the original use of the property commences with the taxpayer. In addition, the property must qualify for depreciation or amortization. Finally, the property must meet performance and quality standards set by the IRS (after consultation with the Department of Energy) and are in effect when the property is acquired.

NEW LAW EXPLAINED

Grants given for specified energy property placed in service in 2009 or 2010 instead of tax credits.—The Secretary of Treasury is authorized to provide a grant to each person who places into service specified energy property that is either: (1) an electricity production facility otherwise eligible for the renewable electricity production credit under Code Sec. 45, or (2) qualifying property otherwise eligible for the energy investment credit under Code Sec. 48 (Act Sec. 1603(a) of the American Recovery and Reinvestment Tax Act of 2009 (P.L. 111-5). Applications must be received by the Secretary of the Treasury by October 1, 2011, for the grant to be made (Act Sec. 1603(j) of the 2009 Recovery Act). However, no grant may be awarded to any

¶515

NEW LAW EXPLAINED

(1) any Federal, state or local government (or any political subdivision, agency or instrumentality thereof);

(2) any Code Sec. 501(c) tax-exempt entity;

(3) any qualified issuer of clean renewable energy bonds under Code Sec. 54(j)(4); or

(4) any partnership or other pass-through entity partner (or holder of an equity or profit interest) described in (1), (2) or (3) above (Act Sec. 1603(g) of the 2009 Recovery Act).

Comment: The 2009 Recovery Act appropriates to the Secretary of Treasury the funds necessary to make the grants under this provision (Act Sec. 1603(i) of the 2009 Recovery Act).

> **Practical Analysis:** Glenn A. Graff, a partner at Applegate & Thorne-Thomsen, P.C., Chicago, observes the law allows projects, which would have qualified for the tax credit under Code Sec. 45 for the production of renewable electricity, to claim the 30-percent investment tax credit under Code Sec. 45. In addition, property electing to receive the investment tax credit can also elect to receive a 30-percent grant rather than the 30-percent tax credit. The receipt of an energy credit or grant rather than the production credit is a significant change for qualifying property. Rather than receiving a production credit over five or 10 years, such property would be eligible to receive a 30-percent credit or 30-percent grant in the year such property is placed in service. The ability to receive the credit or grant at such an early date should help owners finance such projects. In addition, the ability to receive credits on capitalized costs including a development fee may create a significant incentive for property owners to make this election.

Specified energy property. To be eligible, a grant applicant must place into service the following specified property unless depreciation (or amortization in lieu of depreciation) is not allowable with respect to such property:

- certain qualified property (as defined in Code Sec. 48(a)(5)(D)), which is a part of a qualified facility under Code Sec. 45(d) including a wind facility, closed-loop biomass facility, open-loop biomass facility, geothermal energy facility, landfill gas facility, trash combustion facility, qualified hydropower facility, marine and hydrokinetic renewable energy facility;
- qualified fuel cell property (Code Sec. 48(c)(1));
- solar property (Code Sec. 48(a)(3)(A)(i) or (ii));
- qualified small wind energy property (Code Sec. 48(c)(4));
- geothermal property (Code Sec. 48(a)(3)(A)(iii));
- qualified microturbine property (Code Sec. 48(c)(2));
- combined heat and power system property (Code Sec. 48(c)(3)); and
- geothermal heat pump property (Code Sec. 48(a)(3)(A)(vii)) (Act Sec. 1603(d) of the 2009 Recovery Act).

¶515

NEW LAW EXPLAINED

The specified property must be placed in service either during 2009 or 2010, or after 2010 but before the credit termination date for such property if construction for the property began during 2009 or 2010 (Act Sec. 1603(a) of the 2009 Recovery Act). The credit termination date is: January 1, 2013, for a wind facility; January 1, 2014, for a closed-loop biomass facility, open-loop biomass facility, geothermal energy facility, landfill gas facility, trash combustion facility, qualified hydropower facility, marine and hydrokinetic renewable energy facility; and January 17, 2017, for specified property otherwise eligible for the energy credit under Code Sec. 48 (Act Sec. 1603(e) of the 2009 Recovery Act).

> **Practical Analysis:** John P. Gimigliano, a principal in the Sustainability Tax group of the Washington National Tax practice of KPMG LLP, notes that Act Sec. 1104 of the American Recovery and Reinvestment Tax Act of 2009 provides that if a developer of a renewable energy project receives a grant pursuant to Act Sec. 1603 of the 2009 Recovery Act, then the project is not eligible for the production tax credit for electricity produced by certain renewable energy facilities or the investment tax credit for certain renewable energy property.
>
> The 2009 Recovery Act provides that taxpayers that develop renewable energy projects are eligible for a grant equal to up to 30 percent of the basis of property used to produce electricity from wind energy, closed-loop biomass, open-loop biomass, geothermal, landfill gas, trash combustion, incremental hydropower, marine and hydrokinetic energy, fuel cell property, solar property and small wind property. Further, taxpayers that develop renewable energy projects are eligible for a grant equal to up to 10 percent of the basis of property used to produce electricity from geothermal (i.e., property not eligible for the 30 percent rate), microturbines, combined heat and power system property, and geothermal heat pump property. In calculating the potential grant award, taxpayers will need to make an allocation of their capitalized costs between those that are incurred for eligible property (e.g., property that is used to produce electricity from wind energy), and those that are incurred for ineligible property (e.g., land improvements, buildings and structures). Eligible projects must be placed in service after 2008, and before 2014 (before 2013 for wind, and before 2017 for solar). Under the program, construction of the facility must begin before 2011. The grant award is excluded from gross income. The initial adjusted basis of the property must be reduced by one-half of the grant money received.
>
> The grant program was enacted, in part, to respond to inefficiencies in the investment market for renewable energy projects. Developers of renewable energy projects often seek investors (so-called tax investors) that are allocated 99 percent of the income, gains, losses, deductions and tax credits of the project. *See* Rev. Proc. 2007-65, IRB 2007-45, 967, for a description of such ventures. In the current economic environment, potential tax investors may not be paying federal income taxes and therefore may be reluctant to make these investments. The creation of a grant program removes this obstacle by permitting developers to obtain a federal subsidy by means of a government grant instead of a tax credit.
>
> Developers may find that the grant program does not completely eliminate the problem of maximizing available federal subsidies. This is because most renewable

¶515

NEW LAW EXPLAINED

> energy projects are eligible for accelerated cost recovery and, as a result, generally generate tax losses during the first six or seven years of operation. Many developers may not be able to use those tax losses to offset other income on a current basis and may still find it necessary to seek tax investors to maximize the value of these projects.
>
> Furthermore, it is not yet clear how a direct grant paid after the project is placed in service solves the larger problem of obtaining project level financing given the current state of the financial markets.

Grant amount. The amount of the grant will be an applicable percentage of the basis of the specified energy property placed into service (Act Sec. 1603(b)(1) of the 2009 Recovery Act). The applicable percentage is 30 percent for qualified facilities, qualified fuel cell property, solar property, and qualified small wind energy property (Act Sec. 1603(b)(2) of the 2009 Recovery Act). For any other property, the applicable percentage is 10 percent. However, in the case of qualified fuel cell property, qualified microturbine property, or combined heat and power system property, the amount of the grant cannot exceed the credit limitation established, respectively, with respect to such property under Code Sec. 48 (Act Sec. 1603(b)(3) of the 2009 Recovery Act).

Comment: The energy credit for any qualified fuel cell property is limited to $500 ($1,500, effective for periods after October 3, 2008, in tax years ending after that date) for each 0.5 kilowatt of capacity of such property (Code Sec. 48(c)(1)(B)). The energy credit for stationary microturbine power plants is limited to $200 for each kilowatt of capacity of such property (Code Sec. 48(c)(2)(B)).

The otherwise allowable energy credit with respect to combined heat and power system property is reduced to the extent the property has an electrical capacity or mechanical capacity in excess of any applicable limits. For property in excess of the applicable limit (15 megawatts or a mechanical energy capacity of more than 20,000 horsepower or an equivalent combination of electrical and mechanical energy capacities), a fraction of the otherwise allowable credit is allowed. The fraction is equal to the applicable limit divided by the capacity of the property. For example, a 45 megawatt property would be eligible for 15/45ths, or one third, of the otherwise allowable credit. No credit is allowed if the system has a capacity of more than 50 megawatts or 67,000 horsepower (Code Sec. 48(c)(3)(B)).

The grant will be paid during the 60-day period beginning on the later of the date of the application for the grant or the date the property is placed into service (Act Sec. 1603(c) of the 2009 Recovery Act). The amount of the grant received is not includible in the gross income of the taxpayer, but is taken into account for determining the basis of the specified energy property (Code Sec. 48(d)(3) as added by the 2009 Recovery Act). The basis of that property is reduced under rules similar to those that apply for the investment tax credit under Code Sec. 50. Thus, the basis of the specified property for which the grant is made must be reduced by 50 percent of the amount of the grant. Accordingly, the reduction of basis affects the computation of depreciation deductions and the computation of gain or loss upon disposition of the property.

¶515

NEW LAW EXPLAINED

In addition, if the specified property is disposed of by the grant recipient or ceases to be a specified property within five years of being placed in service, some or all of the grant will be subject to recapture. The Secretary of Treasury will provide for appropriate percentage of the grant amount to be recaptured and the manner in which the grant will be recaptured (Act Sec. 1603(f) of the 2009 Recovery Act).

> **Practical Analysis:** Glenn A. Graff, a partner at Applegate & Thorne-Thomsen, P.C., Chicago, explains that Act Sec. 1603 of the American Recovery and Reinvestment Tax Act allows taxpayers to apply to receive a grant of money in lieu of tax credits. Grants are available either equal to 30 percent or 10 percent of the basis of qualifying property. Thirty-percent grants are available for qualified fuel cell property, solar property, qualified small wind property, all as defined under Code Sec. 48. Thirty-percent grants are also available for certain property qualifying for the production tax credit under Code Sec. 45. Ten percent grants are available for geothermal, qualified microturbine, combined heat and power property and geothermal heat pumps.
>
> The current economic climate has significantly reduced or eliminated the tax credit appetite of many of the traditional investors in energy investment credits or energy productions credits. As a result, many projects that are otherwise feasible have not been able to find an investor for their tax credits or have found that the pricing for such credits has decreased. This has resulted in a decrease in the number of energy credit projects under construction. The provision for grant funds in place of tax credits for qualifying properties should be a significant help to projects that are financially feasible but have not been able to begin construction due to the impaired market for energy credits. An additional result may be that the availability of grants in place of credits may result in a significant reduction in the amount of energy credits available to be purchased by syndicators and direct investors in such credits.
>
> Congress has provided for a fairly generous placement in service deadline in order to receive the energy grants. To be eligible for the grants, the property must be placed in service in 2009 or 2010 or the property can be placed in service after 2010 if construction of the property began in 2009 or 2010 and is completed prior to the Credit Termination Date. The Credit Termination Date is (1) January 1, 2013, for qualified wind facilities under Code Sec. 45(d)(1), (2) January 1, 2014, for other Code Sec. 45 properties that are allowed to elect the investment credit under Code Sec. 48, and (3) January 1, 2017, for traditional energy credit properties under Code Sec. 48.
>
> Energy grants are not available for certain nontaxpayers and may create issues that were more easily handled when receiving credits rather than grants. In general, energy grants are not available for (1) Federal, State or local governments (or any political subdivision, agency or instrumentality thereof); (2) 501(c) organizations; and (3) Code Sec. 54(j)(4) issuers, i.e., clean renewable energy bond lenders, cooperative electric companies and governmental bodies. However, the new law specifically disallows the grants for any partnership or pass-through entity any partner (or other holder of an equity or profits interest) of which is described in the foregoing clauses (1)-(3). This means that a partnership or other pass-through entity with a governmental entity or Code Sec. 501(c) organization as a small partner may not qualify for any

NEW LAW EXPLAINED

> grants. This appears to be more restrictive than the restrictions on obtaining tax credits where tax-exempt entities participate in partnerships or pass-through entities. When using credits, the tax-exempt use rules under Code Sec. 168(h)(6) reduce the amount of credits where a tax-exempt entity does not have a "qualified allocation." A qualified allocation exists where for all years that the tax-exempt entity is a member it has an allocation consistent with it receiving the same share of all items of partnership income, gain, loss, deduction, credit and basis. The tax-exempt use rules could also be avoided in the credit context by having the tax-exempt entity participate in the partnership through a taxable corporation that makes an election under Code Sec. 168(h)(6)(F)(ii). Thus it was possible for tax-exempt entities to participate in energy credit projects if the tax-exempt entity limited itself to a qualified allocation or used a Code Sec. 168(h)(6)(F)(ii) structure. However the new grant law does not contain a provision allowing the grants where the tax-exempt entity has a qualified allocation or Code Sec. 168(h)(6)(F)(ii) election. It is possible that the IRS will issue guidance whereby the grants would only be disallowed to the extent of a nontaxpayer does not have a qualified allocation or Code Sec. 168(h)(6)(F)(ii) election. In the absence of such guidance, projects where a nontaxpayer wished to participate may need to claim credits rather than grants and limit the nontaxpayer to qualified allocations or use a Code Sec. 168(h)(6)(F)(ii) structure.

Coordination with credits. If the grant is paid, no renewable electricity credit or energy credit may be claimed with respect to the grant eligible property (Code Sec. 48(d)(1) as added by the 2009 Recovery Act). If a credit was determined for property for a tax year ending before the grant is made, the tax imposed on the taxpayer for that tax year is increased by the amount of the credit allowed under Code Sec. 38 (Code Sec. 48(d)(2)(A) as added by the 2009 Recovery Act). The general business carryforwards under Code Sec. 39 are adjusted to recapture the portion of the credit that was not allowed (Code Sec. 48(d)(2)(B) as added by the 2009 Recovery Act). The amount of the grant, however, is determined without regard to any reduction in the basis of the property because of the credit (Code Sec. 48(d)(2)(C) as added by the 2009 Recovery Act).

▶ **Effective date.** No specific effective date is provided by the Act. The provision is, therefore, considered effective on February 17, 2009, the date of enactment.

Law source: Law at ¶5110. Committee Report at ¶10,130.

— Act Sec. 1104 of the American Recovery and Reinvestment Tax Act of 2009 (P.L. 111-5), adding Code Sec. 48(d);

— Act Sec. 1603 of the American Recovery and Reinvestment Tax Act of 2009.

Reporter references: For further information, consult the following CCH reporters.

— Standard Federal Tax Reporter, ¶4415.01 and ¶4671.01

— Tax Research Consultant, BUSEXP: 51, 105 and BUSEXP: 54,550

— Practical Tax Explanation, § 13,710 and § 14,215

¶520 Renewable Electricity Production Credit

SUMMARY OF NEW LAW

For purposes of the renewable electricity production tax credit, the placed-in-service date has been extended for: qualified wind facilities; qualified closed- and open-loop biomass, geothermal energy, landfill gas, trash, and qualified hydropower facilities; and for marine and hydrokinetic renewable energy facilities. Also, the placed-in-service date for qualified small irrigation power facilities has been changed.

BACKGROUND

An income tax credit is allowed for the production of electricity from certain renewable energy resources at qualified facilities (Code Sec. 45). Qualified energy resources include wind, closed-loop biomass, open-loop biomass, geothermal or solar energy, small irrigation power, municipal solid waste (trash), qualified hydropower production, and marine and hydrokinetic renewable energy (Code Sec. 45(c)). Qualified facilities are generally facilities that generate electricity using these renewable energy resources. To be eligible for the credit, electricity produced from these energy resources at qualified facilities must be sold by the taxpayer to an unrelated person.

The base amount of the electricity production credit is 1.5 cents per kilowatt-hour (indexed annually for inflation) of electricity produced (Code Sec. 45(a)). The credit rate is reduced by one-half for electricity produced from open-loop biomass, small irrigation power, landfill gas, trash combustion and qualified hydropower facilities (Code Sec. 45(b)). The credit amount for 2008 for electricity produced from wind, closed-loop biomass, geothermal or solar qualified energy facilities is 2.1 cents per kilowatt-hour, and for open-loop biomass, small irrigation power, landfill gas, trash combustion, qualified hydropower, and marine and hydrokinetic renewable energy qualified facilities the reduced amount is one cent per kilowatt-hour (Notice 2008-48, I.R.B. 2008-21, 1008). The credit is also reduced for grants, tax-exempt bonds, subsidized energy financing, and other credits (Code Sec. 45(b)(3)).

A taxpayer may generally claim a credit during the 10-year period commencing with the date the qualified facility is placed in service (Code Sec. 45(a)(2)(A)(ii)). The placed-in-service date depends on the qualified facility and the renewable energy resource.

- A wind energy facility is a facility that uses wind to produce electricity. To be a qualified facility, a wind energy facility must be placed in service after December 31, 1993, and before January 1, 2010.

- A closed-loop biomass facility is a facility that uses any organic material from a plant which is planted exclusively for the purpose of being used at a qualifying facility to produce electricity. In addition, a closed-loop biomass facility may be one that is modified to use closed-loop biomass to co-fire with coal, with other biomass, or both, providing the modification meets specified requirements. To be a qualified facility, a closed-loop biomass facility must be placed in service after December 31, 1992, and before January 1, 2011.

BACKGROUND

- A open-loop biomass facility is a facility that uses any agricultural livestock waste nutrients or any solid, nonhazardous, cellulosic waste or any lignin material at a qualifying facility to produce electricity. To be a qualified facility, an open-loop biomass facility using livestock waste nutrients must be placed in service after October 22, 2004, and before January 1, 2011, have a nameplate capacity not less than 150 kilowatts. All other qualified open-loop biomass facilities must be placed in service before January 1, 2011.
- A geothermal facility is a facility that uses geothermal energy to produce electricity. Geothermal energy is energy derived from a geothermal deposit that is a geothermal reservoir consisting of natural heat that is stored in rocks or in an aqueous liquid or vapor (whether or not under pressure). To be a qualified facility, a geothermal facility must be placed in service after October 22, 2004, and before January 1, 2011.
- A solar facility is a facility that uses solar energy to produce electricity. To be a qualified facility, a solar facility must be placed in service after October 22, 2004, and before January 1, 2006.
- A small irrigation power facility is a facility that generates electric power through an irrigation system canal or ditch without any dam or impoundment of water. The installed capacity of a qualified facility must be at least 150 kilowatts but less than five megawatts. To be a qualified facility, a small irrigation facility must be originally placed in service after October 22, 2004, and before January 1, 2011.
- A landfill gas facility is a facility that uses landfill gas to produce electricity. Landfill gas is defined as methane gas derived from the biodegradation of municipal solid waste. To be a qualified facility, a landfill gas facility must be placed in service after October 22, 2004, and before January 1, 2011.
- Trash facilities are facilities that use municipal solid waste (garbage) to produce steam to drive a turbine for the production of electricity. To be a qualified facility, a trash combustion facility must be placed in service after October 22, 2004, and before January 1, 2011. A qualified trash combustion facility includes a new unit, placed in service on or before October 22, 2004, that increases electricity production capacity at an existing trash facility.
- A qualified hydropower facility is: (1) a facility that produced hydroelectric power (a hydroelectric dam) prior to August 8, 2005, at which efficiency improvements or additions to capacity have been made after such date and before January 1, 2011, that enable the taxpayer to produce incremental hydropower, or (2) a facility placed in service before August 8, 2005, that did not produce hydroelectric power (a nonhydroelectric dam) on such date, and to which turbines or other electricity generating equipment have been added after such date and before January 1, 2011.
- A marine and hydrokinetic renewable energy facility is one that produces electric power from energy derived from: (1) waves, tides, and other currents in the ocean, estuaries, and tidal areas, (2) free flowing water in rivers, lakes, and streams, (3) free flowing water in an irrigation system, canal, or other man-made channel, including projects that utilize non-mechanical structures to accelerate the flow of water for electric power production purposes, or (4) differentials in ocean temperature (ocean thermal energy conversion) and that has a nameplate capacity rating of

¶520

BACKGROUND

at least 150 kilowatt hours and is placed in service after October 2, 2008, but before January 1, 2012. Marine and hydrokinetic renewable energy does not include energy generated from any source utilizing a dam, diversionary structure (except for irrigation systems, canals and other man-made channels) or impoundment for electric power production.

NEW LAW EXPLAINED

Renewable electricity credit extended and modified.—The placed-in-service date for purposes of the renewable electricity production tax credit in the case of a qualified wind facility is extended for three years, through December 31, 2012 (Code Sec. 45(d)(1), as amended by the American Recovery and Reinvestment Tax Act of 2009 (P.L. 111-5)). The placed-in-service date for closed- and open-loop biomass, geothermal, landfill gas, trash, and qualified hydropower facilities also is extended for three years, through December 31, 2013. The placed-in-service date for marine and hydrokinetic renewable energy facilities has been extended for two years, through December 31, 2013 (Code Sec. 45(d)(2), (3), (4), (6), (7), (9), and (11)(B), as amended by the 2009 Recovery Act). In addition, the termination placed-in-service date for small irrigation power facilities is amended to before October 3, 2008 (Code Sec. 45(d)(5), as amended by the 2009 Recovery Act). This has been done to correct an overlap of placed-in-service dates given that a qualifying facility for marine and hydrokinetic renewable energy includes irrigation systems. Such facilities must be placed in service after October 2, 2008.

▶ **Effective date.** Generally, the provisions of this section apply to property placed in service after February 17, 2009 (Act Sec. 1101(c)(1) of the American Recovery and Reinvestment Tax Act of 2008 (P.L. 111-5)). The amendment to the placed-in-service date for small irrigation qualified facilities is effective for electricity produced and sold after the October 3, 2008, in tax years ending after such date (Act Sec. 1101(c)(2) of the 2009 Recovery; Act Sec. 102(f) of the Emergency Economic Stabilization Act of 2008 (P.L. 110-343)).

Law source: Law at ¶5090. Committee Report at ¶10,100.

— Act Sec. 1101(a)(1) of the American Recovery and Reinvestment Tax Act of 2008 (P.L. 111-5), amending Code Sec. 45(d)(1);

— Act Sec. 1101(a)(2), amending Code Sec. 45(d)(2), (3), (4), (6), (7), and (9)

— Act Sec. 1101(a)(3), amending Code Sec. 45(d)(11)(B);

— Act Sec. 1101(b), amending Code Sec. 45(d)(5);

— Act Sec. 1101(c), providing the effective dates.

Reporter references: For further information, consult the following CCH reporters.

— Standard Federal Tax Reporter, ¶4415.03

— Tax Research Consultant, BUSEXP: 54,550

— Practical Tax Explanation, § 14,215

¶520

¶525 Credit for Investment in Advanced Energy Facilities

SUMMARY OF NEW LAW

A 30-percent credit is provided for investment in qualified property used in a qualifying advanced energy project. The credit is part of the investment credit and is available only for qualifying projects certified by the Secretary of Treasury Secretary, in consultation with the Secretary of Energy.

BACKGROUND

A nonrefundable income tax credit is allowed for the domestic production of electricity from qualified energy resources at qualified facilities that is sold to unrelated persons (Code Sec. 45). Qualified energy resources comprise wind, closed-loop biomass, open-loop biomass, geothermal energy, solar energy, small irrigation power, municipal solid waste, qualified hydropower production, and marine and hydrokinetic renewable energy. Qualified facilities are, generally, facilities that generate electricity using qualified energy resources. The credit is also allowed for the sale to unrelated persons of certain refined coal produced at a refined coal production facility and coal produced on an Indian reservation. The credit is a component of the general business credit under Code Sec. 38.

An income tax credit is also available for certain qualifying energy property placed in service (Code Sec. 48). For purposes of this credit, qualifying property includes certain fuel cell property, solar property, geothermal power production property, small wind energy property, combined heat and power system property, and geothermal heat pump property. The energy credit equals a specified energy percentage of the basis of each qualified property placed in service during the tax year.

The energy credit is a component of the investment credit under Code Sec. 46, which also includes the rehabilitation credit, the qualifying advanced coal project credit, and the qualifying gasification project credit. The investment credit is allowable in the year that the qualified property is first placed in service. However, under the Code Sec. 49, the investment credit is not allowed for otherwise eligible property to the extent that the property is financed with nonqualified nonrecourse borrowing. As a result, the credit base of the property must be reduced by the amount of nonqualified nonrecourse financing attributable to the property and determined at the close of the tax year in which the property is placed in service. For this purpose, the credit base includes: (1) the portion of the basis of any qualified rehabilitated building attributable to qualified rehabilitation expenditures, (2) the basis of energy property, (3) the basis of any property that is part of a qualifying advanced coal project, and (4) the basis of any property that is part of a qualifying gasification project (Code Sec. 49(a)(1)(C)).

In addition to the above credits, taxpayers may also claim other credits intended to encourage renewable energy production and energy conservation, such as credits for residential energy property and energy efficient property (Code Secs. 25C and 25D), certain alcohol and biodiesel fuels (Code Secs. 40 and 40A), and qualified electric and

BACKGROUND

alternative technology vehicles (Code Secs. 30 and 30B). The current law, however, does not provide for a credit specifically designed to encourage the development of a domestic manufacturing base to support the energy-related industries described above.

NEW LAW EXPLAINED

Credit for investment in advanced energy projects provided.—A tax credit is allowed equal to 30 percent of a taxpayer's qualified investment for the tax year with respect to any qualifying advanced energy project of the taxpayer (Code Sec. 48C(a), as added by the American Recovery and Reinvestment Tax Act of 2009 (P.L. 111-5). The credit is part of the investment credit and the basis of any property that is part of a qualifying advanced energy project is included in the credit base for purposes of applying the investment credit at-risk limitation rules under Code Sec. 49 (Code Secs. 46(5) and 49(a)(1)(C)(v), as added by the 2009 Recovery Act). The credit is not allowed for any qualified investment for which a credit is also allowed for the energy credit (Code Sec. 48, the qualifying advanced coal project credit (Code Sec. 48A), or the qualifying gasification project credit (Code Sec. 48B) (Code Sec. 48C(e), as added by the 2009 Recovery Act).

> **Practical Analysis:** Charles R. Goulding, J.D., CPA, MBA, and President of Energy Tax Savers Inc. of Syosset, New York, observes that the Qualifying Advanced Energy Project Credit added by the American Recovery and Reinvestment Tax Act of 2009 is aimed at encouraging energy-related manufacturing expansion in the United States. This is a very strategic provision because historically, although certain leading alternative energy technologies like solar were developed by U.S. Federal government national laboratory, often the core manufacturing of the resulting products occurred off shore. The same U.S. lab to offshore manufacturing transfer occurred with the original lithium-ion batteries used in notebook computers and cell phones. Many leading U.S. companies are focusing on new battery technologies requiring tremendous manufacturing facility investments. Certain states such as New York and Michigan are also making large investments in battery technology, and this tax incentive should work well in tandem with those initiatives.
>
> Some of the major U.S. manufacturing entrants into the battery area are Eneri, with an Indianapolis, Indiana plant; A123, a Massachusetts Institute of Technology spin-off; and Johnson Controls-Saft, a Franco-American joint venture.
>
> Eneri has applied for Federal loan to build a 600,000 per year battery plant, and A123 of Watertown, Massachusetts has announced plans to build $1.8 billion car battery factory in Michigan. In addition to plug-in vehicles, long-range batteries are the key to widespread implementation of robots and other mobile equipment.

Comment: The credit will apply to qualified property constructed, reconstructed, or erected by the taxpayer after February 18, 2009, to the extent of the cost attributable to construction, reconstruction, or erection of the qualified property after February 18, 2009, and to acquisitions of qualified property made after

¶525

NEW LAW EXPLAINED

February 18, 2009, and placed in service after February 18, (Act Sec. 1302(d) of the 2009 Recovery Act). For any qualified property having a normal construction period of more than two years, the 30 percent credit will apply to expenditures made after February 18, 2009.

A qualified investment for any tax year is the basis of eligible property placed in service during that tax year that is part of a qualifying advanced energy project (Code Sec. 48C(b)(1), as added by the 2009 Recovery Act). For this purpose, a taxpayer can elect to increase the amount of its qualified investment for the tax year by its qualified progress expenditures made during the year (Code Sec. 48C(b)(2), as added by the 2009 Recovery Act). Qualified progress expenditures are amounts paid (paid or incurred in the case of self-constructed property) during the year for the construction of eligible property which has a normal construction period of at least two years and a useful life of seven years or more. However, no qualified progress expenditures may be taken into account in the tax year the property is placed in service. In addition, the credit amount with respect to any qualifying advanced energy project for all tax years cannot exceed the amount designated by the Secretary of Treasury as eligible for the credit (Code Sec. 48C(b)(3), as added by the 2009 Recovery Act).

Comment: The qualified progress expenditure rules are those similar to the rules under Code Sec. 46(c)(4) and (d), as in effect on the day before the enactment of the Revenue Reconciliation Act of 1990 (P.L. 101-508), apply.

A qualifying advanced energy project is a project that re-equips, expands, or establishes a manufacturing facility for the production of:

- property designed to be used to produce energy from the sun, wind, or geothermal deposits (within the meaning of Code Sec. 613(e)(2)) or other renewable resources;
- fuel cells, microturbines, or an energy storage system for use with electric or hybrid-electric motor vehicles;
- electric grids to support the transmission of intermittent sources of renewable energy, including storage of such energy;
- property designed to capture and sequester carbon dioxide emissions;
- property designed to refine or blend renewable fuels or to produce energy conservation technologies (including energy-conserving lighting technologies and smart grid technologies);
- new qualified plug-in electric drive motor vehicles (see ¶345), qualified plug-in electric vehicles (see ¶350), or components which are designed specifically for use with such vehicles, including electric motors, generators, and power control units; or
- other advanced energy property designed to reduce greenhouse gas emissions as may be determined by the Secretary of Treasury (Code Sec. 48C(c)(1)(A)(i), as added by the 2009 Recovery Act).

Any portion of the qualified investment in the qualifying project must be certified by the Secretary of Treasury as eligible for the credit (Code Sec. 48C(c)(1)(A)(ii), as added by the 2009 Recovery Act). A qualifying project does not include any portion of a project for the production of any property used in the refining or blending of any

¶525

NEW LAW EXPLAINED

transportation fuel (other than renewable fuels) (Code Sec. 48C(c)(1)(B), as added by the 2009 Recovery Act).

For purposes of the credit, eligible property is any property (1) that is necessary for the production of property described above; (2) that is tangible personal property or other tangible property (not including a building or its structural components), but only if such property is used as an integral part of the qualified investment credit facility; and (3) with respect to which depreciation (or amortization in lieu of depreciation) is allowable (Code Sec. 48C(c)(2), as added by the 2009 Recovery Act).

Not later than 180 days after February 17, 2009, the date of enactment of this provision, the Secretary of Treasury, in consultation with the Secretary of Energy, will establish a qualifying advanced energy project program to consider and award certifications for qualified investments eligible for credits to qualifying advanced energy project sponsors. The total amount of credits that may be allocated under the program may not exceed $2.3 billion (Code Sec. 48C(d)(1), as added by the 2009 Recovery Act).

Applicants for certification must submit applications containing any required information during the two-year period beginning on the date the qualifying advanced energy project program is established. Each applicant will have one year from the date of the Treasury Secretary's acceptance of the application to provide evidence that the certification requirements have been met. Applicants that receive a certification will have three years from the date of the issuance of the certification to place the project in service. If the project is not placed in service within the three-year period, the certification will no longer be valid (Code Sec. 48C(d)(2), as added by the 2009 Recovery Act).

In determining which qualifying advanced energy projects to certify, the Treasury Secretary will take into consideration only those projects where there is a reasonable expectation of commercial viability. In addition, the Treasury Secretary will consider which projects (1) will provide the greatest domestic job creation (both direct and indirect) during the credit period; (2) will provide the greatest net impact in avoiding or reducing air pollutants or anthropogenic emissions of greenhouse gases; (3) have the greatest potential for technological innovation and commercial deployment; (4) have the lowest levelized cost of generated or stored energy, or of measured reduction in energy consumption or greenhouse gas emission (based on costs of the full supply chain); and (5) have the shortest project time from certification to completion (Code Sec. 48C(d)(3), as added by the 2009 Recovery Act).

Not later than four years after February 17, 2009, the date of enactment of this provision, the Treasury Secretary will review the credits allocated under Code Sec. 48C as of such date. The Treasury Secretary may reallocate any awarded credits if it determines that there is an insufficient quantity of qualifying applications for certification pending at the time of the review or if any certification has been revoked because the project subject to the certification has been delayed as a result of third-party opposition or litigation to the proposed project. If the Treasury Secretary determines that credits are available for reallocation, it is authorized to conduct an additional program for applications for certification (Code Sec. 48C(d)(4), as added by the 2009 Recovery Act).

¶525

NEW LAW EXPLAINED

Upon making certification, the Secretary of Treasury will publicly disclose the identity of the applicant and the amount of the credit with respect to that applicant (Code Sec. 48C(d)(5), as added by the 2009 Recovery Act).

▶ **Effective date.** The amendments made by this section shall apply to periods after February 17, 2009, under rules similar to the rules of Code Sec. 48(m) (as in effect on the day before the date of enactment of the Revenue Reconciliation Act of 1990 (P.L.101-508)) (Act Sec. 1302(d) of the American Recovery and Reinvestment Tax Act of 2009 (P.L. 111-5)).

Law source: Law at ¶5105, ¶5125 and ¶5130. Committee Report at ¶10,340.

— Act Sec. 1302(a) of the American Recovery and Reinvestment Tax Act of 2009 (P.L. 111-5), adding Code Sec. 46(5);

— Act Sec. 1302(b), adding Code Sec. 48C;

— Act Sec. 1302(c), amending Code Sec. 49(a)(1)(C);

— Act Sec. 1302(d), providing the effective date.

Reporter references: For further information, consult the following CCH reporters.

— Standard Federal Tax Reporter, ¶4580.01

— Tax Research Consultant, BUSEXP:51,100

— Practical Tax Explanation, § 13,701

¶530 New Markets Tax Credit

SUMMARY OF NEW LAW

For calendar years 2008 and 2009, the new markets tax credit is modified to increase the maximum amount of qualified equity investments from $3.5 billion to $5 billion. A special rule applies in 2008 for the allocation of the $1.5 billion increase to qualified community development entities.

BACKGROUND

Among the incentives offered to encourage taxpayers to invest in, or make loans to, small businesses located in low-income communities is the new markets tax credit (Code Sec. 45D). The new markets tax credit provides a credit for qualified equity investments made to acquire stock in a corporation, or a capital interest in a partnership, that is a qualified community development entity (CDE). The credit allowable to the investor is (1) a five-percent credit for the first three years from the date that the equity interest was purchased from the CDE, and (2) a six-percent credit for each of the following four years (Code Sec. 45D(a)(2)). The credit is determined by applying the applicable percentage (five or six) to the amount paid to the CDE for the investment at its original issue (Code Sec. 45D(a)(1)). The credit is subject to recapture in certain circumstances (Code Sec. 45D(g)).

BACKGROUND

There is a national limitation with respect to the new markets tax credit. The maximum annual amount of qualified equity investments is capped at $2 billion for calendar years 2004 and 2005. In 2006, 2007, and 2008, the cap is $3.5 billion (Code Sec. 45D(f)(1)). The Secretary of the Treasury is authorized to allocate the amounts among qualified CDEs, giving preference (in part) to any entity with a record of successfully providing capital or technical assistance to disadvantaged businesses or communities (Code Sec. 45D(f)(2)).

A qualified CDE includes any domestic corporation or partnership: (1) whose primary mission is serving or providing investment capital for low-income communities or persons; (2) that maintains accountability to the residents of low-income communities by their representation on any governing board of or any advisory board to the CDE; and (3) that is certified by the Secretary of the Treasury as being a qualified CDE (Code Sec. 45D(c)). A qualified equity investment means stock (other than nonqualified preferred stock) in a corporation or a capital interest in a partnership that is acquired directly from a CDE for cash. Substantially all of the investment proceeds must be used by the CDE to make qualified low-income community investments, as defined in Code Sec. 45D(d) (Code Sec. 45D(b)(1)).

One category of qualified low-income community investments is any capital or equity investment in (or loan to) any qualified active low-income community business (Code Sec. 45D(d)(1)(A)). For purposes of Code Sec. 45D, the term "low-income community" means any population census tract with either (1) a poverty rate of at least 20 percent or (2) median family income that does not exceed 80 percent of metropolitan area median family income (or in the case of a non-metropolitan census tract, does not exceed 80 percent of statewide median family income) (Code Sec. 45D(e)(1)). A modification is made for census tracts within high migration rural counties (Code Sec. 45D(e)(5)).

The Emergency Economic Stabilization Act of 2008 (P.L. 110-343) extended the new markets tax credit through 2009. As a result, up to $3.5 billion in qualified equity investments could be allocated among qualified CDEs for that calendar year (Code Sec. 45D(f)(1)(D)).

NEW LAW EXPLAINED

New markets tax credit modified.—For calendar years 2008 and 2009, the maximum amount of qualified equity investments that can be made is increased by $1.5 billion (to $5 billion for each year) (Code Sec. 45D(f)(1)(E) and (F), as added by the American Recovery and Reinvestment Tax Act of 2009 (P.L. 111-5)). The additional amount for 2008 must be allocated in accordance with Code Sec. 45D(f)(2) to qualified community development entities (CDEs) that submitted an allocation application for calendar year 2008 and either (1) did not receive an allocation for that year, or (2) received an allocation for that year in an amount less than the amount requested in the application (Act Sec. 1403(b), of the 2009 Recovery Act).

> **Comment:** The additional allocation for 2008 must be allocated "in accordance with section 45D(f)(2)." Thus, the rule that priority be given to CDEs that have a successful record of providing capital or technical assistance to disadvantaged

NEW LAW EXPLAINED

businesses or communities or meet other requirements should continue to apply in making the additional allocations among previously unsuccessful applicants.

> **Practical Analysis:** Glenn A. Graff, a partner at Applegate & Thorne-Thomsen, P.C., Chicago, says that the American Recovery and Reinvestment Tax Act of 2009 increases the New Markets Tax Credits for 2008 and 2009 from $3.5 million to $5 million. This substantial increase in credits should provide additional financing for qualifying businesses in low-income communities. However, the credit is still scheduled to expire after 2009. It is hoped that the credit will be continued by legislation passed later in 2009.

▶ **Effective date.** No specific effective date is provided by the Act. The provision is therefore, considered effective on February 17, 2009, the date of enactment.

Law source: Law at ¶5095. Committee Report at ¶10,370.

— Act Sec. 1403(a) of the American Recovery and Reinvestment Tax Act of 2009 (P.L. 111-5), adding Code Sec. 45D(f)(1)(E) and (F);

— Act Sec. 1403(b).

Reporter references: For further information, consult the following CCH reporters.

— Standard Federal Tax Reporter, ¶4490.01
— Tax Research Consultant, BUSEXP: 54,900
— Practical Tax Explanation, § 14,430

¶535 Grants to Provide Financing for Low-Income Housing

SUMMARY OF NEW LAW

The Secretary of the Treasury is authorized to make grants to states in an amount equal to each state's low-income housing grant election amount, in lieu of low-income housing credit allocations for 2009. The otherwise applicable low-income housing credit ceiling for any state for 2009 will be reduced by the amount taken into account in determining the amount of the grant.

BACKGROUND

The owner of a qualified low-income housing project that is constructed, rehabilitated, or acquired may claim the low-income housing credit in each of 10 tax years in an amount equal to the applicable credit percentage appropriate to the type of project, multiplied by the qualified basis allocable to the low-income units in each qualified low-income building. The applicable percentage is generally based on the month the building is placed in service or, at the election of the taxpayer, the month

BACKGROUND

in which the taxpayer and housing credit agency agree to the amount of housing credit allocated to the building (Code Sec. 42(a) and (b)(2)(A)). The IRS prescribes credit percentages which yield, over the 10-year credit period, a credit having a present value equal to 70 percent of the qualified basis of a new building that is not federally subsidized, 30 percent of the qualified basis of a new building that is federally subsidized, and 30 percent of the qualified basis of an existing building (Code Sec. 42(a) and (b)).

State agency credit ceiling. Generally, the amount of the low-income housing credit for any tax year for any building may not exceed the housing credit allocated to that building, although the allocation limitation does not apply to buildings financed with certain tax-exempt obligations (Code Sec. 42(h)(1)(A) and (h)(4)). The allocation is made by a state housing credit agency, which is limited in the dollar amount of housing credit allocations it may make in a year. The allocation must generally be made not later than the close of the calendar year in which the building is placed in service, unless the allocation is subject to one of the exceptions discussed in Code Sec. 42(h)(1)(B). The housing credit agency must allocate credits under a qualified allocation plan which sets selection criteria and provides a procedure for monitoring compliance with credit requirements and reporting noncompliance to the IRS (Code Sec. 42(m)(1)).

Credit apportionment. A state's housing credit allotment for each year must be apportioned among the state and local housing credit agencies within the state. A housing agency may allocate credits only to buildings located within the jurisdiction of the governmental unit of which the agency is a part. Allocations may be received from different agencies with overlapping jurisdictions and can be made for whole projects, as well as separately for individual buildings. At least 10 percent of the state's credit allocation must be set aside for projects in which tax-exempt charitable and social welfare organizations materially participate (Code Sec. 42(h)(5)(B)).

State credit ceiling amount. The housing credit allocations of any state for any calendar year are limited by the state credit ceiling, which is the sum of:

(1) the unused carryforward component, which is the unused state housing credit ceiling for the preceding calendar year;

(2) the population component, which is the greater of: (a) $2 million (adjusted annually for inflation, see below), or (b) the state population multiplied by $1.75 (adjusted annually for inflation);

(3) the returned credit component, which is the amount of housing credit ceiling returned in the calendar year; and

(4) the national pool component, which is the amount of unused credit carryover assigned to the state by the Treasury Secretary (Code Sec. 42(h)(3)(C)).

The IRS publishes in Rev. Proc. 2008-57, I.R.B. 2008-41, 855, each eligible state's annual population and national pool components. Rev. Proc. 2008-66, I.R.B. 2008-45, 1107, contains the inflation adjusted dollar amounts for 2009.

¶535

NEW LAW EXPLAINED

Grants authorized for states' low-income housing projects in lieu of low-income housing credit allocations for 2009.—To provide financing for low-income housing, the Secretary of the Treasury is authorized to make a grant to each state's housing credit agency in an amount equal to the low-income housing grant election amount (Act Sec. 1602(a) of the American Recovery and Reinvestment Tax Act of 2009 (P.L. 111-5)).

Low-income housing grant election amount. The low-income housing grant election amount for a state is an amount elected by the state subject to certain limits. The maximum low-income housing grant election amount for a state may not exceed 85 percent of the product of ten and the sum of the state's:

(1) unused housing credit ceiling for 2008 (Code Sec. 42(h)(3)(C)(i));

(2) amount of housing credit ceiling returned in 2009 (Code Sec. 42(h)(3)(C)(iii));

(3) 40 percent of the state's 2009 housing credit ceiling attributable to the greater of $2,665,000 or the state population multiplied by $2.30 (both dollar amounts are adjusted annually for inflation) (Code Sec. 42(h)(3)(C)(ii); Rev. Proc. 2008-66, I.R.B. 2008-45, 1107); and

(4) 40 percent of the state's unused housing credit carryover for 2009, if any (Code Sec. 42(h)(3)(C)(iv) and (h)(3)(D)) (Act Sec. 1602(b) of the 2009 Recovery Act).

> **Comment:** According to the Joint Committee report, these grants are not taxable income to recipients (Joint Committee on Taxation, Description of Title I of H.R. 598, the American Recovery and Reinvestment Tax Act of 2009 (JCX-5-09), January 21, 2009).

Subawards for low-income buildings. In general, a state housing credit agency receiving a grant under this provision must use it to make subawards to finance the construction or acquisition and rehabilitation of qualified low-income buildings as defined under the low-income housing credit rules of Code Sec. 42. A subaward may be made to finance a qualified low-income building whether or not the building has a low-income housing credit allocation. However, for qualified low-income buildings without a low-income housing credit allocation, the state housing credit agency must make a determination that the subaward with respect to such buildings will increase the total funds available to the state to build and rehabilitate affordable housing. To comply with this determination requirement, the state housing credit agency must establish a process requiring applicants that are allocated credits to demonstrate good faith efforts to obtain investment commitments before the agency makes these subawards (Act Sec. 1602(c)(1) and (e) of the 2009 Recovery Act).

Low-income housing credit rules apply. Any subaward made with respect to any qualified low-income building must be made in the same manner, and be subject to the same limitations (including rent, income, and use restrictions on such building) as provided in the low-income housing credit rules under Code Sec. 42. However, these subawards will not be limited by, or otherwise affect the state housing credit ceiling applicable to such agency (Act Sec. 1602(c)(2) of the 2009 Recovery Act).

> **Comment:** The bill text refers to Code Sec. 42(h)(3)(J), as an exception to the subawards limitation referred to above. This reference appears to be a drafting error because Code Sec. 42(h)(3)(J) does not exist. However, the reference could

¶535

NEW LAW EXPLAINED

be to Code Sec. 42(h)(3)(I), increasing the state housing credit ceiling for 2008 and 2009.

Compliance and asset management. The state housing credit agency must perform asset management functions to ensure compliance with the low-income housing credit rules and the long-term viability of buildings funded by these subawards. The state housing credit agency may collect reasonable fees from a subaward recipient to cover the expenses of the agency's asset management duties. The state housing credit agency may also retain an agent or other private contractor to perform these duties (Act Sec. 1602(c)(3) of the 2009 Recovery Act).

Recapture. Conditions or restrictions, including a requirement providing for recapture, will be imposed by the state housing credit agency on any subaward made so as to assure that the subject building remains a qualified low-income building during the compliance period. Any recapture, enforced by means of liens or other methods that the Secretary of the Treasury (or the Secretary's delegate) deems appropriate, will be payable to the Secretary of the Treasury for deposit in the general fund of the Treasury (Act Sec. 1602(c)(4) and (e) of the 2009 Recovery Act).

Caution: It is important to note that even though the low-income housing credit is claimed over a 10 year period, the compliance period to prevent recapture of the credit is a 15 year period (Code Sec. 42(i)(1)).

Practical Analysis: Glenn A. Graff, a partner at Applegate & Thorne-Thomsen, P.C., Chicago, points out that the current economic crisis has significantly reduced or eliminated the appetite of many traditional investors for Code Sec. 42 low-income housing tax credits. As a result, the price investors are willing to pay for Code Sec. 42 credits has decreased dramatically, resulting in larger gaps in the financing of such projects. Furthermore, in some portions of the country there are no investors interested in such credits.

Act Sec. 1602 of the American Recovery and Reinvestment Tax Act of 2009 ("2009 Recovery Act") gives grant funds in place of tax credits for qualifying properties, which should significantly help projects that are financially feasible but have not been able to begin construction due to the impaired market for credits. An additional result may be that availability of grants in place of credits may result in a significant reduction in the amount of low-income housing credits available to be purchased by investors.

The 2009 Recovery Act allows a state to elect to return (1) up to 100 percent of unused 2008 credits plus 100 percent credits returned to the state in 2009, plus (2) up to 40 percent of a state's 2009 housing credit ceiling plus its share of the national pool. In exchange for the returned credits, the state would receive a grant of funds equal to 85 percent of 10 times the amount of credits returned. This basically equals a purchase price of $0.85 per credit. Note that the "10 times" component makes sense because an award of credits results in 10 years of credits at that amount each year. Thus any credits converted to a grant will result in 10 times less credits over the 10-year credit period.

The 2009 Recovery Act allows for grants to projects that have allocations of credits and for grants to projects that do not have allocations. However, for projects without

NEW LAW EXPLAINED

allocations, a grant may be made only if the state "makes a determination that such use will increase the total funds available to the state to build and rehabilitate affordable housing." The 2009 Recovery Act goes on to state that "in complying with such determination requirement, a state housing credit agency shall establish a process in which applicants that are allocated credits are required to demonstrate good faith efforts to obtain investment commitments for such credits before the agency makes such subawards." It is unclear if a project would have to show that it had no investor interested in its tax credit equity or if a showing that the investor was paying less than the $0.85 per credit provided for in the grant provisions would be sufficient.

It is unclear how the amount of credits that a state wants to exchange for grants is determined. First, it is unclear if a state will be required to identify to the Treasury a fixed amount of grant money at one time or if they can ask for the grant money on a rolling basis as projects are identified for grant proceeds. Second, it remains to be seen how each state will choose which project will receive grants. Clearly for projects for which credits have been allocated but for which there is no current investor interest, there would be an incentive to turn such credits into a grant. However, there are some projects for which an investor may show interest, but the pricing offered may be below $0.85 per credit. If a state can return credits from a project with investor interest, but insufficient pricing (see comment above), then from a purely formula perspective such an approach could work in a state's favor. For example, if a project had $5 million of credits ($5 million of credits over 10 years), but investor pricing for the credits was only $0.75 resulting in only $3.75 million of investor equity, the agency could benefit from taking back the $500,000 of credits and giving a grant of $3.75 million. Because the $5 million of returned credits would generate $4.25 million of grant money, the state would have $500,000 of additional grant funds, which could be used for the project in question or for another project. However, there are other benefits from having a tax credit investor invested in a project that may be significant to the state. One benefit is that credit investors may agree (albeit reluctantly) to put additional money into a project in a future year when problems unexpectedly arise. Tax credit investors often invest in multiple projects and set aside reserves for such contingencies to avoid tax credit recapture. A project that does not have a tax credit investor will instead have to rely on the project's developer, which is unlikely to have the same financial resources as a tax credit investor. Also, tax credit investors are motivated to perform a rigorous financial review and receive a tax opinion from counsel before investing and investors also provide second level of asset management to assist the developer and avoid tax credit recapture. The developer may not provide the same rigorous financial review and would not have the benefit of the investor's asset management review. In addition, for projects receiving grants, the 2009 Recovery Act requires that the state provide its own asset management (or to contract for such asset management). However, it is unclear what leverage a state will have with a developer that owns a project. The investor normally has significant leverage resulting from its ability to seek tax credit adjuster payments from a general partner or even remove a general partner that is mismanaging a project (note that the general partners are usually related to the developer). States would not have the same relationship with developers. While the terms of the grant may come into play, the threat of requiring

¶535

NEW LAW EXPLAINED

repayment or recapture of a grant may turn the asset management function into an adversarial process. Finally, states may desire equity rather than a grant merely to avoid having the state become involved in asset management at all.

The 2009 Recovery Act requires that the state provide its own asset management (or to contract for such asset management) if grants are given. The purpose of this rule is to fill the void normally provided by investors who provide asset management services. It is said that one of the keys to the success of the low-income housing tax credit program is the multiple levels of supervision—i.e., there is supervision at the developer, and syndicator/investor level as well as compliance audits at the state level. The elimination of the syndicator/investor asset management function was seen as a weakness in the grant approach and therefore state asset management was required. However, it is noteworthy that the state asset management function appears to be required even where grants are given to a project that also has an allocation of state credits. This will create a duplication of asset management functions by the state and the syndicator/investor. In addition, because states are separately required to audit projects and file IRS Form 8823 when they observe noncompliance, there may be concerns from project owners as to how the state participation in asset management will interact with state audits and the issuance of Forms 8823. A primary role of syndicator/investor asset management is to proactively identify and correct issues before a state commences an audit. One has to wonder if a states asset management function will similarly work in such a problem avoidance role as opposed to an audit/enforcement role. For example, if a problem during asset management could trigger repayment of a low-income housing grant or soft loan, then the process could become adversarial.

The IRS and states will have to decide if any timing requirements accompany the award of a low-income housing grant or soft loan. Tax credits are commonly received via a carryover allocation requiring the building to be placed in service by the end of two calendar years after the carryover allocation. However, the 2009 Recovery Act does require that funds which have not been used to make subwards by January 1, 2011, must be returned. However, meeting the sub-award requirement does not necessarily mean that a project has been placed in service and the grant provisions do not specifically require that the carryover allocation two-year requirement be followed. It is conceivable for the IRS or state agencies to create a similar deadline as such an approach would be consistent with the overall purpose of the stimulus bill to create projects and jobs quickly. However, timing requirements that are too strict could cause project lenders to be uncomfortable. Thus any desire to impose a time restriction would need to be carefully balanced with reasonable requirements for the project and concerns from lenders and other interested parties and it would be wise for the states to retain discretion with respect to reasonable extensions.

The tax treatment of the low-income housing grants is unclear. The new law is clear that basis of a low-income housing tax credit project is not reduced due to the grant. This is critical for projects that receive an allocation of credit and a grant. However, whether there will be taxable income from the receipt of a grant is less clear. The Joint Explanatory Statement issued by the House and Senate conference committee includes language stating that the receipt of such a grant is not taxable income to the recipient. However, there is no explicit statement in the 2009 Recovery Act itself. This contrasts with the new grant provisions in Act Sec. 1104 of the 2009 Recovery

¶535

NEW LAW EXPLAINED

> Act for energy credits. The energy grant provisions specifically provide that the grants are not includible in the gross income of the taxpayer. Hopefully the IRS will provide guidance showing that low-income housing grants are not taxable income to the recipients.
>
> States may choose to provide grants to building owners in the form of "soft loans," i.e., loans without current debt service with repayment due at maturity. Such loans are already commonplace in the low-income housing field. While soft loans may avoid the issue of whether there is taxable income from receipt of a grant, other issues may be created. For particular projects there may be difficulty showing an ability to repay the loans so that such loans constitute bona fide indebtedness. In addition, recipients of such a loan will one day have to repay the indebtedness or try to work out a refinancing or forgiveness. Repayment is obviously an economic detriment verses tax credit equity, which often does not have to be repaid subject to capital account requirements. Refinancing or forgiveness would bring up tax issues such as original issue discount from non-interest bearing loans or cancellation of indebtedness income. Hopefully the IRS will provide guidance showing that grants in the form of forgivable loans are not taxable income.
>
> The 2009 Recovery Act requires that state housing credit agencies must include a requirement for recapture to ensure that any buildings receiving grants remain qualified low-income buildings during the 15-year compliance period. However, this language is different from tax credit recapture, which is only for one-third of credits and decreases over time. The statutory language could conceivably result in 100 percent recapture in the 14th year whereas tax credit recapture would be much lower. Hopefully the IRS will issue guidance providing that grant recapture will work similarly to tax credit recapture. It is also noteworthy that tax credit recapture occurs merely from a change in a building's applicable fraction, i.e., number of low-income units. If the 2009 Recovery Act is interpreted as requiring recapture only if a building fails to be a qualified low-income building, this would mean that recapture would be avoided merely by meeting the Code Sec. 42 minimum set-aside of either 20 percent of units being rented to persons at 50 percent of area median income or 40 percent of units being rented to persons at 60 percent of area median income. Thus a project receiving a grant could end up with significantly fewer low-income units than expected but still meet the minimum set-aside and not trigger recapture. It is clear that the state will still require an extended use agreement requiring that the promised number of low-income units be delivered. However, extended use agreements are enforced via contractual remedies and the absence of a threat of recapture would be noteworthy. It will be interesting to see if the IRS allows recapture for problems that do not arise to the level of violating the minimum set-aside.

Return of unused grant funds. Any grant funds not used to make subawards before January 1, 2011, and any subawards returned on or after January 1, 2011, must be promptly returned to the Secretary of the Treasury for deposit in the Treasury's general fund (Act Sec. 1602(d) of the 2009 Recovery Act).

Definitions. The terms used in the low-income housing grant provision and also in Code Sec. 42 have the same meaning as when used in Code Sec. 42. Reference to the Secretary of Treasury also refers to those that act as the Secretary's delegates (Act Sec. 1602(e) of the 2009 Recovery Act).

¶535

NEW LAW EXPLAINED

Coordination with low-income housing credit. For purposes of the low-income housing credit, the components of the state housing credit ceiling will each be reduced by the amount that is taken into account in determining the amount of the grant for 2009 (Code Sec. 42(i)(9)(A), as added by the 2009 Recovery Act). However, the basis of a qualified low-income building will not be reduced by the amount of any low-income housing grant received in 2009 (Code Sec. 42(i)(9)(B), as added by the 2009 Recovery Act).

Appropriations. The provision appropriates to the Secretary of the Treasury such sums as may be necessary to carry out this provision (Act Sec. 1602(f) of the 2009 Recovery Act).

▶ **Effective date.** No specific effective date is provided by the Act. The provisions are, therefore, effective on February 17, 2009, the date of enactment.

Law source: Law at ¶5085 and ¶7033. Committee Report at ¶10,380.

— Act Sec. 1404 of the American Recovery and Reinvestment Tax Act of 2009 (P.L. 111-5), adding Code Sec. 42(i)(9);

— Act Sec. 1602.

Reporter references: For further information, consult the following CCH reporters.

— Standard Federal Tax Reporter, ¶4385.035, ¶4385.045 and ¶4385.05

— Tax Research Consultant, BUSEXP: 54,212 and BUSEXP: 54,220

— Practical Tax Explanation, § 14,420

¶540 Incentives to Hire Unemployed Veterans or Disconnected Youth

SUMMARY OF NEW LAW

Unemployed veterans or disconnected youth who begin work in 2009 or 2010 will be treated as members of a targeted group for purposes of the work opportunity tax credit.

BACKGROUND

The work opportunity tax credit is designed to provide an incentive for employers to hire individuals from certain disadvantaged groups (i.e., targeted groups) that have a particularly high unemployment rate. Generally, an employer who hires an individual from one of these targeted groups may claim a tax credit equal to 40 percent of the first $6,000 of qualified wages paid to that individual during the first year of employment. However, the credit is reduced to 25 percent of the qualified first-year wages for an employee who works 400 hours or less during the first year of employment. The employer may not claim the credit for qualified wages paid to an employee who works less than 120 hours in the first year of employment. The

BACKGROUND

employer may elect out of the application of the credit. The credit is scheduled to expire for individuals who begin work after August 31, 2011 (Code Sec. 51).

The targeted groups for which the credit is presently available are as follows:

(1) individuals who are members of families receiving assistance under the Temporary Assistance for Needy Families program (Title IV-A of the Social Security Act) for at least nine months during the 18-month period ending on the hiring date;

(2) qualified veterans who are:

   (a) members of families that receive benefits under a supplemental nutrition assistance program for at least three months ending during the 12-month period ending on the hiring date, or

   (b) entitled to compensation for a service-connected disability and were (A) discharged or released from active duty in the Armed Forces within one year before the hiring date, or (B) unemployed for six months or more during the 12-month period ending on the hiring date;

(3) ex-felons hired within one year after conviction or release from prison;

(4) individuals who have attained age 18, but not 40, on the hiring date and who live in an empowerment zone, enterprise community, renewal community, or rural renewal community;

(5) individuals who have a physical or mental disability that is a substantial handicap to employment and who are referred to the employer upon completion of, or while receiving, vocational rehabilitation;

(6) individuals aged 16 and 17 who are employed for at least 90 days during the summer months (May 1 through September 15) and who live in an empowerment zone, enterprise community, or renewal community;

(7) individuals aged 18 through 39 who are members of families that receive assistance under a supplemental nutrition assistance program during the six-month period ending on the hiring date, or for at least three months of the five-month period ending on the hiring date in the case of a family member who ceases to be eligible for such assistance;

(8) individuals who receive supplemental security income (SSI) benefits under Title XVI of the Social Security Act for any month that ends within the 60-day period ending on the hiring date; and

(9) long-term family assistance recipients who include:

   (a) members of families that receive family assistance under Title IV-A of the Social Security Act during the 18-month period ending on the hiring date;

   (b) members of families that receive such assistance for at least 18 months after August 5, 1997, if the hiring date is within two years after the earliest such 18-month period; or

   (c) members of families that are no longer eligible to receive family assistance under Title IV-A of the Social Security Act due to federal or state time limits

¶540

BACKGROUND

if the hiring date is within two years after the date the family became ineligible (Code Sec. 51(d)).

For purposes of the credit, a veteran is an individual who (a) has served on active duty in the Armed Forces for more than 180 days or has been discharged or released from active duty for a service-connected disability; and (b) is not on an extended active duty (i.e., an active duty for more than 90 days) on any day during the 60-day period ending on the hiring date (Code Sec. 51(d)(3)(B)).

An employer cannot treat an individual as a member of a targeted group unless:

(1) the employer has received certification from a designated local agency (i.e., a state employment agency) on or before the date the individual begins work that the individual is a member of a targeted group; or

(2) a pre-screening notice for the individual has been completed by the employer on or before the date the individual is offered employment, and the employer submits that notice to the designated local agency as part of a certification request by the 28th day after the individual begins work (Code Sec. 51(d)(13)).

NEW LAW EXPLAINED

Work opportunity tax credit allowed for unemployed veterans and disconnected youth.—Unemployed veterans or disconnected youth who begin work for an employer during 2009 or 2010 will be treated as members of a targeted group for whom the employer may claim the work opportunity tax credit (Code Sec. 51(d)(14)(A), as added by the American Recovery and Reinvestment Tax Act of 2009 (P.L. 111-5)).

For this purpose, an unemployed veteran includes any individual who is certified by the designated local agency as:

(1) having served on active duty in the Armed Forces for more than 180 days or having been discharged or released from active duty in the Armed Forces for a service-connected disability;

(2) having been discharged or released from active duty in the Armed Forces at any time during the five-year period ending on the hiring date; and

(3) having received unemployment compensation under state or federal law for at least four weeks during the one-year period ending on the hiring date (Code Sec. 51(d)(14)(B)(i), as added by the 2009 Recovery Act).

Comment: The veteran definition for purposes of the new targeted group is generally the same as the definition used for the existing qualified veteran group, except that it does not require that the individual is not on an extended active duty on any day during the 60-day period ending on the hiring date. Thus, the employer may receive a credit for hiring unemployed veterans from the new targeted group even if they departed from service within the last 60 days before the hiring date.

Disconnected youth includes any individual certified by the designated local agency as:

NEW LAW EXPLAINED

(1) having attained age 16, but not age 25, on the hiring date;

(2) not regularly attending school secondary, technical, or post-secondary school during the six-month period preceding the hiring date;

(3) not being regularly employed during the six-month preceding the hiring date; and

(4) not being readily employable due to the lack of a sufficient number of basic skills (Code Sec. 51(d)(14)(B)(ii), as added by the 2009 Recovery Act).

Comment: The Conference Committee Report clarifies that for purposes of disconnected youths, it is intended that a low-level of formal education may satisfy the requirement that an individual is not readily employable by reason of lacking a sufficient number of skills. In addition, it is intended that the IRS will take into account the administrability of the program by the state agencies when providing general guidance regarding the various new criteria (Conference Report for P.L. 111-5, American Recovery and Reinvestment Act of 2009 (H. Rept. 111-16)).

▶ **Effective date.** The provision applies to individuals who begin work for the employer after December 31, 2008 (Act Sec. 1221(b) of the American Recovery and Reinvestment Tax Act of 2009 (P.L. 111-5)).

Law source: Law at ¶5135. Committee Report at ¶10,260.

— Act Sec. 1221(a) of the American Recovery and Reinvestment Tax Act of 2009 (P.L. 111-5), adding Code Sec. 51(d)(14);

— Act Sec. 1221(b), providing the effective date.

Reporter references: For further information, consult the following CCH reporters.

— Standard Federal Tax Reporter, ¶4803.03
— Tax Research Consultant, BUSEXP: 54,258
— Practical Tax Explanation, § 13,805.10 and § 13,805.15

¶545 Carbon Dioxide Capture Credit

SUMMARY OF NEW LAW

To qualify for the tax credit of $10 per metric ton for the capture of carbon dioxide for use as a tertiary injectant in an enhanced oil or natural gas recovery project, the carbon dioxide must remain sequestered in permanent geologic storage.

BACKGROUND

The carbon dioxide capture credit is a general business credit that was created by the Emergency Economic Stabilization Act of 2008 (P.L. 110-343) (Code Sec. 45Q). In an effort to reduce greenhouse gas emissions, the credit provides incentives to taxpayers that capture carbon dioxide at certain industrial facilities and either permanently

BACKGROUND

dispose of the gas in a geologic formation or use it in certain enhanced oil or natural gas recovery efforts.

The credit applies to carbon dioxide captured at industrial facilities located in the United States or its possessions that (1) are owned by the taxpayer, (2) have carbon capture equipment installed, and (3) capture at least 500,000 metric tons of carbon dioxide during the tax year (Code Sec. 45Q(c) and (d)(1)). The credit provides $20 per metric ton for carbon dioxide that is captured and disposed of in "secure geologic storage" (Code Sec. 45Q(a)(1)). Secure geologic storage includes geologic formations such as deep saline formations and unminable coal seems, subject to regulations to be established by the Secretary of the Treasury and the Administrator of the Environmental Protection Agency (Code Sec. 45Q(d)(2)).

The credit also provides $10 per metric ton for carbon dioxide that is captured and used as a tertiary injectant in a qualified enhanced oil or natural gas recovery project (Code Sec. 45Q(a)(2)). The term tertiary injectant has the same meaning as used in Code Sec. 193(b)(1) and, in the case of an enhanced oil recovery project, refers to the injection of the carbon dioxide into an oil field to increase the amount of oil that can be extracted—a type of enhanced oil recovery. During the tertiary injectant process a portion of the carbon dioxide may dissolve in or return with the newly extracted oil where it is often reinjected into the oil field. The credit, however, only applies to the initial deposit of captured carbon dioxide not to the carbon dioxide that is recaptured, recycled, or reinjected during the enhanced oil and natural gas recovery process (Code Sec. 45Q(b)(2)).

Although both credit amounts were meant to promote carbon sequestration technology to help capture and store carbon dioxide in order to reduce greenhouse gas emissions, there is no requirement that the carbon dioxide used in enhanced oil or natural gas recovery and otherwise eligible for the $10 per metric ton credit remain in the same secure geologic storage that is required for the $20 per metric ton credit.

Both credit amounts are adjusted for inflation (Code Sec. 45Q(d)(7)). The credit expires at the end of the calendar year in which the Secretary of the Treasury and the Environmental Protection Agency certify that 75 million metric tons of carbon dioxide have been captured and disposed of or used as a tertiary injectant (Code Sec. 45Q(e)).

NEW LAW EXPLAINED

Carbon dioxide capture credit modified to require sequestration of carbon dioxide used as a tertiary injectant.—The carbon dioxide capture credit is modified to require that carbon dioxide used as a tertiary injectant and otherwise eligible for the $10 per metric ton credit must be disposed of in secure geologic storage in order to qualify for the credit (Code Sec. 45Q(a)(2), as amended by the American Recovery and Reinvestment Tax Act of 2009 (P.L. 111-5)).

> **Comment:** Although the carbon dioxide capture credit incorporates the definition of a "qualified enhanced oil or natural gas recovery project" from a related credit for enhanced oil recovery projects under Code Sec. 43(c)(2) (Code Sec. 45Q(d)(4)), there are some inconsistencies created by the use of this definition.

NEW LAW EXPLAINED

Most notably, projects under the recovery credit definition must be certified by a petroleum engineer to be "in accordance with sound engineering principles," while the carbon dioxide credit includes non-petroleum applications such as natural gas projects.

Credit overlap. The 2009 Recovery Act clarifies that the $20 credit amount is not available with respect to carbon dioxide that is used as a tertiary injectant (Code Sec. 45Q(a)(1)(B), as amended by the 2009 Recovery Act).

Regulation of geological storage. The Department of Energy and the Department of the Interior are added to the list of government entities responsible for establishing regulations for determining adequate security measures for geological carbon dioxide storage. Previously, only the Department of the Treasury and the Environmental Protection Agency had regulatory authority (Code Sec. 45Q(d)(2), as amended by the 2009 Recovery Act).

> **Practical Analysis:** Charles R. Goulding, J.D., CPA, MBA, and President of Energy Tax Savers Inc. of Syosset, New York, observes that carbon sequestration is a newly developing technology where leading experts consider natural geological formation sequestration as the most promising opportunity. With the focus on natural geological formation carbon storage, the new Section C safe storage requirement is designed to insure that credits are only available where the storage location is documented as secure.

Comment: According to the Conference Committee Report for American Recovery and Reinvestment Act of 2009, the carbon dioxide must be sequestered in "permanent geological storage" to claim the credit. The credit provision, however, uses the phrase "secure geological storage" (Code Sec. 45Q(d)(2)) and while it requires that the carbon dioxide not escape into the atmosphere, it does not address the permanence of the storage.

Types of geological storage. The term "secure geological storage" is clarified to include oil and gas reservoirs in addition to unminable coal seams and deep saline formations (Code Sec. 45Q(d)(2), as amended by the 2009 Recovery Act).

Credit expiration. The 75 million metric tons of carbon dioxide limit that causes the credit to sunset now applies to captured carbon dioxide that is claimed under the credit (Code Sec. 45Q(e), as amended by the 2009 Recovery Act).

▶ **Effective date.** The provision shall apply to carbon dioxide captured after February 17, 2009 (Act Sec. 1131(c) of the American Recovery and Reinvestment Tax Act of 2009 (P.L. 111-5)).

Law source: Law at ¶5100. Committee Report at ¶10,190.

— Act Sec. 1131(a) of the American Recovery and Reinvestment Tax Act of 2009 (P.L. 111-5), adding Code Sec. 45Q(a)(2)(C);

— Act Sec. 1131(b), amending Code Sec. 45Q(a)(1)(B), (d)(2), and (e);

— Act Sec. 1131(c), providing the effective date.

¶545

NEW LAW EXPLAINED

Reporter references: For further information, consult the following CCH reporters.
— Standard Federal Tax Reporter, ¶4500ZL.21
— Tax Research Consultant, BUSEXP: 55,600
— Practical Tax Explanation, § 14,450

Tax Bonds

TAX-CREDIT BONDS

¶605 Build America Bonds
¶610 Credit for Qualified Bonds
¶615 Pass-Through of Tax Credit Bond Credits to Mutual Fund Shareholders
¶625 Recovery Zone Economic Development Bonds
¶630 Qualified School Construction Tax Credit Bonds
¶635 Qualified Zone Academy Bonds (QZAB)
¶640 Qualified Energy Conservation Bonds
¶645 New Clean Renewable Energy Bonds

TAX-EXEMPT BONDS

¶650 Alternative Minimum Tax Limitations on Tax-Exempt Bonds
¶652 Recovery Zone Facility Bonds
¶655 Exempt Facility Bonds for High-Speed Intercity Rail Facilities
¶660 Industrial Development Bond Financing for Production of Intangible Property
¶665 Tribal Economic Development Bonds

TAX-CREDIT BONDS

¶605 Build America Bonds

SUMMARY OF NEW LAW

State and local governments may issue taxable build America bonds before January 1, 2011, that provide bondholders taxable interest payments and a credit against their federal income tax liability. State and local governments may elect to receive a payment credit that replaces the bondholder's tax credit with respect to certain build America bonds.

¶605

BACKGROUND

State and local bonds are classified generally as either governmental bonds or private activity bonds. Governmental bonds are primarily used to finance governmental functions or are repaid with governmental funds. Private activity bonds are bonds that allow the state or local government to serve as a conduit for providing financing to nongovernmental persons, such as private businesses or individuals.

The Code has long contained provisions making the interest on qualifying state and local bonds exempt from federal income tax. This provides an indirect federal subsidy for state and local government operations and activities (Code Sec. 103). Tax-exempt bonds are subject to a number of restrictions intended to insure that their proceeds are indeed used for public purposes.

The exclusion from income for interest on state and local bonds does not apply to private activity bonds, unless the bonds are issued for certain permitted purposes ("qualified private activity bonds") and other Code requirements are met (Code Secs. 103(b)(1) and 141). The exclusion also does not apply to bonds with respect to which the federal government directly or indirectly guarantees the payment of principal or interest ("federally guaranteed bonds") (Code Sec. 149(b)).

Arbitrage bonds are also excluded from the category of tax-exempt bonds (Code Sec. 103(b)(2)). Arbitrage bonds are, most simply, bonds that are issued to directly or indirectly acquire higher yielding investments (Code Sec. 148).

Tax credit bonds. Tax credit bonds offer an alternative means of subsidizing state and local governments. Tax credit bonds are not interest-bearing obligations. Instead, a taxpayer holding a tax credit bond on an allowance date during a tax year is allowed a credit against federal income tax equivalent to the interest that the bond would otherwise pay. The bondholder must include the amount of the credit in gross income and treat it as interest income. The Treasury Secretary determines credit rates for tax credit bonds based on general assumptions about credit quality of the class of potential eligible issuers, and other factors.

Through the tax credit, the federal government effectively pays the interest on the bonds, allowing the issuer to borrow interest free. In return, the issuer must satisfy certain requirements with regard to the form of the bonds and the use of the proceeds.

The types of qualified tax credit bonds include qualified forestry conservation bonds (Code Sec. 54B), new clean renewable energy bonds (Code Sec. 54C), qualified energy conservation bonds (Code Sec. 54D) and qualified zone academy bonds (Code Sec. 54E). General rules that apply to all qualified tax credit bonds include requirements regarding credit allowance dates, the expenditure of available project proceeds, reporting, arbitrage, maturity limitations, and financial conflicts of interest (Code Sec. 54A).

NEW LAW EXPLAINED

Taxable bond option for build America bonds issued by state and local governments.—The American Recovery and Reinvestment Tax Act of 2009 allows state and local governments to issue taxable build America bonds, which provide the bondholder

NEW LAW EXPLAINED

with both taxable interest and a tax credit (Code Sec. 54AA, as added by the American Recovery and Reinvestment Tax Act of 2009 (P.L. 111-5)). For qualified bonds, the issuer can elect to receive a federal payment in lieu of the credit to the bondholder.

> **Practical Analysis:** John O. Everett, Ph.D., CPA, tax professor at Virginia Commonwealth University, Cherie J. Hennig, Ph.D., CPA, tax professor at Florida International University, and William A. Raabe, Ph.D., CPA, tax professor at the Ohio State University, note that the American Recovery and Reinvestment Tax Act of 2009 includes a series of newly created categories of state and local debt securities, the most prominent of which may be the Build America Bond. The various debt issuances authorized by the American Recovery and Reinvestment Tax Act of 2009 provide borrowed funds to target projects encouraged by the federal government but largely paid for at the state and local level, such as infrastructure improvement, control of climate change and the like.
>
> Under the American Recovery and Reinvestment Tax Act of 2009, the state or local jurisdiction can issue, in lieu of bonds whose interest is excluded under Code Sec. 103, a "tax credit bond." Tax credit bonds that are issued in 2009 or 2010 receive the treatment specified in the American Recovery and Reinvestment Tax Act of 2009. The type of bond issued by the jurisdiction, *i.e.*, gaining the investor an exclusion or a credit, is at the preference of the state or local government. Tax-credit bonds result in the following federal income tax treatment for the lender:
>
> Interest paid is included in the investor's gross income.
>
> The investor is allowed a nonrefundable tax credit against the federal income tax liability.
>
> The tax credit process is meant to make the bonds more attractive to investors, in that the after-tax income from the bonds may be greater than would be the case for a traditional municipal bond. As a result, state and local jurisdictions will have access to greater amounts of borrowed funds in the short term, and the net cost of the borrowing to the jurisdiction is reduced because the interest rate that it must pay is lower than that elsewhere in the bond market.
>
> If the state or local government believes that investors will not be attracted by additional nonrefundable tax credits, given the current economic conditions, it can elect that an amount equivalent to the projected credits allowed against the federal income tax will be received as a direct grant from the U.S. Treasury.
>
> "Private activity" bonds, using the definition of such for AMT purposes, cannot qualify as Build America Bonds. Private activity bonds similarly cannot qualify for parallel state and local government debt issuances, such as the Recovery Zone bonds and Tribal Economic Development bonds authorized elsewhere in the American Recovery and Reinvestment Tax Act of 2009.
>
> Profitable, upper-bracket taxpayers are likely to consider purchases of the Build America Bonds, but not if they would trigger a greater AMT liability. Thus, governments should restrict the use of the funds (under the various AMT private activity bond definitions) to governmental functions.

¶605

NEW LAW EXPLAINED

> The various new bond structures constitute a means by which the federal government shares some of the costs of certain state and local government projects. Estimated federal revenue losses attributable to the provision are over $4 billion over the 10-year scoring period, as investors are likely to be attracted to these bonds.

A build America bond is any obligation, other than a private activity bond, that meets these three requirements:

(1) the bond must be issued before January 1, 2011;

(2) the issuer must make an irrevocable election to have Code Sec. 54AA apply to the bond; and

(3) but for that election, the interest on the bond would have been excludable under Code Sec. 103 (Code Sec. 54AA(d)(1), as added by the 2009 Recovery Act).

For purposes of the rules under Code Sec. 149(b) that exclude federally guaranteed bonds from the category of tax-exempt bonds, build America bonds are not treated as federally guaranteed by virtue of their cash payment or credit features. Also, for purposes of the rules under Code Sec. 148 that exclude arbitrage bonds from the category of tax-exempt bonds, the yield on build America bonds must be determined without regard to the credit. Finally, build America bonds cannot have an issue price that has more than a de minimis amount of premium over the stated principal amount of the bond (a de minimis amount is generally ¼ of one percent of the stated redemption price at maturity, multiplied by the number of years to maturity) (Code Sec. 54AA(d)(2), as added by the 2009 Recovery Act; see Code Sec. 1273(a)(3)).

Unlike tax credit bonds, which provide a tax credit in lieu of interest payments, build America bonds pay interest to the bondholders and also provide a tax credit. The bondholder must include the interest in gross income, but is allowed a credit against federal income tax liability for a portion of the interest payments received (Code Sec. 54AA(a) and (f)(1) as added by the 2009 Recovery Act). The credit is itself treated as interest that is includible in gross income (Code Sec. 54AA(f)(2), as added by the 2009 Recovery Act; see Code Sec. 54A(f)).

> **Comment:** Although the interest and the credit are includible in the bondholder's gross income for federal tax purposes, they are treated as exempt from federal income tax for purposes of state income tax laws, unless the state provides otherwise after February 17, 2009, the date of enactment of these provisions (Act § 1531(d) of the 2009 Recovery Act).

The tax credit is equal to 35 percent of the interest payable on the interest payment date of the bond (Code Sec. 54AA(b), as added by the 2009 Recovery Act). The interest payment date is any date on which the bondholder of record is entitled to a payment of interest under the bond (Code Sec. 54AA(e), as added by the 2009 Recovery Act).

> **Comment:** Because the bondholder includes the interest in income, but receives a tax credit equal to 35 percent of the interest payment, the interest rate on build America bonds should be equal to approximately 74.1 percent of the interest on

¶605

NEW LAW EXPLAINED

comparable taxable bonds (Conference Committee Report for American Recovery and Reinvestment Act of 2009).

> **Example:** Assume a taxable bond pays a $1,000 coupon and sells at par. The same sized bond issued as a build America bond with coupon of $741.00 should also sell at par. The holder of the build America bond will receive an interest payment of $741, and is eligible to claim a credit of $259 (35 percent of $741). The credit and the interest payment are both included in the bondholder's income. Thus, the bondholder's taxable income from the instrument would be $1,000, the same taxable income that the bondholder would recognize from acquiring a comparable taxable bond (Conference Committee Report for American Recovery and Reinvestment Act of 2009).

> **Practical Analysis:** Dale S. Collinson, a director in the Financial Institutions and Products group of the Washington National Tax practice of KPMG LLP, notes that interest on bonds issued by States, local governmental units and certain other qualified entities is generally exempt from federal income tax under Code Sec. 103. The availability of the exemption is subject to compliance with a number of rules, including a prohibition on arbitrage bonds and limitations on the use of bond proceeds to finance private entities (private activity bonds). Tax-exempt bonds other than private activity bonds are often called governmental bonds.
>
> New Code Sec. 54AA creates a new category of tax-credit bonds called "Build America Bonds." Build America Bonds are any obligation (other than a private activity bond) where the interest on the obligation would otherwise be excludable from gross income under Code Sec. 103, the obligation is issued before January 1, 2011, and the issuer makes an irrevocable election to have Code Sec. 54AA apply. The holder of a Build America Bond is allowed a credit on each bond equal to 35 percent of the amount of the interest payable by the issuer on each interest payment date. Interest on the bonds and the tax credit amount are both includible in gross income. Build America Bonds may not be issued with more than a *de minimis* amount of premium over the stated principal amount of the bonds. Unlike other tax-credit bonds, Build America Bonds are not subject to a limitation on total bond amount.
>
> Code Sec. 54AA provides an issuer with the option of electing to receive a direct payment (in the form of a refundable credit) in lieu of the holder tax credit. The election is available for a Build America Bond issued before January 1, 2011, if 100 percent of the excess of (1) the available project proceeds of such issue, over (2) the amounts in a reasonably required reserve (within the meaning of Code Sec. 150(a)(3)) with respect to such issue, are to be used for capital expenditures, and the issuer makes an irrevocable election to have the election apply. New Code Sec. 6431 provides that the Treasury Department shall pay (contemporaneously with each interest payment date on the bonds) to the issuer (or to a person responsible for making interest payments on behalf of the issuer) 35 percent of the interest

¶605

NEW LAW EXPLAINED

payable on the bond on that interest date. The Taxable Bond Option Provisions apply to obligations issued after date of enactment.

Issuers of tax-exempt governmental bonds receive a financial benefit that is attributable to interest on the bonds being exempt from federal income tax in that the bonds may be issued at interest rates lower than interest rates on comparable taxable bonds. Proposals have been made over the years to provide issuers of governmental bonds with an option to issue taxable bonds and to receive from the federal government a direct payment to offset the greater interest expense that would result. The proposals stem from a belief such direct payments would be a more efficient way of providing an equivalent financial benefit to issuers.

The American Recovery and Reinvestment Tax Act of 2009 provides alternative methods for implementing a taxable bond option: a tax credit to holders or a tax payment to issuers. Issuers are likely to find the issuer payment provisions financially more attractive than the holder credit provisions, because an investor is likely to demand an overall yield from the combination of the actual interest paid and the tax credit equal to the yield on a comparable corporate tax bond. At the 35-percent holder credit rate, a holder's total yield from a Build America Bond will equal the yield on a comparable corporate taxable bond if the issuer's interest payment equals approximately 74 percent of the interest rate on the comparable taxable bond (74 + (35 × 74, or 25.9) = 99.9). So a governmental issuer's cost for issuing holder tax-credit bonds would be approximately 74 percent of the comparable taxable bond yield. If an issuer elects the issuer payment and sets the rate of interest on the bonds at 100 percent of the rate on a comparable taxable bond, the issuer will receive a payment of 35 percent of the interest paid and will, therefore, have a net interest cost of 65 percent of the taxable rate compared to the 74 percent cost in the case of the holder credit.*

Another advantage of the issuer payment alternative is that it could facilitate a separation of the federal payment from the issuer payments in a coupon stripping transaction. The bonds could be placed in trust and separate trust receipts could be issued for the federal payments. As permitted by new Code Sec. 6431, the issuer could direct that the federal payments be made directly to the trustee holding the bonds. This arrangement should make it possible for the trust receipts representing entitlement to the federal payment to be sold at a lower yield.

The issuer payment alternative also overcomes concerns that holder tax credits may have lesser appeal in the current economic climate in which many potential investors are experiencing such large losses that tax credits have no immediate value.

The amount of the credit cannot exceed the excess of the sum of the bondholder's regular tax liability and alternative minimum tax liability over the sum of the credits allowed under Code Secs. 21 through 54E, not including Code Secs. 31 through 37 and

---

* The issuer credit provisions also provide a greater financial benefit for small issuers, but the difference is somewhat less substantial. At the 40-percent holder credit rate, an issuer would need to set the bond interest rate at approximately 71.4-percent of the comparable taxable rate in order for a holder to have a net yield equal to the yield on a comparable nongovernmental taxable bond.

¶605

NEW LAW EXPLAINED

the build America bond credit itself. Any unused credit may be carried forward to succeeding tax years (Code Sec. 54AA(c), as added by the 2009 Recovery Act).

Rules similar to Code Sec. 54A(g), (h) and (i) apply for purposes of the credit (Code Sec. 54AA(f)(2), as added by the 2009 Recovery Act). Thus, in the case of a build America bond held by an S corporation or partnership, the allocation of the credit to the shareholders or partners is treated as a distribution (see Code Sec. 54A(g)). For build America bonds held by a real estate investment trust (REIT), the credit is allowed to the respective beneficiaries (and any gross income included in income with respect to the credit is treated as distributed to them) under procedures to be prescribed by the Treasury Secretary (see Code Sec. 54A(h)).

Rules similar to those governing REITs are also extended to regulated investment companies (RICs). Thus, a RIC holding build America bonds can elect to include the interest payment in income, increase its dividend paid deduction by the same amount, and pass the credit through proportionately to its respective shareholders (and any gross income included in income with respect to the credit is treated as distributed to those shareholders) (Code Sec. 853A, as added by the 2009 Recovery Act). See ¶ 615 for an explanation of new Code Sec. 853A.

Future regulations may permit interest to be stripped from the bonds. Thus, there could be a separation (including at issuance) of the ownership of a bond and the entitlement to the credit with respect to the bond. The credit would then be allowed to the person who, on the credit allowance date, holds the instrument evidencing the entitlement to the credit, rather than to the holder of the bond (see Code Secs. 54A(i) and 1286).

Qualified bonds issued before 2011. State and local governments may elect to issue certain build America bonds as "qualified bonds" before January 1, 2011. These qualified bonds are issued in exchange for a payment credit, determined in accordance with new Code Sec. 6431 (see ¶ 610 for an explanation of Code Sec. 6431). This credit to the issuer is in lieu of the credit that would otherwise be allowed to the bondholder; and is generally equal to 35 percent of the interest paid on the bond (Code Sec. 54AA(g)(1), as added by the 2009 Recovery Act).

In order to constitute a qualified bond, 100 percent of the available project proceeds of the issue, less a reasonably required reserve (within the meaning of Code Sec. 150(a)(3)) for debt service with respect to the issue, must be used for capital expenditures (Code Sec. 54AA(g)(2), as added by the 2009 Recovery Act). The issuer must also make an irrevocable election to have Code Sec. 54AA(g) apply to the bonds.

> **Comment:** It would appear that the reserve on qualified bonds cannot exceed 10 percent of the available project proceeds. This is because under Code Sec. 148(d)(2), a bond becomes an arbitrage bond when the reserve exceeds 10 percent of the proceeds from the sale of the issue. The interest on an arbitrage bond is not tax-exempt under Code Sec. 103 and, therefore, a bond with a 10-percent reserve is not eligible to be a qualified bond (Conference Committee Report for American Recovery and Reinvestment Act of 2009).

Available project proceeds are proceeds from the sale of the issue less issuance costs (not to exceed two percent), plus any investment earnings on the sale proceeds (Code

¶605

NEW LAW EXPLAINED

Sec. 54A(e)(4)). A capital expenditure is any cost of a type that is properly chargeable to capital account (or would be chargeable with a proper election or with application of the of the "placed in service" definition under Reg. §1.150-2(c)) under general federal income tax principles, applied as if the bond issuer were a C corporation) (Conference Committee Report for American Recovery and Reinvestment Act of 2009).

Regulations. The Treasury Secretary is given the authority to issue regulations and other guidance necessary or appropriate to carry out these provisions and Code Sec. 6431 (Code Sec. 54AA(h), as added by the 2009 Recovery Act).

▶ **Effective date.** The provisions apply to obligations issued after February 17, 2009 (Act Sec. 1531(e) of the American Recovery and Reinvestment Tax Act of 2009 (P.L. 111-5)).

Law source: Law at ¶5145, ¶5150, ¶5155, ¶5300, ¶5310, ¶5375 and ¶5385. Committee Report at ¶10,450.

— Act Sec. 1531(a) of the American Recovery and Reinvestment Tax Act of 2009 (P.L. 111-5), adding Code Sec. 54AA;

— Act Sec. 1531(c), amending Code Secs. 54A(c)(1)(B), 54(c)(2), 1397E(c)(2), 1400N(l)(3)(B), 6211(b)(4)(A) and 6401(b)(1), and 31 U.S.C. Sec. 1324(b)(2);

— Act Sec. 1531(d);

— Act Sec. 1531(e), providing the effective date.

Reporter references: For further information, consult the following CCH reporters.

— Standard Federal Tax Reporter, ¶4888.01

— Tax Research Consultant, BUSEXP: 55,802

— Practical Tax Explanation, §3,105.05

¶610 Credit for Qualified Bonds

SUMMARY OF NEW LAW

State and local governments may elect to issue qualified build America bonds before January 1, 2011, in exchange for a payment credit.

BACKGROUND

The Code has long contained provisions making the interest on qualifying state and local bonds exempt from federal income tax, which provides an indirect federal subsidy for state and local government operations and activities (Code Sec. 103). State and local bonds are classified generally as either governmental bonds or private activity bonds. Governmental bonds are primarily used to finance governmental functions or are repaid with governmental funds. Private activity bonds are bonds in which the state or local government serves as a conduit providing financing to nongovernmental persons (e.g., private businesses or individuals). Tax-exempt bonds

BACKGROUND

are subject to a number of restrictions intended to insure that their proceeds are indeed used for public purposes.

Tax credit bonds generally. A new method of subsidizing state and local governments was introduced with the authorization of tax credit bonds, first exemplified in the form of qualified zone academy bonds, in the Taxpayer Relief Act of 1997 (P.L. 105-34). Tax credit bonds are not interest-bearing obligations. Instead, a taxpayer holding a tax credit bond on one or more allowance dates during a tax year is allowed a credit against federal income tax equivalent to the interest that the bond would otherwise pay. The bondholder must include the amount of the credit in his or her gross income and treat it as interest income. In effect, the federal government pays the interest, allowing the issuer to borrow interest free. In return, the issuer must follow certain requirements with regard to the form of the bonds and the use of the proceeds. The types of qualified tax credit bonds include qualified forestry conservation bonds (Code Sec. 54B), new clean renewable energy bonds (Code Sec. 54C), qualified energy conservation bonds (Code Sec. 54D) and qualified zone academy bonds (Code Sec. 54E).

NEW LAW EXPLAINED

Payment to issuers of qualified bonds.—State and local governments may elect to issue "build America bonds" which provide bondholders taxable interest payments and a credit against their federal income tax liability in lieu of receiving tax-exempt interest payments (Code Sec. 54AA, as added by the American Recovery and Reinvestment Tax Act of 2009 (P.L. 111-5)). A "build America bond" is any obligation issued prior to January 1, 2011, other than a private activity bond, for which interest would have otherwise been excludable from gross income under Code Sec. 103 and for which the issuer makes an irrevocable election to have Code Sec. 54AA apply (Code Sec. 54AA(d)(1), as added by the 2009 Recovery Act). For an explanation of the new build America bonds see ¶ 605.

The bondholder of a build America bond must include the interest received in income, but is allowed a credit against the bondholder's federal income tax liability for a portion of the interest payments received (Code Sec. 54AA(a) and (f)(1) as added by the 2009 Recovery Act). The credit is also treated as interest which is includible in gross income (Code Sec. 54AA(f)(2), as added by the 2009 Recovery Act).

The amount of the credit with respect to any interest payment date for the bond is 35 percent of the amount of interest payable by the bond's issuer with respect to the interest payment date (Code Sec. 54AA(b), as added by the 2009 Recovery Act).

The amount of the credit cannot exceed the excess of the sum of the bondholder's regular tax liability and alternative minimum tax liability over the sum of certain other credits allowable to the bondholder. Any unused credit may be carried forward to each succeeding tax year (Code Sec. 54AA(c), as added by the 2009 Recovery Act). Unless a state provides otherwise, the interest on any build America bond, and the amount of any credit determined with respect to the bond, is treated as exempt from federal income tax for purposes of state income tax laws (Act Sec. 1531(d) of the 2009 Recovery Act).

NEW LAW EXPLAINED

For certain build America bonds, known as "qualified bonds," issued prior to January 1, 2011, state and local governments may elect to issue build America bonds in exchange for a payment credit (Code Secs. 54AA(g) and 6431(a), as added by the 2009 Recovery Act). The credit is 35 percent of the interest payable by the issuer to the holder of the bond on each interest payment date (Code Sec. 6431(b), as added by the 2009 Recovery Act). The "interest payment date" means each date on which interest is payable by the issuer under the terms of the bond (Code Sec. 6431(d), as added by the 2009 Recovery Act).

The credit is paid to the bond issuer (Code Sec. 54AA(g), as added by the 2009 Recovery Act). It is in lieu of the credit otherwise allowed to the holder of the bond.

> **Comment:** Because the market for tax credits is small under current economic conditions, this provision allows state or local governments to elect to receive a direct payment from the federal government equal to the subsidy that would have otherwise been delivered through the federal tax credit for bonds issued in 2009 and 2010 (Committee on Ways and Means, Summary of the Tax Relief Included in the "American Recovery and Reinvestment Plan").

Example: Assume a taxable bond pays a $1,000 coupon and sells at par. If a state or local issuer issues a qualified bond in 2009 with a $1,000 interest coupon, the bondholder would include the $1,000 of interest in taxable income, the same as if the holder had instead purchased the taxable bond. While there is no economic difference to the holder of the bond, with a qualified bond the state or local issuer would receive a payment of $350 for the $1,000 coupon paid to the holder. Thus, the net interest cost to the issuer would be only $650 (Conference Committee Report for American Recovery and Reinvestment Act of 2009).

> **Comment:** Original issue discount, defined in Code Sec. 1273(a) as the excess of an obligation's stated redemption price at maturity over its issue price, is not treated as a payment of interest for purposes of calculating the 35 percent refundable credit (Conference Committee Report for American Recovery and Reinvestment Act of 2009).

One type of bond eligible to be treated as a qualified bond is a taxable recovery zone economic development bond (Code Sec. 1400U-2, as added by the 2009 Recovery Act). The credit to the issuer for such bonds is, however, 45 percent instead of 35 percent (Code Sec. 1400U-2(a)(2), as added by the 2009 Recovery Act). For an explanation of the new taxable recovery zone economic development bonds see ¶625.

In order to constitute a qualified bond, 100 percent of the available project proceeds of the issue, less a reasonably required reserve within the meaning of Code Sec. 150(a)(3) for debt service related to the issue, must used for capital expenditures (Code Secs. 54AA(g) and 6431(e), as added by the 2009 Recovery Act). The issuer must also make an irrevocable election to have Code Sec. 54AA(g) apply.

> **Comment:** It appears that the reserve on qualified bonds cannot exceed 10 percent of the available project proceeds. This is because under Code Sec.

NEW LAW EXPLAINED

148(d)(2), a bond becomes an arbitrage bond when there is a reserve which exceeds 10 percent of the proceeds from the sale of the issue. The interest on an arbitrage bond is not tax-exempt under Code Sec. 103 and, therefore, the bond is not eligible to be a qualified bond. (Conference Committee Report for American Recovery and Reinvestment Act of 2009).

Available project proceeds means proceeds from the sale of the issue less issuance costs (not to exceed two percent) and any investment earnings on the sale proceeds (Code Sec. 54A(e)(4)). Capital expenditure means any cost of a type that is properly chargeable to capital account (or would be chargeable with a proper election or with application of the "placed in service" definition under Reg. § 1.150-2(c)) under general federal income tax principles (Joint Committee on Taxation, Description of Title I of H.R. 598, the American Recovery and Reinvestment Tax Act of 2009 (JCX-5-09), January 21, 2009). For purposes of applying the general federal income tax principles standard, an issuer is generally treated as if it is a corporation subject to taxation under subchapter C of chapter 1 of the Code.

Comment: An example of a capital expenditure would include expenditures made for the purchase of fiber-optic cable to provide municipal broadband service (Joint Committee on Taxation, Description of Title I of H.R. 598, the American Recovery and Reinvestment Tax Act of 2009 (JCX-5-09), January 21, 2009).

The Secretary of the Treasury will pay the 35 or 45 percent credit, as applicable, to the state or local issuer of the bond contemporaneously with each interest payment date (Code Sec. 6431(b), as added by the 2009 Recovery Act). The payment may be made either in advance or as a reimbursement (Joint Committee on Taxation, Description of Title I of H.R. 598, the American Recovery and Reinvestment Tax Act of 2009 (JCX-5-09), January 21, 2009). In lieu of payment to the issuer, the payment may be made to a person making interest payments on behalf of the issuer (Code Sec. 6431(b), as added by the 2009 Recovery Act). For purposes of the arbitrage restrictions of Code Sec. 148, the yield on a qualified bond is reduced by the credit (Code Sec. 6431(c), as added by the 2009 Recovery Act).

Regulations. The Treasury Secretary is given the authority to issue regulations and other guidance necessary or appropriate to carry out these provisions and Code Sec. 54AA (Code Sec. 54AA(h), as added by the 2009 Recovery Act).

▶ **Effective date.** The provisions apply to obligations issued after February 17, 2009 (Act Sec. 1531(e) of the American Recovery and Reinvestment Tax Act of 2009 (P.L. 111-5)).

Law source: Law at ¶5145, ¶5150, ¶5300, ¶5310, ¶5375, ¶5385, and ¶5390. Committee Report at ¶10,450.

— Act Sec. 1531(b) of the American Recovery and Reinvestment Tax Act of 2009 (P.L. 111-5), adding Code Sec. 6431;

— Act Sec. 1531(c), amending Code Secs. 54A(c)(1)(B), 54(c)(2), 1397E(c)(2), 1400N(l)(3)(B), 6211(b)(4)(A) and 6401(b)(1); and 31 U.S.C. Sec. 1324(b)(2);

— Act Sec. 1531(d);

— Act Sec. 1531(e), providing the effective date.

¶610

NEW LAW EXPLAINED

Reporter references: For further information, consult the following CCH reporters.
— Standard Federal Tax Reporter, ¶4888.01
— Tax Research Consultant, BUSEXP: 55,802
— Practical Tax Explanation, §3,105

¶615 Pass-Through of Tax Credit Bond Credits to Mutual Fund Shareholders

SUMMARY OF NEW LAW

Effective for tax years ending after February 17, 2009, regulated investment companies (RICs), commonly known as mutual funds, can elect to pass through to shareholders credits from tax credit bonds, replacing the requirement that the credits be passed through.

BACKGROUND

A regulated investment company (RIC), more commonly known as a mutual fund, is a corporation that acts as an investment agent for its shareholders. A RIC generally operates by investing in and holding government and corporate securities, and passing on interest and dividends to its shareholders. A RIC can typically avoid paying income tax because it can claim a dividends paid deduction against ordinary and capital gain income for distributions to its shareholders.

In order to qualify for this preferred tax treatment, a RIC must satisfy stringent requirements. At least 90 percent of the gross income of a RIC must consist generally of dividends, interest, payments with respect to securities loans and gains from the sale or other disposition of stock, securities or foreign currencies or other income from investments in stock, securities, or foreign currencies (Code Sec. 851(b)(2)). At the close of each quarter of a RIC's tax year, at least 50 percent of the value of a RIC's holdings must consist of cash, government securities, securities of other issuers or a limited amount of other securities, but not more than 25 percent of the value of its total assets can be invested in any one issuer (Code Sec. 851(b)(3)). A RIC is also required to distribute 90 percent of its earnings to shareholders (Code Sec. 852(a)(1)).

While a RIC is not subject to tax on the income it realizes due to the deduction for distributions to shareholders, shareholders are subject to tax on the passed through income when received. However, the dividends received by a shareholder from a RIC retain the character of the income in the hands of the RIC. For example, a dividend received by a shareholder from a RIC that represents the shareholder's proportionate share of income earned by the RIC from the disposition of a capital asset is generally taxed as a long-term capital gain for the shareholder (Code Sec. 852(b)(3)).

Under Code Sec. 853, a RIC may elect to pass through any foreign tax credits for which the RIC is eligible due to income, war profits or excess profits taxes described

BACKGROUND

in Code Sec. 901(b)(1) paid to foreign countries (Code Sec. 853(a)). If so elected, the shareholders are allowed to claim a proportionate share of the foreign tax credit for the amount paid in taxes by the RIC (Code Sec. 853(b)(2). The RIC must provide to the shareholders no later than 60 days after the end of the tax year the amount of the shareholder's proportionate share of the foreign tax credit (Code Sec. 853(c)).

Tax credit bonds generally. Tax credit bonds offer an alternative means of subsidizing state and local governments. Tax credit bonds are not interest-bearing obligations. Instead, a taxpayer holding a tax credit bond on an allowance date during a tax year is allowed a credit against federal income tax equivalent to the interest that the bond would otherwise pay. The bondholder must include the amount of the credit in gross income and treat it as interest income. Through the tax credit, the federal government effectively pays the interest, allowing the issuer to borrow interest free. In return, the issuer must satisfy certain requirements with regard to the form of the bonds and the use of the proceeds.

The types of qualified tax credit bonds include qualified forestry conservation bonds (Code Sec. 54B), new clean renewable energy bonds (Code Sec. 54C), qualified energy conservation bonds (Code Sec. 54D) and qualified zone academy bonds (Code Sec. 54E). General rules that apply to all qualified tax credit bonds include requirements regarding credit allowance dates, the expenditure of available project proceeds, reporting, arbitrage, maturity limitations, and financial conflicts of interest (Code Sec. 54A). Another type of tax credit bond, not under the umbrella of Code Sec. 54A, is the clean renewable energy bond (separate from *new* clean renewable energy bond) (Code Sec. 54).

RICs and tax credit bonds. Where a RIC is a holder of a tax credit bond, the credit is required to be passed through to the shareholders. The manner in which the credit is allowed to shareholders of the RIC is to be determined by the Secretary of the Treasury, but no guidance has yet been provided (Code Sec. 54A(h)).

NEW LAW EXPLAINED

Elective pass through of tax credit bond credits to mutual fund shareholders.—A new provision allows a regulated investment company (RIC) to elect to pass through to shareholders of the RIC credits attributable to tax credit bonds held by the RIC, replacing the required pass-through of the credits (Code Sec. 853A, as added by the American Recovery and Reinvestment Tax Act of 2009 (P.L. 111-5)). If the election is made, the RIC is not allowed any credits attributable to the tax credit bonds and includes in gross income, as interest, the amount of income that the RIC would have included if the election did not apply, increasing the amount of the dividends paid deduction by the same amount (Code Sec. 853A(b)(1) and (2), as added by the 2009 Recovery Act).

In order to qualify for the election, a RIC must hold, directly or indirectly, one or more tax credit bonds on one or more applicable dates during the tax year, and must also meet the 90 percent distribution requirements of a RIC under Code Sec. 852(a)(1). The RIC must also have been taxed as a RIC under Code Sec. 852 for all tax years ending on

NEW LAW EXPLAINED

or after November 8, 1983, or have no accumulated earnings and profits from a tax year to which the RIC provisions did not apply (Code Sec. 853A(a), as added by the 2009 Recovery Act).

> **Comment:** The seemingly complicated process of including the interest in income and then allowing a dividends paid deduction for an equal amount is meant to assist a RIC in satisfying both the 90 percent income requirement of Code Sec. 851(b)(2) and the 90 percent distribution requirement of Code Sec. 852(a)(1). Without this process, a RIC would have to satisfy requirements through other holdings that bear sufficient interest or other similarly passive income. Ultimately, this allows a RIC to be formed that consists entirely of investments in tax credit bonds.

> **Comment:** The requirement that the RIC include interest from the bond in income may at first appear inconsistent with the notion of tax credit bonds. Under the rules for such bonds in place prior to the American Recovery and Reinvestment Tax Act of 2009, tax credit bonds allowed the holder to claim a credit in lieu of receiving interest. However, a new tax credit bond, the "build America bond," provides an interest payment to the holder *in addition* to allowing the holder to claim a tax credit (Code Sec. 54AA, as added by the 2009 Recovery Act), see ¶605. It is this new bond that necessitates the consideration of the receipt of bond interest in the effects of the election.

Where the election is made, shareholders of the RIC are to include in income the shareholder's proportionate share of the interest income attributable to the credits and are simultaneously allowed the proportionate share of credits (Code Sec. 853A(b)(3), as added by the 2009 Recovery Act). A RIC must report to shareholders in a written notice the shareholder's proportionate share of credits and gross income in respect of the credits not later than 60 days after the close of the RIC's tax year. The shareholder's proportionate share of credits and gross income in respect of the credits cannot exceed the amounts so designated by the RIC in the notice (Code Sec. 853A(c), as added by the 2009 Recovery Act).

> **Compliance Pointer:** The manner in which the election is made and the form of the notice to shareholders will be prescribed by the Secretary of the Treasury (Code Sec. 853A(d), as added by the 2009 Recovery Act). Note that the election to pass through to shareholders foreign tax credits under Code Sec. 853 is very similarly drafted, and the manner in which RICs have been making that election and providing notice to shareholders should also suffice here, until formal guidance is provided.

If the ownership of a tax credit bond is separated from the credit with respect to the bond (creating a "stripped tax credit bond"), the election to pass through the credit to RIC shareholders is applied by reference to the instruments evidencing the entitlement to the credit rather than the tax credit bond (Code Sec. 853A(e)(2), as added by the 2009 Recovery Act). Put simply, in the case of a stripped tax credit bond, the election can be made by the taxpayer entitled to receive the credit.

NEW LAW EXPLAINED

Practical Analysis: Deanna Flores, a principal in Financial Institutions and Products group of the Washington National Tax practice of KPMG LLP in San Diego, notes that holders of "qualified tax credit bonds" are entitled to a tax credit on a quarterly basis under Code Sec. 54A. The holders claim the tax credit and include the amount of the credit in gross income as interest.

Act Sec. 1541 of the American Recovery and Reinvestment Tax Act of 2009 adds Code Sec. 853A, which permits regulated investment companies (RICs) directly or indirectly holding tax credit bonds to pass through credits related to the bonds to their shareholders. Code Sec. 853A(e)(2) provides that if a tax credit is separated from ownership of the underlying tax credit bond (a "stripped tax credit bond"), then the pass through rules apply by reference to the terms of the stripped tax credit bond. The procedures for RICs to make the pass through election and notify shareholders are to be provided by later regulations. Regulatory authority also is provided to permit similar pass through treatment for certain tax credit bonds held by real estate investment trusts (REITs) and their beneficiaries.*

RICs generally do not incur an entity-level tax liability under Subchapter M and the excise tax rules of Code Sec. 4982, provided that they distribute their ordinary income and net capital gains to shareholders. This result obtains largely due to the dividends paid deduction provided to RICs under Code Sec. 852 and 561. Absent the special provision in new Code Sec. 853A, a RIC holding a tax credit bond would include the tax credit amount in gross income as interest, like other taxpayers. Unlike other taxpayers, however, the RIC would be required to distribute this "deemed interest" to shareholders, without a corresponding receipt of cash for the distributable amount. Further, a RIC ordinarily would not have an entity-level tax liability to offset with a credit. For these reasons, RICs generally would not be interested in investing in tax-credit bonds.

Code Sec. 853A addresses these tax issues for RICs holding tax credit bonds by permitting an electing RIC to pass the tax credit through to its shareholders, while increasing its dividends paid deduction for the amount of the "deemed interest" includible in the RIC's gross income (without the necessity of a cash distribution). Shareholders of the RIC would receive their share of the tax credit and include in gross income their reported share of the interest income attributable to the credits passed through to them. RICs may find it helpful to offer shareholder education to explain the difference between the cash actually distributed and the amount deemed distributed to shareholders. While this "disconnect" presently exists for a RIC investing in foreign securities that elects to pass through foreign tax credits to shareholders, this would be a new phenomenon for fixed income investors.

An issue could arise under the statute for a RIC purchasing a stripped tax credit bond. In that case, it is unclear whether the RIC would be required to include in gross income the full amount of the credit, or just the excess of the credit amount over the

---

* Prior to the American Recovery and Reinvestment Tax Act of 2009, Code Sec. 54A(h) was added in 2008 to permit pass through of tax credit bond credits by RICs and REITs under procedures prescribed by the IRS. While no formal guidance has been issued, the 2009 instructions to Form 1099-DIV provide for the pass through.

¶615

NEW LAW EXPLAINED

> purchase price for the stripped tax credit bond. It appears that this issue could be resolved by regulation under the authority provided in Code Sec. 853A(f).
>
> Finally, for a small holding of tax credit bonds by a RIC, the administrative costs to administer the Code Sec. 853A election may outweigh any potential tax benefit to the RIC or its shareholders.

Definitions. A tax credit bond, for purposes of this election, is defined as one of three tax credit bonds provided for by the code. The first is a qualified tax credit bond under Code Sec. 54A (Code Sec. 853A(e) (1) (A) (i), as added by the 2009 Recovery Act).

Comment: Effective after February 17, 2009, in addition to the qualified forestry conservation bond, the new clean renewable energy bond, the qualified energy conservation bond and the qualified zone academy bond, Code Sec. 54A also allows for a qualified school construction bond under new Code Sec. 54F, as added by the 2009 Recovery Act. For a discussion of qualified school construction bonds, see ¶630.

The second tax credit bond is a build America bond (Code Sec. 853A(e)(1)(A)(ii), as added by the 2009 Recovery Act).

Comment: A build America bond under new Code Sec. 54AA is a tax credit bond added by the 2009 Recovery Act. There are many requirements for the issuance of the bond and for taxpayers to claim a credit for the bond. For a complete discussion of the build America bond, see ¶605. The credit in the case of these bonds is claimed by the issuer/state; it has no application to this provision.

The third type of tax credit bond is one for which a credit is allowable under chapter 1, subchapter A, part IV, subpart H of the Internal Revenue Code (Code Sec. 853A(e)(1)(A)(iii), as added by the 2009 Recovery Act).

Comment: As of the passage of the 2009 Recovery Act, the only provision in chapter 1, subchapter A, part IV, subpart H of the Internal Revenue Code is Code Sec. 54, allowing a credit to holders of clean renewable energy bonds.

The "applicable date," for purposes of a RIC qualifying to make the election, varies depending on the type of tax credit bond in question. In the case of a qualified tax credit bond under Code Sec. 54A, or for clean renewable energy bonds for which a credit can be claimed under Code Sec. 54, the applicable date is any credit allowance date. The credit allowance date is the fifteenth day of March, June, September and December (Code Sec. 54A(e)(1); Code Sec. 853A(e)(1)(B)(i), as added by the 2009 Recovery Act). In the case of a build America bond, the applicable date is any interest payment date (Code Sec. 853A(e)(1)(B)(ii), as added by the 2009 Recovery Act). The interest payment date is any date on which the holder of record of the build America bond is entitled to a payment of interest (Code Sec. 54AA(c), as added by the 2009 Recovery Act). For a discussion of the interest payment dates for build America bonds, see ¶605.

The Secretary of the Treasury is required to prescribe regulations or other guidance necessary or appropriate to carry out the purposes of the election, including methods

NEW LAW EXPLAINED

for determining a shareholder's proportionate share of credits (Code Sec. 853A(f), as added by the 2009 Recovery Act).

▶ **Effective date.** The provision is applicable to tax years ending after February 17, 2009 (Act Sec. 1541(c) of the American Recovery and Reinvestment Tax Act of 2009 (P.L. 111-5)).

Law source: Law at ¶5145, ¶5150 and ¶5275. Committee Report at ¶10,460.

— Act Sec. 1541(a) of the American Recovery and Reinvestment Tax Act of 2009 (P.L. 111-5), adding Code Sec. 853A;

— Act Sec. 1541(b), amending Code Secs. 54(l) and Code Sec. 54A(h);

— Act Sec. 1541(c), providing the effective date.

Reporter references: For further information, consult the following CCH reporters.

— Standard Federal Tax Reporter, ¶4888.01 and ¶26,433.01

— Tax Research Consultant, RIC: 3,200, RIC: 3,350 and BUSEXP: 55,800

— Practical Tax Explanation, §3105 and §19,205

¶625 Recovery Zone Economic Development Bonds

SUMMARY OF NEW LAW

Up to $10 billion in recovery zone economic development bonds can be issued by counties or large municipalities before January 1, 2011. A recovery zone economic development bond is treated as a type of qualified bond, which entitles the county or municipal issuer to elect to receive a 45 percent tax credit for the interest paid on the bond.

BACKGROUND

The Code has long contained provisions making the interest on qualifying state and local bonds exempt from federal income tax, which provides an indirect federal subsidy for state and local government operations and activities (Code Sec. 103). State and local bonds are classified generally as either governmental bonds or private activity bonds. Governmental bonds are primarily used to finance governmental functions or are repaid with governmental funds. Private activity bonds are bonds in which the state or local government serves as a conduit providing financing to nongovernmental persons (e.g., private businesses or individuals). Tax-exempt bonds are subject to a number of restrictions intended to insure that their proceeds are indeed used for public purposes.

Labor standards. The Davis-Bacon Act (40 U.S.C. §3141), requires that every contract over $2,000 for the construction, alteration or repair of public buildings or public works must contain a clause specifying the minimum wages that will be paid to certain classes of mechanics and laborers employed under the contract. Contractors and their subcontractors are required to pay their workers who are employed on the

BACKGROUND

actual work site no less than the prevailing wages locally, plus the fringe benefits normally paid on similar projects. Two types of local prevailing wage rates are established by the Wage and Hour Division of the U.S. Department of Labor: general wage determinations regarding specific geographical areas for specific types of construction; and project wage determinations applicable only to specific named projects. Generally, the Davis-Bacon prevailing wage requirement is limited to contracts to which the Federal Government is a party. However, Congress has imposed the Davis-Bacon requirements to a number of programs which assist construction projects of State or local governments through grants, loans, loan guarantees, and insurance. Thus, if a construction project is funded or assisted under a Federal statute, the Davis-Bacon prevailing wage requirement may apply to the project.

NEW LAW EXPLAINED

Recovery zone economic development bonds are qualified bonds.—Counties and large municipalities in States in which employment declined during 2008 are authorized to issue $10 billion in recovery zone economic development bonds prior to January 1, 2011. A recovery zone economic development bond is treated as a qualified bond for purposes of new Code Secs. 54AA(g) and Code Sec. 6431 and the applicable credit amount payable to the issuer with respect to the interest paid is 45 percent (Code Sec. 1400U-2, as added by the American Recovery and Reinvestment Tax Act of 2009 (P.L. 111-5)).

> **Comment:** The 45 percent credit rate for issuers of recovery zone economic development bonds is higher than the 35 percent rate that applies to other qualified bonds.

> **Comment:** A related provision of the new law allows the issuers of certain tax-exempt bonds to make an election to treat certain bonds as "build America bonds." If a bond is designated as a build America bond the issuer pays taxable interest and the bondholders also receive a credit against their federal taxes equal to 35 percent of those interest payments (Code Sec. 54AA, as added by the 2009 Recovery Act). A build America bond for this purpose is defined as (1) any obligation (other than a private activity bond) if the interest on the obligation would otherwise be tax-exempt under Code Sec. 103, (2) the bond is issued before January 1, 2011, and (3) the issuer makes the irrevocable election to have Code Sec. 54AA apply (i.e., elects to treat the bond as a build America bond) (Code Sec. 54AA(d), as added by the 2009 Recovery Act). The issuer of a build America bond may make an additional irrevocable election to treat certain build America bonds as "qualified bonds." This election may only be made with respect to a build America bond issued before January 1, 2011. A qualified bond is a build America bond issued as part of an issue if (1) 100 percent of the available project proceeds of the issue, excluding amounts in a reasonably required reserve with respect to the issue, are used for capital expenditures and (2) the issuer makes an irrevocable election to claim the 35 percent credit that the bondholder would otherwise receive (Code Secs. 54AA(g) and 6431, as added by

NEW LAW EXPLAINED

the 2009 Recovery Act). For complete explanations of Code Secs. 54AA and Code Sec. 6431, see ¶605 and ¶610.

Recovery zone economic development bond defined. A recovery zone economic development bond is a "build America bond" issued before January 1, 2011, as part of an issue, if (1) 100 percent of the "available project proceeds" of the issue in excess of amounts in a reasonably required reserve (within the meaning of Code Sec. 150(a)(3)) with respect to the issue are to be used for one or more "qualified economic development purposes," and (2) the issuer designates the bond as a recovery zone economic development bond (Code Sec. 1400U-2(b)(1), as added by the 2009 Recovery Act).

Build America bond defined. A build America bond for this purpose is defined as any obligation (other than a private activity bond) issued before January 1, 2011, if the interest on the obligation would otherwise be tax-exempt under Code Sec. 103, and the issuer makes the irrevocable election to have Code Sec. 54AA apply (Code Sec. 1400U-2(b)(1), as added by the 2009 Recovery Act; Code Sec. 54AA(d), as added by the 2009 Recovery Act).

Available project proceeds. Available project proceeds are defined as the excess of (1) the proceeds from the sale of an issue over (2) the issuance costs financed by the issue (not to exceed two percent of the proceeds). Project proceeds also include any amount earned by investing the net proceeds (Code Sec. 1400U-2(b)(1)(A), as added by the 2009 Recovery Act; Code Sec. 54A(e)(4)).

Qualified economic development purpose. A qualified economic development purpose means expenditures for purposes of promoting development or other economic activity in a "recovery zone," including:

(1) capital expenditures paid or incurred with respect to property located in the zone;

(2) expenditures for public infrastructure and construction of public facilities; and

(3) expenditures for job training and educational programs (Code Sec. 1400U-2(c), as added by the 2009 Recovery Act).

Recovery zone defined. A recovery zone is (1) any area designated by the issuer as having significant poverty, unemployment, rate of home foreclosures, or general distress; (2) any area designated by the issuer as economically distressed by reason of the closure or realignment of a military installation pursuant to the Defense Base Closure and Realignment Act of 1990; and (3) any area for which a designation as an empowerment zone (under Code Sec. 1391(b)(2)) or renewal community (under Code Sec. 1400E) is in effect (Code Sec. 1400U-1(b), as added by the 2009 Recovery Act).

Limitation on amount of bonds designated. An issuer may not designate more bonds as recovery zone economic development bonds than the limitation amount allocated to it by its State (Code Sec. 1400U-2(b)(2), as added by the 2009 Recovery Act).

Allocation of national limitation on recovery zone economic development bonds among States. The national limitation on the amount of recovery zone economic development bonds that may be issued before January 1, 2011 is $10 billion (Code Sec. 1400U-1(a)(4)(A), as added by the 2009 Recovery Act). The limitation will be allocated

¶625

NEW LAW EXPLAINED

by the IRS to the States. The allocation for a State is the amount that bears the same ratio to the total limitation that its employment decline for 2008 bears to the aggregate of the 2008 employment declines for all of the States (Code Sec. 1400U-1(a)(1)(A), as added by the 2009 Recovery Act). A State's employment decline is the difference (if any) between the number of individuals employed in the State in December 2007 and the number of individuals employed in the State in December 2008 (Code Sec. 1400U-1(a)(2), as added by the 2009 Recovery Act). However, no State may be allocated less than 0.9 percent of the $10 billion national limitation (i.e., each State must receive an allocation of at least $90 million). The allocation to each State based on their 2008 employment decline is to be adjusted to the extent necessary to ensure that no State receives less than its 0.9 percent allocation (Code Sec. 1400U-1(a)(1)(B), as added by the 2009 Recovery Act).

> **Example:** State X's total employment in December 2007 was 1 million persons. By December 2008, its total employment had dropped by 100,000 persons to 900,000 persons. Assume that the total employment decline for all States that had an employment decline in 2008 was 3 million. State X's share of the $10 billion national limitation on recovery zone economic development bonds is $333,333,330 (100,000/3,000,000 × $10 billion). However, this amount is subject to reduction in a manner to be determined by the IRS to account for the rule that no State may receive less than 0.9 percent of the $10 billion national limitation.

Reallocation of State's share of national limitation among its counties and large municipalities. A State must reallocate its share of the national limitation among the counties and large municipalities within the State in the proportion that each county's or municipality's 2008 employment decline bears to the aggregate of the 2008 employment declines for all the counties and large municipalities in the State. However, a county or large municipality may waive any some or all of its allocation (Code Sec. 1400U-1(a)(3)(A), as added by the 2009 Recovery Act).

A large municipality is a municipality with a population in excess of 100,000 (Code Sec. 1400U-1(a)(3)(B), as added by the 2009 Recovery Act).

A large municipality's or county's employment decline is calculated in the same manner as the State's employment decline for purposes for determining the State's share of the national limitation. If a large municipality is located in a county, the employment decline within the municipality is not taken into account in determining the county's employment decline (Code Sec. 1400U-1(a)(3)(C), as added by the 2009 Recovery Act).

Prevailing wage requirements. The prevailing wage requirement of the Davis-Bacon Act (40 U.S.C. § 3141) will apply to any project financed with the proceeds of any recovery zone economic development bond (Act Sec. 1601 of the 2009 Recovery Act).

▶ **Effective date.** The provision applies to obligations issued after February 17, 2009 (Act Sec. 1401(c) of the American Recovery and Reinvestment Tax Act of 2009 (P.L. 111-5)).

¶625

NEW LAW EXPLAINED

Law source: Law at ¶5315 and ¶5316. Committee Report at ¶10,350.

— Act Sec. 1401(a) of the American Recovery and Reinvestment Act of 2009 (P.L. 111-5), adding Code Secs. 1400U-1 and 1400U-2;

— Act Sec. 1601;

— Act Sec. 1401(c), providing the effective date.

Reporter references: For further information, consult the following CCH reporters.

— Standard Federal Tax Reporter, ¶4888.01

— Tax Research Consultant, BUSEXP: 55,802

— Practical Tax Explanation, §3,105.05

¶630 Qualified School Construction Tax Credit Bonds

SUMMARY OF NEW LAW

A new category of tax credit bonds, qualified school construction bonds, is authorized for issue in 2009 and 2010, with a national volume cap of $11 billion per year. The bond proceeds must be used to fund the construction, rehabilitation, or repair of a public school, or for the purchase of land on which a funded school will be built.

BACKGROUND

The Code has long contained provisions making the interest on qualifying state and local bonds exempt from federal income tax, which provides an indirect federal subsidy for state and local government operations and activities, including the construction and operation of public schools (Code Sec. 103). Tax-exempt bonds must be registered, and the issuer must meet reporting requirements (Code Sec. 149). Also, arbitrage rules require that the proceeds of a tax-exempt bond issue cannot just be invested to provide income for the issuer arising from the spread between the investment income and the interest paid on the bonds (Code Sec. 148).

A newer method of subsidizing state and local governments is the use of tax credit bonds. Tax credit bonds are not interest-bearing obligations. Instead, a taxpayer holding a tax credit bond on an allowance date during a tax year is allowed a credit against federal income tax equivalent to the interest that the bond would otherwise pay. The bondholder must include the amount of the credit in gross income and treat it as interest income. The credit effectively replaces the interest that would be paid on an exempt bond, allowing the issuer to borrow interest-free. In return, the issuer must follow certain requirements with regard to the form of the bonds and the use of the proceeds.

The Code provisions authorizing the issuance of tax credit bonds for various financing purposes include mechanical provisions, relating to the credit and the application of tax-exempt bond rules, and substantive provisions, which vary depending on what

¶630

BACKGROUND

program or activity the bond proceeds are used to finance. Prior to 2008, tax credit bonds for clean renewable energy purposes and for qualified zone academy purposes were added to the Code separately, each with their own separate substantive and mechanical provisions. The Heartland, Habitat, Harvest, and Horticulture Act of 2008 (P.L. 110-246) added a new Subpart I to Part IV of the Code (regarding credits against tax), placing common mechanical provisions for tax credit bonds in a new Code Sec. 54A, with room for substantive provisions relating to various types of tax credit bonds to follow in succeeding Code Sections.

The common mechanical requirements for tax credit bonds include requirements that:

- the available project proceeds of the bonds be spent for the specified purposes within three years;
- the issuer meet certain reporting and arbitrage requirements generally applicable to tax-exempt bonds;
- the maturity of the bonds not exceed a maximum term to be set each month by the IRS; and
- any applicable conflict-of-interest rules are satisfied (Code Sec. 54A(d)).

Qualified Zone Academy Bonds. Federal support for public schools has been provided in the Internal Revenue Code through the authorization of the issuance of qualified zone academy bonds (QZABs). In the years from 1998 to 2009, $400 million of these tax credit bonds were authorized to be issued in each year. The annual cap is allocated among the states based on their respective populations of individual's below the poverty line.

Projects funded by QZABs must have a significant contribution from the private sector (equal to at least ten percent of the bond proceeds). The proceeds must be used to renovate, provide equipment to, develop course materials for, or train teachers or other personnel in a school that is a qualified zone academy. A qualified zone academy is a public primary or secondary school operating a special program in conjunction with businesses to enhance the curriculum, and is located in an empowerment zone or enterprise community or otherwise has a significant number of economically disadvantaged students.

Prevailing wage requirements. The Davis-Bacon Act (40 U.S.C. §3141) requires that every contract over $2,000 for the construction, alteration or repair of public buildings or public works must contain a clause specifying the minimum wages that will be paid to certain classes of mechanics and laborers employed under the contract. Contractors and their subcontractors are required to pay their workers who are employed on the actual work site no less than the prevailing wages locally, plus the fringe benefits normally paid on similar projects. Two types of local prevailing wage rates are established by the Wage and Hour Division of the U.S. Department of Labor: general wage determinations regarding specific geographical areas for specific types of construction; and project wage determinations applicable only to specific named projects. Generally, the Davis-Bacon prevailing wage requirement is limited to contracts that include the federal government as a party. However, Congress has added the requirement to a number of other laws that provide federal grants to assist

BACKGROUND

construction projects of States or local governments through grants, loans, loan guarantees, and insurance. Thus, the Davis-Bacon prevailing wage requirement may apply to a non-federal construction project that is funded or assisted under a federal statute.

NEW LAW EXPLAINED

Issuance of school construction tax credit bonds authorized.—The American Recovery and Reinvestment Tax Act of 2009 (P.L. 111-5) authorizes the issuance of a new type of tax credit bond called "qualified school construction bonds" during 2009 and 2010 (Code Sec. 54F, as added by the 2009 Recovery Act). These tax credit bonds provide a federal subsidy to assist state and local governments in financing the expenses of public school construction, rehabilitation, and repair.

> **Comment:** Tax credit bonds remain an unexplored territory for most investors. In order to be a competitive option, the credit rate as set by the IRS should yield a return greater than the prevailing municipal bond rate and at least equal to the after-tax rate for corporate bonds of similar maturity and risk. The relatively small volume of tax credit bonds available means there is less incentive for bond analysts to evaluate them ("Tax Credit Bonds: A Brief Explanation," CRS Report for Congress, August 20, 2008). School construction bonds may nevertheless be attractive to some investors for their social benefit.

A bond is a *qualified school construction bond* if:

(1) 100 percent of the available project proceeds of the issue of which it is a part are to be used for the construction, rehabilitation, or repair of a public school facility or to acquire land on which a facility funded by the same issue is to be built;

(2) the bond is issued by a state or local government within the jurisdiction of which the school is located; and

(3) the issuer designates the bond as a qualified school construction bond (Code Sec. 54F(a), as added by the 2009 Recovery Act).

Available project proceeds of an issue are the excess of the proceeds from the sale of the issue over the issuance costs financed by the issue (not to exceed two percent of the proceeds) plus the proceeds from any investment of that excess (Code Sec. 54A(e)(4)).

The *national volume cap* for these bonds is $11 billion for 2009 and another $11 billion for 2010 (Code Sec. 54F(c), as added by the 2009 Recovery Act).

Practical Analysis: Dale S. Collinson, a director in the Financial Institutions and Products group of the Washington National Tax practice of KPMG LLP, notes that under current law interest on bonds issued by States, local governmental units and certain other qualified entities is generally exempt from federal income tax under Code Sec. 103. The availability of the exemption is subject to compliance with a number of rules, including a prohibition on arbitrage bonds and limitations on the use of bond proceeds to finance private entities (private activity bonds).

¶630

NEW LAW EXPLAINED

A tax-credit bond alternative to the interest exemption for bonds that would otherwise qualify for the exemption was created in 1997 with the enactment of provisions for Qualified Zone Academy Bonds (QZABs). Clean renewable energy tax-credit bonds (or "CREBs") were created by the Energy Tax Incentives Act of 2005 (P.L. 109-58), and Gulf tax-credit bonds (or "GOZA bonds") were created by the Gulf Opportunity Zone Act of 2005 (P.L. 109-135). Subsequent legislation has added additional categories of tax-credit bonds.

In earlier legislation, each category of tax-credit bond has been authorized for a limited period and for a maximum amount of bonds (which may be stated in annual amounts). For example, the 1997 QZAB legislation authorized a maximum of $400 million of QZABs in each of 1998 and 1999. The initial authorizations have then been periodically extended, other than for GOZAs. Newer tax-credit bond provisions simply provide an overall limitation on the maximum amount of bonds. Generally, the provisions also provide for the carryover of unused bond limitation amount to subsequent years.

The holder of a tax-credit bond is entitled to a tax credit on a quarterly basis at an annual rate established by a statutory formula. Generally the tax credit rate is a rate determined by the IRS to be a rate that will permit bonds to be issued without discount and without interest cost to the issuer (Code Sec. 54A(b)(3)). In those cases, the bonds will not pay interest; instead, the tax credit functions as interest. The holder claims the tax credit and includes the amount of the credit in gross income.

Each tax credit bond provision generally includes a mechanism for allocating the bond amount limitation among issuers (although the statute itself provides the allocation among States in the case of the GOZA bonds) and a number of other rules, including maximum bond maturity limits.*

Act Sec. 1521 of the American Recovery and Reinvestment Act of 2009 creates a new category of tax credit bonds, Qualified School Construction Bonds (QSCBs). Unless the provision is extended by future legislation, QSCBs may be issued only during 2009 or 2010 (subject to the carryover provision described below). Code Sec. 54F defines a Qualified School Construction Bond as any bond issued as part of an issue if (1) 100 percent of the available project proceeds of the issue are to be used for the construction, rehabilitation or repair of a public school facility or for the acquisition of land on which the facility is to be constructed with part of the proceeds of the issue; (2) the bond is issued by a State or local government having jurisdiction over the place where the school is located; and (3) the issuer makes a QSCB designation.

Code Sec. 54F(c) sets forth a bond issuance limitation for each calendar year as follows: $11 billion for 2009 and $11 billion for 2010. The American Recovery and Reinvestment Act of 2009 establishes a two-part allocation procedure. Under the first part, the IRS is directed to allocate the annual limitation amount among the States and the possessions (other than the Commonwealth of Puerto Rico) generally in

---

* See generally Collinson, *Tax Credit Bonds—Using the IRS to Pay Bond Interest*, 6 J. TAX'N FIN'L PRODUCTS 4, at 51 (2007).

NEW LAW EXPLAINED

> proportion to the respective amounts each State is eligible to receive under Act Sec. 1124 of the Elementary and Secondary Education Act of 1965 (P.L. 89-10) for the most recent fiscal year ending before such calendar year (but with a separate allocation formula for possessions). The second part overrides that initial allocation by directing the IRS to allocate 40 percent of the available limitation for any year to large local educational agencies in proportion to the respective amounts each such agency received under Act Sec. 1124 of the Elementary and Secondary Education Act of 1965. The allocation to any State is then reduced by the aggregate amount of allocations to large local educational agencies within such State.
>
> In addition, $200 million of issuance authority is to be allocated each year for calendar years 2009 and 2010 by the Secretary of the Interior for purposes of the construction, rehabilitation and repair of schools funded by the Bureau of Indian Affairs. Indian tribal governments (as defined in Code Sec. 7701(a)(40)) will be qualified issuers of those bonds. Code Sec. 54F(e) provides for a carryover to the following year of excess bond limitation amount when the amount of bonds issued in a year is less than the amount of the allocated bond limitation amount. Code Sec. 54F will apply to obligations issued after the date of the enactment.
>
> In the past, the implementation of new tax-credit bond provisions has required an initial start-up period for potential issuers to become familiar with the requirements and for the IRS and the States to develop procedures to allocate bond limitation amount, including the submission and review of applications. In addition, many school districts need to obtain voter approval for the issuance of bonds to finance needed capital expenditures. For these districts, the challenge may be to demonstrate that a proposed project has sufficient support to warrant allocation of bond limitation amount for 2009 and 2010. In that event, the carryover allocation provisions will be of major importance.

Allocation of the volume cap. The IRS's allocation of the total annual volume cap for each calendar year is a multi-step process. The first step is a preliminary allocation of the entire amount among the states and U.S. possessions. The $11 billion limit is divided among the states and possessions based on their respective populations of individuals below the poverty line (as defined by the Office of Management and Budget). Each U.S. possession (except Puerto Rico) receives an allocation based on its share of that population (Code Sec. 54F(d)(3), as added by the 2009 Recovery Act). The remaining portion of the cap is then allocated among the states (including Puerto Rico) in proportion to the amounts each is eligible to receive under section 1124 of the Elementary and Secondary Education Act of 1965 (20 U.S.C. § 6333) for the most recent fiscal year ending before the allocation calendar year (Code Sec. 54F(d)(1), as added by the 2009 Recovery Act).

Allocation to school districts. The next step in the process is a separate allocation of 40 percent of the annual cap to local school districts. The IRS will allocate $4.4 billion from the annual cap among participating local school districts in proportion to the amounts each received under section 1124 of the Elementary and Secondary Education Act of 1965 (20 U.S.C. § 6333) for the most recent fiscal year ending before the allocation year (Code Sec. 54F(d)(2), as added by the 2009 Recovery Act). The participating districts,

NEW LAW EXPLAINED

called "large local education agencies," include the 100 local educational agencies with the largest numbers of children aged five through 17 from families living below the poverty level; plus not more than 25 additional local educational agencies determined by the Secretary of Education to be in particular need of assistance, based on a low level of resources for school construction, a high level of enrollment growth, or other factors (Code Sec. 54F(d)(2)(E), as added by the 2009 Recovery Act). Any amount allocated to a large local education agency may be reallocated by the agency to the state in which it is located and reallocated by the state to another issuer (Code Sec. 54F(d)(2)(D), as added by the 2009 Recovery Act).

Allocation to states. Next, the preliminary allocation to each state, determined in the first step above, is reduced by the amount of any allocations, under the second step above, to large local educational agencies within it (Code Sec. 54F(d)(2)(C), as added by the 2009 Recovery Act). Each state then allocates its own share (including any amounts passed along by large local education agencies) to issuers within its borders (Code Sec. 54F(d)(1), as added by the 2009 Recovery Act). A state can carry over any unused allocation for one calendar year to following years (Code Sec. 54F(e), as added by the 2009 Recovery Act).

Indian schools. A separate and additional volume limit of $200 million each year for 2009 and 2010 applies for the issuance of qualified school construction bonds to finance the construction, repair or rehabilitation of schools funded by the Bureau of Indian Affairs. This limit is to be allocated by the Secretary of the Interior. Indian tribal governments can issue these bonds (Code Sec. 54F(d)(4), as added by the 2009 Recovery Act). Unused allocations for any calendar year can be carried over (Code Sec. 54F(e), as added by the 2009 Recovery Act).

Mechanical requirements. Like other tax credit bonds, a qualified school construction bond must satisfy the requirements relating to expenditures, reporting, arbitrage, maturity, and conflicts of interest laid out in Code Sec. 54A (Code Sec. 54A(d)(1)(E), as added by the 2009 Recovery Act).

Prevailing wage requirements. The prevailing wage requirements of the Davis-Bacon Act (40 U.S.C. §3141) apply to any project financed with the proceeds of any qualified school construction bond (Act Sec. 1601 of the 2009 Recovery Act).

▶ **Effective date.** The provisions apply to obligations issued after February 17, 2009 (Act Sec. 1521(c) of the American Recovery and Reinvestment Tax Act of 2009 (P.L. 111-5)).

Law source: Law at ¶5150 and ¶5175. Committee Report at ¶10,430.

— Act Sec. 1521(a) of the American Recovery and Reinvestment Tax Act of 2009 (P.L. 111-5), adding Code Sec. 54F;

— Act Sec. 1521(b), amending Code Sec. 54A(d);

— Act Sec. 1601;

— Act Sec. 1521(c), providing the effective date.

NEW LAW EXPLAINED

Reporter references: For further information, consult the following CCH reporters.
— Standard Federal Tax Reporter, ¶4888.01
— Tax Research Consultant, BUSEXP: 55,800
— Practical Tax Explanation, §3,105

¶635 Qualified Zone Academy Bonds (QZAB)

SUMMARY OF NEW LAW

The authority of state and local governments to issue qualified zone academy bonds ("QZAB") has been extended for one more year through 2010. The new law allows $1.4 billion of QZAB issuing authority to state and local governments in 2009 and 2010, which can be used to finance renovations, equipment purchases, developing course material, and training teachers and personnel at a qualified zone academy.

BACKGROUND

As an alternative to traditional tax-exempt bonds, state and local governments were given the authority to issue qualified zone academy bonds ("QZAB"). $400 million of qualified zone academy bonds is authorized to be issued annually in calendar years 2008 and 2009. The $400 million annual bond cap is allocated each year to the States according to their respective populations of individuals below the poverty line. Each state, in turn allocates the credit authority to qualified zone academies within such state.

A "qualified zone academy bond" is any bond issued as part of an issue if: (1) 100 percent of the available project proceeds of the issue are to be used for a qualified purpose with respect to a qualified zone academy established by an eligible local education agency; (2) the bond is issued by the state or a local government within the jurisdiction of which the academy is located; and (3) the issuer designates the bond as a QZAB, certifies that it has written assurances of the required private contributions with respect to the academy, and certifies that it has the written approval of the eligible local education agency for the bond issuance. In general, a qualified zone academy is any public school (or academic program within a public school) that: (1) provides education and training below the college level; (2) operates a special academic program in cooperation with businesses to enhance the academic curriculum and increase graduation and employment rates; and (3) is either located in an empowerment zone or enterprise community or it is reasonably expected that at least 35 percent of the students at the school will be eligible for free or reduced-cost lunches under the school lunch program established under the National School Lunch Act. A QZAB is a form of tax credit bond which offers the holder a federal tax credit instead of interest.

Labor Standards. The Davis-Bacon Act (40 U.S.C. §3141), requires that every contract over $2,000 for the construction, alteration or repair of public buildings or public

BACKGROUND

works must contain a clause specifying the minimum wages that will be paid to certain classes of mechanics and laborers employed under the contract. Contractors and their subcontractors are required to pay their workers who are employed on the actual work site no less than the prevailing wages locally, plus the fringe benefits normally paid on similar projects. Two types of local prevailing wage rates are established by the Wage and Hour Division of the U.S. Department of Labor (1) general wage determinations regarding specific geographical areas for specific types of construction and (2) project wage determinations applicable only to specific named projects. Generally, the Davis-Bacon prevailing wage requirement is limited to contracts to which the federal government is a party. However, Congress has added the requirement to a number of other laws which assist construction projects of States or local governments through grants, loans, loan guarantees, and insurance. Thus, if a construction project is funded or assisted under a federal statute, the Davis-Bacon prevailing wage requirement may apply to the project.

NEW LAW EXPLAINED

Extension and expansion of qualified zone academy bonds.—The new law has extended the authority of state and local governments to issue qualified zone academy bonds ("QZAB") for one additional year through 2010. The new law allows $1.4 billion of QZAB issuing authority to state and local governments in 2009 and 2010, which can be used to finance renovations, equipment purchases, developing course material, and training teachers and personnel at a qualified zone academy (Code Sec. 54E(c)(1), as amended by the American Recovery and Reinvestment Tax Act of 2009 (P.L. 111-5)).

> **Practical Analysis:** Dale S. Collinson, a director in the Financial Institutions and Products group of the Washington National Tax practice of KPMG LLP, notes that Qualified Zone Academy Bonds (QZABs) were the first tax credit bonds, introduced under the Taxpayer Relief Act of 1997 (P.L. 105-34). Under this program, qualified zone academies, through their state and local governments, use the bond proceeds for school renovations, equipment, teacher training, and course materials.
>
> Qualified zone academies are public schools that provide education and training below the college level; that operate a special program in cooperation with businesses to enhance the academic curriculum and to increase graduation and employment rates; and that meet a location requirement by either being located in an empowerment zone or enterprise community or by reasonably expecting that that at least 35 percent of the students at the school will be eligible for free or reduced-cost lunches under the school lunch program established under the National School Lunch Act.
>
> The QZAB provisions contain a number of eligibility requirements. One such requirement is a private business contribution requirement. The private business contribution requirement is met with respect to any issue if the eligible local education agency that established the qualified zone academy has written commitments from private entities to make qualified contributions having a present value (as of the date of issuance) of not less than 10 percent of the proceeds of the issuance. Section 54E(c)

NEW LAW EXPLAINED

of the Code establishes a national QZAB limitation for each year. Currently, the limitation is $400 million for 2008 and 2009.

The American Recovery and Reinstatement Tax Act of 2009 increases the annual QZAB limitation from $400 million to $1.4 billion for 2009 and creates a new limitation of $1.4 billion for 2010. The new limitation amounts apply to obligations issued after December 31, 2008. It has taken time to develop a market for tax-credit bonds. Traditional investors in tax-exempt bonds, such as tax-exempt bond mutual funds, have generally not been interested because the tax credit is taxable. And traditional investors in taxable bonds have generally been unfamiliar with the matters affecting the credit rating of the issuers, including municipal finance law. Because a large volume of QZABs has been issued since 1998, the market for those bonds is relatively mature. But a study of investor holdings based on 2004 data indicates that the market is still rather thin. Of 115 financial institutions that reported holding QZABs, 68 reported holding only a single QZAB issue. Sixty percent of QZAB issues included in the sample were owned by 10 financial institutions that each had at least $100 billion in assets.[*] These institutions may presently have relatively little tax liability and little appetite for acquiring more QZABs. However, new Code Sec. 853A, which permits a regulated investment company to pass through credits on tax-credit bonds, may led to the creation of one or more regulated investment company specializing in QZABs.

Prevailing wage requirements. The prevailing wage requirement of the Davis-Bacon Act (40 U.S.C. §3141) will apply to any project financed with the proceeds of any qualified zone academy bond issued after February 17, 2009 (Act Sec. 1601 of the 2009 Recovery Act).

▶ **Effective date.** The provision applies to obligations issued after December 31, 2008 (Act Sec. 1522(b) of the American Recovery and Reinvestment Tax Act of 2009 (P.L. 111-5)).

Law source: Law at ¶5170. Committee Report at ¶10,440.

— Act Sec. 1522(a) of the American Recovery and Reinvestment Tax Act of 2009 (P.L. 111-5), amending Code Sec. 54E(c)(1);

— Act Sec. 1601;

— Act Sec. 1522(b), providing the effective date.

Reporter references: For further information, consult the following CCH reporters.

— Standard Federal Tax Reporter, ¶4916.01

— Tax Research Consultant, BUSEXP: 55,810

— Practical Tax Explanation, §3105.15

---

[*] Matheson, *Qualified Academy Bond Issuance and Investment: Evidence from 2004 Form 8860b Data,* Internal Revenue Service, Statistics of Income 155, at 158 (Spring 2007).

¶640 Qualified Energy Conservation Bonds

SUMMARY OF NEW LAW

The qualified energy conservation bond program is expanded, increasing the national limitation on the issuance of qualified energy conservation bonds by an additional $2.4 billion, to finance state, local, and tribal government qualified energy conservation programs that are aimed at reducing greenhouse gas emissions. The definition of "qualified conservation purpose" is broadened to include the use of loans, grants or other repayment mechanisms to implement green community programs. Further, a special rule is added for bonds issued for the purpose of providing loans, grants, or other repayment mechanisms for capital expenditures to implement green community programs. Under this special rule, such bonds are not treated as private activity bonds nor subject to the private activity bond allocation restriction.

BACKGROUND

The Emergency Economic Stabilization Act of 2008 (P.L. 110-343) authorized the issuance of $800 million in a new type of tax credit bond known as a "qualified energy conservation bond" (Code Sec. 54D, as added by the Emergency Economic Stabilization Act of 2008 (P.L. 110-343)). These tax credit bonds provide a federal subsidy to assist state and local governments (including Indian tribal governments) in financing energy conservation projects with respect to capital expenditures, research expenditures, expenses for mass commuting facilities, demonstration projects that promote green building technology and other technologies that promote energy efficiency, and public education campaigns designed to reduce greenhouse gas emissions. The national limit on energy conservation bonds is allocated among the states in proportion to their populations with sub-allocations to large local governments (for allocation purposes, Indian tribal governments are treated, generally, as large local governments).

Labor Standards. The Davis-Bacon Act (40 U.S.C. § 3141), requires that every contract over $2,000 for the construction, alteration or repair of public buildings or public works must contain a clause specifying the minimum wages that will be paid to certain classes of mechanics and laborers employed under the contract. Contractors and their subcontractors are required to pay their workers who are employed on the actual work site no less than the prevailing wages locally, plus the fringe benefits normally paid on similar projects. Two types of local prevailing wage rates are established by the Wage and Hour Division of the U.S. Department of Labor 1) general wage determinations regarding specific geographical areas for specific types of construction and 2) project wage determinations applicable only to specific named projects. Generally, the Davis-Bacon prevailing wage requirement is limited to contracts to which the federal government is a party. However, Congress has added the requirement to a number of other laws which assist construction projects of States or local governments through grants, loans, loan guarantees, and insurance. Thus, if a construction project is funded or assisted under a federal statute, the Davis-Bacon prevailing wage requirement may apply to the project.

NEW LAW EXPLAINED

Increased allocation authorized, green community program bonds clarified.— The qualified energy conservation bond program is expanded, increasing the national limitation on the issuance of qualified energy conservation bonds by an additional $2.4 billion (raising the cap from $800 million to $3.2 billion) to finance state, local, and tribal government qualified energy conservation programs that are aimed at reducing greenhouse gas emissions (Code Sec. 54D(d), as amended by the American Recovery and Reinvestment Tax Act of 2009 (P.L. 111-5)). The definition of "qualified conservation purpose" is broadened to include the use of loans, grants or other repayment mechanisms to implement green community programs (Code Sec. 54D(f)(1)(A)(ii), as amended by the 2009 Recovery Act). Another limitation on qualified energy conservation bonds, the restriction on private activity bonds, is removed for bonds issued for the purpose of providing loans, grants, or other repayment mechanisms for capital expenditures to implement green community programs. Accordingly, such bonds will not be treated as private activity bonds nor be subject to the private activity bond allocation restriction (Code Sec. 54D(e)(4), as added by the 2009 Recovery Act).

> **Practical Analysis:** John P. Gimigliano, a principal in the Sustainability Tax group of the Washington National Tax practice of KPMG LLP, points out that Qualified Energy Conservation Bonds (QECBs) are tax-credit bonds that meet the following requirements: (1) 100 percent of the available project proceeds of such issue are to be used for one ore more qualified conservation purposes, (2) the bond is issued by a State or local government, and (3) the issuer designates such bond as a Qualified Energy Conservation Bond. The bonds are used to fund, among other things, qualified conservation purposes such as reducing energy consumption, supporting research through grants, and promoting energy efficiency through educational campaigns. The QECB bond limitation amount, which is currently $800 million, is allocated to states according to their respective populations with a sub-allocation to large local governments. Not less than 70 percent of the allocation to issuers within a State should be used to designate bonds which are not private activity bonds.
>
> The American Recovery and Reinvestment Tax Act of 2009 increases the QECB bond limitation amount to $3.2 billion. In addition, the 2009 Recovery Act expands the purposes for which QECBs may be issued to include capital expenditures for green community programs. In the case of any bond issued for the purpose of providing loans, grants, or other repayment mechanisms for green community programs, such bond shall not be treated as a private activity bond. These amendments apply to bonds issued after the date of enactment.
>
> Much of the interest in the QECB provision to date has come from municipalities seeking to finance construction of government-owned green buildings and energy efficient retrofits of existing public facilities. The initial bond limitation of $800 million was seen by many as too small to accommodate the national demand for such projects. The additional $2.6 billion in QECB authorization is expected to ease such concerns.

¶640

NEW LAW EXPLAINED

> It remains to be seen, however, whether there are sufficient numbers of tax-motivated investors to allow states and municipalities to issue the large number of tax credit bonds authorized by the 2009 Recovery Act.

Prevailing wage requirements. The prevailing wage requirement of the Davis-Bacon Act (40 U.S.C. § 3141) will apply to any project financed with the proceeds of any qualified energy conservation bond issued after February 17, 2009 (Act Sec. 1601 of the 2009 Recovery Act).

▶ **Effective date.** No specific effective date is provided by the Act. The provision is, therefore, considered effective on February 17, 2009, the date of enactment.

Law source: Law at ¶5165. Committee Report at ¶10,150.

— Act Sec. 1112(a) of the American Recovery and Reinvestment Tax Act of 2009 (P.L. 111-5), amending Code Sec. 54D(d);

— Act Sec. 1112(b)(1), of the 2009 Recovery Act amending Code Sec. 54D(f)(1)(A)(ii);

— Act Sec. 1112(b)(2), of the 2009 Recovery Act adding Code Sec. 54D(e)(4);

— Act Sec. 1601 of the 2009 Recovery Act.

Reporter references: For further information, consult the following CCH reporters.

— Standard Federal Tax Reporter, ¶4908.03

— Tax Research Consultant, BUSEXP: 55,808

— Practical Tax Explanation, § 3,105.35

¶645 New Clean Renewable Energy Bonds

SUMMARY OF NEW LAW

The New Clean Renewable Energy Bonds ("New CREBs") program is expanded, increasing the national limitation on the issuance of new clean renewable energy bonds by an additional $1.6 billion, to finance qualified renewable energy facilities that generate electricity. Up to one-third of the $1.6 billion authorized will be available to qualifying public power providers; up to one-third will be available to qualified projects of governmental bodies (including state or Indian tribal governments, or any political subdivision thereof); and up to one-third will be available to qualifying projects of electric cooperative companies.

BACKGROUND

In order to encourage the generation of electricity from clean, renewable energy sources, the federal government has provided incentives to qualifying for-profit energy companies and non-profit producers of electricity through a number of programs. Tax credits, under Code Sec. 45, for the production of electricity from

BACKGROUND

certain specific renewable sources have been available to for-profit energy companies. Non-profit electricity producers could obtain incentives under the Department of Energy's Renewable Energy Production Incentive Program and by issuing tax credit bonds called clean, renewable energy bonds or "CREBs" under Code Sec. 54. While the incentives available to non-profits were subject to dollar limitations, the production credits that for-profit energy companies could obtain were not.

The Energy Tax Incentives Act of 2005 (P.L. 109-58) authorized the issuance of up to $800 million in CREBs during 2006 and 2007 as a federal subsidy to finance capital expenditures by tax-exempt producers of electricity so that they could increase their production capacity from clean, renewable sources and compete more evenly with for-profit companies that could avail themselves of the existing tax credit under Code Sec. 45. An additional $400 million of CREBs was authorized under the Tax Relief and Health Care Act of 2006 (Code Sec. 54(f)(1), as amended by the Tax Relief and Health Care Act of 2006 (P.L. 109-432)), raising the national limitation on the amount of bonds to $1.2 billion. In addition, the maximum amount of CREBs that could be allocated to finance qualified projects by qualified governmental bodies was increased by $250 million, raising that limitation to $750 million (Code Sec. 54(f)(2)). The authority to issue CREBs was also extended through December 31, 2008 (Code Sec. 54(m)).

The Emergency Economic Stabilization Act of 2008 (P.L. 110-343) extended the authorization for non-profit electricity producers to issue clean, renewable energy bonds under Code Sec. 54 for an additional year, through the end of 2009 (Code Sec. 54(m), as amended by the Emergency Economic Stabilization Act of 2008 (P.L. 110-343)). There was no increase in the dollar amount of CREBs that could be issued. However, after October 3, 2008, the issuance of up to $800 million in a similar category of tax credit bonds called "new clean renewable energy bonds" ("New CREBs") was added by the 2008 Act (Code Sec. 54C, as added by the Emergency Economic Act of 2008). These tax credit bonds provided a federal subsidy to allow non-profit electricity producers, including cooperatives and government-owned utilities, to compete more effectively with for-profit companies that can take advantage of the production tax credit under Code Sec. 45.

In general, holders of tax credit bonds are entitled to an annual tax credit calculated by multiplying the outstanding face amount of the bonds held by the applicable credit rate, as set by the IRS. The credit rate is set so that the bonds can be issued at face value with no interest. However, for New CREBs, the annual tax credit is limited to 70 percent of the face amount times the applicable credit rate (Code Sec. 54C(b), as added by the Emergency Economic Act of 2008).

"Qualified renewable energy issuers" include public power providers, cooperative electric companies, governmental bodies, clean renewable energy bond lenders, and not-for-profit electric utilities that have received a loan or loan guarantee under the Rural Electrification Act (Code Sec. 54C(d)(6)).

"Qualified renewable energy facilities" are those facilities producing electrical power that are owned by a public power provider, a governmental body or a cooperative electric company and that qualify under the renewable electricity production credit (Code Sec. 45) as: 1) wind facilities; 2) closed-loop biomass facilities; 3) open-loop

¶645

BACKGROUND

biomass facilities; 4) geothermal or solar energy facilities; 5) small irrigation power facilities; 6) landfill gas facilities; 7) trash combustion facilities; or 8) qualified hydropower facilities (Code Sec. 54C(d)(1))

Labor Prevailing Wage Requirements. The Davis-Bacon Act (40 U.S.C. § 3141), requires that every contract over $2,000 for the construction, alteration or repair of public buildings or public works must contain a clause specifying the minimum wages that will be paid to certain classes of mechanics and laborers employed under the contract. Contractors and their subcontractors are required to pay their workers who are employed on the actual work site no less than the prevailing wages locally, plus the fringe benefits normally paid on similar projects. Two types of local prevailing wage rates are established by the Wage and Hour Division of the U.S. Department of Labor: 1) general wage determinations regarding specific geographical areas for specific types of construction and 2) project wage determinations applicable only to specific named projects. Generally, the Davis-Bacon prevailing wage requirement is limited to contracts to which the federal government is a party. However, Congress has added the requirement to a number of other laws which assist construction projects of States or local governments through grants, loans, loan guarantees, and insurance. Thus, if a construction project is funded or assisted under a federal statute, the Davis-Bacon prevailing wage requirement may apply to the project.

NEW LAW EXPLAINED

Increased allocation authorized.—The New Clean Renewable Energy Bonds ("New CREBs") program is expanded, increasing the national limitation on the issuance of new clean renewable energy bonds by an additional $1.6 billion, to finance qualified renewable energy facilities that generate electricity. Up to one-third of the $1.6 billion authorized will be available to qualifying public power providers; up to one-third will be available to qualified projects of governmental bodies (including state or Indian tribal governments, or any political subdivision thereof); and up to one-third will be available to qualifying projects of electric cooperative companies. The increase will be allocated among qualified projects of governmental bodies and cooperative electric companies by the Secretary in a manner deemed appropriate by the Secretary (Code Sec. 54C(c)(4), as added by the American Recovery and Reinvestment Tax Act of 2009 (P.L. 111-5)).

> **Practical Analysis:** Dale S. Collinson, a director in the Financial Institutions and Products group of the Washington National Tax practice of KPMG LLP, notes that New Clean Renewable Energy Bonds ("New CREBs") are tax-credit bonds that may be issued to finance qualified energy production projects, which include (1) wind facilities, (2) closed-loop bio-mass facilities, (3) open-loop bio-mass facilities, (4) geothermal or solar energy facilities, (5) small irrigation power facilities, (6) landfill gas facilities, (7) trash combustion facilities, (8) certain hydropower facilities, and (9) marine and hydrokinetic renewable energy facilities. The tax-credit rate is set at 70 percent of the rate that would permit the bonds to be sold at par.

NEW LAW EXPLAINED

> Under current Code Sec. 54C, the national limit on the bonds is $800 million. The available bond limitation amount is allocated one-third for qualifying projects of governmental bodies; one-third for qualifying projects of public power providers; and one-third for qualifying projects of electric cooperatives. Code Sec. 54C does not limit when the bonds may be issued.
>
> The American Recovery and Reinvestment Tax Act of 2009 increases the National New CREB limitation by $1.6 billion. The additional authorization is to be allocated in the same manner as under existing law. New CREBS replace the tax-credit bond provisions enacted in 2004 for Clean Renewable Energy Bonds.
>
> The IRS procedure for allocating bond limitation amount under those provisions sparked substantial controversy. It set a deadline for allocation applications and then awarded the available bond limitation amount to the projects for which the smallest dollar amount of CREB limitation had been requested. The provisions for New CREBs mandate a more complicated allocation procedure. For example, Code Sec. 54C(c)(3)(A) provides as follows with respect to the allocation of bond limitation amount among public power providers:
>
>> After the Secretary determines the qualified projects of public power providers which are appropriate for receiving an allocation of the national clean renewable energy bond limitation, the Secretary shall, to the maximum extent practicable, make allocations among such projects in such manner that the amount allocated to each such project bears the same ratio to the cost of such project as the limitation under paragraph (2)(A) bears to the cost of all such projects.
>
> The implementation of this provision may prove challenging.

Prevailing wage requirements. The prevailing wage requirement of the Davis-Bacon Act (40 U.S.C. § 3141) will apply to any project financed with the proceeds of any qualified clean renewable energy bond issued after February 17, 2009 (Act Sec. 1601 of the 2009 Recovery Act).

▶ **Effective date.** No specific effective date is provided by the Act. The provision is, therefore, considered effective on February 17, 2009, the date of enactment.

Law source: Law at ¶5160. Committee Report at ¶10,140.

— Act Sec. 1111 of the American Recovery and Reinvestment Tax Act of 2009 (P.L. 111-5), adding Code Sec. 54C(c)(4);

— Act Sec. 1601 of the 2009 Recovery Act.

Reporter references: For further information, consult the following CCH reporters.

— Standard Federal Tax Reporter, ¶4900.01

— Tax Research Consultant, BUSEXP: 55,806

— Practical Tax Explanation, § 3,105.30

¶645

TAX-EXEMPT BONDS

¶650 Alternative Minimum Tax Limitations on Tax-Exempt Bonds

SUMMARY OF NEW LAW

Bonds issued in 2009 and 2010 are not private activity bonds for AMT purposes and interest on such bonds is not a tax preference item. In addition, no adjustment is made to a corporation's adjusted current earnings for such tax-exempt interest.

BACKGROUND

The alternative minimum tax (AMT) is designed to assure that high income individuals or corporations with large revenues do not unfairly reduce their tax liability through the extensive use of exclusions and deductions. To achieve this goal, the AMT regime recaptures certain tax savings by requiring taxpayers to modify their regular taxable income to take into account certain preference items and adjustments. The modified taxable income is the alternative minimum taxable income (AMTI) on the basis of which the taxpayers compute their tentative minimum tax. The AMT is the amount by which the tentative minimum tax exceeds the regular income tax (Code Sec. 55).

The tax preference items, which are added back to the taxpayer's taxable income in computing the AMTI, may include portions of deductions taken into account for regular tax purposes or income that is excluded for regular tax purpose (Code Sec. 57). One of the preference items is tax-exempt interest on private activity bonds. Such tax-exempt interest is included in AMTI and is subject to the AMT, although it is excluded from regular taxable income. For purposes of this preference, private activity bonds do not include qualified Code Sec. 501(c)(3) bonds or current or advance refunding bonds if the refunded bonds (or in the case of a series of refundings, the original bonds) were issued before August 8, 1986. Certain housing bonds issued after July 30, 2008, are also excluded by the Housing Assistance Tax Act of 2008 (P.L. 110-289) and tax-exempt interest on such bonds is not a preference item (Code Sec. 57(a)(5)).

A corporation must generally increase its AMTI by 75 percent of the excess of the corporation's adjusted current earnings (ACE) over its pre-adjustment AMTI (which is the AMTI determined without regard to this ACE adjustment and the AMT net operating loss deduction). On the other hand, a corporation's AMTI is reduced by 75 percent of the excess of the corporation's pre-adjustment AMTI over its ACE (Code Sec. 56(g)). In computing ACE, a corporation must make a number of adjustments to the AMTI. One such adjustment is for items, including tax-exempt interest, that are excluded from the pre-adjustment AMTI but are taken into account in determining earnings and profits. The Housing Assistance Tax Act (P.L. 110-289) eliminated the adjustment for tax-exempt interest on certain housing bonds issued after July 30, 2008 (Code Sec. 56(g)(4)(B)).

NEW LAW EXPLAINED

Certain tax-exempt interest not treated as preference item and no ACE adjustment made for it.—For AMT purposes, a private activity bond will not include any bond issued after December 31, 2008, and before January 1, 2011. For purpose of this exception, a refunding bond (whether current or advance refunding) will be treated as issued on the date of issuance of the refunded bond, or, in the case of a series of refundings, on the date of issuance of the original bond. However, this treatment will not apply to any refunding bond issued to refund any bond that was issued after December 31, 2003 and before January 1, 2009 (Code Sec. 57(a)(5)(C)(vi), as added by the American Recovery and Reinvestment Tax Act of 2009 (P.L. 111-5)).

As a result of these temporary modifications to the AMT limitations on tax-exempt interest, tax-exempt interest on private activity bonds issued in 2009 and 2010 will not be treated as a tax preference item for AMT purposes and will not be included in a corporation's AMTI for purposes of computing its ACE.

> **Practical Analysis:** John O. Everett, Ph.D., CPA, tax professor at Virginia Commonwealth University, Cherie J. Hennig, Ph.D., CPA, tax professor at Florida International University, and William A. Raabe, Ph.D., CPA, tax professor at the Ohio State University, observe that interest from state and local bonds generally is excluded from federal gross income, but such interest is included in computing the corporate AMT adjustment for adjusted current earnings (ACE). Included in the AMT tax base for all taxpayers, though, is interest from "private activity" state and local bonds. Such bonds typically are used by the jurisdictions to attract or retain business activity, *e.g.*, by providing benefits to tax-paying commercial entities like making nearby highway improvements, utility and landscaping upgrades, or property acquisitions.
>
> Municipal bonds usually can be issued at interest rates that are significantly lower than that required for corporate or Treasury debt, because of the associated tax exclusion. This rate discount is especially valuable to the state and local jurisdictions that issue bonds, as the cost of borrowing the needed funds is reduced due to the lower interest rates. Purchases of municipal bonds are especially attractive to taxpayers subject to higher marginal federal income tax rates, again because of the income tax exclusion for the interest.
>
> But because "private activity" bonds may be subject to the federal AMT, they typically are issued at an interest rate that exceeds the current market rate for similar bonds, thereby allowing the lender to cover some or all of the resulting tax increases. But this higher interest rate increases to the jurisdictions the cost of acquiring funds.
>
> To eliminate the tax-based detriment to issuing private activity bonds, and to allow state and local jurisdictions potentially to borrow more funds at a lower cost to them, the American Recovery and Reinvestment Tax Act of 2009 allows that securities that otherwise would be private activity bonds and are issued during calendar 2009 and 2010 are not classified as private activity bonds. The exemption also applies to existing bonds that are re-funded by the jurisdiction during 2009 and 2010.
>
> As a result, borrowed funds are likely to flow more freely into state and local governments, and Act Sec. 1503 of the American Recovery and Reinvestment Tax

NEW LAW EXPLAINED

> Act of 2009 exemption will allow a decrease in market and auction interest rates for these bonds. The exemption thus acts as a grant from the federal government to the state and local jurisdictions, through the credit markets. Investors are affected by this scheduled two-year exemption in at least two ways:
>
> > Those who always are subject to the AMT (currently these are upper-middle-income U.S. individual taxpayers) receive an important tax cut, in that the AMT tax base now has been reduced.
> >
> > Those who are never subject to the AMT (most important for this purpose are likely to be very high income individuals) see their after-tax investment income reduced, as market rates for this set of municipal bonds almost certainly will fall for the 2009 and 2010 calendar years.
>
> Corporate taxpayers should keep in mind that private activity bond interest income that is no longer treated as a tax preference will be considered tax-exempt income for purposes of the ACE adjustment. As a result, corporate taxpayers may see only a small reduction in the tentative minimum taxable income.
>
> The result of the provision to the U.S. Treasury is a net decrease in revenues of over $500 million over the 10-year scoring period. Most of this benefit will flow to upper-income individual taxpayers. The projected revenue decrease reflects the anticipated increase in demand for the affected state and local bonds by investors.

In addition, there is no adjustment to a corporation's adjusted current earnings (ACE) for tax-exempt interest on bonds issued after December 31, 2008, and before January 1, 2011. For purposes of this rule, a refunding bond (whether current or advance refunding) will be treated as issued on the date of issuance of the refunded bond, or, in the case of a series of refundings, on the date of issuance of the original bond. However, this treatment will not apply to any refunding bond issued to refund any bond that was issued after December 31, 2003 and before January 1, 2009 (Code Sec. 56(g)(4)(B)(iv), as added by the 2009 Recovery Act).

> **Practical Analysis:** Jeffrey D. Eicher, J.D., CPA, Professor of Finance at Clarion University of Pennsylvania, and Leo N. Hitt, J.D., LL.M., Tax Partner in the Pittsburgh office of Reed Smith, LLP, note that interest on tax-exempt bonds issued in 2009 and 2010 that would otherwise be treated as private activity bonds and, thus, a tax preference for the alternative minimum tax, qualifies for a temporary exception from the application of the alternative minimum tax. Also, the interest on such bonds will be excluded from the determination of adjusted current earnings for corporate taxpayers. These exceptions will not apply to refunding bonds that are issued to refund earlier tax exempt bonds that were issued after 2003 and before 2009.

▶ **Effective date.** The amendments made by this provision apply to obligations issued after December 31, 2008 (Act Sec. 1503(c) of the American Recovery and Reinvestment Tax Act of 2009 (P.L. 111-5)).

¶650

NEW LAW EXPLAINED

Law source: Law at ¶5185 and ¶5190. Committee Report at ¶10,400.

— Act Sec. 1503(a) of the American Recovery and Reinvestment Tax Act of 2009 (P.L. 111-5), adding Code Sec. 57(a)(5)(C)(vi);

— Act Sec. 1503(b), adding Code Sec. 56(g)(4)(B)(iv);

— Act Sec. 1503(c), providing the effective date.

Reporter references: For further information, consult the following CCH reporters.

— Standard Federal Tax Reporter, ¶5210.0535 and ¶5307.035

— Tax Research Consultant, FILEIND: 30,252, SALES: 51,054.45, and STAGES: 9,120.05

— Practical Tax Explanation, § 15,125 and § 15,315

¶652 Recovery Zone Facility Bonds

SUMMARY OF NEW LAW

Up to $15 billion in recovery zone facility bonds can be issued by counties or large municipalities before January 1, 2011. Recovery zone facility bonds are generally treated as exempt facility bonds under the rules that apply to private activity bonds.

BACKGROUND

Private activity bonds are bonds in which a State or local government serves as a conduit to finance nongovernmental persons (e.g., private businesses or individuals). A private activity bond is defined as any bond that satisfies (1) the private business use test (Code Sec. 141(b)(1)) and the private security or payment test (Code Sec. 141(b)(2)) or (2) the private loan financing test (Code Sec. 141(c)) (Code Sec. 141(a)).

The exclusion from income for interest on State and local bonds does not apply to private activity bonds unless the bonds are issued for certain permitted purposes. Such bonds are referred to as "qualified private activity bonds" (Code Sec. 141(d)).

Qualified private activity bonds currently include (Code Sec. 141(e)):

(1) exempt facility bonds (Code Sec. 142)

(2) qualified mortgage bonds (Code Sec. 143)

(3) qualified veterans' bonds (Code Sec. 143)

(4) qualified small issue bonds (Code Sec. 144)

(5) qualified redevelopment bonds (Code Sec. 144)

(6) qualified 501(c)(3) bonds (Code Sec. 145); and

(7) qualified student loan bonds (Code Sec. 144)

Subject to certain exceptions, the aggregate volume of qualified private activity bonds that may be issued within a State during a calendar years is restricted by a "State volume cap" which is announced by the IRS annually (Code Sec. 146).

BACKGROUND

Qualified private activity bonds are subject to restrictions on the use of proceeds for the acquisition of land (Code Sec. 147(c)) and existing property (Code Sec. 147(d)). Qualified private activity bonds also may not be used to finance certain specified facilities (e.g., airplanes, skyboxes, other luxury boxes, health club facilities, gambling facilities, and liquor stores) (Code Sec. 147(e)), The costs of issuance (e.g., bond counsel and underwriter fees) may not be paid for with the proceeds of the bonds (Code Sec. 147(g)).

The term of a qualified private activity bond generally may not exceed 120 percent of the economic life of the property being financed (Code Sec. 147(b)), and certain public approval requirements apply (Code Sec. 147(f)).

Exempt facility bonds includes bonds issued to finance certain transportation facilities (airports, ports, mass commuting, and high-speed intercity rail facilities); qualified residential rental projects; privately owned and/or operated utility facilities (sewage, water, solid waste disposal, and local district heating and cooling facilities, certain private electric and gas facilities, and hydroelectric dam enhancements); public/private educational facilities; qualified green building and sustainable design projects; and qualified highway or surface freight transfer facilities (Code Sec. 142(a)).

NEW LAW EXPLAINED

Recovery zone facility bonds categorized as exempt facility bonds.—Up to $15 billion in recovery zone facility bonds can be issued by counties or large municipalities before January 1, 2011. Recovery zone facility bonds are treated as exempt facility bonds for purposes of the tax-exemption requirements for state and local bonds (Code Sec. 1400U-3, as added by the American Recovery and Reinvestment Tax Act of 2009 (P.L. 111-5)).

A recovery zone facility bond is any bond issued as part of an issue if:

(1) 95 percent or more of the net proceeds (as defined in Code Sec. 150(a)(3)) of the issue are to be used for recovery zone property;

(2) the bond is issued before January 1, 2011; and

(3) the issuer designates the bond as a recovery zone facility bond (Code Sec. 1400U-3(b)(1), as added by the 2009 Recovery Act).

Net proceeds. Net proceeds of an issue are the proceeds of the issue reduced by amounts in a reasonably required reserve or replacement fund (Code Sec. 150(a)(3)).

Recovery zone property defined. Recovery zone property is any property which is depreciable under the Modified Accelerated Cost Recovery System (MACRS) (Code Sec. 168) or would be depreciable under MACRS if its cost had not been expensed under Code Sec. 179 and:

(1) the property was constructed, reconstructed, renovated, or acquired by purchase (within the meaning of Code Sec. 179(d)(2)) by the taxpayer after the date on which the designation of the recovery zone took effect;

¶652

NEW LAW EXPLAINED

(2) the original use of the property in a recovery zone commences with the taxpayer; and

(3) substantially all the use of the property is in a recovery zone and is in the active conduct of a qualified business by the taxpayer in the zone (Code Sec. 1400U-3(c)(1), as added by the 2009 Recovery Act).

Purchase defined. Any acquisition of property is considered to be a purchase except:

(1) acquisitions of property from a person whose relationship to the taxpayer would bar recognition of a loss in any transaction between them under Code Sec. 267 or Code Sec. 707(b);

(2) property transfers between members of a controlled group of corporations (substituting 50 percent for the 80 percent that would otherwise apply with respect to stock ownership requirements);

(3) property that will have a substituted basis (in whole or in part); or

(4) property that has its basis determined under Code Sec. 1014(a) relating to inherited property (Code Sec. 179(d)(2); Reg. § 1.179-4(c)).

Recovery zone defined. A recovery zone is (1) any area designated by the issuer as having significant poverty, unemployment, rate of home foreclosures, or general distress; (2) any area designated by the issuer as economically distressed by reason of the closure or realignment of a military installation pursuant to the Defense Base Closure and Realignment Act of 1990; and (3) any area for which a designation as an empowerment zone (under Code Sec. 1391(b)(2))) or renewal community (under Code Sec. 1400E) is in effect (Code Sec. 1400U-1(b), as added by the 2009 Recovery Act).

Qualified business defined. A qualified business is any trade or business other than (1) the rental of residential rental property (as defined in Code Sec. 168(e)(2)) and (2) the operation of any private or commercial golf course, country club, massage parlor, hot tub facility, suntan facility, racetrack or other facility used for gambling, or any store the principal business of which is the sale of alcoholic beverages for consumption off premises (i.e., the operation of facilities described in Code Sec. 144(c)(6)(B)).

Substantial renovations and sale-leasebacks. Rules similar to the rules for empowerment zone property for substantial renovations (Code Sec. 1397D(a)(2)) and sale-leasebacks (Code Sec. 1397D(b)) apply (Code Sec. 1400U-3(c)(3), as added by the 2009 Recovery Act).

The substantial renovation rules provide that the acquisition by purchase and original use requirements (items (1) and (2) in the list above) are satisfied with respect to any property which is substantially renovated by a taxpayer. Property is treated as substantially renovated by a taxpayer if, during any 24-month period beginning after the date on which the designation of the recovery zone took effect, additions to the basis of property in the hands of the taxpayer exceed the greater of (i) an amount equal to the adjusted basis at the beginning of the 24-month period in the hands of the taxpayer, or (ii) $5,000.

¶652

NEW LAW EXPLAINED

The sale-leaseback rules provide that, for purposes of the original use requirement (item (1) in the list above), if property is sold and leased back by the taxpayer within 3 months after the date the property was originally placed in service, the property is treated as originally placed in service not earlier than the date on which the property is used under the leaseback.

Original use requirement. As noted above, the original use of the recovery zone property in a recovery zone must commence with the taxpayer (Code Sec. 1400U-3(c)(1)(B), as added by the 2009 Recovery Act). Thus, used property located within a recovery zone does not qualify as recovery zone property. However, used property purchased outside of the recovery zone may qualify if its original use within the zone commences with the taxpayer. The rule contained in Code Sec. 147(d), which provides that a private activity bond is not a qualified bond if any portion of the net proceeds of the bond is used for the acquisition of any property (or an interest therein) unless the first use of the property is pursuant to the acquisition does not apply to recovery zone facility bonds (Code Sec. 1400U-3(d), as added by the 2009 Recovery Act).

> **Comment:** As in the case of an exempt facility bond, a recovery zone facility bond is a type of qualified private activity bond. Accordingly, a recovery zone facility bond is subject to any restrictions placed on private activity bonds (or on exempt facility bonds) unless specifically excepted from the restriction.

Practical Analysis: Dale S. Collinson, a director in the Financial Institutions and Products group of the Washington National Tax practice of KPMG LLP, notes that interest on bonds issued by States, local governmental units and certain other qualified entities is generally exempt from federal income tax under Code Sec. 103. The availability of the exemption is subject to compliance with a number of rules, including a prohibition on arbitrage bonds and limitations on the use of bond proceeds to finance private entities (private activity bonds). Under Code Sec. 142, private activity bonds may be issued to finance certain exempt facilities subject to a number of limitations. The limitations include an annual volume cap limitation (Code Sec. 146) and a prohibition on the acquisition of used property, except for certain rehabilitations (Code Sec. 147(d)).

New Code Sec. 1400U-1(a) establishes national limitations of $10 billion for Recovery Zone Economic Development Bonds (RZEDBs) and $15 billion for Recovery Zone Facility Bonds (RZFBs). All of the limitation amounts are allocated among States. The IRS is directed to allocate the limitation in the proportion that each State's 2008 employment decline bears to the aggregate of the 2008 employment declines for all of the States. The IRS is to adjust the allocation to the extent necessary to ensure that no State receives less than 0.9 percent of the bond limitation for both RZEDBs and RFZBs. The limitation amounts are then to be allocated by each State to its counties and large municipalities (population over 100,000) in proportion to their employment declines. The proceeds of RZEDBs and RZFBs are to be used in recovery zones, which Code Sec. 1400U-1(b) defines as (1) any area having significant poverty, unemployment, home foreclosure rates or general distress; (2) any area designated by the issuer as distressed by reason of

NEW LAW EXPLAINED

> the closure of realignment of a military installation pursuant to the Defense Base Realignment Act of 1990; and (3) any area for which a designation as an empowerment zone or renewal community is in effect.
>
> Under new Code Sec. 1400U-2, RZEDBs are Build America Bonds issued before January 1, 2011, if (1) 100 percent of the excess of (a) the available project proceeds of such issue, over (b) the amounts in a reasonably required reserve (within the meaning of Code Sec. 150(a)(3)) with respect to such issue, are to be used for one more qualified economic development purposes; and (2) the issuer designates the bonds as RZEDBs. A qualified economic development purpose means expenditures for "purposes of promoting development or other economic activity in a recovery zone, including (1) capital expenditures paid or incurred with respect to property located in such zone, (2) expenditures for public infrastructure and construction of public facilities, and (3) expenditures for job training and educational programs."
>
> New Code Sec. 1400U-3 creates RZFBs as a new category of "exempt facility bonds." The effect of this designation is that the bonds may provide financing for private purposes and still qualify as tax-exempt bonds. In addition, Code Sec. 1400U-3(d) exempts RZFBs from the limitation on financing existing property in Code Sec. 147(d) and from the general private activity bond volume cap under Code Sec. 146 (although RZFBs have their own volume limitation as described above).
>
> RZFBs are any bond issued as part of an issue if 95 percent or more of the net proceeds are used for recovery zone property, the bonds are issued before January 1, 2011, and the issuer designates the bonds as RZFBs. Recovery zone property is depreciable property acquired by the taxpayer by purchase after the date the designation of the recovery zone took effect, the original use of which within the recovery zone commences with the taxpayer, and substantially all of the use of which is in the active conduct of a qualified business by the taxpayer in the recovery zone. A qualified business is generally any business other than rental of residential rental property and other than any business consisting of the operation of a facility for which private activity bond financing may not be provided under Code Sec. 144(c)(6)(B) (such as a golf course, country club, gambling facility, suntan facility or liquor store). While the general prohibition in Code Sec. 147(d) on financing used property does not apply, RZFBs may not be used to acquire property that has been previously used in the particular recovery zone (subject to special rules for substantial renovations and sale-leasebacks).
>
> The Recovery Zone Bond provisions apply to bonds issued after the date of enactment. The advantage afforded by RZEDBs is that the issuer credit under new Code Sec. 6431 is increased from 35 to 45 percent. In effect, an issuer may choose whether to issue bonds to fund eligible expenditures in recovery zones by issuing traditional tax exempt bonds, by issuing Build America Bonds for which it elects a holder tax credit under new Code Sec. 54AA, or by issuing RZEDBs and electing the enhanced issuer credit under new Code Sec. 6431.

Allocation of national limitation on recovery zone facility bonds among States. The national limitation on the amount of recovery zone facility bonds that may be issued before January 1, 2011 is $15 billion (Code Sec. 1400U-1(a)(4), as added by the 2009 Recovery Act). The $15 billion national limitation will be allocated by the IRS to the

¶652

NEW LAW EXPLAINED

States. The allocation for a State is the amount that bears the same ratio to the total limitation that its employment decline for 2008 bears to the aggregate of the 2008 employment declines for all of the States (Code Sec. 1400U-1(a)(1), as added by the 2009 Recovery Act). A State's employment decline is the difference (if any) between the number of individuals employed in the State in December 2007 and the number of individuals employed in the State in December 2008 (Code Sec. 1400U-1(a)(2), as added by the 2009 Recovery Act). However, no State may be allocated less than 0.9 percent of the $15 billion national limitation (i.e., each State must receive an allocation of at least $135 million). The allocation to each State based on their 2008 employment decline is to be adjusted to the extent necessary to ensure that no State receives less than its 0.9 percent allocation (Code Sec. 1400U-1(a)(1)(B), as added by the 2009 Recovery Act).

> **Example:** State X's total employment in December 2007 was 1 million persons. By December 2008, its total employment had dropped by 100,000 persons to 900,000 persons. Assume that the total employment decline for all States that had an employment decline in 2008 was 3 million. State X's share of the $15 billion national limitation on recovery zone economic development bonds is $500 million (100,000/3,000,000 × 15 billion). However, this amount is subject to reduction in a manner to be determined by the IRS to account for the rule that no State may receive less than 0.9 percent of the $15 billion national limitation.

Reallocation of State's share of national limitation among its counties and large municipalities. A State must reallocate its share of the national limitation among the counties and large municipalities within the State in the proportion that each county's or municipality's 2008 employment decline bears to the aggregate of the 2008 employment declines for all the counties and large municipalities in the State. However, a county or large municipality may waive some or all of its allocation (Code Sec. 1400U-1(a)(3)(A), as added by the 2009 Recovery Act).

A large municipality is a municipality with a population in excess of 100,000 (Code Sec. 1400U-1(a)(3)(B), as added by the 2009 Recovery Act).

Each large municipality's or county's employment decline is determined in the same manner as the State's employment decline. If a large municipality is located in a county, the employment decline within the municipality is not taken into account in determining the county's employment decline (Code Sec. 1400U-1(a)(3)(C), as added by the 2009 Recovery Act).

Limitation on amount of bonds designated as recovery zone facility bonds. The maximum aggregate face amount of bonds that an issuer may designate as recovery zone facility bonds is its share of the State's share of the national $15 billion cap determined pursuant to Code Sec. 1400U-1 (Code Sec. 1400U-3(b)(2), as added by the 2009 Recovery Act). Code Sec. 146, relating to the State volume cap on private activity bonds, does not apply to any recovery zone facility bond (Code Sec. 1400U-3(d), as added by the 2009 Recovery Act).

NEW LAW EXPLAINED

▶ **Effective date.** The provision applies to obligations issued after February 17, 2009 (Act Sec. 1531(c) of the American Recovery and Reinvestment Tax Act of 2009 (P.L. 111-5)).

Law source: Law at ¶5315 and ¶5317. Committee Report at ¶10,350.

— Act Sec. 1401(a) of the American Recovery and Reinvestment Tax Act of 2009 (P.L. 111-5), adding Code Secs. 1400U-1 and 1400U-3;

— Act Sec. 1401(c), providing the effective date.

Reporter references: For further information, consult the following CCH reporters.

— Standard Federal Tax Reporter, ¶7707.01; ¶7752.01

— Tax Research Consultant, SALES: 51,200

— Practical Tax Explanation, §3,105.10

¶655 Exempt Facility Bonds for High-Speed Intercity Rail Facilities

SUMMARY OF NEW LAW

The requirement that high-speed intercity rail transportation facilities use vehicles that are reasonably expected to operate at speeds in excess of 150 miles per hour is modified to require the vehicles to be reasonably expected to be capable of attaining a maximum speed in excess of 150 miles per hour.

BACKGROUND

An exempt facility bond is a type of qualified private activity bond. Private activity bonds are bonds in which the state or local government serves as a conduit to provide financing to nongovernmental persons (e.g., private businesses or individuals). The exclusion from income of interest on state and local bonds does not apply to private activity bonds unless the bonds are issued for certain permitted purposes. Exempt facility bonds can be issued for high-speed intercity rail facilities. The facilities must use vehicles that are reasonably expected to operate at speeds in excess of 150 miles per hour between scheduled stops and the facilities must be made available to members of the general public as passengers. If the bonds are issued for a nongovernmental owner of the facility, such owner must irrevocably elect not to claim depreciation or credits with respect to the property financed by the net proceeds of the bond issue. Any proceeds not used within three years of the date of issuance of the bonds must be used within the following six months to redeem bonds which are part of that issue.

NEW LAW EXPLAINED

Speed requirement modification.—The new law modifies the definition of "high-speed rail facilities" for purposes of exempt facility bonds for providing high-speed intercity rail facilities. The modification requires that the facility for fixed guideway rail transportation use vehicles that are reasonably expected to be able to attain a maximum speed in excess of 150 miles per hour (Code Sec. 142(i)(1), as amended by the American Recovery and Reinvestment Act of 2009 (P.L. 111-5)). Prior to the modification, a facility was required to use vehicles that were reasonably expected to operate at speeds in excess of 150 miles per hour.

> **Comment:** This modification lowers the operating standard for vehicles used in high-speed intercity transportation systems funded by exempt facility bonds. Rather than require that the vehicle be reasonably expected to **operate** at speeds in excess of 150 miles per hour (previous requirement), the new standard requires that the vehicle be reasonably expected to only be **capable** of reaching a top speed in excess of 150 miles per hour.

▶ **Effective date.** The provision is effective for obligations issued after February 17, 2009 (Act Sec. 1504(b) of the American Recovery and Reinvestment Tax Act of 2009 (P.L. 111-5)).

Law source: Law at ¶5220. Committee Report at ¶10,410.

— Act Sec. 1504(a) of the American Recovery and Reinvestment Tax Act of 2009 (P.L. 111-5), amending Code Sec. 142(i)(1);

— Act Sec. 1504(b), providing the effective date.

Reporter references: For further information, consult the following CCH reporters.

— Standard Federal Tax Reporter, ¶7752.03

— Tax Research Consultant, SALES: 51,206.30

— Practical Tax Explanation, § 3,105.10

¶660 Industrial Development Bond Financing for Production of Intangible Property

SUMMARY OF NEW LAW

The definition of manufacturing facilities for purposes of industrial development bonds issued in 2009 and 2010 is expanded to include facilities used in the creation or production of intangible property or facilities that are functionally related and subordinate to a manufacturing facility if such facility is located on the same site as the manufacturing facility. The 25 percent of net proceeds restriction does not apply to such functionally related and subordinate facilities.

BACKGROUND

Qualified small issue bonds, commonly referred to as industrial development bonds, are tax-exempt bonds issued by state and local governments to finance private business manufacturing facilities or the acquisition of land and equipment by certain farmers. In both cases, the bonds are limited in the amount of financing provided for both single borrowing and in the aggregate. Generally, no more than $1 million of small issue bond financing may be outstanding at any time for property of a business (including related parties) located in the same municipality or county. The $1 million limit may be increased to $10 million if, in addition to outstanding bonds, all other capital expenditures of the business in the same municipality or county are counted toward the limit over a six-year period that begins three years before the issue date of the bonds and ends three years after such date. Outstanding aggregate borrowing is limited to $40 million per borrower regardless of where the property is located.

For bonds issued after December 31, 2006, up to $10 million of capital expenditures are disregarded, in effect increasing from $10 million to $20 million the maximum allowable amount of total capital expenditures by an eligible business in the same municipality or county. However, no more than $10 million of bond financing may be outstanding at any time for property of an eligible business (including related parties) located in the same municipality or county.

A manufacturing facility is defined as any facility which is used in the manufacturing or production of tangible personal property (including the processing resulting in a change in the condition of such property). Manufacturing facilities include facilities that are directly related and ancillary to a manufacturing facility if such facilities are located on the same site as the manufacturing facility and not more than 25 percent of the net proceeds of the bond issue are used to provide such facilities.

NEW LAW EXPLAINED

Definition of manufacturing facility temporarily expanded.—For industrial development bonds issued after February 17, 2009 and before January 1, 2011, the definition of manufacturing facilities is expanded to include facilities used in the manufacturing, creation or production of intangible property (Code Sec. 144(a)(12)(C)(iii)(I), as added by the American Recovery and Reinvestment Tax Act 2009 (P.L. 111-5)). For purposes of this provision, intangible property means any patent, copyright, formula, process, design, pattern, knowhow, format, or other similar item (Code Sec. 197(d)(1)(C)(iii)). In addition, for such bonds, facilities that are functionally related and subordinate to a manufacturing facility are treated as a manufacturing facility if such facility is located on the same site as the manufacturing facility (Code Sec. 144(a)(12)(C)(iii)(II) as added by the 2009 Recovery Act). The 25 percent of net proceeds restriction does not apply to such facilities (Code Sec. 144(a)(12)(C)(iii) as added by the 2009 Recovery Act).

> **Comment:** The definition of intangible property is intended to include, among other items, the creation of computer software, and intellectual property associated bio-tech and pharmaceuticals (Conference Committee Report for American Recovery and Reinvestment Act of 2009).

NEW LAW EXPLAINED

▶ **Effective date.** The provision applies to obligations issued after February 17, 2009 (Act Sec. 1301(b) of the American Recovery and Reinvestment Tax Act 2009 (P.L. 111-5)).

Law source: Law at ¶5225. Committee Report at ¶10,330.

— Act Sec. 1301(a)(1) of the American Recovery and Reinvestment Tax Act 2009 (P.L. 111-5), amending Code Sec. 144(a)(12)(C);

— Act Sec. 1301(a)(2) amending Code Sec. 144(a)(12)(C) and adding Code Sec. 144(a)(12)(C)(iii);

— Act Sec. 1301(b), providing the effective date.

Reporter references: For further information, consult the following CCH reporters.

— Standard Federal Tax Reporter, ¶7814.021

— Tax Research Consultant, SALES: 51,300

— Practical Tax Explanation, § 3,105.10

¶665 Tribal Economic Development Bonds

SUMMARY OF NEW LAW

The "essential government function" requirement has been temporarily lifted to allow Indian tribal governments the opportunity to issue up to $2 billion in tax-exempt bonds nationally for projects to spur economic development on tribal lands. Indian tribal governments may not issue tribal economic development bonds to finance construction of buildings conducting or housing class II or class III gaming as defined in the Indian Gaming Regulatory Act of 1988 (P.L. 100-497) or for construction projects not on tribal lands.

BACKGROUND

The Indian Tribal Governmental Tax Status Act of 1982 (P.L. 97-473) clarified the eligibility of Indian tribal governments for treatment as States or similar to States. The provisions applied only to those Indian tribal governments which possessed official recognition as a tribal government by the Treasury Department. Recognition by the Treasury Department, following consultation with the Department of the Interior, specifically included only those tribal governments which have been delegated the right to exercise sovereign powers (Code Sec. 7871(d)). Sovereign powers included the power to tax, the power of eminent domain, and the exercise of police powers as demonstrated by control over zoning and offering police and fire protection.

Congress treats tribal governments as States for tax purposes under certain circumstances. In particular, tribal governments receive treatment as States for transfers to or for use by tribal governments (Code Sec. 7871(a)(1)), including:

BACKGROUND

- income tax deductions of charitable contributions made to a tribe;
- estate tax deductions; and
- gift tax deductions.

A tribal government receives treatment as a State for exemptions from, credit or refund of, and payments toward excise taxes imposed on special fuels, manufacturing, communications, and use of certain highway vehicles (Code Sec. 7871(a)(2)). Tribal governments, however, can only make use of Code Sec. 7871(a)(2) when the transaction involves an "essential governmental function" (Code Sec. 7871(b)). Additionally, tribal governments receive treatment as States for:

- income tax deductions for payment of State and local taxes (Code Sec. 7871(a)(3));
- interest on State and local bonds (Code Sec. 7871(a)(4));
- taxation of tribal colleges and universities (Code Sec. 7871(a)(5));
- taxation of accident and health plans (Code Sec. 7871(a)(6)(A));
- contributions by employers to employee annuities (Code Sec. 7871(a)(6)(B));
- taxation of discounted obligations (Code Sec. 7871(a)(6)(C));
- taxation of excess lobbying expenditures to influence legislation (Code Sec. 7871(a)(7)(A)); and
- tax treatment of private foundation activities (Code Sec. 7871(a)(7)(B))

In the area of public bonds, Code Sec. 7871 grants Indian tribal governments State treatment only if the proceeds of the obligation are used in the exercise of an "essential governmental function" (Code Sec. 7871(c)(1)). Generally, tribal governments do not enjoy State treatment for private activity bonds (Code Sec. 7871(c)(2)). However, tribal governments do have an exemption for a qualified small issue bond, so long as 95 percent of the proceeds of the obligation are applied to the acquisition, construction, reconstruction or improvement of a manufacturing facility (Code Sec. 7871(c)(3)(B)).

NEW LAW EXPLAINED

Tribal economic development bonds created.—Indian tribal governments may now issue tribal economic development bonds (Code Sec. 7871(f), as added by the American Recovery and Reinvestment Tax Act of 2009 (P.L. 111-5)). Typically, a tax-exempt bond issued by a tribal government requires the obligation to serve an "essential governmental function" (Code Sec. 7871(c)(1)). Following the addition of Code Sec. 7871(f), the "essential government function" requirement has been eased for tribal economic development bonds (Code Sec. 7871(f)(2)). An Indian tribal government issuing bonds designated as tribal economic development bonds will now receive treatment as a State as described under Code Sec. 141. Volume limitations under Code Sec. 146 will not apply to tribal economic development bonds (Code Sec. 7871(f)(2)(C)). Going forward, tribal governments can now leverage off of the benefit of the tax-exempt interest generated by tribal economic development bonds to raise funds for economic develop-

¶665

NEW LAW EXPLAINED

ment projects which otherwise might not have fallen within the scope of the "essential government function" requirement.

> **Comment:** Tribal governments must satisfy the "essential governmental function" requirement when issuing tax-exempt bonds. State and local governments issue bonds without the limitation of the "essential governmental function" requirement. Passage of the 2009 Recovery Act provides tribal governments with the ability "to spur economic development" without the restriction of the "essential governmental function" requirement (Committee on Ways and Means, Summary of the Tax Relief Included in the "American Recovery and Reinvestment Plan").

The 2009 Recovery Act places a $2 billion national limitation on the issuance of tribal economic development bonds (Code Sec. 7871(f)(1)(B)). The Treasury Secretary, in consultation with the Secretary of the Interior, will determine the appropriate allocation of the national limitation among the Indian tribal governments (Code Sec. 7871(f)(1)(A)). The amount of bonds designated by any tribal government cannot exceed the bond limitation allocated by the Treasury Secretary to that tribal government (Code Sec. 7871(f)(3)(C)).

Tribal governments may not issue tribal economic development bonds to finance any portion of a building in which class II or class III gaming is conducted or housed (Code Sec. 7871(f)(3)(B)(i)). Class II gaming refers to games of chance such as bingo, lotto, and certain card games (P.L. 100-497). Class III gaming includes casino games such as slot machines, blackjack, and roulette, among others (P.L. 100-497). Also, tribal economic development bonds may not be issued for facilities located outside an Indian reservation as defined in Code Sec. 168(j)(6) (Code Sec. 7871(f)(3)(B)(iii)).

The 2009 Recovery Act tasks the Secretary of the Treasury with conducting a study of the effects of Code Sec. 7871(f). Within one year of February 17, 2009, the date of enactment of the 2009 Recovery Act, the Treasury Secretary, or one delegated by the Secretary, will report to Congress on the results of the study and forward any recommendations regarding the addition of Code Sec. 7871(f).

▶ **Effective date.** The provision applies to obligations issued after February 17, 2009 (Act Sec. 1402(c) of the American Recovery and Reinvestment Tax Act of 2009 (P.L. 111-5)).

Law source: Law at ¶5420. Committee Report at ¶10,360.

— Act Sec. 1402(a) of the American Recovery and Reinvestment Tax Act of 2009 (P.L. 111-5), adding Code Sec. 7871(f);

— Act Sec. 1402(c), providing the effective date.

Reporter references: For further information, consult the following CCH reporters.

— Standard Federal Tax Reporter, ¶43,952.01 and ¶43,952.03

— Tax Research Consultant, INDIV: 12,128 and SALES: 51,056.15

— Practical Tax Explanation, §3,105.05

— Federal Estate and Gift Tax Reporter, ¶18,501.01 and ¶18,501.02

Group Health Insurance and Other Provisions

¶705 COBRA Premium Assistance
¶710 Penalty for Failure to Notify Health Plan of Cessation of Eligibility for COBRA Premium Assistance
¶715 Extension of COBRA Benefits for Certain TAA-Eligible Individuals and PBGC Recipients
¶720 Special Enrollment Period for Group Health Plans for Medicaid or CHIP Coverage
¶725 Health Coverage Tax Credit
¶730 Tobacco Tax Rates and Treasury's Authority Over Permits

¶705 COBRA Premium Assistance

SUMMARY OF NEW LAW

Employers are provided a credit against payroll taxes for amounts of COBRA continuation coverage premiums not paid by involuntarily terminated employees who qualify for premium reductions. Premium reductions are excluded from the employee's gross income. Neither the Health Coverage Tax Credit (HCTC) nor the advance payment program for the HCTC is available for any month that an individual receives a premium reduction for COBRA continuing coverage.

BACKGROUND

A group health plan must offer each qualified beneficiary, who would otherwise lose coverage under the plan as a result of a qualifying event, an opportunity to elect, within the election period, continuation coverage under the plan. If a plan does not comply with these COBRA (Consolidated Omnibus Budget Reconciliation Act of 1985 (P.L. 99-272)) continuation coverage requirements, the IRS imposes an excise tax on the employer maintaining the plan or on the plan itself. A "qualified beneficiary" is any individual who is covered under a group health plan on the day before a qualifying event by virtue of being, on that day, a covered employee, the spouse or the dependent child of a covered employee (Reg. § 54.4980B-3). The plan may require the payment of premiums for the continuation coverage.

BACKGROUND

The Trade Adjustment Assistance Reform Act of 2002 (P.L. 107-210) established the Health Coverage Tax Credit as a benefit available under the Trade Adjustment Assistance (TAA) programs (19 U.S.C. § 2271 et seq.) (Code Sec. 35). The HCTC is a partially refundable tax credit available to eligible individuals to purchase health insurance for eligible coverage months (Code Sec. 35(a)).

An eligible coverage month for purposes of the HCTC is any month if, as of the first day of the month, the taxpayer meets certain requirements. These requirements are met if the taxpayer: (1) is an eligible individual; (2) is covered by qualified health insurance for which the taxpayer pays the premium; (3) does not have other specified coverage; and (4) is not imprisoned under federal, state, or local authority (Code Sec. 35(b)). Some individuals may be enrolled in a form of insurance that is automatically qualified, such as COBRA continuation coverage, certain spousal coverage, or individual health insurance coverage that began at least 30 days prior to separation from employment.

Eligible individuals include: (1) TAA recipients; (2) individuals eligible for alternative trade adjustment assistance (ATAA recipients); and (3) eligible Pension Benefit Guaranty Corporation (PBGC) recipients (i.e., individuals who are at least 55 years old and who receive a benefit that is paid at least in part by the PBGC). In general, TAA recipients are workers who lose their jobs due to increased imports or shifts in production to other countries. The TAA recipient must be receiving a trade readjustment allowance under the TAA Workers program under the Trade Act of 1974. An ATAA recipient is an individual over 50 years old who receives a wage subsidy under the program as a result of being reemployed at a lower wage. The ATAA recipient must be participating in and receiving benefits under the ATAA program (Code Sec. 35(c)). An eligible individual can claim the HCTC for qualifying family members, including the individual's spouse and dependents (Code Sec. 35(d)).

The HCTC is claimed on an individual's tax return. Individuals may, however, elect to have the amount of the credit paid directly to the health insurance provider under an advance payment program (Code Sec. 7527). For the advance payments to be made, a qualified health insurance costs credit eligibility certificate must state that an individual is an eligible individual within the meaning of Code Sec. 35(c) (i.e., a certified individual) (Code Sec. 7527(c) and (d)).

NEW LAW EXPLAINED

COBRA premium assistance tax consequences.—A temporary reduction in premiums for COBRA coverage is provided to assistance eligible individuals who are involuntarily terminated from their employment (Act Sec. 3001 of the American Recovery and Reinvestment Act of 2009 (P.L. 111-5)). An assistance eligible individual is treated for purposes of COBRA continuation coverage as having paid the premium required for coverage if the individual pays 35 percent of the premium. In effect, the individual is provided with a 65-percent reduction in premiums (Act Sec. 3001(a)(1)(A) of the 2009 Recovery Act). An "assistance eligible individual" is defined as any qualified beneficiary if:

¶705

NEW LAW EXPLAINED

(1) at any time during the period beginning on September 1, 2008, and ending on December 31, 2009, the qualified beneficiary is eligible for COBRA continuation coverage;

(2) the beneficiary elects such coverage; and

(3) the qualifying event for which the beneficiary would otherwise lose health plan coverage is the involuntary termination of the covered employee's employment during such period (Act Sec. 3001(a)(3) of the 2009 Recovery Act).

The 65-percent premium reduction or subsidy terminates with the first month beginning on or after the earlier of (1) the date that is nine months after the first day of the first month for which the subsidy applies, (2) the end of the maximum required period of continuation coverage for the beneficiary under the Code's COBRA rules or the applicable state or federal law, or (3) the date the assistance eligible individual is eligible for coverage under Medicare or any other employer-sponsored health plan (Act Sec. 3001(a)(2) of the 2009 Recovery Act). Employees who were terminated between September 1, 2008, and February 17, 2009, but who failed to initially elect COBRA continuation coverage, are given an additional 60 days to elect coverage and receive the subsidy (Act Sec. 3001(a)(4) of the 2009 Recovery Act).

Practical Analysis: Pamela D. Perdue, author of QUALIFIED PENSION AND PROFIT-SHARING PLANS and Of Counsel with Summers, Compton, Wells & Hamburg in St. Louis, Missouri, notes that employers will likely find Act Sec. 3001(a) of the American Recovery and Reinvestment Tax Act of 2009 costly on a number of fronts. First, currently most studies show that only a small percentage of those individuals eligible for COBRA continuation coverage actually elect such coverage due to the cost. By providing subsidized coverage, plans will likely experience a significant increase in those percentages. Since those who elect COBRA coverage on average tend to be those most in need of medical care, this will likely result in increased plan cost, particularly for those large employers that self insure their group health coverage.

While the 2009 Recovery Act allows, but does not require, employers to offer alternative coverage to assist eligible employees (subject to limitations designed to ensure that the alternative coverage is generally as good), nothing in the 2009 Recovery Act suggest that the plan could make such an option available to other qualified beneficiaries not qualifying for the assistance—something that larger employers have previously expressed an interest to do.

Employers, and their third-party COBRA coordinators, as applicable, will need to prepare for additional notice obligations, implement practices and procedures designed to implement the law including adding an additional 60-day election period for those employees who terminated between September 1 and the date of enactment who otherwise have been eligible for the assistance and implement procedures as to how and when to implement the payroll offset.

Therefore, given the cash flow problems experienced by many employers, most will likely prefer to apply the credit as soon as possible against future payroll taxes. However, employers may need to await guidance from the Treasury. This is be-

¶705

NEW LAW EXPLAINED

> cause, under the 2009 Recovery Act, for purposes of reimbursement, the employer is treated as having paid payroll taxes in the amount of the subsidy on the date that the premium payment is received. It will be important to have clarification as to when the premium is deemed to have been received in order to ensure that the correct amount of payroll taxes paid for a period properly aligns with the amount reported on the Schedule B of Form 941 to ensure that no late payment penalty is imposed.
>
> In addition, the IRS will have to fill in the blanks as to how the COBRA credit is to be reported for payroll purposes as well as how to claim a credit or refund of any excess amounts.

A person to whom premiums for COBRA continuation coverage are payable will be reimbursed for the amount of premiums not paid by plan beneficiaries because of the temporary subsidy. The reimbursement will be made in the form of a credit against the person's liability for payroll taxes. If the reimbursement due exceeds the amount of such taxes, the IRS will pay the person the amount of the excess. No payment will made with respect to any assistance eligible individual until after the person has received the reduced premium from the individual (Code Sec. 6432(a), as added by the 2009 Recovery Act).

Elimination of premium subsidy for high-income individuals. If premium assistance is provided for any COBRA continuation coverage that covers a taxpayer, the taxpayer's spouse, or any dependent of the taxpayer during any portion of the tax year, and the taxpayer's modified adjusted gross income for the tax year exceeds $125,000 ($250,000 for joint returns), then the income tax imposed on the taxpayer is increased by the amount of the assistance (Act Sec. 3001(b)(1), as added by the 2009 Recovery Act).

> **Comment:** A recent Commonwealth Fund/Modern Healthcare Health Care Opinion Leaders Survey found that 60 percent said that COBRA premium assistance for recently unemployed workers was very important or an absolutely essential feature of an economic stimulus package.

Payroll taxes. Payroll taxes are defined as amounts:

(1) required to be deducted and withheld for the payroll period under Code Sec. 3402 (wages);

(2) required to be deducted for the payroll period under Code Sec. 3102 (FICA employee); and

(3) of the taxes imposed for the payroll period under Code Sec. 3111 (FICA employer) (Code Sec. 6432(d), as added by the 2009 Recovery Act).

Method of reimbursement. Each person entitled to reimbursements will be treated as having paid, on the date that the assistance eligible individual's premium payment is received, payroll taxes in an amount equal to the unpaid portion of the premium (Code Sec. 6432(c), as added by the 2009 Recovery Act). To the extent that the amount treated as paid exceeds the amount of the person's liability for such taxes, the person will receive a refund or credit in the same manner as if it were an overpayment of taxes.

Reporting. Each person entitled to a reimbursement must submit a report including:

NEW LAW EXPLAINED

(1) an attestation of involuntary termination of employment for each covered employee on the basis of whose termination a claim for reimbursement is made;

(2) a report of the amount of payroll taxes offset for the reporting period and the estimated offsets of such taxes for the subsequent reporting period; and

(3) a report containing the taxpayer identification numbers (TINs) of all covered employees, the amount of subsidy reimbursed with respect to each covered employee and qualified beneficiaries, and a designation with respect to each covered employee as to whether the subsidy reimbursement is for coverage of one individual or two or more individuals (Code Sec. 6432(e), as added by the 2009 Recovery Act).

Regulations. Regulations or other guidance may be issued for carrying out COBRA premium assistance, including (1) the requirement to report information or for the establishment of other methods for verifying the correct amounts of payments and credits and (2) the application of the rules to group health plans that are multi-employer plans (Code Sec. 6432(f), as added by the 2009 Recovery Act).

Income exclusion for plan beneficiaries. A plan beneficiary who qualifies as an "assistance eligible individual" may exclude from gross income the 65-percent premium reduction for COBRA continuation coverage (Code Sec. 139C, as added by the 2009 Recovery Act).

> **Comment:** According to the Joint Committee on Taxation (Description of Title III of H.R. 598, the American Recovery and Reinvestment Act of 2009 (JCX-6-09), January 21, 2009), despite the exclusion from gross income provided for the covered employee and any other assistance eligible individuals, for purposes of determining the gross income of the employer and any welfare benefit plan of which the group health plan is a part, the amount of the premium reduction is meant to be treated as an employee contribution to the group health plan. Further, under the new law, the subsidy is not to be treated as income or resources in determining eligibility for, or the amount of assistance or benefits under, any public benefit provided under federal or state law (including the law of any political subdivision).

Coordination between HCTC and COBRA premium assistance. If an assistance eligible individual receives a premium reduction for COBRA continuation coverage for any month during the tax year, the individual will not be treated as an eligible individual, a certified individual, or a qualifying family member for purposes of the HCTC under Code Sec. 35 or the advance payment program for the credit under Code Sec. 7527 with respect to that month (Code Sec. 35(g)(9), as added by the 2009 Recovery Act).

See ¶725 for a discussion of the HCTC.

▶ **Effective date.** Code Sec. 6432 applies to premiums that are reduced under Act Sec. 3001(a)(1)(A) of the American Recovery and Reinvestment Act of 2009 (P.L. 111-5) (i.e., premiums for a period of coverage beginning on or after February 17, 2009) (Act Sec. 3001(a)(12)(D) of the 2009 Recovery Act). Code Sec. 139C applies to tax years ending after February 17, 2009 (Act Sec. 3001(a)(15)(C) of the 2009 Recovery Act). The coordination provision applies to tax years ending after February 17, 2009 (Act Sec. 3001(a)(14)(B)

¶705

NEW LAW EXPLAINED

of the 2009 Recovery Act). The elimination of the premium subsidy for high-income individuals applies to tax years ending after February 17, 2009 (Act Sec. 3001(b)(7) of the 2009 Recovery Act).

Law source: Law at ¶5065, ¶5215 and ¶5395. Committee Report at ¶10,510.

— Act Sec. 3001(a)(12)(A) of the American Recovery and Reinvestment Act of 2009 (P.L. 111-5), adding Code Sec. 6432;

— Act Sec. 3001(a)(14)(A), redesignating Code Sec. 35(g)(9) as (10) and adding new Code Sec. 35(g)(9);

— Act Sec. 3001(a)(15)(A), adding Code Sec. 139C;

— Act Sec. 3001(b);

— Act Sec. 3001(a)(12)(D), (14)(B) and (15)(C), and Act Sec. 3001(b)(7), providing the effective dates.

Reporter references: For further information, consult the following CCH reporters.

— Standard Federal Tax Reporter, ¶4175.01, ¶34,601.021 and ¶42,816S.01

— Tax Research Consultant, COMPEN: 45,206 and INDIV: 57,600

— Practical Tax Explanation, §13,101 and §20,715.05

¶710 Penalty for Failure to Notify Health Plan of Cessation of Eligibility for COBRA Premium Assistance

SUMMARY OF NEW LAW

A new penalty is imposed on persons who fail to notify health plans that they cease to be eligible for COBRA premium assistance.

BACKGROUND

A group medical plan may require the beneficiary to make a timely election of COBRA continuation coverage. Generally, the employer or plan administrator must determine when a qualifying event that would result in the loss of coverage has occurred, and a covered employee or qualified beneficiary is not required to give notice of the event. Covered employees or qualified beneficiaries, however, must notify the plan administrator of a change in marital or dependent status and of a relevant disability. After receiving notice of the qualifying event, the plan administrator must notify a qualifying beneficiary who is about to lose regular coverage of his right to continuation coverage (Code Sec. 4980B(f)(6) and Reg. §54.4980B-6, Q&A 1-2).

NEW LAW EXPLAINED

Penalty for failure to notify health plan of cessation of COBRA premium assistance eligibility.—An assistance eligible individual paying a reduced premium for COBRA continuation coverage (see ¶ 705) is required to provide written notice to the group health plan of eligibility for coverage under another group health plan or Medicare. The notification by the assistance eligible individual must be provided to the group health plan in the time and manner as is specified by the Secretary of Labor (Act Sec. 3001(a)(2)(C) of the American Recovery and Reinvestment Act of 2009 (P.L. 111-5)).

If an assistance eligible individual fails to provide this notification at the required time and in the required manner, and as a result the individual pays reduced COBRA continuation coverage premiums after the termination of the individual's eligibility for the reduction, a penalty is imposed on the individual equal to 110 percent of the premium reduction after termination of eligibility (Code Sec. 6720C(a), as added by the 2009 Recovery Act).

> **Comment:** This penalty only applies if the premium reduction is actually provided to a qualified beneficiary for a month that the beneficiary is not eligible for the reduction. Thus, if a qualified beneficiary becomes eligible for coverage under another group health plan and stops paying the reduced COBRA continuation premium, the penalty generally will not apply (Joint Committee on Taxation, Description of Title III of H.R. 598, the Health Insurance Assistance for the Unemployed Act of 2009 (JCX-6-09), January 21, 2009).

An "assistance eligible individual" means any qualified beneficiary if:

(1) at any time during the period beginning on September 1, 2008, and ending on December 31, 2009, the qualified beneficiary is eligible for COBRA continuing coverage;

(2) the beneficiary elects COBRA continuation coverage; and

(3) the qualifying event with respect to the COBRA continuation coverage is the involuntary termination of the covered employee's employment during such period (Act Sec. 3001(a)(2)(C) and 3001(a)(3) of the 2009 Recovery Act).

There will be no penalty imposed for any failure to notify if it is shown that the failure is due to reasonable cause and not to willful neglect (Code Sec. 6720C(b), as added by the 2009 Recovery Act).

▶ **Effective date.** The provision applies to failures occurring after February 17, 2009 (Act Sec. 3001(a)(13)(C) of the American Recovery and Reinvestment Act of 2009 (P.L. 111-5)).

Law source: Law at ¶5410. Committee Report at ¶10,510.

— Act Sec. 3001(a)(13)(A) of the American Recovery and Reinvestment Act of 2009 (P.L. 111-5), adding Code Sec. 6720C;

— Act Sec. 3001(a)(13)(C), providing the effective date.

NEW LAW EXPLAINED

Reporter references: For further information, consult the following CCH reporters.
— Standard Federal Tax Reporter, ¶34,601.021
— Tax Research Consultant, COMPEN: 45,206.35
— Practical Tax Explanation, § 20,735

¶715 Extension of COBRA Benefits for Certain TAA-Eligible Individuals and PBGC Recipients

SUMMARY OF NEW LAW

In the case of a qualifying event that is a termination or reduction of hours, COBRA continuation coverage is extended with respect to certain covered employees who are "PBGC recipients" or "TAA-eligible individuals." However, these extensions with respect to PBGC recipients and TAA-eligible individuals do not require any period of coverage to extend beyond December 31, 2010.

BACKGROUND

A group health plan must offer each qualified beneficiary, who would otherwise lose coverage under the plan as a result of a qualifying event, defined in Code Sec. 4980B(f)(3), an opportunity to elect, within the election period, continuation coverage under the plan. If a plan does not comply with the COBRA (Consolidated Omnibus Budget Reconciliation Act of 1985 (P.L. 99-272)) continuation coverage requirements, generally the IRS imposes an excise tax on the employer maintaining the plan or on the plan itself (Code Sec. 4980B). A "qualified beneficiary" is generally any individual who is covered under a group health plan on the day before a qualifying event by virtue of being, on that day, a covered employee or the spouse, or the dependent child, of a covered employee (Reg. § 54.4980B-3). The plan may require the payment of premiums for the continuation coverage.

In the case of a qualifying event that is the termination (other than by reason of the employee's gross misconduct), or reduction of hours, of the covered employee's employment, the "maximum coverage period" generally ends 18 months after termination or reduction of hours (Code Sec. 4980B(f)(2)(B)(i)(I)). If a qualifying event that is a termination or reduction of hours of employment is followed within the 18-month maximum coverage period by a second qualifying event, such as a death or a divorce, the maximum coverage period is generally extended to 36 months (Code Sec. 4980B(f)(2)(B)(i)(II) and (f)(3)(A)-(E)). In the case of a qualifying event that is a termination or reduction of hours of employment that occurs less than 18 months after the date the covered employee became entitled to Medicare benefits under Title XVIII of the Social Security Act, maximum coverage period for qualified beneficiaries other than the covered employee will not terminate before the close of the 36-month period beginning on the date the covered employee became entitled to the Medicare benefits (Code Sec. 4980B(f)(2)(B)(i)(V)). The period of coverage may be shorter if

BACKGROUND

certain events occur, such as a failure to pay premiums under Code Sec. 4980B(f)(2)(B)(iii).

NEW LAW EXPLAINED

Extension of COBRA benefits for certain TAA-eligible individuals and PBGC recipients.—In the case of a qualifying event that is a termination (other than by reason of the employee's gross misconduct), or reduction of hours, of the covered employee's employment under Code Sec. 4980B(f)(3)(B), the maximum required period of coverage under Code Sec. 4980B(f)(2)(B)(i) is changed with respect a covered employee:

(1) who, as of the termination or reduction, has a nonforfeitable right to a benefit, any portion of which is to be paid by the Pension Benefit Guaranty Corporation (PBGC) under Title IV of the Employee Retirement Income Security Act of 1974 (ERISA) ("PBGC recipients") (Code Sec. 4980B(f)(2)(B)(i)(V), as added by the American Recovery and Reinvestment Tax Act of 2009 (P.L. 111-5)); or

(2) who is a TAA-eligible individual, as defined in Code Sec. 4980B(f)(5)(C)(iv)(II), as of the date that the period of coverage would (but for Code Sec. 4980B(f)(2)(B)(i)(VI) or (VII)) otherwise terminate under the 18- or 36-month provisions of Code Sec. 4980B(f)(2)(B)(i)(I) or (II) ("TAA-eligible individuals") (Code Sec. 4980B(f)(2)(B)(i)(VI), as added by the 2009 Recovery Act).

With respect to PBGC recipients, notwithstanding Code Sec. 4980B(f)(2)(B)(i)(I) and (II), the maximum coverage period must end not earlier than the date of death of the covered employee, or, in the case of the surviving spouse or dependent children of the covered employee, not earlier than 24 months after the date of death of the covered employee. However, this provision does not require any period of coverage to extend beyond December 31, 2010 (Code Sec. 4980B(f)(2)(B)(i)(V), as added by the 2009 Recovery Act).

With respect to TAA-eligible individuals, the period of coverage may not terminate by reason of the 18- or 36- month provisions of Code Sec. 4980B(f)(2)(B)(i)(I) or (II), as the case may be, before the later of the date specified in Code Sec. 4980B(f)(2)(B)(i)(I) or (II), as the case may be, or the date on which the individual ceases to be a TAA-eligible individual. However, this provision does not require any period of coverage to extend beyond December 31, 2010 (Code Sec. 4980B(f)(2)(B)(i)(VI), as added by the 2009 Recovery Act).

Provisions similar to new Code Sec. 4980B(f)(2)(B)(i)(V) and (VI) have been added to ERISA (ERISA Sec. 602(2)(A)(v) and (vi), as added by the 2009 Recovery Act) and the Public Health Service Act (PHSA) (PHSA Sec. 2202(2)(A)(iv), as added by the 2009 Recovery Act).

> **Comment:** Although new Code Sec. 4980B(f)(2)(B)(i)(V) and (VI) do not require any period of coverage to extend beyond December 31, 2010, COBRA continuation coverage extensions under new Code Sec. 4980B(f)(2)(B)(i)(V) and (VI) may prove helpful to those who would have otherwise lost COBRA continuation coverage before the end of 2010. See ¶725 for more information on trade adjustment assistance (TAA) for workers.

¶715

NEW LAW EXPLAINED

▶ **Effective date.** This provision applies to periods of coverage which would (without regard to the amendments made by Act Sec. 1899F of the 2009 Recovery Act) end on or after February 17, 2009 (Act Sec. 1899F(d) of the American Recovery and Reinvestment Tax Act of 2009 (P.L. 111-5)).

Law source: Law at ¶5320. Committee Report at ¶10,480.

— Act Sec. 1899F(a) of the American Recovery and Reinvestment Tax Act of 2009 (P.L. 111-5), amending ERISA Sec. 602(2)(A);

— Act Sec. 1899F(b), amending Code Sec. 4980B(f)(2)(B)(i);

— Act Sec. 1899F(c), amending PHSA Sec. 2202(2)(A);

— Act Sec. 1899F(d), providing the effective date.

Reporter references: For further information, consult the following CCH reporters.

— Standard Federal Tax Reporter, ¶34,601.021,

— Tax Research Consultant, COMPEN: 45,206

— Practical Tax Explanation, § 20,730.10

¶720 Special Enrollment Period for Group Health Plans for Medicaid or CHIP Coverage

SUMMARY OF NEW LAW

To reduce barriers to providing premium assistance, termination of Medicaid or CHIP coverage due to ineligibility, or a determination of eligibility for Medicaid or CHIP benefits triggers a 60 day enrollment period during which an unenrolled employee or dependent can apply for coverage under a group health plan. Employers must notify families of their potential eligibility for premium assistance, and must disclose to states, upon request, information about their benefit packages.

BACKGROUND

A group health plan is required to provide special enrollment opportunities to qualified individuals. Such individuals must have lost eligibility for other group coverage, or lost employer contributions towards health coverage, or added a dependent due to marriage, birth, adoption, or placement for adoption, in order to enroll in a group health plan without having to wait until a late enrollment opportunity or open season. The individual must still meet the plan's substantive eligibility requirements, such as being a full-time worker or satisfying a waiting period. Health plans must give qualified individuals at least 30 days after the qualifying event (e.g., loss of eligibility) to make a request for special enrollment (Code Sec. 9801(f)(1), (2); ERISA Sec. 701(f)(1), (2); and Sec. 2701(f)(1), (2) of the Public Health Service Act).

BACKGROUND

A state may establish a Children's Health Insurance Program (CHIP) under title XXI of the Social Security Act, and/or a Medicaid program under title XIX of the Social Security Act.

NEW LAW EXPLAINED

Special enrollment period for group health plans triggered by changes in eligibility for Medicaid and/or CHIP subsidy of employer plan premiums.—Under the Children's Health Insurance Program Reauthorization Act of 2009 (P.L.111-3), a group health plan must permit an employee or dependent of the employee who is eligible, but not enrolled, to enroll in the plan if the employee or dependent applies for coverage not later than 60 days after either:

- The employee's or dependent's Medicaid or CHIP coverage is terminated as a result of loss of eligibility for such coverage (Code Sec. 9801(f)(3)(A)(i), ERISA Sec. 701(f)(3)(A)(i) and PHSA Sec. 2701(f)(3)(A)(i), as added by P.L. 111-3); or

- The employee or dependent is determined to be eligible for employment assistance under Medicaid or CHIP to help pay for coverage under the plan (Code Sec. 9801(f)(3)(A)(ii), ERISA Sec. 701(f)(3)(A)(ii) and PHSA Sec. 2701(f)(3)(A)(ii), as added by P.L. 111-3).

> **Comment:** States may offer a premium assistance subsidy for qualified employer sponsored coverage to all Medicaid and/or CHIP-eligible children, and parents of Medicaid and/or CHIP-eligible children where the family has access to such coverage and the family chooses to participate (Act Sec. 301 of P.L. 111-3). Changes in eligibility under these programs would likely affect an individual's ability to pay for employer coverage. The normal once-a-year employer plan enrollment window would complicate use of these benefits, and this extension of the special enrollment period provision to changes in Medicaid and CHIP eligibility is designed to minimize such concerns.

Employee outreach. Each employer that maintains a group health plan in a state that provides Medicaid or CHIP benefits must provide each employee with a written notice informing the employee of potential opportunities for premium assistance for health coverage for the employee or the employee's dependents currently available in the state in which the employee resides (Code Sec. 9801(f)(3)(B)(i)(I), ERISA Sec. 701(f)(3)(B)(i)(I) and PHSA Sec. 2701(f)(3)(B)(i)(I), as added by P.L. 111-3). Not later than one year after February 4, 2009, the date of enactment of P.L. 111-3, the Secretaries of Labor, and Health and Human Services, in consultation with directors of state Medicaid and CHIP agencies, are to jointly develop national and state-specific model notices for these purposes, and provide them to employers. The model notices must include information regarding how an employee may contact the state in which the employee resides for additional information regarding potential opportunities for premium assistance, including how to apply for such assistance (ERISA Sec. 701(f)(3)(B)(i)(II), as added by P.L. 111-3). Employers must provide the initial annual notices to its employees beginning with the first plan year that begins after

¶720

NEW LAW EXPLAINED

the date on which such initial model notices are first issued (Act Sec. 311(b)(1)(D) of P.L. 111-3).

The notice to employees may be provided with other plan materials, including materials notifying the employee of health plan eligibility, materials provided in connection with an open season or election process conducted under the plan, or the summary plan description (Code Sec. 9801(f)(3)(B)(i)(ll), ERISA Sec. 701(f)(3)(B)(i)(III) and PHSA Sec. 2701(f)(3)(B)(i)(II), as added by P.L. 111-3).

Disclosure of information so states can evaluate the need to provide wraparound coverage. If a participant or beneficiary of a group health plan is covered under a state Medicaid or CHIP plan, the plan administrator must disclose to the state, upon request, information about the benefits available under the group health plan. The Secretaries of Health and Human Services, and Labor are to establish a working group to devise a model coverage coordination disclosure form, which is to be used to allow states to make cost-effectiveness determinations concerning the state providing medical or child health assistance through premium assistance for the purchase of coverage under such group health plan and in order for the state to provide supplemental benefits (Code Sec. 9801(f)(3)(B)(ii), ERISA Sec. 701(f)(3)(B)(ii) and PHSA Sec. 2701(f)(3)(B)(ii), as added by P.L. 111-3). The model coverage coordination disclosure form will apply with respect to requests made by states beginning with the first plan year that begins after the date on which the form is first issued (Act Sec. 311(b)(1)(D) of P.L. 111-3).

Penalties. The Secretary of Labor can assess a civil penalty against (1) any employer of up to $100 a day from the date of the employer's failure to meet the employee notice requirement under ERISA Sec. 701(f)(3)(B)(i)(I); and (2) any plan administrator of up to $100 a day from the date of the plan administrator's failure to timely provide to any state the information required to be disclosed under ERISA Sec. 701(f)(3)(B)(ii). Each violation with respect to any single employee, participant or beneficiary shall be treated as a separate violation (ERISA Sec. 502(a)(9)(A) and (B), as added by P.L. 111-3).

▶ **Effective dates.** The enrollment provision takes effect on April 1, 2009, and shall apply to child health assistance and medical assistance provided on or after that date (Act Sec. 3(a) of the Children's Health Insurance Program Reauthorization Act of 2009 (P.L.111-3)). The Secretary of Labor and the Secretary of Health and Human Services shall develop the initial model notices, and the Secretary of Labor shall provide such notices to employers, not later than the date that is one year after February 4, 2009, the date of enactment of P.L. 111-3, and each employer shall provide the initial annual notices to such employer's employees beginning with the first plan year that begins after the date on which such initial model notices are first issued. The model coverage coordination disclosure form shall apply with respect to requests made by states beginning with the first plan year that begins after the date on which such model coverage coordination disclosure form is first issued (Act Sec. 311(b)(1)(D) of P.L. 111-3).

Law source: Law at ¶5425 and ¶7078.

— Act Sec. 311(a) of the Children's Health Insurance Program Reauthorization Act of 2009 (P.L.111-3), adding Code Sec. 9801(f)(3);

— Act Sec. 311(b)(1)(A), adding ERISA Sec. 701(f)(3);

NEW LAW EXPLAINED

— Act Sec. 311(b)(1)(B), amending ERISA Sec. 102(b);

— Act Sec. 311(b)(1)(E), amending ERISA Sec. 502;

— Act Sec. 311(b)(2), adding PHSA Sec. 2701(f)(3);

— Act Sec. 3(a) and 311(b)(1)(D), providing the effective dates.

Reporter references: For further information, consult the following CCH reporters.

— Standard Federal Tax Reporter, ¶44,053.034

— Tax Research Consultant, COMPEN: 45,216

— Practical Tax Explanation, §20,825.15

¶725 Health Coverage Tax Credit

SUMMARY OF NEW LAW

The Health Coverage Tax Credit (HCTC) is increased to 80 percent of the taxpayer's premiums for qualified health insurance for coverage months beginning on or after May 1, 2009, and before 2011. The increase also applies to the advance payment of the credit under the advance payment program.

BACKGROUND

The Trade Adjustment Assistance (TAA) programs (19 U.S.C. §2271 et seq.) are established under the Fair Trade Act of 1974. The programs provide workers, firms and farmers, who are negatively affected by trade, with government funded adjustment assistance. The TAA programs are administered by the Employment and Training Administration of the U.S. Department of Labor. States act as agents of the Labor Department in administering the programs.

The Trade Adjustment Assistance Reform Act of 2002 (P.L. 107-210) established the Health Coverage Tax Credit (HCTC) as a benefit available under the TAA programs (Code Sec. 35). The HCTC is a 65 percent refundable tax credit for amounts paid by eligible individuals to purchase health insurance for eligible coverage months (Code Sec. 35(a)). Eligible individuals include: (1) TAA recipients and (2) individuals eligible for alternative trade adjustment assistance (ATAA recipients). In general, TAA recipients are workers who lose their jobs due to increased imports or shifts in production to other countries. The TAA recipient must be receiving a trade readjustment allowance (TRA) under Chapter 2 of title II of the Trade Act of 1974. An eligible individual also includes an individual who would be eligible to receive a TRA, but for the requirement to exhaust unemployment benefits before receiving the allowance. An ATAA recipient is an individual over 50 years old who receives a wage subsidy under the program as a result of being reemployed at a lower wage. The ATAA recipient must be participating in and receiving benefits under the ATAA program for older workers established under Act Sec. 246 of the Trade Act of 1974 (19 U.S.C. §2318), as

BACKGROUND

added by P.L.107-210. An eligible individual may also include an eligible Pension Benefit Guaranty Corporation (PBGC) pension recipient (i.e., an individual who is at least 55 years old and who is receiving a benefit that is at least in part paid by the PBGC) (Code Sec. 35(c)).

An eligible individual can claim the HCTC credit for qualifying family members, including the individual's spouse and any person the eligible individual can claim as a dependent (Code Sec. 35(d)). The individual can claim the HCTC for seven categories of state-based coverage (i.e., elected by the states) and three categories of COBRA coverage (Code Sec. 35(e)). Individuals who pay for qualified health coverage for a month are not entitled to claim the HCTC for that month if the individual has other specified coverage on the first day of the month (Code Sec. 35(b)(1)(A)(iii)).

The HCTC is claimed on the individual's tax return; however, an individual can elect advanced payment of the credit under an advance payment program. Under the advance payment program, eligible individuals may elect to have the amount of the credit paid in advance directly to their health insurance provider. A qualified health insurance costs credit eligibility certificate is a written statement that identifies an individual who is eligible or certified under the program (Code Sec. 7527). Health insurance providers are required to file information returns to report any advance payments of the credit under Code Sec. 7527 (Code Sec. 6050T).

The first eligible coverage month for the HCTC was December of 2002. The TAA for Workers program expired on December 31, 2007, but it continued to operate through March 6, 2009, under the appropriations in the Consolidated Security, Disaster Assistance, and Continuing Appropriations Act, 2009, Act Sec. 154 (P.L. 110-329).

NEW LAW EXPLAINED

Health Coverage Tax Credit modified.—A number of changes have been made to the Health Coverage Tax Credit (HCTC) in order to make the credit more favorable for eligible individuals and their qualifying family members. The following modifications are made to the credit and do not extend beyond 2010:

- Increased credit amount;
- Retroactive payments allowed for premiums paid before advance payment of credit begins;
- Expanded eligibility for the credit and types of coverage;
- Favorable pre-certification rule for determining a 63-day lapse in coverage;
- Enhanced notice requirements;
- Surveys, studies and reports to assess the credit.

Increase in amount of HCTC. The amount of the Health Coverage Tax Credit (HCTC) is increased to 80 percent of the premiums paid for qualified health insurance for the taxpayer and qualifying family members, in the case of eligible coverage months beginning on or after May 1, 2009, and before January 1, 2011 (Code Sec. 35(a), as amended by the TAA Health Coverage Improvement Act of 2009 (P.L. 111-5)). Similarly,

¶725

NEW LAW EXPLAINED

the amount of the credit that may be paid in advance directly to the health care provider is 80 percent of the premiums paid by the taxpayer, for qualified health insurance for eligible coverage months beginning on or after May 1, 2009, and before January 1, 2011 (Code Sec. 7527(b) of the 2009 TAA Health Coverage Act).

> **Comment:** An amount of $80,000,000 was appropriated for the period of fiscal years 2009 through 2010 to implement the changes to the HCTC (Act Sec. 1899J of the 2009 TAA Health Coverage Act).

Advance payment program. In the case of eligible coverage months beginning on or after January 1, 2009, and before January 1, 2011, the advance payment program will allow the Secretary of Treasury to make one or more retroactive payments to pay for premiums due before the advance payments begin. Specifically, the payments can be made on behalf of certified individuals in an amount equal to 80 percent of the premiums for coverage of the taxpayer and qualifying family members for qualified health insurance for eligible coverage months, as defined in Code Sec. 35(b), occurring prior to the first month for which an advance payment is made. Note that the amount of the payment must be reduced by the amount of any payment made to the taxpayer under a national emergency grant pursuant to section 173(f) of the Workforce Investment Act of 1998, for a tax year including the eligible coverage months (Code Sec. 7527(e), as added by the 2009 TAA Health Coverage Act). Retroactive payments are not required until after the date that is six months after February 17, 2009, the date of enactment (Act Sec. 1899B(c) of the 2009 TAA Health Coverage Act).

The qualified health insurance costs eligibility certificate that identifies an individual as eligible or certified under the advance payment program must, for statements issued before January 1, 2011, provide the name, address and telephone number of the state office or offices responsible for providing the individual with assistance in his or her enrollment in qualified health insurance under Code Sec. 35(e) (Code Sec. 7527(d), as amended by the 2009 TAA Health Coverage Act).

A list of coverage options that are treated as qualified health insurance defined by the state of residence must also be provided, along with, in the case of a TAA-eligible individual, a statement that the individual has 63 days from the date that is seven days after the date the certificate is issued to enroll in such insurance without a lapse in creditable coverage (the pre-certification rule) (Code Sec. 7527(d), as amended by the 2009 TAA Health Coverage Act, and Code Sec. 9801(c)(2)(D), as added by the 2009 TAA Health Coverage Act). The pre-certification rule also applies for purposes of the Employment Retirement Income Security Act of 1974 (ERISA) and the Public Health Service Act (PHSA) (ERISA Sec. 701(c)(2)(C) and PHSA Sec. 2701(c)(2)(C), as added by the 2009 TAA Health Coverage Act).

Participation in training program not required for credit. Under a special rule, during any eligible coverage month beginning after February 17, 2009 and before January 1, 2011, an eligible TAA recipient is defined as, with respect to any month, an individual who is receiving for any day of the month a trade readjustment allowance (TRA) under chapter 2 of Title II of the Trade Act of 1974 and who would otherwise be eligible to receive the TRA, except that there is a break in training under an approved training program that exceeds the period of weeks during which the worker is receiving on-

¶725

NEW LAW EXPLAINED

the-job training, but is within the period allowed for receiving additional payments for approved training (Code Sec. 35(c)(2), as amended by 2009 TAA Health Coverage Act).

For the same period, an eligible individual is an individual who is receiving for any day of the month a TRA under chapter 2 of Title II of the Trade Act of 1974 and who is receiving unemployment compensation, as defined by Code Sec. 85(b), and who would be eligible to receive the TRA, except for the rules that require that unemployment benefits be exhausted and the individual be enrolled in an approved training program (Code Sec. 35(c)(2), as amended by the 2009 TAA Health Coverage Act).

Continued qualification for family members. The HCTC will continue to apply to family members in the case of eligible coverage months beginning after 2009 and before January 1, 2011, despite the occurrence of a number of events that would otherwise disqualify the coverage. These events include eligibility for Medicare, divorce and death (Code Sec. 35(g)(10), as added by the 2009 TAA Health Coverage Act).

Once an eligible individual qualifies for Medicare, the amount of the credit and advanced payment of the credit will be determined for qualifying family members for 24 months after the individual is first entitled to Medicare benefits (Code Sec. 35(g)(10)(A), as added be the 2009 TAA Health Coverage Act).

After a divorce is finalized between an eligible individual and the individual's spouse, the spouse will be treated as an eligible individual for purposes of determining the credit and the advanced payment of the credit for 24 months after the finalization date. The spouse can calculate the amount of the credit only with respect to premiums paid for those individuals who were qualifying family members immediately before the finalization date (Code Sec. 35(g)(10)(B), as added by the 2009 TAA Health Coverage Act).

After the date of death of an eligible individual, the individual's spouse will be treated as an eligible individual for purposes of determining the credit and advanced payment of the credit, for a period of 24 months beginning with the date of death. Similar to the rule for divorce, the spouse can calculate the amount of the credit only with respect to those individuals who were family members immediately before the date of death (Code Sec. 35(g)(10)(C)(i), as added by the 2009 TAA Health Coverage Act). Any individual who was a qualifying family member before the date of death is treated as an eligible individual for a period of 24 months beginning with the date of death, except that in determining the amount of the credit only amounts paid for the qualifying family member are taken into account. In the case of dependents, the rule applies to the taxpayer to whom the personal exemption deduction under Code Sec. 151 is allowed (Code Sec. 35(g)(10)(C)(ii)),

VEBAs. Qualified health insurance includes, in the case of eligible coverage beginning after February 17, 2009 and before January 1, 2011, coverage under an employee benefit plan funded by a Voluntary Employees' Beneficiary Association (VEBA), as defined in Code Sec. 501(c)(9). The VEBA must be established pursuant to an order of the bankruptcy court, or by an agreement with an authorized representative, as provided in 11 U.S.C. Sec. 1114 (Code Sec. 35(e)(1)(K), as added by the 2009 TAA Health Coverage Act).

¶725

NEW LAW EXPLAINED

Survey, reports and studies. The Secretary of the Treasury will conduct a biennial survey of eligible individuals relating to the HCTC program. With respect to HCTC participants, the survey will gather demographic information and inquire as to whether individuals are satisfied with the enrollment process and with the available health coverage options. With respect to non-HCTC participants, the survey will gather demographic information, inquire as to whether the individual is aware of the HCTC, determine the reason an individual has not enrolled in the program and inquire as to whether the individual has other coverage. The survey may gather any other information the Secretary feels is appropriate (Act Sec. 1899I of the 2009 TAA Health Coverage Act).

No later than December 31 of each year that the survey is required, beginning in 2010, the Secretary of the Treasury will report the findings to the Committee on Finance, Committee on Education, Labor and Pensions of the Senate and the Committee on Ways and Means, Committee on Health, Education and Labor, and the Committee on Energy and Commerce of the House of Representatives. No later than October of each year, beginning in 2010, the Secretary of the Treasury will report to these Committees the number of eligible individuals and the number receiving the HCTC or advance payment of the HCTC through the HCTC program, the average length of participation in the program and the total number of participating eligible individuals in the program who are enrolled in each category of coverage in Code Sec. 35(e)(1). The information is required for each state and nationally. Additionally, an analysis of the range of monthly premiums and the average and median monthly premiums must be made, for self-only coverage and for family coverage, in each state and nationally. Other information must be analyzed and reported for each state and nationally (Act Sec. 1899I of the 2009 TAA Health Coverage Act).

The GAO must also perform a study of the HCTC and provide a report to Congress, no later than March 1, 2010. The report must analyze administrative costs of the federal government and health insurance providers associated with the credit and advance payment program and with providing such insurance. The report must also analyze the health status and relative risk status of eligible individuals and qualifying family members covered, participation or non-participation in the HCTC program and the extent to which these individuals obtained other types of coverage or went without health insurance (Act Sec. 1899L of the 2009 TAA Health Coverage Act).

▶ **Effective date.** The increase in the eligible HCTC credit applies to coverage months beginning on or after the first day of the first month beginning 60 days after February 17, 2009, the date of enactment (Act Sec. 1899A(b) of the TAA Health Coverage Improvement Act of 2009 (P.L. 111-5)). The provision that allows retroactive payments prior to the first month an advance payment is made applies to coverage months beginning after December 31, 2008 (Act Sec. 1899B(b) of the 2009 TAA Health Coverage Act). The notice requirement applies to certificates issued after the date that is six months after February 17, 2009, the date of enactment (Act Sec. 1899H(b) of the 2009 TAA Health Coverage Act). The TAA pre-certification rule applies to plan years beginning after February 17, 2009 (Act Sec. 1899D(d)). The provision for TAA eligible recipients not enrolled in training programs and the VEBA provision apply to coverage months beginning after February 17, 2009 (Act Sec. 1899C(b) and 1899G(b) of the 2009 TAA Health Coverage Act). The provision continuing coverage for family members after certain events applies to months beginning after Decem-

¶725

NEW LAW EXPLAINED

ber 31, 2009 (Act Sec. 1899E(c) of the 2009 TAA Health Coverage Act). The survey, report and study requirements apply on February 17, 2009.

Law source: Law at ¶5065, ¶5320, ¶5415 and ¶5425. Committee Report at ¶10,480.

— Act Sec. 1899A(a), of the TAA Health Coverage Improvement Act of 2009 (P.L. 111-5)), amending Code Sec. 35(a) and Code Sec. 7527(b);

— Act Secs. 1899B(a) and 1899H(a), adding Code Sec. 7527(e) and amending Code Sec. 7527(d), respectively;

— Act Sec. 1899C(a), amending Code Sec. 35(c)(2);

— Act Sec. 1899D(a)-(c), adding Code Sec. 9801(c)(2)(D), ERISA Sec. 701(c)(2)(C) and PHSA Sec. 2701(c)(2)(C);

— Act Sec. 1899E(a), redesignating Code Sec. 35(g)(9) as (10), and adding new Code Sec. 35(g)(9), subsequently redesignated as 35(g)(10) by Act Sec. 3001(a)(14)(A);

— Act Sec. 1899G(a), adding Code Sec. 35(e)(1)(K);

— Act Secs. 1899I, 1899J and 1899L;

— Act Secs. 1899A(b), 1899B(b), 1899C(b), 1899D(d), 1899E(c), 1899G(b) and 1899H(b), providing the effective date.

Reporter references: For further information, consult the following CCH reporters.

— Standard Federal Tax Reporter, ¶4175.01, ¶36,330.01, ¶42,816S.01

— Tax Research Consultant, INDIV: 57,600

— Practical Tax Explanation, § 13,101

¶730 Tobacco Tax Rates and Treasury's Authority Over Permits

SUMMARY OF NEW LAW

The tax rates on tobacco products and cigarette papers and tubes are increased and a floor stocks tax is imposed. The definition of roll-your-own tobacco is modified and the regulatory and enforcement authority of the Treasury with respect to tobacco and alcohol is strengthened.

BACKGROUND

Tobacco products and cigarette papers and tubes manufactured in or imported into the United States are subject to federal excise tax determined at the time of removal (Code Sec. 5701). "Tobacco products" include cigarettes, cigars, smokeless tobacco, pipe tobacco, and roll-your-own tobacco (Code Sec. 5702(c)). "Removal" means the removal of tobacco products or cigarette papers or tubes from the factory or from internal revenue bond, or release from customs custody, and includes smuggling or other unlawful importation of these articles into the United States (Code Sec. 5702(j)).

BACKGROUND

The following federal excise tax rates generally apply to tobacco products and cigarette papers and tubes manufactured in the United States or imported into the United States:

- small cigars: $1.828 cents per thousand
- large cigars: 20.719 percent of the manufacturer's or importer's sales price, but not more than $48.75 per thousand
- small cigarettes: $19.50 per thousand (39 cents per pack)
- large cigarettes: $40.95 per thousand
- cigarette papers: 1.22 cents for 50 papers
- cigarette tubes: 2.44 cents for 50 tubes
- snuff: 58.5 cents per pound
- chewing tobacco: 19.5 cents per pound
- pipe tobacco: $1.0969 cents per pound
- roll-your-own tobacco: $1.0969 cents per pound

Floor stocks taxes. Essentially, a floor stocks tax is an excise tax on the inventory of the taxpayer. The imposition of floor stocks taxes generally accompanies the imposition of a new tax or the expiration and nonretroactive reinstatement of excise taxes by Congress.

Foreign trade zone. The term "foreign trade zone" means a discrete area located at or adjacent to a port of entry that is authorized by Congress to receive preferential treatment under the customs laws of the United States.

Roll-your-own tobacco. "Roll-your-own tobacco" is any tobacco that, because of its appearance, type, packaging, or labeling, is suitable for use and likely to be used by consumers for making cigarettes. Wrappers containing tobacco, because they are usually used to make cigars, not cigarettes, are not generally within the definition of roll-your-own tobacco. Similarly, loose tobacco suitable for roll-your-own cigars is not considered to be roll-your-own tobacco.

Permit and other requirements for manufacturers and importers; denial, suspension and revocation. Manufacturers and importers of tobacco products and export warehouse proprietors must obtain a permit from the Treasury. The Treasury may deny the application under certain conditions (Code Sec. 5712), and may suspend or revoke a permit under certain conditions (Code Sec. 5713), after a notice and hearing. Manufacturers and importers of tobacco products or cigarette papers or tubes, as well as export warehouse proprietors, must also periodically make an inventory and certain reports, and keep certain records (Code Secs. 5721, 5722 and 5741). Further, manufacturers of tobacco products or cigarette papers or tubes and export warehouse proprietors must file a bond and obtain approval of the bond from Treasury.

No immediate tax on tobacco products. Although distilled spirits, wines, and beer produced at any place other than a place required by the Code are subject to tax immediately on production (Code Secs. 5006(c)(2), 5041(f) and 5054(a)(3)), there is no such rule for tobacco products and cigarette papers and tubes.

¶730

BACKGROUND

Statute of limitations. Generally, under the Code, tax must be assessed within three years after a tax return is filed, and without assessment, no court proceeding for collection of tax is allowed after that period has expired (Code Sec. 6501(a)). If a required return is not filed, tax may be assessed, or a collection proceeding may be initiated without assessment, at any time (Code Sec. 6501(c)(3)). In contrast, Customs has one year from the date of entry or removal to fix and assess duties and taxes with respect to an import (19 U.S.C. 1504(a)).

Use of tax information and the Tobacco Trust Fund. Returns and return information generally are confidential and may not be disclosed (Code Sec. 6103). However, return and return information regarding taxes imposed on alcohol, tobacco and firearms may be inspected by or disclosed to officers and employees of a federal agency whose official duties require it (Code Sec. 6103(o)). "Return information" is defined very broadly and includes any information gathered by the IRS with respect to a person's liability or possible liability under the Code.

The Fair and Equitable Tobacco Reform Act of 2004 (P.L. 108-357, Title VI) creates a Tobacco Trust Fund; its purpose is to provide transitional payments to tobacco quota holders and eligible tobacco producers. Quarterly assessments paid by manufacturers and importers of tobacco products fund the trust fund. In administering the Tobacco Trust Fund assessments, the Farm Service Agency receives tax information from Treasury's Alcohol and Tobacco Tax and Trade Bureau.

According to a Department of Agriculture report in September 2008, a number of companies were delinquent in paying their assessments and have been referred to the Department of Justice for debt collection. Code Sec. 6103(o) does not, however, allow tax information to be used in civil actions against delinquent companies (Joint Committee on Taxation, Description of the Revenue Provisions of the Children's Health Insurance Program Reauthorization Act of 2009 (JCX-1-09)).

NEW LAW EXPLAINED

Rates on tobacco products increased; regulatory and enforcement authority over tobacco and alcohol strengthened.—Effective April 1, 2009, the rates of excise tax on tobacco products and cigarette papers and tubes are increased, generally in a proportionate manner, as follows (Code Sec. 5701, as amended by the Children's Health Insurance Program Reauthorization Act of 2009 (P.L. 111-3)):

- small cigars: $50.33 per thousand
- large cigars: 52.75 percent of the manufacturer's or importer's sales price, but not more than 40.26 cents per cigar
- small cigarettes: $50.33 per thousand (over $1.00 per pack)
- large cigarettes: $105.69 per thousand
- cigarette papers: 3.15 cents for each 50 papers
- cigarette tubes: 6.30 cents for each 50 tubes
- snuff: $1.51 per pound

NEW LAW EXPLAINED

- chewing tobacco: 50.33 cents per pound
- pipe tobacco: $2.8311 cents per pound
- roll-your-own tobacco: $24.78 per pound

Floor stocks tax. A floor stocks tax applies to those articles listed above (except for large cigars) that are manufactured in or imported into the United States and which are removed before April 1, 2009, and held on that date for sale. The floor stocks tax is equal to the excess of the applicable tax at the new rates over the applicable tax at the former rates. The person holding the article on April 1, 2009, is liable for tax, but is allowed a $500 credit against the tax. Further, the floor stocks tax generally applies to an article located in a foreign trade zone on April 1, 2009. For purposes of determining the floor stocks tax, component members of a "controlled group" are treated as one taxpayer. The floor stocks tax generally must be paid on or before August 1, 2009 (Act Sec. 701(h) of P.L. 111-3).

Roll-your-own tobacco. Roll-your-own tobacco, effective April 1, 2009, includes any tobacco that, because of its appearance, type, packaging, or labeling, is suitable for use and likely to be used by consumers as tobacco for making cigarettes or cigars, or used as wrappers for making cigars (Code Sec. 5702(o), as amended by P.L. 111-3).

Processed tobacco. Though not subject to federal excise tax, manufacturers and importers of *processed tobacco*, effective April 1, 2009, are subject to existing permit, inventory, reporting, and recordkeeping requirements (Code Secs. 5712, 5713(a), 5721, 5722, 5723 and 5741, as amended by P.L. 111-3). Processed tobacco is any tobacco other than tobacco products. The processing of tobacco, however, does not include farming or growing it, or handling whole tobacco leaf for sale, shipment, or delivery to a manufacturer of tobacco products or processed tobacco (Code Sec. 5702(p), as added by P.L. 111-3). A manufacturer or importer of processed tobacco who submits a permit application within 90 days of April 1, 2009, can continue to stay in business pending final action on the applicant's permit application (Act Sec. 702(g) of P.L. 111-3).

Broader authority over permits. Treasury now has broader authority to deny, suspend, and revoke tobacco permits. An application for a permit may now be denied if the applicant has been convicted of a felony violation of a federal or state criminal law relating to tobacco products or cigarette papers or tubes. In addition, a permit application may be denied if, by reason of previous or current legal proceedings involving a violation of federal criminal felony laws relating to tobacco products or cigarette papers or tubes, the applicant is not likely to maintain operations in compliance with the Code (Code Sec. 5712(3), as amended by P.L. 111-3). Similarly, a permit may be suspended or revoked on these grounds following a hearing (Code Sec. 5713(b), as amended by P.L. 111-3).

Statute of limitations. Notwithstanding customs laws, the general three-year statute of limitations for assessment under Code Sec. 6501 applies with respect to taxes imposed on distilled spirits, wines, and beer, and taxes imposed on tobacco and cigarette papers and tubes (19 U.S.C. 1514(a), as amended by P.L. 111-3).

¶730

NEW LAW EXPLAINED

Immediate tax. For tobacco products or cigarette papers or tubes produced in the United States at any place other than the premises of a manufacturer that has filed the bond and obtained the required permit, the excise tax is due and payable immediately upon manufacture, unless produced solely for personal consumption or use (Code Sec. 5703(b)(2)(F), as added by P.L. 111-3).

Use of tax information. Returns and return information disclosed to a federal agency under Code Sec. 6103(o) may be used in an action or proceeding brought under Sec. 625 of the Fair and Equitable Tobacco Reform Act of 2004 (P.L. 108-357, Title VI) for unpaid assessments or penalties (Code Sec. 6103(o), as amended by P.L. 111-3).

Tobacco smuggling study. The Treasury must conduct a study of the magnitude of tobacco smuggling in the United States and recommend steps to reduce it. The study is to assess how much federal tax is lost due to illicit tobacco trade and the role played by imported tobacco products in that illicit trade (Act Sec. 703 of P.L. 111-3; Joint Committee on Taxation, Description of the Revenue Provisions of the Children's Health Insurance Program Reauthorization Act of 2009 (JCX-1-09), January 13, 2009).

▶ **Effective date.** The provisions effecting tax rate increases and providing for a floor stocks tax apply to articles removed (as defined in Code Sec. 5702(j)) after March 31, 2009 (Act Sec. 701(i) of the Children's Health Insurance Program Reauthorization Act of 2009 (P.L. 111-3)). The provisions relating to processed tobacco take effect on April 1, 2009 (Act Sec. 702(a)(6) of P.L. 111-3). The provisions relating to the denial, suspension and revocation of permits take effect on February 4, 2009, the date of enactment (Act Sec. 702(b)(3) of P.L. 111-3). The provision relating to the statute of limitations for alcohol and tobacco applies to articles imported after February 4, 2009, the date of enactment (Act Sec. 702(c)(2) of P.L. 111-3). The modified definition of roll-your-own tobacco applies to articles removed (as defined in Code Sec. 5702(j)) after March 31, 2009 (Act Sec. 702(d)(2) of P.L. 111-3). The immediate tax on unlawfully manufactured tobacco products takes effect on February 4, 2009, the date of enactment (Act Sec. 702(e)(2) of P.L. 111-3). The provision relating to the use of information in connection with companies delinquent in paying their assessments that fund the Tobacco Trust Fund applies on or after February 4, 2009, the date of enactment (Act Sec. 702(f)(3) of P.L. 111-3).

Law source: Law at ¶5325, ¶5330, ¶5335, ¶5340, ¶5345, ¶5350, ¶5355, ¶5360, ¶5365 and ¶5370. Committee Reports at ¶15,010, ¶15,020, ¶15,030, ¶15,040, ¶15,050, ¶15,060, ¶15,070, ¶15,080 and ¶15,090.

— Act Sec. 701(a)-(g) of the Children's Health Insurance Program Reauthorization Act of 2009 (P.L. 111-3), amending Code Sec. 5701(a)-(g), respectively;

— Act Sec. 702(a)(1)(A) and 702(b)(1), amending Code Sec. 5712 and 5712(3), respectively;

— Act Sec. 702(a)(1)(B) and 702(b)(2), amending Code Sec. 5713(a) and (b), respectively;

— Act Sec. 702(a)(2)(A), amending Code Sec. 5721;

— Act Sec. 702(a)(2)(B), amending Code Sec. 5722;

— Act Sec. 702(a)(2)(C), amending Code Sec. 5723;

— Act Sec. 702(a)(3), amending Code Sec. 5741;

— Act Sec. 702(a)(4), adding Code Sec. 5702(p);

— Act Sec. 702(c), amending Section 514(a) of the Tariff Act of 1930 (19 U.S.C. 1514(a));

¶730

Explanation 299

NEW LAW EXPLAINED

— Act Sec. 702(d), amending Code Sec. 5702(o);
— Act Sec. 702(e)(1), adding Code Sec. 5703(b)(2)(F);
— Act Sec. 702(f)(1), amending Code Sec. 6103(o)(1);
— Act Secs. 701(i), 702(a)(6), 702(b)(3), 702(c)(2), 702(d)(2), 702(e)(2) and 702(f)(3), providing the effective dates.

Reporter references: For further information, consult the following CCH reporters.
— Standard Federal Tax Reporter, ¶129 and ¶36,894
— Tax Research Consultant, IRS: 9,258
— Practical Tax Explanation, §225 and §51,415.10
— Federal Excise Tax Reporter, ¶101 and ¶36,620

¶730

Code Sections Added, Amended Or Repealed

[¶ 5001]

INTRODUCTION.

The Internal Revenue Code provisions amended by the American Recovery and Reinvestment Tax Act of 2009 (P.L. 111-5), and the Children's Health Insurance Program Reauthorization Act of 2009 (P.L. 111-3) are shown in the following paragraphs. Deleted Code material or the text of the Code Section prior to amendment appears in the amendment notes following each amended Code provision. *Any changed or added material is set out in italics.*

[¶ 5005] CODE SEC. 24. CHILD TAX CREDIT.

* * *

(b) Limitations.—

* * *

(3) Limitation based on amount of tax.—In the case of a taxable year to which section 26(a)(2) does not apply, the credit allowed under subsection (a) for any taxable year shall not exceed the excess of—

    (A) the sum of the regular tax liability (as defined in section 26(b)) plus the tax imposed by section 55, over

⟫→ *Caution: Code Sec. 24(b)(3)(B), below, was amended by P.L. 111-5. For sunset provisions, see P.L. 111-5, §§1004(e), 1142(e), and 1144(d), in the amendment notes.*

    (B) the sum of the credits allowable under this subpart (other than this section and sections 23, *25A(i)*, 25B, 25D, *30*, *30B*, and 30D) and section 27 for the taxable year.

* * *

[CCH Explanation at ¶ 330, ¶ 350 and ¶ 360. Committee Reports at ¶ 10,040 and ¶ 10,200.]

Amendments

- **2009, American Recovery and Reinvestment Tax Act of 2009 (P.L. 111-5)**

P.L. 111-5, §1004(b)(1):

Amended Code Sec. 24(b)(3)(B) by inserting "25A(i)," after "23,". **Effective** for tax years beginning after 12-31-2008.

P.L. 111-5, §1004(e), provides:

(e) Application of EGTRRA Sunset.—The amendment made by subsection (b)(1) shall be subject to title IX of the Economic Growth and Tax Relief Reconciliation Act of 2001 in the same manner as the provision of such Act to which such amendment relates.

P.L. 111-5, §1142(b)(1)(A):

Amended Code Sec. 24(b)(3)(B) by inserting "30," after "25D,". **Effective** for vehicles acquired after 2-17-2009. For a transitional rule, see Act Sec. 1142(d) in the amendment notes for Code Sec. 30.

P.L. 111-5, §1142(e), provides:

(e) Application of EGTRRA Sunset.—The amendment made by subsection (b)(1)(A) shall be subject to title IX of the Economic Growth and Tax Relief Reconciliation Act of 2001 in the same manner as the provision of such Act to which such amendment relates.

P.L. 111-5, §1144(b)(1)(A):

Amended Code Sec. 24(b)(3)(B), as amended by this Act, by inserting "30B," after "30,". **Effective** for tax years beginning after 12-31-2008.

P.L. 111-5, §1144(d), provides:

(d) Application of EGTRRA Sunset.—The amendment made by subsection (b)(1)(A) shall be subject to title IX of the Economic Growth and Tax Relief Reconciliation Act of 2001 in the same manner as the provision of such Act to which such amendment relates.

(d) Portion of Credit Refundable.—

* * *

(4) Special rule for 2009 and 2010.—*Notwithstanding paragraph (3), in the case of any taxable year beginning in 2009 or 2010, the dollar amount in effect for such taxable year under paragraph (1)(B)(i) shall be $3,000.*

* * *

[CCH Explanation at ¶315. Committee Reports at ¶10,030.]

Amendments

- 2009, American Recovery and Reinvestment Tax Act of 2009 (P.L. 111-5)

P.L. 111-5, §1003(a):

Amended Code Sec. 24(d)(4). **Effective** for tax years beginning after 12-31-2008. Prior to amendment, Code Sec. 24(d)(4) read as follows:

(4) Special rule for 2008.—Notwithstanding paragraph (3), in the case of any taxable year beginning in 2008, the dollar amount in effect for such taxable year under paragraph (1)(B)(i) shall be $8,500.

[¶5010] CODE SEC. 25. INTEREST ON CERTAIN HOME MORTGAGES.

* * *

(e) Special Rules and Definitions.—For purposes of this section—

(1) Carryforward of Unused Credit.—

* * *

(C) Applicable tax limit.—For purposes of this paragraph, the term "applicable tax limit" means—

* * *

(ii) in the case of a taxable year to which section 26(a)(2) does not apply, the limitation imposed by section 26(a)(1) for the taxable year reduced by the sum of the credits allowable under this subpart (other than this section and sections 23, 24, *25A(i)*, 25B, 25D, *30*, *30B*, 30D, and 1400C).

* * *

[CCH Explanation at ¶330 and ¶350. Committee Reports at ¶10,040 and ¶10,200.]

Amendments

- 2009, American Recovery and Reinvestment Tax Act of 2009 (P.L. 111-5)

P.L. 111-5, §1004(b)(2):

Amended Code Sec. 25(e)(1)(C)(ii) by inserting "25A(i)," after "24,". **Effective** for tax years beginning after 12-31-2008.

P.L. 111-5, §1142(b)(1)(B):

Amended Code Sec. 25(e)(1)(C)(ii) by inserting "30," after "25D,". **Effective** for vehicles acquired after 2-17-2009. For a transitional rule, see Act Sec. 1142(d) in the amendment notes for Code Sec. 30.

P.L. 111-5, §1144(b)(1)(B):

Amended Code Sec. 25(e)(1)(C)(ii), as amended by this Act, by inserting "30B," after "30,". **Effective** for tax years beginning after 12-31-2008.

[¶5015] CODE SEC. 25A. HOPE AND LIFETIME LEARNING CREDITS.

* * *

(i) American Opportunity Tax Credit.—*In the case of any taxable year beginning in 2009 or 2010—*

(1) Increase in credit.—*The Hope Scholarship Credit shall be an amount equal to the sum of—*

(A) 100 percent of so much of the qualified tuition and related expenses paid by the taxpayer during the taxable year (for education furnished to the eligible student during any academic period beginning in such taxable year) as does not exceed $2,000, plus

(B) 25 percent of such expenses so paid as exceeds $2,000 but does not exceed $4,000.

(2) Credit allowed for first 4 years of post-secondary education.—*Subparagraphs (A) and (C) of subsection (b)(2) shall be applied by substituting "4" for "2".*

(3) QUALIFIED TUITION AND RELATED EXPENSES TO INCLUDE REQUIRED COURSE MATERIALS.—Subsection (f)(1)(A) shall be applied by substituting "tuition, fees, and course materials" for "tuition and fees".

(4) INCREASE IN AGI LIMITS FOR HOPE SCHOLARSHIP CREDIT.—In lieu of applying subsection (d) with respect to the Hope Scholarship Credit, such credit (determined without regard to this paragraph) shall be reduced (but not below zero) by the amount which bears the same ratio to such credit (as so determined) as—

(A) the excess of—

(i) the taxpayer's modified adjusted gross income (as defined in subsection (d)(3)) for such taxable year, over

(ii) $80,000 ($160,000 in the case of a joint return), bears to

(B) $10,000 ($20,000 in the case of a joint return).

(5) CREDIT ALLOWED AGAINST ALTERNATIVE MINIMUM TAX.—In the case of a taxable year to which section 26(a)(2) does not apply, so much of the credit allowed under subsection (a) as is attributable to the Hope Scholarship Credit shall not exceed the excess of—

(A) the sum of the regular tax liability (as defined in section 26(b)) plus the tax imposed by section 55, over

(B) the sum of the credits allowable under this subpart (other than this subsection and sections 23, 25D, and 30D) and section 27 for the taxable year.

Any reference in this section or section 24, 25, 26, 25B, 904, or 1400C to a credit allowable under this subsection shall be treated as a reference to so much of the credit allowable under subsection (a) as is attributable to the Hope Scholarship Credit.

(6) PORTION OF CREDIT MADE REFUNDABLE.—40 percent of so much of the credit allowed under subsection (a) as is attributable to the Hope Scholarship Credit (determined after application of paragraph (4) and without regard to this paragraph and section 26(a)(2) or paragraph (5), as the case may be) shall be treated as a credit allowable under subpart C (and not allowed under subsection (a)). The preceding sentence shall not apply to any taxpayer for any taxable year if such taxpayer is a child to whom subsection (g) of section 1 applies for such taxable year.

(7) COORDINATION WITH MIDWESTERN DISASTER AREA BENEFITS.—In the case of a taxpayer with respect to whom section 702(a)(1)(B) of the Heartland Disaster Tax Relief Act of 2008 applies for any taxable year, such taxpayer may elect to waive the application of this subsection to such taxpayer for such taxable year.

[CCH Explanation at ¶330. Committee Reports at ¶10,040.]

Amendments

• **2009, American Recovery and Reinvestment Tax Act of 2009 (P.L. 111-5)**

P.L. 111-5, §1004(a):

Amended Code Sec. 25A by redesignating subsection (i) as subsection (j) and by inserting after subsection (h) a new subsection (i). **Effective** for tax years beginning after 12-31-2008.

(j) REGULATIONS.—The Secretary may prescribe such regulations as may be necessary or appropriate to carry out this section, including regulations providing for a recapture of the credit allowed under this section in cases where there is a refund in a subsequent taxable year of any amount which was taken into account in determining the amount of such credit.

[CCH Explanation at ¶330. Committee Reports at ¶10,040.]

Amendments

• **2009, American Recovery and Reinvestment Tax Act of 2009 (P.L. 111-5)**

P.L. 111-5, §1004(a):

Amended Code Sec. 25A by redesignating subsection (i) as subsection (j). **Effective** for tax years beginning after 12-31-2008.

[¶ 5020] CODE SEC. 25B. ELECTIVE DEFERRALS AND IRA CONTRIBUTIONS BY CERTAIN INDIVIDUALS.

* * *

(g) LIMITATION BASED ON AMOUNT OF TAX.—In the case of a taxable year to which section 26(a)(2) does not apply, the credit allowed under subsection (a) for the taxable year shall not exceed the excess of—

(1) the sum of the regular tax liability (as defined in section 26(b)) plus the tax imposed by section 55, over

(2) the sum of the credits allowable under this subpart (other than this section and sections 23, *25A(i)*, 25D , *30, 30B*, and 30D) and section 27 for the taxable year.

[CCH Explanation at ¶ 330 and ¶ 350. Committee Reports at ¶ 10,040 and ¶ 10,200.]

Amendments

• **2009, American Recovery and Reinvestment Tax Act of 2009 (P.L. 111-5)**

P.L. 111-5, § 1004(b)(4):

Amended Code Sec. 25B(g)(2) by inserting "25A(i)," after "23,". **Effective** for tax years beginning after 12-31-2008.

P.L. 111-5, § 1142(b)(1)(C):

Amended Code Sec. 25B(g)(2) by inserting "30," after "25D,". **Effective** for vehicles acquired after 2-17-2009. For a transitional rule, see Act Sec. 1142(d) in the amendment notes for Code Sec. 30.

P.L. 111-5, § 1144(b)(1)(C):

Amended Code Sec. 25B(g)(2), as amended by this Act, by inserting "30B," after "30,". **Effective** for tax years beginning after 12-31-2008.

[¶ 5025] CODE SEC. 25C. NONBUSINESS ENERGY PROPERTY.

(a) ALLOWANCE OF CREDIT.—In the case of an individual, there shall be allowed as a credit against the tax imposed by this chapter for the taxable year an amount equal to 30 percent of the sum of—

(1) the amount paid or incurred by the taxpayer during such taxable year for qualified energy efficiency improvements, and

(2) the amount of the residential energy property expenditures paid or incurred by the taxpayer during such taxable year.

[CCH Explanation at ¶ 335. Committee Reports at ¶ 10,160.]

Amendments

• **2009, American Recovery and Reinvestment Tax Act of 2009 (P.L. 111-5)**

P.L. 111-5, § 1121(a):

Amended Code Sec. 25C by striking subsections (a) and (b) and inserting new subsections (a) and (b). **Effective** for tax years beginning after 12-31-2008. Prior to being stricken, Code Sec. 25C(a) read as follows:

(a) ALLOWANCE OF CREDIT.—In the case of an individual, there shall be allowed as a credit against the tax imposed by this chapter for the taxable year an amount equal to the sum of—

(1) 10 percent of the amount paid or incurred by the taxpayer for qualified energy efficiency improvements installed during such taxable year, and

(2) the amount of the residential energy property expenditures paid or incurred by the taxpayer during such taxable year.

(b) LIMITATION.—The aggregate amount of the credits allowed under this section for taxable years beginning in 2009 and 2010 with respect to any taxpayer shall not exceed $1,500.

[CCH Explanation at ¶ 335. Committee Reports at ¶ 10,160.]

Amendments

• **2009, American Recovery and Reinvestment Tax Act of 2009 (P.L. 111-5)**

P.L. 111-5, § 1121(a):

Amended Code Sec. 25C by striking subsection (b) and inserting a new subsection (b). **Effective** for tax years beginning after 12-31-2008. Prior to being stricken, Code Sec. 25C(b) read as follows:

(b) LIMITATIONS.—

(1) LIFETIME LIMITATION.—The credit allowed under this section with respect to any taxpayer for any taxable year shall not exceed the excess (if any) of $500 over the aggregate credits allowed under this section with respect to such taxpayer for all prior taxable years.

(2) WINDOWS.—In the case of amounts paid or incurred for components described in subsection (c)(2)(B) by any taxpayer for any taxable year, the credit allowed under this

section with respect to such amounts for such year shall not exceed the excess (if any) of $200 over the aggregate credits allowed under this section with respect to such amounts for all prior taxable years.

(3) LIMITATION ON RESIDENTIAL ENERGY PROPERTY EXPENDITURES.—The amount of the credit allowed under this section by reason of subsection (a)(2) shall not exceed—

(A) $50 for any advanced main air circulating fan,

(B) $150 for any qualified natural gas, propane, or oil furnace or hot water boiler, and

(C) $300 for any item of energy-efficient building property.

(c) QUALIFIED ENERGY EFFICIENCY IMPROVEMENTS.—For purposes of this section—

* * *

(2) BUILDING ENVELOPE COMPONENT.—The term "building envelope component" means—

(A) any insulation material or system which is specifically and primarily designed to reduce the heat loss or gain of a dwelling unit when installed in or on such dwelling unit *and meets the prescriptive criteria for such material or system established by the 2009 International Energy Conservation Code, as such Code (including supplements) is in effect on the date of the enactment of the American Recovery and Reinvestment Tax Act of 2009,*

* * *

(4) QUALIFICATIONS FOR EXTERIOR WINDOWS, DOORS, AND SKYLIGHTS.—*Such term shall not include any component described in subparagraph (B) or (C) of paragraph (2) unless such component is equal to or below a U factor of 0.30 and SHGC of 0.30.*

[CCH Explanation at ¶335. Committee Reports at ¶10,160.]

Amendments

• **2009, American Recovery and Reinvestment Tax Act of 2009 (P.L. 111-5)**

P.L. 111-5, §1121(d)(1):

Amended Code Sec. 25C(c) by adding at the end a new paragraph (4). **Effective** for property placed in service after 2-17-2009.

P.L. 111-5, §1121(d)(2):

Amended Code Sec. 25C(c)(2)(A) by inserting "and meets the prescriptive criteria for such material or system established by the 2009 International Energy Conservation Code, as such Code (including supplements) is in effect on the date of the enactment of the American Recovery and Reinvestment Tax Act of 2009" after "such dwelling unit". **Effective** for property placed in service after 2-17-2009.

(d) RESIDENTIAL ENERGY PROPERTY EXPENDITURES.—For purposes of this section—

* * *

(2) QUALIFIED ENERGY PROPERTY.—

(A) IN GENERAL.—The term "qualified energy property" means—

* * *

(ii) any qualified natural gas furnace, qualified propane furnace, qualified oil furnace, qualified natural gas hot water boiler, qualified propane hot water boiler, or qualified oil hot water boiler, or

* * *

(3) ENERGY-EFFICIENT BUILDING PROPERTY.—The term "energy-efficient building property" means—

(A) an electric heat pump water heater which yields an energy factor of at least 2.0 in the standard Department of Energy test procedure,

(B) *an electric heat pump which achieves the highest efficiency tier established by the Consortium for Energy Efficiency, as in effect on January 1, 2009.*[,]

(C) a central air conditioner which achieves the highest efficiency tier established by the Consortium for Energy Efficiency, as in effect on January 1, 2009,

(D) *a natural gas, propane, or oil water heater which has either an energy factor of at least 0.82 or a thermal efficiency of at least 90 percent.*[, and]

(E) a stove which uses the burning of biomass fuel to heat a dwelling unit located in the United States and used as a residence by the taxpayer, or to heat water for use in such a dwelling unit, and which has a thermal efficiency rating of at least 75 percent, *as measured using a lower heating value.*

(4) QUALIFIED NATURAL GAS, PROPANE, AND OIL FURNACES AND HOT WATER BOILERS.—

(A) QUALIFIED NATURAL GAS FURNACE.—The term "qualified natural gas furnace" means any natural gas furnace which achieves an annual fuel utilization efficiency rate of not less than 95.

(B) QUALIFIED NATURAL GAS HOT WATER BOILER.—The term "qualified natural gas hot water boiler" means any natural gas hot water boiler which achieves an annual fuel utilization efficiency rate of not less than 90.

(C) QUALIFIED PROPANE FURNACE.—The term "qualified propane furnace" means any propane furnace which achieves an annual fuel utilization efficiency rate of not less than 95.

(D) QUALIFIED PROPANE HOT WATER BOILER.—The term "qualified propane hot water boiler" means any propane hot water boiler which achieves an annual fuel utilization efficiency rate of not less than 90.

(E) QUALIFIED OIL FURNACES.—The term "qualified oil furnace" means any oil furnace which achieves an annual fuel utilization efficiency rate of not less than 90.

(F) QUALIFIED OIL HOT WATER BOILER.—The term "qualified oil hot water boiler" means any oil hot water boiler which achieves an annual fuel utilization efficiency rate of not less than 90.

* * *

[CCH Explanation at ¶335. Committee Reports at ¶10,160.]

Amendments

• **2009, American Recovery and Reinvestment Tax Act of 2009 (P.L. 111-5)**

P.L. 111-5, §1121(b)(1):

Amended Code Sec. 25C(d)(3)(B). **Effective** for property placed in service after 2-17-2009. Prior to amendment, Code Sec. 25C(d)(3)(B) read as follows:

(B) an electric heat pump which has a heating seasonal performance factor (HSPF) of at least 9, a seasonal energy efficiency ratio (SEER) of at least 15, and an energy efficiency ratio (EER) of at least 13,

P.L. 111-5, §1121(b)(2):

Amended Code Sec. 25C(d)(3)(C) by striking "2006" and inserting "2009". **Effective** for property placed in service after 2-17-2009.

P.L. 111-5, §1121(b)(3):

Amended Code Sec. 25C(d)(3)(D). **Effective** for property placed in service after 2-17-2009. Prior to amendment, Code Sec. 25C(d)(3)(D) read as follows:

(D) a natural gas, propane, or oil water heater which has an energy factor of at least 0.80 or a thermal efficiency of at least 90 percent, and

P.L. 111-5, §1121(b)(4):

Amended Code Sec. 25C(d)(3)(E) by inserting ", as measured using a lower heating value" after "75 percent". **Effective** for tax years beginning after 12-31-2008.

P.L. 111-5, §1121(c)(1):

Amended Code Sec. 25C(d)(4). **Effective** for property placed in service after 2-17-2009. Prior to amendment, Code Sec. 25C(d)(4) read as follows:

(4) QUALIFIED NATURAL GAS, PROPANE, OR OIL FURNACE OR HOT WATER BOILER.—The term "qualified natural gas, propane, or oil furnace or hot water boiler" means a natural gas, propane, or oil furnace or hot water boiler which achieves an annual fuel utilization efficiency rate of not less than 95.

P.L. 111-5, §1121(c)(2):

Amended Code Sec. 25C(d)(2)(A)(ii). **Effective** for property placed in service after 2-17-2009. Prior to amendment, Code Sec. 25C(d)(2)(A)(ii) read as follows:

(ii) a qualified natural gas, propane, or oil furnace or hot water boiler, or

(e) SPECIAL RULES.—For purposes of this section—

(1) APPLICATION OF RULES.—Rules similar to the rules under paragraphs (4), (5), (6), (7), *and (8)* of section 25D(e) shall apply.

* * *

[CCH Explanation at ¶510. Committee Reports at ¶10,120.]

Amendments

• **2009, American Recovery and Reinvestment Tax Act of 2009 (P.L. 111-5)**

P.L. 111-5, §1103(b)(2)(A):

Amended Code Sec. 25C(e)(1) by striking "(8), and (9)" and inserting "and (8)". **Effective** for tax years beginning after 12-31-2008.

(g) TERMINATION.—This section shall not apply with respect to any property placed in service—

(1) after December 31, 2007, and before January 1, 2009, or

(2) after *December 31, 2010*.

[CCH Explanation at ¶335. Committee Reports at ¶10,160.]

Amendments

• 2009, American Recovery and Reinvestment Tax Act of 2009 (P.L. 111-5)

P.L. 111-5, §1121(e):

Amended Code Sec. 25C(g)(2) by striking "December 31, 2009" and inserting "December 31, 2010". **Effective** for tax years beginning after 12-31-2008.

[¶5030] CODE SEC. 25D. RESIDENTIAL ENERGY EFFICIENT PROPERTY.

* * *

(b) LIMITATIONS.—

(1) MAXIMUM CREDIT FOR FUEL CELLS.—In the case of any qualified fuel cell property expenditure, the credit allowed under subsection (a) (determined without regard to subsection (c)) for any taxable year shall not exceed $500 with respect to each half kilowatt of capacity of the qualified fuel cell property (as defined in section 48(c)(1)) to which such expenditure relates.

* * *

[CCH Explanation at ¶340. Committee Reports at ¶10,170.]

Amendments

• 2009, American Recovery and Reinvestment Tax Act of 2009 (P.L. 111-5)

P.L. 111-5, §1122(a)(1):

Amended Code Sec. 25D(b)(1). **Effective** for tax years beginning after 12-31-2008. Prior to amendment, Code Sec. 25D(b)(1) read as follows:

(1) MAXIMUM CREDIT.—The credit allowed under subsection (a) (determined without regard to subsection (c)) for any taxable year shall not exceed—

(A) $2,000 with respect to any qualified solar water heating property expenditures,

(B) $500 with respect to each half kilowatt of capacity of qualified fuel cell property (as defined in section 48(c)(1)) for which qualified fuel cell property expenditures are made,

(C) $500 with respect to each half kilowatt of capacity (not to exceed $4,000) of wind turbines for which qualified small wind energy property expenditures are made, and

(D) $2,000 with respect to any qualified geothermal heat pump property expenditures.

(e) SPECIAL RULES.—For purposes of this section—

* * *

(4) FUEL CELL EXPENDITURE LIMITATIONS IN CASE OF JOINT OCCUPANCY.—In the case of any dwelling unit with respect to which qualified fuel cell property expenditures are made and which is jointly occupied and used during any calendar year as a residence by two or more individuals, the following rules shall apply:

(A) MAXIMUM EXPENDITURES FOR FUEL CELLS.—The maximum amount of such expenditures which may be taken into account under subsection (a) by all such individuals with respect to such dwelling unit during such calendar year shall be $1,667 in the case of each half kilowatt of capacity of qualified fuel cell property (as defined in section 48(c)(1)) with respect to which such expenditures relate.

* * *

(C) [*Stricken.*]

* * *

(9) [*Stricken.*]

* * *

[CCH Explanation at ¶ 340 and ¶ 510. Committee Reports at ¶ 10,120 and ¶ 10,170.]

Amendments

• **2009, American Recovery and Reinvestment Tax Act of 2009 (P.L. 111-5)**

P.L. 111-5, § 1103(b)(2)(B):

Amended Code Sec. 25D(e) by striking paragraph (9). **Effective** for tax years beginning after 12-31-2008. Prior to being stricken, Code Sec. 25D(e)(9) read as follows:

(9) PROPERTY FINANCED BY SUBSIDIZED ENERGY FINANCING.—For purposes of determining the amount of expenditures made by any individual with respect to any dwelling unit, there shall not be taken into account expenditures which are made from subsidized energy financing (as defined in section 48(a)(4)(C)).

P.L. 111-5, § 1122(a)(2)(A)-(B):

Amended Code Sec. 25D(e)(4) by striking all that precedes subparagraph (B) and inserting "(4) FUEL CELL EXPENDITURE LIMITATIONS IN CASE OF JOINT OCCUPANCY.—", introductory text and new subparagraph (A), and by striking subparagraph (C). **Effective** for tax years beginning after 12-31-2008. Prior to amendment, Code Sec. 25D(e)(4) read as follows:

(4) DOLLAR AMOUNTS IN CASE OF JOINT OCCUPANCY.—In the case of any dwelling unit which is jointly occupied and used during any calendar year as a residence by two or more individuals the following rules shall apply:

(A) MAXIMUM EXPENDITURES.—The maximum amount of expenditures which may be taken into account under subsection (a) by all such individuals with respect to such dwelling unit during such calendar year shall be—

(i) $6,667 in the case of any qualified solar water heating property expenditures,

(ii) $1,667 in the case of each half kilowatt of capacity of qualified fuel cell property (as defined in section 48(c)(1)) for which qualified fuel cell property expenditures are made,

(iii) $1,667 in the case of each half kilowatt of capacity (not to exceed $13,333) of wind turbines for which qualified small wind energy property expenditures are made, and

(iv) $6,667 in the case of any qualified geothermal heat pump property expenditures.

(B) ALLOCATION OF EXPENDITURES.—The expenditures allocated to any individual for the taxable year in which such calendar year ends shall be an amount equal to the lesser of—

(i) the amount of expenditures made by such individual with respect to such dwelling during such calendar year, or

(ii) the maximum amount of such expenditures set forth in subparagraph (A) multiplied by a fraction—

(I) the numerator of which is the amount of such expenditures with respect to such dwelling made by such individual during such calendar year, and

(II) the denominator of which is the total expenditures made by all such individuals with respect to such dwelling during such calendar year.

(C) Subparagraphs (A) and (B) shall be applied separately with respect to expenditures described in paragraphs (1), (2), and (3) of subsection (d).

[¶ 5035] CODE SEC. 26. LIMITATION BASED ON TAX LIABILITY; DEFINITION OF TAX LIABILITY.

(a) LIMITATION BASED ON AMOUNT OF TAX.—

(1) IN GENERAL.—The aggregate amount of credits allowed by this subpart (other than sections 23, 24, *25A(i)*, 25B, 25D, *30*, *30B*, and 30D) for the taxable year shall not exceed the excess (if any) of—

(A) the taxpayer's regular tax liability for the taxable year, over

(B) the tentative minimum tax for the taxable year (determined without regard to the alternative minimum tax foreign tax credit).

For purposes of subparagraph (B), the taxpayer's tentative minimum tax for any taxable year beginning during 1999 shall be treated as being zero.

(2) SPECIAL RULE FOR TAXABLE YEARS 2000 THROUGH *2009*.—For purposes of any taxable year beginning during 2000, 2001, 2002, 2003, 2004, 2005, 2006, 2007, *2008, or 2009*, the aggregate amount of credits allowed by this subpart for the taxable year shall not exceed the sum of—

(A) the taxpayer's regular tax liability for the taxable year reduced by the foreign tax credit allowable under section 27(a), and

(B) the tax imposed by section 55(a) for the taxable year.

* * *

[CCH Explanation at ¶ 240, ¶ 330, ¶ 350 and ¶ 360. Committee Reports at ¶ 10,040, ¶ 10,090 and ¶ 10,200.]

Amendments

• **2009, American Recovery and Reinvestment Tax Act of 2009 (P.L. 111-5)**

P.L. 111-5, § 1004(b)(3):

Amended Code Sec. 26(a)(1) by inserting "25A(i)," after "24,". **Effective** for tax years beginning after 12-31-2008.

P.L. 111-5, § 1011(a)(1)-(2):

Amended Code Sec. 26(a)(2) by striking "or 2008" and inserting "2008, or 2009", and by striking "2008" in the heading thereof and inserting "2009". **Effective** for tax years beginning after 12-31-2008.

P.L. 111-5, § 1142(b)(1)(D):

Amended Code Sec. 26(a)(1) by inserting "30," after "25D,". **Effective** for vehicles acquired after 2-17-2009. For a transitional rule, see Act Sec. 1142(d) in the amendment notes for Code Sec. 30.

P.L. 111-5, § 1144(b)(1)(D):

Amended Code Sec. 26(a)(1), as amended by this Act, by inserting "30B," after "30,". **Effective** for tax years beginning after 12-31-2008.

[¶ 5040] CODE SEC. 30. CERTAIN PLUG-IN ELECTRIC VEHICLES.

(a) ALLOWANCE OF CREDIT.—There shall be allowed as a credit against the tax imposed by this chapter for the taxable year an amount equal to 10 percent of the cost of any qualified plug-in electric vehicle placed in service by the taxpayer during the taxable year.

(b) PER VEHICLE DOLLAR LIMITATION.—The amount of the credit allowed under subsection (a) with respect to any vehicle shall not exceed $2,500.

(c) APPLICATION WITH OTHER CREDITS.—

(1) BUSINESS CREDIT TREATED AS PART OF GENERAL BUSINESS CREDIT.—So much of the credit which would be allowed under subsection (a) for any taxable year (determined without regard to this subsection) that is attributable to property of a character subject to an allowance for depreciation shall be treated as a credit listed in section 38(b) for such taxable year (and not allowed under subsection (a)).

(2) PERSONAL CREDIT.—

(A) IN GENERAL.—For purposes of this title, the credit allowed under subsection (a) for any taxable year (determined after application of paragraph (1)) shall be treated as a credit allowable under subpart A for such taxable year.

(B) LIMITATION BASED ON AMOUNT OF TAX.—In the case of a taxable year to which section 26(a)(2) does not apply, the credit allowed under subsection (a) for any taxable year (determined after application of paragraph (1)) shall not exceed the excess of—

(i) the sum of the regular tax liability (as defined in section 26(b)) plus the tax imposed by section 55, over

(ii) the sum of the credits allowable under subpart A (other than this section and sections 23, 25D, and 30D) and section 27 for the taxable year.

(d) QUALIFIED PLUG-IN ELECTRIC VEHICLE.—For purposes of this section—

(1) IN GENERAL.—The term "qualified plug-in electric vehicle" means a specified vehicle—

(A) the original use of which commences with the taxpayer,

(B) which is acquired for use or lease by the taxpayer and not for resale,

(C) which is made by a manufacturer,

(D) which is manufactured primarily for use on public streets, roads, and highways,

(E) which has a gross vehicle weight rating of less than 14,000 pounds, and

(F) which is propelled to a significant extent by an electric motor which draws electricity from a battery which—

(i) has a capacity of not less than 4 kilowatt hours (2.5 kilowatt hours in the case of a vehicle with 2 or 3 wheels), and

(ii) is capable of being recharged from an external source of electricity.

(2) SPECIFIED VEHICLE.—The term "specified vehicle" means any vehicle which—

(A) is a low speed vehicle within the meaning of section 571.3 of title 49, Code of Federal Regulations (as in effect on the date of the enactment of the American Recovery and Reinvestment Tax Act of 2009), or

(B) has 2 or 3 wheels.

(3) MANUFACTURER.—The term "manufacturer" has the meaning given such term in regulations prescribed by the Administrator of the Environmental Protection Agency for purposes of the administration of title II of the Clean Air Act (42 U.S.C. 7521 et seq.).

(4) BATTERY CAPACITY.—The term "capacity" means, with respect to any battery, the quantity of electricity which the battery is capable of storing, expressed in kilowatt hours, as measured from a 100 percent state of charge to a 0 percent state of charge.

(e) SPECIAL RULES.—

(1) BASIS REDUCTION.—For purposes of this subtitle, the basis of any property for which a credit is allowable under subsection (a) shall be reduced by the amount of such credit so allowed.

(2) NO DOUBLE BENEFIT.—The amount of any deduction or other credit allowable under this chapter for a new qualified plug-in electric drive motor vehicle shall be reduced by the amount of credit allowable under subsection (a) for such vehicle.

(3) PROPERTY USED BY TAX-EXEMPT ENTITY.—In the case of a vehicle the use of which is described in paragraph (3) or (4) of section 50(b) and which is not subject to a lease, the person who sold such vehicle to the person or entity using such vehicle shall be treated as the taxpayer that placed such vehicle in service, but only if such person clearly discloses to such person or entity in a document the amount of any credit allowable under subsection (a) with respect to such vehicle (determined without regard to subsection (c)).

(4) PROPERTY USED OUTSIDE UNITED STATES NOT QUALIFIED.—No credit shall be allowable under subsection (a) with respect to any property referred to in section 50(b)(1).

(5) RECAPTURE.—The Secretary shall, by regulations, provide for recapturing the benefit of any credit allowable under subsection (a) with respect to any property which ceases to be property eligible for such credit.

(6) ELECTION NOT TO TAKE CREDIT.—No credit shall be allowed under subsection (a) for any vehicle if the taxpayer elects to not have this section apply to such vehicle.

(f) TERMINATION.—This section shall not apply to any vehicle acquired after December 31, 2011.

[CCH Explanation at ¶ 350. Committee Reports at ¶ 10,200.]

Amendments

• 2009, American Recovery and Reinvestment Tax Act of 2009 (P.L. 111-5)

P.L. 111-5, § 1142(a):

Amended Code Sec. 30. **Effective** for vehicles acquired after 2-17-2009. For a transitional rule, see Act Sec. 1142(d), below. Prior to amendment, Code Sec. 30 read as follows:

SEC. 30. CREDIT FOR QUALIFIED ELECTRIC VEHICLES.

(a) ALLOWANCE OF CREDIT.—There shall be allowed as a credit against the tax imposed by this chapter for the taxable year an amount equal to 10 percent of the cost of any qualified electric vehicle placed in service by the taxpayer during the taxable year.

(b) LIMITATIONS.—

(1) LIMITATION PER VEHICLE.—The amount of the credit allowed under subsection (a) for any vehicle shall not exceed $4,000.

(2) PHASEOUT.—In the case of any qualified electric vehicle placed in service after December 31, 2005, the credit otherwise allowable under subsection (a) (determined after the application of paragraph (1)) shall be reduced by 75 percent.

(3) APPLICATION WITH OTHER CREDITS.—The credit allowed by subsection (a) for any taxable year shall not exceed the excess (if any) of—

(A) the regular tax for the taxable year reduced by the sum of the credits allowable under subpart A and section 27, over—

(B) the tentative minimum tax for the taxable year.

(c) QUALIFIED ELECTRIC VEHICLE.—For purposes of this section—

(1) IN GENERAL.—The term "qualified electric vehicle" means any motor vehicle—

(A) which is powered primarily by an electric motor drawing current from rechargeable batteries, fuel cells, or other portable sources of electrical current,

(B) the original use of which commences with the taxpayer, and

(C) which is acquired for use by the taxpayer and not for resale.

(2) MOTOR VEHICLE.—For purposes of paragraph (1), the term "motor vehicle" means any vehicle which is manufactured primarily for use on public streets, roads, and highways (not including a vehicle operated exclusively on a rail or rails) and which has at least 4 wheels.

(d) SPECIAL RULES.—

(1) BASIS REDUCTION.—The basis of any property for which a credit is allowable under subsection (a) shall be reduced by the amount of such credit (determined without regard to subsection (b)(3)).

(2) RECAPTURE.—The Secretary shall, by regulations, provide for recapturing the benefit of any credit allowable under subsection (a) with respect to any property which ceases to be property eligible for such credit.

(3) PROPERTY USED OUTSIDE UNITED STATES, ETC., NOT QUALIFIED.—No credit shall be allowed under subsection (a) with respect to any property referred to in section 50(b) or with respect to the portion of the cost of any property taken into account under section 179.

(4) ELECTION TO NOT TAKE CREDIT.—No credit shall be allowed under subsection (a) for any vehicle if the taxpayer elects to not have this section apply to such vehicle.

(e) TERMINATION.—This section shall not apply to any property placed in service after December 31, 2006.

P.L. 111-5, § 1142(d), provides:

(d) TRANSITIONAL RULE.—In the case of a vehicle acquired after the date of the enactment of this Act and before January 1, 2010, no credit shall be allowed under section 30 of the Internal Revenue Code of 1986, as added by this section, if credit is allowable under section 30D of such Code with respect to such vehicle.

[¶ 5045] CODE SEC. 30B. ALTERNATIVE MOTOR VEHICLE CREDIT.

(a) ALLOWANCE OF CREDIT.—There shall be allowed as a credit against the tax imposed by this chapter for the taxable year an amount equal to the sum of—

    (1) the new qualified fuel cell motor vehicle credit determined under subsection (b),

    (2) the new advanced lean burn technology motor vehicle credit determined under subsection (c),

    (3) the new qualified hybrid motor vehicle credit determined under subsection (d),

    (4) the new qualified alternative fuel motor vehicle credit determined under subsection (e), and

    (5) *the plug-in conversion credit determined under subsection (i).*

* * *

[CCH Explanation at ¶ 355. Committee Reports at ¶ 10,200.]

Amendments

• **2009, American Recovery and Reinvestment Tax Act of 2009 (P.L. 111-5)**

P.L. 111-5, § 1143(b):

Amended Code Sec. 30B(a) by striking "and" at the end of paragraph (3), by striking the period at the end of paragraph (4) and inserting ", and", and by adding at the end a new paragraph (5). **Effective** for property placed in service after 2-17-2009.

(d) NEW QUALIFIED HYBRID MOTOR VEHICLE CREDIT.—

* * *

(3) NEW QUALIFIED HYBRID MOTOR VEHICLE.—For purposes of this subsection—

* * *

▶▶▶→ *Caution: Code Sec. 30B(d)(3)(D), below, as amended by P.L. 111-5, applies to vehicles acquired after December 31, 2009.*

    (D) EXCLUSION OF PLUG-IN VEHICLES.—Any vehicle with respect to which a credit is allowable under section 30D (determined without regard to *subsection (c) thereof*) shall not be taken into account under this section.

* * *

[CCH Explanation at ¶ 345. Committee Reports at ¶ 10,200.]

Amendments

• **2009, American Recovery and Reinvestment Tax Act of 2009 (P.L. 111-5)**

P.L. 111-5, § 1141(b)(1):

Amended Code Sec. 30B(d)(3)(D) by striking "subsection (d) thereof" and inserting "subsection (c) thereof". **Effective** for vehicles acquired after 12-31-2009.

    (g) APPLICATION WITH OTHER CREDITS.—

* * *

    (2) PERSONAL CREDIT.—

        (A) IN GENERAL.—For purposes of this title, the credit allowed under subsection (a) for any taxable year (determined after application of paragraph (1)) shall be treated as a credit allowable under subpart A for such taxable year.

(B) LIMITATION BASED ON AMOUNT OF TAX.—In the case of a taxable year to which section 26(a)(2) does not apply, the credit allowed under subsection (a) for any taxable year (determined after application of paragraph (1)) shall not exceed the excess of—

    (i) the sum of the regular tax liability (as defined in section 26(b)) plus the tax imposed by section 55, over

    (ii) the sum of the credits allowable under subpart A (other than this section and sections 23, 25D, 30, and 30D) and section 27 for the taxable year.

[CCH Explanation at ¶360. Committee Reports at ¶10,200.]

Amendments

• 2009, American Recovery and Reinvestment Tax Act of 2009 (P.L. 111-5)

P.L. 111-5, §1144(a):

Amended Code Sec. 30B(g)(2). **Effective** for tax years beginning after 12-31-2008. Prior to amendment, Code Sec. 30B(g)(2) read as follows:

(2) PERSONAL CREDIT.—The credit allowed under subsection (a) (after the application of paragraph (1)) for any taxable year shall not exceed the excess (if any) of—

(A) the regular tax liability (as defined in section 26(b)) reduced by the sum of the credits allowable under subpart A and sections 27 and 30, over

(B) the tentative minimum tax for the taxable year.

(h) OTHER DEFINITIONS AND SPECIAL RULES.—For purposes of this section—

    (1) MOTOR VEHICLE.—The term "motor vehicle" means any vehicle which is manufactured primarily for use on public streets, roads, and highways (not including a vehicle operated exclusively on a rail or rails) and which has at least 4 wheels.

* * *

    (8) RECAPTURE.—The Secretary shall, by regulations, provide for recapturing the benefit of any credit allowable under subsection (a) with respect to any property which ceases to be property eligible for such credit (including recapture in the case of a lease period of less than the economic life of a vehicle)., [sic] except that no benefit shall be recaptured if such property ceases to be eligible for such credit by reason of conversion to a qualified plug-in electric drive motor vehicle.

* * *

[CCH Explanation at ¶350 and ¶355. Committee Reports at ¶10,200.]

Amendments

• 2009, American Recovery and Reinvestment Tax Act of 2009 (P.L. 111-5)

P.L. 111-5, §1142(b)(2):

Amended Code Sec. 30B(h)(1). **Effective** for vehicles acquired after 2-17-2009. For a transitional rule, see Act Sec. 1142(d) in the amendment notes for Code Sec. 30. Prior to amendment, Code Sec. 30B(h)(1) read as follows:

(1) MOTOR VEHICLE.—The term "motor vehicle" has the meaning given such term by section 30(c)(2).

P.L. 111-5, §1143(c):

Amended Code Sec. 30B(h)(8) by adding at the end ", except that no benefit shall be recaptured if such property ceases to be eligible for such credit by reason of conversion to a qualified plug-in electric drive motor vehicle.". **Effective** for property placed in service after 2-17-2009.

(i) PLUG-IN CONVERSION CREDIT.—

    (1) IN GENERAL.—For purposes of subsection (a), the plug-in conversion credit determined under this subsection with respect to any motor vehicle which is converted to a qualified plug-in electric drive motor vehicle is 10 percent of so much of the cost of the [sic] converting such vehicle as does not exceed $40,000.

    (2) QUALIFIED PLUG-IN ELECTRIC DRIVE MOTOR VEHICLE.—For purposes of this subsection, the term "qualified plug-in electric drive motor vehicle" means any new qualified plug-in electric drive motor vehicle (as defined in section 30D, determined without regard to whether such vehicle is made by a manufacturer or whether the original use of such vehicle commences with the taxpayer).

    (3) CREDIT ALLOWED IN ADDITION TO OTHER CREDITS.—The credit allowed under this subsection shall be allowed with respect to a motor vehicle notwithstanding whether a credit has been allowed with respect to such motor vehicle under this section (other than this subsection) in any preceding taxable year.

    (4) TERMINATION.—This subsection shall not apply to conversions made after December 31, 2011.

[CCH Explanation at ¶355. Committee Reports at ¶10,200.]

Amendments

• **2009, American Recovery and Reinvestment Tax Act of 2009 (P.L. 111-5)**

P.L. 111-5, §1143(a):

Amended Code Sec. 30B by redesignating subsections (i) and (j) as subsections (j) and (k), respectively, and by inserting after subsection (h) a new subsection (i). **Effective** for property placed in service after 2-17-2009.

(j) REGULATIONS.—

* * *

[CCH Explanation at ¶355. Committee Reports at ¶10,200.]

Amendments

• **2009, American Recovery and Reinvestment Tax Act of 2009 (P.L. 111-5)**

P.L. 111-5, §1143(a):

Amended Code Sec. 30B by redesignating subsection (i) as subsection (j). **Effective** for property placed in service after 2-17-2009.

(k) TERMINATION.—This section shall not apply to any property purchased after—

(1) in the case of a new qualified fuel cell motor vehicle (as described in subsection (b)), December 31, 2014,

(2) in the case of a new advanced lean burn technology motor vehicle (as described in subsection (c)) or a new qualified hybrid motor vehicle (as described in subsection (d)(2)(A)), December 31, 2010,

(3) in the case of a new qualified hybrid motor vehicle (as described in subsection (d)(2)(B)), December 31, 2009, and

(4) in the case of a new qualified alternative fuel vehicle (as described in subsection (e)), December 31, 2010.

[CCH Explanation at ¶355. Committee Reports at ¶10,200.]

Amendments

• **2009, American Recovery and Reinvestment Tax Act of 2009 (P.L. 111-5)**

P.L. 111-5, §1143(a):

Amended Code Sec. 30B by redesignating subsection (j) as subsection (k). **Effective** for property placed in service after 2-17-2009.

[¶5050] CODE SEC. 30C. ALTERNATIVE FUEL VEHICLE REFUELING PROPERTY CREDIT.

* * *

(d) APPLICATION WITH OTHER CREDITS.—

* * *

(2) PERSONAL CREDIT.—The credit allowed under subsection (a) (after the application of paragraph (1)) for any taxable year shall not exceed the excess (if any) of—

(A) the regular tax liability (as defined in section 26(b)) reduced by the sum of the credits allowable under subpart A and *section 27*, over

(B) the tentative minimum tax for the taxable year.

[CCH Explanation at ¶350. Committee Reports at ¶10,200.]
Amendments

• **2009, American Recovery and Reinvestment Tax Act of 2009 (P.L. 111-5)**

P.L. 111-5, §1142(b)(3):

Amended Code Sec. 30C(d)(2)(A) by striking ", 30," after "sections 27". **Effective** for vehicles acquired after 2-17-2009.

For a transitional rule, see Act Sec. 1142(d) in the amendment notes for Code Sec. 30.

P.L. 111-5, §1144(b)(2):

Amended Code Sec. 30C(d)(2)(A), as amended by this Act, by striking "sections 27 and 30B" and inserting "section 27". **Effective** for tax years beginning after 12-31-2008.

(e) SPECIAL RULES.—For purposes of this section—

* * *

(6) SPECIAL RULE FOR PROPERTY PLACED IN SERVICE DURING 2009 AND 2010.—In the case of property placed in service in taxable years beginning after December 31, 2008, and before January 1, 2011—

(A) in the case of any such property which does not relate to hydrogen—

(i) subsection (a) shall be applied by substituting "50 percent" for "30 percent",

(ii) subsection (b)(1) shall be applied by substituting "$50,000" for "$30,000", and

(iii) subsection (b)(2) shall be applied by substituting "$2,000" for "$1,000", and

(B) in the case of any such property which relates to hydrogen, subsection (b)(1) shall be applied by substituting "$200,000" for "$30,000".

* * *

[CCH Explanation at ¶365. Committee Reports at ¶10,180.]
Amendments

• **2009, American Recovery and Reinvestment Tax Act of 2009 (P.L. 111-5)**

P.L. 111-5, §1123(a):

Amended Code Sec. 30C(e) by adding at the end a new paragraph (6). **Effective** for tax years beginning after 12-31-2008.

»→ Caution: Code Sec. 30D, below, as amended by P.L. 111-5, applies to vehicles acquired after December 31, 2009.

[¶5055] CODE SEC. 30D. NEW QUALIFIED PLUG-IN ELECTRIC DRIVE MOTOR VEHICLES.

(a) ALLOWANCE OF CREDIT.—There shall be allowed as a credit against the tax imposed by this chapter for the taxable year an amount equal to the sum of the credit amounts determined under subsection (b) with respect to each new qualified plug-in electric drive motor vehicle placed in service by the taxpayer during the taxable year.

(b) PER VEHICLE DOLLAR LIMITATION.—

(1) IN GENERAL.—The amount determined under this subsection with respect to any new qualified plug-in electric drive motor vehicle is the sum of the amounts determined under paragraphs (2) and (3) with respect to such vehicle.

(2) BASE AMOUNT.—The amount determined under this paragraph is $2,500.

(3) BATTERY CAPACITY.—In the case of a vehicle which draws propulsion energy from a battery with not less than 5 kilowatt hours of capacity, the amount determined under this paragraph is $417, plus $417 for each kilowatt hour of capacity in excess of 5 kilowatt hours. The amount determined under this paragraph shall not exceed $5,000.

(c) APPLICATION WITH OTHER CREDITS.—

(1) BUSINESS CREDIT TREATED AS PART OF GENERAL BUSINESS CREDIT.—So much of the credit which would be allowed under subsection (a) for any taxable year (determined without regard to this subsection) that is attributable to property of a character subject to an allowance for depreciation shall be treated as a credit listed in section 38(b) for such taxable year (and not allowed under subsection (a)).

(2) PERSONAL CREDIT.—

(A) IN GENERAL.—For purposes of this title, the credit allowed under subsection (a) for any taxable year (determined after application of paragraph (1)) shall be treated as a credit allowable under subpart A for such taxable year.

(B) LIMITATION BASED ON AMOUNT OF TAX.—In the case of a taxable year to which section 26(a)(2) does not apply, the credit allowed under subsection (a) for any taxable year (determined after application of paragraph (1)) shall not exceed the excess of—

(i) the sum of the regular tax liability (as defined in section 26(b)) plus the tax imposed by section 55, over

(ii) the sum of the credits allowable under subpart A (other than this section and sections 23 and 25D) and section 27 for the taxable year.

(d) NEW QUALIFIED PLUG-IN ELECTRIC DRIVE MOTOR VEHICLE.—For purposes of this section—

(1) IN GENERAL.—The term "new qualified plug-in electric drive motor vehicle" means a motor vehicle—

(A) the original use of which commences with the taxpayer,

(B) which is acquired for use or lease by the taxpayer and not for resale,

(C) which is made by a manufacturer,

(D) which is treated as a motor vehicle for purposes of title II of the Clean Air Act,

(E) which has a gross vehicle weight rating of less than 14,000 pounds, and

(F) which is propelled to a significant extent by an electric motor which draws electricity from a battery which—

(i) has a capacity of not less than 4 kilowatt hours, and

(ii) is capable of being recharged from an external source of electricity.

(2) MOTOR VEHICLE.—The term "motor vehicle" means any vehicle which is manufactured primarily for use on public streets, roads, and highways (not including a vehicle operated exclusively on a rail or rails) and which has at least 4 wheels.

(3) MANUFACTURER.—The term "manufacturer" has the meaning given such term in regulations prescribed by the Administrator of the Environmental Protection Agency for purposes of the administration of title II of the Clean Air Act (42 U.S.C. 7521 et seq.).

(4) BATTERY CAPACITY.—The term "capacity" means, with respect to any battery, the quantity of electricity which the battery is capable of storing, expressed in kilowatt hours, as measured from a 100 percent state of charge to a 0 percent state of charge.

(e) LIMITATION ON NUMBER OF NEW QUALIFIED PLUG-IN ELECTRIC DRIVE MOTOR VEHICLES ELIGIBLE FOR CREDIT.—

(1) IN GENERAL.—In the case of a new qualified plug-in electric drive motor vehicle sold during the phaseout period, only the applicable percentage of the credit otherwise allowable under subsection (a) shall be allowed.

(2) PHASEOUT PERIOD.—For purposes of this subsection, the phaseout period is the period beginning with the second calendar quarter following the calendar quarter which includes the first date on which the number of new qualified plug-in electric drive motor vehicles manufactured by the manufacturer of the vehicle referred to in paragraph (1) sold for use in the United States after December 31, 2009, is at least 200,000.

(3) APPLICABLE PERCENTAGE.—For purposes of paragraph (1), the applicable percentage is—

(A) 50 percent for the first 2 calendar quarters of the phaseout period,

(B) 25 percent for the 3d and 4th calendar quarters of the phaseout period, and

(C) 0 percent for each calendar quarter thereafter.

(4) CONTROLLED GROUPS.—Rules similar to the rules of section 30B(f)(4) shall apply for purposes of this subsection.

(f) SPECIAL RULES.—

(1) BASIS REDUCTION.—For purposes of this subtitle, the basis of any property for which a credit is allowable under subsection (a) shall be reduced by the amount of such credit so allowed.

(2) NO DOUBLE BENEFIT.—The amount of any deduction or other credit allowable under this chapter for a new qualified plug-in electric drive motor vehicle shall be reduced by the amount of credit allowed under subsection (a) for such vehicle.

(3) PROPERTY USED BY TAX-EXEMPT ENTITY.—In the case of a vehicle the use of which is described in paragraph (3) or (4) of section 50(b) and which is not subject to a lease, the person who sold such vehicle to the person or entity using such vehicle shall be treated as the taxpayer that placed such vehicle in service, but only if such person clearly discloses to such person or entity in a document the amount of any credit allowable under subsection (a) with respect to such vehicle (determined without regard to subsection (c)).

(4) PROPERTY USED OUTSIDE UNITED STATES NOT QUALIFIED.—No credit shall be allowable under subsection (a) with respect to any property referred to in section 50(b)(1).

(5) RECAPTURE.—The Secretary shall, by regulations, provide for recapturing the benefit of any credit allowable under subsection (a) with respect to any property which ceases to be property eligible for such credit.

(6) ELECTION NOT TO TAKE CREDIT.—No credit shall be allowed under subsection (a) for any vehicle if the taxpayer elects to not have this section apply to such vehicle.

(7) INTERACTION WITH AIR QUALITY AND MOTOR VEHICLE SAFETY STANDARDS.—A motor vehicle shall not be considered eligible for a credit under this section unless such vehicle is in compliance with—

(A) the applicable provisions of the Clean Air Act for the applicable make and model year of the vehicle (or applicable air quality provisions of State law in the case of a State which has adopted such provision under a waiver under section 209(b) of the Clean Air Act), and

(B) the motor vehicle safety provisions of sections 30101 through 30169 of title 49, United States Code.

[CCH Explanation at ¶345. Committee Reports at ¶10,200.]

Amendments

• **2009, American Recovery and Reinvestment Tax Act of 2009 (P.L. 111-5)**

P.L. 111-5, §1141(a):

Amended Code Sec. 30D. **Effective** for vehicles acquired after 12-31-2009. Prior to amendment, Code Sec. 30D read as follows:

CODE SEC. 30D. NEW QUALIFIED PLUG-IN ELECTRIC DRIVE MOTOR VEHICLES.

(a) ALLOWANCE OF CREDIT.—

(1) IN GENERAL.—There shall be allowed as a credit against the tax imposed by this chapter for the taxable year an amount equal to the applicable amount with respect to each new qualified plug-in electric drive motor vehicle placed in service by the taxpayer during the taxable year.

(2) APPLICABLE AMOUNT.—For purposes of paragraph (1), the applicable amount is sum of—

(A) $2,500, plus

(B) $417 for each kilowatt hour of traction battery capacity in excess of 4 kilowatt hours.

(b) LIMITATIONS.—

(1) LIMITATION BASED ON WEIGHT.—The amount of the credit allowed under subsection (a) by reason of subsection (a)(2) shall not exceed—

(A) $7,500, in the case of any new qualified plug-in electric drive motor vehicle with a gross vehicle weight rating of not more than 10,000 pounds,

(B) $10,000, in the case of any new qualified plug-in electric drive motor vehicle with a gross vehicle weight rating of more than 10,000 pounds but not more than 14,000 pounds,

(C) $12,500, in the case of any new qualified plug-in electric drive motor vehicle with a gross vehicle weight rating of more than 14,000 pounds but not more than 26,000 pounds, and

(D) $15,000, in the case of any new qualified plug-in electric drive motor vehicle with a gross vehicle weight rating of more than 26,000 pounds.

(2) LIMITATION ON NUMBER OF PASSENGER VEHICLES AND LIGHT TRUCKS ELIGIBLE FOR CREDIT.—

(A) IN GENERAL.—In the case of a new qualified plug-in electric drive motor vehicle sold during the phaseout period, only the applicable percentage of the credit otherwise allowable under subsection (a) shall be allowed.

(B) PHASEOUT PERIOD.—For purposes of this subsection, the phaseout period is the period beginning with the second calendar quarter following the calendar quarter which includes the first date on which the total number of such new qualified plug-in electric drive motor vehicles sold for use in the United States after December 31, 2008, is at least 250,000.

¶5055 Code Sec. 30D(e)(4)

(C) APPLICABLE PERCENTAGE.—For purposes of subparagraph (A), the applicable percentage is—

(i) 50 percent for the first 2 calendar quarters of the phaseout period,

(ii) 25 percent for the 3d and 4th calendar quarters of the phaseout period, and

(iii) 0 percent for each calendar quarter thereafter.

(D) CONTROLLED GROUPS.—Rules similar to the rules of section 30B(f)(4) shall apply for purposes of this subsection.

(c) NEW QUALIFIED PLUG-IN ELECTRIC DRIVE MOTOR VEHICLE.—For purposes of this section, the term "new qualified plug-in electric drive motor vehicle" means a motor vehicle—

(1) which draws propulsion using a traction battery with at least 4 kilowatt hours of capacity,

(2) which uses an offboard source of energy to recharge such battery,

(3) which, in the case of a passenger vehicle or light truck which has a gross vehicle weight rating of not more than 8,500 pounds, has received a certificate of conformity under the Clean Air Act and meets or exceeds the equivalent qualifying California low emission vehicle standard under section 243(e)(2) of the Clean Air Act for that make and model year, and

(A) in the case of a vehicle having a gross vehicle weight rating of 6,000 pounds or less, the Bin 5 Tier II emission standard established in regulations prescribed by the Administrator of the Environmental Protection Agency under section 202(i) of the Clean Air Act for that make and model year vehicle, and

(B) in the case of a vehicle having a gross vehicle weight rating of more than 6,000 pounds but not more than 8,500 pounds, the Bin 8 Tier II emission standard which is so established,

(4) the original use of which commences with the taxpayer,

(5) which is acquired for use or lease by the taxpayer and not for resale, and

(6) which is made by a manufacturer.

(d) APPLICATION WITH OTHER CREDITS.—

(1) BUSINESS CREDIT TREATED AS PART OF GENERAL BUSINESS CREDIT.—So much of the credit which would be allowed under subsection (a) for any taxable year (determined without regard to this subsection) that is attributable to property of a character subject to an allowance for depreciation shall be treated as a credit listed in section 38(b) for such taxable year (and not allowed under subsection (a)).

(2) PERSONAL CREDIT.—

(A) IN GENERAL.—For purposes of this title, the credit allowed under subsection (a) for any taxable year (determined after application of paragraph (1)) shall be treated as a credit allowable under subpart A for such taxable year.

(B) LIMITATION BASED ON AMOUNT OF TAX.—In the case of a taxable year to which section 26(a)(2) does not apply, the credit allowed under subsection (a) for any taxable year (determined after application of paragraph (1)) shall not exceed the excess of—

(i) the sum of the regular tax liability (as defined in section 26(b)) plus the tax imposed by section 55, over

(ii) the sum of the credits allowable under subpart A (other than this section and sections 23 and 25D) and section 27 for the taxable year.

(e) OTHER DEFINITIONS AND SPECIAL RULES.—For purposes of this section—

(1) MOTOR VEHICLE.—The term "motor vehicle" has the meaning given such term by section 30(c)(2).

(2) OTHER TERMS.—The terms "passenger automobile", "light truck", and "manufacturer" have the meanings given such terms in regulations prescribed by the Administrator of the Environmental Protection Agency for purposes of the administration of title II of the Clean Air Act (42 U.S.C. 7521 et seq.).

(3) TRACTION BATTERY CAPACITY.—Traction battery capacity shall be measured in kilowatt hours from a 100 percent state of charge to a zero percent state of charge.

(4) REDUCTION IN BASIS.—For purposes of this subtitle, the basis of any property for which a credit is allowable under subsection (a) shall be reduced by the amount of such credit so allowed.

(5) NO DOUBLE BENEFIT.—The amount of any deduction or other credit allowable under this chapter for a new qualified plug-in electric drive motor vehicle shall be reduced by the amount of credit allowed under subsection (a) for such vehicle for the taxable year.

(6) PROPERTY USED BY TAX-EXEMPT ENTITY.—In the case of a vehicle the use of which is described in paragraph (3) or (4) of section 50(b) and which is not subject to a lease, the person who sold such vehicle to the person or entity using such vehicle shall be treated as the taxpayer that placed such vehicle in service, but only if such person clearly discloses to such person or entity in a document the amount of any credit allowable under subsection (a) with respect to such vehicle (determined without regard to subsection (b)(2)).

(7) PROPERTY USED OUTSIDE UNITED STATES, ETC., NOT QUALIFIED.—No credit shall be allowable under subsection (a) with respect to any property referred to in section 50(b)(1) or with respect to the portion of the cost of any property taken into account under section 179.

(8) RECAPTURE.—The Secretary shall, by regulations, provide for recapturing the benefit of any credit allowable under subsection (a) with respect to any property which ceases to be property eligible for such credit (including recapture in the case of a lease period of less than the economic life of a vehicle).

(9) ELECTION TO NOT TAKE CREDIT.—No credit shall be allowed under subsection (a) for any vehicle if the taxpayer elects not to have this section apply to such vehicle.

(10) INTERACTION WITH AIR QUALITY AND MOTOR VEHICLE SAFETY STANDARDS.—Unless otherwise provided in this section, a motor vehicle shall not be considered eligible for a credit under this section unless such vehicle is in compliance with—

(A) the applicable provisions of the Clean Air Act for the applicable make and model year of the vehicle (or applicable air quality provisions of State law in the case of a State which has adopted such provision under a waiver under section 209(b) of the Clean Air Act), and

(B) the motor vehicle safety provisions of sections 30101 through 30169 of title 49, United States Code.

(f) REGULATIONS.—

(1) IN GENERAL.—Except as provided in paragraph (2), the Secretary shall promulgate such regulations as necessary to carry out the provisions of this section.

(2) COORDINATION IN PRESCRIPTION OF CERTAIN REGULATIONS.—The Secretary of the Treasury, in coordination with the Secretary of Transportation and the Administrator of the Environmental Protection Agency, shall prescribe such regulations as necessary to determine whether a motor vehicle meets the requirements to be eligible for a credit under this section.

(g) TERMINATION.—This section shall not apply to property purchased after December 31, 2014.

[¶5060] CODE SEC. 32. EARNED INCOME.

* * *

(b) PERCENTAGES AND AMOUNTS.—For purposes of subsection (a)—

* * *

(3) SPECIAL RULES FOR 2009 AND 2010.—In the case of any taxable year beginning in 2009 or 2010—

(A) INCREASED CREDIT PERCENTAGE FOR 3 OR MORE QUALIFYING CHILDREN.—In the case of a taxpayer with 3 or more qualifying children, the credit percentage is 45 percent.

(B) REDUCTION OF MARRIAGE PENALTY.—

(i) IN GENERAL.—The dollar amount in effect under paragraph (2)(B) shall be $5,000.

(ii) INFLATION ADJUSTMENT.—In the case of any taxable year beginning in 2010, the $5,000 amount in clause (i) shall be increased by an amount equal to—

(I) such dollar amount, multiplied by

(II) the cost of living adjustment determined under section 1(f)(3) for the calendar year in which the taxable year begins determined by substituting "calendar year 2008" for "calendar year 1992" in subparagraph (B) thereof.

(iii) ROUNDING.—Subparagraph (A) of subsection (j)(2) shall apply after taking into account any increase under clause (ii).

* * *

[CCH Explanation at ¶320. Committee Reports at ¶10,020.]

Amendments

• 2009, American Recovery and Reinvestment Tax Act of 2009 (P.L. 111-5)

P.L. 111-5, §1002(a):

Amended Code Sec. 32(b) by adding at the end a new paragraph (3). **Effective** for tax years beginning after 12-31-2008.

[¶5065] CODE SEC. 35. HEALTH INSURANCE COSTS OF ELIGIBLE INDIVIDUALS.

(a) IN GENERAL.—In the case of an individual, there shall be allowed as a credit against the tax imposed by subtitle A an amount equal to 65 percent *(80 percent in the case of eligible coverage months beginning before January 1, 2011)* of the amount paid by the taxpayer for coverage of the taxpayer and qualifying family members under qualified health insurance for eligible coverage months beginning in the taxable year.

* * *

[CCH Explanation at ¶725. Committee Reports at ¶10,480.]

Amendments

• 2009, TAA Health Coverage Improvement Act of 2009 (P.L. 111-5)

P.L. 111-5, §1899A(a)(1):

Amended Code Sec. 35(a) by inserting "(80 percent in the case of eligible coverage months beginning before January 1, 2011)" after "65 percent". **Effective** for coverage months beginning on or after the first day of the first month beginning 60 days after 2-17-2009.

(c) ELIGIBLE INDIVIDUAL.—For purposes of this section—

* * *

(2) ELIGIBLE TAA RECIPIENT.—

(A) IN GENERAL.—Except as provided in subparagraph (B), the term "eligible TAA recipient" means, with respect to any month, any individual who is receiving for any day of such month a trade readjustment allowance under chapter 2 of title II of the Trade Act of 1974 or who would be eligible to receive such allowance if section 231 of such Act were applied without regard to subsection (a)(3)(B) of such section. An individual shall continue to be treated as an eligible TAA recipient during the first month that such individual would otherwise cease to be an eligible TAA recipient by reason of the preceding sentence.

(B) SPECIAL RULE.—In the case of any eligible coverage month beginning after the date of the enactment of this paragraph and before January 1, 2011, the term "eligible TAA recipient" means, with respect to any month, any individual who—

(i) is receiving for any day of such month a trade readjustment allowance under chapter 2 of title II of the Trade Act of 1974,

(ii) would be eligible to receive such allowance except that such individual is in a break in training provided under a training program approved under section 236 of such Act that exceeds the period specified in section 233(e) of such Act, but is within the period for receiving such allowances provided under section 233(a) of such Act, or

(iii) is receiving unemployment compensation (as defined in section 85(b)) for any day of such month and who would be eligible to receive such allowance for such month if section 231 of such Act were applied without regard to subsections (a)(3)(B) and (a)(5) thereof.

An individual shall continue to be treated as an eligible TAA recipient during the first month that such individual would otherwise cease to be an eligible TAA recipient by reason of the preceding sentence.

* * *

[CCH Explanation at ¶725. Committee Reports at ¶10,480.]
Amendments

• 2009, TAA Health Coverage Improvement Act of 2009 (P.L. 111-5)

P.L. 111-5, §1899C(a):

Amended Code Sec. 35(c)(2). **Effective** for coverage months beginning after 2-17-2009. Prior to amendment, Code Sec. 35(c)(2) read as follows:

(2) ELIGIBLE TAA RECIPIENT.—The term "eligible TAA recipient" means, with respect to any month, any individual who is receiving for any day of such month a trade readjustment allowance under chapter 2 of title II of the Trade Act of 1974 or who would be eligible to receive such allowance if section 231 of such Act were applied without regard to subsection (a)(3)(B) of such section. An individual shall continue to be treated as an eligible TAA recipient during the first month that such individual would otherwise cease to be an eligible TAA recipient by reason of the preceding sentence.

(e) QUALIFIED HEALTH INSURANCE.—For purposes of this section—

(1) IN GENERAL.—The term "qualified health insurance" means any of the following:

* * *

(K) In the case of eligible coverage months beginning before January 1, 2011, coverage under an employee benefit plan funded by a voluntary employees' beneficiary association (as defined in section 501(c)(9)) established pursuant to an order of a bankruptcy court, or by agreement with an authorized representative, as provided in section 1114 of title 11, United States Code.

* * *

[CCH Explanation at ¶725. Committee Reports at ¶10,490.]
Amendments

• 2009, TAA Health Coverage Improvement Act of 2009 (P.L. 111-5)

P.L. 111-5, §1899G(a):

Amended Code Sec. 35(e)(1) by adding at the end a new subparagraph (K). **Effective** for coverage months beginning after 2-17-2009.

(g) SPECIAL RULES.—

* * *

(9) COBRA PREMIUM ASSISTANCE.—In the case of an assistance eligible individual who receives premium reduction for COBRA continuation coverage under section 3002(a) of the Health Insurance

Assistance for the Unemployed Act of 2009 for any month during the taxable year, such individual shall not be treated as an eligible individual, a certified individual, or a qualifying family member for purposes of this section or section 7527 with respect to such month.

>>>→ *Caution: Former Code Sec. 35(g)(9), as added by P.L. 111-5, §1899E(a), and redesignated as Code Sec. 35(g)(10), below, by P.L. 111-5, §3001(a)(14)(A), applies to months beginning after December 31, 2009.*

(10) CONTINUED QUALIFICATION OF FAMILY MEMBERS AFTER CERTAIN EVENTS.—In the case of eligible coverage months beginning before January 1, 2011—

(A) MEDICARE ELIGIBILITY.—In the case of any month which would be an eligible coverage month with respect to an eligible individual but for subsection (f)(2)(A), such month shall be treated as an eligible coverage month with respect to such eligible individual solely for purposes of determining the amount of the credit under this section with respect to any qualifying family members of such individual (and any advance payment of such credit under section 7527). This subparagraph shall only apply with respect to the first 24 months after such eligible individual is first entitled to the benefits described in subsection (f)(2)(A).

(B) DIVORCE.—In the case of the finalization of a divorce between an eligible individual and such individual's spouse, such spouse shall be treated as an eligible individual for purposes of this section and section 7527 for a period of 24 months beginning with the date of such finalization, except that the only qualifying family members who may be taken into account with respect to such spouse are those individuals who were qualifying family members immediately before such finalization.

(C) DEATH.—In the case of the death of an eligible individual—

(i) any spouse of such individual (determined at the time of such death) shall be treated as an eligible individual for purposes of this section and section 7527 for a period of 24 months beginning with the date of such death, except that the only qualifying family members who may be taken into account with respect to such spouse are those individuals who were qualifying family members immediately before such death, and

(ii) any individual who was a qualifying family member of the decedent immediately before such death (or, in the case of an individual to whom paragraph (4) applies, the taxpayer to whom the deduction under section 151 is allowable) shall be treated as an eligible individual for purposes of this section and section 7527 for a period of 24 months beginning with the date of such death, except that in determining the amount of such credit only such qualifying family member may be taken into account.

(10)[11] REGULATIONS.—The Secretary may prescribe such regulations and other guidance as may be necessary or appropriate to carry out this section, section 6050T, and section 7527.

[CCH Explanation at ¶705 and 725. Committee Reports at ¶10,490 and ¶10,510.]

Amendments

• **2009, TAA Health Coverage Improvement Act of 2009 (P.L. 111-5)**

P.L. 111-5, §1899E(a):

Amended Code Sec. 35(g) by redesignating paragraph (9) as paragraph (10) and inserting after paragraph (8) a new paragraph (9). **Effective** for months beginning after 12-31-2009.

P.L. 111-5, §3001(a)(14)(A):

Amended Code Sec. 35(g) by redesignating paragraph (9) as paragraph (10) and inserting after paragraph (8) a new paragraph (9). **Effective** for tax years ending after 2-17-2009.

[¶5070] CODE SEC. 36. FIRST-TIME HOMEBUYER CREDIT.

* * *

(b) LIMITATIONS.—

(1) DOLLAR LIMITATION.—

(A) IN GENERAL.—Except as otherwise provided in this paragraph, the credit allowed under subsection (a) shall not exceed *$8,000*.

(B) MARRIED INDIVIDUALS FILING SEPARATELY.—In the case of a married individual filing a separate return, subparagraph (A) shall be applied by substituting "*$4,000*" for "*$8,000*".

(C) OTHER INDIVIDUALS.—If two or more individuals who are not married purchase a principal residence, the amount of the credit allowed under subsection (a) shall be allocated among such individuals in such manner as the Secretary may prescribe, except that the total amount of the credits allowed to all such individuals shall not exceed *$8,000*.

* * *

[CCH Explanation at ¶ 310. Committee Reports at ¶ 10,060.]

Amendments

• **2009, American Recovery and Reinvestment Tax Act of 2009 (P.L. 111-5)**

P.L. 111-5, § 1006(b)(1):

Amended Code Sec. 36(b) by striking "$7,500" each place it appears and inserting "$8,000". **Effective** for residences purchased after 12-31-2008.

P.L. 111-5, § 1006(b)(2):

Amended Code Sec. 36(b)(1)(B) by striking "$3,750" and inserting "$4,000". **Effective** for residences purchased after 12-31-2008.

(d) EXCEPTIONS.—No credit under subsection (a) shall be allowed to any taxpayer for any taxable year with respect to the purchase of a residence if—

(1) the taxpayer is a nonresident alien, or

(2) the taxpayer disposes of such residence (or such residence ceases to be the principal residence of the taxpayer (and, if married, the taxpayer's spouse)) before the close of such taxable year.

* * *

[CCH Explanation at ¶ 310. Committee Reports at ¶ 10,060.]

Amendments

• **2009, American Recovery and Reinvestment Tax Act of 2009 (P.L. 111-5)**

P.L. 111-5, § 1006(d)(2):

Amended Code Sec. 36(d) by striking paragraph (1). **Effective** for residences purchased after 12-31-2008. Prior to being stricken, Code Sec. 36(d)(1) read as follows:

(1) a credit under section 1400C (relating to first-time homebuyer in the District of Columbia) is allowable to the taxpayer (or the taxpayer's spouse) for such taxable year or any prior taxable year,

P.L. 111-5, § 1006(e):

Amended Code Sec. 36(d), as amended by Act Sec. 1006(c)(2) [1006(d)(2)], by striking paragraph (2) and by redesignating paragraphs (3) and (4) as paragraphs (1) and (2), respectively. **Effective** for residences purchased after 12-31-2008. Prior to being stricken, Code Sec. 36(d)(2) read as follows:

(2) the residence is financed by the proceeds of a qualified mortgage issue the interest on which is exempt from tax under section 103,

(f) RECAPTURE OF CREDIT.—

* * *

(4) EXCEPTIONS.—

* * *

(D) WAIVER OF RECAPTURE FOR PURCHASES IN 2009.—*In the case of any credit allowed with respect to the purchase of a principal residence after December 31, 2008, and before December 1, 2009—*

(i) paragraph (1) shall not apply, and

(ii) paragraph (2) shall apply only if the disposition or cessation described in paragraph (2) with respect to such residence occurs during the 36-month period beginning on the date of the purchase of such residence by the taxpayer.

* * *

[CCH Explanation at ¶ 310. Committee Reports at ¶ 10,060.]

Amendments

• **2009, American Recovery and Reinvestment Tax Act of 2009 (P.L. 111-5)**

P.L. 111-5, § 1006(c)(1):

Amended Code Sec. 36(f)(4) by adding at the end a new subparagraph (D). **Effective** for residences purchased after 12-31-2008.

(g) ELECTION TO TREAT PURCHASE IN PRIOR YEAR.—In the case of a purchase of a principal residence after December 31, 2008, and before *December 1, 2009*, a taxpayer may elect to treat such purchase as made on December 31, 2008, for purposes of this section (other than *subsections (c) and (f)(4)(D)*).

[CCH Explanation at ¶ 310. Committee Reports at ¶ 10,060.]

Amendments

• **2009, American Recovery and Reinvestment Tax Act of 2009 (P.L. 111-5)**

P.L. 111-5, § 1006(a)(2):

Amended Code Sec. 36(g) by striking "July 1, 2009" and inserting "December 1, 2009". **Effective** for residences purchased after 12-31-2008.

P.L. 111-5, § 1006(c)(2):

Amended Code Sec. 36(g) by striking "subsection (c)" and inserting "subsections (c) and (f)(4)(D)". **Effective** for residences purchased after 12-31-2008.

(h) APPLICATION OF SECTION.—This section shall only apply to a principal residence purchased by the taxpayer on or after April 9, 2008, and before *December 1, 2009*.

[CCH Explanation at ¶ 310. Committee Reports at ¶ 10,060.]

Amendments

• **2009, American Recovery and Reinvestment Tax Act of 2009 (P.L. 111-5)**

P.L. 111-5, § 1006(a)(1):

Amended Code Sec. 36(h) by striking "July 1, 2009" and inserting "December 1, 2009". **Effective** for residences purchased after 12-31-2008.

[¶ 5075] **CODE SEC. 36A. MAKING WORK PAY CREDIT.**

(a) ALLOWANCE OF CREDIT.—*In the case of an eligible individual, there shall be allowed as a credit against the tax imposed by this subtitle for the taxable year an amount equal to the lesser of—*

(1) 6.2 percent of earned income of the taxpayer, or

(2) $400 ($800 in the case of a joint return).

(b) LIMITATION BASED ON MODIFIED ADJUSTED GROSS INCOME.—

(1) IN GENERAL.—The amount allowable as a credit under subsection (a) (determined without regard to this paragraph and subsection (c)) for the taxable year shall be reduced (but not below zero) by 2 percent of so much of the taxpayer's modified adjusted gross income as exceeds $75,000 ($150,000 in the case of a joint return).

(2) MODIFIED ADJUSTED GROSS INCOME.—For purposes of subparagraph (A), the term "modified adjusted gross income" means the adjusted gross income of the taxpayer for the taxable year increased by any amount excluded from gross income under section 911, 931, or 933.

(c) REDUCTION FOR CERTAIN OTHER PAYMENTS.—*The credit allowed under subsection (a) for any taxable year shall be reduced by the amount of any payments received by the taxpayer during such taxable year under section 2201, and any credit allowed to the taxpayer under section 2202, of the American Recovery and Reinvestment Tax Act of 2009.*

(d) DEFINITIONS AND SPECIAL RULES.—*For purposes of this section—*

(1) ELIGIBLE INDIVIDUAL.—

(A) IN GENERAL.—The term "eligible individual" means any individual other than—

(i) any nonresident alien individual,

(ii) any individual with respect to whom a deduction under section 151 is allowable to another taxpayer for a taxable year beginning in the calendar year in which the individual's taxable year begins, and

(iii) an estate or trust.

(B) IDENTIFICATION NUMBER REQUIREMENT.—Such term shall not include any individual who does not include on the return of tax for the taxable year—

(i) such individual's social security account number, and

(ii) in the case of a joint return, the social security account number of one of the taxpayers on such return.

For purposes of the preceding sentence, the social security account number shall not include a TIN issued by the Internal Revenue Service.

(2) EARNED INCOME.—The term "earned income" has the meaning given such term by section 32(c)(2), except that such term shall not include net earnings from self-employment which are not taken into account in computing taxable income. For purposes of the preceding sentence, any amount excluded from gross income by reason of section 112 shall be treated as earned income which is taken into account in computing taxable income for the taxable year.

(e) TERMINATION.—This section shall not apply to taxable years beginning after December 31, 2010.

[CCH Explanation at ¶305. Committee Reports at ¶10,010.]
Amendments
• 2009, American Recovery and Reinvestment Tax Act of 2009 (P.L. 111-5)

P.L. 111-5, §1001(a):

Amended subpart C of part IV of subchapter A of chapter 1 by inserting after Code Sec. 36 a new Code Sec. 36A. **Effective** for tax years beginning after 12-31-2008.

[¶5080] CODE SEC. 38. GENERAL BUSINESS CREDIT.

* * *

(b) CURRENT YEAR BUSINESS CREDIT.—For purposes of this subpart, the amount of the current year business credit is the sum of the following credits determined for the taxable year:

* * *

⇒ *Caution: Code Sec. 38(b)(35), as amended by P.L. 111-5, below, applies to vehicles acquired after December 31, 2009.*

(35) the portion of the new qualified plug-in electric drive motor vehicle credit to which section 30D(c)(1) applies.

* * *

[CCH Explanation at ¶345. Committee Reports at ¶10,200.]
Amendments
• 2009, American Recovery and Reinvestment Tax Act of 2009 (P.L. 111-5)

P.L. 111-5, §1141(b)(2):

Amended Code Sec. 38(b)(35) by striking "30D(d)(1)" and inserting "30D(c)(1)". **Effective** for vehicles acquired after 12-31-2009.

[¶5085] CODE SEC. 42. LOW-INCOME HOUSING CREDIT.

* * *

(i) DEFINITIONS AND SPECIAL RULES.—For purposes of this section—

* * *

(9) COORDINATION WITH LOW-INCOME HOUSING GRANTS.—

(A) REDUCTION IN STATE HOUSING CREDIT CEILING FOR LOW-INCOME HOUSING GRANTS RECEIVED IN 2009.—For purposes of this section, the amounts described in clauses (i) through (iv) of subsection (h)(3)(C) with respect to any State for 2009 shall each be reduced by so much of such amount as is taken into account in determining the amount of any grant to such State under section 1602 of the American Recovery and Reinvestment Tax Act of 2009.

(B) SPECIAL RULE FOR BASIS.—Basis of a qualified low-income building shall not be reduced by the amount of any grant described in subparagraph (A).

* * *

[CCH Explanation at ¶535. Committee Reports at ¶10,380.]
Amendments
• **2009, American Recovery and Reinvestment Tax Act of 2009 (P.L. 111-5)**

P.L. 111-5, §1404:

Amended Code Sec. 42(i) by adding at the end a new paragraph (9). Effective 2-17-2009.

[¶5090] CODE SEC. 45. ELECTRICITY PRODUCED FROM CERTAIN RENEWABLE RESOURCES, etc. [sic]

* * *

(d) QUALIFIED FACILITIES.—For purposes of this section:

(1) WIND FACILITY.—In the case of a facility using wind to produce electricity, the term "qualified facility" means any facility owned by the taxpayer which is originally placed in service after December 31, 1993, and before January 1, *2013*. Such term shall not include any facility with respect to which any qualified small wind energy property expenditure (as defined in subsection (d)(4) of section 25D) is taken into account in determining the credit under such section.

(2) CLOSED-LOOP BIOMASS FACILITY.—

(A) IN GENERAL.—In the case of a facility using closed-loop biomass to produce electricity, the term "qualified facility" means any facility—

(i) owned by the taxpayer which is originally placed in service after December 31, 1992, and before January 1, *2014*, or

(ii) owned by the taxpayer which before January 1, *2014*, is originally placed in service and modified to use closed-loop biomass to co-fire with coal, with other biomass, or with both, but only if the modification is approved under the Biomass Power for Rural Development Programs or is part of a pilot project of the Commodity Credit Corporation as described in 65 Fed. Reg. 63052.

* * *

(3) OPEN-LOOP BIOMASS FACILITIES.—

(A) IN GENERAL.—In the case of a facility using open-loop biomass to produce electricity, the term "qualified facility" means any facility owned by the taxpayer which—

(i) in the case of a facility using agricultural livestock waste nutrients—

(I) is originally placed in service after the date of the enactment of this subclause and before January 1, *2014*, and

(II) the nameplate capacity rating of which is not less than 150 kilowatts, and

(ii) in the case of any other facility, is originally placed in service before January 1, *2014*.

* * *

(4) GEOTHERMAL OR SOLAR ENERGY FACILITY.—In the case of a facility using geothermal or solar energy to produce electricity, the term "qualified facility" means any facility owned by the taxpayer which is originally placed in service after the date of the enactment of this paragraph and before January 1, *2014* (January 1, 2006, in the case of a facility using solar energy). Such term shall not include any property described in section 48(a)(3) the basis of which is taken into account by the taxpayer for purposes of determining the energy credit under section 48.

(5) SMALL IRRIGATION POWER FACILITY.—In the case of a facility using small irrigation power to produce electricity, the term "qualified facility" means any facility owned by the taxpayer which is originally placed in service after the date of the enactment of this paragraph *and before October 3, 2008.*

(6) LANDFILL GAS FACILITIES.—In the case of a facility producing electricity from gas derived from the biodegradation of municipal solid waste, the term "qualified facility" means any facility owned by the taxpayer which is originally placed in service after the date of the enactment of this paragraph and before January 1, *2014.*

(7) TRASH FACILITIES.—In the case of a facility (**other than** a facility described in paragraph (6)) which uses municipal solid waste to produce electricity, the term "qualified facility" means any facility owned by the taxpayer which is originally placed in service after the date of the enactment of this paragraph and before January 1, *2014.* Such term shall include a new unit placed in service in connection with a facility placed in service on or before the date of the enactment of this paragraph, but only to the extent of the increased amount of electricity produced at the facility by reason of such new unit.

* * *

(9) QUALIFIED HYDROPOWER FACILITY.—In the case of a facility producing qualified hydroelectric production described in subsection (c)(8), the term "qualified facility" means—

(A) in the case of any facility producing incremental hydropower production, such facility but only to the extent of its incremental hydropower production attributable to efficiency improvements or additions to capacity described in subsection (c)(8)(B) placed in service after the date of the enactment of this paragraph and before January 1, *2014,* and

(B) any other facility placed in service after the date of the enactment of this paragraph and before January 1, *2014.*

* * *

(11) MARINE AND HYDROKINETIC RENEWABLE ENERGY FACILITIES.—In the case of a facility producing electricity from marine and hydrokinetic renewable energy, the term "qualified facility" means any facility owned by the taxpayer—

(A) which has a nameplate capacity rating of at least 150 kilowatts, and

(B) which is originally placed in service on or after the date of the enactment of this paragraph and before January 1, *2014.*

* * *

[CCH Explanation at ¶ 520. Committee Reports at ¶ 10,100.]
Amendments

- **2009, American Recovery and Reinvestment Tax Act of 2009 (P.L. 111-5)**

P.L. 111-5, § 1101(a)(1)-(3):

Amended Code Sec. 45(d) by striking "2010" in paragraph (1) and inserting "2013", by striking "2011" each place it appears in paragraphs (2), (3), (4), (6), (7) and (9) and inserting "2014", and by striking "2012" in paragraph (11)(B) and inserting "2014". **Effective** for property placed in service after 2-17-2009.

P.L. 111-5, § 1101(b):

Amended Code Sec. 45(d)(5) by striking "and before" and all that follows and inserting "and before October 3, 2008.". **Effective** as if included in section 102 of the Energy Improvement and Extension Act of 2008 (P.L. 110-343) [**effective** for electricity produced and sold after 10-3-2008, in tax years ending after such date.—CCH]. Prior to being stricken, "and before" and all that followed read as follows: and before January 1, 2011.

Code Sec. 45(d)(11)(B) ¶ 5090

[¶5095] CODE SEC. 45D. NEW MARKETS TAX CREDIT.

* * *

(f) NATIONAL LIMITATION ON AMOUNT OF INVESTMENTS DESIGNATED.—

(1) IN GENERAL.—There is a new markets tax credit limitation for each calendar year. Such limitation is—

(A) $1,000,000,000 for 2001,

(B) $1,500,000,000 for 2002 and 2003,

(C) $2,000,000,000 for 2004 and 2005,

(D) $3,500,000,000 for 2006 *and 2007,*

(E) *$5,000,000,000 for 2008, and*

(F) *$5,000,000,000 for 2009.*

* * *

[CCH Explanation at ¶530. Committee Reports at ¶10,370.]

Amendments

• 2009, American Recovery and Reinvestment Tax Act of 2009 (P.L. 111-5)

P.L. 111-5, §1403(a)(1)-(3):

Amended Code Sec. 45D(f)(1) by striking "and" at the end of subparagraph (C), by striking ", 2007, 2008, and 2009." in subparagraph (D), and inserting "and 2007,", and by adding at the end new subparagraphs (E)-(F). **Effective** 2-17-2009.

[¶5100] CODE SEC. 45Q. CREDIT FOR CARBON DIOXIDE SEQUESTRATION.

(a) GENERAL RULE.—For purposes of section 38, the carbon dioxide sequestration credit for any taxable year is an amount equal to the sum of—

(1) $20 per metric ton of qualified carbon dioxide which is—

(A) captured by the taxpayer at a qualified facility, and

(B) disposed of by the taxpayer in secure geological storage *and not used by the taxpayer as described in paragraph (2)(B)*, and

(2) $10 per metric ton of qualified carbon dioxide which is—

(A) captured by the taxpayer at a qualified facility,

(B) used by the taxpayer as a tertiary injectant in a qualified enhanced oil or natural gas recovery project, *and*

(C) *disposed of by the taxpayer in secure geological storage.*

* * *

[CCH Explanation at ¶545. Committee Reports at ¶10,190.]

Amendments

• 2009, American Recovery and Reinvestment Tax Act of 2009 (P.L. 111-5)

P.L. 111-5, §1131(a):

Amended Code Sec. 45Q(a)(2) by striking "and" at the end of subparagraph (A), by striking the period at the end of subparagraph (B) and inserting ", and", and by adding at the end a new subparagraph (C). **Effective** for carbon dioxide captured after 2-17-2009.

P.L. 111-5, §1131(b)(2):

Amended Code Sec. 45Q(a)(1)(B) by inserting "and not used by the taxpayer as described in paragraph (2)(B)" after "storage". **Effective** for carbon dioxide captured after 2-17-2009.

(d) SPECIAL RULES AND OTHER DEFINITIONS.—For purposes of this section—

* * *

(2) SECURE GEOLOGICAL STORAGE.—The Secretary, in consultation with the Administrator of the Environmental Protection Agency[,] *the Secretary of Energy, and the Secretary of the Interior,* [sic], shall establish regulations for determining adequate security measures for the geological storage of carbon dioxide under *paragraph (1)(B) or (2)(C) of subsection (a)* such that the carbon dioxide does not escape into the atmosphere. Such term shall include storage at deep saline

formations, *oil and gas reservoirs, and unminable coal seams* under such conditions as the Secretary may determine under such regulations.

* * *

[CCH Explanation at ¶ 545. Committee Reports at ¶ 10,190.]

Amendments

• **2009, American Recovery and Reinvestment Tax Act of 2009 (P.L. 111-5)**

P.L. 111-5, § 1131(b)(1)(A)-(C):

Amended Code Sec. 45Q(d)(2) by striking "subsection (a)(1)(B)" and inserting "paragraph (1)(B) or (2)(C) of subsection (a)", by striking "and unminable coal seems" and inserting ", oil and gas reservoirs, and unminable coal seams", and by inserting "the Secretary of Energy, and the Secretary of the Interior," after "Environmental Protection Agency". **Effective** for carbon dioxide captured after 2-17-2009.

(e) APPLICATION OF SECTION.—The credit under this section shall apply with respect to qualified carbon dioxide before the end of the calendar year in which the Secretary, in consultation with the Administrator of the Environmental Protection Agency, certifies that 75,000,000 metric tons of qualified carbon dioxide have been *taken into account in accordance with subsection (a)*.

[CCH Explanation at ¶ 545. Committee Reports at ¶ 10,190.]

Amendments

• **2009, American Recovery and Reinvestment Tax Act of 2009 (P.L. 111-5)**

P.L. 111-5, § 1131(b)(3):

Amended Code Sec. 45Q(e) by striking "captured and disposed of or used as a tertiary injectant" and inserting "taken into account in accordance with subsection (a)". **Effective** for carbon dioxide captured after 2-17-2009.

[¶ 5105] CODE SEC. 46. AMOUNT OF CREDIT.

For purposes of section 38, the amount of the investment credit determined under this section for any taxable year shall be the sum of—

(1) the rehabilitation credit,

(2) the energy credit[,]

(3) the qualifying advanced coal project credit,

(4) the qualifying gasification project credit[, and]

(5) *the qualifying advanced energy project credit.*

[CCH Explanation at ¶ 525. Committee Reports at ¶ 10,340.]

Amendments

• **2009, American Recovery and Reinvestment Tax Act of 2009 (P.L. 111-5)**

P.L. 111-5, § 1302(a):

Amended Code Sec. 46 by striking "and" at the end of paragraph (3), by striking the period at the end of paragraph (4), and by adding at the end a new paragraph (5). **Effective** for periods after 2-17-2009, under rules similar to the rules of Code Sec. 48(m) (as in effect on the day before the date of the enactment of the Revenue Reconciliation Act of 1990 [10-30-90]).

[¶ 5110] CODE SEC. 48. ENERGY CREDIT.

(a) ENERGY CREDIT.—

* * *

(4) SPECIAL RULE FOR PROPERTY FINANCED BY SUBSIDIZED ENERGY FINANCING OR INDUSTRIAL DEVELOPMENT BONDS.—

* * *

(D) TERMINATION.—*This paragraph shall not apply to periods after December 31, 2008, under rules similar to the rules of section 48(m) (as in effect on the day before the date of the enactment of the Revenue Reconciliation Act of 1990).*

(5) ELECTION TO TREAT QUALIFIED FACILITIES AS ENERGY PROPERTY.—

(A) IN GENERAL.—In the case of any qualified property which is part of a qualified investment credit facility—

(i) such property shall be treated as energy property for purposes of this section, and

(ii) the energy percentage with respect to such property shall be 30 percent.

(B) DENIAL OF PRODUCTION CREDIT.—No credit shall be allowed under section 45 for any taxable year with respect to any qualified investment credit facility.

(C) QUALIFIED INVESTMENT CREDIT FACILITY.—For purposes of this paragraph, the term "qualified investment credit facility" means any of the following facilities if no credit has been allowed under section 45 with respect to such facility and the taxpayer makes an irrevocable election to have this paragraph apply to such facility:

(i) WIND FACILITIES.—Any qualified facility (within the meaning of section 45) described in paragraph (1) of section 45(d) if such facility is placed in service in 2009, 2010, 2011, or 2012.

(ii) OTHER FACILITIES.—Any qualified facility (within the meaning of section 45) described in paragraph (2), (3), (4), (6), (7), (9), or (11) of section 45(d) if such facility is placed in service in 2009, 2010, 2011, 2012, or 2013.

(D) QUALIFIED PROPERTY.—For purposes of this paragraph, the term "qualified property" means property—

(i) which is—

(I) tangible personal property, or

(II) other tangible property (not including a building or its structural components), but only if such property is used as an integral part of the qualified investment credit facility, and

(ii) with respect to which depreciation (or amortization in lieu of depreciation) is allowable.

* * *

[CCH Explanation at ¶510. Committee Reports at ¶10,110 and ¶10,120.]

Amendments

• **2009, American Recovery and Reinvestment Tax Act of 2009 (P.L. 111-5)**

P.L. 111-5, §1102(a):

Amended Code Sec. 48(a) by adding at the end a new paragraph (5). **Effective** for facilities placed in service after 12-31-2008.

P.L. 111-5, §1103(b)(1):

Amended Code Sec. 48(a)(4) by adding at the end a new subparagraph (D). **Effective** for periods after 12-31-2008, under rules similar to the rules of Code Sec. 48(m) (as in effect on the day before the date of the enactment of the Revenue Reconciliation Act of 1990 [10-30-90]).

(c) DEFINITIONS.—For purposes of this section—

* * *

(4) QUALIFIED SMALL WIND ENERGY PROPERTY.—

* * *

(B) QUALIFYING SMALL WIND TURBINE.—The term "qualifying small wind turbine" means a wind turbine which has a nameplate capacity of not more than 100 kilowatts.

(C) TERMINATION.—The term "qualified small wind energy property" shall not include any property for any period after December 31, 2016.

[CCH Explanation at ¶510. Committee Reports at ¶10,120.]

Amendments

• **2009, American Recovery and Reinvestment Tax Act of 2009 (P.L. 111-5)**

P.L. 111-5, §1103(a):

Amended Code Sec. 48(c)(4) by striking subparagraph (B) and by redesignating subparagraphs (C) and (D) as subparagraphs (B) and (C). **Effective** for periods after 12-31-2008,

under rules similar to the rules of Code Sec. 48(m) (as in effect on the day before the date of the enactment of the Revenue Reconciliation Act of 1990 [10-30-90]). Prior to being stricken, Code Sec. 48(c)(4)(B) read as follows:

(B) LIMITATION.—In the case of qualified small wind energy property placed in service during the taxable year, the credit otherwise determined under subsection (a)(1) for such year with respect to all such property of the taxpayer shall not exceed $4,000.

(d) COORDINATION WITH DEPARTMENT OF TREASURY GRANTS.—In the case of any property with respect to which the Secretary makes a grant under section 1603 of the American Recovery and Reinvestment Tax Act of 2009—

(1) DENIAL OF PRODUCTION AND INVESTMENT CREDITS.—No credit shall be determined under this section or section 45 with respect to such property for the taxable year in which such grant is made or any subsequent taxable year.

(2) RECAPTURE OF CREDITS FOR PROGRESS EXPENDITURES MADE BEFORE GRANT.—If a credit was determined under this section with respect to such property for any taxable year ending before such grant is made—

(A) the tax imposed under subtitle A on the taxpayer for the taxable year in which such grant is made shall be increased by so much of such credit as was allowed under section 38,

(B) the general business carryforwards under section 39 shall be adjusted so as to recapture the portion of such credit which was not so allowed, and

(C) the amount of such grant shall be determined without regard to any reduction in the basis of such property by reason of such credit.

(3) TREATMENT OF GRANTS.—Any such grant shall—

(A) not be includible in the gross income of the taxpayer, but

(B) shall be taken into account in determining the basis of the property to which such grant relates, except that the basis of such property shall be reduced under section 50(c) in the same manner as a credit allowed under subsection (a).

[CCH Explanation at ¶515. Committee Reports at ¶10,130.]

Amendments

• 2009, American Recovery and Reinvestment Tax Act of 2009 (P.L. 111-5)

P.L. 111-5, §1104:

Amended Code Sec. 48 by adding at the end a new subsection (d). **Effective** 2-17-2009.

[¶5115] CODE SEC. 48A. QUALIFYING ADVANCED COAL PROJECT CREDIT.

* * *

(b) QUALIFIED INVESTMENT.—

* * *

(2) SPECIAL RULE FOR CERTAIN SUBSIDIZED PROPERTY.—Rules similar to section 48(a)(4) *(without regard to subparagraph (D) thereof)* shall apply for purposes of this section.

* * *

[CCH Explanation at ¶510. Committee Reports at ¶10,120.]

Amendments

• 2009, American Recovery and Reinvestment Tax Act of 2009 (P.L. 111-5)

P.L. 111-5, §1103(b)(2)(C):

Amended Code Sec. 48A(b)(2) by inserting "(without regard to subparagraph (D) thereof)" after "section 48(a)(4)".

Effective for periods after 12-31-2008, under rules similar to the rules of Code Sec. 48(m) (as in effect on the day before the date of the enactment of the Revenue Reconciliation Act of 1990 [10-30-90]).

[¶5120] CODE SEC. 48B. QUALIFYING GASIFICATION PROJECT CREDIT.

* * *

(b) QUALIFIED INVESTMENT.—

* * *

(2) SPECIAL RULE FOR CERTAIN SUBSIDIZED PROPERTY.—Rules similar to section 48(a)(4) *(without regard to subparagraph (D) thereof)* shall apply for purposes of this section.

* * *

[CCH Explanation at ¶ 510. Committee Reports at ¶ 10,120.]

Amendments

• 2009, American Recovery and Reinvestment Tax Act of 2009 (P.L. 111-5)

P.L. 111-5, § 1103(b)(2)(D):

Amended Code Sec. 48B(b)(2) by inserting "(without regard to subparagraph (D) thereof)" after "section 48(a)(4)".

Effective for periods after 12-31-2008, under rules similar to the rules of Code Sec. 48(m) (as in effect on the day before the date of the enactment of the Revenue Reconciliation Act of 1990 [10-30-90]).

[¶ 5125] CODE SEC. 48C. QUALIFYING ADVANCED ENERGY PROJECT CREDIT.

(a) IN GENERAL.—For purposes of section 46, the qualifying advanced energy project credit for any taxable year is an amount equal to 30 percent of the qualified investment for such taxable year with respect to any qualifying advanced energy project of the taxpayer.

(b) QUALIFIED INVESTMENT.—

(1) IN GENERAL.—For purposes of subsection (a), the qualified investment for any taxable year is the basis of eligible property placed in service by the taxpayer during such taxable year which is part of a qualifying advanced energy project.

(2) CERTAIN QUALIFIED PROGRESS EXPENDITURES RULES MADE APPLICABLE.—Rules similar to the rules of subsections (c)(4) and (d) of section 46 (as in effect on the day before the enactment of the Revenue Reconciliation Act of 1990) shall apply for purposes of this section.

(3) LIMITATION.—The amount which is treated for all taxable years with respect to any qualifying advanced energy project shall not exceed the amount designated by the Secretary as eligible for the credit under this section.

(c) DEFINITIONS.—

(1) QUALIFYING ADVANCED ENERGY PROJECT.—

(A) IN GENERAL.—The term "qualifying advanced energy project" means a project—

(i) which re-equips, expands, or establishes a manufacturing facility for the production of—

(I) property designed to be used to produce energy from the sun, wind, geothermal deposits (within the meaning of section 613(e)(2)), or other renewable resources,

(II) fuel cells, microturbines, or an energy storage system for use with electric or hybrid-electric motor vehicles,

(III) electric grids to support the transmission of intermittent sources of renewable energy, including storage of such energy,

(IV) property designed to capture and sequester carbon dioxide emissions,

(V) property designed to refine or blend renewable fuels or to produce energy conservation technologies (including energy-conserving lighting technologies and smart grid technologies),

(VI) new qualified plug-in electric drive motor vehicles (as defined by section 30D), qualified plug-in electric vehicles (as defined by section 30(d)), or components which are designed specifically for use with such vehicles, including electric motors, generators, and power control units, or

(VII) other advanced energy property designed to reduce greenhouse gas emissions as may be determined by the Secretary, and

(ii) any portion of the qualified investment of which is certified by the Secretary under subsection (d) as eligible for a credit under this section.

(B) EXCEPTION.—Such term shall not include any portion of a project for the production of any property which is used in the refining or blending of any transportation fuel (other than renewable fuels).

(2) ELIGIBLE PROPERTY.—The term "eligible property" means any property—

(A) which is necessary for the production of property described in paragraph (1)(A)(i),

(B) which is—

(i) tangible personal property, or

(ii) other tangible property (not including a building or its structural components), but only if such property is used as an integral part of the qualified investment credit facility, and

(C) with respect to which depreciation (or amortization in lieu of depreciation) is allowable.

(d) QUALIFYING ADVANCED ENERGY PROJECT PROGRAM.—

(1) ESTABLISHMENT.—

(A) IN GENERAL.—Not later than 180 days after the date of enactment of this section, the Secretary, in consultation with the Secretary of Energy, shall establish a qualifying advanced energy project program to consider and award certifications for qualified investments eligible for credits under this section to qualifying advanced energy project sponsors.

(B) LIMITATION.—The total amount of credits that may be allocated under the program shall not exceed $2,300,000,000.

(2) CERTIFICATION.—

(A) APPLICATION PERIOD.—Each applicant for certification under this paragraph shall submit an application containing such information as the Secretary may require during the 2-year period beginning on the date the Secretary establishes the program under paragraph (1).

(B) TIME TO MEET CRITERIA FOR CERTIFICATION.—Each applicant for certification shall have 1 year from the date of acceptance by the Secretary of the application during which to provide to the Secretary evidence that the requirements of the certification have been met.

(C) PERIOD OF ISSUANCE.—An applicant which receives a certification shall have 3 years from the date of issuance of the certification in order to place the project in service and if such project is not placed in service by that time period, then the certification shall no longer be valid.

(3) SELECTION CRITERIA.—In determining which qualifying advanced energy projects to certify under this section, the Secretary—

(A) shall take into consideration only those projects where there is a reasonable expectation of commercial viability, and

(B) shall take into consideration which projects—

(i) will provide the greatest domestic job creation (both direct and indirect) during the credit period,

(ii) will provide the greatest net impact in avoiding or reducing air pollutants or anthropogenic emissions of greenhouse gases,

(iii) have the greatest potential for technological innovation and commercial deployment,

(iv) have the lowest levelized cost of generated or stored energy, or of measured reduction in energy consumption or greenhouse gas emission (based on costs of the full supply chain), and

(v) have the shortest project time from certification to completion.

(4) REVIEW AND REDISTRIBUTION.—

(A) REVIEW.—Not later than 4 years after the date of enactment of this section, the Secretary shall review the credits allocated under this section as of such date.

(B) REDISTRIBUTION.—The Secretary may reallocate credits awarded under this section if the Secretary determines that—

(i) there is an insufficient quantity of qualifying applications for certification pending at the time of the review, or

(ii) any certification made pursuant to paragraph (2) has been revoked pursuant to paragraph (2)(B) because the project subject to the certification has been delayed as a result of third party opposition or litigation to the proposed project.

(C) REALLOCATION.—If the Secretary determines that credits under this section are available for reallocation pursuant to the requirements set forth in paragraph (2), the Secretary is authorized to conduct an additional program for applications for certification.

(5) DISCLOSURE OF ALLOCATIONS.—The Secretary shall, upon making a certification under this subsection, publicly disclose the identity of the applicant and the amount of the credit with respect to such applicant.

(e) DENIAL OF DOUBLE BENEFIT.—A credit shall not be allowed under this section for any qualified investment for which a credit is allowed under section 48, 48A, or 48B.

[CCH Explanation at ¶ 525. Committee Reports at ¶ 10,340.]

Amendments

• **2009, American Recovery and Reinvestment Tax Act of 2009 (P.L. 111-5)**

P.L. 111-5, § 1302(b):

Amended subpart E of part IV of subchapter A of chapter 1 by inserting after Code Sec. 48B a new Code Sec. 48C.

Effective for periods after 2-17-2009, under rules similar to the rules of Code Sec. 48(m) (as in effect on the day before the date of the enactment of the Revenue Reconciliation Act of 1990).

[¶ 5130] CODE SEC. 49. AT-RISK RULES.

(a) GENERAL RULE.—

(1) CERTAIN NONRECOURSE FINANCING EXCLUDED FROM CREDIT BASE.—

* * *

(C) CREDIT BASE DEFINED.—For purposes of this paragraph, the term "credit base" means—

* * *

(iii) the basis of any property which is part of a qualifying advanced coal project under section 48A,

(iv) the basis of any property which is part of a qualifying gasification project under section 48B, *and*

(v) the basis of any property which is part of a qualifying advanced energy project under section 48C.

* * *

[CCH Explanation at ¶ 525. Committee Reports at ¶ 10,340.]

Amendments

• **2009, American Recovery and Reinvestment Tax Act of 2009 (P.L. 111-5)**

P.L. 111-5, § 1302(c)(1):

Amended Code Sec. 49(a)(1)(C) by striking "and" at the end of clause (iii), by striking the period at the end of clause (iv) and inserting ", and", and by adding after clause (iv) a new clause (v). **Effective** for periods after 2-17-2009, under rules similar to the rules of Code Sec. 48(m) (as in effect on the day before the date of the enactment of the Revenue Reconciliation Act of 1990 [10-30-90]).

[¶ 5135] CODE SEC. 51. AMOUNT OF CREDIT.

* * *

(d) MEMBERS OF TARGETED GROUPS.—For purposes of this subpart—

* * *

(14) CREDIT ALLOWED FOR UNEMPLOYED VETERANS AND DISCONNECTED YOUTH HIRED IN 2009 OR 2010.—

(A) IN GENERAL.—Any unemployed veteran or disconnected youth who begins work for the employer during 2009 or 2010 shall be treated as a member of a targeted group for purposes of this subpart.

(B) DEFINITIONS.—For purposes of this paragraph—

(i) UNEMPLOYED VETERAN.—The term "unemployed veteran" means any veteran (as defined in paragraph (3)(B), determined without regard to clause (ii) thereof) who is certified by the designated local agency as—

(I) having been discharged or released from active duty in the Armed Forces at any time during the 5-year period ending on the hiring date, and

(II) being in receipt of unemployment compensation under State or Federal law for not less than 4 weeks during the 1-year period ending on the hiring date.

(ii) DISCONNECTED YOUTH.—The term "disconnected youth" means any individual who is certified by the designated local agency—

(I) as having attained age 16 but not age 25 on the hiring date,

(II) as not regularly attending any secondary, technical, or post-secondary school during the 6-month period preceding the hiring date,

(III) as not regularly employed during such 6-month period, and

(IV) as not readily employable by reason of lacking a sufficient number of basic skills.

* * *

[CCH Explanation at ¶540. Committee Reports at ¶10,260.]

Amendments
• **2009, American Recovery and Reinvestment Tax Act of 2009 (P.L. 111-5)**

P.L. 111-5, §1221(a):

Amended Code Sec. 51(d) by adding at the end a new paragraph (14). **Effective** for individuals who begin work for the employer after 12-31-2008.

[¶5140] CODE SEC. 53. CREDIT FOR PRIOR YEAR MINIMUM TAX LIABILITY.

* * *

(d) DEFINITIONS.—For purposes of this section—

(1) NET MINIMUM TAX.—

* * *

(B) CREDIT NOT ALLOWED FOR EXCLUSION PREFERENCES.—

* * *

(iii) CREDIT ALLOWABLE FOR EXCLUSION PREFERENCES OF CORPORATIONS.—In the case of a corporation—

(I) the preceding provisions of this subparagraph shall not apply, and

(II) the adjusted net minimum tax for any taxable year is the amount of the net minimum tax for such year.

* * *

[CCH Explanation at ¶ 350. Committee Reports at ¶ 10,200.]

Amendments

• 2009, American Recovery and Reinvestment Tax Act of 2009 (P.L. 111-5)

P.L. 111-5, § 1142(b)(4)(A):

Amended Code Sec. 53(d)(1)(B) by striking clause (iii) and redesignating clause (iv) as clause (iii). **Effective** for vehicles acquired after 2-17-2009. For a transitional rule, see Act Sec. 1142(d) in the amendment notes for Code Sec. 30. Prior to being stricken, Code Sec. 53(d)(1)(B)(iii) read as follows:

(iii) SPECIAL RULE.—The adjusted net minimum tax for the taxable year shall be increased by the amount of the credit not allowed under section 30 solely by reason of the application of section 30(b)(3)(B).

P.L. 111-5, § 1142(b)(4)(B):

Amended Code Sec. 53(d)(1)(B)(iii)(II), as redesignated by Act Sec. 1142(b)(4)(A), by striking "increased in the manner provided in clause (iii)" after "such year". **Effective** for vehicles acquired after 2-17-2009. For a transitional rule, see Act Sec. 1142(d) in the amendment notes for Code Sec. 30.

[¶ 5145] CODE SEC. 54. CREDIT TO HOLDERS OF CLEAN RENEWABLE ENERGY BONDS.

* * *

(c) LIMITATION BASED ON AMOUNT OF TAX.—The credit allowed under subsection (a) for any taxable year shall not exceed the excess of—

(1) the sum of the regular tax liability (as defined in section 26(b)) plus the tax imposed by section 55, over

(2) the sum of the credits allowable under this part (other than subparts C, I, *and J*, section 1400N(l), and this section).

* * *

[CCH Explanation at ¶ 605. Committee Reports at ¶ 10,450.]

Amendments

• 2009, American Recovery and Reinvestment Tax Act of 2009 (P.L. 111-5)

P.L. 111-5, § 1531(c)(3):

Amended Code Sec. 54(c)(2) by striking "and I" and inserting ", I, and J". **Effective** for obligations issued after 2-17-2009.

(l) OTHER DEFINITIONS AND SPECIAL RULES.—For purposes of this section—

* * *

(4) RATABLE PRINCIPAL AMORTIZATION REQUIRED.—A bond shall not be treated as a clean renewable energy bond unless it is part of an issue which provides for an equal amount of principal to be paid by the qualified issuer during each calendar year that the issue is outstanding.

(5) REPORTING.—Issuers of clean renewable energy bonds shall submit reports similar to the reports required under section 149(e).

* * *

[CCH Explanation at ¶ 615. Committee Reports at ¶ 10,460.]

Amendments

• 2009, American Recovery and Reinvestment Tax Act of 2009 (P.L. 111-5)

P.L. 111-5, § 1541(b)(1):

Amended Code Sec. 54(l) by striking paragraph (4) and by redesignating paragraphs (5) and (6) as paragraphs (4) and (5), respectively. **Effective** for tax years ending after 2-17-2009. Prior to being stricken, Code Sec. 54(l)(4) read as follows:

(4) BONDS HELD BY REGULATED INVESTMENT COMPANIES.—If any clean renewable energy bond is held by a regulated investment company, the credit determined under subsection (a) shall be allowed to shareholders of such company under procedures prescribed by the Secretary.

[¶ 5150] CODE SEC. 54A. CREDIT TO HOLDERS OF QUALIFIED TAX CREDIT BONDS.

* * *

(c) LIMITATION BASED ON AMOUNT OF TAX.—

(1) IN GENERAL.—The credit allowed under subsection (a) for any taxable year shall not exceed the excess of—

(A) the sum of the regular tax liability (as defined in section 26(b)) plus the tax imposed by section 55, over

(B) the sum of the credits allowable under this part (other than *subparts C and J* and this subpart).

* * *

[CCH Explanation at ¶ 605. Committee Reports at ¶ 10,450.]
Amendments
• **2009, American Recovery and Reinvestment Tax Act of 2009 (P.L. 111-5)**

P.L. 111-5, § 1531(c)(2):

Amended Code Sec. 54A(c)(1)(B) by striking "subpart C" and inserting "subparts C and J". **Effective** for obligations issued after 2-17-2009.

(d) QUALIFIED TAX CREDIT BOND.—For purposes of this section—

(1) QUALIFIED TAX CREDIT BOND.—The term "qualified tax credit bond" means—

(A) a qualified forestry conservation bond,

(B) a new clean renewable energy bond,

(C) a qualified energy conservation bond,

(D) a qualified zone academy bond, *or*

(E) *a qualified school construction bond,*

which is part of an issue that meets requirements of paragraphs (2), (3), (4), (5), and (6).

(2) SPECIAL RULES RELATING TO EXPENDITURES.—

* * *

(C) QUALIFIED PURPOSE.—For purposes of this paragraph, the term "qualified purpose" means—

* * *

(iii) in the case of a qualified energy conservation bond, a purpose specified in section 54D(a)(1),

(iv) in the case of a qualified zone academy bond, a purpose specified in section 54E(a)(1), *and*

(v) *in the case of a qualified school construction bond, a purpose specified in section 54F(a)(1).*

* * *

[CCH Explanation at ¶ 630. Committee Reports at ¶ 10,430.]
Amendments
• **2009, American Recovery and Reinvestment Tax Act of 2009 (P.L. 111-5)**

P.L. 111-5, § 1521(b)(1):

Amended Code Sec. 54A(d)(1) by striking "or" at the end of subparagraph (C), by inserting "or" at the end subparagraph (D), and by inserting after subparagraph (D) a new subparagraph (E). **Effective** for obligations issued after 2-17-2009.

P.L. 111-5, § 1521(b)(2):

Amended Code Sec. 54A(d)(2)(C) by striking "and" at the end of clause (iii), by striking the period at the end clause (iv) and inserting ", and", and by adding at the end a new clause (v). **Effective** for obligations issued after 2-17-2009.

(h) BONDS HELD BY REAL ESTATE INVESTMENT TRUSTS.—*If any qualified tax credit bond is held by a real estate investment trust, the credit determined under subsection (a) shall be allowed to beneficiaries of such trust (and any gross income included under subsection (f) with respect to such credit shall be distributed to such beneficiaries) under procedures prescribed by the Secretary.*

* * *

[CCH Explanation at ¶615. Committee Reports at ¶10,460.]

Amendments

• 2009, American Recovery and Reinvestment Tax Act of 2009 (P.L. 111-5)

P.L. 111-5, §1541(b)(2):

Amended Code Sec. 54A(h). **Effective** for tax years ending after 2-17-2009. Prior to amendment, Code Sec. 54A(h) read as follows:

(h) BONDS HELD BY REGULATED INVESTMENT COMPANIES AND REAL ESTATE INVESTMENT TRUSTS.—If any qualified tax credit bond is held by a regulated investment company or a real estate investment trust, the credit determined under subsection (a) shall be allowed to shareholders of such company or beneficiaries of such trust (and any gross income included under subsection (f) with respect to such credit shall be treated as distributed to such shareholders or beneficiaries) under procedures prescribed by the Secretary.

[¶5155] CODE SEC. 54AA. BUILD AMERICA BONDS.

(a) IN GENERAL.—If a taxpayer holds a build America bond on one or more interest payment dates of the bond during any taxable year, there shall be allowed as a credit against the tax imposed by this chapter for the taxable year an amount equal to the sum of the credits determined under subsection (b) with respect to such dates.

(b) AMOUNT OF CREDIT.—The amount of the credit determined under this subsection with respect to any interest payment date for a build America bond is 35 percent of the amount of interest payable by the issuer with respect to such date.

(c) LIMITATION BASED ON AMOUNT OF TAX.—

(1) IN GENERAL.—The credit allowed under subsection (a) for any taxable year shall not exceed the excess of—

(A) the sum of the regular tax liability (as defined in section 26(b)) plus the tax imposed by section 55, over

(B) the sum of the credits allowable under this part (other than subpart C and this subpart).

(2) CARRYOVER OF UNUSED CREDIT.—If the credit allowable under subsection (a) exceeds the limitation imposed by paragraph (1) for such taxable year, such excess shall be carried to the succeeding taxable year and added to the credit allowable under subsection (a) for such taxable year (determined before the application of paragraph (1) for such succeeding taxable year).

(d) BUILD AMERICA BOND.—

(1) IN GENERAL.—For purposes of this section, the term "build America bond" means any obligation (other than a private activity bond) if—

(A) the interest on such obligation would (but for this section) be excludable from gross income under section 103,

(B) such obligation is issued before January 1, 2011, and

(C) the issuer makes an irrevocable election to have this section apply.

(2) APPLICABLE RULES.—For purposes of applying paragraph (1)—

(A) for purposes of section 149(b), a build America bond shall not be treated as federally guaranteed by reason of the credit allowed under subsection (a) or section 6431,

(B) for purposes of section 148, the yield on a build America bond shall be determined without regard to the credit allowed under subsection (a), and

(C) a bond shall not be treated as a build America bond if the issue price has more than a de minimis amount (determined under rules similar to the rules of section 1273(a)(3)) of premium over the stated principal amount of the bond.

(e) INTEREST PAYMENT DATE.—For purposes of this section, the term "interest payment date" means any date on which the holder of record of the build America bond is entitled to a payment of interest under such bond.

Law Added, Amended or Repealed 337

(f) SPECIAL RULES.—

(1) INTEREST ON BUILD AMERICA BONDS INCLUDIBLE IN GROSS INCOME FOR FEDERAL INCOME TAX PURPOSES.—For purposes of this title, interest on any build America bond shall be includible in gross income.

(2) APPLICATION OF CERTAIN RULES.—Rules similar to the rules of subsections (f), (g), (h), and (i) of section 54A shall apply for purposes of the credit allowed under subsection (a).

(g) SPECIAL RULE FOR QUALIFIED BONDS ISSUED BEFORE 2011.—In the case of a qualified bond issued before January 1, 2011—

(1) ISSUER ALLOWED REFUNDABLE CREDIT.—In lieu of any credit allowed under this section with respect to such bond, the issuer of such bond shall be allowed a credit as provided in section 6431.

(2) QUALIFIED BOND.—For purposes of this subsection, the term "qualified bond" means any build America bond issued as part of an issue if—

(A) 100 percent of the excess of—

(i) the available project proceeds (as defined in section 54A) of such issue, over

(ii) the amounts in a reasonably required reserve (within the meaning of section 150(a)(3)) with respect to such issue,

are to be used for capital expenditures, and

(B) the issuer makes an irrevocable election to have this subsection apply.

(h) REGULATIONS.—The Secretary may prescribe such regulations and other guidance as may be necessary or appropriate to carry out this section and section 6431.

[CCH Explanation at ¶605. Committee Reports at ¶10,450.]

Amendments

• **2009, American Recovery and Reinvestment Tax Act of 2009 (P.L. 111-5)**

P.L. 111-5, §1531(a):

Amended part IV of subchapter A of chapter 1 by adding at the end a new subpart J (Code Sec. 54AA). **Effective** for obligations issued after 2-17-2009.

P.L. 111-5, §1531(d), provides:

(d) TRANSITIONAL COORDINATION WITH STATE LAW.—Except as otherwise provided by a State after the date of the enactment of this Act, the interest on any build America bond (as defined in section 54AA of the Internal Revenue Code of 1986, as added by this section) and the amount of any credit determined under such section with respect to such bond shall be treated for purposes of the income tax laws of such State as being exempt from Federal income tax.

[¶5160] CODE SEC. 54C. NEW CLEAN RENEWABLE ENERGY BONDS.

* * *

(c) LIMITATION ON AMOUNT OF BONDS DESIGNATED.—

* * *

(4) ADDITIONAL LIMITATION.—The national new clean renewable energy bond limitation shall be increased by $1,600,000,000. Such increase shall be allocated by the Secretary consistent with the rules of paragraphs (2) and (3).

* * *

[CCH Explanation at ¶645. Committee Reports at ¶10,140.]

Amendments

• **2009, American Recovery and Reinvestment Tax Act of 2009 (P.L. 111-5)**

P.L. 111-5, §1111:

Amended Code Sec. 54C(c) by adding at the end a new paragraph (4). **Effective** 2-17-2009.

[¶ 5165] CODE SEC. 54D. QUALIFIED ENERGY CONSERVATION BONDS.

* * *

(d) NATIONAL LIMITATION ON AMOUNT OF BONDS DESIGNATED.—There is a national qualified energy conservation bond limitation of *$3,200,000,000*.

[CCH Explanation at ¶ 640. Committee Reports at ¶ 10,150.]

Amendments
• **2009, American Recovery and Reinvestment Tax Act of 2009 (P.L. 111-5)**

P.L. 111-5, § 1112(a):

Amended Code Sec. 54D(d) by striking "$800,000,000" and inserting "$3,200,000,000". **Effective 2-17-2009.**

(e) ALLOCATIONS.—

* * *

(4) SPECIAL RULES FOR BONDS TO IMPLEMENT GREEN COMMUNITY PROGRAMS.—In the case of any bond issued for the purpose of providing loans, grants, or other repayment mechanisms for capital expenditures to implement green community programs, such bond shall not be treated as a private activity bond for purposes of paragraph (3).

[CCH Explanation at ¶ 640. Committee Reports at ¶ 10,150.]

Amendments
• **2009, American Recovery and Reinvestment Tax Act of 2009 (P.L. 111-5)**

P.L. 111-5, § 1112(b)(2):

Amended Code Sec. 54D(e) by adding at the end a new paragraph (4). **Effective 2-17-2009.**

(f) QUALIFIED CONSERVATION PURPOSE.—For purposes of this section—

(1) IN GENERAL.—The term "qualified conservation purpose" means any of the following:

(A) Capital expenditures incurred for purposes of—

(i) reducing energy consumption in publicly-owned buildings by at least 20 percent,

(ii) implementing green community programs *(including the use of loans, grants, or other repayment mechanisms to implement such programs)*,

(iii) rural development involving the production of electricity from renewable energy resources, or

(iv) any qualified facility (as determined under section 45(d) without regard to paragraphs (8) and (10) thereof and without regard to any placed in service date).

* * *

[CCH Explanation at ¶ 640. Committee Reports at ¶ 10,150.]

Amendments
• **2009, American Recovery and Reinvestment Tax Act of 2009 (P.L. 111-5)**

P.L. 111-5, § 1112(b)(1):

Amended Code Sec. 54D(f)(1)(A)(ii) by inserting "(including the use of loans, grants, or other repayment mechanisms to implement such programs)" after "green community programs". **Effective 2-17-2009.**

[¶ 5170] CODE SEC. 54E. QUALIFIED ZONE ACADEMY BONDS.

* * *

(c) LIMITATION ON AMOUNT OF BONDS DESIGNATED.—

(1) NATIONAL LIMITATION.—There is a national zone academy bond limitation for each calendar year. Such limitation is $400,000,000 for 2008 *and $1,400,000,000 for 2009 and 2010*, and, except as provided in paragraph (4), zero thereafter.

* * *

[CCH Explanation at ¶ 635. Committee Reports at ¶ 10,440.]

Amendments

• **2009, American Recovery and Reinvestment Tax Act of 2009 (P.L. 111-5)**

P.L. 111-5, § 1522(a):

Amended Code Sec. 54E(c)(1) by striking "and 2009" and inserting "and $1,400,000,000 for 2009 and 2010". **Effective** for obligations issued after 12-31-2008.

[¶ 5175] CODE SEC. 54F. QUALIFIED SCHOOL CONSTRUCTION BONDS.

(a) QUALIFIED SCHOOL CONSTRUCTION BOND.—*For purposes of this subchapter, the term "qualified school construction bond" means any bond issued as part of an issue if—*

(1) 100 percent of the available project proceeds of such issue are to be used for the construction, rehabilitation, or repair of a public school facility or for the acquisition of land on which such a facility is to be constructed with part of the proceeds of such issue,

(2) the bond is issued by a State or local government within the jurisdiction of which such school is located, and

(3) the issuer designates such bond for purposes of this section.

(b) LIMITATION ON AMOUNT OF BONDS DESIGNATED.—*The maximum aggregate face amount of bonds issued during any calendar year which may be designated under subsection (a) by any issuer shall not exceed the limitation amount allocated under subsection (d) for such calendar year to such issuer.*

(c) NATIONAL LIMITATION ON AMOUNT OF BONDS DESIGNATED.—*There is a national qualified school construction bond limitation for each calendar year. Such limitation is—*

(1) $11,000,000,000 for 2009,

(2) $11,000,000,000 for 2010, and

(3) except as provided in subsection (e), zero after 2010.

(d) ALLOCATION OF LIMITATION.—

(1) ALLOCATION AMONG STATES.—Except as provided in paragraph (2)(C), the limitation applicable under subsection (c) for any calendar year shall be allocated by the Secretary among the States in proportion to the respective amounts each such State is eligible to receive under section 1124 of the Elementary and Secondary Education Act of 1965 (20 U.S.C. 6333) for the most recent fiscal year ending before such calendar year. The limitation amount allocated to a State under the preceding sentence shall be allocated by the State to issuers within such State.

(2) 40 PERCENT OF LIMITATION ALLOCATED AMONG LARGEST SCHOOL DISTRICTS.—

(A) IN GENERAL.—40 percent of the limitation applicable under subsection (c) for any calendar year shall be allocated under subparagraph (B) by the Secretary among local educational agencies which are large local educational agencies for such year.

(B) ALLOCATION FORMULA.—The amount to be allocated under subparagraph (A) for any calendar year shall be allocated among large local educational agencies in proportion to the respective amounts each such agency received under section 1124 of the Elementary and Secondary Education Act of 1965 (20 U.S.C. 6333) for the most recent fiscal year ending before such calendar year.

(C) REDUCTION IN STATE ALLOCATION.—The allocation to any State under paragraph (1) shall be reduced by the aggregate amount of the allocations under this paragraph to large local educational agencies within such State.

(D) ALLOCATION OF UNUSED LIMITATION TO STATE.—The amount allocated under this paragraph to a large local educational agency for any calendar year may be reallocated by such agency to the State in which such agency is located for such calendar year. Any amount reallocated to a State under the preceding sentence may be allocated as provided in paragraph (1).

(E) LARGE LOCAL EDUCATIONAL AGENCY.—For purposes of this paragraph, the term "large local educational agency" means, with respect to a calendar year, any local educational agency if such agency is—

(i) among the 100 local educational agencies with the largest numbers of children aged 5 through 17 from families living below the poverty level, as determined by the Secretary using the most recent data available from the Department of Commerce that are satisfactory to the Secretary, or

(ii) 1 of not more than 25 local educational agencies (other than those described in clause (i)) that the Secretary of Education determines (based on the most recent data available satisfactory to the Secretary) are in particular need of assistance, based on a low level of resources for school construction, a high level of enrollment growth, or such other factors as the Secretary deems appropriate.

(3) ALLOCATIONS TO CERTAIN POSSESSIONS.—The amount to be allocated under paragraph (1) to any possession of the United States other than Puerto Rico shall be the amount which would have been allocated if all allocations under paragraph (1) were made on the basis of respective populations of individuals below the poverty line (as defined by the Office of Management and Budget). In making other allocations, the amount to be allocated under paragraph (1) shall be reduced by the aggregate amount allocated under this paragraph to possessions of the United States.

(4) ALLOCATIONS FOR INDIAN SCHOOLS.—In addition to the amounts otherwise allocated under this subsection, $200,000,000 for calendar year 2009, and $200,000,000 for calendar year 2010, shall be allocated by the Secretary of the Interior for purposes of the construction, rehabilitation, and repair of schools funded by the Bureau of Indian Affairs. In the case of amounts allocated under the preceding sentence, Indian tribal governments (as defined in section 7701(a)(40)) shall be treated as qualified issuers for purposes of this subchapter.

(e) CARRYOVER OF UNUSED LIMITATION.—If for any calendar year—

(1) the amount allocated under subsection (d) to any State, exceeds

(2) the amount of bonds issued during such year which are designated under subsection (a) pursuant to such allocation,

the limitation amount under such subsection for such State for the following calendar year shall be increased by the amount of such excess. A similar rule shall apply to the amounts allocated under subsection (d)(4).

[CCH Explanation at ¶ 630. Committee Reports at ¶ 10,430.]
Amendments
• **2009, American Recovery and Reinvestment Tax Act of 2009 (P.L. 111-5)**

P.L. 111-5, § 1521(a):

Amended subpart I of part IV of subchapter A of chapter 1 by adding at the end a new Code Sec. 54F. **Effective** for obligations issued after 2-17-2009.

[¶ 5180] CODE SEC. 55. ALTERNATIVE MINIMUM TAX IMPOSED.

* * *

(c) REGULAR TAX.—

* * *

(3) CROSS REFERENCES.—

For provisions providing that certain credits are not allowable against the tax imposed by this section, see sections 26(a), 30C(d)(2), and 38(c).

¶5180 Code Sec. 54F(d)(2)(C)

[CCH Explanation at ¶ 350. Committee Reports at ¶ 10,200.]

Amendments

• **2009, American Recovery and Reinvestment Tax Act of 2009 (P.L. 111-5)**

P.L. 111-5, § 1142(b)(5):

Amended Code Sec. 55(c)(3) by striking "30(b)(3)," following "sections 26(a),". **Effective** for vehicles acquired after 2-17-2009. For a transitional rule, see Act Sec. 1142(d) in the amendment notes for Code Sec. 30.

P.L. 111-5, § 1144(b)(3):

Amended Code Sec. 55(c)(3) by striking "30B(g)(2)," before "30C(d)(2)". **Effective** for tax years beginning after 12-31-2008.

(d) EXEMPTION AMOUNT.—For purposes of this section—

(1) EXEMPTION AMOUNT FOR TAXPAYERS OTHER THAN CORPORATIONS.—In the case of a taxpayer other than a corporation, the term "exemption amount" means—

(A) $45,000 *($70,950 in the case of taxable years beginning in 2009)* in the case of—

(i) a joint return, or

(ii) a surviving spouse,

(B) $33,750 *($46,700 in the case of taxable years beginning in 2009)* in the case of an individual who—

(i) is not a married individual, and

(ii) is not a surviving spouse,

(C) 50 percent of the dollar amount applicable under paragraph (1)(A) in the case of a married individual who files a separate return, and

(D) $22,500 in the case of an estate or trust.

For purposes of this paragraph, the term "surviving spouse" has the meaning given to such term by section 2(a), and marital status shall be determined under section 7703.

* * *

[CCH Explanation at ¶ 235. Committee Reports at ¶ 10,090.]

Amendments

• **2009, American Recovery and Reinvestment Tax Act of 2009 (P.L. 111-5)**

P.L. 111-5, § 1012(a)(1)-(2):

Amended Code Sec. 55(d)(1) by striking "($69,950 in the case of taxable years beginning in 2008)" in subparagraph (A) and inserting "($70,950 in the case of taxable years beginning in 2009)", and by striking "($46,200 in the case of taxable years beginning in 2008)" in subparagraph (B) and inserting "($46,700 in the case of taxable years beginning in 2009)". **Effective** for tax years beginning after 12-31-2008.

[¶ 5185] CODE SEC. 56. ADJUSTMENTS IN COMPUTING ALTERNATIVE MINIMUM TAXABLE INCOME.

* * *

(b) ADJUSTMENTS APPLICABLE TO INDIVIDUALS.—In determining the amount of the alternative minimum taxable income of any taxpayer (other than a corporation), the following treatment shall apply (in lieu of the treatment applicable for purposes of computing the regular tax):

(1) LIMITATION ON DEDUCTIONS.—

* * *

(E) STANDARD DEDUCTION AND DEDUCTION FOR PERSONAL EXEMPTIONS NOT ALLOWED.—The standard deduction under section 63(c), the deduction for personal exemptions under section 151, and the deduction under section 642(b) shall not be allowed. The preceding sentence shall not apply to so much of the standard deduction as is determined under *subparagraphs (D) and (E) of section 63(c)(1).*

* * *

[CCH Explanation at ¶230. Committee Reports at ¶10,080.]

Amendments

• **2009, American Recovery and Reinvestment Tax Act of 2009 (P.L. 111-5)**

P.L. 111-5, §1008(d):

Amended the last sentence of Code Sec. 56(b)(1)(E) by striking "section 63(c)(1)(D)" and inserting "subparagraphs (D) and (E) of section 63(c)(1)". **Effective** for purchases on or after 2-17-2009 in tax years ending after such date.

(g) ADJUSTMENTS BASED ON ADJUSTED CURRENT EARNINGS.—

* * *

(4) ADJUSTMENTS.—In determining adjusted current earnings, the following adjustments shall apply:

* * *

(B) INCLUSION OF ITEMS INCLUDED FOR PURPOSES OF COMPUTING EARNINGS AND PROFITS.—

* * *

(iv) TAX EXEMPT INTEREST ON BONDS ISSUED IN 2009 AND 2010.—

(I) IN GENERAL.—Clause (i) shall not apply in the case of any interest on a bond issued after December 31, 2008, and before January 1, 2011.

(II) TREATMENT OF REFUNDING BONDS.—For purposes of subclause (I), a refunding bond (whether a current or advance refunding) shall be treated as issued on the date of the issuance of the refunded bond (or in the case of a series of refundings, the original bond).

(III) EXCEPTION FOR CERTAIN REFUNDING BONDS.—Subclause (II) shall not apply to any refunding bond which is issued to refund any bond which was issued after December 31, 2003, and before January 1, 2009.

* * *

[CCH Explanation at ¶650. Committee Reports at ¶10,400.]

Amendments

• **2009, American Recovery and Reinvestment Tax Act of 2009 (P.L. 111-5)**

P.L. 111-5, §1503(b):

Amended Code Sec. 56(g)(4)(B) by adding at the end a new clause (iv). **Effective** for obligations issued after 12-31-2008.

[¶5190] CODE SEC. 57. ITEMS OF TAX PREFERENCE.

(a) GENERAL RULE.—For purposes of this part, the items of tax preference determined under this section are—

* * *

(5) TAX-EXEMPT INTEREST.—

* * *

(C) SPECIFIED PRIVATE ACTIVITY BONDS.—

* * *

(vi) EXCEPTION FOR BONDS ISSUED IN 2009 AND 2010.—

(I) IN GENERAL.—For purposes of clause (i), the term "private activity bond" shall not include any bond issued after December 31, 2008, and before January 1, 2011.

(II) TREATMENT OF REFUNDING BONDS.—For purposes of subclause (I), a refunding bond (whether a current or advance refunding) shall be treated as issued on the date of the issuance of the refunded bond (or in the case of a series of refundings, the original bond).

(III) EXCEPTION FOR CERTAIN REFUNDING BONDS.—*Subclause (II) shall not apply to any refunding bond which is issued to refund any bond which was issued after December 31, 2003, and before January 1, 2009.*

* * *

[CCH Explanation at ¶ 650. Committee Reports at ¶ 10,400.]
Amendments
• **2009, American Recovery and Reinvestment Tax Act of 2009 (P.L. 111-5)**

P.L. 111-5, § 1503(a):

Amended Code Sec. 57(a)(5)(C) by adding at the end a new clause (vi). **Effective** for obligations issued after 12-31-2008.

[¶ 5195] CODE SEC. 63. TAXABLE INCOME DEFINED.

* * *

(c) STANDARD DEDUCTION.—For purposes of this subtitle—

(1) IN GENERAL.—Except as otherwise provided in this subsection, the term "standard deduction" means the sum of—

    (A) the basic standard deduction,

    (B) the additional standard deduction,

    (C) in the case of any taxable year beginning in 2008 or 2009, the real property tax deduction,

    (D) the disaster loss deduction, *and*

    (E) *the motor vehicle sales tax deduction.*

* * *

(9) MOTOR VEHICLE SALES TAX DEDUCTION.—For purposes of paragraph (1), the term "motor vehicle sales tax deduction" means the amount allowable as a deduction under section 164(a)(6). Such term shall not include any amount taken into account under section 62(a).

* * *

[CCH Explanation at ¶ 230. Committee Reports at ¶ 10,080.]
Amendments
• **2009, American Recovery and Reinvestment Tax Act of 2009 (P.L. 111-5)**

P.L. 111-5, § 1008(c)(1):

Amended Code Sec. 63(c)(1) by striking "and" at the end of subparagraph (C), by striking the period at the end of subparagraph (D) and inserting ", and", and by adding at the end a new subparagraph (E). **Effective** for purchases on or after 2-17-2009 in tax years ending after such date.

P.L. 111-5, § 1008(c)(2):

Amended Code Sec. 63(c) by adding at the end a new paragraph (9). **Effective** for purchases on or after 2-17-2009 in tax years ending after such date.

[¶ 5200] CODE SEC. 85. UNEMPLOYMENT COMPENSATION.

* * *

(c) SPECIAL RULE FOR 2009.—In the case of any taxable year beginning in 2009, gross income shall not include so much of the unemployment compensation received by an individual as does not exceed $2,400.

[CCH Explanation at ¶ 205. Committee Reports at ¶ 10,070.]
Amendments
• **2009, American Recovery and Reinvestment Tax Act of 2009 (P.L. 111-5)**

P.L. 111-5, § 1007(a):

Amended Code Sec. 85 by adding at the end a new subsection (c). **Effective** for tax years beginning after 12-31-2008.

[¶ 5205] CODE SEC. 108. INCOME FROM DISCHARGE OF INDEBTEDNESS.

* * *

(i) DEFERRAL AND RATABLE INCLUSION OF INCOME ARISING FROM BUSINESS INDEBTEDNESS DISCHARGED BY THE REACQUISITION OF A DEBT INSTRUMENT.—

(1) IN GENERAL.—At the election of the taxpayer, income from the discharge of indebtedness in connection with the reacquisition after December 31, 2008, and before January 1, 2011, of an applicable debt instrument shall be includible in gross income ratably over the 5-taxable-year period beginning with—

(A) in the case of a reacquisition occurring in 2009, the fifth taxable year following the taxable year in which the reacquisition occurs, and

(B) in the case of a reacquisition occurring in 2010, the fourth taxable year following the taxable year in which the reacquisition occurs.

(2) DEFERRAL OF DEDUCTION FOR ORIGINAL ISSUE DISCOUNT IN DEBT FOR DEBT EXCHANGES.—

(A) IN GENERAL.—If, as part of a reacquisition to which paragraph (1) applies, any debt instrument is issued for the applicable debt instrument being reacquired (or is treated as so issued under subsection (e)(4) and the regulations thereunder) and there is any original issue discount determined under subpart A of part V of subchapter P of this chapter with respect to the debt instrument so issued—

(i) except as provided in clause (ii), no deduction otherwise allowable under this chapter shall be allowed to the issuer of such debt instrument with respect to the portion of such original issue discount which—

(I) accrues before the 1st taxable year in the 5-taxable-year period in which income from the discharge of indebtedness attributable to the reacquisition of the debt instrument is includible under paragraph (1), and

(II) does not exceed the income from the discharge of indebtedness with respect to the debt instrument being reacquired, and

(ii) the aggregate amount of deductions disallowed under clause (i) shall be allowed as a deduction ratably over the 5-taxable-year period described in clause (i)(I).

If the amount of the original issue discount accruing before such 1st taxable year exceeds the income from the discharge of indebtedness with respect to the applicable debt instrument being reacquired, the deductions shall be disallowed in the order in which the original issue discount is accrued.

(B) DEEMED DEBT FOR DEBT EXCHANGES.—For purposes of subparagraph (A), if any debt instrument is issued by an issuer and the proceeds of such debt instrument are used directly or indirectly by the issuer to reacquire an applicable debt instrument of the issuer, the debt instrument so issued shall be treated as issued for the debt instrument being reacquired. If only a portion of the proceeds from a debt instrument are so used, the rules of subparagraph (A) shall apply to the portion of any original issue discount on the newly issued debt instrument which is equal to the portion of the proceeds from such instrument used to reacquire the outstanding instrument.

(3) APPLICABLE DEBT INSTRUMENT.—For purposes of this subsection—

(A) APPLICABLE DEBT INSTRUMENT.—The term "applicable debt instrument" means any debt instrument which was issued by—

(i) a C corporation, or

(ii) any other person in connection with the conduct of a trade or business by such person.

(B) DEBT INSTRUMENT.—The term "debt instrument" means a bond, debenture, note, certificate, or any other instrument or contractual arrangement constituting indebtedness (within the meaning of section 1275(a)(1)).

(4) REACQUISITION.—For purposes of this subsection—

(A) IN GENERAL.—The term "reacquisition" means, with respect to any applicable debt instrument, any acquisition of the debt instrument by—

(i) the debtor which issued (or is otherwise the obligor under) the debt instrument, or

(ii) a related person to such debtor.

(B) ACQUISITION.—The term "acquisition" shall, with respect to any applicable debt instrument, include an acquisition of the debt instrument for cash, the exchange of the debt instrument for another debt instrument (including an exchange resulting from a modification of the debt instrument), the exchange of the debt instrument for corporate stock or a partnership interest, and the contribution of the debt instrument to capital. Such term shall also include the complete forgiveness of the indebtedness by the holder of the debt instrument.

(5) OTHER DEFINITIONS AND RULES.—For purposes of this subsection—

(A) RELATED PERSON.—The determination of whether a person is related to another person shall be made in the same manner as under subsection (e)(4).

(B) ELECTION.—

(i) IN GENERAL.—An election under this subsection with respect to any applicable debt instrument shall be made by including with the return of tax imposed by chapter 1 for the taxable year in which the reacquisition of the debt instrument occurs a statement which—

(I) clearly identifies such instrument, and

(II) includes the amount of income to which paragraph (1) applies and such other information as the Secretary may prescribe.

(ii) ELECTION IRREVOCABLE.—Such election, once made, is irrevocable.

(iii) PASS-THRU ENTITIES.—In the case of a partnership, S corporation, or other pass-thru entity, the election under this subsection shall be made by the partnership, the S corporation, or other entity involved.

(C) COORDINATION WITH OTHER EXCLUSIONS.—If a taxpayer elects to have this subsection apply to an applicable debt instrument, subparagraphs (A), (B), (C), and (D) of subsection (a)(1) shall not apply to the income from the discharge of such indebtedness for the taxable year of the election or any subsequent taxable year.

(D) ACCELERATION OF DEFERRED ITEMS.—

(i) IN GENERAL.—In the case of the death of the taxpayer, the liquidation or sale of substantially all the assets of the taxpayer (including in a title 11 or similar case), the cessation of business by the taxpayer, or similar circumstances, any item of income or deduction which is deferred under this subsection (and has not previously been taken into account) shall be taken into account in the taxable year in which such event occurs (or in the case of a title 11 or similar case, the day before the petition is filed).

(ii) SPECIAL RULE FOR PASSTHRU ENTITIES.—The rule of clause (i) shall also apply in the case of the sale or exchange or redemption of an interest in a partnership, S corporation, or other passthru entity by a partner, shareholder, or other person holding an ownership interest in such entity.

(6) SPECIAL RULE FOR PARTNERSHIPS.—In the case of a partnership, any income deferred under this subsection shall be allocated to the partners in the partnership immediately before the discharge in the manner such amounts would have been included in the distributive shares of such partners under section 704 if such income were recognized at such time. Any decrease in a partner's share of partnership liabilities as a result of such discharge shall not be taken into account for purposes of section 752 at the time of the discharge to the extent it would cause the partner to recognize gain under section 731. Any decrease in partnership liabilities deferred under the preceding sentence shall be taken into account by such partner at the same time, and to the extent remaining in the same amount, as income deferred under this subsection is recognized.

(7) SECRETARIAL AUTHORITY.—The Secretary may prescribe such regulations, rules, or other guidance as may be necessary or appropriate for purposes of applying this subsection, including—

(A) extending the application of the rules of paragraph (5)(D) to other circumstances where appropriate,

(B) requiring reporting of the election (and such other information as the Secretary may require) on returns of tax for subsequent taxable years, and

(C) rules for the application of this subsection to partnerships, S corporations, and other pass-thru entities, including for the allocation of deferred deductions.

[CCH Explanation at ¶ 405. Committee Reports at ¶ 10,290.]

Amendments
• 2009, American Recovery and Reinvestment Tax Act of 2009 (P.L. 111-5)

P.L. 111-5, § 1231(a):

Amended Code Sec. 108 by adding at the end a new subsection (i). **Effective** for discharges in tax years ending after 12-31-2008.

[¶ 5210] CODE SEC. 132. CERTAIN FRINGE BENEFITS.

* * *

(f) QUALIFIED TRANSPORTATION FRINGE.—

* * *

(2) LIMITATION ON EXCLUSION.— The amount of the fringe benefits which are provided by an employer to any employee and which may be excluded from gross income under subsection (a)(5) shall not exceed—

(A) $100 per month in the case of the aggregate of the benefits described in subparagraphs (A) and (B) of paragraph (1),

(B) $175 per month in the case of qualified parking, and

(C) the applicable annual limitation in the case of any qualified bicycle commuting reimbursement.

In the case of any month beginning on or after the date of the enactment of this sentence and before January 1, 2011, subparagraph (A) shall be applied as if the dollar amount therein were the same as the dollar amount in effect for such month under subparagraph (B).

* * *

[CCH Explanation at ¶ 215. Committee Reports at ¶ 10,210.]

Amendments
• 2009, American Recovery and Reinvestment Tax Act of 2009 (P.L. 111-5)

P.L. 111-5, § 1151(a):

Amended Code Sec. 132(f)(2) by adding at the end a new flush sentence. **Effective** for months beginning on or after 2-17-2009.

[¶ 5215] CODE SEC. 139C. COBRA PREMIUM ASSISTANCE.

In the case of an assistance eligible individual (as defined in section 3002 [3001] of the Health Insurance Assistance for the Unemployed Act of 2009 [American Recovery and Reinvestment Act of 2009]), gross income does not include any premium reduction provided under subsection (a) of such section.

[CCH Explanation at ¶705. Committee Reports at ¶10,510.]

Amendments

• **2009, American Recovery and Reinvestment Tax Act of 2009 (P.L. 111-5)**

P.L. 111-5, §3001(a)(15)(A):

Amended part III of subchapter B of chapter 1 by inserting after Code Sec. 139B a new Code Sec. 139C. **Effective** for tax years ending after 2-17-2009.

[¶5220] CODE SEC. 142. EXEMPT FACILITY BOND.

* * *

(i) HIGH-SPEED INTERCITY RAIL FACILITIES.—

(1) IN GENERAL.—For purposes of subsection (a)(11), the term "high-speed intercity rail facilities" means any facility (not including rolling stock) for the fixed guideway rail transportation of passengers and their baggage between metropolitan statistical areas (within the meaning of section 143(k)(2)(B)) using vehicles that are reasonably expected to *be capable of attaining a maximum speed in excess of* 150 miles per hour between scheduled stops, but only if such facility will be made available to members of the general public as passengers.

* * *

[CCH Explanation at ¶655. Committee Reports at ¶10,410.]

Amendments

• **2009, American Recovery and Reinvestment Tax Act of 2009 (P.L. 111-5)**

P.L. 111-5, §1504(a):

Amended Code Sec. 142(i)(1) by striking "operate at speeds in excess of" and inserting "be capable of attaining a maximum speed in excess of". **Effective** for obligations issued after 2-17-2009.

[¶5225] CODE SEC. 144. QUALIFIED SMALL ISSUE BOND; QUALIFIED STUDENT LOAN BOND; QUALIFIED REDEVELOPMENT BOND.

(a) QUALIFIED SMALL ISSUE BOND.—

* * *

(12) TERMINATION DATES.—

* * *

(C) MANUFACTURING FACILITY.—*For purposes of this paragraph*—

(i) IN GENERAL.—The term "manufacturing facility" means any facility which is used in the manufacturing or production of tangible personal property (including the processing resulting in a change in the condition of such property). A rule similar to the rule of section 142(b)(2) shall apply for purposes of the preceding sentence.

(ii) CERTAIN FACILITIES INCLUDED.—*Such term includes facilities which are directly related and ancillary to a manufacturing facility (determined without regard to this clause) if*—

(I) *such facilities are located on the same site as the manufacturing facility, and*

(II) *not more than 25 percent of the net proceeds of the issue are used to provide such facilities.*

(iii) SPECIAL RULES FOR BONDS ISSUED IN 2009 AND 2010.—*In the case of any issue made after the date of enactment of this clause and before January 1, 2011, clause (ii) shall not apply and the net proceeds from a bond shall be considered to be used to provide a manufacturing facility if such proceeds are used to provide*—

(I) *a facility which is used in the creation or production of intangible property which is described in section 197(d)(1)(C)(iii), or*

(II) a facility which is functionally related and subordinate to a manufacturing facility (determined without regard to this subclause) if such facility is located on the same site as the manufacturing facility.

* * *

[CCH Explanation at ¶ 660. Committee Reports at ¶ 10,330.]

Amendments

• 2009, American Recovery and Reinvestment Tax Act of 2009 (P.L. 111-5)

P.L. 111-5, § 1301(a)(1)-(2):

Amended Code Sec. 144(a)(12)(C) by striking "For purposes of this paragraph, the term" and inserting "For purposes of this paragraph—

"(i) IN GENERAL.—The term", and

by striking the last sentence and inserting new clauses (ii)-(iii). **Effective** for obligations issued after 2-17-2009. Prior to being stricken, the last sentence of Code Sec. 144(a)(12)(C) read as follows:

For purposes of the 1st sentence of this subparagraph, the term "manufacturing facility" includes facilities which are directly related and ancillary to a manufacturing facility (determined without regard to this sentence) if—

(i) such facilities are located on the same site as the manufacturing facility, and

(ii) not more than 25 percent of the net proceeds of the issue are used to provide such facilities.

[¶ 5230] CODE SEC. 163. INTEREST.

* * *

(e) ORIGINAL ISSUE DISCOUNT.—

* * *

(5) SPECIAL RULES FOR ORIGINAL ISSUE DISCOUNT ON CERTAIN HIGH YIELD OBLIGATIONS.—

* * *

(F) SUSPENSION OF APPLICATION OF PARAGRAPH.—

(i) TEMPORARY SUSPENSION.—This paragraph shall not apply to any applicable high yield discount obligation issued during the period beginning on September 1, 2008, and ending on December 31, 2009, in exchange (including an exchange resulting from a modification of the debt instrument) for an obligation which is not an applicable high yield discount obligation and the issuer (or obligor) of which is the same as the issuer (or obligor) of such applicable high yield discount obligation. The preceding sentence shall not apply to any obligation the interest on which is interest described in section 871(h)(4) (without regard to subparagraph (D) thereof) or to any obligation issued to a related person (within the meaning of section 108(e)(4)).

(ii) SUCCESSIVE APPLICATION.—Any obligation to which clause (i) applies shall not be treated as an applicable high yield discount obligation for purposes of applying this subparagraph to any other obligation issued in exchange for such obligation.

(iii) SECRETARIAL AUTHORITY TO SUSPEND APPLICATION.—The Secretary may apply this paragraph with respect to debt instruments issued in periods following the period described in clause (i) if the Secretary determines that such application is appropriate in light of distressed conditions in the debt capital markets.

(G) CROSS REFERENCE.—

For definition of applicable high yield discount obligation, see subsection (i).

* * *

[CCH Explanation at ¶ 440. Committee Reports at ¶ 10,300.]

Amendments

• 2009, American Recovery and Reinvestment Tax Act of 2009 (P.L. 111-5)

P.L. 111-5, § 1232(a):

Amended Code Sec. 163(e)(5) by redesignating subparagraph (F) as subparagraph (G) and by inserting after subparagraph (E) a new subparagraph (F). **Effective** for obligations issued after 8-31-2008, in tax years ending after such date.

(i) APPLICABLE HIGH YIELD DISCOUNT OBLIGATION.—

* * *

⇒ *Caution: Code Sec. 163(i)(1), below, as amended by P.L. 111-5, applies to obligations issued after December 31, 2009, in tax years ending after such date.*

(1) IN GENERAL.—For purposes of this section, the term "applicable high yield discount obligation" means any debt instrument if—

(A) the maturity date of such instrument is more than 5 years from the date of issue,

(B) the yield to maturity on such instrument equals or exceeds the sum of—

(i) the applicable Federal rate in effect under section 1274(d) for the calendar month in which the obligation is issued, plus

(ii) 5 percentage points, and

(C) such instrument has significant original issue discount.

For purposes of subparagraph (B)(i), the Secretary may by regulation *(i)* permit a rate to be used with respect to any debt instrument which is higher than the applicable Federal rate if the taxpayer establishes to the satisfaction of the Secretary that such higher rate is based on the same principles as the applicable Federal rate and is appropriate for the term of the instrument, *or (ii) permit, on a temporary basis, a rate to be used with respect to any debt instrument which is higher than the applicable Federal rate if the Secretary determines that such rate is appropriate in light of distressed conditions in the debt capital markets.*

* * *

[CCH Explanation at ¶ 440. Committee Reports at ¶ 10,300.]

Amendments

• **2009, American Recovery and Reinvestment Tax Act of 2009 (P.L. 111-5)**

P.L. 111-5, § 1232(b)(1)-(2):

Amended the last sentence of Code Sec. 163(i)(1) by inserting "(i)" after "regulation", and by inserting ", or (ii) permit, on a temporary basis, a rate to be used with respect to any debt instrument which is higher than the applicable Federal rate if the Secretary determines that such rate is appropriate in light of distressed conditions in the debt capital markets" before the period at the end. **Effective** for obligations issued after 12-31-2009, in tax years ending after such date.

[¶ 5235] CODE SEC. 164. TAXES.

(a) GENERAL RULE.—Except as otherwise provided in this section, the following taxes shall be allowed as a deduction for the taxable year within which paid or accrued:

* * *

(6) *Qualified motor vehicle taxes.*

* * *

[CCH Explanation at ¶ 230. Committee Reports at ¶ 10,080.]

Amendments

• **2009, American Recovery and Reinvestment Tax Act of 2009 (P.L. 111-5)**

P.L. 111-5, § 1008(a):

Amended Code Sec. 164(a) by inserting after paragraph (5) a new paragraph (6). **Effective** for purchases on or after 2-17-2009 in tax years ending after such date.

(b) DEFINITIONS AND SPECIAL RULES.—For purposes of this section—

* * *

(6) QUALIFIED MOTOR VEHICLE TAXES.—

(A) IN GENERAL.—For purposes of this section, the term "qualified motor vehicle taxes" means any State or local sales or excise tax imposed on the purchase of a qualified motor vehicle.

Code Sec. 164(b)(6)(A)   ¶ 5235

(B) LIMITATION BASED ON VEHICLE PRICE.—The amount of any State or local sales or excise tax imposed on the purchase of a qualified motor vehicle taken into account under subparagraph (A) shall not exceed the portion of such tax attributable to so much of the purchase price as does not exceed $49,500.

(C) INCOME LIMITATION.—The amount otherwise taken into account under subparagraph (A) (after the application of subparagraph (B)) for any taxable year shall be reduced (but not below zero) by the amount which bears the same ratio to the amount which is so treated as—

(i) the excess (if any) of—

(I) the taxpayer's modified adjusted gross income for such taxable year, over

(II) $125,000 ($250,000 in the case of a joint return), bears to

(ii) $10,000.

For purposes of the preceding sentence, the term "modified adjusted gross income" means the adjusted gross income of the taxpayer for the taxable year (determined without regard to sections 911, 931, and 933).

(D) QUALIFIED MOTOR VEHICLE.—For purposes of this paragraph—

(i) IN GENERAL.—The term "qualified motor vehicle" means—

(I) a passenger automobile or light truck which is treated as a motor vehicle for purposes of title II of the Clean Air Act, the gross vehicle weight rating of which is not more than 8,500 pounds, and the original use of which commences with the taxpayer,

(II) a motorcycle the gross vehicle weight rating of which is not more than 8,500 pounds and the original use of which commences with the taxpayer, and

(III) a motor home the original use of which commences with the taxpayer.

(ii) OTHER TERMS.—The terms "motorcycle" and "motor home" have the meanings given such terms under section 571.3 of title 49, Code of Federal Regulations (as in effect on the date of the enactment of this paragraph).

(E) QUALIFIED MOTOR VEHICLE TAXES NOT INCLUDED IN COST OF ACQUIRED PROPERTY.—The last sentence of subsection (a) shall not apply to any qualified motor vehicle taxes.

(F) COORDINATION WITH GENERAL SALES TAX.—This paragraph shall not apply in the case of a taxpayer who makes an election under paragraph (5) for the taxable year.

(G) TERMINATION.—This paragraph shall not apply to purchases after December 31, 2009.

* * *

[CCH Explanation at ¶230. Committee Reports at ¶10,080.]

Amendments

• 2009, American Recovery and Reinvestment Tax Act of 2009 (P.L. 111-5)

P.L. 111-5, §1008(b):

Amended Code Sec. 164(b) by adding at the end a new paragraph (6). **Effective** for purchases on or after 2-17-2009 in tax years ending after such date.

[¶5240] CODE SEC. 168. ACCELERATED COST RECOVERY SYSTEM.

* * *

(k) SPECIAL ALLOWANCE FOR CERTAIN PROPERTY ACQUIRED AFTER DECEMBER 31, 2007, AND BEFORE JANUARY 1, 2010.—

* * *

(2) QUALIFIED PROPERTY.—For purposes of this subsection—

(A) IN GENERAL.—The term "qualified property" means property—

(i)(I) to which this section applies which has a recovery period of 20 years or less,

(II) which is computer software (as defined in section 167(f)(1)(B)) for which a deduction is allowable under section 167(a) without regard to this subsection,

(III) which is water utility property, or

(IV) which is qualified leasehold improvement property,

(ii) the original use of which commences with the taxpayer after December 31, 2007,

(iii) which is—

(I) acquired by the taxpayer after December 31, 2007, and before *January 1, 2010*, but only if no written binding contract for the acquisition was in effect before January 1, 2008, or

(II) acquired by the taxpayer pursuant to a written binding contract which was entered into after December 31, 2007, and before *January 1, 2010*, and

(iv) which is placed in service by the taxpayer before *January 1, 2010*, or, in the case of property described in subparagraph (B) or (C), before *January 1, 2011*.

(B) CERTAIN PROPERTY HAVING LONGER PRODUCTION PERIODS TREATED AS QUALIFIED PROPERTY.—

* * *

(ii) ONLY PRE-*JANUARY 1, 2010*, BASIS ELIGIBLE FOR ADDITIONAL ALLOWANCE.—In the case of property which is qualified property solely by reason of clause (i), paragraph (1) shall apply only to the extent of the adjusted basis thereof attributable to manufacture, construction, or production before *January 1, 2010*.

* * *

(E) SPECIAL RULES.—

(i) SELF-CONSTRUCTED PROPERTY.—In the case of a taxpayer manufacturing, constructing, or producing property for the taxpayer's own use, the requirements of clause (iii) of subparagraph (A) shall be treated as met if the taxpayer begins manufacturing, constructing, or producing the property after December 31, 2007, and before *January 1, 2010*.

* * *

(4) ELECTION TO ACCELERATE THE AMT AND RESEARCH CREDITS IN LIEU OF BONUS DEPRECIATION.—

* * *

(D) ELIGIBLE QUALIFIED PROPERTY.—For purposes of this paragraph, the term "eligible qualified property" means qualified property under paragraph (2), except that in applying paragraph (2) for purposes of this paragraph—

(i) "March 31, 2008" shall be substituted for "December 31, 2007" each place it appears in subparagraph (A) and clauses (i) and (ii) of subparagraph (E) thereof,

(ii) *"April 1, 2008" shall be substituted for "January 1, 2008" in subparagraph (A)(iii)(I) thereof, and*

(iii) only adjusted basis attributable to manufacture, construction, or production after March 31, 2008, and before January 1, *2010*, shall be taken into account under subparagraph (B)(ii) thereof.

* * *

(H) SPECIAL RULES FOR EXTENSION PROPERTY.—

(i) TAXPAYERS PREVIOUSLY ELECTING ACCELERATION.—*In the case of a taxpayer who made the election under subparagraph (A) for its first taxable year ending after March 31, 2008—*

(I) the taxpayer may elect not to have this paragraph apply to extension property, but

(II) if the taxpayer does not make the election under subclause (I), in applying this paragraph to the taxpayer a separate bonus depreciation amount, maximum amount, and maximum increase amount shall be computed and applied to eligible qualified property

which is extension property and to eligible qualified property which is not extension property.

(ii) TAXPAYERS NOT PREVIOUSLY ELECTING ACCELERATION.—In the case of a taxpayer who did not make the election under subparagraph (A) for its first taxable year ending after March 31, 2008—

(I) the taxpayer may elect to have this paragraph apply to its first taxable year ending after December 31, 2008, and each subsequent taxable year, and

(II) if the taxpayer makes the election under subclause (I), this paragraph shall only apply to eligible qualified property which is extension property.

(iii) EXTENSION PROPERTY.—For purposes of this subparagraph, the term "extension property" means property which is eligible qualified property solely by reason of the extension of the application of the special allowance under paragraph (1) pursuant to the amendments made by section 1201(a) of the American Recovery and Reinvestment Tax Act of 2009 (and the application of such extension to this paragraph pursuant to the amendment made by section 1201(b)(1) of such Act).

[CCH Explanation at ¶ 505. Committee Reports at ¶ 10,220.]

Amendments
• **2009, American Recovery and Reinvestment Tax Act of 2009 (P.L. 111-5)**

P.L. 111-5, § 1201(a)(1)(A)-(B):

Amended Code Sec. 168(k)(2) by striking "January 1, 2010" and inserting "January 1, 2011", and by striking "January 1, 2009" each place it appears and inserting "January 1, 2010". **Effective** for property placed in service after 12-31-2008, in tax years ending after such date.

P.L. 111-5, § 1201(a)(2)(A):

Amended the heading for Code Sec. 168(k) by striking "JANUARY 1, 2009" and inserting "JANUARY 1, 2010". **Effective** for property placed in service after 12-31-2008, in tax years ending after such date.

P.L. 111-5, § 1201(a)(2)(B):

Amended the heading for Code Sec. 168(k)(2)(B)(ii) by striking "PRE-JANUARY 1, 2009" and inserting "PRE-JANUARY 1, 2010". **Effective** for property placed in service after 12-31-2008, in tax years ending after such date.

P.L. 111-5, § 1201(a)(3)(A)(i)-(iii):

Amended Code Sec. 168(k)(4)(D) by striking "and" at the end of clause (i), by redesignating clause (ii) as clause (iii), and by inserting after clause (i) a new clause (ii). **Effective** for tax years ending after 3-31-2008.

P.L. 111-5, § 1201(b)(1)(A)-(B):

Amended Code Sec. 168(k)(4) by striking "2009" and inserting "2010" in subparagraph (D)(iii) (as redesignated by Act Sec. 1201(a)(3)), and by adding at the end a new subparagraph (H). **Effective** for property placed in service after 12-31-2008, in tax years ending after such date.

(l) SPECIAL ALLOWANCE FOR CELLULOSIC BIOFUEL PLANT PROPERTY.—

* * *

(5) SPECIAL RULES.—For purposes of this subsection, rules similar to the rules of subparagraph (E) of section 168(k)(2) shall apply, except that such subparagraph shall be applied—

* * *

(B) by substituting "January 1, 2013" for "*January 1, 2010*" in clause (i) thereof, and

* * *

[CCH Explanation at ¶ 415. Committee Reports at ¶ 10,220.]

Amendments
• **2009, American Recovery and Reinvestment Tax Act of 2009 (P.L. 111-5)**

P.L. 111-5, § 1201(a)(2)(C):

Amended Code Sec. 168(l)(5)(B) by striking "January 1, 2009" and inserting "January 1, 2010". **Effective** for property placed in service after 12-31-2008, in tax years ending after such date.

(n) SPECIAL ALLOWANCE FOR QUALIFIED DISASTER ASSISTANCE PROPERTY.—

* * *

(2) QUALIFIED DISASTER ASSISTANCE PROPERTY.—For purposes of this subsection—

* * *

(C) SPECIAL RULES.—For purposes of this subsection, rules similar to the rules of subparagraph (E) of subsection (k)(2) shall apply, except that such subparagraph shall be applied—

* * *

(ii) without regard to "and before *January 1, 2010*" in clause (i) thereof, and

* * *

[CCH Explanation at ¶415 and ¶505. Committee Reports at ¶10,220.]

Amendments
• **2009, American Recovery and Reinvestment Tax Act of 2009 (P.L. 111-5)**

P.L. 111-5, § 1201(a)(2)(D):

Amended Code Sec. 168(n)(2)(C) by striking "January 1, 2009" and inserting "January 1, 2010". **Effective** for property placed in service after 12-31-2008, in tax years ending after such date.

[¶5245] CODE SEC. 172. NET OPERATING LOSS DEDUCTION.

* * *

(b) NET OPERATING LOSS CARRYBACKS AND CARRYOVERS.—

(1) YEARS TO WHICH LOSS MAY BE CARRIED.—

* * *

(H) CARRYBACK FOR 2008 NET OPERATING LOSSES OF SMALL BUSINESSES.—

(i) IN GENERAL.—*If an eligible small business elects the application of this subparagraph with respect to an applicable 2008 net operating loss—*

(I) *subparagraph (A)(i) shall be applied by substituting any whole number elected by the taxpayer which is more than 2 and less than 6 for "2",*

(II) *subparagraph (E)(ii) shall be applied by substituting the whole number which is one less than the whole number substituted under subclause (I) for "2", and*

(III) *subparagraph (F) shall not apply.*

(ii) APPLICABLE 2008 NET OPERATING LOSS.—*For purposes of this subparagraph, the term "applicable 2008 net operating loss" means—*

(I) *the taxpayer's net operating loss for any taxable year ending in 2008, or*

(II) *if the taxpayer elects to have this subclause apply in lieu of subclause (I), the taxpayer's net operating loss for any taxable year beginning in 2008.*

(iii) ELECTION.—*Any election under this subparagraph shall be made in such manner as may be prescribed by the Secretary, and shall be made by the due date (including extension of time) for filing the taxpayer's return for the taxable year of the net operating loss. Any such election, once made, shall be irrevocable. Any election under this subparagraph may be made only with respect to 1 taxable year.*

(iv) ELIGIBLE SMALL BUSINESS.—*For purposes of this subparagraph, the term "eligible small business" has the meaning given such term by subparagraph (F)(iii), except that in applying such subparagraph, section 448(c) shall be applied by substituting "$15,000,000" for "$5,000,000" each place it appears.*

* * *

[CCH Explanation at ¶425. Committee Reports at ¶10,240.]

Amendments

• 2009, American Recovery and Reinvestment Tax Act of 2009 (P.L. 111-5)

P.L. 111-5, §1211(a):

Amended Code Sec. 172(b)(1)(H). **Effective** for net operating losses arising in tax years ending after 12-31-2007. For a transitional rule, see Act Sec. 1211(d)(2), below. Prior to amendment, Code Sec. 172(b)(1)(H) read as follows:

(H) In the case of a net operating loss for any taxable year ending during 2001 or 2002, subparagraph (A)(i) shall be applied by substituting "5" for "2" and subparagraph (F) shall not apply.

P.L. 111-5, §1211(d)(2), provides:

(2) TRANSITIONAL RULE.—In the case of a net operating loss for a taxable year ending before the date of the enactment of this Act—

(A) any election made under section 172(b)(3) of the Internal Revenue Code of 1986 with respect to such loss may (notwithstanding such section) be revoked before the applicable date,

(B) any election made under section 172(b)(1)(H) of such Code with respect to such loss shall (notwithstanding such section) be treated as timely made if made before the applicable date, and

(C) any application under section 6411(a) of such Code with respect to such loss shall be treated as timely filed if filed before the applicable date.

For purposes of this paragraph, the term "applicable date" means the date which is 60 days after the date of the enactment of this Act.

(k) CROSS REFERENCES.—

(1) For treatment of net operating loss carryovers in certain corporate acquisitions, see section 381.

(2) For special limitation on net operating loss carryovers in case of a corporate change of ownership, see section 382.

[CCH Explanation at ¶425. Committee Reports at ¶10,240.]

Amendments

• 2009, American Recovery and Reinvestment Tax Act of 2009 (P.L. 111-5)

P.L. 111-5, §1211(b):

Amended Code Sec. 172 by striking subsection (k) and redesignating subsection (l) as subsection (k). **Effective** for net operating losses arising in tax years ending after 12-31-2007. For a transitional rule, see Act Sec. 1211(d)(2), in the amendment notes for Code Sec. 172(b). Prior to being stricken, Code Sec. 172(k) read as follows:

(k) ELECTION TO DISREGARD 5-YEAR CARRYBACK FOR CERTAIN NET OPERATING LOSSES.—Any taxpayer entitled to a 5-year carryback under subsection (b)(1)(H) from any loss year may elect to have the carryback period with respect to such loss year determined without regard to subsection (b)(1)(H). Such election shall be made in such manner as may be prescribed by the Secretary and shall be made by the due date (including extensions of time) for filing the taxpayer's return for the taxable year of the net operating loss. Such election, once made for any taxable year, shall be irrevocable for such taxable year.

[¶5250] CODE SEC. 179. ELECTION TO EXPENSE CERTAIN DEPRECIABLE BUSINESS ASSETS.

* * *

(b) LIMITATIONS.—

* * *

(7) INCREASE IN LIMITATIONS FOR *2008, AND [SIC] 2009*.—In the case of any taxable year beginning in *2008, or [sic] 2009*—

(A) the dollar limitation under paragraph (1) shall be $250,000,

(B) the dollar limitation under paragraph (2) shall be $800,000, and

(C) the amounts described in subparagraphs (A) and (B) shall not be adjusted under paragraph (5).

* * *

[CCH Explanation at ¶410. Committee Reports at ¶10,230.]

Amendments

• 2009, American Recovery and Reinvestment Tax Act of 2009 (P.L. 111-5)

P.L. 111-5, §1202(a)(1)-(2):

Amended Code Sec. 179(b)(7) by striking "2008" and inserting "2008, or [sic] 2009", and by striking "2008" in the heading thereof and inserting "2008, AND [SIC] 2009". **Effective** for tax years beginning after 12-31-2008.

[¶ 5255] CODE SEC. 265. EXPENSES AND INTEREST RELATING TO TAX-EXEMPT INCOME.

* * *

(b) PRO RATA ALLOCATION OF INTEREST EXPENSE OF FINANCIAL INSTITUTIONS TO TAX-EXEMPT INTEREST.—

* * *

(3) EXCEPTION FOR CERTAIN TAX-EXEMPT OBLIGATIONS.—

* * *

(G) SPECIAL RULES FOR OBLIGATIONS ISSUED DURING 2009 AND 2010.—

(i) INCREASE IN LIMITATION.—In the case of obligations issued during 2009 or 2010, subparagraphs (C)(i), (D)(i), and (D)(iii)(II) shall each be applied by substituting "$30,000,000" for "$10,000,000".

(ii) QUALIFIED 501(C)(3) BONDS TREATED AS ISSUED BY EXEMPT ORGANIZATION.—In the case of a qualified 501(c)(3) bond (as defined in section 145) issued during 2009 or 2010, this paragraph shall be applied by treating the 501(c)(3) organization for whose benefit such bond was issued as the issuer.

(iii) SPECIAL RULE FOR QUALIFIED FINANCINGS.—In the case of a qualified financing issue issued during 2009 or 2010—

(I) subparagraph (F) shall not apply, and

(II) any obligation issued as a part of such issue shall be treated as a qualified tax-exempt obligation if the requirements of this paragraph are met with respect to each qualified portion of the issue (determined by treating each qualified portion as a separate issue which is issued by the qualified borrower with respect to which such portion relates).

(iv) QUALIFIED FINANCING ISSUE.—For purposes of this subparagraph, the term "qualified financing issue" means any composite, pooled, or other conduit financing issue the proceeds of which are used directly or indirectly to make or finance loans to 1 or more ultimate borrowers each of whom is a qualified borrower.

(v) QUALIFIED PORTION.—For purposes of this subparagraph, the term "qualified portion" means that portion of the proceeds which are used with respect to each qualified borrower under the issue.

(vi) QUALIFIED BORROWER.—For purposes of this subparagraph, the term "qualified borrower" means a borrower which is a State or political subdivision thereof or an organization described in section 501(c)(3) and exempt from taxation under section 501(a).

* * *

(7) DE MINIMIS EXCEPTION FOR BONDS ISSUED DURING 2009 OR 2010.—

(A) IN GENERAL.—In applying paragraph (2)(A), there shall not be taken into account tax-exempt obligations issued during 2009 or 2010.

(B) LIMITATION.—The amount of tax-exempt obligations not taken into account by reason of subparagraph (A) shall not exceed 2 percent of the amount determined under paragraph (2)(B).

(C) REFUNDINGS.—For purposes of this paragraph, a refunding bond (whether a current or advance refunding) shall be treated as issued on the date of the issuance of the refunded bond (or in the case of a series of refundings, the original bond).

[CCH Explanation at ¶445. Committee Reports at ¶10,390.]

Amendments

• 2009, American Recovery and Reinvestment Tax Act of 2009 (P.L. 111-5)

P.L. 111-5, §1501(a):

Amended Code Sec. 265(b) by adding at the end a new paragraph (7). **Effective** for obligations issued after 12-31-2008.

P.L. 111-5, §1502(a):

Amended Code Sec. 265(b)(3) by adding at the end a new subparagraph (G). **Effective** for obligations issued after 12-31-2008.

[¶5260] CODE SEC. 291. SPECIAL RULES RELATING TO CORPORATE PREFERENCE ITEMS.

* * *

(e) DEFINITIONS.—For purposes of this section—

(1) FINANCIAL INSTITUTION PREFERENCE ITEM.—The term "financial institution preference item" includes the following:

* * *

(B) INTEREST ON DEBT TO CARRY TAX-EXEMPT OBLIGATIONS ACQUIRED AFTER DECEMBER 31, 1982, AND BEFORE AUGUST 8, 1986.—

* * *

(iv) APPLICATION OF SUBPARAGRAPH TO CERTAIN OBLIGATIONS ISSUED AFTER AUGUST 7, 1986.—For application of this subparagraph to certain obligations issued after August 7, 1986, see section 265(b)(3). *That portion of any obligation not taken into account under paragraph (2)(A) of section 265(b) by reason of paragraph (7) of such section shall be treated for purposes of this section as having been acquired on August 7, 1986.*

* * *

[CCH Explanation at ¶445. Committee Reports at ¶10,390.]

Amendments

• 2009, American Recovery and Reinvestment Tax Act of 2009 (P.L. 111-5)

P.L. 111-5, §1501(b):

Amended Code Sec. 291(e)(1)(B)(iv) by adding at the end a new sentence. **Effective** for obligations issued after 12-31-2008.

[¶5265] CODE SEC. 382. LIMITATION ON NET OPERATING LOSS CARRYFORWARDS AND CERTAIN BUILT-IN LOSSES FOLLOWING OWNERSHIP CHANGE.

* * *

(n) SPECIAL RULE FOR CERTAIN OWNERSHIP CHANGES.—

(1) IN GENERAL.—The limitation contained in subsection (a) shall not apply in the case of an ownership change which is pursuant to a restructuring plan of a taxpayer which—

(A) is required under a loan agreement or a commitment for a line of credit entered into with the Department of the Treasury under the Emergency Economic Stabilization Act of 2008, and

(B) is intended to result in a rationalization of the costs, capitalization, and capacity with respect to the manufacturing workforce of, and suppliers to, the taxpayer and its subsidiaries.

(2) SUBSEQUENT ACQUISITIONS.—Paragraph (1) shall not apply in the case of any subsequent ownership change unless such ownership change is described in such paragraph.

(3) LIMITATION BASED ON CONTROL IN CORPORATION.—

(A) IN GENERAL.—Paragraph (1) shall not apply in the case of any ownership change if, immediately after such ownership change, any person (other than a voluntary employees' beneficiary association under section 501(c)(9)) owns stock of the new loss corporation possessing 50 percent or more of the total combined voting power of all classes of stock entitled to vote, or of the total value of the stock of such corporation.

(B) TREATMENT OF RELATED PERSONS.—

(i) IN GENERAL.—Related persons shall be treated as a single person for purposes of this paragraph.

(ii) RELATED PERSONS.—For purposes of clause (i), a person shall be treated as related to another person if—

(I) such person bears a relationship to such other person described in section 267(b) or 707(b), or

(II) such persons are members of a group of persons acting in concert.

[CCH Explanation at ¶435. Committee Reports at ¶10,280.]
Amendments

• 2009, American Recovery and Reinvestment Tax Act of 2009 (P.L. 111-5)

P.L. 111-5, §1262(a):

Amended Code Sec. 382 by adding at the end a new subsection (n). **Effective** for ownership changes after 2-17-2009.

[¶5270] CODE SEC. 529. QUALIFIED TUITION PROGRAMS.

* * *

(e) OTHER DEFINITIONS AND SPECIAL RULES.—For purposes of this section—

* * *

(3) QUALIFIED HIGHER EDUCATION EXPENSES.—

(A) IN GENERAL.—The term "qualified higher education expenses" means—

(i) tuition, fees, books, supplies, and equipment required for the enrollment or attendance of a designated beneficiary at an eligible educational institution;

(ii) expenses for special needs services in the case of a special needs beneficiary which are incurred in connection with such enrollment or attendance[; *and*]

(iii) *expenses paid or incurred in 2009 or 2010 for the purchase of any computer technology or equipment (as defined in section 170(e)(6)(F)(i)) or Internet access and related services, if such technology, equipment, or services are to be used by the beneficiary and the beneficiary's family during any of the years the beneficiary is enrolled at an eligible educational institution.*

Clause (iii) shall not include expenses for computer software designed for sports, games, or hobbies unless the software is predominantly educational in nature.

* * *

[CCH Explanation at ¶220. Committee Reports at ¶10,050.]
Amendments

• 2009, American Recovery and Reinvestment Tax Act of 2009 (P.L. 111-5)

P.L. 111-5, §1005(a):

Amended Code Sec. 529(e)(3)(A) by striking "and" at the end of clause (i), by striking the period at the end of clause (ii), and by adding at the end a new clause (iii) and flush sentence. **Effective** for expenses paid or incurred after 12-31-2008.

[¶5275] CODE SEC. 853A. CREDITS FROM TAX CREDIT BONDS ALLOWED TO SHAREHOLDERS.

(a) GENERAL RULE.—A regulated investment company—

(1) which holds (directly or indirectly) one or more tax credit bonds on one or more applicable dates during the taxable year, and

(2) which meets the requirements of section 852(a) for the taxable year,

may elect the application of this section with respect to credits allowable to the investment company during such taxable year with respect to such bonds.

(b) EFFECT OF ELECTION.—If the election provided in subsection (a) is in effect for any taxable year—

(1) the regulated investment company shall not be allowed any credits to which subsection (a) applies for such taxable year,

(2) the regulated investment company shall—

(A) include in gross income (as interest) for such taxable year an amount equal to the amount that such investment company would have included in gross income with respect to such credits if this section did not apply, and

(B) increase the amount of the dividends paid deduction for such taxable year by the amount of such income, and

(3) each shareholder of such investment company shall—

(A) include in gross income an amount equal to such shareholder's proportionate share of the interest income attributable to such credits, and

(B) be allowed the shareholder's proportionate share of such credits against the tax imposed by this chapter.

(c) NOTICE TO SHAREHOLDERS.—For purposes of subsection (b)(3), the shareholder's proportionate share of—

(1) credits described in subsection (a), and

(2) gross income in respect of such credits, shall not exceed the amounts so designated by the regulated investment company in a written notice mailed to its shareholders not later than 60 days after the close of its taxable year.

(d) MANNER OF MAKING ELECTION AND NOTIFYING SHAREHOLDERS.—The election provided in subsection (a) and the notice to shareholders required by subsection (c) shall be made in such manner as the Secretary may prescribe.

(e) DEFINITIONS AND SPECIAL RULES.—

(1) DEFINITIONS.—For purposes of this subsection—

(A) TAX CREDIT BOND.—The term "tax credit bond" means—

(i) a qualified tax credit bond (as defined in section 54A(d)),

(ii) a build America bond (as defined in section 54AA(d)), and

(iii) any bond for which a credit is allowable under subpart H of part IV of subchapter A of this chapter.

(B) APPLICABLE DATE.—The term "applicable date" means—

(i) in the case of a qualified tax credit bond or a bond described in subparagraph (A)(iii), any credit allowance date (as defined in section 54A(e)(1)), and

(ii) in the case of a build America bond (as defined in section 54AA(d)), any interest payment date (as defined in section 54AA(e)).

(2) STRIPPED TAX CREDIT BONDS.—If the ownership of a tax credit bond is separated from the credit with respect to such bond, subsection (a) shall be applied by reference to the instruments evidencing the entitlement to the credit rather than the tax credit bond.

(f) REGULATIONS, ETC.—The Secretary shall prescribe such regulations or other guidance as may be necessary or appropriate to carry out the purposes of this section, including methods for determining a shareholder's proportionate share of credits.

¶5275   Code Sec. 853A(b)

[CCH Explanation at ¶ 615. Committee Reports at ¶ 10,460.]

Amendments

• **2009, American Recovery and Reinvestment Tax Act of 2009 (P.L. 111-5)**

P.L. 111-5, §1541(a):

Amended part I of subchapter M of chapter 1 by inserting after Code Sec. 853 a new Code Sec. 853A. **Effective** for tax years ending after 2-17-2009.

[¶ 5280] CODE SEC. 904. LIMITATION ON CREDIT.

* * *

(i) COORDINATION WITH NONREFUNDABLE PERSONAL CREDITS.—In the case of any taxable year of an individual to which section 26(a)(2) does not apply, for purposes of subsection (a), the tax against which the credit is taken is such tax reduced by the sum of the credits allowable under subpart A of part IV of subchapter A of this chapter (other than sections 23, 24, *25A(i), 25B, 30, 30B, and 30D*).

* * *

[CCH Explanation at ¶ 330 and ¶ 350. Committee Reports at ¶ 10,040 and ¶ 10,200.]

Amendments

• **2009, American Recovery and Reinvestment Tax Act of 2009 (P.L. 111-5)**

P.L. 111-5, §1004(b)(5):

Amended Code Sec. 904(i) by inserting "25A(i)," after "24,". **Effective** for tax years beginning after 12-31-2008.

P.L. 111-5, §1142(b)(1)(E):

Amended Code Sec. 904(i) by striking "and 25B" and inserting "25B, 30, and 30D". **Effective** for vehicles acquired after 2-17-2009. For a transitional rule, see Act Sec. 1142(d) in the amendment notes for Code Sec. 30.

P.L. 111-5, §1144(b)(1)(E):

Amended Code Sec. 904(i), as amended by this Act, by inserting "30B," after "30". **Effective** for tax years beginning after 12-31-2008.

[¶ 5285] CODE SEC. 1016. ADJUSTMENTS TO BASIS.

(a) GENERAL RULE.—Proper adjustment in respect of the property shall in all cases be made—

* * *

(25) to the extent provided in *section 30(e)(1)*,

* * *

[CCH Explanation at ¶ 345 and ¶ 350. Committee Reports at ¶ 10,200.]

Amendments

• **2009, American Recovery and Reinvestment Tax Act of 2009 (P.L. 111-5)**

P.L. 111-5, §1141(b)(3):

Amended Code Sec. 1016(a)(25) by striking "section 30D(e)(4)" and inserting "section 30D(f)(1)". [The text "section 30D(e)(4)" does not exist. Therefore, this amendment cannot be made.—CCH] **Effective** for vehicles acquired after 12-31-2009.

P.L. 111-5, §1142(b)(6):

Amended Code Sec. 1016(a)(25) by striking "section 30(d)(1)" and inserting "section 30(e)(1)". **Effective** for vehicles acquired after 2-17-2009. For a transitional rule, see Act Sec. 1142(d) in the amendment notes for Code Sec. 30.

[¶ 5290] CODE SEC. 1202. PARTIAL EXCLUSION FOR GAIN FROM CERTAIN SMALL BUSINESS STOCK.

(a) EXCLUSION.—

* * *

(3) SPECIAL RULES FOR 2009 AND 2010.—*In the case of qualified small business stock acquired after the date of the enactment of this paragraph and before January 1, 2011—*

    (A) paragraph (1) shall be applied by substituting "75 percent" for "50 percent", and

    (B) paragraph (2) shall not apply.

* * *

[CCH Explanation at ¶ 210. Committee Reports at ¶ 10,310.]

Amendments

• 2009, American Recovery and Reinvestment Tax Act of 2009 (P.L. 111-5)

P.L. 111-5, § 1241(a):

Amended Code Sec. 1202(a) by adding at the end a new paragraph (3). Effective for stock acquired after 2-17-2009.

[¶ 5295] CODE SEC. 1374. TAX IMPOSED ON CERTAIN BUILT-IN GAINS.

* * *

(d) DEFINITIONS AND SPECIAL RULES.—For purposes of this section—

* * *

(7) RECOGNITION PERIOD.—

(A) IN GENERAL.—The term "recognition period" means the 10-year period beginning with the 1st day of the 1st taxable year for which the corporation was an S corporation.

(B) SPECIAL RULE FOR 2009 AND 2010.—In the case of any taxable year beginning in 2009 or 2010, no tax shall be imposed on the net recognized built-in gain of an S corporation if the 7th taxable year in the recognition period preceded such taxable year. The preceding sentence shall be applied separately with respect to any asset to which paragraph (8) applies.

(C) SPECIAL RULE FOR DISTRIBUTIONS TO SHAREHOLDERS.—For purposes of applying this section to any amount includible in income by reason of distributions to shareholders pursuant to section 593(e)—

(i) subparagraph (A) shall be applied without regard to the phrase "10-year", and

(ii) subparagraph (B) shall not apply.

* * *

[CCH Explanation at ¶ 420. Committee Reports at ¶ 10,320.]

Amendments

• 2009, American Recovery and Reinvestment Tax Act of 2009 (P.L. 111-5)

P.L. 111-5, § 1251(a):

Amended Code Sec. 1374(d)(7). Effective for tax years beginning after 12-31-2008. Prior to amendment, Code Sec. 1374(d)(7) read as follows:

(7) RECOGNITION PERIOD.—The term "recognition period" means the 10-year period beginning with the 1st day of the 1st taxable year for which the corporation was an S corporation. For purposes of applying this section to any amount includible in income by reason of section 593(e), the preceding sentence shall be applied without regard to the phrase "10-year".

[¶ 5300] CODE SEC. 1397E. CREDIT TO HOLDERS OF QUALIFIED ZONE ACADEMY BONDS.

* * *

(c) LIMITATION BASED ON AMOUNT OF TAX.—The credit allowed under subsection (a) for any taxable year shall not exceed the excess of—

(1) the sum of the regular tax liability (as defined in section 26(b)) plus the tax imposed by section 55, over

(2) the sum of the credits allowable under part IV of subchapter A (other than subpart C thereof, relating to refundable credits, and subparts H, I, and J thereof).

* * *

[CCH Explanation at ¶605. Committee Reports at ¶10,450.]

Amendments

• **2009, American Recovery and Reinvestment Tax Act of 2009 (P.L. 111-5)**

P.L. 111-5, §1531(c)(3):

Amended Code Sec. 1397E(c)(2) by striking "and I" and inserting ", I, and J". **Effective** for obligations issued after 2-17-2009.

[¶5305] CODE SEC. 1400C. FIRST-TIME HOMEBUYER CREDIT FOR DISTRICT OF COLUMBIA.

* * *

(d) CARRYFORWARD OF UNUSED CREDIT.—

* * *

(2) RULE FOR OTHER YEARS.—In the case of a taxable year to which section 26(a)(2) does not apply, if the credit allowable under subsection (a) exceeds the limitation imposed by section 26(a)(1) for such taxable year reduced by the sum of the credits allowable under subpart A of part IV of subchapter A (other than this section and sections 23, 24, *25A(i)*, 25B, *25D, 30, and 30B*, and 30D), such excess shall be carried to the succeeding taxable year and added to the credit allowable under subsection (a) for such taxable year.

[CCH Explanation at ¶330, ¶350 and ¶360. Committee Reports at ¶10,040 and ¶10,200.]

Amendments

• **2009, American Recovery and Reinvestment Tax Act of 2009 (P.L. 111-5)**

P.L. 111-5, §1004(b)(6):

Amended Code Sec. 1400C(d)(2) by inserting "25A(i)," after "24,". **Effective** for tax years beginning after 12-31-2008.

P.L. 111-5, §1142(b)(1)(F):

Amended Code Sec. 1400C(d)(2) by striking "and [sic] 25D" and inserting "25D, and 30". **Effective** for vehicles acquired after 2-17-2009. For a transitional rule, see Act Sec. 1142(d) in the amendment notes for Code Sec. 30.

P.L. 111-5, §1144(b)(1)(F):

Amended Code Sec. 1400C(d)(2), as amended by this Act, by striking "and 30" and inserting "30, and 30B". **Effective** for tax years beginning after 12-31-2008.

(e) SPECIAL RULES.—For purposes of this section—

* * *

(4) COORDINATION WITH NATIONAL FIRST-TIME HOMEBUYERS CREDIT.—No credit shall be allowed under this section to any taxpayer with respect to the purchase of a residence after December 31, 2008, and before December 1, 2009, if a credit under section 36 is allowable to such taxpayer (or the taxpayer's spouse) with respect to such purchase.

* * *

[CCH Explanation at ¶310. Committee Reports at ¶10,060.]

Amendments

• **2009, American Recovery and Reinvestment Tax Act of 2009 (P.L. 111-5)**

P.L. 111-5, §1006(d)(1):

Amended Code Sec. 1400C(e) by adding at the end new paragraph (4). **Effective** for residences purchased after 12-31-2008.

[¶5310] CODE SEC. 1400N. TAX BENEFITS FOR GULF OPPORTUNITY ZONE.

* * *

(d) SPECIAL ALLOWANCE FOR CERTAIN PROPERTY ACQUIRED ON OR AFTER AUGUST 28, 2005.—

* * *

(3) SPECIAL RULES.—For purposes of this subsection, rules similar to the rules of subparagraph (E) of section 168(k)(2) shall apply, except that such subparagraph shall be applied—

(A) by substituting "August 27, 2005" for "December 31, 2007" each place it appears therein,

(B) without regard to "and before *January 1, 2010*" in clause (i) thereof, and

(C) by substituting "qualified Gulf Opportunity Zone property" for "qualified property" in clause (iv) thereof.

* * *

[CCH Explanation at ¶ 415. Committee Reports at ¶ 10,220.]

Amendments

• **2009, American Recovery and Reinvestment Tax Act of 2009 (P.L. 111-5)**

P.L. 111-5, § 1201(a)(2)(E):

Amended Code Sec. 1400N(d)(3)(B) by striking "January 1, 2009" and inserting "January 1, 2010". **Effective** for property placed in service after 12-31-2008, in tax years ending after such date.

(l) CREDIT TO HOLDERS OF GULF TAX CREDIT BONDS.—

* * *

(3) LIMITATION BASED ON AMOUNT OF TAX.—The credit allowed under paragraph (1) for any taxable year shall not exceed the excess of—

(A) the sum of the regular tax liability (as defined in section 26(b)) plus the tax imposed by section 55, over

(B) the sum of the credits allowable under part IV of subchapter A (other than subparts C, *I, and J* and this subsection).

* * *

[CCH Explanation at ¶ 605. Committee Reports at ¶ 10,450.]

Amendments

• **2009, American Recovery and Reinvestment Tax Act of 2009 (P.L. 111-5)**

P.L. 111-5, § 1531(c)(3):

Amended Code Sec. 1400N(l)(3)(B) by striking "and I" and inserting ", I, and J". **Effective** for obligations issued after 2-17-2009.

[¶ 5315] CODE SEC. 1400U-1. ALLOCATION OF RECOVERY ZONE BONDS.

(a) ALLOCATIONS.—

(1) IN GENERAL.—

(A) GENERAL ALLOCATION.—The Secretary shall allocate the national recovery zone economic development bond limitation and the national recovery zone facility bond limitation among the States in the proportion that each such State's 2008 State employment decline bears to the aggregate of the 2008 State employment declines for all of the States.

(B) MINIMUM ALLOCATION.—The Secretary shall adjust the allocations under subparagraph (A) for any calendar year for each State to the extent necessary to ensure that no State receives less than 0.9 percent of the national recovery zone economic development bond limitation and 0.9 percent of the national recovery zone facility bond limitation.

(2) 2008 STATE EMPLOYMENT DECLINE.—For purposes of this subsection, the term "2008 State employment decline" means, with respect to any State, the excess (if any) of—

(A) the number of individuals employed in such State determined for December 2007, over

(B) the number of individuals employed in such State determined for December 2008.

(3) ALLOCATIONS BY STATES.—

(A) IN GENERAL.—Each State with respect to which an allocation is made under paragraph (1) shall reallocate such allocation among the counties and large municipalities in such State in the proportion to each such county's or municipality's 2008 employment decline bears to the aggregate of the 2008 employment declines for all the counties and municipalities in such State. A county or municipality may waive any portion of an allocation made under this subparagraph.

(B) LARGE MUNICIPALITIES.—For purposes of subparagraph (A), the term "large municipality" means a municipality with a population of more than 100,000.

(C) DETERMINATION OF LOCAL EMPLOYMENT DECLINES.—For purposes of this paragraph, the employment decline of any municipality or county shall be determined in the same manner as determining the State employment decline under paragraph (2), except that in the case of a municipality any portion of which is in a county, such portion shall be treated as part of such municipality and not part of such county.

(4) NATIONAL LIMITATIONS.—

(A) RECOVERY ZONE ECONOMIC DEVELOPMENT BONDS.—There is a national recovery zone economic development bond limitation of $10,000,000,000.

(B) RECOVERY ZONE FACILITY BONDS.—There is a national recovery zone facility bond limitation of $15,000,000,000.

(b) RECOVERY ZONE.—For purposes of this part, the term "recovery zone" means—

(1) any area designated by the issuer as having significant poverty, unemployment, rate of home foreclosures, or general distress,

(2) any area designated by the issuer as economically distressed by reason of the closure or realignment of a military installation pursuant to the Defense Base Closure and Realignment Act of 1990, and

(3) any area for which a designation as an empowerment zone or renewal community is in effect.

[CCH Explanation at ¶ 652 and ¶ 625. Committee Reports at ¶ 10,350.]

Amendments

• 2009, American Recovery and Reinvestment Tax Act of 2009 (P.L. 111-5)

P.L. 111-5, § 1401(a):

Amended subchapter Y of chapter 1 by adding at the end a new part III (Code Secs. 1400U-1—1400U-3). Effective for obligations issued after 2-17-2009.

[¶ 5316] CODE SEC. 1400U-2. RECOVERY ZONE ECONOMIC DEVELOPMENT BONDS.

(a) IN GENERAL.—In the case of a recovery zone economic development bond—

(1) such bond shall be treated as a qualified bond for purposes of section 6431, and

(2) subsection (b) of such section shall be applied by substituting "45 percent" for "35 percent".

(b) RECOVERY ZONE ECONOMIC DEVELOPMENT BOND.—

(1) IN GENERAL.—For purposes of this section, the term "recovery zone economic development bond" means any build America bond (as defined in section 54AA(d)) issued before January 1, 2011, as part of issue if—

(A) 100 percent of the excess of—

(i) the available project proceeds (as defined in section 54A) of such issue, over

(ii) the amounts in a reasonably required reserve (within the meaning of section 150(a)(3)) with respect to such issue, are to be used for one or more qualified economic development purposes, and

(B) the issuer designates such bond for purposes of this section.

(2) LIMITATION ON AMOUNT OF BONDS DESIGNATED.—The maximum aggregate face amount of bonds which may be designated by any issuer under paragraph (1) shall not exceed the amount of the recovery zone economic development bond limitation allocated to such issuer under section 1400U-1.

(c) QUALIFIED ECONOMIC DEVELOPMENT PURPOSE.—For purposes of this section, the term "qualified economic development purpose" means expenditures for purposes of promoting development or other economic activity in a recovery zone, including—

(1) capital expenditures paid or incurred with respect to property located in such zone,

(2) expenditures for public infrastructure and construction of public facilities, and

(3) expenditures for job training and educational programs.

[CCH Explanation at ¶ 625. Committee Reports at ¶ 10,350.]
Amendments
• **2009, American Recovery and Reinvestment Tax Act of 2009 (P.L. 111-5)**
P.L. 111-5, § 1401(a):
Amended subchapter Y of chapter 1 by adding at the end a new part III (Code Secs. 1400U-1—1400U-3). **Effective** for obligations issued after 2-17-2009.

[¶ 5317] CODE SEC. 1400U-3. RECOVERY ZONE FACILITY BONDS.

(a) IN GENERAL.—For purposes of part IV of subchapter B (relating to tax exemption requirements for State and local bonds), the term "exempt facility bond" includes any recovery zone facility bond.

(b) RECOVERY ZONE FACILITY BOND.—

(1) IN GENERAL.—For purposes of this section, the term "recovery zone facility bond" means any bond issued as part of an issue if—

(A) 95 percent or more of the net proceeds (as defined in section 150(a)(3)) of such issue are to be used for recovery zone property,

(B) such bond is issued before January 1, 2011, and

(C) the issuer designates such bond for purposes of this section.

(2) LIMITATION ON AMOUNT OF BONDS DESIGNATED.—The maximum aggregate face amount of bonds which may be designated by any issuer under paragraph (1) shall not exceed the amount of recovery zone facility bond limitation allocated to such issuer under section 1400U-1.

(c) RECOVERY ZONE PROPERTY.—For purposes of this section—

(1) IN GENERAL.—The term "recovery zone property" means any property to which section 168 applies (or would apply but for section 179) if—

(A) such property was constructed, reconstructed, renovated, or acquired by purchase (as defined in section 179(d)(2)) by the taxpayer after the date on which the designation of the recovery zone took effect,

(B) the original use of which in the recovery zone commences with the taxpayer, and

(C) substantially all of the use of which is in the recovery zone and is in the active conduct of a qualified business by the taxpayer in such zone.

(2) QUALIFIED BUSINESS.—The term "qualified business" means any trade or business except that—

(A) the rental to others of real property located in a recovery zone shall be treated as a qualified business only if the property is not residential rental property (as defined in section 168(e)(2)), and

(B) such term shall not include any trade or business consisting of the operation of any facility described in section 144(c)(6)(B).

(3) SPECIAL RULES FOR SUBSTANTIAL RENOVATIONS AND SALE-LEASEBACK.—Rules similar to the rules of subsections (a)(2) and (b) of section 1397D shall apply for purposes of this subsection.

(d) NONAPPLICATION OF CERTAIN RULES.—Sections 146 (relating to volume cap) and 147(d) (relating to acquisition of existing property not permitted) shall not apply to any recovery zone facility bond.

[CCH Explanation at ¶652. Committee Reports at ¶10,350.]

Amendments

• 2009, American Recovery and Reinvestment Tax Act of 2009 (P.L. 111-5)

P.L. 111-5, §1401(a):

Amended subchapter Y of chapter 1 by adding at the end a new part III (Code Secs. 1400U-1—1400U-3). **Effective** for obligations issued after 2-17-2009.

[¶5320] CODE SEC. 4980B. FAILURE TO SATISFY CONTINUATION COVERAGE REQUIREMENTS OF GROUP HEALTH PLANS.

* * *

(f) CONTINUATION COVERAGE REQUIREMENTS OF GROUP HEALTH PLANS.—

* * *

(2) CONTINUATION COVERAGE.—For purposes of paragraph (1), the term "continuation coverage" means coverage under the plan which meets the following requirements:

* * *

(B) PERIOD OF COVERAGE.—The coverage must extend for at least the period beginning on the date of the qualifying event and ending not earlier than the earliest of the following:

(i) MAXIMUM REQUIRED PERIOD.—

(I) GENERAL RULE FOR TERMINATIONS AND REDUCED HOURS.—In the case of a qualifying event described in paragraph (3)(B), except as provided in subclause (II), the date which is 18 months after the date of the qualifying event.

(II) SPECIAL RULE FOR MULTIPLE QUALIFYING EVENTS.—If a qualifying event (other than a qualifying event described in paragraph (3)(F)) occurs during the 18 months after the date of a qualifying event described in paragraph (3)(B), the date which is 36 months after the date of the qualifying event described in paragraph (3)(B).

(III) SPECIAL RULE FOR CERTAIN BANKRUPTCY PROCEEDINGS.—In the case of a qualifying event described in paragraph (3)(F) (relating to bankruptcy proceedings), the date of the death of the covered employee or qualified beneficiary (described in subsection (g)(1)(D)(iii)), or in the case of the surviving spouse or dependent children of the covered employee, 36 months after the date of the death of the covered employee.

(IV) GENERAL RULE FOR OTHER QUALIFYING EVENTS.—In the case of a qualifying event not described in paragraph (3)(B) or (3)(F), the date which is 36 months after the date of the qualifying event.

(V) SPECIAL RULE FOR PBGC RECIPIENTS.—*In the case of a qualifying event described in paragraph (3)(B) with respect to a covered employee who (as of such qualifying event) has a nonforfeitable right to a benefit any portion of which is to be paid by the Pension Benefit Guaranty Corporation under title IV of the Employee Retirement Income Security Act of 1974, notwithstanding subclause (I) or (II), the date of the death of the covered employee, or in the case of the surviving spouse or dependent children of the covered employee, 24 months after the date of the death of the covered employee. The preceding sentence shall not require any period of coverage to extend beyond December 31, 2010.*

(VI) SPECIAL RULE FOR TAA-ELIGIBLE INDIVIDUALS.—*In the case of a qualifying event described in paragraph (3)(B) with respect to a covered employee who is (as of the date that the period of coverage would, but for this subclause or subclause (VII), otherwise terminate under subclause (I) or (II)) a TAA-eligible individual (as defined in paragraph*

(5)(C)(iv)(II)), *the period of coverage shall not terminate by reason of subclause (I) or (II), as the case may be, before the later of the date specified in such subclause or the date on which such individual ceases to be such a TAA-eligible individual. The preceding sentence shall not require any period of coverage to extend beyond December 31, 2010.*

(VII) MEDICARE ENTITLEMENT FOLLOWED BY QUALIFYING EVENT.—In the case of a qualifying event described in paragraph (3)(B) that occurs less than 18 months after the date the covered employee became entitled to benefits under title XVIII of the Social Security Act, the period of coverage for qualified beneficiaries other than the covered employee shall not terminate under this clause before the close of the 36-month period beginning on the date the covered employee became so entitled.

(VIII) SPECIAL RULE FOR DISABILITY.—*In the case of a qualified beneficiary* who is determined, under title II or XVI of the Social Security Act, to have been disabled at any time during the first 60 days of continuation coverage under this section, any reference in subclause (I) or (II) to 18 months is deemed a reference to 29 months (with respect to all qualified beneficiaries), but only if the qualified beneficiary has provided notice of such determination under paragraph (6)(C) before the end of such 18 months.

* * *

[CCH Explanation at ¶ 725. Committee Reports at ¶ 10,480.]

Amendments

• **2009, TAA Health Coverage Improvement Act of 2009 (P.L. 111-5)**

P.L. 111-5, § 1899F(b)(1)-(2):

Amended Code Sec. 4980B(f)(2)(B)(i) by striking "In the case of a qualified beneficiary" and inserting "(VI) SPECIAL RULE FOR DISABILITY.—In the case of a qualified beneficiary", and by redesignating subclauses (V) and (VI), as added by Act Sec. 1899F(b)(1), as subclauses (VII) and (VIII), respectively, and by inserting after clause (IV) new subclauses (V)-(VI). **Effective** for periods of coverage which would (without regard to the amendments made by this section) end on or after 2-17-2009.

[¶ 5325] CODE SEC. 5701. RATE OF TAX.

(a) CIGARS.—On cigars, manufactured in or imported into the United States, there shall be imposed the following taxes:

(1) SMALL CIGARS.—On cigars, weighing not more than 3 pounds per thousand, *$50.33 per thousand,*

(2) LARGE CIGARS.—On cigars weighing more than 3 pounds per thousand, a tax equal to 52.75 *percent* of the price for which sold but not more than *40.26 cents per cigar.*

* * *

[CCH Explanation at ¶ 730. Committee Reports at ¶ 15,010.]

Amendments

• **2009, Children's Health Insurance Program Reauthorization Act of 2009 (P.L. 111-3)**

P.L. 111-3, § 701(a)(1)-(3):

Amended Code Sec. 5701(a) by striking "$1.828 cents per thousand ($1.594 cents per thousand on cigars removed during 2000 or 2001)" in paragraph (1) and inserting "$50.33 per thousand", by striking "20.719 percent (18.063 percent on cigars removed during 2000 or 2001)" in paragraph (2) and inserting "52.75 percent", and by striking "$48.75 per thousand ($42.50 per thousand on cigars removed during 2000 or 2001)" in paragraph (2) and inserting "40.26 cents per cigar". **Effective** for articles removed (as defined in Code Sec. 5702(j)) after 3-31-2009.

P.L. 111-3, § 701(h), provides:

(h) FLOOR STOCKS TAXES.—

(1) IMPOSITION OF TAX.—On tobacco products (other than cigars described in section 5701(a)(2) of the Internal Revenue Code of 1986) and cigarette papers and tubes manufactured in or imported into the United States which are removed before April 1, 2009, and held on such date for sale by any person, there is hereby imposed a tax in an amount equal to the excess of—

(A) the tax which would be imposed under section 5701 of such Code on the article if the article had been removed on such date, over

(B) the prior tax (if any) imposed under section 5701 of such Code on such article.

(2) CREDIT AGAINST TAX.—Each person shall be allowed as a credit against the taxes imposed by paragraph (1) an amount equal to $500. Such credit shall not exceed the amount of taxes imposed by paragraph (1) on April 1, 2009, for which such person is liable.

(3) LIABILITY FOR TAX AND METHOD OF PAYMENT.—

(A) LIABILITY FOR TAX.—A person holding tobacco products, cigarette papers, or cigarette tubes on April 1, 2009, to which any tax imposed by paragraph (1) applies shall be liable for such tax.

(B) METHOD OF PAYMENT.—The tax imposed by paragraph (1) shall be paid in such manner as the Secretary shall prescribe by regulations.

(C) TIME FOR PAYMENT.—The tax imposed by paragraph (1) shall be paid on or before August 1, 2009.

(4) ARTICLES IN FOREIGN TRADE ZONES.—Notwithstanding the Act of June 18, 1934 (commonly known as the Foreign Trade Zone Act, 48 Stat. 998, 19 U.S.C. 81a et seq.) or any other provision of law, any article which is located in a foreign trade zone on April 1, 2009, shall be subject to the tax imposed by paragraph (1) if—

(A) internal revenue taxes have been determined, or customs duties liquidated, with respect to such article before such date pursuant to a request made under the 1st proviso of section 3(a) of such Act, or

(B) such article is held on such date under the supervision of an officer of the United States Customs and Border Protection of the Department of Homeland Security pursuant to the 2d proviso of such section 3(a).

(5) DEFINITIONS.—For purposes of this subsection—

(A) IN GENERAL.—Any term used in this subsection which is also used in section 5702 of the Internal Revenue Code of 1986 shall have the same meaning as such term has in such section.

(B) SECRETARY.—The term "Secretary" means the Secretary of the Treasury or the Secretary's delegate.

(6) CONTROLLED GROUPS.—Rules similar to the rules of section 5061(e)(3) of such Code shall apply for purposes of this subsection.

(7) OTHER LAWS APPLICABLE.—All provisions of law, including penalties, applicable with respect to the taxes imposed by section 5701 of such Code shall, insofar as applicable and not inconsistent with the provisions of this subsection, apply to the floor stocks taxes imposed by paragraph (1), to the same extent as if such taxes were imposed by such section 5701. The Secretary may treat any person who bore the ultimate burden of the tax imposed by paragraph (1) as the person to whom a credit or refund under such provisions may be allowed or made.

(b) CIGARETTES.—On cigarettes, manufactured in or imported into the United States, there shall be imposed the following taxes:

(1) SMALL CIGARETTES.—On cigarettes, weighing not more than 3 pounds per thousand, *$50.33 per thousand;*

(2) LARGE CIGARETTES.—On cigarettes, weighing more than 3 pounds per thousand, *$105.69 per thousand;* except that, if more than 6½ inches in length, they shall be taxable at the rate prescribed for cigarettes weighing not more than 3 pounds per thousand, counting each 2¾ inches, or fraction thereof, of the length of each as one cigarette.

[CCH Explanation at ¶730. Committee Reports at ¶15,010.]

Amendments

• 2009, Children's Health Insurance Program Reauthorization Act of 2009 (P.L. 111-3)

P.L. 111-3, §701(b)(1)-(2):

Amended Code Sec. 5701(b) by striking "$19.50 per thousand ($17 per thousand on cigarettes removed during 2000 or 2001)" in paragraph (1) and inserting "$50.33 per thousand", and by striking "$40.95 per thousand ($35.70 per thousand on cigarettes removed during 2000 or 2001)" in paragraph (2) and inserting "$105.69 per thousand". **Effective** for articles removed (as defined in Code Sec. 5702(j)) after 3-31-2009.

(c) CIGARETTE PAPERS.—On cigarette papers, manufactured in or imported into the United States, there shall be imposed a tax of *3.15 cents* for each 50 papers or fractional part thereof; except that, if cigarette papers measure more than 6½ inches in length, they shall be taxable at the rate prescribed, counting each 2¾ inches, or fraction thereof, of the length of each as one cigarette paper.

[CCH Explanation at ¶730. Committee Reports at ¶15,010.]

Amendments

• 2009, Children's Health Insurance Program Reauthorization Act of 2009 (P.L. 111-3)

P.L. 111-3, §701(c):

Amended Code Sec. 5701(c) by striking "1.22 cents (1.06 cents on cigarette papers removed during 2000 or 2001)" and inserting "3.15 cents". **Effective** for articles removed (as defined in Code Sec. 5702(j)) after 3-31-2009.

(d) CIGARETTE TUBES.—On cigarette tubes, manufactured in or imported into the United States, there shall be imposed a tax of *6.30 cents* for each 50 tubes or fractional part thereof, except that if cigarette tubes measure more than 6½ inches in length, they shall be taxable at the rate prescribed, counting each 2¾ inches, or fraction thereof, of the length of each as one cigarette tube.

[CCH Explanation at ¶730. Committee Reports at ¶15,010.]

Amendments

• 2009, Children's Health Insurance Program Reauthorization Act of 2009 (P.L. 111-3)

P.L. 111-3, §701(d):

Amended Code Sec. 5701(d) by striking "2.44 cents (2.13 cents on cigarette tubes removed during 2000 or 2001)" and inserting "6.30 cents". **Effective** for articles removed (as defined in Code Sec. 5702(j)) after 3-31-2009.

(e) SMOKELESS TOBACCO.—On smokeless tobacco, manufactured in or imported into the United States, there shall be imposed the following taxes:

(1) SNUFF.—On snuff, *$1.51* per pound and a proportionate tax at the like rate on all fractional parts of a pound.

(2) CHEWING TOBACCO.—On chewing tobacco, *50.33 cents* per pound and a proportionate tax at the like rate on all fractional parts of a pound.

[CCH Explanation at ¶730. Committee Reports at ¶15,010.]

Amendments

• 2009, Children's Health Insurance Program Reauthorization Act of 2009 (P.L. 111-3)

P.L. 111-3, §701(e)(1)-(2):

Amended Code Sec. 5701(e) by striking "58.5 cents (51 cents on snuff removed during 2000 or 2001)" in paragraph (1) and inserting "$1.51", and by striking "19.5 cents (17 cents on chewing tobacco removed during 2000 or 2001)" in paragraph (2) and inserting "50.33 cents". **Effective** for articles removed (as defined in Code Sec. 5702(j)) after 3-31-2009.

(f) PIPE TOBACCO.—On pipe tobacco, manufactured in or imported into the United States, there shall be imposed a tax of *$2.8311 cents* per pound (and a proportionate tax at the like rate on all fractional parts of a pound).

[CCH Explanation at ¶730. Committee Reports at ¶15,010.]

Amendments

• 2009, Children's Health Insurance Program Reauthorization Act of 2009 (P.L. 111-3)

P.L. 111-3, §701(f):

Amended Code Sec. 5701(f) by striking "$1.0969 cents (95.67 cents on pipe tobacco removed during 2000 or 2001)" and inserting "$2.8311 cents". **Effective** for articles removed (as defined in Code Sec. 5702(j)) after 3-31-2009.

(g) ROLL-YOUR-OWN TOBACCO.—On roll-your-own tobacco, manufactured in or imported into the United States, there shall be imposed a tax of *$24.78* per pound (and a proportionate tax at the like rate on all fractional parts of a pound).

* * *

[CCH Explanation at ¶730. Committee Reports at ¶15,010.]

Amendments

• 2009, Children's Health Insurance Program Reauthorization Act of 2009 (P.L. 111-3)

P.L. 111-3, §701(g):

Amended Code Sec. 5701(g) by striking "$1.0969 cents (95.67 cents on roll-your-own tobacco removed during 2000 or 2001)" and inserting "$24.78". **Effective** for articles removed (as defined in Code Sec. 5702(j)) after 3-31-2009.

[¶5330] CODE SEC. 5702. DEFINITIONS.

When used in this chapter—

* * *

(h) EXPORT WAREHOUSE.—"Export warehouse" means a bonded internal revenue warehouse for the storage of *tobacco products or cigarette papers or tubes or any processed tobacco*, upon which the internal revenue tax has not been paid, for subsequent shipment to a foreign country, Puerto Rico, the Virgin Islands, or a possession of the United States, or for consumption beyond the jurisdiction of the internal revenue laws of the United States.

* * *

[CCH Explanation at ¶730. Committee Reports at ¶15,020.]

Amendments
- 2009, Children's Health Insurance Program Reauthorization Act of 2009 (P.L. 111-3)

P.L. 111-3, §702(a)(5)(A):

Amended Code Sec. 5702(h) by striking "tobacco products and cigarette papers and tubes" and inserting "tobacco products or cigarette papers or tubes or any processed tobacco". Effective 4-1-2009.

(j) REMOVAL OR REMOVE.—"Removal" or "remove" means the removal of tobacco products or cigarette papers or tubes, *or any processed tobacco*, from the factory or from internal revenue bond under section 5704, as the Secretary shall by regulation prescribe, or release from customs custody, and shall also include the smuggling or other unlawful importation of such articles into the United States.

[CCH Explanation at ¶730. Committee Reports at ¶15,020.]

Amendments
- 2009, Children's Health Insurance Program Reauthorization Act of 2009 (P.L. 111-3)

P.L. 111-3, §702(a)(5)(B):

Amended Code Sec. 5702(j) by inserting ", or any processed tobacco," after "tobacco products or cigarette papers or tubes". Effective 4-1-2009.

(k) IMPORTER.—"Importer" means any person in the United States to whom nontaxpaid tobacco products or cigarette papers or tubes, *or any processed tobacco*, manufactured in a foreign country, Puerto Rico, the Virgin Islands, or a possession of the United States are shipped or consigned; any person who removes cigars or cigarettes for sale or consumption in the United States from a customs bonded manufacturing warehouse; and any person who smuggles or otherwise unlawfully brings tobacco products or cigarette papers or tubes, *or any processed tobacco*, into the United States.

* * *

[CCH Explanation at ¶730. Committee Reports at ¶15,020.]

Amendments
- 2009, Children's Health Insurance Program Reauthorization Act of 2009 (P.L. 111-3)

P.L. 111-3, §702(a)(5)(B):

Amended Code Sec. 5702(k) by inserting ", or any processed tobacco," after "tobacco products or cigarette papers or tubes" [each place it appears]. Effective 4-1-2009.

(o) ROLL-YOUR-OWN TOBACCO.—The term "roll-your-own tobacco" means any tobacco which, because of its appearance, type, packaging, or labeling, is suitable for use and likely to be offered to, or purchased by, consumers as tobacco for making cigarettes *or cigars, or for use as wrappers thereof*.

[CCH Explanation at ¶730. Committee Reports at ¶15,050.]

Amendments
- 2009, Children's Health Insurance Program Reauthorization Act of 2009 (P.L. 111-3)

P.L. 111-3, §702(d)(1):

Amended Code Sec. 5702(o) by inserting "or cigars, or for use as wrappers thereof" before the period at the end. Effective for articles removed (as defined in Code Sec. 5702(j)) after 3-31-2009.

(p) MANUFACTURER OF PROCESSED TOBACCO.—

(1) IN GENERAL.—The term *"manufacturer of processed tobacco"* means any person who processes any tobacco other than tobacco products.

(2) PROCESSED TOBACCO.—The processing of tobacco shall not include the farming or growing of tobacco or the handling of tobacco solely for sale, shipment, or delivery to a manufacturer of tobacco products or processed tobacco.

[CCH Explanation at ¶730. Committee Reports at ¶15,020.]

Amendments

- 2009, Children's Health Insurance Program Reauthorization Act of 2009 (P.L. 111-3)

P.L. 111-3, §702(a)(4):

Amended Code Sec. 5702 by adding at the end a new subsection (p). Effective 4-1-2009.

[¶5335] CODE SEC. 5703. LIABILITY FOR TAX AND METHOD OF PAYMENT.

* * *

(b) METHOD OF PAYMENT OF TAX.—

* * *

(2) TIME FOR PAYMENT OF TAXES.—

* * *

(F) SPECIAL RULE FOR UNLAWFULLY MANUFACTURED TOBACCO PRODUCTS.—*In the case of any tobacco products, cigarette paper, or cigarette tubes manufactured in the United States at any place other than the premises of a manufacturer of tobacco products, cigarette paper, or cigarette tubes that has filed the bond and obtained the permit required under this chapter, tax shall be due and payable immediately upon manufacture.*

* * *

[CCH Explanation at ¶730. Committee Reports at ¶15,060.]

Amendments

- 2009, Children's Health Insurance Program Reauthorization Act of 2009 (P.L. 111-3)

P.L. 111-3, §702(e)(1):

Amended Code Sec. 5703(b)(2) by adding at the end a new subparagraph (F). Effective 2-4-2009.

[¶5340] CODE SEC. 5712. APPLICATION FOR PERMIT.

Every person, before commencing business as a manufacturer or importer of tobacco products *or processed tobacco* or as an export warehouse proprietor, and at such other time as the Secretary shall by regulation prescribe, shall make application for the permit provided for in section 5713. The application shall be in such form as the Secretary shall prescribe and shall set forth, truthfully and accurately, the information called for on the form. Such application may be rejected and the permit denied if the Secretary, after notice and opportunity for hearing, finds that—

(1) the premises on which it is proposed to conduct the business are not adequate to protect the revenue;

(2) the activity proposed to be carried out at such premises does not meet such minimum capacity or activity requirements as the Secretary may prescribe, or

(3) *such person (including, in the case of a corporation, any officer, director, or principal stockholder and, in the case of a partnership, a partner)*—

(A) *is, by reason of his business experience, financial standing, or trade connections or by reason of previous or current legal proceedings involving a felony violation of any other provision of Federal criminal law relating to tobacco products, processed tobacco, cigarette paper, or cigarette tubes, not likely to maintain operations in compliance with this chapter,*

(B) *has been convicted of a felony violation of any provision of Federal or State criminal law relating to tobacco products, processed tobacco, cigarette paper, or cigarette tubes, or*

(C) has failed to disclose any material information required or made any material false statement in the application therefor.

[CCH Explanation at ¶ 730. Committee Reports at ¶ 15,020 and ¶ 15,030.]

Amendments

• 2009, Children's Health Insurance Program Reauthorization Act of 2009 (P.L. 111-3)

P.L. 111-3, § 702(a)(1)(A):

Amended Code Sec. 5712 by inserting "or processed tobacco" after "tobacco products". Effective 4-1-2009. For a transitional rule, see Act Sec. 702(g), below.

P.L. 111-3, § 702(b)(1):

Amended Code Sec. 5712(3). Effective 2-4-2009. For a transitional rule, see Act Sec. 702(g), below. Prior to amendment, Code Sec. 5712(3) read as follows:

(3) such person (including, in the case of a corporation, any officer, director, or principal stockholder and, in the case of a partnership, a partner) is, by reason of his business experience, financial standing, or trade connections, not likely to maintain operations in compliance with this chapter, or has failed to disclose any material information required or made any material false statement in the application therefor.

P.L. 111-3, § 702(g), provides:

(g) TRANSITIONAL RULE.—Any person who—

(1) on April 1, 2009 is engaged in business as a manufacturer of processed tobacco or as an importer of processed tobacco, and

(2) before the end of the 90-day period beginning on such date, submits an application under subchapter B of chapter 52 of such Code to engage in such business, may, notwithstanding such subchapter B, continue to engage in such business pending final action on such application. Pending such final action, all provisions of such chapter 52 shall apply to such applicant in the same manner and to the same extent as if such applicant were a holder of a permit under such chapter 52 to engage in such business.

[¶ 5345] CODE SEC. 5713. PERMIT.

(a) ISSUANCE.—A person shall not engage in business as a manufacturer or importer of tobacco products *or processed tobacco* or as an export warehouse proprietor without a permit to engage in such business. Such permit, conditioned upon compliance with this chapter and regulations issued thereunder, shall be issued in such form and in such manner as the Secretary shall by regulation prescribe, to every person properly qualified under sections 5711 and 5712. A new permit may be required at such other time as the Secretary shall by regulation prescribe.

[CCH Explanation at ¶ 730. Committee Reports at ¶ 15,020.]

Amendments

• 2009, Children's Health Insurance Program Reauthorization Act of 2009 (P.L. 111-3)

P.L. 111-3, § 702(a)(1)(B):

Amended Code Sec. 5713(a) by inserting "or processed tobacco" after "tobacco products". Effective 4-1-2009. For a transitional rule, see Act Sec. 702(g), below.

P.L. 111-3, § 702(g), provides:

(g) TRANSITIONAL RULE.—Any person who—

(1) on April 1, 2009 is engaged in business as a manufacturer of processed tobacco or as an importer of processed tobacco, and

(2) before the end of the 90-day period beginning on such date, submits an application under subchapter B of chapter 52 of such Code to engage in such business, may, notwithstanding such subchapter B, continue to engage in such business pending final action on such application. Pending such final action, all provisions of such chapter 52 shall apply to such applicant in the same manner and to the same extent as if such applicant were a holder of a permit under such chapter 52 to engage in such business.

(b) SUSPENSION OR REVOCATION.—

(1) SHOW CAUSE HEARING.—If the Secretary has reason to believe that any person holding a permit—

(A) has not in good faith complied with this chapter, or with any other provision of this title involving intent to defraud,

(B) has violated the conditions of such permit,

(C) has failed to disclose any material information required or made any material false statement in the application for such permit,

(D) has failed to maintain his premises in such manner as to protect the revenue,

(E) is, by reason of previous or current legal proceedings involving a felony violation of any other provision of Federal criminal law relating to tobacco products, processed tobacco, cigarette paper, or cigarette tubes, not likely to maintain operations in compliance with this chapter, or

(F) has been convicted of a felony violation of any provision of Federal or State criminal law relating to tobacco products, processed tobacco, cigarette paper, or cigarette tubes, *the Secretary shall issue an order, stating the facts charged, citing such person to show cause why his permit should not be suspended or revoked.*

(2) ACTION FOLLOWING HEARING.—If, after hearing, the Secretary finds that such person has not shown cause why his permit should not be suspended or revoked, such permit shall be suspended for such period as the Secretary deems proper or shall be revoked.

[CCH Explanation at ¶730. Committee Reports at ¶15,030.]

Amendments

- 2009, Children's Health Insurance Program Reauthorization Act of 2009 (P.L. 111-3)

P.L. 111-3, §702(b)(2):

Amended Code Sec. 5713(b). Effective 2-4-2009. For a transitional rule, see Act Sec. 702(g), below. Prior to amendment, Code Sec. 5713(b) read as follows:

(b) REVOCATION.—If the Secretary has reason to believe that any person holding a permit has not in good faith complied with this chapter, or with any other provision of this title involving intent to defraud, or has violated the conditions of such permit, or has failed to disclose any material information required or made any material false statement in the application for such permit, or has failed to maintain his premises in such manner as to protect the revenue, the Secretary shall issue an order, stating the facts charged, citing such person to show cause why his permit should not be suspended or revoked. If, after hearing, the Secretary finds that such person has not in good faith complied with this chapter or with any other provision of this title involving intent to defraud, has violated the conditions of such permit, has failed to disclose any material information required or made any material false statement in the application therefor, or has failed to maintain his premises in such manner as to protect the revenue, such permit shall be suspended for such period as the Secretary deems proper or shall be revoked.

P.L. 111-3, §702(g), provides:

(g) TRANSITIONAL RULE.—Any person who—

(1) on April 1, 2009 is engaged in business as a manufacturer of processed tobacco or as an importer of processed tobacco, and

(2) before the end of the 90-day period beginning on such date, submits an application under subchapter B of chapter 52 of such Code to engage in such business, may, notwithstanding such subchapter B, continue to engage in such business pending final action on such application. Pending such final action, all provisions of such chapter 52 shall apply to such applicant in the same manner and to the same extent as if such applicant were a holder of a permit under such chapter 52 to engage in such business.

[¶5350] CODE SEC. 5721. INVENTORIES.

Every manufacturer or importer of tobacco products, *processed tobacco*, or cigarette papers and tubes, and every export warehouse proprietor, shall make a true and accurate inventory at the time of commencing business, at the time of concluding business, and at such other times, in such manner and form, and to include such items, as the Secretary shall by regulation prescribe. Such inventories shall be subject to verification by any revenue officer.

[CCH Explanation at ¶730. Committee Reports at ¶15,020.]

Amendments

- 2009, Children's Health Insurance Program Reauthorization Act of 2009 (P.L. 111-3)

P.L. 111-3, §702(a)(2)(A):

Amended Code Sec. 5721 by inserting ", processed tobacco," after "tobacco products". Effective 4-1-2009.

[¶5355] CODE SEC. 5722. REPORTS.

Every manufacturer or importer of tobacco products, *processed tobacco*, or cigarette papers and tubes, and every export warehouse proprietor, shall make reports containing such information, in such form, at such times, and for such periods as the Secretary shall by regulation prescribe.

[CCH Explanation at ¶730. Committee Reports at ¶15,020.]

Amendments

- 2009, Children's Health Insurance Program Reauthorization Act of 2009 (P.L. 111-3)

P.L. 111-3, §702(a)(2)(B):

Amended Code Sec. 5722 by inserting ", processed tobacco," after "tobacco products". Effective 4-1-2009.

[¶5360] CODE SEC. 5723. PACKAGES, MARKS, LABELS, AND NOTICES.

(a) PACKAGES.—All tobacco products, *processed tobacco*, and cigarette papers and tubes shall, before removal, be put up in such packages as the Secretary shall by regulation prescribe.

[CCH Explanation at ¶730. Committee Reports at ¶15,020.]

Amendments

- **2009, Children's Health Insurance Program Reauthorization Act of 2009 (P.L. 111-3)**

P.L. 111-3, §702(a)(2)(C):

Amended Code Sec. 5723 by inserting ", processed tobacco," after "tobacco products" each place it appears. Effective 4-1-2009.

(b) MARKS, LABELS, AND NOTICES.—Every package of tobacco products, *processed tobacco*, or cigarette papers or tubes shall, before removal, bear the marks, labels, and notices, if any, that the Secretary by regulation prescribes.

[CCH Explanation at ¶730. Committee Reports at ¶15,020.]

Amendments

- **2009, Children's Health Insurance Program Reauthorization Act of 2009 (P.L. 111-3)**

P.L. 111-3, §702(a)(2)(C):

Amended Code Sec. 5723 by inserting ", processed tobacco," after "tobacco products" each place it appears. Effective 4-1-2009.

(c) LOTTERY FEATURES.—No certificate, coupon, or other device purporting to be or to represent a ticket, chance, share, or an interest in, or dependent on, the event of a lottery shall be contained in, attached to, or stamped, marked, written, or printed on any package of tobacco products, *processed tobacco*, or cigarette papers or tubes.

[CCH Explanation at ¶730. Committee Reports at ¶15,020.]

Amendments

- **2009, Children's Health Insurance Program Reauthorization Act of 2009 (P.L. 111-3)**

P.L. 111-3, §702(a)(2)(C):

Amended Code Sec. 5723 by inserting ", processed tobacco," after "tobacco products" each place it appears. Effective 4-1-2009.

(d) INDECENT OR IMMORAL MATERIAL PROHIBITED.—No indecent or immoral picture, print, or representation shall be contained in, attached to, or stamped, marked, written, or printed on any package of tobacco products, *processed tobacco*, or cigarette papers or tubes.

[CCH Explanation at ¶730. Committee Reports at ¶15,020.]

Amendments

- **2009, Children's Health Insurance Program Reauthorization Act of 2009 (P.L. 111-3)**

P.L. 111-3, §702(a)(2)(C):

Amended Code Sec. 5723 by inserting ", processed tobacco," after "tobacco products" each place it appears. Effective 4-1-2009.

(e) EXCEPTIONS.—Tobacco products furnished by manufacturers of such products for use or consumption by their employees, or for experimental purposes, and tobacco products, *processed tobacco*, and cigarette papers and tubes transferred to the bonded premises of another manufacturer or export warehouse proprietor or released in bond from customs custody for delivery to a manufacturer of tobacco products, *processed tobacco*, or cigarette papers and tubes, may be exempted from subsections (a) and (b) in accordance with such regulations as the Secretary shall prescribe.

[CCH Explanation at ¶730. Committee Reports at ¶15,020.]

Amendments

• 2009, Children's Health Insurance Program Reauthorization Act of 2009 (P.L. 111-3)

P.L. 111-3, § 702(a)(2)(C):

Amended Code Sec. 5723 by inserting ", processed tobacco," after "tobacco products" each place it appears. Effective 4-1-2009.

[¶5365] CODE SEC. 5741. RECORDS TO BE MAINTAINED.

Every manufacturer of tobacco products, *processed tobacco*, or cigarette papers and tubes, every importer, and every export warehouse proprietor shall keep such records in such manner as the Secretary shall by regulation prescribe. The records required under this section shall be available for inspection by any internal revenue officer during business hours.

[CCH Explanation at ¶730. Committee Reports at ¶15,020.]

Amendments

• 2009, Children's Health Insurance Program Reauthorization Act of 2009 (P.L. 111-3)

P.L. 111-3, § 702(a)(3):

Amended Code Sec. 5741 by inserting ", processed tobacco," after "tobacco products". Effective 4-1-2009.

[¶5370] CODE SEC. 6103. CONFIDENTIALITY AND DISCLOSURE OF RETURNS AND RETURN INFORMATION.

* * *

(o) DISCLOSURE OF RETURNS AND RETURN INFORMATION WITH RESPECT TO CERTAIN TAXES.—

(1) TAXES IMPOSED BY SUBTITLE E.—

(A) IN GENERAL.—Returns and return information with respect to taxes imposed by subtitle E (relating to taxes on alcohol, tobacco, and firearms) shall be open to inspection by or disclosure to officers and employees of a Federal agency whose official duties require such inspection or disclosure.

(B) USE IN CERTAIN PROCEEDINGS.—*Returns and return information disclosed to a Federal agency under subparagraph (A) may be used in an action or proceeding (or in preparation for such action or proceeding) brought under section 625 of the American Jobs Creation Act of 2004 for the collection of any unpaid assessment or penalty arising under such Act.*

* * *

[CCH Explanation at ¶730. Committee Reports at ¶15,070.]

Amendments

• 2009, Children's Health Insurance Program Reauthorization Act of 2009 (P.L. 111-3)

P.L. 111-3, § 702(f)(1):

Amended Code Sec. 6103(o)(1) by designating the text as subparagraph (A), moving such text 2 ems to the right, striking "Returns" and inserting "(A) IN GENERAL.—Returns", and by inserting after subparagraph (A) (as so redesignated) a new subparagraph (B). Effective on or after 2-4-2009.

(p) PROCEDURE AND RECORDKEEPING.—

* * *

(4) SAFEGUARDS.—Any Federal agency described in subsection (h)(2), (h)(5), (i)(1), (2), (3), (5), or (7), (j)(1), (2), or (5) (k)(8) or (10), (l)(1), (2), (3), (5), (10), (11), (13), (14), or (17) or *(o)(1)(A)*, the Government Accountability Office, the Congressional Budget Office, or any agency, body, or commission described in subsection (d), (i)(3)(B)(i) or 7(A)(ii), or (l)(6), (7), (8), (9), (12), (15), or (16), any appropriate State officer (as defined in section 6104(c)), or any other person described in

subsection (l)(10), (16), (18), (19), or (20) shall, as a condition for receiving returns or return information—

(A) establish and maintain, to the satisfaction of the Secretary, a permanent system of standardized records with respect to any request, the reason for such request, and the date of such request made by or of it and any disclosure of return or return information made by or to it;

(B) establish and maintain, to the satisfaction of the Secretary, a secure area or place in which such returns or return information shall be stored;

(C) restrict, to the satisfaction of the Secretary, access to the returns or return information only to persons whose duties or responsibilities require access and to whom disclosure may be made under the provisions of this title;

(D) provide such other safeguards which the Secretary determines (and which he prescribes in regulations) to be necessary or appropriate to protect the confidentiality of the returns or return information;

(E) furnish a report to the Secretary, at such time and containing such information as the Secretary may prescribe, which describes the procedures established and utilized by such agency, body, or commission, the Government Accountability Office, or the Congressional Budget Office for ensuring the confidentiality of returns and return information required by this paragraph; and

(F) upon completion of use of such returns or return information—

(i) in the case of an agency, body, or commission described in subsection (d), (i)(3)(B)(i), or (l)(6), (7), (8), (9), or (16), any appropriate State officer (as defined in section 6104(c)), or any other person described in subsection (l)(10), (16), (18), (19), or (20) return to the Secretary such returns or return information (along with any copies made there-from) or make such returns or return information undisclosable in any manner and furnish a written report to the Secretary describing such manner,

(ii) in the case of an agency described in subsections (h)(2), (h)(5), (i)(1), (2), (3), (5) or (7), (j)(1), (2), or (5), or (k)(8) or (10), (l)(1), (2), (3), (5), (10), (11), (12), (13), (14), (15), or (17) or *(o)(1)(A)*, the Government Accountability Office, or the Congressional Budget Office, either—

(I) return to the Secretary such returns or return information (along with any copies made therefrom),

(II) otherwise make such returns or return information undisclosable, or

(III) to the extent not so returned or made undisclosable, ensure that the conditions of subparagraphs (A), (B), (C), (D), and (E) of this paragraph continue to be met with respect to such returns or return information, and

(iii) in the case of the Department of Health and Human Services for purposes of subsection (m)(6), destroy all such return information upon completion of its use in providing the notification for which the information was obtained, so as to make such information undisclosable;

except that the conditions of subparagraphs (A), (B), (C), (D), and (E) shall cease to apply with respect to any return or return information if, and to the extent that, such return or return information is disclosed in the course of any judicial or administrative proceeding and made a part of the public record thereof. If the Secretary determines that any such agency, body, or commission, including an agency, an appropriate State officer (as defined in section 6104(c)), or any other person described in subsection (l)(10), (16), (18), (19), or (20), or the Government Accountability Office or the Congressional Budget Office, has failed to, or does not, meet the requirements of this paragraph, he may, after any proceedings for review established under paragraph (7), take such actions as are necessary to ensure such requirements are met, including refusing to disclose returns or return information to such agency, body, or commission, including an agency, an appropriate State officer (as defined in section 6104(c)), or any other person described in subsection (l)(10), (16), (18), (19), or (20), or the Government Accountability Office or the Congressional Budget Office, until he determines that such requirements have been or will be met. In the case of any agency which receives any mailing address under paragraph (2), (4), (6), or (7) of subsection (m) and which discloses any such mailing address to any agent or which receives any information under paragraph (6)(A), (10), (12)(B), or (16) of subsection (l) and which discloses any such information to any agent, or any person including an agent described in subsection (l)(10) or (16), this paragraph shall apply to such agency and each such agent or other person (except that, in the case of an agent, or any person including an agent described in subsection (l)(10) or (16), any report to the Secretary or other action with respect to the Secretary shall be made or taken through such agency). For purposes of applying this paragraph in any case to which subsection (m)(6) applies, the term "return information" includes related blood donor records (as defined in section 1141(h)(2) of the Social Security Act).

* * *

[CCH Explanation at ¶730. Committee Reports at ¶15,070.]

Amendments

• **2009, Children's Health Insurance Program Reauthorization Act of 2009 (P.L. 111-3)**

P.L. 111-3, §702(f)(2):

Amended Code Sec. 6103(p)(4) by striking "(o)(1)" both places it appears and inserting "(o)(1)(A)". **Effective** on or after 2-4-2009.

[¶5375] CODE SEC. 6211. DEFINITION OF A DEFICIENCY.

* * *

(b) RULES FOR APPLICATION OF SUBSECTION (a).—For purposes of this section—

* * *

(4) For purposes of subsection (a)—

(A) any excess of the sum of the credits allowable under sections 24(d), *25A by reason of subsection (i)(6) thereof,* 32, 34, 35, 36, *36A,* 53(e), *168(k)(4),* 6428, *and 6431* over the tax imposed by subtitle A (determined without regard to such credits), and

(B) any excess of the sum of such credits as shown by the taxpayer on his return over the amount shown as the tax by the taxpayer on such return (determined without regard to such credits),

shall be taken into account as negative amounts of tax.

* * *

[CCH Explanation at ¶305, ¶330 and ¶505. Committee Reports at ¶10,010, ¶10,040, ¶10,220 and ¶10,450.]

Amendments

• **2009, American Recovery and Reinvestment Tax Act of 2009 (P.L. 111-5)**

P.L. 111-5, §1001(e)(1):

Amended Code Sec. 6211(b)(4)(A) by inserting "36A," after "36,". **Effective** for tax years beginning after 12-31-2008.

P.L. 111-5, §1004(b)(7):

Amended Code Sec. 6211(b)(4)(A) by inserting "25A by reason of subsection (i)(6) thereof," after "24(d),". **Effective** for tax years beginning after 12-31-2008.

P.L. 111-5, §1201(a)(3)(B):

Amended Code Sec. 6211(b)(4)(A) by inserting "168(k)(4)," after "53(e),". **Effective** for tax years ending after 3-31-2008.

P.L. 111-5, §1201(b)(2):

Amended Code Sec. 6211(b)(4)(A) by inserting "168(k)(4)," after "53(e),". **Effective** for tax years ending after 3-31-2008. [This amendment cannot be made because the same amendment was made by P.L. 111-5, §1201(a)(3)(B).—CCH].

P.L. 111-5, §1531(c)(4):

Amended Code Sec. 6211(b)(4)(A) by striking "and 6428" and inserting "6428, and 6431". **Effective** for obligations issued after 2-17-2009.

[¶5380] CODE SEC. 6213. RESTRICTIONS APPLICABLE TO DEFICIENCIES; PETITION TO TAX COURT.

* * *

(g) DEFINITIONS.—For purposes of this section—

* * *

(2) MATHEMATICAL OR CLERICAL ERROR.—The term "mathematical or clerical error" means—

* * *

(L) the inclusion on a return of a TIN required to be included on the return under section 21, 24, 32, or 6428 if—

(i) such TIN is of an individual whose age affects the amount of the credit under such section, and

(ii) the computation of the credit on the return reflects the treatment of such individual as being of an age different from the individual's age based on such TIN,

(M) the entry on the return claiming the credit under section 32 with respect to a child if, according to the Federal Case Registry of Child Support Orders established under section 453(h) of the Social Security Act, the taxpayer is a non-custodial parent of such child, *and*

(N) *an omission of the reduction required under section 36A(c) with respect to the credit allowed under section 36A or an omission of the correct social security account number required under section 36A(d)(1)(B).*

A taxpayer shall be treated as having omitted a correct TIN for purposes of the preceding sentence if information provided by the taxpayer on the return with respect to the individual whose TIN was provided differs from the information the Secretary obtains from the person issuing the TIN.

* * *

[CCH Explanation at ¶ 305. Committee Reports at ¶ 10,010.]

Amendments

• **2009, American Recovery and Reinvestment Tax Act of 2009 (P.L. 111-5)**

P.L. 111-5, § 1001(d):

Amended Code Sec. 6213(g)(2) by striking "and" at the end of subparagraph (L)(ii), by striking the period at the end of subparagraph (M) and inserting ", and", and by adding at the end a new subparagraph (N). **Effective** for tax years beginning after 12-31-2008.

[¶ 5385] CODE SEC. 6401. AMOUNTS TREATED AS OVERPAYMENTS.

* * *

(b) EXCESSIVE CREDITS.—

(1) IN GENERAL.—If the amount allowable as credits under subpart C of part IV of subchapter A of chapter 1 (relating to refundable credits) exceeds the tax imposed by subtitle A (reduced by the credits allowable under subparts A, B, D, G, H, *I, and J* of such part IV), the amount of such excess shall be considered an overpayment.

* * *

[CCH Explanation at ¶ 605. Committee Reports at ¶ 10,450.]

Amendments

• **2009, American Recovery and Reinvestment Tax Act of 2009 (P.L. 111-5)**

P.L. 111-5, § 1531(c)(5):

Amended Code Sec. 6401(b)(1) by striking "and I" and inserting "I, and J". **Effective** for obligations issued after 2-17-2009.

[¶ 5390] *CODE SEC. 6431. CREDIT FOR QUALIFIED BONDS ALLOWED TO ISSUER.*

(a) IN GENERAL.—In the case of a qualified bond issued before January 1, 2011, the issuer of such bond shall be allowed a credit with respect to each interest payment under such bond which shall be payable by the Secretary as provided in subsection (b).

(b) PAYMENT OF CREDIT.—The Secretary shall pay (contemporaneously with each interest payment date under such bond) to the issuer of such bond (or to any person who makes such interest payments on behalf of the issuer) 35 percent of the interest payable under such bond on such date.

(c) APPLICATION OF ARBITRAGE RULES.—For purposes of section 148, the yield on a qualified bond shall be reduced by the credit allowed under this section.

(d) INTEREST PAYMENT DATE.—For purposes of this subsection, the term "interest payment date" means each date on which interest is payable by the issuer under the terms of the bond.

(e) QUALIFIED BOND.—For purposes of this subsection, the term "qualified bond" has the meaning given such term in section 54AA(g).

[CCH Explanation at ¶610. Committee Reports at ¶10,450.]

Amendments

• **2009, American Recovery and Reinvestment Tax Act of 2009 (P.L. 111-5)**

P.L. 111-5, §1531(b):

Amended subchapter B of chapter 65 by adding at the end a new Code Sec. 6431. **Effective** for obligations issued after 2-17-2009.

P.L. 111-5, §1531(d), provides:

(d) TRANSITIONAL COORDINATION WITH STATE LAW.—Except as otherwise provided by a State after the date of the enactment of this Act, the interest on any build America bond (as defined in section 54AA of the Internal Revenue Code of 1986, as added by this section) and the amount of any credit determined under such section with respect to such bond shall be treated for purposes of the income tax laws of such State as being exempt from Federal income tax.

[¶5395] CODE SEC. 6432. COBRA PREMIUM ASSISTANCE.

(a) IN GENERAL.—The person to whom premiums are payable under COBRA continuation coverage shall be reimbursed as provided in subsection (c) for the amount of premiums not paid by assistance eligible individuals by reason of section 3002(a) [3001(a)] of the Health Insurance Assistance for the Unemployed Act of 2009 [American Recovery and Reinvestment Act of 2009].

(b) PERSON ENTITLED TO REIMBURSEMENT.—For purposes of subsection (a), except as otherwise provided by the Secretary, the person to whom premiums are payable under COBRA continuation coverage shall be treated as being—

(1) in the case of any group health plan which is a multiemployer plan (as defined in section 3(37) of the Employee Retirement Income Security Act of 1974), the plan,

(2) in the case of any group health plan not described in paragraph (1)—

(A) which is subject to the COBRA continuation provisions contained in—

(i) the Internal Revenue Code of 1986,

(ii) the Employee Retirement Income Security Act of 1974,

(iii) the Public Health Service Act, or

(iv) title 5, United States Code, or

(B) under which some or all of the coverage is not provided by insurance,

the employer maintaining the plan, and

(3) in the case of any group health plan not described in paragraph (1) or (2), the insurer providing the coverage under the group health plan.

(c) METHOD OF REIMBURSEMENT.—Except as otherwise provided by the Secretary—

(1) TREATMENT AS PAYMENT OF PAYROLL TAXES.—Each person entitled to reimbursement under subsection (a) (and filing a claim for such reimbursement at such time and in such manner as the Secretary may require) shall be treated for purposes of this title and section 1324(b)(2) of title 31, United States Code, as having paid to the Secretary, on the date that the assistance eligible individual's premium payment is received, payroll taxes in an amount equal to the portion of such reimbursement which relates to such premium. To the extent that the amount treated as paid under the preceding sentence exceeds the amount of such person's liability for such taxes, the Secretary shall credit or refund such excess in the same manner as if it were an overpayment of such taxes.

(2) OVERSTATEMENTS.—Any overstatement of the reimbursement to which a person is entitled under this section (and any amount paid by the Secretary as a result of such overstatement) shall be treated as an underpayment of payroll taxes by such person and may be assessed and collected by the Secretary in the same manner as payroll taxes.

(3) REIMBURSEMENT CONTINGENT ON PAYMENT OF REMAINING PREMIUM.—No reimbursement may be made under this section to a person with respect to any assistance eligible individual until after the reduced premium required under section 3002(a)(1)(A) [3001(a)(1)(A)] of such Act with respect to such individual has been received.

(d) DEFINITIONS.—For purposes of this section—

(1) PAYROLL TAXES.—The term "payroll taxes" means—

(A) amounts required to be deducted and withheld for the payroll period under section 3402 (relating to wage withholding),

(B) amounts required to be deducted for the payroll period under section 3102 (relating to FICA employee taxes), and

(C) amounts of the taxes imposed for the payroll period under section 3111 (relating to FICA employer taxes).

(2) PERSON.—The term "person" includes any governmental entity.

(e) REPORTING.—Each person entitled to reimbursement under subsection (a) for any period shall submit such reports (at such time and in such manner) as the Secretary may require, including—

(1) an attestation of involuntary termination of employment for each covered employee on the basis of whose termination entitlement to reimbursement is claimed under subsection (a),

(2) a report of the amount of payroll taxes offset under subsection (a) for the reporting period and the estimated offsets of such taxes for the subsequent reporting period in connection with reimbursements under subsection (a), and

(3) a report containing the TINs of all covered employees, the amount of subsidy reimbursed with respect to each covered employee and qualified beneficiaries, and a designation with respect to each covered employee as to whether the subsidy reimbursement is for coverage of 1 individual or 2 or more individuals.

(f) REGULATIONS.—The Secretary shall issue such regulations or other guidance as may be necessary or appropriate to carry out this section, including—

(1) the requirement to report information or the establishment of other methods for verifying the correct amounts of reimbursements under this section, and

(2) the application of this section to group health plans that are multiemployer plans (as defined in section 3(37) of the Employee Retirement Income Security Act of 1974).

[CCH Explanation at ¶705. Committee Reports at ¶10,510.]

Amendments

• 2009, American Recovery and Reinvestment Tax Act of 2009 (P.L. 111-5)

P.L. 111-5, §3001(a)(12)(A):

Amended subchapter B of chapter 65 [as amended by this Act] by adding at the end a new Code Sec. 6432. **Effective** generally for premiums for a period of coverage beginning on or after 2-17-2009.

[¶5400] CODE SEC. 6501. LIMITATIONS ON ASSESSMENT AND COLLECTION.

* * *

⇛ *Caution: Code Sec. 6501(m), below, as amended by P.L. 111-5, §1142(b)(7), but prior to amendment by P.L. 111-5, §1141(b)(4), applies to vehicles acquired on or before December 31, 2009.*

(m) DEFICIENCIES ATTRIBUTABLE TO ELECTION OF CERTAIN CREDITS.—The period for assessing a deficiency attributable to any election under *section 30(e)(6)*, 30B(h)(9), 30C(e)(5) [30C(e)(4)], 30D(e)(9), 40(f), 43, 45B, 45C(d)(4), 45H(g), or 51(j) (or any revocation thereof) shall not expire before the date 1 year after the date on which the Secretary is notified of such election (or revocation).

>>>→ *Caution: Code Sec. 6501(m), below, as amended by P.L. 111-5, §§1141(b)(4) and 1142(b)(7), applies to vehicles acquired after December 31, 2009.*

(m) DEFICIENCIES ATTRIBUTABLE TO ELECTION OF CERTAIN CREDITS.—The period for assessing a deficiency attributable to any election under *section 30(e)(6)*, 30B(h)(9), 30C(e)(5) [30C(e)(4)], *30D(e)(4)*, 40(f), 43, 45B, 45C(d)(4), 45H(g), or 51(j) (or any revocation thereof) shall not expire before the date 1 year after the date on which the Secretary is notified of such election (or revocation).

* * *

[CCH Explanation at ¶345 and ¶350. Committee Reports at ¶10,200.]

Amendments

• **2009, American Recovery and Reinvestment Tax Act of 2009 (P.L. 111-5)**

P.L. 111-5, §1141(b)(4):

Amended Code Sec. 6501(m) by striking "section [sic] 30D(e)(9)" and inserting "section [sic] 30D(e)(4)". **Effective** for vehicles acquired after 12-31-2009.

P.L. 111-5, §1142(b)(7):

Amended Code Sec. 6501(m) by striking "section 30(d)(4)" and inserting "section 30(e)(6)". **Effective** for vehicles acquired after 2-17-2009. For a transitional rule, see Act Sec. 1142(d) in the amendment notes for Code Sec. 30.

[¶5405] CODE SEC. 6654. FAILURE BY INDIVIDUAL TO PAY ESTIMATED INCOME TAX.

* * *

(d) AMOUNT OF REQUIRED INSTALLMENTS.—For purposes of this section—

(1) AMOUNT.—

* * *

(D) SPECIAL RULE FOR 2009.—

(i) IN GENERAL.—*Notwithstanding subparagraph (C), in the case of any taxable year beginning in 2009, clause (ii) of subparagraph (B) shall be applied to any qualified individual by substituting "90 percent" for "100 percent".*

(ii) QUALIFIED INDIVIDUAL.—*For purposes of this subparagraph, the term "qualified individual" means any individual if—*

(I) the adjusted gross income shown on the return of such individual for the preceding taxable year is less than $500,000, and

(II) such individual certifies that more than 50 percent of the gross income shown on the return of such individual for the preceding taxable year was income from a small business.

A certification under subclause (II) shall be in such form and manner and filed at such time as the Secretary may by regulations prescribe.

(iii) INCOME FROM A SMALL BUSINESS.—For purposes of clause (ii), income from a small business means, with respect to any individual, income from a trade or business the average number of employees of which was less than 500 employees for the calendar year ending with or within the preceding taxable year of the individual.

(iv) SEPARATE RETURNS.—In the case of a married individual (within the meaning of section 7703) who files a separate return for the taxable year for which the amount of the installment is being determined, clause (ii)(I) shall be applied by substituting "$250,000" for "$500,000".

(v) ESTATES AND TRUSTS.—In the case of an estate or trust, adjusted gross income shall be determined as provided in section 67(e).

* * *

[CCH Explanation at ¶465. Committee Reports at ¶10,250.]

Amendments

• 2009, American Recovery and Reinvestment Tax Act of 2009 (P.L. 111-5)

P.L. 111-5, §1212:

Amended Code Sec. 6654(d)(1) by adding at the end a new subparagraph (D). **Effective** 2-17-2009.

[¶5410] CODE SEC. 6720C. PENALTY FOR FAILURE TO NOTIFY HEALTH PLAN OF CESSATION OF ELIGIBILITY FOR COBRA PREMIUM ASSISTANCE.

(a) IN GENERAL.—Any person required to notify a group health plan under section 3002(a)(2)(C) [3001(a)(2)(C)] of the Health Insurance Assistance for the Unemployed Act of 2009 [American Recovery and Reinvestment Act of 2009] who fails to make such a notification at such time and in such manner as the Secretary of Labor may require shall pay a penalty of 110 percent of the premium reduction provided under such section after termination of eligibility under such subsection.

(b) REASONABLE CAUSE EXCEPTION.—No penalty shall be imposed under subsection (a) with respect to any failure if it is shown that such failure is due to reasonable cause and not to willful neglect.

[CCH Explanation at ¶710. Committee Reports at ¶10,510.]

Amendments

• 2009, American Recovery and Reinvestment Tax Act of 2009 (P.L. 111-5)

P.L. 111-5, §3001(a)(13)(A):

Amended part I of subchapter B of chapter 68 by adding at the end a new Code Sec. 6720C. **Effective** for failures occurring after 2-17-2009.

[¶5415] CODE SEC. 7527. ADVANCE PAYMENT OF CREDIT FOR HEALTH INSURANCE COSTS OF ELIGIBLE INDIVIDUALS.

* * *

(b) LIMITATION ON ADVANCE PAYMENTS DURING ANY TAXABLE YEAR.—The Secretary may make payments under subsection (a) only to the extent that the total amount of such payments made on behalf of any individual during the taxable year does not exceed 65 percent *(80 percent in the case of eligible coverage months beginning before January 1, 2011)* of the amount paid by the taxpayer for coverage of the taxpayer and qualifying family members under qualified health insurance for eligible coverage months beginning in the taxable year.

* * *

[CCH Explanation at ¶725. Committee Reports at ¶10,480.]

Amendments

• 2009, TAA Health Coverage Improvement Act of 2009 (P.L. 111-5)

P.L. 111-5, §1899A(a)(2):

Amended Code Sec. 7527(b) by inserting "(80 percent in the case of eligible coverage months beginning before January 1, 2011)" after "65 percent". **Effective** for coverage months beginning on or after the first day of the first month beginning 60 days after 2-17-2009.

⟫→ *Caution: Code Sec. 7527(d), below, as amended by P.L. 111-5, applies to certificates issued after the date that is 6 months after February 17, 2009.*

(d) QUALIFIED HEALTH INSURANCE COSTS ELIGIBILITY CERTIFICATE.—

(1) IN GENERAL.—For purposes of this section, the term "qualified health insurance costs eligibility certificate" means any written statement that an individual is an eligible individual (as defined in section 35(c)) if such statement provides such information as the Secretary may require for purposes of this section and—

(A) in the case of an eligible TAA recipient (as defined in section 35(c)(2)) or an eligible alternative TAA recipient (as defined in section 35(c)(3)), is certified by the Secretary of Labor (or by any other person or entity designated by the Secretary), or

(B) in the case of an eligible PBGC pension recipient (as defined in section 35(c)(4)), is certified by the Pension Benefit Guaranty Corporation (or by any other person or entity designated by the Secretary).

(2) INCLUSION OF CERTAIN INFORMATION.—In the case of any statement described in paragraph (1) which is issued before January 1, 2011, such statement shall not be treated as a qualified health insurance costs credit eligibility certificate unless such statement includes—

(A) the name, address, and telephone number of the State office or offices responsible for providing the individual with assistance with enrollment in qualified health insurance (as defined in section 35(e)),

(B) a list of the coverage options that are treated as qualified health insurance (as so defined) by the State in which the individual resides, and

(C) in the case of a TAA-eligible individual (as defined in section 4980B(f)(5)(C)(iv)(II)), a statement informing the individual that the individual has 63 days from the date that is 7 days after the date of the issuance of such certificate to enroll in such insurance without a lapse in creditable coverage (as defined in section 9801(c)).

[CCH Explanation at ¶725. Committee Reports at ¶10,480.]

Amendments

• 2009, TAA Health Coverage Improvement Act of 2009 (P.L. 111-5)

P.L. 111-5, §1899H(a):

Amended Code Sec. 7527(d). **Effective** for certificates issued after the date that is 6 months after 2-17-2009. Prior to amendment, Code Sec. 7527(d) read as follows:

(d) QUALIFIED HEALTH INSURANCE COSTS CREDIT ELIGIBILITY CERTIFICATE.—For purposes of this section, the term "qualified health insurance costs credit eligibility certificate" means any written statement that an individual is an eligible individual (as defined in section 35(c)) if such statement provides such information as the Secretary may require for purposes of this section and—

(1) in the case of an eligible TAA recipient (as defined in section 35(c)(2)) or an eligible alternative TAA recipient (as defined in section 35(c)(3)), is certified by the Secretary of Labor (or by any other person or entity designated by the Secretary), or

(2) in the case of an eligible PBGC pension recipient (as defined in section 35(c)(4)), is certified by the Pension Benefit Guaranty Corporation (or by any other person or entity designated by the Secretary).

(e) PAYMENT FOR PREMIUMS DUE PRIOR TO COMMENCEMENT OF ADVANCE PAYMENTS.—In the case of eligible coverage months beginning before January 1, 2011—

(1) IN GENERAL.—The program established under subsection (a) shall provide that the Secretary shall make 1 or more retroactive payments on behalf of a certified individual in an aggregate amount equal to 80 percent of the premiums for coverage of the taxpayer and qualifying family members under qualified health insurance for eligible coverage months (as defined in section 35(b)) occurring prior to the first month for which an advance payment is made on behalf of such individual under subsection (a).

(2) REDUCTION OF PAYMENT FOR AMOUNTS RECEIVED UNDER NATIONAL EMERGENCY GRANTS.—The amount of any payment determined under paragraph (1) shall be reduced by the amount of any payment made to the taxpayer for the purchase of qualified health insurance under a national emergency grant pursuant to section 173(f) of the Workforce Investment Act of 1998 for a taxable year including the eligible coverage months described in paragraph (1).

[CCH Explanation at ¶725. Committee Reports at ¶10,480.]

Amendments

• 2009, TAA Health Coverage Improvement Act of 2009 (P.L. 111-5)

P.L. 111-5, §1899B(a):

Amended Code Sec. 7527 by adding at the end a new subsection (e). **Effective** for coverage months beginning after 12-31-2008. For a transitional rule, see Act Sec. 1899B(c), below.

P.L. 111-5, §1899B(c), provides:

(c) TRANSITIONAL RULE.—The Secretary of the Treasury shall not be required to make any payments under section 7527(e) of the Internal Revenue Code of 1986, as added by this section, until after the date that is 6 months after the date of the enactment of this Act.

¶5415 Code Sec. 7527(d)(1)(A)

[¶ 5420] CODE SEC. 7871. INDIAN TRIBAL GOVERNMENTS TREATED AS STATES FOR CERTAIN PURPOSES.

* * *

(f) TRIBAL ECONOMIC DEVELOPMENT BONDS.—

(1) ALLOCATION OF LIMITATION.—

(A) IN GENERAL.—The Secretary shall allocate the national tribal economic development bond limitation among the Indian tribal governments in such manner as the Secretary, in consultation with the Secretary of the Interior, determines appropriate.

(B) NATIONAL LIMITATION.—There is a national tribal economic development bond limitation of $2,000,000,000.

(2) BONDS TREATED AS EXEMPT FROM TAX.—In the case of a tribal economic development bond—

(A) notwithstanding subsection (c), such bond shall be treated for purposes of this title in the same manner as if such bond were issued by a State,

(B) the Indian tribal government issuing such bond and any instrumentality of such Indian tribal government shall be treated as a State for purposes of section 141, and

(C) section 146 shall not apply.

(3) TRIBAL ECONOMIC DEVELOPMENT BOND.—

(A) IN GENERAL.—For purposes of this section, the term "tribal economic development bond" means any bond issued by an Indian tribal government—

(i) the interest on which would be exempt from tax under section 103 if issued by a State or local government, and

(ii) which is designated by the Indian tribal government as a tribal economic development bond for purposes of this subsection.

(B) EXCEPTIONS.—Such term shall not include any bond issued as part of an issue if any portion of the proceeds of such issue are used to finance—

(i) any portion of a building in which class II or class III gaming (as defined in section 4 of the Indian Gaming Regulatory Act) is conducted or housed or any other property actually used in the conduct of such gaming, or

(ii) any facility located outside the Indian reservation (as defined in section 168(j)(6)).

(C) LIMITATION ON AMOUNT OF BONDS DESIGNATED.—The maximum aggregate face amount of bonds which may be designated by any Indian tribal government under subparagraph (A) shall not exceed the amount of national tribal economic development bond limitation allocated to such government under paragraph (1).

[CCH Explanation at ¶ 665. Committee Reports at ¶ 10,360.]

Amendments

• 2009, American Recovery and Reinvestment Tax Act of 2009 (P.L. 111-5)

P.L. 111-5, § 1402(a):

Amended Code Sec. 7871 by adding at the end a new subsection (f). **Effective** for obligations issued after 2-17-2009.

[¶ 5425] CODE SEC. 9801. INCREASED PORTABILITY THROUGH LIMITATION ON PREEXISTING CONDITION EXCLUSIONS.

* * *

(c) RULES RELATING TO CREDITING PREVIOUS COVERAGE.—

* * *

(2) NOT COUNTING PERIODS BEFORE SIGNIFICANT BREAKS IN COVERAGE.—

* * *

(D) TAA-ELIGIBLE INDIVIDUALS.—*In the case of plan years beginning before January 1, 2011*—

(i) TAA PRE-CERTIFICATION PERIOD RULE.—*In the case of a TAA-eligible individual, the period beginning on the date the individual has a TAA-related loss of coverage and ending on the date which is 7 days after the date of the issuance by the Secretary (or by any person or entity designated by the Secretary) of a qualified health insurance costs credit eligibility certificate for such individual for purposes of section 7527 shall not be taken into account in determining the continuous period under subparagraph (A).*

(ii) DEFINITIONS.—*The terms "TAA-eligible individual" and "TAA-related loss of coverage" have the meanings given such terms in section 4980B(f)(5)(C)(iv).*

* * *

[CCH Explanation at ¶725. Committee Reports at ¶10,480.]

Amendments

• **2009, TAA Health Coverage Improvement Act of 2009 (P.L. 111-5)**

P.L. 111-5, §1899D(a):

Amended Code Sec. 9801(c)(2) by adding at the end a new subparagraph (D). **Effective** for plan years beginning after 2-17-2009.

(f) SPECIAL ENROLLMENT PERIODS.—

* * *

(3) SPECIAL RULES RELATING TO MEDICAID AND CHIP.—

(A) IN GENERAL.—*A group health plan shall permit an employee who is eligible, but not enrolled, for coverage under the terms of the plan (or a dependent of such an employee if the dependent is eligible, but not enrolled, for coverage under such terms) to enroll for coverage under the terms of the plan if either of the following conditions is met:*

(i) TERMINATION OF MEDICAID OR CHIP COVERAGE.—*The employee or dependent is covered under a Medicaid plan under title XIX of the Social Security Act or under a State child health plan under title XXI of such Act and coverage of the employee or dependent under such a plan is terminated as a result of loss of eligibility for such coverage and the employee requests coverage under the group health plan not later than 60 days after the date of termination of such coverage.*

(ii) ELIGIBILITY FOR EMPLOYMENT ASSISTANCE UNDER MEDICAID OR CHIP.—*The employee or dependent becomes eligible for assistance, with respect to coverage under the group health plan under such Medicaid plan or State child health plan (including under any waiver or demonstration project conducted under or in relation to such a plan), if the employee requests coverage under the group health plan not later than 60 days after the date the employee or dependent is determined to be eligible for such assistance.*

(B) EMPLOYEE OUTREACH AND DISCLOSURE.—

(i) OUTREACH TO EMPLOYEES REGARDING AVAILABILITY OF MEDICAID AND CHIP COVERAGE.—

(I) IN GENERAL.—*Each employer that maintains a group health plan in a State that provides medical assistance under a State Medicaid plan under title XIX of the Social Security Act, or child health assistance under a State child health plan under title XXI of such Act, in the form of premium assistance for the purchase of coverage under a group health plan, shall provide to each employee a written notice informing the employee of potential opportunities then currently available in the State in which the employee resides for premium assistance under such plans for health coverage of the employee or the employee's dependents. For purposes of compliance with this clause, the employer may use any State-specific model notice developed in accordance with section 701(f)(3)(B)(i)(II) of the Employee Retirement Income Security Act of 1974 (29 U.S.C. 1181(f)(3)(B)(i)(II)).*

(II) OPTION TO PROVIDE CONCURRENT WITH PROVISION OF PLAN MATERIALS TO EMPLOYEE.—An employer may provide the model notice applicable to the State in which an employee resides concurrent with the furnishing of materials notifying the employee of health plan eligibility, concurrent with materials provided to the employee in connection with an open season or election process conducted under the plan, or concurrent with the furnishing of the summary plan description as provided in section 104(b) of the Employee Retirement Income Security Act of 1974 (29 U.S.C. 1024).

(ii) DISCLOSURE ABOUT GROUP HEALTH PLAN BENEFITS TO STATES FOR MEDICAID AND CHIP ELIGIBLE INDIVIDUALS.—In the case of a participant or beneficiary of a group health plan who is covered under a Medicaid plan of a State under title XIX of the Social Security Act or under a State child health plan under title XXI of such Act, the plan administrator of the group health plan shall disclose to the State, upon request, information about the benefits available under the group health plan in sufficient specificity, as determined under regulations of the Secretary of Health and Human Services in consultation with the Secretary that require use of the model coverage coordination disclosure form developed under section 311(b)(1)(C) of the Children's Health Insurance Program Reauthorization Act of 2009, so as to permit the State to make a determination (under paragraph (2)(B), (3), or (10) of section 2105(c) of the Social Security Act or otherwise) concerning the cost-effectiveness of the State providing medical or child health assistance through premium assistance for the purchase of coverage under such group health plan and in order for the State to provide supplemental benefits required under paragraph (10)(E) of such section or other authority.

[CCH Explanation at ¶720.]

Amendments

• 2009, Children's Health Insurance Program Reauthorization Act of 2009 (P.L. 111-3)

P.L. 111-3, §311(a):

Amended Code Sec. 9801(f) by adding at the end a new paragraph (3). For the **effective** date, see Act Sec. 3, below.

P.L. 111-3, §3, provides:

SEC. 3. GENERAL EFFECTIVE DATE; EXCEPTION FOR STATE LEGISLATION; CONTINGENT EFFECTIVE DATE; RELIANCE ON LAW.

(a) GENERAL EFFECTIVE DATE.—Unless otherwise provided in this Act, subject to subsections (b) through (d), this Act (and the amendments made by this Act) shall take effect on April 1, 2009, and shall apply to child health assistance and medical assistance provided on or after that date.

(b) EXCEPTION FOR STATE LEGISLATION.—In the case of a State plan under title XIX or State child health plan under XXI of the Social Security Act, which the Secretary of Health and Human Services determines requires State legislation in order for the respective plan to meet one or more additional requirements imposed by amendments made by this Act, the respective plan shall not be regarded as failing to comply with the requirements of such title solely on the basis of its failure to meet such an additional requirement before the first day of the first calendar quarter beginning after the close of the first regular session of the State legislature that begins after the date of enactment of this Act. For purposes of the previous sentence, in the case of a State that has a 2-year legislative session, each year of the session shall be considered to be a separate regular session of the State legislature.

(c) COORDINATION OF CHIP FUNDING FOR FISCAL YEAR 2009.—Notwithstanding any other provision of law, insofar as funds have been appropriated under section 2104(a)(11), 2104(k), or 2104(l) of the Social Security Act, as amended by section 201 of Public Law 110-173, to provide allotments to States under CHIP for fiscal year 2009—

(1) any amounts that are so appropriated that are not so allotted and obligated before April 1, 2009 are rescinded; and

(2) any amount provided for CHIP allotments to a State under this Act (and the amendments made by this Act) for such fiscal year shall be reduced by the amount of such appropriations so allotted and obligated before such date.

(d) RELIANCE ON LAW.—With respect to amendments made by this Act (other than title VII) that become effective as of a date—

(1) such amendments are effective as of such date whether or not regulations implementing such amendments have been issued; and

(2) Federal financial participation for medical assistance or child health assistance furnished under title XIX or XXI, respectively, of the Social Security Act on or after such date by a State in good faith reliance on such amendments before the date of promulgation of final regulations, if any, to carry out such amendments (or before the date of guidance, if any, regarding the implementation of such amendments) shall not be denied on the basis of the State's failure to comply with such regulations or guidance.

Act Sections Not Amending Code Sections

AMERICAN RECOVERY AND REINVESTMENT ACT OF 2009

DIVISION B—TAX, UNEMPLOYMENT, HEALTH, STATE FISCAL RELIEF, AND OTHER PROVISIONS

TITLE I—TAX PROVISIONS

[¶ 7003] ACT SEC. 1000. SHORT TITLE, ETC.

(a) SHORT TITLE.—This title may be cited as the "American Recovery and Reinvestment Tax Act of 2009".

(b) REFERENCE.—Except as otherwise expressly provided, whenever in this title an amendment or repeal is expressed in terms of an amendment to, or repeal of, a section or other provision, the reference shall be considered to be made to a section or other provision of the Internal Revenue Code of 1986.

* * *

Subtitle A—Tax Relief for Individuals and Families

PART I—GENERAL TAX RELIEF

[¶ 7006] ACT SEC. 1001. MAKING WORK PAY CREDIT.

* * *

(b) TREATMENT OF POSSESSIONS.—

(1) PAYMENTS TO POSSESSIONS.—

(A) MIRROR CODE POSSESSION.—The Secretary of the Treasury shall pay to each possession of the United States with a mirror code tax system amounts equal to the loss to that possession by reason of the amendments made by this section with respect to taxable years beginning in 2009 and 2010. Such amounts shall be determined by the Secretary of the Treasury based on information provided by the government of the respective possession.

(B) OTHER POSSESSIONS.—The Secretary of the Treasury shall pay to each possession of the United States which does not have a mirror code tax system amounts estimated by the Secretary of the Treasury as being equal to the aggregate benefits that would have been provided to residents of such possession by reason of the amendments made by this section for taxable years beginning in 2009 and 2010 if a mirror code tax system had been in effect in such possession. The preceding sentence shall not apply with respect to any possession of the United States unless such possession has a plan, which has been approved by the Secretary of the Treasury, under which such possession will promptly distribute such payments to the residents of such possession.

(2) COORDINATION WITH CREDIT ALLOWED AGAINST UNITED STATES INCOME TAXES.—No credit shall be allowed against United States income taxes for any taxable year under section 36A of the Internal Revenue Code of 1986 (as added by this section) to any person—

(A) to whom a credit is allowed against taxes imposed by the possession by reason of the amendments made by this section for such taxable year, or

Act Sec. 1001(b)(2)(A) ¶ 7006

(B) who is eligible for a payment under a plan described in paragraph (1)(B) with respect to such taxable year.

(3) DEFINITIONS AND SPECIAL RULES.—

(A) POSSESSION OF THE UNITED STATES.—For purposes of this subsection, the term "possession of the United States" includes the Commonwealth of Puerto Rico and the Commonwealth of the Northern Mariana Islands.

(B) MIRROR CODE TAX SYSTEM.—For purposes of this subsection, the term "mirror code tax system" means, with respect to any possession of the United States, the income tax system of such possession if the income tax liability of the residents of such possession under such system is determined by reference to the income tax laws of the United States as if such possession were the United States.

(C) TREATMENT OF PAYMENTS.—For purposes of section 1324(b)(2) of title 31, United States Code, the payments under this subsection shall be treated in the same manner as a refund due from the credit allowed under section 36A of the Internal Revenue Code of 1986 (as added by this section).

(c) REFUNDS DISREGARDED IN THE ADMINISTRATION OF FEDERAL PROGRAMS AND FEDERALLY ASSISTED PROGRAMS.—Any credit or refund allowed or made to any individual by reason of section 36A of the Internal Revenue Code of 1986 (as added by this section) or by reason of subsection (b) of this section shall not be taken into account as income and shall not be taken into account as resources for the month of receipt and the following 2 months, for purposes of determining the eligibility of such individual or any other individual for benefits or assistance, or the amount or extent of benefits or assistance, under any Federal program or under any State or local program financed in whole or in part with Federal funds.

* * *

(f) EFFECTIVE DATE.—This section, and the amendments made by this section, shall apply to taxable years beginning after December 31, 2008.

* * *

[CCH Explanation at ¶305. Committee Reports at ¶10,010.]

[¶7009] ACT SEC. 1004. AMERICAN OPPORTUNITY TAX CREDIT.

* * *

(b) CONFORMING AMENDMENTS.—

* * *

(8) Section 1324(b)(2) of title 31, United States Code, is amended by inserting "25A," before "35".

(c) TREATMENT OF POSSESSIONS.—

(1) PAYMENTS TO POSSESSIONS.—

(A) MIRROR CODE POSSESSION.—The Secretary of the Treasury shall pay to each possession of the United States with a mirror code tax system amounts equal to the loss to that possession by reason of the application of section 25A(i)(6) of the Internal Revenue Code of 1986 (as added by this section) with respect to taxable years beginning in 2009 and 2010. Such amounts shall be determined by the Secretary of the Treasury based on information provided by the government of the respective possession.

(B) OTHER POSSESSIONS.—The Secretary of the Treasury shall pay to each possession of the United States which does not have a mirror code tax system amounts estimated by the Secretary of the Treasury as being equal to the aggregate benefits that would have been provided to residents of such possession by reason of the application of section 25A(i)(6) of such Code (as so added) for taxable years beginning in 2009 and 2010 if a mirror code tax system had been in effect in such possession. The preceding sentence shall not apply with respect to any possession of the United States unless such possession has a plan, which has been approved by the Secretary of the Treasury, under which such possession will promptly distribute such payments to the residents of such possession.

(2) COORDINATION WITH CREDIT ALLOWED AGAINST UNITED STATES INCOME TAXES.—Section 25A(i)(6) of such Code (as added by this section) shall not apply to a bona fide resident of any possession of the United States.

(3) DEFINITIONS AND SPECIAL RULES.—

(A) POSSESSION OF THE UNITED STATES.—For purposes of this subsection, the term "possession of the United States" includes the Commonwealth of Puerto Rico and the Commonwealth of the Northern Mariana Islands.

(B) MIRROR CODE TAX SYSTEM.—For purposes of this subsection, the term "mirror code tax system" means, with respect to any possession of the United States, the income tax system of such possession if the income tax liability of the residents of such possession under such system is determined by reference to the income tax laws of the United States as if such possession were the United States.

(C) TREATMENT OF PAYMENTS.—For purposes of section 1324(b)(2) of title 31, United States Code, the payments under this subsection shall be treated in the same manner as a refund due from the credit allowed under section 25A of the Internal Revenue Code of 1986 by reason of subsection (i)(6) of such section (as added by this section).

(d) EFFECTIVE DATE.—The amendments made by this section shall apply to taxable years beginning after December 31, 2008.

* * *

(f) TREASURY STUDIES REGARDING EDUCATION INCENTIVES.—

(1) STUDY REGARDING COORDINATION WITH NON-TAX STUDENT FINANCIAL ASSISTANCE.—The Secretary of the Treasury and the Secretary of Education, or their delegates, shall—

(A) study how to coordinate the credit allowed under section 25A of the Internal Revenue Code of 1986 with the Federal Pell Grant program under section 401 of the Higher Education Act of 1965 to maximize their effectiveness at promoting college affordability, and

(B) examine ways to expedite the delivery of the tax credit.

(2) STUDY REGARDING INCLUSION OF COMMUNITY SERVICE REQUIREMENTS.—The Secretary of the Treasury and the Secretary of Education, or their delegates, shall study the feasibility of requiring including community service as a condition of taking their tuition and related expenses into account under section 25A of the Internal Revenue Code of 1986.

(3) REPORT.—Not later than 1 year after the date of the enactment of this Act, the Secretary of the Treasury, or the Secretary's delegate, shall report to Congress on the results of the studies conducted under this paragraph.

* * *

[CCH Explanation at ¶ 330. Committee Reports at ¶ 10,040.]

Subtitle C—Tax Incentives for Business
* * *

PART II—SMALL BUSINESS PROVISIONS

[¶ 7012] ACT SEC. 1211. 5-YEAR CARRYBACK OF OPERATING LOSSES OF SMALL BUSINESSES.

* * *

(c) ANTI-ABUSE RULES.—The Secretary of Treasury or the Secretary's designee shall prescribe such rules as are necessary to prevent the abuse of the purposes of the amendments made by this section, including anti-stuffing rules, anti-churning rules (including rules relating to sale-leasebacks), and rules similar to the rules under section 1091 of the Internal Revenue Code of 1986 relating to losses from wash sales.

* * *

[CCH Explanation at ¶425. Committee Reports at ¶10,240.]

PART VII—RULES RELATING TO OWNERSHIP CHANGES

[¶7015] ACT SEC. 1261. CLARIFICATION OF REGULATIONS RELATED TO LIMITATIONS ON CERTAIN BUILT-IN LOSSES FOLLOWING AN OWNERSHIP CHANGE.

(a) FINDINGS.—Congress finds as follows:

(1) The delegation of authority to the Secretary of the Treasury under section 382(m) of the Internal Revenue Code of 1986 does not authorize the Secretary to provide exemptions or special rules that are restricted to particular industries or classes of taxpayers.

(2) Internal Revenue Service Notice 2008–83 is inconsistent with the congressional intent in enacting such section 382(m).

(3) The legal authority to prescribe Internal Revenue Service Notice 2008–83 is doubtful.

(4) However, as taxpayers should generally be able to rely on guidance issued by the Secretary of the Treasury legislation is necessary to clarify the force and effect of Internal Revenue Service Notice 2008–83 and restore the proper application under the Internal Revenue Code of 1986 of the limitation on built-in losses following an ownership change of a bank.

(b) DETERMINATION OF FORCE AND EFFECT OF INTERNAL REVENUE SERVICE NOTICE 2008-83 EXEMPTING BANKS FROM LIMITATION ON CERTAIN BUILT-IN LOSSES FOLLOWING OWNERSHIP CHANGE.—

(1) IN GENERAL.—Internal Revenue Service Notice 2008–83—

(A) shall be deemed to have the force and effect of law with respect to any ownership change (as defined in section 382(g) of the Internal Revenue Code of 1986) occurring on or before January 16, 2009, and

(B) shall have no force or effect with respect to any ownership change after such date.

(2) BINDING CONTRACTS.—Notwithstanding paragraph (1), Internal Revenue Service Notice 2008–83 shall have the force and effect of law with respect to any ownership change (as so defined) which occurs after January 16, 2009, if such change—

(A) is pursuant to a written binding contract entered into on or before such date, or

(B) is pursuant to a written agreement entered into on or before such date and such agreement was described on or before such date in a public announcement or in a filing with the Securities and Exchange Commission required by reason of such ownership change.

* * *

[CCH Explanation at ¶430. Committee Reports at ¶10,310.]

Subtitle E—Economic Recovery Tools
* * *

[¶7018] ACT SEC. 1402. TRIBAL ECONOMIC DEVELOPMENT BONDS.

* * *

(b) STUDY.—The Secretary of the Treasury, or the Secretary's delegate, shall conduct a study of the effects of the amendment made by subsection (a). Not later than 1 year after the date of the enactment of this Act, the Secretary of the Treasury, or the Secretary's delegate, shall report to

Congress on the results of the study conducted under this paragraph, including the Secretary's recommendations regarding such amendment.

* * *

[CCH Explanation at ¶665. Committee Reports at ¶10,360.]

[¶7021] ACT SEC. 1403. INCREASE IN NEW MARKETS TAX CREDIT.

* * *

(b) SPECIAL RULE FOR ALLOCATION OF INCREASED 2008 LIMITATION.—The amount of the increase in the new markets tax credit limitation for calendar year 2008 by reason of the amendments made by subsection (a) shall be allocated in accordance with section 45D(f)(2) of the Internal Revenue Code of 1986 to qualified community development entities (as defined in section 45D(c) of such Code) which—

    (1) submitted an allocation application with respect to calendar year 2008, and

    (2)(A) did not receive an allocation for such calendar year, or

        (B) received an allocation for such calendar year in an amount less than the amount requested in the allocation application.

* * *

[CCH Explanation at ¶530. Committee Reports at ¶10,370.]

Subtitle F—Infrastructure Financing Tools

* * *

PART II—DELAY IN APPLICATION OF WITHHOLDING TAX ON GOVERNMENT CONTRACTORS

[¶7024] ACT SEC. 1511. DELAY IN APPLICATION OF WITHHOLDING TAX ON GOVERNMENT CONTRACTORS.

Subsection (b) of section 511 of the Tax Increase Prevention and Reconciliation Act of 2005 is amended by striking "December 31, 2010" and inserting "December 31, 2011".

• • *TAX INCREASE PREVENTION AND RECONCILIATION ACT OF 2005 ACT SEC. 511(b) AS AMENDED*——————

ACT SEC. 511. IMPOSITION OF WITHHOLDING ON CERTAIN PAYMENTS MADE BY GOVERNMENT ENTITIES.

* * *

    (b) EFFECTIVE DATE.—The amendment made by this section shall apply to payments made after *December 31, 2011*.

[CCH Explanation at ¶460. Committee Reports at ¶10,420.]

PART IV—BUILD AMERICA BONDS

[¶7027] ACT SEC. 1531. BUILD AMERICA BONDS.

* * *

(c) CONFORMING AMENDMENTS.—

(1) Section 1324(b)(2) of title 31, United States Code, is amended by striking "or 6428" and inserting "6428, or 6431,".

* * *

(d) TRANSITIONAL COORDINATION WITH STATE LAW.—Except as otherwise provided by a State after the date of the enactment of this Act, the interest on any build America bond (as defined in section 54AA of the Internal Revenue Code of 1986, as added by this section) and the amount of any credit determined under such section with respect to such bond shall be treated for purposes of the income tax laws of such State as being exempt from Federal income tax.

(e) EFFECTIVE DATE.—The amendments made by this section shall apply to obligations issued after the date of the enactment of this Act.

[CCH Explanations at ¶605 and ¶610. Committee Reports at ¶10,450.]

PART V—REGULATED INVESTMENT COMPANIES ALLOWED TO PASS-THRU TAX CREDIT BOND CREDITS

* * *

Subtitle G—Other Provisions

[¶7030] ACT SEC. 1601. APPLICATION OF CERTAIN LABOR STANDARDS TO PROJECTS FINANCED WITH CERTAIN TAX-FAVORED BONDS.

Subchapter IV of chapter 31 of the title 40, United States Code, shall apply to projects financed with the proceeds of—

(1) any new clean renewable energy bond (as defined in section 54C of the Internal Revenue Code of 1986) issued after the date of the enactment of this Act,

(2) any qualified energy conservation bond (as defined in section 54D of the Internal Revenue Code of 1986) issued after the date of the enactment of this Act,

(3) any qualified zone academy bond (as defined in section 54E of the Internal Revenue Code of 1986) issued after the date of the enactment of this Act,

(4) any qualified school construction bond (as defined in section 54F of the Internal Revenue Code of 1986), and

(5) any recovery zone economic development bond (as defined in section 1400U–2 of the Internal Revenue Code of 1986).

[CCH Explanations at ¶625, ¶630, ¶635, ¶640 and ¶645. Committee Reports at ¶10,470.]

[¶7033] ACT SEC. 1602. GRANTS TO STATES FOR LOW-INCOME HOUSING PROJECTS IN LIEU OF LOW-INCOME HOUSING CREDIT ALLOCATIONS FOR 2009.

(a) IN GENERAL.—The Secretary of the Treasury shall make a grant to the housing credit agency of each State in an amount equal to such State's low-income housing grant election amount.

(b) LOW-INCOME HOUSING GRANT ELECTION AMOUNT.—For purposes of this section, the term "low-income housing grant election amount" means, with respect to any State, such amount as the State may elect which does not exceed 85 percent of the product of—

(1) the sum of—

(A) 100 percent of the State housing credit ceiling for 2009 which is attributable to amounts described in clauses (i) and (iii) of section 42(h)(3)(C) of the Internal Revenue Code of 1986, and

(B) 40 percent of the State housing credit ceiling for 2009 which is attributable to amounts described in clauses (ii) and (iv) of such section, multiplied by

(2) 10.

(c) SUBAWARDS FOR LOW-INCOME BUILDINGS.—

(1) IN GENERAL.—A State housing credit agency receiving a grant under this section shall use such grant to make subawards to finance the construction or acquisition and rehabilitation of qualified low-income buildings. A subaward under this section may be made to finance a qualified low-income building with or without an allocation under section 42 of the Internal Revenue Code of 1986, except that a State housing credit agency may make subawards to finance qualified low-income buildings without an allocation only if it makes a determination that such use will increase the total funds available to the State to build and rehabilitate affordable housing. In complying with such determination requirement, a State housing credit agency shall establish a process in which applicants that are allocated credits are required to demonstrate good faith efforts to obtain investment commitments for such credits before the agency makes such subawards.

(2) SUBAWARDS SUBJECT TO SAME REQUIREMENTS AS LOW-INCOME HOUSING CREDIT ALLOCATIONS.—Any such subaward with respect to any qualified low-income building shall be made in the same manner and shall be subject to the same limitations (including rent, income, and use restrictions on such building) as an allocation of housing credit dollar amount allocated by such State housing credit agency under section 42 of the Internal Revenue Code of 1986, except that such subawards shall not be limited by, or otherwise affect (except as provided in subsection (h)(3)(J) of such section), the State housing credit ceiling applicable to such agency.

(3) COMPLIANCE AND ASSET MANAGEMENT.—The State housing credit agency shall perform asset management functions to ensure compliance with section 42 of the Internal Revenue Code of 1986 and the long-term viability of buildings funded by any subaward under this section. The State housing credit agency may collect reasonable fees from a subaward recipient to cover expenses associated with the performance of its duties under this paragraph. The State housing credit agency may retain an agent or other private contractor to satisfy the requirements of this paragraph.

(4) RECAPTURE.—The State housing credit agency shall impose conditions or restrictions, including a requirement providing for recapture, on any subaward under this section so as to assure that the building with respect to which such subaward is made remains a qualified low-income building during the compliance period. Any such recapture shall be payable to the Secretary of the Treasury for deposit in the general fund of the Treasury and may be enforced by means of liens or such other methods as the Secretary of the Treasury determines appropriate.

(d) RETURN OF UNUSED GRANT FUNDS.—Any grant funds not used to make subawards under this section before January 1, 2011, shall be returned to the Secretary of the Treasury on such date. Any subawards returned to the State housing credit agency on or after such date shall be promptly returned to the Secretary of the Treasury. Any amounts returned to the Secretary of the Treasury under this subsection shall be deposited in the general fund of the Treasury.

(e) DEFINITIONS.—Any term used in this section which is also used in section 42 of the Internal Revenue Code of 1986 shall have the same meaning for purposes of this section as when used in such section 42. Any reference in this section to the Secretary of the Treasury shall be treated as including the Secretary's delegate.

(f) APPROPRIATIONS.—There is hereby appropriated to the Secretary of the Treasury such sums as may be necessary to carry out this section.

[CCH Explanation at ¶ 535. Committee Reports at ¶ 10,380.]

[¶ 7036] ACT SEC. 1603. GRANTS FOR SPECIFIED ENERGY PROPERTY IN LIEU OF TAX CREDITS.

(a) IN GENERAL.—Upon application, the Secretary of the Treasury shall, subject to the requirements of this section, provide a grant to each person who places in service specified energy property to reimburse such person for a portion of the expense of such property as provided in subsection (b). No grant shall be made under this section with respect to any property unless such property—

(1) is placed in service during 2009 or 2010, or

(2) is placed in service after 2010 and before the credit termination date with respect to such property, but only if the construction of such property began during 2009 or 2010.

(b) GRANT AMOUNT.—

(1) IN GENERAL.—The amount of the grant under subsection (a) with respect to any specified energy property shall be the applicable percentage of the basis of such property.

(2) APPLICABLE PERCENTAGE.—For purposes of paragraph (1), the term "applicable percentage" means—

(A) 30 percent in the case of any property described in paragraphs (1) through (4) of subsection (d), and

(B) 10 percent in the case of any other property.

(3) DOLLAR LIMITATIONS.—In the case of property described in paragraph (2), (6), or (7) of subsection (d), the amount of any grant under this section with respect to such property shall not exceed the limitation described in section 48(c)(1)(B), 48(c)(2)(B), or 48(c)(3)(B) of the Internal Revenue Code of 1986, respectively, with respect to such property.

(c) TIME FOR PAYMENT OF GRANT.—The Secretary of the Treasury shall make payment of any grant under subsection (a) during the 60-day period beginning on the later of—

(1) the date of the application for such grant, or

(2) the date the specified energy property for which the grant is being made is placed in service.

(d) SPECIFIED ENERGY PROPERTY.—For purposes of this section, the term "specified energy property" means any of the following:

(1) QUALIFIED FACILITIES.—Any qualified property (as defined in section 48(a)(5)(D) of the Internal Revenue Code of 1986) which is part of a qualified facility (within the meaning of section 45 of such Code) described in paragraph (1), (2), (3), (4), (6), (7), (9), or (11) of section 45(d) of such Code.

(2) QUALIFIED FUEL CELL PROPERTY.—Any qualified fuel cell property (as defined in section 48(c)(1) of such Code).

(3) SOLAR PROPERTY.—Any property described in clause (i) or (ii) of section 48(a)(3)(A) of such Code.

(4) QUALIFIED SMALL WIND ENERGY PROPERTY.—Any qualified small wind energy property (as defined in section 48(c)(4) of such Code).

(5) GEOTHERMAL PROPERTY.—Any property described in clause (iii) of section 48(a)(3)(A) of such Code.

(6) QUALIFIED MICROTURBINE PROPERTY.—Any qualified microturbine property (as defined in section 48(c)(2) of such Code).

(7) COMBINED HEAT AND POWER SYSTEM PROPERTY.—Any combined heat and power system property (as defined in section 48(c)(3) of such Code).

(8) GEOTHERMAL HEAT PUMP PROPERTY.—Any property described in clause (vii) of section 48(a)(3)(A) of such Code.

Such term shall not include any property unless depreciation (or amortization in lieu of depreciation) is allowable with respect to such property.

(e) CREDIT TERMINATION DATE.—For purposes of this section, the term "credit termination date" means—

(1) in the case of any specified energy property which is part of a facility described in paragraph (1) of section 45(d) of the Internal Revenue Code of 1986, January 1, 2013,

(2) in the case of any specified energy property which is part of a facility described in paragraph (2), (3), (4), (6), (7), (9), or (11) of section 45(d) of such Code, January 1, 2014, and

(3) in the case of any specified energy property described in section 48 of such Code, January 1, 2017.

In the case of any property which is described in paragraph (3) and also in another paragraph of this subsection, paragraph (3) shall apply with respect to such property.

(f) APPLICATION OF CERTAIN RULES.—In making grants under this section, the Secretary of the Treasury shall apply rules similar to the rules of section 50 of the Internal Revenue Code of 1986. In applying such rules, if the property is disposed of, or otherwise ceases to be specified energy property, the Secretary of the Treasury shall provide for the recapture of the appropriate percentage of the grant amount in such manner as the Secretary of the Treasury determines appropriate.

(g) EXCEPTION FOR CERTAIN NON-TAXPAYERS.—The Secretary of the Treasury shall not make any grant under this section to—

(1) any Federal, State, or local government (or any political subdivision, agency, or instrumentality thereof),

(2) any organization described in section 501(c) of the Internal Revenue Code of 1986 and exempt from tax under section 501(a) of such Code,

(3) any entity referred to in paragraph (4) of section 54(j) of such Code, or

(4) any partnership or other pass-thru entity any partner (or other holder of an equity or profits interest) of which is described in paragraph (1), (2) or (3).

(h) DEFINITIONS.—Terms used in this section which are also used in section 45 or 48 of the Internal Revenue Code of 1986 shall have the same meaning for purposes of this section as when used in such section 45 or 48. Any reference in this section to the Secretary of the Treasury shall be treated as including the Secretary's delegate.

(i) APPROPRIATIONS.—There is hereby appropriated to the Secretary of the Treasury such sums as may be necessary to carry out this section.

(j) TERMINATION.—The Secretary of the Treasury shall not make any grant to any person under this section unless the application of such person for such grant is received before October 1, 2011.

[CCH Explanation at ¶ 515. Committee Reports at ¶ 10,130.]

[¶ 7039] ACT SEC. 1604. INCREASE IN PUBLIC DEBT LIMIT.

Subsection (b) of section 3101 of title 31, United States Code, is amended by striking out the dollar limitation contained in such subsection and inserting "$12,104,000,000,000".

Subtitle H—Prohibition on Collection of Certain Payments Made Under the Continued Dumping and Subsidy Offset Act of 2000

[¶ 7042] ACT SEC. 1701. PROHIBITION ON COLLECTION OF CERTAIN PAYMENTS MADE UNDER THE CONTINUED DUMPING AND SUBSIDY OFFSET ACT OF 2000.

(a) IN GENERAL.—Notwithstanding any other provision of law, neither the Secretary of Homeland Security nor any other person may—

(1) require repayment of, or attempt in any other way to recoup, any payments described in subsection (b); or

(2) offset any past, current, or future distributions of antidumping or countervailing duties assessed with respect to imports from countries that are not parties to the North American Free Trade Agreement in an attempt to recoup any payments described in subsection (b).

(b) PAYMENTS DESCRIBED.—Payments described in this subsection are payments of antidumping or countervailing duties made pursuant to the Continued Dumping and Subsidy Offset Act of 2000 (section 754 of the Tariff Act of 1930 (19 U.S.C. 1675c; repealed by subtitle F of title VII of the Deficit Reduction Act of 2005 (Public Law 109–171; 120 Stat. 154))) that were—

(1) assessed and paid on imports of goods from countries that are parties to the North American Free Trade Agreement; and

(2) distributed on or after January 1, 2001, and before January 1, 2006.

(c) PAYMENT OF FUNDS COLLECTED OR WITHHELD.—Not later than the date that is 60 days after the date of the enactment of this Act, the Secretary of Homeland Security shall—

(1) refund any repayments, or any other recoupment, of payments described in subsection (b); and

(2) fully distribute any antidumping or countervailing duties that the U.S. Customs and Border Protection is withholding as an offset as described in subsection (a)(2).

(d) LIMITATION.—Nothing in this section shall be construed to prevent the Secretary of Homeland Security, or any other person, from requiring repayment of, or attempting to otherwise recoup, any payments described in subsection (b) as a result of—

(1) a finding of false statements or other misconduct by a recipient of such a payment; or

(2) the reliquidation of an entry with respect to which such a payment was made.

* * *

Subtitle I—Trade Adjustment Assistance

[¶ 7045] ACT SEC. 1800. SHORT TITLE.

This subtitle may be cited as the "Trade and Globalization Adjustment Assistance Act of 2009".

* * *

PART VI—HEALTH COVERAGE IMPROVEMENT

[¶ 7048] ACT SEC. 1899. SHORT TITLE.

This part may be cited as the "TAA Health Coverage Improvement Act of 2009".

* * *

[¶ 7051] ACT SEC. 1899D. TAA PRE-CERTIFICATION PERIOD RULE FOR PURPOSES OF DETERMINING WHETHER THERE IS A 63-DAY LAPSE IN CREDITABLE COVERAGE.

* * *

(b) ERISA AMENDMENT.—Section 701(c)(2) of the Employee Retirement Income Security Act of 1974 (29 U.S.C. 1181(c)(2)) is amended by adding at the end the following new subparagraph:

"(C) TAA-ELIGIBLE INDIVIDUALS.—In the case of plan years beginning before January 1, 2011—

"(i) TAA PRE-CERTIFICATION PERIOD RULE.—In the case of a TAA-eligible individual, the period beginning on the date the individual has a TAA-related loss of coverage and ending on the date that is 7 days after the date of the issuance by the Secretary (or by any person or entity designated by the Secretary) of a qualified health insurance costs credit eligibility certificate for such individual for purposes of section 7527 of the Internal Revenue Code of 1986 shall not be taken into account in determining the continuous period under subparagraph (A).

"(ii) DEFINITIONS.—The terms 'TAA-eligible individual' and 'TAA-related loss of coverage' have the meanings given such terms in section 605(b)(4).".

(c) PHSA AMENDMENT.—Section 2701(c)(2) of the Public Health Service Act (42 U.S.C. 300gg(c)(2)) is amended by adding at the end the following new subparagraph:

"(C) TAA-ELIGIBLE INDIVIDUALS.—In the case of plan years beginning before January 1, 2011—

"(i) TAA PRE-CERTIFICATION PERIOD RULE.—In the case of a TAA-eligible individual, the period beginning on the date the individual has a TAA-related loss of coverage and ending on the date that is 7 days after the date of the issuance by the Secretary (or by any person or entity designated by the Secretary) of a qualified health insurance costs credit eligibility certificate for such individual for purposes of section 7527 of the Internal Revenue Code of 1986 shall not be taken into account in determining the continuous period under subparagraph (A).

"(ii) DEFINITIONS.—The terms 'TAA-eligible individual' and 'TAA-related loss of coverage' have the meanings given such terms in section 2205(b)(4).".

(d) EFFECTIVE DATE.—The amendments made by this section shall apply to plan years beginning after the date of the enactment of this Act.

[CCH Explanation at ¶ 725.]

[¶ 7054] ACT SEC. 1899E. CONTINUED QUALIFICATION OF FAMILY MEMBERS AFTER CERTAIN EVENTS.

* * *

(b) CONFORMING AMENDMENT.—Section 173(f) of the Workforce Investment Act of 1998 (29 U.S.C. 2918(f)) is amended by adding at the end the following:

"(8) CONTINUED QUALIFICATION OF FAMILY MEMBERS AFTER CERTAIN EVENTS.—In the case of eligible coverage months beginning before January 1, 2011—

"(A) MEDICARE ELIGIBILITY.—In the case of any month which would be an eligible coverage month with respect to an eligible individual but for paragraph (7)(B)(i), such month shall be treated as an eligible coverage month with respect to such eligible individual solely for purposes of determining the eligibility of qualifying family members of such individual under this subsection. This subparagraph shall only apply with respect to the first 24 months after such eligible individual is first entitled to the benefits described in paragraph (7)(B)(i).

"(B) DIVORCE.—In the case of the finalization of a divorce between an eligible individual and such individual's spouse, such spouse shall be treated as an eligible individual for purposes of this subsection for a period of 24 months beginning with the date of such finalization, except that the only qualifying family members who may be taken into account with respect to such spouse are those individuals who were qualifying family members immediately before such finalization.

"(C) DEATH.—In the case of the death of an eligible individual—

"(i) any spouse of such individual (determined at the time of such death) shall be treated as an eligible individual for purposes of this subsection for a period of 24 months beginning with the date of such death, except that the only qualifying family members who may be taken into account with respect to such spouse are those individuals who were qualifying family members immediately before such death, and

"(ii) any individual who was a qualifying family member of the decedent immediately before such death shall be treated as an eligible individual for purposes [of] this subsection for a period of 24 months beginning with the date of such death, except that no qualifying family members may be taken into account with respect to such individual.".

(c) EFFECTIVE DATE.—The amendments made by this section shall apply to months beginning after December 31, 2009.

[CCH Explanation at ¶725.]

[¶7057] ACT SEC. 1899F. EXTENSION OF COBRA BENEFITS FOR CERTAIN TAA-ELIGIBLE INDIVIDUALS AND PBGC RECIPIENTS.

(a) ERISA AMENDMENTS.—Section 602(2)(A) of the Employee Retirement Income Security Act of 1974 (29 U.S.C. 1162(2)(A)) is amended—

(1) by moving clause (v) to after clause (iv) and before the flush left sentence beginning with "In the case of a qualified beneficiary";

(2) by striking "In the case of a qualified beneficiary" and inserting the following:

"(vi) SPECIAL RULE FOR DISABILITY.—In the case of a qualified beneficiary"; and

(3) by redesignating clauses (v) and (vi), as amended by paragraphs (1) and (2), as clauses (vii) and (viii), respectively, and by inserting after clause (iv) the following new clauses:

"(v) SPECIAL RULE FOR PBGC RECIPIENTS.—In the case of a qualifying event described in section 603(2) with respect to a covered employee who (as of such qualifying event) has a nonforfeitable right to a benefit any portion of which is to be paid by the Pension Benefit Guaranty Corporation under title IV, notwithstanding clause (i) or (ii), the date of the death of the covered employee, or in the case of the surviving spouse or dependent children of the covered employee, 24 months after the date of the death of the covered employee. The preceding sentence shall not require any period of coverage to extend beyond December 31, 2010.

"(vi) SPECIAL RULE FOR TAA-ELIGIBLE INDIVIDUALS.—In the case of a qualifying event described in section 603(2) with respect to a covered employee who is (as of the date that the period of coverage would, but for this clause or clause (vii), otherwise terminate under clause (i) or (ii)) a TAA-eligible individual (as defined in section 605(b)(4)(B)), the period of coverage shall not terminate by reason of clause (i) or (ii), as the case may be, before the later of the date specified in such clause or the date on which such individual ceases to be such a TAA-eligible individual. The preceding sentence shall not require any period of coverage to extend beyond December 31, 2010.".

* * *

(c) PHSA AMENDMENTS.—Section 2202(2)(A) of the Public Health Service Act (42 U.S.C. 300bb-2(2)(A)) is amended—

(1) by striking "In the case of a qualified beneficiary" and inserting the following:

"(v) SPECIAL RULE FOR DISABILITY.—In the case of a qualified beneficiary"; and

(2) by redesignating clauses (iv) and (v), as amended by paragraph (1), as clauses (v) and (vi), respectively, and by inserting after clause (iii) the following new clause:

"(iv) SPECIAL RULE FOR TAA-ELIGIBLE INDIVIDUALS.—In the case of a qualifying event described in section 2203(2) with respect to a covered employee who is (as of the date that the period of coverage would, but for this clause or clause (v), otherwise terminate under clause (i) or (ii)) a TAA-eligible individual (as defined in section 2205(b)(4)(B)), the period of coverage shall not terminate by reason of clause (i) or (ii), as the case may be, before the later of the date specified in such clause or the date on which such individual ceases to be such a

TAA-eligible individual. The preceding sentence shall not require any period of coverage to extend beyond December 31, 2010.".

(d) EFFECTIVE DATE.—The amendments made by this section shall apply to periods of coverage which would (without regard to the amendments made by this section) end on or after the date of the enactment of this Act.

* * *

[CCH Explanation at ¶725.]

[¶7060] ACT SEC. 1899I. SURVEY AND REPORT ON ENHANCED HEALTH COVERAGE TAX CREDIT PROGRAM.

(a) SURVEY.—

(1) IN GENERAL.—The Secretary of the Treasury shall conduct a biennial survey of eligible individuals (as defined in section 35(c) of the Internal Revenue Code of 1986) relating to the health coverage tax credit under section 35 of the Internal Revenue Code of 1986 (hereinafter in this section referred to as the "health coverage tax credit").

(2) INFORMATION OBTAINED.—The survey conducted under subsection (a) shall obtain the following information:

(A) HCTC PARTICIPANTS.—In the case of eligible individuals receiving the health coverage tax credit (including individuals participating in the health coverage tax credit program under section 7527 of such Code, hereinafter in this section referred to as the "HCTC program")—

(i) demographic information of such individuals, including income and education levels,

(ii) satisfaction of such individuals with the enrollment process in the HCTC program,

(iii) satisfaction of such individuals with available health coverage options under the credit, including level of premiums, benefits, deductibles, cost-sharing requirements, and the adequacy of provider networks, and

(iv) any other information that the Secretary determines is appropriate.

(B) NON-HCTC PARTICIPANTS.—In the case of eligible individuals not receiving the health coverage tax credit—

(i) demographic information of each individual, including income and education levels,

(ii) whether the individual was aware of the health coverage tax credit or the HCTC program,

(iii) the reasons the individual has not enrolled in the HCTC program, including whether such reasons include the burden of the process of enrollment and the affordability of coverage,

(iv) whether the individual has health insurance coverage, and, if so, the source of such coverage, and

(v) any other information that the Secretary determines is appropriate.

(3) REPORT.—Not later than December 31 of each year in which a survey is conducted under paragraph (1) (beginning in 2010), the Secretary of the Treasury shall report to the Committee on Finance and the Committee on Health, Education, Labor, and Pensions of the Senate and the Committee on Ways and Means, the Committee on Education and Labor, and the Committee on Energy and Commerce of the House of Representatives the findings of the most recent survey conducted under paragraph (1).

(b) REPORT.—Not later than October 1 of each year (beginning in 2010), the Secretary of the Treasury (after consultation with the Secretary of Health and Human Services, and, in the case of the information required under paragraph (7), the Secretary of Labor) shall report to the Committee on Finance and the Committee on Health, Education, Labor, and Pensions of the Senate and the Committee on Ways and Means, the Committee on Education and Labor, and the Committee on

Energy and Commerce of the House of Representatives the following information with respect to the most recent taxable year ending before such date:

(1) In each State and nationally—

(A) the total number of eligible individuals (as defined in section 35(c) of the Internal Revenue Code of 1986) and the number of eligible individuals receiving the health coverage tax credit,

(B) the total number of such eligible individuals who receive an advance payment of the health coverage tax credit through the HCTC program,

(C) the average length of the time period of the participation of eligible individuals in the HCTC program, and

(D) the total number of participating eligible individuals in the HCTC program who are enrolled in each category of coverage as described in section 35(e)(1) of such Code,

with respect to each category of eligible individuals described in section 35(c)(1) of such Code.

(2) In each State and nationally, an analysis of—

(A) the range of monthly health insurance premiums, for self-only coverage and for family coverage, for individuals receiving the health coverage tax credit, and

(B) the average and median monthly health insurance premiums, for self-only coverage and for family coverage, for individuals receiving the health coverage tax credit,

with respect to each category of coverage as described in section 35(e)(1) of such Code.

(3) In each State and nationally, an analysis of the following information with respect to the health insurance coverage of individuals receiving the health coverage tax credit who are enrolled in coverage described in subparagraphs (B) through (H) of section 35(e)(1) of such Code:

(A) Deductible amounts.

(B) Other out-of-pocket cost-sharing amounts.

(C) A description of any annual or lifetime limits on coverage or any other significant limits on coverage services, or benefits.

The information required under this paragraph shall be reported with respect to each category of coverage described in such subparagraphs.

(4) In each State and nationally, the gender and average age of eligible individuals (as defined in section 35(c) of such Code) who receive the health coverage tax credit, in each category of coverage described in section 35(e)(1) of such Code, with respect to each category of eligible individuals described in such section.

(5) The steps taken by the Secretary of the Treasury to increase the participation rates in the HCTC program among eligible individuals, including outreach and enrollment activities.

(6) The cost of administering the HCTC program by function, including the cost of subcontractors, and recommendations on ways to reduce administrative costs, including recommended statutory changes.

(7) The number of States applying for and receiving national emergency grants under section 173(f) of the Workforce Investment Act of 1998 (29 U.S.C. 2918(f)), the activities funded by such grants on a State-by-State basis, and the time necessary for application approval of such grants.

[CCH Explanation at ¶725.]

[¶7063] ACT SEC. 1899J. AUTHORIZATION OF APPROPRIATIONS.

There is authorized to be appropriated $80,000,000 for the period of fiscal years 2009 through 2010 to implement the amendments made by, and the provisions of, sections 1899 through 1899I of this part.

[¶7066] ACT SEC. 1899K. EXTENSION OF NATIONAL EMERGENCY GRANTS.

(a) IN GENERAL.—Section 173(f) of the Workforce Investment Act of 1998 (29 U.S.C. 2918(f)), as amended by this Act, is amended—

(1) by striking paragraph (1) and inserting the following new paragraph:

"(1) USE OF FUNDS.—

"(A) HEALTH INSURANCE COVERAGE FOR ELIGIBLE INDIVIDUALS IN ORDER TO OBTAIN QUALIFIED HEALTH INSURANCE THAT HAS GUARANTEED ISSUE AND OTHER CONSUMER PROTECTIONS.—Funds made available to a State or entity under paragraph (4)(A) of subsection (a) may be used to provide an eligible individual described in paragraph (4)(C) and such individual's qualifying family members with health insurance coverage for the 3-month period that immediately precedes the first eligible coverage month (as defined in section 35(b) of the Internal Revenue Code of 1986) in which such eligible individual and such individual's qualifying family members are covered by qualified health insurance that meets the requirements described in clauses (i) through (v) of section 35(e)(2)(A) of the Internal Revenue Code of 1986 (or such longer minimum period as is necessary in order for such eligible individual and such individual's qualifying family members to be covered by qualified health insurance that meets such requirements).

"(B) ADDITIONAL USES.—Funds made available to a State or entity under paragraph (4)(A) of subsection (a) may be used by the State or entity for the following:

"(i) HEALTH INSURANCE COVERAGE.—To assist an eligible individual and such individual's qualifying family members with enrolling in health insurance coverage and qualified health insurance or paying premiums for such coverage or insurance.

"(ii) ADMINISTRATIVE EXPENSES AND START-UP EXPENSES TO ESTABLISH GROUP HEALTH PLAN COVERAGE OPTIONS FOR QUALIFIED HEALTH INSURANCE.—To pay the administrative expenses related to the enrollment of eligible individuals and such individuals' qualifying family members in health insurance coverage and qualified health insurance, including—

"(I) eligibility verification activities;

"(II) the notification of eligible individuals of available health insurance and qualified health insurance options;

"(III) processing qualified health insurance costs credit eligibility certificates provided for under section 7527 of the Internal Revenue Code of 1986;

"(IV) providing assistance to eligible individuals in enrolling in health insurance coverage and qualified health insurance;

"(V) the development or installation of necessary data management systems; and

"(VI) any other expenses determined appropriate by the Secretary, including start-up costs and on going administrative expenses, in order for the State to treat the coverage described in subparagraphs (C) through (H) of section 35(e)(1) of the Internal Revenue Code of 1986 as qualified health insurance under that section.

"(iii) OUTREACH.—To pay for outreach to eligible individuals to inform such individuals of available health insurance and qualified health insurance options, including outreach consisting of notice to eligible individuals of such options made available after the date of enactment of this clause and direct assistance to help potentially eligible individuals and such individual's qualifying family members qualify and remain eligible for the credit established under section 35 of the Internal Revenue Code of 1986 and advance payment of such credit under section 7527 of such Code.

"(iv) BRIDGE FUNDING.—To assist potentially eligible individuals to purchase qualified health insurance coverage prior to issuance of a qualified health insurance costs credit eligibility certificate under section 7527 of the Internal Revenue Code of 1986 and commencement of advance payment, and receipt of expedited payment, under subsections (a) and (e), respectively, of that section.

"(C) RULE OF CONSTRUCTION.—The inclusion of a permitted use under this paragraph shall not be construed as prohibiting a similar use of funds permitted under subsection (g)."; and

(2) by striking paragraph (2) and inserting the following new paragraph:

"(2) QUALIFIED HEALTH INSURANCE.—For purposes of this subsection and subsection (g), the term 'qualified health insurance' has the meaning given that term in section 35(e) of the Internal Revenue Code of 1986.".

(b) FUNDING.—Section 174(c)(1) of the Workforce Investment Act of 1998 (29 U.S.C. 2919(c)(1)) is amended—

(1) in the paragraph heading, by striking "AUTHORIZATION AND APPROPRIATION FOR FISCAL YEAR 2002" and inserting "APPROPRIATIONS"; and

(2) by striking subparagraph (A) and inserting the following new subparagraph:

"(A) to carry out subsection (a)(4)(A) of section 173—

"(i) $10,000,000 for fiscal year 2002; and

"(ii) $150,000,000 for the period of fiscal years 2009 through 2010; and".

[¶ 7069] ACT SEC. 1899L. GAO STUDY AND REPORT.

(a) STUDY.—The Comptroller General of the United States shall conduct a study regarding the health insurance tax credit allowed under section 35 of the Internal Revenue Code of 1986.

(b) REPORT.—Not later than March 1, 2010, the Comptroller General shall submit a report to Congress regarding the results of the study conducted under subsection (a). Such report shall include an analysis of—

(1) the administrative costs—

(A) of the Federal Government with respect to such credit and the advance payment of such credit under section 7527 of such Code, and

(B) of providers of qualified health insurance with respect to providing such insurance to eligible individuals and their qualifying family members,

(2) the health status and relative risk status of eligible individuals and qualifying family members covered under such insurance,

(3) participation in such credit and the advance payment of such credit by eligible individuals and their qualifying family members, including the reasons why such individuals did or did not participate and the effect of the amendments made by this part on such participation, and

(4) the extent to which eligible individuals and their qualifying family members—

(A) obtained health insurance other than qualifying health insurance, or

(B) went without health insurance coverage.

(c) ACCESS TO RECORDS.—For purposes of conducting the study required under this section, the Comptroller General and any of his duly authorized representatives shall have access to, and the right to examine and copy, all documents, records, and other recorded information—

(1) within the possession or control of providers of qualified health insurance, and

(2) determined by the Comptroller General (or any such representative) to be relevant to the study.

The Comptroller General shall not disclose the identity of any provider of qualified health insurance or any eligible individual in making any information obtained under this section available to the public.

(d) DEFINITIONS.—Any term which is defined in section 35 of the Internal Revenue Code of 1986 shall have the same meaning when used in this section.

TITLE II—ASSISTANCE FOR UNEMPLOYED WORKERS AND STRUGGLING FAMILIES

* * *

SUBTITLE C—Economic Recovery Payments to Certain Individuals

* * *

[¶ 7070] ACT SEC. 2201. ECONOMIC RECOVERY PAYMENT TO RECIPIENTS OF SOCIAL SECURITY, SUPPLEMENTAL SECURITY INCOME, RAILROAD RETIREMENT BENEFITS, AND VETERANS DISABILITY COMPENSATION OR PENSION BENEFITS.

(a) AUTHORITY TO MAKE PAYMENTS.—

(1) ELIGIBILITY.—

(A) IN GENERAL.—Subject to paragraph (5)(B), the Secretary of the Treasury shall disburse a $250 payment to each individual who, for any month during the 3-month period ending with the month which ends prior to the month that includes the date of the enactment of this Act, is entitled to a benefit payment described in clause (i), (ii), or (iii) of subparagraph (B) or is eligible for a SSI cash benefit described in subparagraph (C).

(B) BENEFIT PAYMENT DESCRIBED.—For purposes of subparagraph (A):

(i) TITLE II BENEFIT.—A benefit payment described in this clause is a monthly insurance benefit payable (without regard to sections 202(j)(1) and 223(b) of the Social Security Act (42 U.S.C. 402(j)(1), 423(b)) under—

(I) section 202(a) of such Act (42 U.S.C. 402(a));

(II) section 202(b) of such Act (42 U.S.C. 402(b));

(III) section 202(c) of such Act (42 U.S.C. 402(c));

(IV) section 202(d)(1)(B)(ii) of such Act (42 U.S.C. 402(d)(1)(B)(ii));

(V) section 202(e) of such Act (42 U.S.C. 402(e));

(VI) section 202(f) of such Act (42 U.S.C. 402(f));

(VII) section 202(g) of such Act (42 U.S.C. 402(g));

(VIII) section 202(h) of such Act (42 U.S.C. 402(h));

(IX) section 223(a) of such Act (42 U.S.C. 423(a));

(X) section 227 of such Act (42 U.S.C. 427); or

(XI) section 228 of such Act (42 U.S.C. 428).

(ii) RAILROAD RETIREMENT BENEFIT.—A benefit payment described in this clause is a monthly annuity or pension payment payable (without regard to section 5(a)(ii) of the Railroad Retirement Act of 1974 (45 U.S.C. 231d(a)(ii))) under—

(I) section 2(a)(1) of such Act (45 U.S.C. 231a(a)(1));

(II) section 2(c) of such Act (45 U.S.C. 231a(c));

(III) section 2(d)(1)(i) of such Act (45 U.S.C. 231a(d)(1)(i));

(IV) section 2(d)(1)(ii) of such Act (45 U.S.C. 231a(d)(1)(ii));

(V) section 2(d)(1)(iii)(C) of such Act to an adult disabled child (45 U.S.C. 231a(d)(1)(iii)(C));

(VI) section 2(d)(1)(iv) of such Act (45 U.S.C. 231a(d)(1)(iv));

(VII) section 2(d)(1)(v) of such Act (45 U.S.C. 231a(d)(1)(v)); or

(VIII) section 7(b)(2) of such Act (45 U.S.C. 231f(b)(2)) with respect to any of the benefit payments described in clause (i) of this subparagraph.

(iii) VETERANS BENEFIT.—A benefit payment described in this clause is a compensation or pension payment payable under—

(I) section 1110, 1117, 1121, 1131, 1141, or 1151 of title 38, United States Code;

(II) section 1310, 1312, 1313, 1315, 1316, or 1318 of title 38, United States Code;

(III) section 1513, 1521, 1533, 1536, 1537, 1541, 1542, or 1562 of title 38, United States Code; or

(IV) section 1805, 1815, or 1821 of title 38, United States Code, to a veteran, surviving spouse, child, or parent as described in paragraph (2), (3), (4)(A)(ii), or (5) of section 101, title 38, United States Code, who received that benefit during any month within the 3 month period ending with the month which ends prior to the month that includes the date of the enactment of this Act.

(C) SSI CASH BENEFIT DESCRIBED.—A SSI cash benefit described in this subparagraph is a cash benefit payable under section 1611 (other than under subsection (e)(1)(B) of such section) or 1619(a) of the Social Security Act (42 U.S.C. 1382, 1382h).

(2) REQUIREMENT.—A payment shall be made under paragraph (1) only to individuals who reside in 1 of the 50 States, the District of Columbia, Puerto Rico, Guam, the United States Virgin Islands, American Samoa, or the Northern Mariana Islands. For purposes of the preceding sentence, the determination of the individual's residence shall be based on the current address of record under a program specified in paragraph (1).

(3) NO DOUBLE PAYMENTS.—An individual shall be paid only 1 payment under this section, regardless of whether the individual is entitled to, or eligible for, more than 1 benefit or cash payment described in paragraph (1).

(4) LIMITATION.—A payment under this section shall not be made—

(A) in the case of an individual entitled to a benefit specified in paragraph (1)(B)(i) or paragraph (1)(B)(ii)(VIII) if, for the most recent month of such individual's entitlement in the 3-month period described in paragraph (1), such individual's benefit under such paragraph was not payable by reason of subsection (x) or (y) of section 202 [of] the Social Security Act (42 U.S.C. 402) or section 1129A of such Act (42 U.S.C. 1320a-8a);

(B) in the case of an individual entitled to a benefit specified in paragraph (1)(B)(iii) if, for the most recent month of such individual's entitlement in the 3 month period described in paragraph (1), such individual's benefit under such paragraph was not payable, or was reduced, by reason of section 1505, 5313, or 5313B of title 38, United States Code;

(C) in the case of an individual entitled to a benefit specified in paragraph (1)(C) if, for such most recent month, such individual's benefit under such paragraph was not payable by reason of subsection (e)(1)(A) or (e)(4) of section 1611 (42 U.S.C. 1382) or section 1129A of such Act (42 U.S.C. 1320a-8a); or

(D) in the case of any individual whose date of death occurs before the date on which the individual is certified under subsection (b) to receive a payment under this section.

(5) TIMING AND MANNER OF PAYMENTS.—

(A) IN GENERAL.—The Secretary of the Treasury shall commence disbursing payments under this section at the earliest practicable date but in no event later than 120 days after the date of enactment of this Act. The Secretary of the Treasury may disburse any payment electronically to an individual in such manner as if such payment was a benefit payment or cash benefit to such individual under the applicable program described in subparagraph (B) or (C) of paragraph (1).

(B) DEADLINE.—No payments shall be disbursed under this section after December 31, 2010, regardless of any determinations of entitlement to, or eligibility for, such payments made after such date.

(b) IDENTIFICATION OF RECIPIENTS.—The Commissioner of Social Security, the Railroad Retirement Board, and the Secretary of Veterans Affairs shall certify the individuals entitled to receive payments under this section and provide the Secretary of the Treasury with the information needed to disburse such payments. A certification of an individual shall be unaffected by any subsequent determination or redetermination of the individual's entitlement to, or eligibility for, a benefit specified in subparagraph (B) or (C) of subsection (a)(1).

(c) TREATMENT OF PAYMENTS.—

(1) PAYMENT TO BE DISREGARDED FOR PURPOSES OF ALL FEDERAL AND FEDERALLY ASSISTED PROGRAMS.—A payment under subsection (a) shall not be regarded as income and shall not be

regarded as a resource for the month of receipt and the following 9 months, for purposes of determining the eligibility of the recipient (or the recipient's spouse or family) for benefits or assistance, or the amount or extent of benefits or assistance, under any Federal program or under any State or local program financed in whole or in part with Federal funds.

(2) PAYMENT NOT CONSIDERED INCOME FOR PURPOSES OF TAXATION.—A payment under subsection (a) shall not be considered as gross income for purposes of the Internal Revenue Code of 1986.

(3) PAYMENTS PROTECTED FROM ASSIGNMENT.—The provisions of sections 207 and 1631(d)(1) of the Social Security Act (42 U.S.C. 407, 1383(d)(1)), section 14(a) of the Railroad Retirement Act of 1974 (45 U.S.C. 231m(a)), and section 5301 of title 38, United States Code, shall apply to any payment made under subsection (a) as if such payment was a benefit payment or cash benefit to such individual under the applicable program described in subparagraph (B) or (C) of subsection (a)(1).

(4) PAYMENTS SUBJECT TO OFFSET.—Notwithstanding paragraph (3), for purposes of section 3716 of title 31, United States Code, any payment made under this section shall not be considered a benefit payment or cash benefit made under the applicable program described in subparagraph (B) or (C) of subsection (a)(1) and all amounts paid shall be subject to offset to collect delinquent debts.

(d) PAYMENT TO REPRESENTATIVE PAYEES AND FIDUCIARIES.—

(1) IN GENERAL.—In any case in which an individual who is entitled to a payment under subsection (a) and whose benefit payment or cash benefit described in paragraph (1) of that subsection is paid to a representative payee or fiduciary, the payment under subsection (a) shall be made to the individual's representative payee or fiduciary and the entire payment shall be used only for the benefit of the individual who is entitled to the payment.

(2) APPLICABILITY.—

(A) PAYMENT ON THE BASIS OF A TITLE II OR SSI BENEFIT.—Section 1129(a)(3) of the Social Security Act (42 U.S.C. 1320a-8(a)(3)) shall apply to any payment made on the basis of an entitlement to a benefit specified in paragraph (1)(B)(i) or (1)(C) of subsection (a) in the same manner as such section applies to a payment under title II or XVI of such Act.

(B) PAYMENT ON THE BASIS OF A RAILROAD RETIREMENT BENEFIT.—Section 13 of the Railroad Retirement Act (45 U.S.C. 231l) shall apply to any payment made on the basis of an entitlement to a benefit specified in paragraph (1)(B)(ii) of subsection (a) in the same manner as such section applies to a payment under such Act.

(C) PAYMENT ON THE BASIS OF A VETERANS BENEFIT.—Sections 5502, 6106, and 6108 of title 38, United States Code, shall apply to any payment made on the basis of an entitlement to a benefit specified in paragraph (1)(B)(iii) of subsection (a) in the same manner as those sections apply to a payment under that title.

(e) APPROPRIATION.—Out of any sums in the Treasury of the United States not otherwise appropriated, the following sums are appropriated for the period of fiscal years 2009 through 2011, to remain available until expended, to carry out this section:

(1) For the Secretary of the Treasury, $131,000,000 for administrative costs incurred in carrying out this section, section 2202, section 36A of the Internal Revenue Code of 1986 (as added by this Act), and other provisions of this Act or the amendments made by this Act relating to the Internal Revenue Code of 1986.

(2) For the Commissioner of Social Security—

(A) such sums as may be necessary for payments to individuals certified by the Commissioner of Social Security as entitled to receive a payment under this section; and

(B) $90,000,000 for the Social Security Administration's Limitation on Administrative Expenses for costs incurred in carrying out this section.

(3) For the Railroad Retirement Board—

(A) such sums as may be necessary for payments to individuals certified by the Railroad Retirement Board as entitled to receive a payment under this section; and

(B) $1,400,000 to the Railroad Retirement Board's Limitation on Administration for administrative costs incurred in carrying out this section.

(4)(A) For the Secretary of Veterans Affairs—

(i) such sums as may be necessary for the Compensation and Pensions account, for payments to individuals certified by the Secretary of Veterans Affairs as entitled to receive a payment under this section; and

(ii) $100,000 for the Information Systems Technology account and $7,100,000 for the General Operating Expenses account for administrative costs incurred in carrying out this section.

(B) The Department of Veterans Affairs Compensation and Pensions account shall hereinafter be available for payments authorized under subsection (a)(1)(A) to individuals entitled to a benefit payment described in subsection (a)(1)(B)(iii).

[CCH Explanation at ¶225. Committee Reports at ¶10,490.]

[¶7071] ACT SEC. 2202. SPECIAL CREDIT FOR CERTAIN GOVERNMENT RETIREES.

(a) IN GENERAL.—In the case of an eligible individual, there shall be allowed as a credit against the tax imposed by subtitle A of the Internal Revenue Code of 1986 for the first taxable year beginning in 2009 an amount equal $250 ($500 in the case of a joint return where both spouses are eligible individuals).

(b) ELIGIBLE INDIVIDUAL.—For purposes of this section—

(1) IN GENERAL.—The term "eligible individual" means any individual—

(A) who receives during the first taxable year beginning in 2009 any amount as a pension or annuity for service performed in the employ of the United States or any State, or any instrumentality thereof, which is not considered employment for purposes of chapter 21 of the Internal Revenue Code of 1986, and

(B) who does not receive a payment under section 2201 during such taxable year.

(2) IDENTIFICATION NUMBER REQUIREMENT.—Such term shall not include any individual who does not include on the return of tax for the taxable year—

(A) such individual's social security account number, and

(B) in the case of a joint return, the social security account number of one of the taxpayers on such return.

For purposes of the preceding sentence, the social security account number shall not include a TIN (as defined in section 7701(a)(41) of the Internal Revenue Code of 1986) issued by the Internal Revenue Service. Any omission of a correct social security account number required under this subparagraph shall be treated as a mathematical or clerical error for purposes of applying section 6213(g)(2) of such Code to such omission.

(c) TREATMENT OF CREDIT.—

(1) REFUNDABLE CREDIT.—

(A) IN GENERAL.—The credit allowed by subsection (a) shall be treated as allowed by subpart C of part IV of subchapter A of chapter 1 of the Internal Revenue Code of 1986.

(B) APPROPRIATIONS.—For purposes of section 1324(b)(2) of title 31, United States Code, the credit allowed by subsection (a) shall be treated in the same manner [as] a refund from the credit allowed under section 36A of the Internal Revenue Code of 1986 (as added by this Act).

(2) DEFICIENCY RULES.—For purposes of section 6211(b)(4)(A) of the Internal Revenue Code of 1986, the credit allowable by subsection (a) shall be treated in the same manner as the credit allowable under section 36A of the Internal Revenue Code of 1986 (as added by this Act).

(d) REFUNDS DISREGARDED IN THE ADMINISTRATION OF FEDERAL PROGRAMS AND FEDERALLY ASSISTED PROGRAMS.—Any credit or refund allowed or made to any individual by reason of this section shall not be taken into account as income and shall not be taken into account as resources for the month of receipt and the following 2 months, for purposes of determining the eligibility of such individual or any other individual for benefits or assistance, or the amount or extent of benefits or assistance, under any Federal program or under any State or local program financed in whole or in part with Federal funds.

[CCH Explanation at ¶325. Committee Reports at ¶10,500.]

TITLE III—PREMIUM ASSISTANCE FOR COBRA BENEFITS
* * *

[¶7072] ACT SEC. 3001. PREMIUM ASSISTANCE FOR COBRA BENEFITS.

(a) PREMIUM ASSISTANCE FOR COBRA CONTINUATION COVERAGE FOR INDIVIDUALS AND THEIR FAMILIES.—

(1) PROVISION OF PREMIUM ASSISTANCE.—

(A) REDUCTION OF PREMIUMS PAYABLE.—In the case of any premium for a period of coverage beginning on or after the date of the enactment of this Act for COBRA continuation coverage with respect to any assistance eligible individual, such individual shall be treated for purposes of any COBRA continuation provision as having paid the amount of such premium if such individual pays (or a person other than such individual's employer pays on behalf of such individual) 35 percent of the amount of such premium (as determined without regard to this subsection).

(B) PLAN ENROLLMENT OPTION.—

(i) IN GENERAL.—Notwithstanding the COBRA continuation provisions, an assistance eligible individual may, not later than 90 days after the date of notice of the plan enrollment option described in this subparagraph, elect to enroll in coverage under a plan offered by the employer involved, or the employee organization involved (including, for this purpose, a joint board of trustees of a multiemployer trust affiliated with one or more multiemployer plans), that is different than coverage under the plan in which such individual was enrolled at the time the qualifying event occurred, and such coverage shall be treated as COBRA continuation coverage for purposes of the applicable COBRA continuation coverage provision.

(ii) REQUIREMENTS.—An assistance eligible individual may elect to enroll in different coverage as described in clause (i) only if—

(I) the employer involved has made a determination that such employer will permit assistance eligible individuals to enroll in different coverage as provided for [in] this subparagraph;

(II) the premium for such different coverage does not exceed the premium for coverage in which the individual was enrolled at the time the qualifying event occurred;

(III) the different coverage in which the individual elects to enroll is coverage that is also offered to the active employees of the employer at the time at which such election is made; and

(IV) the different coverage is not—

(aa) coverage that provides only dental, vision, counseling, or referral services (or a combination of such services);

(bb) a flexible spending arrangement (as defined in section 106(c)(2) of the Internal Revenue Code of 1986); or

(cc) coverage that provides coverage for services or treatments furnished in an on-site medical facility maintained by the employer and that consists

Act Sec. 3001(a)(1)(B)(ii)(IV)(cc) ¶7072

primarily of first-aid services, prevention and wellness care, or similar care (or a combination of such care).

(C) PREMIUM REIMBURSEMENT.—For provisions providing the balance of such premium, see section 6432 of the Internal Revenue Code of 1986, as added by paragraph (12).

(2) LIMITATION OF PERIOD OF PREMIUM ASSISTANCE.—

(A) IN GENERAL.—Paragraph (1)(A) shall not apply with respect to any assistance eligible individual for months of coverage beginning on or after the earlier of—

(i) the first date that such individual is eligible for coverage under any other group health plan (other than coverage consisting of only dental, vision, counseling, or referral services (or a combination thereof), coverage under a flexible spending arrangement (as defined in section 106(c)(2) of the Internal Revenue Code of 1986), or coverage of treatment that is furnished in an on-site medical facility maintained by the employer and that consists primarily of first-aid services, prevention and wellness care, or similar care (or a combination thereof)) or is eligible for benefits under title XVIII of the Social Security Act, or

(ii) the earliest of—

(I) the date which is 9 months after the first day of the first month that paragraph (1)(A) applies with respect to such individual,

(II) the date following the expiration of the maximum period of continuation coverage required under the applicable COBRA continuation coverage provision, or

(III) the date following the expiration of the period of continuation coverage allowed under paragraph (4)(B)(ii).

(B) TIMING OF ELIGIBILITY FOR ADDITIONAL COVERAGE.—For purposes of subparagraph (A)(i), an individual shall not be treated as eligible for coverage under a group health plan before the first date on which such individual could be covered under such plan.

(C) NOTIFICATION REQUIREMENT.—An assistance eligible individual shall notify in writing the group health plan with respect to which paragraph (1)(A) applies if such paragraph ceases to apply by reason of subparagraph (A)(i). Such notice shall be provided to the group health plan in such time and manner as may be specified by the Secretary of Labor.

(3) ASSISTANCE ELIGIBLE INDIVIDUAL.—For purposes of this section, the term "assistance eligible individual" means any qualified beneficiary if—

(A) at any time during the period that begins with September 1, 2008, and ends with December 31, 2009, such qualified beneficiary is eligible for COBRA continuation coverage,

(B) such qualified beneficiary elects such coverage, and

(C) the qualifying event with respect to the COBRA continuation coverage consists of the involuntary termination of the covered employee's employment and occurred during such period.

(4) EXTENSION OF ELECTION PERIOD AND EFFECT ON COVERAGE.—

(A) IN GENERAL.—For purposes of applying section 605(a) of the Employee Retirement Income Security Act of 1974, section 4980B(f)(5)(A) of the Internal Revenue Code of 1986, section 2205(a) of the Public Health Service Act, and section 8905a(c)(2) of title 5, United States Code, in the case of an individual who does not have an election of COBRA continuation coverage in effect on the date of the enactment of this Act but who would be an assistance eligible individual if such election were so in effect, such individual may elect the COBRA continuation coverage under the COBRA continuation coverage provisions containing such sections during the period beginning on the date of the enactment of this Act and ending 60 days after the date on which the notification required under paragraph (7)(C) is provided to such individual.

(B) COMMENCEMENT OF COVERAGE; NO REACH-BACK.—Any COBRA continuation coverage elected by a qualified beneficiary during an extended election period under subparagraph (A)—

(i) shall commence with the first period of coverage beginning on or after the date of the enactment of this Act, and

(ii) shall not extend beyond the period of COBRA continuation coverage that would have been required under the applicable COBRA continuation coverage provision if the coverage had been elected as required under such provision.

(C) PREEXISTING CONDITIONS.—With respect to a qualified beneficiary who elects COBRA continuation coverage pursuant to subparagraph (A), the period—

(i) beginning on the date of the qualifying event, and

(ii) ending with the beginning of the period described in subparagraph (B)(i),

shall be disregarded for purposes of determining the 63-day periods referred to in section 701(c)(2) of the Employee Retirement Income Security Act of 1974, section 9801(c)(2) of the Internal Revenue Code of 1986, and section 2701(c)(2) of the Public Health Service Act.

(5) EXPEDITED REVIEW OF DENIALS OF PREMIUM ASSISTANCE.—In any case in which an individual requests treatment as an assistance eligible individual and is denied such treatment by the group health plan, the Secretary of Labor (or the Secretary of Health and Human Services in connection with COBRA continuation coverage which is provided other than pursuant to part 6 of subtitle B of title I of the Employee Retirement Income Security Act of 1974), in consultation with the Secretary of the Treasury, shall provide for expedited review of such denial. An individual shall be entitled to such review upon application to such Secretary in such form and manner as shall be provided by such Secretary. Such Secretary shall make a determination regarding such individual's eligibility within 15 business days after receipt of such individual's application for review under this paragraph. Either Secretary's determination upon review of the denial shall be de novo and shall be the final determination of such Secretary. A reviewing court shall grant deference to such Secretary's determination. The provisions of this paragraph, paragraphs (1) through (4), and paragraph (7) shall be treated as provisions of title I of the Employee Retirement Income Security Act of 1974 for purposes of part 5 of subtitle B of such title.

(6) DISREGARD OF SUBSIDIES FOR PURPOSES OF FEDERAL AND STATE PROGRAMS.—Notwithstanding any other provision of law, any premium reduction with respect to an assistance eligible individual under this subsection shall not be considered income or resources in determining eligibility for, or the amount of assistance or benefits provided under, any other public benefit provided under Federal law or the law of any State or political subdivision thereof.

(7) NOTICES TO INDIVIDUALS.—

(A) GENERAL NOTICE.—

(i) IN GENERAL.—In the case of notices provided under section 606(a)(4) of the Employee Retirement Income Security Act of 1974 (29 U.S.C. 1166(4)), section 4980B(f)(6)(D) of the Internal Revenue Code of 1986, section 2206(4) of the Public Health Service Act (42 U.S.C. 300bb-6(4)), or section 8905a(f)(2)(A) of title 5, United States Code, with respect to individuals who, during the period described in paragraph (3)(A), become entitled to elect COBRA continuation coverage, the requirements of such sections shall not be treated as met unless such notices include an additional notification to the recipient of—

(I) the availability of premium reduction with respect to such coverage under this subsection, and

(II) the option to enroll in different coverage if the employer permits assistance eligible individuals to elect enrollment in different coverage (as described in paragraph (1)(B)).

(ii) ALTERNATIVE NOTICE.—In the case of COBRA continuation coverage to which the notice provision under such sections does not apply, the Secretary of Labor, in consultation with the Secretary of the Treasury and the Secretary of Health and Human Services, shall, in consultation with administrators of the group health plans (or other entities) that provide or administer the COBRA continuation coverage involved, provide rules requiring the provision of such notice.

(iii) FORM.—The requirement of the additional notification under this subparagraph may be met by amendment of existing notice forms or by inclusion of a separate document with the notice otherwise required.

(B) SPECIFIC REQUIREMENTS.—Each additional notification under subparagraph (A) shall include—

(i) the forms necessary for establishing eligibility for premium reduction under this subsection,

(ii) the name, address, and telephone number necessary to contact the plan administrator and any other person maintaining relevant information in connection with such premium reduction,

(iii) a description of the extended election period provided for in paragraph (4)(A),

(iv) a description of the obligation of the qualified beneficiary under paragraph (2)(C) to notify the plan providing continuation coverage of eligibility for subsequent coverage under another group health plan or eligibility for benefits under title XVIII of the Social Security Act and the penalty provided under section 6720C of the Internal Revenue Code of 1986 for failure to so notify the plan,

(v) a description, displayed in a prominent manner, of the qualified beneficiary's right to a reduced premium and any conditions on entitlement to the reduced premium, and

(vi) a description of the option of the qualified beneficiary to enroll in different coverage if the employer permits such beneficiary to elect to enroll in such different coverage under paragraph (1)(B).

(C) NOTICE IN CONNECTION WITH EXTENDED ELECTION PERIODS.—In the case of any assistance eligible individual (or any individual described in paragraph (4)(A)) who became entitled to elect COBRA continuation coverage before the date of the enactment of this Act, the administrator of the group health plan (or other entity) involved shall provide (within 60 days after the date of enactment of this Act) for the additional notification required to be provided under subparagraph (A) and failure to provide such notice shall be treated as a failure to meet the notice requirements under the applicable COBRA continuation provision.

(D) MODEL NOTICES.—Not later than 30 days after the date of enactment of this Act—

(i) the Secretary of the Labor, in consultation with the Secretary of the Treasury and the Secretary of Health and Human Services, shall prescribe models for the additional notification required under this paragraph (other than the additional notification described in clause (ii)), and

(ii) in the case of any additional notification provided pursuant to subparagraph (A) under section 8905a(f)(2)(A) of title 5, United States Code, the Office of Personnel Management shall prescribe a model for such additional notification.

(8) REGULATIONS.—The Secretary of the Treasury may prescribe such regulations or other guidance as may be necessary or appropriate to carry out the provisions of this subsection, including the prevention of fraud and abuse under this subsection, except that the Secretary of Labor and the Secretary of Health and Human Services may prescribe such regulations (including interim final regulations) or other guidance as may be necessary or appropriate to carry out the provisions of paragraphs (5), (7), and (9).

(9) OUTREACH.—The Secretary of Labor, in consultation with the Secretary of the Treasury and the Secretary of Health and Human Services, shall provide outreach consisting of public education and enrollment assistance relating to premium reduction provided under this subsection. Such outreach shall target employers, group health plan administrators, public assistance programs, States, insurers, and other entities as determined appropriate by such Secretaries. Such outreach shall include an initial focus on those individuals electing continuation coverage who

are referred to in paragraph (7)(C). Information on such premium reduction, including enrollment, shall also be made available on websites of the Departments of Labor, Treasury, and Health and Human Services.

(10) DEFINITIONS.—For purposes of this section—

(A) ADMINISTRATOR.—The term "administrator" has the meaning given such term in section 3(16)(A) of the Employee Retirement Income Security Act of 1974.

(B) COBRA CONTINUATION COVERAGE.—The term "COBRA continuation coverage" means continuation coverage provided pursuant to part 6 of subtitle B of title I of the Employee Retirement Income Security Act of 1974 (other than under section 609), title XXII of the Public Health Service Act, section 4980B of the Internal Revenue Code of 1986 (other than subsection (f)(1) of such section insofar as it relates to pediatric vaccines), or section 8905a of title 5, United States Code, or under a State program that provides comparable continuation coverage. Such term does not include coverage under a health flexible spending arrangement under a cafeteria plan within the meaning of section 125 of the Internal Revenue Code of 1986.

(C) COBRA CONTINUATION PROVISION.—The term "COBRA continuation provision" means the provisions of law described in subparagraph (B).

(D) COVERED EMPLOYEE.—The term "covered employee" has the meaning given such term in section 607(2) of the Employee Retirement Income Security Act of 1974.

(E) QUALIFIED BENEFICIARY.—The term "qualified beneficiary" has the meaning given such term in section 607(3) of the Employee Retirement Income Security Act of 1974.

(F) GROUP HEALTH PLAN.—The term "group health plan" has the meaning given such term in section 607(1) of the Employee Retirement Income Security Act of 1974.

(G) STATE.—The term "State" includes the District of Columbia, the Commonwealth of Puerto Rico, the Virgin Islands, Guam, American Samoa, and the Commonwealth of the Northern Mariana Islands.

(H) PERIOD OF COVERAGE.—Any reference in this subsection to a period of coverage shall be treated as a reference to a monthly or shorter period of coverage with respect to which premiums are charged with respect to such coverage.

(11) REPORTS.—

(A) INTERIM REPORT.—The Secretary of the Treasury shall submit an interim report to the Committee on Education and Labor, the Committee on Ways and Means, and the Committee on Energy and Commerce of the House of Representatives and the Committee on Health, Education, Labor, and Pensions and the Committee on Finance of the Senate regarding the premium reduction provided under this subsection that includes—

(i) the number of individuals provided such assistance as of the date of the report; and

(ii) the total amount of expenditures incurred (with administrative expenditures noted separately) in connection with such assistance as of the date of the report.

(B) FINAL REPORT.—As soon as practicable after the last period of COBRA continuation coverage for which premium reduction is provided under this section, the Secretary of the Treasury shall submit a final report to each Committee referred to in subparagraph (A) that includes—

(i) the number of individuals provided premium reduction under this section;

(ii) the average dollar amount (monthly and annually) of premium reductions provided to such individuals; and

(iii) the total amount of expenditures incurred (with administrative expenditures noted separately) in connection with premium reduction under this section.

(12) COBRA PREMIUM ASSISTANCE.—

* * *

(B) SOCIAL SECURITY TRUST FUNDS HELD HARMLESS.—In determining any amount transferred or appropriated to any fund under the Social Security Act, section 6432 of the Internal Revenue Code of 1986 shall not be taken into account.

(E) SPECIAL RULE.—

(i) IN GENERAL.—In the case of an assistance eligible individual who pays, with respect to the first period of COBRA continuation coverage to which subsection (a)(1)(A) applies or the immediately subsequent period, the full premium amount for such coverage, the person to whom such payment is payable shall—

(I) make a reimbursement payment to such individual for the amount of such premium paid in excess of the amount required to be paid under subsection (a)(1)(A); or

(II) provide credit to the individual for such amount in a manner that reduces one or more subsequent premium payments that the individual is required to pay under such subsection for the coverage involved.

(ii) REIMBURSING EMPLOYER.—A person to which clause (i) applies shall be reimbursed as provided for in section 6432 of the Internal Revenue Code of 1986 for any payment made, or credit provided, to the employee under such clause.

(iii) PAYMENT OR CREDITS.—Unless it is reasonable to believe that the credit for the excess payment in clause (i)(II) will be used by the assistance eligible individual within 180 days of the date on which the person receives from the individual the payment of the full premium amount, a person to which clause (i) applies shall make the payment required under such clause to the individual within 60 days of such payment of the full premium amount. If, as of any day within the 180-day period, it is no longer reasonable to believe that the credit will be used during that period, payment equal to the remainder of the credit outstanding shall be made to the individual within 60 days of such day.

* * *

(b) ELIMINATION OF PREMIUM SUBSIDY FOR HIGH-INCOME INDIVIDUALS.—

(1) RECAPTURE OF SUBSIDY FOR HIGH-INCOME INDIVIDUALS.—If—

(A) premium assistance is provided under this section with respect to any COBRA continuation coverage which covers the taxpayer, the taxpayer's spouse, or any dependent (within the meaning of section 152 of the Internal Revenue Code of 1986, determined without regard to subsections (b)(1), (b)(2), and (d)(1)(B) thereof) of the taxpayer during any portion of the taxable year, and

(B) the taxpayer's modified adjusted gross income for such taxable year exceeds $125,000 ($250,000 in the case of a joint return),

then the tax imposed by chapter 1 of such Code with respect to the taxpayer for such taxable year shall be increased by the amount of such assistance.

(2) PHASE-IN OF RECAPTURE.—

(A) IN GENERAL.—In the case of a taxpayer whose modified adjusted gross income for the taxable year does not exceed $145,000 ($290,000 in the case of a joint return), the increase in the tax imposed under paragraph (1) shall not exceed the phase-in percentage of such increase (determined without regard to this paragraph).

(B) PHASE-IN PERCENTAGE.—For purposes of this subsection, the term "phase-in percentage" means the ratio (expressed as a percentage) obtained by dividing—

(i) the excess of [sic] described in subparagraph (B) of paragraph (1), by

(ii) $20,000 ($40,000 in the case of a joint return).

(3) OPTION FOR HIGH-INCOME INDIVIDUALS TO WAIVE ASSISTANCE AND AVOID RECAPTURE.—Notwithstanding subsection (a)(3), an individual shall not be treated as an assistance eligible individual for purposes of this section and section 6432 of the Internal Revenue Code of 1986 if such individual—

(A) makes a permanent election (at such time and in such form and manner as the Secretary of the Treasury may prescribe) to waive the right to the premium assistance provided under this section, and

(B) notifies the entity to whom premiums are reimbursed under section 6432(a) of such Code of such election.

(4) MODIFIED ADJUSTED GROSS INCOME.—For purposes of this subsection, the term "modified adjusted gross income" means the adjusted gross income (as defined in section 62 of the Internal Revenue Code of 1986) of the taxpayer for the taxable year increased by any amount excluded from gross income under section 911, 931, or 933 of such Code.

(5) CREDITS NOT ALLOWED AGAINST TAX, ETC.—For purposes [of] determining regular tax liability under section 26(b) of such Code, the increase in tax under this subsection shall not be treated as a tax imposed under chapter 1 of such Code.

(6) REGULATIONS.—The Secretary of the Treasury shall issue such regulations or other guidance as are necessary or appropriate to carry out this subsection, including requirements that the entity to whom premiums are reimbursed under section 6432(a) of the Internal Revenue Code of 1986 report to the Secretary, and to each assistance eligible individual, the amount of premium assistance provided under subsection (a) with respect to each such individual.

(7) EFFECTIVE DATE.—The provisions of this subsection shall apply to taxable years ending after the date of the enactment of this Act.

* * *

[CCH Explanation at ¶705. Committee Reports at ¶10,510.]

TITLE VII—LIMITS ON EXECUTIVE COMPENSATION

* * *

[¶7075] SEC. 7001. EXECUTIVE COMPENSATION AND CORPORATE GOVERNANCE.

Section 111 of the Emergency Economic Stabilization Act of 2008 (12 U.S.C. 5221) is amended to read as follows:

"SEC. 111. EXECUTIVE COMPENSATION AND CORPORATE GOVERNANCE.

"(a) DEFINITIONS.—For purposes of this section, the following definitions shall apply:

"(1) SENIOR EXECUTIVE OFFICER.—The term 'senior executive officer' means an individual who is 1 of the top 5 most highly paid executives of a public company, whose compensation is required to be disclosed pursuant to the Securities Exchange Act of 1934, and any regulations issued thereunder, and non-public company counterparts.

"(2) GOLDEN PARACHUTE PAYMENT.—The term 'golden parachute payment' means any payment to a senior executive officer for departure from a company for any reason, except for payments for services performed or benefits accrued.

"(3) TARP RECIPIENT.—The term 'TARP recipient' means any entity that has received or will receive financial assistance under the financial assistance provided under the TARP.

"(4) COMMISSION.—The term 'Commission' means the Securities and Exchange Commission.

"(5) PERIOD IN WHICH OBLIGATION IS OUTSTANDING; RULE OF CONSTRUCTION.—For purposes of this section, the period in which any obligation arising from financial assistance provided under the TARP remains outstanding does not include any period during which the Federal Government only holds warrants to purchase common stock of the TARP recipient.

"(b) EXECUTIVE COMPENSATION AND CORPORATE GOVERNANCE.—

"(1) ESTABLISHMENT OF STANDARDS.—During the period in which any obligation arising from financial assistance provided under the TARP remains outstanding, each TARP recipient shall be subject to—

"(A) the standards established by the Secretary under this section; and

"(B) the provisions of section 162(m)(5) of the Internal Revenue Code of 1986, as applicable.

"(2) STANDARDS REQUIRED.—The Secretary shall require each TARP recipient to meet appropriate standards for executive compensation and corporate governance.

"(3) SPECIFIC REQUIREMENTS.—The standards established under paragraph (2) shall include the following:

"(A) Limits on compensation that exclude incentives for senior executive officers of the TARP recipient to take unnecessary and excessive risks that threaten the value of such recipient during the period in which any obligation arising from financial assistance provided under the TARP remains outstanding.

"(B) A provision for the recovery by such TARP recipient of any bonus, retention award, or incentive compensation paid to a senior executive officer and any of the next 20 most highly-compensated employees of the TARP recipient based on statements of earnings, revenues, gains, or other criteria that are later found to be materially inaccurate.

"(C) A prohibition on such TARP recipient making any golden parachute payment to a senior executive officer or any of the next 5 most highly-compensated employees of the TARP recipient during the period in which any obligation arising from financial assistance provided under the TARP remains outstanding.

"(D)(i) A prohibition on such TARP recipient paying or accruing any bonus, retention award, or incentive compensation during the period in which any obligation arising from financial assistance provided under the TARP remains outstanding, except that any prohibition developed under this paragraph shall not apply to the payment of long-term restricted stock by such TARP recipient, provided that such long-term restricted stock—

"(I) does not fully vest during the period in which any obligation arising from financial assistance provided to that TARP recipient remains outstanding;

"(II) has a value in an amount that is not greater than $1/3$ of the total amount of annual compensation of the employee receiving the stock; and

"(III) is subject to such other terms and conditions as the Secretary may determine is in the public interest.

"(ii) The prohibition required under clause (i) shall apply as follows:

"(I) For any financial institution that received financial assistance provided under the TARP equal to less than $25,000,000, the prohibition shall apply only to the most highly compensated employee of the financial institution.

"(II) For any financial institution that received financial assistance provided under the TARP equal to at least $25,000,000, but less than $250,000,000, the prohibition shall apply to at least the 5 most highly-compensated employees of the financial institution, or such higher number as the Secretary may determine is in the public interest with respect to any TARP recipient.

"(III) For any financial institution that received financial assistance provided under the TARP equal to at least $250,000,000, but less than $500,000,000, the prohibition shall apply to the senior executive officers and at least the 10 next most highly-compensated employees, or such higher number as the Secretary may determine is in the public interest with respect to any TARP recipient.

"(IV) For any financial institution that received financial assistance provided under the TARP equal to $500,000,000 or more, the prohibition shall apply to the senior executive officers and at least the 20 next most highly-compensated employees, or such higher number as the Secretary may determine is in the public interest with respect to any TARP recipient.

"(iii) The prohibition required under clause (i) shall not be construed to prohibit any bonus payment required to be paid pursuant to a written employment contract executed on or before February 11, 2009, as such valid employment contracts are determined by the Secretary or the designee of the Secretary.

"(E) A prohibition on any compensation plan that would encourage manipulation of the reported earnings of such TARP recipient to enhance the compensation of any of its employees.

"(F) A requirement for the establishment of a Board Compensation Committee that meets the requirements of subsection (c).

"(4) CERTIFICATION OF COMPLIANCE.—The chief executive officer and chief financial officer (or the equivalents thereof) of each TARP recipient shall provide a written certification of compliance by the TARP recipient with the requirements of this section—

"(A) in the case of a TARP recipient, the securities of which are publicly traded, to the Securities and Exchange Commission, together with annual filings required under the securities laws; and

"(B) in the case of a TARP recipient that is not a publicly traded company, to the Secretary.

"(c) BOARD COMPENSATION COMMITTEE.—

"(1) ESTABLISHMENT OF BOARD REQUIRED.—Each TARP recipient shall establish a Board Compensation Committee, comprised entirely of independent directors, for the purpose of reviewing employee compensation plans.

"(2) MEETINGS.—The Board Compensation Committee of each TARP recipient shall meet at least semiannually to discuss and evaluate employee compensation plans in light of an assessment of any risk posed to the TARP recipient from such plans.

"(3) COMPLIANCE BY NON-SEC REGISTRANTS.—In the case of any TARP recipient, the common or preferred stock of which is not registered pursuant to the Securities Exchange Act of 1934, and that has received $25,000,000 or less of TARP assistance, the duties of the Board Compensation Committee under this subsection shall be carried out by the board of directors of such TARP recipient.

"(d) LIMITATION ON LUXURY EXPENDITURES.—The board of directors of any TARP recipient shall have in place a company-wide policy regarding excessive or luxury expenditures, as identified by the Secretary, which may include excessive expenditures on—

"(1) entertainment or events;

"(2) office and facility renovations;

"(3) aviation or other transportation services; or

"(4) other activities or events that are not reasonable expenditures for staff development, reasonable performance incentives, or other similar measures conducted in the normal course of the business operations of the TARP recipient.

"(e) SHAREHOLDER APPROVAL OF EXECUTIVE COMPENSATION.—

"(1) ANNUAL SHAREHOLDER APPROVAL OF EXECUTIVE COMPENSATION.—Any proxy or consent or authorization for an annual or other meeting of the shareholders of any TARP recipient during the period in which any obligation arising from financial assistance provided under the TARP remains outstanding shall permit a separate shareholder vote to approve the compensation of executives, as disclosed pursuant to the compensation disclosure rules of the Commission (which disclosure shall include the compensation discussion and analysis, the compensation tables, and any related material).

"(2) NONBINDING VOTE.—A shareholder vote described in paragraph (1) shall not be binding on the board of directors of a TARP recipient, and may not be construed as overruling a decision by such board, nor to create or imply any additional fiduciary duty by such board, nor shall such vote be construed to restrict or limit the ability of shareholders to make proposals for inclusion in proxy materials related to executive compensation.

Act Sec. 7001 ¶7075

"(3) DEADLINE FOR RULEMAKING.—Not later than 1 year after the date of enactment of the American Recovery and Reinvestment Act of 2009, the Commission shall issue any final rules and regulations required by this subsection.

"(f) REVIEW OF PRIOR PAYMENTS TO EXECUTIVES.—

"(1) IN GENERAL.—The Secretary shall review bonuses, retention awards, and other compensation paid to the senior executive officers and the next 20 most highly-compensated employees of each entity receiving TARP assistance before the date of enactment of the American Recovery and Reinvestment Act of 2009, to determine whether any such payments were inconsistent with the purposes of this section or the TARP or were otherwise contrary to the public interest.

"(2) NEGOTIATIONS FOR REIMBURSEMENT.—If the Secretary makes a determination described in paragraph (1), the Secretary shall seek to negotiate with the TARP recipient and the subject employee for appropriate reimbursements to the Federal Government with respect to compensation or bonuses.

"(g) NO IMPEDIMENT TO WITHDRAWAL BY TARP RECIPIENTS.—Subject to consultation with the appropriate Federal banking agency (as that term is defined in section 3 of the Federal Deposit Insurance Act), if any, the Secretary shall permit a TARP recipient to repay any assistance previously provided under the TARP to such financial institution, without regard to whether the financial institution has replaced such funds from any other source or to any waiting period, and when such assistance is repaid, the Secretary shall liquidate warrants associated with such assistance at the current market price.

"(h) REGULATIONS.—The Secretary shall promulgate regulations to implement this section.".

* * *

[CCH Explanation at ¶ 705. Committee Reports at ¶ 10,520.]

CHILDREN'S HEALTH INSURANCE PROGRAM REAUTHORIZATION ACT OF 2009

[¶ 7076] ACT SEC. 1. SHORT TITLE; AMENDMENTS TO SOCIAL SECURITY ACT; REFERENCES; TABLE OF CONTENTS.

(a) SHORT TITLE.—This Act may be cited as the "Children's Health Insurance Program Reauthorization Act of 2009.

(b) AMENDMENTS TO SOCIAL SECURITY ACT.—Except as otherwise specifically provided, whenever in this Act an amendment is expressed in terms of an amendment to or repeal of a section or other provision, the reference shall be considered to be made to that section or other provision of the Social Secuirty Act.

(c) REFERENCES TO CHIP; MEDICAID; SECRETARY.—In this Act:

(1) CHIP.—The term "CHIP" means the State Children's Health Insurance Program established under title XXI of the Social Security Act (42 U.S.C. 1397aa et seq.).

(2) MEDICAID.—The term "Medicaid" means the program for medical assistance established under title XIX of the Social Seecurity Act (42 U.S.C. 1396 et seq.).

(3) SECRETARY.—The term "Secretary" means the Secretary of Health and Human Services.

* * *

[¶ 7077] ACT SEC. 3. GENERAL EFFECTIVE DATE; EXCEPTION FOR STATE LEGISLATION; CONTINGENT EFFECTIVE DATE; RELIANCE ON LAW.

(a) GENERAL EFFECTIVE DATE.—Unless otherwise provided in this Act, subject to subsections (b) through (d), this Act (and the amendments made by this Act) shall take effect on April 1, 2009, and shall apply to child health assistance and medical assistance provided on or after that date.

* * *

TITLE III—REDUCING BARRIERS TO PROVIDING PREMIUM ASSISTANCE

* * *

Subtitle B—Coordinating Premium Assistance With Private Coverage

[¶ 7078] ACT SEC. 311. SPECIAL ENROLLMENT PERIOD UNDER GROUP HEALTH PLANS IN CASE OF TERMINATION OF MEDICAID OR CHIP COVERAGE OR ELIGIBILITY FOR ASSISTANCE IN PURCHASE OF EMPLOYMENT-BASED COVERAGE; COORDINATION OF COVERAGE.

* * *

(b) CONFORMING AMENDMENTS.—

(1) AMENDMENTS TO EMPLOYEE RETIREMENT INCOME SECURITY ACT.—

(A) IN GENERAL.—Section 701(f) of the Employee Retirement Income Security Act of 1974 (29 U.S.C. 1181(f)) is amended by adding at the end the following new paragraph:

"(3) SPECIAL RULES FOR APPLICATION IN CASE OF MEDICAID AND CHIP.—

"(A) IN GENERAL.—A group health plan, and a health insurance issuer offering group health insurance coverage in connection with a group health plan, shall permit an employee who is eligible, but not enrolled, for coverage under the terms of the plan (or a dependent of such an employee if the dependent is eligible, but not enrolled, for coverage under such terms) to enroll for coverage under the terms of the plan if either of the following conditions is met:

"(i) TERMINATION OF MEDICAID OR CHIP COVERAGE.—The employee or dependent is covered under a Medicaid plan under title XIX of the Social Security Act or under a State child health plan under title XXI of such Act and coverage of the employee or dependent under such a plan is terminated as a result of loss of eligibility for such coverage and the employee requests coverage under the group health plan (or health insurance coverage) not later than 60 days after the date of termination of such coverage.

"(ii) ELIGIBILITY FOR EMPLOYMENT ASSISTANCE UNDER MEDICAID OR CHIP.—The employee or dependent becomes eligible for assistance, with respect to coverage under the group health plan or health insurance coverage, under such Medicaid plan or State child health plan (including under any waiver or demonstration project conducted under or in relation to such a plan), if the employee requests coverage under the group health plan or health insurance coverage not later than 60 days after the date the employee or dependent is determined to be eligible for such assistance.

"(B) COORDINATION WITH MEDICAID AND CHIP.—

"(i) OUTREACH TO EMPLOYEES REGARDING AVAILABILITY OF MEDICAID AND CHIP COVERAGE.—

"(I) IN GENERAL.—Each employer that maintains a group health plan in a State that provides medical assistance under a State Medicaid plan under title XIX of the Social Security Act, or child health assistance under a State child health plan under title XXI of such Act, in the form of premium assistance for the purchase of coverage under a group health plan, shall provide to each employee a written notice informing the employee of potential opportunities then currently available in the State in which the employee resides for premium assistance under such plans for health coverage of the employee or the employee's dependents.

"(II) MODEL NOTICE.—Not later than 1 year after the date of enactment of the Children's Health Insurance Program Reauthorization Act of 2009, the Secretary and the Secretary of Health and Human Services, in consultation with Directors of State Medicaid agencies under title XIX of the Social Security

Act and Directors of State CHIP agencies under title XXI of such Act, shall jointly develop national and State-specific model notices for purposes of subparagraph (A). The Secretary shall provide employers with such model notices so as to enable employers to timely comply with the requirements of subparagraph (A). Such model notices shall include information regarding how an employee may contact the State in which the employee resides for additional information regarding potential opportunities for such premium assistance, including how to apply for such assistance.

"(III) OPTION TO PROVIDE CONCURRENT WITH PROVISION OF PLAN MATERIALS TO EMPLOYEE.—An employer may provide the model notice applicable to the State in which an employee resides concurrent with the furnishing of materials notifying the employee of health plan eligibility, concurrent with materials provided to the employee in connection with an open season or election process conducted under the plan, or concurrent with the furnishing of the summary plan description as provided in section 104(b).

"(ii) DISCLOSURE ABOUT GROUP HEALTH PLAN BENEFITS TO STATES FOR MEDICAID AND CHIP ELIGIBLE INDIVIDUALS.—In the case of a participant or beneficiary of a group health plan who is covered under a Medicaid plan of a State under title XIX of the Social Security Act or under a State child health plan under title XXI of such Act, the plan administrator of the group health plan shall disclose to the State, upon request, information about the benefits available under the group health plan in sufficient specificity, as determined under regulations of the Secretary of Health and Human Services in consultation with the Secretary that require use of the model coverage coordination disclosure form developed under section 311(b)(1)(C) of the Children's Health Insurance Program Reauthorization Act of 2009, so as to permit the State to make a determination (under paragraph (2)(B), (3), or (10) of section 2105(c) of the Social Security Act or otherwise) concerning the cost-effectiveness of the State providing medical or child health assistance through premium assistance for the purchase of coverage under such group health plan and in order for the State to provide supplemental benefits required under paragraph (10)(E) of such section or other authority.".

(B) CONFORMING AMENDMENT.—Section 102(b) of the Employee Retirement Income Security Act of 1974 (29 U.S.C. 1022(b)) is amended—

(i) by striking "and the remedies" and inserting ", the remedies"; and

(ii) by inserting before the period the following: ", and if the employer so elects for purposes of complying with section 701(f)(3)(B)(i), the model notice applicable to the State in which the participants and beneficiaries reside".

(C) WORKING GROUP TO DEVELOP MODEL COVERAGE COORDINATION DISCLOSURE FORM.—

(i) MEDICAID, CHIP, AND EMPLOYER-SPONSORED COVERAGE COORDINATION WORKING GROUP.—

(I) IN GENERAL.—Not later than 60 days after the date of enactment of this Act, the Secretary of Health and Human Services and the Secretary of Labor shall jointly establish a Medicaid, CHIP, and Employer-Sponsored Coverage Coordination Working Group (in this subparagraph referred to as the "Working Group"). The purpose of the Working Group shall be to develop the model coverage coordination disclosure form described in subclause (II) and to identify the impediments to the effective coordination of coverage available to families that include employees of employers that maintain group health plans and members who are eligible for medical assistance under title XIX of the Social Security Act or child health assistance or other health benefits coverage under title XXI of such Act.

(II) MODEL COVERAGE COORDINATION DISCLOSURE FORM DESCRIBED.—The model form described in this subclause is a form for plan administrators of group health plans to complete for purposes of permitting a State to determine the availability and cost-effectiveness of the coverage available under such plans to employees who have family members who are eligible for premium assistance offered under a State plan under title XIX or XXI of such Act and to allow for coordination of coverage for enrollees of such plans. Such form shall provide the following information in addition to such other information as the Working Group determines appropriate:

(aa) A determination of whether the employee is eligible for coverage under the group health plan.

(bb) The name and contract information of the plan administrator of the group health plan.

(cc) The benefits offered under the plan.

(dd) The premiums and cost-sharing required under the plan.

(ee) Any other information relevant to coverage under the plan.

(ii) MEMBERSHIP.—The Working Group shall consist of not more than 30 members and shall be composed of representatives of—

(I) the Department of Labor;

(II) the Department of Health and Human Services;

(III) State directors of the Medicaid program under title XIX of the Social Security Act;

(IV) State directors of the State Children's Health Insurance Program under title XXI of the Social Security Act;

(V) employers, including owners of small businesses and their trade or industry representatives and certified human resource and payroll professionals;

(VI) plan administrators and plan sponsors of group health plans (as defined in section 607(1) of the Employee Retirement Income Security Act of 1974);

(VII) health insurance issuers; and

(VIII) children and other beneficiaries of medical assistance under title XIX of the Social Security Act or child health assistance or other health benefits coverage under title XXI of such Act.

(iii) COMPENSATION.—The members of the Working Group shall serve without compensation.

(iv) ADMINISTRATIVE SUPPORT.—The Department of Health and Human Services and the Department of Labor shall jointly provide appropriate administrative support to the Working Group, including technical assistance. The Working Group may use the services and facilities of either such Department, with or without reimbursement, as jointly determined by such Departments.

(v) REPORT.—

(I) REPORT BY WORKING GROUP TO THE SECRETARIES.—Not later than 18 months after the date of the enactment of this Act, the Working Group shall submit to the Secretary of Labor and the Secretary of Health and Human Services the model form described in clause (i)(II) along with a report containing recommendations for appropriate measures to address the impediments to the effective coordination of coverage between group health plans and the State plans under titles XIX and XXI of the Social Security Act.

(II) REPORT BY SECRETARIES TO THE CONGRESS.—Not later than 2 months after receipt of the report pursuant to subclause (I), the Secretaries shall jointly submit a report to each House of the Congress regarding the recommendations contained in the report under such subclause.

(vi) TERMINATION.—The Working Group shall terminate 30 days after the date of the issuance of its report under clause (v).

(D) EFFECTIVE DATES.—The Secretary of Labor and the Secretary of Health and Human Services shall develop the initial model notices under section 701(f)(3)(B)(i)(II) of the Employee Retirement Income Security Act of 1974, and the Secretary of Labor shall provide such notices to employers, not later than the date that is 1 year after the date of enactment of this Act, and each employer shall provide the initial annual notices to such employer's employees beginning with the first plan year that begins after the date on which such initial model notices are first issued. The model coverage coordination disclosure form developed under subparagraph (C) shall apply with respect to requests made by States beginning with the first plan year that begins after the date on which such model coverage coordination disclosure form is first issued.

(E) ENFORCEMENT.—Section 502 of the Employee Retirement Income Security Act of 1974 (29 U.S.C. 1132) is amended—

(i) in subsection (a)(6), by striking "or (8)" and inserting "(8), or (9)"; and

(ii) in subsection (c), by redesignating paragraph (9) as paragraph (10), and by inserting after paragraph (8) the following:

"(9)(A) The Secretary may assess a civil penalty against any employer of up to $100 a day from the date of the employer's failure to meet the notice requirement of section 701(f)(3)(B)(i)(I). For purposes of this subparagraph, each violation with respect to any single employee shall be treated as a separate violation."

"(B) The Secretary may assess a civil penalty against any plan administrator of up to $100 a day from the date of the plan administrator's failure to timely provide to any State the information required to be disclosed under section 701(f)(3)(B)(ii). For purposes of this subparagraph, each violation with respect to any single participant or beneficiary shall be treated as a separate violation.".

(2) AMENDMENTS TO PUBLIC HEALTH SERVICE ACT.—Section 2701(f) of the Public Health Service Act (42 U.S.C. 300gg(f)) is amended by adding at the end the following new paragraph:

"(3) SPECIAL RULES FOR APPLICATION IN CASE OF MEDICAID AND CHIP.—

"(A) IN GENERAL.—A group health plan, and a health insurance issuer offering group health insurance coverage in connection with a group health plan, shall permit an employee who is eligible, but not enrolled, for coverage under the terms of the plan (or a dependent of such an employee if the dependent is eligible, but not enrolled, for coverage under such terms) to enroll for coverage under the terms of the plan if either of the following conditions is met:

"(i) TERMINATION OF MEDICAID OR CHIP COVERAGE.—The employee or dependent is covered under a Medicaid plan under title XIX of the Social Security Act or under a State child health plan under title XXI of such Act and coverage of the employee or dependent under such a plan is terminated as a result of loss of eligibility for such coverage and the employee requests coverage under the group health plan (or health insurance coverage) not later than 60 days after the date of termination of such coverage.

"(ii) ELIGIBILITY FOR EMPLOYMENT ASSISTANCE UNDER MEDICAID OR CHIP.—The employee or dependent becomes eligible for assistance, with respect to coverage under the group health plan or health insurance coverage, under such Medicaid plan or State child health plan (including under any waiver or demonstration project conducted under or in relation to such a plan), if the employee requests coverage under the group health plan or health insurance coverage not later than 60 days after the date the employee or dependent is determined to be eligible for such assistance.

"(B) COORDINATION WITH MEDICAID AND CHIP.—

"(i) OUTREACH TO EMPLOYEES REGARDING AVAILABILITY OF MEDICAID AND CHIP COVERAGE.—

"(I) IN GENERAL.—Each employer that maintains a group health plan in a State that provides medical assistance under a State Medicaid plan under title XIX of the Social Security Act, or child health assistance under a State child health plan under title XXI of such Act, in the form of premium assistance for the purchase of coverage under a group health plan, shall provide to each employee a written notice informing the employee of potential opportunities then currently available in the State in which the employee resides for premium assistance under such plans for health coverage of the employee or the employee's dependents. For purposes of compliance with this subclause, the employer may use any State-specific model notice developed in accordance with section 701(f)(3)(B)(i)(II) of the Employee Retirement Income Security Act of 1974 (29 U.S.C. 1181(f)(3)(B)(i)(II)).

"(II) OPTION TO PROVIDE CONCURRENT WITH PROVISION OF PLAN MATERIALS TO EMPLOYEE.— An employer may provide the model notice applicable to the State in which an employee resides concurrent with the furnishing of materials notifying the employee of health plan eligibility, concurrent with materials provided to the employee in connection with an open season or election process conducted under the plan, or concurrent with the furnishing of the summary plan description as provided in section 104(b) of the Employee Retirement Income Security Act of 1974.

"(ii) DISCLOSURE ABOUT GROUP HEALTH PLAN BENEFITS TO STATES FOR MEDICAID AND CHIP ELIGIBLE INDIVIDUALS.—In the case of an enrollee in a group health plan who is covered under a Medicaid plan of a State under title XIX of the Social Security Act or under a State child health plan under title XXI of such Act, the plan administrator of the group health plan shall disclose to the State, upon request, information about the benefits available under the group health plan in sufficient specificity, as determined under regulations of the Secretary of Health and Human Services in consultation with the Secretary that require use of the model coverage coordination disclosure form developed under section 311(b)(1)(C) of the Children's Health Insurance Reauthorization Act of 2009, so as to permit the State to make a determination (under paragraph (2)(B), (3), or (10) of section 2105(c) of the Social Security Act or otherwise) concerning the cost-effectiveness of the State providing medical or child health assistance through premium assistance for the purchase of coverage under such group health plan and in order for the State to provide supplemental benefits required under paragraph (10)(E) of such section or other authority.".

* * *

[CCH Explanation at ¶720.]

TITLE VII—REVENUE PROVISIONS

[¶7081] ACT SEC. 701. INCREASE IN EXCISE TAX RATE ON TOBACCO PRODUCTS.

* * *

(h) FLOOR STOCKS TAXES.—

(1) IMPOSITION OF TAX.—On tobacco products (other than cigars described in section 5701(a)(2) of the Internal Revenue Code of 1986) and cigarette papers and tubes manufactured in or imported into the United States which are removed before April 1, 2009, and held on such date for sale by any person, there is hereby imposed a tax in an amount equal to the excess of—

(A) the tax which would be imposed under section 5701 of such Code on the article if the article had been removed on such date, over

(B) the prior tax (if any) imposed under section 5701 of such Code on such article.

(2) CREDIT AGAINST TAX.—Each person shall be allowed as a credit against the taxes imposed by paragraph (1) an amount equal to $500. Such credit shall not exceed the amount of taxes imposed by paragraph (1) on April 1, 2009, for which such person is liable.

(3) LIABILITY FOR TAX AND METHOD OF PAYMENT.—

(A) LIABILITY FOR TAX.—A person holding tobacco products, cigarette papers, or cigarette tubes on April 1, 2009, to which any tax imposed by paragraph (1) applies shall be liable for such tax.

(B) METHOD OF PAYMENT.—The tax imposed by paragraph (1) shall be paid in such manner as the Secretary shall prescribe by regulations.

(C) TIME FOR PAYMENT.—The tax imposed by paragraph (1) shall be paid on or before August 1, 2009.

(4) ARTICLES IN FOREIGN TRADE ZONES.—Notwithstanding the Act of June 18, 1934 (commonly known as the Foreign Trade Zone Act, 48 Stat. 998, 19 U.S.C. 81a et seq.) or any other provision of law, any article which is located in a foreign trade zone on April 1, 2009, shall be subject to the tax imposed by paragraph (1) if—

(A) internal revenue taxes have been determined, or customs duties liquidated, with respect to such article before such date pursuant to a request made under the 1st proviso of section 3(a) of such Act, or

(B) such article is held on such date under the supervision of an officer of the United States Customs and Border Protection of the Department of Homeland Security pursuant to the 2d proviso of such section 3(a).

(5) DEFINITIONS.—For purposes of this subsection—

(A) IN GENERAL.—Any term used in this subsection which is also used in section 5702 of the Internal Revenue Code of 1986 shall have the same meaning as such term has in such section.

(B) SECRETARY.—The term "Secretary" means the Secretary of the Treasury or the Secretary's delegate.

(6) CONTROLLED GROUPS.—Rules similar to the rules of section 5061(e)(3) of such Code shall apply for purposes of this subsection.

(7) OTHER LAWS APPLICABLE.—All provisions of law, including penalties, applicable with respect to the taxes imposed by section 5701 of such Code shall, insofar as applicable and not inconsistent with the provisions of this subsection, apply to the floor stocks taxes imposed by paragraph (1), to the same extent as if such taxes were imposed by such section 5701. The Secretary may treat any person who bore the ultimate burden of the tax imposed by paragraph (1) as the person to whom a credit or refund under such provisions may be allowed or made.

(i) EFFECTIVE DATE.—The amendments made by this section shall apply to articles removed (as defined in section 5702(j) of the Internal Revenue Code of 1986) after March 31, 2009.

[CCH Explanation at ¶730. Committee Reports at ¶15,010.]

[¶7084] ACT SEC. 702. ADMINISTRATIVE IMPROVEMENTS.

* * *

(c) APPLICATION OF INTERNAL REVENUE CODE STATUTE OF LIMITATIONS FOR ALCOHOL AND TOBACCO EXCISE TAXES.—

(1) IN GENERAL.—Section 514(a) of the Tariff Act of 1930 (19 U.S.C. 1514(a)) is amended by striking "and section 520 (relating to refunds)" and inserting "section 520 (relating to refunds), and section 6501 of the Internal Revenue Code of 1986 (but only with respect to taxes imposed under chapters 51 and 52 of such Code)".

(2) EFFECTIVE DATE.—The amendment made by this subsection shall apply to articles imported after the date of the enactment of this Act.

* * *

[CCH Explanation at ¶730. Committee Reports at ¶15,040.]

[¶7087] ACT SEC. 703. TREASURY STUDY CONCERNING MAGNITUDE OF TOBACCO SMUGGLING IN THE UNITED STATES.

Not later than one year after the date of the enactment of this Act, the Secretary of the Treasury shall conduct a study concerning the magnitude of tobacco smuggling in the United States and submit to Congress recommendations for the most effective steps to reduce tobacco smuggling. Such study shall also include a review of the loss of Federal tax receipts due to illicit tobacco trade in the United States and the role of imported tobacco products in the illicit tobacco trade in the United States.

[CCH Explanation at ¶730. Committee Reports at ¶15,080.]

[¶7090] ACT SEC. 704. TIME FOR PAYMENT OF CORPORATE ESTIMATED TAXES.

The percentage under subparagraph (C) of section 401(1) of the Tax Increase Prevention and Reconciliation Act of 2005 in effect on the date of the enactment of this Act is increased by 0.5 percentage point.

[CCH Explanation at ¶470. Committee Reports at ¶15,090.]

Committee Reports

American Recovery and Reinvestment Act of 2009

¶10,001 Introduction

The American Recovery and Reinvestment Act of 2009 (P.L. 111-5) was passed by Congress on February 13, 2009. President Obama signed the Act on February 17, 2009. This Act represents a final consensus on one of the largest spending bills in U. S. history, and contains numerous tax-related provisions. A Joint Explanatory Statement of the bill, Conference Report (H. REPT. 111-16), was issued by the Conference Committee of the House and Senate on February 12, 2009. This statement is the official report of the Conference Committee, and it is cited as the "Conference Report." This report is included to aid the reader's understanding of the new law. At the end of each section, references are provided to the corresponding CCH explanations and Internal Revenue Code provisions. Subscribers to the electronic version can link from these references to the corresponding material. *The pertinent sections of the Conference Report appear in Act Section order beginning at ¶10,010.*

¶10,005 Background

The American Recovery and Reinvestment Act of 2009 was introduced in the House of Representatives on January 26, 2009. The House passed the bill by a vote of 244 to 188 on January 28, 2009. It was then agreed to by the Senate on February 10, 2009, by a vote of 61 to 37. The Conference Report was filed on February 12, 2009, and was agreed to by the House on February 13, 2009, by a vote of 246 to 183 (with one member voting present). The Conference Report was agreed to by the Senate later that day by a vote of 60 to 38. The Act was signed into law by the President on February 17, 2009.

References are to the following report:

• Joint Explanatory Statement of the American Recovery and Reinvestment Act of 2009, is referred to as Conference Report (H. REPT. 111-16).

[¶ 10,010] Act Sec. 1001. Making work pay credit

Conference Report (H. REPT. 111-16)

[New Code Sec. 36A]

Present Law

Earned income tax credit

Low-and moderate-income workers may be eligible for the refundable earned income tax credit ("EITC"). Eligibility for the EITC is based on earned income, adjusted gross income, investment income, filing status, and immigration and work status in the United States. The amount of the EITC is based on the presence and number of qualifying children in the worker's family, as well as on adjusted gross income and earned income.

The EITC generally equals a specified percentage of earned income[1] up to a maximum dollar amount. The maximum amount applies over a certain income range and then diminishes to zero over a specified phaseout range. For taxpayers with earned income (or adjusted gross income ("AGI"), if greater) in excess of the beginning of the phaseout range, the maximum EITC amount is reduced by the phaseout rate multiplied by the amount of earned income (or AGI, if greater) in excess of the beginning of the phaseout range. For taxpayers with earned income (or AGI, if greater) in excess of the end of the phaseout range, no credit is allowed.

The EITC is a refundable credit, meaning that if the amount of the credit exceeds the taxpayer's Federal income tax liability, the excess is payable to the taxpayer as a direct transfer payment. Under an advance payment system, eligible taxpayers may elect to receive the credit in their paychecks, rather than waiting to claim a refund on their tax returns filed by April 15 of the following year.

Child credit

An individual may claim a tax credit for each qualifying child under the age of 17. The amount of the credit per child is $1,000 through 2010 and $500 thereafter. A child who is not a citizen, national, or resident of the United States cannot be a qualifying child.

The credit is phased out for individuals with income over certain threshold amounts. Specifically, the otherwise allowable child tax credit is reduced by $50 for each $1,000 (or fraction thereof) of modified adjusted gross income over $75,000 for single individuals or heads of households, $110,000 for married individuals filing joint returns, and $55,000 for married individuals filing separate returns. For purposes of this limitation, modified adjusted gross income includes certain otherwise excludable income earned by U.S. citizens or residents living abroad or in certain U.S. territories.

The credit is allowable against the regular tax and the alternative minimum tax. To the extent the child credit exceeds the taxpayer's tax liability, the taxpayer is eligible for a refundable credit (the additional child tax credit) equal to 15 percent of earned income in excess of a threshold dollar amount (the "earned income" formula). The threshold dollar amount is $12,550 (for 2009), and is indexed for inflation.

Families with three or more children may determine the additional child tax credit using the "alternative formula," if this results in a larger credit than determined under the earned income formula. Under the alternative formula, the additional child tax credit equals the amount by which the taxpayer's social security taxes exceed the taxpayer's earned income tax credit.

Earned income is defined as the sum of wages, salaries, tips, and other taxable employee compensation plus net self-employment earnings. Unlike the EITC, which also includes the preceding items in its definition of earned income, the additional child tax credit is based only on earned income to the extent it is included in computing taxable income. For example, some ministers' parsonage allowances are considered self-employment income, and thus are considered earned income for purposes of computing the EITC, but the allowances are excluded from gross income for individual income tax purposes, and thus are not considered earned income for purposes of the additional child tax credit.

House Bill

In general

The provision provides eligible individuals a refundable income tax credit for two years (taxable years beginning in 2009 and 2010).

---

[1] Earned income is defined as (1) wages, salaries, tips, and other employee compensation, but only if such amounts are includible in gross income, plus (2) the amount of the individual's net self-employment earnings.

The credit is the lesser of (1) 6.2 percent of an individual's earned income or (2) $500 ($1,000 in the case of a joint return). For these purposes, the earned income definition is the same as for the earned income tax credit with two modifications. First, earned income for these purposes does not include net earnings from self-employment which are not taken into account in computing taxable income. Second, earned income for these purposes includes combat pay excluded from gross income under section 112.[2]

The credit is phased out at a rate of two percent of the eligible individual's modified adjusted gross income above $75,000 ($150,000 in the case of a joint return). For these purposes an eligible individual's modified adjusted gross income is the eligible individual's adjusted gross income increased by any amount excluded from gross income under sections 911, 931, or 933. An eligible individual means any individual other than: (1) a nonresident alien; (2) an individual with respect to whom another individual may claim a dependency deduction for a taxable year beginning in a calendar year in which the eligible individual's taxable year begins; and (3) an estate or trust. Each eligible individual must satisfy identical taxpayer identification number requirements to those applicable to the earned income tax credit.

Treatment of the U.S. possessions

Mirror code possessions[3]

The U.S. Treasury will make payments to each mirror code possession in an amount equal to the aggregate amount of the credits allowable by reason of the provision to that possession's residents against its income tax. This amount will be determined by the Treasury Secretary based on information provided by the government of the respective possession. For purposes of these payments, a possession is a mirror code possession if the income tax liability of residents of the possession under that possession's income tax system is determined by reference to the U.S. income tax laws as if the possession were the United States.

Non-mirror code possessions[4]

To each possession that does not have a mirror code tax system, the U.S. Treasury will make two payments (for 2009 and 2010, respectively) in an amount estimated by the Secretary as being equal to the aggregate credits that would have been allowed to residents of that possession if a mirror code tax system had been in effect in that possession. Accordingly, the amount of each payment to a non-mirror Code possession will be an estimate of the aggregate amount of the credits that would be allowed to the possession's residents if the credit provided by the provision to U.S. residents were provided by the possession to its residents. This payment will not be made to any U.S. possession unless that possession has a plan that has been approved by the Secretary under which the possession will promptly distribute the payment to its residents.

General rules

No credit against U.S. income tax is permitted under the provision for any person to whom a credit is allowed against possession income taxes as a result of the provision (for example, under that possession's mirror income tax). Similarly, no credit against U.S. income tax is permitted for any person who is eligible for a payment under a non-mirror code possession's plan for distributing to its residents the payment described above from the U.S. Treasury.

For purposes of the payments to the possessions, the Commonwealth of Puerto Rico and the Commonwealth of the Northern Mariana Islands are considered possessions of the United States.

For purposes of the rule permitting the Treasury Secretary to disburse appropriated amounts for refunds due from certain credit provisions of the Internal Revenue Code of 1986, the payments required to be made to possessions under the provision are treated in the same manner as a refund due from the credit allowed under the provision.

Federal programs or Federally-assisted programs

Any credit or refund allowed or made to an individual under this provision (including to any resident of a U.S. possession) is not taken into account as income and shall not be taken into account as resources for the month of receipt and the following two months for purposes of determining eligibility of such individual or any other individual for benefits or assistance, or the amount or extent of benefits or assistance, under any Federal program or under any State or local

---

[2] Unless otherwise stated, all section references are to the Internal Revenue Code of 1986, as amended (the "Code").

[3] Possessions with mirror code tax systems are the United States Virgin Islands, Guam, and the Commonwealth of the Northern Mariana Islands.

[4] Possessions that do not have mirror code tax systems are Puerto Rico and American Samoa.

Act Sec. 1001   ¶10,010

program financed in whole or in part with Federal funds.

Income tax withholding

Taxpayers' reduced tax liability under the provision shall be expeditiously implemented through revised income tax withholding schedules produced by the Internal Revenue Service. These revised income tax withholding schedules should be designed to reduce taxpayers' income tax withheld for each remaining pay period in the remainder of 2009 by an amount equal to the amount that withholding would have been reduced had the provision been reflected in the income tax withholding schedules for the entire taxable year.

Effective date

The provision applies to taxable years beginning after December 31, 2008.

Senate Amendment

In general

The Senate is the same as the House bill, except that the credit is phased out at a rate of four percent (rather than two percent) of the eligible individual's modified adjusted gross income above $70,000 ($140,000 in the case of a joint return).

Also, the Senate amendment provides that the otherwise allowable credit allowed under the provision is reduced by the amount of any payment received by the taxpayer pursuant to the provisions of the bill providing economic recovery payments under the Veterans Administration, Railroad Retirement Board, and the Social Security Administration. The provision treats the failure to reduce the credit by the amount of these payments, and the omission of the correct TIN, as clerical errors. This allows the IRS to assess any tax resulting from such failure or omission without the requirement to send the taxpayer a notice of deficiency allowing the taxpayer the right to file a petition with the Tax Court.

Income tax withholding

The Senate amendment also provides for a more accelerated delivery of the credit in 2009 through revised income tax withholding schedules produced by the Department of the Treasury. Under the Senate amendment, these revised income tax withholding schedules would be designed to reduce taxpayers' income tax withheld for the remainder of 2009 in such a manner that the full annual benefit of the provision is reflected in income tax withheld during the remainder of 2009.

Conference Agreement

In general

The provision provides eligible individuals a refundable income tax credit for two years (taxable years beginning in 2009 and 2010).

The credit is the lesser of (1) 6.2 percent of an individual's earned income or (2) $400 ($800 in the case of a joint return). For these purposes, the earned income definition is the same as for the earned income tax credit with two modifications. First, earned income for these purposes does not include net earnings from self-employment which are not taken into account in computing taxable income. Second, earned income for these purposes includes combat pay excluded from gross income under section 112.

The credit is phased out at a rate of two percent of the eligible individual's modified adjusted gross income above $75,000 ($150,000 in the case of a joint return). For these purposes an eligible individual's modified adjusted gross income is the eligible individual's adjusted gross income increased by any amount excluded from gross income under sections 911, 931, or 933. An eligible individual means any individual other than: (1) a nonresident alien; (2) an individual with respect to whom another individual may claim a dependency deduction for a taxable year beginning in a calendar year in which the eligible individual's taxable year begins; and (3) an estate or trust.

Also, the conference agreement provides that the otherwise allowable making work pay credit allowed under the provision is reduced by the amount of any payment received by the taxpayer pursuant to the provisions of the bill providing economic recovery payments under the Veterans Administration, Railroad Retirement Board, and the Social Security Administration and a temporary refundable tax credit for certain government retirees.[5] The conference agreement treats the failure to reduce the making work pay

---

[5] The credit for certain government employees is available for 2009. The credit is $250 ($500 for a joint return where both spouses are eligible individuals). An eligible individual for these purposes is an individual: (1) who receives an amount as a pension or annuity for service performed in the employ of the United States or any State or any instrumentality thereof, which is not considered employment for purposes of Social Security taxes; and (2) who does not receive an economic recovery payment under the Veterans Administration, Railroad Retirement Board, or the Social Security Administration.

credit by the amount of such payments or credit, and the omission of the correct TIN, as clerical errors. This allows the IRS to assess any tax resulting from such failure or omission without the requirement to send the taxpayer a notice of deficiency allowing the taxpayer the right to file a petition with the Tax Court.

Each tax return on which this credit is claimed must include the social security number of the taxpayer (in the case of a joint return, the social security number of at least one spouse).

Treatment of the U.S. possessions

The conference agreement follows the House bill and the Senate amendment.

Federal programs or Federally-assisted programs

The conference agreement follows the House bill and the Senate amendment.

Income tax withholding

The conference agreement follows the Senate amendment.

Effective date

The provision applies to taxable years beginning after December 31, 2008.

[Law at ¶ 5075, ¶ 5375, ¶ 5380 and ¶ 7006. CCH Explanation at ¶ 305.]

[¶ 10,020] Act Sec. 1002. Increase in the earned income tax credit

Conference Report (H. Rept. 111-16)

[Code Sec. 32]

Present Law

Overview

Low-and moderate-income workers may be eligible for the refundable earned income tax credit ("EITC"). Eligibility for the EITC is based on earned income, adjusted gross income, investment income, filing status, and immigration and work status in the United States. The amount of the EITC is based on the presence and number of qualifying children in the worker's family, as well as on adjusted gross income and earned income.

The EITC generally equals a specified percentage of earned income[6] up to a maximum dollar amount. The maximum amount applies over a certain income range and then diminishes to zero over a specified phaseout range. For taxpayers with earned income (or adjusted gross income (AGI), if greater) in excess of the beginning of the phaseout range, the maximum EITC amount is reduced by the phaseout rate multiplied by the amount of earned income (or AGI, if greater) in excess of the beginning of the phaseout range. For taxpayers with earned income (or AGI, if greater) in excess of the end of the phaseout range, no credit is allowed.

An individual is not eligible for the EITC if the aggregate amount of disqualified income of the taxpayer for the taxable year exceeds $3,100

(for 2009). This threshold is indexed for inflation. Disqualified income is the sum of: (1) interest (taxable and tax exempt); (2) dividends; (3) net rent and royalty income (if greater than zero); (4) capital gains net income; and (5) net passive income (if greater than zero) that is not self-employment income.

The EITC is a refundable credit, meaning that if the amount of the credit exceeds the taxpayer's Federal income tax liability, the excess is payable to the taxpayer as a direct transfer payment. Under an advance payment system, eligible taxpayers may elect to receive the credit in their paychecks, rather than waiting to claim a refund on their tax returns filed by April 15 of the following year.

Filing status

An unmarried individual may claim the EITC if he or she files as a single filer or as a head of household. Married individuals generally may not claim the EITC unless they file jointly. An exception to the joint return filing requirement applies to certain spouses who are separated. Under this exception, a married taxpayer who is separated from his or her spouse for the last six months of the taxable year shall not be considered as married (and, accordingly, may file a return as head of household and claim the EITC), provided that the taxpayer maintains a household that constitutes the principal place of abode for a dependent child (including a son,

---

[6] Earned income is defined as (1) wages, salaries, tips, and other employee compensation, but only if such amounts are includible in gross income, plus (2) the amount of the individual's net self-employment earnings.

stepson, daughter, stepdaughter, adopted child, or a foster child) for over half the taxable year,[7] and pays over half the cost of maintaining the household in which he or she resides with the child during the year.

Presence of qualifying children and amount of the earned income credit

Three separate credit schedules apply: one schedule for taxpayers with no qualifying children, one schedule for taxpayers with one qualifying child, and one schedule for taxpayers with more than one qualifying child.[8]

Taxpayers with no qualifying children may claim a credit if they are over age 24 and below age 65. The credit is 7.65 percent of earnings up to $5,970, resulting in a maximum credit of $457 for 2009. The maximum is available for those with incomes between $5,970 and $7,470 ($10,590 if married filing jointly). The credit begins to phase down at a rate of 7.65 percent of earnings above $7,470 ($10,590 if married filing jointly) resulting in a $0 credit at $13,440 of earnings ($16,560 if married filing jointly).

Taxpayers with one qualifying child may claim a credit in 2009 of 34 percent of their earnings up to $8,950, resulting in a maximum credit of $3,043. The maximum credit is available for those with earnings between $8,950 and $16,420 ($19,540 if married filing jointly). The credit begins to phase down at a rate of 15.98 percent of earnings above $16,420 ($19,540 if married filing jointly). The credit is phased down to $0 at $35,463 of earnings ($38,583 if married filing jointly).

Taxpayers with more than one qualifying child may claim a credit in 2009 of 40 percent of earnings up to $12,570, resulting in a maximum credit of $5,028. The maximum credit is available for those with earnings between $12,570 and $16,420 ($19,540 if married filing jointly). The credit begins to phase down at a rate of 21.06 percent of earnings above $16,420 ($19,540 if married filing jointly). The credit is phased down to $0 at $40,295 of earnings ($43,415 if married filing jointly).

If more than one taxpayer lives with a qualifying child, only one of these taxpayers may claim the child for purposes of the EITC. If multiple eligible taxpayers actually claim the same qualifying child, then a tiebreaker rule determines which taxpayer is entitled to the EITC with respect to the qualifying child. Any eligible taxpayer with at least one qualifying child who does not claim the EITC with respect to qualifying children due to failure to meet certain identification requirements with respect to such children (i.e., providing the name, age and taxpayer identification number of each of such children) may not claim the EITC for taxpayers without qualifying children.

House Bill

Three or more qualifying children

The provision increases the EITC credit percentage for families with three or more qualifying children to 45 percent for 2009 and 2010. For example, in 2009 taxpayers with three or more qualifying children may claim a credit of 45 percent of earnings up to $12,570, resulting in a maximum credit of $5,656.50.

Provide additional marriage penalty relief through higher threshold phase-out amounts for married couples filing joint returns

The provision increases the threshold phase-out amounts for married couples filing joint returns to $5,000[9] above the threshold phase-out amounts for singles, surviving spouses, and heads of households) for 2009 and 2010. For example, in 2009 the maximum credit of $3,043 for one qualifying child is available for those with earnings between $8,950 and $16,420 ($21,420 if married filing jointly). The credit begins to phase down at a rate of 15.98 percent of earnings above $16,420 ($21,420 if married filing jointly). The credit is phased down to $0 at $35,463 of earnings ($40,463 if married filing jointly).

Effective date

The provision is effective for taxable years beginning after December 31, 2008.

Senate Amendment

The Senate amendment is the same as the House bill.

Conference Agreement

The conference agreement follows the House bill and the Senate amendment.

[Law at ¶ 5060. CCH Explanation at ¶ 320.]

---

[7] A foster child must reside with the taxpayer for the entire taxable year.

[8] All income thresholds are indexed for inflation annually.

[9] The $5,000 is indexed for inflation in the case of taxable years beginning in 2010.

[¶ 10,030] Act Sec. 1003. Increase of refundable portion of the child credit

Conference Report (H. REPT. 111-16)

[Code Sec. 24]

Present Law

An individual may claim a tax credit for each qualifying child under the age of 17. The amount of the credit per child is $1,000 through 2010, and $500 thereafter. A child who is not a citizen, national, or resident of the United States cannot be a qualifying child.

The credit is phased out for individuals with income over certain threshold amounts. Specifically, the otherwise allowable child tax credit is reduced by $50 for each $1,000 (or fraction thereof) of modified adjusted gross income over $75,000 for single individuals or heads of households, $110,000 for married individuals filing joint returns, and $55,000 for married individuals filing separate returns. For purposes of this limitation, modified adjusted gross income includes certain otherwise excludable income earned by U.S. citizens or residents living abroad or in certain U.S. territories.

The credit is allowable against the regular tax and the alternative minimum tax. To the extent the child credit exceeds the taxpayer's tax liability, the taxpayer is eligible for a refundable credit (the additional child tax credit) equal to 15 percent of earned income in excess of a threshold dollar amount (the "earned income" formula). The threshold dollar amount is $12,550 (for 2009), and is indexed for inflation.

Families with three or more children may determine the additional child tax credit using the "alternative formula," if this results in a larger credit than determined under the earned income formula. Under the alternative formula, the additional child tax credit equals the amount by which the taxpayer's social security taxes exceed the taxpayer's earned income tax credit ("EITC").

Earned income is defined as the sum of wages, salaries, tips, and other taxable employee compensation plus net self-employment earnings. Unlike the EITC, which also includes the preceding items in its definition of earned income, the additional child tax credit is based only on earned income to the extent it is included in computing taxable income. For example, some ministers' parsonage allowances are considered self-employment income and thus, are considered earned income for purposes of computing the EITC, but the allowances are excluded from gross income for individual income tax purposes and thus, are not considered earned income for purposes of the additional child tax credit.

Any credit or refund allowed or made to an individual under this provision (including to any resident of a U.S. possession) is not taken into account as income and shall not be taken into account as resources for the month of receipt and the following two months for purposes of determining eligibility of such individual or any other individual for benefits or assistance, or the amount or extent of benefits or assistance, under any Federal program or under any State or local program financed in whole or in part with Federal funds.

House Bill

The provision modifies the earned income formula for the determination of the refundable child credit to apply to 15 percent of earned income in excess of $0 for taxable years beginning in 2009 and 2010.

Effective date

The provision is effective for taxable years beginning after December 31, 2008.

Senate Amendment

The Senate amendment is the same as the House bill except that the refundable child credit is calculated to apply to 15 percent of earned income in excess of $8,100 for taxable years beginning in 2009 and 2010.

Conference Agreement

The conference agreement follows the House bill and the Senate amendment except that the refundable child credit is calculated to apply to 15 percent of earned income in excess of $3,000 for taxable years beginning in 2009 and 2010.

[Law at ¶ 5005. CCH Explanation at ¶ 315.]

[¶ 10,040] Act Sec. 1004. American opportunity tax credit

Conference Report (H. Rept. 111-16)

[New Code Sec. 25A]

Present Law

Individual taxpayers are allowed to claim a nonrefundable credit, the Hope credit, against Federal income taxes of up to $1,800 (for 2009) per eligible student per year for qualified tuition and related expenses paid for the first two years of the student's post-secondary education in a degree or certificate program.[10] The Hope credit rate is 100 percent on the first $1,200 of qualified tuition and related expenses, and 50 percent on the next $1,200 of qualified tuition and related expenses; these dollar amounts are indexed for inflation, with the amount rounded down to the next lowest multiple of $100. Thus, for example, a taxpayer who incurs $1,200 of qualified tuition and related expenses for an eligible student is eligible (subject to the adjusted gross income phaseout described below) for a $1,200 Hope credit. If a taxpayer incurs $2,400 of qualified tuition and related expenses for an eligible student, then he or she is eligible for a $1,800 Hope credit.

The Hope credit that a taxpayer may otherwise claim is phased out ratably for taxpayers with modified adjusted gross income between $50,000 and $60,000 ($100,000 and $120,000 for married taxpayers filing a joint return) for 2009. The adjusted gross income phaseout ranges are indexed for inflation, with the amount rounded down to the next lowest multiple of $1,000.

The qualified tuition and related expenses must be incurred on behalf of the taxpayer, the taxpayer's spouse, or a dependent of the taxpayer. The Hope credit is available with respect to an individual student for two taxable years, provided that the student has not completed the first two years of post-secondary education before the beginning of the second taxable year.

The Hope credit is available in the taxable year the expenses are paid, subject to the requirement that the education is furnished to the student during that year or during an academic period beginning during the first three months of the next taxable year. Qualified tuition and related expenses paid with the proceeds of a loan generally are eligible for the Hope credit. The repayment of a loan itself is not a qualified tuition or related expense.

A taxpayer may claim the Hope credit with respect to an eligible student who is not the taxpayer or the taxpayer's spouse (e.g., in cases in which the student is the taxpayer's child) only if the taxpayer claims the student as a dependent for the taxable year for which the credit is claimed. If a student is claimed as a dependent, the student is not entitled to claim a Hope credit for that taxable year on the student's own tax return. If a parent (or other taxpayer) claims a student as a dependent, any qualified tuition and related expenses paid by the student are treated as paid by the parent (or other taxpayer) for purposes of determining the amount of qualified tuition and related expenses paid by such parent (or other taxpayer) under the provision. In addition, for each taxable year, a taxpayer may elect either the Hope credit, the Lifetime Learning credit, or an above-the-line deduction for qualified tuition and related expenses with respect to an eligible student.

The Hope credit is available for "qualified tuition and related expenses," which include tuition and fees (excluding nonacademic fees) required to be paid to an eligible educational institution as a condition of enrollment or attendance of an eligible student at the institution. Charges and fees associated with meals, lodging, insurance, transportation, and similar personal, living, or family expenses are not eligible for the credit. The expenses of education involving sports, games, or hobbies are not qualified tuition and related expenses unless this education is part of the student's degree program.

Qualified tuition and related expenses generally include only out-of-pocket expenses. Qualified tuition and related expenses do not include expenses covered by employer-provided educational assistance and scholarships that are not required to be included in the gross income of either the student or the taxpayer claiming the credit. Thus, total qualified tuition and related expenses are reduced by any scholarship or fellowship grants excludable from gross income under section 117 and any other tax-free educational benefits received by the student (or the taxpayer claiming the credit) during the taxable year. The Hope credit is not allowed with respect to any education expense for which a deduction

---

[10] Sec. 25A. The Hope credit generally may not be claimed against a taxpayer's alternative minimum tax liability. However, the credit may be claimed against a taxpayer's alternative minimum tax liability for taxable years beginning prior to January 1, 2009.

is claimed under section 162 or any other section of the Code.

An eligible student for purposes of the Hope credit is an individual who is enrolled in a degree, certificate, or other program (including a program of study abroad approved for credit by the institution at which such student is enrolled) leading to a recognized educational credential at an eligible educational institution. The student must pursue a course of study on at least a half-time basis. A student is considered to pursue a course of study on at least a half-time basis if the student carries at least one half the normal full-time work load for the course of study the student is pursuing for at least one academic period that begins during the taxable year. To be eligible for the Hope credit, a student must not have been convicted of a Federal or State felony consisting of the possession or distribution of a controlled substance.

Eligible educational institutions generally are accredited post-secondary educational institutions offering credit toward a bachelor's degree, an associate's degree, or another recognized post-secondary credential. Certain proprietary institutions and post-secondary vocational institutions also are eligible educational institutions. To qualify as an eligible educational institution, an institution must be eligible to participate in Department of Education student aid programs.

Effective for taxable years beginning after December 31, 2010, the changes to the Hope credit made by the Economic Growth and Tax Relief Reconciliation Act of 2001 ("EGTRRA") no longer apply. The principal EGTRRA change scheduled to expire is the change that permitted a taxpayer to claim a Hope credit in the same year that he or she claimed an exclusion from a Coverdell education savings account. Thus, after 2010, a taxpayer cannot claim a Hope credit in the same year he or she claims an exclusion from a Coverdell education savings account.

House Bill

The provision modifies the Hope credit for taxable years beginning in 2009 or 2010. The modified credit is referred to as the American Opportunity Tax credit. The allowable modified credit is up to $2,500 per eligible student per year for qualified tuition and related expenses paid for each of the first four years of the student's post-secondary education in a degree or certificate program. The modified credit rate is 100 percent on the first $2,000 of qualified tuition and related expenses, and 25 percent on the next $2,000 of qualified tuition and related expenses. For purposes of the modified credit, the definition of qualified tuition and related expenses is expanded to include course materials.

Under the provision, the modified credit is available with respect to an individual student for four years, provided that the student has not completed the first four years of post-secondary education before the beginning of the fourth taxable year. Thus, the modified credit, in addition to other modifications, extends the application of the Hope credit to two more years of post-secondary education.

The modified credit that a taxpayer may otherwise claim is phased out ratably for taxpayers with modified adjusted gross income between $80,000 and $90,000 ($160,000 and $180,000 for married taxpayers filing a joint return). The modified credit may be claimed against a taxpayer's alternative minimum tax liability.

Forty percent of a taxpayer's otherwise allowable modified credit is refundable. However, no portion of the modified credit is refundable if the taxpayer claiming the credit is a child to whom section 1(g) applies for such taxable year (generally, any child under age 18 or any child under age 24 who is a student providing less than one-half of his or her own support, who has at least one living parent and does not file a joint return).

In addition, the provision requires the Secretary of the Treasury to conduct two studies and submit a report to Congress on the results of those studies within one year after the date of enactment. The first study shall examine how to coordinate the Hope and Lifetime Learning credits with the Pell grant program. The second study shall examine requiring students to perform community service as a condition of taking their tuition and related expenses into account for purposes of the Hope and Lifetime Learning credits.

Effective date

The provision is effective with respect to taxable years beginning after December 31, 2008.

Senate Amendment

The Senate amendment is the same as the House bill, except that the Senate amendment provides that only 30 percent of a taxpayer's otherwise allowable modified credit is refundable.

Conference Agreement

The conference agreement follows the House bill, with the following modifications. Under the conference agreement, bona fide re-

Act Sec. 1004 ¶10,040

sidents of the U.S. possessions (American Samoa, Commonwealth of the Northern Mariana Islands, Commonwealth of Puerto Rico, Guam, Virgin Islands) are not permitted to claim the refundable portion of the American opportunity credit in the United States. Rather, a bona fide resident of a mirror code possession (Commonwealth of the Northern Mariana Islands, Guam, Virgin Islands) may claim the refundable portion of the credit in the possession in which the individual is a resident. Similarly, a bona fide resident of a non-mirror code possession (Commonwealth of Puerto Rico, American Samoa) may claim the refundable portion of the credit in the possession in which the individual is a resident, but only if that possession establishes a plan for permitting the claim under its internal law.

The conference agreement provides that the U.S. Treasury will make payments to the possessions in respect of credits allowable to their residents under their internal laws. Specifically, the U.S. Treasury will make payments for to each mirror code possession in an amount equal to the aggregate amount of the refundable portion of the credits allowable by reason of the provision to that possession's residents against its income tax. This amount will be determined by the Treasury Secretary based on information provided by the government of the respective possession. To each possession that does not have a mirror code tax system, the U.S. Treasury will make two payments (for 2009 and 2010, respectively) in an amount estimated by the Secretary as being equal to the aggregate amount of the refundable portion of the credits that would have been allowed to residents of that possession if a mirror code tax system had been in effect in that possession. Accordingly, the amount of each payment to a non-mirror code possession will be an estimate of the aggregate amount of the refundable portion of the credits that would be allowed to the possession's residents if the credit provided by the provision to U.S. residents were provided by the possession to its residents. This payment will not be made to any U.S. possession unless that possession has a plan that has been approved by the Secretary under which the possession will promptly distribute the payment to its residents.

[Law at ¶5005, ¶5010, ¶5015, ¶5020, ¶5035, ¶5280, ¶5305, ¶5375 and ¶7009. CCH Explanation at ¶330.]

[¶10,050] Act Sec. 1005. Temporarily allow computer technology and equipment as a qualified higher education expense for qualified tuition programs

Conference Report (H. REPT. 111-16)

[Code Sec. 529]

Present Law

Section 529 provides specified income tax and transfer tax rules for the treatment of accounts and contracts established under qualified tuition programs.[11] A qualified tuition program is a program established and maintained by a State or agency or instrumentality thereof, or by one or more eligible educational institutions, which satisfies certain requirements and under which a person may purchase tuition credits or certificates on behalf of a designated beneficiary that entitle the beneficiary to the waiver or payment of qualified higher education expenses of the beneficiary (a "prepaid tuition program"). In the case of a program established and maintained by a State or agency or instrumentality thereof, a qualified tuition program also includes a program under which a person may make contributions to an account that is established for the purpose of satisfying the qualified higher education expenses of the designated beneficiary of the account, provided it satisfies certain specified requirements (a "savings account program"). Under both types of qualified tuition programs, a contributor establishes an account for the benefit of a particular designated beneficiary to provide for that beneficiary's higher education expenses.

For this purpose, qualified higher education expenses means tuition, fees, books, supplies, and equipment required for the enrollment or attendance of a designated beneficiary at an eligible educational institution, and expenses for special needs services in the case of a special needs beneficiary that are incurred in connection with such enrollment or attendance. Qualified higher education expenses generally also include

---

[11] For purposes of this description, the term "account" is used interchangeably to refer to a prepaid tuition benefit contract or a tuition savings account established pursuant to a qualified tuition program.

room and board for students who are enrolled at least half-time.

Contributions to a qualified tuition program must be made in cash. Section 529 does not impose a specific dollar limit on the amount of contributions, account balances, or prepaid tuition benefits relating to a qualified tuition account; however, the program is required to have adequate safeguards to prevent contributions in excess of amounts necessary to provide for the beneficiary's qualified higher education expenses. Contributions generally are treated as a completed gift eligible for the gift tax annual exclusion. Contributions are not tax deductible for Federal income tax purposes, although they may be deductible for State income tax purposes. Amounts in the account accumulate on a tax-free basis (i.e., income on accounts in the plan is not subject to current income tax).

Distributions from a qualified tuition program are excludable from the distributee's gross income to the extent that the total distribution does not exceed the qualified higher education expenses incurred for the beneficiary. If a distribution from a qualified tuition program exceeds the qualified higher education expenses incurred for the beneficiary, the portion of the excess that is treated as earnings generally is subject to income tax and an additional 10-percent tax. Amounts in a qualified tuition program may be rolled over to another qualified tuition program for the same beneficiary or for a member of the family of that beneficiary without income tax consequences.

In general, prepaid tuition contracts and tuition savings accounts established under a qualified tuition program involve prepayments or contributions made by one or more individuals for the benefit of a designated beneficiary, with decisions with respect to the contract or account to be made by an individual who is not the designated beneficiary. Qualified tuition accounts or contracts generally require the designation of a person (generally referred to as an "account owner") whom the program administrator (oftentimes a third party administrator retained by the State or by the educational institution that established the program) may look to for decisions, recordkeeping, and reporting with respect to the account established for a designated beneficiary. The person or persons who make the contributions to the account need not be the same person who is regarded as the account owner for purposes of administering the account. Under many qualified tuition programs, the account owner generally has control over the account or contract, including the ability to change designated beneficiaries and to withdraw funds at any time and for any purpose. Thus, in practice, qualified tuition accounts or contracts generally involve a contributor, a designated beneficiary, an account owner (who oftentimes is not the contributor or the designated beneficiary), and an administrator of the account or contract.[12]

House Bill

No provision.

Senate Amendment

The provision expands the definition of qualified higher education expenses for expenses paid or incurred in 2009 and 2010 to include expenses for certain computer technology and equipment to be used by the designated beneficiary while enrolled at an eligible educational institution.

Effective date

The provision is effective for expenses paid or incurred after December 31, 2008.

Conference Agreement

The conference agreement follows the Senate amendment.

[Law at ¶ 5270. CCH Explanation at ¶ 220.]

[¶ 10,060] Act Sec. 1006. Modifications to homebuyer credit

Conference Report (H. Rept. 111-16)

[Code Sec. 36]

Present Law

A taxpayer who is a first-time homebuyer is allowed a refundable tax credit equal to the lesser of $7,500 ($3,750 for a married individual filing separately) or 10 percent of the purchase price of a principal residence. The credit is allowed for the tax year in which the taxpayer purchases the home unless the taxpayer makes an election as described below. The credit is allowed for qualifying home purchases on or

---

[12] Section 529 refers to contributors and designated beneficiaries, but does not define or otherwise refer to the term account owner, which is a commonly used term among qualified tuition programs.

after April 9, 2008 and before July 1, 2009 (without regard to whether there was a binding contract to purchase prior to April 9, 2008).

The credit phases out for individual taxpayers with modified adjusted gross income between $75,000 and $95,000 ($150,000 and $170,000 for joint filers) for the year of purchase.

A taxpayer is considered a first-time homebuyer if such individual had no ownership interest in a principal residence in the United States during the three-year period prior to the purchase of the home to which the credit applies.

No credit is allowed if the D.C. homebuyer credit is allowable for the taxable year the residence is purchased or a prior taxable year. A taxpayer is not permitted to claim the credit if the taxpayer's financing is from tax-exempt mortgage revenue bonds, if the taxpayer is a nonresident alien, or if the taxpayer disposes of the residence (or it ceases to be a principal residence) before the close of a taxable year for which a credit otherwise would be allowable.

The credit is recaptured ratably over fifteen years with no interest charge beginning in the second taxable year after the taxable year in which the home is purchased. For example, if the taxpayer purchases a home in 2008, the credit is allowed on the 2008 tax return, and repayments commence with the 2010 tax return. If the taxpayer sells the home (or the home ceases to be used as the principal residence of the taxpayer or the taxpayer's spouse) prior to complete repayment of the credit, any remaining credit repayment amount is due on the tax return for the year in which the home is sold (or ceases to be used as the principal residence). However, the credit repayment amount may not exceed the amount of gain from the sale of the residence to an unrelated person. For this purpose, gain is determined by reducing the basis of the residence by the amount of the credit to the extent not previously recaptured. No amount is recaptured after the death of a taxpayer. In the case of an involuntary conversion of the home, recapture is not accelerated if a new principal residence is acquired within a two year period. In the case of a transfer of the residence to a spouse or to a former spouse incident to divorce, the transferee spouse (and not the transferor spouse) will be responsible for any future recapture.

An election is provided to treat a home purchased in the eligible period in 2009 as if purchased on December 31, 2008 for purposes of claiming the credit on the 2008 tax return and for establishing the beginning of the recapture period. Taxpayers may amend their returns for this purpose.

House Bill

The provision waives the recapture of the credit for qualifying home purchases after December 31, 2008 and before July 1, 2009. This waiver of recapture applies without regard to whether the taxpayer elects to treat the purchase in 2009 as occurring on December 31, 2008. If the taxpayer disposes of the home or the home otherwise ceases to be the principal residence of the taxpayer within 36 months from the date of purchase, the present law rules for recapture of the credit will still apply.

Effective date.–The provision applies to residences purchased after December 31, 2008.

Senate Amendment

The Senate amendment repeals the existing section 36 for purchases on or after the date of enactment of the American Recovery and Reinvestment Act of 2009.

A taxpayer is allowed a new nonrefundable tax credit equal to the lesser of $15,000 ($7,500 for a married individual filing separately) or 10 percent of the purchase price of a principal residence. The credit is allowed for the tax year in which the taxpayer purchases the home unless the taxpayer makes an election as described below. The credit is allowed for qualifying home purchases after the date of enactment of the American Recovery and Reinvestment Act and on or before the date that is one year after such date of enactment.

The credit is limited to the excess of regular tax liability plus alternative minimum tax liability over the sum of other nonrefundable personal credits.

No credit is allowed for any purchase for which the section 36 first-time homebuyer credit or the D.C. homebuyer credit is allowable. If a credit is allowed under this provision in the case of any individual (and such individual's spouse, if married) with respect to the purchase of any principal residence, no credit is allowed with respect to the purchase of any other principal residence by such individual or a spouse of such individual.

If the taxpayer disposes of the residence (or it ceases to be a principal residence) at any time within 24 months after the date on which the taxpayer purchased the residence, then the credit shall be subject to recapture for the taxable year in which such disposition occurred (or in which the taxpayer failed to occupy the residence as a principal residence). No amount is recaptured after the death of a taxpayer or in the case of a member of the Armed Forces of the United States on active duty who fails to meet the residency requirement pursuant to a military order and incident to a permanent change of station. In the case of an involuntary conversion of the home, recapture is not accelerated if a new principal residence is acquired within a two year period. In the case of a transfer of the residence to a spouse or to a former spouse incident to divorce, the transferee spouse (and not the transferor spouse) will be responsible for any future recapture.

A further election is provided to treat a home purchased in the eligible period as if purchased on December 31, 2008 for purposes of claiming the credit on the 2008 tax return. Taxpayers may amend their returns for this purpose.

Effective date.–The provision applies to purchases after the date of enactment.

Conference Agreement

The conference agreement extends the existing homebuyer credit for qualifying home purchases before December 1, 2009. In addition, it increases the maximum credit amount to $8,000 ($4,000 for a married individual filing separately) and waives the recapture of the credit for qualifying home purchases after December 31, 2008 and before December 1, 2009. This waiver of recapture applies without regard to whether the taxpayer elects to treat the purchase in 2009 as occurring on December 31, 2008. If the taxpayer disposes of the home or the home otherwise ceases to be the principal residence of the taxpayer within 36 months from the date of purchase, the present law rules for recapture of the credit will apply.

The conference agreement modifies the coordination with the first-time homebuyer credit for residents of the District of Columbia under section 1400C. No credit under section 1400C shall be allowed to any taxpayer with respect to the purchase of a residence during 2009 if a credit under section 36 is allowable to such taxpayer (or the taxpayer's spouse) with respect to such purchase. Taxpayers thus qualify for the more generous national first-time homebuyer credit rather than the D.C. homebuyer credit for qualifying purchases in 2009. No credit under section 36 is allowed for a taxpayer who claimed the D.C. homebuyer credit in any prior taxable year.

The conference agreement removes the prohibition on claiming the credit if the residence is financed by the proceeds of a mortgage revenue bond, a qualified mortgage issue the interest on which is exempt from tax under section 103.

Effective date

The provision applies to residences purchased after December 31, 2008.

[Law at ¶5070. CCH Explanation at ¶310.]

[¶10,070] Act Sec. 1007. Exclusion from gross income for unemployment compensation benefits

Conference Report (H. REPT. 111-16)

[Code Sec. 85]

Present Law

An individual must include in gross income any unemployment compensation benefits received under the laws of the United States or any State.

House Bill

No provision.

Senate Amendment

The Senate amendment provides that up to $2,400 of unemployment compensation benefits received in 2009 are excluded from gross income by the recipient.

Effective date

The provision is effective for taxable years beginning after December 31, 2008.

Conference Agreement

The conference agreement follows the Senate amendment.

[Law at ¶5200. CCH Explanation at ¶205.]

[¶10,080] Act Sec. 1008. Deduction for state sales tax and excise tax on the purchase of qualified motor vehicles

Conference Report (H. REPT. 111-16)

[Code Secs. 63 and 164]

Present Law

In general, a deduction from gross income is allowed for certain taxes for the taxable year within which the taxes are paid or accrued. These include State and local, and foreign, real property taxes; State and local personal property taxes; State, local, and foreign income, war profits, and excess profit taxes; generation skipping transfer taxes; environmental taxes imposed by section 59A; and taxes paid or accrued within the taxable year in carrying on a trade or business or an activity described in section 212 (relating to the expenses for production of income). At the election of the taxpayer for the taxable year, a taxpayer may deduct State and local sales taxes in lieu of State and local income taxes. No deduction is allowed for any general sales tax imposed with respect to an item at a rate other than the general rate of tax, except in the case of a lower rate of tax applicable to items of food, clothing, medical supplies, and motor vehicles. In the case of motor vehicles, if the rate of tax exceeds the general rate, such excess shall be disregarded and the general rate shall be treated as the rate of tax.

House Bill

No provision.

Senate Amendment

The Senate amendment provides an above-the-line deduction for qualified motor vehicle taxes. Qualified motor vehicle taxes include any State or local sales or excise tax imposed on the purchase of a qualified motor vehicle. A qualified motor vehicle means a passenger automobile or light truck acquired for use by the taxpayer and not for resale after November 12, 2008 and before January 1, 2010, the original use of which commences with the taxpayer and which has a gross vehicle weight rating of not more than 8,500 pounds.

The deduction is limited to sales tax of up to $49,500.

The deduction is phased out for taxpayers with modified adjusted gross income between $125,000 and $135,000 ($250,000 and $260,000 in the case of a joint return).

Notwithstanding other provisions of present law, qualified motor vehicle taxes are not treated as part of the cost of acquired property or, in the case of a disposition, as a reduction in the amount realized on the disposition.

A taxpayer who makes an election to deduct State and local sales taxes for the taxable year shall not be allowed the above-the-line deduction for qualified motor vehicle taxes.

If the indebtedness described in section 163(h)(5)(A) includes the amounts of any State or local sales or excise taxes paid or accrued by the taxpayer in connection with the acquisition of a qualified motor vehicle, the aggregate amount of such indebtedness taken into account shall be reduced, but not below zero, by the amount of any such taxes for which a deduction is allowed.

Effective date.–The provision is effective for taxable years beginning after December 31, 2008.

Conference Agreement

The conference agreement does not include the House bill or the Senate amendment. The conference agreement provides a deduction for qualified motor vehicle taxes. It expands the definition of taxes allowed as a deduction to include qualified motor vehicle taxes paid or accrued within the taxable year. A taxpayer who itemizes and makes an election to deduct State and local sales taxes for qualified motor vehicles for the taxable year shall not be allowed the increased standard deduction for qualified motor vehicle taxes.

Qualified motor vehicle taxes include any State or local sales or excise tax imposed on the purchase of a qualified motor vehicle. A qualified motor vehicle means a passenger automobile, light truck, or motorcycle which has a gross vehicle weight rating of not more than 8,500 pounds, or a motor home acquired for use by the taxpayer after the date of enactment and before January 1, 2010, the original use of which commences with the taxpayer.

The deduction is limited to the tax on up to $49,500 of the purchase price of a qualified motor vehicle. The deduction is phased out for taxpayers with modified adjusted gross income between $125,000 and $135,000 ($250,000 and $260,000 in the case of a joint return).

Effective date

The provision is effective for purchases on or after the date of enactment and before January 1, 2010.

[Law at ¶5195 and ¶5235. CCH Explanation at ¶230.]

[¶ 10,090] Act Secs. 1011 and 1012. Extend alternative minimum tax relief for individuals

Conference Report (H. Rept. 111-16)

[Code Secs. 26 and 55]

Present Law

Present law imposes an alternative minimum tax ("AMT") on individuals. The AMT is the amount by which the tentative minimum tax exceeds the regular income tax. An individual's tentative minimum tax is the sum of (1) 26 percent of so much of the taxable excess as does not exceed $175,000 ($87,500 in the case of a married individual filing a separate return) and (2) 28 percent of the remaining taxable excess. The taxable excess is so much of the alternative minimum taxable income ("AMTI") as exceeds the exemption amount. The maximum tax rates on net capital gain and dividends used in computing the regular tax are used in computing the tentative minimum tax. AMTI is the individual's taxable income adjusted to take account of specified preferences and adjustments.

The exemption amounts are: (1) $69,950 for taxable years beginning in 2008 and $45,000 in taxable years beginning after 2008 in the case of married individuals filing a joint return and surviving spouses; (2) $46,200 for taxable years beginning in 2008 and $33,750 in taxable years beginning after 2008 in the case of other unmarried individuals; (3) $34,975 for taxable years beginning in 2008 and $22,500 in taxable years beginning after 2008 in the case of married individuals filing separate returns; and (4) $22,500 in the case of an estate or trust. The exemption amount is phased out by an amount equal to 25 percent of the amount by which the individual's AMTI exceeds (1) $150,000 in the case of married individuals filing a joint return and surviving spouses, (2) $112,500 in the case of other unmarried individuals, and (3) $75,000 in the case of married individuals filing separate returns or an estate or a trust. These amounts are not indexed for inflation.

Present law provides for certain nonrefundable personal tax credits (i.e., the dependent care credit, the credit for the elderly and disabled, the adoption credit, the child credit, the credit for interest on certain home mortgages, the Hope Scholarship and Lifetime Learning credits, the credit for savers, the credit for certain nonbusiness energy property, the credit for residential energy efficient property, the credit for plug-in electric drive motor vehicles, and the D.C. first-time homebuyer credit).

For taxable years beginning before 2009, the nonrefundable personal credits are allowed to the extent of the full amount of the individual's regular tax and alternative minimum tax.

For taxable years beginning after 2008, the nonrefundable personal credits (other than the adoption credit, the child credit, the credit for savers, the credit for residential energy efficient property, and the credit for plug-in electric drive motor vehicles) are allowed only to the extent that the individual's regular income tax liability exceeds the individual's tentative minimum tax, determined without regard to the minimum tax foreign tax credit. The adoption credit, the child credit, the credit for savers, the credit for residential energy efficient property, and the credit for plug-in electric drive motor vehicles are allowed to the full extent of the individual's regular tax and alternative minimum tax.[18]

House Bill

No provision.

Senate Amendment

The Senate amendment provides that the individual AMT exemption amount for taxable years beginning in 2009 is $70,950, in the case of married individuals filing a joint return and surviving spouses; (2) $46,700 in the case of other unmarried individuals; and (3) $35,475 in the case of married individuals filing separate returns.

For taxable years beginning in 2009, the provision allows an individual to offset the entire regular tax liability and alternative minimum tax liability by the nonrefundable personal credits.

Effective date

The provision is effective for taxable years beginning in 2009.

---

[18] The rule applicable to the adoption credit and child credit is subject to the EGTRRA sunset.

Conference Agreement

The conference agreement follows the Senate amendment.

[Law at ¶5035 and ¶5180. CCH Explanation at ¶235 and ¶240.]

[¶10,100] Act Sec. 1101. Extension of the renewable electricity production credit

Conference Report (H. Rept. 111-16)

[Code Sec. 45]

Present Law

In general

An income tax credit is allowed for the production of electricity from qualified energy resources at qualified facilities (the "renewable electricity production credit").[167] Qualified energy resources comprise wind, closed-loop biomass, open-loop biomass, geothermal energy, solar energy, small irrigation power, municipal solid waste, qualified hydropower production, and marine and hydrokinetic renewable energy. Qualified facilities are, generally, facilities that generate electricity using qualified energy resources. To be eligible for the credit, electricity produced from qualified energy resources at qualified facilities must be sold by the taxpayer to an unrelated person.

Credit amounts and credit period

In general

The base amount of the electricity production credit is 1.5 cents per kilowatt-hour (indexed annually for inflation) of electricity produced. The amount of the credit was 2.1 cents per kilowatt-hour for 2008. A taxpayer may generally claim a credit during the 10-year period commencing with the date the qualified facility is placed in service. The credit is reduced for grants, tax-exempt bonds, subsidized energy financing, and other credits.

Credit phaseout

The amount of credit a taxpayer may claim is phased out as the market price of electricity exceeds certain threshold levels. The electricity production credit is reduced over a 3-cent phaseout range to the extent the annual average contract price per kilowatt-hour of electricity sold in the prior year from the same qualified energy resource exceeds 8 cents (adjusted for inflation; 11.8 cents for 2008).

Reduced credit periods and credit amounts

Generally, in the case of open-loop biomass facilities (including agricultural livestock waste nutrient facilities), geothermal energy facilities, solar energy facilities, small irrigation power facilities, landfill gas facilities, and trash combustion facilities placed in service before August 8, 2005, the 10-year credit period is reduced to five years, commencing on the date the facility was originally placed in service. However, for qualified open-loop biomass facilities (other than a facility described in section 45(d)(3)(A)(i) that uses agricultural livestock waste nutrients) placed in service before October 22, 2004, the five-year period commences on January 1, 2005. In the case of a closed-loop biomass facility modified to co-fire with coal, to co-fire with other biomass, or to co-fire with coal and other biomass, the credit period begins no earlier than October 22, 2004.

In the case of open-loop biomass facilities (including agricultural livestock waste nutrient facilities), small irrigation power facilities, landfill gas facilities, trash combustion facilities, and qualified hydropower facilities the otherwise allowable credit amount is 0.75 cent per kilowatt-hour, indexed for inflation measured after 1992 (1 cent per kilowatt-hour for 2008).

Other limitations on credit claimants and credit amounts

In general, in order to claim the credit, a taxpayer must own the qualified facility and sell the electricity produced by the facility to an unrelated party. A lessee or operator may claim the credit in lieu of the owner of the qualifying facility in the case of qualifying open-loop biomass facilities and in the case of closed-loop biomass facilities modified to co-fire with coal, to co-fire with other biomass, or to co-fire with coal and other biomass. In the case of a poultry waste facility, the taxpayer may claim the credit as a

---

[167] Sec. 45. In addition to the renewable electricity production credit, section 45 also provides income tax credits for the production of Indian coal and refined coal at qualified facilities.

lessee or operator of a facility owned by a governmental unit.

For all qualifying facilities, other than closed-loop biomass facilities modified to co-fire with coal, to co-fire with other biomass, or to co-fire with coal and other biomass, the amount of credit a taxpayer may claim is reduced by reason of grants, tax-exempt bonds, subsidized energy financing, and other credits, but the reduction cannot exceed 50 percent of the otherwise allowable credit. In the case of closed-loop biomass facilities modified to co-fire with coal, to co-fire with other biomass, or to co-fire with coal and other biomass, there is no reduction in credit by reason of grants, tax-exempt bonds, subsidized energy financing, and other credits.

The credit for electricity produced from renewable resources is a component of the general business credit.[168] Generally, the general business credit for any taxable year may not exceed the amount by which the taxpayer's net income tax exceeds the greater of the tentative minimum tax or 25 percent of so much of the net regular tax liability as exceeds $25,000. However, this limitation does not apply to section 45 credits for electricity or refined coal produced from a facility (placed in service after October 22, 2004) during the first four years of production beginning on the date the facility is placed in service.[169] Excess credits may be carried back one year and forward up to 20 years.

Qualified facilities

Wind energy facility

A wind energy facility is a facility that uses wind to produce electricity. To be a qualified facility, a wind energy facility must be placed in service after December 31, 1993, and before January 1, 2010.

Closed-loop biomass facility

A closed-loop biomass facility is a facility that uses any organic material from a plant which is planted exclusively for the purpose of being used at a qualifying facility to produce electricity. In addition, a facility can be a closed-loop biomass facility if it is a facility that is modified to use closed-loop biomass to co-fire with coal, with other biomass, or with both coal and other biomass, but only if the modification is approved under the Biomass Power for Rural Development Programs or is part of a pilot project of the Commodity Credit Corporation.

To be a qualified facility, a closed-loop biomass facility must be placed in service after December 31, 1992, and before January 1, 2011. In the case of a facility using closed-loop biomass but also co-firing the closed-loop biomass with coal, other biomass, or coal and other biomass, a qualified facility must be originally placed in service and modified to co-fire the closed-loop biomass at any time before January 1, 2011.

A qualified facility includes a new power generation unit placed in service after October 3, 2008, at an existing closed-loop biomass facility, but only to the extent of the increased amount of electricity produced at the existing facility by reason of such new unit.

Open-loop biomass (including agricultural livestock waste nutrients) facility

An open-loop biomass facility is a facility that uses open-loop biomass to produce electricity. For purposes of the credit, open-loop biomass is defined as (1) any agricultural livestock waste nutrients or (2) any solid, nonhazardous, cellulosic waste material or any lignin material that is segregated from other waste materials and which is derived from:

* forest-related resources, including mill and harvesting residues, precommercial thinnings, slash, and brush;

* solid wood waste materials, including waste pallets, crates, dunnage, manufacturing and construction wood wastes, and landscape or right-of-way tree trimmings; or

* agricultural sources, including orchard tree crops, vineyard, grain, legumes, sugar, and other crop by-products or residues.

Agricultural livestock waste nutrients are defined as agricultural livestock manure and litter, including bedding material for the disposition of manure. Wood waste materials do not qualify as open-loop biomass to the extent they are pressure treated, chemically treated, or painted. In addition, municipal solid waste, gas derived from the biodegradation of solid waste, and paper which is commonly recycled do not qualify as open-loop biomass. Open-loop biomass does not include closed-loop biomass or any biomass burned in conjunction with fossil fuel (co-firing) beyond such fossil fuel required for start up and flame stabilization.

In the case of an open-loop biomass facility that uses agricultural livestock waste nutrients, a

---

[168] Sec. 38(b)(8).

[169] Sec. 38(c)(4)(B)(ii).

qualified facility is one that was originally placed in service after October 22, 2004, and before January 1, 2009, and has a nameplate capacity rating which is not less than 150 kilowatts. In the case of any other open-loop biomass facility, a qualified facility is one that was originally placed in service before January 1, 2011. A qualified facility includes a new power generation unit placed in service after October 3, 2008, at an existing open-loop biomass facility, but only to the extent of the increased amount of electricity produced at the existing facility by reason of such new unit.

Geothermal facility

A geothermal facility is a facility that uses geothermal energy to produce electricity. Geothermal energy is energy derived from a geothermal deposit that is a geothermal reservoir consisting of natural heat that is stored in rocks or in an aqueous liquid or vapor (whether or not under pressure). To be a qualified facility, a geothermal facility must be placed in service after October 22, 2004, and before January 1, 2011.

Solar facility

A solar facility is a facility that uses solar energy to produce electricity. To be a qualified facility, a solar facility must be placed in service after October 22, 2004, and before January 1, 2006.

Small irrigation facility

A small irrigation power facility is a facility that generates electric power through an irrigation system canal or ditch without any dam or impoundment of water. The installed capacity of a qualified facility must be at least 150 kilowatts but less than five megawatts. To be a qualified facility, a small irrigation facility must be originally placed in service after October 22, 2004, and before October 3, 2008. Marine and hydrokinetic renewable energy facilities, described below, subsume small irrigation power facilities after October 2, 2008.

Landfill gas facility

A landfill gas facility is a facility that uses landfill gas to produce electricity. Landfill gas is defined as methane gas derived from the biodegradation of municipal solid waste. To be a qualified facility, a landfill gas facility must be placed in service after October 22, 2004, and before January 1, 2011.

Trash combustion facility

Trash combustion facilities are facilities that use municipal solid waste (garbage) to produce steam to drive a turbine for the production of electricity. To be a qualified facility, a trash combustion facility must be placed in service after October 22, 2004, and before January 1, 2011. A qualified trash combustion facility includes a new unit, placed in service after October 22, 2004, that increases electricity production capacity at an existing trash combustion facility. A new unit generally would include a new burner/boiler and turbine. The new unit may share certain common equipment, such as trash handling equipment, with other pre-existing units at the same facility. Electricity produced at a new unit of an existing facility qualifies for the production credit only to the extent of the increased amount of electricity produced at the entire facility.

Hydropower facility

A qualifying hydropower facility is (1) a facility that produced hydroelectric power (a hydroelectric dam) prior to August 8, 2005, at which efficiency improvements or additions to capacity have been made after such date and before January 1, 2011, that enable the taxpayer to produce incremental hydropower or (2) a facility placed in service before August 8, 2005, that did not produce hydroelectric power (a nonhydroelectric dam) on such date, and to which turbines or other electricity generating equipment have been added after such date and before January 1, 2011.

At an existing hydroelectric facility, the taxpayer may claim credit only for the production of incremental hydroelectric power. Incremental hydroelectric power for any taxable year is equal to the percentage of average annual hydroelectric power produced at the facility attributable to the efficiency improvement or additions of capacity determined by using the same water flow information used to determine an historic average annual hydroelectric power production baseline for that facility. The Federal Energy Regulatory Commission will certify the baseline power production of the facility and the percentage increase due to the efficiency and capacity improvements.

Nonhydroelectric dams converted to produce electricity must be licensed by the Federal Energy Regulatory Commission and meet all other applicable environmental, licensing, and regulatory requirements.

For a nonhydroelectric dam converted to produce electric power before January 1, 2009, there must not be any enlargement of the diversion structure, construction or enlargement of a bypass channel, or the impoundment or any withholding of additional water from the natural stream channel.

For a nonhydroelectric dam converted to produce electric power after December 31, 2008, the nonhydroelectric dam must have been (1) placed in service before October 3, 2008, (2) operated for flood control, navigation, or water supply purposes and (3) did not produce hydroelectric power on October 3, 2008. In addition, the hydroelectric project must be operated so that the water surface elevation at any given location and time that would have occurred in the absence of the hydroelectric project is maintained, subject to any license requirements imposed under applicable law that change the water surface elevation for the purpose of improving environmental quality of the affected waterway. The Secretary, in consultation with the Federal Energy Regulatory Commission, shall certify if a hydroelectric project licensed at a nonhydroelectric dam meets this criteria.

Marine and hydrokinetic renewable energy facility

A qualified marine and hydrokinetic renewable energy facility is any facility that produces electric power from marine and hydrokinetic renewable energy, has a nameplate capacity rating of at least 150 kilowatts, and is placed in service after October 2, 2008, and before January 1, 2012. Marine and hydrokinetic renewable energy is defined as energy derived from (1) waves, tides, and currents in oceans, estuaries, and tidal areas; (2) free flowing water in rivers, lakes, and streams; (3) free flowing water in an irrigation system, canal, or other man-made channel, including projects that utilize nonmechanical structures to accelerate the flow of water for electric power production purposes; or (4) differentials in ocean temperature (ocean thermal energy conversion). The term does not include energy derived from any source that uses a dam, diversionary structure (except for irrigation systems, canals, and other man-made channels), or impoundment for electric power production.

Summary of credit rate and credit period by facility type

Table 1.-Summary of Section 45 Credit for Electricity Produced from Certain Renewable Resources

Eligible electricity production activity	Credit amount for 2008 (cents per kilowatt-hour)	Credit period for facilities placed in service on or before August 8, 2005 (years from placed-in-service date)	Credit period for facilities placed in service after August -8, 2005 (years from placed-in-service date)
Wind	2.1	10	10
Closed-loop biomass	2.1	10[1]	10
Open-loop biomass (including agricultural livestock waste nutrient facilities)	1.0	5[2]	10
Geothermal	2.1	5	10
Solar (pre-2006 facilities only)	2.1	5	10
Small irrigation power	1.0	5	10
Municipal solid waste (including landfill gas facilities and trash combustion facilities)	1.0	5	10
Qualified hydropower	1.0	N/A	10
Marine and hydrokinetic	1.0	N/A	10

[1] In the case of certain co-firing closed-loop facilities, the credit period begins no earlier than October 22, 2004.
[2] For certain facilities placed in service before October 22, 2004, the five-year credit period commences on January 1, 2005.

Taxation of cooperatives and their patrons

For Federal income tax purposes, a cooperative generally computes its income as if it were a taxable corporation, with one exception: the cooperative may exclude from its taxable income distributions of patronage dividends. Generally, a cooperative that is subject to the cooperative tax rules of subchapter T of the Code[170] is permitted a deduction for patronage dividends paid only to the extent of net income that is derived from transactions with patrons who are members of the cooperative.[171] The availability of such deductions from taxable income has the effect of allowing the cooperative to be treated like a conduit with respect to profits derived

---

[170] Secs. 1381-1383.

[171] Sec. 1382.

from transactions with patrons who are members of the cooperative.

Eligible cooperatives may elect to pass any portion of the credit through to their patrons. An eligible cooperative is defined as a cooperative organization that is owned more than 50 percent by agricultural producers or entities owned by agricultural producers. The credit may be apportioned among patrons eligible to share in patronage dividends on the basis of the quantity or value of business done with or for such patrons for the taxable year. The election must be made on a timely filed return for the taxable year and, once made, is irrevocable for such taxable year.

House Bill

The provision extends for three years (generally, through 2013; through 2012 for wind facilities) the period during which qualified facilities producing electricity from wind, closed-loop biomass, open-loop biomass, geothermal energy, municipal solid waste, and qualified hydropower may be placed in service for purposes of the electricity production credit. The provision extends for two years (through 2013) the placed-in-service period for marine and hydrokinetic renewable energy resources.

The provision also makes a technical amendment to the definition of small irrigation power facility to clarify its integration into the definition of marine and hydrokinetic renewable energy facility.

Effective date

The extension of the electricity production credit is effective for property placed in service after the date of enactment. The technical amendment is effective as if included in section 102 of the Energy Improvement and Extension Act of 2008.

Senate Amendment

The Senate amendment is the same as the House bill.

Conference Agreement

The conference agreement follows the House bill and the Senate amendment.

[Law at ¶ 5090. CCH Explanation at ¶ 520.]

[¶ 10,110] Act Sec. 1102. Election of investment credit in lieu of production tax credits

Conference Report (H. REPT. 111-16)

[Code Secs. 45 and 48]

Present Law

Renewable electricity credit

An income tax credit is allowed for the production of electricity from qualified energy resources at qualified facilities.[172] Qualified energy resources comprise wind, closed-loop biomass, open-loop biomass, geothermal energy, solar energy, small irrigation power, municipal solid waste, qualified hydropower production, and marine and hydrokinetic renewable energy. Qualified facilities are, generally, facilities that generate electricity using qualified energy resources. To be eligible for the credit, electricity produced from qualified energy resources at qualified facilities must be sold by the taxpayer to an unrelated person. The credit amounts, credit periods, definitions of qualified facilities, and other rules governing this credit are described more fully in section D.1 of this document.

Energy credit

An income tax credit is also allowed for certain energy property placed in service. Qualifying property includes certain fuel cell property, solar property, geothermal power production property, small wind energy property, combined heat and power system property, and geothermal heat pump property.[173] The amounts of credit, definitions of qualifying property, and other rules governing this credit are described more fully in section D.3 of this document.

House Bill

The House bill allows the taxpayer to make an irrevocable election to have certain qualified facilities placed in service in 2009 and 2010 be

---

[172] Sec. 45. In addition to the electricity production credit, section 45 also provides income tax credits for the production of Indian coal and refined coal at qualified facilities.

[173] Sec. 48.

treated as energy property eligible for a 30 percent investment credit under section 48. For this purpose, qualified facilities are facilities otherwise eligible for the section 45 production tax credit (other than refined coal, Indian coal, and solar facilities) with respect to which no credit under section 45 has been allowed. A taxpayer electing to treat a facility as energy property may not claim the production credit under section 45.

Effective date

The provision applies to facilities placed in service after December 31, 2008.

Senate Amendment

The Senate amendment is similar to the House bill, but with a modification with respect to the placed in service period that determines eligibility for the election. Under the Senate amendment, facilities are eligible if placed in service during the extension period of section 45 as provided in the Senate amendment (generally, through 2013; through 2012 for wind facilities), and with respect to which no credit under section 45 has been allowed.

Conference Agreement

The conference agreement generally follows the Senate amendment. Property eligible for the credit is tangible personal or other tangible property (not including a building or its structural components), and with respect to which depreciation or amortization is allowable but only if such property is used as an integral part of the qualified facility. For example, in the case of a wind facility, the conferees intend that only property eligible for five-year depreciation under section 168(e)(3)(b)(vi) is treated as credit-eligible energy property under the election.

[Law at ¶ 5110. CCH Explanation at ¶ 510.]

[¶ 10,120] Act Sec. 1103. Modification of energy credit[174]

Conference Report (H. REPT. 111-16)

[Code Sec. 48]

Present Law

In general

A nonrefundable, 10-percent business energy credit[175] is allowed for the cost of new property that is equipment that either (1) uses solar energy to generate electricity, to heat or cool a structure, or to provide solar process heat, or (2) is used to produce, distribute, or use energy derived from a geothermal deposit, but only, in the case of electricity generated by geothermal power, up to the electric transmission stage. Property used to generate energy for the purposes of heating a swimming pool is not eligible solar energy property.

The energy credit is a component of the general business credit.[176] An unused general business credit generally may be carried back one year and carried forward 20 years.[177] The taxpayer's basis in the property is reduced by one-half of the amount of the credit claimed. For projects whose construction time is expected to equal or exceed two years, the credit may be claimed as progress expenditures are made on the project, rather than during the year the property is placed in service. The credit is allowed against the alternative minimum tax for credits determined in taxable years beginning after October 3, 2008.

Property financed by subsidized energy financing or with proceeds from private activity bonds is subject to a reduction in basis for purposes of claiming the credit. The basis reduction is proportional to the share of the basis of the property that is financed by the subsidized financing or proceeds. The term "subsidized energy financing" means financing provided under a Federal, State, or local program a principal purpose of which is to provide subsidized financing for projects designed to conserve or produce energy.

Special rules for solar energy property

The credit for solar energy property is increased to 30 percent in the case of periods prior to January 1, 2017. Additionally, equipment that uses fiber-optic distributed sunlight to illuminate

---

[174] Additional provisions that (1) allow section 45 facilities to elect to be treated as section 48 energy property, and (2) allow section 45 and 48 facilities to elect to receive a grant from the Department of the Treasury rather than the section 45 production credit or the section 48 energy credit, are described in sections D.2 and D.4 of this document.

[175] Sec. 48.
[176] Sec. 38(b)(1).
[177] Sec. 39.

the inside of a structure is solar energy property eligible for the 30-percent credit.

Fuel cells and microturbines

The energy credit applies to qualified fuel cell power plants, but only for periods prior to January 1, 2017. The credit rate is 30 percent.

A qualified fuel cell power plant is an integrated system composed of a fuel cell stack assembly and associated balance of plant components that (1) converts a fuel into electricity using electrochemical means, and (2) has an electricity-only generation efficiency of greater than 30 percent and a capacity of at least one-half kilowatt. The credit may not exceed $1,500 for each 0.5 kilowatt of capacity.

The energy credit applies to qualifying stationary microturbine power plants for periods prior to January 1, 2017. The credit is limited to the lesser of 10 percent of the basis of the property or $200 for each kilowatt of capacity.

A qualified stationary microturbine power plant is an integrated system comprised of a gas turbine engine, a combustor, a recuperator or regenerator, a generator or alternator, and associated balance of plant components that converts a fuel into electricity and thermal energy. Such system also includes all secondary components located between the existing infrastructure for fuel delivery and the existing infrastructure for power distribution, including equipment and controls for meeting relevant power standards, such as voltage, frequency and power factors. Such system must have an electricity-only generation efficiency of not less than 26 percent at International Standard Organization conditions and a capacity of less than 2,000 kilowatts.

Geothermal heat pump property

The energy credit applies to qualified geothermal heat pump property placed in service prior to January 1, 2017. The credit rate is 10 percent. Qualified geothermal heat pump property is equipment that uses the ground or ground water as a thermal energy source to heat a structure or as a thermal energy sink to cool a structure.

Small wind property

The energy credit applies to qualified small wind energy property placed in service prior to January 1, 2017. The credit rate is 30 percent. The credit is limited to $4,000 per year with respect to all wind energy property of any taxpayer. Qualified small wind energy property is property that uses a qualified wind turbine to generate electricity. A qualifying wind turbine means a wind turbine of 100 kilowatts of rated capacity or less.

Combined heat and power property

The energy credit applies to combined heat and power ("CHP") property placed in service prior to January 1, 2017. The credit rate is 10 percent.

CHP property is property: (1) that uses the same energy source for the simultaneous or sequential generation of electrical power, mechanical shaft power, or both, in combination with the generation of steam or other forms of useful thermal energy (including heating and cooling applications); (2) that has an electrical capacity of not more than 50 megawatts or a mechanical energy capacity of no more than 67,000 horsepower or an equivalent combination of electrical and mechanical energy capacities; (3) that produces at least 20 percent of its total useful energy in the form of thermal energy that is not used to produce electrical or mechanical power, and produces at least 20 percent of its total useful energy in the form of electrical or mechanical power (or a combination thereof); and (4) the energy efficiency percentage of which exceeds 60 percent. CHP property does not include property used to transport the energy source to the generating facility or to distribute energy produced by the facility.

The otherwise allowable credit with respect to CHP property is reduced to the extent the property has an electrical capacity or mechanical capacity in excess of any applicable limits. Property in excess of the applicable limit (15 megawatts or a mechanical energy capacity of more than 20,000 horsepower or an equivalent combination of electrical and mechanical energy capacities) is permitted to claim a fraction of the otherwise allowable credit. The fraction is equal to the applicable limit divided by the capacity of the property. For example, a 45 megawatt property would be eligible to claim 15/45ths, or one third, of the otherwise allowable credit. Again, no credit is allowed if the property exceeds the 50 megawatt or 67,000 horsepower limitations described above.

Additionally, the provision provides that systems whose fuel source is at least 90 percent open-loop biomass and that would qualify for the credit but for the failure to meet the efficiency standard are eligible for a credit that is reduced in proportion to the degree to which the system fails to meet the efficiency standard. For example, a system that would otherwise be required to meet the 60-percent efficiency standard, but which only achieves 30-percent efficiency, would be permitted a credit equal to one-half of the otherwise allowable credit (i.e., a 5-percent credit).

House Bill

The House bill eliminates the credit cap applicable to qualified small wind energy property. The House bill also removes the rule that reduces the basis of the property for purposes of claiming the credit if the property is financed in whole or in part by subsidized energy financing or with proceeds from private activity bonds.

Effective date

The provision applies to periods after December 31, 2008, under rules similar to the rules of section 48(m) of the Code (as in effect on the day before the enactment of the Revenue Reconciliation Act of 1990).

Senate Amendment

The Senate amendment is the same as the House bill.

Conference Agreement

The conference agreement follows the House bill and the Senate amendment.

[Law at ¶ 5025, ¶ 5030, ¶ 5110, ¶ 5115, and ¶ 5120. CCH Explanation at ¶ 510.]

[¶ 10,130] Act Sec. 1104. Grants for specified energy property in lieu of tax credits

Conference Report (H. Rept. 111-16)

[Code Secs. 45 and 48]

Present Law

Renewable electricity production credit

An income tax credit is allowed for the production of electricity from qualified energy resources at qualified facilities (the "renewable electricity production credit").[178] Qualified energy resources comprise wind, closed-loop biomass, open-loop biomass, geothermal energy, solar energy, small irrigation power, municipal solid waste, qualified hydropower production, and marine and hydrokinetic renewable energy. Qualified facilities are, generally, facilities that generate electricity using qualified energy resources. To be eligible for the credit, electricity produced from qualified energy resources at qualified facilities must be sold by the taxpayer to an unrelated person. The credit amounts, credit periods, definitions of qualified facilities, and other rules governing this credit are described more fully in section D.1 of this document.

Energy credit

An income tax credit is also allowed for certain energy property placed in service. Qualifying property includes certain fuel cell property, solar property, geothermal power production property, small wind energy property, combined heat and power system property, and geothermal heat pump property.[179] The amounts of credit, definitions of qualifying property, and other rules governing this credit are described more fully in section D.3 of this document.

House Bill

The provision authorizes the Secretary of Energy to provide a grant to each person who places in service during 2009 or 2010 energy property that is either (1) an electricity production facility otherwise eligible for the renewable electricity production credit or (2) qualifying property otherwise eligible for the energy credit. In general, the grant amount is 30 percent of the basis of the property that would (1) be eligible for credit under section 48 or (2) comprise a section 45 credit-eligible facility. For qualified microturbine, combined heat and power system, and geothermal heat pump property, the amount is 10 percent of the basis of the property.

It is intended that the grant provision mimic the operation of the credit under section 48. For example, the amount of the grant is not includable in gross income. However, the basis of the property is reduced by fifty percent of the amount of the grant. In addition, some or all of each grant is subject to recapture if the grant eligible property is disposed of by the grant recipient within five years of being placed in service.[180]

Nonbusiness property and property that would not otherwise be eligible for credit under

---

[178] Sec. 45. In addition to the renewable electricity production credit, section 45 also provides income tax credits for the production of Indian coal and refined coal at qualified facilities.

[179] Sec. 48.
[180] Section 1604 of the House bill.

section 48 or part of a facility that would be eligible for credit under section 45 is not eligible for a grant under the provision. The grant may be paid to whichever party would have been entitled to a credit under section 48 or section 45, as the case may be.

Under the provision, if a grant is paid, no renewable electricity credit or energy credit may be claimed with respect to the grant eligible property. In addition, no grant may be awarded to any Federal, State, or local government (or any political subdivision, agency, or instrumentality thereof) or any section 501(c) tax-exempt entity.

The provision appropriates to the Secretary of Energy the funds necessary to make the grants. No grant may be made unless the application for the grant has been received before October 1, 2011.

Effective date

The provision is effective on date of enactment.

Senate Amendment

No provision.

Conference Agreement

The conference agreement generally follows the House bill with the following modifications. The conference agreement clarifies that qualifying property must be depreciable or amortizable to be eligible for a grant. The conference agreement also permits taxpayers to claim the credit with respect to otherwise eligible property that is not placed in service in 2009 and 2010 so long as construction begins in either of those years and is completed prior to 2013 (in the case of wind facility property), 2014 (in the case of other renewable power facility property eligible for credit under section 45), or 2017 (in the case of any specified energy property described in section 48). The conference agreement also provides that the grant program be administered by the Secretary of the Treasury.

[Law at ¶ 5110. CCH Explanation at ¶ 515.]

[¶10,140] Act Sec. 1111. Expand new clean renewable energy bonds

Conference Report (H. REPT. 111-16)

[Code Sec. 54C]

Present Law

New Clean Renewable Energy Bonds

New clean renewable energy bonds ("New CREBs") may be issued by qualified issuers to finance qualified renewable energy facilities.[181] Qualified renewable energy facilities are facilities that: (1) qualify for the tax credit under section 45 (other than Indian coal and refined coal production facilities), without regard to the placed-in-service date requirements of that section; and (2) are owned by a public power provider, governmental body, or cooperative electric company.

The term "qualified issuers" includes: (1) public power providers; (2) a governmental body; (3) cooperative electric companies; (4) a not-for-profit electric utility that has received a loan or guarantee under the Rural Electrification Act; and (5) clean renewable energy bond lenders. The term "public power provider" means a State utility with a service obligation, as such terms are defined in section 217 of the Federal Power Act (as in effect on the date of the enactment of this paragraph). A "governmental body" means any State or Indian tribal government, or any political subdivision thereof. The term "cooperative electric company" means a mutual or cooperative electric company (described in section 501(c)(12) or section 1381(a)(2)(C)). A clean renewable energy bond lender means a cooperative that is owned by, or has outstanding loans to, 100 or more cooperative electric companies and is in existence on February 1, 2002 (including any affiliated entity which is controlled by such lender).

There is a national limitation for New CREBs of $800 million. No more than one third of the national limit may be allocated to projects of public power providers, governmental bodies, or cooperative electric companies. Allocations to governmental bodies and cooperative electric companies may be made in the manner the Secretary determines appropriate. Allocations to projects of public power providers shall be made, to the extent practicable, in such manner that the amount allocated to each such project

---

[181] Sec. 54C.

bears the same ratio to the cost of such project as the maximum allocation limitation to projects of public power providers bears to the cost of all such projects.

New CREBs are a type of qualified tax credit bond for purposes of section 54A of the Code. As such, 100 percent of the available project proceeds of New CREBs must be used within the three-year period that begins on the date of issuance. Available project proceeds are proceeds from the sale of the bond issue less issuance costs (not to exceed two percent) and any investment earnings on such sale proceeds. To the extent less than 100 percent of the available project proceeds are used to finance qualified projects during the three-year spending period, bonds will continue to qualify as New CREBs if unspent proceeds are used within 90 days from the end of such three-year period to redeem bonds. The three-year spending period may be extended by the Secretary upon the qualified issuer's request demonstrating that the failure to satisfy the three-year requirement is due to reasonable cause and the projects will continue to proceed with due diligence.

New CREBs generally are subject to the arbitrage requirements of section 148. However, available project proceeds invested during the three-year spending period are not subject to the arbitrage restrictions (i.e., yield restriction and rebate requirements). In addition, amounts invested in a reserve fund are not subject to the arbitrage restrictions to the extent: (1) such fund is funded at a rate not more rapid than equal annual installments; (2) such fund is funded in a manner reasonably expected to result in an amount not greater than an amount necessary to repay the issue; and (3) the yield on such fund is not greater than the average annual interest rate of tax-exempt obligations having a term of 10 years or more that are issued during the month the New CREBs are issued.

As with other tax credit bonds, a taxpayer holding New CREBs on a credit allowance date is entitled to a tax credit. However, the credit rate on New CREBs is set by the Secretary at a rate that is 70 percent of the rate that would permit issuance of such bonds without discount and interest cost to the issuer.[182] The Secretary determines credit rates for tax credit bonds based on general assumptions about credit quality of the class of potential eligible issuers and such other factors as the Secretary deems appropriate. The Secretary may determine credit rates based on general credit market yield indexes and credit ratings.[183]

The amount of the tax credit is determined by multiplying the bond's credit rate by the face amount of the holder's bond. The credit accrues quarterly, is includible in gross income (as if it were an interest payment on the bond), and can be claimed against regular income tax liability and alternative minimum tax liability. Unused credits may be carried forward to succeeding taxable years. In addition, credits may be separated from the ownership of the underlying bond similar to how interest coupons can be stripped for interest-bearing bonds.

An issuer of New CREBs is treated as meeting the "prohibition on financial conflicts of interest" requirement in section 54A(d)(6) if it certifies that it satisfies (i) applicable State and local law requirements governing conflicts of interest and (ii) any additional conflict of interest rules prescribed by the Secretary with respect to any Federal, State, or local government official directly involved with the issuance of New CREBs.

House Bill

In general

The provision expands the New CREBs program. The provision authorizes issuance of up to an additional $1.6 billion of New CREBs.

Effective date

The provision applies to obligations issued after the date of enactment.

Senate Amendment

The Senate amendment is the same as the House bill.

Conference Agreement

The conference agreement follows the House bill and the Senate amendment.

[Law at ¶ 5160. CCH Explanation at ¶ 645.]

---

[182] Given the differences in credit quality and other characteristics of individual issuers, the Secretary cannot set credit rates in a manner that will allow each issuer to issue tax credit bonds at par.

[183] See Internal Revenue Service, Notice 2009-15, *Credit Rates on Tax Credit Bonds*, 2009-6 I.R.B. 1 (January 22, 2009).

[¶10,150] Act Sec. 1112. Expand qualified energy conservation bonds

Conference Report (H. REPT. 111-16)

[Code Sec. 54D]

Present Law

Qualified energy conservation bonds may be used to finance qualified conservation purposes.

The term "qualified conservation purpose" means:

1. Capital expenditures incurred for purposes of reducing energy consumption in publicly owned buildings by at least 20 percent; implementing green community programs; rural development involving the production of electricity from renewable energy resources; or any facility eligible for the production tax credit under section 45 (other than Indian coal and refined coal production facilities);

2. Expenditures with respect to facilities or grants that support research in: (a) development of cellulosic ethanol or other nonfossil fuels; (b) technologies for the capture and sequestration of carbon dioxide produced through the use of fossil fuels; (c) increasing the efficiency of existing technologies for producing nonfossil fuels; (d) automobile battery technologies and other technologies to reduce fossil fuel consumption in transportation; and (E) technologies to reduce energy use in buildings;

3. Mass commuting facilities and related facilities that reduce the consumption of energy, including expenditures to reduce pollution from vehicles used for mass commuting;

4. Demonstration projects designed to promote the commercialization of: (a) green building technology; (b) conversion of agricultural waste for use in the production of fuel or otherwise; (c) advanced battery manufacturing technologies; (D) technologies to reduce peak-use of electricity; and (d) technologies for the capture and sequestration of carbon dioxide emitted from combusting fossil fuels in order to produce electricity; and

5. Public education campaigns to promote energy efficiency (other than movies, concerts, and other events held primarily for entertainment purposes).

There is a national limitation on qualified energy conservation bonds of $800 million. Allocations of qualified energy conservation bonds are made to the States with sub-allocations to large local governments. Allocations are made to the States according to their respective populations, reduced by any sub-allocations to large local governments (defined below) within the States. Sub-allocations to large local governments shall be an amount of the national qualified energy conservation bond limitation that bears the same ratio to the amount of such limitation that otherwise would be allocated to the State in which such large local government is located as the population of such large local government bears to the population of such State. The term "large local government" means: any municipality or county if such municipality or county has a population of 100,000 or more. Indian tribal governments also are treated as large local governments for these purposes (without regard to population).

Each State or large local government receiving an allocation of qualified energy conservation bonds may further allocate issuance authority to issuers within such State or large local government. However, any allocations to issuers within the State or large local government shall be made in a manner that results in not less than 70 percent of the allocation of qualified energy conservation bonds to such State or large local government being used to designate bonds that are not private activity bonds (i.e., the bond cannot meet the private business tests or the private loan test of section 141).

Qualified energy conservations bonds are a type of qualified tax credit bond for purposes of section 54A of the Code. As a result, 100 percent of the available project proceeds of qualified energy conservation bonds must be used for qualified conservation purposes. In the case of qualified conservation bonds issued as private activity bonds, 100 percent of the available project proceeds must be used for capital expenditures. In addition, qualified energy conservation bonds only may be issued by Indian tribal governments to the extent such bonds are issued for purposes that satisfy the present law requirements for tax-exempt bonds issued by Indian tribal governments (i.e., essential governmental functions and certain manufacturing purposes).

Under present law, 100 percent of the available project proceeds of qualified energy conservation bonds to be used within the three-year period that begins on the date of issuance. Available project proceeds are proceeds from the sale of the issue less issuance costs (not to exceed two percent) and any investment earnings on such sale proceeds. To the extent less than 100 percent of the available project proceeds are used to finance qualified conservation purposes during the three-year spending period, bonds will continue to qualify as qualified energy conservation bonds if unspent proceeds are used within 90 days from the end of such three-year period to redeem bonds. The three-year spending period may be extended by the Secretary upon the issuer's request demonstrating that the failure to satisfy the three-year requirement is due to reasonable cause and the projects will continue to proceed with due diligence.

Qualified energy conservation bonds generally are subject to the arbitrage requirements of section 148. However, available project proceeds invested during the three-year spending period are not subject to the arbitrage restrictions (i.e., yield restriction and rebate requirements). In addition, amounts invested in a reserve fund are not subject to the arbitrage restrictions to the extent: (1) such fund is funded at a rate not more rapid than equal annual installments; (2) such fund is funded in a manner reasonably expected to result in an amount not greater than an amount necessary to repay the issue; and (3) the yield on such fund is not greater than the average annual interest rate of tax-exempt obligations having a term of 10 years or more that are issued during the month the qualified energy conservation bonds are issued.

The maturity of qualified energy conservation bonds is the term that the Secretary estimates will result in the present value of the obligation to repay the principal on such bonds being equal to 50 percent of the face amount of such bonds, using as a discount rate the average annual interest rate of tax-exempt obligations having a term of 10 years or more that are issued during the month the qualified energy conservation bonds are issued.

As with other tax credit bonds, the taxpayer holding qualified energy conservation bonds on a credit allowance date is entitled to a tax credit. The credit rate on the bonds is set by the Secretary at a rate that is 70 percent of the rate that would permit issuance of such bonds without discount and interest cost to the issuer.[184] The Secretary determines credit rates for tax credit bonds based on general assumptions about credit quality of the class of potential eligible issuers and such other factors as the Secretary deems appropriate. The Secretary may determine credit rates based on general credit market yield indexes and credit ratings.[185] The amount of the tax credit is determined by multiplying the bond's credit rate by the face amount on the holder's bond. The credit accrues quarterly, is includible in gross income (as if it were an interest payment on the bond), and can be claimed against regular income tax liability and alternative minimum tax liability. Unused credits may be carried forward to succeeding taxable years. In addition, credits may be separated from the ownership of the underlying bond similar to how interest coupons can be stripped for interest-bearing bonds.

Issuers of qualified energy conservation bonds are required to certify that the financial disclosure requirements that applicable State and local law requirements governing conflicts of interest are satisfied with respect to such issue, as well as any other additional conflict of interest rules prescribed by the Secretary with respect to any Federal, State, or local government official directly involved with the issuance of qualified energy conservation bonds.

House Bill

In general

The provision expands the present-law qualified energy conservation bond program. The provision authorizes issuance of an additional $2.4 billion of qualified energy conservation bonds. The provision expands eligibility for these tax credit bonds to include loans and grants for capital expenditures as part of green community programs. For example, this expansion will enable States to issue these tax credit bonds to finance loans and/or grants to individual homeowners to retrofit existing housing. The use of bond proceeds for such loans and grants will not cause such bond to be treated as a private activity bond for purposes of the private activity bond restrictions contained in the qualified energy conservation bond provisions.

Effective date

The provision is effective for bonds issued after the date of enactment.

Senate Amendment

In general

The provision expands the present-law qualified energy conservation bond program. The provision authorizes issuance of an additional $2.4 billion of qualified energy conservation bonds. The provision clarifies that capital expenditures to implement green community programs, includes grants, loans and other re-

---

[184] Given the differences in credit quality and other characteristics of individual issuers, the Secretary cannot set credit rates in a manner that will allow each issuer to issue tax credit bonds at par.

[185] See Internal Revenue Service, Notice 2009-15, *Credit Rates on Tax Credit Bonds*, 2009-6 I.R.B. 1 (January 22, 2009).

payment mechanisms for capital expenditures to implement such programs.

Effective date

The provision is effective for bonds issued after the date of enactment.

Conference Agreement

In general

The provision expands the present-law qualified energy conservation bond program. The provision authorizes issuance of an additional $2.4 billion of qualified energy conservation bonds. Also, the provision clarifies that capital expenditures to implement green community programs includes grants, loans and other repayment mechanisms to implement such programs. For example, this expansion will enable States to issue these tax credit bonds to finance retrofits of existing private buildings through loans and/or grants to individual homeowners or businesses, or through other repayment mechanisms. Other repayment mechanisms can include periodic fees assessed on a government bill or utility bill that approximates the energy savings of energy efficiency or conservation retrofits. Retrofits can include heating, cooling, lighting, water-saving, storm water-reducing, or other efficiency measures.

Finally, the provision clarifies that any bond used for the purpose of providing grants, loans or other repayment mechanisms for capital expenditures to implement green community programs is not treated as a private activity bond for purposes of determining whether the requirement that not less than 70 percent of allocations within a State or large local government be used to designate bonds that are not private activity bonds (sec. 54D(e)(3)) has been satisfied.

Effective date

The conference agreement follows the House bill and the Senate amendment.

[Law at ¶ 5165. CCH Explanation at ¶ 640.]

[¶ 10,160] Act Sec. 1121. Extension and modification of credit for nonbusiness energy property

Conference Report (H. REPT. 111-16)

[Code Sec. 25C]

Present Law

Section 25C provides a 10-percent credit for the purchase of qualified energy efficiency improvements to existing homes. A qualified energy efficiency improvement is any energy efficiency building envelope component (1) that meets or exceeds the prescriptive criteria for such a component established by the 2000 International Energy Conservation Code as supplemented and as in effect on August 8, 2005 (or, in the case of metal roofs with appropriate pigmented coatings, meets the Energy Star program requirements); (2) that is installed in or on a dwelling located in the United States and owned and used by the taxpayer as the taxpayer's principal residence; (3) the original use of which commences with the taxpayer; and (4) that reasonably can be expected to remain in use for at least five years. The credit is nonrefundable.

Building envelope components are: (1) insulation materials or systems which are specifically and primarily designed to reduce the heat loss or gain for a dwelling; (2) exterior windows (including skylights) and doors; and (3) metal or asphalt roofs with appropriate pigmented coatings or cooling granules that are specifically and primarily designed to reduce the heat gain for a dwelling.

Additionally, section 25C provides specified credits for the purchase of specific energy efficient property. The allowable credit for the purchase of certain property is (1) $50 for each advanced main air circulating fan, (2) $150 for each qualified natural gas, propane, or oil furnace or hot water boiler, and (3) $300 for each item of qualified energy efficient property.

An advanced main air circulating fan is a fan used in a natural gas, propane, or oil furnace originally placed in service by the taxpayer during the taxable year, and which has an annual electricity use of no more than two percent of the total annual energy use of the furnace (as determined in the standard Department of Energy test procedures).

A qualified natural gas, propane, or oil furnace or hot water boiler is a natural gas, propane, or oil furnace or hot water boiler with an annual fuel utilization efficiency rate of at least 95.

Qualified energy-efficient property is: (1) an electric heat pump water heater which yields an energy factor of at least 2.0 in the standard Department of Energy test procedure, (2) an electric heat pump which has a heating seasonal performance factor (HSPF) of at least 9, a seasonal energy efficiency ratio (SEER) of at least 15, and an energy efficiency ratio (EER) of at least 13, (3) a central air conditioner with energy efficiency of at least the highest efficiency tier established by the Consortium for Energy Efficiency as in effect on Jan. 1, 2006[186], (4) a natural gas, propane, or oil water heater which has an energy factor of at least 0.80 or thermal efficiency of at least 90 percent, and (5) biomass fuel property.

Biomass fuel property is a stove that burns biomass fuel to heat a dwelling unit located in the United States and used as a principal residence by the taxpayer, or to heat water for such dwelling unit, and that has a thermal efficiency rating of at least 75 percent. Biomass fuel is any plant-derived fuel available on a renewable or recurring basis, including agricultural crops and trees, wood and wood waste and residues (including wood pellets), plants (including aquatic plants, grasses, residues, and fibers.

Under section 25C, the maximum credit for a taxpayer with respect to the same dwelling for all taxable years is $500, and no more than $200 of such credit may be attributable to expenditures on windows.

The taxpayer's basis in the property is reduced by the amount of the credit. Special proration rules apply in the case of jointly owned property, condominiums, and tenant-stockholders in cooperative housing corporations. If less than 80 percent of the property is used for nonbusiness purposes, only that portion of expenditures that is used for nonbusiness purposes is taken into account.

For purposes of determining the amount of expenditures made by any individual with respect to any dwelling unit, there shall not be taken into account expenditures which are made from subsidized energy financing. The term "subsidized energy financing" means financing provided under a Federal, State, or local program a principal purpose of which is to provide subsidized financing for projects designed to conserve or produce energy.

The credit applies to expenditures made after December 31, 2008 for property placed in service after December 31, 2008, and prior to January 1, 2010.

House Bill

The House bill raises the 10 percent credit rate to 30 percent. Additionally, all energy property otherwise eligible for the $50, $100, or $150 credits is instead eligible for a 30 percent credit on expenditures for such property.

The House bill additionally extends the provision for one year, through December 31, 2010. Finally, the $500 lifetime cap (and the $200 lifetime cap with respect to windows) is eliminated and replaced with an aggregate cap of $1,500 in the case of property placed in service after December 31, 2008 and prior to January 1, 2011.

The present law rule related to subsidized energy financing is eliminated.

Effective date.-The provision is effective for taxable years beginning after December 31, 2008.

Senate Amendment

The Senate amendment is similar to the House bill, but modifies the efficiency standards for qualifying property.

Specifically, the Senate amendment updates the building insulation requirements to follow the prescriptive criteria of the 2009 International Energy Conservation Code. Additionally, qualifying exterior windows, doors, and skylights must have a U-factor at or below 0.30 and a seasonal heat gain coefficient ("SHGC") at or below 0.30.

Electric heat pumps must achieve the highest efficiency tier of Consortium for Energy Efficiency, as in effect on January 1, 2009. These standards are a SEER greater than or equal to 15, EER greater than or equal to 12.5, and HSPF greater than or equal to 8.5 for split heat pumps, and SEER greater than or equal to 14, EER greater than or equal to 12, and HSPF greater than or equal to 8.0 for packaged heat pumps.

Central air conditioners must achieve the highest efficiency tier of Consortium for Energy Efficiency, as in effect on January 1, 2009. These standards are a SEER greater than or equal to 16 and EER greater than or equal to 13 for split systems, and SEER greater than or equal to 14 and EER greater than or equal to 12 for packaged systems.

Natural gas, propane, or oil water heaters must have an energy factor greater than or equal

---

[186] The highest tier in effect at this time was tier 2, requiring SEER of at least 15 and EER of at least 12.5 for split central air conditioning systems and SEER of at least 14 and EER of at least 12 for packaged central air conditioning systems.

to 0.82 or a thermal efficiency of greater than or equal to 90 percent. Natural gas, propane, or oil water boilers must achieve an annual fuel utilization efficiency rate of at least 90. Qualified oil furnaces must achieve an annual fuel utilization efficiency rate of at least 90.

Lastly, the requirement that biomass fuel property have a thermal efficiency rating of at least 75 percent is modified to be a thermal efficiency rating of at least 75 percent as measured using a lower heating value.

Effective date

The provision is generally effective for taxable years beginning after December 31, 2008. The provisions that alter the efficiency standards of qualifying property, other than biomass fuel property, apply to property placed in service after December 31, 2009. The modification with respect to biomass fuel property is effective for taxable years beginning after December 31, 2008.

Conference Agreement

The conference agreement follows the Senate amendment, with the exception that the new efficiency standards for qualifying property, other than those for biomass fuel property, apply to property placed in service after the date of enactment.

[Law at ¶ 5025. CCH Explanation at ¶ 335.]

[¶ 10,170] Act Sec. 1122. Credit for residential energy efficient property

Conference Report (H. REPT. 111-16)

[Code Sec. 25D]

Present Law

Section 25D provides a personal tax credit for the purchase of qualified solar electric property and qualified solar water heating property that is used exclusively for purposes other than heating swimming pools and hot tubs. The credit is equal to 30 percent of qualifying expenditures, with a maximum credit of $2,000 with respect to qualified solar water heating property. There is no cap with respect to qualified solar electric property.

Section 25D also provides a 30 percent credit for the purchase of qualified geothermal heat pump property, qualified small wind energy property, and qualified fuel cell power plants. The credit for geothermal heat pump property is capped at $2,000, the credit for qualified small wind energy property is limited to $500 with respect to each half kilowatt of capacity, not to exceed $4,000, and the credit for any fuel cell may not exceed $500 for each 0.5 kilowatt of capacity.

The credit with respect to all qualifying property may be claimed against the alternative minimum tax.

Qualified solar electric property is property that uses solar energy to generate electricity for use in a dwelling unit. Qualifying solar water heating property is property used to heat water for use in a dwelling unit located in the United States and used as a residence if at least half of the energy used by such property for such purpose is derived from the sun.

A qualified fuel cell power plant is an integrated system comprised of a fuel cell stack assembly and associated balance of plant components that (1) converts a fuel into electricity using electrochemical means, (2) has an electricity-only generation efficiency of greater than 30 percent. The qualified fuel cell power plant must be installed on or in connection with a dwelling unit located in the United States and used by the taxpayer as a principal residence.

Qualified small wind energy property is property that uses a wind turbine to generate electricity for use in a dwelling unit located in the U.S. and used as a residence by the taxpayer.

Qualified geothermal heat pump property means any equipment which (1) uses the ground or ground water as a thermal energy source to heat the dwelling unit or as a thermal energy sink to cool such dwelling unit, (2) meets the requirements of the Energy Star program which are in effect at the time that the expenditure for such equipment is made, and (3) is installed on or in connection with a dwelling unit located in the United States and used as a residence by the taxpayer.

The credit is nonrefundable, and the depreciable basis of the property is reduced by the amount of the credit. Expenditures for labor costs allocable to onsite preparation, assembly, or original installation of property eligible for the credit are eligible expenditures.

Special proration rules apply in the case of jointly owned property, condominiums, and tenant-stockholders in cooperative housing corporations. If less than 80 percent of the property is used for nonbusiness purposes, only that portion of expenditures that is used for nonbusiness purposes is taken into account.

For purposes of determining the amount of expenditures made by any individual with respect to any dwelling unit, there shall not be taken into account expenditures which are made from subsidized energy financing. The term "subsidized energy financing" means financing provided under a Federal, State, or local program a principal purpose of which is to provide subsidized financing for projects designed to conserve or produce energy.

The credit applies to property placed in service prior to January 1, 2017.

House Bill

The House bill eliminates the credit caps for solar hot water, geothermal, and wind property and eliminates the reduction in credits for property using subsidized energy financing.

Effective date

The provision applies to taxable years beginning after December 31, 2008.

Senate Amendment

The Senate amendment is the same as the House bill.

Conference Agreement

The conference agreement follows the House bill and the Senate amendment.

[Law at ¶ 5030. CCH Explanation at ¶ 340.]

[¶ 10,180] Act Sec. 1123. Temporary increase in credit for alternative fuel vehicle refueling property

Conference Report (H. REPT. 111-16)

[Code Sec. 30C]

Present Law

Taxpayers may claim a 30-percent credit for the cost of installing qualified clean-fuel vehicle refueling property to be used in a trade or business of the taxpayer or installed at the principal residence of the taxpayer.[187] The credit may not exceed $30,000 per taxable year per location, in the case of qualified refueling property used in a trade or business and $1,000 per taxable year per location, in the case of qualified refueling property installed on property which is used as a principal residence.

Qualified refueling property is property (not including a building or its structural components) for the storage or dispensing of a clean-burning fuel or electricity into the fuel tank or battery of a motor vehicle propelled by such fuel or electricity, but only if the storage or dispensing of the fuel or electricity is at the point of delivery into the fuel tank or battery of the motor vehicle. The use of such property must begin with the taxpayer.

Clean-burning fuels are any fuel at least 85 percent of the volume of which consists of ethanol, natural gas, compressed natural gas, liquefied natural gas, liquefied petroleum gas, or hydrogen. In addition, any mixture of biodiesel and diesel fuel, determined without regard to any use of kerosene and containing at least 20 percent biodiesel, qualifies as a clean fuel.

Credits for qualified refueling property used in a trade or business are part of the general business credit and may be carried back for one year and forward for 20 years. Credits for residential qualified refueling property cannot exceed for any taxable year the difference between the taxpayer's regular tax (reduced by certain other credits) and the taxpayer's tentative minimum tax. Generally, in the case of qualified refueling property sold to a tax-exempt entity, the taxpayer selling the property may claim the credit.

A taxpayer's basis in qualified refueling property is reduced by the amount of the credit. In addition, no credit is available for property used outside the United States or for which an election to expense has been made under section 179.

The credit is available for property placed in service after December 31, 2005, and (except in the case of hydrogen refueling property) before

---

[187] Sec. 30C.

January 1, 2011. In the case of hydrogen refueling property, the property must be placed in service before January 1, 2015.

House Bill

For property placed in service in 2009 or 2010, the provision increases the maximum credit available for business property to $200,000 for qualified hydrogen refueling property and to $50,000 for other qualified refueling property. For nonbusiness property, the maximum credit is increased to $2,000. In addition, the credit rate is increased from 30 percent to 50 percent, except in the case of hydrogen refueling property.

Effective date

The provision is effective for taxable years beginning after December 31, 2008.

Senate Amendment

The Senate amendment is the same as the House bill, except that it adds interoperability, public access, and other standards to qualified refueling property that is used for recharging electric or hybrid-electric motor vehicles.

Conference Agreement

The conference agreement follows the House bill.

[Law at ¶ 5050. CCH Explanation at ¶ 365.]

[¶ 10,190] Act Sec. 1131. Modification of credit for carbon dioxide sequestration

Conference Report (H. REPT. 111-16)

[Code Sec. 45Q]

Present Law

A credit of $20 per metric ton is available for qualified carbon dioxide captured by a taxpayer at a qualified facility and disposed of by such taxpayer in secure geological storage (including storage at deep saline formations and unminable coal seams under such conditions as the Secretary may determine).[208] In addition, a credit of $10 per metric ton is available for qualified carbon dioxide that is captured by the taxpayer at a qualified facility and used by such taxpayer as a tertiary injectant (including carbon dioxide augmented waterflooding and immiscible carbon dioxide displacement) in a qualified enhanced oil or natural gas recovery project. Both credit amounts are adjusted for inflation after 2009.

Qualified carbon dioxide is defined as carbon dioxide captured from an industrial source that (1) would otherwise be released into the atmosphere as an industrial emission of greenhouse gas, and (2) is measured at the source of capture and verified at the point or points of injection. Qualified carbon dioxide includes the initial deposit of captured carbon dioxide used as a tertiary injectant but does not include carbon dioxide that is recaptured, recycled, and reinjected as part of an enhanced oil or natural gas recovery project process. A qualified enhanced oil or natural gas recovery project is a project that would otherwise meet the definition of an enhanced oil recovery project under section 43, if natural gas projects were included within that definition.

A qualified facility means any industrial facility (1) which is owned by the taxpayer, (2) at which carbon capture equipment is placed in service, and (3) which captures not less than 500,000 metric tons of carbon dioxide during the taxable year. The credit applies only with respect to qualified carbon dioxide captured and sequestered or injected in the United States[209] or one of its possessions.[210]

Except as provided in regulations, credits are attributable to the person that captures and physically or contractually ensures the disposal, or use as a tertiary injectant, of the qualified carbon dioxide. Credits are subject to recapture, as provided by regulation, with respect to any qualified carbon dioxide that ceases to be recaptured, disposed of, or used as a tertiary injectant in a manner consistent with the rules of the provision.

The credit is part of the general business credit. The credit sunsets at the end of the calendar year in which the Secretary, in consultation with the Administrator of the Environmental Protection Agency, certifies that 75 million met-

---

[208] Sec. 45Q.
[209] Sec. 638(1).
[210] Sec. 638(2).

ric tons of qualified carbon dioxide have been captured and disposed of or used as a tertiary injectant.

House Bill

No provision.

Senate Amendment

The provision requires that carbon dioxide used as a tertiary injectant and otherwise eligible for a $10 per metric ton credit must be sequestered by the taxpayer in permanent geological storage in order to qualify for such credit. The Senate amendment also clarifies that the term permanent geological storage includes oil and gas reservoirs in addition to unminable coal seams and deep saline formations. In addition, the Senate amendment requires that the Secretary of the Treasury consult with the Secretary of Energy and the Secretary of the Interior, in addition to the Administrator of the Environmental Protection Agency, in promulgating regulations relating to the permanent geological storage of carbon dioxide.

Effective date

The provision is effective for carbon dioxide captured after the date of enactment.

Conference Agreement

The conference agreement follows the Senate amendment.

[Law at ¶ 5100. CCH Explanation at ¶ 545.]

[¶ 10,200] Act Secs. 1141, 1142, 1143 and 1144. Modification of the plug-in electric drive motor vehicle credit

Conference Report (H. Rept. 111-16)

[Code Secs. 30B and 30D]

Present Law

Alternative motor vehicle credit

A credit is available for each new qualified fuel cell vehicle, hybrid vehicle, advanced lean burn technology vehicle, and alternative fuel vehicle placed in service by the taxpayer during the taxable year.[211] In general, the credit amount varies depending upon the type of technology used, the weight class of the vehicle, the amount by which the vehicle exceeds certain fuel economy standards, and, for some vehicles, the estimated lifetime fuel savings. The credit generally is available for vehicles purchased after 2005. The credit terminates after 2009, 2010, or 2014, depending on the type of vehicle. The alternative motor vehicle credit is not allowed against the alternative minimum tax.

Plug-in electric drive motor vehicle credit

A credit is available for each qualified plug-in electric drive motor vehicle placed in service. A qualified plug-in electric drive motor vehicle is a motor vehicle that has at least four wheels, is manufactured for use on public roads, meets certain emissions standards (except for certain heavy vehicles), draws propulsion using a traction battery with at least four kilowatt-hours of capacity, and is capable of being recharged from an external source of electricity.

The base amount of the plug-in electric drive motor vehicle credit is $2,500, plus another $417 for each kilowatt-hour of battery capacity in excess of four kilowatt-hours. The maximum credit for qualified vehicles weighing 10,000 pounds or less is $7,500. This maximum amount increases to $10,000 for vehicles weighing more than 10,000 pounds but not more than 14,000 pounds, to $12,500 for vehicles weighing more than 14,000 pounds but not more than 26,000 pounds, and to $15,000 for vehicle weighing more than 26,000 pounds.

In general, the credit is available to the vehicle owner, including the lessor of a vehicle subject to lease. If the qualified vehicle is used by certain tax-exempt organizations, governments, or foreign persons and is not subject to a lease, the seller of the vehicle may claim the credit so long as the seller clearly discloses to the user in a document the amount that is allowable as a credit. A vehicle must be used predominantly in the United States to qualify for the credit.

Once a total of 250,000 credit-eligible vehicles have been sold for use in the United States, the credit phases out over four calendar quarters. The phaseout period begins in the second calendar quarter following the quarter during which the vehicle cap has been reached. Taxpayers may claim one-half of the otherwise allowable credit during the first two calendar quarters of the phaseout period and twenty-five percent of the

---

[211] Sec. 30B.

otherwise allowable credit during the next two quarters. After this, no credit is available. Regardless of the phase-out limitation, no credit is available for vehicles purchased after 2014.

The basis of any qualified vehicle is reduced by the amount of the credit. To the extent a vehicle is eligible for credit as a qualified plug-in electric drive motor vehicle, it is not eligible for credit as a qualified hybrid vehicle under section 30B. The portion of the credit attributable to vehicles of a character subject to an allowance for depreciation is treated as part of the general business credit; the nonbusiness portion of the credit is allowable to the extent of the excess of the regular tax over the alternative minimum tax (reduced by certain other credits) for the taxable year.

House Bill

No provision.

Senate Amendment

Credit for electric drive low-speed vehicles, motorcycles, and three-wheeled vehicles

The Senate amendment creates a new 10-percent credit for low-speed vehicles, motorcycles, and three-wheeled vehicles that would otherwise meet the criteria of a qualified plug-in electric drive motor vehicle but for the fact that they are low-speed vehicles or do not have at least four wheels. The maximum credit for such vehicles is $4,000. Basis reduction and other rules similar to those found in section 30 apply under the provision. The new credit is part of the general business credit. The new credit is not available for vehicles sold after December 31, 2011.

Credit for converting a vehicle into a plug-in electric drive motor vehicle

The Senate amendment also creates a new 10-percent credit, up to $4,000, for the cost of converting any motor vehicle into a qualified plug-in electric drive motor vehicle. To be eligible for the credit, a qualified plug-in traction battery module must have a capacity of at least 2.5 kilowatt-hours. In the case of a leased traction battery module, the credit may be claimed by the lessor but not the lessee. The credit is not available for conversions made after December 31, 2012.

Modification of plug-in electric drive motor vehicle credit

The Senate amendment modifies the plug-in electric drive motor vehicle credit by increasing the 250,000 vehicle limitation to 500,000. It also modifies the definition of qualified plug-in electric drive motor vehicle to exclude low-speed vehicles.

Effective date

The Senate amendment is generally effective for vehicles sold after December 31, 2009. The credit for plug-in vehicle conversion is effective for property placed in service after December 31, 2008, in taxable years beginning after such date.

Conference Agreement

The conference agreement follows the Senate amendment with substantial modifications.

Credit for electric drive low-speed vehicles, motorcycles, and three-wheeled vehicles

With respect to electric drive low-speed vehicles, motorcycles, and three-wheeled vehicles, the conference agreement follows the Senate amendment with the following modifications. Under the conference agreement, the maximum credit available is $2,500. The conference agreement also makes other technical changes.

Credit for converting a vehicle into a plug-in electric drive motor vehicle

With respect to plug-in vehicle conversions, the conference agreement follows the Senate amendment but increases the minimum capacity of a qualified battery module to four kilowatt-hours, changes the effective date to property placed in service after the date of enactment, and eliminates the credit for plug-in conversions made after December 31, 2011. The conference agreement also removes the rule permitting lessors of battery modules to claim the plug-in conversion credit.

Modification of the plug-in electric drive motor vehicle credit

The conference agreement modifies the plug-in electric drive motor vehicle credit by limiting the maximum credit to $7,500 regardless of vehicle weight. The conference agreement also eliminates the credit for low speed plug-in vehicles and for plug-in vehicles weighing 14,000 pounds or more.

The conference agreement replaces the 250,000 total plug-in vehicle limitation with a 200,000 plug-in vehicles per manufacturer limitation. The credit phases out over four calendar quarters beginning in the second calendar quarter following the quarter in which the manufacturer limit is reached. The conference agreement also makes other technical changes.

The changes to the plug-in electric drive motor vehicle credit are effective for vehicles acquired after December 31, 2009.

Treatment of alternative motor vehicle credit as a personal credit allowed against the alternative minimum tax

The conference agreement provides that the alternative motor vehicle credit is a personal credit allowed against the alternative minimum tax. The provision is effective for taxable years beginning after December 31, 2008.

[Law at ¶5005, ¶5010, ¶5020, ¶5035, ¶5040, ¶5045, ¶5050, ¶5055, ¶5080, ¶5140, ¶5180, ¶5280, ¶5285, ¶5305 and ¶5400. CCH Explanation at ¶345, ¶350, ¶355 and ¶360.]

[¶10,210] Act Sec. 1151. Parity for qualified transportation fringe benefits

Conference Report (H. REPT. 111-16)

[Code Sec. 132]

Present Law

Qualified transportation fringe benefits provided by an employer are excluded from an employee's gross income for income tax purposes and from an employee's wages for payroll tax purposes.[212] Qualified transportation fringe benefits include parking, transit passes, vanpool benefits, and qualified bicycle commuting reimbursements. Up to $230 (for 2009) per month of employer-provided parking is excludable from income. Up to $120 (for 2009) per month of employer-provided transit and vanpool benefits are excludable from gross income. These amounts are indexed annually for inflation, rounded to the nearest multiple of $5. No amount is includible in the income of an employee merely because the employer offers the employee a choice between cash and qualified transportation fringe benefits. Qualified transportation fringe benefits also include a cash reimbursement by an employer to an employee. However, in the case of transit passes, a cash reimbursement is considered a qualified transportation fringe benefit only if a voucher or similar item which may be exchanged only for a transit pass is not readily available for direct distribution by the employer to the employee.

House Bill

No provision.

Senate Amendment

The provision increases the monthly exclusion for employer-provided transit and vanpool benefits to the same level as the exclusion for employer-provided parking.

Effective date

The provision is effective for months beginning on or after date of enactment. The proposal does not apply to tax years beginning after December 31, 2010.

Conference Agreement

The conference agreement follows the Senate amendment.

[Law at ¶5210. CCH Explanation at ¶215.]

---

[212] Code secs. 132(f), 3121(b)(2), 3306(b)(16), and 3401(a)(19).

[¶10,220] Act Sec. 1201. Special allowance for certain property acquired during 2009 and extension of election to accelerate AMT and research credits in lieu of bonus depreciation

Conference Report (H. Rept. 111-16)

[Code Sec. 168(k)]

Present Law

An additional first-year depreciation deduction is allowed equal to 50 percent of the adjusted basis of qualified property placed in service during 2008 (and 2009 for certain longer-lived and transportation property).[19] The additional first-year depreciation deduction is allowed for both regular tax and alternative minimum tax purposes for the taxable year in which the property is placed in service.[20] The basis of the property and the depreciation allowances in the year of purchase and later years are appropriately adjusted to reflect the additional first-year depreciation deduction. In addition, there are no adjustments to the allowable amount of depreciation for purposes of computing a taxpayer's alternative minimum taxable income with respect to property to which the provision applies. The amount of the additional first-year depreciation deduction is not affected by a short taxable year. The taxpayer may elect out of additional first-year depreciation for any class of property for any taxable year.

The interaction of the additional first-year depreciation allowance with the otherwise applicable depreciation allowance may be illustrated as follows. Assume that in 2008, a taxpayer purchases new depreciable property and places it in service.[21] The property's cost is $1,000, and it is five-year property subject to the half-year convention. The amount of additional first-year depreciation allowed is $500. The remaining $500 of the cost of the property is deductible under the rules applicable to 5-year property. Thus, 20 percent, or $100, is also allowed as a depreciation deduction in 2008. The total depreciation deduction with respect to the property for 2008 is $600. The remaining $400 cost of the property is recovered under otherwise applicable rules for computing depreciation.

In order for property to qualify for the additional first-year depreciation deduction it must meet all of the following requirements. First, the property must be (1) property to which MACRS applies with an applicable recovery period of 20 years or less, (2) water utility property (as defined in section 168(e)(5)), (3) computer software other than computer software covered by section 197, or (4) qualified leasehold improvement property (as defined in section 168(k)(3)).[22] Second, the original use[23] of the property must commence with the taxpayer after December 31, 2007.[24] Third, the taxpayer must purchase the property within the applicable time period. Finally, the property must be placed in service after December 31, 2007, and before January 1, 2009. An extension of the placed in service date of one year (i.e., to January 1, 2010) is provided for certain property with a recovery period of ten years or longer and certain transportation prop-

---

[19] Sec. 168(k). The additional first-year depreciation deduction is subject to the general rules regarding whether an item is deductible under section 162 or instead is subject to capitalization under section 263 or section 263A.

[20] However, the additional first-year depreciation deduction is not allowed for purposes of computing earnings and profits.

[21] Assume that the cost of the property is not eligible for expensing under section 179.

[22] A special rule precludes the additional first-year depreciation deduction for any property that is required to be depreciated under the alternative depreciation system of MACRS.

[23] The term "original use" means the first use to which the property is put, whether or not such use corresponds to the use of such property by the taxpayer.

If in the normal course of its business a taxpayer sells fractional interests in property to unrelated third parties, then the original use of such property begins with the first user of each fractional interest (i.e., each fractional owner is considered the original user of its proportionate share of the property).

[24] A special rule applies in the case of certain leased property. In the case of any property that is originally placed in service by a person and that is sold to the taxpayer and leased back to such person by the taxpayer within three months after the date that the property was placed in service, the property would be treated as originally placed in service by the taxpayer not earlier than the date that the property is used under the leaseback.

If property is originally placed in service by a lessor (including by operation of section 168(k)(2)(D)(i)), such property is sold within three months after the date that the property was placed in service, and the user of such property does not change, then the property is treated as originally placed in service by the taxpayer not earlier than the date of such sale.

erty.[25] Transportation property is defined as tangible personal property used in the trade or business of transporting persons or property.

The applicable time period for acquired property is (1) after December 31, 2007, and before January 1, 2009, but only if no binding written contract for the acquisition is in effect before January 1, 2008, or (2) pursuant to a binding written contract which was entered into after December 31, 2007, and before January 1, 2009.[26] With respect to property that is manufactured, constructed, or produced by the taxpayer for use by the taxpayer, the taxpayer must begin the manufacture, construction, or production of the property after December 31, 2007, and before January 1, 2009. Property that is manufactured, constructed, or produced for the taxpayer by another person under a contract that is entered into prior to the manufacture, construction, or production of the property is considered to be manufactured, constructed, or produced by the taxpayer. For property eligible for the extended placed in service date, a special rule limits the amount of costs eligible for the additional first-year depreciation. With respect to such property, only the portion of the basis that is properly attributable to the costs incurred before January 1, 2009 ("progress expenditures") is eligible for the additional first-year depreciation.[27]

Property does not qualify for the additional first-year depreciation deduction when the user of such property (or a related party) would not have been eligible for the additional first-year depreciation deduction if the user (or a related party) were treated as the owner. For example, if a taxpayer sells to a related party property that was under construction prior to January 1, 2008, the property does not qualify for the additional first-year depreciation deduction. Similarly, if a taxpayer sells to a related party property that was subject to a binding written contract prior to January 1, 2008, the property does not qualify for the additional first-year depreciation deduction. As a further example, if a taxpayer (the lessee) sells property in a sale-leaseback arrangement, and the property otherwise would not have qualified for the additional first-year depreciation deduction if it were owned by the taxpayer-lessee, then the lessor is not entitled to the additional first-year depreciation deduction.

The limitation on the amount of depreciation deductions allowed with respect to certain passenger automobiles (sec. 280F) is increased in the first year by $8,000 for automobiles that qualify (and do not elect out of the increased first year deduction). The $8,000 increase is not indexed for inflation.

Corporations otherwise eligible for additional first year depreciation under section 168(k) may elect to claim additional research or minimum tax credits in lieu of claiming depreciation under section 168(k) for "eligible qualified property" placed in service after March 31, 2008 and before December 31, 2008.[28] A corporation making the election forgoes the depreciation deductions allowable under section 168(k) and instead increases the limitation under section 38(c) on the use of research credits or section 53(c) on the use of minimum tax credits.[29] The increases in the allowable credits are treated as refundable for purposes of this provision. The depreciation for qualified property is calculated for both regular tax and AMT purposes using the straight-line method in place of the method that would otherwise be used absent the election under this provision.

The research credit or minimum tax credit limitation is increased by the bonus depreciation amount, which is equal to 20 percent of bonus depreciation[30] for certain eligible qualified property that could be claimed absent an election under this provision. Generally, eligible qualified property included in the calculation is bonus depreciation property that meets the following requirements: (1) the original use of the property must commence with the taxpayer after March 31, 2008; (2) the taxpayer must

---

[25] In order for property to qualify for the extended placed in service date, the property is required to have an estimated production period exceeding one year and a cost exceeding $1 million.

[26] Property does not fail to qualify for the additional first-year depreciation merely because a binding written contract to acquire a component of the property is in effect prior to January 1, 2008.

[27] For purposes of determining the amount of eligible progress expenditures, it is intended that rules similar to sec. 46(d)(3) as in effect prior to the Tax Reform Act of 1986 shall apply.

[28] Sec. 168(k)(4). In the case of an electing corporation that is a partner in a partnership, the corporate partner's distributive share of partnership items is determined as if section 168(k) does not apply to any eligible qualified property and the straight line method is used to calculate depreciation of such property.

[29] Special rules apply to an applicable partnership.

[30] For this purpose, bonus depreciation is the difference between (i) the aggregate amount of depreciation for all eligible qualified property determined if section 168(k)(1) applied using the most accelerated depreciation method (determined without regard to this provision), and shortest life allowable for each property, and (ii) the amount of depreciation that would be determined if section 168(k)(1) did not apply using the same method and life for each property.

purchase the property either (a) after March 31, 2008, and before January 1, 2009, but only if no binding written contract for the acquisition is in effect before April 1, 2008,[31] or (b) pursuant to a binding written contract which was entered into after March 31, 2008, and before January 1, 2009;[32] and (3) the property must be placed in service after March 31, 2008, and before January 1, 2009 (January 1, 2010 for certain longer-lived and transportation property).

The bonus depreciation amount is limited to the lesser of: (1) $30 million, or (2) six percent of the sum of research credit carryforwards from taxable years beginning before January 1, 2006 and minimum tax credits allocable to the adjusted minimum tax imposed for taxable years beginning before January 1, 2006. All corporations treated as a single employer under section 52(a) are treated as one taxpayer for purposes of the limitation, as well as for electing the application of this provision.

House Bill

The provision extends the additional first-year depreciation deduction for one year, generally through 2009 (through 2010 for certain longer-lived and transportation property).[33]

Effective date.–The provision is effective for property placed in service after December 31, 2008.

Senate Amendment

The provision extends the additional first-year depreciation deduction for one year, generally through 2009 (through 2010 for certain longer-lived and transportation property).

The provision generally permits corporations to increase the research credit or minimum tax credit limitation by the bonus depreciation amount with respect to certain property placed in service in 2009 (2010 in the case of certain longer-lived and transportation property). The provision applies with respect to extension property, which is defined as property that is eligible qualified property solely because it meets the requirements under the extension of the special allowance for certain property acquired during 2009.

Under the provision, a taxpayer that has made an election to increase the research credit or minimum tax credit limitation for eligible qualified property for its first taxable year ending after March 31, 2008, may choose not to make this election for extension property. Further, the provision allows a taxpayer that has not made an election for eligible qualified property for its first taxable year ending after March 31, 2008, to make the election for extension property for its first taxable year ending after December 31, 2008, and for each subsequent year. In the case of a taxpayer electing to increase the research or minimum tax credit for both eligible qualified property and extension property, a separate bonus depreciation amount, maximum amount, and maximum increase amount is computed and applied to each group of property.[34]

Effective date

The extension of the additional first-year depreciation deduction is generally effective for property placed in service after December 31, 2008.

The extension of the election to accelerate AMT and research credits in lieu of bonus depreciation is effective for taxable years ending after December 31, 2008.

Conference Agreement

The conference agreement follows the Senate amendment.

[Law at ¶ 5240 and ¶ 5375. CCH Explanation at ¶ 415 and ¶ 505.]

---

[31] In the case of passenger aircraft, the written binding contract limitation does not apply.

[32] Special rules apply to property manufactured, constructed, or produced by the taxpayer for use by the taxpayer.

[33] The provision does not modify the property eligible for the election to accelerate AMT and research credits in lieu of bonus depreciation under section 168(k)(4). However, the provision includes a technical amendment to section 168(k)(4)(D) providing that no written binding contract for the acquisition of eligible qualified property may be in effect before April 1, 2008 (effective for taxable years ending after March 31, 2008).

[34] In computing the maximum amount, the maximum increase amount for extension property is reduced by bonus depreciation amounts for preceding taxable years only with respect to extension property.

[¶ 10,230] Act Sec. 1202. Temporary increase in limitations on expensing of certain depreciable business assets

Conference Report (H. Rept. 111-16)

[Code Sec. 179]

Present Law

In lieu of depreciation, a taxpayer with a sufficiently small amount of annual investment may elect to deduct (or "expense") such costs under section 179. Present law provides that the maximum amount a taxpayer may expense for taxable years beginning in 2008 is $250,000 of the cost of qualifying property placed in service for the taxable year.[35] For taxable years beginning in 2009 and 2010, the limitation is $125,000. In general, qualifying property is defined as depreciable tangible personal property that is purchased for use in the active conduct of a trade or business. Off-the-shelf computer software placed in service in taxable years beginning before 2011 is treated as qualifying property. For taxable years beginning in 2008, the $250,000 amount is reduced (but not below zero) by the amount by which the cost of qualifying property placed in service during the taxable year exceeds $800,000. For taxable years beginning in 2009 and 2010, the $125,000 amount is reduced (but not below zero) by the amount by which the cost of qualifying property placed in service during the taxable year exceeds $500,000. The $125,000 and $500,000 amounts are indexed for inflation in taxable years beginning in 2009 and 2010.

The amount eligible to be expensed for a taxable year may not exceed the taxable income for a taxable year that is derived from the active conduct of a trade or business (determined without regard to this provision). Any amount that is not allowed as a deduction because of the taxable income limitation may be carried forward to succeeding taxable years (subject to similar limitations). No general business credit under section 38 is allowed with respect to any amount for which a deduction is allowed under section 179. An expensing election is made under rules prescribed by the Secretary.[36]

For taxable years beginning in 2011 and thereafter (or before 2003), the following rules apply. A taxpayer with a sufficiently small amount of annual investment may elect to deduct up to $25,000 of the cost of qualifying property placed in service for the taxable year. The $25,000 amount is reduced (but not below zero) by the amount by which the cost of qualifying property placed in service during the taxable year exceeds $200,000. The $25,000 and $200,000 amounts are not indexed for inflation. In general, qualifying property is defined as depreciable tangible personal property that is purchased for use in the active conduct of a trade or business (not including off-the-shelf computer software). An expensing election may be revoked only with consent of the Commissioner.[37]

House Bill

The provision extends the $250,000 and $800,000 amounts to taxable years beginning in 2009.

Effective date

The provision is effective for taxable years beginning after December 31, 2008.

Senate Amendment

The Senate amendment is the same as the House bill.

Conference Agreement

The conference agreement follows the House bill and the Senate amendment.

[Law at ¶ 5250. CCH Explanation at ¶ 410.]

---

[35] Additional section 179 incentives are provided with respect to qualified property meeting applicable requirements that is used by a business in an empowerment zone (sec. 1397A) or a renewal community (sec. 1400J), qualified section 179 Gulf Opportunity Zone property (sec. 1400N(e)), qualified Recovery Assistance property placed in service in the Kansas disaster area (Pub. L. No. 110-234, sec. 15345 (2008)), and qualified disaster assistance property (sec. 179(e)).

[36] Sec. 179(c)(1). Under Treas. Reg. sec. 1.179-5, applicable to property placed in service in taxable years beginning after 2002 and before 2008, a taxpayer is permitted to make or revoke an election under section 179 without the consent of the Commissioner on an amended Federal tax return for that taxable year. This amended return must be filed within the time prescribed by law for filing an amended return for the taxable year. T.D. 9209, July 12, 2005.

[37] Sec. 179(c)(2).

[¶ 10,240] Act Sec. 1211. Five-year carryback of operating losses

Conference Report (H. Rept. 111-16)

[Code Sec. 172]

Present Law

Under present law, a net operating loss ("NOL") generally means the amount by which a taxpayer's business deductions exceed its gross income. In general, an NOL may be carried back two years and carried over 20 years to offset taxable income in such years.[38] NOLs offset taxable income in the order of the taxable years to which the NOL may be carried.[39]

The alternative minimum tax rules provide that a taxpayer's NOL deduction cannot reduce the taxpayer's alternative minimum taxable income ("AMTI") by more than 90 percent of the AMTI.

Different rules apply with respect to NOLs arising in certain circumstances. A three-year carryback applies with respect to NOLs (1) arising from casualty or theft losses of individuals, or (2) attributable to Presidentially declared disasters for taxpayers engaged in a farming business or a small business. A five-year carryback applies to NOLs (1) arising from a farming loss (regardless of whether the loss was incurred in a Presidentially declared disaster area), (2) certain amounts related to Hurricane Katrina, Gulf Opportunity Zone, and Midwestern Disaster Area, or (3) qualified disaster losses.[40] Special rules also apply to real estate investment trusts (no carryback), specified liability losses (10-year carryback), and excess interest losses (no carryback to any year preceding a corporate equity reduction transaction). Additionally, a special rule applies to certain electric utility companies.

In the case of a life insurance company, present law allows a deduction for the operations loss carryovers and carrybacks to the taxable year, in lieu of the deduction for net operation losses allowed to other corporations.[41] A life insurance company is permitted to treat a loss from operations (as defined under section 810(c)) for any taxable year as an operations loss carryback to each of the three taxable years preceding the loss year and an operations loss carryover to each of the 15 taxable years following the loss year.[42] Special rules apply to new life insurance companies.

House Bill

The House bill provides an election[43] to increase the present-law carryback period for an applicable 2008 or 2009 NOL from two years to any whole number of years elected by the taxpayer which is more than two and less than six. An applicable NOL is the taxpayer's NOL for any taxable year ending in 2008 or 2009, or if elected by the taxpayer, the NOL for any taxable year beginning in 2008 or 2009. If an election is made to increase the carryback period, the applicable NOL is permanently reduced by 10 percent.

These provisions may be illustrated by the following example. Taxpayer incurs a $100 NOL for its taxable year ended January 31, 2008 and elects to carryback the NOL five years to its taxable year ended January 31, 2003. Under the provision, Taxpayer must first permanently reduce the NOL by 10 percent, or $10, and then may carryback the $90 NOL to its taxable year ended January 31, 2003.

The provision also suspends the 90-percent limitation on the use of any alternative tax NOL deduction attributable to carrybacks of losses from taxable years ending during 2008 or 2009, and carryovers of losses to such taxable years (this rule applies to taxable years beginning in 2008 or 2009 if an election is in place to use such years as applicable NOLs).

For life insurance companies, the provision provides an election to increase the present-law carryback period for an applicable loss from operations from three years to four or five years. An applicable loss from operations is the taxpayer's loss from operations for any taxable year ending in 2008 or 2009, or if elected by the taxpayer, the loss from operations for any taxable year beginning in 2008 or 2009. If an election is made to increase the carryback period, the appli-

---

[38] Sec. 172(b)(1)(A).
[39] Sec. 172(b)(2).
[40] Sec. 172(b)(1)(J).
[41] Secs. 810, 805(a)(5).
[42] Sec. 810(b)(1).

[43] For all elections under this provision, the common parent of a group of corporations filing a consolidated return makes the election, which is binding on all such corporations.

cable loss from operations is permanently reduced by 10 percent.

The provision does not apply to: (1) any taxpayer if (a) the Federal Government acquires, at any time,[44] an equity interest in the taxpayer pursuant to the Emergency Economic Stabilization Act of 2008, or (b) the Federal Government acquires, at any time, any warrant (or other right) to acquire any equity interest with respect to the taxpayer pursuant to such Act; (2) the Federal National Mortgage Association and the Federal Home Loan Mortgage Corporation; or (3) any taxpayer that in 2008 or 2009[45] is a member of the same affiliated group (as defined in section 1504 without regard to subsection (b) thereof) as a taxpayer to which the provision does not otherwise apply.

Effective date.–The provision is generally effective for net operating losses arising in taxable years ending after December 31, 2007. The modification to the alternative tax NOL deduction applies to taxable years ending after 1997.[46] The modification with respect to operating loss deductions of life insurance companies applies to losses from operations arising in taxable years ending after December 31, 2007.

For an NOL or loss from operations for a taxable year ending before the enactment of the provision, the provision includes the following transition rules: (1) any election to waive the carryback period under either sections 172(b)(3) or 810(b)(3) with respect to such loss may be revoked before the applicable date; (2) any election to increase the carryback period under this provision is treated as timely made if made before the applicable date; and (3) any application for a tentative carryback adjustment under section 6411(a) with respect to such loss is treated as timely filed if filed before the applicable date. For purposes of the transition rules, the applicable date is the date which is 60 days after the date of the enactment of the provision.

Senate Amendment

The Senate amendment is generally the same as the House bill, except that the Senate amendment does not include the permanent reduction of the NOL for taxpayers electing to increase the carryback period.

Effective date.–The effective date follows the House bill.

Conference Agreement

The conference agreement provides an eligible small business with an election[47] to increase the present-law carryback period for an applicable 2008 NOL from two years to any whole number of years elected by the taxpayer that is more than two and less than six. An eligible small business is a taxpayer meeting a $15,000,000 gross receipts test.[48] An applicable NOL is the taxpayer's NOL for any taxable year ending in 2008, or if elected by the taxpayer, the NOL for any taxable year beginning in 2008. However, any election under this provision may be made only with respect to one taxable year.

Effective date

The conference agreement provision is effective for net operating losses arising in taxable years ending after December 31, 2007.

For an NOL for a taxable year ending before the enactment of the provision, the provision includes the following transition rules: (1) any election to waive the carryback period under either section 172(b)(3) with respect to such loss may be revoked before the applicable date; (2) any election to increase the carryback period under this provision is treated as timely made if made before the applicable date; and (3) any application for a tentative carryback adjustment under section 6411(a) with respect to such loss is treated as timely filed if filed before the applicable date. For purposes of the transition rules, the

---

[44] For example, if the Federal government acquires an equity interest in the taxpayer during 2010, or in later years, the taxpayer is not entitled to the extended carryback rules under this provision. If the carryback has previously been claimed, amended filings may be necessary to reflect this disallowance.

[45] For example, a taxpayer with an NOL in 2008 that in 2010 joins an affiliated group with a member in which the Federal Government has an equity interest pursuant to the Emergency Economic Stabilization Act of 2008 may not utilize the extended carryback rules under this provision with regard to the 2008 NOL. The taxpayer is required to amend prior filings to reflect the permitted carryback period.

[46] NOL deductions from as early as taxable years ending after 1997 may be carried forward to 2008 and utilize the provision suspending the 90 percent limitation on alternative tax NOL deductions.

[47] For all elections under this provision, the common parent of a group of corporations filing a consolidated return makes the election, which is binding on all such corporations.

[48] For this purpose, the gross receipt test of sec. 448(c) is applied by substituting $15,000,000 for $5,000,000 each place it appears.

Act Sec. 1211 ¶10,240

applicable date is the date which is 60 days after the date of the enactment of the provision.

[Law at ¶ 5245 and ¶ 7012. CCH Explanation at ¶ 425.]

[¶ 10,250] Act Sec. 1212. Estimated tax payments

Conference Report (H. Rept. 111-16)

[Code Sec. 6654]

Present Law

Under present law, the income tax system is designed to ensure that taxpayers pay taxes throughout the year based on their income and deductions. To the extent that tax is not collected through withholding, taxpayers are required to make quarterly estimated payments of tax, the amount of which is determined by reference to the required annual payment. The required annual payment is the lesser of 90 percent of the tax shown on the return or 100 percent of the tax shown on the return for the prior taxable year (110 percent if the adjusted gross income for the preceding year exceeded $150,000). An underpayment results if the required payment exceeds the amount (if any) of the installment paid on or before the due date of the installment. The period of the underpayment runs from the due date of the installment to the earlier of (1) the 15th day of the fourth month following the close of the taxable year or (2) the date on which each portion of the underpayment is made. If a taxpayer fails to pay the required estimated tax payments under the rules, a penalty is imposed in an amount determined by applying the underpayment interest rate to the amount of the underpayment for the period of the underpayment. The penalty for failure to pay estimated tax is the equivalent of interest, which is based on the time value of money.

Taxpayers are not liable for a penalty for the failure to pay estimated tax in certain circumstances. The statute provides exceptions for U.S. persons who did not have a tax liability the preceding year, if the tax shown on the return for the taxable year (or, if no return is filed, the tax), reduced by withholding, is less than $1,000, or the taxpayer is a recently retired or disabled person who satisfies the reasonable cause exception.

House Bill

No provision.

Senate Amendment

No provision.

Conference Agreement

The conference agreement provides that the required annual estimated tax payments of a qualified individual for taxable years beginning in 2009 is not greater than 90 percent of the tax liability shown on the tax return for the preceding taxable year. A qualified individual means any individual if the adjusted gross income shown on the tax return for the preceding taxable year is less than $500,000 ($250,000 if married filing separately) and the individual certifies that at least 50 percent of the gross income shown on the return for the preceding taxable year was income from a small trade or business. For purposes of this provision, a small trade or business means any trade or business that employed no more than 500 persons, on average, during the calendar year ending in or with the preceding taxable year.

Effective date

The proposal is effective on the date of enactment.

[Law at ¶ 5405. CCH Explanation at ¶ 465.]

[¶ 10,260] Act Sec. 1221. Modification of work opportunity tax credit

Conference Report (H. Rept. 111-16)

[Code Sec. 51]

Present Law

In general

The work opportunity tax credit is available on an elective basis for employers hiring individuals from one or more of nine targeted groups. The amount of the credit available to an employer is determined by the amount of qualified wages paid by the employer. Generally, qualified wages consist of wages attributable to service rendered by a member of a targeted group

¶ 10,250 Act Sec. 1212

during the one-year period beginning with the day the individual begins work for the employer (two years in the case of an individual in the long-term family assistance recipient category).

Targeted groups eligible for the credit

Generally an employer is eligible for the credit only for qualified wages paid to members of a targeted group.

(1) Families receiving TANF

An eligible recipient is an individual certified by a designated local employment agency (e.g., a State employment agency) as being a member of a family eligible to receive benefits under the Temporary Assistance for Needy Families Program ("TANF") for a period of at least nine months part of which is during the 18-month period ending on the hiring date. For these purposes, members of the family are defined to include only those individuals taken into account for purposes of determining eligibility for the TANF.

(2) Qualified veteran

There are two subcategories of qualified veterans related to eligibility for Food stamps and compensation for a service-connected disability.

Food stamps

A qualified veteran is a veteran who is certified by the designated local agency as a member of a family receiving assistance under a food stamp program under the Food Stamp Act of 1977 for a period of at least three months part of which is during the 12-month period ending on the hiring date. For these purposes, members of a family are defined to include only those individuals taken into account for purposes of determining eligibility for a food stamp program under the Food Stamp Act of 1977.

Entitled to compensation for a service-connected disability

A qualified veteran also includes an individual who is certified as entitled to compensation for a service-connected disability and: (1) having a hiring date which is not more than one year after having been discharged or released from active duty in the Armed Forces of the United States; or (2) having been unemployed for six months or more (whether or not consecutive) during the one-year period ending on the date of hiring.

Definitions

For these purposes, being entitled to compensation for a service-connected disability is defined with reference to section 101 of Title 38, U.S. Code, which means having a disability rating of 10 percent or higher for service connected injuries.

For these purposes, a veteran is an individual who has served on active duty (other than for training) in the Armed Forces for more than 180 days or who has been discharged or released from active duty in the Armed Forces for a service-connected disability. However, any individual who has served for a period of more than 90 days during which the individual was on active duty (other than for training) is not a qualified veteran if any of this active duty occurred during the 60-day period ending on the date the individual was hired by the employer. This latter rule is intended to prevent employers who hire current members of the armed services (or those departed from service within the last 60 days) from receiving the credit.

(3) Qualified ex-felon

A qualified ex-felon is an individual certified as: (1) having been convicted of a felony under any State or Federal law; and (2) having a hiring date within one year of release from prison or the date of conviction.

(4) Designated community residents

A designated community resident is an individual certified as being at least age 18 but not yet age 40 on the hiring date and as having a principal place of abode within an empowerment zone, enterprise community, renewal community or a rural renewal community. For these purposes, a rural renewal county is a county outside a metropolitan statistical area (as defined by the Office of Management and Budget) which had a net population loss during the five-year periods 1990-1994 and 1995-1999. Qualified wages do not include wages paid or incurred for services performed after the individual moves outside an empowerment zone, enterprise community, renewal community or a rural renewal community.

(5) Vocational rehabilitation referral

A vocational rehabilitation referral is an individual who is certified by a designated local agency as an individual who has a physical or mental disability that constitutes a substantial handicap to employment and who has been referred to the employer while receiving, or after completing: (a) vocational rehabilitation services under an individualized, written plan for employment under a State plan approved under the Rehabilitation Act of 1973; (b) under a rehabilitation plan for veterans carried out under Chapter

Act Sec. 1221   ¶10,260

31 of Title 38, U.S. Code; or (c) an individual work plan developed and implemented by an employment network pursuant to subsection (g) of section 1148 of the Social Security Act. Certification will be provided by the designated local employment agency upon assurances from the vocational rehabilitation agency that the employee has met the above conditions.

(6) Qualified summer youth employee

A qualified summer youth employee is an individual: (a) who performs services during any 90-day period between May 1 and September 15; (b) who is certified by the designated local agency as being 16 or 17 years of age on the hiring date; (c) who has not been an employee of that employer before; and (d) who is certified by the designated local agency as having a principal place of abode within an empowerment zone, enterprise community, or renewal community (as defined under Subchapter U of Subtitle A, Chapter 1 of the Internal Revenue Code). As with designated community residents, no credit is available on wages paid or incurred for service performed after the qualified summer youth moves outside of an empowerment zone, enterprise community, or renewal community. If, after the end of the 90-day period, the employer continues to employ a youth who was certified during the 90-day period as a member of another targeted group, the limit on qualified first year wages will take into account wages paid to the youth while a qualified summer youth employee.

(7) Qualified food stamp recipient

A qualified food stamp recipient is an individual at least age 18 but not yet age 40 certified by a designated local employment agency as being a member of a family receiving assistance under a food stamp program under the Food Stamp Act of 1977 for a period of at least six months ending on the hiring date. In the case of families that cease to be eligible for food stamps under section 6(o) of the Food Stamp Act of 1977, the six-month requirement is replaced with a requirement that the family has been receiving food stamps for at least three of the five months ending on the date of hire. For these purposes, members of the family are defined to include only those individuals taken into account for purposes of determining eligibility for a food stamp program under the Food Stamp Act of 1977.

(8) Qualified SSI recipient

A qualified SSI recipient is an individual designated by a local agency as receiving supplemental security income ("SSI") benefits under Title XVI of the Social Security Act for any month ending within the 60-day period ending on the hiring date.

(9) Long-term family assistance recipients

A qualified long-term family assistance recipient is an individual certified by a designated local agency as being: (a) a member of a family that has received family assistance for at least 18 consecutive months ending on the hiring date; (b) a member of a family that has received such family assistance for a total of at least 18 months (whether or not consecutive) after August 5, 1997 (the date of enactment of the welfare-to-work tax credit)[49] if the individual is hired within two years after the date that the 18-month total is reached; or (c) a member of a family who is no longer eligible for family assistance because of either Federal or State time limits, if the individual is hired within two years after the Federal or State time limits made the family ineligible for family assistance.

Qualified wages

Generally, qualified wages are defined as cash wages paid by the employer to a member of a targeted group. The employer's deduction for wages is reduced by the amount of the credit.

For purposes of the credit, generally, wages are defined by reference to the FUTA definition of wages contained in sec. 3306(b) (without regard to the dollar limitation therein contained). Special rules apply in the case of certain agricultural labor and certain railroad labor.

Calculation of the credit

The credit available to an employer for qualified wages paid to members of all targeted groups except for long-term family assistance recipients equals 40 percent (25 percent for employment of 400 hours or less) of qualified first-year wages. Generally, qualified first-year wages are qualified wages (not in excess of $6,000) attributable to service rendered by a member of a targeted group during the one-year period beginning with the day the individual began work for the employer. Therefore, the maximum credit per employee is $2,400 (40 percent of the first

---

[49] The welfare-to-work tax credit was consolidated into the work opportunity tax credit in the Tax Relief and Health Care Act of 2006, for qualified individuals who begin to work for an employer after December 31, 2006.

$6,000 of qualified first-year wages). With respect to qualified summer youth employees, the maximum credit is $1,200 (40 percent of the first $3,000 of qualified first-year wages). Except for long-term family assistance recipients, no credit is allowed for second-year wages.

In the case of long-term family assistance recipients, the credit equals 40 percent (25 percent for employment of 400 hours or less) of $10,000 for qualified first-year wages and 50 percent of the first $10,000 of qualified second-year wages. Generally, qualified second-year wages are qualified wages (not in excess of $10,000) attributable to service rendered by a member of the long-term family assistance category during the one-year period beginning on the day after the one-year period beginning with the day the individual began work for the employer. Therefore, the maximum credit per employee is $9,000 (40 percent of the first $10,000 of qualified first-year wages plus 50 percent of the first $10,000 of qualified second-year wages).

In the case of a qualified veteran who is entitled to compensation for a service connected disability, the credit equals 40 percent of $12,000 of qualified first-year wages. This expanded definition of qualified first-year wages does not apply to the veterans qualified with reference to a food stamp program, as defined under present law.

Certification rules

An individual is not treated as a member of a targeted group unless: (1) on or before the day on which an individual begins work for an employer, the employer has received a certification from a designated local agency that such individual is a member of a targeted group; or (2) on or before the day an individual is offered employment with the employer, a pre-screening notice is completed by the employer with respect to such individual, and not later than the 28th day after the individual begins work for the employer, the employer submits such notice, signed by the employer and the individual under penalties of perjury, to the designated local agency as part of a written request for certification. For these purposes, a pre-screening notice is a document (in such form as the Secretary may prescribe) which contains information provided by the individual on the basis of which the employer believes that the individual is a member of a targeted group.

Minimum employment period

No credit is allowed for qualified wages paid to employees who work less than 120 hours in the first year of employment.

Other rules

The work opportunity tax credit is not allowed for wages paid to a relative or dependent of the taxpayer. No credit is allowed for wages paid to an individual who is a more than fifty-percent owner of the entity. Similarly, wages paid to replacement workers during a strike or lockout are not eligible for the work opportunity tax credit. Wages paid to any employee during any period for which the employer received on-the-job training program payments with respect to that employee are not eligible for the work opportunity tax credit. The work opportunity tax credit generally is not allowed for wages paid to individuals who had previously been employed by the employer. In addition, many other technical rules apply.

Expiration

The work opportunity tax credit is not available for individuals who begin work for an employer after August 31, 2011.

House Bill

In general

The provision creates a new targeted group for the work opportunity tax credit. That new category is unemployed veterans and disconnected youth who begin work for the employer in 2009 or 2010.

An unemployed veteran is defined as an individual certified by the designated local agency as someone who: (1) has served on active duty (other than for training) in the Armed Forces for more than 180 days or who has been discharged or released from active duty in the Armed Forces for a service-connected disability; (2) has been discharged or released from active duty in the Armed Forces during 2008, 2009, or 2010; and (3) has received unemployment compensation under State or Federal law for not less than four weeks during the one-year period ending on the hiring date.

A disconnected youth is defined as an individual certified by the designated local agency as someone: (1) at least age 16 but not yet age 25 on the hiring date; (2) not regularly attending any secondary, technical, or post-secondary school during the six-month period preceding the hiring date; (3) not regularly employed during the six-month period preceding the hiring date; and (4) not readily employable by reason of lacking a sufficient number of skills.

Effective date

The provisions are effective for individuals who begin work for an employer after December 31, 2008.

Senate Amendment

The Senate amendment is the same as the House bill except that the otherwise applicable definition of unemployed veterans is expanded to include individuals who were discharged or released from active duty in the Armed Forces during the period beginning on September 1, 2001 and ending on December 31, 2010.

Conference Agreement

The conference agreement follows the House bill and the Senate amendment with one modification. Under this modification a unemployed veteran for purposes of this new targeted group is defined below:

An unemployed veteran is defined as an individual certified by the designated local agency as someone who: (1) has served on active duty (other than for training) in the Armed Forces for more than 180 days or who has been discharged or released from active duty in the Armed Forces for a service-connected disability; (2) has been discharged or released from active duty in the Armed Forces during the five-year period ending on the hiring date; and (3) has received unemployment compensation under State or Federal law for not less than four weeks during the one-year period ending on the hiring date.

For purposes of the disconnected youths, it is intended that a low-level of formal education may satisfy the requirement that an individual is not readily employable by reason of lacking a sufficient number of skills. Further, it is intended that the Internal Revenue Service, when providing general guidance regarding the various new criteria, shall take into account the administrability of the program by the State agencies.

[Law at ¶ 5135. CCH Explanation at ¶ 540.]

[¶ 10,270] Act Sec. 1231. Deferral of certain income from the discharge of indebtedness

Conference Report (H. Rept. 111-16)

[Code Sec. 108]

Present Law

In general, gross income includes income that is realized by a debtor from the discharge of indebtedness, subject to certain exceptions for debtors in title 11 bankruptcy cases, insolvent debtors, certain student loans, certain farm indebtedness, certain real property business indebtedness, and certain qualified principal residence indebtedness.[81] In cases involving discharges of indebtedness that are excluded from gross income under the exceptions to the general rule, taxpayers generally are required to reduce certain tax attributes, including net operating losses, general business credits, minimum tax credits, capital loss carryovers, and basis in property, by the amount of the discharge of indebtedness.[82]

The amount of discharge of indebtedness excluded from income by an insolvent debtor not in a title II bankruptcy case cannot exceed the amount by which the debtor is insolvent. In the case of a discharge in bankruptcy or where the debtor is insolvent, any reduction in basis may not exceed the excess of the aggregate bases of properties held by the taxpayer immediately after the discharge over the aggregate of the liabilities of the taxpayer immediately after the discharge.[83]

For all taxpayers, the amount of discharge of indebtedness generally is equal to the excess of the adjusted issue price of the indebtedness being satisfied over the amount paid (or deemed paid) to satisfy such indebtedness.[84] This rule generally applies to (1) the acquisition by the debtor of its debt instrument in exchange for cash, (2) the issuance of a debt instrument by the debtor in satisfaction of its indebtedness, including a modification of indebtedness that is treated as an exchange (a debt-for-debt exchange), (3) the transfer by a debtor corporation of stock, or a debtor partnership of a capital or profits interest in such partnership, in satisfaction of its indebtedness (an equity-for-debt exchange), and (4) the acquisition by a debtor corporation of its indebt-

---

[81] See sections 61(a)(12) and 108. But see sec. 102 (a debt cancellation which constitutes a gift or bequest is not treated as income to the donee debtor).

[82] Sec. 108(b).

[83] Sec. 1017.

[84] Treas. Reg. sec. 1.61-12(c)(2)(ii). Treas. Reg. sec. 1.1275-1(b) defines "adjusted issue price."

edness from a shareholder as a contribution to capital.

Debt-for-debt exchanges

If a debtor issues a debt instrument in satisfaction of its indebtedness, the debtor is treated as having satisfied the indebtedness with an amount of money equal to the issue price of the newly issued debt instrument.[85] The issue price of such newly issued debt instrument generally is determined under sections 1273 and 1274.[86] Similarly, a "significant modification" of a debt instrument, within the meaning of Treas. Reg. sec. 1.1001-3, results in an exchange of the original debt instrument for a modified instrument. In such cases, where the issue price of the modified debt instrument is less than the adjusted issue price of the original debt instrument, the debtor will have income from the cancellation of indebtedness.

If any new debt instrument is issued (including as a result of a significant modification to a debt instrument), such debt instrument will have original issue discount equal to the excess (if any) of such debt instrument's stated redemption price at maturity over its issue price.[87] In general, an issuer of a debt instrument with original issue discount may deduct for any taxable year, with respect to such debt instrument, an amount of original issue discount equal to the aggregate daily portions of the original issue discount for days during such taxable year.[88]

Equity-for-debt exchanges

If a corporation transfers stock, or a partnership transfers a capital or profits interest in such partnership, to a creditor in satisfaction of its indebtedness, then such corporation or partnership is treated as having satisfied its indebtedness with an amount of money equal to the fair market value of the stock or interest.[89]

Related party acquisitions

Indebtedness directly or indirectly acquired by a person who bears a relationship to the debtor described in section 267(b) or section 707(b) is treated as if it were acquired by the debtor.[90] Thus, where a debtor's indebtedness is acquired for less than its adjusted issue price by a person related to the debtor (within the meaning of section 267(b) or 707(b)), the debtor recognizes income from the cancellation of indebtedness. Regulations under section 108 provide that the indebtedness acquired by the related party is treated as new indebtedness issued by the debtor to the related holder on the acquisition date (the deemed issuance).[91] The new indebtedness is deemed issued with an issue price equal to the amount used under regulations to compute the amount of cancellation of indebtedness income realized by the debtor (i.e., either the holder's adjusted basis or the fair market value of the indebtedness, as the case may be).[92] The indebtedness deemed issued pursuant to the regulations has original issue discount to the extent its stated redemption price at maturity exceeds its issue price.

In the case of a deemed issuance under Treas. Reg. sec. 1.108-2(g), the related holder does not recognize any gain or loss, and the related holder's adjusted basis in the indebtedness remains the same as it was immediately before the deemed issuance.[93] The deemed issuance is treated as a purchase of the indebtedness by the related holder for purposes of section 1272(a)(7) (pertaining to reduction of original issue discount where a subsequent holder pays acquisition premium) and section 1276 (pertaining to acquisitions of debt at a market discount).[94]

Contribution of a debt instrument to capital of a corporation

Where a debtor corporation acquires its indebtedness from a shareholder as a contribution to capital, section 118[95] does not apply, but the corporation is treated as satisfying such indebtedness with an amount of money equal to the shareholder's adjusted basis in the indebtedness.

House Bill

No provision.

Senate Amendment

The provision permits a taxpayer to elect to defer income from cancellation of indebtedness recognized by the taxpayer as a result of a repurchase by (1) the taxpayer or (2) a person who bears a relationship to the taxpayer described in

---

[85] Sec. 108(e)(10)(A).
[86] Sec. 108(e)(10)(B).
[87] Sec. 1273.
[88] Sec. 163(e).
[89] Sec. 108(e)(8).
[90] Sec. 108(e)(4).
[91] Treas. Reg. sec. 1.108-2(g).

[92] Id.
[93] Treas. Reg. sec. 1.108-2(g)(2).
[94] Id.
[95] Section 118 provides, in general, that in the case of a corporation, gross income does not include any contribution to the capital of the taxpayer.

section 267(b) or section 707(b), of a "debt instrument" that was issued by the taxpayer. The provision applies only to repurchases of debt that (1) occur after December 31, 2008, and prior to January 1, 2011, and (2) are repurchases for cash. Thus, for example, the provision does not apply to a debt-for-debt exchange or to any exchange of the taxpayer's equity for a debt instrument of the taxpayer. For purposes of the provision, a "debt instrument" is broadly defined to include any bond, debenture, note, certificate or any other instrument or contractual arrangement constituting indebtedness.

Income from the discharge of indebtedness in connection with the repurchase of a debt instrument in 2009 or 2010 must be included in the gross income of the taxpayer ratably in the eight taxable years beginning with (1) for repurchases in 2009, the second taxable year following the taxable year in which the repurchase occurs or (2) for repurchases in 2010, the taxable year following the taxable year in which the repurchase occurs. The provision authorizes the Secretary of the Treasury to prescribe such regulations as may be necessary or appropriate for purposes of applying the provision.

Effective date.—The provision applies to discharges in taxable years ending after December 31, 2008.

Conference Agreement

The conference agreement follows the Senate amendment with modifications. The provision permits a taxpayer to elect to defer cancellation of indebtedness income arising from a "reacquisition" of "an applicable debt instrument" after December 31, 2008, and before January 1, 2011. Income deferred pursuant to the election must be included in the gross income of the taxpayer ratably in the five taxable years beginning with (1) for repurchases in 2009, the fifth taxable year following the taxable year in which the repurchase occurs or (2) for repurchases in 2010, the fourth taxable year following the taxable year in which the repurchase occurs.

An "applicable debt instrument" is any debt instrument issued by (1) a C corporation or (2) any other person in connection with the conduct of a trade or business by such person. For purposes of the provision, a "debt instrument" is broadly defined to include any bond, debenture, note, certificate or any other instrument or contractual arrangement constituting indebtedness (within the meaning of section 1275(a)(1)).

A "reacquisition" is any "acquisition" of an applicable debt instrument by (1) the debtor that issued (or is otherwise the obligor under) such debt instrument or (2) any person related to the debtor within the meaning of section 108(c)(4). For purposes of the provision, an "acquisition" includes, without limitation, (1) an acquisition of a debt instrument for cash, (2) the exchange of a debt instrument for another debt instrument (including an exchange resulting from a modification of a debt instrument), (3) the exchange of corporate stock or a partnership interest for a debt instrument, (4) the contribution of a debt instrument to the capital of the issuer, and (5) the complete forgiveness of a debt instrument by a holder of such instrument.

Special rules for debt-for-debt exchanges

If a taxpayer makes the election provided by the provision for a debt-for-debt exchange in which the newly issued debt instrument issued (or deemed issued, including by operation of the rules in Treas. Reg. sec. 1.108-2(g)) in satisfaction of an outstanding debt instrument of the debtor has original issue discount, then any otherwise allowable deduction for original issue discount with respect to such newly issued debt instrument that (1) accrues before the first year of the five-taxable-year period in which the related, deferred discharge of indebtedness income is included in the gross income of the taxpayer and (2) does not exceed such related, deferred discharge of indebtedness income, is deferred and allowed as a deduction ratably over the same five-taxable-year period in which the deferred discharge of indebtedness income is included in gross income.

This rule can apply also in certain cases when a debtor reacquires its debt for cash. If the taxpayer issues a debt instrument and the proceeds of such issuance are used directly or indirectly to reacquire a debt instrument of the taxpayer, the provision treats the newly issued debt instrument as if it were issued in satisfaction of the retired debt instrument. If the newly issued debt instrument has original issue discount, the rule described above applies. Thus, all or a portion of the interest deductions with respect to original issue discount on the newly issued debt instrument are deferred into the five-taxable-year period in which the discharge of indebtedness income is recognized. Where only a portion of the proceeds of a new issuance are used by a taxpayer to satisfy outstanding debt, then the deferral rule applies to the portion of the original issue discount on the newly issued debt instrument that is equal to the portion of the proceeds of such newly issued instrument used to retire outstanding debt of the taxpayer.

Acceleration of deferred items

Cancellation of indebtedness income and any related deduction for original issue discount that is deferred by an electing taxpayer (and has not previously been taken into account) generally is accelerated and taken into income in the taxable year in which the taxpayer: (1) dies, (2) liquidates or sells substantially all of its assets (including in a title 11 or similar case), (3) ceases to do business, or (4) or is in similar circumstances. In a case under title 11 or a similar case, any deferred items are taken into income as of the day before the petition is filed. Deferred items are accelerated in a case under Title 11 where the taxpayer liquidates, sells substantially all of its assets, or ceases to do business, but not where a taxpayer reorganizes and emerges from the Title 11 case. In the case of a pass thru entity, this acceleration rule also applies to the sale, exchange, or redemption of an interest in the entity by a holder of such interest.

Special rule for partnerships

In the case of a partnership, any income deferred under the provision is allocated to the partners in the partnership immediately before the discharge of indebtedness in the manner such amounts would have been included in the distributive shares of such partners under section 704 if such income were recognized at the time of the discharge. Any decrease in a partner's share of liabilities as a result of such discharge is not taken into account for purposes of section 752 at the time of the discharge to the extent the deemed distribution under section 752 would cause the partner to recognize gain under section 731. Thus, the deemed distribution under section 752 is deferred with respect to a partner to the extent it exceeds such partner's basis. Amounts so deferred are taken into account at the same time, and to the extent remaining in the same amount, as income deferred under the provision is recognized by the partner.

Coordination with section 108(a) and procedures for election

Where a taxpayer makes the election provided by the provision, the exclusions provided by section 108(a)(1)(A), (B), (C), and (D) shall not apply to the income from the discharge of indebtedness for the year in which the taxpayer makes the election or any subsequent year. Thus, for example, an insolvent taxpayer may elect under the provision to defer income from the discharge of indebtedness rather than excluding such income and reducing tax attributes by a corresponding amount. The election is to be made on an instrument by instrument basis; once made, the election is irrevocable. A taxpayer makes an election with respect to a debt instrument by including with its return for the taxable year in which the reacquisition of the debt instrument occurs a statement that (1) clearly identifies the debt instrument and (2) includes the amount of deferred income to which the provision applies and such other information as may be prescribed by the Secretary. The Secretary is authorized to require reporting of the election (and other information with respect to the reacquisition) for years subsequent to the year of the reacquisition.

Regulatory authority

The provision authorizes the Secretary of the Treasury to prescribe such regulations as may be necessary or appropriate for purposes of applying the provision, including rules extending the acceleration provisions to other circumstances where appropriate, rules requiring reporting of the election and such other information as the Secretary may require on returns of tax for subsequent taxable years, rules for the application of the provision to partnerships, S corporations, and other pass thru entities, including for the allocation of deferred deductions.

Effective date

The provision is effective for discharges in taxable years ending after December 31, 2008.

[Law at ¶ 5205. CCH Explanation at ¶ 405.]

[¶10,280] Act Sec. 1232. Modifications of rules for original issue discount on certain high yield obligations

Conference Report (H. REPT. 111-16)

[Code Sec. 163]

Present Law

In general, the issuer of a debt instrument with original issue discount may deduct the portion of such original issue discount equal to the aggregate daily portions of the original issue discount for days during the taxable year.[96] However, in the case of an applicable high-yield discount obligation (an "AHYDO") issued by a corporate issuer: (1) no deduction is allowed for the "disqualified portion" of the original issue discount on such obligation, and (2) the remainder of the original issue discount on any such obligation is not allowable as a deduction until paid by the issuer.[97]

An AHYDO is any debt instrument if (1) the maturity date on such instrument is more than five years from the date of issue; (2) the yield to maturity on such instrument exceeds the sum of (a) the applicable Federal rate in effect under section 1274(d) for the calendar month in which the obligation is issued and (b) five percentage points, and (3) such instrument has "significant original issue discount."[98] An instrument is treated as having "significant original issue discount" if the aggregate amount of interest that would be includible in the gross income of the holder with respect to such instrument for periods before the close of any accrual period (as defined in section 1272(a)(5)) ending after the date five years after the date of issue, exceeds the sum of (1) the aggregate amount of interest to be paid under the instrument before the close of such accrual period, and (2) the product of the issue price of such instrument (as defined in sections 1273(b) and 1274(a)) and its yield to maturity.[99]

The disqualified portion of the original issue discount on an AHYDO is the lesser of (1) the amount of original issue discount with respect to such obligation or (2) the portion of the "total return" on such obligation which bears the same ratio to such total return as the "disqualified yield" (i.e., the excess of the yield to maturity on the obligation over the applicable Federal rate plus six percentage points) on such obligation bears to the yield to maturity on such obligation.[100] The term "total return" means the amount which would have been the original issue discount of the obligation if interest described in section 1273(a)(2) were included in the stated redemption to maturity.[101] A corporate holder treats the disqualified portion of original issue discount as a stock distribution for purposes of the dividend received deduction.[102]

House Bill

No provision.

Senate Amendment

No provision.

Conference Agreement

The conference agreement adds a provision that suspends the rules in section 163(e)(5) for certain obligations issued in a debt-for-debt exchange, including an exchange resulting from a significant modification of a debt instrument, after August 31, 2008, and before January 1, 2010.

In general, the suspension does not apply to any newly issued debt instrument (including any debt instrument issued as a result of a significant modification of a debt instrument) that is issued for an AHYDO. However, any newly issued debt instrument (including any debt instrument issued as a result of a significant modification of a debt instrument) for which the AHYDO rules are suspended under the provision is not treated as an AHYDO for purposes of a subsequent application of the suspension rule. Thus, for example, if a new debt instrument that would be an AHYDO under present law is issued in exchange for a debt instrument that is not an AHYDO, and the provision suspends application of section 163(e)(5), another new debt instrument, issued during the suspension period in exchange for the instrument with respect to which the rule in section 163(e)(5) was suspended, would be eligible for the relief provided

---

[96] Sec. 163(e)(1). For purposes of section 163(e)(1), the daily portion of the original issue discount for any day is determined under section 1272(a) (without regard to paragraph (7) thereof and without regard to section 1273(a)(3)).
[97] Sec. 163(e)(5).
[98] Sec. 163(i)(1).
[99] Sec. 163(i)(2).
[100] Sec. 163(e)(5)(C).
[101] Sec. 163(e)(5)(C)(ii).
[102] Sec. 163(e)(5)(B).

by the provision despite the fact that it is issued for an instrument that is an AHYDO under present law.

In addition, the suspension does not apply to any newly issued debt instrument (including any debt instrument issued as a result of a significant modification of a debt instrument) that is (1) described in section 871(h)(4) (without regard to subparagraph (D) thereof) (i.e., certain contingent debt) or (2) issued to a person related to the issuer (within the meaning of section 108(e)(4)).

The provision provides authority to the Secretary to apply the suspension rule to periods after December 31, 2009, where the Secretary determines that such application is appropriate in light of distressed conditions in the debt capital markets. In addition, the provision grants authority to the Secretary to use a rate that is higher than the applicable Federal rate for purposes of applying section 163(e)(5) for obligations issued after December 31, 2009, in taxable years ending after such date if the Secretary determines that such higher rate is appropriate in light of distressed conditions in the debt capital markets.

Effective date

The temporary suspension of section 163(e)(5) applies to obligations issued after August 31, 2008, in taxable years ending after such date. The additional authority granted to the Secretary to use a rate higher than the applicable Federal rate for purposes of applying section 163(e)(5) applies to obligations issued after December 31, 2009, in taxable years ending after such date.

[Law at ¶ 5230. CCH Explanation at ¶ 440.]

[¶ 10,290] Act Sec. 1241. Special rules applicable to qualified small business stock for 2009 and 2010

Conference Report (H. REPT. 111-16)

[Code Sec. 1202]

Present Law

Under present law, individuals may exclude 50 percent (60 percent for certain empowerment zone businesses) of the gain from the sale of certain small business stock acquired at original issue and held for at least five years.[103] The portion of the gain includible in taxable income is taxed at a maximum rate of 28 percent under the regular tax.[104] A percentage of the excluded gain is an alternative minimum tax preference;[105] the portion of the gain includible in alternative minimum taxable income is taxed at a maximum rate of 28 percent under the alternative minimum tax.

Thus, under present law, gain from the sale of qualified small business stock is taxed at effective rates of 14 percent under the regular tax[106] and (i) 14.98 percent under the alternative minimum tax for dispositions before January 1, 2011; (ii) 19.98 percent under the alternative minimum tax for dispositions after December 31, 2010, in the case of stock acquired before January 1, 2001; and (iii) 17.92 percent under the alternative minimum tax for dispositions after December 31, 2010, in the case of stock acquired after December 31, 2000.[107]

The amount of gain eligible for the exclusion by an individual with respect to any corporation is the greater of (1) ten times the taxpayer's basis in the stock or (2) $10 million. In order to qualify as a small business, when the stock is issued, the gross assets of the corporation may not exceed $50 million. The corporation also must meet certain active trade or business requirements.

House Bill

No provision.

---

[103] Sec. 1202.

[104] Sec. 1(h).

[105] Sec. 57(a)(7). In the case of qualified small business stock, the percentage of gain excluded from gross income which is an alternative minimum tax preference is (i) seven percent in the case of stock disposed of in a taxable year beginning before 2011; (ii) 42 percent in the case of stock acquired before January 1, 2001, and disposed of in a taxable year beginning after 2010; and (iii) 28 percent in the case of stock acquired after December 31, 2000, and disposed of in a taxable year beginning after 2010.

[106] The 50 percent of gain included in taxable income is taxed at a maximum rate of 28 percent.

[107] The amount of gain included in alternative minimum tax is taxed at a maximum rate of 28 percent. The amount so included is the sum of (i) 50 percent (the percentage included in taxable income) of the total gain and (ii) the applicable preference percentage of the one-half gain that is excluded from taxable income.

Senate Amendment

Under the Senate amendment, the percentage exclusion for qualified small business stock sold by an individual is increased from 50 percent (60 percent for certain empowerment zone businesses) to 75 percent.

As a result of the increased exclusion, gain from the sale of qualified small business stock to which the provision applies is taxed at effective rates of seven percent under the regular tax[108] and 12.88 percent under the alternative minimum tax.[109]

Effective date

The provision is effective for stock issued after the date of enactment and before January 1, 2011.

Conference Agreement

The conference agreement follows the Senate amendment.

[Law at ¶ 5290. CCH Explanation at ¶ 210.]

[¶ 10,300] Act Sec. 1251. Temporary reduction in recognition period for S corporation built-in gains tax

Conference Report (H. Rept. 111-16)

[Code Sec. 1374]

Present Law

A "small business corporation" (as defined in section 1361(b)) may elect to be treated as an S corporation. Unlike C corporations, S corporations generally pay no corporate-level tax. Instead, items of income and loss of an S corporation pass though to its shareholders. Each shareholder takes into account separately its share of these items on its individual income tax return.[110]

A corporate level tax, at the highest marginal rate applicable to corporations (currently 35 percent) is imposed on an S corporation's gain that arose prior to the conversion of the C corporation to an S corporation and is recognized by the S corporation during the recognition period, i.e., the first 10 taxable years that the S election is in effect.[111]

Gains recognized in the recognition period are not built-in gains to the extent they are shown to have arisen while the S election was in effect or are offset by recognized built-in losses. The built-in gains tax also applies to gains with respect to net recognized built-in gain attributable to property received by an S corporation from a C corporation in a carryover basis transaction.[112] The amount of the built-in gains tax is treated as a loss taken into account by the shareholders in computing their individual income tax.[113]

House Bill

No provision.

Senate Amendment

The Senate amendment provides that, for any taxable year beginning in 2009 and 2010, no tax is imposed on an S corporation under section 1374 if the seventh taxable year in the corporation's recognition period preceded such taxable year. Thus, with respect to gain that arose prior to the conversion of a C corporation to an S corporation, no tax will be imposed under section 1374 after the seventh taxable year the S corporation election is in effect. In the case of built-in gain attributable to an asset received by an S corporation from a C corporation in a carryover basis transaction, no tax will be imposed under section 1374 if such gain is recognized after the date that is seven years following the date on which such asset was acquired.[114]

---

[108] The 25 percent of gain included in taxable income is taxed at a maximum rate of 28 percent.

[109] The 46 percent of gain included in alternative minimum tax is taxed at a maximum rate of 28 percent. Forty-six percent is the sum of 25 percent (the percentage of total gain included in taxable income) plus 21 percent (the percentage of total gain which is an alternative minimum tax preference).

[110] Sec. 1366.

[111] Sec. 1374.

[112] Sec. 1374(d)(8). With respect to such assets, the recognition period runs from the day on which such assets were acquired (in lieu of the beginning of the first taxable year for which the corporation was an S corporation). Sec. 1374(d)(8)(B).

[113] Sec. 1366(f)(2).

[114] Shareholders will continue to take into account all items of gain and loss under section 1366.

Effective Date

The provision applies to taxable years beginning after December 31, 2008.

Conference Agreement

The conference agreement follows the Senate amendment.

[¶ 10,310] Act Sec. 1261. Clarification of regulations related to limitations on certain built-in losses following an ownership change

Conference Report (H. REPT. 111-16)

[Code Sec. 382]

Present Law

Section 382 limits the extent to which a "loss corporation" that experiences an "ownership change" may offset taxable income in any post-change taxable year by pre-change net operating losses, certain built-in losses, and deductions attributable to the pre-change period.[50] In general, the amount of income in any post-change year that may be offset by such net operating losses, built-in losses and deductions is limited to an amount (referred to as the "section 382 limitation") determined by multiplying the value of the loss corporation immediately before the ownership change by the long-term tax-exempt interest rate.[51]

A "loss corporation" is defined as a corporation entitled to use a net operating loss carryover or having a net operating loss carryover for the taxable year in which the ownership change occurs. Except to the extent provided in regulations, such term includes any corporation with a "net unrealized built-in loss" (or NUBIL),[52] defined as the amount by which the fair market value of the assets of the corporation immediately before an ownership change is less than the aggregate adjusted basis of such assets at such time. However, if the amount of the NUBIL does not exceed the lesser of (i) 15 percent of the fair market value of the corporation's assets or (ii) $10,000,000, then the amount of the NUBIL is treated as zero.[53]

An ownership change is defined generally as an increase by more than 50-percentage points in the percentage of stock of a loss corporation that is owned by any one or more five-percent (or greater) shareholders (as defined) within a three-year period.[54] Treasury regulations provide generally that this measurement is to be made as of any "testing date," which is any date on which the ownership of one or more persons who were or who become five-percent shareholders increases.[55]

---

[50] Sec. 383 imposes similar limitations, under regulations, on the use of carryforwards of general business credits, alternative minimum tax credits, foreign tax credits, and net capital loss carryforwards. Sec. 383 generally refers to sec. 382 for the meanings of its terms, but requires appropriate adjustments to take account of its application to credits and net capital losses.

[51] If the loss corporation had a "net unrealized built-in gain" (or NUBIG) at the time of the ownership change, then the sec. 382 limitation for any taxable year may be increased by the amount of the "recognized built-in gains" (discussed further below) for that year. A NUBIG is defined as the amount by which the fair market value of the assets of the corporation immediately before an ownership change exceeds the aggregate adjusted basis of such assets at such time. However, if the amount of the NUBIG does not exceed the lesser of (i) 15 percent of the fair market value of the corporation's assets or (ii) $10,000,000, then the amount of the NUBIG is treated as zero. Sec. 382(h)(3)(B).

[52] Sec. 382(k)(1).

[53] Sec. 382(h)(3).

[54] Determinations of the percentage of stock of any corporation held by any person are made on the basis of value. Sec. 382(k)(6)(C).

[55] See Treas. Reg. sec. 1.382-2(a)(4) (providing that "a loss corporation is required to determine whether an ownership change has occurred immediately after any owner shift, or issuance or transfer (including an issuance or transfer described in Treas. Reg. sec. 1.382-4(d)(8)(i) or (ii)) of an option with respect to stock of the loss corporation that is treated as exercised under Treas. Reg. sec. 1.382-4(d)(2)" and defining a "testing date" as "each date on which a loss corporation is required to make a determination of whether an ownership change has occurred") and Temp. Treas. Reg. sec. 1.382-2T(e)(1) (defining an "owner shift" as "any change in the ownership of the stock of a loss corporation that affects the percentage of such stock owned by any 5-percent shareholder"). Treasury regulations under section 382 provide that, in computing stock ownership on specified testing dates, certain unexercised options must be treated as exercised if certain ownership, control, or income tests are met. These tests are met only if "a principal purpose of the

Section 382(h) governs the treatment of certain built-in losses and built-in gains recognized with respect to assets held by the loss corporation at the time of the ownership change. In the case of a loss corporation that has a NUBIL (measured immediately before an ownership change), section 382(h)(1) provides that any "recognized built-in loss" (or RBIL) for any taxable year during a "recognition period" (consisting of the five years beginning on the ownership change date) is subject to the section 382 limitation in the same manner as if it were a pre-change net operating loss.[56] An RBIL is defined for this purpose as any loss recognized during the recognition period on the disposition of any asset held by the loss corporation immediately before the ownership change date, to the extent that such loss is attributable to an excess of the adjusted basis of the asset on the change date over its fair market value on that date.[57] An RBIL also includes any amount allowable as depreciation, amortization or depletion during the recognition period, to the extent that such amount is attributable to the excess of the adjusted basis of the asset over its fair market value on the ownership change date.[58] In addition, any amount that is allowable as a deduction during the recognition period (determined without regard to any carryover) but which is attributable to periods before the ownership change date is treated as an RBIL for the taxable year in which it is allowable as a deduction.[59]

As indicated above, section 382(h)(1) provides in the case of a loss corporation that has a NUBIG that the section 382 limitation may be increased for any taxable year during the recognition period by the amount of recognized built-in gains (or RBIGs) for such taxable year.[60] An RBIG is defined for this purpose as any gain recognized during the recognition period on the disposition of any asset held by the loss corporation immediately before the ownership change date, to the extent that such gain is attributable to an excess of the fair market value of the asset on the change date over its adjusted basis on that date.[61] In addition, any item of income that is properly taken into account during the recognition period but which is attributable to periods before the ownership change date is treated as an RBIG for the taxable year in which it is properly taken into account.[62]

Internal Revenue Service Notice 2003-65[63] provides two alternative safe harbor approaches for the identification of built-in items for pur-

---

(Footnote Continued)

issuance, transfer, or structuring of the option (alone or in combination with other arrangements) is to avoid or ameliorate the impact of an ownership change of the loss corporation." Treas. Reg. sec. 1.382-4(d). Compare prior temporary regulations, Temp. Reg. sec. 1.382-2T(h)(4) ("Solely for the purpose of determining whether there is an ownership change on any testing date, stock of the loss corporation that is subject to an option shall be treated as acquired on any such date, pursuant to an exercise of the option by its owner on that date, if such deemed exercise would result in an ownership change."). Internal Revenue Service Notice 2008-76, I.R.B. 2008-39 (September 29, 2008), released September 7, 2008, provides that the Treasury Department intends to issue regulations modifying the term "testing date" under sec. 382 to exclude any date on or after which the United States acquires stock or options to acquire stock in certain corporations with respect to which there is a "Housing Act Acquisition" pursuant to the Housing and Economic Recovery Act of 2008 (P.L. 110-289). The Notice states that the regulations will apply on and after September 7, 2008, unless and until there is additional guidance. Internal Revenue Service Notice 2008-84, I.R.B. 2008-41 (October 14, 2008), provides that the Treasury Department intends to issue regulations modifying the term "testing date" under sec. 382 to exclude any date as of the close of which the United States owns, directly or indirectly, a more than 50 percent interest in a loss corporation, which regulations will apply unless and until there is additional guidance. Internal Revenue Service Notice 2008-100, 2008-14 I.R.B. 1081 (released October 15, 2008) provides that the Treasury Department intends to issue regulations providing, among other things, that certain instruments acquired by the Treasury Department under the Capital Purchase Program (CPP) pursuant to the Emergency Economic Stabilization Act of 2008 (P.L. 100-343)("EESA") shall not be treated as stock for certain purposes. The Notice also provides that certain capital contributions made by Treasury pursuant to the CPP shall not be considered to have been made as part of a plan the principal purpose of which was to avoid or increase any sec. 382 limitation (for purposes of section 382(l)(1)). The Notice states that taxpayers may rely on the rules described unless and until there is further guidance; and that any contrary guidance will not apply to instruments (i) held by Treasury that were acquired pursuant to the CCP prior to publication of that guidance, or (ii) issued to Treasury pursuant to the CCP under written binding contracts entered into prior to the publication of that guidance. Internal Revenue Service Notice 2009-14, 2009-7 I.R.B. 1 (January 30, 2009) amplifies and supersedes Notice 2008-100, and provides additional guidance regarding the application of sec. 382 and other provisions of law to corporations whose instruments are acquired by the Treasury Department under certain programs pursuant to EESA.

[56] Sec. 382(h)(2). The total amount of the loss corporation's RBILs that are subject to the section 382 limitation cannot exceed the amount of the corporation's NUBIL.

[57] Sec. 382(h)(2)(B).

[58] Id.

[59] Sec. 382(h)(6)(B).

[60] The total amount of such increases cannot exceed the amount of the corporation's NUBIG.

[61] Sec. 382(h)(2)(A).

[62] Sec. 382(h)(6)(A).

[63] 2003-2 C.B. 747.

poses of section 382(h): the "1374 approach" and the "338 approach."

Under the 1374 approach,[64] NUBIG or NUBIL is the net amount of gain or loss that would be recognized in a hypothetical sale of the assets of the loss corporation immediately before the ownership change.[65] The amount of gain or loss recognized during the recognition period on the sale or exchange of an asset held at the time of the ownership change is RBIG or RBIL, respectively, to the extent it is attributable to a difference between the adjusted basis and the fair market value of the asset on the change date, as described above. However, the 1374 approach generally relies on the accrual method of accounting to identify items of income or deduction as RBIG or RBIL, respectively. Generally, items of income or deduction properly included in income or allowed as a deduction during the recognition period are considered attributable to period before the change date (and thus are treated as RBIG or RBIL, respectively), if a taxpayer using an accrual method of accounting would have included the item in income or been allowed a deduction for the item before the change date. However, the 1374 approach includes a number of exceptions to this general rule, including a special rule dealing with bad debt deductions under section 166. Under this special rule, any deduction item properly taken into account during the first 12 months of the recognition period as a bad debt deduction under section 166 is treated as RBIL if the item arises from a debt owed to the loss corporation at the beginning of the recognition period (and deductions for such items properly taken into account after the first 12 months of the recognition period are not RBILs).[66]

The 338 approach identifies items of RBIG and RBIL generally by comparing the loss corporation's actual items of income, gain, deduction and loss with those that would have resulted if a section 338 election had been made with respect to a hypothetical purchase of all of the outstanding stock of the loss corporation on the change date. Under the 338 approach, NUBIG or NUBIL is calculated in the same manner as it is under the 1374 approach.[67] The 338 approach identifies RBIG or RBIL by comparing the loss corporation's actual items of income, gain, deduction and loss with the items of income, gain, deduction and loss that would result if a section 338 election had been made for the hypothetical purchase. The loss corporation is treated for this purpose as using those accounting methods that the loss corporation actually uses. The 338 approach does not include any special rule with regard to bad debt deductions under section 166.

Section 166 generally allows a deduction in respect of any debt that becomes worthless, in whole or in part, during the taxable year.[68] The determination of whether a debt is worthless, in whole or in part, is a question of fact. However, in the case of a bank or other corporation that is subject to supervision by Federal authorities, or by State authorities maintaining substantially equivalent standards, the Treasury regulations under section 166 provide a presumption of worthlessness to the extent that a debt is charged off during the taxable year pursuant to a specific order of such an authority or in accordance with established policies of such an authority (and in the latter case, the authority confirms in writing upon the first subsequent audit of the bank or other corporation that the charge-off would have been required if the audit had been made at the time of the charge-off). The presumption does not apply if the taxpayer does not claim the amount so charged off as a deduction for the taxable year in which the charge-off takes place. In that case, the charge-off is treated as having been involuntary; however, in order to claim the section 166 deduction in a later taxable year, the taxpayer must produce sufficient evidence to

---

[64] The 1374 approach generally incorporates rules similar to those of section 1374(d) and the Treasury regulations thereunder in calculating NUBIG and NUBIL and identifying RBIG and RBIL.

[65] More specifically, NUBIG or NUBIL is calculated by determining the amount that would be realized if immediately before the ownership change the loss corporation had sold all of its assets, including goodwill, at fair market value to a third party that assumed all of its liabilities, decreased by the sum of any deductible liabilities of the loss corporation that would be included in the amount realized on the hypothetical sale and the loss corporation's aggregate adjusted basis in all of its assets, increased or decreased by the corporation's section 481 adjustments that would be taken into account on a hypothetical sale, and increased by any RBIL that would not be allowed as a deduction under section 382, 383 or 384 on the hypothetical sale.

[66] Notice 2003-65, section III.B.2.b.

[67] Accordingly, unlike the case in which a section 338 election is actually made, contingent consideration (including a contingent liability) is taken into account in the initial calculation of NUBIG or NUBIL, and no further adjustments are made to reflect subsequent changes in deemed consideration.

[68] Section 166 does not apply, however, to a debt which is evidenced by a security, defined for this purpose (by cross-reference to section 165(g)(2)(C)) as a bond, debenture, note or certificate or other evidence of indebtedness issued by a corporation or by a government or political subdivision thereof, with interest coupons or in registered form. Sec. 166(e).

show that the debt became partially worthless in the later year or became recoverable only in part subsequent to the taxable year of the charge-off, as the case may be, and to the extent that the deduction claimed in the later year for a partially worthless debt was not involuntarily charged off in prior taxable years, it was charged off in the later taxable year.[69]

The Treasury regulations also permit a bank (generally as defined for purposes of section 581, with certain modifications) that is subject to supervision by Federal authorities, or State authorities maintaining substantially equivalent standards, to make a "conformity election" under which debts charged off for regulatory purposes during a taxable year are conclusively presumed to be worthless for tax purposes to the same extent, provided that the charge-off results from a specific order of the regulatory authority or corresponds to the institution's classification of the debt as a "loss asset" pursuant to loan loss classification standards that are consistent with those of certain specified bank regulatory authorities. The conformity election is treated as the adoption of a method of accounting.[70]

Internal Revenue Service Notice 2008-83,[71] released on October 1, 2008, provides that "[f]or purposes of section 382(h), any deduction properly allowed after an ownership change (as defined in section 382(g)) to a bank with respect to losses on loans or bad debts (including any deduction for a reasonable addition to a reserve for bad debts) shall not be treated as a built-in loss or a deduction that is attributable to periods before the change date."[72] The Notice further states that the Internal Revenue Service and the Treasury Department are studying the proper treatment under section 382(h) of certain items of deduction or loss allowed after an ownership change to a corporation that is a bank (as defined in section 581) both immediately before and after the change date, and that any such corporation may rely on the treatment set forth in Notice 2008-83 unless and until there is additional guidance.

House Bill

The provision states that Congress finds as follows: (1) The delegation of authority to the Secretary of the Treasury, or his delegate, under section 382(m) does not authorize the Secretary to provide exemptions or special rules that are restricted to particular industries or classes of taxpayers; (2) Internal Revenue Service Notice 2008-83 is inconsistent with the congressional intent in enacting such section 382(m); (3) the legal authority to prescribe Notice 2008-83 is doubtful; (4) however, as taxpayers should generally be able to rely on guidance issued by the Secretary of the Treasury, legislation is necessary to clarify the force and effect of Notice 2008-83 and restore the proper application under the Internal Revenue Code of the limitation on built-in losses following an ownership change of a bank.

Under the provision, Treasury Notice 2008-83 shall be deemed to have the force and effect of law with respect to any ownership change (as defined in section 382(g)) occurring on or before January 16, 2009, and with respect to any ownership change (as so defined) which occurs after January 16, 2009, if such change (1) is pursuant to a written binding contract entered in to on or before such date or (2) is pursuant to a written agreement entered into on or before such date and such agreement was described on or before such date in a public announcement or in a filing with the Securities and Exchange Commission required by reason of such ownership change, but shall otherwise have no force or effect with respect to any ownership change after such date.

Effective date

The provision is effective on the date of enactment.

Senate Amendment

The Senate amendment is the same as the House bill.

Conference Agreement

The conference agreement follows the House bill and the Senate amendment.

[Law at ¶ 7015. CCH Explanation at ¶ 430.]

---

[69] See Treas. Reg. sec. 1.166-2(d)(1) and (2).
[70] See Treas. Reg. sec. 1.166-2(d)(3); of. Priv. Let. Rul. 9248048 (July 7, 1992); Tech. Ad. Mem. 9122001 (Feb. 8, 1991).
[71] 2008-42 I.R.B. 2008-42 (Oct. 20, 2008).
[72] Notice 2008-83, section 2.

[¶ 10,320] Act Sec. 1262. Treatment of certain ownership changes for purposes of limitations on net operating loss carryforwards and certain built-in losses

Conference Report (H. REPT. 111-16)

[Code Sec. 382]

Present Law

Section 382 limits the extent to which a "loss corporation" that experiences an "ownership change" may offset taxable income in any post-change taxable year by pre-change net operating losses, certain built-in losses, and deductions attributable to the pre-change period.[73] In general, the amount of income in any post-change year that may be offset by such net operating losses, built-in losses and deductions is limited to an amount (referred to as the "section 382 limitation") determined by multiplying the value of the loss corporation immediately before the ownership change by the long-term tax-exempt interest rate.[74]

A "loss corporation" is defined as a corporation entitled to use a net operating loss carryover or having a net operating loss carryover for the taxable year in which the ownership change occurs. Except to the extent provided in regulations, such term includes any corporation with a "net unrealized built-in loss" (or NUBIL),[75] defined as the amount by which the fair market value of the assets of the corporation immediately before an ownership change is less than the aggregate adjusted basis of such assets at such time. However, if the amount of the NUBIL does not exceed the lesser of (i) 15 percent of the fair market value of the corporation's assets or (ii) $10,000,000, then the amount of the NUBIL is treated as zero.[76]

An ownership change is defined generally as an increase by more than 50-percentage points in the percentage of stock of a loss corporation that is owned by any one or more five-percent (or greater) shareholders (as defined) within a three year period.[77] Treasury regulations provide generally that this measurement is to be made as of any "testing date," which is any date on which the ownership of one or more persons who were or who become five-percent shareholders increases.[78]

---

[73] Section 383 imposes similar limitations, under regulations, on the use of carryforwards of general business credits, alternative minimum tax credits, foreign tax credits, and net capital loss carryforwards. Section 383 generally refers to section 382 for the meanings of its terms, but requires appropriate adjustments to take account of its application to credits and net capital losses.

[74] If the loss corporation had a "net unrealized built in gain" (or NUBIG) at the time of the ownership change, then the section 382 limitation for any taxable year may be increased by the amount of the "recognized built-in gains" (discussed further below) for that year. A NUBIG is defined as the amount by which the fair market value of the assets of the corporation immediately before an ownership change exceeds the aggregate adjusted basis of such assets at such time. However, if the amount of the NUBIG does not exceed the lesser of (i) 15 percent of the fair market value of the corporation's assets or (ii) $10,000,000, then the amount of the NUBIG is treated as zero. Sec. 382(h)(1).

[75] Sec. 382(k)(1).

[76] Sec. 382(h)(3).

[77] Determinations of the percentage of stock of any corporation held by any person are made on the basis of value. Sec. 382(k)(6)(C).

[78] See Treas. Reg. sec. 1.382-2(a)(4) (providing that "a loss corporation is required to determine whether an ownership change has occurred immediately after any owner shift, or issuance or transfer (including an issuance or transfer described in Treas. Reg. sec. 1.382-4(d)(8)(i) or (ii)) of an option with respect to stock of the loss corporation that is treated as exercised under Treas. Reg. sec. 1.382-4(d)(2)" and defining a "testing date" as "each date on which a loss corporation is required to make a determination of whether an ownership change has occurred") and Temp. Treas. Reg. sec. 1.382-2T(e)(1) (defining an "owner shift" as "any change in the ownership of the stock of a loss corporation that affects the percentage of such stock owned by any 5-percent shareholder"). Treasury regulations under section 382 provide that, in computing stock ownership on specified testing dates, certain unexercised options must be treated as exercised if certain ownership, control, or income tests are met. These tests are met only if "a principal purpose of the issuance, transfer, or structuring of the option (alone or in combination with other arrangements) is to avoid or ameliorate the impact of an ownership change of the loss corporation." Treas. Reg. sec. 1.382-4(d). Compare prior temporary regulations, Temp. Treas. Reg. sec. 1.382-2T(h)(4) ("Solely for the purpose of determining whether there is an ownership change on any testing date, stock of the loss corporation that is subject to an option shall be treated as acquired on any such date, pursuant to an exercise of the option by its owner on that date, if such deemed exercise would result in an ownership change."). Internal Revenue Service Notice 2008-76, I.R.B. 2008-39 (September 29, 2008), released September 7, 2008, provides that the Treasury Department intends to issue regulations modifying the term "testing date" under section 382 to exclude any date on or after which the United States acquires stock or options to acquire stock in certain corporations with respect to which there is a "Housing Act Acquisition" pursuant to the Housing and Economic Recovery Act of 2008 (P.L. 110-289). The Notice states that the regulations will apply on and after September 7, 2008, unless and until there is additional guidance. Internal

House Bill

No provision.

Senate Amendment

No provision.

Conference Agreement

The conference agreement amends section 382 of the Code to provide an exception from the application of the section 382 limitation. Under the provision, the section 382 limitation that would otherwise arise as a result of an ownership change shall not apply in the case of an ownership change that occurs pursuant to a restructuring plan of a taxpayer which is required under a loan agreement or commitment for a line of credit entered into with the Department of the Treasury under the Emergency Economic Stabilization Act of 2008, and is intended to result in a rationalization of the costs, capitalization, and capacity with respect to the manufacturing workforce of, and suppliers to, the taxpayer and its subsidiaries.[79]

However, an ownership change that would otherwise be excepted from the section 382 limitation under the provision will instead remain subject to the section 382 limitation if, immediately after such ownership change, any person (other than a voluntary employees' beneficiary association within the meaning of section 501(c)(9)) owns stock of the new loss corporation possessing 50 percent or more of the total combined voting power of all classes of stock entitled to vote or of the total value of the stock of such corporation. For purposes of this rule, persons who bear a relationship to one another described in section 267(b) or 707(b)(1), or who are members of a group of persons acting in concert, are treated as a single person.

The exception from the application of the section 382 limitation under the provision does not change the fact that an ownership change has occurred for other purposes of section 382.[80]

Effective date

The conference agreement applies to ownership changes after the date of enactment.

[Law at ¶ 5265. CCH Explanation at ¶ 435.]

[¶ 10,330] Act Sec. 1301. Temporary expansion of availability of industrial development bonds to facilities creating intangible property and other modifications

Conference Report (H. REPT. 111-16)

[Code Sec. 144(a)]

Present Law

Qualified small issue bonds (commonly referred to as "industrial development bonds" or "small issue IDBs") are tax-exempt bonds issued by State and local governments to finance private business manufacturing facilities (including certain directly related and ancillary facilities) or the acquisition of land and equipment by certain

---

(Footnote Continued)

Revenue Service Notice 2008-84, I.R.B. 2008-41 (October 14, 2008), provides that the Treasury Department intends to issue regulations modifying the term "testing date" under section 382 to exclude any date as of the close of which the United States owns, directly or indirectly, a more than 50 percent interest in a loss corporation, which regulations will apply unless and until there is additional guidance. Internal Revenue Service Notice 2008-100, 2008-14 I.R.B. 1081 (released October 15, 2008) provides that the Treasury Department intends to issue regulations providing, among other things, that certain instruments acquired by the Treasury Department under the Capital Purchase Program (CPP) pursuant to the Emergency Economic Stabilization Act of 2008 (P.L. 100-343)("EESA") shall not be treated as stock for certain purposes. The Notice also provides that certain capital contributions made by Treasury pursuant to the CPP shall not be considered to have been made as part of a plan the principal purpose of which was to avoid or increase any section 382 limitation (for purposes of section 382(1)(1)). The Notice states that taxpayers may rely on the rules described unless and until there is further guidance; and that any contrary guidance will not apply to instruments (i) held by Treasury that were acquired pursuant to the CCP prior to publication of that guidance, or (ii) issued to Treasury pursuant to the CCP under written binding contracts entered into prior to the publication of that guidance. Internal Revenue Service Notice 2009-14, 2009-7 I.R.B. 1 (January 30, 2009) amplifies and supersedes Notice 2008-100, and provides additional guidance regarding the application of section 382 and other provisions of law to corporations whose instruments are acquired by the Treasury Department under certain programs pursuant to EESA.

[79] This exception shall not apply in the case of any subsequent ownership change unless such subsequent ownership change also meets the requirements of the exception.

[80] For example, an ownership change has occurred for purposes of determining the testing period. under section 382(i)(2).

farmers. In both instances, these bonds are subject to limits on the amount of financing that may be provided, both for a single borrowing and in the aggregate. In general, no more than $1 million of small-issue bond financing may be outstanding at any time for property of a business (including related parties) located in the same municipality or county. Generally, this $1 million limit may be increased to $10 million if, in addition to outstanding bonds, all other capital expenditures of the business (including related parties) in the same municipality or county are counted toward the limit over a six-year period that begins three years before the issue date of the bonds and ends three years after such date. Outstanding aggregate borrowing is limited to $40 million per borrower (including related parties) regardless of where the property is located.

The Code permits up to $10 million of capital expenditures to be disregarded, in effect increasing from $10 million to $20 million the maximum allowable amount of total capital expenditures by an eligible business in the same municipality or county. However, no more than $10 million of bond financing may be outstanding at any time for property of an eligible business (including related parties) located in the same municipality or county. Other limits (e.g., the $40 million per borrower limit) also continue to apply.

A manufacturing facility is any facility which is used in the manufacturing or production of tangible personal property (including the processing resulting in a change in the condition of such property). Manufacturing facilities include facilities that are directly related and ancillary to a manufacturing facility (as described in the previous sentence) if (1) such facilities are located on the same site as the manufacturing facility and (2) not more than 25 percent of the net proceeds of the issue are used to provide such facilities.[126]

House Bill

No provision.

Senate Amendment

In general

For bonds issued after the date of enactment and before January 1, 2011, the provision expands the definition of manufacturing facilities to mean any facility that is used in the manufacturing, creation, or production of tangible property or intangible property (within the meaning of section 197(d)(1)(C)(iii)). For this purpose, intangible property means any patent, copyright, formula, process, design, knowhow, format, or other similar item. It is intended to include among other items, the creation of computer software, and intellectual property associated bio-tech and pharmaceuticals.

In lieu of the directly related and ancillary test of present law, the provision provides a special rule for bonds issued after the date of enactment and before January 1, 2011. For these bonds, the provision provides that facilities that are functionally related and subordinate to the manufacturing facility are treated as a manufacturing facility and the 25 percent of net proceeds restriction does not apply to such facilities.[127] Functionally related and subordinate facilities must be located on the same site as the manufacturing facility.

Effective date

The provision is effective for bonds issued after the date of enactment and before January 1, 2011.

Conference Agreement

The conference agreement follows the Senate amendment.

[Law at ¶ 5225. CCH Explanation at ¶ 660.]

---

[126] The 25 percent restriction was enacted by the Technical and Miscellaneous Tax Act of 1988 because of concern over the scope of the definition of manufacturing facility. See H.R. Rpt. No. 100-795 (1988). The amendment was intended to clarify that while the manufacturing facility definition does not preclude the financing of ancillary activities, the 25 percent restriction was intended to limit the use of bond proceeds to finance facilities other than for "core manufacturing." The conference agreement followed the House bill, which the conference report described as follows: "The House bill clarifies that up to 25 percent of the proceeds of a qualified small issue may be used to finance ancillary activities which are carried out at the manufacturing site. All such ancillary activities must be subordinate and integral to the manufacturing process."

[127] The provision is based in part on a similar rule applicable to exempt facility bonds. Treas. Reg. sec. 1.103-8(a)(3) provides: "(3) Functionally related and subordinate. An exempt facility includes any land, building, or other property functionally related and subordinate to such facility. Property is not functionally related and subordinate to a facility if it is not of a character and size commensurate with the character and size of such facility."

Act Sec. 1301   ¶10,330

[¶ 10,340] Act Sec. 1302. Credit for investment in advanced energy property

Conference Report (H. REPT. 111-16)

[New Code Sec. 48C]

Present Law

An income tax credit is allowed for the production of electricity from qualified energy resources at qualified facilities.[213] Qualified energy resources comprise wind, closed-loop biomass, open-loop biomass, geothermal energy, solar energy, small irrigation power, municipal solid waste, qualified hydropower production, and marine and hydrokinetic renewable energy. Qualified facilities are, generally, facilities that generate electricity using qualified energy resources.

An income tax credit is also allowed for certain energy property placed in service. Qualifying property includes certain fuel cell property, solar property, geothermal power production property, small wind energy property, combined heat and power system property, and geothermal heat pump property.[214]

In addition to these, numerous other credits are available to taxpayers to encourage renewable energy production and energy conservation, including, among others, credits for certain biofuels, plug-in electric vehicles, and energy efficient appliances, and for improvements to heating, air conditioning, and insulation.

No credit is specifically designed under present law to encourage the development of a domestic manufacturing base to support the industries described above.

House Bill

No provision.

Senate Amendment

The Senate amendment establishes a 30 percent credit for investment in qualified property used in a qualified advanced energy manufacturing project. A qualified advanced energy project is a project that re-equips, expands, or establishes a manufacturing facility for the production: (1) property designed to be used to produce energy from the sun, wind, or geothermal deposits (within the meaning of section 613(e)(2)), or other renewable resources; (2) fuel cells, microturbines, or an energy storage system for use with electric or hybrid-electric motor vehicles; (3) electric grids to support the transmission of intermittent sources of renewable energy, including storage of such energy; (4) property designed to capture and sequester carbon dioxide; (5) property designed to refine or blend renewable fuels (but not fossil fuels) or to produce energy conservation technologies (including energy-conserving lighting technologies and smart grid technologies; or (6) other advanced energy property designed to reduce greenhouse gas emissions as may be determined by the Secretary.

Qualified property must be depreciable (or amortizable) property used in a qualified advanced energy project. Qualified property does not include property designed to manufacture equipment for use in the refining or blending of any transportation fuel other than renewable fuels. The basis of qualified property must be reduced by the amount of credit received.

Credits are available only for projects certified by the Secretary of Treasury, in consultation with the Secretary of Energy. The Secretary of Treasury must establish a certification program no later than 180 days after date of enactment, and may allocate up to $2 billion in credits.

In selecting projects, the Secretary may consider only those projects where there is a reasonable expectation of commercial viability. In addition, the Secretary must consider other selection criteria, including which projects (1) will provide the greatest domestic job creation; (2) will provide the greatest net impact in avoiding or reducing air pollutants or anthropogenic emissions of greenhouse gases; (3) have the greatest readiness for commercial employment, replication, and further commercial use in the United States, (4) will provide the greatest benefit in terms of newness in the commercial market; (5) have the lowest levelized cost of generated or stored energy, or of measured reduction in energy consumption or greenhouse gas emission; and (6) have the shortest project time from certification to completion.

Each project application must be submitted during the three-year period beginning on the date such certification program is established. An applicant for certification has two years from the date the Secretary accepts the application to provide the Secretary with evidence that the requirements for certification have been met. Upon certification, the applicant has five years from the date of issuance of the certification to place

---

[213] Sec. 45. In addition to the electricity production credit, section 45 also provides income tax credits for the production of Indian coal and refined coal at qualified facilities.

[214] Sec. 48.

the project in service. Not later than six years after the date of enactment of the credit, the Secretary is required to review the credit allocations and redistribute any credits that were not used either because of a revoked certification or because of an insufficient quantity of credit applications.

Effective date

The provision is effective on the date of enactment.

Conference Agreement

The conference agreement follows the Senate amendment with the following modifications. The conference agreement increases by $300 million (to $2.3 billion) the amount of credits that may be allocated by the Secretary. The conference agreement expands the list of qualifying advance energy projects to include projects designed to manufacture any new qualified plug-in electric drive motor vehicle (as defined by section 30D(c)), any specified vehicle (as defined by section 30D(f)(2)), or any component which is designed specifically for use with such vehicles, including any electric motor, generator, or power control unit. The conference agreement also replaces the third and fourth project selection criteria with a requirement that the Secretary, in addition to the remaining criteria, consider projects that have the greatest potential for technological innovation and commercial deployment.

In addition, the conference agreement shortens to two years the period during which project applications may be submitted, shortens to one year the period during which the project applicants must provide evidence that the certification requirements have been met, and shortens to three years the period during which certified projects must be placed in service. The conference agreement also shortens the period after which the Secretary must review the credit allocations from six to four years. Finally, the conference agreement clarifies that only tangible personal property and other tangible property (not including a building or its structural components) is credit-eligible.

[Law at ¶ 5105, ¶ 5125 and ¶ 5130. CCH Explanation at ¶ 525.]

[¶ 10,350] Act Sec. 1401. Recovery zone bonds

Conference Report (H. REPT. 111-16)

[New Code Secs. 1400U-1, 1400U-2, and 1400U-3]

Present Law

In general

Under present law, gross income does not include interest on State or local bonds. State and local bonds are classified generally as either governmental bonds or private activity bonds. Governmental bonds are bonds the proceeds of which are primarily used to finance governmental functions or which are repaid with governmental funds. Private activity bonds are bonds in which the State or local government serves as a conduit providing financing to nongovernmental persons (e.g., private businesses or individuals). The exclusion from income for State and local bonds does not apply to private activity bonds unless the bonds are issued for certain permitted purposes ("qualified private activity bonds") and other Code requirements are met.

Private activity bonds

The Code defines a private activity bond as any bond that satisfies (1) the private business use test and the private security or payment test ("the private business test"); or (2) "the private loan financing test."[151]

Private business test

Under the private business test, a bond is a private activity bond if it is part of an issue in which:

1. More than 10 percent of the proceeds of the issue (including use of the bond-financed property) are to be used in the trade or business of any person other than a governmental unit ("private business use"); and

2. More than 10 percent of the payment of principal or interest on the issue is, directly or indirectly, secured by (a) property used or to be used for a private business use or (b) to be

---

[151] Sec. 141.

derived from payments in respect of property, or borrowed money, used or to be used for a private business use ("private payment test").[152]

A bond is not a private activity bond unless both parts of the private business test (i.e., the private business use test and the private payment test) are met. Thus, a facility that is 100 percent privately used does not cause the bonds financing such facility to be private activity bonds if the bonds are not secured by or paid with private payments. For example, land improvements that benefit a privately-owned factory may be financed with governmental bonds if the debt service on such bonds is not paid by the factory owner or other private parties and such bonds are not secured by the property.

Private loan financing test

A bond issue satisfies the private loan financing test if proceeds exceeding the lesser of $5 million or five percent of such proceeds are used directly or indirectly to finance loans to one or more nongovernmental persons. Private loans include both business and other (e.g., personal) uses and payments to private persons; however, in the case of business uses and payments, all private loans also constitute private business uses and payments subject to the private business test.

Arbitrage restrictions

The exclusion from income for interest on State and local bonds does not apply to any arbitrage bond.[153] An arbitrage bond is defined as any bond that is part of an issue if any proceeds of the issue are reasonably expected to be used (or intentionally are used) to acquire higher yielding investments or to replace funds that are used to acquire higher yielding investments.[154] In general, arbitrage profits may be earned only during specified periods (e.g., defined "temporary periods") before funds are needed for the purpose of the borrowing or on specified types of investments (e.g., "reasonably required reserve or replacement funds"). Subject to limited exceptions, investment profits that are earned during these periods or on such investments must be rebated to the Federal Government.

Qualified private activity bonds

Qualified private activity bonds permit States or local governments to act as conduits providing tax-exempt financing for certain private activities. The definition of qualified private activity bonds includes an exempt facility bond, or qualified mortgage, veterans' mortgage, small issue, redevelopment, 501(c)(3), or student loan bond (sec. 141(e)).

The definition of an exempt facility bond includes bonds issued to finance certain transportation facilities (airports, ports, mass commuting, and high-speed intercity rail facilities); qualified residential rental projects; privately owned and/or operated utility facilities (sewage, water, solid waste disposal, and local district heating and cooling facilities, certain private electric and gas facilities, and hydroelectric dam enhancements); public/private educational facilities; qualified green building and sustainable design projects; and qualified highway or surface freight transfer facilities (sec. 142(a)).

In most cases, the aggregate volume of qualified private activity bonds is restricted by annual aggregate volume limits imposed on bonds issued by issuers within each State ("State volume cap"). For calendar year 2007, the State volume cap, which is indexed for inflation, equals $85 per resident of the State, or $256.24 million, if greater. Exceptions to the State volume cap are provided for bonds for certain governmentally owned facilities (e.g., airports, ports, high-speed intercity rail, and solid waste disposal) and bonds which are subject to separate local, State, or national volume limits (e.g., public/private educational facility bonds, enterprise zone facility bonds, qualified green building bonds, and qualified highway or surface freight transfer facility bonds).

Qualified private activity bonds generally are subject to restrictions on the use of proceeds for the acquisition of land and existing property. In addition, qualified private activity bonds generally are subject to restrictions on the use of proceeds to finance certain specified facilities (e.g., airplanes, skyboxes, other luxury boxes, health club facilities, gambling facilities, and liquor stores), and use of proceeds to pay costs of issuance (e.g., bond counsel and underwriter fees). Small issue and redevelopment bonds also are subject to additional restrictions on the use of proceeds for certain facilities (e.g., golf courses and massage parlors).

Moreover, the term of qualified private activity bonds generally may not exceed 120 per-

---

[152] The 10 percent private business test is reduced to five percent in the case of private business uses (and payments with respect to such uses) that are unrelated to any governmental use being financed by the issue.

[153] Sec. 103(a) and (b)(2).
[154] Sec. 148.

cent of the economic life of the property being financed and certain public approval requirements (similar to requirements that typically apply under State law to issuance of governmental debt) apply under Federal law to issuance of private activity bonds.

Qualified tax credit bonds

In lieu of interest, holders of qualified tax credit bonds receive a tax credit that accrues quarterly. The following bonds are qualified tax credit bonds: qualified forestry conservation bonds, new clean renewable energy bonds, qualified energy conservation bonds, and qualified zone academy bonds.[155]

Section 54A of the Code sets forth general rules applicable to qualified tax credit bonds. These rules include requirements regarding the expenditure of available project proceeds, reporting, arbitrage, maturity limitations, and financial conflicts of interest, among other special rules.

A taxpayer who holds a qualified tax credit bond on one or more credit allowance dates of the bond during the taxable year shall be allowed a credit against the taxpayer's income tax for the taxable year. In general, the credit amount for any credit allowance date is 25 percent of the annual credit determined with respect to the bond. The annual credit is determined by multiplying the applicable credit rate by the outstanding face amount of the bond. The applicable credit rate for the bond is the rate that the Secretary estimates will permit the issuance of the qualified tax credit bond with a specified maturity or redemption date without discount and without interest cost to the qualified issuer.[156] The Secretary determines credit rates for tax credit bonds based on general assumptions about credit quality of the class of potential eligible issuers and such other factors as the Secretary deems appropriate. The Secretary may determine credit rates based on general credit market yield indexes and credit ratings. The credit is included in gross income and, under regulations prescribed by the Secretary, may be stripped.

Section 54A of the Code requires that 100 percent of the available project proceeds of qualified tax credit bonds must be used within the three-year period that begins on the date of issuance. Available project proceeds are proceeds from the sale of the bond issue less issuance costs (not to exceed two percent) and any investment earnings on such sale proceeds. To the extent less than 100 percent of the available project proceeds are used to finance qualified projects during the three-year spending period, bonds will continue to qualify as qualified tax credit bonds if unspent proceeds are used within 90 days from the end of such three-year period to redeem bonds. The three-year spending period may be extended by the Secretary upon the issuer's request demonstrating that the failure to satisfy the three-year requirement is due to reasonable cause and the projects will continue to proceed with due diligence.

Qualified tax credit bonds generally are subject to the arbitrage requirements of section 148. However, available project proceeds invested during the three-year spending period are not subject to the arbitrage restrictions (i.e., yield restriction and rebate requirements). In addition, amounts invested in a reserve fund are not subject to the arbitrage restrictions to the extent: (1) such fund is funded at a rate not more rapid than equal annual installments; (2) such fund is funded in a manner reasonably expected to result in an amount not greater than an amount necessary to repay the issue; and (3) the yield on such fund is not greater than the average annual interest rate of tax-exempt obligations having a term of 10 years or more that are issued during the month the qualified tax credit bonds are issued.

The maturity of qualified tax credit bonds is the term that the Secretary estimates will result in the present value of the obligation to repay the principal on such bonds being equal to 50 percent of the face amount of such bonds, using as a discount rate the average annual interest rate of tax-exempt obligations having a term of 10 years or more that are issued during the month the qualified tax credit bonds are issued.

House Bill

In general

The provision permits an issuer to designate one or more areas as recovery zones. The area must have significant poverty, unemployment, general distress, or home foreclosures, or be any area for which a designation as an empowerment zone or renewal community is in effect. Issuers may issue recovery zone economic development bonds and recovery zone facility bonds with respect to these zones.

---

[155] See secs. 54B, 54C, 54D, and 54E.
[156] Given the differences in credit quality and other characteristics of individual issuers, the Secretary cannot set credit rates in a manner that will allow each issuer to issue tax credit bonds at par.

There is a national recovery zone economic development bond limitation of $10 billion. In addition, there is a separate national recovery zone facility bond limitation of $15 billion. The Secretary is to separately allocate the bond limitations among the States in the proportion that each State's employment decline bears to the national decline in employment (the aggregate 2008 State employment declines for all States). In turn each State is to reallocate its allocation among the counties (parishes) and large municipalities in such State in the proportion that each such county or municipality's 2008 employment decline bears to the aggregate employment declines for all counties and municipalities in such State. In calculating the local employment decline with respect to a county, the portion of such decline attributable to a large municipality is disregarded for purposes of determining the county's portion of the State employment decline and is attributable to the large municipality only.

For purposes of the provision "2008 State employment decline" means, with respect to any State, the excess (if any) of (i) the number of individuals employed in such State as determined for December 2007, over (ii) the number of individuals employed in such State as determined for December 2008. The term "large municipality" means a municipality with a population of more than 100,000.

Recovery Zone Economic Development Bonds

New section 54AA(h) of the House bill creates a special rule for qualified bonds (a type of taxable governmental bond) issued before January 1, 2011, that entitles the issuer of such bonds to receive an advance tax credit equal to 35 percent of the interest payable on an interest payment date. For taxable governmental bonds that are designated recovery zone economic development bonds, the applicable percentage is 55 percent.

A recovery zone economic development bond is a taxable governmental bond issued as part of an issue if 100 percent of the available project proceeds of such issue are to be used for one or more qualified economic development purposes and the issuer designates such bond for purposes of this section. A qualified economic development purpose means expenditures for purposes of promoting development or other economic activity in a recovery zone, including (1) capital expenditures paid or incurred with respect to property located in such zone, (2) expenditures for public infrastructure and construction of public facilities located in a recovery zone.

The aggregate face amount of bonds which may be designated by any issuer cannot exceed the amount of the recovery zone economic development bond limitation allocated to such issuer.

Recovery Zone Facility Bonds

The provision creates a new category of exempt facility bonds, "recovery zone facility bonds." A recovery zone facility bond means any bond issued as part of an issue if: (1) 95 percent or more of the net proceeds of such issue are to be used for recovery zone property and (2) such bond is issued before January 1, 2011, and (3) the issuer designates such bond as a recovery zone facility bond. The aggregate face amount of bonds which may be designated by any issuer cannot exceed the amount of the recovery zone facility bond limitation allocated to such issuer.

Under the provision, the term "recovery zone property" means any property subject to depreciation to which section 168 applies (or would apply but for section 179) if (1) such property was acquired by the taxpayer by purchase after the date on which the designation of the recovery zone took effect; (2) the original use of such property in the recovery zone commences with the taxpayer; and (3) substantially all of the use of such property is in the recovery zone and is in the active conduct of a qualified business by the taxpayer in such zone. The term "qualified business" means any trade or business except that the rental to others of real property located in a recovery zone shall be treated as a qualified business only if the property is not residential rental property (as defined in section 168(e)(2)) and does not include any trade or business consisting of the operation of any facility described in section 144(c)(6)(B) (i.e., any private or commercial golf course, country club, massage parlor, hot tub facility, suntan facility, racetrack or other facility used for gambling, or any store the principal purpose of which is the sale of alcoholic beverages for consumption off premises).

Subject to the following exceptions and modifications, issuance of recovery zone facility bonds is subject to the general rules applicable to issuance of qualified private activity bonds:

1. Issuance of the bonds is not subject to the aggregate annual State private activity bond volume limits (sec. 146);

2. The restriction on acquisition of existing property does not apply (sec. 147(d));

Effective date

The provision is effective for obligations issued after the date of enactment.

Senate Amendment

In general

The Senate amendment is the same as the House bill with a modification for allocating the bonds between the States. Under the Senate amendment each State receives a minimum allocation of one percent of the national recovery zone economic development bond limitation and one percent of the national recovery zone facility bond limitation. The remainder of each bond limitation is separately allocated among the States in the proportion that each State's employment decline bears to the national decline in employment (the aggregate 2008 State employment declines for all States).

Recovery Zone Economic Development Bonds

New section 54AA(g) of the Senate amendment creates a special rule for qualified bonds (a type of Build America Bond) issued before January 1, 2011, that entitles the issuer of such bonds to receive an advance tax credit equal to 35 percent of the interest payable on an interest payment date. For Build America Bonds that are designated recovery zone economic development bonds, the applicable percentage is 40 percent. In other respects the Senate amendment is the same as the House bill.

Recovery Zone Facility Bonds

The Senate amendment is the same as the House bill.

Effective date

The Senate amendment is the same as the House bill.

Conference Agreement

In general

The conference agreement follows the House bill, with a modification for allocating the bond limitations among the States. Under the conference agreement the national recovery zone economic development bond limitation and national recovery zone facility bond limitation are allocated among the States in the proportion that each State's employment decline bears to the national decline in employment (the aggregate 2008 State employment declines for all States).[157] The Secretary is to adjust each State's allocation for a calendar year such that no State receives less than 0.9 percent of the national recovery zone economic development bond limitation and no less than 0.9 percent of the national recovery zone facility bond limitation. The conference agreement also permits a county or large municipality to waive all or part of its allocation of the State bond limitations to allow further allocation within that State. With respect to all other aspects of the allocation of the bond limitations, the conference agreement follows the House bill.

The conference agreement also provides that a "recovery zone" includes any area designated by the issuer as economically distressed by reason of the closure or realignment of a military installation pursuant to the Defense Base Closure and Realignment Act of 1990.

Recovery Zone Economic Development Bonds

The conference agreement follows the House bill, except the issuer of recovery zone economic development bonds is entitled to receive an advance tax credit equal to 45 percent of the interest payable on an interest payment date and the conference agreement allows for a reasonably required reserve fund to be funded from the proceeds of a recovery zone economic development bond.

Recovery Zone Facility Bonds

The conference agreement follows the House bill, except "recovery zone property" is defined as any property subject to depreciation to which section 168 applies (or would apply but for section 179) if (1) such property was constructed, reconstructed, renovated, or acquired by purchase by the taxpayer after the date on which the designation of the recovery zone took effect; (2) the original use of such property in the recovery zone commences with the taxpayer; and (3) substantially all of the use of such property is in the recovery zone and is in the active conduct of a qualified business by the taxpayer in such zone.

Effective date

The conference agreement follows the House bill and the Senate amendment.

[Law at ¶ 5315, ¶ 5316 and ¶ 5317. CCH Explanation at ¶ 625 and ¶ 652.]

---

[157] The Bureau of Labor Statistics prepares data on regional and State employment and unemployment. See e.g., Bureau of Labor Statistics, USDL 09-0093, *Regional and State Employment and Unemployment: December 2008* (January 27, 2009) <http://www.bls.gov/news.release/laus.nr0.htm>.

[¶ 10,360] Act Sec. 1402. Tribal economic development bonds

Conference Report (H. Rept. 111-16)

[Code Sec. 7871(f)]

Present Law

Under present law, gross income does not include interest on State or local bonds.[158] State and local bonds are classified generally as either governmental bonds or private activity bonds. Governmental bonds are bonds the proceeds of which are primarily used to finance governmental facilities or the debt is repaid with governmental funds. Private activity bonds are bonds in which the State or local government serves as a conduit providing financing to nongovernmental persons. For these purposes, the term "nongovernmental person" includes the Federal government and all other individuals and entities other than States or local governments.[159] Interest on private activity bonds is taxable, unless the bonds are issued for certain purposes permitted by the Code and other requirements are met.[160]

Although not States or subdivisions of States, Indian tribal governments are provided with a tax status similar to State and local governments for specified purposes under the Code.[161] Among the purposes for which a tribal government is treated as a State is the issuance of tax-exempt bonds. Under section 7871(c), tribal governments are authorized to issue tax-exempt bonds only if substantially all of the proceeds are used for essential governmental functions.[162] The term essential governmental function does not include any function that is not customarily performed by State and local governments with general taxing powers. Section 7871(c) further prohibits Indian tribal governments from issuing tax-exempt private activity bonds (as defined in section 141(a) of the Code) with the exception of certain bonds for manufacturing facilities.

House Bill

Tribal Economic Development Bonds

The provision allows Indian tribal governments to issue "tribal economic development bonds." There is a national bond limitation of $2 billion, to be allocated as the Secretary determines appropriate, in consultation with the Secretary of the Interior. Tribal economic development bonds issued by an Indian tribal government are treated as if such bond were issued by a State except that section 146 (relating to State volume limitations) does not apply.

A tribal economic development bond is any bond issued by an Indian tribal government (1) the interest on which would be tax-exempt if issued by a State or local government but would be taxable under section 7871(c), and (2) that is designated by the Indian tribal government as a tribal economic development bond. The aggregate face amount of bonds that may be designated by any Indian tribal government cannot exceed the amount of national tribal economic development bond limitation allocated to such government.

Tribal economic development bonds cannot be used to finance any portion of a building in which class II or class III gaming (as defined in section 4 of the Indian Gaming Regulatory Act) is conducted, or housed, or any other property used in the conduct of such gaming. Nor can tribal economic development bonds be used to finance any facility located outside of the Indian reservation.

Treasury study

The provision requires that the Treasury Department study the effects of tribal economic development bonds. One year after the date of enactment, a report is to be submitted to Congress providing the results of such study along with any recommendations, including whether the restrictions of section 7871(c) should be eliminated or otherwise modified.

Effective date

The provision applies to obligations issued after the date of enactment.

Senate Amendment

The Senate amendment is the same as the House bill except the Senate amendment defines a tribal economic development bond as any bond issued by an Indian tribal government (1) the interest on which would be tax-exempt if issued by a State or local government, and (2)

---

[158] Sec. 103.
[159] Sec. 141(b)(6); Treas. Reg. sec. 1.141-1(b).
[160] Secs. 103(b)(1) and 141.
[161] Sec. 7871.
[162] Sec. 7871(c).

that is designated by the Indian tribal government as a tribal economic development bond.

The Senate amendment also clarifies that for purposes of section 141 of the Code, use of bond proceeds by an Indian tribe, or instrumentality thereof, is treated as use by a State.

Conference Agreement

The conference agreement follows the Senate amendment.

[Law at ¶5420 and ¶7018. CCH Explanation at ¶665.]

[¶10,370] Act Sec. 1403. Extend and modify the new markets tax credit

Conference Report (H. REPT. 111-16)

[Code Sec. 45D]

Present Law

Section 45D provides a new markets tax credit for qualified equity investments made to acquire stock in a corporation, or a capital interest in a partnership, that is a qualified community development entity ("CDE").[165] The amount of the credit allowable to the investor (either the original purchaser or a subsequent holder) is (1) a five-percent credit for the year in which the equity interest is purchased from the CDE and for each of the following two years, and (2) a six-percent credit for each of the following four years. The credit is determined by applying the applicable percentage (five or six percent) to the amount paid to the CDE for the investment at its original issue, and is available for a taxable year to the taxpayer who holds the qualified equity investment on the date of the initial investment or on the respective anniversary date that occurs during the taxable year. The credit is recaptured if, at any time during the seven-year period that begins on the date of the original issue of the qualified equity investment, the issuing entity ceases to be a qualified CDE, the proceeds of the investment cease to be used as required, or the equity investment is redeemed.

A qualified CDE is any domestic corporation or partnership: (1) whose primary mission is serving or providing investment capital for low-income communities or low-income persons; (2) that maintains accountability to residents of low-income communities by providing them with representation on any governing board of or any advisory board to the CDE; and (3) that is certified by the Secretary as being a qualified CDE. A qualified equity investment means stock (other than nonqualified preferred stock) in a corporation or a capital interest in a partnership that is acquired directly from a CDE for cash, and includes an investment of a subsequent purchaser if such investment was a qualified equity investment in the hands of the prior holder. Substantially all of the investment proceeds must be used by the CDE to make qualified low-income community investments. For this purpose, qualified low-income community investments include: (1) capital or equity investments in, or loans to, qualified active low-income community businesses; (2) certain financial counseling and other services to businesses and residents in low-income communities; (3) the purchase from another CDE of any loan made by such entity that is a qualified low-income community investment; or (4) an equity investment in, or loan to, another CDE.

A "low-income community" is a population census tract with either (1) a poverty rate of at least 20 percent or (2) median family income which does not exceed 80 percent of the greater of metropolitan area median family income or statewide median family income (for a non-metropolitan census tract, does not exceed 80 percent of statewide median family income). In the case of a population census tract located within a high migration rural county, low-income is defined by reference to 85 percent (rather than 80 percent) of statewide median family income. For this purpose, a high migration rural county is any county that, during the 20-year period ending with the year in which the most recent census was conducted, has a net out-migration of inhabitants from the county of at least 10 percent of the population of the county at the beginning of such period.

The Secretary has the authority to designate "targeted populations" as low-income communities for purposes of the new markets tax credit. For this purpose, a "targeted population" is defined by reference to section 103(20) of the Riegle

---

[165] Section 45D was added by section 121(a) of the Community Renewal Tax Relief Act of 2000, Pub. L. No. 106-554 (2000).

Community Development and Regulatory Improvement Act of 1994 (12 U.S.C. 4702(20)) to mean individuals, or an identifiable group of individuals, including an Indian tribe, who (A) are low-income persons; or (B) otherwise lack adequate access to loans or equity investments. Under such Act, "low-income" means (1) for a targeted population within a metropolitan area, less than 80 percent of the area median family income; and (2) for a targeted population within a non-metropolitan area, less than the greater of 80 percent of the area median family income or 80 percent of the statewide non-metropolitan area median family income.[166] Under such Act, a targeted population is not required to be within any census tract. In addition, a population census tract with a population of less than 2,000 is treated as a low-income community for purposes of the credit if such tract is within an empowerment zone, the designation of which is in effect under section 1391, and is contiguous to one or more low-income communities.

A qualified active low-income community business is defined as a business that satisfies, with respect to a taxable year, the following requirements: (1) at least 50 percent of the total gross income of the business is derived from the active conduct of trade or business activities in any low-income community; (2) a substantial portion of the tangible property of such business is used in a low-income community; (3) a substantial portion of the services performed for such business by its employees is performed in a low-income community; and (4) less than five percent of the average of the aggregate unadjusted bases of the property of such business is attributable to certain financial property or to certain collectibles.

The maximum annual amount of qualified equity investments is capped at $3.5 billion per year for calendar years 2006 through 2009. Lower caps applied for calendar years 2001 through 2005.

House Bill

No provision.

Senate Amendment

For calendar years 2008 and 2009, the Senate amendment increases the maximum amount of qualified equity investments by $1.5 billion (to $5 billion for each year). The Senate amendment requires that the additional amount for 2008 be allocated to qualified CDEs that submitted an allocation application with respect to calendar year 2008 and either (1) did not receive an allocation for such calendar year, or (2) received an allocation for such calendar year in an amount less than the amount requested in the allocation application. The Senate amendment also provides alternative minimum tax relief for equity investment allocations subject to the 2009 annual limitation.

Effective date

The provision is effective on the date of enactment.

Conference Agreement

The conference agreement generally follows the Senate amendment but does not provide for any alternative minimum tax relief.

[Law at ¶ 5095 and ¶ 7021. CCH Explanation at ¶ 530.]

[¶ 10,380] Act Secs. 1404 and 1602. Election to substitute grants to states for low-income housing projects in lieu of low-income housing credit allocation for 2009

Conference Report (H. Rept. 111-16)

[Code Sec. 42]

Present Law

In general

The low-income housing credit may be claimed over a 10-year period by owners of certain residential rental property for the cost of rental housing occupied by tenants having incomes below specified levels.[13] The amount of the credit for any taxable year in the credit period is the applicable percentage of the qualified basis of each qualified low-income building. The qualified basis of any qualified low-income building for any taxable year equals the applicable fraction of the eligible basis of the building.

---

[166] 12 U.S.C. sec. 4702(17) (defines "low-income" for purposes of 12 U.S.C. sec. 4702(20)).

[13] Sec. 42.

Volume limits

A low-income housing credit is allowable only if the owner of a qualified building receives a housing credit allocation from the State or local housing credit agency. Generally, the aggregate credit authority provided annually to each State for calendar year 2009 is $2.30 per resident, with a minimum annual cap of $2,665,000 for certain small population States.[14] These amounts are indexed for inflation. Projects that also receive financing with proceeds of tax-exempt bonds issued subject to the private activity bond volume limit do not require an allocation of the low-income housing credit.

Basic rule for Federal grants

The basis of a qualified building must be reduced by the amount of any federal granty with respect to such building.

House Bill

Low-income housing grant election amount

The Secretary of the Treasury shall make a grant to the State housing credit agency of each State in an amount equal to the low-income housing grant election amount.

The low-income housing grant election amount for a State is an amount elected by the State subject to certain limits. The maximum low-income housing grant election amount for a State may not exceed 85 percent of the product of ten and the sum of the State's: (1) unused housing credit ceiling for 2008; (2) any returns to the State during 2009 of credit allocations previously made by the State; (3) 40 percent of the State's 2009 credit allocation; and (4) 40 percent of the State's share of the national pool allocated in 2009, if any).

Grants under this provision are not taxable income to recipients.

Subawards to low-income housing credit buildings

A State receiving a grant under this provision is to use these monies to make subawards to finance the construction, or acquisition and rehabilitation of qualified low-income buildings as defined under the low-income housing credit. A subaward may be made to finance a qualified low-income building regardless of whether the building has an allocation of low-income housing credit. However, in the case of qualified low-income buildings without allocations of the low-income housing credit, the State housing credit agency must make a determination that the subaward with respect to such building will increase the total funds available to the State to build and rehabilitate affordable housing. In conjunction with this determination the State housing credit agency must establish a process in which applicants for the subawards must demonstrate good faith efforts to obtain investment commitments before the agency makes such subawards.

Any building receiving grant money from a subaward is required to satisfy the low-income housing credit rules. The State housing credit agency shall perform asset management functions to ensure compliance with the low-income housing credit rules and the long-term viability of buildings financed with these subawards.[15] Failure to satisfy the low-income housing credit rules will result in recapture enforced by means of liens or other methods that the Secretary of the Treasury (or delegate) deems appropriate. Any such recapture will be payable to the Secretary of the Treasury for deposit in the general fund of the Treasury.

Any grant funds not used to make subawards before January 1, 2011 and any grant monies from subawards returned on or after January 1, 2011 must be returned to the Secretary of the Treasury.

Basic rule for Federal grants

The grants received under this provision do not reduce tax basis of a qualified low-income building.

Reduction in low-income housing credit volume limit for 2009

The otherwise applicable low-income housing credit volume limit for any State for 2009 is reduced by the amount taken into account in determining the low-income housing grant election amount.

Appropriations

The provision appropriates to the Secretary of the Treasury such sums as may be necessary to carry out this provision.

---

[14] Rev. Proc. 2008-66.

[15] The State housing credit agency may collect reasonable fees from subaward recipients to cover the expenses of the agency's asset management duties. Alternatively, the State housing credit agency may retain a thirdparty to perform these asset management duties.

Effective date

The provision is effective on the date of enactment.

Senate Amendment

No provision.

Conference Agreement

The conference agreement follows the House bill.

[Law at ¶5085 and ¶7033. CCH Explanation at ¶535.]

[¶10,390] Act Sec. 1501. De minimis safe harbor exception for tax-exempt interest expense of financial institutions and modification of small issuer exception to tax-exempt interest expense allocation rules for financial institutions

Conference Report (H. Rept. 111-16)

[Code Secs. 265 and 291]

Present Law

Present law disallows a deduction for interest on indebtedness incurred or continued to purchase or carry obligations the interest on which is exempt from tax.[116] In general, an interest deduction is disallowed only if the taxpayer has a purpose of using borrowed funds to purchase or carry tax-exempt obligations; a determination of the taxpayer's purpose in borrowing funds is made based on all of the facts and circumstances.[117]

Two-percent rule for individuals and certain nonfinancial corporations

In the absence of direct evidence linking an individual taxpayer's indebtedness with the purchase or carrying of tax-exempt obligations, the Internal Revenue Service takes the position that it ordinarily will not infer that a taxpayer's purpose in borrowing money was to purchase or carry tax-exempt obligations if the taxpayer's investment in tax-exempt obligations is "insubstantial."[118] An individual's holdings of tax-exempt obligations are presumed to be insubstantial if during the taxable year the average adjusted basis of the individual's tax-exempt obligations is two percent or less of the average adjusted basis of the individual's portfolio investments and assets held by the individual in the active conduct of a trade or business.

Similarly, in the case of a corporation that is not a financial institution or a dealer in tax-exempt obligations, where there is no direct evidence of a purpose to purchase or carry tax-exempt obligations, the corporation's holdings of tax-exempt obligations are presumed to be insubstantial if the average adjusted basis of the corporation's tax-exempt obligations is two percent or less of the average adjusted basis of all assets held by the corporation in the active conduct of its trade or business.

Financial institutions

In the case of a financial institution, the Code generally disallows that portion of the taxpayer's interest expense that is allocable to tax-exempt interest.[119] The amount of interest that is disallowed is an amount which bears the same ratio to such interest expense as the taxpayer's average adjusted bases of tax-exempt obligations acquired after August 7, 1986, bears to the average adjusted bases for all assets of the taxpayer.

Exception for certain obligations of qualified small issuers

The general rule in section 265(b), denying financial institutions' interest expense deductions allocable to tax-exempt obligations, does not apply to "qualified tax-exempt obligations."[120] Instead, as discussed in the next section, only 20 percent of the interest expense allocable to "qualified tax-exempt obligations" is disallowed.[121] A "qualified tax-exempt obligation" is a tax-exempt obligation that (1) is issued after August 7, 1986, by a qualified small issuer, (2) is not a private activity bond, and (3) is designated by the issuer as qualifying for the exception from the general rule of section 265(b).

---

[116] Sec. 265(a).
[117] See Rev. Proc. 72-18, 1972-1 C.B. 740.
[118] Id.
[119] Sec. 265(b)(1). A "financial institution" is any person that (1) accepts deposits from the public in the ordinary course of such person's trade or business and is subject to Federal or State supervision as a financial institution or (2) is a corporation described in section 585(a)(2). Sec. 265(b)(5).
[120] Sec. 265(b)(3).
[121] Secs. 265(b)(3)(A), 291(a)(3) and 291(e)(1).

A "qualified small issuer" is an issuer that reasonably anticipates that the amount of tax-exempt obligations that it will issue during the calendar year will be $10 million or less.[122] The Code specifies the circumstances under which an issuer and all subordinate entities are aggregated.[123] For purposes of the $10 million limitation, an issuer and all entities that issue obligations on behalf of such issuer are treated as one issuer. All obligations issued by a subordinate entity are treated as being issued by the entity to which it is subordinate. An entity formed (or availed of) to avoid the $10 million limitation and all entities benefiting from the device are treated as one issuer.

Composite issues (i.e., combined issues of bonds for different entities) qualify for the "qualified tax-exempt obligation" exception only if the requirements of the exception are met with respect to (1) the composite issue as a whole (determined by treating the composite issue as a single issue) and (2) each separate lot of obligations that is part of the issue (determined by treating each separate lot of obligations as a separate issue).[124] Thus a composite issue may qualify for the exception only if the composite issue itself does not exceed $10 million, and if each issuer benefitting from the composite issue reasonably anticipates that it will not issue more than $10 million of tax-exempt obligations during the calendar year, including through the composite arrangement.

Treatment of financial institution preference items

Section 291(a)(3) reduces by 20 percent the amount allowable as a deduction with respect to any financial institution preference item. Financial institution preference items include interest on debt to carry tax-exempt obligations acquired after December 31, 1982, and before August 8, 1986.[125] Section 265(b)(3) treats qualified tax-exempt obligations as if they were acquired on August 7, 1986. As a result, the amount allowable as a deduction by a financial institution with respect to interest incurred to carry a qualified tax-exempt obligation is reduced by 20 percent.

House Bill

Two-percent safe harbor for financial institutions

The provision provides that tax-exempt obligations issued during 2009 or 2010 and held by a financial institution, in an amount not to exceed two percent of the adjusted basis of the financial institution's assets, are not taken into account for the purpose of determining the portion of the financial institution's interest expense subject to the pro rata interest disallowance rule of section 265(b). For purposes of this rule, a refunding bond (whether a current or advance refunding) is treated as issued on the date of the issuance of the refunded bond (or in the case of a series of refundings, the original bond).

The provision also amends section 291(e) to provide that tax-exempt obligations issued during 2009 and 2010, and not taken into account for purposes of the calculation of a financial institution's interest expense subject to the pro rata interest disallowance rule, are treated as having been acquired on August 7, 1986. As a result, such obligations are financial institution preference items, and the amount allowable as a deduction by a financial institution with respect to interest incurred to carry such obligations is reduced by 20 percent.

Modifications to qualified small issuer exception

With respect to tax-exempt obligations issued during 2009 and 2010, the provision increases from $10 million to $30 million the annual limit for qualified small issuers.

In addition, in the case of "qualified financing issue" issued in 2009 or 2010, the provision applies the $30 million annual volume limitation at the borrower level (rather than at the level of the pooled financing issuer). Thus, for the purpose of applying the requirements of the section 265(b)(3) qualified small issuer exception, the portion of the proceeds of a qualified financing issue that are loaned to a "qualified borrower" that participates in the issue are treated as a separate issue with respect to which the qualified borrower is deemed to be the issuer.

A "qualified financing issue" is any composite, pooled or other conduit financing issue the proceeds of which are used directly or indirectly to make or finance loans to one or more ultimate borrowers all of whom are qualified borrowers. A "qualified borrower" means (1) a State or political subdivision of a State or (2) an organization described in section 501(c)(3) and exempt from tax under section 501(a). Thus, for example, a $100 million pooled financing issue that was issued in 2009 could qualify for the section 265(b)(3) exception if the proceeds of such issue were used to make four equal loans of $25 mil-

---

[122] Sec. 265(b)(3)(C).
[123] Sec. 265(b)(3)(E).
[124] Sec. 265(b)(3)(F).
[125] Sec. 291(e)(1).

lion to four qualified borrowers. However, if (1) more than $30 million were loaned to any qualified borrower, (2) any borrower were not a qualified borrower, or (3) any borrower would, if it were the issuer of a separate issue in an amount equal to the amount loaned to such borrower, fail to meet any of the other requirements of section 265(b)(3), the entire $100 million pooled financing issue would fail to qualify for the exception.

For purposes of determining whether an issuer meets the requirements of the small issuer exception, qualified 501(c)(3) bonds issued in 2009 or 2010 are treated as if they were issued by the 501(c)(3) organization for whose benefit they were issued (and not by the actual issuer of such bonds). In addition, in the case of an organization described in section 501(c)(3) and exempt from taxation under section 501(a), requirements for "qualified financing issues" shall be applied as if the section 501(c)(3) organization were the issuer. Thus, in any event, an organization described in section 501(c)(3) and exempt from taxation under section 501(a) shall be limited to the $30 million per issuer cap for qualified tax exempt obligations described in section 265(b)(3).

Effective Date

The provisions are effective for obligations issued after December 31, 2008.

Senate Amendment

The Senate amendment is the same as the House bill.

Conference Agreement

The conference agreement follows the House bill and the Senate amendment.

[Law at ¶5255 and ¶5260. CCH Explanation at ¶445 and ¶450.]

[¶10,400] Act Sec. 1503. Temporary modification of alternative minimum tax limitations on tax-exempt bonds

Conference Report (H. REPT. 111-16)

[Code Secs. 56 and 57]

Present Law

Present law imposes an alternative minimum tax ("AMT") on individuals and corporations. AMT is the amount by which the tentative minimum tax exceeds the regular income tax. The tentative minimum tax is computed based upon a taxpayer's alternative minimum taxable income ("AMTI"). AMTI is the taxpayer's taxable income modified to take into account certain preferences and adjustments. One of the preference items is tax-exempt interest on certain tax-exempt bonds issued for private activities (sec. 57(a)(5)). Also, in the case of a corporation, an adjustment based on current earnings is determined, in part, by taking into account 75 percent of items, including tax-exempt interest, that are excluded from taxable income but included in the corporation's earnings and profits (sec. 56(g)(4)(B)).

House Bill

The House bill provides that tax-exempt interest on private activity bonds issued in 2009 and 2010 is not an item of tax preference for purposes of the alternative minimum tax and interest on tax exempt bonds issued in 2009 and 2010 is not included in the corporate adjustment based on current earnings. For these purposes, a refunding bond is treated as issued on the date of the issuance of the refunded bond (or in the case of a series of refundings, the original bond).

Effective date.—The provision applies to interest on bonds issued after December 31, 2008.

Senate Amendment

The Senate amendment is the same as the House. bill.

Conference Agreement

The conference agreement provides that tax-exempt interest on private activity bonds issued in 2009 and 2010 is not an item of tax preference for purposes of the alternative minimum tax and interest on tax exempt bonds issued in 2009 and 2010 is not included in the corporate adjustment based on current earnings. For these purposes, a refunding bond is treated as issued on the date of the issuance of the refunded bond (or in the case of a series of refundings, the original bond).

The conference agreement also provides that tax-exempt interest on private activity bonds issued in 2009 and 2010 to currently refund a private activity bond issued after December 31, 2003, and before January 1, 2009, is not an item of tax preference for purposes of the alternative minimum tax. Also tax-exempt interest on bonds

¶10,400 Act Sec. 1503

issued in 2009 and 2010 to currently refund a bond issued after December 31, 2003, and before January 1, 2009, is not included in the corporate adjustment based on current earnings.

[Law at ¶ 5185 and ¶ 5190. CCH Explanation at ¶ 650.]

Effective date

The provision applies to interest on bonds issued after December 31, 2008.

[¶ 10,410] Act Sec. 1504. Modification to high-speed intercity rail facility bonds

Conference Report (H. REPT. 111-16)

[Code Sec. 142(j)]

Present Law

In general

Under present law, gross income does not include interest on State or local bonds. State and local bonds are classified generally as either governmental bonds or private activity bonds. Governmental bonds are bonds the proceeds of which are primarily used to finance governmental functions or which are repaid with governmental funds. Private activity bonds are bonds in which the State or local government serves as a conduit providing financing to nongovernmental persons (e.g., private businesses or individuals). The exclusion from income for State and local bonds does not apply to private activity bonds unless the bonds are issued for certain permitted purposes ("qualified private activity bonds") and other Code requirements are met.

High-speed rail

An exempt facility bond is a type of qualified private activity bond. Exempt facility bonds can be issued for high-speed intercity rail facilities. A facility qualifies as a high-speed intercity rail facility if it is a facility (other than rolling stock) for fixed guideway rail transportation of passengers and their baggage between metropolitan statistical areas. The facilities must use vehicles that are reasonably expected to operate at speeds in excess of 150 miles per hour between scheduled stops and the facilities must be made available to members of the general public as passengers. If the bonds are to be issued for a nongovernmental owner of the facility, such owner must irrevocably elect not to claim depreciation or credits with respect to the property financed by the net proceeds of the issue.

The Code imposes a special redemption requirement for these types of bonds. Any proceeds not used within three years of the date of issuance of the bonds must be used within the following six months to redeem such bonds.

Seventy-five percent of the principal amount of the bonds issued for high-speed rail facilities is exempt from the volume limit. If all the property to be financed by the net proceeds of the issue is to be owned by a governmental unit, then such bonds are completely exempt from the volume limit.

House Bill

No provision.

Senate Amendment

In general

The provision modifies the requirement that high-speed intercity rail transportation facilities use vehicles that are reasonably expected to operate at speeds in excess of 150 miles per hour. Instead, under the provision such facilities must use vehicles capable of attaining a maximum speed in excess of 150 miles per hour.

Effective date

The provision is effective for obligations issued after the date of enactment.

Conference Agreement

The conference agreement follows the Senate amendment.

[Law at ¶ 5220. CCH Explanation at ¶ 655.]

[¶ 10,420] Act Sec. 1511. Delay in implementation of withholding tax on government contractors

Conference Report (H. Rept. 111-16)

[Code Sec. 3402(t)]

Present Law

For payments made after December 31, 2010, the Code imposes a withholding requirement at a three-percent rate on certain payments to persons providing property or services made by the Government of the United States, every State, every political subdivision thereof, and every instrumentality of the foregoing (including multi-State agencies). The withholding requirement applies regardless of whether the government entity making such payment is the recipient of the property or services. Political subdivisions of States (or any instrumentality thereof) with less than $100 million of annual expenditures for property or services that would otherwise be subject to withholding are exempt from the withholding requirement.

Payments subject to the three-percent withholding requirement include any payment made in connection with a government voucher or certificate program which functions as a payment for property or services. For example, payments to a commodity producer under a government commodity support program are subject to the withholding requirement. Present law also imposes information reporting requirements on the payments that are subject to withholding requirement.

The three-percent withholding requirement does not apply to any payments made through a Federal, State, or local government public assistance or public welfare program for which eligibility is determined by a needs or income test. The three-percent withholding requirement also does not apply to payments of wages or to any other payment with respect to which mandatory (e.g., U.S.-source income of foreign taxpayers) or voluntary (e.g., unemployment benefits) withholding applies under present law. Although the withholding requirement applies to payments that are potentially subject to backup withholding under section 3406, it does not apply to those payments from which amounts are actually being withheld under backup withholding rules.

The three-percent withholding requirement also does not apply to the following: payments of interest; payments for real property; payments to tax-exempt entities or foreign governments; intra-governmental payments; payments made pursuant to a classified or confidential contract (as defined in section 6050M(e)(3)), and payments to government employees that are not otherwise excludable from the new withholding proposal with respect to the employees' services as employees.

House Bill

The provision repeals the three-percent withholding requirement on government payments.

Effective date

The provision is effective on the date of enactment.

Senate Amendment

The provision delays the implementation of the three percent withholding requirement by one year to apply to payments after December 31, 2011.

Effective date

The provision is effective on the date of enactment.

Conference Agreement

The conference agreement follows the Senate amendment.

[Law at ¶ 7024. CCH Explanation at ¶ 460.]

[¶ 10,430] Act Sec. 1521. Qualified school construction bonds

Conference Report (H. Rept. 111-16)

[New Code Sec. 54F]

Present Law

Tax-exempt bonds

Interest on State and local governmental bonds generally is excluded from gross income for Federal income tax purposes if the proceeds of the bonds are used to finance direct activities of these governmental units or if the bonds are repaid with revenues of the governmental units. These can include tax-exempt bonds which finance public schools.[128] An issuer must file with

---

[128] Sec. 103.

the Internal Revenue Service certain information about the bonds issued in order for that bond issue to be tax-exempt.[129] Generally, this information return is required to be filed no later than the 15th day of the second month after the close of the calendar quarter in which the bonds were issued.

The tax exemption for State and local bonds does not apply to any arbitrage bond.[130] An arbitrage bond is defined as any bond that is part of an issue if any proceeds of the issue are reasonably expected to be used (or intentionally are used) to acquire higher yielding investments or to replace funds that are used to acquire higher yielding investments.[131] In general, arbitrage profits may be earned only during specified periods (e.g., defined "temporary periods") before funds are needed for the purpose of the borrowing or on specified types of investments (e.g., "reasonably required reserve or replacement funds"). Subject to limited exceptions, investment profits that are earned during these periods or on such investments must be rebated to the Federal Government.

Qualified zone academy bonds

As an alternative to traditional tax-exempt bonds, States and local governments were given the authority to issue "qualified zone academy bonds."[132] A total of $400 million of qualified zone academy bonds is authorized to be issued annually in calendar years 1998 through 2009. The $400 million aggregate bond cap is allocated each year to the States according to their respective populations of individuals below the poverty line. Each State, in turn, allocates the credit authority to qualified zone academies within such State.

A taxpayer holding a qualified zone academy bond on the credit allowance date is entitled to a credit. The credit is includible in gross income (as if it were a taxable interest payment on the bond), and may be claimed against regular income tax and alternative minimum tax liability.

The Treasury Department sets the credit rate at a rate estimated to allow issuance of qualified zone academy bonds without discount and without interest cost to the issuer.[133] The Secretary determines credit rates for tax credit bonds based on general assumptions about credit quality of the class of potential eligible issuers and such other factors as the Secretary deems appropriate. The Secretary may determine credit rates based on general credit market yield indexes and credit ratings. The maximum term of the bond is determined by the Treasury Department, so that the present value of the obligation to repay the principal on the bond is 50 percent of the face value of the bond.

"Qualified zone academy bonds" are defined as any bond issued by a State or local government, provided that (1) at least 95 percent of the proceeds are used for the purpose of renovating, providing equipment to, developing course materials for use at, or training teachers and other school personnel in a "qualified zone academy" and (2) private entities have promised to contribute to the qualified zone academy certain equipment, technical assistance or training, employee services, or other property or services with a value equal to at least 10 percent of the bond proceeds.

A school is a "qualified zone academy" if (1) the school is a public school that provides education and training below the college level, (2) the school operates a special academic program in cooperation with businesses to enhance the academic curriculum and increase graduation and employment rates, and (3) either (a) the school is located in an empowerment zone or enterprise community designated under the Code, or (b) it is reasonably expected that at least 35 percent of the students at the school will be eligible for free or reduced-cost lunches under the school lunch program established under the National School Lunch Act.

The arbitrage requirements which generally apply to interest-bearing tax-exempt bonds also generally apply to qualified zone academy bonds. In addition, an issuer of qualified zone academy bonds must reasonably expect to and actually spend 100 percent of the proceeds of such bonds on qualified zone academy property within the three years period that begins on the date of issuance. To the extent less than 100 percent of the proceeds are used to finance qualified zone academy property during the three years spending period, bonds will continue to qualify as qualified zone academy bonds if unspent proceeds are used within 90 days from the end of such three years period to redeem any nonqualified bonds. The three years spending period may be extended by the Secretary if the

---

[129] Sec. 149(e).
[130] Sec. 103(a) and (b)(2).
[131] Sec. 148.
[132] Sec. 1397E.

[133] Given the differences in credit quality and other characteristics of individual issuers, the Secretary cannot set credit rates in a manner that will allow each issuer to issue tax credit bonds at par.

issuer establishes that the failure to meet the spending requirement is due to reasonable cause and the related purposes for issuing the bonds will continue to proceed with due diligence.

Two special arbitrage rules apply to qualified zone academy bonds. First, available project proceeds invested during the three-year period beginning on the date of issue are not subject to the arbitrage restrictions (i.e., yield restriction and rebate requirements). Available project proceeds are proceeds from the sale of an issue of qualified zone academy bonds, less issuance costs (not to exceed two percent) and any investment earnings on such proceeds. Thus, available project proceeds invested during the three-year spending period may be invested at unrestricted yields, but the earnings on such investments must be spent on qualified zone academy property. Second, amounts invested in a reserve fund are not subject to the arbitrage restrictions to the extent: (1) such fund is funded at a rate not more rapid than equal annual installments; (2) such fund is funded in a manner reasonably expected to result in an amount not greater than an amount necessary to repay the issue; and (3) the yield on such fund is not greater than the average annual interest rate of tax-exempt obligations having a term of 10 years or more that are issued during the month the qualified zone academy bonds are issued.

Issuers of qualified zone academy bonds are required to report issuance to the Internal Revenue Service in a manner similar to the information returns required for tax-exempt bonds.

House Bill

In general

The provision creates a new category of tax-credit bonds: qualified school construction bonds. Qualified school construction bonds must meet three requirements: (1) 100 percent of the available project proceeds of the bond issue is used for the construction, rehabilitation, or repair of a public school facility or for the acquisition of land on which such a bond-financed facility is to be constructed; (2) the bond is issued by a State or local government within which such school is located; and (3) the issuer designates such bonds as a qualified school construction bond.

National limitation

There is a national limitation on qualified school construction bonds of $11 billion for calendar years 2009 and 2010, respectively. Allocations of the national limitation of qualified school construction bonds are divided between the States and certain large school districts. The States receive 60 percent of the national limitation for a calendar year and the remaining 40 percent of the national limitation for a calendar year is allocated to certain of the largest school districts.

Allocation to the States

Generally allocations are made to the States under the 60 percent allocation according to their respective populations of children aged five through seventeen. However, the Secretary of the Treasury shall adjust the annual allocations among the States to ensure that for each State the sum of its allocations under the 60 percent allocation plus any allocations to large educational agencies within the States is not less than a minimum percentage. A State's minimum percentage for a calendar year is a product of 1.68 and the minimum percentage described in section 1124(d) of the Elementary and Secondary Education Act of 1965 for such State for the most recent fiscal year ending before such calendar year.

For allocation purposes, a State includes the District of Columbia and any possession of the United States. The provision provides a special allocation for possessions of the United States other than Puerto Rico under the 60 percent share of the national limitation for States. Under this special rule an allocation to a possession other than Puerto Rico is made on the basis of the respective populations of individuals below the poverty line (as defined by the Office of Management and Budget) rather than respective populations of children aged five through seventeen. This special allocation reduces the State allocation share of the national limitation otherwise available for allocation among the States. Under another special rule the Secretary of the Interior may allocate $200 million of school construction bonds for 2009 and 2010, respectively, to Indian schools. This special allocation for Indian schools is to be used for purposes of the construction, rehabilitation, and repair of schools funded by the Bureau of Indian Affairs. For purposes of such allocations Indian tribal governments are qualified issuers. The special allocation for Indian schools does not reduce the State allocation share of the national limitation otherwise available for allocation among the States.

If an amount allocated under this allocation to the States is unused for a calendar year it may be carried forward by the State to the next calendar year.

Allocation to large school districts

The remaining 40 percent of the national limitation for a calendar year is allocated by the Secretary of the Treasury among local educational agencies which are large local educational agencies for such year. This allocation is made in proportion to the respective amounts each agency received for Basic Grants under subpart 2 of Part A of Title I of the Elementary and Secondary Education Act of 1965 for the most recent fiscal year ending before such calendar year. Any unused allocation of any agency within a State may be allocated by the agency to such State. With respect to a calendar year, the term large local educational agency means any local educational agency if such agency is: (1) among the 100 local educational agencies with the largest numbers of children aged 5 through 17 from families living below the poverty level, or (2) one of not more than 25 local educational agencies (other than in 1, immediately above) that the Secretary of Education determines are in particular need of assistance, based on a low level of resources for school construction, a high level of enrollment growth, or other such factors as the Secretary of Education deems appropriate. If any amount allocated to large local educational agency is unused for a calendar year the agency may reallocate such amount to the State in which the agency is located.

The provision makes qualified school construction bonds a type of qualified tax credit bond for purposes of section 54A. In addition, qualified school construction bonds may be issued by Indian tribal governments only to the extent such bonds are issued for purposes that satisfy the present law requirements for tax-exempt bonds issued by Indian tribal governments (i.e., essential governmental functions and certain manufacturing purposes).

The provision requires 100 percent of the available project proceeds of qualified school construction bonds to be used within the three-year period that begins on the date of issuance. Available project proceeds are proceeds from the sale of the issue less issuance costs (not to exceed two percent) and any investment earnings on such sale proceeds. To the extent less than 100 percent of the available project proceeds are used to finance qualified purposes during the three-year spending period, bonds will continue to qualify as qualified school construction bonds if unspent proceeds are used within 90 days from the end of such three-year period to redeem bonds. The three-year spending period may be extended by the Secretary upon the issuer's request demonstrating that the failure to satisfy the three-year requirement is due to reasonable cause and the projects will continue to proceed with due diligence.

Qualified school construction bonds generally are subject to the arbitrage requirements of section 148. However, available project proceeds invested during the three-year spending period are not subject to the arbitrage restrictions (i.e., yield restriction and rebate requirements). In addition, amounts invested in a reserve fund are not subject to the arbitrage restrictions to the extent: (1) such fund is funded at a rate not more rapid than equal annual installments; (2) such fund is funded in a manner reasonably expected to result in an amount not greater than an amount necessary to repay the issue; and (3) the yield on such fund is not greater than the average annual interest rate of tax-exempt obligations having a term of 10 years or more that are issued during the month the qualified school construction bonds are issued.

The maturity of qualified school construction bonds is the term that the Secretary estimates will result in the present value of the obligation to repay the principal on such bonds being equal to 50 percent of the face amount of such bonds, using as a discount rate the average annual interest rate of tax-exempt obligations having a term of 10 years or more that are issued during the month the qualified school construction bonds are issued.

As with present-law tax credit bonds, the taxpayer holding qualified school construction bonds on a credit allowance date is entitled to a tax credit. The credit rate on the bonds is set by the Secretary at a rate that is 100 percent of the rate that would permit issuance of such bonds without discount and interest cost to the issuer. The amount of the tax credit is determined by multiplying the bond's credit rate by the face amount on the holder's bond. The credit accrues quarterly, is includible in gross income (as if it were an interest payment on the bond), and can be claimed against regular income tax liability and alternative minimum tax liability. Unused credits may be carried forward to succeeding taxable years. In addition, credits may be separated from the ownership of the underlying bond in a manner similar to the manner in which interest coupons can be stripped from interest-bearing bonds.

Issuers of qualified school construction bonds are required to certify that the financial disclosure requirements and applicable State and local law requirements governing conflicts of interest are satisfied with respect to such issue, as well as any other additional conflict of interest rules prescribed by the Secretary with respect to

Act Sec. 1521 ¶10,430

any Federal, State, or local government official directly involved with the issuance of qualified school construction bonds.

Effective date

The provision is effective for bonds issued after December 31, 2008.

Senate Amendment

In general

The Senate amendment is the same as the House bill.

National limitation

There is a national limitation on qualified school construction bonds of $5 billion for calendar years 2009 and 2010, respectively. Also, allocations of the national limitation of qualified school construction bonds are divided between the States with no special allocations to certain large school districts.

Allocation to the States

The allocations are made to the States according to their respective populations of children aged five through seventeen. However, the Secretary of the Treasury shall adjust the annual allocations among the States to ensure that for each State is not less than a minimum percentage. A State's minimum percentage for a calendar year is calculated by dividing (1) the amount the State is eligible to receive under section 1124(d) of the Elementary and Secondary Education Act of 1965 for such State for the most recent fiscal year ending before such calendar year by (2) the amount all States are eligible to received under section 1124(d) of the Elementary and Secondary Education Act of 1965 for such fiscal year, and then multiplying the result by 100.

Allocation to large school districts

No portion of the national limitation for a calendar year is allocated by the Secretary of the Treasury among local educational agencies which are large local educational agencies for such year.

Effective Date

The provision is effective for obligations issued after the date of enactment.

Conference Agreement

In general

The provision creates a new category of tax-credit bonds: qualified school construction bonds. Qualified school construction bonds must meet three requirements: (1) 100 percent of the available project proceeds of the bond issue is used for the construction, rehabilitation, or repair of a public school facility or for the acquisition of land on which such a bond-financed facility is to be constructed; (2) the bond is issued by a State or local government within which such school is located; and (3) the issuer designates such bonds as a qualified school construction bond.

National limitation

There is a national limitation on qualified school construction bonds of $11 billion for calendar years 2009 and 2010, respectively.

Allocation to the States

The national limitation is tentatively allocated among the States in proportion to respective amounts each such State is eligible to receive under section 1124 of the Elementary and Secondary Education Act of 1965 for the most recent fiscal year ending before such calendar year. The amount each State is allocated under the above formula is then reduced by the amount received by any local large educational agency within the State.

For allocation purposes, a State includes the District of Columbia and any possession of the United States. The provision provides a special allocation for possessions of the United States other than Puerto Rico under the national limitation for States. Under this special rule an allocation to a possession other than Puerto Rico is made on the basis of the respective populations of individuals below the poverty line (as defined by the Office of Management and Budget) rather than respective populations of children aged five through seventeen. This special allocation reduces the State allocation share of the national limitation otherwise available for allocation among the States. Under another special rule the Secretary of the Interior may allocate $200 million of school construction bonds for 2009 and 2010, respectively, to Indian schools. This special allocation for Indian schools is to be used for purposes of the construction, rehabilitation, and repair of schools funded by the Bureau of Indian Affairs. For purposes of such allocations Indian tribal governments are qualified issuers. The special allocation for Indian schools does not reduce the State allocation share of the national limitation otherwise available for allocation among the States.

If an amount allocated under this allocation to the States is unused for a calendar year it may be carried forward by the State to the next calendar year.

Allocation to large school districts

Forty percent of the national limitation is allocated among large local educational agencies in proportion to the respective amounts each agency received under section 1124 of the Elementary and Secondary Education Act of 1965 for the most recent fiscal year ending before such calendar year. Any unused allocation of any agency within a State may be allocated by the agency to such State. With respect to a calendar year, the term large local educational agency means any local educational agency if such agency is: (1) among the 100 local educational agencies with the largest numbers of children aged 5 through 17 from families living below the poverty level, or (2) one of not more than 25 local educational agencies (other than in 1, immediately above) that the Secretary of Education determines are in particular need of assistance, based on a low level of resources for school construction, a high level of enrollment growth, or other such factors as the Secretary of Education deems appropriate. If any amount allocated to large local educational agency is unused for a calendar year the agency may reallocate such amount to the State in which the agency is located.

Application of qualified tax credit bond rules

The provision makes qualified school construction bonds a type of qualified tax credit bond for purposes of section 54A. In addition, qualified school construction bonds may be issued by Indian tribal governments only to the extent such bonds are issued for purposes that satisfy the present law requirements for tax-exempt bonds issued by Indian tribal governments (i.e., essential governmental functions and certain manufacturing purposes).

The provision requires 100 percent of the available project proceeds of qualified school construction bonds to be used within the three-year period that begins on the date of issuance. Available project proceeds are proceeds from the sale of the issue less issuance costs (not to exceed two percent) and any investment earnings on such sale proceeds. To the extent less than 100 percent of the available project proceeds are used to finance qualified purposes during the three-year spending period, bonds will continue to qualify as qualified school construction bonds if unspent proceeds are used within 90 days from the end of such three-year period to redeem bonds. The three-year spending period may be extended by the Secretary upon the issuer's request demonstrating that the failure to satisfy the three-year requirement is due to reasonable cause and the projects will continue to proceed with due diligence.

Qualified school construction bonds generally are subject to the arbitrage requirements of section 148. However, available project proceeds invested during the three-year spending period are not subject to the arbitrage restrictions (i.e., yield restriction and rebate requirements). In addition, amounts invested in a reserve fund are not subject to the arbitrage restrictions to the extent: (1) such fund is funded at a rate not more rapid than equal annual installments; (2) such fund is funded in a manner reasonably expected to result in an amount not greater than an amount necessary to repay the issue; and (3) the yield on such fund is not greater than the average annual interest rate of tax-exempt obligations having a term of 10 years or more that are issued during the month the qualified school construction bonds are issued.

The maturity of qualified school construction bonds is the term that the Secretary estimates will result in the present value of the obligation to repay the principal on such bonds being equal to 50 percent of the face amount of such bonds, using as a discount rate the average annual interest rate of tax-exempt obligations having a term of 10 years or more that are issued during the month the qualified school construction bonds are issued.

As with present-law tax credit bonds, the taxpayer holding qualified school construction bonds on a credit allowance date is entitled to a tax credit. The credit rate on the bonds is set by the Secretary at a rate that is 100 percent of the rate that would permit issuance of such bonds without discount and interest cost to the issuer. The amount of the tax credit is determined by multiplying the bond's credit rate by the face amount on the holder's bond. The credit accrues quarterly, is includible in gross income (as if it were an interest payment on the bond), and can be claimed against regular income tax liability and alternative minimum tax liability. Unused credits may be carried forward to succeeding taxable years. In addition, credits may be separated from the ownership of the underlying bond in a manner similar to the manner in which interest coupons can be stripped from interest-bearing bonds.

Issuers of qualified school construction bonds are required to certify that the financial disclosure requirements and applicable State and local law requirements governing conflicts of interest are satisfied with respect to such issue, as well as any other additional conflict of interest rules prescribed by the Secretary with respect to

Act Sec. 1521   ¶10,430

any Federal, State, or local government official directly involved with the issuance of qualified school construction bonds.

[Law at ¶ 5150 and ¶ 5175. CCH Explanation at ¶ 630.]

Effective date

The provision is effective for obligations issued after the date of enactment.

[¶ 10,440] Act Sec. 1522. Extend and expand qualified zone academy bonds

Conference Report (H. REPT. 111-16)

[Code Sec. 54E]

Present Law

Tax-exempt bonds

Interest on State and local governmental bonds generally is excluded from gross income for Federal income tax purposes if the proceeds of the bonds are used to finance direct activities of these governmental units or if the bonds are repaid with revenues of the governmental units. These can include tax-exempt bonds which finance public schools.[134] An issuer must file with the Internal Revenue Service certain information about the bonds issued in order for that bond issue to be tax-exempt.[135] Generally, this information return is required to be filed no later than the 15th day of the second month after the close of the calendar quarter in which the bonds were issued.

The tax exemption for State and local bonds does not apply to any arbitrage bond.[136] An arbitrage bond is defined as any bond that is part of an issue if any proceeds of the issue are reasonably expected to be used (or intentionally are used) to acquire higher yielding investments or to replace funds that are used to acquire higher yielding investments.[137] In general, arbitrage profits may be earned only during specified periods (e.g., defined "temporary periods") before funds are needed for the purpose of the borrowing or on specified types of investments (e.g., "reasonably required reserve or replacement funds"). Subject to limited exceptions, investment profits that are earned during these periods or on such investments must be rebated to the Federal Government.

Qualified zone academy bonds

As an alternative to traditional tax-exempt bonds, States and local governments were given the authority to issue "qualified zone academy bonds."[138] A total of $400 million of qualified zone academy bonds is authorized to be issued annually in calendar years 1998 through 2009. The $400 million aggregate bond cap is allocated each year to the States according to their respective populations of individuals below the poverty line. Each State, in turn, allocates the credit authority to qualified zone academies within such State.

A taxpayer holding a qualified zone academy bond on the credit allowance date is entitled to a credit. The credit is includible in gross income (as if it were a taxable interest payment on the bond), and may be claimed against regular income tax and alternative minimum tax liability.

The Treasury Department sets the credit rate at a rate estimated to allow issuance of qualified zone academy bonds without discount and without interest cost to the issuer.[139] The Secretary determines credit rates for tax credit bonds based on general assumptions about credit quality of the class of potential eligible issuers and such other factors as the Secretary deems appropriate. The Secretary may determine credit rates based on general credit market yield indexes and credit ratings. The maximum term of the bond is determined by the Treasury Department, so that the present value of the obligation to repay the principal on the bond is 50 percent of the face value of the bond.

---

[134] Sec. 103.
[135] Sec. 149(e).
[136] Sec. 103(a) and (b)(2).
[137] Sec. 148.
[138] See secs. 54E and 1397E.

[139] Given the differences in credit quality and other characteristics of individual issuers, the Secretary cannot set credit rates in a manner that will allow each issuer to issue tax credit bonds at par.

"Qualified zone academy bonds" are defined as any bond issued by a State or local government, provided that (1) at least 95 percent of the proceeds are used for the purpose of renovating, providing equipment to, developing course materials for use at, or training teachers and other school personnel in a "qualified zone academy" and (2) private entities have promised to contribute to the qualified zone academy certain equipment, technical assistance or training, employee services, or other property or services with a value equal to at least 10 percent of the bond proceeds.

A school is a "qualified zone academy" if (1) the school is a public school that provides education and training below the college level, (2) the school operates a special academic program in cooperation with businesses to enhance the academic curriculum and increase graduation and employment rates, and (3) either (a) the school is located in an empowerment zone or enterprise community designated under the Code, or (b) it is reasonably expected that at least 35 percent of the students at the school will be eligible for free or reduced-cost lunches under the school lunch program established under the National School Lunch Act.

The arbitrage requirements which generally apply to interest-bearing tax-exempt bonds also generally apply to qualified zone academy bonds. In addition, an issuer of qualified zone academy bonds must reasonably expect to and actually spend 100 percent or more of the proceeds of such bonds on qualified zone academy property within the three-year period that begins on the date of issuance. To the extent less than 100 percent of the proceeds are used to finance qualified zone academy property during the three-year spending period, bonds will continue to qualify as qualified zone academy bonds if unspent proceeds are used within 90 days from the end of such three-year period to redeem any nonqualified bonds. The three-year spending period may be extended by the Secretary if the issuer establishes that the failure to meet the spending requirement is due to reasonable cause and the related purposes for issuing the bonds will continue to proceed with due diligence.

Two special arbitrage rules apply to qualified zone academy bonds. First, available project proceeds invested during the three-year period beginning on the date of issue are not subject to the arbitrage restrictions (i.e., yield restriction and rebate requirements). Available project proceeds are proceeds from the sale of an issue of qualified zone academy bonds, less issuance costs (not to exceed two percent) and any investment earnings on such proceeds. Thus, available project proceeds invested during the three-year spending period may be invested at unrestricted yields, but the earnings on such investments must be spent on qualified zone academy property. Second, amounts invested in a reserve fund are not subject to the arbitrage restrictions to the extent: (1) such fund is funded at a rate not more rapid than equal annual installments; (2) such fund is funded in a manner reasonably expected to result in an amount not greater than an amount necessary to repay the issue; and (3) the yield on such fund is not greater than the average annual interest rate of tax-exempt obligations having a term of 10 years or more that are issued during the month the qualified zone academy bonds are issued.

Issuers of qualified zone academy bonds are required to report issuance to the Internal Revenue Service in a manner similar to the information returns required for tax-exempt bonds.

House Bill

In general

The provision extends and expands the present-law qualified zone academy bond program. The provision authorizes issuance of up to $1.4 billion of qualified zone academy bonds annually for 2009 and 2010, respectively.

Effective date

The provision applies to obligations issued after December 31, 2008.

Senate Amendment

The Senate amendment is the same as the House bill.

Conference Agreement

The conference agreement follows the House bill and the Senate amendment.

[Law at ¶5170. CCH Explanation at ¶635.]

Act Sec. 1522   ¶10,440

[¶ 10,450] Act Sec. 1531. Build America bonds

Conference Report (H. Rept. 111-16)

[New Code Secs. 54AA and 6431]

Present Law

In general

Under present law, gross income does not include interest on State or local bonds. State and local bonds are classified generally as either governmental bonds or private activity bonds. Governmental bonds are bonds the proceeds of which are primarily used to finance governmental functions or which are repaid with governmental funds. Private activity bonds are bonds in which the State or local government serves as a conduit providing financing to nongovernmental persons (e.g., private businesses or individuals). The exclusion from income for State and local bonds does not apply to private activity bonds, unless the bonds are issued for certain permitted purposes ("qualified private activity bonds") and other Code requirements are met.

Private activity bonds

The Code defines a private activity bond as any bond that satisfies (1) the private business use test and the private security or payment test ("the private business test"); or (2) "the private loan financing test."[140]

Private business test

Under the private business test, a bond is a private activity bond if it is part of an issue in which:

1. More than 10 percent of the proceeds of the issue (including use of the bond-financed property) are to be used in the trade or business of any person other than a governmental unit ("private business use"); and

2. More than 10 percent of the payment of principal or interest on the issue is, directly or indirectly, secured by (a) property used or to be used for a private business use or (b) to be derived from payments in respect of property, or borrowed money, used or to be used for a private business use ("private payment test").[141]

A bond is not a private activity bond unless both parts of the private business test (i.e., the private business use test and the private payment test) are met. Thus, a facility that is 100 percent privately used does not cause the bonds financing such facility to be private activity bonds if the bonds are not secured by or paid with private payments. For example, land improvements that benefit a privately-owned factory may be financed with governmental bonds if the debt service on such bonds is not paid by the factory owner or other private parties.

Private loan financing test

A bond issue satisfies the private loan financing test if proceeds exceeding the lesser of $5 million or five percent of such proceeds are used directly or indirectly to finance loans to one or more nongovernmental persons. Private loans include both business and other (e.g., personal) uses and payments by private persons; however, in the case of business uses and payments, all private loans also constitute private business uses and payments subject to the private business test.

Arbitrage restrictions

The exclusion from income for interest on State and local bonds does not apply to any arbitrage bond.[142] An arbitrage bond is defined as any bond that is part of an issue if any proceeds of the issue are reasonably expected to be used (or intentionally are used) to acquire higher yielding investments or to replace funds that are used to acquire higher yielding investments.[143] In general, arbitrage profits may be earned only during specified periods (e.g., defined "temporary periods") before funds are needed for the purpose of the borrowing or on specified types of investments (e.g., "reasonably required reserve or replacement funds"). Subject to limited exceptions, investment profits that are earned during these periods or on such investments must be rebated to the Federal Government.

---

[140] Sec. 141.

[141] The 10 percent private business test is reduced to five percent in the case of private business uses (and payments with respect to such uses) that are unrelated to any governmental use being financed by the issue.

[142] Sec. 103(a) and (b)(2).

[143] Sec. 148.

Qualified tax credit bonds

In lieu of interest, holders of qualified tax credit bonds receive a tax credit that accrues quarterly. The following bonds are qualified tax credit bonds: qualified forestry conservation bonds, new clean renewable energy bonds, qualified energy conservation bonds, and qualified zone academy bonds.[144]

Section 54A of the Code sets forth general rules applicable to qualified tax credit bonds. These rules include requirements regarding credit allowance dates, the expenditure of available project proceeds, reporting, arbitrage, maturity limitations, and financial conflicts of interest, among other special rules.

A taxpayer who holds a qualified tax credit bond on one or more credit allowance dates of the bond during the taxable year shall be allowed a credit against the taxpayer's income tax for the taxable year. In general, the credit amount for any credit allowance date is 25 percent of the annual credit determined with respect to the bond. The annual credit is determined by multiplying the applicable credit rate by the outstanding face amount of the bond. The applicable credit rate for the bond is the rate that the Secretary estimates will permit the issuance of the qualified tax credit bond with a specified maturity or redemption date without discount and without interest cost to the qualified issuer.[145] The Secretary determines credit rates for tax credit bonds based on general assumptions about credit quality of the class of potential eligible issuers and such other factors as the Secretary deems appropriate. The Secretary may determine credit rates based on general credit market yield indexes and credit ratings.

The credit is included in gross income and, under regulations prescribed by the Secretary, may be stripped (a separation (including at issuance) of the ownership of a qualified tax credit bond and the entitlement to the credit with respect to such bond).

Section 54A of the Code requires that 100 percent of the available project proceeds of qualified tax credit bonds must be used within the three-year period that begins on the date of issuance. Available project proceeds are proceeds from the sale of the bond issue less issuance costs (not to exceed two percent) and any investment earnings on such sale proceeds. To the extent less than 100 percent of the available project proceeds are used to finance qualified projects during the three-year spending period, bonds will continue to qualify as qualified tax credit bonds if unspent proceeds are used within 90 days from the end of such three-year period to redeem bonds. The three-year spending period may be extended by the Secretary upon the issuer's request demonstrating that the failure to satisfy the three-year requirement is due to reasonable cause and the projects will continue to proceed with due diligence.

Qualified tax credit bonds generally are subject to the arbitrage requirements of section 148. However, available project proceeds invested during the three-year spending period are not subject to the arbitrage restrictions (i.e., yield restriction and rebate requirements). In addition, amounts invested in a reserve fund are not subject to the arbitrage restrictions to the extent: (1) such fund is funded at a rate not more rapid than equal annual installments; (2) such fund is funded in a manner reasonably expected to result in an amount not greater than an amount necessary to repay the issue; and (3) the yield on such fund is not greater than the average annual interest rate of tax-exempt obligations having a term of 10 years or more that are issued during the month the qualified tax credit bonds are issued.

The maturity of qualified tax credit bonds is the term that the Secretary estimates will result in the present value of the obligation to repay the principal on such bonds being equal to 50 percent of the face amount of such bonds, using as a discount rate the average annual interest rate of tax-exempt obligations having a term of 10 years or more that are issued during the month the qualified tax credit bonds are issued.

House Bill

In general

The provision permits an issuer to elect to have an otherwise tax-exempt bond treated as a "taxable governmental bond." A "taxable governmental bond" is any obligation (other than a private activity bond) if the interest on such obligation would be (but for this provision) excludable from gross income under section 103 and the issuer makes an irrevocable election to have the provision apply. In determining if an obligation would be tax-exempt under section 103, the credit (or the payment discussed below

---

[144] See secs. 54B, 54C, 54D, and 54E.
[145] Given the differences in credit quality and other characteristics of individual issuers, the Secretary cannot set credit rates in a manner that will allow each issuer to issue tax credit bonds at par.

for qualified bonds) is not treated as a Federal guarantee. Further, the yield on a taxable governmental bond is determined without regard to the credit. A taxable governmental bond does not include any bond if the issue price has more than a de minimis amount of premium over the stated principal amount of the bond.

The holder of a taxable governmental bond will accrue a tax credit in the amount of 35 percent of the interest paid on the interest payment dates of the bond during the calendar year.[146] The interest payment date is any date on which the holder of record of the taxable governmental bond is entitled to a payment of interest under such bond. The sum of the accrued credits is allowed against regular and alternative minimum tax. Unused credit may be carried forward to succeeding taxable years. The credit, as well as the interest paid by the issuer, is included in gross income and the credit may be stripped under rules similar to those provided in section 54A regarding qualified tax credit bonds. Rules similar to those that apply for S corporations, partnerships and regulated investment companies with respect to qualified tax credit bonds also apply to the credit.

Unlike the tax credit for bonds issued under section 54A, the credit rate would not be calculated by the Secretary, but rather would be set by law at 35 percent. The actual credit that a taxpayer may claim is determined by multiplying the interest payment that the taxpayer receives from the issuer (i.e., the bond coupon payment) by 35 percent. Because the credit that the taxpayer claims is also included in income, the Committee anticipates that State and local issuers will issue bonds paying interest at rates approximately equal to 74.1 percent of comparable taxable bonds. The Committee anticipates that if an issuer issues a taxable governmental bond with coupons at 74.1 percent of a comparable taxable bond's coupon that the issuer's bond should sell at par. For example, if a taxable bond of comparable risk pays a $1,000 coupon and sells at par, then if a State or local issuer issues an equal-sized bond with coupon of $741.00, such a bond should also sell at par. The taxpayer who acquires the latter bond will receive an interest payment of $741 and may claim a credit of $259 (35 percent of $741). The credit and the interest payment are both included in the taxpayer's income. Thus, the taxpayer's taxable income from this instrument would be $1,000. This is the same taxable income that the taxpayer would recognize from holding the comparable taxable bond. Consequently the issuer's bond should sell at the same price as would the taxable bond.

Special rule for qualified bonds issued during 2009 and 2010

A "qualified bond" is any taxable governmental bond issued as part of an issue if 100 percent of the available project proceeds of such issue are to be used for capital expenditures.[147] The bond must be issued after the date of enactment of the provision and before January 1, 2011. The issuer must make an irrevocable election to have the special rule for qualified bonds apply.

Under the special rule for qualified bonds, in lieu of the tax credit to the holder, the issuer is allowed a credit equal to 35 percent of each interest payment made under such bond.[148] If in 2009 or 2010, the issuer elects to receive the credit, in the example above, for the State or local issuer's bond to sell at par, the issuer would have to issue the bond with a $1,000 interest coupon. The taxpayer who holds such a bond would include $1,000 on interest in his or her income. From the taxpayer's perspective the bond is the same the taxable bond in the example above and the taxpayer would be willing to pay par for the bond. However, under the provision the State or local issuer would receive a payment of $350 for each $1,000 coupon paid to bondholders. (The net interest cost to the issuer would be $650.)

The payment by the Secretary is to be made contemporaneously with the interest payment made by the issuer, and may be made either in advance or as reimbursement. In lieu of payment to the issuer, the payment may be made to a person making interest payments on behalf of the issuer. For purposes of the arbitrage rules,

---

[146] Original issue discount (OID) is not treated as a payment of interest for purposes of determining the credit under the provision. OID is the excess of an obligation's stated redemption price at maturity over the obligation's issue price (sec. 1273(a)).

[147] Under Treas. Reg. sec. 150-1(b), capital expenditure means any cost of a type that is properly chargeable to capital account (or would be so chargeable with a proper election or with the application of the definition of placed in service under Treas. Reg. sec. 1.150-2(c)) under general Federal income tax principles. For purposes of applying the "general Federal income tax principles" standard, an issuer should generally be treated as if it were a corporation subject to taxation under subchapter C of chapter 1 of the Code. An example of a capital expenditure would include expenditures made for the purchase of fiber-optic cable to provide municipal broadband service.

[148] Original issue discount (OID) is not treated as a payment of interest for purposes of calculating the refundable credit under the provision.

the yield on a qualified bond is reduced by the amount of the credit/payment.

Transitional coordination with State law

As noted above, interest on a taxable governmental bond and the related credit are includible in gross income to the holder for Federal tax purposes. The provision provides that until a State provides otherwise, the interest on any taxable governmental bond and the amount of any credit determined with respect to such bond shall be treated as being exempt from Federal income tax for purposes of State income tax laws.

Effective date

The provision is effective for obligations issued after the date of enactment.

Senate Amendment

In general

The Senate amendment is the same as the House bill except that it renames these bonds "Build America Bonds."

The Senate amendment also restricts these bonds to obligations issued before January 1, 2011.

For bonds issued by small issuers,[149] the credit rate is 40 percent instead of 35 percent.

Special rule for qualified bonds issued during 2009 and 2010

The Senate amendment is the same as the House bill, except for bonds issued by small issuers, the credit rate is 40 percent instead of 35 percent.

Transitional coordination with State law

The Senate amendment is the same as the House bill.

Effective date

The Senate amendment is the same as the House bill.

Conference Agreement

In general

The conference agreement follows the House bill except that it renames these bonds "Build America Bonds."

The conference agreement restricts these bonds to obligations issued before January 1, 2011.

Special rule for qualified bonds issued during 2009 and 2010

The conference agreement follows the House bill, except that it allows for a reasonably required reserve fund to be funded from bond proceeds.[150]

Transitional coordination with State law

The conference agreement follows the House bill and the Senate amendment.

Effective date

The conference agreement follows the House bill and the Senate amendment.

[Law at ¶ 5145, ¶ 5150, ¶ 5155, ¶ 5300, ¶ 5310, ¶ 5375, ¶ 5385, and ¶ 5390. CCH Explanation at ¶ 605 and ¶ 610.]

[¶ 10,460] Act Sec. 1541. Pass-through of credits on tax credit bonds held by regulated investment companies

Conference Report (H. REPT. 111-16)

[New Code Sec. 853A]

Present Law

In lieu of interest, holders of qualified tax credit bonds receive a tax credit that accrues quarterly. The credit is treated as interest that is includible in gross income. The following bonds are qualified tax credit bonds: qualified forestry conservation bonds, new clean renewable energy bonds, qualified energy conservation bonds, and qualified zone academy bonds.[163] The Code provides that in the case of a qualified tax credit

---

[149] Small issuer status is determined generally by reference to the rules of sec. 148(f)(4)(D)) and increasing the aggregate face amount of all tax-exempt governmental bonds reasonably expected to be issued during the calendar year from $5 million to $30 million.

[150] Under section 148(d)(2), a bond is an arbitrage bond if the amount of the proceeds from the sale of such issue that is part or any reserve or replacement fund exceeds 10 percent of the proceeds. As such the interest on such bond would not be tax-exempt under section 103 and thus would not be a qualified bond for purposes of the provision.

[163] See secs. 54B, 54C, 54D, and 54E.

bond held by a regulated investment company, the credit is allowed to shareholders of such company (and any gross income included with respect to such credit shall be treated as distributed to such shareholders) under procedures prescribed by the Secretary.[164] The Secretary has not prescribed procedures for the pass through of the credit to regulated investment company shareholders.

House Bill

No provision.

Senate Amendment

No provision.

Conference Agreement

The conference agreement provides procedures for passing though credits on "tax credit bonds" to the shareholders of an electing regulated investment company. In general, an electing regulated investment company is not allowed any credits with respect to any tax credit bonds it holds during any year for which an election is in effect. The company is treated as having an amount of interest included in its gross income in an amount equal that which would have been included if no election were in effect, and a dividends paid deduction in the same amount is allowed to the company. Each shareholder of the electing regulated investment company is (1) required to include in gross income an amount equal to the shareholder's proportional share of the interest attributable to its credits and (2) allowed such proportional share as a credit against such shareholder's Federal income tax. In order to pass through tax credits to a shareholder, a regulated investment company is required to mail a written notice to such shareholder not later than 60 days after the close of the regulated investment company's taxable year, designating the shareholder's proportionate share of passed-through credits and the shareholder's gross income in respect of such credits.

A tax credit bond means a qualified tax credit bond as defined in section 54A(d), a build America bond (as defined in section 54AA(d)), and any other bond for which a credit is allowable under subpart H of part IV of subchapter A of the Code.

The provision gives the Secretary authority to prescribe the time and manner in which a regulated investment company makes the election to pass through credits on tax credit bonds. In addition, the provision requires the Secretary to prescribe such guidance as may be necessary to carry out the provision, including prescribing methods for determining a shareholder's proportionate share of tax credits.

Effective date.

The provision is applicable to taxable years ending after the date of enactment.

[Law at ¶ 5145, ¶ 5150, and ¶ 5275. CCH Explanation at ¶ 615.]

[¶ 10,470] Act Sec. 1601. Application of certain labor standards to projects financed with certain tax-favored bonds

Conference Report (H. REPT. 111-16)

[Act Sec. 1601]

Present Law

The United States Code (Subchapter IV of Chapter 31 of Title 40) applies a prevailing wage requirement to certain contracts to which the Federal Government is a party.

House Bill

The provision provides that Subchapter IV of Chapter 31 of Title 40 of the U.S. Code shall apply to projects financed with the proceeds of:

1. any qualified clean renewable energy bond (as defined in sec. 54C of the Code) issued after the date of enactment;

2. any qualified energy conservation bond (as defined in sec. 54D of the Code) issued after the date of enactment;;

3. any qualified zone academy bond (as defined in sec. 54E of the Code) issued after the date of enactment;

4. any qualified school construction bond (as defined in sec. 54F of the Code); and

---

[164] See sec. 54A(h), which also covers real estate investment trusts.

5. any recovery zone economic development bond (as defined in sec. 1400U-2 of the Code).

Effective date

The provision is effective on the date of enactment.

Senate Amendment

The Senate amendment is the same as the House bill except it makes a technical correction to change "qualified clean renewable energy bond" to "new clean renewable energy bond."

Conference Agreement

The conference agreement follows the Senate amendment.

[Law at ¶ 7030. CCH Explanation at ¶ 625, ¶ 630, ¶ 635, ¶ 640 and ¶ 645.]

[¶ 10,480] Act Secs. 1899 through 1899L. Modify the health coverage tax credit

Conference Report (H. Rept. 111-16)

[Code Secs. 35, 4980B, 7527 and 9801]

Present Law

In general

Under the Trade Act of 2002,[248] in the case of taxpayers who are eligible individuals, a refundable tax credit is provided for 65 percent of the taxpayer's premiums for qualified health insurance of the taxpayer and qualifying family members for each eligible coverage month beginning in the taxable year. The credit is commonly referred to as the health coverage tax credit ("HCTC"). The credit is available only with respect to amounts paid by the taxpayer. The credit is available on an advance basis.[249]

Qualifying family members are the taxpayer's spouse and any dependent of the taxpayer with respect to whom the taxpayer is entitled to claim a dependency exemption. Any individual who has other specified coverage is not a qualifying family member.

Persons eligible for the credit

Eligibility for the credit is determined on a monthly basis. In general, an eligible coverage month is any month if, as of the first day of the month, the taxpayer (1) is an eligible individual, (2) is covered by qualified health insurance, (3) does not have other specified coverage, and (4) is not imprisoned under Federal, State, or local authority.[250] In the case of a joint return, the eligibility requirements are met if at least one spouse satisfies the requirements.

An eligible individual is an individual who is (1) an eligible TAA recipient, (2) an eligible alternative Trade Adjustment Assistance ("TAA") recipient, or (3) an eligible Pension Benefit Guaranty Corporation ("PBGC") pension recipient.

An individual is an eligible TAA recipient during any month if the individual (1) is receiving for any day of such month a trade readjustment allowance[251] or who would be eligible to receive such an allowance but for the requirement that the individual exhaust unemployment benefits before being eligible to receive an allowance and (2) with respect to such allowance, is covered under a certification issued under subchapter A or D of chapter 2 of title II of the Trade Act of 1974. An individual is treated as an eligible TAA recipient during the first month that such individual would otherwise cease to be an eligible TAA recipient.

An individual is an eligible alternative TAA recipient during any month if the individual (1) is a worker described in section 246(a)(3)(B) of the Trade Act of 1974 who is participating in the program established under section 246(a)(1) of such Act, and (2) is receiving a benefit for such month under section 246(a)(2) of such Act. An

---

[248] Pub. L. No. 107-210 (2002).

[249] An individual is eligible for the advance payment of the credit once a qualified health insurance costs credit eligibility certificate is in effect. Sec. 7527. Unless otherwise indicated, all "section" references are to the Internal Revenue Code of 1986, as amended.

[250] An eligible month must begin after November 4, 2002. This date is 90 days after the date of enactment of the Trade Act of 2002, which was August 6, 2002.

[251] The eligibility rules and conditions for such an allowance are specified in chapter 2 of title II of the Trade Act of 1974. Among other requirements, payment of a trade readjustment allowance is conditioned upon the individual enrolling in certain training programs or receiving a waiver of training requirements.

individual is treated as an eligible alternative TAA recipient during the first month that such individual would otherwise cease to be an eligible TAA recipient.

An individual is a PBGC pension recipient for any month if he or she (1) is age 55 or over as of the first day of the month, and (2) is receiving a benefit any portion of which is paid by the PBGC. The IRS has interpreted the definition of PBGC pension recipient to also include certain alternative recipients and recipients who have received certain lump-sum payments on or after August 6, 2002. A person is not an eligible individual if he or she may be claimed as a dependent on another person's tax return.

An otherwise eligible taxpayer is not eligible for the credit for a month if, as of the first day of the month, the individual has other specified coverage. Other specified coverage is (1) coverage under any insurance which constitutes medical care (except for insurance substantially all of the coverage of which is for excepted benefits)[252] maintained by an employer (or former employer) if at least 50 percent of the cost of the coverage is paid by an employer[253] (or former employer) of the individual or his or her spouse or (2) coverage under certain governmental health programs. Specifically, an individual is not eligible for the credit if, as of the first day of the month, the individual is (1) entitled to benefits under Medicare Part A, enrolled in Medicare Part B, or enrolled in Medicaid or SCHIP, (2) enrolled in a health benefits plan under the Federal Employees Health Benefit Plan, or (3) entitled to receive benefits under chapter 55 of title 10 of the United States Code (relating to military personnel). An individual is not considered to be enrolled in Medicaid solely by reason of receiving immunizations.

A special rule applies with respect to alternative TAA recipients. For eligible alternative TAA recipients, an individual has other specified coverage if the individual is (1) eligible for coverage under any qualified health insurance (other than coverage under a COBRA continuation provision, State-based continuation coverage, or coverage through certain State arrangements) under which at least 50 percent of the cost of coverage is paid or incurred by an employer of the taxpayer or the taxpayer's spouse or (2) covered under any such qualified health insurance under which any portion of the cost of coverage is paid or incurred by an employer of the taxpayer or the taxpayer's spouse.

Qualified health insurance

Qualified health insurance eligible for the credit is: (1) COBRA continuation[254] coverage; (2) State-based continuation coverage provided by the State under a State law that requires such coverage; (3) coverage offered through a qualified State high risk pool; (4) coverage under a health insurance program offered to State employees or a comparable program; (5) coverage through an arrangement entered into by a State and a group health plan, an issuer of health insurance coverage, an administrator, or an employer; (6) coverage offered through a State arrangement with a private sector health care coverage purchasing pool; (7) coverage under a State-operated health plan that does not receive any Federal financial participation; (8) coverage under a group health plan that is available through the employment of the eligible individual's spouse; and (9) coverage under individual health insurance if the eligible individual was covered under individual health insurance during the entire 30-day period that ends on the date the individual became separated from the employment which qualified the individual for the TAA allowance, the benefit for an eligible alternative TAA recipient, or a pension benefit from the PBGC, whichever applies.[255]

Qualified health insurance does not include any State-based coverage (i.e., coverage described in (2)-(7) in the preceding paragraph),

---

[252] Excepted benefits are: (1) coverage only for accident or disability income or any combination thereof; (2) coverage issued as a supplement to liability insurance; (3) liability insurance, including general liability insurance and automobile liability insurance; (4) worker's compensation or similar insurance; (5) automobile medical payment insurance; (6) credit-only insurance; (7) coverage for on-site medical clinics; (8) other insurance coverage similar to the coverages in (1)-(7) specified in regulations under which benefits for medical care are secondary or incidental to other insurance benefits; (9) limited scope dental or vision benefits; (10) benefits for long-term care, nursing home care, home health care, community-based care, or any combination thereof; and (11) other benefits similar to those in (9) and (10) as specified in regulations; (12) coverage only for a specified disease or illness; (13) hospital indemnity or other fixed indemnity insurance; and (14) Medicare supplemental insurance.

[253] An amount is considered paid by the employer if it is excludable from income. Thus, for example, amounts paid for health coverage on a salary reduction basis under an employer plan are considered paid by the employer. A rule aggregating plans of the same employer applies in determining whether the employer pays at least 50 percent of the cost of coverage.

[254] COBRA continuation is defined in section 9832(d)(1).

[255] For this purpose, "individual health insurance" means any insurance which constitutes medical care offered to individuals other than in connection with a group health plan. Such term does not include Federal- or State-based health insurance coverage.

unless the State has elected to have such coverage treated as qualified health insurance and such coverage meets certain requirements.[256] Such State coverage must provide that each qualifying individual is guaranteed enrollment if the individual pays the premium for enrollment or provides a qualified health insurance costs eligibility certificate and pays the remainder of the premium. In addition, the State-based coverage cannot impose any pre-existing condition limitation with respect to qualifying individuals. State-based coverage cannot require a qualifying individual to pay a premium or contribution that is greater than the premium or contribution for a similarly situated individual who is not a qualified individual. Finally, benefits under the State-based coverage must be the same as (or substantially similar to) benefits provided to similarly situated individuals who are not qualifying individuals.

A qualifying individual is an eligible individual who seeks to enroll in the State-based coverage and who has aggregate periods of creditable coverage[257] of three months or longer, does not have other specified coverage, and who is not imprisoned. In general terms, creditable coverage includes health care coverage without a gap of more than 63 days. Therefore, if an individual's qualifying coverage were terminated more than 63 days before the individual enrolled in the State-based coverage, the individual would not be a qualifying individual and would not be entitled to the State-based protections. A qualifying individual also includes qualified family members of such an eligible individual.

Qualified health insurance does not include coverage under a flexible spending or similar arrangement or any insurance if substantially all of the coverage is for excepted benefits.

Other rules

Amounts taken into account in determining the credit may not be taken into account in determining the amount allowable under the itemized deduction for medical expenses or the deduction for health insurance expenses of self-employed individuals. Amounts distributed from a medical savings account or health savings accounts are not eligible for the credit. The amount of the credit available through filing a tax return is reduced by any credit received on an advance basis. Married taxpayers filing separate returns are eligible for the credit; however, if both spouses are eligible individuals and the spouses file separate returns, then the spouse of the taxpayer is not a qualifying family member.

The Secretary of the Treasury is authorized to prescribe such regulations and other guidance as may be necessary or appropriate to carry out the credit provision.

COBRA

The Consolidated Omnibus Reconciliation Act of 1985 ("COBRA") requires that a group health plan must offer continuation coverage to qualified beneficiaries in the case of a qualifying event. An excise tax under the Code applies on the failure of a group health plan to meet the requirement.[258] Qualifying events include the death of the covered employee, termination of the covered employee's employment, divorce or legal separation of the covered employee, and certain bankruptcy proceedings of the employer. In the case of termination from employment, the coverage must be extended for a period of not less than 18 months. In certain other cases, coverage must be extended for a period of not less than 36 months. Under such period of continuation coverage, the plan may require payment of a premium by the beneficiary of up to 102 percent of the applicable premium for the period.

House Bill

No provision.

Senate Amendment

No provision.[259]

Conference Agreement

Increase in credit percentage amount

The provision increases the amount of the HCTC to 80 percent of the taxpayer's premiums for qualified health insurance of the taxpayer and qualifying family members.

Effective date.—The provision is effective for coverage months beginning on or after the first day of the first month beginning 60 days after date of enactment. The increased credit rate does not apply to months beginning after December 31, 2010.

---

[256] For guidance on how a State elects a health program to be qualified health insurance for purposes of the credit, see Rev. Proc. 2004-12, 2004-1 C.B. 528.

[257] Creditable coverage is determined under the Health Insurance Portability and Accountability Act. Sec. 9801(c).

[258] Sec. 4980B.

[259] The Senate amendment did not amend the HCTC, but section 1701 of the Senate amendment provided for a temporary extension of the Trade Adjustment Assistance Program (generally until December 31, 2010). Certain beneficiaries of this program are eligible for the HCTC.

Payment for monthly premiums paid prior to commencement of advance payment of credit

The provision provides that the Secretary of Treasury shall make one or more retroactive payments on behalf of certified individuals equal to 80 percent of the premiums for coverage of the taxpayer and qualifying family members for qualified health insurance for eligible coverage months occurring prior to the first month for which an advance payment is made on behalf of such individual. The amount of the payment must be reduced by the amount of any payment made to the taxpayer under a national emergency grant pursuant to section 173(f) of the Workforce Investment Act of 1998 for a taxable year including such eligible coverage months.

Effective date.—The provision is effective for eligible coverage months beginning after December 31, 2008. The Secretary of the Treasury, however, is not required to make any payments under the provision until after the date that is six months after the date of enactment. The provision does not apply to months beginning after December 31, 2010.

TAA recipients not enrolled in training programs eligible for credit

The provision modifies the definition of an eligible TAA recipient to eliminate the requirement that an individual be enrolled in training in the case of an individual receiving unemployment compensation. In addition, the provision clarifies that the definition of an eligible TAA recipient includes an individual who would be eligible to receive a trade readjustment allowance except that the individual is in a break in training that exceeds the period specified in section 233(c) of the Trade Act of 1974, but is within the period for receiving the allowance.

Effective date.—The provision is effective for months beginning after the date of enactment in taxable years ending after such date. The provision does not apply to months beginning after December 31, 2010.

TAA pre-certification period rule for purposes of determining whether there is a 63-day lapse in creditable coverage

Under the provision, in determining if there has been a 63-day lapse in coverage (which determines, in part, if the State-based consumer protections apply), in the case of a TAA-eligible individual, the period beginning on the date the individual has a TAA-related loss of coverage and ending on the date which is seven days after the date of issuance by the Secretary (or by any person or entity designated by the Secretary) of a qualified health insurance costs credit eligibility certificate (under section 7527) for such individual is not taken into account.

Effective date.—The provision is effective for plan years beginning after the date of enactment. The provision does not apply to plan years beginning after December 31, 2010.

Continued qualification of family members after certain events

The provision provides continued eligibility for the credit for family members after certain events. The rule applies in the case of (1) the eligible individual becoming entitled to Medicare, (2) divorce and (3) death.

In the case of a month which would be an eligible coverage month with respect to an eligible individual except that the individual is entitled to benefits under Medicare Part A or enrolled in Medicare Part B, the month is treated as an eligible coverage month with respect to the individual solely for purposes of determining the amount of the credit with respect to qualifying family members (i.e., the credit is allowed for expenses paid for qualifying family members after the eligible individual is eligible for Medicare). Such treatment applies only with respect to the first 24 months after the eligible individual is first entitled to benefits under Medicare Part A or enrolled in Medicare Part B.

In the case of the finalization of a divorce between an eligible individual and the individual's spouse, the spouse is treated as an eligible individual for a period of 24 months beginning with the date of the finalization of the divorce. Under such rule, the only family members that may be taken into account with respect to the spouse as qualifying family members are those individuals who were qualifying family members immediately before such divorce finalization.

In the case of the death of an eligible individual, the spouse of such individual (determined at the time of death) is treated as an eligible individual for a period of 24 months beginning with the date of death. Under such rule, the only qualifying family members that may be taken into account with respect to the spouse are those individuals who were qualifying family members immediately before such death. In addition, any individual who was a qualifying family member of the decedent immediately before such death[260] is treated as an eligible individual for a period of 24 months beginning with the date of death, except that in determining the amount of the HCTC only such qualifying family member may be taken into account.

Effective date.—The provision is effective for months beginning after December 31, 2009. The provision does not apply to months that begin after December 31, 2010.

Alignment of COBRA coverage

The maximum required COBRA continuation coverage period is modified by the provision with respect to certain individuals whose qualifying event is a termination of employment or a reduction in hours. First, in the case of such a qualifying event with respect to a covered employee who has a nonforfeitable right to a benefit any portion of which is paid by the PBGC, the maximum coverage period must end not earlier than the date of death of the covered employee (or in the case of the surviving spouse or dependent children of the covered employee, not earlier than 24 months after the date of death of the covered employee). Second, in the case of such a qualifying event where the covered employee is a TAA eligible individual as of the date that the maximum coverage period would otherwise terminate, the maximum coverage period must extend during the period that the individual is a TAA eligible individual.

Effective date.—The provision is effective for periods of coverage that would, without regard to the provision, end on or after the date of enactment, provided that the provision does not extend any periods of coverage beyond December 31, 2010.

Addition of coverage through voluntary employees' beneficiary associations

The provision expands the definition of qualified health insurance by including coverage under an employee benefit plan funded by a voluntary employees' beneficiary association ("VEBA", as defined in section 501(c)(9)) established pursuant to an order of a bankruptcy court, or by agreement with an authorized representative, as provided in section 1114 of title 11, United States Code.

Effective date.—The provision is effective on the date of enactment. The provision does not apply with respect to certificates of eligibility issued after December 31, 2010.

Notice requirements

The provision requires that the qualified health insurance costs credit eligibility certificate provided in connection with the advance payment of the HCTC must include (1) the name, address, and telephone number of the State office or offices responsible for providing the individual with assistance with enrollment in qualified health insurance, (2) a list of coverage options that are treated as qualified health insurance by the State in which the individual resides, (3) in the case of a TAA-eligible individual, a statement informing the individual that the individual has 63 days from the date that is seven days after the issuance of such certificate to enroll in such insurance without a lapse in creditable coverage, and (4) such other information as the Secretary may provide.

Effective date. The provision is effective for certificates issued after the date that is six months after the date of enactment. The provision does not apply to months beginning after December 31, 2010.

Survey and report on enhanced health coverage tax credit program

Survey

The provision requires that the Secretary of the Treasury must conduct a biennial survey of eligible individuals containing the following information:

1. In the case of eligible individuals receiving the HCTC (including those participating in the advance payment program (the "HCTC program")) (A) demographic information of such individuals, including income and education levels, (B) satisfaction of such individuals with the enrollment process in the HCTC program, (C) satisfaction of such individuals with available health coverage options under the credit, including level of premiums, benefits, deductibles, cost-sharing requirements, and the adequacy of provider networks, and (D) any other information that the Secretary determines is appropriate.

2. In the case of eligible individuals not receiving the HCTC (A) demographic information on each individual, including income and education levels, (B) whether the individ-

---

[260] In the case of a dependent, the rule applies to the taxpayer to whom the personal exemption deduction under section 151 is allowable.

ual was aware of the HCTC or the HCTC program, (C) the reasons the individual has not enrolled in the HCTC program, including whether such reasons include the burden of process of enrollment and the affordability of coverage, (D) whether the individual has health insurance coverage, and, if so, the source of such coverage, and (E) any other information that the Secretary determines is appropriate.

Not later than December 31 of each year in which a survey described above is conducted (beginning in 2010), the Secretary of Treasury must report to the Committee on Finance and the Committee on Health, Education, Labor, and Pensions of the Senate and the Committee on Ways and Means and the Committee on Education and Labor of the House of Representatives the findings of the most recent survey.

Report

Not later than October 1 of each year (beginning in 2010), the Secretary of Treasury must report to the Committee on Finance and the Committee on Health, Education, Labor, and Pensions of the Senate and the Committee on Ways and Means and the Committee on Education and Labor of the House of Representatives the following information with respect to the most recent taxable year ending before such date:

1. In each State and nationally (A) the total number of eligible individuals and the number of eligible individuals receiving the HCTC, (B) the total number of such eligible individuals who receive an advance payment of the HCTC through the HCTC program, (C) the average length of the time period of participation of eligible individuals in the HCTC program, and (D) the total number of participating eligible individuals in the HCTC program who are enrolled in each category of qualified health insurance with respect to each category of eligible individuals.

2. In each State and nationality, an analysis of (A) the range of monthly health insurance premiums, for self-only coverage and for family coverage, for individuals receiving the benefit of the HCTC and (B) the average and median monthly health insurance premiums, for self-only coverage and for family coverage, for individuals receiving the HCTC with respect to each category of qualified health insurance.

3. In each State and nationally, an analysis of the following information with respect to the health insurance coverage of individuals receiving the HCTC who are enrolled in State-based coverage: (A) deductible amounts, (B) other out-of-pocket cost-sharing amounts, and (C) a description of any annual or lifetime limits on coverage or any other significant limits on coverage services or benefits. The information must be reported with respect to each category of coverage.

4. In each State and nationally, the gender and average age of eligible individuals who receive the HCTC in each category of qualified health insurance with respect to each category of eligible individuals.

5. The steps taken by the Secretary of the Treasury to increase the participation rates in the HCTC program among eligible individuals, including outreach and enrollment activities.

6. The cost of administering the HCTC program by function, including the cost of subcontractors, and recommendations on ways to reduce the administrative costs, including recommended statutory changes.

7. After consultation with the Secretary of Labor, the number of States applying for and receiving national emergency grants under section 173(f) of the Workforce Investment Act of 1998, the activities funded by such grants on a State-by-State basis, and the time necessary for application approval of such grants.

Other non-revenue provisions

The provision also authorizes appropriations for implementation of the revenue provisions of the provision and provides grants under the Workforce Investment Act of 1998 for purposes related to the HCTC.

GAO study

The provision requires the Comptroller General of the United States to conduct a study regarding the HCTC to be submitted to Congress no later than March 31, 2010. The study is to include an analysis of (1) the administrative costs of the Federal government with respect to the credit and the advance payment of the credit and of providers of qualified health insurance with respect to providing such insurance to eligible individuals and their families, (2) the health status and relative risk status of eligible individuals and qualified family members covered under such insurance, (3) participation in the credit and the advance payment of the credit by eligible individuals and their qualifying family members, including the reasons why such individuals did or did not participate and the effects of the provision on participation, and (4) the extent to which eligible individuals and their qualifying family members obtained health insurance other than qualifying insurance or went without insurance coverage. The provision provides the Comptroller General access to the records within the possession or control of providers of qualified health insurance if determined relevant to the study. The Comptroller General may not disclose the identity of any provider of qualified health insurance or eligible individual in making information available to the public.

Effective Date

The provision is generally effective upon the date of enactment, excepted as otherwise noted above.

[Law at ¶5065, ¶5320, ¶5415, ¶5425, ¶7048, ¶7051, ¶7054, ¶7057, ¶7060, ¶7063, ¶7066 and ¶7069. CCH Explanation at ¶725.]

[¶10,490] Act Sec. 2201. Economic recovery payments to recipients of social security, supplemental security income, railroad retirement benefits, and veterans disability compensation or pension benefits

Conference Report (H. REPT. 111-16)

[Act Sec. 2201]

Current Law

Title II of the Social Security Act authorizes cash benefits for retired and disabled workers and their dependents and survivors under the Old Age and Survivors Insurance (OASI) and Disability Insurance (DI) programs. Title XVI of the Social Security Act authorizes monthly cash benefits for blind and disabled persons and persons age 65 or over who have limited income and resources under the Supplemental Security Income (SSI) program.

The Railroad Retirement Act of 1974 authorizes cash benefits for retired and disabled railroad workers and their dependents and survivors.

Title 38 of the United States Code authorizes cash benefits for certain veterans and their dependents and survivors.

Current law does not authorize any one-time emergency payments for any of these programs.

Under Title II of the Social Security Act, a person is eligible for Social Security benefits only if he or she has insured status as the result of sufficient employment that was covered by the Social Security system and for which Social Security payroll taxes were paid. Federal employees hired before 1983 were covered by the Civil Service Retirement System (CSRS) and, unless they were eligible for the CSRS-Offset or elected to enroll in the Federal Employees Retirement System (FERS), they are not eligible for Social Security benefits on the basis of their federal service. In addition, some state and local government employees are not covered by the Social Security system and thus are not eligible for Social Security benefits on the basis of their public service.

Current law does not authorize any one-time tax credit for government retirees who are not eligible for Social Security benefits.

House Bill

The House bill authorizes a one-time emergency payment to be made to SSI recipients. This payment must be made by the Social Security Administration (SSA) at the earliest practical date and no more than 120 days after enactment of the law. The amount of this one-time emergency payment would be equal to the average monthly amount of federal SSI benefits paid to an individual (approximately $456) or a married couple (approximately $637) in the most recent month for which data are available.

To be eligible for the one-time emergency payment, a person must be eligible for an SSI benefit, other than a personal needs allowance, for at least one day during the month of the payment. A person who was eligible for an SSI benefit, other than a personal needs allowance, for at least one day during the two-month period preceding the month of the emergency payment and their SSI eligibility ended during the two-month period solely because their income exceeded the SSI income guidelines is also eligible for the one-time emergency payment.

Only persons who are determined by the Commissioner of Social Security in calendar year 2009 to fall into one of the categories described above are eligible for the emergency payment. Thus, a person who is awarded SSI benefits anytime after 2009 would not be eligible for the emergency payment, even if he or she is awarded benefits retroactive to a date before the date of the emergency payment.

The one-time emergency payment would be protected from garnishment and assignment and would not be considered income in the month of receipt and the following 6 months for the purposes of determining eligibility of the recipient (or the recipient's spouse or family) for any means-tested program funded entirely or in part with federal funds.

The House bill provides an appropriation of such sums as may be necessary to carry out this section, including any administrative costs associated with the payment.

Senate Bill

The Senate bill provides for a one-time economic recovery payment of $300 to adult Social Security (Old Age and Survivors Insurance and Disability Insurance) and Railroad Retirement beneficiaries, Supplemental Security Income (SSI) recipients, and veterans receiving compensation or pension benefits from the Department of Veterans Affairs.

The economic recovery payment would be made by the Secretary of the Treasury after eligible beneficiaries are identified by the Social Security Administration (SSA), the Railroad Retirement Board, and the Department of Veterans Affairs. Payments are to be made at the earliest practicable date and in no event later than 120 days after enactment.

To be eligible for the economic recovery payment, a person must have been during the three-month period prior to the month of the enactment: an adult Social Security Old Age and Survivors Insurance (OASI) or Disability Insurance (DI) beneficiary (including adults eligible for child's benefits on the basis of as disability that began before the age of 22, persons eligible under transitional insured status, and persons eligible under special rules for uninsured persons over the age of 72), an adult Railroad Retirement or disability beneficiary (including dependents, survivors, and disabled adult children), a veterans pension or compensation beneficiary, or an SSI recipient (excluding persons who only receive a personal needs allowance).

The Senate bill requires that economic recovery payment recipients live in the United States or its territories. The Senate bill prohibits any person from receiving more than one economic recovery payment regardless of whether the individual is entitled to, or eligible for, more than one benefit or cash payment under this section.

The Senate bill prohibits the payment of an economic recovery payment to any Social Security beneficiary or person eligible for Social Security benefits paid by the Railroad Retirement Board, or SSI recipient, if, for the most recent month of the three-month period prior to enactment the person's benefits were not payable due to his or her status as a prisoner, inmate in a public institute, illegal alien, or fugitive felon.

The bill prohibits an economic recovery payment to any veterans compensation or pension beneficiary if, for the most recent month of the three-month period prior to enactment, the person's benefits were not payable due to his or her status as a prisoner or fugitive felon. It also prohibits the payment of an economic recovery payment to any person who dies before the date he or she is certified as eligible to receive a payment.

The bill limits the applicability of the economic recovery payments to retroactive beneficiaries by providing that no payment may be made for any reason after December 31, 2010.

The economic recovery payment would not be considered income in the month of receipt and the following 9 months for the purposes of determining eligibility of the recipient (or the recipient's spouse or family) for any means-tested program funded entirely or in part with federal funds. The payment would not be considered income for the purposes of taxation and would be protected from garnishment and assignment. However, the payment could be used to collect debts owed to the federal government. Electronic payments and payments to representative payees and fiduciaries would be authorized.

The Senate bill provides additional appropriations for the period from fiscal year 2009 through fiscal year 2011 in the amounts of: $57,000,000 to the Department of the Treasury; $90,000,000 to the SSA; $1,000,000 to the Railroad Retirement Board; and $7,200,000 to the Department of Veterans Affairs for administrative expenses associated with the one-time economic recovery payment. Of the money appropriated to the Department of Veterans Affairs, $100,000 shall be for the Information Systems Technology Account and $7,100,000 for general expenses related to the administration of the economic recovery payment. It also appropriates to the Department of the Treasury such sums as may be necessary for making economic recovery payments.

The Senate bill provides that the amount of a person's Making Work Pay tax credit authorized by Section 1001 of Division A of the Senate bill would be offset by the amount of any economic recovery payment that person receives.

Conference Agreement

The conference agreement follows the Senate bill, with some modifications. The conference agreement directs the Secretary of the Treasury to disburse a onetime Economic Recovery Payment of $250 to adults who were eligible for Social Security benefits, Railroad Retirement benefits, or veteran's compensation or pension benefits; or individuals who were eligible for Supplemental Security Income (SSI) benefits (excluding individuals who receive SSI while in a Medicaid institution). Only individuals who were eligible for one of the four programs for any of the three months prior to the month of enactment shall receive an Economic Recovery Payment.

The provision stipulates that Economic Recovery Payments will only be made to individuals whose address of record is in 1 of the 50 states, the District of Columbia, Puerto Rico, Guam, the United States Virgin Islands, American Samoa, or the Northern Mariana Islands.

An individual shall only receive one $250 Economic Recovery Payment under this section regardless of whether the individual is eligible for a benefit from more than one of the four federal programs. If the individual is also eligible for the "Making Work Pay" credit from Section 1001, that credit shall be reduced by the Economic Recovery Payment made under this section.

Individuals who are otherwise eligible for an Economic Recovery Payment will not receive a payment if their federal program benefits have been suspended because they are in prison, a fugitive, a probation or parole violator, have committed fraud, or are no longer lawfully present in the United States.

The provision directs the Commissioner of Social Security, the Railroad Retirement Board, and the Secretary of Veterans Affairs to provide the Secretary of the Treasury with information and data to send the payments to eligible individuals and to disburse the payments.

The provision provides that the Economic Recovery Payments shall not be taken into account as income, or taken into account as resources for the month of receipt and the following 9 months, for purposes of determining the eligibility of such individual or any other individual for benefits or assistance, or the amount or extent of benefits or assistance, under any Federal program or under any State or local program financed in whole or in part with Federal funds.

The provision provides that Economic Recovery Payments shall not be considered gross income for income tax purposes and that the payments are protected by the assignment and garnishment provisions of the four federal benefit programs. The payments will be subject to the Treasury Offset Program.

The provision stipulates that if an individual who is eligible for an Economic Recovery Payment has a representative payee, the payment shall be made to the representative payee and the entire payment shall only be used for the benefit of the individual who is entitled to the Economic Recovery Payment.

The provision appropriates the following amounts for FY2009 through FY2011: to the Secretary of the Treasury, $131 million for administrative costs to carry out the provisions of this section and the new Section 36A (the Making Work Pay credit); to the Commissioner of Social Security, such funds as are necessary to make the payments and $90 million to carry out the provisions of this section; to the Railroad Retirement Board, such funds as are necessary to make the payments and $1.4 million to carry out the provisions of this section; and to the Secretary of Veterans Affairs, such funds as are necessary to make the payments, $100,000 for the Information Systems Technology account and $7,100,000 to the General Operating Expenses account.

The Secretary of the Treasury shall commence making payments as soon as possible, but no later than 120 days after the date of enactment. No Economic Recovery Payments shall be made after December 31, 2010.

[Law at ¶7070. CCH Explanation at ¶225.]

Act Sec. 2201　¶10,490

[¶ 10,500] Act Sec. 2202. Special credit for certain government retirees

Conference Report (H. Rept. 111-16)

[Act Sec. 2202]

Current Law

No provision.

House Bill

No provision.

Senate Bill

No provision.

Conference Agreement

The conference agreement creates a $250 credit ($500 for a joint return where both spouses are eligible) against income taxes owed for tax year 2009 for individuals who receive a government pension or annuity from work not covered by Social Security, and were not eligible to receive a payment under section 2201. If the individual is also eligible for the "Making Work Pay" credit from Section 1001, that credit shall be reduced by the credit made under this section.

Each tax return on which this credit is claimed must include the social security number of the taxpayer (in the case of a joint return, the social security number of at least one spouse). The provision states that the credit under this section shall be a refundable credit.

The provision provides that any credit or refund allowed or made by this provision shall not be taken into account as income and shall not be taken into account as resources for the month of receipt and the following two months for purposes of determining the eligibility of such individual or any other individual for benefits or assistance, or the amount or extent of benefits or assistance, under any Federal program or under any State or local program financed in whole or in part with Federal funds.

The provision is effective on the date of enactment.

[Law at ¶ 7071. CCH Explanation at ¶ 325.]

[¶ 10,510] Act Sec. 3001. Assistance for COBRA continuation coverage

Conference Report (H. Rept. 111-16)

[Code Sec. 4980B and New Code Secs. 139C, 6432 and 6720C]

Present Law

In general

The Code contains rules that require certain group health plans to offer certain individuals ("qualified beneficiaries") the opportunity to continue to participate for a specified period of time in the group health plan ("continuation coverage") after the occurrence of certain events that otherwise would have terminated such participation ("qualifying events").[228] These continuation coverage rules are often referred to as "COBRA continuation coverage" or "COBRA," which is a reference to the acronym for the law that added the continuation coverage rules to the Code.[229]

The Code imposes an excise tax on a group health plan if it fails to comply with the COBRA continuation coverage rules with respect to a qualified beneficiary. The excise tax with respect to a qualified beneficiary generally is equal to $100 for each day in the noncompliance period with respect to the failure. A plan's noncompliance period generally begins on the date the failure first occurs and ends when the failure is corrected. Special rules apply that limit the amount of the excise tax if the failure would not have been discovered despite the exercise of reasonable diligence or if the failure is due to reasonable cause and not willful neglect.

---

[228] Sec. 4980B.

[229] The COBRA rules were added to the Code by the Consolidated Omnibus Budget Reconciliation Act of 1985, Pub. L. No. 99-272. The rules were originally added as Code sections 162(i) and (k). The rules were later restated as Code section 4980B, pursuant to the Technical and Miscellaneous Revenue Act of 1988, Pub. L. No. 100-647.

¶ 10,500 Act Sec. 2202

In the case of a multiemployer plan, the excise tax generally is imposed on the group health plan. A multiemployer plan is a plan to which more than one employer is required to contribute, that is maintained pursuant to one or more collective bargaining agreements between one or more employee organizations and more than one employer, and that satisfies such other requirements as the Secretary of Labor may prescribe by regulation. In the case of a plan other than a multiemployer plan (a "single employer plan"), the excise tax generally is imposed on the employer.

Plans subject to COBRA

A group health plan is defined as a plan of, or contributed to by, an employer (including a self-employed person) or employee organization to provide health care (directly or otherwise) to the employees, former employees, the employer, and others associated or formerly associated with the employer in a business relationship, or their families. A group health plan includes a self-insured plan. The term group health plan does not, however, include a plan under which substantially all of the coverage is for qualified long-term care services.

The following types of group health plans are not subject to the Code's COBRA rules: (1) a plan established and maintained for its employees by a church or by a convention or association of churches which is exempt from tax under section 501 (a "church plan"); (2) a plan established and maintained for its employees by the Federal government, the government of any State or political subdivision thereof, or by any instrumentality of the foregoing (a "governmental plan");[230] and (3) a plan maintained by an employer that normally employed fewer than 20 employees on a typical business day during the preceding calendar year[231] (a "small employer plan").

Qualifying events and qualified beneficiaries

A qualifying event that gives rise to COBRA continuation coverage includes, with respect to any covered employee, the following events which would result in a loss of coverage of a qualified beneficiary under a group health plan (but for COBRA continuation coverage): (1) death of the covered employee; (2) the termination (other than by reason of such employee's gross misconduct), or a reduction in hours, of the covered employee's employment; (3) divorce or legal separation of the covered employee; (4) the covered employee becoming entitled to Medicare benefits under title XVIII of the Social Security Act; (5) a dependent child ceasing to be a dependent child under the generally applicable requirements of the plan; and (6) a proceeding in a case under the U.S. Bankruptcy Code commencing on or after July 1, 1986, with respect to the employer from whose employment the covered employee retired at any time.

A "covered employee" is an individual who is (or was) provided coverage under the group health plan on account of the performance of services by the individual for one or more persons maintaining the plan and includes a self-employed individual. A "qualified beneficiary" means, with respect to a covered employee, any individual who on the day before the qualifying event for the employee is a beneficiary under the group health plan as the spouse or dependent child of the employee. The term qualified beneficiary also includes the covered employee in the case of a qualifying event that is a termination of employment or reduction in hours.

Continuation coverage requirements

Continuation coverage that must be offered to qualified beneficiaries pursuant to COBRA must consist of coverage which, as of the time coverage is being provided, is identical to the coverage provided under the plan to similarly situated non-COBRA beneficiaries under the plan with respect to whom a qualifying event has not occurred. If coverage under a plan is modified for any group of similarly situated non-COBRA beneficiaries, the coverage must also be modified in the same manner for qualified beneficiaries. Similarly situated non-COBRA beneficiaries means the group of covered employees, spouses of covered employees, or dependent children of covered employees who (i) are receiving coverage under the group health plan for a reason other than pursuant to COBRA, and (ii) are the most similarly situated to the situation of the qualified beneficiary immediately before the qualifying event, based on all of the facts and circumstances.

The maximum required period of continuation coverage for a qualified beneficiary (i.e., the minimum period for which continuation cover-

---

[230] A governmental plan also includes certain plans established by an Indian tribal government.

[231] If the plan is a multiemployer plan, then each of the employers contributing to the plan for a calendar year must normally employ fewer than 20 employees during the preceding calendar year.

Act Sec. 3001 ¶10,510

age must be offered) depends upon a number of factors, including the specific qualifying event that gives rise to a qualified beneficiary's right to elect continuation coverage. In the case of a qualifying event that is the termination, or reduction of hours, of a covered employee's employment, the minimum period of coverage that must be offered to the qualified beneficiary is coverage for the period beginning with the loss of coverage on account of the qualifying event and ending on the date that is 18 months[232] after the date of the qualifying event. If coverage under a plan is lost on account of a qualifying event but the loss of coverage actually occurs at a later date, the minimum coverage period may be extended by the plan so that it is measured from the date when coverage is actually lost.

The minimum coverage period for a qualified beneficiary generally ends upon the earliest to occur of the following events: (1) the date on which the employer ceases to provide any group health plan to any employee, (2) the date on which coverage ceases under the plan by reason of a failure to make timely payment of any premium required with respect to the qualified beneficiary, and (3) the date on which the qualified beneficiary first becomes (after the date of election of continuation coverage) either (i) covered under any other group health plan (as an employee or otherwise) which does not include any exclusion or limitation with respect to any preexisting condition of such beneficiary or (ii) entitled to Medicare benefits under title XVIII of the Social Security Act. Mere eligibility for another group health plan or Medicare benefits is not sufficient to terminate the minimum coverage period. Instead, the qualified beneficiary must be actually covered by the other group health plan or enrolled in Medicare. Coverage under another group health plan or enrollment in Medicare does not terminate the minimum coverage period if such other coverage or Medicare enrollment begins on or before the date that continuation coverage is elected.

Election of continuation coverage

The COBRA rules specify a minimum election period under which a qualified beneficiary is entitled to elect continuation coverage. The election period begins not later than the date on which coverage under the plan terminates on account of the qualifying event, and ends not earlier than the later of 60 days or 60 days after notice is given to the qualified beneficiary of the qualifying event and the beneficiary's election rights.

Notice requirements

A group health plan is required to give a general notice of COBRA continuation coverage rights to employees and their spouses at the time of enrollment in the group health plan.

An employer is required to give notice to the plan administrator of certain qualifying events (including a loss of coverage on account of a termination of employment or reduction in hours) generally within 30 days of the qualifying event. A covered employee or qualified beneficiary is required to give notice to the plan administrator of certain qualifying events within 60 days after the event. The qualifying events giving rise to an employee or beneficiary notification requirement are the divorce or legal separation of the covered employee or a dependent child ceasing to be a dependent child under the terms of the plan. Upon receiving notice of a qualifying event from the employer, covered employee, or qualified beneficiary, the plan administrator is then required to give notice of COBRA continuation coverage rights within 14 days to all qualified beneficiaries with respect to the event.

Premiums

A plan may require payment of a premium for any period of continuation coverage. The amount of such premium generally may not exceed 102 percent[233] of the "applicable premium" for such period and the premium must be payable, at the election of the payor, in monthly installments.

The applicable premium for any period of continuation coverage means the cost to the plan for such period of coverage for similarly situated non-COBRA beneficiaries with respect to whom a qualifying event has not occurred, and is determined without regard to whether the cost is paid by the employer or employee. The determination of any applicable premium is made for a period of 12 months (the "determination period") and is

---

[232] In the case of a qualified beneficiary who is determined, under Title II or XVI of the Social Security Act, to have been disabled during the first 60 days of continuation coverage, the 18 month minimum coverage period is extended to 29 months with respect to all qualified beneficiaries if notice is given before the end of the initial 18 month continuation coverage period.

[233] In the case of a qualified beneficiary whose minimum coverage period is extended to 29 months on account of a disability determination, the premium for the period of the disability extension may not exceed 150 percent of the applicable premium for the period.

required to be made before the beginning of such 12 month period.

In the case of a self-insured plan, the applicable premium for any period of continuation coverage of qualified beneficiaries is equal to a reasonable estimate of the cost of providing coverage during such period for similarly situated non-COBRA beneficiaries which is determined on an actuarial basis and takes into account such factors as the Secretary of Treasury prescribes in regulations. A self-insured plan may elect to determine the applicable premium on the basis of an adjusted cost to the plan for similarly situated non-COBRA beneficiaries during the preceding determination period.

A plan may not require payment of any premium before the day which is 45 days after the date on which the qualified beneficiary made the initial election for continuation coverage. A plan is required to treat any required premium payment as timely if it is made within 30 days after the date the premium is due or within such longer period as applies to, or under, the plan.

Other continuation coverage rules

Continuation coverage rules which are parallel to the Code's continuation coverage rules apply to group health plans under the Employee Retirement Income Security Act of 1974 (ERISA).[234] ERISA generally permits the Secretary of Labor and plan participants to bring a civil action to obtain appropriate equitable relief to enforce the continuation coverage rules of ERISA, and in the case of a plan administrator who fails to give timely notice to a participant or beneficiary with respect to COBRA continuation coverage, a court may hold the plan administrator liable to the participant or beneficiary in the amount of up to $110 a day from the date of such failure.

Although the Federal government and State and local governments are not subject to the Code and ERISA's continuation coverage rules, other laws impose similar continuation coverage requirements with respect to plans maintained by such governmental employers.[235] In addition, many States have enacted laws or promulgated regulations that provide continuation coverage rights that are similar to COBRA continuation coverage rights in the case of a loss of group health coverage. Such State laws, for example, may apply in the case of a loss of coverage under a group health plan maintained by a small employer.

House Bill

Reduced COBRA premium

The provision provides that, for a period not exceeding 12 months, an assistance eligible individual is treated as having paid any premium required for COBRA continuation coverage under a group health plan if the individual pays 35 percent of the premium.[236] Thus, if the assistance eligible individual pays 35 percent of the premium, the group health plan must treat the individual as having paid the full premium required for COBRA continuation coverage, and the individual is entitled to a subsidy for 65 percent of the premium. An assistance eligible individual is any qualified beneficiary who elects COBRA continuation coverage and satisfies two additional requirements. First, the qualifying event with respect to the covered employee for that qualified beneficiary must be a loss of group health plan coverage on account of an involuntary termination of the covered employee's employment. However, a termination of employment for gross misconduct does not qualify (since such a termination under present law does not qualify for COBRA continuation coverage). Second, the qualifying event must occur during the period beginning September 1, 2008 and ending with December 31, 2009 and the qualified beneficiary must be eligible for COBRA continuation coverage during that period and elect such coverage.

An assistance eligible individual can be any qualified beneficiary associated with the relevant covered employee (e.g., a dependent of an employee who is covered immediately prior to a qualifying event), and such qualified beneficiary can independently elect COBRA (as provided under present law COBRA rules) and independently receive a subsidy. Thus, the subsidy for

---

[234] Secs. 601 to 608 of ERISA.

[235] Continuation coverage rights similar to COBRA continuation coverage rights are provided to individuals covered by health plans maintained by the Federal government. 5 U.S.C. sec. 8905a. Group health plans maintained by a State that receives funds under Chapter 6A of Title 42 of the United States Code (the Public Health Service Act) are required to provide continuation coverage rights similar to COBRA continuation coverage rights for individuals covered by plans maintained by such State (and plans maintained by political subdivisions of such State and agencies and instrumentalities of such State or political subdivision of such State). 42 U.S.C. sec. 300bb-1.

[236] For this purpose, payment by an assistance eligible individual includes payment by another individual paying on behalf of the individual, such as a parent or guardian, or an entity paying on behalf of the individual, such as a State agency or charity. Further, the amount of the premium used to calculate the reduced premium is the premium amount that the employee would be required to pay for COBRA continuation coverage absent this premium reduction (e.g. 102 percent of the "applicable premium" for such period).

Act Sec. 3001   ¶10,510

an assistance eligible individual continues after an intervening death of the covered employee.

Under the provision, any subsidy provided is excludible from the gross income of the covered employee and any assistance eligible individuals. However, for purposes of determining the gross income of the employer and any welfare benefit plan of which the group health plan is a part, the amount of the premium reduction is intended to be treated as an employee contribution to the group health plan. Finally, under the provision, notwithstanding any other provision of law, the subsidy is not permitted to be considered as income or resources in determining eligibility for, or the amount of assistance or benefits under, any public benefit provided under Federal or State law (including the law of any political subdivision).

Eligible COBRA continuation coverage

Under the provision, continuation coverage that qualifies for the subsidy is not limited to coverage required to be offered under the Code's COBRA rules but also includes continuation coverage required under State law that requires continuation coverage comparable to the continuation coverage required under the Code's COBRA rules for group health plans not subject to those rules (e.g., a small employer plan) and includes continuation coverage requirements that apply to health plans maintained by the Federal government or a State government. Comparable continuation coverage under State law does not include every State law right to continue health coverage, such as a right to continue coverage with no rules that limit the maximum premium that can be charged with respect to such coverage. To be comparable, the right generally must be to continue substantially similar coverage as was provided under the group health plan (or substantially similar coverage as is provided to similarly situated beneficiaries) at a monthly cost that is based on a specified percentage of the group health plan's cost of providing such coverage.

The cost of coverage under any group health plan that is subject to the Code's COBRA rules (or comparable State requirements or continuation coverage requirement under health plans maintained by the Federal government or any State government) is eligible for the subsidy, except contributions to a health flexible spending account.

Termination of eligibility for reduced premiums

The assistance eligible individual's eligibility for the subsidy terminates with the first month beginning on or after the earlier of (1) the date which is 12 months after the first day of the first month for which the subsidy applies, (2) the end of the maximum required period of continuation coverage for the qualified beneficiary under the Code's COBRA rules or the relevant State or Federal law (or regulation), or (3) the date that the assistance eligible individual becomes eligible for Medicare benefits under title XVIII of the Social Security Act or health coverage under another group health plan (including, for example, a group health plan maintained by the new employer of the individual or a plan maintained by the employer of the individual's spouse). However, eligibility for coverage under another group health plan does not terminate eligibility for the subsidy if the other group health plan provides only dental, vision, counseling, or referral services (or a combination of the foregoing), is a health flexible spending account or health reimbursement arrangement, or is coverage for treatment that is furnished in an on-site medical facility maintained by the employer and that consists primarily of first-aid services, prevention and wellness care, or similar care (or a combination of such care).

If a qualified beneficiary paying a reduced premium for COBRA continuation coverage under this provision becomes eligible for coverage under another group health plan or Medicare, the provision requires the qualified beneficiary to notify, in writing, the group health plan providing the COBRA continuation coverage with the reduced premium of such eligibility under the other plan or Medicare. The notification by the assistance eligible individual must be provided to the group health plan in the time and manner as is specified by the Secretary of Labor. If an assistance eligible individual fails to provide this notification at the required time and in the required manner, and as a result the individual's COBRA continuation coverage continues to be subsidized after the termination of the individual's eligibility for such subsidy, a penalty is imposed on the individual equal to 110 percent of the subsidy provided after termination of eligibility.

This penalty only applies if the subsidy in the form of the premium reduction is actually provided to a qualified beneficiary for a month that the beneficiary is not eligible for the reduction. Thus, for example, if a qualified beneficiary becomes eligible for coverage under another group health plan and stops paying the reduced COBRA continuation premium, the penalty generally will not apply. As discussed below, under the provision, the group health plan is reimbursed for the subsidy for a month (65 percent of the amount of the premium for the month) only after receipt of the qualified beneficiary's portion (35 percent of the premium amount). Thus, the penalty generally will only arise when the qualified beneficiary continues to pay the reduced premium and does not notify the group health plan providing COBRA continuation coverage of the beneficiary's eligibility under another group health plan or Medicare.

Special COBRA election opportunity

The provision provides a special 60 day election period for a qualified beneficiary who is eligible for a reduced premium and who has not elected COBRA continuation coverage as of the date of enactment. The 60 day election period begins on the date that notice is provided to the qualified beneficiary of the special election period. However, this special election period does not extend the period of COBRA continuation coverage beyond the original maximum required period (generally 18 months after the qualifying event) and any COBRA continuation coverage elected pursuant to this special election period begins on the date of enactment and does not include any period prior to that date. Thus, for example, if a covered employee involuntarily terminated employment on September 10, 2008, but did not elect COBRA continuation coverage and was not eligible for coverage under another group health plan, the employee would have 60 days after date of notification of this new election right to elect the coverage and receive the subsidy. If the employee made the election, the coverage would begin with the date of enactment and would not include any period prior to that date. However, the coverage would not be required to last for 18 months. Instead the maximum required COBRA continuation coverage period would end not later than 18 months after September 10, 2008.

The special enrollment provision applies to a group health plan that is subject to the COBRA continuation coverage requirements of the Code, ERISA, Title 5 of the United States Code (relating to plans maintained by the Federal government), or the Public Health Service Act ("PHSA").

With respect to an assistance eligible individual who elects coverage pursuant to the special election period, the period beginning on the date of the qualifying event and ending with the day before the date of enactment is disregarded for purposes of the rules that limit the group health plan from imposing pre-existing condition limitations with respect to the individual's coverage.[237]

Reimbursement of group health plans

The provision provides that the entity to which premiums are payable (determined under the applicable COBRA continuation coverage requirement)[238] shall be reimbursed by the amount of the premium for COBRA continuation coverage that is not paid by an assistance eligible individual on account of the premium reduction. An entity is not eligible for subsidy reimbursement, however, until the entity has received the reduced premium payment from the assistance eligible individual. To the extent that such entity has liability for income tax withholding from wages[239] or FICA taxes[240] with respect to its employees, the entity is reimbursed by treating the amount that is reimbursable to the entity as a credit against its liability for these payroll taxes.[241] To the extent that such amount exceeds the amount of the entity's liability for these payroll taxes, the Secretary shall reimburse the entity for the excess directly. The provision requires any entity entitled to such reimbursement to submit such reports as the Secretary of Treasury may require, including an attestation of the involuntary termination of employment of each covered employee on the basis of whose termination entitlement to reimbursement of premiums is claimed, and a report of the amount of payroll taxes offset for a reporting period and the estimated offsets of such taxes for the next reporting period. This report is required to be

---

[237] Section 9801 provides that a group health plan may impose a pre-existing condition exclusion for no more than 12 months after a participant or beneficiary's enrollment date. Such 12-month period must be reduced by the aggregate period of creditable coverage (which includes periods of coverage under another group health plan). A period of creditable coverage can be disregarded if, after the coverage period and before the enrollment date, there was a 63-day period during which the individual was not covered under any creditable coverage. Similar rules are provided under ERISA and PHSA.

[238] Applicable continuation coverage that qualifies for the subsidy and thus for reimbursement is not limited to coverage required to be offered under the Code's COBRA rules but also includes continuation coverage required under State law that requires continuation coverage comparable to the continuation coverage required under the Code's COBRA rules for group health plans not subject to those rules (e.g., a small employer plan) and includes continuation coverage requirements that apply to health plans maintained by the Federal government or a State government.

[239] Sec. 3401.

[240] Sec. 3102 (relating to FICA taxes applicable to employees) and sec. 3111 (relating to FICA taxes applicable to employers).

[241] In determining any amount transferred or appropriated to any fund under the Social Security Act, amounts credited against an employer's payroll tax obligations pursuant to the provision shall not be taken into account.

provided at the same time as the deposits of the payroll taxes would have been required, absent the offset, or such times as the Secretary specifies.

Notice requirements

The notice of COBRA continuation coverage that a plan administrator is required to provide to qualified beneficiaries with respect to a qualifying event under present law must contain, under the provision, additional information including, for example, information about the qualified beneficiary's right to the premium reduction (and subsidy) and the conditions on the subsidy, and a description of the obligation of the qualified beneficiary to notify the group health plan of eligibility under another group health plan or eligibility for Medicare benefits under title XVIII of the Social Security Act, and the penalty for failure to provide this notification. The provision also requires a new notice to be given to qualified beneficiaries entitled to a special election period after enactment. In the case of group health plans that are not subject to the COBRA continuation coverage requirements of the Code, ERISA, Title 5 of the United States Code (relating to plans maintained by the Federal government), or PHSA, the provision requires that notice be given to the relevant employees and beneficiaries as well, as specified by the Secretary of Labor. Within 30 days after enactment, the Secretary of Labor is directed to provide model language for the additional notification required under the provision. The provision also provides an expedited 10-day review process by the Department of Labor, under which an individual may request review of a denial of treatment as an assistance eligible individual by a group health plan.

Regulatory authority

The provision provides authority to the Secretary of the Treasury to issue regulations or other guidance as may be necessary or appropriate to carry out the provision, including any reporting requirements or the establishment of other methods for verifying the correct amounts of payments and credits under the provision. For example, the Secretary of the Treasury might require verification on the return of an assistance eligible individual who is the covered employee that the individual's termination of employment was involuntary. The provision directs the Secretary of the Treasury to issue guidance or regulations addressing the reimbursement of the subsidy in the case of a multiemployer group health plan. The provision also provides authority to the Secretary of the Treasury to promulgate rules, procedures, regulations, and other guidance as is necessary and appropriate to prevent fraud and abuse in the subsidy program, including the employment tax offset mechanism.

Reports

The provision requires the Secretary of the Treasury to submit an interim and a final report regarding the implementation of the premium reduction provision. The interim report is to include information about the number of individuals receiving assistance, and the total amount of expenditures incurred, as of the date of the report. The final report, to be issued as soon as practicable after the last period of COBRA continuation coverage for which premiums are provided, is to include similar information as provided in the interim report, with the addition of information about the average dollar amount (monthly and annually) of premium reductions provided to such individuals. The reports are to be given to the Committee on Ways and Means, the Committee on Energy and Commerce, the Committee on Health Education, Labor and Pensions and the Committee on Finance.

Effective date

The provision is effective for premiums for months of coverage beginning on or after the date of enactment. However, it is intended that a group health plan will not fail to satisfy the requirements for COBRA continuation coverage merely because the plan accepts payment of 100 percent of the premium from an assistance eligible employee during the first two months beginning on or after the date of enactment while the premium reduction is being implemented, provided the amount of the resulting premium overpayment is credited against the individual's premium (35 percent of the premium) for future months or the overpayment is otherwise repaid to the employee as soon as practical.

Senate Amendment

The Senate amendment is the same as the House bill with certain modifications. The amount of the COBRA the premium reduction (or subsidy) is 50 percent of the required premium under the Senate amendment (rather than 65 percent as provided under the House bill).

In addition, a group health plan is permitted to provide a special enrollment right to assistance-eligible individuals to allow them to change coverage options under the plan in conjunction with electing COBRA continuation coverage. Under this special enrollment right, the assistance eligible individual must only be offered the option to change to any coverage option offered to employed workers that provides the same or lower health insurance premiums than the individual's group health plan coverage as of the date of the covered employee's qualifying event. If the individual elects a different coverage option under this special enrollment right in conjunction with electing COBRA continuation coverage, this is the coverage that must be provided for purposes of satisfying the COBRA continuation coverage requirement. However the coverage plan option into which the individual must be given the opportunity to enroll under this special enrollment right does not include the following: a coverage option providing only dental, vision, counseling, or referral services (or a combination of the foregoing); a health flexible spending account or health reimbursement arrangement; or coverage for treatment that is furnished in an on-site medical facility maintained by the employer and that consists primarily of first-aid services, prevention and wellness care, or similar care (or a combination of such care).

Effective date

The provision is effective for months of coverage beginning after the date of enactment. In addition, the Senate amendment specifically provides rules for reimbursement of an assistance eligible individual if such individual pays 100 percent of the premium required for COBRA continuation coverage for any month during the 60-day period beginning on the first day of the first month after the date of enactment. The person who receives the premium overpayment is permitted to provide a credit to the assistance eligible individual for the amount overpaid against one or more subsequent premiums (subject to the 50 percent payment rule) for COBRA continuation coverage, but only if it is reasonable to believe that the credit for the excess will be used by the assistance eligible individual within 180 days of the individual's overpayment. Otherwise, the person must make a reimbursement payment to the individual for the amount of the premium overpayment within 60 days of receiving the overpayment. Further, if as of any day during the 180-day period it is no longer reasonable to believe that the credit will be used during that period by the assistance eligible individual (e.g., the individual ceases to be eligible for COBRA continuation coverage), payment equal to the remainder of the credit outstanding must be made to the individual within 60 days of such day.

Conference Agreement

In general

The conference agreement generally follows the House bill. Thus, as under the House bill, the rate of the premium subsidy is 65 percent of the premium for a period of coverage. However, the period of the premium subsidy is limited to a maximum of 9 months of coverage (instead of a maximum of 12 months). As under the House bill and Senate amendment, the premium subsidy is only provided with respect to involuntary terminations that occur on or after September 1, 2008, and before January 1, 2010.

The conference agreement includes the provision in the Senate amendment that permits a group health plan to provide a special enrollment right to assistance eligible individuals to allow them to change coverage options under the plan in conjunction with electing COBRA continuation coverage.[242] This provision only allows a group health plan to offer additional coverage options to assistance eligible individuals and does not change the basic requirement under Federal COBRA continuation coverage requirements that a group health plan must allow an assistance eligible individual to choose to continue with the coverage in which the individual is enrolled as of the qualifying event.[243] However, once the election of the other coverage is made, it becomes COBRA continuation coverage under the applicable COBRA continuation provisions, Thus, for example, under the Federal COBRA continuation coverage provisions, if a covered employee chooses different coverage pursuant to being provided this option, the different coverage elected must generally be permitted to be continued for the applicable required period (generally 18 months or 36 months, absent an event that permits coverage to be terminated under the Federal COBRA continuation provisions) even though the premium subsidy is only for nine months.

The conference agreement adds an income threshold as an additional condition on an individual's entitlement to the premium subsidy during any taxable year. The income threshold applies based on the modified adjusted gross

---

[242] An employer can make this option available to covered employees under current law.

[243] All references to "Federal COBRA continuation coverage" mean the COBRA continuation coverage provisions of the Code, ERISA, and PHSA.

income for an individual income tax return for the taxable year in which the subsidy is received (i.e., either 2009 or 2010) with respect to which the assistance eligible individual is the taxpayer, the taxpayer's spouse or a dependent of the taxpayer (within the meaning of section 152 of the Code, determined without regard to sections 152(b)(1), (b)(2) and (d)(1)(B)). Modified adjusted gross income for this purpose means adjusted gross income as defined in section 62 of the Code increased by any amount excluded from gross income under section 911, 931, or 933 of the Code. Under this income threshold, if the premium subsidy is provided with respect to any COBRA continuation coverage which covers the taxpayer, the taxpayer's spouse, or any dependent of the taxpayer during a taxable year and the taxpayer's modified adjusted gross income exceeds $145,000 (or $290,000 for joint filers), then the amount of the premium subsidy for all months during the taxable year must be repaid. The mechanism for repayment is an increase in the taxpayer's income tax liability for the year equal to such amount. For taxpayers with adjusted gross income between $125,000 and $145,000 (or $250,000 and $290,000 for joint filers), the amount of the premium subsidy for the taxable year that must be repaid is reduced proportionately.

Under this income threshold, for example, an assistance eligible individual who is eligible for Federal COBRA continuation coverage based on the involuntary termination of a covered employee in August 2009 but who is not entitled to the premium subsidy for the periods of coverage during 2009 due to having income above the threshold, may nevertheless be entitled to the premium subsidy for any periods of coverage in the remaining period (e.g. 5 months of coverage) during 2010 to which the subsidy applies if the modified adjusted gross income for 2010 of the relevant taxpayer is not above the income threshold.

The conference report allows an individual to make a permanent election (at such time and in such form as the Secretary of Treasury may prescribe) to waive the right to the premium subsidy for all periods of coverage. For the election to take effect, the individual must notify the entity (to which premiums are reimbursed under section 6432(a) of the Code) of the election. This waiver provision allows an assistance eligible individual who is certain that the modified adjusted gross income limit prevents the individual from being entitled to any premium subsidy for any coverage period to decline the subsidy for all coverage periods and avoid being subject to the recapture tax. However, this waiver applies to all periods of coverage (regardless of the tax year of the coverage) for which the individual might be entitled to the subsidy. The premium subsidy for any period of coverage cannot later be claimed as a tax credit or otherwise be recovered, even if the individual later determines that the income threshold was not exceeded for a relevant tax year. This waiver is made separately by each qualified beneficiary (who could be an assistance eligible individual) with respect to a covered employee.

Technical changes

The conference agreement makes a number of technical changes to the COBRA premium subsidy provisions in the House bill. The conference agreement clarifies that a reference to a period of coverage in the provision is a reference to the monthly or shorter period of coverage with respect to which premiums are charged with respect to such coverage. For example, the provision is effective for a period of coverage beginning after the date of enactment. In the case of a plan that provides and charges for COBRA continuation coverage on a calendar month basis, the provision is effective for the first calendar month following date of enactment.

The conference agreement specifically provides that if a person other than the individual's employer pays on the individual's behalf then the individual is treated as paying 35 percent of the premium, as required to be entitled to the premium subsidy. Thus, the conference agreement makes clear that, for this purpose, payment by an assistance eligible individual includes payment by another individual paying on behalf of the individual, such as a parent or guardian, or an entity paying on behalf of the individual, such as a State agency or charity.

The conference agreement clarifies that, for the special 60 day election period for a qualified beneficiary who is eligible for a reduced premium and who has not elected COBRA continuation coverage as of the date of enactment provided in the House bill, the election period begins on the date of enactment and ends 60 days after the notice is provided to the qualified beneficiary of the special election period. In addition, the conference agreement clarifies that coverage elected under this special election right begins with the first period of coverage beginning on or after the date of enactment. The conference agreement also extends this special COBRA election opportunity to a qualified beneficiary who elected COBRA coverage but who is no longer enrolled on the date of enactment, for example, because the beneficiary was unable to continue paying the premium.

The conference agreement clarifies that a violation of the new notice requirements is also a violation of the notice requirements of the underlying COBRA provision. As under the House bill, a notice must be provided to all individuals who terminated employment during the applicable time period, and not just to individuals who were involuntarily terminated.

As under the House bill, coverage under a flexible spending account ("FSA") is not eligible for the subsidy. The conference agreement clarifies that a FSA is defined as a health flexible spending account offered under a cafeteria plan within the meaning of section 125 of the Code.[244]

As under the House bill, there is a provision for expedited review, by the Secretary of Labor or Health and Human Services (in consultation with the Secretary of the Treasury), of denials of the premium subsidy. Under the conference agreement, such reviews must be completed within 15 business days (rather than 10 business days as provided in the House bill) after receipt of the individual's application for review. The conference agreement is intended to give the Secretaries the flexibility necessary to make determinations within 15 business days based upon evidence they believe, in their discretion, to be appropriate. Additionally, the conference agreement intends that, if an individual is denied treatment as an assistance eligible individual and also submits a claim for benefits to the plan that would be denied by reason of not being eligible for Federal COBRA continuation coverage (or failure to pay full premiums), the individual would be eligible to proceed with expedited review irrespective of any claims for benefits that may be pending or subject to review under the provisions of ERISA 503. Under the conference agreement, either Secretary's determination upon review is de novo and is the final determination of such Secretary.

The conference agreement clarifies the reimbursement mechanism for the premium subsidy in several respects. First, it clarifies that the person to whom the reimbursement is payable is either (1) the multiemployer group health plan, (2) the employer maintaining the group health plan subject to Federal COBRA continuation coverage requirements, and (3) the insurer providing coverage under an insured plan. Thus, this is the person who is eligible to offset its payroll taxes for purposes of reimbursement. It also clarifies that the credit for the reimbursement is treated as a payment of payroll taxes. Thus, it clarifies that any reimbursement for an amount in excess of the payroll taxes owed is treated in the same manner as a tax refund. Similarly, it clarifies that overstatement of reimbursement is a payroll tax violation. For example, IRS can assert appropriate penalties for failing to truthfully account for the reimbursement. However, it is not intended that any portion of the reimbursement is taken into account when determining the amount of any penalty to be imposed against any person, required to collect, truthfully account for, and pay over any tax under section 6672 of the Code.

It is intended that reimbursement not be mirrored in the U.S. possessions that have mirror income tax codes (the Commonwealth of the Northern Mariana Islands, Guam, and the Virgin Islands). Rather, the intent of Congress is that reimbursement will have direct application to persons in those possessions. Moreover, it is intended that income tax withholding payable to the government of any possession (American Samoa, the Commonwealth of the Northern Mariana Islands, the Commonwealth of Puerto Rico, Guam, or the Virgin Islands) (in contrast with FICA withholding payable to the U.S. Treasury) will not be reduced as a result of the application of this provision. A person liable for both FICA withholding payable to the U.S. Treasury and income tax withholding payable to a possession government will be credited or refunded any excess of (1) the amount of FICA taxes treated as paid under the reimbursement rule of the provision over (2) the amount of the person's liability for those FICA taxes.

Effective date

The provision is effective for periods of coverage beginning after the date of enactment. In addition, specific rules are provided in the case of an assistance eligible individual who pays 100 percent of the premium required for COBRA continuation coverage for any coverage period during the 60-day period beginning on the first day of the first coverage period after the date of enactment. Such rules follow the Senate amendment.

[Law at ¶5065, ¶5215, ¶5395, ¶5410 and ¶7072. CCH Explanation at ¶705.]

---

[244] Other FSA coverage does not terminate eligibility for coverage. Coverage under another group Health Reimbursement Account ("HRA") will not terminate an individual's eligibility for the subsidy as long as the HRA is properly classified as an FSA under relevant IRS guidance. See Notice 2002-45, 2002-2 CB 93.

Act Sec. 3001   ¶10,510

[¶ 10,520] Act Sec. 7001. Executive compensation oversight

Conference Report (H. Rept. 111-16)

[Act Sec. 7001]

Present Law

An employer generally may deduct reasonable compensation for personal services as an ordinary and necessary business expense. Section 162(m) (relating to remuneration expenses for certain executives that are in excess of $1 million) and section 280G (relating to excess parachute payments) provide explicit limitations on the deductibility of certain compensation expenses in the case of corporate employers, and section 4999 imposes an additional tax of 20 percent on the recipient of an excess parachute payment. The Emergency Economic Stabilization Act of 2008 ("EESA") limits the amount of payments that may be deducted as reasonable compensation by certain financial institutions ("TARP recipients") that receive financial assistance from the United States pursuant to the troubled asset relief program ("TARP") established under EESA by modifying the section 162(m) and section 280G limits. EESA also provided non-tax rules relating to the compensation that is payable by such a financial institution (the "TARP executive compensation rules").

House Bill

No provision.

Senate Amendment

The provision modifies and expands the present law non-tax TARP executive compensation rules. The modifications include: (1) expanding the requirement of recovery of a bonus, retention award, or incentive compensation paid to a senior executive officer based on statements of earnings, revenues, gains, or other criteria that are found to be materially inaccurate to the next 20 most highly compensated employees of a TARP recipient; (2) expanding the prohibition on the payment of golden parachute payments from senior executive officers to the next five most highly compensated employees of the TARP recipient, and defining the term "golden parachute payment" as any payment to a senior executive officer for departure from a company for any reason, except for payments for services performed or benefits accrued; and (3) prohibiting a TARP recipient from paying or accruing any bonus, retention award, or incentive compensation to at least the 25 most highly compensated employees; and (4) prohibiting any compensation plan that would encourage manipulation of the reported earnings of a TARP recipient to enhance the compensation of any of its employees. The provision also provides rules relating to the compensation committees of TARP recipients, nonbinding shareholder votes on executive compensation payable by a TARP recipient, and the adoption by TARP recipients of policies regarding luxury expenditures such as entertainment, aviation, and office renovation expenses.

Conference Agreement

The conference agreement follows the Senate amendment with several modifications. Among the modifications are (1) a rule that provides that financial assistance under TARP is not treated as outstanding for a period in which the United States only holds warrants to purchase common stock of the TARP recipient; (2) rules that phase-in the restriction on bonuses, retention awards, and other incentive compensation by the amount of financial assistance received by the entity receiving TARP assistance, and that permit compensation to be paid in the form of restricted stock; and (3) and a directive to the Secretary of the Treasury to review compensation paid to senior executive officers and the next 20 most highly compensated employees of an entity receiving TARP assistance before the date of enactment to determine whether such payments were inconsistent with the provision, the TARP, or public interest.

[Law at ¶ 7075. CCH Explanation at ¶ 455.]

Committee Reports

Children's Health Insurance Program Reauthorization Act of 2009

¶15,001 Introduction

The "Children's Health Insurance Program Reauthorization Act of 2009" (P.L.111-3) was passed by Congress and was signed into law on February 4, 2009. The Joint Committee on Taxation prepared a Technical Explanation, JCX-1-09, "Description of the Revenue Provisions of the 'Children's Health Insurance Program Reauthorization Act of 2009,'" which was released on January 13, 2009. This Technical Explanation explains the intent of Congress regarding the provisions of the Act. There was no Conference Report issued for this Act. The Technical Explanation from the Joint Committee on Taxation is included in this section to aid the reader's understanding, but may not be cited as an official House, Senate, or Conference Committee Report accompanying the 2009 Act. At the end of each section, references are provided to the corresponding CCH explanations and Internal Revenue Code provisions. Subscribers to the electronic version can link from these references to the corresponding material. *The pertinent sections of the Technical Explanation appear in Act Section order beginning at ¶15,010.*

¶15,005 Background

The "Children's Health Insurance Program Reauthorization Act of 2009," H.R. 2, was introduced in the House of Representatives, and was referred to several different House Committees, on January 13, 2009. It was passed by the House the next day, January 14, 2009, by a vote of 289 to 139. On that day, the bill was received in the Senate. On January 29, 2009, the bill, with amendment, was passed by the Senate by a vote of 66 to 32. On February 4, 2009, the House approved the bill as amended by the Senate by a vote of 290 to 135. It was presented to the President and signed by him on that day, and was enrolled as Public Law 111-3.

References are to the following report:

- Description of the Revenue Provisions of the "Children's Health Insurance Program Reauthorization Act of 2009" is referred to as Joint Committee on Taxation (J.C.T. Rep. No. JCX-1-09).

[¶ 15,010] Act Sec. 701. Increase excise tax rates on tobacco products and cigarette papers and tubes

Joint Committee on Taxation (J.C.T. Rep. No. JCX-1-09)

[Code Sec. 5701]

Present Law

Rates of excise tax on tobacco products and cigarette papers and tubes

Tobacco products and cigarette papers and tubes manufactured in the United States or imported into the United States are subject to Federal excise tax at the following rates:[2]

- Cigars weighing not more than three pounds per thousand ("small cigars") are taxed at the rate of $1.828 per thousand;

- Cigars weighing more than three pounds per thousand ("large cigars") are taxed at the rate equal to 20.719 percent of the manufacturer's or importer's sales price but not more than $48.75 per thousand;

- Cigarettes weighing not more than three pounds per thousand ("small cigarettes") are taxed at the rate of $19.50 per thousand ($0.39 per pack);

- Cigarettes weighing more than three pounds per thousand ("large cigarettes") are taxed at the rate of $40.95 per thousand, except that, if they measure more than six and one-half inches in length, they are taxed at the rate applicable to small cigarettes, counting each two and three-quarter inches (or fraction thereof) of the length of each as one cigarette;

- Cigarette papers are taxed at the rate of $0.0122 for each 50 papers or fractional part thereof, except that, if they measure more than six and one-half inches in length, they are taxable by counting each two and three-quarter inches (or fraction thereof) of the length of each as one cigarette paper;

- Cigarette tubes are taxed at the rate of $0.0244 for each 50 tubes or fractional part thereof, except that, if they measure more than six and one-half inches in length, they are taxable by counting each two and three-quarter inches (or fraction thereof) of the length of each as one cigarette tube;

- Snuff is taxed at the rate of $0.585 per pound, and proportionately at that rate on all fractional parts of a pound;

- Chewing tobacco is taxed at the rate of $0.195 per pound, and proportionately at that rate on all fractional parts of a pound;

- Pipe tobacco is taxed at the rate of $1.0969 per pound, and proportionately at that rate on all fractional parts of a pound; and

- Roll-your-own tobacco is taxed at the rate of $1.0969 per pound, and proportionately at that rate on all fractional parts of a pound.

In general, excise taxes on tobacco products and cigarette papers and tubes manufactured in the United States are determined at the time of removal.

Floor stocks tax and foreign trade zones

Special tax and duty rules apply with respect to foreign trade zones. In general, merchandise may be brought into a foreign trade zone without being subject to the general customs laws of the United States. Such merchandise may be stored in a foreign trade zone or may be subjected to manufacturing or other processes there. The United States Customs and Border Protection agency of the Department of Homeland Security ("Customs") may determine internal revenue taxes and liquidate duties imposed on foreign merchandise in such foreign trade zones. Articles on which such taxes and applicable duties have already been paid, or which have been admitted into the United States free of tax, that have been taken into a foreign trade zone from inside the United States, may be held under the supervision of a customs officer. Such articles may later be released back into the United States free of further taxes and duties.[3]

Description of Proposal

Rate increases

Under the provision, the rates of excise tax on tobacco products and cigarette papers and

---

[2] Sec. 5701. Except where otherwise stated, all section references are to the Internal Revenue Code of 1986, as amended (the "Code").

[3] 19 U.S.C. sec. 81c(a).

tubes are increased, generally in a proportionate manner. The special rules relating to the application of the tax rates to large cigarettes and cigarette papers and tubes longer than six and one-half inches apply under the provision in the same manner as under present law. The rates under the provision are as follows:

- Small cigars are taxed at the rate of $50.00 per thousand ($1.00 per pack);

- Large cigars are taxed at the rate equal to 52.4 percent of the manufacturer's or importer's sales price but not more than $0.40 per cigar;

- Small cigarettes are taxed at the rate of $50.00 per thousand ($1.00 per pack);

- Large cigarettes are taxed at the rate of $105.00 per thousand;

- Cigarette papers are taxed at the rate of $0.0313 for each 50 papers or fractional part thereof;

- Cigarette tubes are taxed at the rate of $0.0626 for each 50 tubes or fractional part thereof;

- Snuff is taxed at the rate of $1.50 per pound, and proportionately at that rate on all fractional parts of a pound;

- Chewing tobacco is taxed at the rate of $0.50 per pound, and proportionately at that rate on all fractional parts of a pound;

- Pipe tobacco is taxed at the rate of $2.8126 per pound, and proportionately at that rate on all fractional parts of a pound; and

- Roll-your-own tobacco is taxed at the rate of $24.62 per pound, and proportionately at that rate on all fractional parts of a pound. The rate for roll-your-own tobacco is intended to approximate the rate for small cigarettes.

Floor stocks tax and foreign trade zone treatment

The provision imposes a tax on floor stocks. Taxable articles (i.e., those articles listed above), except for large cigars, manufactured in the United States or imported into the United States which are removed before April 1, 2009 and held on that date for sale by any person are subject to a floor stocks tax. The floor stocks tax is equal to the excess of the applicable tax under the new rates over the applicable tax at the present-law rates. The person holding the article on April 1, 2009 to which the floor stocks tax applies is liable for the tax. Each such person is allowed a $500 credit against the floor stocks tax.

Notwithstanding any other provision of law, the floor stocks tax applies to an article located in a foreign trade zone on April 1, 2009, provided that internal revenue taxes have been determined, or customs duties have been liquidated, with respect to such article before such date, or such article is held on a tax-and-duty-paid basis on such date under the supervision of a customs officer.

For purposes of determining the floor stocks tax, component members of a "controlled group" (as modified) are treated as one taxpayer.[4] "Controlled group" for these purposes means a parent-subsidiary, brother-sister, or combined corporate group with more than 50-percent ownership with respect to either combined voting power or total value. Under regulations, similar principles may apply to a group of persons under common control where one or more persons are not a corporation.

The floor stocks tax shall be paid on or before August 1, 2009, in the manner prescribed by Treasury regulations. In general, all of the rules, including penalties, applicable with respect to taxes on tobacco products and cigarette papers and tubes apply to the floor stocks tax. The Secretary of the Treasury or his delegate ("Secretary") may treat person who bore the ultimate burden of the floor stocks tax as the person entitled to a credit of refund of such tax.

Effective Date

The provision applies to articles removed after March 31, 2009.

[Law at ¶ 5325. CCH Explanation at ¶ 730.]

---

[4] Controlled group is defined in section 1563.

Act Sec. 701   ¶15,010

[¶ 15,020] Act Sec. 702(a). Permit, inventory, reporting, and recordkeeping requirements for manufacturers and importers of processed tobacco

Joint Committee on Taxation (J.C.T. REP. NO. JCX-1-09)

[Code Secs. 5712 and 5713]

Present Law

Tobacco products and cigarette papers and tubes are subject to Federal excise tax.[7] Tobacco products are cigars, cigarettes, smokeless tobacco, pipe tobacco, and roll-your-own tobacco.[8] Manufacturers and importers of tobacco products and export warehouse proprietors must obtain a permit from the Secretary of the Treasury or his delegate ("Secretary").[9] Manufacturers and importers of tobacco products or cigarette papers or tubes, and export warehouse proprietors, must also periodically make an inventory and certain reports and keep certain records, all as prescribed by the Secretary.[10]

Description of Proposal

The provision creates a new category of manufacturers and importers who are subject to regulation but not to Federal excise tax. Under the provision, manufacturers and importers of "processed tobacco" are subject to the present-law permit, inventory, reporting, and recordkeeping requirements. Processed tobacco is any tobacco other than tobacco products.[11] A manufacturer of processed tobacco is any person who processes any tobacco other than tobacco products, and an importer includes an importer of processed tobacco. However, the processing of tobacco does not include the farming or growing of tobacco or the handling of whole tobacco leaf solely for sale, shipment, or delivery to a manufacturer of tobacco products or processed tobacco. For example, under the provision an importer of "cut rag" tobacco or a leaf processor that manufactures such tobacco is subject to the general permit, inventory, reporting, and recordkeeping requirements of the Code but is not subject to Federal excise tax (unless it also imports or manufactures tobacco products or cigarette papers or tubes).

Under the provision, any person who is engaged in business as a manufacturer or importer of processed tobacco on the effective date of the provision and who submits a permit application within 90 days of the effective date of this provision may continue to engage in such business pending action on their permit application. Such persons will be subject to the requirements of this provision to the same extent as if the person was a permit holder while final action on the permit application is pending.

Effective Date

The provision is effective on April 1, 2009.

[Law at ¶ 5330, ¶ 5340, ¶ 5345, ¶ 5350, ¶ 5355, ¶ 5360 and ¶ 5365. CCH Explanation at ¶ 730.]

[¶ 15,030] Act Sec. 702(b). Broaden authority to deny, suspend, and revoke tobacco permits

Joint Committee on Taxation (J.C.T. REP. NO. JCX-1-09)

[Code Sec. 5712(3)]

Present Law

Manufacturers and importers of tobacco products and proprietors of export warehouses must obtain a permit to engage in such businesses.[12] A permit is obtained by application to the Secretary. The Secretary may deny the application if (1) the business premises are inadequate to protect the revenue; (2) the activity to be carried out at the business premises does not meet such minimum capacity or activity requirements as prescribed by the Secretary; (3) the applicant is, by reason of his business experience, financial

---

[7] Sec. 5701.
[8] Sec. 5702.
[9] Sec. 5713.
[10] Sec. 5721 (inventories); sec. 5722 (reports); sec. 5741 (records).
[11] Sec. 5702(c) defines tobacco products as cigars, cigarettes, smokeless tobacco, pipe tobacco, and roll-your-own tobacco.
[12] Sec. 5713.

standing, or trade connections, not likely to maintain operations in compliance with the applicable provisions of the Code; or (4) such applicant has failed to disclose any material information required or made any material false statement in the application.[13] In the case of a corporation, an applicant includes any officer, director, or principal stockholder and, in the case of a partnership, a partner.

A permit is conditioned upon compliance with the rules of the Code and related regulations pertaining to taxes and regulation of tobacco products and cigarette papers and tubes. The Secretary may suspend or revoke a permit after a notice and hearing if the holder (1) has not in good faith complied with those rules or has violated any other provision of the Code involving intent to defraud; (2) has violated the conditions of the permit; (3) has failed to disclose any material information required or made any material false statement in the permit application; or (4) has failed to maintain the business premises in such a manner as to protect the revenue.[14]

Description of Proposal

The provision broadens the present-law authority of the Secretary to deny, suspend, and revoke tobacco permits. Under the provision, the Secretary may deny an application for a permit if the applicant has been convicted of a felony violation of a Federal or State criminal law relating to tobacco products or cigarette papers or tubes, or if, by reason of previous or current legal proceedings involving a violation of Federal criminal felony laws relating to tobacco products or cigarette papers or tubes, such applicant is not likely to maintain operations in compliance with the applicable provisions of the Code.

Similarly, a permit may be suspended or revoked if the holder is convicted of a felony violation of a Federal or State criminal law relating to tobacco products or cigarette papers or tubes, or if, by reason of previous or current legal proceedings involving a violation of Federal criminal felony laws relating to tobacco products or cigarette papers or tubes, such applicant is not likely to maintain operations in compliance with the applicable provisions of the Code.

Effective Date

The provision is effective on the date of enactment.

[Law at ¶ 5340 and ¶ 5345. CCH Explanation at ¶ 730.]

[¶ 15,040] Act Sec. 702(c). Clarify statute of limitations pertaining to excise taxes imposed on imported alcohol, tobacco products and cigarette papers and tubes

Joint Committee on Taxation (J.C.T. REP. NO. JCX-1-09)

[Act Sec. 702(c)]

Present Law

Under the Code, amounts of tax must generally be assessed within three years after a tax return is filed, and no proceeding in court without assessment for the collection of such tax may begin after such period has expired.[15] If no return is filed (but is required), the tax may be assessed, or a proceeding in court for the collection of such tax may be initiated without assessment, at any time.[16]

Customs collects duties and excise taxes on imports. Importers of taxable articles relating to tobacco and alcohol must file a tax return with Customs.[17] In general, the limitations period for fixing and assessing duties and taxes with respect to an import is one year from the date of entry or removal.[18] Under the applicable customs law, with some limited exceptions, any duty or tax imposed on an import is final and conclusive upon all persons, including the United States, unless a protest is filed within 180 days or a court action is timely commenced.[19]

---

[13] Sec. 5712.
[14] Sec. 5713.
[15] Sec. 6501(a).
[16] Sec. 6501(c)(3).
[17] 24 C.F.R. sec. 41.81(b) (tobacco products and cigarette papers and tubes); sec. 5061(a) (distilled spirits, wines, and beer).

[18] 19 U.S.C. sec. 1504(a). The Secretary may extend this period under certain circumstances and with notice to the importer.
[19] 19 U.S.C. sec. 1514(a) & (c)(3).

Description of Proposal

The provision clarifies the tax and customs law in the area of alcohol and tobacco products by providing that, notwithstanding customs law, the general statute of limitations for assessment under the Code (sec. 6501) applies with respect to taxes imposed under chapters 51 (relating to distilled spirits, wines, and beer) and 52 (relating to tobacco products and cigarette papers and tubes) of the Code.

No inference is intended regarding the applicability of the statute of limitations under the Code to pending cases or to excise taxes imposed other than under chapters 51 and 52 of the Code.

Effective Date

The provision is effective for articles imported into the United States after the date of enactment.

[Law at ¶7084. CCH Explanation at ¶730.]

[¶15,050] Act Sec. 702(d). Modify definition of roll-your-own tobacco

Joint Committee on Taxation (J.C.T. Rep. No. JCX-1-09)

[Code Sec. 5702(o)]

Present Law

Federal excise taxes are imposed upon tobacco products and cigarette papers and tubes.[5] Tobacco products are cigars, cigarettes, snuff, chewing tobacco, pipe tobacco, and roll-your-own tobacco. A "cigar" is any roll of tobacco wrapped in leaf tobacco or in any substance containing tobacco, other than any roll of tobacco which is a cigarette. A "cigarette" is (i) any roll of tobacco wrapped in paper or in any substance not containing tobacco; and (ii) any roll of tobacco wrapped in any substance containing tobacco which, because of its appearance, the type of tobacco used in the filler, or its packaging and labeling, is likely to be offered to, or purchased by, consumers as a cigarette. "Roll-your-own tobacco" is any tobacco, which because of its appearance, type, packaging, or labeling, is suitable for use and likely to be offered to, or purchased by, consumers as tobacco for making cigarettes. "Cigarette paper" is paper, or any other material except tobacco, prepared for use as a cigarette wrapper. A "cigarette tube" is cigarette paper made into a hollow cylinder for use in making cigarettes.[6]

Wrappers containing tobacco are not within the definition of cigarette papers or tubes because they contain tobacco. They are also not generally within the definition of roll-your-own tobacco because they are usually used to make cigars, not cigarettes. For the same reason, loose tobacco suitable for making roll-your-own cigars is not considered to be roll-your-own tobacco.

Description of Proposal

Under the provision, roll-your-own tobacco also includes any tobacco, which because of its appearance, type, packaging, or labeling, is suitable for use and likely to be offered to, or purchased by, consumers as tobacco for making cigars, or for use as wrappers for making cigars.

Effective Date

The provision applies to articles removed after March 31, 2009.

[Law at ¶5330. CCH Explanation at ¶730.]

[¶15,060] Act Sec. 702(e). Impose immediate tax on unlawfully manufactured tobacco products and cigarette papers and tubes

Joint Committee on Taxation (J.C.T. Rep. No. JCX-1-09)

[Code Sec. 5702(b)(2)]

Present Law

Manufacturers and importers of tobacco products and proprietors of export warehouses must obtain a permit to engage in such busi-

---

[5] Sec. 5701.

[6] Sec. 5702.

nesses.[20] A permit is obtained by application to the Secretary.[21] A manufacturer of tobacco products or cigarette papers or tubes, or an export warehouse proprietor, must file a bond and obtain approval of such bond from the Secretary.[22] In general, excise taxes on tobacco products and cigarette papers and tubes manufactured in the United States are determined at the time of removal. In the case of taxes on tobacco products and cigarette papers and tubes removed during any semimonthly period under bond for deferred payment of tax, payment is due no later than the 14th day after the last day of such semimonthly period.[23]

Distilled spirits, wines, and beer produced at any place other than a place required by the Code are subject to tax immediately on production.[24] There is no such rule imposing immediate tax on tobacco products and cigarette papers and tubes that are produced by an out-ofcompliance manufacturer.

Description of Proposal

Under the provision, in the case of any tobacco products or cigarette papers or tubes produced in the United States at any place other than the premises of a manufacturer that has obtained a permit (if required) and approval of a bond, the excise tax is due and payable immediately upon manufacture, unless they are produced solely for the person's own personal consumption or use.

Effective Date

The provision is effective on the date of enactment.

[Law at ¶5335. CCH Explanation at ¶730.]

[¶15,070] Act Sec. 702(f). Use of tax information in tobacco assessments

Joint Committee on Taxation (J.C.T. REP. No. JCX-1-09)

[Code Sec. 6103(o)]

Present Law

Section 6103 provides that returns and return information are confidential and may not be disclosed by the IRS, other Federal employees, State employees, and certain others having access to the information except as provided in the Code.[25] A "return" is any tax or information return, declaration of estimated tax, or claim for refund required by, or permitted under, the Code, that is filed with the Secretary by, on behalf of, or with respect to any person.[26] "Return" also includes any amendment or supplement thereto, including supporting schedules, attachments, or lists which are supplemental to, or part of, the return so filed.

The definition of "return information" is very broad and includes any information gathered by the IRS with respect to a person's liability or possible liability under the Code.[27]

However, data in a form that cannot be associated with, or otherwise identify, directly or indirectly a particular taxpayer is not "return information" for section 6103 purposes.

---

[20] Sec. 5713. A "manufacturer of tobacco products" does not include (1) a person who produces tobacco products solely for the person's own personal consumption or use, and (2) a proprietor of a customs bonded manufacturing warehouse with respect to the operation of such warehouse. Sec. 5702(d).

[21] Sec. 5712.

[22] Sec. 5711.

[23] Sec. 5703.

[24] Sec. 5006(c)(2) (distilled spirits); sec. 5041(f) (wines); sec. 5054(a)(3) (beer).

[25] Sec. 6103(a).

[26] Sec. 6103(b)(1).

[27] Sec. 6103(b)(2). Return information is:

- a taxpayer's identity, the nature, source, or amount of his income, payments, receipts, deductions, exemptions, credits, assets, liabilities, net worth, tax liability, tax withheld, deficiencies, overassessments, or tax payments, whether the taxpayer's return was, is being, or will be examined or subject to other investigation or processing, or any other data, received by, recorded by, prepared by, furnished to, or collected by the Secretary with respect to a return or with respect to the determination of the existence, or possible existence, of liability (or the amount thereof) of any person under this title for any tax, penalty, interest, fine, forfeiture, or other imposition, or offense,

- any part of any written determination or any background file document relating to such written determination (as such terms are defined in section 6110(b)) which is not open to public inspection under section 6110,

- any advance pricing agreement entered into by a taxpayer and the Secretary and any background information related to such agreement or any application for an advance pricing agreement, and

- any closing agreement under section 7121, and any similar agreement, and any background information related to such an agreement or request for such an agreement.

Section 6103 contains a number of exceptions to the general rule of confidentiality, which permit disclosure in specifically identified circumstances when certain conditions are satisfied.[28]

For example, under section 6103(o) of the Code, returns and return information with respect to the taxes imposed on alcohol, tobacco and firearms are open to inspection by or disclosure to officers and employees of a Federal agency whose official duties require such inspection or disclosure.

The Fair and Equitable Tobacco Reform Act of 2004[29] repealed the Federal tobacco support program and created a Tobacco Trust Fund. Funds from the Tobacco Trust Fund are used to provide transitional payments to tobacco quota holders and eligible tobacco producers. The Tobacco Trust Fund is funded by quarterly assessments paid by manufacturers and importers of tobacco products. The Farm Service Agency receives tax information from the Department of the Treasury's Alcohol and Tobacco Tax and Trade Bureau as part of its administration of the Tobacco Trust Fund assessments.

A September 2008 Department of Agriculture inspector general report indicated that a number of companies were delinquent in paying their assessments and have been referred to the Department of Justice for debt collection.[30] Section 6103(o) does not provide for the use of the tax information received in civil actions against the delinquent companies. The Department of Justice could proceed with the lawsuits based on information provided by other entities, other than the tax data.

Description of Proposal

The proposal provides that returns and return information provided to a Federal agency under section 6103(o) may be used in an action or proceeding, or in the preparation for an action or proceeding, brought under section 625 the Fair and Equitable Tobacco Reform Act of 2004 for any unpaid assessments or penalties arising under such Act.

Effective Date

The proposal is effective on and after the date of enactment.

[Law at ¶ 5370. CCH Explanation at ¶ 730.]

[¶ 15,080] Act Sec. 703. Study concerning magnitude of tobacco smuggling in the United States

Joint Committee on Taxation (J.C.T. REP. NO. JCX-1-09)

[Act Sec. 703]

Present Law

Present law does not require the Secretary to submit a tobacco smuggling study to Congress.

Description of Proposal

The provision requires the Secretary to submit to Congress a study concerning the magnitude of tobacco smuggling in the United States and to recommend the most effective steps to reduce it. The study would include a review of the loss of Federal tax revenue due to illicit tobacco trade in the United States, and the role of imported tobacco products in such illicit trade.

Effective Date

The study will be completed no later than one year after the date of enactment.

[Law at ¶ 7087. CCH Explanation at ¶ 730.]

---

[28] Sec. 6103(c) - (o). Such exceptions include disclosures by consent of the taxpayer, disclosures to State tax officials, disclosures to the taxpayer and persons having a material interest, disclosures to Committees of Congress, disclosures to the President, disclosures to Federal employees for tax administration purposes, disclosures to Federal employees for nontax criminal law enforcement purposes and to the Government Accountability Office, disclosures for statistical purposes, disclosures for miscellaneous tax administration purposes, disclosures for purposes other than tax administration, disclosures of taxpayer identity information, disclosures to tax administration contractors and disclosures with respect to wagering excise taxes.

[29] Title VI of the American Jobs Creation Act of 2004 (Pub. L. No. 108-357).

[30] U.S. Department of Agriculture, Office of Inspector General, Southeast Region, Report No. 03601-15-At, *Audit Report: Tobacco Transition Payment Program Tobacco Assessments Against Tobacco Manufacturers and Importers (September 2008).*

[¶15,090] Act Sec. 704. Modifications to corporate estimated tax payments

Joint Committee on Taxation (J.C.T. Rep. No. JCX-1-09)

[Act Sec. 704]

Present Law

In general, corporations are required to make quarterly estimated tax payments of their income tax liability. For a corporation whose taxable year is a calendar year, these estimated payments must be made by April 15, June 15, September 15, and December 15. For tax years beginning on any date other than January 1, the payments are due in months of the fiscal year that correspond to the calendar year payment months.

Under the Tax Increase Prevention Act of 2005 ("TIPRA"), as amended, in the case of a corporation with assets of at least $1 billion, the payments due in July, August, and September, 2013, shall be increased to 120.00 percent of the payment otherwise due and the next required payment shall be reduced accordingly.

Explanation of Provision

The provision increases the otherwise applicable percentage for 2013 (120.00) by 0.5 percentage points.

Effective Date

The provision is effective on the date of enactment.

[Law at ¶7090. CCH Explanation at ¶470.]

¶20,001 Effective Dates

American Recovery and Reinvestment Act of 2009

This CCH-prepared table presents the general effective dates for major law provisoins added, amended or repealed by the American Recovery and Reinvestment Act of 2009 (P.L. 111-5), enacted February 17, 2009. Entries are listed in Code Section order.

Code Sec.	Act Sec.	Act Provision Subject	Effective Date
24(b)(3)(B)	1004(b)(1)	American Opportunity Tax Credit—Conforming Amendments	Tax years beginning after December 31, 2008
24(b)(3)(B)	1142(b)(1)(A)	Credit for Certain Plug-In Electric Vehicles—Conforming Amendments	Vehicles acquired after February 17, 2009
24(b)(3)(B)	1144(b)(1)(A)	Treatment of Alternative Motor Vehicle Credit as a Personal Credit Allowed Against AMT—Conforming Amendments	Tax years beginning after December 31, 2008
24(d)(4)	1003(a)	Temporary Increase of Refundable Portion of Child Credit	Tax years beginning after December 31, 2008
25(e)(1)(C)(ii)	1004(b)(2)	American Opportunity Tax Credit—Conforming Amendments	Tax years beginning after December 31, 2008
25(e)(1)(C)(ii)	1142(b)(1)(B)	Credit for Certain Plug-In Electric Vehicles—Conforming Amendments	Vehicles acquired after February 17, 2009
25(e)(1)(C)(ii)	1144(b)(1)(B)	Treatment of Alternative Motor Vehicle Credit as a Personal Credit Allowed Against AMT—Conforming Amendments	Tax years beginning after December 31, 2008
25A(i)-(j)	1004(a)	American Opportunity Tax Credit	Tax years beginning after December 31, 2008
25B(g)(2)	1004(b)(4)	American Opportunity Tax Credit—Conforming Amendments	Tax years beginning after December 31, 2008
25B(g)(2)	1142(b)(1)(C)	Credit for Certain Plug-In Electric Vehicles—Conforming Amendments	Vehicles acquired after February 17, 2009
25B)(g)(2)	1144(b)(1)(C)	Treatment of Alternative Motor Vehicle Credit as a Personal Credit Allowed Against AMT—Conforming Amendments	Tax years beginning after December 31, 2008
25C(a)-(b)	1121(a)	Extension and Modification of Credit for Nonbusiness Energy Property	Tax years beginning after December 31, 2008
25C(c)(2)(A)	1121(d)(2)	Extension and Modification of Credit for Nonbusiness Energy Property—Modifications of Standards for Qualified Energy Efficient Improvements—Additional Qualification for Insulation	Property placed in service after February 17, 2009
25C(c)(4)	1121(d)(1)	Extension and Modification of Credit for Nonbusiness Energy Property—Modifications of Standards for Qualified Energy Efficient Improvements—Qualifications for Exterior Windows, Doors, and Skylights	Property placed in service after February 17, 2009

Code Sec.	Act Sec.	Act Provision Subject	Effective Date
25C(d)(2)(A)(ii)	1121(c)(2)	Extension and Modification of Credit for Nonbusiness Energy Property—Modifications of Standards for Oil Furnaces and Hot Water Boilers—Conforming Amendment	Property placed in service after February 17, 2009
25C(d)(3)(B)	1121(b)(1)	Extension and Modification of Credit for Nonbusiness Energy Property—Modifications of Standards for Energy-Efficient Building Property—Electric Heat Pumps	Property placed in service after February 17, 2009
25C(d)(3)(C)	1121(b)(2)	Extension and Modification of Credit for Nonbusiness Energy Property—Modifications of Standards for Energy-Efficient Building Property—Central Air Conditioners	Property placed in service after February 17, 2009
25C(d)(3)(D)	1121(b)(3)	Extension and Modification of Credit for Nonbusiness Energy Property—Modifications of Standards for Energy-Efficient Building Property—Water Heaters	Property placed in service after February 17, 2009
25C(d)(3)(E)	1121(b)(4)	Extension and Modification of Credit for Nonbusiness Energy Property—Modifications of Standards for Energy-Efficient Building Property—Wood Stoves	Tax years beginning after December 31, 2008
25C(d)(4)	1121(c)(1)	Extension and Modification of Credit for Nonbusiness Energy Property—Modifications of Standards for Oil Furnaces and Hot Water Boilers	Property placed in service after February 17, 2009
25C(e)(1)	1103(b)(2)(A)	Repeal of Certain Limitations on Credit for Renewable Energy Property—Repeal of Limitation on Property Financed by Subsidized Energy Financing—Conforming Amendments	Tax years beginning after December 31, 2008
25C(g)(2)	1121(e)	Extension and Modification of Credit for Nonbusiness Energy Property—Extension	Tax years beginning after December 31, 2008
25D(b)(1)	1122(a)(1)	Modification of Credit for Residential Energy Efficient Property—Removal of Credit Limitation for Property Placed in Service	Tax years beginning after December 31, 2008
25D(e)(4)	1122(a)(2)(A)	Modification of Credit for Residential Energy Efficient Property—Removal of Credit Limitation for Property Placed in Service—Conforming Amendment	Tax years beginning after December 31, 2008
25D(e)(4)(C)	1122(a)(2)(B)	Modification of Credit for Residential Energy Efficient Property—Removal of Credit Limitation for Property Placed in Service—Conforming Amendment	Tax years beginning after December 31, 2008

¶20,001

Effective Dates

Code Sec.	Act Sec.	Act Provision Subject	Effective Date
25D(e)(9)	1103(b)(2)(B)	Repeal of Certain Limitations on Credit for Renewable Energy Property—Repeal of Limitation on Property Financed by Subsidized Energy Financing—Conforming Amendments	Tax years beginning after December 31, 2008
26(a)(1)	1004(b)(3)	American Opportunity Tax Credit—Conforming Amendments	Tax years beginning after December 31, 2008
26(a)(1)	1142(b)(1)(D)	Credit for Certain Plug-In Electric Vehicles—Conforming Amendments	Vehicles acquired after February 17, 2009
26(a)(1)	1144(b)(1)(D)	Treatment of Alternative Motor Vehicle Credit as a Personal Credit Allowed Against AMT—Conforming Amendments	Tax years beginning after December 31, 2008
26(a)(2)	1011(a)(1)-(2)	Extension of Alternative Minimum Tax Relief for Nonrefundable Personal Credits	Tax years beginning after December 31, 2008
30	1142(a)	Credit for Certain Plug-In Electric Vehicles	Vehicles acquired after February 17, 2009
30B(a)(3)-(5)	1143(b)	Conversion Kits—Credit Treated as Part of Alternative Motor Vehicle Credit	Property placed in service after February 17, 2009
30B(d)(3)(D)	1141(b)(1)	Credit for New Qualified Plug-In Electric Drive Motor Vehicles—Conforming Amendments	Vehicles acquired after December 31, 2009
30B(g)(2)	1144(a)	Treatment of Alternative Motor Vehicle Credit as a Personal Credit Allowed Against AMT	Tax years beginning after December 31, 2008
30B(h)(1)	1142(b)(2)	Credit for Certain Plug-In Electric Vehicles—Conforming Amendments	Vehicles acquired after February 17, 2009
30B(h)(8)	1143(c)	Conversion Kits—No Recapture for Vehicles Converted to Qualified Plug-In Electric Drive Motor Vehicles	Property placed in service after February 17, 2009
30B(i)-(k)	1143(a)	Conversion Kits	Property placed in service after February 17, 2009
30C(d)(2)(A)	1142(b)(3)	Credit for Certain Plug-In Electric Vehicles—Conforming Amendments	Vehicles acquired after February 17, 2009
30C(d)(2)(A)	1144(b)(2)	Treatment of Alternative Motor Vehicle Credit as a Personal Credit Allowed Against AMT—Conforming Amendments	Tax years beginning after December 31, 2008
30C(e)(6)	1123(a)	Temporary Increase in Credit for Alternative Fuel Vehicle Refueling Property	Tax years beginning after December 31, 2008
30D	1141(a)	Credit for New Qualified Plug-In Electric Drive Motor Vehicles	Vehicles acquired after December 31, 2009
32(b)(3)	1002(a)	Temporary Increase in Earned Income Tax Credit	Tax years beginning after December 31, 2008
35(a)	1899A(a)(1)	Improvement of the Affordability of the Credit—Improvement of Affordability	Coverage months beginning or or after the first day of the first month beginning 60 days after February 17, 2009, the date of enactment

¶20,001

American Recovery and Reinvestment Act of 2009

Code Sec.	Act Sec.	Act Provision Subject	Effective Date
35(c)(2)	1899C(a)	TAA Recipients Not Enrolled in Training Programs Eligible for Credit	Coverage months beginning after February 17, 2009
35(e)(1)(K)	1899G(a)	Addition of Coverage Through Voluntary Employees' Beneficiary Associations	Coverage months beginning after February 17, 2009
35(g)(9)-(10)	1899E(a)	Continued Qualification of Family Members After Certain Events	Months beginning after December 31, 2009
35(g)(9)-(10)	3001(a)(14)(A)	Premium Assistance for COBRA Benefits—Premium Assistance for COBRA Continuation Coverage for Individuals and Their Families—Coordination with HCTC	Tax years ending after February 17, 2009
36(b)	1006(b)(1)	Extension of and Increase in First-Time Homebuyer Credit; Waiver of Requirement to Pay—Increase	Residences purchased after December 31, 2008
36(b)(1)(B)	1006(b)(2)	Extension of and Increase in First-Time Homebuyer Credit; Waiver of Requirement to Pay—Increase—Conforming Amendment	Residences purchased afterDecember 31, 2008
36(d)(1)	1006(d)(2)	Extension of and Increase in First-Time Homebuyer Credit; Waiver of Requirement to Pay—Coordination with First-Time Homebuyer Credit for District of Columbia—Conforming Amendment	Residences purchased after December 31, 2008
36(d)(1)-(4)	1006(e)	Extension of and Increase in First-Time Homebuyer Credit; Waiver of Requirement to Pay—Removal of Prohibition on Financing by Mortgage Revenue Bonds	Residences purchased after December 31, 2008
36(f)(4)(D)	1006(c)(1)	Extension of and Increase in First-Time Homebuyer Credit; Waiver of Requirement to Pay—Waiver of Recapture	Residences purchased after December 31, 2008
36(g)	1006(a)(2)	Extension of and Increase in First-Time Homebuyer Credit; Waiver of Requirement to Pay—Extension—Conforming Amendment	Residences purchased after December 31, 2008
36(g)	1006(c)(2)	Extension of and Increase in First-Time Homebuyer Credit; Waiver of Requirement to Pay—Waiver of Recapture—Conforming Amendment	Residences purchased after December 31, 2008
36(h)	1006(a)(1)	Extension of and Increase in First-Time Homebuyer Credit; Waiver of Requirement to Pay—Extension	Residences purchased after December 31, 2008
36A	1001(a)	Making Work Pay Credit	Tax years beginning after December 31, 2008
38(b)(35)	1141(b)(2)	Credit for New Qualified Plug-In Electric Drive Motor Vehicles—Conforming Amendments	Vehicles acquired after December 31, 2009
42(i)(9)	1404	Coordination of Low-Income Housing Credit and Low-Income Housing Grants	February 17, 2009

¶20,001

Effective Dates

Code Sec.	Act Sec.	Act Provision Subject	Effective Date
45(d)(1)	1101(a)(1)	Extension of Credit for Electricity Produced from Certain Renewable Resources	Property placed in service after February 17, 2009
45(d)(2)-(4), (6)-(7), (9)	1101(a)(2)	Extension of Credit for Electricity Produced from Certain Renewable Resources	Property placed in service after February 17, 2009
45(d)(5)	1101(b)	Extension of Credit for Electricity Produced from Certain Renewable Resources—Technical Amendment	Electricity produced and sold after October 3, 2008, in taxable years ending after such date
45(d)(11)(B)	1101(a)(3)	Extension of Credit for Electricity Produced from Certain Renewable Resources	Property placed in service after February 17, 2009
45D(f)(1)(C)-(F)	1403(a)(1)-(3)	Increase in New Markets Tax Credit	February 17, 2009
45Q(a)(1)(B)	1131(b)(2)	Application of Monitoring Requirements to Carbon Dioxide Used as a Tertiary Injectant—Conforming Amendments	Carbon dioxide captured after February 17, 2009
45Q(a)(2)(A)-(C)	1131(a)	Application of Monitoring Requirements to Carbon Dioxide Used as a Tertiary Injectant	Carbon dioxide captured after February 17, 2009
45Q(d)(2)	1131(b)(1)(A)-(C)	Application of Monitoring Requirements to Carbon Dioxide Used as a Tertiary Injectant—Conforming Amendments	Carbon dioxide captured after February 17, 2009
45Q(e)	1131(b)(3)	Application of Monitoring Requirements to Carbon Dioxide Used as a Tertiary Injectant—Conforming Amendments	Carbon dioxide captured after February 17, 2009
46(3)-(5)	1302(a)	Credit for Investment in Advanced Energy Facilities	Periods after February 17, 2009 under rules similar to rules of Code Sec. 48(m) in effect on October 29, 1990
48(a)(4)(D)	1103(b)(1)	Repeal of Certain Limitations on Credit for Renewable Energy Property—Repeal of Limitation on Property Financed by Subsidized Energy Financing	Periods after December 31, 2008, under rules similar to the rules of Code Sec. 48(m) (as in effect on October 29, 1990)
48(a)(5)	1102(a)	Election of Investment Credit in Lieu of Production Credit	Facilities placed in service after December 31, 2008
48(c)(4)(B)-(D)	1103(a)	Repeal of Certain Limitations on Credit for Renewable Energy Property—Repeal of Limitation on Credit for Qualified Small Wind Energy Property	Periods after December 31, 2008, under rules similar to the rules of Code Sec. 48(m) (as in effect on October 29, 1990)
48(d)	1104	Coordination with Renewable Energy Grants	February 17, 2009
48A(b)(2)	1103(b)(2)(C)	Repeal of Certain Limitations on Credit for Renewable Energy Property—Repeal of Limitation on Property Financed by Subsidized Energy Financing—Conforming Amendments	Periods after December 31, 2008, under rules similar to the rules of Code Sec. 48(m) (as in effect on October 29, 1990)

¶20,001

Code Sec.	Act Sec.	Act Provision Subject	Effective Date
48B(b)(2)	1103(b)(2)(D)	Repeal of Certain Limitations on Credit for Renewable Energy Property—Repeal of Limitation on Property Financed by Subsidized Energy Financing—Conforming Amendments	Periods after December 31, 2008, under rules similar to the rules of Code Sec. 48(m) (as in effect on October 29, 1990
48C	1302(b)	Credit for Investment in Advanced Energy Facilities—Amount of Credit	Periods after February 17, 2009 under rules similar to rules of Code Sec. 48(m) in effect on October 29, 1990
49(a)(1)(C)((iii)-(v)	1302(c)(1)	Credit for Investment in Advanced Energy Facilities—Conforming Amendments	Periods after February 17, 2009 under rules similar to rules of Code Sec. 48(m) in effect on October 29, 1990
51(d)(14)	1221(a)	Incentives to Hire Uemployed Veterans and Disconnected Youth	Individuals who begin work for the employer after December 31, 2008
53(d)(1)(B)(iii)(II)	1142(b)(4)(B)	Credit for Certain Plug-In Electric Vehicles—Conforming Amendments	Vehicles acquired after February 17, 2009
53(d)(1)(B)(iii)-(iv)	1142(b)(4)(A)	Credit for Certain Plug-In Electric Vehicles—Conforming Amendments	Vehicles acquired after February 17, 2009
54(c)(2)	1531(c)(3)	Build America Bonds—Conforming Amendments	Obligations issued after February 17, 2009
54(l)(4)-(6)	1541(b)(1)	Regulated Investment Companies Allowed to Pass-Thru Tax Credit Bond Credits—Conforming Amendments	Tax years ending after February 17, 2009
54A(c)(1)(B)	1531(c)(2)	Build America Bonds—Conforming Amendments	Obligations issued after February 17, 2009
54A(d)(1)(C)-(E)	1521(b)(1)	Qualified School Construction Bonds—Conforming Amendments	Obligations issued after February 17, 2009
54A(d)(2)(C)(iii)-(v)	1521(b)(2)	Qualified School Construction Bonds—Conforming Amendments	Obligations issued after February 17, 2009
54A(h)	1541(b)(2)	Regulated Investment Companies Allowed to Pass-Thru Tax Credit Bond Credits—Conforming Amendments	Tax years ending after February 17, 2009
54AA	1531(a)	Build America Bonds	Obligations issued after February 17, 2009
54C(c)(4)	1111	Increased Limitation on Issuance of New Clean Renewable Energy Bonds	February 17, 2009
54D(d)	1112(a)	Increased Limitation on Issuance of Qualified Energy Conservation Bonds	February 17, 2009
54D(e)(4)	1112(b)(2)	Increased Limitation on Issuance of Qualified Energy Conservation Bonds—Clarification with Respect to Green Community Programs—Special Rules for Bonds to Implement Green Community Programs	February 17, 2009
54D(f)(1)(A)(ii)	1112(b)(1)	Increased Limitation on Issuance of Qualified Energy Conservation Bonds—Clarification with Respect to Green Community Programs	February 17, 2009

¶20,001

Effective Dates

Code Sec.	Act Sec.	Act Provision Subject	Effective Date
54E(c)(1)	1522(a)	Extension and Expansion of Qualified Zone Academy Bonds	Obligations issued after December 31, 2008
54F	1521(a)	Qualified School Construction Bonds	Obligations issued after February 17, 2009
55(c)(3)	1142(b)(5)	Credit for Certain Plug-In Electric Vehicles—Conforming Amendments	Vehicles acquired after February 17, 2009
55(c)(3)	1144(b)(3)	Treatment of Alternative Motor Vehicle Credit as a Personal Credit Allowed Against AMT—Conforming Amendments	Tax years beginning after December 31, 2008
55(d)(1)(A)-(B)	1012(a)(1)-(2)	Extension of Increased Alternative Minimum Tax Exemption Amount	Tax years beginning after December 31, 2008
56(b)(1)(E)	1008(d)	Additional Deduction for State Sales Tax and Excise Tax on the Purchase of Certain Motor Vehicles—Treatment of Deduction Under Alternative Minimum Tax	Purchases on or after date of enactment in tax years ending after such date
56(g)(4)(B)(iv)	1503(b)	Temporary Modification of Alternative Minimum Tax Limitations on Tax-Exempt Bonds—No Adjustment to Adjusted Current Earnings for Interest on Tax-Exempt Bonds Issued During 2009 and 2010	Obligations issued after December 31, 2008
57(a)(5)(C)(vi)	1503(a)	Temporary Modification of Alternative Minimum Tax Limitations on Tax-Exempt Bonds—Interest on Private Activity Bonds Issued During 2009 and 2010 Not Treated as Tax Preference Item	Obligations issued after December 31, 2008
63(c)(1)(C)-(E)	1008(c)(1)	Additional Deduction for State Sales Tax and Excise Tax on the Purchase of Certain Motor Vehicles—Deduction Allowed to Nonitemizers	Purchases on or after date of enactment in tax years ending after such date
63(c)(9)	1008(c)(2)	Additional Deduction for State Sales Tax and Excise Tax on the Purchase of Certain Motor Vehicles—Deduction Allowed to Nonitemizers—Definition	Purchases on or after date of enactment in tax years ending after such date
85(c)	1007(a)	Suspension of Tax on Portion of Unemployment Compensation	Tax years beginning after December 31, 2008
108(i)	1231(a)	Deferral and Ratable Inclusion of Income Arising from Business Indebtedness Discharged by the Reacquisition of a Debt Instrument	Discharges in tax years ending after December 31, 2008
132(f)(2)	1151(a)	Increased Exclusion Amount for Commuter Transit Benefits and Transit Passes	Months beginning on or after February 17, 2009
139C	3001(a)(15)(A)	Premium Assistance for COBRA Benefits—Premium Assistance for COBRA Continuation Coverage for Individuals and Their Families—Exclusion of COBRA Premium Assistance from Gross Income	Tax years ending after February 17, 2009
142(i)(1)	1504(a)	Modification to High Speed Intercity Rail Facility Bonds	Obligations issued after February 17, 2009

¶20,001

Code Sec.	Act Sec.	Act Provision Subject	Effective Date
144(a)(12)(C)	1301(a)(1)-(2)	Temporary Expansion of Availability of Industrial Development Bonds to Facilities Manufacturing Intangible Property	Obligations issued after February 17, 2009
163(e)(5)(F)-(G)	1232(a)	Modifications of Rules for Original Issue Discount on Certain High Yield Obligations—Suspension of Special Rules	Obligations issued after August 31, 2008, in tax years ending after such date
163(i)(1)	1232(b)(1)-(2)	Modifications of Rules for Original Issue Discount on Certain High Yield Obligations—Interest Rate Used in Determinig High Yield Obligations	Obligations issued after December 31, 2009, in tax years ending after such date
164(a)(6)	1008(a)	Additional Deduction for State Sales Tax and Excise Tax on the Purchase of Certain Motor Vehicles	Purchases on or after date of enactment in tax years ending after such date
164(b)(6)	1008(b)	Additional Deduction for State Sales Tax and Excise Tax on the Purchase of Certain Motor Vehicles—Qualified Motor Vehicle Taxes	Purchases on or after date of enactment in tax years ending after such date
168(k)	1201(a)(2)(A)	Special Allowance for Certain Property Acquired During 2009—Extension of Special Allowance—Conforming Amendments	Property placed in service after December 31, 2008, in tax years ending after such date
168(k)(2)	1201(a)(1)(A)-(B)	Special Allowance for Certain Property Acquired During 2009—Extention of Special Allowance	Property placed in service after December 31, 2008, in tax years ending after such date
168(k)(2)(B)(ii)	1201(a)(2)(B)	Special Allowance for Certain Property Acquired During 2009—Extension of Special Allowance—Conforming Amendments	Property placed in service after December 31, 2008, in tax years ending after such date
168(k)(4)(D)(i)-(iii)	1201(a)(3)(A)(i)-(iii)	Special Allowance for Certain Property Acquired During 2009—Extension of Special Allowance—Technical Amendments	Tax years ending after March 31, 2008
168(k)(4)(D)(iii)	1201(b)(1)(A)	Special Allowance for Certain Property Acquired During 2009—Extension of Election to Accelerate the AMT and Research Credits in Lieu of Bonus Depreciation	Property placed in service after December 31, 2008, in tax years ending after such date
168(k)(4)(H)	1201(b)(1)(B)	Special Allowance for Certain Property Acquired During 2009—Extension of Election to Accelerate the AMT and Research Credits in Lieu of Bonus Depreciation	Property placed in service after December 31, 2008, in tax years ending after such date
168(l)(5)(B)	1201(a)(2)(C)	Special Allowance for Certain Property Acquired During 2009—Extension of Special Allowance—Conforming Amendments	Property placed in service after December 31, 2008, in tax years ending after such date

¶20,001

Effective Dates

Code Sec.	Act Sec.	Act Provision Subject	Effective Date
168(n)(2)(C)	1201(a)(2)(D)	Special Allowance for Certain Property Acquired During 2009—Extension of Special Allowance—Conforming Amendments	Property placed in service after December 31, 2008, in tax years ending after such date
172(b)(1)(H)	1211(a)	5-Year Carryback of Operating Losses of Small Businesses	Net operating losses arising in tax years ending after December 31, 2007, in general
172(k)-(l)	1211(b)	5-Year Carryback of Operating Losses of Small Businesses—Conforming Amendment	Net operating losses arising in tax years ending after December 31, 2007, in general
179(b)(7)	1202(a)(1)-(2)	Temporary Increase in Limitations on Expensing of Certain Depreciable Business Assets	Tax years beginning after December 31, 2008
265(b)(3)(G)	1502(a)	Modification of Small Issuer Exception to Tax-Exempt Interest Expense Allocation Rules for Financial Institutions	Obligations issued after December 31, 2008
265(b)(7)	1501(a)	De Minimis Safe Harbor Exception for Tax-Exempt Interest Expense of Financial Institutions	Obligations issued after December 31, 2008
291(e)(1)(B)(iv)	1501(b)	De Minimis Safe Harbor Exception for Tax-Exempt Interest Expense of Financial Institutions—Treatment as Financial Institution Preference Item	Obligations issued after December 31, 2008
382(n)	1262(a)	Treatment of Certain Ownership Changes for Purposes of Limitations on Net Operating Loss Carryforwards and Certain Built-In Losses	Ownership changes after February 17, 2009
529(e)(3)(A)(i)-(iii)	1005(a)	Computer Technology and Equipment Allowed as a Qualified Higher Education Expense for Section 529 Accounts in 2009 and 2010	Expenses paid or incurred after December 31, 2008
853A	1541(a)	Regulated Investment Companies Allowed to Pass-Thru Tax Credit Bond Credits	Tax years ending after February 17, 2009
904(i)	1004(b)(5)	American Opportunity Tax Credit—Conforming Amendments	Tax years beginning after December 31, 2008
904(i)	1142(b)(1)(E)	Credit for Certain Plug-In Electric Vehicles—Conforming Amendments	Vehicles acquired after February 17, 2009
904(i)	1144(b)(1)(E)	Treatment of Alternative Motor Vehicle Credit as a Personal Credit Allowed Against AMT—Conforming Amendments	Tax years beginning after December 31, 2008
1016(a)(25)	1141(b)(3)	Credit for New Qualified Plug-In Electric Drive Motor Vehicles—Conforming Amendments	Vehicles acquired after December 31, 2009
1016(a)(25)	1142(b)(6)	Credit for Certain Plug-In Electric Vehicles—Conforming Amendments	Vehicles acquired after February 17, 2009
1202(a)(3)	1241(a)	Special Rules Applicable to Qualified Small Business Stock for 2009 and 2010	Stock acquired after date of enactment
1374(d)(7)	1251(a)	Temporary Reduction in Recognition Period for Built-In Gains Tax	Tax years beginning after December 31, 2008

¶20,001

Code Sec.	Act Sec.	Act Provision Subject	Effective Date
1397E(c)(2)	1531(c)(3)	Build America Bonds—Conforming Amendments	Obligations issued after February 17, 2009
1400C(d)(2)	1004(b)(6)	American Opportunity Tax Credit—Conforming Amendments	Tax years beginning after December 31, 2008
1400C(d)(2)	1142(b)(1)(F)	Credit for Certain Plug-In Electric Vehicles—Conforming Amendments	Vehicles acquired after February 17, 2009
1400C(d)(2)	1144(b)(1)(F)	Treatment of Alternative Motor Vehicle Credit as a Personal Credit Allowed Against AMT—Conforming Amendments	Tax years beginning after December 31, 2008
1400C(e)(4)	1006(d)(1)	Extension of and Increase in First-Time Homebuyer Credit; Waiver of Requirement to Pay—Coordination with First-Time Homebuyer Credit for District of Columbia	Residences purchased after December 31, 2008
1400N(d)(3)(B)	1201(a)(2)(E)	Special Allowance for Certain Property Acquired During 2009—Extension of Special Allowance—Conforming Amendments	Property placed in service after December 31, 2008, in tax years ending after such date
1400N(l)(3)(B)	1531(c)(3)	Build America Bonds—Conforming Amendments	Obligations issued after February 17, 2009
1400U-1—U-3	1401(a)	Recovery Zone Bonds	Obligations issued after February 17, 2009
4980B(f)(2)(B)(i)(V)-(VIII)	1899F(b)(1)-(2)	Extension of COBRA Benefits for Certain TAA-Eligible Individuals and PBGC Recipients—IRC Amendments	Periods of coverage which would (without regard to amendments made by this section) end or or after date of enactment
6211(b)(4)(A)	1001(e)(1)	Making Work Pay Credit—Conforming Amendments	Tax years beginning after December 31, 2008
6211(b)(4)(A)	1004(b)(7)	American Opportunity Tax Credit—Conforming Amendments	Tax years beginning after December 31, 2008
6211(b)(4)(A)	1201(a)(3)(B)	Special Allowance for Certain Property Acquired During 2009—Extension of Special Allowance—Technical Amendments	Tax years ending after March 31, 2008
6211(b)(4)(A)	1201(b)(2)	Special Allowance for Certain Property Acquired During 2009—Extension of Election to Accelerate the AMT and Research Credits in Lieu of Bonus Depreciation—Technical Amendment	Tax years ending after March 31, 2008
6211(b)(4)(A)	1531(c)(4)	Build America Bonds—Conforming Amendments	Obligations issued after February 17, 2009
6213(g)(2)(L)-(N)	1001(d)	Making Work Pay Credit—Authority Relating to Clerical Errors	Tax years beginning after December 31, 2008
6401(b)(1)	1531(c)(5)	Build America Bonds—Conforming Amendments	Obligations issued after February 17, 2009
6431	1531(b)	Build America Bonds—Credit for Qualified Bonds Issued Before 2011	Obligations issued after February 17, 2009

¶20,001

Effective Dates

Code Sec.	Act Sec.	Act Provision Subject	Effective Date
6432	3001(a)(12)(A)	Premium Assistance for COBRA Benefits—Premium Assistance for COBRA Continuation Coverage for Individuals and Their Families—COBRA Premium Assistance	Premium for a period of coverage beginning on or after February 17, 2009, generallly
6501(m)	1141(b)(4)	Credit for New Qualified Plug-In Electric Drive Motor Vehicles—Conforming Amendments	Vehicles acquired after December 31, 2009
6501(m)	1142(b)(7)	Credit for Certain Plug-In Electric Vehicles—Conforming Amendments	Vehicles acquired after February 17, 2009
6654(d)(1)(D)	1212	Decreased Required Estimated Tax Payment in 2009 for Certain Small Businesses	February 17, 2009
6720C	3001(a)(13)(A)	Premium Assistance for COBRA Benefits—Premium Assistance for COBRA Continuation Coverage for Individuals and Their Families—Penalty for Failure to Notify Health Plan of Cessation of Eligibility for Premium Assistance	Failures occurring after February 17, 2009
7527(b)	1899A(a)(2)	Improvement of the Affordability of the Credit—Improvement of Affordability—Conforming Amendment	Coverage months beginning or or after the first day of the first month beginning 60 days after February 17, 2009, the date of enactment
7527(d)	1899H(a)	Notice Requirements	Certificates issued after the date that is 6 months after February 17, 2009, the date of enactment
7527(e)	1899B(a)	Payment for Monthly Premiums Paid Prior to Commencement of Advance Payments of Credit—Payment for Premiums Due Prior to Commencement of Advance Payments of Credit	Coverage months beginning after December 31, 2008
7871(f)	1402(a)	Tribal Economic Development Bonds	Obligations issued after February 17, 2009
9801(c)(2)(D)	1899D(a)	TAA Pre-Certification Period Rule for Purposes of Determining Whether There is a 63-Day Lapse in Creditable Coverage	Plan years beginning after February 17, 2009
...	1001(e)(2)	Making Work Pay Credit—Conforming Amendments	Tax years beginning after December 31, 2008
...	1001(e)(3)	Making Work Pay Credit—Conforming Amendments	Tax years beginning after December 31, 2008
...	1004(b)(8)	American Opportunity Tax Credit—Conforming Amendments	Tax years beginning after December 31, 2008
...	1142(b)(8)	Credit for Certain Plug-In Electric Vehicles—Conforming Amendments	February 17, 2009
...	1302(c)(2)	Credit for Investment in Advanced Energy Facilities—Conforming Amendments	February 17, 2009

¶20,001

American Recovery and Reinvestment Act of 2009

Code Sec.	Act Sec.	Act Provision Subject	Effective Date
...	1401(b)	Recovery Zone Bonds—Clerical Amendment	February 17, 2009
...	1403(b)	Increase in New Markets Tax Credit—Special Rule for Allocation of Increased 2008 Limitation	February 17, 2009
...	1521(b)(3)	Qualified School Construction Bonds—Conforming Amendments	February 17, 2009
...	1531(c)(1)	Build America Bonds—Conforming Amendments	Obligations issued after February 17, 2009
...	1531(c)(6)	Build America Bonds—Conforming Amendments	February 17, 2009
...	1531(c)(7)	Build America Bonds—Conforming Amendments	February 17, 2009
...	1541(b)(3)	Regulated Investment Companies Allowed to Pass-Thru Tax Credit Bond Credits—Conforming Amendments	February 17, 2009
...	3001(a)(12)(B)	Premium Assistance for COBRA Benefits—Premium Assistance for COBRA Continuation Coverage for Individuals and Their Families—COBRA Premium Assistance—Social Security Trust Funds Held Harmless	February 17, 2009
...	3001(a)(12)(C)	Premium Assistance for COBRA Benefits—Premium Assistance for COBRA Continuation Coverage for Individuals and Their Families—COBRA Premium Assistance—Clerical Amendment	February 17, 2009
...	3001(a)(13)(B)	Premium Assistance for COBRA Benefits—Premium Assistance for COBRA Continuation Coverage for Individuals and Their Families—Penalty for Failure to Notify Health Plan of Cessation of Eligibility for Premium Assistance—Clerical Amendment	February 17, 2009
...	3001(a)(15)(B)	Premium Assistance for COBRA Benefits—Premium Assistance for COBRA Continuation Coverage for Individuals and Their Families—Exclusion of COBRA Premium Assistance from Gross Income—Clerical Amendment	February 17, 2009

¶20,001

¶20,005 Effective Dates

Children's Health Insurance Program Reauthorization Bill of 2009

This CCH-prepared table presents the general effective dates for major law provisoins added, amended or repealed by the Children's Health Insurance Program Reauthorization Bill of 2009 (P.L. 111-3), enacted February 4, 2009. Entries are listed in Code Section order.

Code Sec.	Act Sec.	Act Provision Subject	Effective Date
5701(a)(1)-(2)	701(a)(1)-(3)	Increase in the Excise Tax Rate on Tobacco Products—Cigars	Articles removed (as defined in section 5702(j) of the Internal Revenue Code of 1986) after March 31, 2009
5701(b)(1)-(2)	701(b)(1)-(2)	Increase in the Excise Tax Rate on Tobacco Products—Cigarettes	Articles removed (as defined in section 5702(j) of the Internal Revenue Code of 1986) after March 31, 2009
5701(c)	701(c)	Increase in the Excise Tax Rate on Tobacco Products—Cigarette Papers	Articles removed (as defined in section 5702(j) of the Internal Revenue Code of 1986) after March 31, 2009
5701(d)	701(d)	Increase in the Excise Tax Rate on Tobacco Products—Cigarette Tubes	Articles removed (as defined in section 5702(j) of the Internal Revenue Code of 1986) after March 31, 2009
5701(e)(1)-(2)	701(e)(1)-(2)	Increase in the Excise Tax Rate on Tobacco Products—Smokeless Tobacco	Articles removed (as defined in section 5702(j) of the Internal Revenue Code of 1986) after March 31, 2009
5701(f)	701(f)	Increase in the Excise Tax Rate on Tobacco Products—Pipe Tobacco	Articles removed (as defined in section 5702(j) of the Internal Revenue Code of 1986) after March 31, 2009
5701(g)	701(g)	Increase in the Excise Tax Rate on Tobacco Products—Roll-Your-Own Tobacco	Articles removed (as defined in section 5702(j) of the Internal Revenue Code of 1986) after March 31, 2009

Code Sec.	Act Sec.	Act Provision Subject	Effective Date
5702(h)	702(a)(5)	Administrative Improvements—Permit, Inventories, Reports, and Records Requirements for Manufacturers and Importers of Processed Tobacco—Conforming Amendments	April 1, 2009
5702(j)-(k)	702(a)(5)(B)	Administrative Improvements—Permit, Inventories, Reports, and Records Requirements for Manufacturers and Importers of Processed Tobacco—Conforming Amendments	April 1, 2009
5702(o)	702(d)(1)	Administrative Improvements—Expansion of Definition of Roll-Your-Own Tobacco	Articles removed (as defined in section 5702(j) of the Internal Revenue Code of 1986) after March 31, 2009
5702(p)	702(a)(4)	Administrative Improvements—Permit, Inventories, Reports, and Records Requirements for Manufacturers and Importers of Processed Tobacco—Manufacturer of Processed Tobacco	April 1, 2009
5703(b)(2)(F)	702(e)(1)	Administrative Improvements—Time of Tax for Unlawfully Manufactured Tobacco Products	February 4, 2009
5712	702(a)(1)(A)	Administrative Improvements—Permit, Inventories, Reports, and Records Requirements for Manufacturers and Importers of Processed Tobacco—Permit—Application	April 1, 2009
5712(3)	702(b)(1)	Administrative Improvements—Basis for Denial, Suspension, or Revocation of Permits—Denial	February 4, 2009
5713(a)	702(a)(1)(B)	Administrative Improvements—Permit, Inventories, Reports, and Records Requirements for Manufacturers and Importers of Processed Tobacco—Permit—Issuance	April 1, 2009
5713(b)	702(b)(2)	Administrative Improvements—Basis for Denial, Suspension, or Revocation of Permits—Suspension or Revocation	February 4, 2009
5721	702(a)(2)(A)	Administrative Improvements—Permit, Inventories, Reports, and Records Requirements for Manufacturers and Importers of Processed Tobacco—Inventories, Reports, and Packages—Inventories	April 1, 2009
5722	702(a)(2)(B)	Administrative Improvements—Permit, Inventories, Reports, and Records Requirements for Manufacturers and Importers of Processed Tobacco—Inventories, Reports, and Packages—Reports	April 1, 2009

Effective Dates

Code Sec.	Act Sec.	Act Provision Subject	Effective Date
5723	702(a)(2)(C)	Administrative Improvements—Permit, Inventories, Reports, and Records Requirements for Manufacturers and Importers of Processed Tobacco—Inventories, Reports, and Packages—Packages, Marks, Labels, and Notices	April 1, 2009
5741	702(a)(3)	Administrative Improvements—Permit, Inventories, Reports, and Records Requirements for Manufacturers and Importers of Processed Tobacco—Records	April 1, 2009
6103(o)(1)(A)-(B)	702(f)(1)	Administrative Improvements—Disclosure	On or after February 4, 2009
6103(p)(4)	702(f)(2)	Administrative Improvements—Disclosure—Conforming Amendment	On or after February 4, 2009
9801(f)(3)	311(a)	Special Enrollment Period Under Group Health Plans in Case of Termination of Medicaid or CHIP Coverage or Eligibility for Assistance in Purchase of Employment-Based Coverage; Coordination of Coverage—Amendments to the Internal Revenue Code of 1986	April 1, 2009
...	701(h)(1)(A)-(B)	Increase in the Excise Tax Rate on Tobacco Products—Floor Stock Taxes—Imposition of Tax	Articles removed (as defined in section 5702(j) of the Internal Revenue Code of 1986) after March 31, 2009
...	701(h)(2)	Increase in the Excise Tax Rate on Tobacco Products—Floor Stock Taxes—Credit Against Tax	Articles removed (as defined in section 5702(j) of the Internal Revenue Code of 1986) after March 31, 2009
...	701(h)(3)(A)	Increase in the Excise Tax Rate on Tobacco Products—Floor Stock Taxes—Liability for Tax and Method of Payment—Liability for Tax	Articles removed (as defined in section 5702(j) of the Internal Revenue Code of 1986) after March 31, 2009
...	701(h)(3)(B)	Increase in the Excise Tax Rate on Tobacco Products—Floor Stock Taxes—Liability for Tax and Method of Payment—Method of Payment	Articles removed (as defined in section 5702(j) of the Internal Revenue Code of 1986) after March 31, 2009
...	701(h)(3)(C)	Increase in the Excise Tax Rate on Tobacco Products—Floor Stock Taxes—Liability for Tax and Method of Payment—Time for Payment	Articles removed (as defined in section 5702(j) of the Internal Revenue Code of 1986) after March 31, 2009

¶20,005

Code Sec.	Act Sec.	Act Provision Subject	Effective Date
...	701(h)(4)(A)-(B)	Increase in the Excise Tax Rate on Tobacco Products—Floor Stock Taxes—Articles in Foreign Trade Zones	Articles removed (as defined in section 5702(j) of the Internal Revenue Code of 1986) after March 31, 2009
...	701(h)(5)(A)	Increase in the Excise Tax Rate on Tobacco Products—Floor Stock Taxes—Definitions—In General	Articles removed (as defined in section 5702(j) of the Internal Revenue Code of 1986) after March 31, 2009
...	701(h)(5)(B)	Increase in the Excise Tax Rate on Tobacco Products—Floor Stock Taxes—Definitions—Tax Increase Date	Articles removed (as defined in section 5702(j) of the Internal Revenue Code of 1986) after March 31, 2009
...	701(h)(5)(C)	Increase in the Excise Tax Rate on Tobacco Products—Floor Stock Taxes—Definitions—Secretary	Articles removed (as defined in section 5702(j) of the Internal Revenue Code of 1986) after March 31, 2009
..	701(h)(6)	Increase in the Excise Tax Rate on Tobacco Products—Floor Stock Taxes—Controlled Groups	Articles removed (as defined in section 5702(j) of the Internal Revenue Code of 1986) after March 31, 2009
...	701(h)(7)	Increase in the Excise Tax Rate on Tobacco Products—Floor Stock Taxes—Other Laws Applicable	Articles removed (as defined in section 5702(j) of the Internal Revenue Code of 1986) after March 31, 2009
...	702(c)(1)	Administrative Improvements—Application of Internal Revenue Code Statute of Limitations for Alcohol and Tobacco Excise Taxes	Articles imported after February 41 1, 2009
...	702(g)(1)-(2)	Administrative Improvements—Transitional Rule	April 1, 2009
...	704	Time for Payment of Corporate Estimated Taxes	April 1, 2009

¶20,005

¶25,001 Code Section to Explanation Table

Code Sec.	Explanation
24(b)(3)(B)	¶330; ¶350
24(d)(4)	¶315
25(e)(1)(C)(ii)	¶330; ¶350
25A(i)	¶330
25A(j)	¶330
25B(g)(2)	¶330; ¶350
25C(a)-(b)	¶335
25C(c)(2)(A)	¶335
25C(c)(4)	¶335
25C(d)(2)(A)(ii)	¶335
25C(d)(3)(B)-(E)	¶335
25C(d)(4)	¶335
25C(e)(1)	¶510
25C(g)(2)	¶335
25D(b)(1)	¶340
25D(e)	¶510
25D(e)(4)	¶340
26(a)(1)	¶330; ¶350
26(a)(2)	¶240
30	¶350
30B(a)	¶355
30B(d)(3)(D)	¶345
30B(g)(2)	¶360
30B(h)	¶350
30B(h)(8)	¶355
30B(i)-(k)	¶355
30C(d)(2)(A)	¶350
30C(e)(6)	¶365
30D	¶345
32(b)(3)	¶320
35(a)	¶725
35(c)(2)	¶725
35(e)(1)(K)	¶725
35(g)(9)-(10)	¶705; ¶725
36(b)	¶310
36(d)(1)-(2)	¶310
36(f)(4)(D)	¶310
36(g)	¶310
36(h)	¶310
36A	¶305
38(b)(35)	¶345
42(i)(9)	¶535
45(d)(1)-(7)	¶520
45(d)(9)	¶520
45(d)(11)(B)	¶520
45D(f)(1)(E)-(F)	¶530
45Q(a)(1)(B)	¶545
45Q(a)(2)	¶545
45Q(a)(2)(C)	¶545
45Q(d)(2)	¶545
45Q(e)	¶545
46(5)	¶525
48(a)(4)(D)	¶510
48(a)(5)	¶510
48(c)(4)(B)-(C)	¶510
48(d)	¶515
48A(b)(2)	¶510
48B(b)(2)	¶510
48C	¶525
49(a)(1)(C)	¶525
51(d)(14)	¶540
53(d)(1)(B)	¶350
54(c)(2)	¶605; ¶610
54(l)	¶615
54A(c)(1)(B)	¶605; ¶610
54A(d)	¶630
54A(h)	¶615
54AA	¶605
54C(c)(4)	¶645
54D(d)	¶640
54D(e)(4)	¶640
54D(f)(1)(A)(ii)	¶640
54E(c)(1)	¶635
54F	¶630
55(c)(3)	¶350
55(d)(1)(A)	¶235
55(d)(1)(B)	¶235
56(b)(1)(E)	¶230
56(g)(4)(B)(iv)	¶650
57(a)(5)(C)(vi)	¶650
63(c)	¶230
85(c)	¶205
108(i)	¶405
132(f)(2)	¶215
139C	¶705
142(i)(1)	¶655
144(a)(12)(C)	¶660
144(a)(12)(C)(iii)	¶660
163(e)(5)(F)-(G)	¶440
163(i)(1)	¶440
164(a)(6)	¶230
164(b)(6)	¶230
168(k)	¶415
168(k)(2)	¶415

Code Sec.	Explanation	Code Sec.	Explanation
168(k)(4)	¶505	5702(o)	¶730
168(k)(4)(D)(ii)-(iii)	¶505	5702(p)	¶730
168(l)(5)(B)	¶415	5703(b)(2)(F)	¶730
168(n)(2)(C)	¶415	5712	¶730
172(b)(1)(H)	¶425	5712(3)	¶730
172(k)	¶425	5713(a)-(b)	¶730
179(b)(7)	¶410	5721	¶730
265(b)(3)(G)	¶450	5722	¶730
265(b)(7)	¶445	5723	¶730
291(e)(1)(B)	¶445	5741	¶730
382(n)	¶435	6103(o)(1)	¶730
529(e)(3)(A)	¶220	6211(b)(4)(A)	¶305; ¶330; ¶505; ¶605; ¶610
853A	¶615		
904(i)	¶330; ¶350		
1016(a)(25)	¶345; ¶350	6213(g)(2)(N)	¶305
1202(a)(3)	¶210	6401(b)(1)	¶605; ¶610
1374(d)(7)	¶420	6431	¶610
1397E(c)(2)	¶605; ¶610	6432	¶705
1400C(d)(2)	¶330; ¶350	6501(m)	¶345; ¶350
1400C(e)(4)	¶310	6654(d)(1)(D)	¶465
1400N(d)(3)(B)	¶415	6720C	¶710
1400N(l)(3)(B)	¶605; ¶610	7527(b)	¶725
1400U-1	¶625; ¶652	7527(d)-(e)	¶725
1400U-2	¶625	7871(f)	¶665
1400U-3	¶652	9801(c)(2)(D)	¶725
4980B(f)(2)(B)(i)	¶715	9801(f)(3)	¶720
5701(a)-(g)	¶730		

¶25,001

¶25,005 Code Sections Added, Amended or Repealed

The list below notes all the Code Sections or subsections of the Internal Revenue Code that were added, amended or repealed by the American Recovery and Reinvestment Act of 2009 (P.L. 111-5), enacted February 17, 2009 and the Children's Health Insurance Program Reauthorization Bill of 2009 (P.L. 111-3), enacted February 4, 2009. The first column indicates the Code Section added, amended or repealed, and the second column indicates the Act Section.

American Recovery and Reinvestment Act of 2009

Code Sec.	Act Sec.	Code Sec.	Act Sec.
24(b)(3)(B)	1004(b)(1)	30C(e)(6)	1123(a)
24(b)(3)(B)	1142(b)(1)(A)	30D	1141(a)
24(b)(3)(B)	1144(b)(1)(A)	32(b)(3)	1002(a)
24(d)(4)	1003(a)	35(a)	1899A(a)(1)
25(e)(1)(C)(ii)	1004(b)(2)	35(c)(2)	1899C(a)
25(e)(1)(C)(ii)	1142(b)(1)(B)	35(e)(1)(K)	1899G(a)
25(e)(1)(C)(ii)	1144(b)(1)(B)	35(g)(9)-(10)	1899E(a)
25A(i)-(j)	1004(a)	35(g)(9)-(10)	3001(a)(14)(A)
25B(g)(2)	1004(b)(4)	36(b)	1006(b)(1)
25B(g)(2)	1142(b)(1)(C)	36(b)(1)(B)	1006(b)(2)
25B(g)(2)	1144(b)(1)(C)	36(d)(1)	1006(d)(2)
25C(a)-(b)	1121(a)	36(d)(1)-(4)	1006(e)
25C(c)(2)(A)	1121(d)(2)	36(f)(4)(D)	1006(c)(1)
25C(c)(4)	1121(d)(1)	36(g)	1006(a)(2)
25C(d)(2)(A)(ii)	1121(c)(2)	36(g)	1006(c)(2)
25C(d)(3)(B)	1121(b)(1)	36(h)	1006(a)(1)
25C(d)(3)(C)	1121(b)(2)	36A	1001(a)
25C(d)(3)(D)	1121(b)(3)	38(b)(35)	1141(b)(2)
25C(d)(3)(E)	1121(b)(4)	42(i)(9)	1404
25C(d)(4)	1121(c)(1)	45(d)	1101(a)(1)-(3)
25C(e)(1)	1103(b)(2)(A)	45(d)(5)	1101(b)
25C(g)(2)	1121(e)	45D(f)(1)(C)-(F)	1403(a)(1)-(3)
25D(b)(1)	1122(a)(1)	45Q(a)(1)(B)	1131(b)(2)
25D(e)(4)	1122(a)(2)(A)-(B)	45Q(a)(2)(A)-(C)	1131(a)
25D(e)(9)	1103(b)(2)(B)	45Q(d)(2)	1131(b)(1)(A)-(C)
26(a)(1)	1004(b)(3)	45Q(e)	1131(b)(3)
26(a)(1)	1142(b)(1)(D)	46(3)-(5)	1302(a)
26(a)(1)	1144(b)(1)(D)	48(a)(4)(D)	1103(b)(1)
26(a)(2)	1011(a)(1)-(2)	48(a)(5)	1102(a)
30	1142(a)	48(c)(4)(B)-(D)	1103(a)
30B(a)(3)-(5)	1143(b)	48(d)	1104
30B(d)(3)(D)	1141(b)(1)	48A(b)(2)	1103(b)(2)(C)
30B(g)(2)	1144(a)	48B(b)(2)	1103(b)(2)(D)
30B(h)(1)	1142(b)(2)	48C	1302(b)
30B(h)(8)	1143(c)	49(a)(1)(C)(iii)-(v)	1302(c)(1)
30B(i)-(k)	1143(a)	51(d)(14)	1221(a)
30C(d)(2)(A)	1142(b)(3)	53(d)(1)(B)(iii)(II)	1142(b)(4)(B)
30C(d)(2)(A)	1144(b)(2)	53(d)(1)(B)(iii)-(iv)	1142(b)(4)(A)

¶25,005

Code Sec.	Act Sec.	Code Sec.	Act Sec.
54(c)(2)	1531(c)(3)	265(b)(7)	1501(a)
54(l)(4)-(6)	1541(b)(1)	291(e)(1)(B)(iv)	1501(b)
54A(c)(1)(B)	1531(c)(2)	382(n)	1262(a)
54A(d)(1)(C)-(E)	1521(b)(1)	529(e)(3)(A)	1005(a)
54A(d)(2)(C)(iii)-(v)	1521(b)(2)	853A	1541(a)
54A(h)	1541(b)(2)	904(i)	1004(b)(5)
54AA	1531(a)	904(i)	1142(b)(1)(E)
54C(c)(4)	1111	904(i)	1144(b)(1)(E)
54D(d)	1112(a)	1016(a)(25)	1141(b)(3)
54D(e)(4)	1112(b)(2)	1016(a)(25)	1142(b)(6)
54D(f)(1)(A)(ii)	1112(b)(1)	1202(a)(3)	1241(a)
54E(c)(1)	1522(a)	1374(d)(7)	1251(a)
54F	1521(a)	1397E(c)(2)	1531(c)(3)
55(c)(3)	1142(b)(5)	1400C(d)(2)	1004(b)(6)
55(c)(3)	1144(b)(3)	1400C(d)(2)	1142(b)(1)(F)
55(d)(1)(A)-(B)	1012(a)(1)-(2)	1400C(d)(2)	1144(b)(1)(F)
56(b)(1)(E)	1008(d)	1400C(e)(4)	1006(d)(1)
56(g)(4)(B)(iv)	1503(b)	1400N(d)(3)(B)	1201(a)(2)(E)
57(a)(5)(C)(vi)	1503(a)	1400N(l)(3)(B)	1531(c)(3)
63(c)(1)(C)-(E)	1008(c)(1)	1400U-1	1401(a)
63(c)(9)	1008(c)(2)	1400U-2	1401(a)
85(c)	1007(a)	1400U-3	1401(a)
108(i)	1231(a)	4980B(f)(2)(B)(i)	1899F(b)(1)-(2)
132(f)(2)	1151(a)	6211(b)(4)(A)	1001(e)(1)
139C	3001(a)(15)(A)	6211(b)(4)(A)	1004(b)(7)
142(i)(1)	1504(a)	6211(b)(4)(A)	1201(a)(3)(B)
144(a)(12)(C)	1301(a)(1)-(2)	6211(b)(4)(A)	1201(b)(2)
163(e)(5)(F)-(G)	1232(a)	6211(b)(4)(A)	1531(c)(4)
163(i)(1)	1232(b)(1)-(2)	6213(g)(2)(L)-(N)	1001(d)
164(a)(6)	1008(a)	6401(b)(1)	1531(c)(5)
164(b)(6)	1008(b)	6431	1531(b)
168(k)	1201(a)(2)(A)	6432	3001(a)(12)(A)
168(k)(2)	1201(a)(1)(A)-(B)	6501(m)	1141(b)(4)
168(k)(2)(B)(ii)	1201(a)(2)(B)	6501(m)	1142(b)(7)
168(k)(4)	1201(b)(1)(A)-(B)	6654(d)(1)(D)	1212
168(k)(4)(D)(i)-(iii)	1201(a)(3)(A)(i)-(iii)	6720C	3001(a)(13)(A)
168(l)(5)(B)	1201(a)(2)(C)	7527(b)	1899A(a)(2)
168(n)(2)(C)	1201(a)(2)(D)	7527(d)	1899H(a)
172(b)(1)(H)	1211(a)	7527(e)	1899B(a)
172(k)-(l)	1211(b)	7871(f)	1402(a)
179(b)(7)	1202(a)(1)-(2)	9801(c)(2)(D)	1899D(a)
265(b)(3)(G)	1502(a)		

¶25,005

Children's Health Insurance Program Reauthorization Bill of 2009

Code Sec.	Act Sec.	Code Sec.	Act Sec.
5701(a)(1)-(2)	701(a)(1)-(3)	5712	702(a)(1)(A)
5701(b)(1)-(2)	701(b)(1)-(2)	5712(3)	702(b)(1)
5701(c)	701(c)	5713(a)	702(a)(1)(B)
5701(d)	701(d)	5713(b)	702(b)(2)
5701(e)(1)-(2)	701(e)(1)-(2)	5721	702(a)(2)(A)
5701(f)	701(f)	5722	702(a)(2)(B)
5701(g)	701(g)	5723	702(a)(2)(C)
5702(h)	702(a)(5)(A)	5741	702(a)(3)
5702(j)-(k)	702(a)(5)(B)	6103(o)(1)	702(f)(1)
5702(o)	702(d)(1)	6103(p)(4)	702(f)(2)
5702(p)	702(a)(4)	9801(f)(3)	311(a)
5703(b)(2)(F)	702(e)(1)		

¶25,010 Table of Amendments to Other Acts

American Recovery and Reinvestment Act of 2009

Amended Act Sec.	H.R. 1 Sec.	Par. (¶)	Amended Act Sec.	H.R. 1 Sec.	Par. (¶)
			\multicolumn{3}{l}{**Public Health Service Act**}		
\multicolumn{3}{l}{**Tax Increase Prevention and Reconciliation Act of 2005**}		2202(2)(A)	1899F(c)	¶7057
			2701(c)(2)	1899D(c)	¶7051
511(b)	1511	¶7024	\multicolumn{3}{l}{**Workforce Investment Act of 1998**}		
			174(c)(1)	1899K(b)	¶7066
\multicolumn{3}{l}{**Title 31, United States Code**}		173(f)(8)	1899E(b)	¶7054
			173(f)(1)	1899K(a)(1)	¶7066
1324(b)(2)	1004(b)(8)	¶7009	173(f)(2)	1899K(a)(2)	¶7066
1324(b)(2)	1531(c)(1)	¶7027	\multicolumn{3}{l}{**Emergency Economic Stabilization Act of 2008**}		
3101(b)	1604	¶7039			
			111	7001	¶7075
\multicolumn{3}{l}{**Employee Retirement Income Security Act of 1974**}				
602(2)(A)	1899F(a)	¶7057			
701(c)(2)	1899D(b)	¶7051			

Children's Health Insurance Program Reauthorization Act of 2009

Amended Act Sec.	P.L. 111-3 Sec.	Par. (¶)	Amended Act Sec.	P.L. 111-3 Sec.	Par. (¶)
			\multicolumn{3}{l}{**Public Health Service Act**}		
\multicolumn{3}{l}{**Employee Retirement Income Security Act of 1974**}		2701(f)(3)	311(b)(2)	¶7078
			\multicolumn{3}{l}{**Tariff Act of 1930**}		
102(b)	311(b)(1)(B)	¶7078	514(a)	702(c)	¶7084
502(a)(6)	311(b)(1)(E)(i)	¶7078			
502(c)	311(b)(1)(E)(ii)	¶7078			
701(f)(3)	311(b)(1)(A)	¶7078			

¶25,010

¶25,015 Table of Act Sections Not Amending Internal Revenue Code Sections

American Recovery and Reinvestment Act of 2009

	Paragraph
Sec. 1000. Short title, etc.	¶7003
Sec. 1001. Making work pay credit	¶7006
Sec. 1004. American opportunity tax credit	¶7009
Sec. 1211. 5-year carryback of operating losses of small businesses	¶7012
Sec. 1261. Clarification of regulations related to limitations on certain built-in losses following an ownership change	¶7015
Sec. 1402. Tribal economic development bonds	¶7018
Sec. 1403. Increase in new markets tax credit	¶7021
Sec. 1531. Build America bonds	¶7027
Sec. 1601. Application of certain labor standards to projects financed with certain tax-favored bonds	¶7030
Sec. 1602. Grants to states for low-income housing projects in lieu of low-income housing credit allocations for 2009	¶7033
Sec. 1603. Grants for specified energy property in lieu of tax credits	¶7036

	Paragraph
Sec. 1701. Prohibition on collection of certain payments made under the Continued Dumping and Subsidy Offset Act of 2000	¶7042
Sec. 1800. Short title	¶7045
Sec. 1899. Short title	¶7048
Sec. 1899I. Survey and report on enhanced health coverage tax credit program	¶7060
Sec. 1899J. Authorization of appropriations	¶7063
Sec. 1899L. GAO study and report	¶7069
Sec. 2201. Economic recovery payment to recipients of social security, supplemental security income, railroad retirement benefits, and veterans disability compensation or pension benefits	¶7070
Sec. 2202. Special credit for certain government retirees	¶7071
Sec. 3001. Premium assistance for COBRA benefits	¶7072
Sec. 7001. Executive compensation and corporate governance	¶7075

Children's Health Insurance Program Reauthorization Act of 2009

	Paragraph
Sec. 1. Short title; amendments to Social Security Act; references; table of contents	¶7076
Sec. 3. General effective date, exception for state legislation; contingent effective date; reliance on law	¶7077
Sec. 311. Special enrollment period under group health plans in case of termination of Medicaid or CHIP coverage or eligibility for assistance in purchase of employment-based coverage; coordination of coverage	¶7078

	Paragraph
Sec. 701. Increase in excise tax rate on tobacco products	¶7081
Sec. 703. Treasury study concerning magnitude of tobacco smuggling in the United States	¶7087
Sec. 704. Time for payment of corporate estimated taxes	¶7090

¶25,020 Act Sections Amending Code Sections

American Recovery and Reinvestment Act of 2009

Act Sec.	Code Sec.	Act Sec.	Code Sec.
1001(a)	36A	1121(b)(1)	25C(d)(3)(B)
1001(d)	6213(g)(2)(L)-(N)	1121(b)(2)	25C(d)(3)(C)
1001(e)(1)	6211(b)(4)(A)	1121(b)(3)	25C(d)(3)(D)
1002(a)	32(b)(3)	1121(b)(4)	25C(d)(3)(E)
1003(a)	24(d)(4)	1121(c)(1)	25C(d)(4)
1004(a)	25A(i)-(j)	1121(c)(2)	25C(d)(2)(A)(ii)
1004(b)(1)	24(b)(3)(B)	1121(d)(1)	25C(c)(4)
1004(b)(2)	25(e)(1)(C)(ii)	1121(d)(2)	25C(c)(2)(A)
1004(b)(3)	26(a)(1)	1121(e)	25C(g)(2)
1004(b)(4)	25B(g)(2)	1122(a)(1)	25D(b)(1)
1004(b)(5)	904(i)	1122(a)(2)(A)-(B)	25D(e)(4)
1004(b)(6)	1400C(d)(2)	1123(a)	30C(e)(6)
1004(b)(7)	6211(b)(4)(A)	1131(a)	45Q(a)(2)(A)-(C)
1005(a)	529(e)(3)(A)	1131(b)(1)(A)-(C)	45Q(d)(2)
1006(a)(1)	36(h)	1131(b)(2)	45Q(a)(1)(B)
1006(a)(2)	36(g)	1131(b)(3)	45Q(e)
1006(b)(1)	36(b)	1141(a)	30D
1006(b)(2)	36(b)(1)(B)	1141(b)(1)	30B(d)(3)(D)
1006(c)(1)	36(f)(4)(D)	1141(b)(2)	38(b)(35)
1006(c)(2)	36(g)	1141(b)(3)	1016(a)(25)
1006(d)(1)	1400C(e)(4)	1141(b)(4)	6501(m)
1006(d)(2)	36(d)(1)	1142(a)	30
1006(e)	36(d)(1)-(4)	1142(b)(1)(A)	24(b)(3)(B)
1007(a)	85(c)	1142(b)(1)(B)	25(e)(1)(C)(ii)
1008(a)	164(a)(6)	1142(b)(1)(C)	25B(g)(2)
1008(b)	164(b)(6)	1142(b)(1)(D)	26(a)(1)
1008(c)(1)	63(c)(1)(C)-(E)	1142(b)(1)(E)	904(i)
1008(c)(2)	63(c)(9)	1142(b)(1)(F)	1400C(d)(2)
1008(d)	56(b)(1)(E)	1142(b)(2)	30B(h)(1)
1011(a)(1)-(2)	26(a)(2)	1142(b)(3)	30C(d)(2)(A)
1012(a)(1)-(2)	55(d)(1)(A)-(B)	1142(b)(4)(A)	53(d)(1)(B)(iii)-(iv)
1101(a)(1)-(3)	45(d)	1142(b)(4)(B)	53(d)(1)(B)(iii)(II)
1101(b)	45(d)(5)	1142(b)(5)	55(c)(3)
1102(a)	48(a)(5)	1142(b)(6)	1016(a)(25)
1103(a)	48(c)(4)(B)-(D)	1142(b)(7)	6501(m)
1103(b)(1)	48(a)(4)(D)	1143(a)	30B(i)-(k)
1103(b)(2)(A)	25C(e)(1)	1143(b)	30B(a)(3)-(5)
1103(b)(2)(B)	25D(e)(9)	1143(c)	30B(h)(8)
1103(b)(2)(C)	48A(b)(2)	1144(a)	30B(g)(2)
1103(b)(2)(D)	48B(b)(2)	1144(b)(1)(A)	24(b)(3)(B)
1104	48(d)	1144(b)(1)(B)	25(e)(1)(C)(ii)
1111	54C(c)(4)	1144(b)(1)(C)	25B(g)(2)
1112(a)	54D(d)	1144(b)(1)(D)	26(a)(1)
1112(b)(1)	54D(f)(1)(A)(ii)	1144(b)(1)(E)	904(i)
1112(b)(2)	54D(e)(4)	1144(b)(1)(F)	1400C(d)(2)
1121(a)	25C(a)-(b)	1144(b)(2)	30C(d)(2)(A)

¶25,020

Act Sec.	Code Sec.	Act Sec.	Code Sec.
1144(b)(3)	55(c)(3)	1501(b)	291(e)(1)(B)(iv)
1151(a)	132(f)(2)	1502(a)	265(b)(3)(G)
1201(a)(1)(A)-(B)	168(k)(2)	1503(a)	57(a)(5)(C)(vi)
1201(a)(2)(A)	168(k)	1503(b)	56(g)(4)(B)(iv)
1201(a)(2)(B)	168(k)(2)(B)(ii)	1504(a)	142(i)(1)
1201(a)(2)(C)	168(l)(5)(B)	1521(a)	54F
1201(a)(2)(D)	168(n)(2)(C)	1521(b)(1)	54A(d)(1)(C)-(E)
1201(a)(2)(E)	1400N(d)(3)(B)	1521(b)(2)	54A(d)(2)(C)(iii)-(v)
1201(a)(3)(A)(i)-(iii)	168(k)(4)(D)(i)-(iii)	1522(a)	54E(c)(1)
1201(a)(3)(B)	6211(b)(4)(A)	1531(a)	54AA
1201(b)(1)(A)-(B)	168(k)(4)	1531(b)	6431
1201(b)(2)	6211(b)(4)(A)	1531(c)(2)	54A(c)(1)(B)
1202(a)(1)-(2)	179(b)(7)	1531(c)(3)	54(c)(2)
1211(a)	172(b)(1)(H)	1531(c)(3)	1397E(c)(2)
1211(b)	172(k)-(l)	1531(c)(3)	1400N(l)(3)(B)
1212	6654(d)(1)(D)	1531(c)(4)	6211(b)(4)(A)
1221(a)	51(d)(14)	1531(c)(5)	6401(b)(1)
1231(a)	108(i)	1541(a)	853A
1232(a)	163(e)(5)(F)-(G)	1541(b)(1)	54(l)(4)-(6)
1232(b)(1)-(2)	163(i)(1)	1541(b)(2)	54A(h)
1241(a)	1202(a)(3)	1899A(a)(1)	35(a)
1251(a)	1374(d)(7)	1899A(a)(2)	7527(b)
1262(a)	382(n)	1899B(a)	7527(e)
1301(a)(1)-(2)	144(a)(12)(C)	1899C(a)	35(c)(2)
1302(a)	46(3)-(5)	1899D(a)	9801(c)(2)(D)
1302(b)	48C	1899E(a)	35(g)(9)-(10)
1302(c)(1)	49(a)(1)(C)(iii)-(v)	1899F(b)(1)-(2)	4980B(f)(2)(B)(i)
1401(a)	1400U-1	1899G(a)	35(e)(1)(K)
1401(a)	1400U-2	1899H(a)	7527(d)
1401(a)	1400U-3	3001(a)(12)(A)	6432
1402(a)	7871(f)	3001(a)(13)(A)	6720C
1403(a)(1)-(3)	45D(f)(1)(C)-(F)	3001(a)(14)(A)	35(g)(9)-(10)
1404	42(i)(9)	3001(a)(15)(A)	139C
1501(a)	265(b)(7)		

Children's Health Insurance Program Reauthorization Bill of 2009

Act Sec.	Code Sec.	Act Sec.	Code Sec.
311(a)	9801(f)(3)	702(a)(2)(C)	5723
701(a)(1)-(3)	5701(a)(1)-(2)	702(a)(3)	5741
701(b)(1)-(2)	5701(b)(1)-(2)	702(a)(4)	5702(p)
701(c)	5701(c)	702(a)(5)(A)	5702(h)
701(d)	5701(d)	702(a)(5)(B)	5702(j)-(k)
701(e)(1)-(2)	5701(e)(1)-(2)	702(b)(1)	5712(3)
701(f)	5701(f)	702(b)(2)	5713(b)
701(g)	5701(g)	702(d)(1)	5702(o)
702(a)(1)(A)	5712	702(e)(1)	5703(b)(2)(F)
702(a)(1)(B)	5713(a)	702(f)(1)	6103(o)(1)
702(a)(2)(A)	5721	702(f)(2)	6103(p)(4)
702(a)(2)(B)	5722		

¶25,020

¶27,001 Client Letters

¶27,005 CLIENT LETTER #1
Re: 2009 Recovery Act – General Information

Dear Client:

Acting quickly to jump start the economy, Congress has passed a massive economic stimulus package: the *American Recovery and Reinvestment Act of 2009*. As you probably have heard, the new law weighs in at nearly $800 billion. Roughly one-third is comprised of tax incentives for individuals and businesses. Congress made many of the tax incentives retroactive to January 1, 2009.

The tax incentives in the stimulus package can be broken down into two broad categories: individuals and business. Let's take a look at the individual incentives first.

Individual Incentives

Making Work Pay credit. Starting later this year, eligible wage earners will see an increase in their take-home pay. The new law provides a credit against income tax in an amount equal to the lesser of 6.2 percent of the individual's earned income or $400 ($800 for married couples filing jointly). However, income limitations apply so the credit is unavailable to higher income wage earners. The Making Work Pay credit will be applied retroactively to January 1, 2009 and prospectively to December 31, 2010. One delay in getting the credit to wage earners is the need for the IRS to revise the payroll tax withholding tables. Some observers predict that the IRS will not be able to revise the tables until June. We will keep you posted of developments.

Seniors and others. Individuals receiving Social Security benefits, disabled veterans and others on fixed incomes will receive one-time payments of $250. If the individual also qualifies for the Making Work pay credit, his or her credit will be reduced by the $250 payment.

First-time homebuyer tax credit. In 2008, Congress enacted the first-time homebuyer tax credit. Unlike other credits, this one had to be repaid, making it unattractive to many taxpayers. The new law removes the repayment requirement for homes purchased by first-time buyers between January 1, 2009 and December 1, 2009. The enhanced credit equals 10 percent of the purchase price of a home up to $8,000 ($4,000 for married individuals filing separately). There are income limitations, which preclude higher-income individuals and couples from taking advantage of the credit.

New car deduction. Automobile sales, like new home sales, have plummeted in recent months. In response, Congress has created an above-the-line deduction for state and local sales taxes or excise taxes paid on qualified purchases of new motor vehicles. This deduction is temporary and is also prospective from the date of enactment of the new law. It will expire at the end of 2009. Income thresholds and other limitations apply.

AMT patch. Every year, bills are introduced in Congress to abolish the alternative minimum tax (AMT). This year is no different but because the federal budget deficit, Congress cannot eliminate the AMT without finding an equivalent source of revenue. However, there is some good news. The new law increases the AMT exemption amounts and allows taxpayers to take most personal credits to reduce AMT liability for 2009.

Child tax credit. The current $1,000 child tax credit is one of the most popular incentives in the Tax Code. The new law increases the refundable portion of the child tax credit for 2009 and 2010. Taxpayers are eligible for a refundable credit equal to 15 percent of their earned income in excess of $3,000 subject to certain restrictions and phase-outs.

Unemployment compensation. Many individuals are surprised to learn that unemployment benefits are taxable. The new law excludes up to $2,400 in unemployment compensation from a recipient's gross income in 2009.

Education. The Tax Code includes a number of incentives to help bring down the cost of education. The new law expands the current Hope education credit (and renames it the American Opportunity Tax Credit). More individuals will be able to take advantage of this credit because of expanded income phase-outs. The new law also raises the maximum credit, extends it over four years of post-secondary school education, and makes 40 percent of the credit refundable. In a related development, the new law also permits beneficiaries of qualified tuition plans (known as "529" plan) to use tax-free distributions to pay for computers and computer technology.

Transit benefits. Individuals who take public transportation to work or van pool may benefit from enhanced transit incentives in the new law. Congress increased the income exclusion amount for transit passes and van pooling from $120 per month to $230 per month for 2009 (starting in March 2009) and through 2010 with an inflation adjustment. However, these benefits must be offered by your employer to take advantage of them.

EITC. The earned income tax credit (EITC) is a refundable tax credit targeted to lower and middle income wage earners and families. When the EITC exceeds the amount of taxes owed, it generates a refund. The new law enhances the EITC for taxpayers with three or more qualifying children and helps eliminate an existing "marriage penalty" across the board.

Energy Incentives. The new law enhances several energy tax incentives that reward taxpayers for installing energy-efficient property and alternative sources of energy in their homes. Among the types of energy-efficient property that may qualify for a tax break are certain heat pumps, furnaces, windows and doors. There's also a tax break for purchasers of plug-in electric vehicles.

Business Incentives

Although the business incentives in the new law are not as expansive as in some recent tax acts, they are still valuable.

Bonus depreciation. Bonus depreciation is one of Congress' favorite mechanisms (along with Code Sec. 179 expensing) to encourage business spending. The new law extends 50 percent bonus depreciation that expired at the end of 2008. Businesses can take advantage of bonus depreciation throughout 2009 (and longer for certain types of property). Bonus depreciation is taken on top of regular depreciation. While it can be valuable in the short term, keep in mind that a large current depreciation deduction results in smaller future deductions. Also good news in applying bonus depreciation to vehicles, the new law raises the first-year depreciation cap limits by $8,000. The new law also allows eligible businesses to monetize accumulated AMT and research tax credits in lieu of taking bonus depreciation for 2009.

Code Sec. 179 expensing. Like bonus depreciation, increased Code Sec. 179 expensing expired at the end of 2008. The new law revives it for 2009. Under the new law, Code Sec. 179 expensing for 2009 is $250,000 and the threshold for reducing the deduction is $800,000.

Net operating losses. Because of the economic downturn, many businesses are in a loss position. The Tax Code generally allows eligible taxpayers to carry back net operating losses (NOLs) two years with some exceptions. The new law increases the carryback period to five years for small businesses (which the new law defines as businesses with average gross receipts of $15million or less). The treatment is also temporary, applying only to 2008 NOLs. Businesses that qualifying can apply for an immediate refund of taxes paid during the extended carryback period.

Work Opportunity Tax Credit. The Work Opportunity Tax Credit rewards employers that hire individuals from targeted groups, such as veterans and young people. The new law modifies the definitions of eligible veterans and disconnected youth for purposes of the credit.

Cancellation of indebtedness. Eligible businesses will be able to recognize cancellation of certain indebtedness over five years, beginning in 2014, under the new law. This treatment applies to specified types of business debt repurchased or forgiven by the business after December 31, 2008 and before January 1, 2011.

Energy incentives. The new law extends and enhances many energy tax incentives for developers and producers of alternative and renewable energy. Examples are wind, biomass and solar power. The incentives are temporary and are intended to boost production of energy from renewable sources.

More business incentives. The new law also allows qualified individuals to exclude 75 percent of the gain from the sale of certain small business stock. Additionally, Congress shortened the holding period for the S corp built-in gain period, prospectively revoked a controversial IRS notice affecting NOL limitations on banks and enhanced COBRA coverage and the health coverage tax credit. The new law also increases the New Markets Tax Credit program, decreases estimated tax payments for certain individuals whose incomes come from small businesses and delays withholding on government contractors. Congress also enhanced many tax-exempt and tax-credit bond rules to help states and local governments generate revenue.

The scope of the American Recovery and Reinvestment Act is broad. Please contact our office to discuss how the tax incentives in the new law may benefit you.

Sincerely yours,

¶27,005

¶27,010 CLIENT LETTER #2

Re: 2009 Recovery Act – Individuals

Dear Client:

Congress has just passed the largest spending bill in U.S. history, including some significant tax incentives for individuals. The nearly $800 billion American Recovery and Reinvestment Act is roughly two-thirds spending and one-third tax cuts. The massive infusion of spending and tax incentives is designed to jump start the troubled U.S. economy. Many of the tax incentives are retroactive to January 1, 2009. This letter examines the individual tax incentives in the new law.

Making Work Pay credit. The centerpiece of the new law is the Making Work Pay credit. Wage earners will see an increase in their take-home pay. The new law allows a credit against income tax in an amount equal to the lesser of 6.2 percent of the individual's earned income or $400 ($800 for married couples filing jointly). Income limitations apply so the credit will not be available to higher income wage earners. Under the new law, the Making Work Pay credit will be applied retroactively to January 1, 2009 and prospectively to December 31, 2010. Additionally, individuals, disabled veterans and others on fixed incomes will receive one-time payments of $250. At this time, it is likely that the Making Work Pay credit will not appear in workers' paychecks until late spring as it may take that long for the IRS to revise the payroll tax withholding tables. President Obama and many members of Congress want the IRS to move more quickly. We'll keep you posted of developments.

Homebuyer tax credit. Home sales are at record lows in most parts of the country. The new law extends and enhances a tax credit put in place last year to encourage home sales. The credit gives first-time homebuyers a temporary refundable tax credit equal to 10 percent of the purchase price of a home up to $8,000 ($4,000 for married individuals filing separately) The credit begins to phase out for higher-income taxpayers. Initially, the credit was effective for homes purchased on or after April 9, 2008, and before July 1, 2009. The new law extends the credit through November 30, 2009. Moreover, the new law eliminates the repayment requirement for homes purchased after December 31, 2008 and before December 1, 2009. This is a significant enhancement. Please contact our office for details.

New car deduction. Automobile sales, like new home sales, have plummeted in recent months. Congress has created an above-the-line deduction for state and local sales taxes or excise taxes paid on qualified purchases of new motor vehicles. Income limits and other restrictions apply so please contact our office before you purchase a new vehicle. This deduction is temporary and also prospective. It will expire at the end of 2009. Because it is an above-the-line deduction, itemizers and non-itemizers can take advantage of it.

AMT patch. The alternative minimum tax (AMT) was created to ensure that very wealthy individuals pay their fair share of federal taxes. Over time, the AMT has encroached on middle income taxpayers, largely because it was not indexed for inflation. Many in Congress would like to abolish the AMT but it generates huge amounts of revenue. To help middle income taxpayers avoid the AMT, the new law increases the AMT exemption amounts and allows taxpayers to take most personal credits to reduce AMT liability for 2009.

Unemployment compensation. Sadly, the number of Americans receiving unemployment benefits is at record numbers. Many individuals are surprised to learn that unemployment benefits are taxable. The new law excludes up to $2,400 in unemployment compensation from a recipient's gross income in 2009.

Education. Education expenses are increasing faster than the rate of inflation in many cases. The Tax Code includes a number of incentives to help bring down the cost of education. The new law expands the current Hope education credit (and renames it the American Opportunity Tax Credit). More individuals will be able to take advantage of this credit because of expanded income phase-outs. The new law also raises the maximum credit, extends it over four years of post-secondary school education, and makes 40 percent of the credit refundable. In a related development, the new law also permits beneficiaries of qualified tuition plans (known as "529" plan) to use tax-free distributions to pay for computers and computer technology. The education credits in the Tax Code are omplex and made more so by the new law. Please contact our office and we'll be happy to explain them in detail.

Child tax credit. Congress has tinkered with the current $1,000 child tax credit many times in recent years. The new law increases the refundable portion of the child tax credit for 2009 and 2010. Taxpayers are eligible for a refundable credit equal to 15 percent of their earned income in excess of $3,000 subject to certain restrictions and phase-outs.

Transit benefits. Transit benefits, such as bus/subway passes and van pooling payments, are very popular with employers and employees. The new law increases the income exclusion amount for transit passes and van pooling from $120 per month to $230 per month for 2009 (starting in March) and 2010 (with an inflation adjustment for 2010).

EITC. The earned income tax credit (EITC) is a refundable tax credit targeted to lower and middle income wage earners and families. When the EITC exceeds the amount of taxes owed, it generates a refund. The new law enhances the EITC for taxpayers with three or more qualifying children.

Energy Incentives. Did you know that you might qualify for a tax break for installing energy-efficient windows, doors, furnaces, and other items in your home? The new law enhances several energy tax incentives that reward taxpayers for installing energy-efficient property and alternative sources of energy in their homes. Before you invest in energy-efficient property, contact our office and we can review the various tax breaks available. Some state tax incentives may piggyback on the federal ones.

More incentives. The new law also increases the health coverage tax credit (HCTC) for, among others, individuals receiving Trade Adjustment Assistance benefits. The new law also decreases estimated tax payments for certain individuals whose incomes come from a small business in 2009. Dislocated workers who apply for COBRA coverage will benefit from an enhanced but temporary subsidy.

Please contact our office if you have any questions about the tax incentives in the American Recovery and Reinvestment Act. Because many of the tax incentives are temporary, don't delay. We don't want you to miss out on any tax savings.

Sincerely yours,

¶27,010

¶27,015 CLIENT LETTER #3

Re: 2009 Recovery Act – Businesses

Dear Client:

Since the inauguration of Barack Obama as our nation's 44th president, everyone's attention has been focused on what he and lawmakers in Congress will do to turn around the distressed U.S. economy. The daily drumbeat of bad economic news is drowning out almost everything else. Business owners know first hand the challenges of trying to increase sales in a slowing economy and at the same time avoid layoffs.

On February ___, President Obama signed a massive $800 billion economic stimulus package, which Congress had passed a few days earlier. The American Recovery and Reinvestment Act is a mixture of tax incentives, including business tax cuts, and direct spending. Although the business tax cuts are not as numerous as many taxpayers may have hoped, they are nonetheless valuable. In this letter, we'll highlight the key incentives targeted to businesses. As always, please contact our office if you have any questions.

Bonus depreciation. Bonus depreciation is back for 2009. The new law extends the 50 percent bonus depreciation authorized by the Economic Stimulus Act of 2008, which generally expired at the end of 2008. Businesses can take advantage of bonus depreciation throughout 2009 (and longer for certain types of property). Bonus depreciation is taken on top of regular depreciation. Keep in mind that a large current depreciation deduction results in smaller future deductions so careful planning is an absolute must. To allow vehicles to continue to be depreciated at a higher level, the new law also adds $8,000 to the "caps" ordinarily placed on such deductions. Especially useful to businesses with accumulated AMT and research tax credits on their tax book,s the new law also allows eligible businesses to monetize these credits in lieu of taking bonus depreciation for 2009.

Code Sec. 179 expensing. Increased Code Sec. 179 expensing is also back for 2009. The Economic Stimulus Act of 2008 increased Code Sec. 179 expensing for 2008 to $250,000 and the threshold for reducing the deduction to $800,000. However, the enhanced provision expired at the end of 2008. The new law revives it for 2009.

Net operating losses. Many taxpayers expected Congress to extend the carryback period for net operating losses (NOLs) to five years. The new law expands the carryback period to five years for qualified small businesses (businesses with average gross receipts of $15 million or less). The treatment is also temporary and only applies to NOLs for any tax year beginning or ending in 2008. Qualified businesses can choose to carry back NOLs three, four or five years. Immediate refunds are available to businesses that qualify.

Cancellation of indebtedness. Many taxpayers also expected Congress to provide tax relief for companies that purchase their own or related party debt at a discount. The new law addresses cancellation of indebtedness but not as generously as many taxpayers had hoped. Eligible businesses will be able to recognize cancellation of certain indebtedness over five years, beginning in 2014, under the new law. This treatment applies to specified types of business debt repurchased or forgiven by the business after December 31, 2008 and before January 1, 2011.

Work Opportunity Tax Credit. Congress has taken a special interest in the Work Opportunity Tax Credit (WOTC) as a mechanism to encourage employers to hire individuals who are economically-challenged. The new law modifies the definitions of eligible veterans and disconnected youth to bring more individuals under the WOTC. This treatment is temporary.

S corporations. A built-in gains tax applies to corporations that make an S corporation election. The tax is computed by applying the highest corporate tax rate to the net recognized built-in gain of the S corporation for the tax year. The new law reduces the recognition period for assets subject to the built-in gains tax from 10 to seven years.

Small business stock. Generally, an investor other than an entity doing business as a C corporation, may exclude 50 percent of the gain from the sale or exchange of "qualified small business stock." The new law raises the 50 percent exclusion to 75 percent. However, the increase is temporary and applies to stock acquired after the date of enactment and before January 1, 2011. Holding period rules also apply.

Executive compensation. The economic slowdown cast a spotlight on the executive compensation practices of Wall Street firms and many lawmakers are unhappy with what they see as "excessive" compensation. The new law reflects the changing mood in Congress. Lawmakers especially singled-out expenditures for luxury items by companies receiving financial assistance from the government's Troubled Asset Relief Program (TARP) for more regulation. Congress also directed the Treasury Secretary to review bonuses, awards and other incentives paid to senior executives at these firms and determine if the payments were contrary to public interest. Separately, the Treasury Administration has recently heightened its oversight of these firms and placed additional limits on executive compensation.

COBRA. Individuals who are involuntarily separated from employment between September 1, 2008 and January 1, 2010 can elect to pay 35 percent of their premiums for COBRA coverage and will be treated under the new law as paying the full amount. The former employer will pay the remaining 65 percent of the premium. In return, the employer will be able to credit its share of this temporary COBRA subsidy against wage withholdings and payroll taxes. The new law is extremely technical application, especially with notice requirements and timeframes for eligibility for coverage.

Energy incentives. Producers of alternative and renewable energy are definite winners under the new law. Congress has rewarded them with significant increases in energy tax incentives. Among the incentives are an enhanced renewable electricity production tax credit, an expanded energy investment tax credit, an increased alternative fuel pump tax credit, and an investment credit election. The incentives are temporary.

First-time homebuyer credit. While the first-time homebuyer credit is thought of as being targeted to individuals, it will impact businesses, especially home construction. The U.S. housing market is in one of its steepest slumps in recent memory. The new law extends the first-time homebuyer tax credit through November 30, 2009, raises it to $8,000 and eliminates the repayment requirement. Home builders, sellers and others in the housing industry need to market this credit aggressively.

More incentives. The new law also prospectively revokes a controversial IRS notice affecting NOL limitations on banks and expands the health coverage tax credit for eligible taxpayers. The new law also increases the New Markets Tax Credit program, modifies the low income housing credit, decreases estimated tax payments for certain individuals whose incomes come from small businesses and delays withholding on government contractors. Congress also enhanced many tax-exempt and tax-credit bond rules to help states and local governments generate revenue.

This letter is just a brief snapshot of the business incentives. As you've noted, most are temporary. Don't delay in contacting our office to learn more about these tax incentives. We're ready to help you maximize your tax savings.

Sincerely yours,

¶27,020 CLIENT LETTER #4

Re: 2009 Recovery Act – Making Work Pay Tax Credit

Dear Client:

The *American Recovery and Reinvestment Tax Act of 2009* (2009 Recovery Act) provides billions of dollars of tax relief for individuals, businesses, and state and local governments. Fortunately, you may qualify for one of these tax cutting provisions.

The 2009 Recovery Act provides a refundable credit of up to $400 for working individuals and $800 for working families. The credit is calculated at 6.2% of earned income, and phases out for taxpayers with modified adjusted gross income in excess of $75,000 (or $150,000 for married couples filing jointly). Nonresident aliens and individuals who can be claimed as a dependent do not qualify for the credit.

The new "Making Work Pay" tax credit benefits 95% of working families in the United States. Taxpayers can receive this benefit by reducing the amount of income tax that is withheld from their paychecks, or through claiming the credit on their tax returns.

The "Making Work Pay" tax credit is only one provision of the 2009 Recovery Act for which you may benefit. We will be happy to discuss other tax relief provisions that may be available to you. Please call our office to arrange an appointment at your earliest convenience.

Sincerely yours,

¶27,025 CLIENT LETTER #5

Re: 2009 Recovery Act – Increase in Earned Income Credit

Dear Client:

The *American Recovery and Reinvestment Tax Act of 2009* (2009 Recovery Act) provides tax relief for many individuals. As a taxpayer with three or more children, you may benefit from a temporary increase in the earned income tax credit.

The earned income credit (EIC) is a refundable tax credit for eligible low-income workers. The credit is based on "earned income," which includes wages, salaries, and other employee compensation, plus earnings from self-employment. The amount of the credit is determined by multiplying an individual's earned income by a credit percentage, subject to a possible phaseout.

The earned income and adjusted gross income limits and the phaseout thresholds applicable to the EIC vary according to whether the taxpayer has one qualifying child, two or more qualifying children, or no qualifying children. The 2009 Recovery Act increases the earned income credit to 45% of a family's first $12,570 of earned income for families with three or more children and increases the beginning point of the phase-out range for all married couples filing a joint return, regardless of the number of children.

To be a qualifying child, an individual must satisfy a relationship test, a residency test, and an age test. A taxpayer cannot claim the EIC if they are a qualifying child for another taxpayer. In addition, a return claiming the EIC based on a qualifying child or children must include each qualifying child's name, age and social security number.

If you have any questions regarding the earned income tax credit and whether or not you qualify, please call our office at your earliest convenience.

Sincerely yours,

¶27,030 CLIENT LETTER #6

Re: 2009 Recovery Act – Increased Eligibility for the Refundable Portion of the Child Tax Credit

Dear Client:

The *American Recovery and Reinvestment Tax Act of 2009* (2009 Recovery Act) provides a temporary increase in the refundable portion of the child tax credit for the 2009 and 2010 tax years, which is accomplished by a reduction in the earned income floor for claiming the credit to $3,000.

In general, individuals with dependent children under age 17 at the close of a calendar year are entitled to a $1,000 credit per child through 2010, although the credit is phased out with income over certain threshold amounts. For 2008, individuals were eligible for a refundable credit (the additional child tax credit) equal to 15 percent of their earned income in excess of $8,500, up to the child credit amount, if the total amount of their allowable credit exceeded their total tax liability (regular and AMT).

Families with three or more children may determine the additional child tax credit under an alternative formula if this results in a larger credit. Under this formula, the additional child tax credit equals the amount by which the taxpayer's social security taxes exceed the taxpayer's earned income credit.

The 2009 Recovery Act changes the minimum earned income threshold for 2009 and 2010 to $3,000, and therefore extends the benefit of this credit to a greater number of families than previous law afforded.

You and your family may qualify for the refundable child tax credit. Please contact our office so that we may discuss how you may take advantage of this tax benefit.

Sincerely yours,

¶27,035 CLIENT LETTER #7
Re: 2009 Recovery Act – American Opportunity Education Credit

Dear Client:

The *American Recovery and Reinvestment Tax Act of 2009* (2009 Recovery Act), which provides billions of dollars of tax relief, includes a tax credit for individuals seeking a college education. This provision may benefit you as a parent of a child working toward a college degree.

There are many federal tax incentives available to help reduce the costs of higher education. Some of these incentives offer tax breaks for current educational expenses, such as the above-the-line deduction for qualified tuition and related expenses, and the Hope scholarship and lifetime learning credits. In lieu of claiming the Hope scholarship credit, the 2009 Recovery Act provides an "American Opportunity" tax credit for 2009 and 2010.

Eligible taxpayers may claim an American Opportunity tax credit up to $2,500. The credit is determined as 100% of the first $2,000, and 25% of the next $2,000 of tuition and related expenses paid during the year. Forty percent of the credit is refundable.

Unlike the Hope credit, the American Opportunity credit is not limited to the first two years of post-secondary education. Also, the American Opportunity credit covers "course materials" such as books. This credit phases out for taxpayers with adjusted gross income in excess of $80,000 ($160,000 for married couples filing jointly).

Educational incentives can provide significant tax relief for families. The American Opportunity credit is one of several tax options related to saving and paying for higher education. Some may be more beneficial than others in your specific circumstances. Maximizing the benefits of the education tax breaks requires careful planning, particularly because of the interrelationship between the rules that apply to each provision. We can help you sort through the options. Please call our office to arrange an appointment at your earliest convenience.

Sincerely yours,

¶27,040 CLIENT LETTER #8

Re: 2009 Recovery Act – Extension of Bonus Depreciation and Code Sec. 179 Expense Deduction

Dear Client:

Congress has passed the *American Recovery and Reinvestment Tax Act of 2009* (2009 Recovery Act), which provides several incentives for business investment in capital and equipment. These provisions extend prior law increases in the limitation on expense deductions for depreciable assets and allowable 50% bonus depreciation on new equipment for the year it is placed in service. More specifically, the 2009 Recovery Act extends the available expense deduction limitation under Code Sec. 179 of $250,000, and the phase-out amount of $800,000, through tax years beginning in 2009. Bonus depreciation is also extended through 2009 (through 2010 for certain longer-lived and transportation property).

Because these extensions are temporary and generally apply only to tax years beginning in 2009, new purchases should be made and placed in service accordingly. The increased expense deduction will revert back to $125,000 (as indexed for inflation) for qualifying assets after 2009. Further, the $125,000 deduction (as adjusted for inflation) is scheduled to revert back to $25,000 for tax years beginning after 2011. Similarly, in 2010, the phase-out amount, which begins with every dollar spent over $800,000, reverts back to $500,000, as adjusted for inflation, and is scheduled to revert to $200,000 after 2011.

If you have any questions about how this development applies to you, or about any other aspects of this legislation, please contact our office at your convenience.

Sincerely yours,

¶27,045 CLIENT LETTER #9

Re: 2009 Recovery Act – NOL Carryback Period Extended

Dear Client:

As you may know, NOLs can generally be carried back two years and forward 20 years. The carryback and carryover periods are determined by the law applicable to the year in which the NOL arises, rather than any of the years to which it is carried back or forward. An NOL that is not utilized within its statutory timeframe expires without providing any tax benefit.

The *American Recovery and Reinvestment Tax Act of 2009* (2009 Recovery Act) provides relief for small businesses by extending the maximum carryback period for 2008 net operating losses (NOLs) from two years to any number of years greater than two and less than six (i.e., three, four, or five years). The number of years selected for the carryback is discretionary within these parameters, but the election must be properly executed in a timely manner and cannot be revoked.

Fiscal-year businesses can apply these rules either to NOLs generated in tax years ending in 2008, or to NOLs generated in tax years *beginning* in 2008. If a small business has already waived an NOL carryback for the applicable 2008 tax year, the election can be revoked in order to obtain NOL carryback relief under the 2009 Recovery Act provisions. However, the prior election must be revoked and the new election executed within 60 days of the legislation's enactment.

Because you sustained an NOL this tax year, these provisions present an opportunity for an immediate refund of prior year taxes paid. Please call us at your earliest convenience to discuss the various alternatives that can be used to optimize your tax savings and cash flow.

Sincerely yours,

¶27,050 CLIENT LETTER #10

Re: 2009 Recovery Act – WOTC for Veterans and Disconnected Youth

Dear Client:

The *American Recovery and Reinvestment Tax Act of 2009* (2009 Recovery Act) has modified the rules for eligible taxpayers to claim the Work Opportunity Tax Credit (WOTC) by creating two new categories of targeted groups for 2009 and 2010, unemployed veterans and disconnected youth.

As you may know, the WOTC was previously extended for employers who hire qualified individuals that begin work before September 1, 2011. Prior to the 2009 Recovery Act, the WOTC was available on an elective basis for employers hiring individuals from the following specified targeted groups:

- families eligible to receive benefits under the Temporary Assistance for Needy Families Program (TANF);
- qualified military veterans;
- qualified ex-felons;
- certified "designated community residents;"
- certified "vocational rehabilitation referrals;"
- qualified summer youth employees;
- qualified food stamp recipients;
- qualified Supplemental Security Income (SSI) recipients; and
- qualified long-term family assistance recipients.

The 2009 Recovery Act defines the new targeted groups as individuals who begin work for the employer after December 31, 2008 and meet the following guidelines:

- Unemployed veterans must be discharged from active duty in the Armed Forces at any time during the five-year period ending on the hiring date, and receive unemployment compensation for at least four weeks during the year prior to being hired by the employer.
- A "disconnected youth" must be between the ages of 16 and 24 on the hiring date and lack basic skills that would make him or her readily employable. In addition, during the six-month period preceding the hiring date, the "disconnected youth" must not be regularly employed nor attending secondary, technical, or post-secondary school.

As an employer, you may be interested in claiming the WOTC for current or future employees. If you would like additional information on qualified wages or employee certification requirements, please call us at your earliest convenience to arrange an appointment.

Sincerely yours,

¶27,055 CLIENT LETTER #11

Re: 2009 Recovery Act – Renewable Energy Production Facilities

Dear Client:

The *American Recovery and Reinvestment Tax Act of 2009* (2009 Recovery Act) extends the placed-in-service date for renewable energy production facilities and allows certain facilities an election to claim the investment tax credit in lieu of the production credit.

Qualified facilities are generally facilities that generate electricity using qualified energy resources. Qualified energy resources include wind, refined coal, closed-loop biomass, open-loop biomass, geothermal energy, solar energy, small irrigation power, municipal solid waste, and qualified hydropower production. To be eligible for the renewable electricity production credit (REPC), electricity produced from qualified energy resources at qualified facilities must be sold by the taxpayer to an unrelated person. In addition, these facilities must be placed in service by a certain date.

Highlights of the 2009 Recovery Act provisions related to renewable energy production facilities include the following:

Long-term extension and modification of renewable energy production tax credit. The 2009 Recovery Act extends the placed-in-service date for wind facilities for three years, through December 31, 2012. The 2009 Recovery Act also extends the placed-in-service date for closed-loop biomass, open-loop biomass, geothermal, small irrigation, hydropower, landfill gas, waste-to-energy, and marine renewable facilities for three years, through December 31, 2013.

Temporary election to claim the investment tax credit in lieu of the production tax credit. Facilities that produce electricity from wind, closed-loop biomass, open-loop biomass, geothermal, small irrigation, hydropower, landfill gas, waste-to-energy, and marine renewable energy are eligible for the production credit. However, the 2009 Recovery Act allows wind property that is placed in service in 2009 through 2012, and other renewable energy property placed in service in 2009 through 2013, an election to claim the investment tax credit in lieu of the production tax credit.

Subsidized energy financing limitation on the investment tax credit repealed. The 2009 Recovery Act repeals the subsidized energy financing limitation on the investment tax credit even if such property is financed with industrial development bonds or through any other subsidized energy financing. This provision is in effect for periods after December 31, 2008.

As you may know, the rules relating to the renewable electricity production credit are quite complex. We can help you determine whether you are eligible to claim the REPC or the investment tax credit, and guide you in documenting your claim. Please call our office at your earliest convenience to arrange an appointment.

Sincerely yours,

¶27,060 CLIENT LETTER #12

Re: 2009 Recovery Act – Residential Energy Credits Modified

Dear Client:

The *American Recovery and Reinvestment Tax Act of 2009* (2009 Recovery Act) provides benefits to homeowners like you by reinstating the Credit for Nonbusiness Energy Property (CNEP) for 2009 and 2010, and enhancing the Residential Energy Efficient Property (REEP) credit.

As you may know, the CNEP can be taken when qualified energy efficient improvements or expenditures are made for your principal residence, including new insulation; replacement windows, skylights and doors; central air conditioners; certain water heaters, furnaces or boilers; and a new metal or asphalt roof specifically treated to reduce heat loss. The CNEP, which was not available for the 2008 tax year, has been reinstated for eligible property placed in service after December 31, 2008, and before January 1, 2011. The 2009 Recovery Act also:

- eliminates the lifetime limitation for the CNEP (previously $500);
- increases the credit from 10 percent to 30 percent of qualified expenses; and
- increases the maximum CNEP amount for 2009 and 2010 installations to $1,500.

The REEP credit is allowed for qualified expenditures that produce energy for home use, such as for solar energy and fuel cell energy property. The REEP was previously extended through the 2016 tax year, and applies not only to your principal residence, but also to your vacation home. Although the maximum credit for qualified fuel cell property remains unchanged ($500 for each half kilowatt of capacity), the 2009 Recovery Act removes the maximum credit amounts for the following qualified property expenditures for tax years beginning after December 31, 2008:

- solar electric (previously capped at $2,000);
- small wind energy (previously capped at $500 for each half kilowatt of capacity of wind turbines (not to exceed $4,000)); and
- geothermal heat pump (previously capped at $2,000).

If you want to install energy-saving improvements or alternative energy property to your home, we can help you categorize your expenses and plan the timing of your energy-saving projects to maximize your overall tax savings. Please call our office at your earliest convenience to arrange an appointment.

Sincerely yours,

¶27,065 CLIENT LETTER #13

Re: 2009 Recovery Act – Modified Alternative Minimum Tax

Dear Client:

As you know, the alternative minimum tax (AMT) is trapping more middle income taxpayers every year. To partially alleviate this tax burden, Congress has enacted annual "patches" to the AMT to increase exemption amounts and provide other relief. *The American Recovery and Reinvestment Tax Act of 2009* (2009 Recovery Act) increases the AMT exemption amounts for 2009 to $70,950 for married couples filing jointly and surviving spouses, $46,700 for single taxpayers and heads of households, and $35,475 for married couples filing separately.

Tax planning strategies can be used to reduce the impact of the AMT. As a general rule, taxpayers subject to the AMT should accelerate income into AMT years and postpone deductions into non-AMT years. We believe that a thorough analysis of your current and projected tax situation could minimize or eliminate your exposure to AMT liability. Please contact our office to make an appointment to discuss this important tax planning opportunity.

Sincerely yours,

¶27,070 CLIENT LETTER #14

Re: 2009 Recovery Act – Increased Tax Credit for Alternative Fueling Property

Dear Client:

The *American Recovery and Reinvestment Tax Act of 2009* (2009 Recovery Act) increases the credit for alternative fuel vehicle refueling property for businesses and individuals. Before this increase, the credit equaled 30 percent of the cost of qualified alternative fuel vehicle (QAFV) refueling property placed in service during the tax year, limited to $30,000 per property for property subject to depreciation, and $1,000 per property for other property.

QAFV refueling property is property, excluding buildings and structures, the original use of which begins with the taxpayer, and that is not used predominately outside of the United States. The property must be subject to depreciation or installed on property that is used as the taxpayer's principal residence. Use of the property must be either for storing alternative fuel at the point where the fuel is delivered into the fuel tank of a motor vehicle propelled by the fuel, or to dispense alternative fuel at that point into the fuel tank of a motor vehicle propelled by the fuel.

Under the 2009 Recovery Act, the credit for QAFV refueling property placed in service in 2009 and 2010 by businesses is increased to 50 percent for a maximum credit of $50,000. For individuals, the credit is also increased to 50% for 2009 and 2010, for a maximum credit of $2,000. For hydrogen refueling property, the 30% rate continues to apply, but the maximum credit is raised to $200,000.

Because your most recent tax returns have indicated that you are in the gas station industry and may own qualifying alternative vehicle refueling property, the enhancement in this credit could apply to you. Please call us so that we may discuss how you can maximize your tax benefit from this enhanced credit.

Sincerely yours,

Treasury and IRS Guidance

¶28,001 Introduction

In 2008, Congress enacted several pieces of legislation to address the downturn in the housing market and U.S. economy, including the Economic Stimulus Act of 2008 (P.L. 110-185), the Housing Assistance Tax Act of 2008 (P.L. 110-289) and the Emergency Economic Stabilization Act of 2008 (P.L. 110-343). The Treasury and IRS have also responded with guidance both on the 2008 legislation and to provide flexibility in the application of federal tax laws to taxpayers impacted by the economic downturn.

Reproduced, below, are selected items of guidance issued by the Treasury and IRS. Use CCH Tax Tracker News and other CCH Tax and Accounting products to keep up-to-date with all of the recently issued guidance.

INDIVIDUALS

¶28,005 IRS News Release IR-2008-141, December 16, 2008

The Internal Revenue Service announced an expedited process that will make it easier for financially distressed homeowners to avoid having a federal tax lien block refinancing of mortgages or the sale of a home.

If taxpayers are looking to refinance or sell a home and there is a federal tax lien filed, there are options. Taxpayers or their representatives, such as their lenders, may request that the IRS make a tax lien secondary to the lien by the lending institution that is refinancing or restructuring a loan. Taxpayers or their representatives may request that the IRS discharge its claim if the home is being sold for less than the amount of the mortgage lien under certain circumstances.

The process to request a discharge or a subordination of a tax lien takes approximately 30 days after the submission of the completed application, but the IRS will work to speed those requests in wake of the economic downturn.

"We don't want the IRS to be a barrier to people saving or selling their homes. We want to raise awareness of these lien options and to speed our decision-making process so people can refinance their mortgages or sell their homes," said Doug Shulman, IRS commissioner.

"We realize these are difficult times for many Americans," Shulman said. "We will ensure we have the resources in place to resolve these issues quickly and homeowners can complete their transactions."

Filing a *Notice of Federal Tax Lien* is a formal process by which the government makes a legal claim to property as security or payment for a tax debt. It serves as a public notice to other creditors that the government has a claim on the property.

In some cases, a federal tax lien can be made secondary to another lien, such as a lending institution's, if the IRS determines that taking a secondary position ultimately will help with collection of the tax debt. That process is called subordination. Taxpayers or their representatives may apply for a subordination of a federal tax lien if they are refinancing or restructuring their mortgage. Without lien subordination, taxpayers may be unable to borrow funds or reduce their payments. Lending institutions generally want their lien to have priority on the home being used as collateral.

To apply for a certificate of lien subordination, people must follow directions in *Publication 784*, How to Prepare an Application for a Certificate of Subordination of a Federal Tax Lien. Again, there is no form but there must be a typed letter of request and certain documentation. The request should be mailed to one of 40 Collection Advisory Groups nationwide. See *Publication 4235*, Collection Advisory Group Addresses, for address information.

Taxpayers or their representatives may apply for a certificate of discharge of a tax lien if they are giving up ownership of the property, such as

¶28,005

selling the property, at an amount less than the mortgage lien if the mortgage lien is senior to the tax lien. The IRS may also issue a certificate of discharge in other circumstances if the taxpayer has sufficient equity in other assets, can substitute other assets, or is able to pay the IRS its equity in the property. Without a tax lien discharge, the taxpayer may be unable to complete the home ownership change and the ownership title will remain clouded.

To apply for a tax lien discharge, applicants must follow directions in *Publication 783*, Instructions on How to Apply for a Certificate of Discharge of a Federal Tax Lien. There is no form but there must be a typed letter of request and certain documentation. The request should be mailed to one of 40 Collection Advisory Groups nationwide. See *Publication 4235* for address information.

The IRS also urges people to contact the agency's Collection Advisory Group early in the home sale or refinancing process so that it can begin work on their requests. People sometimes delay informing lenders of the tax liens, which only serves to delay the transaction.

Currently, there are more than 1 million federal tax liens outstanding tied to both real and personal property. The IRS issues more than 600,000 federal tax lien notices annually.

¶28,010   IRS News Release IR-2009-2, January 6, 2009

The Internal Revenue Service kicked off the 2009 tax filing season by announcing a number of new steps to help financially distressed taxpayers maximize their refunds and speed payments while providing additional help to people struggling to meet their tax obligations.

IRS Commissioner Doug Shulman encouraged taxpayers to take advantage of several new tax credits and deductions this filing season and announced a major enhancement to the Free File program that will allow nearly all taxpayers to *e-file* for free and accelerate their refunds.

"With so many people facing financial difficulties, we want taxpayers to get all the tax credits they're entitled to as quickly as they can," Shulman said. "In addition, we are creating new protections to help people trying to meet their tax obligations. The IRS will do everything it can to help during these tough times."

Help for People Who Owe Taxes

With many people facing additional financial difficulties, the IRS is taking several additional steps to help people who owe back taxes.

"We need to ensure that we balance our responsibility to enforce the law with the economic realities facing many American citizens today," Shulman said. "We want to go the extra mile to help taxpayers, especially those who've done the right thing in the past and are facing unusual hardships."

On a wide range of situations, IRS employees have flexibility to work with struggling taxpayers to assist them with their situation. Depending on the circumstances, taxpayers in hardship situations may be able to adjust payments for back taxes, avoid defaulting on payment agreements or possibly defer collection action.

The IRS reminds taxpayers who are behind on tax payments and need assistance to contact the phone numbers listed on their IRS correspondence. There could be additional help available for these taxpayers facing unusual hardship situations.

Among the areas where the IRS can provide assistance:

- **Postponement of Collection Actions:** IRS employees will have greater authority to suspend collection actions in certain hardship cases where taxpayers are unable to pay. This includes instances when the taxpayer has recently lost a job, is relying solely on Social Security or welfare income or is facing devastating illness or significant medical bills. If an individual has recently encountered this type of financial problem, IRS assistors may be able to suspend collection without documentation to minimize burden on the taxpayer.

- **Added Flexibility for Missed Payments:** The IRS is allowing more flexibility for previously compliant individuals in existing Installment Agreements who have difficulty making payments because of a job loss or other financial hardship. The IRS may allow a skipped payment or a reduced monthly payment amount without automatically suspending the Installment Agreement. Taxpayers in a difficult financial situation should contact the IRS.

- **Additional Review for Offers in Compromise on Home Values:** An Offer in Compromise (OIC), an agreement between a taxpayer and the IRS that settles the taxpayer's tax debt for less than the full amount owed, may be a viable option for taxpayers experiencing economic difficulties. However, the equity taxpayers have in real property can be a barrier to an OIC being accepted. With the uncertainty in the housing market, the IRS recognizes that the real-estate valuations used to assess ability to pay may not be accurate. So in instances where the accuracy of local real-estate valuations is in question or other unusual hardships exist, the IRS is creating a new second review of the information to determine if accepting an offer is appropriate.

- **Prevention of Offer in Compromise Defaults:** Taxpayers who are unable to meet the periodic payment terms of an accepted OIC will be able to contact the IRS office handling the offer for available options to help them avoid default.

- **Expedited Levy Releases:** The IRS will speed the delivery of levy releases by easing requirements on taxpayers who request expedited levy releases for hardship reasons. Taxpayers seeking expedited releases for levies to an employer or bank should contact the IRS number shown on the notice of levy to discuss available options. When calling, taxpayers requesting a levy release due to hardship should be prepared to provide the IRS with the fax number of the bank or employer processing the levy.

Taxpayers with financial problems who discover they can't pay when they file their 2008 tax returns also have options available. IRS.gov has a list of "What If?" scenarios that deal with payment and other financial problems. These scenarios, in question-and-answer format, provide information on specific actions taxpayers can take. Taxpayers unable to pay in full can likewise contact the IRS to discuss additional options to pay.

Maximizing Refunds and Speeding Refund Delivery

This filing season, there are several steps taxpayers can take to maximize their refunds and speed the delivery of money from the IRS.

Taxpayers should look into the numerous tax breaks available and take every credit, deduction and exclusion for which they qualify. People who had less income in 2008 could find they qualify for credits for which they previously did not qualify. And there are several new benefits this year:

- **First-Time Homebuyer Credit:** Those who bought a principal residence recently or are considering buying one should take note. This unique credit of up to $7,500 works much like a 15-year interest-free loan. IRS.gov has more details and answers to common questions.

- **The Recovery Rebate Credit:** This credit is figured like last year's Economic Stimulus Payment except that Recovery Rebate Credit amounts are based on tax year 2008 instead of 2007. Most people already received their full benefit in the form of the Economic Stimulus Payment. However, a taxpayer may qualify for the Recovery Rebate Credit, if, for example, he or she did not get an Economic Stimulus Payment, had a child in 2008 or had a change in income level. If you receive this credit, it will be included in your refund and will not be issued as a separate payment. See the Form 1040 Instructions, Fact Sheet 2009-3 or the *information center* on IRS.gov for details.

- **Standard Deduction for Real Estate Taxes:** Taxpayers can claim an additional standard deduction, based on the state or local real estate taxes paid in 2008. The maximum deduction is $500, or $1,000 for joint filers.

- **Mortgage Workouts and Foreclosures:** For most homeowners, these are now tax-free. Eligible homeowners can exclude debt forgiven on their principal residence if the balance of the loan was less than $2 million. The limit is $1 million for a married person filing a separate return. See Form 982 and its instructions for details.

IRS.gov, the official IRS Web site, has more information on these and other popular credits, such as the child tax credit, the Earned Income Tax Credit and alternative fuel vehicle credit.

E-File, E-Pay and Direct Deposit

This year, electronic filing options will speed the payment of refunds to millions of taxpayers. Taxpayers who e-file and choose direct deposit for their refunds, for example, will get their refunds in as few as 10 days. That compares to approximately six weeks for people who file a paper return and get a traditional paper check.

This year, taxpayers can begin filing electronically on Jan. 16.

The IRS in 2009 is again offering free tax preparation and filing through the Free File program. Anyone with an adjusted gross income up to $56,000 can use the standard Free File options this year — that is approximately 98 million Americans. The program also has usability improvements, including a standardized set of electronic forms that are most frequently used by Free File-eligible taxpayers.

¶ 28,010

This year the IRS and its partners are offering a new option, Free File Fillable Tax Forms, that opens up Free File to virtually everyone, even those whose incomes exceed $56,000.

Free File Fillable Tax Forms allows taxpayers to fill out and file their tax forms electronically, just as they would on paper. This option does not include an "interview" process like the other Free File offerings, but it does allow taxpayers to enter their tax data, perform basic math calculations, sign electronically, print their returns for recordkeeping and e-file their returns. It may be just right for those who are comfortable with the tax law or those who use electronic software to prepare their returns but file using paper forms.

Both the fillable-forms option and the previously available Free File offerings are available only through the IRS.gov Web site. More information will be available in mid-January.

1040 Central and Taxpayer-Friendly Features

When they visit the IRS.gov Web site this filing season, taxpayers may notice the new "rotating spotlight" feature on the homepage. The *spotlights*, which change every few seconds, give the taxpaying public direct access to more of the IRS Web site's vast amount of content.

Also on the homepage, taxpayers can click on *1040 Central* to find help preparing and filing their tax returns. Like last year, this popular section of IRS.gov has a wide range of offerings that address taxpayer needs.

Finally, the IRS is producing a number of podcasts this filing season that will be available on *IRS.gov*. In addition to Tax Tips, Fact Sheets and News Releases, these short audio interviews cover a wide range of topics and are a way for the IRS to reach out to a new generation of taxpayers.

¶28,015 IRS News Release IR-2009-3, January 7, 2009

National Taxpayer Advocate Nina E. Olson released her annual report, urging Congress to greatly simplify the tax code and recommending measures to reduce the burden on taxpayers who are struggling to pay their tax bills.

The report takes note of the serious financial difficulties facing many Americans in light of the ongoing economic downturn. "It is imperative for the IRS to consider the circumstances of taxpayers facing economic hardship before initiating enforcement actions," Olson wrote.

When the IRS contemplates taking an enforced collection action such as a levy, a lien or an asset seizure, both the tax code and IRS procedures require that IRS personnel consider whether the collection action will impose an economic hardship on the taxpayer. Despite these requirements, "current IRS guidance provides little direction to help IRS employees identify taxpayers who are experiencing economic hardship and prevent undue economic burden," Olson wrote.

Call for Tax Simplification

The report designates the complexity of the tax code as the most serious problem facing taxpayers. According to data compiled by Olson's office, U.S. taxpayers and businesses spend about 7.6 billion hours a year complying with tax-filing requirements. "If tax compliance were an industry, it would be one of the largest in the United States," the report says. "To consume 7.6 billion hours, the 'tax industry' requires the equivalent of 3.8 million full-time workers."

The report estimates that U.S. taxpayers spend $193 billion a year complying with income tax requirements, an amount that equals 14 percent of the total amount of income taxes collected. One count shows the number of words in the tax code has reached 3.7 million, and over the past eight years, changes to the tax code have been made at a rate of more than one a day - including more than 500 changes in 2008 alone. Individual taxpayers now find the tax rules so overwhelming that more than 80 percent pay transaction fees to help them file their returns - about 60 percent pay a preparer to do the job and another 22 percent purchase tax software.

Two examples of tax law complexity:

- The Alternative Minimum Tax (AMT) effectively requires taxpayers to compute their taxes twice - once under the regular rules and again under the AMT regime - and then to pay the higher of the two amounts. Absent repeal or continuing AMT patches, the AMT will affect 33 million taxpayers in 2010. Although the AMT was originally conceived to prevent wealthy taxpayers from escaping tax liability through the use of tax-avoidance transactions, 77 percent of the additional income subject to tax under the AMT today is attributable to the disallowance of deductions otherwise allowed for state and local taxes and personal and dependency exemptions. "Few people think of having children or living in a high-tax state as a tax-avoidance maneuver, but under the unique logic of the AMT, that is essentially how those actions are treated," the report notes.

- The tax code provides tax breaks to encourage taxpayers to save for education and retirement. However, the number of such tax incentives has grown to at least 27 and the eligibility requirements, definitions of common terms, income-level thresholds, phase-out ranges and inflation adjustments vary among the provisions. This complexity undermines the intent of the incentives, as taxpayers can only respond to incentives if they know they exist and understand them.

Olson recommends that Congress substantially simplify the tax code. The report includes a series of recommendations, including recommendations to repeal the Alternative Minimum Tax; streamline education and retirement savings tax incentives; simplify the family status provisions of the tax code; simplify the rules under which workers are classified as employees or independent contractors; reduce sunset and phase-out provisions and revise the overall penalty structure. More broadly, Olson recommends six core principles on which fundamental tax reform should be based. (For details, see Most Serious Problem: *The Complexity of the Tax Code* and corresponding items in the *Legislative Recommendations* section of the report.)

Working with Taxpayers Who Are Experiencing Financial Difficulties

The report makes three principal recommendations to reduce burden on financially struggling taxpayers:

1. *Make greater use of collection alternatives when economic hardship is present.* While enforced collection actions like levy and seizure authority are important collection tools that allow the IRS to address serious incidents of noncompliance, a review of IRS historical enforcement data show that more enforcement actions do not translate into commensurate increases in revenue collection. One example: The number of levies issued by the IRS increased by 1,608 percent from FY 2000 to FY 2007 - from 220,000 levies to about 3.76 million levies - yet the increase in the total collection yield during the period was slightly less than 45 percent. By contrast, historical enforcement data indicate that collection alternatives, such as offers in compromise and partial-payment installment agreements, may be more effective at collecting liabilities from taxpayers having difficulty paying their tax debts. (For details, *see* Most Serious Problem: *The IRS Needs to More Fully Consider the Impact of Collection Enforcement Actions on Taxpayers Experiencing Economic Difficulties.*)

2. *Simplify the "cancellation of debt" minefield that many taxpayers who default on debts must navigate.* Most financially distressed individuals who lose their homes to foreclosure or cannot pay off their car loans, credit card balances, student loans, or medical bills probably do not realize that their delinquency may increase their tax liabilities, but it often does. If a creditor writes off a debt, the tax code generally treats the amount of the canceled debt as taxable income to the debtor. Congress has carved out a number of exclusions, including an exclusion for "insolvency" and a recently enacted exclusion to help some (but not all) homeowners whose mortgage debts are canceled when their houses are foreclosed upon and sold or whose loan balances are reduced as part of a mortgage loan modification. However, taxpayers do not receive the benefit of these exclusions automatically. A taxpayer must file Form 982, *Reduction of Tax Attributes Due to Discharge of Indebtedness (and Section 1082 Basis Adjustment)*, to claim an exclusion. Form 982 is extremely complex, and very few taxpayers or preparers are familiar with it.

IRS data show that approximately two million Forms 1099-C, *Cancellation of Debt*, are issued to taxpayers and the IRS each year reporting canceled debts. In an economic downturn, the number of taxpayers defaulting on credit card bills, car loans, home mortgages and other debts can be expected to rise. Olson estimates that tens of thousands and possibly hundreds of thousands of taxpayers who qualify to exclude canceled debts from gross income do not file Form 982 to claim allowable exclusions. Instead, some of these taxpayers unnecessarily include the amount of the canceled debt in gross income, and other taxpayers who fail to include it unnecessarily face IRS examinations and tax assessments.

Olson recommends that Congress change the law to remove taxpayers with modest amounts of debt cancellation from the cancellation of debt income regime, and she recommends that the IRS develop an insolvency worksheet that taxpayers can file with their returns and create a centralized unit dedicated to handling cancellation of debt issues. (For details, *see* Legislative Recommendation: *Simplify the Tax Treatment of Cancellation of Debt Income* and Most Serious Problem: *Understanding and Reporting the Tax Consequences of Cancellation of Debt Income.*)

3. *Implement a "screen" to protect low income Social Security recipients from continuous, automated tax levies.* Under the Federal Payment Levy Program, the IRS is authorized to "levy" (or withhold) 15 percent of any federal payment made to a delinquent taxpayer. Using this au-

¶28,015

thority, the IRS levied against 1.8 million payments to Social Security recipients in 2008. TAS estimates that more than 25 percent of these taxpayers had incomes below the poverty level and more than one-third would likely be classified by the IRS as unable to pay if their cases were subject to human review. However, the automated levy system does not use built-in screens to identify and shield these taxpayers. The report contains a research study recommending the implementation of such a screen. (For details, see Research Study: *Building a Better Filter: Protecting Lower Income Social Security Recipients from the Federal Payment Levy Program*.)

Finally, taxpayers who are unable to make their tax payments and face enforced collection action will generally qualify for assistance from the Taxpayer Advocate Service (TAS), which Olson heads. (See information below about contacting TAS.)

Other Issues

Olson reiterates her longstanding recommendation that Congress regulate unenrolled tax preparers to protect taxpayers from preparer errors and exploitation. She notes that 62 percent of taxpayers use preparers, yet anyone can now be a "preparer" - with no training, no licensing and no oversight required.

The report also proposes a comprehensive framework for reforming the penalty provisions in the tax code, which have increased from about 14 in 1954 to more than 130 today. More specifically, the report recommends quick congressional action to remedy particularly harsh consequences of a penalty enacted in 2004 to combat tax shelters. Section 6707A of the tax code imposes a penalty of $100,000 per individual per year and $200,000 per entity per year for failure to make special disclosures of a "listed transaction." The penalty creates what Olson calls "unconscionable" results and may have the effect of bankrupting middle class families who had no intention of entering into a tax shelter. Under the law, the IRS *must* impose the penalty where a taxpayer fails to make the special disclosures - even if the taxpayer had no knowledge that the transaction was listed or even questionable, even if the taxpayer derived no tax savings from the transaction, and even if the transaction is not "listed" until years after the taxpayer entered into it and filed a return reflecting the transaction. A taxpayer who does business through a wholly owned S corporation is subject to a penalty of $300,000 ($200,000 at the entity level and $100,000 at the individual level) for each year in which the transaction is reflected on a return. The IRS is currently considering this penalty in hundreds of cases.

Overall, the report discusses 21 problems facing taxpayers, makes dozens of recommendations for administrative change, proposes 17 recommendations for legislative change and analyzes the 10 tax issues most frequently litigated in the federal courts during the past fiscal year. It also contains a second volume that presents in-depth studies on three subjects - the penalty regime in the tax code, the development of a "filter" to protect low income Social Security recipients from automated levies and strategies to improve tax compliance by tax preparers and their clients.

About the Taxpayer Advocate Service

The Taxpayer Advocate Service (TAS) is an independent organization within the IRS whose employees assist taxpayers who are experiencing economic harm, who are seeking help in resolving tax problems that have not been resolved through normal channels or who believe that an IRS system or procedure is not working as it should. If you believe you are eligible for TAS assistance, you can reach TAS by calling the TAS toll-free case intake line at 1-877-777-4778 or TTY/TDD 1-800-829-4059. For more information, go to *www.irs.gov/advocate*.

¶28,020 Notice 2009-12, I.R.B. 2009-6, January 15, 2009

PURPOSE

This notice provides guidance under §36(b)(1)(C) of the Internal Revenue Code (Code) for allocating the first-time homebuyer credit between taxpayers who are not married.

LAW

Section 36 was added to the Code by section 3011 of the Housing and Economic Recovery Act of 2008, Pub. L. No. 110-289, 122 Stat. 2654, 2888 (2008). Section 36(a) provides that a taxpayer who is a first-time homebuyer of a principal residence (as defined in §121) may claim a credit on the taxpayer's income tax return equal to 10 percent of the purchase price of the residence. Section 36(c)(1) defines "first-time homebuyer" as any individual (and if married, the individual's spouse) who has not had an ownership interest in any principal residence during the three-year period ending on the date of the purchase of the principal residence. Section 36(c)(3) defines "purchase" as any acquisition, but only if (i) the taxpayer did not acquire the property from a related person, and (ii) the taxpayer's basis in the property is not determined, in whole or in part, by reference to the adjusted basis of the property in the hands of the person from whom the taxpayer acquired the property, or determined under § 1014(a) (relating to property acquired from a decedent). For purposes of § 36(c)(3)(i), § 36(c)(5) provides that a person is treated as related to another person if the relationship would result in the disallowance of losses under § 267 or § 707, except that members of a family of an individual include only the individual's spouse, ancestors, and lineal descendants.

Pursuant to § 36(h), the first-time homebuyer credit applies to a home purchased on or after April 9, 2008, and before July 1, 2009. The maximum amount of the credit is $7,500 ($3,750 for a married taxpayer filing a separate return), as provided in § 36(b)(1)(A) and (B). Under § 36(b)(2), the credit begins to phase out for a taxpayer whose modified adjusted gross income (MAGI) is $75,000 ($150,000 for married taxpayers filing a joint return) ("MAGI threshold"). The allowable credit is reduced by an amount equal to:

Maximum Allowable Credit × MAGI in excess of $75,000 ($150,000 for married filing jointly). / $20,000

The credit is completely phased out for a taxpayer whose MAGI is $95,000 ($170,000 for married taxpayers filing a joint return) ("MAGI cap").

Section 36(f) generally requires a taxpayer who claims the first-time homebuyer credit to repay the credit allowed in 15 equal annual installments beginning with the second taxable year after the taxable year in which the taxpayer claims the credit. This repayment obligation may be accelerated or forgiven under certain exceptions as provided in § 36(f).

For eligible purchases in 2008, a taxpayer claims the credit by attaching Form 5405, "First-Time Homebuyer Credit," to the taxpayer's 2008 tax return. For eligible purchases in 2009, a taxpayer may elect to claim the credit for 2008 or 2009 by attaching Form 5405 to the taxpayer's original or amended 2008 tax return or 2009 tax return.

APPLICATION

Section 36(b)(1)(C) provides that the Secretary may prescribe the manner in which the first-time homebuyer credit is allocated between two or more taxpayers who are not married and who purchase a principal residence. The total credit allocated between the taxpayers cannot exceed $7,500. For purposes of § 36(b)(1)(C), if two or more taxpayers who are not married purchase (within the meaning of § 36(c)(3)) a principal residence and otherwise satisfy the requirements of § 36, the first-time homebuyer credit may be allocated between the taxpayers using any reasonable method. A reasonable method is any method that does not allocate any portion of the credit to a taxpayer not eligible to claim that portion. A reasonable method includes allocating the credit between taxpayers who are eligible to claim the credit based on (1) the taxpayers' contributions towards the purchase price of a residence as tenants in common or joint tenants, or (2) the taxpayers' ownership interests in a residence as tenants in common.

EXAMPLES

The examples illustrate how the first-time homebuyer credit may be allocated when A and B purchase a principal residence as tenants in common. The rules illustrated in the examples also apply in a similar manner to taxpayers who purchase a principal residence as joint tenants. Unless otherwise indicated, assume that in each example A and B (i) purchase a principal residence on May 1, 2008, (ii) are not married to each other, (iii) do not have MAGI in excess of the MAGI threshold, and (iv) are first-time homebuyers who otherwise satisfy the requirements of § 36.

Example 1.

A contributes $45,000 and B contributes $15,000 towards the $60,000 purchase price of a residence. Each owns a one-half interest in the residence as tenants in common. Under § 36(a), the allowable credit is limited to 10 percent of the purchase price, or $6,000. A and B may allocate the allowable $6,000 credit three-fourths to A and one-fourth to B based on their contributions toward the purchase price of the residence, one-half to each based on their ownership interests in the residence, or using any other reasonable method (for example, the entire credit to A or B because both A and B are eligible to claim the entire allowable credit).

¶28,020

Example 2.

A contributes $10,000 for a down payment towards the $100,000 purchase price of a residence, and A and B obtain and are jointly liable for a $90,000 mortgage for the remainder of the purchase price. Each owns a one-half interest in the residence as tenants in common. Under § 36(b)(1)(A), the allowable credit is not $10,000 (10 percent of the purchase price) but is limited to $7,500. A and B may allocate the allowable $7,500 credit 55 percent to A and 45 percent to B based on their contributions toward the purchase price, one-half to each based on their ownership interests in the residence, or using any other reasonable method (for example, the entire credit to A or B because both A and B are eligible to claim the entire allowable credit).

Example 3.

On April 15, 2008, A pays the entire $100,000 purchase price of a residence and is the sole owner. Under § 36(b)(1)(A), the allowable credit is not $10,000 (10 percent of the purchase price) but is limited to $7,500. On May 12, 2008, A transfers a one-half interest in the residence to B as a tenant in common for $10,000. A may claim the entire allowable $7,500 credit. Because B acquired B's interest in the residence from A in part by gift, B's basis in the residence is determined under § 1015 by reference to A's basis in the residence. Therefore, B did not purchase an interest in the residence within the meaning of § 36(c)(3), and no portion of the credit may be allocated to B because B is not eligible to claim any portion of the credit.

Example 4.

A and B each contributes $50,000 towards the $100,000 purchase price of a residence and owns a one-half interest in the residence as tenants in common. Under § 36(b)(1)(A), the allowable credit is not $10,000 (10 percent of the purchase price) but is limited to $7,500. However, B is not a first-time homebuyer within the meaning of § 36(c)(1). Therefore, no portion of the credit may be allocated to B because B is not eligible to claim any portion of the credit. A may claim the entire allowable $7,500 credit.

Example 5.

A contributes $75,000 and B contributes $25,000 towards the $100,000 purchase price of a residence, and each owns a one-half interest in the residence as tenants in common. Under § 36(b)(1)(A), the allowable credit is not $10,000 (10 percent of the purchase price) but is limited to $7,500. A's MAGI is $100,000 and B's MAGI is $60,000. Because A's MAGI exceeds the $95,000 MAGI cap, any portion of the credit allocated to A would be reduced to $0. A and B may allocate the entire allowable $7,500 credit to B because B's MAGI is less than the $75,000 MAGI threshold and, therefore, B is eligible to claim the entire allowable credit.

Example 6.

A and B each contributes $50,000 towards the $100,000 purchase price of a residence and owns a one-half interest in the residence as tenants in common. Under § 36(b)(1)(A), the allowable credit is not $10,000 (10 percent of the purchase price) but is limited to $7,500. A's MAGI is $80,000 and B's MAGI is $60,000. Because A's MAGI exceeds the $75,000 MAGI threshold by $5,000, any portion of the allowable credit allocated to A will be reduced by one-quarter, $5,000 (MAGI in excess of $75,000) / $20,000. A and B may allocate the allowable $7,500 credit one-half to A and one-half to B ($3,750 each) based on their contributions toward the purchase price of the residence or their ownership interests in the residence. However, A's $3,750 portion of the credit is limited by § 36(b)(2) and is reduced by one-quarter ($3,750 × .25 = $937.50) to $2,812.50 ($3,750 − 937.50). Alternatively, A and B may allocate the allowable $7,500 credit using any other reasonable method (for example, the entire credit to B because B's MAGI is less than the $75,000 MAGI threshold and, therefore, B is eligible to claim the entire allowable credit).

Example 7.

A and B, who are sisters, each contributes $50,000 towards the $100,000 purchase price of a residence and each owns a one-half interest as tenants in common. Under § 36(b)(1)(A), the allowable credit is not $10,000 (10 percent of the purchase price) but is limited to $7,500. A and B purchase the residence from their cousin, C. A, B, and C are not related persons within the meaning of § 36(c)(5). Therefore, A and B may allocate the allowable $7,500 credit one-half to A and one-half to B based on their contributions toward the purchase price of the residence or their ownership interests in the residence. Alternatively, A and B may allocate the allowable $7,500 credit using any other reasonable method (for example, the entire credit to A or B because both A and B are eligible to claim the entire allowable credit).

DRAFTING INFORMATION

The principal author of this notice is Christina M. Glendening of the Office of Associate Chief Counsel (Income Tax & Accounting). For further information regarding this notice, contact Ms. Glendening at (202) 622-4920 (not a toll-free call).

¶28,025 IRS News Release, IR-2009-10, January 30, 2009

In response to errors showing up on early tax filings, the Internal Revenue Service urged taxpayers and tax preparers to make sure they properly determine eligibility for the recovery rebate credit before they file their 2008 federal tax returns.

Some individuals who did not get the economic stimulus payment, and a smaller number of those who did, may be eligible for the recovery rebate credit. However, most taxpayers who received the economic stimulus payment last year will not qualify for the recovery rebate credit on their 2008 federal income tax return.

An early sampling of tax returns shows about 15 percent have errors involving the recovery rebate credit. Some tax returns erroneously claim the credit, do not claim the proper amount of recovery rebate credit or mistakenly enter the amount of the stimulus payment they received on the recovery rebate credit line.

To avoid delays in tax refunds, it is critical that taxpayers know the correct amount of the stimulus payment they received last year, if any, to help determine whether they qualify for the recovery rebate credit now.

The amount of the stimulus payment will not be entered directly on the tax return. For people using a paper tax return, the stimulus payment amount will be required when completing a related worksheet. For people using tax software, the stimulus payment amount will be needed as part of the return preparation process.

How to Get the Recovery Rebate Credit Right

The IRS sent taxpayers nearly 119 million stimulus payments last year. There are three ways individuals can find out how much they received:

- Check the amount listed on Notice 1378, which the IRS mailed last year to individuals who received the economic stimulus payment.
- Go to the *How Much Was My Stimulus Payment?* tool that is available on the IRS Web site, IRS.gov. This can provide the correct amount in a matter of a few seconds.
- Individuals can call the IRS at 1-866-234-2942. After a brief recorded announcement they can select option one to find out the amount of their economic stimulus payment. They will need to provide their filing status, Social Security Number and number of exemptions.

With the amount of last year's economic stimulus payment in hand, the taxpayer can then enter the figure on the recovery rebate credit worksheet or in the appropriate location when tax preparation software requests it.

If the taxpayer or preparer is using tax software, the amount of the rebate recovery credit will automatically be calculated and reported properly. If the taxpayer is using the paper method, the rebate recovery credit, as determined through the worksheet, should be reported on Line 70 of Form 1040, Line 42 of Form 1040A or Line 9 of Form 1040EZ.

For most taxpayers, the correct entry for the recovery rebate credit will either be blank or zero.

If there is any question at all as to the amount that should be reported for the recovery rebate credit, the taxpayer or preparer should enter a zero on the appropriate line above, and the IRS will determine whether a recovery rebate credit is due, and, if so, how much.

Some of the major factors that could qualify you for the recovery rebate credit include:

- Your financial situation changed dramatically from 2007 to 2008.
- You did not file a 2007 tax return.
- Your family gained an additional qualifying child in 2008.
- You were claimed as a dependent on someone else's return in 2007 but cannot be claimed as dependent by someone else in 2008.

Stimulus Payments Not Taxable; Reports of Extensive Refund Delays False

The IRS has received a number of recurring questions involving stimulus payments and the recovery rebate credit. Here are some important tips to keep in mind:

Taxability. The economic stimulus payment is not taxable and it should not be reported as income on the 2008 Form 1040, 1040A or 1040EZ.

Refund delays. IRS personnel are aware of reports that errors in claiming the recovery rebate credit could delay tax refunds for as much as eight to 12 weeks. These reports are false. As the IRS detects and corrects return errors concerning the recovery rebate credit, refund delays are currently no longer than about one week.

One payment. In addition, the IRS notes taxpayers will receive a single refund that includes any recovery rebate credit to which they are entitled. The IRS will not be issuing separate recovery rebate credit payments.

Refund amounts. The IRS reminds taxpayers they should not use their regular refund from last year in calculating the recovery rebate credit. Some taxpayers may be confusing their regular tax refunds with the economic stimulus payment they received when completing their 2008 tax return.

Direct Deposit Requests. Taxpayers who request a direct deposit will receive the refund in the form of a direct deposit even if errors are detected.

For more information, visit the Recovery Rebate Credit Information Center as well as the rebate questions and answers on IRS.gov.

DEPRECIATION

¶28,030 Rev. Proc. 2008-65, I.R.B. 2008-44, 1082, supplemented by Rev. Proc. 2009-16 (see ¶28,035)

SECTION 1. PURPOSE

This revenue procedure provides guidance under § 3081 of the Housing and Economic Recovery Act of 2008, Pub. L. No. 110-289, 122 Stat. 2654 (July 30, 2008) (Housing Act). Section 3081(a) of the Housing Act amends § 168(k) of the Internal Revenue Code by adding § 168(k)(4), allowing corporations to elect not to claim the 50-percent additional first year depreciation for certain new property acquired after March 31, 2008, and placed in service generally before January 1, 2009, and instead to increase their business credit limitation under § 38(c) or alternative minimum tax (AMT) credit limitation under § 53(c). This revenue procedure clarifies the rules regarding the effects of making the § 168(k)(4) election, the property eligible for the election, and the computation of the amount by which the business credit limitation and AMT credit limitation may be increased if the election is made. The Internal Revenue Service (IRS) and Treasury Department intend to publish future guidance regarding the time and manner for making the § 168(k)(4) election, for allocating the credit limitation increases allowed by the election, and for making the election to apply § 3081(b) of the Housing Act by certain automotive partnerships, and regarding the procedures applicable to partnerships with corporate partners that make the § 168(k)(4) election (see § 168(k)(4)(G)(ii)).

SECTION 2. BACKGROUND

.01 Section 168(k), amended by § 103 of the Economic Stimulus Act of 2008, Pub. L. No. 110-185, 122 Stat. 613 (February 13, 2008) (Stimulus Act), allows a 50-percent additional first year depreciation deduction (Stimulus additional first year depreciation deduction) for certain new property acquired by a taxpayer after 2007 and placed in service by the taxpayer before 2009 (before 2010 in the case of property described in § 168(k)(2)(B) or (C)).

.02 Section 3081(a) of the Housing Act added § 168(k)(4) to the Code. If a corporation elects to apply § 168(k)(4), § 168(k)(4)(A) provides that, for the corporation's first taxable year ending after March 31, 2008, and for any subsequent taxable year, the corporation forgoes the Stimulus additional first year depreciation deduction allowable under § 168(k) for eligible qualified property placed in service by the taxpayer and increases each of the limitations described in § 38(c) (relating to the general business credit) and § 53(c) (relating to the AMT credit). As a result, the corporation will be able to claim unused credits from taxable years beginning before January 1, 2006, that are allocable to research expenditures or AMT liabilities. This revenue procedure clarifies which depreciable property is eligible qualified property (see section 3 of this revenue procedure) and clarifies the effects of making the election to apply § 168(k)(4) (see section 4 of this revenue procedure).

.03 Section 38(c)(1) limits the general business credit allowed under § 38(a) to the excess (if any) of the taxpayer's net income tax (generally, the sum of the taxpayer's regular tax liability and AMT liability less certain credits) over the greater of (i) the tentative minimum tax for the taxable year or (ii) 25 percent of so much of the taxpayer's net regular tax liability (generally, the taxpayer's regular tax liability less certain credits) as exceeds $25,000. Under § 38(b)(4), the gen-

¶28,030

eral business credit includes the research credit determined under §41. Section 53(c) provides that the amount of the minimum tax credit allowed for any taxable year shall not exceed the excess (if any) of the regular tax liability of the taxpayer (reduced by certain credits) over the tentative minimum tax for the taxable year. In general, a taxpayer that makes the election to apply §168(k)(4) increases the limitations under §§38(c) and 53(c) by the bonus depreciation amount. In general, the amount by which the bonus depreciation amount increases each of the credit limitations under §§38(c) and 53(c) is determined by the portion of the bonus depreciation amount that the taxpayer allocates to each credit limitation for the taxable year. This revenue procedure clarifies the computation of the bonus depreciation amount (see section 5 of this revenue procedure) and the limitations on a taxpayer's allocation of the bonus depreciation amount between §§38(c) and 53(c) (see section 6 of this revenue procedure).

.04 To the extent that a taxpayer is allowed the business credit or AMT credit in an amount allocable to the aggregate increases in the business credit limitation and the AMT credit limitation that result from the § 168(k)(4) election, such amount(s) are treated as overpayments within the meaning of §6401(b) that are refundable to the taxpayer. See §168(k)(4)(F).

.05 Section 168(m), added by §308(a) of the Energy Improvement and Extension Act of 2008, Pub. L. No. 110-343, __ Stat. __ (October 3, 2008), allows a 50-percent additional first year depreciation deduction for qualified reuse and recycling property placed in service after August 31, 2008. Section 168(n), added by §710(a) of the Heartland Disaster Tax Relief Act of 2008, Pub. L. No. 110-343, __ Stat. __ (October 3, 2008), allows a 50-percent additional first year depreciation deduction for qualified disaster assistance property placed in service after December 31, 2007, with respect to federally declared disasters occurring after 2007 and before 2010. Both new Code provisions provide that property described in such provisions does not include property to which §168(k) applies. Therefore, eligible qualified property for which a taxpayer makes the §168(k)(4) election does not qualify for the 50-percent additional first year depreciation deduction allowed under § 168(m) and (n).

SECTION 3. ELIGIBLE QUALIFIED PROPERTY

.01 *In General.* With the exception of revised dates, eligible qualified property for purposes of §168(k)(4) is qualified property under §168(k)(2). Consequently, the property must be placed in service by the taxpayer before January 1, 2009. *See* § 168(k)(4)(D)(i) and (k)(2)(A)(iv). The placed-in-service-date deadline is extended to before January 1, 2010, for property that meets the requirements of §168(k)(2)(B) (long production period property) and property that meets the requirements of §168(k)(2)(C) (certain aircraft). *See* §168(k)(4)(D)(i) and (k)(2)(A)(iv). Pursuant to section 5.01 of Rev. Proc. 2008-54, 2008-38 I.R.B. 722, 723, rules similar to the rules in §1.168(k)-1 of the Income Tax Regulations for "qualified property" or for "30-percent additional first year depreciation deduction" apply for determining whether depreciable property is qualified property under §168(k)(2).

.02 *Application of Revised Dates.* In applying §168(k)(2) to determine whether depreciable property is eligible qualified property for purposes of §168(k)(4), §168(k)(4)(D)(i) provides that "March 31, 2008" is substituted for "December 31, 2007" each place it appears in §168(k)(2)(A) and §168(k)(2)(E)(i) and (ii). Accordingly, the affected requirements of §168(k)(2) are modified as follows for determining whether depreciable property that is qualified property under §168(k)(2) also is eligible qualified property for purposes of §168(k)(4):

(1) Original use of the property commences with the taxpayer after March 31, 2008. Section 168(k)(4)(D)(i) and (k)(2)(A)(ii);

(2) The property (a) is acquired by the taxpayer after March 31, 2008, and before January 1, 2009, but only if no written binding contract for the acquisition was in effect before January 1, 2008, or (b) is acquired by the taxpayer pursuant to a written binding contract which was entered into after March 31, 2008, and before January 1, 2009. Section 168(k)(4)(D)(i) and (k)(2)(A)(iii). However, see section 3.03 of this revenue procedure for an exception to this rule;

(3) In the case of a taxpayer manufacturing, constructing, or producing property for the taxpayer's own use, the requirements of section 3.02(2) of this revenue procedure are treated as met if the taxpayer begins manufacturing, constructing, or producing the property after March 31, 2008, and before January 1, 2009. Section 168(k)(4)(D)(i) and (k)(2)(E)(i); and

(4) If new property is originally placed in service by a person after March 31, 2008, and is sold to a taxpayer and leased back to the person by the taxpayer within three months after the date the property was originally placed in service by the person, the taxpayer-lessor is considered the original user of the property under section 3.02(1) of this revenue procedure and, for purposes of the placed-in-service date requirement in §168(k)(2)(A)(iv), the property is treated as

¶28,030

originally placed in service by the taxpayer-lessor not earlier than the date on which the property is used by the lessee under the leaseback. Section 168(k)(4)(D)(i) and (k)(2)(E)(ii); *see also* § 1.168(k)-1(b)(3)(iii)(A) and (b)(5)(ii)(A).

.03 *Passenger Aircraft.* For passenger aircraft, the binding contract requirement in § 168(k)(2)(A)(iii)(I) does not apply for determining whether the passenger aircraft is eligible qualified property. Section 168(k)(4)(G)(iii). Accordingly, a passenger aircraft is eligible qualified property if the aircraft is acquired by the taxpayer (1) after March 31, 2008, and before January 1, 2009, or (2) pursuant to a written binding contract entered into after March 31, 2008, and before January 1, 2009 (assuming all other requirements for qualified property under § 168(k)(2) are met).

SECTION 4. SECTION 168(k)(4) ELECTION

.01 *In General.* Except as provided in § 3081(b) of the Housing Act (relating to certain automotive partnerships), only a corporation may elect to apply § 168(k)(4). This election is made by the corporate taxpayer for its first taxable year ending after March 31, 2008. If the election to apply § 168(k)(4) is made, the election applies to all eligible qualified property placed in service by the taxpayer in the taxpayer's first taxable year ending after March 31, 2008, and in any subsequent taxable year. Even if a taxpayer does not place in service any eligible qualified property in its first taxable year ending after March 31, 2008, the taxpayer must make the election to apply § 168(k)(4) for that taxable year if it wishes to apply the election to eligible qualified property placed in service in a subsequent taxable year.

.02 *Controlled Group of Corporations.* All corporations which are treated as a single employer under § 52(a) (generally any controlled group of corporations within the meaning of § 1563(a), determined by substituting "more than 50 percent" for "more than 80 percent" each place it appears in that section) shall be treated as one taxpayer for purposes of § 168(k)(4) and as having elected to apply § 168(k)(4) if any such corporation so elects. Section 168(k)(4)(C)(iv). For example, if the common parent of an affiliated group of corporations filing a consolidated return makes the election to apply § 168(k)(4) for one member of the affiliated group, then all members of the affiliated group are treated as one taxpayer for purposes of § 168(k)(4) and as having made the election.

.03 *Applicable Depreciation Method.* If a taxpayer elects to apply § 168(k)(4), the applicable depreciation method under § 168(b) for all eligible qualified property is the straight line method. Section 168(k)(4)(A)(ii).

.04 *Ordering Rules for Applying Elections under § 168(k).* Under § 168(k), there are two elections: the election not to claim the Stimulus additional first year depreciation for all property in a particular class of property (*see* § 168(k)(2)(D)(iii)) and the election to apply § 168(k)(4) for all eligible qualified property. If a taxpayer makes both elections, the taxpayer applies § 168(k)(2)(D)(iii) first. Any class of property (as defined in § 1.168(k)-1(e)(2)) for which a § 168(k)(2)(D)(iii) election has been made is not qualified property under § 168(k)(2) nor eligible qualified property under § 168(k)(4). For example, if a calendar-year taxpayer for its taxable year ending December 31, 2008, makes the election to apply § 168(k)(4) and also elects not to claim the Stimulus additional first year depreciation deduction for 7-year property, the taxpayer first applies § 168(k)(2)(D)(iii) to all of its 7-year property acquired and placed in service in 2008. All eligible qualified property (excluding the 7-year property) will be included in the taxpayer's § 168(k)(4) election.

.05 *Time and Manner for Making Election.* The IRS and Treasury intend to publish separate guidance on the time and manner of making the election.

.06 *Revocation of Election.* Once made, the election to apply § 168(k)(4) may be revoked only with the written consent of the Commissioner of Internal Revenue. *See* § 168(k)(4)(G)(i). To seek the Commissioner's consent, the taxpayer must submit a request for a letter ruling. *See* Rev. Proc. 2008-1, 2008-1 I.R.B. 1 (or any successor).

SECTION 5. BONUS DEPRECIATION AMOUNT

01. *In General.* Except as limited by section 5.03, the bonus depreciation amount for any taxable year is equal to 20 percent of the excess (if any) of —

(1) the aggregate amount of depreciation that would be allowable under § 168 for eligible qualified property placed in service by the taxpayer during the taxable year if the Stimulus additional first year depreciation deduction applied to all such property, over

(2) the aggregate amount of depreciation that would be allowable under § 168 for eligible qualified property placed in service by the taxpayer during the taxable year if the Stimulus additional first year depreciation deduction did not apply to any such property. Section 168(k)(4)(C)(i)(I) and (II).

.02 *Special Rules for Determining Bonus Depreciation Amount.* For purposes of sections 5.01(1) and (2) of this revenue procedure, the following rules apply:

(1) The aggregate amounts of depreciation computed under sections 5.01(1) and (2) of this revenue procedure are made without regard to any election made under § 168(b)(2)(C) (relating to the 150 percent declining balance method), § 168(b)(3)(D) (relating to the straight line method election), § 168(g)(7) (relating to the alternative depreciation system election), and the requirement under section 4.03 of this revenue procedure that eligible qualified property must be depreciated using the straight line method if the taxpayer makes the election to apply § 168(k)(4). Section 168(k)(4)(C)(i).

(2) If a corporation makes the election to apply § 168(k)(4) and is a partner in a partnership, property placed in service by the partnership is not taken into account in determining the corporation's aggregate amounts of depreciation computed under sections 5.01(1) and (2) of this revenue procedure.

(3) The applicable convention rules under § 168(d) (including the mid-quarter convention for property placed in service during the last three months of a taxable year) apply in determining the aggregate depreciation amounts under sections 5.01(1) and (2) of this revenue procedure.

(4) For passenger aircraft, the binding contract requirement in § 168(k)(2)(A)(iii)(I) does not apply for determining the aggregate depreciation amount under section 5.01(1) of this revenue procedure. Section 168(k)(4)(G)(iii). Accordingly, for determining the aggregate depreciation amount under section 5.01(1) of this revenue procedure, a passenger aircraft is taken into account if the aircraft is acquired by the taxpayer (1) after March 31, 2008, and before January 1, 2009, or (2) pursuant to a written binding contract entered into after March 31, 2008, and before January 1, 2009 (assuming all other requirements for qualified property under § 168(k)(2) are met).

(5) With respect to long production period property, only the adjusted basis of such property attributable to manufacture, construction, or production after March 31, 2008, and before January 1, 2009, is taken into account in determining the aggregate depreciation amounts under sections 5.01(1) and (2) of this revenue procedure. Section 168(k)(4)(D)(ii). The amounts of adjusted basis of the property attributable to manufacture, construction, or production after March 31, 2008, and before January 1, 2009, are referred to as "progress expenditures." For purposes of determining progress expenditures under this section 5.02(5), rules similar to the rules in section 4.02(1)(b) of Notice 2007-36, 2007-17 I.R.B. 1000, 1001 (relating to progress expenditures for GO Zone extension real property), apply.

.03 *Maximum Amount.* The bonus depreciation amount for any taxable year shall not exceed the maximum increase amount (as computed under section 5.04 of this revenue procedure) reduced (but not below zero) by the sum of the bonus depreciation amounts determined under § 168(k)(4)(C) for all preceding taxable years. Section 168(k)(4)(C)(i) and (ii).

.04 *Maximum Increase Amount.* For purposes of section 5.03 of this revenue procedure, the maximum increase amount for any taxpayer means the lesser of (1) $30,000,000, or (2) 6 percent of the sum of the business credit increase amount (as computed under section 5.05 of this revenue procedure) and the AMT credit increase amount (as computed under section 5.06 of this revenue procedure). Section 168(k)(4)(C)(iii)(I) and (II).

.05 *Business Credit Increase Amount.* The business credit increase amount means the portion of the credit allowable under § 38 (without regard to § 38(c)) for the first taxable year ending after March 31, 2008, that is allocable to business credit carryforwards to such taxable year that are (1) from taxable years beginning before January 1, 2006, and (2) properly allocable (considering the application of § 38(d) to credits used in prior taxable years) to the research credit determined under § 41(a). Section 168(k)(4)(E)(iii). For purposes of this section 5.05, a business credit carryforward allocable to the research credit that was from a taxable year beginning before January 1, 2006, but has expired before the first taxable year ending after March 31, 2008, is not taken into account in determining the business credit increase amount.

.06 *AMT Credit Increase Amount.* The AMT credit increase amount means the portion of the minimum tax credit under § 53(b) for the first taxable year ending after March 31, 2008, determined by taking into account only the adjusted minimum tax for taxable years beginning before January 1, 2006. Section 168(k)(4)(E)(iv). For purposes of this section 5.06, minimum tax credits shall be treated as allowed on a first-in, first-out basis. Section 168(k)(4)(E)(iv).

SECTION 6. ALLOCATION OF BONUS DEPRECIATION AMOUNTS

.01 *In General.* Except as limited by section 6.02 of this revenue procedure, the taxpayer shall specify the portion (if any) of the bonus depreciation amount for the taxable year that is to be allocated to each of the business credit limitation under § 38(c) and the AMT credit limitation under § 53(c).

.02 *Limitation on Allocations.*

(1) For any taxable year, the portion of the bonus depreciation amount that may be allocated to the business credit limitation under § 38(c) shall not exceed the excess of the business credit increase amount (determined under section 5.05 of this revenue procedure) over the bonus depreciation amount allocated by the taxpayer to such limitation for all preceding taxable years.

(2) For any taxable year, the portion of the bonus depreciation amount that may be allocated to the AMT credit limitation under § 53(c) shall not exceed the excess of the AMT tax credit increase amount (determined under section 5.06 of this revenue procedure) over the bonus depreciation amount allocated by the taxpayer to such limitation for all preceding taxable years.

.03 *Time and Manner for Specifying Allocation.* The IRS and Treasury intend to publish separate guidance on the time and manner for specifying the allocation.

.04 *Example.* Y, a calendar-year corporation, makes the election to apply § 168(k)(4) for its taxable year ending December 31, 2008. Because § 168(k)(4) was not available prior to 2008, Y has no bonus depreciation amounts (as defined in § 168(k)(4)(C)) for preceding taxable years. Assume that (1) under section 5.01 of this revenue procedure, Y's bonus depreciation amount is $100 million, (2) under section 5.05 of this revenue procedure, Y's business credit increase amount is $10 million, and (3) under section 5.06 of this revenue procedure, Y's AMT credit increase amount is $590 million. Consequently, under section 5.04 of this revenue procedure, Y's maximum increase amount is $30 million (the lesser of (1) $30 million and (2) .06 X ($10 million + $590 million), or $36 million). Therefore, under section 5.03 of this revenue procedure, Y's bonus depreciation amount that may be allocated to increase the credit limitations under § § 38(c) and 53(c) is $30 million. Pursuant to section 6.01 of this revenue procedure, as limited by section 6.02 of this revenue procedure, the portion of the bonus depreciation amount ($30 million) that Y allocates to the credit limitation under § 38(c) is $10 million (the maximum amount that Y may allocate to its § 38(c) credit limitation under section 6.02(1) of this revenue procedure) and the portion of the bonus depreciation amount that Y allocates to the credit limitation under § 53(c) is $20 million.

In addition, during its taxable year ending December 31, 2009, Y places in service long production period property or certain aircraft that is eligible qualified property. Y's 2008 § 168(k)(4) election remains in effect. For the 2009 taxable year, assume that (1) under section 5.01 of this revenue procedure, Y's bonus depreciation amount is $100 million and (2) under section 5.04 of this revenue procedure, Y's maximum increase amount is $30 million. Therefore, under section 5.03 of this revenue procedure, Y's bonus depreciation amount for the taxable year ending December 31, 2009, is $0 ($30 million (maximum increase amount) less $30 million (the bonus depreciation amount that Y allocated to increase its § § 38(c) and 53(c) credit limitations for 2008)).

SECTION 7. EFFECTIVE DATE

This revenue procedure is effective October 10, 2008.

SECTION 8. DRAFTING INFORMATION

The principal author of this revenue procedure is Jeffrey T. Rodrick of the Office of Associate Chief Counsel (Income Tax & Accounting). For further information regarding this revenue procedure contact Jeffrey T. Rodrick on (202) 622-4930 (not a toll free call).

¶ 28,035 Rev. Proc. 2009-16, I.R.B. 2009-6, January 23, 2009, supplementing Rev. Proc. 2008-65 (see ¶ 28,030)

SECTION 1. PURPOSE

This revenue procedure supplements Rev. Proc. 2008-65, 2008-44 I.R.B. 1082, to provide additional guidance under § 3081 of the Housing and Economic Recovery Act of 2008, Pub. L. No. 110-289, 122 Stat. 2654 (July 30, 2008) (Housing Act). Section 3081(a) of the Housing Act amends § 168(k) of the Internal Revenue Code by adding § 168(k)(4), allowing corporations to elect not to claim the 50-percent additional first year depreciation for certain new property acquired after March 31, 2008, and placed in service generally before January 1, 2009, and instead to increase their business credit limitation under § 38(c) and alternative minimum tax (AMT) credit limitation under § 53(c). Section 3081(b) of the Housing Act allows certain automotive partnerships to elect to be treated as making a refundable deemed payment of income tax in a certain amount. Rev. Proc. 2008-65 provides guidance regarding the effects of making the § 168(k)(4) election, the property eligible for this election, and the computation of the amount by which the business credit limitation and AMT credit limitation may be increased if the § 168(k)(4) election is made. This revenue procedure provides guidance regarding the time and manner for making the § 168(k)(4) election, the allocation of the credit limitation increases allowed by this election among members of a controlled group, the effect of the election on partnerships with corporate partners that make the § 168(k)(4) election, the application of § 168(k)(4) to S corporations, and the election under § 3081(b) of the Housing Act by certain automotive partnerships.

SECTION 2. BACKGROUND

.01 Section 168(k), amended by § 103 of the Economic Stimulus Act of 2008, Pub. L. No. 110-185, 122 Stat. 613 (February 13, 2008) (Stimulus Act), allows a 50-percent additional first year depreciation deduction (Stimulus additional first year depreciation deduction) for certain new property acquired by a taxpayer after 2007 and placed in service by the taxpayer before 2009 (before 2010 in the case of property described in § 168(k)(2)(B) or (C)).

.02 Section 3081(a) of the Housing Act added § 168(k)(4) to the Code. If a corporation elects to apply § 168(k)(4), § 168(k)(4)(A) provides that, for the corporation's first taxable year ending after March 31, 2008, and for any subsequent taxable year, the corporation forgoes the Stimulus additional first year depreciation deduction allowable under § 168(k) for eligible qualified property placed in service by the taxpayer and increases the limitations described in § 38(c) (relating to the general business credit) and § 53(c) (relating to the AMT credit). As a result, the corporation will be able to claim unused credits from taxable years beginning before January 1, 2006, that are allocable to research expenditures or AMT liabilities. Rev. Proc. 2008-65 clarifies which depreciable property is eligible qualified property for purposes of the § 168(k)(4) election and clarifies the effects of making the § 168(k)(4) election.

.03 In general, the amount by which the § 168(k)(4) election increases the business credit limitation under § 38(c) and the AMT credit limitation under § 53(c) is the bonus depreciation amount. See § 168(k)(4)(A)(iii). Except as provided below, the bonus depreciation amount generally is equal to 20 percent of the excess of the aggregate amount of depreciation that would be allowable for eligible qualified property if the Stimulus additional first year depreciation deduction applied to all such property, over the aggregate amount of depreciation that would be allowable for all such property if the Stimulus additional first year depreciation deduction did not apply. See § 168(k)(4)(C)(i). However, the bonus depreciation amount for any taxable year must not exceed the maximum increase amount reduced by the sum of the bonus depreciation amounts determined for all prior taxable years. See § 168(k)(4)(C)(ii). In general, the maximum increase amount is equal to the lesser of $30 million, or 6 percent of the sum of the unexpired and unused pre-2006 business credit carryforwards allocable to the research credit and AMT credit carryforwards to the current taxable year. See § 168(k)(4)(C)(iii). For any taxable year, the bonus depreciation amount allocated to either the business credit limitation or AMT credit limitation must not exceed the amount of unexpired and unused pre-2006 business credit carryforwards allocable to the research credit or AMT credit carryforwards less bonus depreciation amounts allocated to each limitation, respectively, for all prior taxable years. See § 168(k)(4)(E)(ii). To the extent that a taxpayer is allowed the business credit or AMT credit in an amount allocable to the aggregate increases in the business credit limitation or AMT credit limitation that result from the § 168(k)(4) election, such amount(s) are treated as overpayments within the meaning of § 6401(b) that are refundable to the taxpayer. See § 168(k)(4)(F).

.04 Rev. Proc. 2008-65 states that the Internal Revenue Service (IRS) and Treasury Department intend to publish separate guidance on the time and manner for making the § 168(k)(4) election and for specifying the allocation of the bonus depreciation amount to increase the business and AMT credit limitations under, respectively, §§ 38(c) and 53(c). This revenue procedure provides the time and manner for making the § 168(k)(4) election (see section 3 of this revenue procedure) and provides guidance on making and reporting the allocation of the bonus depreciation amount to increase the business and AMT credit limitations (see section 4 of this revenue procedure).

.05 Section 168(k)(4)(C)(iv) provides that all corporations that are treated as a single employer under § 52(a) (generally any controlled group of corporations within the meaning of § 1563(a), determined by substituting "more than 50 percent" for "more than 80 percent" each place it appears in § 1563(a)(1)) (hereinafter such group of corporations is referred to as a "controlled group") are treated as one taxpayer for purposes of § 168(k)(4) and as having elected to

¶28,035

apply § 168(k)(4) if any member of such controlled group so elects. This revenue procedure provides guidance regarding the allocation of the bonus depreciation amount to increase the business and AMT credit limitations among members of a controlled group (see section 4.02 of this revenue procedure).

.06 Under § 168(k)(4)(G)(ii), if a corporation that makes the § 168(k)(4) election is a partner in a partnership, the electing corporate partner's distributive share of partnership items under § 702 for any eligible qualified property placed in service by the partnership must be computed by using the straight line method and without claiming the Stimulus additional first year depreciation deduction. This revenue procedure provides guidance regarding partnerships with corporate partners that make the § 168(k)(4) election (see section 5 of this revenue procedure).

.07 Except as provided in § 3081(b) of the Housing Act, only a corporation may elect to apply § 168(k)(4). Some S corporations and their shareholders are uncertain about whether § 168(k)(4) applies to them. This revenue procedure clarifies the application of § 168(k)(4) to S corporations and their shareholders (see section 6 of this revenue procedure).

.08 Section 3081(b)(1) of the Housing Act provides that an applicable partnership may elect to be treated as making a refundable deemed payment of income tax in a certain amount. This revenue procedure provides guidance regarding this election (see section 7 of this revenue procedure).

.09 Section 168(k)(4) does not modify the rules under §§ 383 and 1502. Section 383 limitations do not affect the credit amounts that a taxpayer takes into consideration in calculating its maximum increase amount under section 5.04 of Rev. Proc. 2008-65. However, the increases in the business credit limitation under § 38(c) and AMT credit limitation under § 53(c) that result from a § 168(k)(4) election do not allow a taxpayer to utilize credit carryforwards that are otherwise limited by § 383.

SECTION 3. TIME AND MANNER FOR MAKING THE § 168(k)(4) ELECTION

.01 *In General.* Except as provided in sections 3.02 and 3.03 of this revenue procedure, a corporate taxpayer must make the § 168(k)(4) election by the due date (including extensions) of the federal income tax return for the taxpayer's first taxable year ending after March 31, 2008. Even if the taxpayer does not place in service any eligible qualified property during its first taxable year ending after March 31, 2008, the taxpayer must make the § 168(k)(4) election for that taxable year if the taxpayer wishes to apply the election to eligible qualified property placed in service in subsequent taxable years. If a taxpayer is not a member of a controlled group, the taxpayer makes the § 168(k)(4) election in the manner provided in either sections 3.02, 3.03, or 3.04 of this revenue procedure. If a taxpayer is a member of a controlled group, the taxpayer makes the § 168(k)(4) election in the manner provided in section 3.05 of this revenue procedure. Failure to comply with any of the reporting or notification requirements provided by this section 3 will nullify a taxpayer's attempted § 168(k)(4) election.

.02 *Taxpayer's First Taxable Year Ending After March 31, 2008, Ends Before December 31, 2008.*

(1) *In general.* Except as provided in section 3.03 of this revenue procedure, if a taxpayer's first taxable year ending after March 31, 2008, ends before December 31, 2008, and:

(a) If the taxpayer has not filed its original federal income tax return for such taxable year on or before March 11, 2009, the taxpayer makes the § 168(k)(4) election:

(i) Either:

(I) By claiming the Stimulus additional first year depreciation deduction for any eligible qualified property placed in service by the taxpayer during such taxable year on its timely-filed federal income tax return for such taxable year. Such property must not be property in a class for which the taxpayer elects out of the Stimulus additional first year depreciation deduction under § 168(k)(2)(D)(iii); or

(II) By filing with its timely-filed federal income tax return for such taxable year the 2007 Form 4562, Depreciation and Amortization (Including Information on Listed Property), indicating that the taxpayer used the straight line method and did not claim the Stimulus additional first year depreciation deduction for all eligible qualified property. Taxpayers that choose to follow this section 3.02(1)(a)(i)(II) must not claim a refundable credit on their original federal income tax return. To claim the refundable credit, see section 3.02(1)(a)(ii).

(ii) By filing an amended federal income tax return for such taxable year in the manner described in section 3.02(2) on or before the due date (without regard to extensions) of the taxpayer's federal income tax return for the succeeding taxable year; and

¶28,035

(iii) If the taxpayer is a partner in a partnership, by notifying the partnership in accordance with section 5.02 of this revenue procedure.

(b) If the taxpayer has filed its original federal income tax return for such taxable year on or before March 11, 2009, the taxpayer makes the § 168(k)(4) election by following the procedures set forth in section 3.02(1)(a)(ii) and (iii) of this revenue procedure.

(2) *Special rules for filing amended return.* If the taxpayer filing the amended federal income tax return under section 3.02(1)(a)(ii) of this revenue procedure:

(a) is not an S corporation, the taxpayer (i) includes the amount of the refundable credit allowed by the § 168(k)(4) election on Line 5g of the Form 1120X, Amended U.S. Corporation Income Tax Return, (ii) makes appropriate adjustments to Lines 2, 3, and 4 of the Form 1120X to reflect the requirements of § 168(k)(4)(A) (requiring that the depreciation deduction for all eligible qualified property be determined by using the straight line method and by not claiming the Stimulus additional first year depreciation deduction), and (iii) indicates in Part II of the Form 1120X that the taxpayer is making the § 168(k)(4) election. The taxpayer should refer to the instructions to the 2008 Form 1120, U.S. Corporation Income Tax Return, the 2008 Form 3800, General Business Credit, and the 2008 Form 8827, Credit for Prior Year Minimum Tax - Corporations, for guidance regarding computation of the refundable credit and allocation of the bonus depreciation amount between the business and AMT credit limitations; or

(b) is an S corporation, the taxpayer (i) makes appropriate adjustments to Line 22b of the amended Form 1120S, U.S. Income Tax Return for an S Corporation, to reflect the results described in section 6.02 of this revenue procedure from making the § 168(k)(4) election, (ii) makes appropriate adjustments on the amended Form 1120S to reflect the requirements of § 168(k)(4)(A) (requiring that the depreciation deduction for all eligible qualified property be determined by using the straight line method and by not claiming the Stimulus additional first year depreciation deduction), and (iii) attaches a statement to the amended Form 1120S indicating that the taxpayer is making the § 168(k)(4) election and a statement showing the computation of the increases to the business credit and AMT credit limitations under, respectively, §§ 38(c) and 53(c) resulting from making the § 168(k)(4) election. The S corporation also should follow the instructions to the Form 1120S for filing an amended return.

.03 *Special Rules for Taxpayers Whose First Taxable Year Ending After March 31, 2008, Ends Before December 31, 2008.*

(1) If a taxpayer described in section 3.02(1)(b) of this revenue procedure makes the § 168(k)(4) election on its timely-filed original federal income tax return and receives a refundable credit attributable to the § 168(k)(4) election made on such return, such taxpayer must not file the amended federal income tax return required by section 3.02(1)(a)(ii) and 3.02(1)(b) of this revenue procedure. However, such taxpayer must follow the notification procedures described in section 3.02(1)(a)(iii) of this revenue procedure.

(2) If a taxpayer described in section 3.02(1) of this revenue procedure wishes to make the § 168(k)(4) election but has not placed in service any eligible qualified property during its first taxable year ending after March 31, 2008, the taxpayer makes the § 168(k)(4) election by attaching a statement to its timely-filed federal income tax return for that taxable year, indicating that the taxpayer is making the § 168(k)(4) election. If a taxpayer described in section 3.02(1)(b) of this revenue procedure wishes to make the § 168(k)(4) election but has not placed in service any eligible qualified property during its first taxable year ending after March 31, 2008, and did not attach a statement to its original federal income tax return for such taxable year indicating that the taxpayer is making the § 168(k)(4) election, the taxpayer must attach such statement to the amended federal income tax return required by section 3.02(1)(a)(ii) and 3.02(1)(b) of this revenue procedure and follow the notification procedures described in section 3.02(1)(a)(iii) of this revenue procedure.

.04 *Taxpayer's First Taxable Year Ending After March 31, 2008, Ends on or After December 31, 2008.*

(1) *C corporations.* Except as provided in section 3.04(3) of this revenue procedure, if a taxpayer's first taxable year ending after March 31, 2008, ends on or after December 31, 2008, a C corporation makes the § 168(k)(4) election by:

(a) Claiming the refundable credit on Line 32g of the 2008 Form 1120;

(b) Filing the 2008 Form 3800 or Form 8827, or both, as applicable. Taxpayers should refer to the applicable instructions to the 2008 Forms 3800 and 8827 for guidance regarding computation of the refundable credit and allocation of the bonus depreciation amount between the business credit limitation and AMT credit limitation;

(c) Filing the 2008 Form 4562, Depreciation and Amortization (Including Information on Listed Property), indicating that the taxpayer used the straight line method and did not claim the Stimulus additional first year depreciation deduction for all eligible qualified property; and

(d) Notifying any partnership in which the C corporation is a partner, in accordance with section 5.02 of this revenue procedure.

(2) *S corporations.* Except as provided in section 3.04(3) of this revenue procedure, if a taxpayer's first taxable year ending after March 31, 2008, ends on or after December 31, 2008, an S corporation makes the § 168(k)(4) election by:

(a) Making appropriate adjustments to Line 22b of the 2008 Form 1120S to reflect the results described in section 6.02 of this revenue procedure from making the § 168(k)(4) election;

(b) Attaching to the Form 1120S a statement indicating that the taxpayer is making the § 168(k)(4) election and a statement showing the computation of the increases to the business credit and AMT credit limitations under, respectively, §§ 38(c) and 53(c) resulting from making the § 168(k)(4) election;

(c) Filing the 2008 Form 4562 indicating that the taxpayer used the straight line method and did not claim the Stimulus additional first year depreciation deduction for all eligible qualified property; and

(d) Notifying any partnership in which the S corporation is a partner, in accordance with section 5.02 of this revenue procedure.

(3) *No eligible qualified property placed in service during first taxable year ending after March 31, 2008, ending on or after December 31, 2008.* If a taxpayer's first taxable year ending after March 31, 2008, ends on or after December 31, 2008, and the taxpayer has not placed in service any eligible qualified property during such taxable year, the taxpayer makes the § 168(k)(4) election by attaching a statement to its timely-filed federal income tax return for that taxable year, indicating that the taxpayer is making the § 168(k)(4) election.

.05 *Controlled Groups.*

(1) *Determination of Controlled Group Members.*

(a) *First taxable year ending after March 31, 2008.* For purposes of applying § 168(k)(4) and this revenue procedure for the first taxable year ending after March 31, 2008, § 168(k)(4)(C)(iv) is applied to determine the members of a controlled group (as defined in section 2.05 of this revenue procedure) on December 31, 2008, and all such members on that date are treated as a controlled group and as one taxpayer. However, if the first taxable year ending after March 31, 2008, ends on the same date for all members of a controlled group (as defined in section 2.05 of this revenue procedure), all members on such ending date are treated as a controlled group and as one taxpayer for purposes of applying § 168(k)(4) and this revenue procedure for the first taxable year ending after March 31, 2008.

(b) *Subsequent taxable years.* For purposes of applying § 168(k)(4) and this revenue procedure for any taxable year subsequent to a taxpayer's first taxable year ending after March 31, 2008, § 168(k)(4)(C)(iv) is applied to determine the members of a controlled group (as defined in section 2.05 of this revenue procedure) on December 31. However, if a taxable year subsequent to the first taxable year ending after March 31, 2008, ends on the same date for all members of a controlled group (as defined in section 2.05 of this revenue procedure), all members on such ending date are treated as a controlled group and as one taxpayer for purposes of applying § 168(k)(4) and this revenue procedure for that subsequent taxable year.

(2) *Time and manner of making the § 168(k)(4) election.*

(a) *In general.* A § 168(k)(4) election made by any member of a controlled group (as determined under section 3.05(1)(a) of this revenue procedure) is binding on all other members of the controlled group for all members' first taxable year ending after March 31, 2008. If in a subsequent taxable year, a controlled group determined under section 3.05(1)(b) of this revenue procedure (the second controlled group) includes 2 or more members of a controlled group determined under 3.05(1)(a) of this revenue procedure (the first controlled group), all members of the second controlled group that were members of the first controlled group are deemed to have made (or not made, as the case may be) the § 168(k)(4) election of the first controlled group. Whether members of the second controlled group that were not members of the first controlled group are bound by a § 168(k)(4) election made by the first controlled group (or bound by the first controlled group's lack of a § 168(k)(4) election) is determined under the rules of section 3.05(2)(d) of this revenue procedure.

(b) *All members of a controlled group constitute a single consolidated group.* If all members of a controlled group are members of an affiliated group of corporations that file a consolidated return (hereinafter, a "consolidated group"), the common parent (within the meaning of § 1.1502-77(a)(1)(i)) of the consolidated group makes the § 168(k)(4) election on behalf of all members of the consolidated group. The common parent makes this election within the time and in the manner provided in sections 3.01, 3.02, 3.03, or 3.04 of this revenue procedure, as applicable.

(c) *All members of a controlled group do not constitute a single consolidated group.*

(i) *In general.* This section 3.05(2)(c) applies when separate federal income tax returns are filed by some or all members of a controlled group. If a controlled group includes, but is not limited to, members of a consolidated group, the consolidated group is treated as a single member of the controlled group. A member of the controlled group makes the § 168(k)(4) election by:

(I) Following the procedures in section 3.05(2)(c)(ii) or (iii) of this revenue procedure, as applicable; and

(II) Notifying all other members of the controlled group that the § 168(k)(4) election has been made. This notification must be made before the due date (excluding extensions) of the member's federal income tax return for the first taxable year ending after March 31, 2008. If the electing member makes the § 168(k)(4) election by filing an amended return under sections 3.02(1)(a)(ii) or 3.03(2) of this revenue procedure, as applicable, the electing member must notify the other members no later than the date it files an amended return containing the § 168(k)(4) election. If the electing member is described in section 3.03(1) of this revenue procedure, the electing member must notify the other members on or before March 11, 2009.

(ii) *Controlled group member's first taxable year ending after March 31, 2008, ends before December 31, 2008.* If a controlled group member's first taxable year ending after March 31, 2008, ends before December 31, 2008, that member makes the § 168(k)(4) election within the time and in the manner provided in sections 3.02 or 3.03(2) of this revenue procedure, as applicable. In addition, the member must attach to the amended federal income tax return:

(I) a statement describing the computation of the group bonus depreciation amount (as provided in section 4.02(3)(b)(ii) of this revenue procedure); and

(II) Schedule O (Form 1120X), Consent Plan and Apportionment Schedule for a Controlled Group, and indicating in column (f) of Part IV that the controlled group has made the § 168(k)(4) election and the portion of the group bonus depreciation amount allocated to the member (as provided in section 4.02 of this revenue procedure).

(iii) *Controlled group member's first taxable year ending after March 31, 2008, ends on or after December 31, 2008.* If a controlled group member's first taxable year ending after March 31, 2008, ends on or after December 31, 2008, that member makes the § 168(k)(4) election within the time provided in section 3.01 of this revenue procedure and in the manner provided in section 3.04 of this revenue procedure. In addition, the member must attach to the federal income tax return:

(I) a statement describing the computation of the group bonus depreciation amount (as provided in section 4.02(3)(b)(ii) of this revenue procedure); and

(II) Schedule O (Form 1120) and indicating in column (f) of Part IV that the controlled group has made the § 168(k)(4) election and the portion of the group bonus depreciation amount allocated to the member (as provided in section 4.02 of this revenue procedure).

(d) *Effect of § 168(k)(4) election for members entering or leaving a controlled group.*

(i) *Member leaves controlled group that made § 168(k)(4) election.* If a taxpayer is a member of a controlled group that makes the § 168(k)(4) election (the old group), and in a subsequent taxable year becomes a member of another controlled group that has not made the § 168(k)(4) election (the new group), the § 168(k)(4) election of the old group is not binding on the new group. The taxpayer, however, continues to be treated as having made the § 168(k)(4) election and must continue to apply §§ 167(f)(1) and 168 as if the § 168(k)(4) election was made. Similarly, if a taxpayer is a member of a controlled group that makes the § 168(k)(4) election (the old group), and in a subsequent taxable year leaves the old group and does not become a member of another controlled group, the taxpayer continues to be treated as having made the § 168(k)(4) election and must continue to apply §§ 167(f)(1) and 168 as if the § 168(k)(4) election was made.

(ii) *Taxpayer becomes a member of a controlled group after § 168(k)(4) election is made.* If a taxpayer was not a member of any controlled group when the taxpayer made the § 168(k)(4) election and in a subsequent taxable year becomes a member of a controlled group that did not make the § 168(k)(4) election, the taxpayer's election is not binding on the controlled group. The taxpayer, however, continues to be treated as having made the § 168(k)(4) election and must continue to apply §§ 167(f)(1) and 168 as if the §

¶28,035

168(k)(4) election was made. If a taxpayer neither made the § 168(k)(4) election nor was a member of a controlled group that made the § 168(k)(4) election, and in a subsequent taxable year becomes a member of a controlled group that made the § 168(k)(4) election, the controlled group's election does not apply to the taxpayer.

(iii) *Special rule for consolidated groups.* Notwithstanding section 3.05(2)(d)(i) and (ii) of this revenue procedure, a § 168(k)(4) election (or the lack of a § 168(k)(4) election) made by a consolidated group (or a controlled group in which the consolidated group is a member) applies to any eligible qualified property placed in service by a member of the consolidated group during a consolidated return year, even if such member is not a member of the consolidated group on the date that controlled group membership is determined under section 3.05(1)(a) of this revenue procedure.

(iv) *Special rule for new taxpayers.* If a taxpayer was not in existence for the first taxable year for which the § 168(k)(4) election is made by a controlled group (as defined in section 3.05(1)(a) of this revenue procedure), immediately after the taxpayer's formation the taxpayer is a member of that controlled group, and the taxpayer is a member of that controlled group as determined under section 3.05(1)(b) of this revenue procedure, that controlled group's § 168(k)(4) election, if any election is made, applies to the taxpayer. For example, if a controlled group makes the § 168(k)(4) election and subsequently transfers eligible qualified property to a newly formed member of the same controlled group (on the day of its formation and on the determination date under section 3.05(1)(b) of this revenue procedure), such property remains eligible qualified property to which the § 168(k)(4) election applies and must be depreciated using the straight line method.

(v) *Overlapping groups.* For purposes of this revenue procedure, for any taxable year a taxpayer will not be considered a member of more than one controlled group. A taxpayer is considered a member of a single controlled group in accordance with the principles of § 1.1563-1T(c) of the temporary Income Tax Regulations.

.06 *Limited Relief for Late Election.*

(1) *Automatic 6-Month Extension.* Pursuant to § 301.9100-2(b) of the Procedure and Administration Regulations, an automatic extension of 6 months from the due date of the federal tax return (*excluding* extensions) for the taxpayer's first taxable year ending after March 31, 2008, is granted to make the § 168(k)(4) election, provided the taxpayer timely filed the taxpayer's federal tax return for the taxpayer's first taxable year ending after March 31, 2008, and the taxpayer satisfies the requirements in § 301.9100-2(c) and (d).

(2) *Other Extensions.* A taxpayer that fails to make the § 168(k)(4) election for the taxpayer's first taxable year ending after March 31, 2008, as provided in section 3.01, 3.02, 3.03, 3.04, 3.05, or 3.06(1) of this revenue procedure but wants to do so must file a request for an extension of time to make the election under the rules in § 301.9100-3.

SECTION 4. ALLOCATION OF THE BONUS DEPRECIATION AMOUNT

.01 *In General.* A taxpayer allocates the bonus depreciation amount between the business credit limitation under § 38(c) and the AMT credit limitation under § 53(c) by the due date (including extensions) of the taxpayer's federal income tax return for the taxable year. Except as provided in section 4.02 of this revenue procedure, the taxpayer specifies this allocation by reporting the amounts on the appropriate lines of the Forms 3800 and 8827. However, if a taxpayer's first taxable year ending after March 31, 2008, ends before December 31, 2008, the taxpayer makes and specifies the allocation for such taxable year on the amended federal income tax return filed pursuant to section 3.02(1)(a)(ii) or 3.03(2) of this revenue procedure. A different allocation may be used for different taxable years.

.02 *Controlled Groups.*

(1) *In general.* If a taxpayer is a member of a controlled group (as determined under section 3.05(1) of this revenue procedure) and any member of the controlled group makes the § 168(k)(4) election, the allocation of the group bonus depreciation amount to each member of the controlled group must be determined in accordance with section 4.02(2) or 4.02(3) of this revenue procedure, as applicable. This allocation of the group bonus depreciation amount for any taxable year is reported on Schedule O (Form 1120) (or a similar statement) that is attached to the federal income tax return or amended federal income tax return for that taxable year, as the case may be, filed by each member of the controlled group within the time provided in section 4.01 of this revenue procedure. However, if a member of a controlled group does not have the information necessary to allocate the group bonus depreciation amount for a taxable year on or before the due date (including extensions) of the member's federal income tax return for the taxable year, the member must make and specify the alloca-

¶ 28,035

tion for that taxable year on an amended federal income tax return for that taxable year that is filed on or before the due date (including extensions) of the member's federal income tax return for the succeeding taxable year. The allocation described in this section 4.02 of this revenue procedure applies to all controlled group members who have made a section 168(k)(4) election or who are treated as having made such an election pursuant to section 3.05 of this revenue procedure.

(2) *All members of a controlled group constitute a single consolidated group.* If all members of a controlled group are members of a consolidated group (as defined in section 3.05(2)(b) of this revenue procedure), the consolidated group determines its bonus depreciation amount in accordance with section 5 of Rev. Proc. 2008-65, treating the consolidated group as a single taxpayer. The allocation of the bonus depreciation amount among the members of the consolidated group must be pursuant to an allocation by the common parent in accordance with the principles of § 1502 and its accompanying regulations.

(3) *All members of a controlled group do not constitute a single consolidated group.*

(a) *In general.* This section 4.02(3) applies when separate federal income tax returns are filed by some or all members of a controlled group. If a controlled group includes, but is not limited to, members of a consolidated group, the consolidated group is treated as a single member of the controlled group. The allocation of the bonus depreciation amount among the members of the controlled group must be made pursuant to section 4.02(3)(b) or (c) of this revenue procedure, as applicable. Any group bonus depreciation amount allocated to a consolidated group under this section 4.02(3) is allocated among the members of the consolidated group pursuant to an allocation by the common parent in accordance with the principles of § 1502 and its accompanying regulations.

(b) *Allocation of group bonus depreciation amount.*

(i) *In general.* The bonus depreciation amount allocable to a member of a controlled group is determined by arriving at each member's proportionate share of the group bonus depreciation amount, unless all members of the group agree to an alternative allocation under section 4.02(3)(c) of this revenue procedure.

(ii) *Computation of group bonus depreciation amount.* The group bonus depreciation amount is computed as follows:

(A) First, calculate the bonus depreciation amount in the manner provided in sections 5.01 and 5.02 of Rev. Proc. 2008-65 treating the controlled group as a single taxpayer. To calculate this amount, the eligible qualified property placed in service by each member of the controlled group during the taxable year is taken into account. However, if some or all members of the controlled group have different taxable years, the eligible qualified property to be taken into account is such property placed in service by each member of the controlled group after March 31, 2008, and before January 1, 2009 (or, for taxable years ending in 2009 or thereafter, during such calendar year);

(B) Second, calculate the maximum increase amount in section 5.04 of Rev. Proc. 2008-65, the business credit increase amount in section 5.05 of Rev. Proc. 2008-65, and the AMT credit increase amount in section 5.06 of Rev. Proc. 2008-65 by taking into account the sum of all member's pre-2006 unexpired and unused research credits and AMT credits as of the last day of the taxable year. However, if the taxable years of some or all members of the controlled group end on different dates, the sum of all members' pre-2006 unexpired and unused research credits and AMT credits as of the last day of each member's last taxable year ending on or before December 31 (determined for each calendar year) are taken into account; and

(C) Finally, calculate the maximum amount in section 5.03 of Rev. Proc. 2008-65 to arrive at the group bonus depreciation amount for the taxable year.

(iii) *Member's proportionate share of group bonus depreciation amount.* Each member's proportionate share of the group bonus depreciation amount is equal to the group bonus depreciation amount determined under section 4.02(3)(b)(ii)(C) of this revenue procedure multiplied by a fraction, the numerator of which is the amount such member contributed to the total computed under section 4.02(3)(b)(ii)(A) of this revenue procedure and the denominator of which is the total computed under section 4.02(3)(b)(ii)(A) of this revenue procedure. If the taxable years of some or all members of the controlled group end on different dates, all (if any) of a member's proportionate share of group bonus depreciation amount must be claimed by such member in the taxable year of the member to which such share relates (determined by reference to the eligible qualified property's placed in service date).

(c) *Allocation agreement.* In lieu of the method provided in section 4.02(3)(b) of this revenue procedure, the controlled group may allocate the group bonus depreciation amount (computed as

¶28,035

provided in section 4.02(3)(b)(ii) of this revenue procedure) to any member in any proportion that all members of the controlled group agree. Any agreement, and the amounts allocated to all members pursuant to such agreement, must be shown on Schedule O (Form 1120) (or a similar statement) within the time and in the manner provided in section 4.02(1) of this revenue procedure. A subsequent agreement may be filed (shown on Schedule O (or similar statement) within the time and in the manner provided in section 4.01(1) of this revenue procedure) that varies the group bonus depreciation amounts allocated to controlled group members in taxable years after the group's first taxable year ending after March 31, 2008.

.04 *Example 1.* A, B, and C are corporations that, on December 31, 2008, are the only members of the ABC controlled group. A's first taxable year ending after March 31, 2008, ends on June 30, 2008. B and C's first taxable year ending after March 31, 2008, ends on December 31, 2008. As of June 30, 2008, A has $300 million of unexpired and unused pre-2006 research and AMT credit carryforwards. As of December 31, 2008, B and C each have $300 million of unexpired and unused pre-2006 research and AMT credit carryforwards. Therefore, as of December 31, 2008, the ABC controlled group has $900 million of unexpired and unused pre-2006 research and AMT credit carryforwards.

On May 1, 2008, A and B each placed in service eligible qualified property that costs $50 million and is 5-year property under § 168(e). On September 1, 2008, A also placed in service eligible qualified property that costs $100 million and is 5-year property under § 168(e). A, B, and C depreciate their 5-year property using the optional depreciation table that corresponds with the general depreciation system, the 200-percent declining balance method, a 5-year recovery period, and the half-year convention. For each of the properties placed in service on May 1, 2008, the difference between the aggregate amount of depreciation that would be allowable for the property if the Stimulus additional first year depreciation deduction applied over the aggregate amount of depreciation that would be allowable for the property if the Stimulus additional first year depreciation deduction did not apply is $20 million. That amount for the property placed in service by A on September 1, 2008, is $40 million.

For its taxable year ending June 30, 2008, A makes the § 168(k)(4) election by filing an amended federal income tax return (Form 1120X) on January 15, 2009, in the manner provided by section 3.05(2)(c)(ii) of this revenue procedure. At the time A's Form 1120X is filed, A, B, and C have not entered into any agreement regarding the allocation of the bonus depreciation amount among them.

(1) Under section 4.02(3)(b)(ii) of this revenue procedure, the ABC controlled group's group bonus depreciation amount is 20 percent of $80 million, or $16 million. Under section 4.02(3)(b)(ii) of this revenue procedure, because $16 million is less than (i) $30 million and (ii) 6 percent of the ABC controlled group aggregate unexpired and unused pre-2006 research and AMT credits (.06 × $900 million, or $54 million), the ABC controlled group is not limited by the maximum increase amount. Thus, under section 4.02(3)(b)(ii)(C) of this revenue procedure, the ABC controlled group's group bonus depreciation amount for the period ending on December 31, 2008, is $16 million.

(2) Under section 4.02(3)(b)(iii) of this revenue procedure, A's proportionate share of the group bonus depreciation amount is $12 million ($16 million × ($60 million/$80 million)). For its taxable year ending June 30, 2008, A may increase its business credit and AMT credit limitations under, respectively, §§ 38(c) and 53(c) by, and claim a refundable credit of, $4 million ($12 million × ($20 million/$60 million)) on its Form 1120X. For its taxable year ending June 30, 2009, A may increase its business credit and AMT credit limitations by $8 million ($12 million × ($40 million/$60 million)) (plus any group bonus depreciation amount calculated for the group and allocated to A for the period January 1, 2009, through December 31, 2009). In addition, B's proportionate share of the group bonus depreciation amount is $4 million ($16 million × ($20 million/$80 million)). B may increase its business credit and AMT credit limitations under, respectively, §§ 38(c) and 53(c) by, and claim a refundable credit of, $4 million on its original federal income tax return for its taxable year ending December 31, 2008. The ABC controlled group then has a maximum amount of $14 million of bonus depreciation amount ($30 million less the $16 million allocated to A and B) remaining to be used for eligible qualified property placed in service by the ABC controlled group after December 31, 2008 (*e.g.*, long-lived property or certain aircraft). The result of this Example is the same if, instead of a single corporation, A represents a consolidated group of corporations, except the $12 million of group bonus depreciation amount allocated to A is reallocated within the A consolidated group pursuant to an allocation by the common parent in accordance with the principles of § 1502 and its accompanying regulations.

¶28,035

(b) *Example 2.* The facts are the same as in *Example 1*, except A has no pre-2006 business credit or AMT credit carryforwards as of the last day of its June 30, 2008, taxable year and C has $600 million of pre-2006 research credit and AMT credit carryforwards as of December 31, 2008. Although A may increase its §§ 38(c) and 53(c) credit limitations for its taxable year ending June 30, 2008, A has no credit carryforwards that A may use to claim a refundable credit. Absent an allocation agreement, B and C may not be allocated any portion of the bonus depreciation amount that was allocated to A under section 4.02(3)(b)(iii) of this revenue procedure. The ABC controlled group, therefore, has $26 million of group bonus depreciation ($30 million less the $4 million allocated to B) remaining to be used for eligible qualified property placed in service by the ABC controlled group after December 31, 2008.

(c) *Example 3.* The facts are the same as *Example 2*, except A, B, and C have entered into an agreement regarding the allocation of the group bonus depreciation amount. The agreement provides that C will be allocated all of the group bonus depreciation amount. C, therefore, may increase its business and AMT credit limitations under, respectively, §§ 38(c) and 53(c) by, and claim a refundable credit of, $16 million on its original income tax return for its taxable year ending December 31, 2008. Neither A nor B may claim the refundable credit for their taxable years ending June 30, 2008, and December 31, 2008, respectively. The ABC controlled group has a maximum amount of $14 million of bonus depreciation amount ($30 million less the $16 million allocated to C) remaining to be used for eligible qualified property placed in service by the ABC controlled group after December 31, 2008.

SECTION 5. PARTNERSHIPS WITH CORPORATE PARTNERS THAT MAKE THE § 168(k)(4) ELECTION

.01 *Partnership's Information to Partner.*

(1) *In general.* If a corporation makes the § 168(k)(4) election and is a partner in a partnership (electing corporate partner), the partnership must provide the electing corporate partner with sufficient information to apply § 168(k)(4)(G)(ii) in determining its distributive share of partnership items under § 702 relating to any eligible qualified property placed in service by the partnership during the taxable year. This information must be provided in the time and manner required by § 6031(b) and § 1.6031(b)-1T(a)(3)(ii) and (b). If the partnership has filed its federal tax return for its first taxable year ending after March 31, 2008, on or before February 9, 2009, and did not provide the electing corporate partner with sufficient information to apply § 168(k)(4)(G)(ii), the partnership must provide such information to the electing corporate partner by the later of May 11, 2009, or 90 calendar days after receiving the corporate partner's notification as required by section 5.02 of this revenue procedure.

(2) *Determination of Electing Corporate Partner's Distributive Share.* A partnership must compute an electing corporate partner's distributive share of depreciation and make other correlative adjustments attributable to eligible qualified property placed in service by the partnership using any reasonable method that is consistent with the intent of § 168(k)(4)(G)(ii). For example, the partnership may apply principles similar to those in § 743(b) and the regulations thereunder to the extent appropriate to make adjustments to the basis of the eligible qualified property and the electing corporate partner's distributive share of depreciation attributable to such property.

.02 *Electing Corporate Partner's Notification to Partnership.* An electing corporate partner must notify the partnership, in writing, that the corporate partner is making the § 168(k)(4) election. This notification must be made on or before the due date (including extensions) of the electing corporate partner's federal income tax return for its first taxable year ending after March 31, 2008. If the electing corporate partner makes the § 168(k)(4) election by filing an amended return under sections 3.02(1)(a)(ii) or 3.03(2) of this revenue procedure, as applicable, the electing corporate partner must notify the partnership on or before the date it files an amended return containing the § 168(k)(4) election. If the electing corporate partner is described in section 3.03(1) of this revenue procedure, the electing corporate partner must notify the partnership on or before March 11, 2009. Failure to comply with the notification requirement provided by this section 5.02 will nullify a taxpayer's attempted § 168(k)(4) election.

SECTION 6. APPLICATION OF § 168(k)(4) TO S CORPORATIONS AND THEIR SHAREHOLDERS

.01 *In General.* An S corporation is allowed to make the § 168(k)(4) election. However, any business or AMT credit limitation increases that result from a § 168(k)(4) election are applied at the corporate level and not at the shareholder level. Thus, a shareholder of an S corporation must not increase the shareholder's business or AMT credit limitations under, respectively, §§ 38(c)

¶28,035

and 53(c) by the bonus depreciation amount that results from a § 168(k)(4) election made by the S corporation.

.02 *Applicability to S Corporations.* Under § 1374(a), an S corporation is subject to tax on its recognized built-in gains during its taxable year. In general, under § 1374(b)(3)(B), an S corporation is allowed as a credit against the § 1374(a) tax any business and AMT credit carryforwards that arose in a taxable year in which the corporation was a C corporation. The credits allowed by § 1374(b)(3)(B) are subject to three limitations: the business credit limitation in § 38(c), the AMT credit limitation in § 53(c), and the amount of the § 1374(a) tax. Sections 1374(b)(3)(B) and 1.1374-6(b). If an S corporation makes the § 168(k)(4) election, the S corporation calculates its bonus depreciation amount as provided in section 5 of Rev. Proc. 2008-65, increases its business and AMT credit limitations, uses the straight line method for depreciating its eligible qualified property, and must not claim the Stimulus additional first year depreciation deduction for such property. However, the § 168(k)(4) election does not increase the S corporation's § 1374(b)(3)(B) limitation. Therefore, if the § 168(k)(4) election is made, an S corporation may not claim business credits or AMT credits in excess of its § 1374(a) tax for the taxable year. Any credits allowed as a result of the increase in the business or AMT credit limitations, which may be used only as an additional credit against the § 1374(a) tax, are not refundable to the S corporation.

.03 *Time and Manner for Making the § 168(k)(4) Election.* An S corporation makes the § 168(k)(4) election within the time and in the manner provided in section 3 of this revenue procedure.

SECTION 7. APPLICATION OF § 3081(b) OF THE HOUSING ACT

.01 *In General.* Section 3081(b)(1) of the Housing Act allows an applicable partnership to elect to be treated as making a deemed payment of income tax (the "deemed payment") in the amount determined under section 7.03 of this revenue procedure. This election applies to any taxable year during which eligible qualified property is placed in service by the applicable partnership. See section 3 of Rev. Proc. 2008-65 for determining which depreciable property qualifies as eligible qualified property. Notwithstanding any other provision of the Code, the deemed payment is refundable to the applicable partnership and may not be treated as an offset or credit against any tax liability of the applicable partnership or any partner. Section 3081(b)(2)(A) of the Housing Act.

.02 *Definition of Applicable Partnership.* An applicable partnership is a domestic partnership that was formed effective on August 3, 2007, and will produce in excess of 675,000 automobiles during the period beginning on January 1, 2008, and ending on June 30, 2008. Section 3081(b)(4)(A) of the Housing Act.

.03 *Computation of the Deemed Payment.* Pursuant to § 3081(b)(1)(A) and (b)(3) of the Housing Act, the amount of the deemed payment for the taxable year is equal to the lesser of:

(1) 20 percent of the excess (if any) of the aggregate amount of depreciation that would be allowable for eligible qualified property placed in service by the applicable partnership during the taxable year if the Stimulus additional first year depreciation deduction applied to all such property, over the aggregate amount of depreciation that would be allowable for all eligible qualified property placed in service by the applicable partnership during the taxable year if the Stimulus additional first year depreciation deduction did not apply to any such property. For purposes of computing this amount, the rules in section 5.02 of Rev. Proc. 2008-65 apply;

(2) the applicable partnership's research credit (determined under § 41) for the taxable year; or

(3) $30 million less any deemed payments made by the applicable partnership under § 3081(b) of the Housing Act for all prior taxable years.

.04 *Effect of Making Election under § 3081(b) of the Housing Act.* If an applicable partnership makes the election to apply § 3081(b) of the Housing Act (the "§ 3081(b) Housing Act election"), the applicable partnership (1) must determine the depreciation deduction for any eligible qualified property placed in service by the partnership during the taxable year by using the straight line method and by not claiming the Stimulus additional first year depreciation deduction, and (2) must reduce the amount of its research credit for the taxable year by the amount of the deemed payment for the taxable year. Section 3081(b)(1)(B) and (C).

.05 *Time and Manner of Making § 3081(b) Housing Act Election.*

(1) *Time for making election.* An applicable partnership must make the § 3081(b) Housing Act election by the due date (including extensions) of the Form 1065, U.S. Return of Partnership Income, for the partnership's first taxable year ending after March 31, 2008. Even if an applicable partnership does not place in service any eligible qualified property during its first taxable

year ending after March 31, 2008, the partnership must make the § 3081(b) Housing Act election for that taxable year if the partnership wishes to apply the election to eligible qualified property placed in service in subsequent taxable years.

(2) *Manner of making election.* An applicable partnership makes the § 3081(b) Housing Act election by making the following statement (printed legibly or typed) on its timely-filed Form 1065 for the first taxable year ending after March 31, 2008, in the space below the signature section of the Form 1065: "A refund in the amount of $[*Insert Amount*] is requested pursuant to Section 3081(b)(1) of P.L. 110-289, the Housing and Economic Recovery Act of 2008."

(3) *Limited Relief for Late Election.*

(a) *Automatic 6-Month Extension.* Pursuant to § 301.9100-2(b) of the Procedure and Administration Regulations, an automatic extension of 6 months from the due date of the federal tax return (*excluding* extensions) for the applicable partnership's first taxable year ending after March 31, 2008, is granted to make the § 3081(b) Housing Act election, provided the applicable partnership timely filed its federal tax return for its first taxable year ending after March 31, 2008, and the applicable partnership satisfies the requirements in § 301.9100-2(c) and (d).

(b) *Other Extensions.* An applicable partnership that fails to make the § 3081(b) Housing Act election for the applicable partnership's first taxable year ending after March 31, 2008, as provided in section 7.05(1) and (2) of this revenue procedure or in section 7.05(3)(a) of this revenue procedure but wants to do so must file a request for an extension of time to make the election under the rules in § 301.9100-3.

.06 *Filing of Form 1065.*

(1) *In general.* For the taxable year in which the § 3081(b) Housing Act election is made (the "year of election") and for any subsequent taxable year in which an applicable partnership is claiming a refundable deemed payment under § 3081(b) of the Housing Act, the partnership's Form 1065 and related forms and schedules (including Schedules K-1) must not be filed electronically. Further, the applicable partnership must mail the Form 1065 and related forms and schedules (including Schedules K-1) to: Internal Revenue Service, 1973 N. Rulon White Blvd., Attn: Audrey Martinez Mail Stop 1120, Ogden, UT 84201.

(2) *Taxable years subsequent to the year of election.* If the applicable partnership claims a refundable deemed payment under § 3081(b) of the Hous-ing Act for any taxable year subsequent to the year of election, the partnership must make the following statement (printed legibly or typed) on its Form 1065 for that taxable year in the space below the signature section of the Form 1065: "A refund in the amount of $[*Insert Amount*] is requested pursuant to Section 3081(b)(1) of P.L. 110-289, the Housing and Economic Recovery Act of 2008."

SECTION 8. EFFECT ON OTHER DOCUMENTS

Rev. Proc. 2008-65 is amplified and supplemented.

SECTION 9. PAPERWORK REDUCTION ACT

The collections of information contained in this revenue procedure have been reviewed and approved by the Office of Management and Budget in accordance with the Paperwork Reduction Act (44 U.S.C. 3507) under control number 1545-2133. An agency may not conduct or sponsor, and a person is not required to respond to, a collection of information unless the collection of information displays a valid OMB control number.

The collections of information in this revenue procedure are in sections 3, 4, 5, and 7. This information is necessary and will be used to determine whether the taxpayer is eligible to make the § 168(k)(4) election and the amount by which the election increases the taxpayer's applicable credit limitations. The collections of information are required for the taxpayer to make the § 168(k)(4) election. The likely respondents are the following: business and other for-profit institutions.

The estimated total annual reporting and/or recordkeeping burden is 2,700 hours.

The estimated annual burden per respondent/recordkeeper varies from 0.25 hours to 1 hour, depending on individual circumstances, with an estimated average of 0.5 hours. The estimated number of respondents is 5,400. The estimated annual frequency of responses is on occasion.

SECTION 10. EFFECTIVE DATE

This revenue procedure is effective January 23, 2009.

SECTION 11. DRAFTING INFORMATION

The principal author of this revenue procedure is Jeffrey T. Rodrick of the Office of Associate Chief Counsel (Income Tax & Accounting). For further information regarding this revenue procedure, contact Mr. Rodrick on (202) 622-4930 (not a toll free call).

EXECUTIVE COMPENSATION

¶ 28,040   Treasury Department News Release, TDNR HP-1364, January 16, 2009

Treasury Issues Additional Executive Compensation Rules Under TARP

The U.S. Department of the Treasury today issued interim final rules for reporting and recordkeeping requirements under the executive compensation standards of the Troubled Asset Relief Program's (TARP) Capital Purchase Program (CPP).

The new rule issued today requires the chief executive officer (CEO) to certify annually within 135 days after the financial institution's fiscal year end that the financial institution and its compensation committee have complied with these executive compensation standards.

In addition, within 120 days of the closing date of the Securities Purchase Agreement between the financial institution and the Treasury, the CEO is required to certify that the compensation committee has reviewed the senior executives' incentive compensation arrangements with the senior risk officers to ensure that these arrangements do not encourage senior executives to take unnecessary and excessive risks that could threaten the value of the financial institution.

The CEO must provide the 120-day and annual certifications to the TARP Chief Compliance Officer.

The financial institution is also required to keep records to substantiate these certifications for at least six years following each certification and provide these records to the TARP Chief Compliance Officer upon request.

Treasury *originally published executive compensation standards* for CPP last October. The rules generally apply to the chief executive officer, chief financial officer, plus the next three most highly compensated executive officers. These standards include:

- ensuring that incentive compensation for senior executives does not encourage unnecessary and excessive risks that threaten the value of the financial institution;

- requiring clawback of any bonus or incentive compensation paid to a senior executive based on statements of earnings, gains, or other criteria that are later proven to be materially inaccurate;

- prohibiting the financial institution from making any golden parachute payment (based on the Internal Revenue Code provision) to a senior executive; and

- agreeing not to deduct for tax purposes executive compensation in excess of $500,000 for each senior executive.

The rule also makes a few clarifications and a technical amendment to the October interim final rule.

Treasury also issued today a revised version of the executive compensation guidelines applicable to financial institutions participating in programs for Systemically Significant Failing Institutions (Treasury Notice 2008-PSSFI) to add similar compliance reporting and recordkeeping requirements as in today's Interim Final Rule.

In addition, Treasury is also issuing Frequently Asked Questions relating to the executive compensation standards to assist financial institutions' compliance with these standards.

¶ 28,045   Notice 2008-94, I.R.B. 2008-44, 1070

I. PURPOSE

This notice provides guidance on certain executive compensation provisions of the Emergency Economic Stabilization Act of 2008, Div. A of Pub. Law No. 110-343 (EESA), which was enacted on October 3, 2008. Section 302 of EESA added new §§ 162(m)(5) and 280G(e) to the Internal Revenue Code. Section 162(m) generally limits the deductibility of compensation paid to certain corporate executives and § 280G provides that a corporate executive's excess parachute payments are not deductible and imposes (under § 4999) an excise tax on the executive for those amounts.

New §§ 162(m)(5) and 280G(e) provide additional limitations on the deductibility of compensation paid to certain executives by employers who sell "troubled assets" in the "troubled assets relief program" included in EESA. Section 162(m)(5) generally reduces the $1 million deduction limitation to $500,000 for certain taxable years and provides that certain exceptions to the deduction limitation, including the exception for performance-based compensation, are not applicable. Section 280G(e) generally expands the definition of a parachute payment to include certain payments made contingent on severance from employment.

II. BACKGROUND RELATING TO EESA EXECUTIVE COMPENSATION PROVISIONS

Section 101(a) of EESA authorizes the Secretary of the Treasury to establish a Troubled Assets Relief Program (TARP) to "purchase, and to make and fund commitments to purchase, troubled assets from any financial institution, on such terms and conditions as are determined by the Secretary, and in accordance with this Act and policies and procedures developed and published by the Secretary." Section 120 of EESA provides that the TARP authorities terminate on December 31, 2009, unless extended upon certification by the Secretary of the Treasury to Congress, but in no event later than two years from the date of enactment (October 3, 2008) (the TARP authorities period). Thus, the TARP authorities period is the period from October 3, 2008 to December 31, 2009 or, if extended, the period from October 3, 2008 to the date so extended, but no later than October 3, 2010.

EESA includes two sections that directly address executive compensation. Section 302 of EESA enacted tax provisions as amendments to §§ 162(m) and 280G that address compensation paid to certain executive officers employed by financial institutions that sell assets under TARP. This notice addresses these tax provisions.

Section 111 of EESA subjects certain financial institutions that sell assets to the Treasury Department to specified executive compensation standards. In the case of a direct purchase the standards under section 111(b) of EESA include: (a) limits on compensation that exclude incentives on senior executive officers of financial institutions to take unnecessary and excessive risks that threaten the value of the financial institution during the period that the Treasury Department holds an equity or debt position, (b) recovery of any bonus or incentive compensation paid to a senior executive officer based on statements of earnings, gains, or other criteria that are later proven to be materially inaccurate, and (c) a prohibition on making any golden parachute payment to any of its senior executive officers during the period that the Treasury Department holds an equity or debt position. In the case of a financial institution that has sold assets under TARP in sales that are not solely direct purchases and the amount sold (including direct purchases) exceeds $300 million in the aggregate, the financial institution is prohibited under section 111(c) during the TARP authorities period from entering into any new employment contract with a senior executive officer that provides a golden parachute in the event of involuntary termination from employment, bankruptcy filing, insolvency, or receivership. See Interim final regulations issued by the Treasury under section 111(b) of EESA at 31 CFR part 30, Notice 2008-PSSFI under section 111(b) of EESA, and Notice 2008-TAAP under section 111(c) of EESA.

III. SECTION 302(a) OF EESA ADDING NEW § 162(m)(5)

A. Section 162(m) Background

Section 162(m) generally limits the otherwise allowable deduction for compensation paid or accrued with respect to a covered employee of a publicly held corporation to no more than $1 million per year.[1] Section 162(m)(3) defines a covered employee as (1) the chief executive officer of the corporation (or an individual acting in such capacity) as of the close of the taxable year, or (2) one of the four most highly compensated officers for the taxable year (other than the chief executive officer) required to be reported to the shareholders under the Securities Exchange Act of 1934 (the Exchange Act).

In 2006, the Securities and Exchange Commission amended the rules related to executive compensation disclosure. In response to the 2006 amendment, the Treasury Department and the Service issued Notice 2007-49, 2007-1 C.B. 1429, which provides that "covered employee" means any employee who is (1) the principal executive officer (or an individual acting in such capacity) defined by reference to the Exchange Act or (2) among the three most highly compensated officers for the taxable year (other than the principal executive officer or the principal financial officer), again defined by reference to the Ex-

---

[1] A corporation is treated as publicly held if it has a class of equity securities that is required to be registered under section 12 of Securities Exchange Act of 1934.

change Act. Section 1.162-27(c)(2) of the Treasury Regulations provides that the individual must meet the criteria of chief executive officer or be among the highest compensated officers as of the last day of the taxable year in order to be a covered employee.

If an individual is a covered employee for a taxable year, then a deduction limit applies to all compensation not explicitly excluded from the deduction limit, regardless of whether the compensation is for services as a covered employee and regardless of when the compensation was earned. The $1 million limit is reduced by excess parachute payments (as defined in § 280G) that are not deductible by the corporation. Under § 162(m) as in effect prior to the amendment included in EESA, the following types of compensation generally are not subject to the deduction limit and are not taken into account in determining whether other compensation exceeds $1 million: (1) remuneration payable on a commission basis; (2) remuneration payable solely on account of the attainment of one or more performance goals if certain outside director and shareholder approval requirements are met ("performance-based compensation"); (3) payments to a tax-qualified retirement plan (including salary reduction contributions); (4) amounts that are excludable from the executive's gross income; and (5) any remuneration payable under a written binding contract that was in effect on February 17, 1993 and that was not materially modified thereafter. Because remuneration generally does not include compensation for which a deduction is allowable after a covered employee ceases to be a covered employee, the deduction limit does not apply to compensation that is deferred until after termination of employment.

B. Section 302(a) of EESA: Amendment adding § 162(m)(5)

Section 302(a) of EESA amended § 162(m) to add § 162(m)(5), which reduces the deduction limit to $500,000 in the case of "executive remuneration" and "deferred deduction executive remuneration." This limit applies only to certain employers (an "applicable employer") for remuneration paid to certain executives ("covered executives) during certain taxable years (an "applicable taxable year"). Employers covered under § 162(m)(5) are not limited to publicly held corporations (nor even to corporations). The exception for performance-based compensation and certain other exceptions do not apply in the case of executive compensation covered under § 162(m)(5).

Q&A-1 and Q&A-2 of this notice provide guidance on when an employer is an applicable employer, Q&A-3 provides guidance on when a taxable year is an applicable taxable year, Q&A-4 provides guidance on the determination of who is a covered executive, Q&A-5 provides guidance on mergers and acquisitions, Q&A-6 provides guidance on executive remuneration, and Q&A-7 through Q&A-10 provide guidance on deferred deduction executive remuneration.

Q-1: What is an applicable employer under § 162(m)(5)?

A-1: (a) *General definition.* An "applicable employer" is any financial institution that is an employer from whom one or more troubled assets are acquired under TARP, but only if the aggregate amount of the assets acquired exceeds $300 million. The assets that are counted for the $300 million threshold include assets that are acquired under TARP in accordance with section 101(a) of EESA. However, if the only such acquisitions from a financial institution are through a direct purchase, the financial institution is not an applicable employer. (For special rules with respect to employers that sell assets through a direct purchase, see section 111(b) of EESA, Interim final regulations issued by the Treasury under section 111(b) of EESA at 31 CFR part 30, and Notice 2008-PSSFI under section 111(b) of EESA.)

(b) *Controlled group rules.* For purposes of § 162(m)(5), including the determination of whether the aggregate amount of assets acquired from an employer exceeds $300 million, two or more persons who are treated as a single employer under § 414(b) (employees of a controlled group of corporations) and § 414(c) (employees of partnerships, proprietorships, etc., that are under common control) are treated as a single employer. However, for purposes of applying the aggregation rules to determine an applicable employer, the rules for brother-sister controlled groups and combined groups are disregarded (including disregarding the rules in § 1563(a)(2) and (a)(3) with respect to corporations and the parallel rules that are in § 1.414(c)-2(c) of the Treasury Regulations with respect to other organizations conducting trades or businesses). See Q&A-4 of this notice regarding the determination of a covered executive in a controlled group, and see Q&A-5 of this notice for special rules where a financial institution has acquired another financial institution through an acquisition.

(c) *Example.* Bank holding company X is the sole owner of banks A, B, and C. In December of

¶ 28,045

2008, bank A sells $150 million of assets under a TARP auction purchase. In February of 2009, bank B sells $100 million of assets under a TARP auction purchase. On August 14, 2009, bank C sells $100 million of assets under a TARP auction purchase. Bank holding company X, along with banks A, B, and C, plus any other entity that is treated as the same employer under the rules described in paragraph (b) of this Q&A-1, constitute a single applicable employer that has sold in excess of $300 million of assets under a TARP auction purchase. As provided in Q&A-4 of this notice, the chief executive officer and chief financial officer of bank holding company X and the three other most highly compensated officers of the bank holding company X controlled group are "covered executives."

Q-2: Can a corporation that is not publicly traded, or an entity that is not a corporation, be an "applicable employer"?

A-2: (a) *General rule.* Yes. An applicable employer for purposes of § 162(m)(5) is not limited to a publicly traded corporation or even to the corporate business form. Thus, an entity, whether or not publicly traded, is an applicable employer if the entity is described in Q&A-1 of this notice regardless of whether the entity is a corporation, a partnership (or taxed as a partnership for federal tax purposes), or a trust.

(b) *Special rule for partnerships, grantor trusts, and similar entities.* In the case of a partnership, grantor trust, or similar entity, the determination of whether more than $300 million of assets has been sold is generally made at the level of the selling entity (taking into account all entities that are treated as the same employer under the controlled group rules described in Q&A-1(b) of this notice). However, if the selling entity has no employees who are officers (or acting in the capacity of an officer), then the owner of the entity that manages the selling entity's assets is the entity that may be the applicable employer (along with all entities that are treated as the same employer as the selling entity under the controlled group rules described in Q&A-1(b) of this notice).

Q-3: What is an applicable taxable year to which the $500,000 deduction limit imposed by § 162(m)(5) applies?

A-3: Section 162(m)(5) does not apply to an employer unless, during a taxable year of the employer that includes any portion of the TARP authorities period, the aggregate amount of the troubled assets acquired under TARP from the employer in that taxable year, when added to the amount acquired from the employer under TARP for all preceding taxable years, exceeds $300 million (unless all such acquisitions are through a direct purchase. If the condition in the preceding sentence is satisfied, then § 162(m)(5) applies to that taxable year and to any subsequent taxable year of the employer that includes any portion of the TARP authorities period. (See Q&A-10 regarding the applicability of § 162(m)(5) to deferred deduction executive compensation after the TARP authorities period.) If the entities that are treated as a single applicable employer under the controlled group rules described in Q&A-1(b) of this notice do not have the same taxable year, the relevant taxable year is the taxable year of the parent entity in the controlled group.

Q-4: Who is a covered executive under § 162(m)(5)?

A-4: (a) *General definition.* A "covered executive" means an individual described in the following sentence who is employed by a financial institution that is an applicable employer at any time during an applicable taxable year. Covered executives are limited to: (i) the chief executive officer (CEO) and the chief financial officer (CFO) (or an individual acting in either of those capacities) of the applicable employer during the taxable year that includes any portion of the TARP authorities period, and (ii) the three highest compensated officers of the applicable employer (including the entire controlled group) other than the CEO or CFO, taking into account only employees employed during the taxable year that includes any portion of the TARP authorities period (the high three officers).

(b) *Determination of high three officers.* For corporations that are subject to the Exchange Act (as defined in section III.A. of this notice), the high three officers are determined on the basis of the shareholder disclosure rules under the Exchange Act with one difference. In accordance with the Exchange Act disclosure rules, the term "officer" means those "executive officers" whose compensation is subject to reporting under the Exchange Act. For the purpose of determining the high three officers, compensation is defined as it is in the Exchange Act disclosure rules to include total compensation without regard to whether the compensation is includible in an executive officer's gross income. However, unlike the Exchange Act disclosure rules that determine the high three officers by reference to total compensation for the last completed fiscal year, the measurement period for purposes of determining the high three officers for an applicable taxable year is that taxable year.

(c) *Application to private employers and noncorporate entities.* Rules analogous to the rules in paragraphs (a) and (b) of this Q&A-4 apply to employers that are not subject to the Exchange Act disclosure rules, including employers whose stock is not publicly traded and employers that are not corporations.

(d) *Time period as a covered executive.* If an employee is a covered executive with respect to an applicable employer for any applicable taxable year, the executive is a covered executive for any subsequent applicable taxable year, including being a covered executive in any later taxable year for purposes of the special rule for deferred deduction executive remuneration (described in Q&A-10 of this notice). (See Q&A-5 of this notice for special rules that apply in connection with an acquisition.)

Q-5: How do the rules apply in connection with an acquisition, merger, or reorganization?

A-5: (a) *Special rules for acquisitions, mergers, or reorganizations.* In the event that a financial institution (target) that sold troubled assets under TARP is acquired by an entity that is not related to target (acquirer) in an acquisition of any form, the troubled assets sold under TARP by target prior to the acquisition are not aggregated with any assets sold by acquirer prior to or after the acquisition. For this purpose, acquirer is related to target if stock or other interests of target are treated (under § 318(a) other than paragraph (4) thereof) as owned by acquirer.

If, after an acquisition, troubled assets of target are sold by acquirer's controlled group (including target in the case of a stock acquisition), those assets must be aggregated with any assets sold by acquirer, whether prior to or after the acquisition, for purposes of determining whether acquirer is an applicable employer.

If target was an applicable employer at the time of the acquisition, acquirer will not become an applicable employer merely as a result of the acquisition. Further, if target was an applicable employer at the time of the acquisition, a covered executive of target will continue to be a covered executive during the TARP authorities period if he or she is employed by the controlled group of which target is a member, regardless of whether acquirer is an applicable employer and regardless of whether the target covered executive is a covered executive of the acquirer. However, if, after an acquisition, a target covered executive ceases employment with the controlled group of which target is a member, no new executive of target will be a covered executive merely because of such termination, unless such executive is a covered executive of acquirer.

(b) *Example.* In 2008, financial institution A sells $100 million of troubled assets under TARP and financial institution B sells $350 million of troubled assets under TARP. In January 2009, financial institution A acquires financial institution B in a stock purchase transaction, with the result that financial institution B becomes a wholly-owned subsidiary of financial institution A. In February 2009, financial institution A sells an additional $100 million of its troubled assets under TARP, and in March 2009 financial institution B (when it is a wholly owned subsidiary of A) sells an additional $150 million of troubled assets. Neither the sale of troubled assets by financial institution A nor the sale of troubled assets by financial institution B are solely through direct purchases. Based on the rules in paragraph (a) of this Q&A-5, financial institution A is not an applicable employer as a result of the acquisition of B, or as a result of the assets sold in February 2009, because the $350 million of troubled assets sold by financial institution B prior to the acquisition are not aggregated with the troubled assets sold by financial institution A's controlled group prior to and after the acquisition of financial institution B. However, financial institution A becomes an applicable employer in March 2009 when the amount of troubled assets sold by financial institution A's controlled group (without regard to the sales by financial institution B prior to the acquisition of B by A) total $350 million. Further, because 2009 is an applicable taxable year with respect to financial institution B, the officers of financial institution B who are covered executives on the date financial institution B was acquired continue to be covered executives during any subsequent applicable taxable year that includes any portion of the TARP authorities period, as long as they are employed by financial institution A's controlled group. Similarly, the CEO, CFO, and high three officers of financial institution A become covered executives in 2009 when financial institution A becomes an applicable employer.

Q-6: What constitutes executive remuneration to which the $500,000 limit imposed by § 162(m)(5) applies?

A-6: (a) *General definition.* For the purposes of the § 162(m)(5) $500,000 deduction limit, except as provided in paragraph (b) of this Q&A-6, executive remuneration means applicable employee remuneration, as determined under § 162(m)(4), but without regard to the following subparagraphs of § 162(m)(4): (B) (remuneration payable on a commission basis), (C) (performance-based compensation), or (D) (exception for existing binding contracts). Under § 162(m)(4), applicable employee remuneration for a year is based on the year in which the remuneration is deductible (whether or not the remuneration is paid in that year or is includible in the employee's income in that year). For example, payments that are deductible by the employer in an applicable taxable year, but are paid to the covered executive by the 15th day of the third month after the end of that year (as described in § 1.404(b)-1T, Q&A-2(b)(1) of the Treasury Regulations), are executive remuneration for that applicable taxable year.

(b) *Remuneration only for the applicable taxable year.* The $500,000 deduction limit in § 162(m)(5)(A) applies to executive remuneration and deferred deduction executive remuneration attributable to services performed by a covered executive during an applicable taxable year. Under this rule, payments of remuneration that are deductible in an applicable taxable year for services performed by the covered executive in a prior taxable year are not treated as executive remuneration for purposes of § 162(m)(5). (See Q&A-7 through Q&A-10 of this notice for rules related to deferred deduction executive remuneration.)

Q-7: How does the $500,000 deduction limitation imposed by § 162(m)(5) apply with respect to deferred deduction executive remuneration?

A-7: (a) *General rule.* No deduction is allowed for any taxable year for deferred deduction executive remuneration for services performed during any applicable taxable year by a covered executive, to the extent that the amount of the deferred deduction executive remuneration exceeds $500,000, minus the sum of: (i) the executive remuneration for that applicable taxable year, plus (ii) the portion of the deferred deduction executive remuneration for such services taken into account in a preceding taxable year. Under this rule, the unused portion (if any) of the $500,000 limit for the applicable taxable year that has not been taken into account (and so is unused) is carried forward until the year in which the deferred deduction executive remuneration allocable to that applicable taxable year is otherwise deductible, and the remaining unused limit is then applied to the payment of the deferred deduction executive remuneration.

(b) *Examples.* (1) Covered executive A is paid $400,000 in salary by an applicable employer in 2009 (an applicable taxable year) and A obtains a legally binding right attributable to services performed in 2009 to receive a payment of $250,000 in 2015. The full $400,000 in cash salary is deductible under the $500,000 limit in 2009. In 2015, the employer's deduction with respect to the $250,000 is limited to $100,000, which represents the unused portion of the $500,000 limit from 2009 (and no deduction will be allowed for the remaining $150,000).

(2) Covered executive B is paid $400,000 salary by an applicable employer in 2009 (an applicable taxable year) and B obtains a legally binding right attributable to services performed in 2009 to be paid $250,000 in 2010 (which is also an applicable taxable year), and B is paid $500,000 in salary in 2010. Accordingly, the employer's deduction in 2010 for the $250,000 payment made in 2010 (attributable to services performed in 2009) is limited to $100,000. The entire $500,000 of salary earned in 2010 is deductible in 2010 (assuming other deduction requirements are satisfied).

Q-8: What is "deferred deduction executive remuneration" for purposes of § 162(m)(5)?

A-8: Deferred deduction executive remuneration means remuneration that would be executive remuneration for services performed by a covered executive in an applicable taxable year but for the fact that the deduction is allowable in a subsequent taxable year (determined without regard to § 162(m)(5)). The amount paid as deferred deduction executive remuneration is taken into account, without distinction between the amount deferred in the taxable year in which the services were performed and earnings thereon.

Q-9: How are the services to which deferred deduction executive remuneration is allocable determined?

A-9: (a) *Period during which services are performed.* For purposes of the $500,000 limit on the deductibility of deferred deduction executive remuneration under § 162(m)(5)(A), the period during which the services are performed by a covered executive to which the remuneration is allocable is determined in accordance with this Q&A-9. (See Q&A-7 of this notice regarding the application of the deduction limits to deferred deduction executive remuneration.)

(b) *Services to which deferred deduction executive remuneration is allocable.* (1) *General rule:* Remuneration allocable to a service period based on plan formula. If an employee obtains a legally binding right to remuneration under a plan, agreement, or arrangement (plan) and that plan provides for benefit payments under a formula that relates to a specific period of service in a year (such as relating to compensation paid during that period), the deferred deduction executive remuneration is generally allocable to that specific period. To the extent that, based on the terms of the plan, deferred deduction executive remuner-

¶ 28,045

ation is not allocable to services performed in a particular taxable year, then the remuneration generally is for services performed during the taxable year in which the employee obtains the legally binding right to the remuneration.

(2) *Legally binding right.* Deferred deduction executive remuneration is not allocable to a period prior to the date the employee is employed by the employer and obtains a legally binding right to the remuneration. An employee does not have a legally binding right to remuneration to the extent that compensation may be reduced unilaterally or eliminated by the employer or other person after the services creating the right to the remuneration have been performed. However, if the facts and circumstances indicate that the discretion to reduce or eliminate the remuneration is available or exercisable only upon a condition, or the discretion to reduce or eliminate the compensation lacks substantive significance, then the employee has a legally binding right to the remuneration. For this purpose, remuneration is not considered subject to unilateral reduction or elimination merely because it may be reduced or eliminated by operation of the objective terms of the plan, such as the application of a nondiscretionary, objective provision creating a substantial risk of forfeiture. (See §§ 1.409A-1(b)(1) and 31.3121(v)(2)-1(b)(3)(i) of the Treasury Regulations for additional rules regarding when an employee obtains a legally binding right to remuneration.)

(3) *Substantial risk of forfeiture.* To the extent that an employee's right to remuneration is subject to a substantial risk of forfeiture (as determined in accordance with the rules under § 1.409A-1(d) of the Treasury Regulations) in the form of a requirement to continue to perform substantial future services for the employer, the remuneration generally is for services performed over the period of time that the employee is required to continue to perform substantial future services for the employer and is allocated to that period on a pro rata basis, unless the remuneration is allocable to a different period under the rule in paragraph (b)(1) of this Q&A-9. If the substantial risk of forfeiture lapses early (such as due to death or disability), then the allocation is prorated over the period from when the employee obtained the legally binding right to the payment to the date that the substantial risk of forfeiture lapses. The only substantial risk of forfeiture taken into account for purposes of this paragraph (b)(3) is a requirement that the employee perform substantial future services. Any other condition related to the purpose of the remuneration that may constitute a substantial risk of forfeiture is disregarded.

(c) *Examples.* (1) Employee A obtains on January 1, 2006 a legally binding right to be paid $400,000 at the end of December, 2010, but only if A continues to be employed on the date of payment. In this case, a pro rata portion of the remuneration is for services performed during 2006, 2007, 2008, 2009, and 2010 ($80,000 per year). If 2009 and 2010 are applicable taxable years for A's employer and A is a covered executive in those years, then, for purposes of the $500,000 deductible limitation for 2009 and 2010, $80,000 of the $400,000 paid in 2010 would be deferred deduction executive remuneration allocable to services rendered in 2009 and $80,000 of the $400,000 paid in 2010 would be allocable to services rendered in 2010.

(2) Employee B obtains a legally binding right in 2008 to receive a payment of $100,000 in 2012 (without regard to continued employment) in the event that an asset is sold by that date for a price at or above a specified dollar amount, which, under the circumstances is a substantial risk of forfeiture. The risk of forfeiture is disregarded and the $100,000 payment is for services performed in 2008. The $100,000 payment made in 2012 is deferred deduction executive remuneration allocable to 2008 and is subject to the 2008 $500,000 deduction limitation.

(3) Employee C obtains on December 31, 2008 a legally binding right to be paid on February 1, 2011 an amount equal to 10 percent of employee C's salary during the period from January 1, 2009 through December 31, 2010, and employee C's salary is $400,000 for each of 2009 and 2010. Under the terms of the plan in this case, the remuneration is allocable pro rata to services performed in 2009 and 2010, so that half of the $80,000 payment made on February 1, 2011 is for services performed in 2009 and the other half is for services performed in 2010.

(4) Employee D obtains on December 31, 2008 a legally binding right to be paid on January 1, 2015 an amount equal to 20 percent of D's highest annual salary times the number of years of service completed by D before January 1, 2011, but only if D remains employed through December 31, 2010. Employee D remains employed through December 31, 2010 and has an annual salary of $400,000 in 2009 and $450,000 in 2010. Accordingly, Employee D receives a payment of $180,000 on January 1, 2015 (20 percent times 2 years of service times $450,000, D's highest annual salary). Under the terms of the plan in this case, under the rule in paragraph (b)(1) of this Q&A-9, the remuneration allocable to services performed in 2009 is $80,000 (20 percent of Employee D's annual salary in 2009 times 1 year of

¶ 28,045

service). The remuneration allocable to services performed in 2010 is $100,000 (20 percent of $450,000, times 2 years of service, reduced by the remuneration allocable to services performed in 2009).

(5) Employee E obtains on December 31, 2008 a legally binding right to be paid $400,000 on February 1, 2011 (without any requirement of continued employment). Under these facts and circumstances, the remuneration is not allocable to services performed in a period of time after December 31, 2008, so that the $400,000 paid on February 1, 2011 is for services performed during the taxable year that includes December 31, 2008.

(6) Employee F obtains on December 31, 2008 a legally binding right to acquire stock (a stock option) with an exercise price equal to the fair market value of the stock on December 31, 2008 (without any requirement of continued employment in order to be able to exercise the right and retain the shares). The remuneration is not allocable to services performed in a period of time after December 31, 2008, so that the remuneration resulting from exercise of the stock option is for services performed in the taxable year that includes December 31, 2008.

(7) Employee G obtains on January 1, 2009 a legally binding right to acquire stock (a stock option) over the next 10 years with an exercise price equal to the fair market value of the stock on January 1, 2009, but the stock option can be exercised only after the employee has continued his or her employment for three more years (through December 31, 2011). The employee exercises the right in 2014 resulting in income of $210,000. In this case, the payment of $210,000 is allocable to services performed from January 1, 2009 through December 31, 2011, of which $70,000 is allocable to services rendered in 2009, $70,000 is allocable to services rendered in 2010, and $70,000 is allocable to services performed in 2011.

Q-10: How long does the limit imposed by § 162(m)(5) apply?

A-10: While the limit imposed by § 162(m)(5) only applies to remuneration for services performed in an applicable taxable year, the limit with respect to deferred deduction executive remuneration for services performed in an applicable taxable year applies for deductions in all subsequent taxable years (until the deferred deduction executive remuneration for services performed in that applicable taxable year is completely paid).

IV. SECTION 302(b) OF EESA ADDING NEW § 280G(e)

A. Section 280G Background

Section 280G, as in effect prior to the addition of § 280G(e) made by section 302(b) of EESA, provides that certain payments in excess of certain limits, referred to as "excess parachute payments," are not deductible by a corporation. In addition, § 4999 imposes an excise tax on the recipient of any excess parachute payment equal to 20 percent of the amount of such payment.

Subject to certain exceptions, § 280G(b)(2) defines a "parachute payment" as any payment in the nature of compensation to (or for the benefit of) a disqualified individual that is contingent on a change in the ownership or effective control of a corporation or on a change in the ownership of a substantial portion of the assets of a corporation ("acquired corporation") if the aggregate present value of all such payments made or to be made to the disqualified individual equals or exceeds three times the individual's "base amount." Section 280G(b)(3) defines the individual's base amount as the average annual compensation payable by the acquired corporation and includible in the individual's gross income over the five taxable years of such individual preceding the individual's taxable year in which the change in ownership or control occurs.

A disqualified individual is any individual who is an employee, independent contractor, or other person specified in Treasury regulations who performs personal services for the corporation and who is an officer, shareholder, or highly compensated individual of the corporation.

B. Section 302(b) OF EESA: Amendment of § 280G

Section 302(b) of EESA amended § 280G by expanding the definition of a parachute payment to include certain severance payments made to a covered executive of an applicable employer participating in TARP. As defined in § 280G(e)(2)(B), an applicable severance from employment is any severance from employment of a covered executive: (1) by reason of an involuntary termination of the executive by the employer or (2) in connection with a bankruptcy, liquidation, or receivership of the employer.

New § 280G(e) is effective for payments made during an applicable taxable year with respect to severances occurring during the TARP authorities period.

¶28,045

Q-11: Who is subject to the special rules in §280G(e)?

A-11: The special rules in §280G(e) apply to any covered executive of an applicable employer who has a severance from employment during an applicable taxable year that is treated as an "applicable severance from employment," as defined in Q&A-12 of this notice. For purposes of §280G(e), the terms "applicable employer," "applicable taxable year," and "covered executive" have the same meaning as under §162(m)(5) (as those terms are described in Q&A-1 through Q&A-4 of this notice, and taking into account the special rule in Q&A-5 of this notice). However, §280G(d)(5) (treatment of affiliated groups) and other provisions do not apply.

Q-12: What is an applicable severance from employment of a covered executive for purposes of §280G(e)?

A-12: (a) *Applicable severance from employment defined.* An applicable severance from employment means any covered executive's severance from employment with the applicable employer: (1) by reason of involuntary termination of employment with an entity that is an applicable employer or (2) in connection with any bankruptcy, liquidation, or receivership of an entity that is an applicable employer.

(b) *Involuntary termination.* (i) An involuntary termination from employment means a severance from employment due to the independent exercise of the unilateral authority of the applicable employer to terminate the covered executive's services, other than due to the covered executive's implicit or explicit request, where the covered executive was willing and able to continue performing services. An involuntary termination from employment may include the applicable employer's failure to renew a contract at the time such contract expires, provided that the covered executive was willing and able to execute a new contract providing terms and conditions substantially similar to those in the expiring contract and able to continue providing such services. In addition, a covered executive's voluntary termination from employment constitutes an involuntary termination from employment if the termination from employment constitutes a termination for good reason due to a material negative change in the covered executive's employment relationship. See §1.409A-1(n)(2) of the Treasury Regulations.

(ii) A severance from employment by a covered executive is by reason of involuntary termination even if the covered executive has voluntarily terminated employment in any case where the facts and circumstances indicate that absent such voluntary termination the applicable employer would have terminated the covered executive's employment and the covered executive had knowledge that he or she would be so terminated. (See §280G(e)(2)(C)(ii)(III).)

Q-13: What is a "parachute payment" for purposes of §280G(e)?

A-13: (a) *General definition.* For purposes of §280G(e), a "parachute payment" means any payment in the nature of compensation to (or for the benefit of) a covered executive made during an applicable taxable year on account of an applicable severance from employment during the TARP authorities period if the aggregate present value of such payments equals or exceeds an amount equal to three times the covered executive's base amount. (See Q&A-14 of this notice for a definition of an excess parachute payment.)

(b) *Payment on account of an applicable severance from employment.* A payment on account of an applicable severance from employment means a payment that would not have been payable if no applicable severance from employment had occurred (including amounts that would otherwise have been forfeited due to severance from employment) and amounts that are accelerated on account of the applicable severance from employment. (See §1.280G-1, Q&A-24(b) of the Treasury Regulations for rules regarding the determination of the amount that is on account of an acceleration.) Further, for purposes of §280G(e), the exclusions under §280G(b)(2)(C) (payments under certain contracts entered into within 1 year of the change); §280G(b)(4) (payment of amount determined to be reasonable compensation); §280G (b)(5) (exceptions for small business corporations); and §280G(d)(5) (treatment of affiliated groups) do not apply.

(c) *Excluded amounts.* Payments on account of an applicable severance from employment do not include amounts paid to a covered executive under a tax-qualified retirement plan.

(d) *Base amount defined.* For purposes of §280G(e), the "base amount" for a covered executive has the meaning set forth in §280G(b)(3) and §1.280G-1, Q&A-34, of the Treasury Regulations, except that references to "change in ownership or control" are treated as referring to an "applicable severance from employment."

Q-14: What is an "excess parachute payment" for purposes of §280G(e)?

A-14: For purposes of §280G(e), an excess parachute payment is any parachute payment (as defined in Q&A-13 of this notice) in excess of the base amount allocated to the payment.

¶28,045

Q-15: What are the consequences of an excess parachute payment?

A-15: (a) *General rule.* No deduction is allowed for an excess parachute payment. Further, a tax equal to 20 percent of the excess parachute payment is imposed on a covered executive who receives an excess parachute payment.

(b) *Example.* In 2008, which is an applicable taxable year for the employer, a covered executive has an applicable severance from employment. The covered executive's base amount is $1 million and the covered executive receives a lump sum payment of $5 million on account of an involuntary termination of employment. The lump sum payment qualifies as a parachute payment since the amount of the lump sum payment ($5 million) is not less than three times the covered executive's base amount (3 times $1 million equals $3 million). The amount of the excess parachute payment is equal to $4 million ($5 million payment less the covered executive's $1 million base amount). Thus, under § 280G(e), the $4 million excess parachute payment is not deductible by the applicable employer. Further, the $4 million excess parachute payment is subject to a 20 percent tax payable by the covered executive.

Q-16: What if a payment treated as a parachute payment under § 280G(e) is also determined to be a parachute payment under § 280G without regard to § 280G(e)?

A-16: If a payment treated as a parachute payment under § 280G(e) is a parachute payment under § 280G on account of a change in control without regard to § 280G(e), then § 280G(e) does not apply to the payment.

Q-17: To which years does the deduction limit imposed by § 280G(e) apply?

A-17: The limit imposed by § 280G(e) applies to remuneration paid in an applicable taxable year. (See Q&A-3 of this notice for additional information, including the definition of an applicable taxable year.)

REQUEST FOR COMMENTS

The Treasury Department and the Service anticipate issuing additional guidance with respect to § § 162(m)(5) and 280G(e). The Treasury Department and the Service request comments on the topics addressed in this notice. All materials submitted will be available for public inspection and copying.

Comments may be submitted to Internal Revenue Service, CC:PA:LPD:PR (Notice 2008-94), Room 5203, PO Box 7604, Ben Franklin Station, Washington, DC 20044. Submissions may also be hand-delivered Monday through Friday between the hours of 8 a.m. and 4 p.m. to the Couriers Desk at 1111 Constitution Avenue, NW, Washington, DC 20224, Attn:CC:PA:LPD:PR (Notice 2008-94), Room 5203. Submissions may also be sent electronically via the internet to the following email address: *Notice.comments@irscounsel.treas.gov.* Include the notice number (Notice 2008-94) in the subject line.

EFFECTIVE DATE

Until further guidance is issued, taxpayers may rely on the rules in this notice for purposes of § § 162(m)(5) and 280G(e) effective from October 3, 2008 (the date of enactment of EESA). Further guidance will be prospective to the extent that it is more restrictive.

CONTACT INFORMATION

For further information regarding this notice, contact Ilya Enkishev of the Office of Division Counsel/Associate Chief Counsel (Tax Exempt & Government Entities) at (202) 622-6030 (not a toll-free call).

¶ 28,050 Treasury Department News Release, TDNR TG-15, February 4, 2009

Treasury Announces New Restrictions On Executive Compensation

Today, the Treasury Department is issuing a new set of guidelines on executive pay for financial institutions that are receiving government assistance to address our current financial crisis. These measures are designed to ensure that public funds are directed only toward the public interest in strengthening our economy by stabilizing our financial system and not toward inappropriate private gain. The measures announced today are designed to ensure that the compensation of top executives in the financial community is closely aligned not only with the interests of shareholders and financial institutions, but with the taxpayers providing assistance to those companies.

The Treasury guidelines on executive pay seek to strike the correct balance between the need for strict monitoring and accountability on executive pay and the need for financial institutions to fully function and attract the talent pool that will maximize the chances of financial recovery and taxpayers being paid back on their investments. The proposals below, such as emphasizing restricted stock that vests as the government is repaid with interest, seek to strike exactly that balance.

The guidelines distinguish between banks participating in any new *generally available capital access program* and banks needing *"exceptional assistance."* Generally available programs have the same terms for all recipients, with limits on the amount each institution may receive and specified returns for taxpayers. The goal of these programs is to help ensure the financial system as a whole can provide the credit necessary for recovery, including providing capital to smaller community banks that play a critical role in lending to small businesses, families and others. The previously announced Capital Purchase Program is an example of a generally available capital access program.

If a firm needs more assistance than is allowed under a widely available standard program, then that is exceptional assistance. Banks falling under the "exceptional assistance" standard have bank-specific negotiated agreements with Treasury. Examples include AIG, and the Bank of America and Citi transactions under the Targeted Investment Program.

As part of President Obama's efforts to promote systemic regulatory reform, the standards today mark the beginning of a long-term effort to examine both the degree that executive compensation structures at financial institutions contributed to our current financial crisis and how corporate governance and compensation rules can be reformed to better promote long-term value and growth for shareholders, companies, workers and the economy at large and to prevent such financial crises from occurring again.

I. COMPLIANCE AND CERTIFICATION:

All Companies Receiving Government Assistance Must Ensure Compliance with Executive Compensation Provisions: The chief executive officers of all companies that have to this point received or do receive any form of government assistance must provide certification that the companies have strictly complied with statutory, Treasury, and contractual executive compensation restrictions. Chief executive officers must recertify compliance with these restrictions on an annual basis. In addition, the compensation committees of all companies receiving government assistance must provide an explanation of how their senior executive compensation arrangements do not encourage excessive and unnecessary risk-taking.

II. ENHANCED CONDITIONS ON EXECUTIVE COMPENSATION GOING FORWARD:

A. *Companies Receiving Exceptional Financial Recovery Assistance:*

- **Limit Senior Executives to $500,000 in Total Annual Compensation - Other than Restricted Stock:** Current programs providing exceptional assistance to financial institutions forbid recipients of government funds from taking a tax deduction for senior executive compensation above $500,000. Today's guidance takes this restriction further by limiting the total amount of compensation to no more than $500,000 for these senior executives except for restricted stock awards.

- **Any Additional Pay for Senior Executives Must Be in Restricted Stock that Vests When the Government Has Been Repaid with Interest:** Any pay to a senior executive of a company receiving exceptional assistance beyond $500,000 *must be made in restricted stock* or other similar long-term incentive arrangements. The senior executive receiving such restricted stock will only be able to cash in either after the government has been repaid - including the contractual dividend payments that ensure taxpayers are compensated for the time value of their money - or after a specified period according to conditions that consider among other factors the degree a company has satisfied repayment obligations, protected taxpayer interests or met lending and stability standards. Such a restricted stock strategy will help assure that senior executives of companies receiving exceptional assistance have incentives aligned with both the long-term interests of shareholders as well as minimizing the costs to taxpayers.

- **Executive Compensation Structure and Strategy Must be Fully Disclosed and Subject to a "Say on Pay" Shareholder Resolution:** The senior executive compensation structure and the rationale for how compensation is tied to sound risk management must be submitted to a non-binding shareholder resolution. There are no "Say on Pay" provisions in the existing programs.

- **Require Provisions to Clawback Bonuses for Top Executives Engaging in Deceptive Practices:** Under the existing programs providing exceptional assistance, only the top

¶ 28,050

five senior executives were subject to a clawback provision. Going forward, a company receiving exceptional assistance must have in place provisions to claw back bonuses and incentive compensation from any of the next twenty senior executives if they are found to have knowingly engaged in providing inaccurate information relating to financial statements or performance metrics used to calculate their own incentive pay.

- **Increase Ban on Golden Parachutes for Senior Executives:** The existing programs providing exceptional assistance to financial institutions prohibited the top five senior executives from receiving any golden parachute payment upon severance from employment, a ban that will be expanded to include the top ten senior executives. In addition, and at a minimum, the next twenty-five executives will be prohibited from receiving any golden parachute payment greater than one year's compensation upon severance from employment.

- **Require Board of Directors' Adoption of Company Policy Relating to Approval of Luxury Expenditures:** The boards of directors of companies receiving exceptional assistance from the government must adopt a company-wide policy on any expenditures related to aviation services, office and facility renovations, entertainment and holiday parties, and conferences and events. This policy is not intended to cover reasonable expenditures for sales conferences, staff development, reasonable performance incentives and other measures tied to a company's normal business operations. These new rules go beyond current guidelines, and would require certification by chief executive officers for expenditures that could be viewed as excessive or luxury items. Companies should also now post the text of the expenditures policy on their web sites.

B. *Financial Institutions Participating in Generally Available Capital Access Programs:*

The Treasury intends to issue proposed guidance subject to public comment on the following executive compensation requirements relating to future generally available capital access programs.

- **Limit Senior Executives to $500,000 in Total Annual Compensation Plus Restricted Stock - Un less Waived with Full Public Disclosure and Shareholder Vote:** Companies that participate in generally available capital access programs may waive the $500,000 plus restricted stock rule only by disclosure of their compensation and, if requested, a non-binding "say on pay" shareholder resolution. All firms participating in a future capital access program must review and disclose the reasons that compensation arrangements of both the senior executives and other employees do not encourage excessive and unnecessary risk taking. Under the current Capital Purchase Program, the companies were only required to review and certify that the top five executives' compensation arrangements did not encourage excessive and unnecessary risk-taking.

- **Require Provisions to Clawback Bonuses for Top Executives Engaging in Deceptive Practices:** The same clawback provision that applies to companies receiving exceptional assistance will apply to those in generally available capital access programs. Thus, in addition to the clawback provision applicable to the top five executives as under the Capital Purchase Program, a company receiving assistance must have in place provisions to claw back bonuses and incentive compensation from any of the next twenty senior executives if they are found to have knowingly engaged in providing inaccurate information relating to financial statements or performance metrics used to calculate their own incentive pay.

- **Increase Ban on Golden Parachutes for Senior Executives:** Even under generally available capital access programs, the golden parachute ban will be strengthened: Upon a severance from employment, the top five senior executives will not be allowed a golden parachute payment greater than one year's compensation, as opposed to three years under the current Capital Purchase Program.

- **Require Board of Directors' Adoption of Company Policy Relating to Approval of Luxury Expenditures:** This policy will be the same for companies accessing generally available capital programs as it is for those receiving exceptional assistance. There are no guidelines on luxury expenditures under the current Capital Purchase Program.

[*These new standards will not apply retroactively to existing investments or to programs already announced such as the Capital Purchase Program and the Term Asset-Backed Securities Loan Facility.*]

¶28,050

III. LONG-TERM REGULATORY REFORM: COMPENSATION STRATEGIES ALIGNED WITH PROPER RISK MANAGEMENT AND LONG-TERM VALUE AND GROWTH:

Even as we work to recover from current market events, it is not too early to begin a serious effort to both examine how company-wide compensation strategies at financial institutions - not just those related to top executives - may have encouraged excessive risk-taking that contributed to current market events and to begin developing model compensation policies for the future. Such steps should include:

- *Requiring all Compensation Committees of Public Financial Institutions to Review and Disclose Strategies for Aligning Compensation with Sound Risk-Management:* The Secretary of the Treasury and the Chairman of the Securities and Exchange Commission should work together to require compensation committees of all public financial institutions - not just those receiving government assistance - to review and disclose executive and certain employee compensation arrangements and explain how these compensation arrangements are consistent with promoting sound risk management and long-term value creation for their companies and their shareholders.

- *Compensation of Top Executives Should Include Incentives That Encourage a Long-Term Perspective:* Over the last decade there has been an emerging consensus that top executives should receive compensation that encourages more of a long-term perspective on creating economic value for their shareholders and the economy at large. One idea worthy of serious consideration is requiring top executives at financial institutions to hold stock for several years after it is awarded before it can be cashed-out as this would encourage a more long-term focus on the economic interests of the firm.

- *Pass Say on Pay Shareholder Resolutions on Executive Compensation:* Even beyond companies receiving financial recovery assistance, owners of financial institutions - the shareholders -should have a non-binding resolution on both the levels of executive compensation as well as how the structure of compensation incentives help promote risk management and long-term value creation for the firm and the economy as a whole.

- *White House -Treasury Conference on Long-Term Executive Pay Reform:* The Secretary of the Treasury will host a conference with shareholder advocates, major public pension and institutional investor leaders, policymakers, executives, academics, and others on executive pay reform at financial institutions. Treasury will seek testimony, comment, and white papers on model executive pay initiatives in the cause of establishing best practices and guidelines on executive compensation arrangements for financial institutions.

CORPORATE LOSS LIMITATION RULES

¶28,055   Notice 2008-76, I.R.B. 2008-39, 768

SECTION 1. OVERVIEW

This notice announces that the Internal Revenue Service (IRS) and the Treasury Department (Treasury) will issue regulations under section 382(m) of the Internal Revenue Code (Code) that address the application of section 382 in the case of certain acquisitions made pursuant to the Housing and Economic Recovery Act of 2008.

Pursuant to section 1117(a) and (b) of the Housing and Economic Recovery Act of 2008, Pub. L. No. 110-289 (2008), the Secretary of the Treasury is authorized to purchase any obligations and other securities issued by certain entities under the Housing and Economic Recovery Act of 2008. A purchase that is made pursuant to this authority is hereinafter referred to as a "Housing Act Acquisition."

SECTION 2. REGULATIONS TO BE ISSUED UNDER SECTION 382(m)

The IRS and Treasury will issue regulations under section 382(m) providing that notwithstanding any other provision of the Code or the regulations thereunder, for purposes of section 382 and the regulations thereunder, with respect to a corporation as to which there is a Housing Act Acquisition, the term "testing date" (as defined in § 1.382-2(a)(4)) shall not include any date on or after the date on which the United States (or any agency or instrumentality thereof) (United States) acquires, in a Housing Act Acquisition, stock (including stock described in section 1504(a)(4)) or an option to acquire stock in the corporation.

¶28,055

SECTION 3. EFFECTIVE DATE

The regulations to be issued under section 382(m) that are described in section 2 of this notice will apply on or after September 7, 2008, and will apply unless and until there is additional guidance.

¶28,060 Notice 2008-78, I.R.B. 2008-41, 851

This notice provides guidance regarding capital contributions under section 382(l)(1) of the Internal Revenue Code and the request comments on the subject.

I. Purpose.

The Internal Revenue Service (Service) and Treasury Department (Treasury) intend to issue regulations under section 382(l)(1) as described below. Pending the issuance of further guidance, taxpayers may rely on the rules set forth in this notice to the extent provided herein.

II. Background.

Section 382(a) of the Internal Revenue Code (Code), as amended, provides that the taxable income of a loss corporation for a year following an ownership change that may be offset by pre-change losses cannot exceed the section 382 limitation for such year. Similarly, section 383 limits the use of certain credits and net capital losses based on the principles applicable under section 382.

The section 382 limitation for a post-change year is generally equal to the fair market value of the stock of the loss corporation immediately before the ownership change multiplied by the applicable long-term tax-exempt rate. Section 382(l)(1)(A) provides that for purposes of section 382 any capital contribution received by a loss corporation as part of a plan a principal purpose of which is to avoid or increase any limitation under section 382 is not taken into account. Under section 382(l)(1)(B), any capital contribution made during the two-year period ending on the change date (as defined in section 382(j)) is, except as provided in regulations, treated as part of a plan described in section 382(l)(1)(A). Therefore, the value of any such capital contribution is excluded from the computation of the section 382 limitation.

Section 382(m) provides that the Secretary shall prescribe such regulations as may be necessary or appropriate to carry out the purposes of sections 382 and 383.

III. Guidance Under Section 382(l)(1) Regarding Capital Contributions.

The Service and Treasury intend to issue regulations regarding the application of section 382(l)(1). These regulations are expected to set forth the rules described in this section of this Notice.

DEFINITIONS.

Except as otherwise provided, any definitions and terms used herein have the same meaning as they do in section 382 and the regulations thereunder.

In addition, any reference herein to terms and definitions in § 1.355-7 have the same meaning as they do in § 1.355-7, taking into account all other terms and definitions in § 1.355-7, but substituting, in each instance, "contribution" for "distribution," "loss corporation" for "Distributing and/or Controlled," and "ownership change" for "acquisition." For example, the phrase "agreement, understanding, arrangement, or substantial negotiations" as used herein has the same meaning as it does in § 1.355-7, taking into account other terms in § 1.355-7 (such as the definition of "controlling shareholder" in § 1.355-7(h)(3)). In addition, for purposes of substituting "ownership change" for "acquisition," any reference in § 1.355-7 to "the acquisition" shall be treated as a reference to "any acquisition."

A "related party" is a party related to the loss corporation (within the meaning of section 267(b), and determined immediately after a capital contribution) or one or more persons that, pursuant to a formal or informal understanding, would be treated as becoming a related party under the principles of § 1.355-7(h)(4) (i.e., a "co-ordinating group"). The phrase "capital contribution" includes a series of related capital contributions.

RULES.

A. Section 382(l)(1)(B).

Notwithstanding section 382(l)(1)(B), a capital contribution shall not be presumed to be part of a plan a principal purpose of which is to avoid or increase a section 382 limitation solely as a result of having been made during the two-year period ending on the change date.

B. Section 382(l)(1)(A).

(1) *In general.* A capital contribution received by an old loss corporation shall be taken into

account (and will not reduce the value of the old loss corporation for purposes of section 382(e)(1)) unless the contribution is part of a plan a principal purpose of which is to avoid or increase a section 382 limitation (hereinafter, a plan). Whether a capital contribution is part of a plan is determined based on all the facts and circumstances, unless the contribution is described in one of the safe harbors in Section III.B.2 below or section 382(l)(1) does not apply to the contribution pursuant to § 1.382-9(k). The fact that a contribution is not described in a safe harbor does not constitute evidence that the contribution is part of a plan.

(2) *Safe harbors.* A capital contribution will not be considered part of a plan if -

(a) The contribution is made by a person who is neither a controlling shareholder (determined immediately before the contribution) nor a related party, no more than 20% of the total value of the loss corporation's outstanding stock is issued in connection with the contribution, there was no agreement, understanding, arrangement, or substantial negotiations at the time of the contribution regarding a transaction that would result in an ownership change, and the ownership change occurs more than six months after the contribution.

(b) The contribution is made by a related party but no more than 10% of the total value of the loss corporation's stock is issued in connection with the contribution, or the contribution is made by a person other than a related party, and in either case there was no agreement, understanding, arrangement, or substantial negotiations at the time of the contribution regarding a transaction that would result in an ownership change, and the ownership change occurs more than one year after the contribution.

(c) The contribution is made in exchange for stock issued in connection with the performance of services, or stock acquired by a retirement plan, under the terms and conditions of § 1.355-7(d)(8) or (9), respectively.

(d) The contribution is received on the formation of a loss corporation (not accompanied by the incorporation of assets with a net unrealized built in loss) or it is received before the first year from which there is a carryforward of a net operating loss, capital loss, excess credit, or excess foreign taxes (or in which a net unrealized built-in loss arose).

C. Coordination of Sections 382(l)(1) and 382(l)(4).

If the value of the old loss corporation is subject to reduction under both sections 382(l)(1) and 382(l)(4), appropriate adjustments must be made to ensure that a reduction in value is not duplicated.

IV. Reliance on Notice.

The Service and Treasury intend to issue regulations under section 382(l)(1) that set forth the rules described in Section III of this notice. Taxpayers may rely on the rules described in Section III for purposes of determining whether a capital contribution is part of a plan with respect to an ownership change that occurs in any taxable year ending on or after September 26, 2008, and these rules will continue to apply unless and until there is additional guidance.

V. Request for Comments.

The Service and Treasury request comments regarding (i) the appropriate scope and application of section 382(l)(1) generally, (ii) the appropriate factors that may tend to show that a capital contribution is or is not made as part of a plan, including standards for contributions made by related parties, (iii) the desirability of applying similar standards in § 1.355-7 as safe harbors for purposes of section 382(l)(1), and whether additional safe harbors are needed, and (iv) the appropriate treatment under section 382(l)(1) of options and conversion rights in general, and whether coordinating rules should be issued under § 1.382-4(d).

VI. Instructions.

Comments should be submitted on or before December 22, 2008, and should include a reference to Notice 2008-78. Send submissions to CC:PA:LPD:PR (Notice 2008-78), Room 5203, Internal Revenue Service, P.O. Box 7604, Ben Franklin Station, Washington, D.C. 20044. Submissions may be hand-delivered Monday through Friday between the hours of 8:00 a.m. and 4:00 p.m. to CC:PA:LPD:PR (Notice 2008-78), Courier's Desk, Internal Revenue Service, 1111 Constitution Avenue, NW, Washington, DC 20224, or sent electronically via the following email address: Notice. Comments@ irscounsel.treas.gov. Please include the notice number 2008-78 in the subject line of any electronic communication. All materials submitted will be available for public inspection and copying.

The principal author of this notice is Michael J. Wilder of the Office of Associate Chief Counsel (Corporate). For further information regarding this notice contact Michael J. Wilder on (202) 622-7700 (not a toll-free call).

¶ 28,060

¶28,065 Notice 2008-83, I.R.B. 2008-42, 905

SECTION 1. OVERVIEW

The Internal Revenue Service and Treasury Department are studying the proper treatment under section 382(h) of the Internal Revenue Code (Code) of certain items of deduction or loss allowed after an ownership change to a corporation that is a bank (as defined in section 581) both immediately before and after the change date (as defined in section 382(j)). As described below under the heading Reliance on Notice, such banks may rely upon this guidance unless and until there is additional guidance.

SECTION 2. TREATMENT OF DEDUCTIONS UNDER SECTION 382(h)

For purposes of section 382(h), any deduction properly allowed after an ownership change (as defined in section 382(g)) to a bank with respect to losses on loans or bad debts (including any deduction for a reasonable addition to a reserve for bad debts) shall not be treated as a built-in loss or a deduction that is attributable to periods before the change date.

SECTION 3. RELIANCE ON NOTICE

Corporations described in section 1 of this notice may rely on the treatment set forth in this notice, unless and until there is additional guidance.

SECTION 4. SCOPE

This notice does not address the application of any provision of the Code other than section 382.

The principal author of this notice is Mark S. Jennings of the Office of Associate Chief Counsel (Corporate). For further information regarding this notice contact Mark S. Jennings on (202) 622-7750 (not a toll-free call).

¶28,070 Notice 2008-84, I.R.B. 2008-41, 855

SECTION 1. OVERVIEW

This notice announces that the Internal Revenue Service (IRS) and the Treasury Department (Treasury) will issue regulations under section 382(m) of the Internal Revenue Code (Code) that address the application of section 382 in the case of certain acquisitions not described in Notice 2008-76, I.R.B. 2008-39, in which the United States (or any agency or instrumentality thereof) (United States) becomes a direct or indirect owner of a more-than-50-percent interest in a loss corporation. For this purpose, a "more-than-50-percent interest" is stock of the loss corporation possessing more than 50 percent of the total value of shares of all classes of stock (excluding stock described in section 1504(a)(4)) or more than 50 percent of the total combined voting power of all classes of stock entitled to vote, or an option to acquire such stock.

SECTION 2. REGULATIONS TO BE ISSUED UNDER SECTION 382(m)

The IRS and Treasury will issue regulations under section 382(m) providing that notwithstanding any other provision of the Code or the regulations thereunder, for purposes of section 382 and the regulations thereunder, with respect to a loss corporation, the term "testing date" (as defined in §1.382-2(a)(4)) shall not include any date as of the close of which the United States directly or indirectly owns a more-than-50-percent interest in the loss corporation. Thus, the loss corporation will be required to determine whether there is a testing date and, if so, whether there has been an ownership change for purposes of section 382, on any date as of the close of which the United States does not directly or indirectly own a more-than-50-percent interest in the loss corporation.

SECTION 3. EFFECTIVE DATE

The regulations to be issued under section 382(m) that are described in section 2 of this notice will apply for any taxable year ending on or after September 26, 2008, and will apply unless and until there is additional guidance.

¶ 28,075 Notice 2008-100, I.R.B. 2008-44, 1081, amplified and superseded by Notice 2009-14 (see ¶ 28,080)

This notice provides guidance regarding the application of section 382 to loss corporations whose instruments are acquired by the Treasury Department (Treasury) under the Capital Purchase Program (CPP) pursuant to the Emergency Economic Stabilization Act of 2008, P.L. 110-343 (the "Act").

I. PURPOSE

The Internal Revenue Service (Service) and Treasury intend to issue regulations regarding the application of section 382 with respect to the CPP pursuant to the Act. Pending the issuance of further guidance, taxpayers may rely on the rules set forth in this notice to the extent provided herein.

II. BACKGROUND

Section 382(a) of the Internal Revenue Code (Code) provides that the taxable income of a loss corporation for a year following an ownership change that may be offset by pre-change losses cannot exceed the section 382 limitation for such year. An ownership change occurs with respect to a corporation if it is a loss corporation on a testing date and, immediately after the close of the testing date, the percentage of stock of the corporation owned by one or more 5-percent shareholders has increased by more than 50 percentage points over the lowest percentage of stock of such corporation owned by such shareholders at any time during the testing period. See § 1.382-2T(a)(1) of the Income Tax Regulations.

Section 101(a)(1) of the Act authorizes the Secretary to establish the Troubled Asset Relief Program. Under the CPP, Treasury will acquire preferred stock and warrants from qualifying financial institutions.

Section 101(c)(5) of the Act provides that the Secretary is authorized to issue such regulations and other guidance as may be necessary or appropriate to carry out the purposes of the Act. Section 382(m) of the Code provides that the Secretary shall prescribe such regulations as may be necessary or appropriate to carry out the purposes of sections 382 and 383.

Except as otherwise provided, any definitions and terms used herein have the same meaning as they do in section 382 of the Code and the regulations thereunder or in the CPP.

III. GUIDANCE REGARDING THE APPLICATION OF SECTION 382 TO LOSS CORPORATIONS WHOSE INSTRUMENTS ARE ACQUIRED BY TREASURY PURSUANT TO THE CPP

The Service and Treasury intend to issue regulations that set forth rules described in this Section III. Taxpayers may rely on the rules described in this Section III to the extent provided below.

RULES:

A. *General rule.* With respect to any shares of stock of a loss corporation acquired by Treasury pursuant to the CPP (either directly or upon the exercise of an option), the ownership represented by such shares on any date on which they are held by Treasury shall not be considered to have caused Treasury's ownership in the loss corporation to have increased over its lowest percentage owned on any earlier date. Except as provided in Sections III.B and III.C below, such shares are considered outstanding for purposes of determining the percentage of loss corporation stock owned by other 5-percent shareholders on a testing date.

B. *Redemptions of stock owned by Treasury.* For purposes of measuring shifts in ownership by any 5-percent shareholder on any testing date occurring on or after the date on which the loss corporation redeems shares of its stock held by Treasury that were acquired pursuant to the CPP, the shares so redeemed shall be treated as if they had never been outstanding.

C. *Treatment of preferred stock acquired by Treasury pursuant to the CPP.* For all Federal income tax purposes, any preferred stock of a loss corporation acquired by Treasury pursuant to the CPP, whether owned by Treasury or another person, shall be treated as stock described in section 1504(a)(4) of the Code.

D. *Treatment of warrants acquired by Treasury pursuant to the CPP.* For all Federal income tax purposes, any warrant to purchase stock of a loss corporation that is acquired by Treasury pursuant to the CPP, whether held by Treasury or another person, shall be treated as an option (and not as stock).

E. *Options held by Treasury not deemed exercised.* For purposes of § 1.382-4(d), any option (within the meaning of § 1.382-4(d)(9)) held by Treasury that is acquired pursuant to the CPP will not be deemed exercised under § 1.382-4(d)(2).

F. *Section 382(l)(1) not applicable with respect to capital contributions made by Treasury to a loss corporation pursuant to the CPP.* For purposes of section 382(l)(1) of the Code, any capital contribution made by Treasury to a loss corporation pursuant to the CPP shall not be considered to have been made as part of a plan a principal purpose of which was to avoid or increase any section 382 limitation.

IV. RELIANCE ON NOTICE

The Service and Treasury intend to issue regulations that set forth rules described in Section III of this notice. Taxpayers may rely on the rules described in Section III for purposes of applying section 382 with respect to loss corporations whose instruments are acquired by Treasury pursuant to the CPP. These rules will continue to apply unless and until there is additional guidance. Any future contrary guidance will not apply to instruments (i) held by Treasury that were acquired pursuant to the CPP prior to the publication of that guidance, or (ii) issued to Treasury pursuant to the CPP under written binding contracts entered into prior to the publication of that guidance.

DRAFTING INFORMATION

The principal author of this notice is Keith E. Stanley of the Office of Associate Chief Counsel (Corporate). For further information regarding this notice contact Keith E. Stanley on (202) 622-7700 (not a toll-free call).

¶ 28,080   Notice 2009-14, I.R.B. 2009-7, January 30, 2009, amplifies and supersedes Notice 2008-100 (see ¶ 28,075)

This notice provides additional guidance regarding the application of section 382 and other provisions of law to corporations whose instruments are acquired by the Treasury Department (Treasury) pursuant to the Emergency Economic Stabilization Act of 2008, P.L. 110-343 (EESA). This notice amplifies and supersedes Notice 2008-100, 2008-44 I.R.B. 1081, to address other EESA programs.

I. Purpose.

The Internal Revenue Service (Service) and Treasury Department (Treasury) intend to issue regulations implementing certain of the rules as described below. Pending the issuance of further guidance, taxpayers may rely on the rules set forth in this notice to the extent provided herein.

Section 101(a)(1) of EESA authorizes the Secretary to establish the Troubled Asset Relief Program (TARP). This notice provides guidance to corporate issuers with respect to five programs established under EESA: (i) the Capital Purchase Program for publicly-traded issuers (Public CPP); (ii) the Capital Purchase Program for private issuers (Private CPP); (iii) the Capital Purchase Program for S corporations (S Corp CPP); (iv) the Targeted Investment Program (TARP TIP); and (v) the Automotive Industry Financing Program (TARP Auto). Unless otherwise specified below, a reference to "the Programs" shall include any of the various EESA programs described in the preceding sentence.

II. Background.

Section 382(a) of the Internal Revenue Code (Code) provides that the taxable income of a loss corporation for a year following an ownership change that may be offset by pre-change losses cannot exceed the section 382 limitation for such year. An ownership change occurs with respect to a corporation if it is a loss corporation on a testing date and, immediately after the close of the testing date, the percentage of stock of the corporation owned by one or more 5-percent shareholders has increased by more than 50 percentage points over the lowest percentage of stock of such corporation owned by such shareholders at any time during the testing period. See § 1.382-2T(a)(1) of the Income Tax Regulations. Section 382(m) of the Code provides that the Secretary shall prescribe such regulations as may be necessary or appropriate to carry out the purposes of sections 382 and 383.

Section 101(c)(5) of EESA provides that the Secretary is authorized to issue such regulations and other guidance as may be necessary or appropriate to carry out the purposes of EESA.

Except as otherwise provided, any definitions and terms used herein have the same meaning as they do in section 382 of the Code and the regulations thereunder or in EESA. Unless otherwise specified, a reference herein to "section" is to the particular section of the Code or regulations thereunder.

III. Guidance Regarding Corporations Whose Instruments are Acquired by the Treasury Pursuant to EESA

Taxpayers may rely on the rules described in this Section III to the extent provided below.

RULES:

A. *Treatment of indebtedness and preferred stock acquired by Treasury.* For all Federal income tax purposes, any instrument issued to Treasury pursuant to the Programs, whether owned by Treasury or subsequent holders, shall be treated as an instrument of indebtedness if denominated as such, and as stock described in section 1504(a)(4) if denominated as preferred stock. Any amount received by an issuer under the Programs shall be treated as received, in its entirety, as consideration in exchange for the instruments issued. No such instrument shall be treated as stock for purposes of section 382 while held by Treasury or by other holders, except that preferred stock will be treated as stock for purposes of section 382(e)(1).

B. *Treatment of warrants acquired by Treasury.* For all Federal income tax purposes, any warrant to purchase stock acquired by Treasury pursuant to the Public CPP, TARP TIP, and TARP Auto, whether owned by Treasury or subsequent holders, shall be treated as an option (and not as stock). While held by Treasury, such warrant will not be deemed exercised under § 1.382-4(d)(2). For all Federal income tax purposes, any warrant to purchase stock acquired by Treasury pursuant to the Private CPP shall be treated as an ownership interest in the underlying stock, which shall be treated as preferred stock described in section 1504(a)(4). For all Federal income tax purposes, any warrant acquired by Treasury pursuant to the S Corp CPP shall be treated as an ownership interest in the underlying indebtedness.

C. *Section 382 treatment of stock acquired by Treasury.* For purposes of section 382, with respect to any stock (other than preferred stock) acquired by Treasury pursuant to the Programs (either directly or upon the exercise of a warrant), the ownership represented by such stock on any date on which it is held by Treasury shall not be considered to have caused Treasury's ownership in the issuing corporation to have increased over its lowest percentage owned on any earlier date. Except as described below, such stock is considered outstanding for purposes of determining the percentage of stock owned by other 5-percent shareholders on a testing date.

D. *Section 382 treatment of redemptions of stock from Treasury.* For purposes of measuring shifts in ownership by any 5-percent shareholder on any testing date occurring on or after the date on which the issuing corporation redeems stock held by Treasury that was acquired pursuant to the Programs (either directly or upon the exercise of a warrant), the stock so redeemed shall be treated as if it had never been outstanding.

E. *Section 382(l)(1) not applicable with respect to capital contributions made by Treasury pursuant to the Programs.* For purposes of section 382(l)(1), any capital contribution made by Treasury pursuant to the Programs shall not be considered to have been made as part of a plan a principal purpose of which was to avoid or increase any section 382 limitation.

IV. Reliance on Notice.

Taxpayers may rely on the rules described in Section III. These rules will continue to apply unless and until there is additional guidance. Any future contrary guidance will not apply to instruments (i) held by Treasury that were acquired pursuant to the Programs prior to the publication of that guidance, or (ii) issued to Treasury pursuant to the Programs under binding contracts entered into prior to the publication of that guidance. In exercising its authority under EESA in this notice, the Treasury and the Service do not intend to suggest that similar Federal income tax results would obtain with respect to instruments similar to those described herein that are not issued under the Programs. Accordingly, the Federal income tax consequences of instruments not issued under the Programs should continue to be determined based upon specific facts and circumstances.

The principal author of this notice is Keith Stanley of the Office of Associate Chief Counsel (Corporate). For further information regarding this notice, contact Keith Stanley on (202) 622-7750 (not a toll-free call).

CONTROLLED FOREIGN CORPORATION LOANS

¶28,085   Rev. Proc. 2008-26, I.R.B. 2008-21, 1014 (see also Notice 2009-10, ¶28,095)

SECTION 1. PURPOSE

This revenue procedure sets forth circumstances in which the Internal Revenue Service (Service) will not challenge whether a security is a "readily marketable security" for purposes of section 956(c)(2)(J) of the Internal Revenue Code (Code). No inference should be drawn regarding whether a security would be described in section 956(c)(2)(J) if it falls outside the scope of this revenue procedure. Furthermore, there should be no inference regarding whether securities within the scope of this revenue procedure

¶28,085

would be readily marketable or would not be readily marketable for purposes of section 956(c)(2)(J) but for this revenue procedure. In addition, this revenue procedure does not address any United States federal income tax issue arising under any other section of the Code.

SECTION 2. BACKGROUND

Section 951(a)(1) requires that a United States shareholder of a controlled foreign corporation include in gross income for his taxable year in which or with which such taxable year of the corporation ends certain amounts including the amount determined under section 956 with respect to such shareholder for such year. Section 951(a)(1)(B).

The amount determined under section 956 is generally the lesser of (i) the excess (if any) of the United States shareholder's pro rata share of the average of the amounts of United States property held (directly or indirectly) by the controlled foreign corporation as of the close of each quarter of the controlled foreign corporation's taxable year over the amount of earnings and profits described in section 959(c)(1)(A) with respect to such shareholder or (ii) the United States shareholder's pro rata share of the applicable earnings (as defined in section 956(b)(1)) of such controlled foreign corporation. Section 956(a).

The term United States property includes an obligation of a United States person, excluding, however:

> an obligation of a United States person to the extent the principal amount of the obligation does not exceed the fair market value of *readily marketable securities* sold or purchased pursuant to a sale and repurchase agreement or otherwise posted or received as collateral for the obligation in the ordinary course of its business by a United States or foreign person which is a dealer in securities or commodities.

Section 956(c)(2)(J) (emphasis added).

Current market conditions and liquidity constraints are creating some uncertainty regarding whether a security is "readily marketable" for purposes of section 956(c)(2)(J). For example, the market for certain securities that were readily marketable in the past has become severely curtailed. As a result, there is uncertainty whether many securities are readily marketable in the current economic environment even though they are of a type that are readily marketable under ordinary market conditions. In response to taxpayers' concerns, this revenue procedure provides certainty to taxpayers by setting forth circumstances under which the Service will not challenge whether a security is "readily marketable" for purposes of section 956(c)(2)(J) to the extent that it is of a type that would be readily marketable under ordinary market conditions.

SECTION 3. SCOPE

This revenue procedure applies to determine whether securities are "readily marketable" for purposes of section 956(c)(2)(J) for any day during calendar years 2007 or 2008 for which it is relevant whether securities are readily marketable for purposes of that section.

SECTION 4. APPLICATION

With respect to a determination within the scope of this revenue procedure, the Service will not challenge whether a security is readily marketable for purposes of section 956(c)(2)(J) if the security is of a type that was readily marketable at any time within three years prior to the effective date of this revenue procedure. For example, the Service will not challenge whether a mortgage-backed security or corporate debt security (whether secured or unsecured) is "readily marketable" if such a security is described in Section 3 of this revenue procedure and is of a type that was readily marketable at any time within three years prior to the effective date of this revenue procedure.

This revenue procedure does not address any other issue relating to the qualification of a transaction under section 956(c)(2)(J) (e.g., whether the transaction is undertaken in the ordinary course of business by a dealer in securities or commodities).

SECTION 5. EFFECTIVE DATE

This revenue procedure is effective May 12, 2008.

SECTION 6. DRAFTING INFORMATION

The principal author of this revenue procedure is John H. Seibert of the Office of Associate Chief Counsel (International). For further information regarding this revenue procedure contact Mr. Seibert at (202) 622-0171 (not a toll-free call).

¶ 28,090 Notice 2008-91, I.R.B. 2008-43, 1001 (see also Notice 2009-10, ¶ 28,095)

SECTION 1. OVERVIEW

Section 956(c) defines United States property generally to include an obligation of a United States person. On September 16, 1988, the Internal Revenue Service and the Treasury Department published Notice 88-108, 1988-2 C.B. 445, which announced that final regulations issued under section 956 will exclude from the definition of the term "obligation" an obligation that would constitute an investment in United States property if held at the end of the controlled foreign corporation's taxable year, so long as the obligation is collected within 30 days from the time it is incurred. This exclusion shall not apply, however, if the controlled foreign corporation holds for 60 or more calendar days during such taxable year obligations which, without regard to the 30 day rule described in the preceding sentence, would constitute an investment in United States property if held at the end of the controlled foreign corporation's taxable year. See S. Rep. No. 103-37, at 178 (1993) ("The bill is not intended to change the measurement of U.S. property that may apply, for example, in the case of short-term obligations, as provided in IRS Notice 88-108").

SECTION 2. TREATMENT OF CERTAIN OBLIGATIONS UNDER SECTION 956(c)

Recently, circumstances affecting liquidity have made it difficult for taxpayers to fund their operations. To facilitate liquidity in the near term, this notice announces that the Internal Revenue Service and the Treasury Department will issue regulations under section 956(e) that, for purposes of section 956, a controlled foreign corporation (within the meaning of section 957(a)) may choose to exclude from the definition of the term "obligation" an obligation held by the controlled foreign corporation that would constitute an investment in United States property provided the obligation is collected within 60 days from the time it is incurred. This exclusion shall not apply, however, if the controlled foreign corporation holds for 180 or more calendar days during its taxable year obligations that, without regard to the 60 day rule described in the preceding sentence, would constitute an investment in United States property.

This notice does not otherwise affect the application of Notice 88-108. A controlled foreign corporation may apply this notice or Notice 88-108, but not both.

SECTION 3. RELIANCE ON NOTICE

This notice shall only apply for the first two taxable years of a foreign corporation ending after October 3, 2008. However, this notice shall not apply to taxable years of a foreign corporation beginning after December 31, 2009. Thus, if a foreign corporation has a calendar tax year, this notice shall apply for the foreign corporation's taxable years ending December 31, 2008, and December 31, 2009.

SECTION 4. DRAFTING INFORMATION

The principal author of this notice is Ethan A. Atticks of the Office of Associate Chief Counsel (International). For further information regarding this notice contact Mr. Atticks at (202) 622-3840 (not a toll free call).

¶ 28,095 Notice 2009-10, I.R.B. 2009-5, 419

1. On October 27, 2008, the Treasury Department and the Internal Revenue Service (Service) published Notice 2008-91. *See* Notice 2008-91, 2008-43 I.R.B. 1001. This notice provides that the regulations described in Notice 2008-91 will apply (in addition to the period described in Notice 2008-91) to the third consecutive taxable year of a foreign corporation, if any, (including any short taxable year) that ends after October 3, 2008, and that ends on or before December 31, 2009.

2. On May 27, 2008, the Treasury Department and the Service published Rev. Proc. 2008-26, 2008-21 I.R.B. 1014, which applies to determine whether securities are "readily marketable" for purposes of section 956(c)(2)(J) for any day during calendar years 2007 or 2008, for which it is relevant whether securities are readily marketable for purposes of that section. This notice extends the application of Rev. Proc. 2008-26 to any day during calendar year 2009, for which it is relevant whether securities are readily marketable for purposes of section 956(c)(2)(J) (in addition to any day during calendar years 2007 or 2008).

DRAFTING INFORMATION

The principal author of this notice is Ethan A. Atticks of the Office of Associate Chief Counsel (International). For further information regarding this notice contact Mr. Atticks at (202) 622-3840 (not a toll-free call).

TAX-EXEMPT BONDS

¶28,100 Notice 2008-27, I.R.B. 2008-10, 543, clarified, amended, supplemented and superseded by Notice 2008-41 (see ¶28,105)

SECTION 1. Purpose. The Internal Revenue Service ("IRS") and the Treasury Department expect to issue regulations under § 150 of the Internal Revenue Code of 1986 to modify and clarify the determination of when tax-exempt bonds are treated as reissued or retired solely for purposes of § 103 and §§ 141 through 150. This Notice provides interim guidance until the promulgation of such regulations. This Notice modifies certain special reissuance standards for "qualified tender bonds" under IRS Notice 88-130, 1988-2 C.B. 530. This Notice also modifies certain aspects of the application of § 1.1001-3 of the Income Tax Regulations on debt modifications as they apply to tax-exempt bonds solely for purposes of § 103 and §§ 141 through 150. This Notice provides three special rules which address certain temporary waivers of interest rate caps, certain nonrecourse debt, and certain modifications of qualified hedges. In part, this Notice is intended to provide greater certainty and flexibility to address certain potential Federal tax issues that have arisen in the tax-exempt bond market as a result of recent rating agency downgrades of major municipal bond insurers and failures of auctions in the auction rate bond sector of the tax-exempt bond market.

This Notice applies solely for purposes of § 103 and §§ 141 through 150 of the Code. No inference should be drawn regarding whether a debt modification described in this Notice would constitute an exchange for purposes of § 1001 of the Code. In addition, no inference should be drawn about whether similar consequences would obtain if a transaction falls outside the scope of this Notice.

This Notice invites public comment on the guidance provided herein.

SECTION 2. Background

Reissuance

Reissuance of a tax-exempt bond for purposes of the tax-exempt bond provisions triggers retesting of all the various program requirements for new issues of tax-exempt bonds. A reissuance of an issue of tax-exempt bonds may result in various negative consequences to a bond issuer, including, among other things, changes in yield for purposes of the arbitrage investment restrictions, acceleration of arbitrage rebate payment obligations, deemed terminations of integrated interest rate swaps under the qualified hedge rules for arbitrage purposes, new public approval requirements for qualified private activity bonds, and change in law risk.

In general, the standard for determining whether tax-exempt bonds are reissued, retired, or otherwise modified significantly enough to trigger a retesting of the program requirements for new issues of tax-exempt bonds under the tax-exempt bond provisions of the Code is based on the general Federal tax standards for debt exchanges under § 1001 and regulations thereunder.

In general, § 1.1001-3 of the Income Tax Regulations employs a significant modification standard to determine whether modifications to a debt instrument in any form are sufficiently significant to cause the debt instrument to be treated as reissued or exchanged for purposes of § 1001. Section 1.1001-3 applies to modifications in the form of amendments to the terms of an existing debt instrument and to modifications in the form of an actual exchange of an existing debt instrument for a different debt instrument. The determination of whether the resulting debt instrument is treated as a reissued new debt instrument or a continuation of the original debt instrument depends on whether the result represents a "significant modification" of the original debt instrument, as defined in § 1.1001-3.

Notice 88-130 provides certain special reissuance rules for certain eligible tax-exempt bonds that are "qualified tender bonds," as defined therein. Notice 88-130 provides that qualified tender bonds will not be treated as reissued for purposes of § 103 and §§ 141 through 150 as a result of certain tender rights and certain changes in interest rate modes and other terms of bonds that are covered specifically by the detailed rules and limitations set forth in Notice 88-130.

Interest Rate Modes—Tender Option Modes and Auction Rate Modes

Issuers may issue fixed rate tax-exempt bonds that bear interest at fixed rates to maturity or variable rate bonds that bear interest at variable rates which float periodically in accordance with various market-based interest-rate setting mechanisms. Issuers often include multi-modal interest rate features in the preauthorized terms of the bond documents which provide issuers with the flexibility to change interest rate modes under parameters set forth in the bond documents.

One common interest rate mode employed with tax-exempt bonds is a tender option mode. "Tender option bonds" are also referred to commonly as "variable rate demand bonds." Tender option bonds have short-term interest rate features tied to current market rates necessary to remarket the bonds at par. Tender option bonds have ongoing tender options or put options associated with the interest rate-setting mechanism which allow bondholders to tender their bonds for purchase at par at specified intervals, typically every seven days. Tender option bonds generally have creditworthy third-party liquidity facilities from banks or other liquidity providers to support the tender options and may have credit enhancement from bond insurers or other providers. Tender option bonds also may have interest mode conversion options which grant to the issuer or a conduit borrower an option to change the interest rate mode on the bonds from a tender option mode to another short-term interest rate mode or to a fixed interest rate to maturity. At the time of a conversion to another interest rate mode, tender option bonds typically are subject to a mandatory tender for purchase but a bondholder may be allowed to elect to retain the bonds. Upon the exercise of ongoing tender options associated with the short-term interest rate-setting mechanism for tender option bonds and upon any mandatory or optional tender upon conversion of the interest rate on the bonds to another interest rate mode, a remarketing agent or a liquidity provider typically will acquire the bonds subject to the tender at par and resell the bonds either to the same bondholders or to others willing to purchase such bonds. In general, Notice 88-130 provides guidance for when the tenders associated with tender option bonds will not constitute reissuances if they meet the specific detailed eligibility requirements for "qualified tender bonds," as defined in Notice 88-130.

Another interest rate mode used with tax-exempt bonds is an auction rate mode. The interest rate on auction rate bonds is reset at predetermined intervals (generally under one year) using a modified Dutch auction process. Auction rate bonds generally trade at par and are callable at par on any interest payment date at the option of the issuer. Unlike bonds in a tender option mode, however, bonds in an auction rate mode have no ongoing tender options or put options to support the interest rate-setting process. Thus, auction rate bonds are viewed as long-term investments with a short-term interest rate-setting process. Auction rate bonds generally have maximum rates based on state law restrictions or certain formulas, such as a multiple of a tax-exempt or taxable index. Auction rate bonds may have credit enhancement from bond insurers or other providers. Auction rate bonds also may have interest mode conversion options similar to tender option bonds which grant to the issuer or a conduit borrower an option to change the interest rate mode on the bonds from an auction rate mode to another short-term interest rate mode or to a fixed interest rate to maturity. At the time of a conversion to another interest rate mode, auction rate bonds typically are subject to a mandatory tender for purchase in a process similar to mandatory tenders on conversions of interest rate modes used with tender option bonds. Questions have arisen regarding whether or to what extent auction rate bonds can be treated as qualified tender bonds for purposes of the provisions of Notice 88-130.

Approach of Guidance

This Notice modifies and expands the protection afforded by Notice 88-130 to provide that authorized changes in additional interest rate modes and certain optional or mandatory tenders of the bonds will not result in a reissuance of the tax-exempt bonds solely for purposes of § 103 and §§ 141 through 150. This Notice provides that other types of changes to tax-exempt bonds are tested for reissuance purposes under the significant modification standard under § 1.1001-3. In addition, this Notice also provides special rules for certain issues that have arisen as a result of recent ratings downgrades of the bond insurers and auction failures on auction rate bonds.

SECTION 3. Scope and Application

3.1. *Scope and General Rules.* The IRS and the Treasury Department expect to promulgate regulations under § 150 to provide guidance on whether tax-exempt bonds are treated as reissued or retired solely for purposes of § 103 and §§ 141 through 150. Specifically, for purposes of § 103 and §§ 141 through 150 only, in the case of a qualified tender bond (as defined herein), any qualified interest rate mode change (as defined herein) and any qualified tender (as defined herein) will not be treated as a modification under § 1.1001-3. Therefore, for these purposes, a qualified tender bond will not be treated as reissued or retired solely as a result of a qualified interest rate mode change or the existence or exercise of any qualified tender. Further, in applying § 1.1001-3 to modifications of tax-exempt bonds, any interest rate variance directly related to a qualified interest rate mode change will not be treated as a modification under § 1.1001-3, and thus such interest rate variances need not be tested under the change in yield rule for determining significant modifications under § 1.1001-3(e)(2). Except as otherwise specially provided in this Notice, the determination of whether any modification to an issue of tax-exempt bonds causes a reissuance or retirement of the tax-exempt bonds for purposes of § 103 and §§ 141 through 150 is based on whether the modifications are significant modifications under § 1.1001-3.

Similar to the treatment under Notice 88-130, and except as expressly provided herein with respect to the treatment of "qualified interest rate mode changes" and "qualified tenders" on "qualified tender bonds" (all as redefined herein), a tax-exempt bond generally is treated as reissued or retired on the first date on which: (1) a significant modification to the terms of the bond occurs under § 1.1001-3 or a disposition of the bond otherwise occurs under section 1001; (2) the bond is purchased or otherwise acquired by or on behalf of the issuer or a true obligor which is a governmental unit or an agency or instrumentality thereof; or (3) the bond is otherwise retired or redeemed. For these purposes, except as otherwise expressly provided herein, a bond is treated as purchased or otherwise acquired by or on behalf of a person if the bond is purchased or otherwise acquired (other than pursuant to the terms of a third party guarantee, liquidity facility, or remarketing arrangement) by that person in a manner that liquidates the bondholder's investment.

3.2. *Definitions.* The following definitions apply for purposes of this Notice only:

(1). *Qualified Tender Bond.* The term "qualified tender bond" means a tax-exempt bond that is part of an issue which has all of the following features: (a) for each interest rate mode that is preauthorized under the terms of the bond considered separately, the bond bears interest during the allowable term of that interest rate mode at either a fixed interest rate or a variable interest rate that constitutes a qualified floating rate on a variable rate debt instrument for a tax-exempt bond under § 1.1275-5(e) (e.g., various interest rate indexes and rate-setting mechanisms that reasonably can be expected to measure contemporaneous variations in the cost of newly-borrowed funds, including, without limitation, interest rates determined by reference to eligible interest rate indexes (e.g., the SIFMA index), tender option-based interest rate measures, or a Dutch auction process); (b) interest on the bond is unconditionally payable at periodic intervals at least annually; and (c) the final maturity date of the bond is no longer than the lesser of 40 years after the issue date of the bond or the latest date that is reasonably expected as of the issue date of the bond to be necessary to carry out the governmental purpose of the bond (with the 120 percent weighted average economic life of financed facilities test under Section 147(b) being treated as a safe harbor for this purpose).

(2). *Qualified Interest Rate Mode Change.* In general, a "qualified interest rate mode change" is a change in the interest rate mode on a bond that is authorized under the terms of the bond upon its original issuance. Further, in order to be a qualified interest rate mode change, the terms of the bond must require that the bond be resold at a price equal to par upon conversion to a new interest rate mode, except that, upon a conversion to an interest rate mode that is a fixed interest rate for the remaining term of the bond to maturity, the bond may be resold at a market premium or a market discount from the stated principal amount of that bond.

(3). *Qualified Tender.* A "qualified tender" is either a tender option or a mandatory tender requirement that is authorized under the terms of the bond upon its original issuance and that meets the requirements of this Section 3.2(3). A bond is subject to a tender option or a tender requirement if the bondholder either has the option at specified times (e.g., an ongoing tender option as part of the interest rate-setting process for tender option bonds) or the mandatory requirement upon specified occurrences (e.g., a mandatory tender upon conversion from one interest rate mode to a different interest rate mode) to tender the bond for purchase or redemption at a price equal to par (which may include any accrued interest) pursuant to the terms of the bond on one or more tender dates before the final stated maturity date. A purchase of a bond pursuant to a tender option or mandatory tender requirement is treated as part of a qualified tender if the purchase occurs under the terms of the bond (regardless of whether the purchase is by the issuer, a liquidity provider, a remarketing agent, a bond trustee, a conduit borrower, or an agent of any of them), the terms of the bond require that at least best efforts be used to remarket the bond, and the bond is remarketed no later than 90 days after the date of such purchase.

3.3. *Special Rule for Nonrecourse Debt.* Solely for purposes of § 103 and §§ 141 through 150, in applying § 1.1001-3(e)(4)(iv)(B) to determine whether a modification of the security or credit enhancement on a tax-exempt bond that is a nonrecourse debt instrument is a significant modification, such a modification is treated as a significant modification only if the modification results in a change in payment expectations under § 1.1001-3(e)(4)(vi).

3.4. *Special Temporary Relief for Certain Waivers of Interest Rate Caps on Auction Rate Bonds.* Solely for purposes of § 103 and §§ 141 through 150, in applying § 1.1001-3(e)(2) to determine whether a modification to the yield on tax-exempt bonds that bear interest based on an auction rate constitutes a significant modification, a temporary waiver, in whole or in part, of the terms of a cap on the maximum interest rate on such auction rate bonds is disregarded to the extent that any agreement to waive such a cap and the period during which such a waiver is in effect both are within the period between November 1, 2007 and July 1, 2008. Except for the special relief provided in this section, a waiver of a cap on an interest rate on a tax-exempt bond generally is required to be tested for whether it causes a significant modification under § 1.1001-3.

3.5 *Certain Modifications of Qualified Hedges for Arbitrage Purposes.* Solely for purposes of the arbitrage investment restrictions under § 148, in determining whether a modification of a qualified hedge results in a termination of the hedge under § 1.148-4(h), such a modification is not treated as a termination of the hedge if both: (1) the modification is not reasonably expected as of the date of the modification to change the yield on the affected hedged bonds over the remaining term of the hedged bonds by more than one quarter of one percent (.25 percent or twenty-five basis points) per annum; and (2) the payments and receipts on the qualified hedge, as modified, are fully taken into account as adjustments to the yield on those hedged bonds for arbitrage purposes under § 148.

3.6 *Examples.* The following examples illustrate the application of certain principles in this Notice and § 1.1001-3 as they apply to tax-exempt bonds for purposes of this Notice.

Example 1. Insignificant Change in Credit Enhancement and Impact on Floating Interest Rate. On July 1, 2007, a municipality (the "Issuer") issued $1 million in tax-exempt bonds that bear interest at an auction interest rate and that mature in 40 years (the "Bonds"). The Bonds are recourse obligations that are secured by the issuer's underlying primary A-rated investment grade credit. The Bonds are secured further by credit enhancement under a bond insurance policy provided by a AAA-rated bond insurer. Pursuant to the terms of the Bonds, the auction interest rate on the Bonds resets every 7 days. The terms of the Bonds grant the issuer the option to convert the interest rate mode on the Bonds from an auction rate mode to either a 7-day tender option rate mode or to a long-term fixed interest rate to maturity, subject to a mandatory tender of the Bonds upon such a conversion. The Bonds are qualified tender bonds under § 3.2 of the Notice.

On January 3, 2008, the auction interest rate on the Bonds is set at 10% as a consequence of a downgrade in the bond insurer's credit rating from a AAA rating to a AA rating and associated market disruption. On January 10, 2008, the issuer amended the terms of the Bonds to replace the now AA-rated bond insurance with a AAA-rated bank letter of credit as credit enhancement, but otherwise made no other changes to the terms of the Bonds. On January 10, 2008, the auction rate on the Bonds floated down to 3% primarily as a result of the change in credit enhancement on the Bonds.

The amendment to the terms of the Bonds to change the credit enhancement is a modification to a recourse debt instrument that must be tested for significance under the change in security or credit enhancement rule in § 1.1001-3(e)(4)(iv). Because the change in security or credit enhancement did not cause a change in payment expectations on the Bonds (i.e., the Bonds had an investment grade payment expectation before and after the change in credit enhancement), this change in credit enhancement is not a significant modification of the Bonds under § 1.1001-3 and thus does not cause a reissuance of the Bonds under § 103 and §§ 141 through 150. Further, the fact that the market impact of the change in credit enhancement caused the floating interest rate on the Bonds to float down from 10% to 3% is not required to be tested under the 25-basis point change in yield rule for significant modifications under § 1.1001-3(e)(2) because the Issuer has made no change to the interest rate-setting mechanism under the terms of the Bonds.

Example 2. Exchange of Bonds to Remove Bond Insurance. Assume the same facts as in *Example 1* above, except that, instead of amending the terms of the existing Bonds (the "Old Bonds") to change the credit enhancement, on January 10, 2008, the Issuer issued new bonds with new Cusip numbers (the "New Bonds") and did an actual exchange of the New Bonds for the Old Bonds. The New Bonds are not backed by any bond insurance or other credit enhancement. The New Bonds without the bond insurance have an A credit rating. There are no other differences between the New Bonds and the Old Bonds. The result would be the same as in *Example 1* and no reissuance of the Bonds would occur. Section 1.1001-3 applies the same significant modification standard to amendments to the terms of an

¶28,100

existing debt instrument and to actual exchanges of an existing debt instruments for a different debt instrument. Further, the same modification analysis under § 1.1001-3 would apply to an acquisition of an existing debt instrument for cash by an intermediary purchaser who is not an agent of or otherwise related to the issuer from an existing bondholder, an exchange of that acquired debt instrument for a modified debt instrument between such intermediary purchaser and the issuer and a subsequent sale by that intermediary purchaser to a different bondholder.

Example 3. Impact of Authorized Changes in Interest Rate Modes and Associated Mandatory Tenders. Assume the same facts as in *Example 1* above, except that, on January 10, 2008, the Issuer also exercised its option under the terms of the Bonds to convert the interest rate mode on the Bonds from an auction rate mode to a fixed interest rate of 5% for the remaining term of the Bonds. The terms of the Bonds also required a mandatory tender and remarketing of the Bonds in connection with this interest rate mode change. The mandatory tender is a qualified tender and the change in the interest rate mode is a qualified interest rate mode change. Thus, the Bonds are qualified tender bonds, as defined in § 3.2 of the Notice, the conversion of the interest rate on the Bonds from an auction rate mode to a fixed interest rate is pursuant to a qualified interest rate mode change" and the associated tender is qualified tender, all as defined in § 3.2 of the Notice. Thus, under § 3.1 of the Notice, in determining whether the Bonds are reissued for purposes of the tax-exempt bond provisions of the Code, the qualified interest rate mode change and the qualified tenders are not treated as modifications under § 1.1001-3. Furthermore, the interest rate change on the Bonds from a floating auction rate of 10% to a fixed interest rate of 5% was directly related to the qualified interest rate mode change and, under § 3.1 of the Notice, also is not treated as a modification under § 1.1001-3. Finally, as in *Example 1*, no reissuance of the Bonds occurred for purposes of § 103 and §§ 141 to § 150 as a result of the change in credit enhancement.

Example 4. Impact of Unauthorized Changes. Assume the same facts as in *Example 1*, except that the terms of the Bonds do not provide for any conversions of the interest rate modes. On January 7, 2008, Issuer amends the Bond documents to allow the Issuer to convert the interest rate mode on the Bonds from an auction rate mode to either a 7-day tender option rate mode or to a long-term fixed interest rate to maturity, subject to a mandatory tender of the Bonds upon such a conversion. On January 10, 2008, Issuer exercised its option under the amended terms of the Bonds to convert the interest rate mode on the Bonds from an auction rate mode to a fixed interest rate of 5% for the remaining term of the Bonds. The Issuer also required a mandatory tender and remarketing of the Bonds in connection with this interest rate mode change.

Because the change in interest rate mode is not pursuant to the terms of the Bonds when originally issued, it is not a qualified interest rate mode change within the meaning of this Notice. Similarly, the tender of the Bonds on January 10, 2008 was not pursuant to the terms of the Bond as originally issued and therefore was not a qualified tender within the meaning of this Notice. Accordingly, the provisions of this Notice are not applicable either to the interest rate mode change on the Bonds or to the tender of the Bonds. Thus, to determine whether these modifications cause a reissuance or retirement of the Bonds for purposes of § 103 and §§ 141 through § 150, the impact of these modifications must be analyzed under § 1.1001-3 to determine whether a significant modification of the terms of the Bonds occurred.

SECTION 4. Interim Guidance and Reliance

This Notice provides interim guidance. Issuers of tax-exempt bonds may rely on this Notice for any actions taken with respect to tax-exempt bonds on or after November 1, 2007 and before the effective date of future regulations under § 150 that implement the guidance in this Notice. Issuers also may continue to rely on Notice 88-130 until the effective date of such future regulations. The IRS and the Treasury Department may amend or supplement the guidance in this Notice as circumstances warrant.

SECTION 5. Request for Comments

Before any notice of proposed rulemaking is issued with respect to the guidance provided in this Notice, consideration will be given to any written public comments on this Notice that are submitted timely by May 19, 2008, and a signed original and eight (8) copies of such comments should be sent to the IRS. Send submissions to: CC:PA:LPD:PR (NOT-), room 5203, IRS, P.O. Box 7604, Ben Franklin Station, Washington, DC 20044. Submissions may be sent electronically, via the IRS Internet site at www.irs.gov/regs or via the Federal eRulemaking Portal at www.regulations.gov (indicate IRS and REG-118788-06). All comments will be available for public inspection and copying.

¶ 28,100

SECTION 6. Drafting Information

The principal author of this Notice is Aviva M. Roth, Office of the Chief Counsel (Financial Institutions and Products). However, other personnel from the IRS and the Treasury Department participated in its development. For further information regarding this Notice, contact Aviva M. Roth at (202) 622-3980 (not a toll-free call).

¶ 28,105 Notice 2008-41, I.R.B. 2008-15, 742, clarifying, amending, supplementing and superseding Notice 2008-27 (see ¶ 28,100)

SECTION 1. Purpose.

This Notice clarifies, amends, supplements, and supersedes Notice 2008-27, 2008-10 I.R.B. 543 (March 10, 2008), regarding reissuance standards for tax-exempt bonds. The Internal Revenue Service ("IRS") and the Treasury Department expect to issue regulations under § 150 of the Internal Revenue Code of 1986, as amended ("Code") to modify and clarify the determination of when tax-exempt bonds are treated as reissued or retired solely for purposes of § 103 and §§ 141 through 150. (Except as noted, section references in this Notice are to the Code and the Income Tax Regulations). This Notice provides interim guidance until the promulgation of such regulations. In part, this Notice is intended to provide greater certainty and flexibility to address certain potential Federal tax issues that have arisen in the tax-exempt bond market as a result of recent rating agency downgrades of major municipal bond insurers and failures of auctions in the auction rate bond sector of the tax-exempt bond market.

In general, this Notice clarifies, amends, supplements, and supersedes Notice 2008-27, which modified certain special reissuance standards for "qualified tender bonds" under IRS Notice 88-130, 1988-2 C.B. 530 for purposes of § 103 and §§ 141 through 150, and modified certain aspects of the application of § 1.1001-3 of the Income Tax Regulations as they apply to tax-exempt bonds.

The following discussion summarizes the changes and clarifications to Notice 2008-27 made in this Notice:

Qualified Tender Bond Rules. With respect to the qualified tender bond provisions, this Notice does the following: (1) it clarifies that the determination of whether a bond is a "qualified tender bond" is generally applied on a bond-by-bond basis, except to the extent that such test requires a determination of the weighted average maturity of the entire issue; (2) it adds qualified inflation rates and qualified inverse floating rates under § 1.1275-5(c) as eligible interest rates for qualified tender bonds; and (3) it clarifies how the 90-day remarketing requirement in the definition of a qualified tender right operates but also provides a temporary 180-day remarketing requirement.

New Temporary Rule Allowing Governmental Issuers to Purchase Their Own Auction Rate Bonds. In order to facilitate liquidity in the tax-exempt market in light of current market conditions, this Notice introduces a temporary rule which allows a governmental issuer to purchase its own tax-exempt auction rate bonds on a temporary basis without causing a retirement or extinguishment of the debt represented by the purchased tax-exempt bonds.

Certain Arbitrage Rules. This Notice also adds several rules which address the consequences of certain actions for purposes of the arbitrage investment restrictions under § 148, including actions taken pursuant to this Notice relating to qualified hedges, purchases of tax-exempt bonds by conduit borrowers, and sales of bonds at a market premium pursuant to a qualified interest rate mode change under this Notice. This Notice supplements the arbitrage rule on the treatment of minor modifications of qualified hedges from Notice 2008-27 with a rule which provides that a deemed termination of an otherwise qualified hedge under § 1.148-4(h) will not result from bonds being held by or on behalf of a governmental issuer during the 90-day permitted holding period or the temporary 180-day permitted holding period for remarketing pursuant to a qualified tender right or during the 180-day permitted holding period for temporary purchases of auction rate bonds. With respect to a conduit borrower's purchase of tax-exempt bonds, the Notice adds a special rule which provides that such a purchase will not cause a violation of a technical arbitrage restriction against purchases of tax-exempt bonds by conduit borrowers under the "program investment" definition in § 1.148-1(b) in certain circumstances. Further, with respect to certain permitted resales of bonds at a market premium upon a conversion of the interest rate to a fixed interest rate to maturity, this Notice provides that, solely for arbitrage purposes, any premium properly received by an issuer pursuant to a qualified interest rate mode change is treated as additional sale proceeds (as defined in § 1.148-1(b)).

Certain Special Rules. Finally, with respect to two special rules from Notice 2008-27 which address certain temporary waivers of interest rate caps and certain nonrecourse debt, this Notice continues those rules and extends the period during which interest rate caps may be waived without resulting in a significant modification under § 1.1001-3 until October 1, 2008.

Changes to Example s

This Notice removes certain language from Example 2 of Notice 2008-27, because that language has proven confusing. No other inference should be drawn with respect to the transaction. In addition, this Notice contains an additional example illustrating the temporary 180-day qualified tender bond remarketing requirement.

Scope and Effective Date. This Notice applies solely for purposes of § 103 and § § 141 through 150. No inference should be drawn regarding whether a debt modification described in this Notice would constitute an exchange for purposes of § 1001. In addition, no inference should be drawn about whether similar consequences would obtain if a transaction falls outside the scope of this Notice.

This Notice is effective as of March 25, 2008. For the scope of application of this Notice, see § 8 of this Notice.

This Notice invites public comment on the guidance provided herein.

SECTION 2. Background

Reissuance

Reissuance of a tax-exempt bond for purposes of the tax-exempt bond provisions triggers retesting of all the various program requirements for new issues of tax-exempt bonds. A reissuance of an issue of tax-exempt bonds may result in various negative consequences to a bond issuer, including, among other things, changes in yield for purposes of the arbitrage investment restrictions, acceleration of arbitrage rebate payment obligations, deemed terminations of integrated interest rate swaps under the qualified hedge rules for arbitrage purposes, new public approval requirements for qualified private activity bonds, and change in law risk.

In general, the standard for determining whether tax-exempt bonds are reissued, retired, or otherwise modified significantly enough to trigger a retesting of the program requirements for new issues of tax-exempt bonds under the tax-exempt bond provisions of the Code is based on the general Federal tax standards for debt exchanges under § 1001 and regulations thereunder.

In general, § 1.1001-3 employs a significant modification standard to determine whether modifications to a debt instrument in any form are sufficiently significant to cause the debt instrument to be treated as reissued or exchanged for purposes of § 1001. Section 1.1001-3 applies to modifications in the form of amendments to the terms of an existing debt instrument and to modifications in the form of actual exchanges of existing debt instruments for different debt instruments. The determination of whether a resulting debt instrument is treated as a reissued new debt instrument or a continuation of the original debt instrument depends on whether the result represents a "significant modification" of the original debt instrument, as defined in § 1.1001-3.

Notice 88-130 provides certain special reissuance rules for certain eligible tax-exempt bonds that are "qualified tender bonds," as defined therein. Notice 88-130 provides that qualified tender bonds will not be treated as reissued for purposes of § 103 and § § 141 through 150 as a result of certain tender rights and certain changes in interest rate modes and other terms of bonds that are covered specifically by the detailed rules and limitations set forth in Notice 88-130.

Debt Extinguishment

Subject to limited exceptions, a debt instrument generally is treated as retired or extinguished when, among other circumstances, an issuer acquires its own debt because a merger of the interests of the issuer and the holder occurs. Notice 88-130 reflects this debt extinguishment principle in § 2.2(d) thereof, which generally treats a tax-exempt qualified tender bond as retired if it is purchased or otherwise acquired by or on behalf of an issuer which is a governmental unit or an agency or instrumentality thereof. If tax-exempt bonds treated as retired as a result of a debt extinguishment upon a governmental issuer's purchase of the tax-exempt bonds, that treatment may have different consequences depending on whether it is retired with the proceeds of another debt instrument or whether it is retired from equity or other non-borrowed funds.

A borrowing, whether taxable or tax-exempt, that is treated as retiring or reissuing a separate borrowing, generally constitutes an issue of refunding bonds which are viewed as financing the same governmental purpose or project as the original bonds (or "stepping into the shoes" of the original bonds) and trigger consequences involving the need to retest certain tax-exempt bond program requirements.

Tax-exempt bonds that are treated as retired through a debt extinguishment without a link to another borrowing, such as potentially an issuer's purchase of its own tax-exempt bonds using equity or other non-borrowed funds, may trigger additional consequences, including the potential adverse consequence of generally limiting the ability to refinance those extinguished bonds later with tax-exempt refunding bonds for the same governmental purpose as the original bonds.

Interest Rate Modes—Tender Option Modes and Auction Rate Modes

Issuers may issue fixed rate tax-exempt bonds that bear interest at fixed rates to maturity or variable rate bonds that bear interest at variable rates which float periodically in accordance with various market-based interest-rate setting mechanisms. Issuers often include multi-modal interest rate features in the preauthorized terms of the bond documents which provide issuers with the flexibility to change interest rate modes under parameters set forth in the bond documents.

One common interest rate mode employed with tax-exempt bonds is a tender option mode. "Tender option bonds" are also referred to commonly as "variable rate demand bonds." Tender option bonds have short-term interest features tied to current market rates necessary to remarket the bonds at par. Tender option bonds have ongoing tender options or put options associated with the interest rate-setting mechanism which allow bondholders to tender their bonds for purchase at par at specified intervals, typically every seven days. Tender option bonds generally have creditworthy third-party liquidity facilities from banks or other liquidity providers to support the tender options and may have credit enhancement from bond insurers or other providers. Tender option bonds also may have interest mode conversion options which grant to the issuer or a conduit borrower an option to change the interest rate mode on the bonds from a tender option mode to another short-term interest rate mode or to a fixed interest rate to maturity. At the time of a conversion to another interest rate mode, tender option bonds typically are subject to a mandatory tender for purchase but a bondholder may be allowed to elect to retain the bonds. Upon the exercise of ongoing tender options associated with the short-term interest rate-setting mechanism for tender option bonds and upon any mandatory or optional tender upon conversion of the interest rate on the bonds to another interest rate mode, a remarketing agent or a liquidity provider typically will acquire the bonds subject to the tender at par and resell the bonds either to the same bondholders or to others willing to purchase such bonds. In general, Notice 88-130 provides guidance for when the tenders associated with tender option bonds will not constitute reissuances if they meet the specific detailed eligibility requirements for "qualified tender bonds," as defined in Notice 88-130.

Another interest rate mode used with tax-exempt bonds is an auction rate mode. The interest rate on auction rate bonds is reset at predetermined intervals (generally under one year) using a modified Dutch auction process. Auction rate bonds generally trade at par and are callable at par on any interest payment date at the option of the issuer. Unlike bonds in a tender option mode, however, bonds in an auction rate mode have no ongoing tender options or put options to support the interest rate-setting process. Thus, auction rate bonds are viewed as long-term investments with a short-term interest rate-setting process. Auction rate bonds generally have maximum rates based on state law restrictions or certain formulas, such as a multiple of a tax-exempt or taxable index. Auction rate bonds may have credit enhancement from bond insurers or other providers. Auction rate bonds also may have interest mode conversion options similar to tender option bonds which grant to the issuer or a conduit borrower an option to change the interest rate mode on the bonds from an auction rate mode to another short-term interest rate mode or to a fixed interest rate to maturity. At the time of a conversion to another interest rate mode, auction rate bonds typically are subject to a mandatory tender for purchase in a process similar to mandatory tenders on conversions of interest rate modes used with tender option bonds.

Questions have arisen regarding whether or to what extent auction rate bonds can be treated as qualified tender bonds for purposes of Notice 88-130. In addition, in light of recent guidance by the Securities and Exchanges Commission which authorizes issuers of tax-exempt bonds to bid on and acquire their own auction rate bonds in an auction in certain circumstances, additional questions have arisen regarding the tax consequences of such acquisitions in various circumstances and whether such acquisitions would result in a retirement or extinguishment of such bonds.

SECTION 3. Reissuance Standards for State and Local Bonds

3.1. *Scope and General Rules.* The IRS and the Treasury Department expect to promulgate regulations under §150 to provide guidance on whether tax-exempt bonds are treated as reissued or retired solely for purposes of §103 and §§141 through 150. Specifically, for purposes of §103 and §§141 through 150 only, in the case of a qualified tender bond (as defined herein), any qualified interest rate mode change (as defined herein) and any qualified tender right (as defined herein) will not be treated as a modification under §1.1001-3. Therefore, for these purposes, a qualified tender bond will not be treated as reissued or retired solely as a result of a qualified interest rate mode change or the existence or exercise of any qualified tender right. Further, in applying §1.1001-3 to modifications of tax-exempt bonds, any interest rate variance directly resulting from a qualified interest rate mode change will not be treated as a modification under §1.1001-3, and thus such interest rate variances need not be tested under the change in yield rule for determining significant modifications under §1.1001-3(e)(2). Except as otherwise specifically provided in this Notice, the determination of whether any modification to an issue of tax-exempt bonds causes a reissuance or retirement of the tax-exempt bonds for purposes of §103 and §§141 through 150 is based on whether the modifications are significant modifications under §1.1001-3.

Except as expressly provided herein in the special rules for the treatment of "qualified interest rate mode changes" and "qualified tender rights" on "qualified tender bonds" (all as redefined herein) under §3 of this Notice, the special temporary rule allowing governmental issuers to purchase their own tax-exempt auction rate bonds for a limited holding period under §4 of this Notice, the special arbitrage rules under §5 of this Notice, and the other special rules under §6 of this Notice, a tax-exempt bond generally is treated as reissued or retired on the first date on which: (1) a significant modification to the terms of the bond occurs under §1.1001-3 or a disposition of the bond otherwise occurs under section 1001; (2) the bond is purchased or otherwise acquired by or on behalf of a governmental issuer (as defined herein); or (3) the bond is otherwise retired or redeemed.

For purposes of determining whether a bond is purchased or otherwise acquired by or on behalf of a governmental issuer, except as otherwise expressly provided in §3.2(3) and §4 of this Notice, a bond is treated as purchased or otherwise acquired by or on behalf of a person if the bond is purchased or otherwise acquired by that person in a manner that liquidates the bondholder's investment.

A purchase of a tax-exempt bond by a third-party guarantor or third-party liquidity facility provider pursuant to the terms of a third-party guarantee or third-party liquidity facility is not treated as a purchase or other acquisition by or on behalf of a governmental issuer. Similarly, a purchase of a tax-exempt bond by a conduit borrower that is not a governmental issuer is not treated as a purchase or other acquisition by or on behalf of the governmental issuer.

3.2. *Definitions and Operating Rules.* The following definitions and special operating rules apply for purposes of this Notice only:

(1). *Qualified Tender Bond.* The term "qualified tender bond" means a tax-exempt bond that has all of the following features: (a) for each interest rate mode that is preauthorized under the terms of the bond considered separately, the bond bears interest during the allowable term of that interest rate mode at either a fixed interest rate, a variable interest rate that constitutes a qualified floating rate on a variable rate debt instrument for a tax-exempt bond under §1.1275-5(b) (e.g., various interest rate indexes and rate-setting mechanisms that reasonably can be expected to measure contemporaneous variations in the cost of newly-borrowed funds, including, without limitation, interest rates determined by reference to eligible interest rate indexes (e.g., the SIFMA index), tender option-based interest rate measures, or a Dutch auction process), or a variable interest rate that constitutes an eligible objective rate for a variable rate debt instrument that is a tax-exempt bond under §1.1275-5(c)(5) (i.e., a qualified inflation rate or a qualified inverse floating rate); (b) interest on the bond is unconditionally payable at periodic intervals at least annually; (c) the final maturity date of the bond is no longer than the lesser of 40 years after the issue date of the bond or the latest date that is reasonably expected as of the issue date of the issue of which the bond is a part to be necessary to carry out the governmental purpose of the issue of which the bond is a part (with the 120 percent weighted average economic life of financed facilities test under Section 147(b) with respect to the issue of which the bond is a part being treated as a safe harbor for this purpose); and (d) the bond is subject to an optional tender right or a mandatory tender requirement which allows or requires a bondholder to tender the bond for purchase in one or more prescribed circumstances under the terms of the bond.

(2). *Qualified Interest Rate Mode Change.* In general, a "qualified interest rate mode change" is a change in the interest rate mode on a bond that is authorized under the terms of the bond upon its original issuance. Further, in order to be a qualified interest rate mode change, the terms of the bond must require that the bond be purchased and resold at a price equal to par upon conversion to a new interest rate mode, except only that, upon a conversion to an interest rate mode that is a fixed interest rate for the remaining term of the bond to maturity, the bond may be resold at a market premium or a market discount from the stated principal amount of that bond.

(3). *Qualified Tender Right.*

(a) *In General.* A "qualified tender right" is a tender right for the purchase of a bond (regardless of whether the purchase is by or on behalf of a governmental issuer) that is authorized under the terms of a bond upon its original issuance and that meets all of the requirements of this § 3.2(3)(a). The tender right must involve either an optional tender right or a mandatory tender requirement which allows or requires the bondholder to tender the bond for purchase on at least one tender date before the final stated maturity date. The tender right must entitle a tendering bondholder to receive a purchase price equal to par (which may include any accrued interest). The terms of the tender right must require the issuer or its remarketing agent to use at least best efforts to remarket a bond upon a purchase pursuant to the tender right.

(b) *Operating Rules for Purchases Pursuant to a Qualified Tender Right.* A bond purchased by or on behalf of a governmental issuer pursuant to a qualified tender right is treated as not retired pursuant to and as a result of the qualified tender right until not later than the end of the 90-day period from and after the date of such purchase, and subsequent to the end of this 90-day period, a governmental issuer generally may not hold its own bond without causing a retirement of such bond under the general rules in § 3.1 of this Notice. This 90-day period is extended to 180-days, however, with respect to any purchase by or on behalf of a governmental issuer pursuant to a qualified tender right as long as such purchase occurs before October 1, 2008.

Thus, with respect to such bonds purchased before October 1, 2008, during this 180-day period, a governmental issuer or its agent may hold the bond under the terms of the bond without causing a retirement of the bond. In addition, recognizing that the bond is treated as outstanding during this 180-day period, the governmental issuer may refund the bond with a refunding bond during this period upon a failed remarketing.

By contrast, third-party guarantors, third-party liquidity facility providers, and conduit borrowers (other than a conduit borrower that is a governmental issuer) are not treated as purchasers by or on behalf of a governmental issuer under the general rules in § 3.1 of this Notice, and, accordingly, any such person may hold a bond purchased pursuant to the exercise of a qualified tender right for an unlimited holding period without causing a retirement of such bond. Further, for example, a governmental issuer may hold a bond purchased before October 1, 2008, pursuant to the exercise of a qualified tender right for a holding period of 179 days while using best efforts under the terms of the bonds to remarket the bond and then resell the bond to a third-party guarantor, third-party liquidity facility provider, or other independent third party before the expiration of the 180-day period in compliance with the operating rules in this § 3.2(3)(b).

(4) *Governmental issuer.* A "governmental issuer" is an issuer of a tax-exempt bond that is a governmental unit or an agency or instrumentality thereof.

SECTION 4. Temporary Rule Allowing Governmental Issuers to Purchase Their Own Auction Rate Bonds

Solely for purposes of § 103 and §§ 141 through 150, a governmental issuer may purchase its own tax-exempt auction rate bond on a temporary basis without resulting in a reissuance or retirement of the purchased tax-exempt bond if it meets the following requirements: (1) the governmental issuer holds the bond for not more than a 180-day period from and after the date of purchase; and (2) the governmental issuer purchases the bond before October 1, 2008. Similar to the treatment of a bond purchased pursuant to a qualified tender right under the operating rule in § 3.2(3)(b) of this Notice, an auction rate bond purchased by a governmental issuer pursuant to this § 4 is treated as not retired pursuant to and as a result of this special rule until not later than the end of this 180-day period, and, subsequent to the end of this 180-day period, a governmental issuer generally may not hold its own bond without causing a retirement of such bond under the general rules in § 3.1 of this Notice.

Thus, recognizing that the bond is treated as not retired during this 180-day period, the governmental issuer may refund the bond with a refunding bond, tender the bond for purchase in a qualified tender right in its capacity as a bondholder, or otherwise resell the bond during this 180-day period. After the end of this 180-day period, however, a governmental issuer generally may not hold its own bond without causing a retirement of such bond under the general rules in § 3.1 of this Notice.

SECTION 5. Arbitrage Provisions

5.1. *Certain Special Rules on Qualified Hedges for Arbitrage Purposes.* Solely for purposes of the arbitrage investment restrictions (including, without limitation, both yield restriction and rebate) under § 148, in determining whether a modification of a qualified hedge results in a termination of the hedge under § 1.148-4(h), such a modification is not treated as a termination of the hedge if both: (1) the modification is not reasonably expected as of the date of the modification to change the yield on the affected hedged bonds over the remaining term of the hedged bonds by more than one quarter of one percent (.25 percent or twenty-five basis points) per annum; and (2) the payments and receipts on the qualified hedge, as modified, are fully taken into account as adjustments to the yield on those hedged bonds for arbitrage purposes under § 148. Further, for arbitrage purposes under § 148, a qualified hedge with respect to bonds is not deemed terminated under § 1.148-4(h) as a result of the governmental issuer's holding of the hedged bonds during either the 90-day permitted holding period or the 180-day temporary permitted holding period under § 3.2(3), or the 180-day permitted holding period under § 4 of this Notice during which the governmental issuer is permitted to hold such bonds without resulting in a reissuance or retirement of such bonds.

5.2. *Special Rule for Certain Purchases by Conduit Borrowers.* In applying the special arbitrage rule for "program investments" under § 1.148-1(b) which restricts a conduit borrower's purchase of tax-exempt bonds for a governmental program in an amount "related" to the amount of its purpose investment financed by the program, a conduit borrower's purchase of a tax-exempt auction rate bond that financed its loan to facilitate liquidity under adverse market conditions is treated as not being so "related" for this purpose.

5.3. *Treatment of Certain Premiums as Proceeds for Arbitrage Purposes.* Solely for purposes of the arbitrage investment restrictions under § 148, any premium received by an issuer pursuant to a conversion of the interest rate on a qualified tender bond to a fixed interest rate for the remaining term of the bond to maturity in a qualified interest rate mode change under § 3.2(2) of this Notice is treated as additional sale proceeds (as defined in § 1.148-1(b)) of such bonds.

SECTION 6. Special Rules

6.1 *Special Rule for Nonrecourse Debt.* Solely for purposes of § 103 and §§ 141 through 150, in applying § 1.1001-3(e)(4)(iv)(B) to determine whether a modification of the security or credit enhancement on a tax-exempt bond that is a nonrecourse debt instrument is a significant modification, such a modification is treated as a significant modification only if the modification results in a change in payment expectations under § 1.1001-3(e)(4)(vi).

6.2. *Special Temporary Relief for Certain Waivers of Interest Rate Caps on Auction Rate Bonds.* Solely for purposes of § 103 and §§ 141 through 150, in applying § 1.1001-3(e)(2) to determine whether a modification to the yield on tax-exempt bonds that bear interest based on an auction rate constitutes a significant modification, a temporary waiver, in whole or in part, of the terms of a cap on the maximum interest rate on such auction rate bonds is disregarded to the extent that any agreement to waive such a cap and the period during which such a waiver is in effect both are within the period between November 1, 2007 and October 1, 2008. Except for the special relief provided in this section, a waiver of a cap on an interest rate on a tax-exempt bond generally is required to be tested for whether it causes a significant modification under § 1.1001-3.

SECTION 7. Examples

The following examples illustrate the application of certain principles in this Notice and § 1.1001-3 as they apply to tax-exempt bonds for purposes of this Notice.

Example 1. Insignificant Change in Credit Enhancement and Impact on Floating Interest Rate. On July 1, 2007, a municipality (the "Issuer") issued $1 million in tax-exempt bonds that bear interest at an auction interest rate and that mature in 40 years (the "Bonds"). The Bonds are recourse obligations that are secured by the issuer's underlying primary A-rated investment grade credit. The Bonds are secured further by credit enhancement under a bond insurance policy provided by a AAA-rated bond insurer. Pursuant to the terms of the Bonds, the auction interest rate on the Bonds resets every 7 days. The terms of the Bonds grant the issuer the option to convert the interest rate mode on the Bonds from an auction rate mode to either a 7-day tender option rate mode or to a long-term fixed interest rate to

¶ 28,105

maturity, subject to a mandatory tender of the Bonds upon such a conversion. The Bonds are qualified tender bonds under §3.2 of this Notice.

On January 3, 2008, the auction interest rate on the Bonds is set at 10% as a consequence of a downgrade in the bond insurer's credit rating from a AAA rating to a AA rating and associated market disruption. On January 10, 2008, the issuer amended the terms of the Bonds to replace the now AA-rated bond insurance with a AAA-rated bank letter of credit as credit enhancement, but otherwise made no other changes to the terms of the Bonds. On January 10, 2008, the auction rate on the Bonds floated down to 3% primarily as a result of the change in credit enhancement on the Bonds.

The amendment to the terms of the Bonds to change the credit enhancement is a modification to a recourse debt instrument that must be tested for significance under the change in security or credit enhancement rule in §1.1001-3(e)(4)(iv). Because the change in security or credit enhancement did not cause a change in payment expectations on the Bonds (i.e., the Bonds had an investment grade payment expectation before and after the change in credit enhancement), this change in credit enhancement is not a significant modification of the Bonds under §1.1001-3 and thus does not cause a reissuance of the Bonds under §103 and §§141 through 150. Further, the fact that the market impact of the change in credit enhancement caused the floating interest rate on the Bonds to float down from 10% to 3% is not required to be tested under the 25-basis point change in yield rule for significant modifications under §1.1001-3(e)(2) because the Issuer has made no change to the interest rate-setting mechanism under the terms of the Bonds.

Example 2. Exchange of Bonds to Remove Bond Insurance.

Assume the same facts as in *Example 1* above, except that, instead of amending the terms of the existing Bonds (the "Old Bonds") to change the credit enhancement, on January 10, 2008, the Issuer issued new bonds with new Cusip numbers (the "New Bonds") and did an actual exchange of the New Bonds for the Old Bonds. The New Bonds are not backed by any bond insurance or other credit enhancement. The New Bonds without the bond insurance have an A credit rating. There are no other differences between the New Bonds and the Old Bonds. The result would be the same as in *Example 1* and no reissuance of the Bonds would occur. Section 1.1001-3 applies the same significant modification standard to amendments to the terms of an existing debt instrument and to actual exchanges of an existing debt instruments for a different debt instrument.

Example 3. Impact of Authorized Changes in Interest Rate Modes and Associated Mandatory Tenders and Effect of Serialization.

(i) Assume the same facts as in *Example 1* above, except that, on January 10, 2008, the Issuer also exercised its option under the terms of the Bonds to convert the interest rate mode on the Bonds from an auction rate mode to a fixed interest rate of 5% for the remaining term of the Bonds. The terms of the Bonds also required a mandatory tender and remarketing of the Bonds in connection with this interest rate mode change. The mandatory tender is a qualified tender right and the change in the interest rate mode is a qualified interest rate mode change. Thus, the Bonds are qualified tender bonds, as defined in §3.2 of the Notice, the conversion of the interest rate on the Bonds from an auction rate mode to a fixed interest rate is pursuant to a qualified interest rate mode change" and the associated tender is a qualified tender right, all as defined in §3.2 of the Notice. Thus, under §3.1 of the Notice, in determining whether the Bonds are reissued for purposes of the tax-exempt bond provisions of the Code, the qualified interest rate mode change and the qualified tender right are not treated as modifications under §1.1001-3. Furthermore, the interest rate change on the Bonds from a floating auction rate of 10% to a fixed interest rate of 5% directly resulted from the qualified interest rate mode change and, under §3.1 of the Notice, also is not treated as a modification under §1.1001-3. Finally, as in *Example 1*, no reissuance of the Bonds occurred for purposes of §103 and §§141 through 150 as a result of the change in credit enhancement.

(ii) Assume the same facts as paragraph (i) above except that the Issuer also amended the terms of the Bonds to modify a term Bond which had a prescribed mandatory sinking fund redemption schedule with alternative Bonds with "serial" maturities instead of the sinking fund redemption schedule. This "serialization" of the term Bond does not directly result from the qualified interest rate mode change. Subject to the particular terms of the Bonds, the serialization of the term Bond generally would be a modification under §1.1001-3 which would be required to be analyzed for significance under the change in yield rule in §1.1001-3(e)(2) and the change in the timing of payments rule in §1.1001-3(e)(3).

¶28,105

Example 4. Impact of Unauthorized Changes.

Assume the same facts as in *Example 1*, except that the terms of the Bonds do not provide for any conversions of the interest rate modes. On January 7, 2008, Issuer amends the Bond documents to allow the Issuer to convert the interest rate mode on the Bonds from an auction rate mode to either a 7-day tender option rate mode or to a long-term fixed interest rate to maturity, subject to a mandatory tender of the Bonds upon such a conversion. On January 10, 2008, Issuer exercised its option under the amended terms of the Bonds to convert the interest rate mode on the Bonds from an auction rate mode to a fixed interest rate of 5% for the remaining term of the Bonds. The Issuer also required a mandatory tender and remarketing of the Bonds in connection with this interest rate mode change. Because the change in interest rate mode is not pursuant to the terms of the Bonds when originally issued, it is not a qualified interest rate mode change within the meaning of this Notice. Similarly, the tender of the Bonds on January 10, 2008 was not pursuant to the terms of the Bond as originally issued and therefore was not a qualified tender right within the meaning of this Notice. Accordingly, the provisions of this Notice are not applicable either to the interest rate mode change on the Bonds or to the tender of the Bonds. Thus, to determine whether these modifications cause a reissuance or retirement of the Bonds for purposes of §103 and §§141 through 150, the impact of these modifications must be analyzed under §1.1001-3 to determine whether a significant modification of the terms of the Bonds occurred.

Example 5. Operation of the 180-Day Temporary Rule for Qualified Tender Rights.

(i) On July 1, 2007, a municipality (the "Issuer") issued $1 million in tax-exempt bonds that bear interest initially at a variable rate demand rate and that mature in 40 years (the "Bonds"). The interest rate on the Bonds resets every 7 days at the minimum interest rate necessary to remarket the Bonds at par. The Bonds have seven-day tender options exercisable by the holders while the Bonds are in the variable rate demand interest rate mode. The Bonds give the Issuer an option to convert the interest rate on the Bonds to other interest rate modes. The Bonds have a mandatory tender requirement upon an interest rate mode conversion. The Bonds are secured by a third-party liquidity facility in the form of a letter of credit (the "Liquidity Facility") from a bank (the "Bank"). The Bonds are further secured by a third-party guarantee in the form of a bond insurance policy from a bond insurer (the "Bond Insurer"). An investment bank serves as a remarketing agent ("Remarketing Agent") for the Issuer with respect to the Bonds. The terms of the remarketing arrangement require the Remarketing Agent to use at least its best efforts to remarket tendered Bonds. On May 1, 2008, the Issuer exercises its option to convert the interest rate on the Bonds to a fixed interest rate to maturity and the Bonds are subject to mandatory tender by the Bondholders. The Bonds are qualified tender bonds which have a qualified tender right and a qualified interest rate mode change within the meaning of §3.2 of this Notice. During the 180-day period after the date of purchase of the bonds pursuant to the qualified tender right, as a result of difficult market conditions and despite best efforts required pursuant to the terms of the Bonds, the Issuer and the Remarketing Agent are unsuccessful in remarketing the Bonds. The particular terms of the Liquidity Facility require that the qualified tender right be funded by the Bank under the Liquidity Facility, but that the Bank not hold the Bonds upon a draw on the Liquidity Facility. Instead, the Bank merely receives a pledge of the Bonds as collateral for the draw on the Liquidity Facility and the Issuer holds the Bonds upon a draw on the Liquidity Facility. During this 180-day period, the Bonds are treated as outstanding under the operating rules for qualified tender rights in §3.2(3)(b) even if the Bonds are held by or on behalf of the Issuer. Thus, during this 180-day period, the Issuer may hold the Bonds under the terms of the Bonds without causing a retirement of the Bonds. In addition, recognizing that the Bonds are treated as outstanding during this 180-day period, the Issuer may refund the Bonds with proceeds from refunding bonds during this period or resell the bonds to a third party.

(ii) Assume the same facts as in paragraph (i), but further assume that the Issuer retains the Bonds beyond the 180-day permitted holding period for a governmental issuer under §3.2(3)(b) of this Notice. The Bonds are treated as retired as the end of the 180\th/ day from and after the date of the purchase of the Bonds pursuant to the exercise of the qualified tender right. Thus, the count of the 180-day permitted holding period for the Issuer starts on the date of the purchase pursuant to the qualified tender right (here, starting May 1, 2008) and ends at the end of the 180\th/ day from and after the date of purchase (here, ending at the end of the day on October 27, 2008).

(iii) Assume the same facts as in paragraph (i), but further assume that the terms of the Liquidity Facility provide that the Bank will hold the Bonds upon a draw on the Liquidity Facility, rather than merely receive a pledge of the Bonds as collateral while the Issuer or its agent holds the Bonds. Here, since a third-party liquidity facility provider is not treated as a purchaser by or on behalf of a governmental issuer under the general rules in § 3.1 of this Notice, the Bank may hold the Bonds during and beyond the 180-day period after the date of the purchase pursuant to the qualified tender right without causing a retirement of the Bonds.

(iv) Assume the same facts as in paragraph (i), but further assume that the Issuer holds the Bonds for 179 days after purchase of the Bonds pursuant to the exercise of a qualified tender right while using best efforts under the terms of the Bonds to remarket the bond, and then sells the Bonds to the Bank pursuant to the Liquidity Facility. This transaction complies with the operating rules for qualified tender rights in § 3.2(3)(b) of this Notice and does not result in a retirement of the Bonds.

SECTION 8. Interim Guidance and Reliance

The effective date of this Notice is March 25, 2008. This Notice provides interim guidance. Issuers of tax-exempt bonds may apply and rely on this Notice for any actions taken with respect to tax-exempt bonds on or after November 1, 2007 and before the effective date of any future regulation under § 150 that implement the guidance with respect to any particular applicable provision in this Notice or other public guidance that withdraws or supersedes any particular applicable provision in this Notice. Issuers also may continue to rely on Notice 88-130 until the effective date of such future regulations. Notice 2008-27 is superseded and may not be relied upon after the effective date of this Notice. The IRS and the Treasury Department may amend or supplement the guidance in this Notice as circumstances warrant.

SECTION 9. Request for Comments

Before any notice of proposed rulemaking is issued with respect to the guidance provided in this Notice, consideration will be given to any written public comments on this Notice that are submitted timely by May 19, 2008, and a signed original and eight (8) copies of such comments should be sent to the IRS. Send submissions to: CC:PA:LPD:PR (NOT-), room 5203, IRS, P.O. Box 7604, Ben Franklin Station, Washington, DC 20044. Submissions may be sent electronically, via the IRS Internet site at *www.irs.gov/regs* or via the Federal eRulemaking Portal at *www.regulations.gov* (indicate IRS and REG-118788-06). All comments will be available for public inspection and copying.

SECTION 10. Drafting Information

The principal author of this Notice is Aviva M. Roth, Office of the Chief Counsel (Financial Institutions and Products). However, other personnel from the IRS and the Treasury Department participated in its development. For further information regarding this Notice, contact Aviva M. Roth at (202) 622-3980 (not a toll-free call).

¶ 28,110   Notice 2008-80, I.R.B. 2008-40, 820

SECTION 1. Purpose.

In order to provide greater administrative certainty in a major short-term sector of the tax-exempt bond market in response to taxpayer requests and to promote stability in this sector of the market, the Treasury Department and the Internal Revenue Service ("IRS") propose to issue a revenue procedure substantially in the form included in section 5 of this Notice. The proposed revenue procedure would modify and supersede Rev. Proc. 2003-84, 2003-2 C.B. 1159. The proposed revenue procedure would provide certain more specific eligibility criteria that partnerships that invest in tax-exempt bonds must meet to qualify for monthly closing elections to allow the partners to take into account monthly the inclusions required under §§ 702 and 707(c) of the Internal Revenue Code of 1986, as amended (the "Code"). The Treasury Department and the IRS are issuing this guidance in proposed form to afford an opportunity for public comment and to limit any potential impact on the current market.

SECTION 2. Request for Comments.

The Treasury Department and the IRS seek public comments on all aspects of the proposed revenue procedure, including comments on ways to facilitate market innovation consistent with promoting administrative certainty and sound tax policy. The Treasury Department and the IRS seek specific public comment on whether or under what circumstances the proposed revenue procedure should apply when the variable interest holder has a minimum gain share percentage of less than five percent, such as circumstances in which the variable-rate interest holders receive particular rights to control sales of underlying tax-exempt bond assets held by a tax-exempt bond partnership. The Treasury Department and the IRS also seek specific comment on whether or under what circumstances the proposed revenue procedure should be expanded to allow qualifying income from assets beyond original assets of the partnership referred to in § 4.02(3) of the proposed revenue procedure. The Treasury Department and the IRS also seek specific comment on whether or under what circumstances the proposed revenue procedure should be expanded to allow application to any other types of transactions besides the contemplated tax-exempt bond partnerships.

Before the proposed revenue procedure described in this Notice is made effective, consideration will be given to any written public comments on this Notice that are submitted in a timely fashion by December 15, 2008. A signed original and eight (8) copies of public comments should be sent by mail to the IRS at CC:PA:LPD:PR (reference IRS Notice 2008-80), Room 5203, Internal Revenue Service, PO Box 7604, Ben Franklin Station, Washington, DC 20044. Public comments also may be sent electronically, via the IRS Internet site at *www.irs.gov/regs* or via the Federal eRulemaking portal at *www.regulations.gov* (reference IRS Notice 2008-80). All comments will be available for public inspection and copying.

SECTION 3. Effective Date and Immediate Elective Reliance.

This Notice is effective on September 17, 2008. The proposed revenue procedure is proposed to apply generally to tax-exempt bond partnerships with a start-up date that occurs on or after the date that is 30 days after the final revenue procedure is released to the public, subject to the special rules set forth in the effective date provisions in section 9 of the proposed revenue procedure.

At their option, eligible tax-exempt bond partnerships may rely immediately on the proposed revenue procedure to make monthly closing elections in accordance with the proposed revenue procedure effective with respect to any such monthly closing elections that are made on or after September 17, 2008. Eligible tax-exempt bond partnerships also may continue to rely on Rev. Proc. 2003-84 until the proposed revenue procedure is finalized and made effective.

SECTION 4. Drafting Information.

The principal author of this Notice is Frank J. Fisher of the Office of Associate Chief Counsel (Passthroughs & Special Industries). For further information regarding this revenue procedure, contact Frank J. Fisher at (202) 622-3050 (not a toll free call).

SECTION 5. Form of Proposed Revenue Procedure.

Set forth below is the form of the proposed revenue procedure that is proposed in this Notice:

Form of Proposed Revenue Procedure

Part III

Administrative, Procedural, and Miscellaneous

26 CFR 1.706-1: Taxable years of partner and partnership.

(Also Part I, Section(s) 103, 171, 702, 704, 706, 708, 851, 852, 1275, 6001, 6031, 6229, 6231, 6233, 6698, 6722; 301.6031(a)-1, 601.105.

Rev. Proc. 2009-XX

SECTION 1. Purpose.

In order to provide greater administrative certainty in a major short-term sector of the tax-exempt bond market in response to taxpayer requests and to promote stability in this sector of the market, this revenue procedure modifies and supersedes Rev. Proc. 2003-84, 2003-2 C.B. 1159. This revenue procedure provides certain more specific eligibility criteria that partnerships that invest in tax-exempt bonds must meet to qualify for monthly closing elections to allow the partners to take into account monthly the inclusions required under §§ 702 and 707(c) of the Internal Revenue Code of 1986, as amended (the "Code"). (Except as noted, section references in this revenue procedure are to the Code and the Income Tax Regulations.) This revenue procedure provides rules for partnership income tax reporting under § 6031 for such partnerships.

SECTION 2. Background.

This revenue procedure provides a means for certain partnerships that invest in state or local governmental debt obligations the interest on which is excludable from gross income under § 103 ("tax-exempt bonds") to elect to allow the partners to take into account monthly the inclusions required under §§ 702 and 707(c). This revenue procedure applies to certain partnerships used to create the economic equivalent of a variable-rate tax-exempt bond. To create this instrument, a sponsor that holds a tax-exempt bond may transfer the tax-exempt bond to an entity that qualifies as a partnership for federal tax purposes ("tax-exempt bond partnership"). The tax-exempt bond partnership issues two classes of equity interests: (1) interests that are entitled to a preferred variable return on its capital payable out of partnership income ("variable-rate interests"); and (2) interests that are entitled to all of the remaining income of the partnership ("inverse interests"). Owners of variable-rate interests and inverse interests are referred to as "variable-rate interest holders" and "inverse interest holders," respectively. The variable return on the variable-rate interests tracks current short-term tax-exempt bond yields. Under § 702(b), tax-exempt interest income received by a partnership retains its character when the partnership allocates the income to a partner.

Under § 706(a), a partner generally includes in income for a taxable year the partner's allocable share of items of partnership income, gain, loss, deduction, and credit for the partnership's taxable year ending within or with the partner's taxable year. A partner must also include in income for a taxable year guaranteed payments under § 707(c) that are taken into account by the partnership under its method of accounting in the partnership's taxable year ending within or with the partner's taxable year. Moreover, for each taxable year in which a partnership has income, deductions, or credits, § 6031(a) and (b) requires the partnership to file a Form 1065, U.S. Return of Partnership Income, and to issue Schedules K-1 (Form 1065) to each partner.

Annual inclusion of income under § 706(a) can be incompatible with the needs of money market funds and certain other investors that invest in tax-exempt bonds. To assist tax-exempt bond partnerships to meet the needs of the market for tax-exempt bonds within the requirements of the Code, the Treasury Department and the Internal Revenue Service ("IRS") are issuing this revenue procedure to allow partners in tax-exempt bond partnerships to take into account on a monthly basis their distributive shares of partnership items ("monthly closing") if the partnership has made an effective monthly closing election with the consent of all partners ("monthly closing election"). A partnership may make a monthly closing election by including a binding provision to that effect in the partnership's governing documents. A partnership that has a monthly closing election in effect for the partnership's entire taxable year and that meets the other applicable requirements is not required to file a Form 1065, U.S. Return of Partnership Income, or to issue Schedules K-1 (Form 1065) to its partners for the taxable year.

In the past, to resolve the annual inclusion of income problem, many tax-exempt-bond partnerships attempted to make an election under § 761(a) to be excluded from the provisions of subchapter K. A tax-exempt-bond partnership is not eligible to elect to be wholly or partially excluded from subchapter K, however, and an attempted election has no effect. Two of the requirements for eligibility to make an election under § 761(a) are that the partners must own the partnership property as co-owners and the partners must be able to compute their income without the necessity of computing partnership taxable income. See § 1.761-2(a)(1) and (2) of the Income Tax Regulations. If a business entity (classified as a partnership) owns a tax-exempt bond and issues membership interests that apportion the benefits and burdens of that bond to its members in a manner that differs significantly from direct investment in the bond, the holders of those membership interests do not satisfy the requirement that they own the partnership property as co-owners. Cf. § 301.7701-4(c) of the Procedure and Administration Regulations. Moreover, if one class of partners has a right to partnership income that is superior to the right of another class of partners, then the net partnership income or loss allocated to the partners with inferior rights to partnership income can be determined only by computing the net income or loss of the partnership and then by reducing that net income by income allocable to partners with superior rights to partnership income. Such a partnership does not meet the requirement of § 1.761-2(a)(1) that the members of the organization be able to compute their incomes without the necessity of computing partnership income.

To assist tax-exempt-bond partnerships to meet the needs of the market for tax-exempt obligations within the requirements of the Internal Revenue Code, the IRS previously issued three revenue procedures on this topic of monthly closing elections. Rev. Proc. 2002-16, 2002-1 C.B. 572, was issued to allow money market fund partners in tax-exempt-bond partnerships to take into account on a monthly basis their distributive shares of partnership items (monthly closing) if the partnership made an effective election under that revenue procedure (monthly closing election). Rev. Proc. 2002-68, 2002-2 C.B. 753, modified and superseded Rev. Proc. 2002-16 to extend the monthly closing election to all partners in tax-exempt-bond partnerships and established certain transition rules. Rev. Proc. 2003-84 modified and superseded Rev. Proc. 2002-68 to provide certain simplified income tax reporting procedures in response to public comment. This revenue procedure modifies and supersedes Rev. Proc. 2003-84 to provide certain additional eligibility conditions and to promote greater administrative certainty.

This revenue procedure generally is intended to cover tax-exempt bond partnerships with certain common characteristics. These tax-exempt bond partnerships create variable-rate interests that have characteristics of investment grade, highly-liquid, short-term tax-exempt bonds. These features often are intended to make the variable-rate interests eligible for investment by money market funds under Rule 2a-7, 17 C.F.R. § 270.2a-7, under the Investment Company Act of 1940 ("Rule 2a-7"). The holders of the variable-rate interests generally invest a substantial majority of the capital in the partnership (for example, often 99 percent of such capital) and the holders of the inverse interests invest the balance of such capital.

In general, the variable-rate interest holders are substantially protected against risk of loss of their capital investment, plus accrued distributive shares in the partnership by short-term tender option rights (for example, seven-day demand purchase options) supported by a creditworthy liquidity provider. The liquidity provider may be an unrelated third party, an affiliate of the partnership's sponsor, or the inverse interest holder. If the liquidity provider purchases variable-rate interests under the liquidity facility, it typically has rights to reimbursement either from the inverse interest holder or from sales of partnership assets in its capacity as a partner. The variable-rate interest holders, however, typically are not fully protected against risk of loss of their capital investments because such tender options terminate if certain extraordinary events occur.

A tax-exempt bond partnership eligible for simplified reporting under this revenue procedure is a partnership whose primary purpose is to invest in a relatively fixed portfolio of investments in tax-exempt bonds, as contrasted with a partnership whose primary purpose is to engage in an active bond trading business which involves frequent trading in tax-exempt bond investments.

Tax-exempt bond partnerships have various unique features that provide broad benefits to the investing public. Tax-exempt bond partnerships efficiently respond to a need in the tax-exempt bond market to address an imbalance between the traditional preferences of State and local governments to issue long-term, fixed-rate tax-exempt bonds and the significant demands of institutional investors, particularly money market funds, to purchase high-quality, short-term, variable-rate tax-exempt bonds. Tax-exempt bond partnerships also expand the investor base in, and enhance liquidity and investor pricing to, the tax-exempt bond market.

SECTION 3. Summary of Changes.

This revenue procedure modifies and supersedes Rev. Proc. 2003-84. This section briefly summarizes the changes.

3.01 *Background.* Section 2 of this revenue procedure provides additional background regarding certain characteristics of partnerships intended to be covered by this revenue procedure.

3.02. *Additional Eligibility Conditions.* Sections 4.01(5), (6), and (7), respectively, of this revenue procedure provide additional conditions to eligibility for a partnership to make a monthly closing election under § 4.01 of this revenue procedure, including additional conditions with respect to tender option termination events, five percent minimum gain shares to the variable-interest holders, and an eighty percent weighted average bond maturity date by which variable-interest holders must have a right to realize any such gains.

3.03. *Effective Dates.* Section 9 of this revenue procedure provides effective date rules, including a general prospective effective date, a rule for certain existing partnerships which receive new capital, and certain grandfathering rules.

SECTION 4. Scope.

This revenue procedure applies to eligible partnerships under § 4.01 of this revenue procedure that make a monthly closing election under § 5 of this revenue procedure).

4.01 *Eligible Partnership.* An entity is an eligible partnership for a calendar month if all of the following conditions are met:

(1) *Test Dates for Income and Expense Test.* As of the election test date and as of every operational test date that occurs on or before the end of such calendar month, the partnership satisfies both the income test and the expense test. The test dates are described in § 4.05 of this revenue procedure, and the income test and the expense test are described in §§ 4.02 and 4.03 of this revenue procedure, respectively.

(2) *Partnership Entity.* The entity is a partnership for federal tax purposes.

(3) *Allocations.* All allocations of income, gain, loss, deduction, and credit of the partnership are made in accordance with § 704(b).

(4) *Partnership Agreement.* A written partnership agreement (or other governing document) provides that (a) the entity is making the

¶ 28,110

monthly closing election under this revenue procedure; and (b) all partners consent to the election.

(5) *Tender option termination events.* The tender option or put option rights provided to the variable-rate interest holders are subject to termination without notice upon the occurrence of one of the following events with respect to a tax-exempt bond held by the partnership: (i) a bankruptcy filing by or against a tax-exempt bond issuer; (ii) a downgrade in the credit rating of a tax-exempt bond and a downgrade in the credit rating of any guarantor of the tax-exempt bond, if applicable, to a rating or ratings, as applicable, below investment grade; (iii) a payment default on a tax-exempt bond; or (iv) a final judicial determination or a final IRS administrative determination of taxability of a tax-exempt bond for Federal income tax purposes under § 103.

(6) *Share in Appreciation.* Upon any sale or other disposition of any tax-exempt bond held by the partnership, the variable-rate interest holders shall have the right to receive a share of the gain from any such sale or other disposition in an amount equal to not less than five percent (5%) of such gain. The partnership shall pay each required gain share to the variable-rate interest holders by distributing the proceeds of the sale or other disposition within a reasonable period.

(7) *Gain Share Realization Event by 80 Percent of Remaining Weighted Average Maturity Date.* In order to provide variable-rate interest holders a reasonable opportunity to realize potential appreciation in the value of tax-exempt bonds held by a tax-exempt bond partnership, the partnership shall terminate or otherwise provide to such holders a right to require a sale, redemption, or other disposition of such tax-exempt bonds, with attendant gain share realization potential, by a date that is no later than the date that represents 80 percent of the remaining weighted average maturity of the tax-exempt bonds held by the partnership, measured from the date of the partnership's acquisition of the tax-exempt bonds, as determined generally in any reasonable manner that takes into account the parameters set forth in this § 4.01(7) (the "80 percent WAM test"). For this purpose, the weighted average maturity of applicable tax-exempt bonds generally shall be determined in a manner similar to the determination of the weighted average maturity of tax-exempt bonds under § 147(b), determined generally based on issue prices and mandatory sinking fund redemptions, with further adjustments to take into account optional redemptions at the first optional par redemption date and to take into account the partnership's date or dates of acquisition of the tax-exempt bonds. Further, any reasonable, consistently applied measure may be used to weight the bonds in lieu of issue price, if different than the partnership's acquisition price (for example, issue price, principal amount, cost, or fair market value). Further, for this purpose, a partnership may apply the 80 percent WAM test either separately on a "bond-by-bond" basis to each group of substantially identical tax-exempt bonds of the same maturity within the same "issue" (as defined in § 1.150-1(c)) held by the partnership, or collectively on a "portfolio" basis to all tax-exempt bonds held by the partnership.

4.02 *Income Test.* At least 95 percent of the partnership's gross income (computed without regard to items described in § 4.04 of this revenue procedure) is or is reasonably expected to be from the following eligible sources:

(1) *Tax-exempt Interest.* Interest on tax-exempt obligations as defined in § 1275(a)(3) and § 1.1275-1(e).

(2) *Exempt-interest Dividends.* "Exempt-interest dividends," as defined in § 852(b)(5), that are paid by a "regulated investment company" ("RIC"), as defined in § 851(a).

(3) *Gains from Eligible Source Income.* Gains from the sale, redemption, or other disposition of assets generating the income described in §§ 4.02(1) and (2) of this revenue procedure and income from the temporary investment (for a period no greater than 7 months) of the proceeds of such a disposition; but only if the assets that are sold, redeemed, or disposed are original assets of the partnership. For this purpose, an asset is an original asset of the partnership if the asset is contributed to the partnership or is acquired with capital contributed to the partnership (and not with the proceeds of the sale, redemption, or other disposition of a partnership asset).

4.03 *Expense Test.* Substantially all of the partnership's expenses and deductions (computed without regard to items described in § 4.04 of this revenue procedure) are properly allocable to the following eligible expense activities:

(1) *Expenses for Certain Income.* Producing, collecting, managing, protecting, and conserving the income described in §§ 4.02(1), (2), or (3) of this revenue procedure or the assets generating the income.

(2) *Expenses for Certain Property.* Acquiring, managing, conserving, maintaining, or disposing of property held for the production of the income described in §§ 4.02(1), (2), or (3) of this revenue procedure.

¶ 28,110

(3) *Expenses for Servicing.* Servicing the equity in the partnership.

4.04 *Exclusion.* For the purposes of §§ 4.02 and 4.03 of this revenue procedure, reasonable amounts charged to persons requesting information from the partnership under § 8.03 of this revenue procedure and the costs of collecting, managing, computing, and supplying the information are not taken into account.

4.05 *Test Dates and Test Periods.* The income test described in § 4.02 of this revenue procedure and the expense test described in § 4.03 of this revenue procedure must be satisfied both as of the first day of the first month for which the partnership's monthly closing election is effective (the "election test date") and, beginning with the fourth month after the partnership's monthly closing election becomes effective, on the last day of each month (the "operational test date"). The partnership determines whether the income test and the expense test are satisfied as of the election test date by reference to the election test period. The partnership determines whether the income test and expense test are satisfied as of each operational test date by reference to the operational test period. In applying the income and expense tests for a test period, a termination of the partnership under § 708(b)(1)(B) during that period is ignored.

(1) *The Election Test Period and Start-up Date.* This § 4.05(1) defines the terms "election test period" and "start-up date." The election test period differs depending upon how long the partnership has been in existence (determined from its start-up date). A partnership's "start-up date" ("start-up date") is the later of the date the entity had more than one owner and the date the entity had more than a de minimis amount of assets. If, on the election test date, the partnership has been in existence for at least six full calendar months, then the "election test period" is the longer of the six full calendar months preceding the election test date and the portion of the partnership's taxable year that precedes the election test date. If, on the election test date, the partnership has not been in existence for at least six full calendar months, then the "election test period" is the first six full calendar months of the partnership's existence.

(2) *The Operational Test Period.* The "operational test period" is the three-calendar-month period consisting of the calendar month within which the operational test date falls and the preceding two calendar months.

SECTION 5. Making a Monthly Closing Election.

5.01 *Manner of Making the Election.* An eligible partnership makes a monthly closing election by providing in the entity's governing documents that (a) the partnership is making a monthly closing election that is effective as provided under § 5.02 of this revenue procedure, and (b) all partners consent to the election.

5.02 *Effective Date of the Election.* The monthly closing election is effective on the later of: (a) the start-up date of the partnership (as defined in § 4.05(1) of this revenue procedure); or (b) the first day of the month in which the provision described in § 5.01 of this revenue procedure is first included in the entity's governing documents.

5.03 *Partnership Terminations under § 708(b)(1)(B).* A termination of the partnership under § 708(b)(1)(B) does not terminate the monthly closing election and does not cause the partnership to close its books under § 1.706-1(c) other than as described in § 6 of this revenue procedure.

SECTION 6. Monthly Closing of the Books.

If, at the end of any calendar month, an eligible partnership has a monthly closing election in effect, then, with respect to each partner, the partnership must close its books as described in § 1.706-1(c)(2) as if each partner had sold its entire interest in the partnership on the last day of that month. Each partner must include in its taxable income for that month both the partner's distributive share of items described in § 702(a) with respect to the partner that were earned by the partnership since either the last closing of the books or the first day of the partnership's taxable year (whichever is later) and any guaranteed payments under § 707(c) to the partner that are taken into account by the partnership since the last closing of the books. If a partner is on a 52-53 week taxable year, then the provisions of § 1.441-2(e) apply as if the last day of the month were the last day of the partnership's taxable year.

SECTION 7. Termination of Monthly Closing Election and Re-election after Termination.

7.01 *Termination of Monthly Closing Election.* A partnership's monthly closing election terminates as of the first day of the month during which a partnership first fails to be an eligible

¶ 28,110

partnership under § 4.01 of this revenue procedure.

7.02. *Consent of Commissioner for Another Election.* If the partnership's monthly closing election terminates, the partnership may not make another monthly closing election without the consent of the Commissioner.

7.03. *Revocation of Election with Commissioner's Consent.* A partnership's monthly closing election may be revoked only with the consent of the Commissioner.

SECTION 8. Reporting Requirements.

8.01. *Initial Filing Requirement.* A partnership must file an abbreviated Form 1065, U.S. Return of Partnership Income, for the first taxable year during which the monthly closing election was in effect. The abbreviated Form 1065 must be filed by the date that the partnership's income tax return for that taxable year would ordinarily be due and must be signed by a person with the authority to sign the partnership's Form 1065. The words "Filed in Accordance with Rev. Proc. 2009-[INSERT NUMBER OF THIS REVENUE PROCEDURE]" must be typed or printed across the top of the form. The partnership is required to provide only the following information on the abbreviated Form 1065:

(1) A statement that the partnership has made an election under this revenue procedure to which all present and future partners consent;

(2) Identification of the partnership by name, address, and EIN;

(3) The name, title, address, and phone number of the contact person from whom partners, beneficial owners, middlemen, and the IRS may request information about the partnership;

(4) The issue date of the partnership interests and the CUSIP (Committee on Uniform Securities Identification Procedures) number or other identification of each class of partnership interest;

(5) A statement that the entity's governing documents expressly provide that the entity is making a monthly closing election; and

(6) The effective month of the election and the start-up date of the partnership. See § 4.05(1) of this revenue procedure for a definition of the start-up date.

8.02 *Annual Filing Requirements.*

(1) *Elimination of Annual Filing Requirements.* A partnership is not required to file a Form 1065, U.S. Return of Partnership Income, or to issue Schedules K-1 (Form 1065) to its partners for any taxable year if the following requirements are satisfied:

(a) The partnership's monthly closing election is effective for the partnership's entire taxable year;

(b) The partnership makes the initial filing described in § 8.01 of this revenue procedure;

(c) A written partnership agreement (or other governing document) provides that (i) the entity and its partners will comply with the reporting requirements of §§ 8.02, 8.03, and 8.04 of this revenue procedure in lieu of complying with the requirements of § 6031(a) through (d); and (ii) all partners consent to such reporting; and

(d) The partnership complies with the requirements of §§ 8.03 and 8.04 of this revenue procedure.

(2) *Effect of Elimination of Annual Filing Requirement.* An entity that is not required to file a partnership return under this revenue procedure is not required to file a partnership return under § 6031(a) and, as a result, is not a partnership as defined under § 6231(a)(1). Consequently, the entity and its members will not be subject to the provisions of subchapter C of chapter 63. An abbreviated Form 1065 used to make the initial filing described in § 8.01 of this revenue procedure is not considered to be a partnership return for purposes of § 6233.

(3) *Monthly Closing Election Effective for Portion of Taxable Year.* A partnership that makes a monthly closing election that is effective after the first day of its taxable year must comply with the partnership reporting rules of § 6031(a) for that taxable year (but is still permitted to close its books on a monthly basis). If the partnership also makes the initial filing described in § 8.01 of this revenue procedure by the due date for its return for the first full taxable year during which the monthly closing election is in effect, then the partnership qualifies for elimination of annual filing requirements under § 8.01 of this revenue procedure for subsequent taxable years.

(4) *Annual Reporting Required.* Failure to qualify for the elimination of annual filing requirements under § 8.02(1) of this revenue procedure does not terminate the partnership's monthly closing election. However, a partnership that fails to satisfy all of the requirements of § 8.02(1) of this revenue procedure is required to file a complete (not abbreviated) Form 1065 and to issue Schedules K-1 (Form 1065) to its partners as required by § 6031(a). A partnership that fails to file a Form 1065 or to issue Schedules K-1 as required is subject to the applicable penalties

¶ 28,110

under §§ 6698 and 6722 for failure to file a partnership return and to furnish payee statements, as well as any other applicable penalties. Moreover, if a partnership is required to file a return under § 6031(a) but fails to do so, the period of limitations on assessment of tax attributable to items of that partnership remains open indefinitely under § 6229(a).

8.03. *Requests for Information.* Within 45 days of a request by the IRS or a partner (or a beneficial owner or a nominee of a beneficial owner), the partnership must make available all the information necessary to compute a partner's taxable income, tax-exempt income, gain, loss, deduction, or credit, including sufficient information for a partner to determine the portion of the tax-exempt interest that may be subject to the alternative minimum tax and information regarding each partner's share of any bond premium amortization under § 171, any market or original issue discount, and capital gain or loss.

8.04. *Nominee and Beneficial Ownership Reporting.*

(1) If an eligible electing partnership complies with the requirements of §§ 8.02 and 8.03 of this revenue procedure, the nominee reporting requirements of § 6031(c) and the regulations thereunder do not apply. In place of those requirements, the partnership and the partners must comply with this § 8.04. See § 1.6001-1(a) and (e) for rules that apply to recordkeeping requirements.

(2) Any person on whose behalf another person holds as a nominee an interest in an eligible partnership (a beneficial owner), other than a beneficial owner for which the relevant advisor or manager agrees to comply with § 8.04(3) of this revenue procedure, shall notify the partnership of its beneficial ownership status and provide the partnership with:

(a) its name, address, and taxpayer identification number and the name, address, and taxpayer identification number of its nominee; and

(b) the name of the partnership, its CUSIP number or other information sufficient to identify the partnership interest, and the amount of the partnership interest.

(3) In the case of a group of RICs that is managed or advised by a common, or affiliated, manager or advisor (the manager), the manager may elect to be responsible for collecting, retaining, and providing the IRS upon demand the beneficial ownership information. To make such an election, the manager must provide each eligible partnership in which any of the RICs has an equity interest a statement indicating that it is responsible for collecting, retaining, and providing the IRS upon demand the beneficial ownership information that otherwise would be required to be provided directly to the eligible partnerships by the beneficial owners. In addition, the manager must provide the partnership with:

(a) its name, address, and taxpayer identification number and contact information for the person from whom the IRS can request beneficial ownership information; and

(b) the name of the partnership, its CUSIP number or other information sufficient to identify the partnership interests, and the amount of the partnership interests.

SECTION 9. Effective Date.

9.01. *In General.* Except as otherwise expressly provided, this revenue procedure applies prospectively to any tax-exempt bond partnership with a "start-up date" under § 4.05(1) of this revenue procedure (that is, generally the later of the date the entity has more than one owner or more than a *de minimis* amount of assets) that occurs on or after [DATE THAT IS 30 DAYS AFTER THE DATE THAT THE FINAL VERSION OF THIS DOCUMENT IS RELEASED TO THE PUBLIC]. Further, except as otherwise expressly provided, this revenue procedure applies to any tax-exempt bond partnership without regard to its start-up date if new capital is originally contributed to the partnership on or after [DATE THAT IS 30 DAYS AFTER THE DATE THAT THE FINAL VERSION OF THIS DOCUMENT IS RELEASED TO THE PUBLIC] in an amount which has an aggregate fair market value that is greater than ten percent of the aggregate fair market value of the total assets owned by the partnership on the day before [DATE THAT IS 30 DAYS AFTER THE DATE THAT THE FINAL VERSION OF THIS DOCUMENT IS RELEASED TO THE PUBLIC]. For purposes of applying the 10 percent new capital test in the preceding sentence, deemed capital contributions to a reconstituted partnership as a result of a partnership termination under § 708(b)(1)(B) upon the sale or exchange of more than 50 percent of the total interests in a partnership's capital and profits within a 12-month period are disregarded. The IRS will not challenge any tax-exempt bond partnership's eligibility to use a monthly closing election on the grounds that such partnership failed to follow specific modifications made to Rev. Proc. 2003-84 by this revenue procedure with respect to additional eligibility conditions added in §§ 4.01(5), (6), or (7) of this revenue procedure (for example, the 5% minimum gain share condition) to the extent that such modifications are inapplicable to the partnership under the effective date provisions in this § 9.

9.02 *Grandfathering Rules.*

(1) *Rev. Proc. 2003-84 Grandfathering Rules.* The grandfathering rules in § 9.02 of Rev. Proc. 2003-84 continue to apply to matters covered by such grandfathering rules.

(2) *Partnerships under IRS Notice 2008-55.* In the case of a partnership that meets the requirements of § 3.8 of IRS Notice 2008-55, 2008-27 I.R.B. (July 7, 2008), regarding certain partnerships that hold certain auction rate preferred stock and that have certain prescribed liquidity facilities, this revenue procedure shall apply for purposes of § 3.8 of IRS Notice 2008-55 as the successor to Rev. Proc. 2003-84, and in applying this revenue procedure to a partnership under § 3.8 of IRS Notice 2008-55, the partnership eligibility conditions in § 4.01(5) and § 4.01(7) of this revenue procedure shall be inapplicable.

SECTION 10. Effect on Other Documents.

Rev. Proc. 2003-84 is modified and superseded.

SECTION 11. Paperwork Reduction Act.

The collection of information contained in this revenue procedure, carried forward without change from Rev. Proc. 2003-84, has been reviewed and approved by the Office of Management and Budget in accordance with the Paperwork Reduction Act (44 U.S.C. 3507) under control number 1545-1768. An agency may not conduct or sponsor, and a person is not required to respond to, a collection of information unless the collection of information displays a valid OMB control number. The collection of information is in section 8 of this revenue procedure. The collection of information is required to obtain a benefit, and is required to inform the Service which partnerships are making the monthly closing election. The likely respondents are businesses. The estimated total annual reporting and recordkeeping burden is 500 hours. The estimated annual burden per respondent/record keeper is 1/2 hour. The estimated number of respondents and record keepers is 1,000. The estimated annual frequency of responses (used for reporting requirements only) is once. Books or records relating to a collection of information must be retained as long as their contents may become material in the administration of any internal revenue law. Generally tax returns and tax return information are confidential, as required by 26 U.S.C. 6103.

SECTION 12. No Inferences on Law.

This revenue procedure provides administrative relief to address a special need in the tax-exempt bond market in furtherance of public policy. No inferences should be drawn from this revenue procedure regarding any general principle of substantive law with respect to partner status or the debt or equity character of any security.

¶ 28,115 Notice 2008-88, I.R.B. 2008-42, 933

SECTION 1. Purpose

This Notice amends and supplements Notice 2008-41, 2008-15 I.R.B. 742 (April 14, 2008), regarding reissuance standards for tax-exempt bonds. (Defined terms in Notice 2008-41 shall have the same meanings when used in this Notice.) This Notice expands the circumstances and time periods during which the Treasury Department and the Internal Revenue Service ("IRS") will treat a tax-exempt bond that is purchased by its state or local governmental issuer as continuing in effect without resulting in a reissuance or retirement of the purchased tax-exempt bond solely for purposes of § 103 and §§ 141 through 150 of the Internal Revenue Code, as amended ("Code"). (Except as noted, section references in this Notice are to the Code and the Income Tax Regulations.) This Notice is intended to provide flexibility to assist state and local governments in efforts to facilitate liquidity and stability in the short-term sector of the tax-exempt bond market.

SECTION 2. Background

In response to auction failures and liquidity constraints in the auction rate bond sector of the tax-exempt bond market, § 4 of Notice 2008-41 provides a special temporary rule which allows governmental issuers to purchase their own tax-exempt auction rate bonds on a temporary basis without resulting in a reissuance or retirement of the purchased tax-exempt bonds solely for purposes of § 103 and §§ 141 to 150. To be eligible for that special rule, a governmental issuer must purchase the tax-exempt auction rate bonds before October 1, 2008, and hold those bonds for not more than a 180-day period from the date of purchase.

Recently, circumstances affecting liquidity and stability in the credit markets have extended beyond the auction rate bond sector to affect other sectors of the short-term tax-exempt bond market, including other "qualified tender bonds" (as defined in § 3.2 of Notice 2008-41) (e.g., variable rate demand bonds with seven-day put options) and tax-exempt commercial paper. In the case of commercial paper, a special rule under § 1.150-1(c)(4)(ii) allows certain short-term tax-exempt bonds issued pursuant to the same commercial paper program to be treated as part of the same issue. For purposes of this Notice, references to "tax-exempt commercial paper" means tax-exempt bonds issued pursuant to the same commercial paper program that are treated as a single issue under this special rule in § 1.150-1(c)(4)(ii).

This Notice expands the circumstances and time periods during which governmental issuers may purchase their own tax-exempt bonds to include the purchase and holding of all qualified tender bonds and tax-exempt commercial paper through the end of 2009. This Notice also extends certain other time deadlines for special rules in Notice 2008-41.

SECTION 3. Scope and Application

3.1 *Expanded Temporary Rule Allowing Governmental Issuers to Purchase Their Own Tax-Exempt Bonds.* Solely for purposes of § 103 and §§ 141 through 150, the Treasury Department and the IRS will treat a tax-exempt "qualified tender bond" (as defined in Notice 2008-41) or "tax-exempt commercial paper" (as defined in § 2 of this Notice) that is purchased by its "governmental issuer" (as defined in Notice 2008-41) on a temporary basis as continuing in effect without resulting in a reissuance or retirement of the purchased tax-exempt bond if, irrespective of when the governmental issuer purchases the bond (including a purchase of a bond before October 1, 2008), the governmental issuer holds the bond until not later than December 31, 2009. Subsequent to the end of this period, a governmental issuer generally may not hold its own bond without causing a reissuance or retirement of such bond under the general rules in § 3.1 of Notice 2008-41 and other applicable law.

Thus, recognizing that the purchased bond is treated as continuing in effect without resulting in a reissuance or retirement of that bond solely for purposes of § 103 and §§ 141 through 150 during the permitted holding period until not later than December 31, 2009 ("permitted holding period"), the governmental issuer may refund the purchased bond with a refunding bond, tender the purchased bond for purchase in a qualified tender right in its capacity as a bondholder, or otherwise resell the purchased bond during this permitted holding period. Further, in the case of the purchase of any particular obligation of tax-exempt commercial paper, including a purchase of such a particular obligation at maturity, a refinancing of that purchased tax-exempt commercial paper during the permitted holding period will be treated as part of the same issue as the issue of which the purchased tax-exempt commercial paper was a part. After the end of this permitted holding period, however, a governmental issuer generally may not hold its own bond without causing a reissuance or retirement of such bond under the general rules in Notice 2008-41 and other applicable law.

3.2 *Extension of Certain Other Time Limits for Special Rules in Notice 2008-41.* Section 3.2(3)(b) of Notice 2008-41 regarding operating rules for qualified tender rights is amended to extend the final date for purchase of bonds pursuant to qualified tender rights for which the special 180-day holding period applies (in lieu of the general 90-day holding period rule for this purpose) from October 1, 2008 to December 31, 2009. Section 6.2 of Notice 2008-41 regarding the treatment of certain waivers of interest rate caps on tax-exempt auction rate bonds is amended to extend the final date on which covered waivers of interest rate caps are disregarded from October 1, 2008 to December 31, 2009.

3.3 *No Inferences on Law.* This Notice provides administrative relief in furtherance of public policy to promote liquidity and stability in the short-term tax-exempt bond market. Except with respect to the administrative relief expressly provided in this Notice, no inference should be drawn from this Notice regarding any other Federal tax issues affecting tax-exempt bonds or any other security. In addition, this Notice is not intended to address any other Federal tax issue implicated in the transactions described in this Notice allowing governmental issuers to purchase their own tax-exempt bonds on a temporary basis in prescribed circumstances.

SECTION 4. Effect on other Documents

This Notice amends and supplements Notice 2008-41.

SECTION 5. Effective Date

This Notice is effective as of March 25, 2008, which is the effective date of Notice 2008-41. Issuers of tax-exempt bonds may apply and rely on this Notice to the same extent and in the same manner as provided in § 8 of Notice 2008-41.

SECTION 6. Drafting Information

The principal author of this Notice is Timothy L. Jones, of the Office of Associate Chief Counsel (Financial Institutions and Products). However, other personnel from the IRS and the Treasury

Department participated in its development. For further information regarding this Notice, contact Mr. Jones at (202) 622-3980 (not a toll-free call).

FINANCIAL INSTITUTIONS

¶28,120 Notice 2008-101, I.R.B. 2008-44, 1082

The purpose of this notice is to provide clarification on the treatment under section 597 of the Internal Revenue Code (Code) of amounts furnished to a financial institution pursuant to the Troubled Asset Relief Program (TARP) of the Emergency Economic Stabilization Act of 2008, Div. A of Pub. Law No. 110-343 (EESA), which was enacted on October 3, 2008.

Unless and until guidance is issued by the Department of the Treasury and the Internal Revenue Service to the contrary, no amount furnished by the Department of the Treasury to a financial institution pursuant to the TARP established by the Secretary under EESA will be treated as the provision of Federal financial assistance within the meaning of section 597 of the Code and the regulations thereunder. Any future contrary guidance will not apply to transactions with the Department of the Treasury, or to securities issued by financial institutions to the Department of the Treasury, prior to the publication of that guidance, or pursuant to written binding contracts entered into prior to that date.

Except with respect to the treatment of amounts furnished pursuant to TARP as expressly described in this notice, no inference should be drawn from this notice regarding the treatment under section 597 of the Code or the regulations thereunder of any other program or payments.

SECURITIES

¶28,125 Rev. Proc. 2008-58, I.R.B. 2008-41, 856

SECTION 1. PURPOSE

This revenue procedure provides guidance regarding the treatment of taxpayers receiving certain offers relating to auction rate securities.

SECTION 2. BACKGROUND

.01 In general, an auction rate security is a security in which the payment rate is reset periodically (typically every seven to 28 days), pursuant to an auction rate-setting process or a similar remarketing agent rate-setting process that is designed to produce the minimum payment rate necessary to enable all interested sellers to sell the security to willing buyers at a price equal to the par amount of the security, plus accrued but unpaid periodic payments. A "failed" auction or remarketing occurs if the auction or remarketing fails to produce buyers for all interested sellers at a payment rate that is at or below the maximum payment rate specified by the terms of the auction rate security. Upon a failed auction or remarketing, the periodic payment rate is reset at a prescribed maximum rate until the next auction or remarketing. In addition, in the case of some issues of auction rate securities, the periodic payment rate may escalate further to prescribed increasing maximum rates based on the continued occurrence of failed auctions or remarketings for increasing periods of time. *See, e.g.,* Notice 2008-55, 2008-27 I.R.B. 11.

.02 On February 12, 2008, auctions with respect to auction rate securities began to fail. Thereafter, as a result of auction failures, many taxpayers were unable to sell auction rate securities for the par amount of the securities.

.03 Taxpayers may assert legal claims against another person (hereinafter, "Corporation X") for its conduct as it relates to auction rate securities. For example, a taxpayer might allege that Corporation X improperly failed to disclose (1) at the time of the taxpayer's purchase, the potential that the auction rate security could become illiquid, or (2) subsequent to the taxpayer's purchase, information relating to the market for auction rate securities which might have suggested it would soon become illiquid.

.04 Corporation X may make an offer (the "Settlement Offer") to affected taxpayers. Pursuant to the terms of the Settlement Offer, the taxpayer will have the right during a specified period (the "Window Period") to cause Corporation X to buy the taxpayer's auction rate securi-

¶28,120

ties for the par amount of the securities, upon the taxpayer's giving notice to Corporation X. If the taxpayer receives the Settlement Offer, subject to the possible existence (and exercise) of the mitigation provision described in section 2.06 of this revenue procedure, so long as auctions continue to fail (and the taxpayer does not direct Corporation X to purchase the security), the taxpayer will continue to receive the maximum payment rate specified by the terms of the auction rate security.

.05 In the event the auction rate-setting process begins to succeed during the Window Period, so long as the taxpayer does not direct Corporation X to purchase the security (and the taxpayer does not sell in the auction), the taxpayer's return will fluctuate with that process, such that as the reset rates go up or down, this variation directly affects the taxpayer's economic return. If the taxpayer continues to hold the security after the Window Period, the taxpayer's entitlements are determined exclusively under the provisions of the auction rate security (e.g., if rates go up or down, or the security becomes worthless, the taxpayer experiences the full economic impact). During the Window Period (and thereafter, if Corporation X does not purchase the security during the Window Period), the taxpayer is entitled to (1) exercise all voting rights associated with the security, and (2) sell the security to a third party. By its terms, the auction rate security is not redeemable on a fixed date (or, if it is, the redemption date is at least two years later than the end of the Window Period).

.06 The Settlement Offer may also contain a provision which has the effect of allowing Corporation X to mitigate its potential economic losses during the Window Period. If the taxpayer accepts a Settlement Offer with such a provision, Corporation X will be authorized to effect sales or dispositions of the security to the market during the Window Period (so long as the taxpayer receives the par amount of the security upon the sale or disposition). Thus, for example, if, during the Window Period, Corporation X finds a person willing to purchase an auction rate security with a par amount of $100x for $99x, Corporation X can purchase the security from the taxpayer for $100x, sell the security for $99x, and limit its economic loss to $1x (rather than risk a larger, or smaller, loss). If Corporation X buys the security under this provision, it will not hold the security for investment purposes.

.07 The Settlement Offer may also permit the taxpayer to elect to "borrow" (in form) the par amount of the auction rate security from Corporation X before the Window Period begins (or during the Window Period). In this case, the taxpayer's obligation to return the cash amount advanced by Corporation X in the form of a "loan" is secured (in form) by the auction rate security. Taxpayers who accept the Settlement Offer are not required to make this election or otherwise participate in this feature of the Settlement Offer.

SECTION 3. SCOPE

This revenue procedure applies to taxpayers who, before June 30, 2009, receive Settlement Offers generally described in section 2 of this revenue procedure that (1) include Window Periods that do not extend beyond December 31, 2012, and (2) require that the taxpayer deliver an auction rate security that the taxpayer purchased on or before February 13, 2008.

SECTION 4. APPLICATION

For taxpayers within the scope of this revenue procedure, the Internal Revenue Service will not challenge the following positions:

.01 The position that the taxpayer continues to own the auction rate security upon receiving or accepting (or "opting into") the Settlement Offer (but not after tendering the security).

.02 The position that the taxpayer does not realize any income as a result of receiving or accepting (or "opting into") the Settlement Offer and does not reduce the basis of the auction rate security from its original purchase price.

.03 The position that the taxpayer's amount realized from the sale of the auction rate security during the Window Period to the person offering the settlement (Corporation X in this revenue procedure) is the full amount of the cash proceeds received from that person.

SECTION 5. NO INFERENCE

This revenue procedure provides administrative guidance in light of the significant number of taxpayers affected by auction failures and the potential litigation resulting therefrom. Except with respect to the administrative guidance expressly provided in this revenue procedure, no inferences should be drawn from this revenue procedure in any other context regarding the ownership of any other security (or the effect of a loan secured by such security), the application of the replacement or restoration of capital doctrine, or any other federal tax issues.

SECTION 6. CONTACT INFORMATION

For further information regarding this revenue procedure, contact William E. Blanchard of the Office of Associate Chief Counsel (Financial Institutions and Products) at (202) 622-3950 or Andrew J. Keyso of the Office of Associate Chief Counsel (Income Tax and Accounting) at (202) 622-4800.

¶ 28,130   Rev. Proc. 2008-63, I.R.B. 2008-42, 946

SECTION 1. PURPOSE

This revenue procedure provides guidance with respect to the application of § 1058(a) of the Internal Revenue Code to situations in which securities are originally transferred pursuant to an agreement that meets the requirements of § 1058(b), the transferee subsequently defaults under the agreement as a direct or indirect result of its bankruptcy (or the bankruptcy of an affiliate), and as soon as is commercially practicable (but in no event more than 30 days following the default), the transferor uses collateral provided pursuant to the agreement to purchase identical securities.

SECTION 2. BACKGROUND

.01 Section 1058(a) provides that in the case of a taxpayer who transfers securities (as defined in § 1236(c)) pursuant to an agreement which meets the requirements of § 1058(b), no gain or loss shall be recognized on the exchange of such securities by the taxpayer for an obligation under such agreement, or on the exchange of rights under such agreement by that taxpayer for securities identical to the securities transferred by that taxpayer.

.02 In adding § 1058 to the Code, Congress intended to provide nonrecognition treatment to securities loans in which "the contractual obligation [to return identical securities] does not differ materially either in kind or in extent from the securities exchanged. . . ." S. Rep. No. 762, 95\th/ Cong., 2d Sess. 7 (1978); 1978-2 C.B. 357, 361 ("Senate Report"). Congress also sought to encourage securities holders to make their securities available for loans. Congress explained:

> Under present law, uncertainty has developed as to the correct income tax treatment of certain securities lending transactions. As a result, some owners of securities are reluctant to enter into such transactions.

Senate Report at 3; 1978-2 C.B. 359.

Because of time delays which a broker may face in obtaining securities (from the seller or transfer agent) to deliver to a purchaser, brokers are frequently required to borrow securities from organizations and individuals with investment portfolios for use in completing these market transactions. It is generally thought to be desirable to encourage organizations and individuals with securities holdings to make the securities available for such loans since the greater the volume of securities available for loan the less frequently will brokers fail to deliver a security to a purchaser within the time required by the relevant market rules.

Senate Report at 5; 1978-2 C.B 360.

.03 Recently, a significant number of securities loans have terminated as a result of a default by the borrower of the securities. These defaults are often the direct or indirect result of the bankruptcy of the borrower (or an affiliate of the borrower). For example, the bankruptcy of the borrower might, by itself, constitute an event of default under the securities loan agreement. Likewise, the bankruptcy of an affiliate of the borrower might indirectly prevent the borrower from returning identical securities upon notice of termination by the lender, if, for example, such a bankruptcy affects the borrower's liquidity and practical ability to acquire identical securities in the secondary market. In many of these situations, the lender thereafter purchases identical securities and applies collateral provided by the borrower pursuant to the securities loan agreement against the purchase price (and the borrower's obligation to return identical securities is terminated).

SECTION 3. SCOPE

This revenue procedure applies to taxpayers ("Lenders") who have transferred securities to an unrelated person ("Borrower") in a securities loan in which—

.01 The securities loan agreement ("Agreement") satisfies the requirements of § 1058(b);

.02 The Agreement requires that the Borrower transfer collateral to secure the Borrower's obligations under the Agreement;

.03 The Borrower defaults under the Agreement as a direct or indirect result of its bankruptcy (or the bankruptcy of an affiliate); and

.04 As soon as is commercially practicable after the default (but in no event more than 30 days following the default), the Lender applies collateral provided under the Agreement (or cash generated by the sale of such collateral) to the purchase of identical securities.

SECTION 4. APPLICATION

For taxpayers within the scope of this revenue procedure, the Internal Revenue Service will treat the purchase described in section 3.04 of this revenue procedure as an exchange of rights under the Agreement for identical securities to which § 1058(a) applies.

SECTION 5. EFFECTIVE DATE

This revenue procedure is effective for taxable years ending on or after January 1, 2008.

SECTION 6. NO INFERENCE

This revenue procedure provides guidance with respect to certain federal income tax issues involving securities loans described in section 3 of this revenue procedure. No inference should be drawn about whether similar consequences will obtain if a securities loan falls outside the scope of this revenue procedure.

SECTION 7. DRAFTING INFORMATION

The principal author of this revenue procedure is Charles W. Culmer of the Office of Associate Chief Counsel (Financial Institutions & Products). For further information regarding this revenue procedure contact Mr. Culmer on (202) 622-3950 (not a toll-free call).

MONEY MARKET FUNDS

¶ 28,135   Notice 2008-81, I.R.B. 2008-41, 852

SECTION 1. Purpose

This Notice relates to a program being provided by the United States Department of the Treasury (the "Treasury Department") in response to the credit market instability to make available certain funds from its Exchange Stabilization Fund on a temporary basis upon prescribed terms and conditions (as described further below, the "Program"), to money market funds that are regulated under the Security and Exchange Commission's Rule 2a-7, 17 C.F.R. 270.2a-7, under the Investment Company Act of 1940 ("Rule 2a-7") to enable money market funds to maintain stable $1.00 per share net asset values. The Program is available to both money market funds holding assets subject to Federal income taxation and to money market funds holding assets that include State and local governmental debt obligations the interest on which is excludable from gross income ("tax-exempt bonds") under § 103 of the Internal Revenue Code, as amended (the "Code"). (Except as noted, section references herein are to the Code.) Money market funds that hold a sufficient portion of their total assets in tax-exempt bonds to be eligible to pay exempt interest dividends under § 852(b)(5) are referred to herein as "tax-exempt money market funds." This Notice provides guidance to the effect that the Program will not result in any violation of the restrictions against federal guarantees of tax-exempt bonds with respect to the tax-exempt bond assets of tax-exempt money market funds which would impair the tax-exempt status of dividends received by their shareholders.

SECTION 2. Background

2.1. *The Program.* In general, under the Program, the Treasury Department plans to make available its Exchange Stabilization Fund on a temporary basis to assist participating money market funds in maintaining $1.00 per share net asset values and in paying their shareholders $1.00 per share upon liquidation of shares. The Program will be limited to assets in money market funds as of the close of business on September 19, 2008, and to investors of record as of that date. Participating money market funds are required to make premium payments to participate in the Program. Payments to a money market fund under the Program are tied to the per share net asset value of the money market fund itself. Payments to a money market fund under the Program are not tied to the terms or performance of any particular assets held by the money market fund, such as tax-exempt bond assets held by a tax-exempt money market fund. The general description of certain aspects of the Program herein is subject fully to the specific terms, conditions, maximum size limitations, and other limitations to be set forth in the operative legal documents for the Program.

2.2. *The Restrictions Against Federal Guarantees of Tax-exempt Bonds.* Section 149(b) provides generally that, subject to certain specific exceptions, the interest on State or local governmental bonds is not excludable from gross income under § 103(a) if the bonds are federally guaranteed. Section 149(b)(2) provides generally that a bond is federally guaranteed if: (A) the payment of principal or interest with respect to such bond is guaranteed (in whole or in part) by the United States (or any agency or instrumentality thereof)); (B) such bond is issued as part of an issue and five (5) percent or more of the proceeds of such issue is to be (i) used in making loans the payment of principal or interest with respect to which are to be guaranteed (in whole or in part) by the United States (or any agency or instrumentality thereof), or (ii) invested (directly or indirectly) in federally insured deposits or accounts; or (C) the payment of principal or interest on such bond is otherwise indirectly guaranteed (in whole or in part) by the United States (or any agency or instrumentality thereof).

SECTION 3. Scope and Application

3.1 *No Violation of Restrictions Against Federal Guarantees of Tax-exempt Bonds.* The Treasury Department and the Internal Revenue Service ("IRS") will not assert that the Program causes any violation of the restrictions against Federal guarantees of tax-exempt bonds under § 149(b) with respect to any tax-exempt bond assets held by tax-exempt money market funds participating in the Program. In addition, the Treasury Department and the IRS will not assert that the Program impairs the ability either of a money market fund participating in the Program to designate exempt interest dividends under § 852(b)(5) or of the shareholders of such a fund to claim the benefits of tax exemption with respect to such exempt interest dividends under § 852(b)(5)(B).

3.2 *No Inferences on Law.* This Notice provides administrative relief in furtherance of public policy to promote stability in the market for money market funds. Except with respect to the administrative relief expressly provided in this Notice, no inference should be drawn from this Notice regarding any other Federal tax issues affecting tax-exempt bonds, money market funds, or any other security. In addition, this Notice is not intended to address any other Federal tax issue implicated in the described transactions under the Program.

SECTION 4. Effective Date

This Notice is effective on September 22, 2008.

¶ 28,140 Notice 2008-92, I.R.B. 2008-43, 1001

SECTION 1. PURPOSE

This Notice relates to the Temporary Guarantee Program for Money Market Funds (the "Program"), which is provided by the Treasury Department in response to the credit market instability to make available certain funds from its Exchange Stabilization Fund, upon prescribed terms and conditions, to money market funds that are regulated under the Security and Exchange Commission's Rule 2a-7, 17 C.F.R. 270.2a-7, under the Investment Company Act of 1940 ("Rule 2a-7"). Some practitioners have expressed concern that participation in the Program may raise certain potential tax issues for money market funds whose beneficial interests are held exclusively by one or more segregated asset accounts of one or more insurance companies (or other investors permitted under § 1.817-5(f)(3) of the Income Tax Regulations) ("Insurance-Dedicated Money Market Funds"). This Notice provides certainty with respect to those issues, as described below.

SECTION 2. BACKGROUND

.01 *The Program.* In general, under the Program, the Treasury Department is making available its Exchange Stabilization Fund on a temporary basis to assist participating money market funds in repaying shareholders upon liquidation of their shares. The Program is limited to assets in money market funds as of the close of business on September 19, 2008, and to investors of record as of that date. The Program is available to both Insurance-Dedicated Money Market Funds and money market funds that are available to the general public. Participating money market funds are required to make premium payments to participate in the Program. Payments to a money market fund under the Program are tied to the per share net asset value of the money market fund itself. Payments to a money market fund under the Program are not tied to the terms or performance of any particular assets held by the money market fund. The general description of certain aspects of the Program herein is subject fully to the specific terms, conditions, maximum size limitations, and other limitations set forth in the operative legal documents for the Program.

.02 *Diversification requirement for variable contracts.* Section 817(h) of the Internal Revenue Code provides that a variable life insurance or annuity contract that is based on a segregated asset account is not treated as a life insurance or annuity contract for any period (and any subsequent period) for which the investments of the account are not adequately diversified. For purposes of determining whether a segregated asset account is adequately diversified, each United States government agency or instrumentality is treated as a separate issuer. In addition, to the extent that a segregated asset account with respect to a variable life insurance contract invests in securities issued by the United States Treasury, the investments made by the account are treated as adequately diversified. The rule in the previous sentence does not apply with respect to a variable annuity contract. Section 1.817-5(h)(1) defines "government security" to mean any security that is issued, guaranteed or insured by the United States or any instrumentality.

.03 *Investor control.* The holder of a variable contract may be treated as an owner of the assets of a segregated asset account funding that contract if (1) the holder exercises sufficient control over the assets to be deemed the owner; or (2) the assets are not available exclusively through the purchase of a life insurance or annuity contract. *See* Rev. Rul. 2003-92, 2003-2 C.B. 350; Rev. Rul. 2003-91, 2003-2 C.B. 347; Rev. Rul. 81-225, 1981-2 C.B. 13; Rev. Rul. 80-274, 1980-2 C.B. 27; Rev. Rul. 77-85, 1977-1 C.B. 12.

SECTION 3. SCOPE AND APPLICATION

.01 *No Violation of Diversification Requirements; No Assertion of Investor Control.* The Treasury Department and the Internal Revenue Service ("IRS") will not assert that participation in the Program by an Insurance-Dedicated Money Market Fund causes a violation of the diversification requirements of § 817(h) in the case of a segregated asset account that invests in the Insurance-Dedicated Money Market Fund. In addition, the Treasury Department and the IRS will not assert that such a fund's participation in the Program causes the holder of a variable contract supported by a segregated asset account that invests in the fund to be treated as an owner of the fund.

.02 *No Inferences on Law.* This Notice provides administrative relief in furtherance of public policy to promote stability in the market for money market funds. Except with respect to the administrative relief expressly provided in this Notice, no inference should be drawn from this Notice regarding any other Federal tax issues affecting variable contracts, money market funds, or any other security. In addition, this Notice is not intended to address any other Federal tax issue implicated in the described transactions under the Program.

DRAFTING INFORMATION

The principal author of this notice is Sheryl B. Flum of the Office of Associate Chief Counsel (Financial Institutions & Products). For further information regarding this notice, contact Ms. Flum at (202) 622-3970 (not a toll-free call).

QUALIFIED TUITION PROGRAMS

¶28,145 Notice 2009-1, I.R.B. 2009-2, 250

This notice provides guidance to qualified tuition programs described in section 529 of the Internal Revenue Code and participants in section 529 programs regarding the restriction on investment direction described in section 529(b)(4). This notice sets forth a special rule under which a program may permit investments in a section 529 account to be changed during 2009 on a more frequent basis than under current rules.

Section 529(b)(4) states that a program shall not be treated as a section 529 qualified tuition program unless it provides that any contributor to, or designated beneficiary under, such program may not directly or indirectly direct the investment of any contributions to the program (or any earnings thereon). The proposed regulations under section 529, which were published in the Federal Register on August 24, 1998 (63 F.R. 45019), provide that a program does not violate this requirement if it permits a person who establishes a section 529 account to select among different investment strategies designed exclusively by the program, only at the time when the initial contribution is made establishing the account. Prop. Treas. Reg. § 1.529-2(g).

Notice 2001-55, 2001-2 CB 299, was issued in response to comments on those proposed regulations, and acknowledged that there are a number of situations that might warrant a change in the investment strategy for a section 529 account. In that Notice, the Treasury Department and the Internal Revenue Service (IRS) expressed an expectation that the final regulations under section 529 will provide that a program does not violate the investment restriction under section 529(b)(4) if it permits a change in the investment strategy selected for a section 529 account once per calendar year, and upon a change in the designated beneficiary of the account. The Notice conditioned the applicability of this special rule on the program's compliance with a requirement that the program must (1) allow participants to select only from among broad-based investment strategies designed exclusively by the program, and (2) establish procedures and maintain appropriate records to prevent a change in investment options from occurring more frequently than once per calendar year or upon a change in the designated beneficiary of the account.

In response to concerns that have been caused by the recent condition of the financial markets, commentators have requested more flexibility in this special rule, specifically the ability to change the investment strategies more frequently. Those commentators expressed concern that the inability to do so may interfere with the preservation of the value of a section 529 account in the face of changes in the markets.

Accordingly, this notice amends the provisions of Notice 2001-55 to further provide that a program does not violate the investment restriction under section 529(b)(4) if it permits a change in the investment strategy selected for a section 529 account twice per calendar year for calendar year 2009, as well as upon a change in the designated beneficiary of the account, subject to the program requirements as detailed in Notice 2001-55. The Treasury Department and the IRS expect that final regulations will incorporate this special rule for 2009.

Section 529 programs and their participants may rely on this notice pending the issuance of final regulations under section 529.

The Treasury Department and the IRS invite comments on the matter described in this notice and any other comments relating to section 529. Comments may be submitted to Internal Revenue Service, CC:PA:LPD:PR (Notice 2009-1), Room 5203, PO Box 7604, Ben Franklin Station, Washington, DC 20044. Submissions may also be hand-delivered Monday through Friday between the hours of 8 a.m. and 4 p.m. to the Courier's Desk at 1111 Constitution Avenue, NW, Washington, DC 20224, Attn:CC:PA:LPD:PR (Notice 2009-1), Room 5203. Submissions may also be sent electronically via the internet to the following email address: Notice.comments@irscounsel.treas.gov. Include the notice number (Notice 2009-1) in the subject line.

EFFECT ON OTHER DOCUMENTS

Notice 2001-55 is modified.

DRAFTING INFORMATION:

The principal author of this notice is Monice Rosenbaum of the Office of Division Counsel/Associate Chief Counsel (Tax Exempt and Government Entities). For further information regarding this notice, contact Ms. Rosenbaum at (202) 622-6070 (not a toll-free number).

REMICs

¶28,150 Rev. Proc. 2008-47, I.R.B. 2008-31, 272

SECTION 1. PURPOSE

This revenue procedure describes the conditions under which modifications to certain subprime mortgage loans will not cause the Internal Revenue Service (Service) to challenge the tax status of certain securitization vehicles that hold the loans or to assert that those modifications create a liability for tax on a prohibited transaction.

The purpose of this revenue procedure is to provide certainty in the current economic environment with respect to certain potential tax issues that may be implicated by fast track loan modifications, as described below. No inference should be drawn about whether similar consequences would obtain if a transaction falls outside the limited scope of this revenue procedure. Furthermore, there should be no inference that, in the absence of this revenue procedure, transactions within its scope would have impaired the tax status of securitization vehicles or would have created liability for tax on a prohibited transaction.

Rev. Proc. 2007-72, 2007-52 I.R.B. 1257, provided similar guidance regarding fast-track loan modifications that were effected in a manner consistent with certain principles, recommendations, and guidelines (the "Original Framework"), which the American Securitization Forum ("ASF") released on December 6, 2007. In July 2008, the ASF released an updated Framework, which covers additional fast-track loan modifications.

This revenue procedure amplifies and supersedes Rev. Proc. 2007-72 by extending its provisions to these additional loan modifications.

¶28,150

SECTION 2. BACKGROUND—THE ASF "JULY 2008 FRAMEWORK"

.01 On July 8, 2008, the American Securitization Forum ("ASF") released a document entitled, "Statement of Principles, Recommendations and Guidelines for a Streamlined Foreclosure and Loss Avoidance Framework for Securitized Subprime Adjustable Rate Mortgage Loans" (the "July 2008 Framework"). An Executive Summary of the July 2008 Framework (entitled "Streamlined Foreclosure and Loss Avoidance Framework for Securitized Subprime Adjustable Rate Mortgage Loans") was released simultaneously and is attached as an Appendix to this revenue procedure.

.02 Both the Original Framework and the July 2008 Framework have been broadly supported as appropriate steps in addressing certain risks in the current economic environment.

.03 The July 2008 Framework applies to first-lien subprime residential adjustable rate mortgage (ARM) loans that—

(1) Have an initial fixed rate period of 36 months or less (including "2/28s" and "3/27s");

(2) Were originated between January 1, 2005, and July 31, 2007;

(3) Are included in securitized pools; and

(4) Have an initial interest rate reset date between January 1, 2008, and July 31, 2010.

This revenue procedure refers to these instruments as "Loans."

.04 The July 2008 Framework provides a "fast track" procedure for modifying Loans in advance of an initial, or any subsequent, interest rate reset date and details the criteria for determining which Loans are eligible for the procedure. Modifications pursuant to the procedure are referred to as "fast track modifications."

.05 A fast track modification affects the interest rate on the Loan, generally for five years following the date on which the rate would have reset in the absence of the modification. During the period affected by the modification, the interest rate on the modified Loan is generally fixed at the rate in effect prior to the upcoming reset date.

SECTION 3. BACKGROUND—REMICS

.01 Real Estate Mortgage Investment Conduits (REMICs) are widely used securitization vehicles for mortgages. REMICs are governed by sections 860A through 860G of the Internal Revenue Code.

.02 For an organization to qualify as a REMIC, all of the interests in the organization must consist of one or more classes of regular interests and a single class of residual interests, *see* section 860D(a), and those interests must be issued on the startup day, within the meaning of § 1.860G-2(k) of the Income Tax Regulations.

.03 A regular interest is one that is designated as a regular interest and whose terms are fixed on the startup day. Section 860G(a)(1). In addition, a regular interest must (1) unconditionally entitle the holder to receive a specified principal amount (or other similar amount), and (2) provide that interest payments, if any, at or before maturity are based on a fixed rate (or to the extent provided in regulations, at a variable rate).

.04 An interest issued after the startup day does not qualify as a REMIC regular interest.

.05 Under section 860D(a)(4), an entity qualifies as a REMIC only if, among other things, as of the close of the third month beginning after the startup day and at all times thereafter, substantially all of its assets consist of qualified mortgages and permitted investments. This asset test is satisfied if the entity owns no more than a *de minimis* amount of other assets. See § 1.860D-1(b)(3)(i). As a safe harbor, the amount of assets other than qualified mortgages and permitted investments is *de minimis* if the aggregate of the adjusted bases of those assets is less than one percent of the aggregate of the adjusted bases of all of the entity's assets. § 1.860D-1(b)(3)(ii).

.06 With limited exceptions, a mortgage loan is not a qualified mortgage unless it is transferred to the REMIC on the startup day in exchange for regular or residual interests in the REMIC. *See* section 860G(a)(3)(A)(i).

.07 The legislative history of the REMIC provisions indicates that Congress intended the provisions to apply only to an entity that holds a substantially fixed pool of real estate mortgages and related assets and that "has no powers to vary the composition of its mortgage assets." S. Rep. No. 99-313, 99\th/ Cong., 2\d/ Sess. 791-92; 1986-3 (Vol. 3) C.B. 791-92.

.08 Section 1.1001-3(c)(1)(i) defines a "modification" of a debt instrument as any alteration, including any deletion or addition, in whole or in part, of a legal right or obligation of the issuer or holder of a debt instrument, whether the alteration is evidenced by an express agreement (oral or written), conduct of the parties, or otherwise. Section 1.1001-3(e) governs which modifications of debt instruments are "significant." Under

§ 1.1001-3(b), for most federal income tax purposes, a significant modification produces a deemed exchange of the original debt instrument for a new debt instrument.

.09 Under § 1.860G-2(b), related rules apply to determine REMIC qualification. Except as specifically provided in § 1.860G-2(b)(3), if there is a significant modification of an obligation that is held by a REMIC, then the modified obligation is treated as one that was newly issued in exchange for the unmodified obligation that it replaced. See § 1.860G-2(b)(1). For this purpose, the rules in § 1.1001-3(e) determine whether a modification is "significant." See § 1.860G-2(b)(2). Thus, even if an entity initially qualifies as a REMIC, one or more significant modifications of loans held by the entity may terminate the qualification if the modifications cause less than substantially all of the entity's assets to be qualified mortgages.

.10 Certain loan modifications, however, are not significant for purposes of § 1.860G-2(b)(1), even if the modifications are significant under the rules in § 1.1001-3. In particular, under § 1.860G-2(b)(3)(i), if a change in the terms of an obligation is "occasioned by default or a reasonably foreseeable default," the change is not a significant modification for purposes of § 1.860G-2(b)(1), regardless of the modification's status under § 1.1001-3.

.11 Section 860F(a)(1) imposes a tax on REMICs equal to 100 percent of the net income derived from "prohibited transactions." The disposition of a qualified mortgage is a prohibited transaction unless the "disposition [is] pursuant to—(i) the substitution of a qualified replacement mortgage for a qualified mortgage . . . , (ii) a disposition incident to the foreclosure, default, or imminent default of the mortgage, (iii) the bankruptcy or insolvency of the REMIC, or (iv) a qualified liquidation." Section 860F(a)(2)(A).

SECTION 4. BACKGROUND—TRUSTS

.01 Section 301.7701-2(a) of the Procedure and Administration Regulations defines a "business entity" as any entity recognized for federal tax purposes (including an entity with a single owner that may be disregarded as an entity separate from its owner under § 301.7701-3) that is not properly classified as a trust under § 301.7701-4 or otherwise subject to special treatment under the Code.

.02 Section 301.7701-4(a) provides that an arrangement is treated as a trust if the purpose of the arrangement is to vest in trustees responsibility for the protection and conservation of property for beneficiaries who cannot share in the discharge of this responsibility and, therefore, are not associates in a joint enterprise for the conduct of business for profit.

.03 Section 301.7701-4(c) provides that an "investment" trust is not classified as a trust if there is a power under the trust agreement to vary the investment of the certificate holders.

SECTION 5. SCOPE

.01 This revenue procedure applies to the following transactions occurring on or before July 31, 2010—

(1) A fast track modification of a Loan pursuant to the July 2008 Framework; and

(2) A second-lien holder's action of subordinating its lien to any new lien that may arise under a Loan as the result of such a fast track modification.

.02 If the July 2008 Framework is materially modified after July 8, 2008, this revenue procedure does not necessarily apply to fast track modifications under the modified Framework or to second-lien subordinations to accommodate those modifications.

SECTION 6. APPLICATION

In the case of one or more transactions to which this revenue procedure applies—

.01 The Service will not challenge a securitization vehicle's qualification as a REMIC on the grounds that the transactions are not among the exceptions listed in § 1.860G-2(b)(3);

.02 The Service will not contend that the transactions are prohibited transactions under section 860F(a)(2) on the grounds that the transactions resulted in one or more dispositions of qualified mortgages and that the dispositions are not among the exceptions listed in section 860F(a)(2)(A)(i)-(iv);

.03 The Service will not challenge a securitization vehicle's classification as a trust under § 301.7701-4(c) on the grounds that the transactions manifest a power to vary the investment of the certificate holders; and

.04 The Service will not challenge a securitization vehicle's qualification as a REMIC on the grounds that the transactions resulted in a deemed reissuance of the REMIC regular interests.

SECTION 7. OTHER GUIDANCE

For the treatment of mortgage loans modified pursuant to certain foreclosure prevention programs, see Rev. Proc. 2008-28, 2008-23 I.R.B. 1054.

¶ 28,150

SECTION 8. EFFECT ON OTHER DOCUMENTS

Rev. Proc. 2007-72 is amplified and, as amplified, is superseded.

SECTION 9. EFFECTIVE DATE

This revenue procedure is effective on July 8, 2008.

SECTION 10. DRAFTING INFORMATION

The principal author of this revenue procedure is Diana Imholtz of the Office of Associate Chief Counsel (Financial Institutions and Products). For further information, contact Ms. Imholtz on (202) 622-3930 (not a toll-free call).

Appendix to Revenue Procedure 2008-47

American Securitization Forum

Streamlined Foreclosure and Loss Avoidance Framework for Securitized Subprime Adjustable Rate Mortgage Loans

Executive Summary

July 8, 2008

Scope:

This streamlined framework applies to all first lien subprime residential adjustable rate mortgage (ARM) loans that have an initial fixed rate period of 36 months or less (including "2/28s" and "3/27s"), referred to below as "subprime ARM loans" that:

- were originated between January 1, 2005 and July 31, 2007;
- are included in securitized pools; and
- have an initial interest rate reset between January 1, 2008 and July 31, 2010.

This streamlined framework may be applied to subprime ARM loans in advance of an initial, or any subsequent, reset date. Typically, servicer/borrower communication should begin 120 days prior to the initial reset date.

As a general overview, under this streamlined framework, if the loan is current and is eligible for refinance, then it should be refinanced. If the loan is current but is not eligible for a refinance, then it would be eligible for a streamlined modification if: the property is occupied as the borrower's primary residence; the borrower meets the "FICO test"; and the payment amount would go up by more than 10% over the current payment amount at the upcoming reset.

Overarching Principles:

- The servicer will not take any action that is prohibited by the pooling and servicing agreement ("PSA") or other applicable securitization governing document, or that would violate applicable laws, regulations, or accounting standards. ASF's Statement of Principles, Recommendations and Guidelines for a Streamlined Foreclosure and Loss Avoidance Framework for Securitized Subprime Adjustable Rate Mortgage Loans, published concurrently with this document, analyzes how the framework described in the Executive Summary is consistent with typical PSA provisions. The ASF urges readers of this Executive Summary to review the full Statement.

- The ASF believes that this framework is consistent with the authority granted to a servicer to modify subprime mortgage loans in typical PSAs. The ASF expects that the procedures in this framework will constitute standard and customary servicing procedures for subprime loans.

- The servicer will expeditiously implement the ASF Investor Reporting Guidelines for the Modification of Subprime ARM Loans recommended by the ASF, which is simultaneously released with this framework.

- LTV and CLTV will be determined based on information at origination. If an origination LTV is below 97%, a servicer may obtain an updated home value by obtaining an AVM, BPO or other means.

- All servicers of second liens to subprime borrowers should cooperate fully with this framework by providing information needed by first lien servicers and by agreeing to subordinate the second lien to any new first lien resulting from a refinance (with no cash out) under this framework.

- All existing contractual obligations and remedies related to fraudulent mortgage origination activity should be strictly enforced.

- The streamlined framework outlined in this framework represents the consensus view of the membership of the ASF, acting through its Board of Directors, as to the parameters used to determine the segmentation of subprime ARM loans, including the numeric values included in those parameters. It is understood by the ASF's members that the numeric values included in the parameters are not based on historic data, but rather simply represent a consensus view as to ap-

¶28,150

propriate numeric values for use within this framework for the purpose of supporting a streamlined approach to loan modifications that complies with typical securitization governing documents. The ASF, acting through its Board of Directors, may in the future change these numeric values or further refine these parameters as experience is gained and market conditions evolve.

Borrower Segmentation:

Under this framework, subprime ARM loans are divided into 3 segments.

Segment 1 includes current (as defined below) loans where the borrower is likely to be able to refinance into any available mortgage product, including FHA, FHA Secure or readily available mortgage industry products.

- Generally, the servicer will determine whether loans may be eligible for refinancing into readily available mortgage industry products based on ascertainable data not requiring direct communication with the borrower, such as LTV, loan amount, FICO and payment history. Servicers will generally not determine current income or DTI to determine initial eligibility for refinancing.

- If the borrower also has a second lien on the property, this framework contemplates that the borrower is able to refinance the first lien only, on a no cash out basis. In order for the loan to fall into this segment, the second lien does not have to be refinanced; however, any second lien holder will need to agree to subordinate their interest to the refinanced first lien.

Segment 2 includes current loans where the borrower is unlikely to be able to refinance into any readily available mortgage industry product.

- *Current*: For purposes of this framework "current" means the loan must be not more than 30 days delinquent, and must not have been more than 1 x 60 days delinquent in the last 12 months, both under the OTS method. Corresponding tests would apply under the MBA method if the servicer uses that standard.

- *Not eligible for refinance*: All current loans that do not satisfy FHA Secure requirements, including delinquency history, DTI at origination, LTV (97% is the maximum LTV allowed under FHA Secure) and loan amount standards for this program, are within Segment 2; unless the servicer can determine whether they may meet eligibility criteria for another product, by reviewing eligibility criteria without performing an underwriting analysis.

Segment 3 includes loans where the borrower is not current as defined above, demonstrating difficulty meeting the introductory rate.

Segment 1 - Refinance:

- It is expected that borrowers in this category should refinance their loans, if they are unable or unwilling to meet their reset payment. However, a servicer may evaluate each borrower in this category on a case by case basis or apply any framework consistent with the applicable servicing standard in the transaction documents for a loan modification or other loss mitigation outcome.

- The servicer will facilitate a refinance in a manner that avoids the imposition of prepayment penalties wherever feasible. This may be accomplished by timing the refinance to occur after the upcoming reset date.

- Servicers should take all reasonable steps permitted under the PSA and other governing documents to encourage or facilitate refinancing for borrowers in Segment 1, or to borrowers in Segment 2 who become eligible for a refinance, including, where permitted, providing borrowers with information about FHA, FHA Secure and other readily available mortgage industry products, even if that servicer is not able to provide those products through any affiliated originator.

Segment 2 - Loan Modification:

- The servicer will determine the following for each Segment 2 borrower: current owner occupancy status (based on information known to the servicer, including billing and property address), current FICO score and the FICO score at origination of the loan.

- FICO test:

○ If the current FICO score is less than 660 and is less than a score 10% higher than the FICO score at origination, the borrower is considered to have met the "FICO test." If the borrower meets the FICO test, the servicer will generally not determine the borrower's current income.

○ If either a) the current FICO score is 660 or higher, or b) the current FICO is at least 10% higher than the FICO score at origination, the borrower is considered to not meet the "FICO

¶28,150

test." If the borrower does not meet the FICO test, the servicer will use an alternate analysis to determine if the borrower is eligible for a loan modification.

- Segment 2 loans will only be eligible for a fast track loan modification if:

○ The borrower currently occupies the property as his or her primary residence;

○ The borrower meets the FICO test; and

○ The servicer determines that, at the upcoming reset, the payment amount would go up by more than 10% over the current payment amount.

- Borrowers in this segment and eligible for a fast track loan modification as described above may be offered a loan modification under which the interest rate will be kept at the existing rate in effect prior to the upcoming reset, generally for 5 years following the upcoming reset.

- As to Segment 2 loans eligible for a fast track loan modification, the servicer may make the following presumptions:

○ The borrower is able and willing to pay under the loan modification based on his or her current payment history prior to the reset date.

○ The borrower is unable to pay (and default is reasonably foreseeable) after the upcoming reset under the original loan terms, based on the size of the payment increase that would otherwise apply.

○ The modification maximizes the net present value of recoveries to the securitization trust and is in the best interests of investors in the aggregate, because refinancing opportunities are likely not available and the borrower is able and willing to pay under the modified terms.

○ The terms of the loan modification shall be binding on the servicer and the borrower, if there is no signed modification agreement, so long as a) the terms of such loan modification are more favorable to the borrower than the existing terms, and b) the servicer sends a written notice to the borrower describing the terms of the modification.

- For borrowers that do not meet the FICO test, the servicer will use an alternate analysis to determine if the borrower is eligible for a loan modification, as well as the terms of the modification (which may vary). This may include a) conducting an individual review of current income and debt obligations, debt-to-income analysis, and considering a tailored modification for a borrower, or b) applying any other framework consistent with the applicable servicing standard in the transaction documents to determine if a borrower is eligible for a loan modification.

- For borrowers that are eligible for a fast track modification, the fast track option is non-exclusive and does not preclude a servicer from using an alternate analysis to determine if a borrower is eligible for a loan modification, as well as the terms of the modification.

Segment 3 - Loss Mitigation:

- For loans in this category, the servicer will determine the appropriate loss mitigation approach in a manner consistent with the applicable servicing standard in the transaction documents, but without employing the fast tracking procedures described under Segment 2. The approach chosen should maximize the net present value of the recoveries to the securitization trust. The available approaches may include loan modification (including rate reduction and/or principal forgiveness), forbearance, short sale, short payoff, or foreclosure.

- These borrowers will require a more intensive analysis, including where appropriate current debt and income analysis, to determine the appropriate loss mitigation approach.

¶ 29,001 Provisions Dropped in Conference

American Recovery and Reinvestment Act of 2009

The following proposed law changes originally included in either the House or Senate version of the American Recovery and Reinvestment Act of 2009 were dropped during conference committee negotiations.

Tax Relief for Individuals and Families
- Above-the-line deduction for interest on indebtedness for the purchase of certain motor vehicles (Senate Bill Sec. 1008).
- Election to accelerate the low-income housing credit allocation (Senate Bill Sec. 1903).

Tax Incentives for Business
- Broadband internet access tax credit (Senate Bill Sec. 1271).
- Modifications to general business credit (Senate Finance Committee Bill Secs. 1141 and 1142).
- Bonus depreciation for qualified film (Senate Finance Committee Bill Sec. 1201(c)).

Energy Incentives
- Accelerated recovery period for depreciation of smart meters (Senate Bill Sec. 1124).
- Increased energy research credit (House Bill Sec. 1631 and Senate Bill Sec. 1131).
- Expensing for manufacturing facilities producing plug-in electric drive motor vehicles and components (Senate Bill Sec. 1303).

Group Health Insurance and Other Provisions
- Extension of COBRA benefits for older or long-term employees (House Bill Sec. 3002(b)(2)).
- Excise tax on TARP companies that fail to redeem certain securities from the United States (Senate Bill Sec. 6021).

Topical Index

References are to paragraph (¶) numbers

A

Advanced energy project credit . . . 525
Alcohol taxes
. assessment
. . statute of limitations . . . 730
Alternative fuel vehicle refueling property credit
. credit percentage and dollar limitations increased . . . 365
Alternative minimum tax
. bonus depreciation . . . 415
. exemption amounts increased . . . 235
. nonrefundable personal credits
. . alternative motor vehicle credit . . . 360
. . extension . . . 240
. prior year liability
. . accelerated credit election, extension . . . 505
. private activity bonds
. . temporary modification . . . 650
Alternative motor vehicle credit
. alternative minimum tax offset . . . 360
American opportunity credit
. modification of Hope credit . . . 330
Automobiles
. alternative motor vehicle credit
. . alternative minimum tax offset . . . 360
. . plug-in conversion credit . . . 355
. bonus depreciation . . . 415
. plug-in electric drive motor vehicle credit
. . modification . . . 345
. plug-in electric vehicle credit
. . low speed and 2- and 3-wheeled vehicles . . . 350
. state and local sales and excise taxes on purchase
. . deduction . . . 230

B

Banks
. ownership change
. . built-in losses, application of Notice 2008-83 . . . 430
Biomass property
. election to claim energy investment credit . . . 510
. grants in lieu of credits . . . 515
. renewable electricity production credit
. . extension . . . 520
Bonds
. build America bonds . . . 605
. . issuer payment credit . . . 610
. . recovery zone economic development bonds . . . 625
. clean renewable energy bonds
. . expansion . . . 645
. energy conservation bonds
. . expansion . . . 640
. exempt facility bonds
. . high-speed intercity rail facilities . . . 655
. . recovery zone facility bonds . . . 652
. green community program bonds . . . 640

Bonds—continued
. industrial development bonds
. . production of intangible property . . . 660
. interest expenses, tax-exempt
. . financial institutions, deduction safe harbor . . . 445
. . financial institutions, small issuer exception . . . 450
. private activity bonds
. . alternative minimum tax modification . . . 650
. . green community program bonds . . . 640
. . recovery zone facility bonds . . . 652
. . small issue bonds, production of intangible property . . . 660
. recovery zone economic development bonds . . . 625
. recovery zone facility bonds . . . 652
. school construction bonds . . . 630
. small issue bonds
. . production of intangible property . . . 660
. tax credit bonds
. . build America bonds . . . 605; 610; 625
. . clean renewable energy bonds . . . 645
. . energy conservation bonds . . . 640
. . mutual funds, election to pass through to shareholders . . . 615
. . recovery zone economic development bonds . . . 625
. . school construction bonds . . . 630
. . zone academy bonds . . . 635
. tribal economic development bonds . . . 665
. zone academy bonds
. . extension and modification . . . 635
Bonus depreciation
. extension . . . 415
. prior year minimum tax credit
. . accelerated credit in lieu of deduction . . . 505
. research credit
. . accelerated credit in lieu of deduction . . . 505
Build America bonds . . . 605
. issuer payment credit . . . 610
. recovery zone economic development bonds . . . 625
Built-in gains or losses
. ownership change, loss limitation
. . banks . . . 430
. . TARP restructuring plans . . . 435
. S corporations
. . reduction in gain recognition period . . . 420

C

Cancellation of debt income
. deferral
. . reacquisition of business debt . . . 405
Carbon dioxide capture credit
. modification . . . 545
Child tax credit
. refundable portion
. . threshold reduced . . . 315
Clean renewable energy bonds
. expansion . . . 645

CLE

Topical Index

References are to paragraph (¶) numbers

COBRA continuation coverage
. PBGC recipients
. . extension . . . 715
. premium assistance
. . cessation of eligibility, notice . . . 710
. . coordination with health coverage tax credit . . . 705
. . employer payroll tax credit . . . 705
. . exclusion from income . . . 705
. TAA-eligible individuals
. . extension . . . 715

Combined heat and power system property
. grants in lieu of credits . . . 515

Compensation
. TARP recipients
. . bonus restrictions . . . 139
. . deduction limit extended . . . 455

Corporations
. alternative minimum tax
. . adjusted current earnings, private activity bonds . . . 650
. corporate equity reduction transactions
. . net operating loss carryback period extended . . . 425
. estimated tax
. . larger payment requirement . . . 470
. net operating losses and net unrealized built-in losses
. . ownership change, banks . . . 430
. . ownership change, TARP restructuring plans . . . 435
. original issue discount
. . applicable high-yield discount obligations, deduction limits suspended . . . 440

Credits against tax
. advanced energy project credit . . . 525
. alternative fuel vehicle refueling property credit
. . credit percentage and dollar limitations increased . . . 365
. alternative minimum tax
. . accelerated credit election, extension . . . 505
. . personal credit offsets, alternative motor vehicle credit . . . 360
. . personal credit offsets, extension . . . 240
. alternative motor vehicle credit
. . alternative minimum tax offset . . . 360
. . plug-in conversion credit . . . 355
. American opportunity credit
. . modification of Hope Credit . . . 330
. build America bonds . . . 605
. . issuer payment credit . . . 610
. . recovery zone economic development bonds . . . 625
. carbon dioxide capture credit
. . modification . . . 545
. child tax credit
. . refundable portion, threshold reduced . . . 315
. clean renewable energy bonds . . . 645
. earned income credit
. . amounts increased . . . 320
. energy conservation bonds
. . expansion . . . 640
. energy investment credit
. . election to claim in lieu of renewable electricity production credit . . . 510
. . grants in lieu of credit . . . 515

Credits against tax—continued
. energy investment credit—continued
. . modification . . . 510
. first-time homebuyer credit
. . expansion . . . 310
. government retirees
. . refundable credit . . . 325
. health coverage tax credit
. . coordination with COBRA premium assistance . . . 705
. . modification . . . 725
. Hope credit
. . modification . . . 330
. investment tax credit
. . advanced energy project credit . . . 525
. . energy credit, election to claim in lieu of renewable electricity production credit . . . 510
. . energy credit, grants in lieu of . . . 515
. . energy credit, modification . . . 510
. low-income housing credit
. . grants to states . . . 535
. making work pay credit . . . 305
. new markets tax credit
. . modification . . . 530
. plug-in conversion credit . . . 355
. plug-in electric drive motor vehicle credit
. . modification . . . 345
. plug-in electric vehicle credit
. . low speed and 2- and 3-wheeled vehicles . . . 350
. recovery zone economic development bonds . . . 625
. refundable credits
. . child tax credit, threshold reduced . . . 315
. . earned income credit, amounts increased . . . 320
. . first-time homebuyer credit, expansion . . . 310
. . government retirees . . . 325
. . Hope credit, partially refundable . . . 330
. . making work pay credit . . . 305
. renewable electricity production credit
. . election to claim energy investment credit in lieu of . . . 510
. . extension and modification . . . 520
. . grants in lieu of credit . . . 515
. research credit
. . accelerated credit election, extension . . . 505
. residential alternative energy credit
. . solar hot water, wind and geothermal property . . . 340
. residential energy property credit
. . expansion . . . 335
. school construction bonds . . . 630
. tax credit bonds
. . build America bonds . . . 605; 610; 625
. . clean renewable energy bonds . . . 645
. . energy conservation bonds . . . 640
. . mutual funds, election to pass through to shareholders . . . 615
. . recovery zone economic development bonds . . . 625
. . school construction bonds . . . 630
. . zone academy bonds . . . 635
. work opportunity credit
. . unemployed veterans and disconnected youth . . . 540
. zone academy bonds
. . extension and modification . . . 635

Topical Index

References are to paragraph (¶) numbers

D

Depreciation
. bonus depreciation
. . extension . . . 415
. . prior year minimum tax credit, accelerated credit in lieu of deduction . . . 505
. . research credit, accelerated credit in lieu of deduction . . . 505
. Sec. 179 deduction
. . increased limits, extension . . . 410

E

Earned income credit
. amounts increased . . . 320
Economic recovery payments
. social security recipients and veterans . . . 225
Education
. American opportunity credit
. . modification of Hope Credit . . . 330
. 529 plans
. . computer and internet access expenses . . . 220
. Hope credit
. . modification . . . 330
. school construction bonds
. . credit against tax . . . 630
. zone academy bonds
. . extension and modification . . . 635
Electric cooperative companies
. clean renewable energy bonds
. . expansion . . . 645
Electric energy
. advanced energy project credit . . . 525
. clean renewable energy bonds
. . expansion . . . 645
. renewable electricity production credit
. . election to claim energy investment credit in lieu of . . . 510
. . extension and modification . . . 520
. . grants in lieu of credit . . . 515
. residential alternative energy credit
. . annual limits, solar hot water, wind and geothermal property . . . 340
Energy conservation bonds
. expansion . . . 640
Energy incentives
. advanced energy project credit . . . 525
. alternative fuel vehicle refueling property credit
. . credit percentage and dollar limitations increased . . . 365
. alternative motor vehicle credit
. . alternative minimum tax offset . . . 360
. . plug-in conversion credit . . . 355
. carbon dioxide capture credit
. . modification . . . 545
. clean renewable energy bonds
. . expansion . . . 645
. energy conservation bonds
. . expansion . . . 640
. energy investment credit
. . election to claim in lieu of renewable electricity production credit . . . 510
. . grants in lieu of credit . . . 515
. . modification . . . 510

Energy incentives—continued
. plug-in conversion credit . . . 355
. plug-in electric drive motor vehicle credit
. . modification . . . 345
. plug-in electric vehicle credit
. . low speed and 2- and 3-wheeled vehicles . . . 350
. renewable electricity production credit
. . election to claim energy investment credit in lieu of . . . 510
. . extension and modification . . . 520
. . grants in lieu of credit . . . 515
. residential alternative energy credit
. . solar hot water, wind and geothermal property . . . 340
. residential energy property credit
. . expansion . . . 335
Energy investment credit
. election to claim in lieu of renewable electricity production credit . . . 510
. grants in lieu of credit . . . 515
. modification . . . 510
Estimated tax
. corporations
. . larger payment requirement . . . 470
. small businesses
. . penalty exception, payment of 90-percent of prior year tax . . . 465
Excise taxes
. alcohol
. . statute of limitations . . . 730
. purchase of motor vehicles
. . deduction . . . 230
. tobacco products
. . rates increased . . . 730
Executive compensation
. TARP recipients
. . bonus restrictions . . . 139
. . deduction limit extended . . . 455
Exempt facility bonds
. high-speed intercity rail facilities
. . speed requirement modified . . . 655
. recovery zone facility bonds . . . 652

F

Financial institutions
. banks
. . ownership change, built-in losses . . . 430
. TARP recipients
. . bonus restrictions . . . 139
. . compensation deduction limit . . . 455
. . net operating losses and net unrealized built-in losses . . . 435
. tax-exempt interest expenses
. . safe harbor exception . . . 445
. . small issuer exception . . . 450
First-time homebuyer credit
. expansion . . . 310
529 plans
. higher education expenses
. . computer and internet access expenses . . . 220
Fringe benefits
. van pools and transit passes
. . monthly exclusion increased . . . 215

FRI

Topical Index

References are to paragraph (¶) numbers

Fuel cell property
. advanced energy project credit . . . 525
. grants in lieu of credits . . . 515

G

Geothermal energy property
. advanced energy project credit . . . 525
. election to claim energy investment credit . . . 510
. grants in lieu of credits . . . 515
. renewable electricity production credit
. . extension . . . 520

Geothermal heat pump property
. grants in lieu of credits . . . 515
. residential alternative energy credit
. . annual limits removed . . . 340

Government employees
. retired employees
. . credit against tax . . . 325

Green community program bonds . . . 640

H

Health and accident plans
. COBRA continuation coverage
. . premium assistance . . . 705; 710
. enrollment period
. . Medicaid or CHIP coverage, change in eligibility . . . 720
. health coverage tax credit
. . coordination with COBRA premium assistance . . . 705
. . modification . . . 725

Hope credit
. modification . . . 330

Hydropower property
. election to claim energy investment credit . . . 510
. grants in lieu of credits . . . 515
. renewable electricity production credit
. . extension . . . 520

I

Indian tribal governments
. clean renewable energy bonds . . . 645
. energy conservation bonds . . . 640
. school construction bonds . . . 630
. tribal economic development bonds . . . 665

Industrial development bonds
. manufacturing facilities
. . production of intangible property . . . 660

Investment tax credit
. advanced energy project credit . . . 525
. energy credit
. . election to claim in lieu of renewable electricity production credit . . . 510
. . grants in lieu of credit . . . 515
. . modification . . . 510

L

Landfill gas energy property
. election to claim energy investment credit . . . 510
. grants in lieu of credits . . . 515

Landfill gas energy property—continued
. renewable electricity production credit
. . extension . . . 520

Low-income housing credit
. grants to states . . . 535

M

Making work pay credit . . . 305

Marine and hydrokinetic energy property
. election to claim energy investment credit . . . 510
. grants in lieu of credits . . . 515
. renewable electricity production credit
. . extension . . . 520

Microturbine property
. advanced energy project credit . . . 525
. grants in lieu of credits . . . 515

Municipal solid waste energy property
. election to claim energy investment credit . . . 510
. grants in lieu of credits . . . 515
. renewable electricity production credit
. . extension . . . 520

Mutual funds
. build America bonds . . . 605
. tax credit bonds
. . election to pass through credits to shareholders . . . 615

N

Net operating losses
. ownership change
. . banks . . . 430
. . TARP restructuring plans . . . 435
. small businesses
. . carryback period extended . . . 425

Net unrealized built-in losses
. ownership change
. . banks . . . 430
. . TARP restructuring plans . . . 435

New markets tax credit
. modification . . . 530

O

Original issue discount
. applicable high-yield discount obligations
. . limits on deduction suspended . . . 440
. cancellation of debt income
. . reacquisition of business debt, deferral . . . 405

P

Partnerships
. build America bonds . . . 605
. cancellation of debt income
. . deferral . . . 405

Pension Benefit Guaranty Corporation (PBGC)
. benefit recipients
. . COBRA continuation coverage, extension . . . 715
. . COBRA continuation coverage, premium assistance . . . 705
. . health coverage tax credit, modification . . . 725

FUE

Topical Index

References are to paragraph (¶) numbers

Plug-in electric vehicles
. credits against tax
. . conversion costs . . . 355
. . low speed and 2- and 3-wheeled vehicles . . . 350
. . modification . . . 345

Principal residence
. first-time homebuyer credit
. . expansion . . . 310

Private activity bonds
. alternative minimum tax
. . temporary modification . . . 650
. green community program bonds . . . 652
. recovery zone facility bonds . . . 652
. small issue bonds
. . production of intangible property . . . 660

Q

Qualified energy conservation bonds
. expansion . . . 640

Qualified school construction bonds . . . 630

Qualified small issue bonds
. production of intangible property . . . 660

Qualified tuition programs
. higher education expenses
. . computer and internet access expenses . . . 220

Qualified zone academy bonds
. extension and modification . . . 635

R

Railroads
. high-speed intercity rail facilities
. . exempt facility bonds . . . 655
. retirement benefit recipients
. . economic recovery payments . . . 225

Real estate investment trusts (REITs)
. build America bonds . . . 605

Recovery zone economic development bonds . . . 625

Recovery zone facility bonds . . . 652

Regulated investment companies (RICs)
. tax credit bonds
. . build America bonds . . . 605
. . election to pass through credits to shareholders . . . 615

Renewable electricity production credit
. election to claim energy investment credit in lieu of . . . 510
. extension and modification . . . 520
. grants in lieu of credit . . . 515

Research credit
. accelerated credit election
. . extension . . . 505

Residential alternative energy credit
. annual limits
. . solar hot water, wind and geothermal property . . . 340

Residential energy property credit
. expansion and modification . . . 335

S

S corporations
. build America bonds . . . 605
. built-in gains
. . reduction in recognition period . . . 420

Sales taxes
. purchase of motor vehicles
. . deduction . . . 230

School construction bonds . . . 630

Sec. 179 deduction
. increased limits
. . extension . . . 410

Small businesses
. estimated tax
. . penalty exception, payment of 90-percent of prior year tax . . . 465
. net operating losses
. . carryback period extended . . . 425
. small business stock
. . exclusion of gain, percentage increased . . . 210

Small irrigation power property
. renewable electricity production credit
. . placed in service date modified . . . 520

Small issue bonds
. manufacturing facilities
. . production of intangible property . . . 660

Small wind energy property
. energy investment credit
. . annual limit removed . . . 510
. grants in lieu of credits . . . 515

Social security benefit recipients
. economic recovery payments . . . 225

Solar energy property
. advanced energy project credit . . . 525
. grants in lieu of credits . . . 515
. hot water heaters
. . residential alternative energy credit, annual limits removed . . . 340

State and local taxes . . . 197
. sales and excise taxes
. . purchase of motor vehicles, deduction . . . 230

Students
. American opportunity credit
. . modification of Hope Credit . . . 330
. 529 plans
. . computer and internet access expenses . . . 220

T

Tax credit bonds
. build America bonds . . . 605
. . issuer payment credit . . . 610
. . recovery zone economic development bonds . . . 625
. clean renewable energy bonds . . . 645
. energy conservation bonds . . . 640
. mutual funds, election to pass through to shareholders . . . 615
. recovery zone economic development bonds . . . 625
. school construction bonds . . . 630

TAX

Topical Index

References are to paragraph (¶) numbers

Tax credit bonds—continued
. zone academy bonds
. . extension and modification . . . 635

Tobacco taxes
. rates increased . . . 730

Trade Adjustment Assistance program
. COBRA continuation coverage
. . extension . . . 715
. . premium assistance . . . 705
. health coverage tax credit
. . modification . . . 725

Transit passes
. fringe benefit
. . monthly exclusion increased . . . 215

Tribal economic development bonds . . . 665

Troubled Asset Relief Program (TARP)
. executive compensation
. . deduction limit extended . . . 455
. ownership changes
. . net operating losses and net unrealized built-in losses . . . 435

U

Unemployment compensation
. partial exclusion from gross income . . . 205

U.S. possessions
. economic recovery payments
. . social security recipients and veterans . . . 225
. Hope credit . . . 330
. making work pay credit . . . 305

V

Van pools
. fringe benefit
. . monthly exclusion increased . . . 215

Vehicles
. alternative motor vehicle credit
. . alternative minimum tax offset . . . 360

Vehicles—continued
. alternative motor vehicle credit—continued
. . plug-in conversion credit . . . 355
. . bonus depreciation . . . 415
. plug-in electric drive motor vehicle credit
. . modification . . . 345
. plug-in electric vehicle credit
. . low speed and 2- and 3-wheeled vehicles . . . 350
. state and local sales and excise taxes on purchase
. . deduction . . . 230

Veterans
. economic recovery payments . . . 225
. unemployed veterans
. . work opportunity credit . . . 540

W

Wind energy property
. advanced energy project credit . . . 525
. election to claim energy investment credit . . . 510
. grants in lieu of credits . . . 515
. renewable electricity production credit
. . extension . . . 520
. residential alternative energy credit
. . annual limits removed . . . 340

Withholding of tax
. government entities
. . withholding requirement delayed . . . 460
. reduced withholding
. . making work pay credit . . . 305

Work opportunity credit
. unemployed veterans and disconnected youth . . . 540

Z

Zone academy bonds
. extension and modification . . . 635

TOB